A COMPANION TO THE ROMAN EMPIRE

BLACKWELL COMPANIONS TO THE ANCIENT WORLD

This series provides sophisticated and authoritative overviews of periods of ancient history, genres of classical literature, and the most important themes in ancient culture. Each volume comprises between twenty-five and forty concise essays written by individual scholars within their area of specialization. The essays are written in a clear, provocative, and lively manner, designed for an international audience of scholars, students, and general readers.

ANCIENT HISTORY

Published

A Companion to the Roman Army
Edited by Paul Erdkamp

A Companion to the Roman Republic
Edited by Nathan Rosenstein and Robert Morstein-Marx

A Companion to the Roman Empire
Edited by David S. Potter

A Companion to the Classical Greek World
Edited by Konrad H. Kinzl

A Companion to the Ancient Near East
Edited by Daniel C. Snell

A Companion to the Hellenistic World
Edited by Andrew Erskine

A Companion to Late Antiquity
Edited by Philip Rousseau

A Companion to Ancient History
Edited by Andrew Erskine

A Companion to Archaic Greece
Edited by Kurt A. Raaflaub and Hans van Wees

A Companion to Julius Caesar
Edited by Miriam Griffin

In preparation

A Companion to Byzantium
Edited by Elizabeth James

A Companion to Ancient Macedonia
Edited by Ian Worthington and Joseph Roisman

A Companion to the Punic Wars
Edited by Dexter Hoyos

A Companion to Ancient Egypt
Edited by Alan Lloyd

A Companion to Sparta
Edited by Anton Powell

LITERATURE AND CULTURE

Published

A Companion to Classical Receptions
Edited by Lorna Hardwick and Christopher Stray

A Companion to Greek and Roman Historiography
Edited by John Marincola

A Companion to Catullus
Edited by Marilyn B. Skinner

A Companion to Roman Religion
Edited by Jörg Rüpke

A Companion to Greek Religion
Edited by Daniel Ogden

A Companion to the Classical Tradition
Edited by Craig W. Kallendorf

A Companion to Roman Rhetoric
Edited by William Dominik and Jon Hall

A Companion to Greek Rhetoric
Edited by Ian Worthington

A Companion to Ancient Epic
Edited by John Miles Foley

A Companion to Greek Tragedy
Edited by Justina Gregory

A Companion to Latin Literature
Edited by Stephen Harrison

A Companion to Greek and Roman Political Thought
Edited by Ryan K. Balot

A Companion to Ovid
Edited by Peter E. Knox

In preparation

A Companion to the Ancient Greek Language
Edited by Egbert Bakker

A Companion to Hellenistic Literature
Edited by Martine Cuypers and James J. Clauss

A Companion to Horace
Edited by N. Gregson Davis

A Companion to Food in the Ancient World
Edited by John Wilkins

A Companion to the Latin Language
Edited by James Clackson

A Companion to Classical Mythology
Edited by Ken Dowden and Niall Livingstone

A Companion to Sophocles
Edited by Kirk Ormand

A Companion to Aeschylus
Edited by Peter Burian

A Companion to Vergil and the Vergilian Tradition
Edited by Joseph Farrell and Michael Putnam

A Companion to Greek Art
Edited by Tyler Jo Smith and Dimitris Plantzos

A Companion to Families in the Greek and Roman World
Edited by Beryl Rawson

A Companion to Tacitus
Edited by Victoria Pagán

A Companion to the Archaeology of the Ancient Near East
Edited by Daniel Potts

A COMPANION TO THE ROMAN EMPIRE

Edited by

David S. Potter

WILEY-BLACKWELL
A John Wiley & Sons, Ltd., Publication

This paperback edition first published 2010
© 2010 Blackwell Publishing Ltd

Edition history: Blackwell Publishing Ltd (hardback, 2006)

Blackwell Publishing was acquired by John Wiley & Sons in February 2007. Blackwell's publishing program has been merged with Wiley's global Scientific, Technical, and Medical business to form Wiley-Blackwell.

Registered Office
John Wiley & Sons Ltd, The Atrium, Southern Gate, Chichester, West Sussex, PO19 8SQ, United Kingdom

Editorial Offices
350 Main Street, Malden, MA 02148-5020, USA
9600 Garsington Road, Oxford, OX4 2DQ, UK
The Atrium, Southern Gate, Chichester, West Sussex, PO19 8SQ, UK

For details of our global editorial offices, for customer services, and for information about how to apply for permission to reuse the copyright material in this book please see our website at www.wiley.com/wiley-blackwell.

The right of David S. Potter to be identified as the author of the editorial material in this work has been asserted in accordance with the Copyright, Designs and Patents Act 1988.

All rights reserved. No part of this publication may be reproduced, stored in a retrieval system, or transmitted, in any form or by any means, electronic, mechanical, photocopying, recording or otherwise, except as permitted by the UK Copyright, Designs and Patents Act 1988, without the prior permission of the publisher.

Wiley also publishes its books in a variety of electronic formats. Some content that appears in print may not be available in electronic books.

Designations used by companies to distinguish their products are often claimed as trademarks. All brand names and product names used in this book are trade names, service marks, trademarks or registered trademarks of their respective owners. The publisher is not associated with any product or vendor mentioned in this book. This publication is designed to provide accurate and authoritative information in regard to the subject matter covered. It is sold on the understanding that the publisher is not engaged in rendering professional services. If professional advice or other expert assistance is required, the services of a competent professional should be sought.

Library of Congress Cataloging-in-Publication Data

A companion to the Roman Empire / edited by David Potter.
    p. cm. — (Blackwell companions to the ancient world. Ancient history)
  Includes bibliographical references and index.
    ISBN: 978-0-631-22644-4 (hard cover : alk. paper) ISBN: 978-1-4051-9918-6 (pbk. : alk. paper)
1. Rome—History—Empire, 30 B.C.–476 A.D. 2. Rome—History—Empire, 30 B.C.–476 A.D.—Sources. 3. Rome—Civilization. I. Potter, D. S. (David Stone), 1957– II. Series.

DG311.P68 2006
937'.06–dc22
                                           2005015454

A catalogue record for this book is available from the British Library.

Set in 10/12pt Galliard by SPi Publisher Services, Pondicherry, India

2 2011

For Claire and Natalie

Contents

List of Illustrations	x
List of Tables	xiii
Notes on Contributors	xiv
Acknowledgments	xvi
Reference works: Abbreviations	xvii
Ancient authors: Abbreviations and Glossary	xx
The Emperors of Rome from Augustus to Constantine	xxix
Introduction: The Shape of Roman History: The Fate of the Governing Class *David S. Potter*	1

PART I THE SOURCES   21

1	Constructing a Narrative *Cynthia Damon*	23
2	Roman Imperial Numismatics *William E. Metcalf*	35
3	Documents *Traianos Gagos and David S. Potter*	45
4	Art, Architecture, and Archaeology in the Roman Empire *Lea Stirling*	75
5	Interdisciplinary Approaches *James B. Rives*	98

Part II Narrative — 113

6 The Emergence of Monarchy: 44 BCE–96 CE — 115
  Greg Rowe

7 Rome the Superpower: 96–235 CE — 126
  Michael Peachin

8 The Transformation of the Empire: 235–337 CE — 153
  David S. Potter

Part III Administration — 175

9 The Administration of the Provinces — 177
  Clifford Ando

10 The Transformation of Government under Diocletian and Constantine — 193
  Hugh Elton

11 The Roman Army — 206
  Nigel Pollard

12 Greek Cities Under Roman Rule — 228
  Maud W. Gleason

13 Cities and Urban Life in the Western Provinces of the Roman Empire 30 BCE–250 CE — 250
  Jonathan Edmondson

Part IV Social and Economic Life — 281

14 The Imperial Economy — 283
  David Mattingly

15 Landlords and Tenants — 298
  Dennis P. Kehoe

16 The Family — 312
  Judith Evans Grubbs

17 Sexuality in the Roman Empire — 327
  Amy Richlin

18 On Food and the Body — 354
  Veronika E. Grimm

19 Leisure — 369
  Garrett G. Fagan

20 Spectacle — 385
  David S. Potter

Part V Intellectual Life — 409

21 The Construction of the Past in the Roman Empire — 411
Rowland Smith

22 Imperial Poetry — 439
K. Sara Myers

23 Greek Fiction — 453
Joseph L. Rife

24 Roman Law and Roman History — 477
John Matthews

25 Roman Medicine — 492
Ann Hanson

26 Philosophy in the Roman Empire — 524
Sara Ahbel-Rappe

Part VI Religion — 541

27 Traditional Cult — 543
David Frankfurter

28 Jews and Judaism 70–429 CE — 565
Yaron Z. Eliav

29 Christians in the Roman Empire in the First Three Centuries CE — 587
Paula Fredriksen

30 Christian Thought — 607
Mark Edwards

Bibliography — 620

Index — 681

Illustrations

Maps

1	Provinces of the Roman Empire at the death of Trajan (AD 117)	xxxi
2	Dioceses and provinces of the Roman Empire according to the Verona List (c. AD 303–324)	172

Figures

2.1	"Crocodile" *as* from Nîmes	39
2.2	*Aureus* of Octavian 28 BCE	43
4.1	Portrait of Livia, wife of Augustus	78
4.2	Roman forum at Chemtou, with foundations of Numidian tombs exposed at the center	81
4.3	The Colosseum at Rome	82
4.4	Statue of Artemis at the Hunt next to a wall painting of a muse in apartment 4 of Terrace House 2, Ephesos	87
4.5	Infant buried in amphora at Leptiminus (Tunisia)	90
4.6a	Statuette of the weary Hercules discovering son Telephos, found in a late-antique suburban villa at Corinth	95
4.6b	Colossal statue of the Weary Hercules found in the Baths of Caracalla, Rome	96
6.1a–e	The Julio-Claudian house: (a) Augustus; (b) Tiberius; (c) Caligula; (d) Claudius; (e) Nero	119
6.2a and b	The propaganda of the Galban revolution	124

Illustrations

6.3a–c	The Flavians: (a) Vespasian; (b) Titus; (c) Domitian	125
7.1a–f	The Antonines: (a) Nerva; (b) Trajan; (c) Hadrian; (d) Antoninus Pius; (e) Marcus Aurelius; (f) Commodus	134
7.2a–d	The Severans: (a) Septimius Severus; (b) Caracalla; (c) Elagabalus; (d) Alexander	142
8.1a–j	Sapor and his enemies. (a) Sapor I; (b) Gordian III; (c) Philip I; d) Decius; (e) Trebonianus Gallus; (f) Aemilianus; (g) Valerian; (h) Gallienus; (i) Claudius II; (j) Aurelian	159
10.1a–d	The tetrarchs: (a) Diocletian; (b) Maximian; (c) Constantius I; (d) Galerius	195
12.1a	The entrance to the agora at Ephesus	236
12.1b	The marble street at Ephesus	236
12.2a	The theater at Ephesus	238
12.2b	Tetrapylon at Aphrodisias	238
13.1a and b	Relief from Avezzano, Italy, showing city and surrounding countryside	252
13.2a and b	Colonia Augusta Emerita (Mérida, Spain): (a) plan of the city and environs; (b) reconstruction of the monumental center	262–3
13.3a and b	*Forum adiectum*, Emerita: (a) general view; (b) reconstruction of R. Mesa	264–5
13.4	Reconstruction of statue-group of Aeneas (center), Ascanius (left), and Anchises (right) from the *forum adiectum*, Emerita	266
13.5	Colonia Iulia Urbs Triumphalis Tarraco	266
13.6	Glanum: plan of the Roman forum and twin temples, surrounded by U-shaped portico	267
13.7a and b	Conimbriga: Forum (a) in Augustan period and (b) as later remodeled after Flavian grant of the *ius Latii*	268
13.8a and b	Cities remodeled by emperors: (a) Italica; (b) Lepcis Magna	270–1
19.1a	Ostia, tavern on the Via di Diana, exterior view	374
19.1b	Ostia, tavern on the Via di Diana, interior view	374
19.2a	Suburban baths, Pompeii	380
19.2b	Suburban baths, Herculaneum	380
25.1a	Relief of Scribonia Attice assisting with a birth	504

25.1b	Relief of Marcus Ulpius Amerimnus drawing blood	504
25.2	An *okytokia*, or "quick birth" amulet	518–19
28.1a	Mosaic "carpet" from the fourth-century synagogue at Ḥamat Tiberieas	569
28.1b	The interior of a fourth-century synagogue at Sardis	570
28.2a	Imperial celebration of the capture of Jerusalem is reflected in the issue of Judaea Capta coinage under Vespasian	572
28.2b	Coin of Caesarea	572
28.3	An Aramaic letter written on papyrus from the so called "Cave of the Letters" at the Judaean Desert	575

Tables

1.1	Coverage of Roman history by historians	25
3.1	The bureaucracy of Roman Egypt	65
7.1	Emperors, AD 96–235	130
7.2	Nerva, Trajan, Hadrian, and Lucius Verus	132
7.3	Antoninus Pius, Marcus Aurelius, Commodus	133
7.4	The Severan emperors	137
11.1	The deployment of the legions in the principate	210
23.1	Timeline of Greek fiction under the Roman Empire	454
26.1	Names and dates of important philosophers	526

Notes on Contributors

Sara Ahbel-Rappe is Associate Professor of Greek and Latin in the Department of Classical Studies at the University of Michigan.

Clifford Ando is Associate Professor in the Classics Department at the University of Southern California.

Cynthia Damon is Associate Professor in the Classics Department at Amherst College.

Jonathan Edmondson is Associate Professor in the Department of History at York University.

Mark Edwards is Lecturer in Patristics at the University of Oxford and Student of Christ Church.

Yaron Z. Eliav is Jean and Samuel Frankel Assistant Professor of Rabbinic Literature and Jewish History of Late Antiquity in the Department of Near Eastern Studies at the University of Michigan.

Hugh Elton is Director of the British Institute at Ankara.

Garrett G. Fagan is Associate Professor of Classics and Ancient Mediterranean Studies and History at Pennsylvania State University.

David Frankfurter is Professor of History and Religious Studies in the Department of History at the University of New Hampshire.

Paula Fredriksen is William Goodwin Aurelio Professor of the Appreciation of Scripture, Social and Intellectual History of Early Christianity in the Department of Religion at Boston University.

Judith Evans Grubbs is Professor of Classics in the Department of Classics at Washington University in St. Louis.

Traianos Gagos is Associate Professor of Papyrology and Greek in the Department of Classical Studies, and Archivist in the Papyrology Collection at the University of Michigan.

Maud W. Gleason is Lecturer in Classics in the Department of Classics at Stanford University.

Notes on Contributors

Veronika E. Grimm is Lecturer in the Department of Classics at Yale University.

Ann Hanson is Senior Research Scholar/Senior Lector in the Department of Classics at Yale University.

Dennis P. Kehoe is Professor of Classics in the Department of Classics at Tulane University.

John Matthews is John M. Schiff Professor of History and Classics in the Department of Classics at Yale University.

David Mattingly is Professor of Roman Archaeology in the School of Archaeology and Ancient History at the University of Leicester.

William E. Metcalf is Adjunct Professor in the Department of Classics and Curator of Coins and Medals, Yale University Art Gallery, at Yale University.

K. Sara Myers is Associate Professor of Classics in the Department of Classics at the University of Virginia.

Michael Peachin is Professor of Classics in the Department of Classics at New York University.

Nigel Pollard is Lecturer in the Faculty of Classics and Ancient History at the University of Swansea.

David S. Potter is Professor of Greek and Latin in the Department of Classical Studies at the University of Michigan.

Amy Richlin is Professor of Classics in the Department of Classics at UCLA.

Joseph L. Rife is Assistant Professor of Classics in the Department of Classics at Macalester College.

James B. Rives is Associate Professor in the Program in Classical Studies at York University.

Greg Rowe is Associate Professor in the Department of Greek and Roman Studies at the University of Victoria.

Lea Stirling is Canada Research Chair in Roman Archaeology in the Department of Classics at the University of Manitoba.

Rowland Smith is Lecturer in the School of Historical Studies at the University of Newcastle upon Tyne.

Acknowledgments

It is a pleasure to thank the many people who made this volume possible. First and foremost my gratitude to the diverse contributors is enormous. I have learned a very great deal from them, and owe them all many thanks, especially those who turned in their chapters as long ago as 2001, for the extreme patience that they have shown in the long process of completion. I can only hope that they will think that the final product has been worth the wait.

For help in the final preparation of this book, I would first like to thank my chairman, Richard Janko, and my colleagues in the Department of Classical Studies for releasing the substantial research funds that enabled me to collect many of the illustrations that appear here, and to pay for the enormous help provided by my two assistants. Professor Kendra Eshleman brought order to the manuscript after completing her dissertation in the summer of 2004, and prepared the list of Classical authors. In the winter of 2005, Robert Chenault assisted mightily with the final preparation of the manuscript in every area, taking on responsibilities that went well beyond what I could have reasonably expected to enormously improve the accuracy of the volume. I also want to thank Professor Yaron Eliav for his assistance with the non-Classical texts that are quoted in this volume. I am responsible for any and all errors that remain.

I am also very grateful to Al Bertrand at Blackwell, firstly for thinking of me as the editor of this volume, and secondly for the gentle, patient encouragement that he has provided in the long process of getting it ready to go to press. In addition, I am grateful to Louise Spencely, who saw the book through its final stages before publication.

The greatest debt that I owe is, as always, to my family, to my wife Ellen, and to our daughters, Claire and Natalie, who brighten every hour of our lives. The pleasure that Claire and Natalie take in seeing the typescript leave the house (and their hope that they will hear less about the $%#$«$ Romans in the future) makes it only right to dedicate this book to them.

David S. Potter, 2006

Reference Works: Abbreviations

ABD	*Anchor Bible Dictionary*
Acts of the Ecumenical Councils	J. Harduin. *Acta Conciliorum.* 4 vols. Paris. 1714–15
AE	*L'Année épigraphique*, published in *Revue Archéologique* and separately. 1888–
AJA	*American Journal of Archaeology*
AJAH	*American Journal of Ancient History*
AJN	*American Journal of Numismatics*
AJP	*American Journal of Philology*
AnalRom	*Analecta Romana*
ANRW	*Aufstieg und Niedergang der römischen Welt.* Berlin. 1972–
ANSMN	*Museum Notes* (American Numismatic Society)
Ant. Afr.	*Antiquités Africaines*
ASP	*American Studies in Papyrology*
BASP	*Bulletin of the American Society of Papyrologists*
BCH	*Bulletin de correspondance hellénique*
BE	*Bulletin épigraphique*, published in *REG*
BGU	*Berliner Griechische Urkunden* (*Ägyptische Urkunden aus den Kgl. Museen zu Berlin*)
BICS	*Bulletin of the Institute for Classical Studies*
CA	*Classical Antiquity*
CAH²	*Cambridge Ancient History.* 2nd edn. 1961–
CEFR	*Collection de l'École française de Rome.* 1976–
CIL	*Corpus Inscriptionum Latinarum.* 1863–
CIS	*Corpus Inscriptionum Semiticarum.* 1881–
C.Pap.Jud.	*Corpus Papyrorum Judaicarum.* 1957–64
CPh	*Classical Philology*
CQ	*Classical Quarterly*
CRAI	*Comptes rendues de l'Académie des Inscriptions et Belles-lettres*
CW	*Classical World*
EchCl	*Echos du monde classique/Classical Views*

EJ	V. Ehrenberg and A. H. M. Jones. *Documents Illustrating the Reigns of Augustus and Tiberius*. 2nd edn. 1976
FIRA	S. Riccobono. *Fontes Iuris Romani AnteIustiniani*. 1941
FIRA^7	Bruns, K. G. *Fontes Iuris Romani Antiqui* (7th edn. by O. Gradenwitz). 1909
FHG	C. Müller. *Fragmenta Historicorum Graecorum*. 1841–70
FGrH	F. Jacoby. *Die Fragmente der griechischen Historiker*. 1923–
GRBS	*Greek, Roman and Byzantine Studies*
HAE	*Hispania Antiqua Epigraphica*
HSCP	*Harvard Studies in Classical Philology*
HTR	*Harvard Theological Review*
I. Ephesus	H. Wankel, R. Merkelback, et al., eds. *Die Inscriften von Ephesos*. 1979–81
IAM	*Inscriptions antiques du Maroc*
IG	*Inscriptiones Graecae*. 1873–
IGLS	*Inscriptions grecques et latines de la Syrie*
IGRR	R. Cagnat. *Inscriptiones Graecae ad Res Romanas Pertinentes*. Paris. 1906–27
ILA	*Inscriptions latines d'Aquitaine*
ILAfr	*Inscriptions latines d'Afrique*
ILCV	*Inscriptiones Latinae Christianae Veterae*
ILS	H. Dessau. *Inscriptiones Latinae Selectae*. Berlin. 1892–1916.
Inscr. It.	*Inscriptiones Italiae*
IRC	G. Fabre, M. Mayer, and I. Rodà. *Inscriptions romaines de Catalogne*. Paris. 1984–2002
IRT	J. M. Reynolds and J. B. Ward-Perkins. *The Inscriptions of Roman Tripolitania*. Rome. 1952
JARCE	*Journal of the American Research Center in Egypt*
JECS	*Journal of Early Christian Studies*
JHS	*Journal of Hellenic Studies*
JNG	*Jahrbuch für Numismatik und Geldgeschichte*
JRA	*Journal of Roman Archaeology*
JRS	*Journal of Roman Studies*
JTS	*Journal of Theological Studies*
LR^3	N. Lewis and M. Reinhold. *Roman Civilization: Selected Readings*. 3rd edn. New York and Oxford. 1990
LTUR	E. M. Steinby, ed. *Lexicon Topographicum Urbis Romae*. 6 vols. Rome. 1992–2002
MAMA	*Monumenta Asiae Minoris Antiquae*. 1928–
MEFRA	*Mélanges de l'École Française de Rome*
NC	*Numismatic Chronicle*
NPNF	*Nicene and Post-Nicene Fathers*
P.Amh.	B. P. Grenfell and A. S. Hunt, eds. *Amherst Papyri*. London. 1900–1
Pap.Brux.	*Papyrologica Bruxellensia*. Brussels. 1962–
P.Fam.Tebt.	B. A. van Groningen. *A Family Archive from Tebtunis*. Pap.Lugd.Bat. VI. Leiden. 1950
P.Panop.Beatty	T. C. Skeat. *Papyri from Panopolis in the Chester Beatty Library Dublin*. Chester Beatty Monographs I. Dublin. 1964
P.Bostra	J. Gascou. Unités administratives locales et fonctionnaires romains. In Eck and Müller-Luckner 1999: 61–73
P.Cair. Isid.	A. E. R. Boak and H. C. Youtie, eds. *The Archive of Aurelius Isidorus in the Egyptian Museum, Cairo, and the University of Michigan*
P.Dura	C. B. Welles et al., eds. *The Excavations at Dura-Europos conducted by Yale University and the French Academy of Inscriptions and Letters*. Final Report 5 pt. 1: *The Parchments and Papyri*. 1959
P.Euphr.	D. Feissel and J. Gascou. Documents d'archives romains inédits du Moyen Euphrate (III^c s. après J.C.). *Journal des Savants*: 65–119. 1995

P.Gen.Lat.	J. Nicole and C. Morel, eds. *Archives militaires du 1er siècle* (*Texte inédit du Papyrus Latin de Genève No. 1*). Geneva. 1900
P.Lond.	*Greek Papyri in the British Museum*. London. 1893–
P.Mich.	*Michigan Papyri*. 1931–
P.Oxy.	*The Oxyrhynchus Papyri*. London. 1898–
P.Thmouis I	S. Kambitsis. *Le Papyrus Thmouis I, colonnes 68–160*. Paris. 1985
P.Yadin	N. Lewis, Y. Yadin, and J. Greenfield. *The Documents from the Bar Kochba Period in the Cave of Letters*. Jerusalem. 1989–2002
P.Yale I	J. F. Oates, A. E. Samuel, and C. B. Welles. *Yale Papyri in the Beinecke Rare Book and Manuscript Library*. ASP 2. New Haven and Toronto. 1967
PBSR	*Papers of the British School at Rome*
PCPS	*Proceedings of the Cambridge Philological Society*
PG	Migne. *Patrologia Graeca*
PGM	K. Preisendanz, ed. *Papyri Graecae Magicae*. Leipzig-Berlin. 1928–31. (Trans. H. D. Betz, *The Magical Papyri in Translation*. Chicago. 1985.)
PSI	*Papiri Greci e Latini, Pubblicazioni della Società italiana per la ricerca dei papiri greci e latini in Egitto*. 1912–
RDGE	R. K. Sherk. *Roman Documents from the Greek East: Senatus Consulta and Epistulae to the Age of Augustus*. Baltimore. 1969
RA	*Revue archéologique*
REA	*Revue des études anciennes*
REG	*Revue des études grecques*
RIB	R. G. Collingwood, R. P. Wright, et. al. *The Roman Inscriptions of Britain*. 1965–
RIC	*Roman Imperial Coinage*
RIN	*Rivista italiana di numismatica e scienze affini*
RIT	G. Alföldy. *Die römischen Inschriften von Tarraco*. Berlin. 1975
RN	*Revue numismatique*
RPC	*Roman Provincial Coinage*
RS	M. H. Crawford. *Roman Statutes*. BICS Suppl. 64. London. 1996
SB	F. Preisigke et al. *Sammelbuch griechischen Urkunden aus Ägypten*. 1915–
SCI	*Scripta Classica Israelica*
SEG	*Supplementum Epigraphicum Graecum*. 1923–
Sel. Pap.	A. S. Hunt, C. C. Edgar, and D. L. Page. *Select Papyri*. 4 vols. Cambridge, MA. 1950
*SIG*³	W. Dittenberger. *Sylloge Inscriptionum Graecarum*. 3rd edn. Leipzig. 1915–24
SNR	*Schweizerische Numismatische Rundschau = Revue suisse de numismatique*
Tab. Vindol.	A. K. Bowman and J. D. Thomas, eds. *Vindolanda: the Latin Writing Tablets*. 1983–2003
TrGF	B. Snell, R. Kannicht, and S. Radt, eds. *Tragicorum Graecorum Fragmenta*. 4 vols. 1971–85; vol. 1² 1986
TSAJ	*Texte und Studien zum Antiken Judentum*
VC	*Vigiliae Christianae*
YCS	*Yale Classical Studies*
ZPE	*Zeitschrift für Papyrologie und Epigraphik*
ZSS	*Zeitschrift der Savigny-Stiftung für Rechtsgeschichte*

Ancient Authors: Abbreviations and Glossary

A. Paul. et Thecl.	*Acts of Paul and Thecla*
A. Pion.	*Acts of Pionius*
Ach. Tat.	Achilles Tatius, Alexandrian novelist, 2nd c. CE, *Leucippe and Cleitophon*
Ael.	Aelian, Latin writer, c.165/70–230/5 CE, *Letters*
Alciphr.	Alciphron, Greek sophist, 2nd/3rd c. CE, *Letters*
Alex. Aphr.	Alexander of Aphrodisias, Aristotelian philosopher, late 2nd c. CE
Amm. Marc.	Ammianus Marcellinus, Latin historian, 4th c. CE, *History*
Antyllus in Orib. *Coll.*	(see Oribasius of Pergamum, *Collectiones medicae*)
AP	Anthologia Palatina (*Greek Anthology*)
Apicius	Apicius, author of (undated) handbook *On Cooking*
Apophth. Patr.	Apophthegmata Patrum (*Sayings of the Desert Fathers*)
App., *BC*	Appian, Greek historian, 2nd c. CE, *Bella Civilia* (*Civil Wars*)
Apul.	Apuleius of Madaura, Latin prose writer, 2nd c. CE
Met.	*Metamorphoses*, or *The Golden Ass*
Aristid., *Or.*	Aelius Aristides, Greek orator, 2nd c. CE, *Orations*
Arr.	Arrian, Greek historian, c.86–160 CE
Alan.	*Expeditio contra Alanos* (*Order of Battle against the Alans*)
Anab.	*Anabasis*
Epict.	*Discourses of Epictetus*
Artem.	Artemidorus Daldianus, author of a work on the dream interpretation, 2nd c. CE, *Oneirocritica* (*The Interpretation of Dreams*)
Ath., *Deip.*	Athenaeus, 3rd c. CE, *Deipnosophistae* (*Doctors at Dinner*)
Ath., *V. Ant.*	Athanasius, bishop of Alexandria, 4th c. CE, *Life of Saint Antony*
August.	Augustine of Hippo, bishop and writer, 354–430 CE
Conf.	*Confessions*
De Trin.	*De Trinitate* (*On the Trinity*)
Serm.	*Sermons*
Aur. Vict., *Caes.*	Aurelius Victor, Latin historian, 4th c. CE, *de Caesaribus* (*Book on the Emperors*)
Auson.	D. Ausonius Magnus, statesman, teacher and writer, 4th c. CE
Ep.	*Epigrams*
Mos.	*Mosella*

Ancient Authors: Abbreviations and Glossary

Barn.	Letter of Barnabas
Basil, *Ep.*	Basil, bishop of Caesarea in Cappadocia, 329–79 CE, *Letters*
Caes.	C. Julius Caesar, 100–44 BCE
BC	*Bellum Civile* (*Civil War*)
BG	*de Bello Gallico* (*Gallic War*)
[Caes.] *B. Afr.*	*Bellum Africum* (*African War*)
Cato, *Agr.*	Cato the Elder, Roman politician and writer, 234–149 BCE, *On Agriculture*
Celsus, *Med.*	A. Cornelius Celsus, 1st c. CE, *Concerning Medicine*
Char.	Chariton, Greek novelist, before mid-2nd c. CE, *Chaereas and Callirhoë*
Chron. Pasc.	*Chronicon Paschale* (*Easter Chronicle*), universal history from Creation to c.630 CE
Cic.	M. Tullius Cicero, Roman politician and writer, 106–43 BCE
Ac.	*Academica*
Att.	*Letters to Atticus*
Brut.	*Brutus*
Cael.	*On Behalf of Caelius*
de Orat.	*de Oratore*
Div.	*On Divination*
Fam.	*Letters to Friends*
Fin.	*de Finibus Bonorum et Malorum*
Flac.	*On Behalf of Flaccus*
Font.	*On Behalf of Fonteius*
Leg.	*de Legibus* (*On Laws*)
Mur.	*On Behalf of Murena*
Off.	*de Officiis* (*On Duties*)
Orat.	*Orator*
Phil.	*Philippics*
Pis.	*Against Piso*
Q. fr.	*Letters to Quintus*
Rep.	*Republic*
Rull.	*Against Rullus*
Tusc.	*Tusculan Disputations*
Ver.	*Against Verres*
Col., *Rust.*	Columella, 1st c. CE, *de Re Rustica*, an agricultural manual
Copa	*The Proprietress*, poem ascribed to Vergil
1–2 Cor	*First and Second Letters to the Corinthians*
CJust.	*Code of Justinian*
CTh.	*Code of Theodosius II*
Cyril, *Ep.*	Cyril, bishop of Alexandria, 5th c. CE, *Letters*
D.	*Digest of Justinian*
Dn	*Daniel*
D.Chr.	Dio Chrysostom, Greek orator and philosopher, mid-1st c.–early 2nd c. CE
Dict. Cret.	Dictys of Crete, supposed companion of Idomeneus at Troy, alleged author of the *Memoirs of the Trojan War*
D.L.	Diogenes Laertius, Greek biographer, 3rd c. CE, *De clarorum philosophorum vitis* (*Concerning the Lives of Famous Philosophers*)
Dio	Cassius Dio, Greek historian of Rome, c.164–after 229 CE, *Roman History*
Enn.	Ennius, Latin poet, 239–169 BCE
Ep. Aristeas	*Letter of Aristeas*, 2nd c. BCE
Epict.	Epictetus, Stoic philosopher, mid-1st–2nd c. CE
Ench.	*Encheiridion* (*Handbook*)
Epitome	*Epitome on the Emperors*, anon. history of Rome, 4th c. CE

Eun., *VS*	Eunapius, Greek sophist and historian, 4th c. CE, *Vitae Sophistarum* (*Lives of the Sophists*)
Eur.	Euripides, Athenian tragedian, c.480s–407/6 BCE
Hec.	*Hecuba*
Tr.	*Trojan Women*
Euseb.	Eusebius of Caesarea, bishop and scholar, c.260–339 CE
Eccl. Hist.	*Ecclesiastical History*
Hierocl.	*Against Hierocles*
LC	*de Laudibus Constantini* (*In Praise of Constantine*)
Mart. Pal.	*Martyrs of Palestine*
VC	*Vita Constantini* (*Life of Constantine*)
Eust., *Comm. Od.*	Eustathius, bishop and scholar, 12th c. CE, *Commentary on the Odyssey*
Eutrop.	Eutropius, Latin historian, 4th c. CE, *Abbreviated History of Rome*
Ex	*Exodus*
Festus	Festus, Latin historian, 4th c. CE, *Abbreviated History*
Florus	L. Annaeus Florus, Latin historian, 2nd. c. CE, *Epitome of Seven Hundred Years' Worth of Wars*
Fron.	S. Julius Frontinus, Roman politician and writer, d. 103/4 CE
Aq.	*On Aqueducts*
Str.	*Strategemata*
Fronto	M. Cornelius Fronto, orator and tutor of Marcus Aurelius, c.95–c.166 CE (the letters are referred to in the ordering of M. Van den Hout, *M. Cornelii Frontonis Epistulae* [Leiden, 1954])
Ant.	*Letters to Antoninus Pius*
Aur.	*Letters to Marcus Aurelius*
Ep. Add.	*Appendix of Letters without Addresses*
Prin. hist.	*Principia historiae*
Gaius, *Inst.*	Gaius, Roman jurist, 2nd c. CE, *Institutes*
Gal	*Letter to the Galatians*
Galen	Galen, Greek medical writer, 2nd c. CE
Anat. admin.	*On Anatomical Procedures*
Antid.	*On Antidotes*
Caus. puls.	*On Causes of Pulses*
Comp. med. per gen.	*On Compound Drugs by Type*
Diff. puls.	*On Differences in Pulses*
Diff. resp.	*On Difficult Breathing*
Examin.	*Examinations of the Best Physicians*
Hipp. Fract. comment.	*Commentary to the Hippocratic "Fractures"*
Introd.	[Galen], *Introduction [to Medicine] or the Doctor*
Libr. Propr.	*On his Own Books*
Loc. affect.	*On the Affected Parts*
Meth. med.	*Methods of Healing*
Mor.	*Habits*; J. N. Mattock, ed., "A Translation of the Arabic of Galen's Book *Peri èthôn*" in S. M. Stern et al., editors, *Islamic Philosophy and The Classical Tradition* (Festschrift R. Walzer), Columbia, SC: 1972. 235–60
Nat. fac.	*On Natural Faculties*
Praecog.	*Prognosis*
Puls. diff.	*On Differences in Pulses*
Sanit.	*Hygiene*
Sem.	*On Generating Seed*
Simpl. med. temp.	*On the Powers of Simples*
Ther. ad Pis.	*On Theriacs, dedicated to Piso*
Usu puls.	*On Usefulness of the Pulse*

Gel.	Aulus Gellius, Roman miscellanist, 2nd c. CE, *Attic Nights*
Greg. Naz. *Ep.*	Gregory, c.325–389 CE, bishop of Nazianzus, *Letters*
HA	*Historia Augusta*, anon. collection of imperial biographies, 4th or 5th c. CE
Ant. Pius	*Life of Antoninus Pius*
Avid. Cass.	*Life of Avidius Cassius*
Carac.	*Life of Caracalla*
Claud.	*Life of Claudius II*
Comm.	*Life of Commodus*
Did. Jul.	*Life of Didius Julianus*
Had.	*Life of Hadrian*
Heliogab.	*Life of Elagabalus*
Marc.	*Life of Marcus Aurelius*
Pert.	*Life of Pertinax*
Sev.	*Life of Septimius Severus*
Hdt.	Herodotus of Halicarnassus, Greek historian, 5th c. BCE
Heb	*Letter to the Hebrews*
Heliod.	Heliodorus, Greek novelist, probably fl. c.230 CE, *The Ethiopian Story of Theagenes and Charicleia*
Hermog., *Prog.*	Hermogenes, Greek rhetorical writer, 2nd c. CE, *Progymnasmata (Preliminary Exercises)*
Herod.	Herodian, Greek historian, 3rd c. CE, *History of the Empire from the Time of Marcus*
Hipp., *Ref.*	Hippolytus of Rome, Christian apologist, fl. c.180–238 CE, *Refutation of all Heresies.*
Hippoc.	*Hippocrates of Cos, Greek medical writer, 5th c. BCE*
Art	*De Articulis (On Joints)*
Epid.	*Epidemiae (Epidemics)*
Morb. mul.	*De morbis mulierum (On the Diseases of Women)*
Nat. puer	*De natura pueri (On the Nature of the Child)*
Hom.	Homer
Il.	*Iliad*
Od.	*Odyssey*
Hor.	Q. Horatius Flaccus, Latin poet, 65–8 BCE
Ars	*Ars Poetica*
Sat.	*Satires*
Hyginus	author of a treatise on categories of land and land disputes, c.100 CE, *On Establishing Boundaries*
Iamb.	Iamblichus, Neoplatonist philosopher, c.245–c.325 CE
Myst.	*On the Mysteries of the Egyptians*
Prot.	*Protrepticus (Exhortation to Philosophy)*
VP	*Vita Pythagorica (Life of Pythagoras)*
Iamb., *Bab.*	Iamblichus, Greek novelist, fl. c.165–80 CE, *The Babylonian History*
Ign.,	Ignatius of Antioch, Christian theologian, fl. c.100 CE
Eph.	*Letter to the Ephesians*
Mg.	*Letter to the Magnesians*
Phld.	*Letter to the Philadelphians*
Sm.	*Letter to the Smyrnaeans*
Tr.	*Letter to the Trallians*
Iren., *AH*	Irenaeus of Lyons, bishop and heresiologist, c.130–c.202 CE, *Against Heresies*
Jas	*Letter of James*
Jer.	Jerome, Christian scholar and ascetic, c.347–420 CE
Chron.	*Chronicle*
Ep.	*Letters*
V.Paul	*Life of Paul*

Jn.	*Gospel according to John*
Jo.Chr.	John Chrysostom, bishop, c.354–407 CE, *de Studio praesentium* (*On the Zeal of those Present*)
Jos.	Flavius Josephus, Jewish historian, 37–c.100 CE
AJ	*Jewish Antiquities*
BJ	*Bellum Judaicum* (*Jewish War*)
Jul.	Julian "the Apostate," emperor 361–3 CE
Caes.	*Caesars*
Ep.	*Letters*
Julian	Salvius Julianus, Roman jurist, 2nd c. CE
Justin	Justin Martyr, Christian teacher and apologist, c.100–65 CE
Trypho	*Dialogue with Trypho*
1 Apol.	*First Apology*
2 Apol.	*Second Apology*
Juv., *Sat.*	Juvenal, Latin poet, 1st–2nd c. CE, *Satires*
Lact., *DMP*	Lactantius, Christian apologist, c.240–c.320 CE, *de Mortibus Persecutorum* (*On the Deaths of the Persecutors*)
Largus	Scribonius Largus, c.1–50 CE, *Compositiones*
Laudatio	*Laudatio Turiae* (*In Praise of "Turia"*)
Lex Irnitana	Municipal Law for Irni in Spain (J. González, *JRS* 76 [1986])
Lex de Provinciis Praetoriis	Law on the praetorian provinces of 100 BCE (M. H. Crawford, *Roman Statutes* no. 12)
Lex Ursonensis	*Lex coloniae Genetivae Iuliae* (Municipal code for Urso in Spain, M. H. Crawford, *Roman Statutes* no. 25)
Lib., *Or.*	Libanius, Greek rhetorician, 314–c.393 CE, *Orations*
Livy	Livy, Latin historian, probably 59 BCE–17 CE; *Ab Urbe Condita* (*From the Foundation of the City*)
Per.	*Periochae* (*Summaries*)
Lk	*Gospel according to Luke*
Long.	Longus, Greek novelist, late 2nd or early 3rd c. CE, *Daphnis and Chloe*
Luc.	Lucian of Samosata, Greek prose writer, b. c.120 CE
Alex.	*Alexander the False Prophet*
Amatores	*The Lovers*
Apol.	*Apologia* (*Defense*)
Peregr.	*De morte Peregrini*
Gall.	*Gallus* (*The Rooster*)
Hist. Conscr.	*Quomodo historia conscribenda sit* (*How to Write History*)
Imag.	*Images*
Laps.	*de Lapsu inter salutandum* (*Concerning a Slip*)
Nav.	*Navigium* (*The Ship*)
Pr.Im.	*pro Imaginibus* (*Concerning Images*)
Rh. Pr.	*Rhetorum praeceptor* (*Teacher of Orators*)
Salt.	*de Saltatione* (*About Dancing*)
Syr. D.	*de Syria Dea* (*On the Syrian Goddess*)
Ver. Hist.	*Verae Historiae* (*True Histories*)
Lucil.	Lucilius, Latin satirist, probably c.180–102/1 BCE
M. Pol.	*Martyrdom of Polycarp*
Mc	*Maccabees*
Malal.	John Malalas, Greek historian, c.490–570s CE, *Chronicle*
Macrob.	Macrobius, Roman politician and scholar, 5th c. CE
In Somn.	*Commentary on the Dream of Scipio*
Sat.	*Saturnalia*
Marc. Aurel.	Marcus Aurelius, Roman emperor 161–80 CE
Med.	*Meditations*

Ancient Authors: Abbreviations and Glossary

Marcian	Aelius Marcianus, Roman jurist, early 3rd c. CE
Mart.	M. Valerius Martialis, Latin poet, c.38/41–101/4 CE
Ep.	*Epigrams*
Sp.	*Spectacles*
Martin of Braga	Martin of Braga, bishop, 6th c. CE
de Corr. Rust.	*de Correctione Rusticorum*
Mela	Pomponius Mela
Men. Rh.	Menander Rhetor, Greek rhetorical writer, probably 3rd c. CE
Mk	*Gospel according to Mark*
Mt	*Gospel according to Matthew*
Muson.	C. Musonius Rufus, Stoic philosopher, before 30–before 101/2 CE
Mustio (or Muscio)	
Gyn.	*Gynecology*
NTh.	*Novels of Theodosius*
Nep.	Cornelius Nepos, Latin biographer, c.110–24 BCE
Att.	*Atticus*
Nm	*Numbers*
Numen.	Numenius of Apamea, Middle Platonist/Pythagorean philosopher, 2nd c. CE, *On the Divergence of the Academy from Plato*
Opt.	Optatus of Miletus, *Against the Donatists*
Orib.	Oribasius of Pergamum, c.325–400 CE
Coll.	*Medical Collections*
Origen	Origen, Alexandrian priest and scholar, probably 184/5–254/5 CE
C. Cels.	*Against Celsus*
De princ.	*On First Principles*
In Joh.	*Commentary on the Gospel of John*
Ph.	*Philokalia*
Ov.	P. Ovidius Naso, Latin poet, 43 BCE–17 CE
Ars	*Art of Love*
Fast.	*Fasti*
Her.	*Heroides*
Met.	*Metamorphoses*
Tr.	*Tristia*
P. Perp.	*Passion of Perpetua and Felicitas*
Pan.	*Latin Panegyrics*
Paul	Iulius Paulus, Roman jurist, early 3rd c. CE, *Sententiae*
Paus.	Pausanias, Greek traveler, 2nd c. CE, *Description of Greece*
Peripl. M. Rubr.	Anonymous, 1st c. CE, *Sailing Around the Red Sea*
Pers.	A. Persius Flaccus, Latin poet, 34–62 CE, *Satires*
Petron., *Sat.*	Petronius, Roman prose writer, d. 66 CE, *Satyricon*
Phaedr.	Phaedrus, 1st c. CE, *Fabulae (Stories)*
Phil	*Letter to the Philippians*
Philo	Philo of Alexandria, Jewish writer, 1st c. CE
Abr.	*On Abraham*
Conf.Ling.	*de Confusione linguarum (On the Confusion of Languages)*
Det.	*Quod deterius potiori insidiari soleat (The Worse Attacks the Better)*
Deus	*Quod Deus sit immutabilis (On the Unchangeableness of God)*
Ebr.	*de Ebrietate (On Drunkenness)*
Gig.	*de Gigantibus (On the Giants)*
Quis Her.	*Quis rerum divinarum heres sit (Who is the Heir?)*
Leg.	*Legatio ad Gaium (Embassy to Gaius)*
Op.	*de Opificio Mundi (On the Creation of the World)*
Som.	*de Somniis (On Dreams)*
Spec.Leg.	*de Specialibus legibus (On the Special Laws)*
Vit.Cont.	*de Vita Contemplativa (On the Contemplative Life)*

Philostr.	Philostratus of Athens, Greek sophist and writer, d. c.244–9 CE
Ep.	Letters
Her.	Heroic Discourse
VA	Vita Apollonii (In honor of Apollonius of Tyana)
VS	Vitae Sophistarum (Lives of the Sophists)
Philostr.Jun.	Philostratus (Iunior) of Lemnos, Greek sophist and writer, 3rd c. CE
Imag.	Imagines (Pictures)
[Phoc.]	[Phocylides], Sententiae
Phot., Bib.	Photius, bishop and scholar, c.810–c.893 CE, Bibliotheca (Library)
Pl.	Plato, Athenian philosopher, c.429–347 BCE
Prm.	Parmenides
Rep.	Republic
Ti.	Timaeus
Plaut.	Plautus, Latin comic playwright, fl. c.205–184 BCE
Men.	Menaechmi (The Menaechmus Twins)
Mil.	Miles Gloriosus (The Braggart Soldier)
Rud.	Rudens (The Rope)
Plin., Nat.	Pliny the Elder, Roman politician and scholar, 23/4–79 CE, Natural History
Pliny	Pliny the Younger, Roman politician, c.61–c.112 CE
Ep.	Letters
Pan.	Panegyric
Plot., Enn.	Plotinus, Neoplatonist philosopher, 205–69/70 CE, Enneads
Plut.	Plutarch, Greek biographer and philosopher, mid-1st–2nd c. CE
Caes.	Life of Caesar
Lyc.	Life of Lycurgus
Mor.	Moralia
Amat.	Amatorius (The Lover)
de Def. or.	de Defectu oraculorum (On the Failure of Oracles)
de Is. et Os.	de Iside et Osiride (On Isis and Osiris)
Prae. ger. reip.	Praecepta gerendae reipublicae (Rules for Politicians)
Rom.	Life of Romulus
Sol.	Life of Solon
Thes.	Life of Theseus
Polyb.	Polybius, Greek historian, c.200–c.118 BCE
Pomponius	S. Pomponius, Roman jurist, mid-2nd c. CE
Porph.	Porphyry, scholar and philosopher, 234–c.305 CE
Abst.	On Abstention from Animal Food
VP	Life of Plotinus
Procl.	Proclus, Neoplatonist philosopher, c.412–85 CE
in Prm.	Commentary on Plato's Parmenides
in Ti.	Commentary on Plato's Timaeus
PT	Platonic Theology
Procop.	Procopius, Greek historian, 6th c. CE
Arc.	Arcana Historia (Secret History)
Goth.	de Bello Gothico (On the Gothic War)
Prop.	Propertius, Latin poet, 1st c. BCE
Ps	Psalms
Q.S.	Quintus of Smyrna, Greek poet, probably 3rd c. CE, Posthomerica
Quint.	Quintilian, Roman rhetorician, c.35–96 CE
Inst.	Orator's Education
[Quint.], Decl.	[Quintilian], Declamations
Rv	Revelation
RG	Res Gestae (Deeds of the Divine Augustus)
Rom	Letter to the Romans
1–2 Sm	First and Second Samuel

Sall.	C. Sallustius Crispus, Latin historian, probably 86–35 BCE
Cat.	*Catiline*
SC de Pisone Patre	*Senatus consultum on the elder Piso*
Schol. ad Juv.	*Scholia on Juvenal*
Sen.	Seneca the Elder, Latin rhetorical writer, c.50 BCE–c.40 CE
Con.	*Controversiae*
Sen.	Seneca the Younger, Roman politician, philosopher and tragedian, 4 BCE/1 CE–65 CE
Ben.	*De Beneficiis* (*On Benefits*)
Dial.	*Dialogues*
Ep.	*Letters*
S.E., M.	Sextus Empiricus, Skeptical philosopher and physician, probably late 2nd c. CE, *Adversus Mathematicos* (*Against the Professors*)
Sid. Apoll., *Carm.*	Sidonius Apollinaris, politician and writer, 5th c. CE, *Carmina*
Sirm.	*Sirmondian Constitutions*
Socr. *Hist. Eccl.*	Socrates of Constantinople, Greek historian, 5th c. CE, *Ecclesiastical History*
Sopater	Sopater, Greek rhetorical writer, 4th c. CE
Soranus	Soranus, Greek doctor, c.60–130 CE
Gyn.	*Gynecology*
Quaest. med.	[Soranus] *Medical questions*
Soz., *Hist. Eccl.*	Sozomen, Greek historian, 5th c. CE, *Ecclesiastical History*
Stat.	P. Papinius Statius, Latin poet, c.45–96 CE
Silv.	*Silvae*
Theb.	*Thebaid*
Stob.	Joannes Stobaeus, Greek anthologist, probably early 5th c. CE
Strabo	Strabo, c.64 BCE–after 20 CE, *Geography*
Suet.	*Suetonius, Latin biographer, c.70–c.130 CE*
Aug.	*Augustus*
Cal.	*Caligula*
Claud.	*Claudius*
Dom.	*Domitian*
Gal.	*Galba*
Jul.	*Julius Caesar*
Nero	*Nero*
Otho	*Otho*
Tib.	*Tiberius*
Ves.	*Vespasian*
Vit.	*Vitellius*
Tac.	Tacitus, Latin historian, c.56–after c.118 CE
Agr.	*Agricola*
Ann.	*Annals*
Dial.	*Dialogue on Orators*
Germ.	*Germania*
Hist.	*Histories*
Tert.	Tertullian, Latin Christian writer, c.160–c.240 CE
Adv. Prax.	*Against Praxeas*
An.	*de Anima* (*On the Soul*)
Apol.	*Apology*
Spec.	*On Spectacles*
1–2 Thes	*First and Second Letters to the Thessalonians*
Thom. Mag.	Thomas Magister, Byzantine scholar, 12th–13th c. CE
Thuc.	Thucydides, Athenian historian, 5th c. BCE
Ulpian	Domitius Ulpianus, Roman jurist, early 3rd c. CE
Val. Max.	Valerius Maximus, Latin writer, 1st c. CE

Varro	M. Terentius Varro, Latin scholar, 116–27 BCE
Rust.	*de Re Rustica* (*Concerning Rural Life*)
Veg., *Mil.*	Flavius Vegetius Renatus, Latin military writer, probably late 4th c. CE, *de Re Militari*
Vell. Pat.	C. Velleius Paterculus, Latin historian, b. c.19 BCE, *Roman History*
Verg.	Vergil, Latin poet, 70–19 BCE
Aen.	*Aeneid*
G.	*Georgics*
Ecl.	*Eclogues*
Victorinus	Victorinus of Pettau, bishop and scholar, d. c.303 BCE, *On the Book of the Apocalypse*
Xen. Eph.	Xenophon of Ephesus, Greek novelist, 2nd c. CE, *The Ephesian Story*
Zonaras	Johannes Zonaras, Byzantine historian, 12th c. CE, *Epitome of the Histories from the Creation to 1118*
Zos.	Zosimus, Greek historian, late 5th–6th c. CE, *New History*

Jewish Sources for the Roman Imperial Period in Languages other than Greek and Latin

[*2 Bar*] *2 Baruch* (*Syriac*) – R.H. Charles, *The Apocalypse of Baruch* (London: Macmillan, 1918)

[*b* with name of tractate] *Babylonian Talmud* – Printed edition (Wilna: Romm, 1880–6)

Mishnah [*m* with name of tractate] – Based on Ms. Kn, Hungarian Academy of Sciences, Ms. A 50, from the library of David Kaufmann; facsimile edition by George Beer, The Hague, 1929; reprinted in smaller format (Jerusalem: Mekorot, 1968); Herbert Danby, *The Mishnah* (Oxford: Oxford University Press, 1933)

MMT (*Miqts'at ma'assei ha-torah; 4Q394-9*) – Elisha Qimron and John Strugnell, eds., *Qumran Cave 4* (Discoveries in the Judaean Desert 10. Oxford: Clarendon Press, 1994)

Sifra – Isaac H. Weiss, *Sifra de-ve Rav hu sefer Torat kohanim* (Vienna: Shlosberg, 1862); Jacob Neusner, *Sifra: An analytical translation* (2 vols.; BJS 138–40; Atlanta: Scholars, 1988)

[*Sir*] Ben Sira, *Wisdom of Ben Sira* – Joseph Ziegler, *Sapientia Iesu Filii Sirach* (Septuaginta: Vetus Testamentum Graecum 12:2. Göttingen: Vandenhoeck and Ruprecht, 1965)

[*t* with name of tractate] *Tosefta* – Saul Lieberman, *The Tosefta* (5 vols. New York: Jewish Theological Seminary, 1955–88)

Yerushalmi (*Palestinian Talmud*) [*y* with name of tractate] – Printed edition (Venice: Bomberg, 1523–4); Jacob Neusner, ed., *The Talmud of the Land of Israel: A preliminary translation and explanation* (35 vols. Chicago: University of Chicago Press, 1982–94)

GenR (*Genesis Rabbah*) – J. Theodor and Ch. Albeck, *Midrash Bereshit Rabba: Critical edition with notes and commentary*, 3 vols., Jerusalem 1965

The Emperors of Rome from Augustus to Constantine

(excluding minor children raised to the rank of Augustus who did not reign as Augustus in their own right)

Augustus	31 BCE–14 CE
Tiberius	14–37
Caligula	37–41
Claudius	41–54
Nero	54–68
Galba	68–69
Otho	69
Vitellius	69
Vespasian	69–79
Titus	79–81
Domitian	81–96
Nerva	96–98
Trajan	98–117
Hadrian	117–137
Antoninus Pius	137–161
Marcus Aurelius	161–180
Lucius Verus (co-emperor with Marcus)	161–167
Commodus	180–192
Pertinax	193
Didius Julianus	193
Septimius Severus	193–211
Caracalla	211–217
Geta (co-emperor with Caracalla)	211
Macrinus	217–218
Elagabalus	218–222
Alexander Severus	222–235
Maximinus	235–238
Gordian I	

The Emperors of Rome

Gordian II (co-emperor with Gordian I)	238
Pupienus and Balbinus	238
Gordian III (Caesar to Pupienus and Balbinus)	238
Gordian III	238–244
Philip	244–249
Decius	249–251
Gallus	251–253
Aemilianus	253
Valerian	253–260
Gallienus (as co-emperor with Valerian)	253–260
(as sole emperor)	260–268[i]
Claudius II	268–270
Vaballathus	269–271[ii]
Aurelian	270–275
Tacitus	275–276
Probus	276–282
Carus	282–283
Carinus	283–285
Numerian (co-emperor with Carinus)	283–284
Diocletian	284–305[iii]
Maximian (as Caesar)	285–286
(as Augustus)	286–305
Constantius I (as Caesar)	293–305
Galerius (as Caesar)	293–305
Constantius I (as Augustus)	305–306
Galerius (as Augustus)	305–311[iv]
Severus (as Caesar)	305–306
Maximin Daia (as Caesar)	305–310
Constantine (as Caesar)	306–308
Severus (as Augustus)	306–307
Maximin Daia (as Augustus)	310–313
Licinius (as Augustus)	308–324
Constantine (as Augustus)	308–337
Crispus (son of Constantine Augustus) (as Caesar)	317–326
Licinius (son of Licinius Augustus) (as Caesar)	317–324
Constantine (son of Constantine Augustus) (as Caesar)	317–337
Constantius II (son of Constantine Augustus) (as Caesar)	324–337
Constans (son of Constantine Augustus) (as Caesar)	333–337
Dalmatius (nephew of Constantine Augustus) (as Caesar)	335–337

i   From 260–274 large portions of the empire to the west and north of the Alps were subject to a breakaway regime consisting of Postumus (260–269), Marius (269), Victorinus (269–271), and Tetricus (271–274). Two other individuals, Laelianus (269) and Domitianus (271?) also claimed authority in this part of the empire, but Laelianus was killed by Postumus and actual evidence for Domitianus is presently limited to two coins and a passing reference in two texts, both of which claim that he rebelled against Aurelian, which may imply that his "reign" should be dated to 274 rather than 271.
ii Only in the eastern provinces.
iii From 286–296 portions of the western provinces were controlled by Carausius (286–293) and Allectus (293–296; Britain only).
iv Maxentius claimed the title Augustus in Italy from 306–312, he was not recognized as a member of the official college of Augusti.

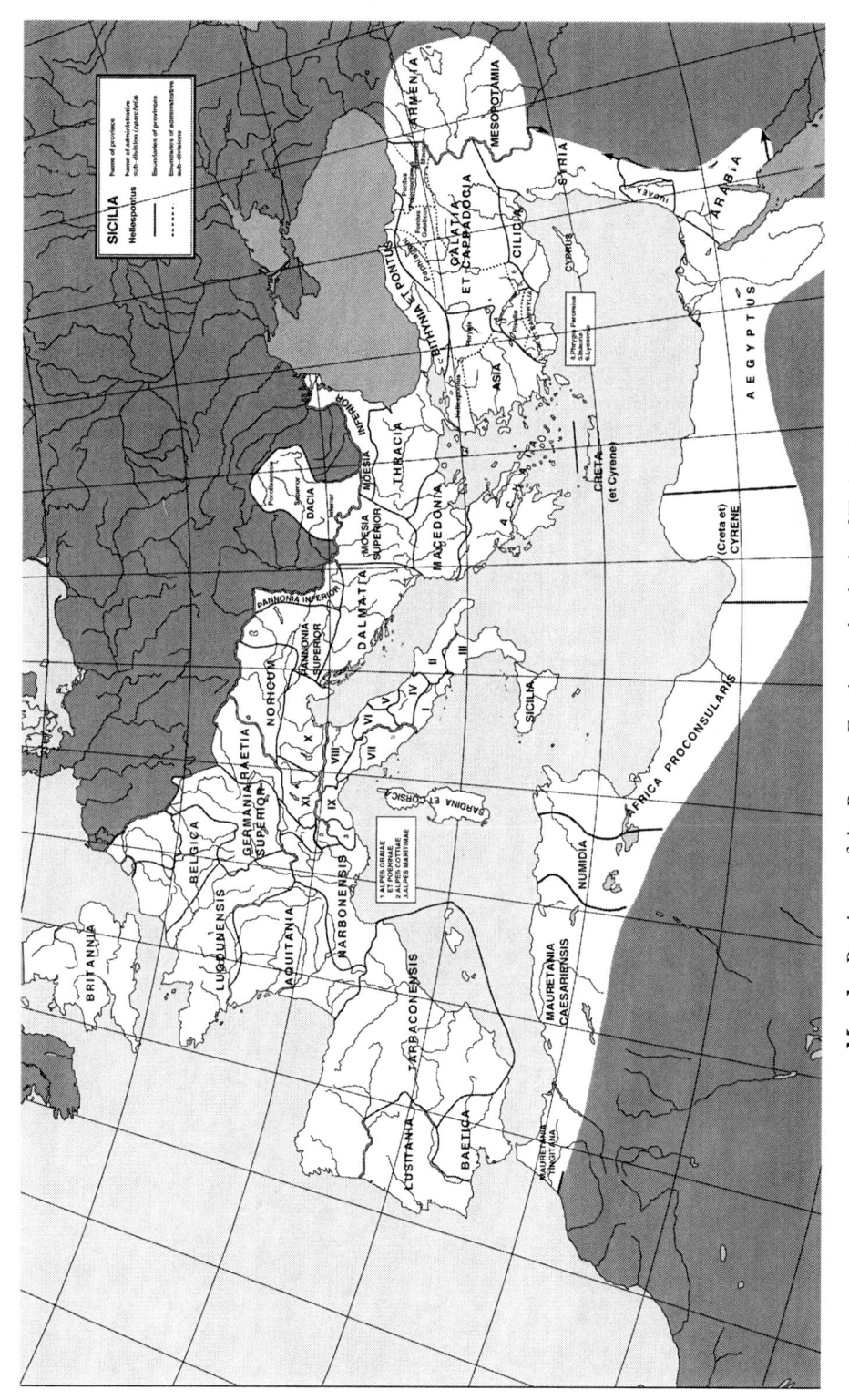

Map 1 Provinces of the Roman Empire at the death of Trajan (AD 117)

INTRODUCTION

The Shape of Roman History: The Fate of the Governing Class

David S. Potter

If this book had been commissioned in the late eighties as opposed to the late nineties, it would have had a very different shape. Fifteen years ago, historians of the Roman world were in the process of dismantling the hierarchical structure of their subject that had endured since the beginning of scholarly discourse about the Roman Empire. In the late sixties and early seventies, scholars began to move away from work concentrating on the dominant social and political group that had produced the bulk of the surviving literature. They were experimenting with the possibility that groups such as women, slaves, children, peasants, the urban poor, and even soldiers might have a history that was not dictated solely by the interests of people like the younger Pliny. Work by archaeologists, epigraphists and papyrologists had begun to show how it was possible to recover voices from outside the literary tradition. Even within the traditional, philological core of the subject there were signs of change. It was in the late sixties that lively debate erupted over the nature of the Greek literature of the Roman Empire. Characters like Galen, Aelius Aristides, and Pausanias became worthy subjects of research as excavation and epigraphic discovery restored the cities in which they had lived and worked. In the late seventies biographical approaches to Roman emperors encountered a massive challenge in Fergus Millar's *Emperor in the Roman World*, which proposed, for the first time, a model for the interaction between emperor and subject that transcended the personalities of individual rulers (Millar 1977). At roughly the same time, two other developments were changing the scope of the subject. One was the growth of interest in "Late Antiquity," which fueled interest in broad areas of social and intellectual history. The other was Moses Finley's work on the economy of the ancient world. His work became the focal point of a debate between archaeologists who studied the evidence for trade and historians who questioned whether any amount of empirical data could overthrow an approach based on a theoretical model.

Recent approaches to the Roman Empire, drawing as they do upon work done in other areas, continue a long tradition of cross fertilization and methodological innovation. The reason for this is that much of the most important work in the past century has been done by scholars who have been able to stand outside the standard curricula of the institutions where they have been employed. They have had to do so because interest in the period after Augustus, or, at least, after the death of Trajan, rarely corresponded to any course of study routinely offered to undergraduates. Lacking literature that was deemed "great" after the death of Tacitus, the study of Rome in later periods nevertheless attracted attention because it raised profound historical questions: how did the empire sustain itself, why did it fail, and how did it deal with the diverse peoples that had come under its rule?

1 Ronald Syme and the Study of the Elite

Interest in the Roman Empire as a model for other empires goes a long way towards explaining traditional concern with the governing class. In the past century, the most substantial contributions in this area came from the pen of Ronald Syme. His brilliantly erudite studies both of the members of this class, and of the ways in which they described their interests, set a standard against which other work was measured. In 1939 Syme shattered prevailing modes of thought about Roman history that were based upon the constitutional theories of Theodor Mommsen, which had been dominant for the previous half century. In Mommsen's view the Romans had elaborate constitutional rules, and the crisis of the late republic stemmed from efforts of democratic reformers to overthrow a corrupt aristocracy. This was the theme of his Nobel Prize-winning *Römische Geschichte*. When it came to the imperial period, as John Matthews shows in his chapter in this volume, Mommsen's great contribution was his *Römisches Staatsrecht*, which traced the evolution of public law and administration from the republic to the empire.

It was to the structures that Mommsen created in the *Staatsrecht* that Syme reacted. Syme felt that rules mattered little, that the constitution was no more than a "screen and sham"; reformers and their enemies were cut from the same cloth, for "whatever the form and name of government, be it monarchy, republic or democracy, an oligarchy lurks behind the façade" (Syme 1939: 15, 7). Because his Augustus was a thug who seized power in a civil war, and held on to it through the careful manipulation of factional politics, he was comprehensible in a world where the naked exercise of power was coming ever more to be the norm, where meaningful historical study needed to cut through layers of propaganda to get at hidden truths. The painstaking study of the people who controlled land and offices, and of how they passed power among themselves replaced analyses of legal questions, because legality seemed to matter little to a generation that had seen Stalin promulgate a constitution for the Soviet Union, Mussolini proclaim a new vision of the Italian future that drew on the reconstructed physical remains of Rome's past, and Hitler's democratically elected government come to power in Germany.

Influential though his work would become, Syme would always remain something of an outsider to the Oxford establishment. He had come from New Zealand, and he remained deeply conscious of his origins. Before he wrote the *Roman Revolution*, he drafted a book on provincials at Rome, and would later produce an eloquent series of essays comparing the experiences of provincials under Roman rule with those of

Spanish and British colonists in America (Syme 1958b, 1999). But that was still to come. When he arrived at Oxford in the early twenties, he rapidly attracted the hostility of Hugh Last, then the dominant figure in Oxford Roman history and devoted to Mommsen's mode of analysis (Bowersock 1994: 548, 552); consequently, he derived inspiration more from the work of continental scholars than from his colleagues.

When Syme began his career, a number of scholars were making the transition from traditional constitutional history to the study of dynamic interactions between members of the governing class, and, in what is a remarkable fact of intellectual history, there was no identifiable connection between the leaders of this movement. The reason for this is that all were reacting in their own way to the same perceived crisis in the historical profession, which

> Stemmed from the near exhaustion of the great tradition of Western historical scholarship established in the nineteenth century. Based on a very close study of the archives of the state, its glories had been institutional, administrative, constitutional, and diplomatic history. But the great advances in these areas had been made... (L. Stone 1972: 113)

The new movement began to take shape in 1913 when Charles Beard antagonized the American historical community by producing his brilliant *An Economic Interpretation of the Constitution of the United States*, in which he argued that responses to federalism in the United States were closely linked to the economic interests of those participating in the debate (Novick 1988: 96–7). Although Beard's book created a stir in the United States, none of the major players in Europe seem to have read it. His concerns were not those of Friedrich Münzer, another, albeit wealthy, outsider to the establishment – he would end his life in a concentration camp – who was even then transforming the study of ancient prosopography from an antiquarian to an historical enterprise. His work was an imaginative development emerging from countless articles on members of the Roman aristocracy for the *Real Encyclopaedie der Klassischen Alterumswissenschaft*, as well as the masterful work of Paul de Rhoden and Hermann Dessau on the first edition of the *Prosopographia Imperii Romani*, which was completed in 1898. Münzer sought patterns linking different groups within the aristocracy, for ways that aristocratic groups could dominate the political scene across generations through extra-constitutional means. He knew, perhaps better than anyone, that certain families could control the highest offices of the Roman state for generation after generation. They did not do so from deep-seated attachment to the principles of law, but rather through their ability to create factions that enabled them to exert control. The result of Münzer's analysis, *Römische Adelsparteien und Adelsfamilien*, was published in 1920, and remained unknown to Lewis Namier, who developed his own style of prosopographical analysis to study the parliaments of the mid-eighteenth century. Syme had not read Namier's fundamental *The Structure of Politics at the Accession of George III* when it appeared in 1929, and would not read it until after he had finished *The Roman Revolution* (Bowersock 1994: 548–9). Even the most casual reader of the two books will see that they are very different in scope. Namier does not attempt a narrative; rather, he studies the diverse reasons that men entered parliament, the different sorts of people to be found there, and the interests that drove each group. In so doing, he undermined the notion that parliament was divided strictly between Whigs and Tories – but no master narrative emerges from his study. In a sense Namier's book is closer in style to yet another book that Namier had not read (though Münzer and Syme did), Matthias Gelzer's *Die Nobilität des römischen Republik* of 1912, a masterful study of the structures of family power and aristocratic interaction in both the public and private spheres. It was Syme's genius that enabled him to join contemporary German scholarship with English traditions of narrative historiography, and it was his profound interest in the literary quality of narrative that set his work apart from that of Münzer, and, indeed, of Gelzer, whose later books on major figures of the late republic seem rarely to unite the conclusions of *Die Nobilität* with his own narratives. The extraordinary ability to combine social analysis with narrative that is characteristic of Syme's early work is equally evident in his masterful *Tacitus* (1958a), a book that remains fundamental to all studies of Roman historiography (Bowersock 1994: 556).

2 Michael Rostovtzeff: The Clash of Town and Country

For Syme, Roman history was shaped by the people at the top. Women, slaves, peasants and the like existed to buttress their power. The sheer brilliance of his analysis cast into the shadows an earlier work that was no less influenced by the catastrophic events of the earlier twentieth century, Michael Rostovtzeff's *Social and Economic History of the Roman Empire* (Rostovtzeff 1957, originally published in 1926).

While Syme's style of historiography could flatter the egos of scholars who might insist on passing judgment upon the foibles of great figures of the past, it also offered some comfort to all who wished to see evil as the product of individuals. By focusing attention on the emperors and those around them, Roman historians tended not to ask how they got away with it. Surely Tacitus saw through it all, and his history could be read as if it were the work of some proto-Solzhenitsyn, exposing foibles of the regime that all discerning observers could agree upon. Sadly such a view would not have much in common with that of Tacitus. Tacitus thought that the imperial system was the inevitable result of the failure of government in the last centuries BCE. His governing class was complicit in the acts of Tiberius, Claudius, and Nero. Tacitus saw the structure of imperial power arise from a dialogue between emperors and their subjects. Tacitus' vision shared a great deal with that of Rostovtzeff, whose basic thesis was that power arose from the people. In the first two centuries CE, Rostovtzeff's emperors supported the interests of what he termed the urban bourgeoisie, before switching direction and becoming the tools of the peasant armies they had previously kept in check, armies that shared the rural population's class hatred for those in the cities. Exploitation of the peasantry led to revolution and military dictatorship. Rostovtzeff's vision, born, as he made very clear, of his experience of the Russian revolution, and less explicitly, perhaps, of his personal relationships with some early leaders of the Bolshevik movement, did not let the people off the hook so easily as did Syme's. If things went wrong, the average person was complicit to the historical process. In Rostovtzeff's view of the empire, the peasant was just as worthy of study as was the senator.

In a sense, Rostovtzeff could be more easily dismissed than Syme. For while Syme possessed an unrivalled mastery of the details of his subject, Rostovtzeff's use of ill-defined modern terminology and admitted tendency to get his facts wrong from time to time invited dismissal of his broader vision. He could easily appear antiquated, and perhaps even a bit amateurish in his use of early twentieth-century sociology. But, even though they rarely admitted it, his critics still tended to operate within the parameters set by Rostovtzeff. One could deny that long distance trade was important, could argue that the empire existed basically at the subsistence level, but the destruction of Rostovtzeff's version of the economy left further questions in its wake. What did matter and how could historical change be explained? At the same time, some scholars began to wonder if Rostovtzeff's understanding of the ancient world, based upon personal experience of a society making a rapid transition from medieval to modern times, was all that inaccurate. Unlike many of his critics, Rostovtzeff had met illiterate peasants striving to make a living with inadequate tools, and felt the contempt of the urban dweller for the rural. Conditions of life in late nineteenth-century rural Russia were closer to those in the Roman Empire than they were to those of the mid-twentieth century.

3 The Ancient Economy: Hugo Jones, Peter Brunt, and Moses Finley

The real strength of Rostovtzeff's work was his sense that the ancient economy had to be treated within the context of ancient social relations. It took a scholar with the vast intellectual range of A. H. M. Jones to understand the true power of Rostovtzeff's analysis and attempt a creative reformation of his understanding of the ancient economy as a tool for analyzing the institutional structures of social control (A. H. M. Jones 1952: 359; Crook 1971: 426).

Jones himself was something of an outsider, though more out of choice than training or background. A product of New College, Oxford, whose brilliance won him immediate election to All Souls after he took his degree in 1926, Jones did not hold a regular academic appointment in England until 1939 (he had taught in Cairo from 1929 to 1934). That appointment, at Wadham College, Oxford, did not survive the outbreak of war (Crook 1971: 426–9). Jones returned to teaching in 1946, this time as Professor of Ancient History at University College, London, and then, from 1951 until his death in 1970 as Professor of Ancient History at Cambridge. In the mid-sixties, he was joined at Cambridge by another scholar who was also somewhat eccentric in his career choices: Peter Brunt.

Peter Brunt, who succeeded Syme as Camden Professor of Ancient History at Oxford in 1971, was unlike his predecessor in that he had an affection for Hugh Last, and a strong interest in the history of ideas as well as the structures of Roman society. Like Syme, however, Brunt was something of an outsider, the son of a Methodist minister and a scholarship student at Oriel College, Oxford. Indeed, it was discomfort with the prevailing trend of Roman history at Oxford in the fifties and sixties that caused him to resign his tutorial fellowship in ancient history at Oriel to take up the position of bursar at Gonville and Caius College, Cambridge. Armed with a sympathy for members of the lower class, and a powerful analytic capacity whose resources he readily deployed to demolish the fanciful constructions of others while offering potent alternatives of his own, his work spanned Classical Greek, republican Roman, and imperial history. It was a span very similar to that of Jones, whom he greatly admired. For, although Jones may be primarily remembered for his monumental study of the institutional history of the later Roman Empire, his studies of the Greek city and various aspects of the economy were markedly different in tone and direction from Syme's, and resonated with Brunt's concern for the lower classes of republican Italy.

Brunt differed from both Jones and Syme in his belief that the history of ideas could be written independently of the people who had those ideas – that there were traditions of Stoic thought, for instance, that could shape the way that people explained the world around them, and motivated their actions (not surprisingly, perhaps, Brunt had been, in his youth, a much better student of philosophy than many ancient historians). The interests of Jones and Brunt melded with the interests of Moses Finley (more below) to suggest a middle ground between Syme's style of analysis and Rostovtzeff's. In a series of brilliant articles Brunt began to ask just how the government managed. What did procurators really do? What did senators do? And, in his great work on Roman population of 1971, Brunt offered an empirical look at the issue of Roman demography. While the demographic aspects of this book now seem dated in light of the application of modern demographic methods to the ancient evidence pioneered by Bruce Frier, and now championed by a new generation of scholars, the originality of Brunt's questions at the time that he asked them cannot be underestimated (Bagnall and Frier 1994; Frier 1982). Demography had previously been the province of Karl Julius Beloch, a genius who was kept from an appointment in his native land by Mommsen, and Arnold Toynbee, who had brilliantly, if improbably, argued that the destruction of Italy under Hannibal led inexorably to the fall of the Roman Republic even as Brunt was writing *Italian Manpower* (Momigliano 1966b [1994]: 104; A. J. Toynbee 1965). Unlike either of his predecessors, Brunt used the study of census returns as the basis for studying how Roman society extended across Italy and into the provinces.

Moses Finley was, like Brunt, a man whose contributions to ancient history range far beyond the Roman imperial period. His intellectual precocity is evident from the fact that he took a degree in psychology at Syracuse University at the age of fifteen (Whittaker 1996: 460). Moving on to Columbia, where he took an MA in public law, he met his future wife, a classicist, and enrolled in the PhD program in ancient history (Whittaker 1996: 461). At the time that he finished his graduate work, Jews were not readily welcomed in the East Coast establishment that dominated American academe in the first part of the century. The consequence was that he obtained a position at Rutgers in 1946 rather than at a major research university, and that he was left unprotected when the scourge of McCarthyism struck (Whittaker 1996: 462–4). In the wake of his genuinely heroic resistance to McCarthyism, which cost him his job at Rutgers, he moved into the little more welcoming environment of the British university. The move was possible thanks to the intervention of the brilliant Greek historian, Tony Andrewes, a product of Winchester and New College, who lived up to his liberal ideals (and was, at the same time, supporting the career of another brilliant

Jewish scholar, the epigraphist David Lewis). Indeed, Finley finished second to Lewis for the studentship (as tutorial fellowships are termed there) at Christ Church in 1955, the same year that he was elected to a lectureship at Cambridge, conjoined, two years later, with a fellowship at Jesus College.

Finley arrived in England with a mind unfettered by the constraints of the British curriculum. He had initially been trained in the study of modern, and then ancient, law at Columbia, and his first book had been on Greek boundary stones. But he had rapidly moved beyond his training, aided by conversations with others at Columbia, and made his reputation with a brilliant study of the economic attitudes evident in the Homeric poems. He was a natural comparative historian. His greatest contribution to the subject was not his use of the work of Karl Polanyi to study the ancient economy; it was rather his ability to inspire others to take equally innovative approaches. In terms of the study of the ancient economy, the chapters that David Mattingly and Dennis Kehoe have contributed to this volume show how the evidence does not sustain the strict "primitivist" line advocated by Finley, who essentially theorized A. H. M. Jones' observation that wealth was held in land, or the "modernist" approach suggested by Rostovtzeff's overt comparisons with the modern world. Mattingly argues from the archaeological evidence for the movement of goods that the economy of the Roman Empire was extraordinary by the standards of the pre-modern world in terms of the links that it forged between regions, a view that largely supports Rostovtzeff's arguments, while conceding that the attitudes towards the accumulation of capital were far different from those of early modern Europe. Kehoe's chapter traces the conservative attitudes of landholders who saw their investments in land as preserving social status, and prevented the Roman economy from developing to its full potential.

Despite criticisms that may be leveled at their conclusions, the work of Syme, Finley, and Rostovtzeff retains the interest of current practitioners because of their ability to achieve the seamless unity of different styles of scholarship. In Rostovtzeff's case, his lasting contribution to scholarship was his insistence on studying material culture alongside the evidence of texts of all sorts (Rives, this volume). By the time he arrived at Wisconsin, having been turned down in his application for the Camden chair of Ancient History in Oxford, Rostovtzeff was already at work on the Zenon archive, had written on Roman art, and made his reputation as an original scholar in a study of the late Roman colonate. His last years before retirement from Yale, where he greeted at least one new student with the statement that she needed to know epigraphy and he would teach her, were spent directing the excavation of Dura Europus (Potter 2001: 320).

4 Arnaldo Momigliano and the History of Ideas

The weakness most evident in the work of Syme, Rostovtzeff, and Finley is in the history of ideas. This is most striking in Syme's work as, unlike the others, he wrote so often about the practice of history, but only in relation to the study of politics. Less convincing, from a literary point of view, were his comments on Augustan poetry in *The Roman Revolution*, or his studies of Ovid's exile poetry. While *History in Ovid* remains a vital study of the circumstances under which Ovid wrote, Syme demonstrated no interest in the actual interpretation of his poetry (Syme 1978). So too, while he often offered stimulating remarks on other writers of the imperial period, these were largely restricted to analysis of the circumstances of composition and literary influences. The history of ideas in antiquity was much more the province of Peter Brunt, and, above all, of yet another displaced person, Arnaldo Momigliano. Perhaps the greatest strength of Momigliano's work was his ability to place ancient thought in the context of the overall history of ideas. In so doing he often directed attention away from the dominant classes, and towards those excluded from the discourse of power.

An early dalliance with fascism ended when Momigliano's Jewish ancestry became known to the authorities (Bowersock 1991: 35). He was fired from his position at the University of Turin and sought refuge at Oxford in 1939, where he joined a remarkable community of exiles, and received assistance from, among others, Hugh Last, who appears to have seen Momigliano as a sort of antidote to Syme (Bowersock 1993: 548; Murray 1991: 52). Momigliano more than lived up to Last's hopes, even though, for several decades, his seemed a lone voice crying in the wilderness. In the end, however, his efforts shaped a new area of inquiry for Roman historians. Momigliano's interest in ideas for their own sake led him away from "mainstream" classics into the history of religion, especially Judaism and Christianity. He made the study of Christianity a subject that historians of antiquity could no longer ignore, and his influence sparked interest on the part of a new generation of historians in what had previously been labeled the later Roman Empire. Although the study of "Late Antiquity," as the history of Rome after Constantine came to be called under the influence of Momigliano and Peter Brown, lies outside the scope of this volume, it is impossible to think about the subject as it now stands without considering the impact of this development on Roman history as a whole. The term itself derives from the realm of art historians, and that points perhaps to one of the most important aspects of its study – for in the hands of late-antique historians, the study of the visual assumed a vastly greater place in mainstream studies of social consciousness than it had in the past (Rives, this volume). This is not to say that some historians, especially Rostovtzeff, did not have an eye for ancient art, or a sense for the importance of iconography – Stephan Weinstock's extraordinary *Divus Julius* is a case in point – but it tended to be relegated to the fringes, and Weinstock himself was a refugee from Nazi Germany (Weinstock 1971). A sense of how radical a step this was may be gleaned from the pages of Jones' *The Later Roman Empire*, a two-volume work with no plates and no index entries for "art" or "iconography" (A. H. M. Jones 1964). Likewise Syme, although he did publish an article on the identification of young men on the *Ara Pacis*, had only a minimal interest in the subject (Syme 1984). For scholars of their generation the study of the physical remains of antiquity was essentially a study of topography, as may be seen in Jones' *Cities of the Eastern Roman Provinces*, or Syme's *Anatolica*, a work that he never finished (A. H. M. Jones 1971; Syme 1995). A consequence of this disinterest was that the study of iconography by English-speaking historians of the high empire lagged far behind that of the late empire, where it had come to the fore under the influence of Peter Brown, until Paul Zanker's splendid *Augustus und die Macht der Bilder*, appeared as *The Power of Images in the Age of Augustus* in 1988.

The interdisciplinary approach to late antiquity that was pioneered by Momigliano and Brown resonated with the work that Finley inspired in Cambridge. Although

Finley's own essays on Roman history were largely concerned with slavery and the economy (barring a very early piece on Roman law that he wrote while he was a student at Columbia), his broad interests inspired students to look beyond the ancient world. Like Momigliano, he invited scholars to think of ancient history as participating in a dialogue with other forms of pre-modern historiography. In yet another instance of the importance of disciplinary cross-fertilization for the development of Roman imperial history, the historiography of those whose voices have only indistinctly survived took on new immediacy for the study of the imperial period thanks largely to work in Greek and late antique history. Another crucial aspect of Momigliano's legacy was simply the fact that historians could no longer ignore either the history of religion, or of non-Roman peoples living in the empire. They had especially to become aware of the vast bulk of literature that survived within the Jewish tradition. In this volume Yaron Eliav offers a splendid analysis of the ways in which the historiography of Judaism in the Roman world developed and how the multiple Judaisms that flourished under Roman rule were shaped through dialogue with the imperial power. We have now to be aware of autonomous developments within the Jewish community, and of developments that were shaped by contact with classical culture. The same issue affects the history of Christianity. In the pages that follow we may see approaches to Christianity that stress its sociological and intellectual dimensions, offered by Paula Fredriksen and Mark Edwards. Even more strikingly, as Sara Ahbel-Rappe shows in her chapter on philosophy, the willingness to take religion seriously as a feature of the intellectual and social history of the empire enables us to understand how philosophy took on radically new dimensions in the course of the second and third centuries CE. Momigliano's influence may likewise be felt in the way that scholars might now want to examine historiography and fiction, two topics that are far less distinct than generic distinctions would make them seen. As Rowland Smith reminds us, historiography is not simply the product of books, but of social consciousness formed by an intellectual and physical environment. As Maud Gleason and Joseph Rife remind us, Roman hegemony could actually foster a sense of Greekness, for instance, as being something to be proud of. Cultural traditions could help shape the imaginative world of the Greek novel, whose dichotomies mirror those of the social world in which they were composed every bit as much as do the attitudes that Smith describes.

5 Louis Robert and the Greek World of the Roman Empire

Our ability to understand the dynamic nature of imperial culture owes a great deal not only to Momigliano, but also to the work of a great French epigraphist, Louis Robert. In many ways, Robert's ability to integrate realia of all sorts to recreate the social imagination of residents of Roman Asia Minor has done more than anything to lay the foundation for contemporary work on Rome's relationship with its subjects. Robert inherited traditions of epigraphic analysis from scholars such as Adolph Wilhelm and his own teacher, Maurice Holleaux, but he took it to new heights. It was largely thanks to Robert's work that it became possible for scholars to see how the careful study of groups of inscriptions could transform their knowledge of social relationships within the ancient city. Robert showed how seemingly mundane events like athletic contests, gladiatorial combats, or the establishment of a festival could illuminate the concerns of ancient society as a whole. He showed how the evidence of different media could be combined to recreate the experience of ancient life. His studies of civic cult rewrote not only the religious history of the empire, but also our understanding of how different groups within the empire interacted with each other. His examination of decrees for governors enabled scholars to think in new ways about the impact of imperial government, while his analysis of cities revealed the real impact of the Roman peace, as ever more people came to participate in and define for themselves the culture of the elite. In terms of the history of religion, Robert made it absolutely clear that the traditional view that new religious movements arose when civic cult ceased to answer the basic needs of its practitioners is simply false. In this volume, Fredriksen, Eliav, and David Frankfurter allow us to gain a sense of how traditional cult continued to flourish and how it shaped other traditions. Robert also showed how the study of literature could benefit from detailed understanding of the civic society that supported its authors. In the English-speaking world, understanding of this point was vastly enhanced by the work of Glen Bowersock, whose wide ranging intellectual interests, extending from Classical Greece to the Islamic world, have helped shape debate on topics as diverse as the nature of Greek literature under Roman rule, the relationship between Hellenism and the Semitic world, and the interaction between paganism and Christianity. It is a corpus of work that shows the creative integration of many trends that have broadened the scope of Roman history.

6 The Roman Empire in the United States

Although Bowersock has spent most of his career in the United States, the influences that helped him develop his interests, those of Momigliano, Brown, Robert, and Syme, were European. It is yet another sign of the fact that the subject as practiced in the English-speaking world has been shaped in British universities, albeit often by professors from abroad. The failure of the United States to produce a similar ferment derives from a number of factors. One was the abiding influence of Tenney Frank, the most significant American-trained historian of the first half of the twentieth century. Although known these days as the editor of the multi-volume *An Economic Survey of Ancient Rome* (1936–40), Frank was primarily interested in the history of the Roman Republic. This interest was shared by his two great pupils, Lily Ross Taylor and Bob Broughton, both at Bryn Mawr College, until Broughton's departure for the University of North Carolina in the mid-sixties (Potter 2001: 317–21). A separate tradition would soon afterwards begin to take shape at Berkeley, where Erich Gruen, an iconoclastic student of Harvard's Mason Hammond, inspired a generation of students to share his interests in both Republican and Hellenistic history.

Concentration on the republic was a natural development of the North American undergraduate curriculum, in which authors from the "central period" of Latin literature were the primary fare. Unlike European universities, where ancient historians worked within their own faculties, most ancient historians in the United States worked in departments of classics. What is more, even though most history departments had an ancient historian (sometimes two) on their faculties, the linguistic demands of the subject made the training of graduate students largely the business of classics departments. Before the 1980s, when classics departments discovered that teaching classics in translation could save them from budget cuts, many ancient historians in these departments did not teach ancient history except in courses on ancient authors, while those who taught in history departments were constrained by the need to offer survey courses for history concentrators. When historians of either stripe sought to teach upper level courses, those courses needed to suit the curricular demands of classics departments. Even in the mid-eighties the view that Roman history ended with the death of Nero was not considered a joke in at least one major American classics department. The result was that when American universities wanted to hire historians of the Roman Empire, they had to turn to foreign universities to fill their staffing needs. The sixties and early seventies saw the arrival of a remarkably talented group of scholars at major graduate institutions such as Berkeley, Harvard, Princeton, Toronto, Chicago, North Carolina, and Columbia who were able to breathe new life into the subject. The one notable exception to this rule was at Yale, where another former Harvardian, Ramsey MacMullen, gradually won the admiration of his colleagues abroad with an astonishing output of extraordinarily original scholarship. Finally, of course, there was the issue of the budget. The old style courses on Greek and Roman civilization gave rise to demands for more – for courses on women, sexuality, slavery, religion, law, and spectacle to name but a few – with the result that American universities have now become hotbeds of innovation.

The growth of interest in social history that has helped shape the study of the ancient world in American universities has led to profound changes in the way the subject is now viewed. As I suggested above, if I had been asked to edit this book in 1990 rather than 1999 there would have been chapters on women, slaves, children, peasants, the urban poor, etc.; that is to say, it would have looked rather more like Andrea Giardina's volume, *The Romans* (1993a), than it does. The reason for this is simple. The evidence for diverse groups in the Roman world has been assembled. The thrust of work for the future seems to me to be the interaction between different groups, and the closer collaboration between colleagues working in areas that have, for one reason or another, remained distinct. Roman historians can no longer afford to ignore the vast bulk of Roman legal writings, literary scholars are increasingly drawn to the study of literature within its social context, and documentary papyrologists no longer confine themselves to the realm of paleography, where the great Herbert Youtie once placed them, but have moved into social history, as Traianos Gagos shows in his contribution. We have learned that we cannot readily write about the experience of women or slaves without consideration of social class and physical location. We cannot assume that there was a single experience of slavery, gender, or rural or urban poverty. In the chapters that make up this volume, the authors have sought to stress interactions. As Veronika Grimm shows, for instance, the study of food now more often becomes the study of its consumption, and the study of its consumption reveals a great deal about those who are doing the eating. As she points out, dining was central to religious, family, and social life. The study of dining cannot simply be dealt with through the analysis of food production, for which there are, in any event, no statistics, but rather must be examined as a function of social, political, and ideological discourse. Only then may we gain some understanding of the basic question of "who ate what." The experience of gender identity may now be profitably studied through examination of sexuality or the institution of marriage, as Amy Richlin and Judith Evans Grubbs both show. Equally importantly, as Richlin and Evans Grubbs show in their very different ways, there is no single set of attitudes towards sexuality, and there is no single model for married life. Indeed, Richlin's "Kinsey" report on sexuality in the Roman world is a stunning antidote to many earlier approaches. Even a subject such as the Roman army, once almost a subdiscipline hermetically sealed off from all others in the field has now come, as Nigel Pollard shows, to offer a paradigm for social relations of all sorts. In addition to the stress on dynamic interaction, one theme that ties many of the chapters in this volume together, thereby differentiating it from what might have been done earlier, and will, perhaps, be done at another time, is that we have shifted from the study of dominance alone to the discourse of dominance and inferiority.

7 Dominance and Inferiority: The Case of the Senate

What is the difference between narratives of dominance and narratives of dominance and inferiority? It is the difference between a narrative that stresses the activities of the powerful as opposed to the negotiation of power between the powerful and the less powerful. It is to stress that the exercise of power was not straightforward, that what often seem to be straightforward relationships are, on further reflection, bound by complex rules of engagement between different groups and individuals within them.

The importance of seeing relationships between different groups as existing outside "the external structures of law and economy," was stressed in a crucial article on the *Life of Aesop* by Keith Hopkins in 1994 (Hopkins 1994: 27). Hopkins argued that the *Life of Aesop*, the only work to preserve a slave's perspective, revealed that "each master and slave had some freedom of maneuver to act in accord with his or her capacities, opportunities and interests" (Hopkins 1994: 27). Hopkins' observation crystallized thinking about the negotiation of power relationships that had begun to have a significant place in scholarship during the previous decade, as evidenced in a brilliant study of slaves in the Roman family by Richard Saller, of literary patronage by Jasper Griffin, or analyses of political patronage and client choice by Peter Brunt and Andrew Wallace-Hadrill (Saller 1987; J. Griffin 1984; Brunt 1988: 351–81, 382–442; Wallace-Hadrill 1990). Many of the chapters in this volume offer a sense of discourse about power, or the structures that distinguished the obviously powerful from the less obviously so.

In traditional terms, it is established that a person who pursued a senatorial career would follow a set path, established in the course of the reign of Augustus. A young man who desired to do this would have to come from a family with property valued at either 1 or 1.2 million sesterces, with his landed property divided up into a number of different estates, consisting, as Dennis Kehoe shows, of a central villa staffed by slaves set amidst a group of tenant farms. These estates guaranteed family status, and the protection of that status often dictated a rather conservative economic outlook: the primary concern of the largest landholders was to preserve what they had. If they sought to increase their wealth, they would most likely do so through marriage to another wealthy family in their home district, a pattern illustrated in Evans Grubbs' discussion of the multiple marriages of the younger Pliny. These links were extremely important in creating a nexus of relationships that drew the local aristocracies, both eastern and western, into direct relationship with the governing class and helped shape the ambitions of these classes. Even though, as the chapters by Jonathon Edmondson and Maud Gleason show, the history of urbanization in the eastern and western parts of the empire was very different, there was a powerful urge for local magnates to ensure that their cities were felt worthy of respect in the imperial system. To do so the members of these elites sought private links with members of the imperial aristocracy, and at the same time sought to make their cities worthy of those links by enhancing the urban space.

If a young man chose to enter the Senate, and the emperor felt that he was worthy, he would be given the right to wear the *latus clavus*, or broad stripe, with his toga, and would be expected to hold a preliminary position, one of a group of 20 minor officeholders on one of four boards. These included the board of three for overseeing the mint, the board of four for overseeing the streets of Rome, the board of ten for judging inheritance cases, or the board of three for overseeing executions. He might also be expected to serve as a military tribune (this seems certainly to have been the case prior to the mid-second century). At age twenty-five all members of one year's class of minor magistrates would be entitled to hold one of the 20 quaestorships that were available. In the next five years, the majority of ex-quaestors would hold further office, either as tribune of the plebs (there were still ten of these, the number inherited from the republic) or the aedileship (of which there were six under the Augustan dispensation), and possibly command a legion as a legate of the emperor. At the end of the five year period after the quaestorship, a man could hold one of the 12 available praetorships (as of 14 CE; there were 18 by the end of the century). The years after the quaestorship were plainly the "make or break" point in a career. Even though it might be expected that one in a class of 20, given ancient conditions of mortality, would not live to age 30, there were too few offices to go around. Forty percent of the men who entered the Senate could not rise to the praetorship After the praetorship, there was even greater attrition. A man of patrician standing might expect rapid preferment and a consulship; if he did not achieve this, there was a further ten-year gap before he could hope for the office that traditionally marked the culmination of a successful public life. Although Augustus had begun the practice of appointing replacement (suffect) consuls so that four men might attain the office in one year, a number that expanded to six by the time of Nero and seven under the Flavians, the majority of praetors would still never ascend so high. Only a third could do so under the Augustan dispensation, and still usually fewer than half in later periods. In the interim, ex-praetors were the backbone of the administration in jobs ranging from road commissioner to treasury officer or even general. These jobs were not easy, and determination of success or failure resided with the emperor alone.

In light of the emperor's control over the markers of aristocratic success, it is not surprising that we may detect various efforts to control his reactions. As both Greg Rowe and Michael Peachin show, there was enormous pressure from below to define the imperial state and exercise control of the broad outlines of its development. The idea of the "good emperor" who took his responsibilities towards the senatorial class seriously and showed respect for the traditions of the Senate, remained a powerful force from the first century to the end of the second. The space between the emperor's needs and those of senators, keen to preserve their status, was a matter for constant negotiation. Thus, for instance, Asinius Gallus asked Tiberius to nominate 12 candidates for the praetorship five years in advance of the time that they would hold office, at the time in which they were assigned legionary commands. Tacitus said that there was no doubt but that this proposal went deeper than the surface and probed the secrets of imperial power. The point that Tacitus was making – and presumably Gallus as well – was affirmed by Tiberius in his response:

> It was a matter disagreeable to his modesty to reward and disappoint so many. It was scarcely possible to avoid offense in a single year, even though one year's disappointment could be made good the next: how much greater would the offense be to men who were put off beyond the five year period? How was it possible to foresee what the mental capacity, family situation and fortune of each man would be so far in advance? Men became arrogant even when they were designated for office a year in advance: what would happen if they had the office for five years? The number of magistrates would be quintupled, the laws stipulated the time for exercising the industry expected of candidates for soliciting or enjoying preferment would be subverted. (*Ann.* 2.36.2–3)

Tiberius was being rather more clear than Tacitus allows (he said that Tiberius was concealing the secret of power through his refusal of the proposal). An emperor was bound by his word, just as Tiberius says. Once he had made an appointment he was expected to live up to it. To grant favors so far in advance would do precisely what Tiberius said it would do: it would enable people to take preferment for granted. As Gallus realized, the Augustan system meant that members of the aristocracy had to compete for the emperor's favor in order to gain further office. The point of the Augustan creation of a host of new positions reserved only for senators of a certain rank was to transfer the arbitration of senatorial success from the Roman people to the emperor. Members of the Senate plainly found the long periods between offices in which they would be expected to prove themselves, over and over again, tedious. In 16 CE when Gallus made this motion, Tiberius was only in the third year of his reign, and men may already have been finding it difficult to discern what his mood would be. His managerial style was different from that of Augustus, who was notably accessible to members of the upper class. Tiberius was less open, and seemed prone to take offense. It was also the case, in the wake of the massive disaster that the Roman army under Varus had suffered in Germany at the end of 9 CE, that any job as a legionary legate was likely to be especially dangerous. The danger was compounded by the fact that Germanicus Caesar, the emperor's adoptive son was, with erratic success, commanding a third of the army in Germany, an army that had mutinied two years before; another significant portion of the army, now commanded by the emperor's biological son, Drusus, had mutinied at the same time. By appointing young men to legionary commands, Tiberius was asking a great deal of them, and Gallus was simply asking that he recognize this by relieving them of the additional fear that some failure would not end their careers. What Gallus was asking was typical of what the slaves in the *Life of Aesop* asked of their masters: that they set reasonable expectations, that they establish clear rules, and that they abide by them. It was true in an even broader way that these slaves might share with their masters (tacitly) an understanding that their sense of self-worth and future prospects were out of their control if these rules did not exist.

The speech that Tacitus attributes to Tiberius gets at the heart of senatorial self-understanding in yet another way, for the Tacitean Tiberius seems aware that office holding and preferment define the self-worth of the individual. Disgruntled men who are passed over were no figment of the imagination. For some, of course, a career that ended with the praetorship could be a very fine thing. It seems to have been so for Velleius Paterculus who saw the joint nomination of himself and his brother to that office in 14 CE by Augustus as a great moment (Vell. Pat. 2.124.4). For others, as Werner Eck has shown in a masterful treatment of the evolution of senatorial self-understanding, inscriptions commemorating a career through detailed enumeration of offices attested to the importance of each rung on the ladder (Eck 1984). Such texts were unknown in the republic; their style might have been inspired by the *elogia* that Augustus had inscribed on the bases of the statues of the "greatest men" in Roman history with which he decorated his forum. But the Augustan decision to inscribe memorials of the dead in this way can only go so far in explaining the habit of the living to make sure that the same was done for them. There could be no greater disgrace than to have one's name removed from records of one's accomplishments. Thus it was that erasure, virtually unknown to the republic, became a regular feature of penalties stemming from the declaration of the condemned as an enemy of the state. The point of an erasure was not simply to eliminate a monument – this could more readily be done by destruction and/or reinscription without the offending name. It was rather to leave a memorial of the fact of the disgrace in public places.

To the senatorial mind the holding of offices, if successfully accomplished, should necessarily entail imperial respect. The virtues of the senator were hard work and frugality. They earned their offices by working at the jobs that were necessary to learn their craft. There was something wrong if they did not. Dio notes that Avidius Cassius, who briefly led a revolt against Marcus Aurelius, was a good man in every way, save that his father, Heliodorus, had achieved the prefecture of Egypt (one of the highest posts available to an equestrian) as a reward for his oratorical talent alone (72.22.2). Contrast the brothers Quintilius Condianus and Quintilius Maximus who "had the greatest fame for learning, military skill, mutual affection and wealth" (73.5.3). He admired Clodius Pompeianus, a man so respected by Marcus that he allowed him to marry his widowed daughter Lucilla, formerly wife of Marcus' co-emperor, Lucius Verus. Even Commodus at his worst had to respect him. Pompeianus alone refused to attend the *ludi Romani* in which Commodus acted the part of both a beast hunter (*venator*) and gladiator on the grounds that he could not bear to see a son of Marcus act that way (73.21.1). Cassius Dio did go to the games and noted a colossal breakdown in the mutual respect owed the Senate by the emperor and vice-versa. Commodus waved the head of an ostrich at the portion of the stands occupied by the Senate, suggesting that he could do to them what he had done to the ostrich. Disgraceful as the emperor's conduct may have been, it would have been wrong – dangerous in Dio's view – to laugh at him (73.21.2). When Commodus was murdered, his successor, Pertinax, himself a senator whose ability enabled him to rise to the highest rank despite the fact that his grandfather had been a slave, displayed the appropriate conduct. He brought Clodius Pompeianus to the

Senate – Dio records that this was the only time that he actually saw the great man in the flesh – and treated him with honor (74.3.2–4). Just as Commodus had to allow Pompeianus to offer him a moderate insult (Pompeianus did at least send his sons to the *ludi Romani* to avoid a total rupture in the relationship) because of his standing, so too were all emperors supposed to be governed by the collective judgment of merit. Tacitus tells of a moment in 21 CE when Sextus Pompeius, consul in 14 CE, tried to have Manius Lepidus removed from the lottery for the provinces of Africa and Asia on the ground that his personal life made him unworthy of the office – but the Senate opposed him because the majority took a different view (*Ann.* 3.32.2). Tiberius respected the view of the Senate and let Lepidus stand for Asia. Lots for these provincial offices were now cast for only one man at a time: the rank of the province was supposed to match the collective judgment of the worth of the man.

The issue of one's right to office remained important for centuries after Tiberius. In the brief reign of Macrinus (217–18 CE), Dio tells of Domitius Florus, "who should by right have been appointed aedile" and was deprived of all hope because he had been too close to Plautianus. Plautianus had been praetorian prefect and chief advisor to Severus, before he was suddenly deprived of his office and life on a bogus charge of conspiracy. In 217, 12 years after the fall of Plautianus, Florus finally achieved the next rank on the ladder of preferment – a tribunate of the plebs. Both he and the men who supported his claim clearly cared deeply about this (79.22.2). Severus' judgment was felt to have been unfair. In another case, however, Severus' judgment plainly conformed to the general opinion. Severus had passed over a man named Anicius Faustus when he was eligible to become governor of Asia. Dio says that Macrinus offered a terrible affront to Julius Asper when he appointed Faustus in Asper's place. Asper had been twice consul and previously governed the province of Africa. Since two emperors had judged him worthy of the highest offices, and his peers agreed that he deserved them, Macrinus had no business demoting him. Furthermore, since he had so fouled up the appointment process, he allowed Faustus a second year to make up for the short term. This meant that he had to deny the office to Aufidius Fronto, who had been appointed to the post by Caracalla. Worse still, he tried to mollify Fronto by offering him the salary that would have gone with the job, a million sesterces, to stay at home. Fronto refused, saying that he wanted the office rather than the money (79.22.3). Equestrian offices – Macrinus had never been a senator – were graded by salary, and Macrinus clearly thought that the gift of the salary would stand for the office. This was a clear sign to Dio that Macrinus simply did not understand how senators thought.

To achieve distinction was no easy thing. Dio makes it plain that a senator needed both to be respected by his peers and to have that respect recognized by the ruler. Their lives were filled with constant testing, and occasionally desperate balancing acts between the interests of class and those of the ruler. To prosecute another senator on a potentially capital charge was a very dangerous thing. It could gain the favor of an emperor who was interested in making sure that his subjects were well ruled, but it could alienate colleagues who realized that the government of a province was fraught with social peril. The jurist Ulpian, who wrote a handbook on how to govern a province, quoted the emperor Septimius Severus as advising that a governor should not remain aloof from his subjects, but that he should be careful when taking gifts: neither everything, nor all the time, nor from everyone (*D.* 2.6.3). Ulpian elsewhere stresses both that the governor is second only to the emperor in the province, and that he is constrained to respect his subjects in a wide range of official and semi-official interactions. If a man put his foot wrong too many times, he could be ruined. As Maud Gleason suggests, "mutual suspicion and the power imbalance tended to poison relations between the governors and the governed." Furthermore, as Clifford Ando shows, mutual suspicion was compounded by the tendency of local elites to try and draw the imperial authorities into disputes where they had very little background, and where the support staff would be totally inadequate to find out everything that needed to be known.

The issues for locals who felt that they were being oppressed, and for senators who had to adjudicate their complaints, were often very different. For senators, trials raised questions not only of proper moral behavior, but also of the standing of the body as a whole. Even in the case of a man whom all could see was guilty, senators had to be careful not to be seen to be "piling on," lest it look like they were currying favor rather than doing their job: if a man was guilty it was sufficient simply to make the case; people need not line up to acquire credit by adding their redundant voices to the prosecution. This would seem to be the point that Tacitus made in describing the trial of Gaius Silanus, a former governor of Asia. The man was plainly guilty of brutality and corruption, "but many things were piled on that would have been dangerous even to an innocent man" (*Ann.* 3.67.2). Tacitus' point was not that Silanus should have been released, but that the feeding frenzy was excessive. Tacitus knew well of what he spoke: he was the prosecutor in the case of Marius Priscus, a notoriously corrupt governor of Africa (Pliny *Ep.* 2.11).

The danger inherent in overstepping the bounds of propriety are evident in a letter that the younger Pliny wrote about his prosecution of Caecilius Classicus for corruption as governor of Baetica. Pliny goes to great lengths to show that he was not a willing participant in the action. First of all the province, remembering his service as prosecutor of Baebius Massa, a previous governor, whom Pliny claimed was even worse than Priscus, asked him to serve. Pliny's colleagues in the prefecture of the treasury, a post-praetorian office he was then holding, told him not to touch the case. Although Pliny does not say as much, this would have been three prosecutions in three years, possibly giving the impression that he liked this sort of thing. Then, however, the Senate passed a decree saying that Pliny should be prosecutor, which got him off the hook for being too willing. Finally, he adds, there were two other considerations. One was that having been a patron of the province he had to continue doing so, "for it is well known that you undercut earlier favors, if you do not add new ones to them. For, no matter how often you are asked, if you deny just one request, the only thing people remember is what you refused to do" (*Ep.* 3.4.6). Finally, Pliny notes that there was an advantage in that the defendant was dead, "and thus was removed that which is most pitiful in cases of this sort: the peril of a senator" (*Ep.* 2.4.7).

Pliny's comments reflect yet another concern that afflicted senators in the struggle to maintain reputation and influence. They were expected to act as patrons for people coming up behind them. Patronage was anything but a one act show. As Pliny says, once you start doing favors, you have to continue to do so, or your clients will complain that you aren't doing your job. People had to be seen to be supporting other good people. It was through the process of recommendation that a record of senatorial opinion was constructed. In some cases we know that efforts at patronage failed. We have, for instance, a letter of the younger Pliny asking Trajan to grant the *latus clavus* to an equestrian named Voconius Romanus. He had previously asked this favor of Nerva and been turned down on the ground that Voconius was not rich enough. Nerva had noted that he would agree once Voconius had received an inheritance of 400,000 sesterces from his mother. This had come through and Pliny was trying again (*Ep.* 10.4). Pliny also asked that Trajan grant Alexandrian citizenship to his masseur, a man to whom Trajan had already granted Roman citizenship (*Ep.* 10.6). Trajan responds that he will do this once Pliny follows the proper form (*Ep.* 10.7; 10). When he was governor of Bithynia, Pliny asked an old friend of equestrian rank to join his staff because he was keen to have the help of experienced men in a province with a long history of prosecuting its governors. In repayment for the favor, this friend appears to have asked Pliny to see if he could speed up his son's promotion to the rank of military tribune, enabling him to aspire to a senatorial career. Pliny writes to Trajan that he is not alone in supporting this young man, that the man's commanders when he was prefect of a cavalry cohort thought he was a good officer (*Ep.* 10.87). In another case, Pliny asks Trajan to grant the privileges accorded the father of three children to Suetonius Tranquillus, the future biographer of the Caesars (for the technical aspects of this request see Evans Grubbs, this volume). Pliny is quite specific that Suetonius has married, but that he and his wife have been unable to have the requisite number of children. As Trajan makes plain in granting the request, this is not something that he usually does, and it is clear that if Suetonius had not met the minimum qualification of having been unfortunate in his efforts to have a family, this would have been a non-starter (*Ep.* 10.94–5). In each case therefore we can see that favors could only be asked within reason, that a person could ordinarily hope only to advance a certain distance with each request and that he had to have preliminary qualifications if the request were to be successful.

Pliny's relationship with Suetonius raises a further complexity in the business of patronage. Years earlier, Pliny had sought a military tribunate for Suetonius from Neratius Marcellus when the latter was governor of Britain in 103. The request was granted, but Suetonius decided that he did not want the office and asked Pliny to get it transferred to a man named Caesennius Silanus (*Ep.* 3.8). In other words, Suetonius was using Pliny's connections to build his own patronage network. But Suetonius would not stop there. In the first years of the reign of Hadrian he became the emperor's secretary in charge of answering letters in Latin, a far more influential position than Pliny would ever hold. It looks very much as if Pliny's patronage of Suetonius was a relationship that could potentially have benefited Pliny more than it benefited Suetonius, since the latter would some day be in a position to do greater favors for Pliny. As soon as we cease to assume that promotion within the empire was governed by rules, and assume instead that it was part of a process of establishing reputations for both patron and client, we begin to gain further insight into the dynamic process by which members of the upper class acquired status. The interest in procedure and precedent that is evident in these relationships is very much a feature of the cast of mind that Matthews detects in the officials who created Roman law. As Gleason, Edmondson, and Ando all show in their very different ways, these relationships affected not only individuals, but whole communities. We might extend this analogy somewhat further to the literary studies contributed to this volume by Sara Myers, Rowland Smith, and Joseph Rife, for they all show us how imperial authors and their audiences dealt with existing traditions to create something new. The interest in the creative handling of precedent enabled the creation of fresh visions of the past, and new forms of pleasure, as discussed by Garrett Fagan and myself in our contributions on leisure and spectacle. It is by seeing connections between modes of conduct in areas that often seem quite distinct from each other that the subject is now advancing. In a sense the history of the governing class is not so much fading away as changing to allow us to visualize broader forms of social and intellectual relationships within the empire.

PART I

The Sources

CHAPTER ONE

Constructing a Narrative

Cynthia Damon

A narrative, you notice, not *the* narrative. The object of inquiry in this opening chapter is the literary material available to a historian desiring to produce a narrative history of the Roman Empire between the assassination of Julius Caesar (44 BCE) and the death of Constantine (337 CE), the sort of thing you'll find, in fact, in Part II, "The Narrative," where the demonstrative pronoun indicates "the narrative used in this book," not "the one and only narrative." A glance at that section will make it immediately clear that literary material is only one of many components currently used in constructing a narrative, but it is an appropriate place to begin, largely because it comes closest to supplying the organizational structure essential to any narrative, namely, a chronologically-arranged account of historically significant events. Such an account will almost certainly not be an adequate history of a period (hence Parts III, IV, and V), but it is generally a useful beginning. We will see below, however, that this linear structure sometimes fails even as a beginning, that there are periods when equally significant events are occurring in two or more areas simultaneously.

The narrative that our literary sources support most readily is the sort that the ancient authors were themselves trying to produce, namely, a narrative of power. Historically significant events were, to their way of thinking, either political or military. The historian asked Who had power? and How was power used, both internally and externally? In the imperial period such questions took him straight to the emperor, the "guiding spirit," as one of Tacitus' characters put it, of "the single body of the empire" (*Ann.* 1.12.3). Tacitus himself discusses the consequence of the political structure for historiography later in the work (*Ann.* 4.32–3):

> I am well aware that many of the incidents I have narrated (and intend to narrate) seem unimportant and even trivial for a history. But one should not compare my *Annals* with the works of those who wrote on the affairs of the Roman people long ago. They treated great wars, cities being sacked, kings defeated and captured, and, when they turned to internal affairs, conflict between consuls and tribunes, laws about land ownership and the

grain dole, the struggle between the plebeian and elite orders, all with a free hand. My task, however, is narrow in compass and without glory.... Now that the nature of our state is different, and security lies only in the rule of one man, it is worthwhile investigating and reporting these things.

With "these things" he refers to events from the narrative that preceded this digression, some trials of men charged (rightly or wrongly) with various offenses against the emperor, a sorry spectacle of ambition, betrayal, fear, favoritism, obsequiousness, and hidden agendas. In other words, a far cry from victorious battles and political convulsions. But however much Tacitus may regret the focus on the emperor and the diminution of the historian's opportunities, these realities could not be denied. The literary sources examined in the balance of this chapter are grouped by genre (history, biography, summary history, limited history), but in all of them the historically significant event is generally connected with the center of power, i.e. with the emperor (Pelling 1997).

The exceptions only prove the rule. Suppose, for example, you want to know about the political situation in January of 69 CE. Tracking the emperor, Galba, will take you to Rome. There you will find that his hold on power is tenuous, since a coup is being planned under his very nose. The machinations of an erstwhile supporter and some praetorian guardsmen go unnoticed, however, since Galba's attention is drawn to another challenge to his power, this one mounted by the legions in Germany and a provincial governor. Galba's rivals, Otho and Vitellius respectively, are not acting in tandem, so the historian cannot subordinate one to the other. But a text, at least as texts are traditionally presented, cannot narrate simultaneous events simultaneously. In the best surviving account of this period, Tacitus' *Histories*, the historian reports the two coups sequentially, as he must, putting first the coup that came to fruition first, Otho's (*Hist.* 1.21–47; Vitellius' movement begins at 1.51). A different arrangement was possible. Indeed when Tacitus is faced with another set of parallel events, the two-pronged invasion of Italy by Vitellius' two commanders, Valens and Caecina, he puts second the narrative of Caecina's route, which reached Italy first (Valens: 1.63–6; Caecina: 1.67–70). Tacitus deals perfectly competently with these small challenges to the single linear narrative format. Both Otho's coup and Vitellius' were decided within a span of a few months, and the invasion of Italy took less time than that. But the political chaos of the mid-third century, roughly 235–84, posed a far greater challenge to linear narrative, with consequences to the literary tradition that will become apparent below (Potter, this volume).

1 The Sources

Roman histories, 44 BCE–337 CE

Most helpful for the construction of a narrative are works that themselves give a narrative. Those covering the period of this study are few in number and lacunose. (The coverage of the sources discussed in these first three sub-sections IA–C is summarized in Table 1.1).

Table 1.1 Coverage of Roman history by historians

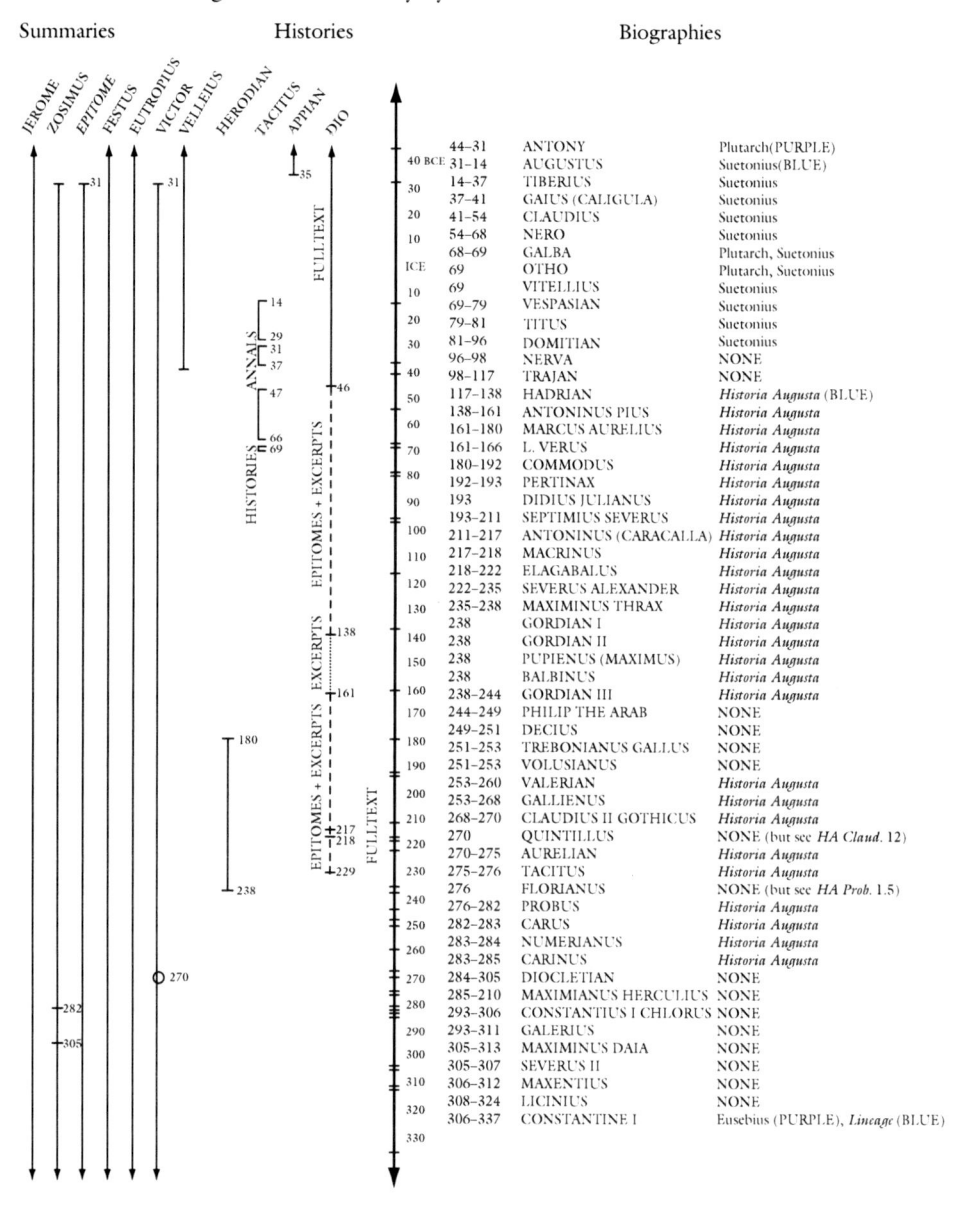

Summaries	Histories	Biographies

Date	Emperor	Biographer
44–31	ANTONY	Plutarch (PURPLE)
40 BCE 31–14	AUGUSTUS	Suetonius (BLUE)
14–37	TIBERIUS	Suetonius
37–41	GAIUS (CALIGULA)	Suetonius
41–54	CLAUDIUS	Suetonius
54–68	NERO	Suetonius
68–69	GALBA	Plutarch, Suetonius
69	OTHO	Plutarch, Suetonius
69	VITELLIUS	Suetonius
69–79	VESPASIAN	Suetonius
79–81	TITUS	Suetonius
81–96	DOMITIAN	Suetonius
96–98	NERVA	NONE
98–117	TRAJAN	NONE
117–138	HADRIAN	Historia Augusta (BLUE)
138–161	ANTONINUS PIUS	Historia Augusta
161–180	MARCUS AURELIUS	Historia Augusta
161–166	L. VERUS	Historia Augusta
180–192	COMMODUS	Historia Augusta
192–193	PERTINAX	Historia Augusta
193	DIDIUS JULIANUS	Historia Augusta
193–211	SEPTIMIUS SEVERUS	Historia Augusta
211–217	ANTONINUS (CARACALLA)	Historia Augusta
217–218	MACRINUS	Historia Augusta
218–222	ELAGABALUS	Historia Augusta
222–235	SEVERUS ALEXANDER	Historia Augusta
235–238	MAXIMINUS THRAX	Historia Augusta
238	GORDIAN I	Historia Augusta
238	GORDIAN II	Historia Augusta
238	PUPIENUS (MAXIMUS)	Historia Augusta
238	BALBINUS	Historia Augusta
238–244	GORDIAN III	Historia Augusta
244–249	PHILIP THE ARAB	NONE
249–251	DECIUS	NONE
251–253	TREBONIANUS GALLUS	NONE
251–253	VOLUSIANUS	NONE
253–260	VALERIAN	Historia Augusta
253–268	GALLIENUS	Historia Augusta
268–270	CLAUDIUS II GOTHICUS	Historia Augusta
270	QUINTILLUS	NONE (but see HA Claud. 12)
270–275	AURELIAN	Historia Augusta
275–276	TACITUS	Historia Augusta
276	FLORIANUS	NONE (but see HA Prob. 1.5)
276–282	PROBUS	Historia Augusta
282–283	CARUS	Historia Augusta
283–284	NUMERIANUS	Historia Augusta
283–285	CARINUS	Historia Augusta
284–305	DIOCLETIAN	NONE
285–210	MAXIMIANUS HERCULIUS	NONE
293–306	CONSTANTIUS I CHLORUS	NONE
293–311	GALERIUS	NONE
305–313	MAXIMINUS DAIA	NONE
305–307	SEVERUS II	NONE
306–312	MAXENTIUS	NONE
308–324	LICINIUS	NONE
306–337	CONSTANTINE I	Eusebius (PURPLE), *Lineage* (BLUE)

For the triumviral period and the reign of Augustus the best surviving narrative source is the *Roman History* of Cassius Dio, an 80-book work written in Greek by a senator and consul from Bithynia in the early part of the third century. The *History* began with the foundation of the city and ended in 229 CE, the year of its author's second consulship. Much of it is now lost, but for 44–10 BCE (books 45–54) the text is complete, and for 9 BCE–14 CE (books 55–6) it is nearly so. Dio lived some two centuries after the reign of Augustus but based his narrative on sources written nearly contemporaneously with these events. For the early part of the triumviral period (44–35 BCE) we also have Appian's *Civil Wars* (books 2.118–5.145), which end with the death of Sextus Pompeius after his defeat at the hands of Octavian. The *Civil Wars* constitute a section of Appian's *Roman History*, a war-centered narrative that takes as its theme the way Rome's wars contributed to the growth of its empire (pr. 14) and, in the case of its civil wars, to the origins of the principate (*BC* 1.6). Like Dio, but writing under the Antonine emperors, Appian was from the Greek part of the Roman world (Alexandria) and wrote in Greek. Like Dio again he had experience of public life, though his perspective was that of a financial official (he was a *procurator*), rather than of a senator and consul.

For the reigns of Tiberius, Claudius, and Nero the fullest history is the *Annals* of Tacitus, written in Latin early in the second century CE. Tacitus, too, was a senator of consular rank; his origin seems to have been in the western part of the empire (Syme 1958a: 611–24). As the title suggests, the *Annals* present Roman history in a year-by-year format within the larger division of imperial reigns (Tiberius in books 1–6, Claudius in books 11–12, Nero in books 13–16). The narratives for each year vary in length (the longest is 49 chapters [14 CE], the shortest, three chapters [57 CE]; the average is 17 chapters per year) and focus (domestic politics: Senate meetings, trials; imperial bureaucracy; dynastic intrigues; diplomatic efforts; military affairs: campaigns, seditions, foreign invasions, etc.), but are fuller than anything else we have. To a greater degree even than in Dio's *History* the senatorial viewpoint of the author dominates the selection and presentation of material, so that there is a constant tension between the necessary focus on the emperor and the historian's sense of Rome's political past, when the Senate and an ever-changing parade of aristocrats ran the state (Smith, this volume). The *Annals* have come down to us missing a section of Tiberius' reign (29–31 CE), all of Gaius' and the beginning of Claudius' (37–47), and the end of Nero's (66–8). Where Dio's *Roman History* is substantially complete (14–46 CE, books 57–60) the gaps in Tacitus can be filled. But after book 60 the manuscript tradition of Dio lapses and our "text" becomes a congeries of excerpts and summaries preserved by other authors (see further below).

Tacitus also supplies, in his *Histories*, a detailed account of the troubled year 69 CE with its four emperors (Galba, Otho, Vitellius, Vespasian) and the beginning of the Flavian dynasty. The *Histories'* five extant books (389 chapters) go only as far as the autumn of 70; for the rest of the Flavian dynasty (69–96: Vespasian, Titus, Domitian), and for the Antonine (96–192: Nerva, Trajan, Hadrian, Pius, Marcus Aurelius, Commodus), and part of the Severan periods (193–235: Septimius Severus, Caracalla, Macrinus, Elagabalus, Severus Alexander) we rely again on the remnants of Dio's *Roman History*. Dio's record of the reign of Pius (138–61), in particular, is very thin indeed, owing to the loss of this section in the work of his principal epitomator, Zonaras (see Dio 70.1.1). For the latter part of this period Dio was himself a participant in public affairs; starting with the reign of Commodus, he says, his facts are drawn "not from the accounts of others but from my own observation" (72.4.2).

For the reigns of Commodus, the Severans, and the short-lived emperors who preceded Gordian III (238) there is also contemporary testimony in Herodian's *History of the Empire from the Time of Marcus,* a work written in Greek, perhaps under Gordian's successor, Philip the Arab (244–9): "a systematic account of events...covering the reigns of several emperors, of which I have personal experience" (2.15.7). As with all of the authors discussed so far, so with Herodian public service informed his history (1.2.5), but we cannot now ascertain his office(s) or rank. He mentions, as an additional guarantee of fidelity, that his initial audience was itself familiar with the events reported (1.1.3), but neither his access to information (via personal experience and written sources) nor his rhetorical style (which tends to the colorful) is such as to make his work as useful a source for the purposes of constructing a chronological narrative as others in this section.

Our list of narrative histories ends here, nearly a century before the death of Constantine. In the middle of the third century the historiographical tradition in which Tacitus, Appian, Dio, and Herodian wrote fell into abeyance, not to be revived until the end of the fourth century, with Ammianus Marcellinus, whose *History* began (in its original state) with Nerva (31.16.9), where Tacitus' *Histories* (again, in their original state) left off. (The former has lost its beginning, the latter its end.) Another type of source helps fill some of the large gaps in the narrative tradition.

Biographies

The biographical tradition is a rich one. The concentration on the emperor noted above in connection with the narrative tradition is given free rein in imperial biographies, which survive for every emperor from Augustus to Constantine except Nerva, Trajan, a cluster of short-lived emperors in the middle of the third century (see Table 1.1), and Diocletian and the Tetrarchs. Their quality varies enormously (see below). The principal collections are Suetonius' *Caesars* (Julius Caesar to Domitian) and the *Historia Augusta* (Hadrian to Carinus). Plutarch adds *Lives* of Galba and Otho, and, for the triumviral period, an important biography of Octavian's opponent Antony. Constantine is the subject of two biographies, one by his contemporary Eusebius, Bishop of Caesarea, the other by a now-unknown author writing at the end of the fourth century (oddly titled *The Lineage of the Emperor Constantine*, since it focuses on the years of Constantine's reign, 305–37). Besides the imperial biographies (and the fairly unreliable biographies of imperial heirs and rivals in the *Historia Augusta*; see below) there is also a biography of C. Julius Agricola by his son-in-law Tacitus, which focuses on Agricola's conquests in Britain under the Flavians (77–84).

Biography is a less-than-ideal contributor to narrative since its organizational principle is generally topical (background, education, career, achievements, virtues, vices, idiosyncrasies, personal appearance, etc.) rather than chronological. And biographies of successive emperors inevitably overlap. The information considered relevant may also be different from that suitable to histories: Plutarch, for example, eschews "the accurate reporting of everything that occurred," which he calls "the stuff of political history," in favor of the memorable deeds and experiences of the emperors (*Life of Galba* 2.3). Not surprisingly, both he and Suetonius omit from their respective biographies of Otho military campaigns led by subordinates rather than by the emperor himself, while Tacitus in the *Histories* records both (1.79, 2.12–15). At the other end of our period we find that the political history of the last decade of Constantine's reign cannot be reconstructed from the literary sources alone, despite his two biographies (Averil Cameron 1997). On the other hand, the biographical genre allows for the inclusion of documents in a way that history proper does not, a feature to which we owe some precious items preserved by Suetonius (especially letters of Augustus) and some wild forgeries in the *Historia Augusta* (see, e.g., Syme 1968: 60–5 on a "letter of Hadrian" and Potter 1999a: 200 n. 86 for a partial list).

Suetonius' 11 imperial biographies – the 12 *Caesars* commence with Julius – supply some of the history that is lost in the gaps in the texts of Dio and Tacitus for the period from Augustus to Domitian. Like Tacitus, Suetonius wrote in the early second century CE. He was not a senator, but a man of equestrian rank who rose through the imperial bureaucracy to be an important secretary ("head of department") under Hadrian (Wallace-Hadrill 1983). The *Lives* are fullest at the beginning of the series, while the treatment of the Flavians (where Dio is fragmentary and Tacitus lost) is disappointingly brief. Much of historiographical value can be learned by comparing Suetonius' biographies of Galba and Otho with those of Plutarch and with Tacitus' narrative treatment of the same period (*Hist.* books 1–2; Damon 2003, Appendix 1).

Forged documents are only the tip of the problematical iceberg that is the *Historia Augusta*. Though it offers *Lives* of some 20 emperors, five imperial heirs who never became emperor, and 40 pretenders to imperial power (the first and last numbers are rounded because the labels "emperor" and "pretender" are artificially simplistic in this period), and though it is the fullest source for many of these reigns, it has to be used with great caution. To list the problems briefly:

1 Authorship and Date: Although the *Historia Augusta* purports to be written by six different authors in the time of Diocletian and Constantine, it is now agreed, with few dissenters, that the work was written at the end of the fourth century by a now unknown author under six different pseudonyms.

2 Purpose: Why this elaborate charade? No good answer has been found.

3 Sources: Citations are given both to actual (now lost) sources and to sources that never existed (Syme 1971a: 1–16; 1983: 98–108). Furthermore, some of the work's sources (e.g. Herodian) are not named (Potter 1999a: 146). There may have been no useful sources for short-lived emperors such as Quintillus (whose very brief reign is incorporated in that of his brother Claudius II Gothicus [*HA Claud.* 12]) and for imperial heirs and rivals, whose *Lives* tend to be derived from the *Life* of the relevant emperor. But an absence of information did not prevent composition. The *Lives* of emperors in the Antonine and early Severan periods are generally accounted more reliable than the later ones; the *Lives* of Macrinus (an interloper in the Severan dynasty) and the last of the Severans, Alexander, are counted with the latter group. Scholarship on the *Historia Augusta* and on the history of the third century has done much to identify the facts in this work that stand up to scrutiny, facts that are of some use for the purpose of constructing a chronological narrative (Peachin and Potter, this volume). Extensive reliance on this source, however, is certainly perilous.

Between them narrative histories and imperial biographies provide us with information (of varying quality) about most of the years between the death of Julius

Caesar and the death of Constantine. To fill in the remaining gaps (the reigns of Philip the Arab and his successors, and of Diocletian and his co-rulers) and to supplement the record where it is thin (on Nerva, Trajan, Pius, and the whole period for which the *Historia Augusta* is the sole authority), we have recourse to texts that cover the whole of this period (and a good deal more) within an abbreviated (sometimes extremely brief) narrative.

Summary histories

The earliest of the summary histories belongs to the reign of Tiberius. In the space of two books Velleius Paterculus, a soldier and senator, treats the history of Rome from the mythological period to 29 CE. The scale of discussion expands as he gets closer to his own time; the chapters relevant to our period are 2.59–131. The work is dedicated to one of the consuls of 30, a family connection, and is highly flattering to the emperor Tiberius, under whom Velleius served on numerous campaigns. Its contemporary and pro-Tiberius point of view makes a sharp and useful contrast with the darker colors of the Tiberian books of Tacitus, Dio, and Suetonius (Smith, this volume).

Not until the fourth century is there an extant successor to Velleius for the imperial period, but here we find four. The first (by ending point) is Sextus Aurelius Victor's *Book on the Emperors*, which runs from Augustus through Constantius II (361, with a small gap in the text around 270 (from the end of Claudius II through Quintillus to the beginning of Aurelian). Victor was a member of the imperial bureaucracy and served as governor of a Pannonian province (360s) and as urban prefect in Rome (388/9). The starting point for his work is "the end of Livy" (preface; actually, 31 BCE), but its scope is much reduced: each emperor gets about a paragraph (long or short). Eutropius' *Abbreviated History of Rome* is about half the length of Victor's book for the imperial period, but begins with the foundation of the city and carries the narrative up to (but not into) the reign of Valens (364–78), by whom it was commissioned (preface), covering in all 1118 years (10.18). He describes his work as a chronological arrangement of "the outstanding achievements of the Romans, in war and peace ... and the distinctive elements in the lives of the emperors" (preface). Valens also commissioned the third work, the even shorter *Abbreviated History* of Festus, which has the same *termini* as Eutropius' work and was completed in 369/70. Festus promises a text so brief that Valens will be able to "count the years and events of Roman history" without having the trouble of reading much about them (ch. 1). Besides being brief, Festus' work is uneven in its coverage, allotting more space to the provinces and conflicts with Parthia/Persia than to Rome and Italy. Hence it is (relatively) abundant on Augustus and Trajan (see below), but omits the long reign of Antoninus Pius (138–61) altogether. From the very end of the fourth century comes the *Epitome on the Emperors*, a work similar in scope to Victor's by a now unknown author. Beginning with the reign of Augustus, it continues into that of Theodosius, ending in 395. A later work in this category is the early sixth-century *New History* of Zosimus, written after the dissolution of the Western Empire by a pagan author to chronicle, in a mirror-image of Polybius on Rome's growth, Rome's decline. From Augustus through the Severan dynasty its coverage is very brief indeed; thereafter it is increasingly (but irregularly) detailed, and has lost its section on Diocletian. The work ends, unfinished, at 410 CE.

Just how abbreviated these summary histories are can be seen from the number of *words* they devote to the reigns of a sampling of emperors:

Trajan (98–117): Victor 312, Eutropius 405, Festus 86, *Epitome* 298, Zosimus 1
Pius (138–61): Victor 92, Eutropius 137, Festus 0, *Epitome* 222, Zosimus 4
Philip the Arab (244–9): Victor 222, Eutropius 50, Festus 9, *Epitome* 72, Zosimus 477 Diocletian (284–305): Victor 1058, Eutropius 775, Festus 126, *Epitome* 176, Zosimus 0 (lost)

Some patterns emerge (e.g. Festus is always briefer than Eutropius, Zosimus' detail increases as time goes on; his narrative on Diocletian is a particularly unfortunate loss), but variation is also evident, as in Victor's surprisingly voluminous (relatively speaking) narrative on Philip the Arab and the *Epitome*'s surprisingly brief section on Diocletian. All of these accounts are interrelated by derivation from common sources, but each contributes unique information – sometimes erroneous or fictitious, but more often useful – to our understanding of the imperial period.

Even briefer than the summary history is the "chronicle" genre, the most influential representative of which for our period is Jerome's Latin translation of (and supplement to) Eusebius' (lost) Greek *Chronological Canons with an Epitome of Universal History, both Greek and Barbarian*. For a period running from the birth of Abraham (2016 BCE) to 378 CE Jerome gives synchronized timelines (e.g., for the imperial period, Olympiads, an emperor's regnal year, years from the birth of Abraham) accompanied by brief notes on political and cultural history. His criteria for selection are somewhat broader than those of the summary historians – the emperors yield a little historiographical territory here – but his reports are generally very brief. Under Tiberius' reign, for example, consecutive entries include: a fire in the Theater of Pompey at Rome, the political advancement of Tiberius' son Drusus, Drusus' death by poison, the death of a noted orator at the age of 90, the suicide of someone on trial, city foundations by a client king in the Near East, and the appointment of Pontius Pilate as governor of Judaea. Jerome's report is complete in 57 words, exactly as many as I have used here. Eusebius' chronicle ended at 326; in about 380 Jerome supplemented the historical portion of the work and added the years 327–78.

Somewhat different in nature from both summary history and chronicle is the epitome, an abbreviated version of (generally) a single source. An early example is the book-by-book epitome of Livy known as the *Periochae* (*Summaries*). Livy's books on the triumviral and early Augustan periods are lost, but the *Periochae* give us a glimpse of them – only the merest glimpse, however, since a whole book of Livy is sometimes summarized in as little as a sentence or two. From book 138, for instance, all that remains is "The Raeti were defeated by Tiberius Nero and Drusus, Augustus' stepsons. Agrippa, Augustus' son-in-law, died. A census was conducted by Drusus." Another epitome source for the triumviral period is Florus' *Epitome of Seven Hundred Years' Worth of Wars*, which begins with Romulus and ends in the reign of Augustus (2.13–34 is the portion relevant to this book). Florus, who wrote in the second century, focuses on Rome's wars and applauds their renewal under Trajan after a too-long period of peace (pr. 8). Where possible he arranges his material by the theater of war: under Augustus, for example, he has separate sections on wars in Noricum,

Illyricum, Pannonia, Dalmatia, Dacia, Sarmatia, Germany, Spain (two sections), and Armenia. On the Alpine campaign mentioned in the epitome of Livy 138 he reports, "Augustus pacified all the peoples in that part of the world – the Breuni, Ucenni, and Vindelici – through the wars of his stepson Claudius Drusus," and adds a brief anecdote about the ferocity of Alpine women. Dates are few. Much more useful than either of the above is the *Epitome of the Histories from the Creation to 1118* by John Zonaras. Writing in twelfth-century Byzantium, Zonaras draws on several texts, including Dio for long stretches, and abbreviates less severely. Where Zonaras' text has gaps our knowledge of Dio becomes vanishingly small (e.g. the reign of Pius), but his is one of the longest reports on the reign of Diocletian (12.31–2).

Limited histories

Long or short, full or thin, the works mentioned in the preceding sections all treat wide swaths of imperial history and, with the exception of Jerome, focus on things Roman. The works mentioned briefly and for the sake of example here lack one or the other trait, or both. An important work with a narrow chronological scope is Josephus' *Jewish War*, which narrates a single war in a single Roman province, but does so with the advantage of personal involvement (Josephus commanded troops against the Romans at the beginning of the war and spent its later years as a prisoner in the Roman general's entourage). The bulk of the work (books 1–6) is spent on five years' events (66–70); Book 7 continues the narrative of the rebellion's somewhat sporadic course (including the siege of Masada) subsequent to the fall of Jerusalem (see further Smith, this volume). Narrowness of focus rather than chronological scope characterizes works such as Eusebius' *Ecclesiastical History* (from Jesus to the fourth century) and Orosius' *History against the Pagans* (from creation to the early fifth century). In both works the events of Roman history reported are tangential to the author's main purpose: Eusebius was sketching the history of the church, Orosius trying to show that life was worse before Christianity. Lactantius' *On the Deaths of the Persecutors* is limited in both temporal scope – principally 303–13 CE – and purpose: pointing to the moral that those emperors who persecute the Christians pay in the end. It is nevertheless an important source for the political history of Rome in that period, giving, to cite just one example, a detailed account of the abdication of Diocletian in 305 (18–19). Many more works could of course be mentioned here, but it is sufficient to have indicated the category.

Reckoning together all of the literary sources, we have some information about the whole of the period between the death of Caesar and the death of Constantine. Most richly documented is the early Julio-Claudian period, for which we have Tacitus' *Annals*, Dio (complete), biographies by Suetonius, the contemporary report of Velleius, and two epitomes of Livy's last books (not to mention all of the later summary histories). Next best is the period from Commodus to Elagabalus, where in addition to contemporary reports by Dio (whose full text of the years 217–18 is preserved in a somewhat damaged manuscript of 79.2–80.10) and Herodian, we have reasonably reliable biographies in the *Historia Augusta* and six summary histories. In about 222, however, the evidence begins to thin: first the *Historia Augusta*'s quality falls off, then Dio's text ends, then Herodian ends. From 238 up to the reign of Constantine the literary sources are frustratingly scant.

2 Source Criticism

Beyond determining the genre, length, and focus of the various strands of the literary tradition, the historian needs to assess their reliability. What is a text's purpose? What are its sources of information? How good are those sources? How does it use the sources? What is the state of its transmission and preservation? And so on. This scrutiny, or source criticism, allows the modern student to use the available information effectively and to cope with conflicting information. A historian's answers to source criticism questions will of course depend on his or her own purpose in writing. Our focus here is simply on the capacity of the sources mentioned above to supply the chronological backbone, so to speak, of the imperial period (for a broader treatment see Smith, this volume).

The question of purpose is basic. Sometimes an author supplies the answer, or at least *an* answer. Eusebius' *Life of Constantine*, for example, was written as "an unstinting account of good things" (1.10.2), particularly of deeds "dear to God" that fell outside the normal scope of political and military history (1.11.1). Eusebius' purpose is explicitly laudatory ("unrestrained praises in varying words" 1.11.2) and the work as a whole is designed as a counterweight to the histories that record the misdeeds of emperors such as Nero (1.10.2). "Good things" do not include the execution of Constantine's eldest son Crispus or the (forced?) suicide of his first wife Fausta, which are accordingly absent from the biography, though attested elsewhere (e.g. Jerome on 328 CE "Constantine killed his wife Fausta," one of three entries for the year). Given Eusebius' purpose in writing, the omission of these events in the *Life* does not in itself cast doubt on the authenticity of reports elsewhere on the deaths of Crispus and Fausta. The dedications to the emperor Valens that open the summary histories of Eutropius and Festus provide similarly helpful information (see above). Frequently, however, and particularly with full-scale histories, there is less to guide us. Reputable historians, as Tacitus tells us in the preface to his *Histories*, are responsible to the truth (1.1.4), not to a patron or the powerful. We would like to believe him, but at no period during the empire does a historian give evidence of being able to feel what he wants and say what he feels, particularly about contemporary events. Tacitus, who asserts that such was the happy condition of the historian under Nerva and Trajan (*Hist.* 1.1.4), did not write about Nerva or Trajan. And Tacitus was aware that there was danger in writing even on non-contemporary events, as is shown by his extended discussion (*Ann.* 4.34–5) of the fate of the historian Cremutius Cordus, who died under Tiberius for his history of the end of the republic. The first question to ask, then, is whether the writer can tell the truth about an event, should he happen to know it.

The second, of course, is whether he can know it (Potter 1999a: 79–119). We do have some contemporary reports: Velleius on parts of the reigns of Augustus and Tiberius, Dio and Herodian on the reigns of Commodus and the Severan emperors, Eusebius on Constantine. Josephus was a participant in the Jewish War of 66–70, Lactantius a contemporary of the persecutions he reports in the greatest detail. Tacitus, Plutarch, and Suetonius were alive, but not yet adult, during some of the periods they reported on; they will have had access to surviving contemporaries. But contemporary evidence, even when obtainable, is necessarily shaped by the prevailing political climate, particularly in authors (e.g. Velleius and Josephus) writing about emperors who are still alive. Few did so.

Authors writing and publishing after their subjects are safely dead depended on earlier (now lost) narrative sources, sometimes a chain of such sources. If these were modern historians we would begin our assessment of their reliability by looking to the sources they cite. But generic decorum discouraged citation of sources in the historians (the biographers, as we have seen, had a little more freedom here). Occasionally Dio will cite a source by name (e.g. the memoirs of Septimius Severus at 75.7.3), but usually to challenge its information. On the victory in 197 CE for which he cites Severus, for example, he says, "my account represents not what Severus wrote about it, but what actually happened." How he knows what actually happened he does not say. (Similarly for a reference to Augustus' memoirs at 44.35.3.) More common are general references to "earlier accounts," which are often occasioned by implausible or discrepant stories. On the identity of Galba's assassin, for example, in Tacitus: "There is no agreement as to the killer. Some say it was a bodyguard named Terentius, others one Laecanius; the more common report says that a soldier of the 15th legion named Camurius applied his sword and slit Galba's throat" (*Hist.* 1.41.3). This kind of citation does little to help us identify Tacitus' sources. In fact this particular passage looks even less helpful when we set beside it Plutarch's report: "The man who killed him, according to most writers, was a certain Camurius from the 15th legion. Some report that it was Terentius, others Lecaenius, still others Fabius Fabullus" (*Life of Galba* 27.2). We have to conclude that both authors took the reference to conflicting reports from their common source. The content of the statement – that Galba's assassin was variously identified – may well be true, but there is nothing to suggest that either Tacitus or Plutarch verified it for himself. In fact, the identification of a literary source's own sources, a procedure known by its German name "Quellenforschung," relies less on the rare specific or general references in a work than on a painstaking analysis of the content-based and thematic and stylistic "fingerprints" of those sources (the introductions to commentaries on historical works generally supply details and bibliography on these sources).

References to documentary information are even rarer than references to literary sources, in part for the same reasons of stylistic decorum, but also because historians of the empire were conditioned to disbelief in official records. Appian, for example, reports that in 35 BCE Octavian ordered written records of the civil wars then ending (so he thought) to be destroyed (*BC* 5.132), thereby ensuring that his version of events had the advantage in future histories. And Tacitus, when faced with the official record of the Senate's implicit verdict on the death of Tiberius' heir Germanicus (natural causes, despite Germanicus' belief, which the Senate duly records, that one Gnaeus Piso caused his death; we have a version of this document in the recently published *Decree of the Senate on Cn. Piso the Elder*), could see as clearly as we can that it offered not the truth about events, but rather the truth about what the Senate felt it could safely and appropriately say on that occasion (Damon and Takács 1999: 143–62). The involvement of Piso in the prince's death, though discredited by the Senate's verdict, is attested in literary sources (Suet. *Cal.* 2, *Tib.* 52.3; Dio 57.9) and survived as a rumor down to Tacitus' own day:

> [Germanicus'] death was the subject of all sorts of rumors not only among his contemporaries but for subsequent generations as well. So much in the dark are we about even the most important events, since some people treat what they hear as the truth, no

matter the source, and others take the truth and turn it into lies. And the stories continue to develop as they are handed down. (*Ann.* 3.19.2)

Tacitus accepted neither the Senate's verdict nor the rumor, but gave both an airing in his narrative. In a similar circumstance Dio can be more decisive, since he was himself present at a Senate meeting that produced some highly dubious official documents in 205. Presented with trumped-up evidence "justifying" the summary execution of a praetorian prefect, the Senate issued decrees praising its authors (76.3–5). In fact, it was clear to all concerned that such decrees were liable to have been issued "under the influence of necessity or awe" (Suet. *Aug.* 57.1).

In general the ancient historian staked his authority, his claim to a reader's belief, on the *persona* he conveyed as an author – his moral character, analytical power, and literary skill – not on his sources, literary or documentary. We prefer to have evidence, especially non-literary evidence, providing independent confirmation. Thus we believe the *Historia Augusta*'s unique report that Hadrian built a wall 80 miles long in Britain (*HA Had.* 11.2) because the troops to whom Hadrian gave the task left records of their progress, including dates and segments built, at the wall itself. Source criticism requires asking many more questions than those illustrated here, particularly when one wants to go beyond simply establishing a chronological sequence, but for these the detailed studies of the various sources for imperial history listed in the bibliography are a more appropriate venue.

3 Conclusion

After adding up all the sources and doing everything possible to assess their reliability, the historian is still faced with the unpalatable fact that there is a limit to how much of the political history of the empire can be known. This limit was already felt, clearly and disturbingly, by ancient writers. Dio's statement of the problem is the most famous:

> Actions taken after this date (27 BCE) cannot be reported in the same way as what went before. Formerly all matters were brought before the senate and the people, even things that occurred far away. Therefore everyone learned about them and many recorded them, and for this reason the truth of the accounts, even if they generally spoke out of fear or favor, friendship or enmity, could after a fashion be found by comparing them with others written on the same subject and with official records. But from that time things began to be done secretly and in a manner not to be made public. (53.19.1–3)

Dio dates this fundamental shift to the reign of Augustus, and to judge by Tacitus' *Annals*, the cloud cloaking the emperor was already quite opaque by the time of Tiberius, as we saw above. To a greater degree than ever before in Roman history public events of a political nature (elections, Senate meetings, trials, etc.) were for show, while the real business of power was transacted "in a manner not to be made public." Like Dio, we have to use "what we have read and seen and heard" (53.19.6) to assess the evidence that survives.

CHAPTER TWO

Roman Imperial Numismatics

William E. Metcalf

"The proper use of the Republican coinage as a historical source," wrote Michael Crawford (1974) "depends on the fulfillment of three conditions – a full and accurate account must be given of its contents, a chronological framework must be provided, and the mints at which it was produced must be identified." He then set out, in a magisterial work, to establish an enduring framework for the study of republican coinage that despite some imperfections (Hersh 1977; H. B. Mattingly 1977), and some revisions necessitated by the discovery of new material (Hersh and Walker 1984), has been the basis for all work since.

The same strictures might have been applied to the coinage of the empire, although here the groundwork had been much more carefully laid. Long before 1974 one of the world's principal collections had been described in detail (H. Mattingly 1923; Carson 1962), and handbooks describing the principal varieties of known coins existed for most of the period. Though the British Museum Catalogue has advanced no further, steadily higher standards for the handbooks, and their extension to cover the entire empire (Sutherland 1967; Bruun 1966; Kent 1981, 1994) have made the need for detailed descriptions of major collections less pressing, and only Paris has subsequently embarked on publication of its extensive holdings (Giard 1976–98).

The traditional, hellenocentric definition treated as Greek coins all coins of Greek city-states and their successors and all coins not bearing Latin legends, whatever their language. The most important development of the last few decades has been an expansion of the definition of what constitutes Roman coinage. A step in this direction was taken by Crawford in a synthetic treatment (1985); and while all the handbooks and most catalogues of collections follow the older tradition, describing coins of the denarius system and its lineal successors, there has been increasing recognition that this provides only a partial view of the currency of the Roman world (Harl 1987; Howgego 1995). Roman provincial coins – some of them indeed minted at the capital – have generated enormous bibliography and a union catalogue of this material, based on the ten major collections of the world, is in progress (Burnett and Amandry 1992, 1999).

1 Historical Survey

The *denarial* (or, to use Crawford's term, "mainstream") coinage is based on the denarius as the principal silver coin, its multiple the *aureus*, and its fractions *sestertius*, *dupondius, as, semis*, and *quadrans*. It was produced at Rome and elsewhere mainly, it is thought, to pay state expenditures. The *provincial* coinage, usually distinguished by the use of Greek legends, was struck to a variety of local standards by a variety of issuing authorities. This coinage was produced mainly to meet local (occasionally provincial) needs, and there was no uniform standard. The two categories are embraced in *Roman Imperial Coinage* and *Roman Provincial Coinage* respectively. Although a glance at the early volumes of either series will suggest the areas of overlap between the two categories, it remains easiest to treat them separately.

The "mainstream" coinage

The death of Antony left Octavian effectively ruler of the western Mediterranean and heir to a chaotic currency situation. The waning years of the republic and the civil wars witnessed the striking of gold at Rome on an unprecedented scale, though most emissions were small. The denarius was the linchpin of the coinage. It was struck throughout Rome's orbit by the most diverse authorities: Brutus, Cassius, the triumvirs jointly and individually, and ultimately, in huge numbers, Octavian and Antony themselves. The "constitutional" moneyers at Rome still held office, but unless the CAESAR DIVI F and IMP CAESAR coins were produced at Rome (which is hard to prove), they had had nothing to do since 42 BCE. There was other silver: Antony had chosen to fully Romanize the *cistophori* of Asia Minor (long under Roman management, even signed by proconsuls). The copper currency was a mess. Its progressive decline in weight had led to the obvious outcome – a complete halt of production – in the eighties; the closest thing to a systematic currency was Antony's "fleet" series, matched in bulk only by Octavian's DIVOS IVLIVS and DIVI F issues.

The Augustan response was nothing if not deliberate. The years down to 23 BCE saw little change: the emperor's portrait was standard even before his recognition as Augustus, but gold and denarii were struck only sporadically and all copper was local. There is nothing which can be attributed with certainty to the mint of Rome.

In 23 BCE the imperial coinage first becomes recognizable as something fully distinct from the republican and triumviral tradition. The signatures of the *triumviri monetales*, unheard of since the forties, reappear, allowing us with some confidence to identify the issues of Rome. The *aureus* stabilizes at 41 to the pound (7.87 gm.), and appears with some regularity; the denarii, struck on the late Republican standard of 84 to the pound, were produced almost annually for 12 years, and revive republican forms (Duncan-Jones 1994: 213–20 with a discussion of the Roman pound). But while one face of the coin may make reference to the moneyer's family or a contemporary event, the emperor's image almost invariably occupies the obverse.

The biggest change is in the base metal. The semuncial *as* is revived at c.12.5 gm. *Orichalcum*, which had not been employed for coinage in republican times, is introduced at a tariff of 5:2 vis-à-vis copper, and with it a coin of one *uncia*, the *sestertius*, which replaced the old, easily lost, silver *sestertius* of one gram silver. The half was the *dupondius*, or two-*as* piece, and in copper there were the *as*, the *semis*, and the *quadrans*. The coins from Rome bear the legend S C, probably indicating senatorial endorsement of the change, and the names of the moneyers (Bay 1972).

In 16 BCE the mint of Lugdunum began producing gold and silver, as well as large bronze coins analogous to the Roman *sestertius* and *as*; Strabo's testimony (4.3.2) that "the Roman emperors coin gold and silver there" strictly applies to Tiberius (and probably Augustus), but in fact it seems that from 12 BCE–64 CE virtually all imperial gold and silver was produced there, and occasionally the mint ventured into *aes* coinage as well (Metcalf 1989; Wolters 1999). The Augustan reform constituted the basis of the imperial system for nearly three centuries. Coincidentally the creation of the *sestertius* was a turning point in numismatic art: given a field large enough to work in, engravers undertook more ambitious compositions, and were able to execute them in more detail. The Augustan mint of Rome produced huge quantities of *aes* and issued gold and silver, regularly but in small quantity, from c.23–12 BCE. Later the *aes* is episodic, and completely lacking for Otho; the gold and silver only slightly less so. The only issues that survive in large numbers are the C L CAESARES of Augustus and the "tribute penny" of Tiberius; while the former is probably the product of a single year, stylistic considerations suggest that the latter may have been produced for Tiberius' whole reign. Externally the coins underwent little change for nearly 90 years following the "Augustan reform." But in 64 CE there was a significant weight reduction in the gold and silver: from (by now) c.1/42 to 1/44 lb. in gold, and from c.1/90 to 1/100 lb. in silver (Duncan-Jones 1994: 217–18). We do not know the tariff of the two coins at this period, but there is no reason to suppose that it changed; nor do we know the reason for the reduction, though the mere recovery of 4.5 percent of gold and 11 percent of silver may have been a motive. The effect is soon apparent in hoards: by the end of the century earlier coins had all but disappeared except for denarii of Mark Antony, which lasted in circulation into the third century.

The weight changes of 64 CE were accompanied by a return of the mint to the capital and the production of *aes* in larger quantity. From this point on there is hardly a year when nothing is produced. Vespasian experiments with striking gold and silver at several eastern mints (Antioch, Ephesus, one uncertain) (Metcalf 1982), there are Italian(?) branch mints under Claudius, and Titus and Domitian may have experimented with *aes* in the Balkans (Burnett and Amandry 1999: 88–9; cf. Komnick 2000), but for most of the early empire Rome is the only mint for denarial coinage.

The purity of the gold and silver was maintained for a time, but eventually the silver began to slide – at first slowly, then more precipitously. But the extensive analyses of Walker (1976, 1977, and 1978), which seemed to indicate frequent and subtle manipulations of silver content as well as an over-tariffing of Roman silver vis-à-vis that of the provinces, have been called into question (Butcher and Ponting 1995), and new analyses will have to be undertaken. The slide in purity is accompanied by a slow erosion of weight as well, but in fact the silver coinage remained remarkably stable for a very long time. The debasement of the so-called "antoninianus" in 215

CE was temporary, and it has been doubted whether the coin, which weighed 1.5 denarii, was really tariffed at two (Carson 1965); the two denominations are hoarded together from the beginning, which is counterintuitive if the silver of one was heavily overvalued. In its first incarnation the denomination did not survive Elagabalus. Its revival is the only legacy of the ill-starred Balbinus and Pupienus, and this time it spelled the end of the denarius as the empire's principal silver coin. The denomination, which had been introduced four and a half centuries before, disappeared virtually overnight from the hoards and remained only vestigially as a unit of account. The period after 240 CE was one of rapid debasement and genuine cynicism: even as he was striking the coins of the "Divi," the emperor Trajan Decius was allowing earlier denarii to be overstruck by *antoniniani*, thus with a blow of the hammer doubling the nominal value of the silver. The silver content seems to stabilize, albeit at a very low level, during the lifetime of Valerian; but by the time of Gallienus' death it had fallen to perhaps 2 percent of a shoddily-produced *antoninianus*.

There is sporadic evidence for the operation of provincial mints coining denarii during the second century, but oddly the permanent establishment of eastern mints can be traced to the usurper Pescennius Niger (Buttrey 1992). It is clear that his two mints were at Antioch and Caesarea in Cappadocia, and Antioch continued to strike denarii for Septimius while the identity of the latter's second denarius mint is uncertain; Caesarea itself reverted to the manufacture of drachms. From this point on Antioch is a major producer of Roman silver coinage; the overall identity of its types with those of Rome makes its output difficult to identify, at least in older hoards published without full illustration. The mint undergoes a hiatus in production in the early 250s CE owing to the city's capture by Sapor I; by the time it resumed coinage other mints, both east and west, were in operation. These can be distinguished on the basis of style and of *officina*-markings, which were introduced under Philip I and became regular on the coinage of all mints by the sole reign of Gallienus, never again to disappear.

The debasement of the third-century coinage was offset by a huge increase in its size. The expansion was made possible by the proliferation of mints, which must also have speeded delivery of coin in response to local demand. The officinal coinage was widely imitated and had a rival first in the coinage of the "Gallic Empire," then in the issues of the British usurpers Carausius and Allectus. The "reform of Aurelian," which occurred in the context of the "revolt of the moneyers" at Rome, altered the tariff and improved the appearance of the coinage (Crawford 1975); the fineness of the "aurelianianus" was set at a silver:copper ratio of 1:20 (4.8 percent silver). This temporarily made the coinage more respectable in appearance but had, apparently, no lasting effect on its intrinsic value; thus we may well believe that underneath the rhetoric of Diocletian's edict on maximum prices lay a crippling inflation that no succession of reforms could abate (Crawford 1975; Bagnall 1985).

Diocletian imposed a new system of denominations and a system of production of uniform coins at multiple mints, the latter linked to the new division of the empire into dioceses (Crawford 1975; Hendy 1970, 1985; Elton, this volume); this put an end to provincial coin production, even at Alexandria. Though Diocletian's new denominations soon became unrecognizable, the mint arrangements he put in place would linger, albeit on a much reduced scale, through the fall of the empire.

The fourth and fifth centuries are a period of slow decline followed by collapse. Gold replaced silver as the fundamental unit of the system. The solidus of 1/72 lb. succeeded the *aureus* as the standard gold denomination. Virtually all the entries pertaining to counterfeiting or fraud in the Theodosian Code refer to gold, in which taxes were paid and revenues forwarded to Rome. Its purity was therefore of utmost concern, and the maintenance of that purity formed the basis of the later Byzantine solidus. Repeated attempts to integrate a silver currency into the system failed, and use of the metal does not seem to have been widespread after the end of the fourth century. The tiny *nummus* (often called a "minimus") had to do for small exchanges; its size ultimately became so small that it could hardly be recognized as an official mint product, and indeed imitation was widespread. These circumstances set the stage for the reforms of Anastasius, which for numismatists constitute the beginning of the Byzantine coinage.

Provincial coinage

It is easy to see the Julio-Claudian *aes* as the successor to that of Augustus, whose emission from Rome seems guaranteed by the presence of the moneyers' names. But as Grant (1946, 1953) showed long ago and has since been abundantly confirmed in *Roman Provincial Coinage,* traditional catalogues oversimplify the situation. Many regions of the empire did not even use the reformed denominations, much less the coins themselves. A glance through the plates of *RPC* suffices to dramatize the Roman indifference to the currency of outlying regions. In some cases – e.g. the "Altar" series of Lugdunum and the "Crocodiles" of Nemausus (Figure 2.1) – the mass of coin was about as great as that emanating from Rome. These large scale mints were joined, on occasion, by short-term ones, coining on the Roman standard, whose purpose is generally unclear.

Rome's *laissez-faire* attitude towards monetary arrangements in the provinces is evident already in the republic, when for example Attalid *cistophori* continue to be the

Figure 2.1 "Crocodile" *as* from Nîmes. The obverse shows heads of Agrippa and Augustus, back to back, with Agrippa facing left wearing a combined rostral crown and olive wreath. The head of Augustus is bare. The reverse shows a crocodile chained to a palm branch, evoking the conquest of Egypt (*RIC* Augustus n. 155 editor's collection)

currency of Asia long after its organization into a province. After some experimentation (C. E. King and D. R. Walker 1976) the coinage of Egypt stabilizes along Ptolemaic lines; other less isolated provinces continue to possess and produce their own silver.

The best summary of what can be known of the early provincial coinage is provided by *RPC*; where the volumes do not exist students have to rely on the rather uneven coverage provided by regional surveys, mint studies, or corpora. Already the arrangement of the material has departed from the traditional classification by "province" (Ionia, Caria, Lydia, etc.) to a more fluid one that recognizes regional influence and proximity of towns, *à la* Louis Robert; but for Asia the classification by *conventus* (provincial administrative center) is no improvement as a recognition of the authority behind issues. The picture will get more complicated still as *RPC* reaches the late second and third centuries; not only does the volume of material increase vastly (the editors of vol. 4, the Antonines, have recorded nearly 40,000 coins of over 12,000 types from 388 cities), but its interrelationship is marked by frequent die links between coins of different authorities – the "Werkstätte" identified by Kraft (1972; cf. Johnston 1974) whose products and relationship to one another has not been fully articulated.

The steady debasement of the imperial coinage must have had much to do with the collapse of the coinage in the provinces; presumably the baseness of the nominally silver coinage drove the heavier but nominally fractional denominations from circulation. By the reign of Gordian III, only Antioch and Caesarea in Cappadocia continued to produce silver (Bland 1991), and the number of authorities producing copper was declining from its peak under Septimius Severus. The period of greatest decline seems to have been the sole reign of Gallienus, when the silver coinage reached its nadir. Only a few mints continued to strike as late as Tacitus (275 CE) and the only one that continues beyond him is Alexandria, by now producing, albeit on a grand scale, only very debased *tetradrachms*. The coinage reform of Diocletian, which took effect in the west in early 293 and expanded eastward, introduced uniform denominations throughout the empire and brought an end to coinage in Alexandria, too.

The relationship of the provincial coinage to the mainstream gold and silver is not easily apprehended. There is some evidence for solicitation of permission to strike coins directly from the emperor (Robert 1960), but more likely the usual authority came from the provincial governor filtered through local magistrates. While the portrait of the emperor is the commonest obverse type, this is by no means as universal as it was at Rome, and *boulê, hiera synklêtos, demos*, and other personifications find their place: these of course are difficult to date with precision. The reverse types occasionally derive from Roman prototypes, but more often local gods and heroes, events and institutions dictate the themes.

As noted already, sometimes the mint of Rome itself engaged in producing provincial denominations, mainly in precious metal, so there must have been some apprehension at the center of needs on the periphery. But no analysis that sees the provincial money as centrally controlled, or contrarily as purely the product of local initiative, will be wholly satisfactory. On the whole there is better evidence for a local initiative (Harl 1987) than for central management (Price 1984). The answer lies somewhere in between, and has to be determined on a case-by-case basis.

2 Some Current Issues

Study of the denarial coinage and that of the provinces is at two distinct stages of development. The former has long been known in great detail, with standard catalogues listing its varieties and few new discoveries; this has facilitated further recording by defining what is *not* known and easing cataloguing of well-known varieties. Even such primitive tools as the alphabetical listing of Cohen (1880–92) facilitated abbreviated recording of coin hoards and finds, an aspect of the discipline that has reached maturity in the last two decades: new discoveries help refine, in ever greater detail, the chronology and structure of imperial mints (e.g. the Eauze hoard: Schaad 1992; Venerà hoard: Estiot 1987, 1995; Giard 1995; Gricourt 2000; Normanby hoard: Bland 1988; Cunetio hoard: Besly and Bland 1983). The same cannot be said of the provincial coinage, for which there is not yet a standard work of reference and much new material continues to emerge. This disparity dictates different strategies of study.

No official document survives in anything like the quantities of imperial coinage; and as it is money, it is natural to try to count it. In perhaps the most influential piece of work ever addressed to numismatists, A. H. M. Jones wrote as follows (1956: 23):

> Could it be estimated how many aurei and denarii were annually minted in the reigns of the successive emperors from Augustus to Septimius Severus relatively to the number of aurei and antoniniani (or denarii) minted annually from the reign of Caracalla to that of Aurelian? Was there, as the literary sources would suggest, an abnormally heavy output of aurei in the latter part of Trajan's reign? Again, what was the relative volume of Diocletian's gold and silver issues to those of Constantine?

Numismatists generally estimate the relative commonness of coins by looking at their occurrence in hoards. For portions of the coinage in which the hoard evidence is abundant (and where the sample has not been altered by recall or suppression) this method, though crude, seems reliable as far as it goes; despite the efforts of Duncan-Jones and others, no satisfactory way has been found of establishing mint output in any absolute sense of the term (Duncan-Jones 1994, with Metcalf 1995; Buttrey 1993, 1994; de Callataÿ 1995).

As far as we can now see, the curve of output is steadily upward in the silver coinage; it reaches a peak during the Antonine period in *aes*, then declines, then rises again before the effective end of the coinage under Valerian and Gallienus. In the second century the output of gold peaks under M. Aurelius; for the third the amount of evidence available is insufficient to form any reliable conclusions (but see Bland 1996).

Most of this coinage is the product of a fairly small minting operation at Rome: inscriptions of Trajanic date seem to represent that portion of the mint given over to actual manufacture of the coins, and their numbers are small, including only 22 *malleatores* whose work was the essential step in production (Carson 1956; Alföldi 1958/9). This mint, in addition to producing the "mainstream" coinage of Rome, took a sporadic role in making coinage for the provinces as well. It is now generally agreed that some of the imperial coinage once attributed to Caesarea in Cappadocia was produced there, and there are clear cases in which Rome struck for other provinces as well: Alexandria under Severus Alexander, Antioch under Philip I (Metcalf 1996; Burnett and Craddock 1983; Baldus 1969). This is quite apart from the question of "consignment" of batches of coins from Rome to designated areas, a phenomenon most clearly documented for Britain (Walker 1988). Why these interventions occurred, and why, once undertaken, they were not continued, remains a mystery.

The types and legends of the imperial coinage were the principal impetus to its early study; after a long quiescence (for which see A. H. M. Jones 1956) these continue to excite interest. The authority behind the coinage, in its early stages, has been debated: the almost invariable occurrence of S C on *aes* coinage has been taken to lie behind the original Augustan reform (Bay 1972) or to reflect continuing senatorial involvement in coin production (Burnett 1977). Clearly the individual object gained its authority from the imperial image (Wallace-Hadrill 1986), but this cannot be taken literally as an expression of the inspiration of the content. The debate goes on: one interesting reading suggests that many coin types were devised to please the emperor himself as the most important member of the audience (Levick 1982).

The impact of the coinage is another matter. The work of Paul Zanker (1988) has shown that a whole atmosphere can be created through management of art, and coinage is a part of this; but its workings in detail are hard to track and attempts to distinguish the audience for coinage on the basis of its likely users have been less than wholly successful (Metcalf 1993). The problem is complicated because we cannot really estimate the size of any particular component of the coinage in any more than a relative way, and it is impossible to gauge the relative size of, say, the gold and silver as against the *aes*. Diametrically opposed views can still be expressed (Ehrhardt 1984; Crawford 1983).

Recent years have seen two significant efforts to address coin imagery. One has to do with a single new discovery: an *aureus* of Octavian struck, probably in Asia, during his sixth consulship (28 BCE) and proclaiming LEGES ET IVRA P R RESTITVIT and showing Octavian seated on a curule chair with a *scrinium* by his side, into which he is about to place a roll (see Rowe, this volume and Figure 2.2). The subject of the sentence is provided by the obverse legend of the coin (IMP CAESAR DIVI F COS VI) but no words were necessary to apprehend its import. The coin – whose verbiage might have been lifted, *mutatis mutandis*, from Augustus' *Res Gestae* – is an ideal reflection of the symbolic equality of obverse and reverse: the words themselves invite the user to turn over the coin, and the message may be read beginning on either side. More than this, the coin is a genuine historical document whose official utterance is above question; it demands modification of the view, based on Cassius Dio, that the "constitutional settlement of 27 BCE" was a monolith. In fact its origins are to be sought, as the coin shows, a year earlier (Rich and Williams 1999). Who knows what this sort of study might reveal, drawing on the vast body of material already known but only superficially explored? The work of Sabine MacCormack (1981) is just one example of what can be done with rigorous attention to the nuances of coin evidence.

Work on mint output has revealed the possibilities of addressing coin types in quantity. The question of who initiated designs is irrelevant – we can at least say that no coin presents the emperor in a negative light – and it is an obvious inference that the content of the coinage was subject to high-level review. Thus coins have their role

Figure 2.2 *Aureus* of Octavian 28 BCE. The obverse shows the head of Augustus with the legend *imp. Caesar Divi f. cos. vi*, the reverse shows Augustus seated with *scrinium* and the legend *leges et iura R.P. restituit* (BMC 1995-4-1-1). Photo courtesy of the British Museum

to play in the study of imperial self-representation, and this has been taken up in an important article based on the silver coins (Noreña 2001).

For the provinces much basic work remains to be done. The older catalogues and "corpora" are all incomplete, having foundered under the sheer mass of material, and long out of date. There are significant studies of individual mints in the provinces, e.g. Corinth (Amandry 1988), Thessalonica (Touratsoglou 1988), Smyrna (Klose 1987), Anazarbos (Ziegler 1993), Balkan mints (Schönert-Geiss 1965, 1970, 1975, 1987, 1991; Youroukova 1973, 1982) and Asian mints (von Aulock 1968, 1969, 1970, 1977, 1979, 1980), and of individual problems (Howgego 1985 on countermarks; Johnston 1985 on portraits, etc.), but these only scratch the surface. Plenty of mints await the detailed study that would constitute dissertation work if numismatics had the relationship it deserves to the mainstream of classical studies.

3 Conclusion

The outlines of the imperial coinage are becoming tolerably clear, and the effort required to refine the picture of production and impact is staggering. It might seem that the investment of effort has reached the point of diminishing returns: hardly anyone outside the field appreciates the labor involved in producing even the simplest mint study, which involves internal comparison of a mint's products and their arrangement by die. These have to be viewed in person or in reproduction not only in public and private collections, but ideally in the commercial auction literature as well; this last is often difficult to access and even offensive to some scholars. The nature of the case may require extension of the study beyond the confines of the mint, but in any case appreciation of the historical significance often involves immersion in geography, literature, archaeology, epigraphy, prosopography, even ancient religion.

So why does anyone pursue the study of coinage? At the most basic level, each coin represents a whole object produced by an artist – and how many of these do we possess in other media? – terse testimony not only to the bureaucratic state of mind but to contemporary artistic taste and accomplishment, even technical expertise. That alone might be regarded as sufficient. But there is one paramount consideration that sets coinage apart from other realia: its "official" character and its unique stature as primary source material. In the Roman world mainstream coinage was produced on high authority and by workmen whose output was carefully supervised and controlled; even in the provinces minters were responsible to local officials and ultimately to Roman magistrates as well. The consistency of the coinage is testimony to the control exercised over it. No imperial portrait or monument, not the *SC de Pisone Patre* or the *Lex Irnitana* (much less the text of, say, Cicero) has such proximity to its source or is so inherently entitled to authority. With this in mind numismatists will continue to go about their work, attempting to set out the evidence to facilitate its proper employment in writing the history of the Roman world.

CHAPTER THREE

Documents

Traianos Gagos and David S. Potter

The Roman Empire was an empire of cities. As urban culture spread, especially into the western provinces, it brought with it a more intensely documentary habit, meaning that the study of the Roman Empire after Augustus is distinguished by the vast increase in the documentary record. Fortuitous discoveries such as the Vindolanda writing tablets, bits of bark preserved in a bog, that contain records from northern Britain, the Babatha archive from Judaea, and the third century documents emanating from Dura Europus and the nearby village of Appadana in Syria attest the spread of an increasingly documentary habit away from urban to rural centers (Bowman 1994; Feissel and Gascou 1995; Cotton 1995). These finds may be paralleled by the rise of the epigraphic habit in regions where public inscription had not been a feature of life previously.

The purpose of this chapter is to illustrate the contributions that papyrologists and epigraphists make to the study of the Roman Empire, and to explore the methodological issues with which they deal. Both papyrologists and epigraphists have some issues in common since their material is documentary in the sense that it was not transmitted through the manuscript tradition, and that its primary function in antiquity was to provide a record of action rather than to entertain a reader (M. H. Hansen 2001: 322–4). That said, there are several fundamental distinctions between the evidence available from inscriptions and papyri. The first is that the former, by their very nature, are limited to only a handful of standardized types of documents meant for wider public display and government propaganda. The second is that inscriptions ordinarily represent the end of a process, or, in cases such as erasure or reuse, an implicit judgment on the relevance of an earlier process. Papyri, on the other hand, may record either completed or in-progress actions. They reveal horizontal and vertical interfaces of administrative operations, both between officials of similar rank and officials all the way through the multi-tiered system of the Roman imperial administration, from Alexandria down to the smallest administrative offices in the countryside. Papyri also offer a picture of everyday interactions outside the official sphere, while inscriptions will only record events that people wish to place on public display. In a word, whereas inscriptions provide a series of isolated, static and premeditated snapshots of concerns, papyri offer a more seamless, dynamic, and spontaneous sequence of interactions. Without papyri we would know something about imperial policy and the actions of the prefect of Egypt and his procurators, but little about the structure, levels, effectiveness, and daily operation of the Roman provincial administration, or how the people of Egypt perceived the system. That said, inscriptions and papyri should not be studied separately or in isolation; their greatest impact comes when they are studied in combination with other types of evidence, including coins and other remnants of material culture (Bowman 2001).

1 Collections

Epigraphy

Epigraphy is the study of writing on non-perishable materials, and virtually all societies that have used writing have had some epigraphic practice, but the extent of that practice varies enormously from place to place and time to time. From the fourth century BCE onwards, for instance, the practice of epigraphy becomes so pronounced in Greek cities that it becomes a useful marker for the extension of Hellenic civilization (Robert 1961: 6). Widespread use of inscription developed later in Roman Italy and the western provinces of Rome's empire, becoming more and more pronounced during the century before the reign of Augustus as the impact of Greek urban culture became ever more prevalent in Roman life. From the reign of Augustus through the beginning of the fourth century CE, there is an epigraphic explosion in western Europe, unparalleled in earlier and later centuries (Woolf 1996). The result of the link between the epigraphic habit and urban culture is that the range of inscribed materials extends across the range of social activities in antiquity, from acts of government to private acts of cursing and/or marking. When these documents are read in large numbers – the first rule of epigraphy is that inscriptions must not be read in isolation from other inscriptions – they enable us to look at the deep structures of ancient life (Robert 1961: 23). For this to be possible, however, we are dependent upon the extraordinary projects that have systematized our knowledge of the texts.

Inscriptions, archives, and dossiers

Ever since the early nineteenth century, historians have looked to archives to correct the inherent biases of narrative history. Inscriptions look as if they should have the status of archival documents, and, at times, they even appear to be related to archival collections since there are some inscriptions that reflect the nature of public archives, or are themselves extracts from civic archives. Other texts, such as the decree of the Senate of 177 CE on the prices of public combatants are similarly archival in that they contain the actual *acta* of a meeting of the Senate, and provide important evidence for the way in which records were kept (the extract from a speech by Marcus Aurelius that is said to be "verbatim" is in fact severely truncated in summary) (*ILS* 5163).

An inscription from Dmeir in Syria reflecting a dispute over the priesthood of the temple of Zeus is simply an extract from the imperial *acta* of the event, while the text contained on the *tabula Siarensis* appears to contain both the *senatus consultum* that summarized possible honors for Germanicus and the final *lex* establishing what those honors would be (*SEG* 17 no. 746, with Stolte 2003; Crawford 1996: nos. 37–8).

Elsewhere the fact that government was conducted domestically by public decree, and internationally through the exchange of letters, meant that selections from state archives might be inscribed in public places. The earliest examples of this sort of activity derive from fifth-century Athens – the public inscription of a series of decrees in favor of Methone in Macedonia – and fourth-century Caria, in the form of a series of decrees concerning attempts on the life of the satrap Mausolus (*ML* 65; *GHI*² 54, with J. K. Davies 2005: 332–4). Extant examples increase in frequency after Alexander, and include not only related dossiers such as that concerning tyrants at Eresus (*GHI* 191), but now as well collections of letters from kings, emperors, and other peoples that reflect upon the standing of a community (S. M. Sherwin-White 1985: 74–5). The typical "history wall," as many of these publications may reasonably be termed, was inscribed on part of a centrally located public monument, such as the wall of a temple, the entrance to a theater, or outside a shrine to the emperors (S. M. Sherwin-White 1985: 69–72; J. Reynolds 1982: 33–7; J. Reynolds 1978; Oliver and Clinton 1989 nos. 8–12, 108–18; Chaniotis 2003; J. K. Davies 2005: 334 n. 32). The functional aspect of these walls is underlined by texts inscribed on a wall of the temple of Zeus at Baetocaece that included a dossier of letters from Hellenistic kings that proclaimed the temple's privileges, below a favorable response from Valerian asserting that the ancient benefits that the temple had obtained from these kings must be maintained in the face of a challenge from an "adversary" (*IGLS* 4028). In a less spectacular, but equally telling instance, an inscription from the Esquiline Hill in Rome offers what appears to be a verbatim transcript of a hearing before *praefecti vigilum* who held in favor of the association of fullers (*FIRA*⁷ no. 188). In this case, of course, it is the fullers who are interested in making sure that the record of their success is visible to all.

"History walls" differ from ordinary civic decrees and letters in that they were assembled over a period of time to form a coherent group. Also, unlike civic decrees and important letters, they were not necessarily verbatim transcripts of the original (J. Reynolds 1978: 113–14). The fact that these texts are selected for publication means that they are not true archives; public inscription was a selective process and we cannot directly access the content of any public or private archive through this medium (Boffo 1995: 97). The problem with ancient collections underlines a difficulty no less characteristic of modern collections of inscriptions: they are a record of fortuitous discoveries. While we may learn a great deal from these collections, we also need to be conscious that we can only rarely, and for only very short periods of time, examine specific practices within specific locations. As we shall see when we turn to papyri, all of these collections are better referred to as dossiers than actual archives, a distinction that papyrologists draw between texts that were once part of a group and that have been found in their original context (an archive) as opposed to those that have been grouped together by the work of modern scholars (a dossier) (p. 61–2 below).

Modern collections of inscriptions

Despite the inherently problematic nature of modern document collections, it is fair to say that the massive work of cataloguing inscriptions has transformed the discipline of ancient history. Without these collections, we would be left with a literary tradition that is heavily biased in terms of class, gender, and location. For all their limitations, epigraphic corpora make it possible to engage in studies of ancient society that would be impossible otherwise (Syme 1973: 585).

Volumes one and two of Karl August Boeckh's *Corpus Inscriptionum Graecarum* initiated the modern study of epigraphy between 1828 and 1844. These two volumes represented the first systematic effort to collect all known Greek inscriptions from the Mediterranean world. Although there were earlier collections of inscriptions, as well as of coins and ancient art, these had only minimal impact on the way history was written prior to the emergence of set curricula for the study of the ancient world in German universities during the first part of the nineteenth century (Rives, this volume; Matthews, this volume). Boeckh understood that the evidence of inscriptions could only be fully exploited if they could be read in bulk through organized corpora. Even though *CIG*, as Boeckh's project is known, was badly out of date by the time the last two volumes (including the indices) were published in 1878, it established the basic principle that comprehensive collections of inscriptions should be organized according to location. Within each location inscriptions are generally subdivided according to date and the bodies responsible for the text, with inscriptions connected with civic administration preceding those connected with cults and then those erected by private associations or individuals.

Boeckh's work on Greek inscriptions had an immediate impact on the study of Latin epigraphy. Theodor Mommsen began work on the great corpus of Latin inscriptions, the *Corpus Inscriptionum Latinarum* (*CIL*) in 1853. Work on *CIL* continues to this day, and at the time this chapter is being written (April 2005), there are 17 volumes in 70 fascicles containing a total of 180,000 inscriptions, along with 13 supplemental volumes of tables and indices (www.cil.bbaw.de/dateien/forschung.html). The organization of the series reflects basic problems in epigraphy – namely how best to present the information. Mommsen decided, quite reasonably, that it was best to handle different topics in different ways. Thus, while the bulk of *CIL* (volumes 2–14) are organized by location, volume 1 is devoted to all Latin inscriptions prior to Augustus, and volumes 15–17 deal, respectively, with instruments of daily use (*instrumenta domestica*), military *diplomata* (on which see Pollard, this volume), and milestones. The regional volumes are organized as follows:

volume 2: Spain
volume 3: central Europe and the eastern provinces
volume 4: Pompeii and other places buried by Vesuvius
volume 5: northern Italy
volume 6: Rome itself (this volume contains nearly a third of all known Latin inscriptions)
volume 7: Britain
volume 8: Africa

volume 9: Calabria, Apulia, Samnium, Sabine territory, and Picenum
volume 10: Bruttium, Lucania, Campania, Sicily, and Sardinia
volume 11: Aemilia, Etruria, and Umbria
volume 12: Gallia Narbonensis
volume 13: the three Gauls and Germany
volume 14: Latium

In a number of cases the volumes of *CIL* were superseded by other projects: *CIL* 7 was replaced in 1965 by *The Roman Inscriptions of Britain*; volume 8 by René Cagnat, et al. *Inscriptions latines d'Afrique*; and the volumes for Italy by the series *Inscriptiones Italiae*, begun in 1931, though only two volumes, one of them Atilio Degrassi's invaluable work on the *Fasti*, were published, and, since 1981 the series *Supplementa Italiae* has filled in the gap.

As the efforts to update *CIL* show, print collections tend to be dated by the time they appear. Even as *CIL* was underway, Mommsen realized that the aim of comprehensive treatment was futile, and in 1873 began to publish supplements to *CIL* in the series *Ephemeris Epigraphica*. This series died out after nine volumes were published in two series, the last in 1909. By that time the French project, *L'Année épigraphique* (*AE*), initiated under the direction of René Cagnat in 1888 as an appendix to the *Revue archéologique*, had filled the need for an annual review of new publications of Latin inscriptions (albeit in a less than systematic way at first). As is appropriate to a series that began life as a supplement to *CIL*, the organization of texts in *AE* is by location. This principle is also maintained in the two publications that offer annual reviews of newly discovered or re-edited Greek inscriptions, the *Bulletin épigraphique* (*BE*), which appears as a regular section in the *Revue des études grecques* and the *Supplementum Epigraphicum Graecum* (*SEG*), which began publication in 1923. The publication of *SEG* was interrupted in 1971, and resumed, with a new editorial team, in 1979 (beginning with publications from 1976–7). The very high current standard for all three reviews was established by *BE*, which was, from 1938 to 1984, edited by Jean and Louis Robert.

In 1903 the Akademie der Wissenschaften at Berlin, which also oversees the ongoing work on *CIL*, undertook a systematic publication of inscriptions from the Greek world in the series *Inscriptiones Graecae* (*IG*). The project was originally envisaged in 15 volumes; although several of these volumes were never completed, the project currently runs to 49 fascicles with around 50,000 texts (information on the current state of the project may be obtained at www.bbaw.de/forschung/ig/index.html):

volumes 1–3: Attica
volume 4: the Argolid
volume 5: Laconia, Messenia, and Arcadia
volume 6: Achaea and Elis
volume 7: the Megarid and Boeotia
volume 8: Delphi
volume 9: northern Greece
volume 10: Macedonia
volume 11: Delos
volume 12: islands of the Aegean other than Delos

volume 13: Crete
volume 14: Sicily and Italy
volume 15: Cyprus

Many of these volumes are in multiple fascicles (especially volume 12) and many of the older ones are badly out of date, and, at major sites, easily surpassed by volumes produced in conjunction with ongoing excavations. Most notable in this regard, for mainland Greece, are the series for Delphi and for Delos (*Fouilles de Delphes* [*FD*], *Inscriptions de Délos* [*ID*]). Volumes of *IG* for areas outside of Europe were never produced at all, so scholars must work from a number of regional corpora. The most notable of these are, for Asia Minor, *Monumenta Asiae Minoris Antiquae* (*MAMA*), now in ten volumes; *Tituli Asiae Minoris* (*TAM*), five volumes in 12 fascicles with five supplemental volumes, and the ever expanding series of *Inschriften griechischer Städte aus Kleinasien* (*IK* followed by the name of the city); and, for Syria, the excellent *Inscriptions grecques et latines de la Syrie* (*IGLS*). These corpora, as Louis Robert has observed, enable a partial reconstruction of the life of a region in antiquity, especially when used, as they must be, with the evidence from coins, literary texts, monuments and of geography (Robert 1961: 26).

Florilegia

The problem with regional corpora is that they are very hard to use, even in cases where they have been well indexed. The consequence is that scholars have often turned to volumes that might be termed "greatest hits" of epigraphy, or, in technical parlance, *florilegia*. The problem with the comprehensive collections for the Greek world was recognized even as the later volumes of *CIG* were in preparation, which is why, in 1877, the German publisher Georg Hirzel invited Wilhelm Dittenberger to produce a collection of texts that would be "especially useful for the study of Greek history and institutions." Dittenberger responded with the first edition of his *Sylloge Inscriptionum Graecarum* (*SIG*).

The history of *SIG* is something of a paradigm for the expanding scope of classical studies during the second half of the nineteenth century. In the first edition, completed in 1883, Dittenberger restricted himself to texts relating to regions that were Greek prior to the time of Alexander, from earliest times to Justinian's closure of the philosophical schools in Athens. He also decided to exclude all verse inscriptions on the grounds that they were already being edited by Georg Kaibel. He retained his organizing principle in the second edition of 1898, though in that volume he eliminated texts from Hellenistic times, deciding instead to produce a supplement, in two volumes, that would accommodate the Greek east after Alexander. The result is the second of the great collections, *Orientis Graeci Inscriptiones Selectae* (*OGIS*), published in two volumes and containing 775 texts. Dittenberger completed work on *OGIS* in 1903 and died three years later. In 1911, a new team of scholars set to work updating and expanding *SIG*, adding new sections that included civic decrees, texts relating to religious institutions and to private life. The third edition, which includes 1,268 texts, was completed in 1920. Although many of the texts included in *SIG* and *OGIS* have subsequently been re-edited, both collections retain immense value because of the extraordinarily astute annotation, philological and historical, with which Dittenberger and his later editors equipped their texts.

Shortly after Dittenberger completed *OGIS*, René Cagnat began a collection of Greek texts relating to the Roman Empire, *Inscriptiones Graecae ad res Romanas Pertinentes* (*IGR*). The project, originally conceived in four volumes, was never completed – volume 2 on mainland Greece was not done at all, and volume 4 was published as it stood when its editor, George Lefaye, died, despite the fact that he had not been able to cover many major cities of the eastern empire. Despite the fact that neither the annotation or proof-reading attain the consistent level of excellence found in Dittenberger's work, *IGR*'s attempt at comprehensive coverage of civic epigraphy and broad geographic coverage make it a valuable guide to the Greek epigraphy of the Roman world.

The inspiration for Dittenberger's *SIG* came from earlier *florilegia* devoted to Latin inscriptions. Wilhelm Henzen began work on a collection to replace those of Orellius (with whom he had worked as an assistant) and a subsequent work by Gustav Wilmanns, *Exempla inscriptionum latinarum*, which appeared in 1878. Henzen died in 1887 with the work as yet incomplete, and, after consultation amongst his friends, the project was given over to Hermann Dessau, another scholar of immense talent. As Dessau himself wrote, *Inscriptiones Latinae Selectae* (*ILS*) represents the progress of epigraphy during the nineteenth century (*ILS* pref., iii). The earlier collection of Orellius was hampered by the fact that Orellius himself had seen very few actual inscriptions, and had to work from texts collected by a number of authors of dubious ability, or published in journals, "by authors of whose faith and learning there was no evidence...now, with the *Corpus Inscriptionum Latinarum* almost complete, with supplements published without delay, we have arrived at a point where, in cases of inscriptions once seen but subsequently lost, there is scarcely any doubt" (*ILS* pref., iv). He is quite frank that the book as it stands really is a summary of the historically significant inscriptions published in *CIL*.

Dessau's *ILS* contains 9,400 Latin texts with an appendix of 150 Greek inscriptions in three volumes divided into five parts. The first volume is in ten chapters, of which the first two contain monuments of historical significance from the republican period and inscriptions relating to the imperial house from Augustus to the Byzantine emperor Constans II (641–68 CE) (*ILS* 839). The third chapter includes foreign kings from Juba (*ILS* 840) to the Vandal king Gelimer (*ILS* 860). Chapters four and five deal with senators from the late republic to Basilus, the last consul (in 541), and with men and women of equestrian rank. In the case of equestrians the texts are divided according to the highest rank that the person held, with praetorian prefects (*ILS* 1321–34) preceding prefects of Egypt, the *annona* and the *vigiles* (*ILS* 1335–47), and then procurators (*ILS* 1348–472). Imperial freedmen and women are the subject of chapter six, followed by magisterial assistants and public slaves in chapter seven. Chapter eight deals with grants of citizenship. Chapter nine is concerned with inscriptions relating to soldiers, while chapter ten collects inscriptions relating to famous men of letters (*ILS* 2915–56). The first part of volume two consists of four chapters: inscriptions relating to cults, organized by cult (*ILS* 2957–5050a), texts relating to public entertainments, organized according to type (*ILS* 5051–316), public works, boundary stones, and private projects (*ILS* 5317–6043), and texts relating to municipal government (*ILS* 6044–7209), a selection that ranges from municipal codes (*ILS* 6085–9) and imperial letters on matters pertaining to civic institutions (*ILS* 6090–2), to Pompeian graffiti (*ILS* 6398–445f). Volume two, part two contains five chapters including inscriptions relating to *collegia* (*ILS* 7211–365), texts relating to private slaves and members of various urban professions (*ILS* 7366–817), funerary monuments (*ILS* 7818a–8560), inscriptions on various tools and other instruments of private life, including brick stamps, amphorae, lamps etc. (*ILS* 8561–742), and inscriptions that are otherwise unclassifiable, ranging from an inscribed divinatory model of a liver (*ILS* 8743), calendars (*ILS* 8744–5), curse tablets (*ILS* 8746–57), texts carved on Egyptian monuments (*ILS* 8758–60) and what appears to be a *lex convivialis* (*ILS* 8761). There follows a brief collection of Greek inscriptions relating to Roman administration (*ILS* 8762–883). The collection concludes with an appendix of texts that came to light after work on the collection began (*ILS* 8884–9522) along with addenda and corrigenda and two volumes of excellent indices.

The basic principle upon which the *florilegia* are organized is that texts relating to specific types of activity should be read together. In the case of wide ranging works such as *ILS*, *OGIS*, and *SIG* this does cause some problems, especially in attempting to categorize inscriptions: how to deal with texts that fit into more than one category? To take just a few of the most obvious issues, important texts for the relationship between emperor and Senate, such as the decree of 177 CE relating to prices for public performers, is placed amongst inscriptions relating to entertainers (*ILS* 5163); one of the most important statements of Constantine's religious policy, the letter to Orcistus, is relegated to the section on imperial letters to cities (*ILS* 6091); the acts of the Arval brethren, which offer crucial information on the structure of the upper class, are placed with religious texts (*ILS* 5026–41); the texts relating to centurions all deal with equestrians, most of the famous literary figures are senators, and so forth. None of these are unreasonable choices, but they are all choices that distort the information offered in other parts of the collection.

Insofar as inscriptions necessarily reflect the totality of relationships connected with any public statement, they inevitably reflect interrelationships between groups in Roman society. For that reason it often makes more sense to collect all texts concerned with specific types of activity regardless of formal type (Robert 1961: 25). There is perhaps no better example of why this should be so than Robert's own masterful study of gladiators in the Greek East (supplemented by a series of publications of work done in subsequent seminars) (Robert 1940). In the area of Roman administration, Michael Crawford's collection of Roman laws and statutes from the early republic through Tiberius has become a crucial starting point for the study of Roman procedure (Crawford 1996). Even though it is now somewhat dated, Robert Sherk's collection of Roman documents from the Greek east remains an invaluable guide to the way in which Roman administration was received in the Greek east (*RDGE*), while John Oliver's collection of epigraphic and papyrological constitutions of Roman emperors is a crucial tool for the study of the role of the emperor in the government of the empire (Oliver and Clinton 1989), especially now that it can be supplemented by Tor Hauken's collection of petitions to emperors (Hauken 1998). The study of the governing classes, which likewise must begin with epigraphy, has been reshaped by work such as Werner Eck's studies of senators from Vespasian to Hadrian (Eck 1970) or his work on the organization of Italy (Eck 1979), or of Roman women by Raepsaet-Charlier (1987). We will return shortly to the way in which H.-G. Pflaum's extraordinary epigraphic study of imperial procurators (Pflaum 1950; 1960–1) has enabled us to see structures that are largely invisible from other sources.

Papyrological corpora and tools

The need to create proper corpora has driven research in papyrology every bit as much as it has the work of epigraphists. In the course of the last century, papyrologists have been collecting information in special corpora and creating tools both in conventional and electronic form. Most papyri are published in series named either after the geographic location of the collection (e.g. *P.Mich.* for the collection at the University of Michigan) or after the place of origin of a collection (e.g. *P.Oxy.* for the papyri from the site of Oxyrhynchus). Several thousand texts, however, have been published in journals. Those have been collected and reprinted in the *Sammelbuch griechischer Urkunden aus Ägypten* (1915–; various editors; currently consisting of 24 volumes, with an index). Below, we provide highlights of the corpora and research tools that are relevant for the Roman period. For more information readers are advised to use the on-line *Checklist of Editions* at www.scriptorium.lib.duke.edu/papyrus/texts/clist.html.

Corpora:

- L. Mitteis and U. Wilcken, *Grundzüge und Chrestomathie der Papyruskunde* (*M.Chr.* and *W.Chr.*) (1912): two vols. of introduction, two of selected texts, one pair each for history and law. Still the fundamental introduction to documents.
- *Chartae Latinae Antiquiores* (*ChLA*), established by A. Bruckner and R. Marichal (1954–). Currently 49 vols. collecting all known Latin texts.
- *Corpus Papyrorum Judaicarum* (*C.Pap.Jud.*). Three vols. by V. A. Tcherikover published in 1957, 1960 (with A. Fuks) and 1964 (with A. Fuks and M. Stern), containing papyri that witness the presence of Jews in Graeco-Roman Egypt.
- *New Documents Illustrating Early Christianity* (*New Docs*). Various editors. (1981–). Eight vols. to date.
- K. Preisendanz, *Papyri Graecae Magicae* (*PGM*). Two vols. (Leipzig-Berlin 1928, 1931). Collects magical texts. Photostatic copies of proofs of an unpublished third volume exist in some libraries. A reprint including texts from the projected third volume with revisions by A. Henrichs was published in 1974. For more recent work on magical papyri, see R. W. Daniel and F. Maltomini, *Supplementum Magicum* (*Suppl.Mag.*). 2 vols. (Opladen 1990, 1992).

There are several collections of letters, such as:

- S. Witkowski, *Epistulae privatae graecae quae in papyris aetatis Lagidarum servantur*. Leipzig 1911 (2nd edn.) for private letters.
- M. Naldini, *Il Cristianesimo in Egitto: Lettere private nei papiri dei secoli II–IV*. Florence 1968, 2nd edn. Fiesole 1998, with addenda but no additional texts. Useful for studying early Christianity through private letters.

- G. Tibiletti, *Le Lettere private nei papiri greci del III e IV secolo d.C.* Milan 1979. Scienze filologiche e letteratura XV. Useful for private letters of the third and fourth centuries.

Research tools

For searching the documentary Greek and Latin texts papyrologists rely on the invaluable "Duke Data Bank of Documentary Papyri" (DDBDP) which at present contains all texts published to June 1996. Available on Packard Humanities CD-ROM #7 and on-line at: www.perseus.tufts.edu/Texts/papyri.html. An updated on-line version including all texts to 2005 is scheduled to be available by the spring of 2006. The DDBDP will undergo major changes in the next two years. For word lists of recent volumes of papyri and ostraca consult the *Wörterliste* of D. Hagedorn at: www.uni-heidelberg.de/institute/Fak8/papy/WL/WL.html.

For tracking corrections to previously published papyri, one must consult the *Berichtigungsliste der griechischen Papyrusurkunden aus Ägypten* (*BL*). Various editors (1922–). At present ten volumes plus a volume of concordances to vols. 1–7.

The main bibliographic tool in the field of papyrology is the *Bibliographie Papyrologique* which covers all publications from 1930 to date. Available on CD-ROM "Subsidia Papyrologica 2.0." Those not familiar with Greek or Papyrology may wish to consult the on-line "Advanced Papyrological Information System" (APIS) at: www.columbia.edu/cu/lweb/projects/digital/apis/ which provides descriptive metadata and some translations for thousands of papyri in North American and some European collections. For geographical names encountered in papyri, one should consult A. Calderini and S. Daris, *Dizionario dei nomi geografici e topografici dell'Egitto greco-romano*. Several vols., fascicles, and supplements (1935–).

2 The Use of Inscriptions and Papyri

Restoration

Inscriptions and papyri share the problem that they are rarely found intact, and, even when they are, the more complex a document is, the more likely that it will contain errors. The people who actually placed inscriptions on stone or bronze tablets were quite good at recognizing forms that were familiar, but often less good at dealing with extended prose. It is more than a bit disturbing to find that there are 178 textual divergences in the two copies of the *senatus consultum Pisonianum* of 20 CE, and that both contain one obvious, and as yet irreparable, textual corruption (Eck et al. 1996: 67–70). The tendency towards error in antiquity, together with breakage in transmission, are the primary issues that epigraphists and papyrologists must face. Like scholars who work with the manuscript tradition, they have to correct errors and fill in lacunae with likely restorations. In the case of inscriptions, as Louis Robert has written, it is the business of the epigraphist to know what can and cannot be reasonably restored (Robert 1961: 29–32). If a portion of a stone has been completely lost, there is no point in trying to reconstitute what is lost – this is especially true if the missing portion is at the top or bottom (Robert 1961: 28). If, however, portions of lines, either on the left or right hand sides have been preserved, there are techniques that permit restoration with a high degree of probability; the key distinction here is between reestablishing and remaking the document. Re-manufacture is a waste of time, while restoration is the process of recovering that which has been lost – or, at least, the sense of what has been lost.

The editorial work of a papyrologist is not dissimilar from that of the epigraphist, except that the former deals with a much broader range of types of text: literature of known or unknown authorship, a variety of subliterary texts such as oracles, prophecies, medical recipes, magic, etc. and primarily documentary material dealing with every aspect of everyday life. In transliterating a text, papyrologists use a uniform system of critical signs that was accepted in 1931 at a meeting of papyrologists at Leiden (the Leiden Convention System). This system has been in use ever since (van Groningen 1932), and is now used by epigraphists as well. With the help of these critical signs papyrologists and epigraphists indicate the following:

- dots under letters: the letters are doubtful, either because of damage or because they are otherwise difficult to read
- just dots: a corresponding number of letters remain unread by the editor
- letters in [ ]: the letters are lost, but restored from a parallel or by conjecture
- dots in [ ]: a corresponding number of letters are lost, but not restored
- ( ): round brackets indicate the resolution of an abbreviation
- letters in [[ ]]: the letters are deleted on the document
- letters in \ /: the letters are added above the line on the papyrus
- letters in < >: the letters are added by the editor
- letters in { }: the letters are regarded as mistaken and rejected by the editor

In addition to visually representing the condition of the original text, this system represents the interpretation of the text, serving as a warning to the reader. According to Herbert Youtie, the proper work of the papyrologist is the creation of the transcribed and edited text. He is the "artificer of fact," namely of "dependable facts" that he "draws from them" and presents "to the substantive disciplines" (H. C. Youtie 1973a: 21; 1973b). Indeed, the "creation" of a text is a mental process in which reading and interpretation are inextricably interwoven. As Peter Parsons has pointed out recently, "our activities fit with curious aptness into modernist discourse: in the most literal way, our texts are artifacts, our readings are creative. The construction of a text is itself a critical act: decipherment determines supplement, supplements build up context, contexts combine in form, form interrogates readings and supplements, and so circularly; eye and understanding provoke each other" (Parsons 1994: 122).

Some historians, as Robert noted, object to any effort at restoration on the grounds that it involves writing history from "square brackets." The expression itself is owed to a scholar who attempted to refute an argument based on literary texts to justify a restoration in an inscription (Badian 1989). The restoration may or may not be correct, but that was not the point; the historical argument did not stand or fall on the basis of the restoration, and historians need to be wary of bogus assertions of caution in dealing with such arguments (Robert 1961: 28). The point is that proper restorations begin with what is available on the surviving document and offer supplements on the basis of parallels with other texts – they explicate rather than create.

Reconstruction

The issue of the restoration of inscriptions and papyri is bound up with the much broader question of how inscriptions are used to further historical arguments. There are no simple rules that can govern all situations. Sometimes it is sufficient to work from within a specific corpus of texts. More often than not, however, inscriptions cannot be allowed to bear the brunt of a case without reference to other categories of evidence, as we shall see in reviewing some of the (excellent) work that has been done in the areas of the Roman family and Roman public administration.

In 1984 Brent Shaw and Richard Saller published a study of family structure in the western empire based on the evidence provided by an extremely large sample of funerary epitaphs (12–13,000 out of 25,000 read) (Saller and Shaw 1984: 125 n. 8). In this survey they divided the sample between texts commemorating relationships within the nuclear family and relationships outside of it (non-kin, heirs, and the extended family). In civilian populations they showed that in 75–90 percent of the texts that listed commemorators, the commemorators came from the nuclear family of the deceased. They compared these results with military populations in the western empire, noting that in some areas (especially North Africa, the Pannonias, and Spain), the military pattern conformed to the civilian, a fact that could be explained for North Africa and Spain by the fact that these legions tended to be stationary and not to engage in major wars. In north-western Europe, however, the pattern was quite different, suggesting, quite reasonably, that the commemorative evidence revealed different patterns of recruitment in the army (Saller and Shaw 1984: 145). They concluded that "though on the narrowest view these tombstone inscriptions tell us only who fulfilled the duty of providing a memorial to the deceased, there are strong reasons for believing that fulfillment of this duty was closely related to transmission of property, to a sense of familial duty and feelings of affection" (Saller and Shaw 1984: 145). This is reasonable as far as it goes. But they went beyond this to argue that the nuclear family was the main form of familial organization in many regions of western Europe as early as the Roman Empire (Saller and Shaw 1984: 146), and Saller went on to assert that Romans "drew a conceptual circle around the mother–father–children triad and made it the center of primary obligations" (Saller 1984: 355).

There are plainly two very different questions here, and neither of them can really be answered on the basis of inscriptions alone: first, what is the relationship between commemorative pattern and household organization?; second, is household organization prescriptive of affectionate patterns? In 1996, Dale Martin published a valuable study of funerary inscriptions from Asia Minor in which he showed that there was considerable regional variation in commemorative patterns, and questioned whether the dichotomy between the nuclear and extended family was useful, suggesting that a better model would be to think in terms of degrees of intimacy within the household (D. Martin 1996: 57–8). While Martin's approach is thoroughly reasonable and will be, as we shall see, supported by a significant body of alternative evidence, his discussion failed to answer the question of why the commemorative pattern in the west should be so overwhelmingly that of the nuclear family. Is the reason ideological? This very issue was raised by Greg Woolf in the same volume of the *Journal of Roman Studies* that contains Martin's essay. Woolf noted an issue that neither Saller and Shaw nor Martin had observed, but which is pertinent to both of their studies. This is the fact that many tombstones are not inscribed at all. In some parts of the empire tombstones tend to contain a relief that is not accompanied by a text (Woolf 1996: 27). He suggested instead that we need to think of all monuments as seeking to establish false claims of permanency in an ever-changing world (Woolf 1996: 39). In this article, Woolf was expanding upon a study by Elizabeth Meyer, who had suggested that the practice of inscription should be linked not so much with family relationship as with status. In their study, Saller and Shaw paid no attention to the issue of date (something that is likewise true of Martin's study). In Meyer's view, there was a massive upsurge in the epigraphic habit in the western empire during the second century CE. This was a period in which many people were acquiring the privileged status of Roman citizenship, even though Roman citizens arguably remained a minority in any provincial population. As she correctly noted, the distinction between public and private is hard to maintain in any epigraphic context since, by their very nature, inscriptions are public. She suggested instead that epitaphic commemoration reached a peak in the later second century, before Caracalla's grant of citizenship to almost all free inhabitants of the empire in 212 meant that there was no longer any point to advertising this status on tombstones. If that is true, then it logically follows that the nature of commemoration in epitaphs is related to Roman rules of inheritance, which left the primary responsibility for commemoration with the heirs (Meyer 1990: 95–6). Although there are problems with Meyer's style of analysis, the most important being that our ability to date funerary epitaphs is vastly less accurate than she asserts (Bodel 2001: 38), it is nevertheless true that, on the basis of inscriptions alone, we cannot be certain whether the evidence they provide is essentially a reflection of ideology or of actual family structure. This point is not affected by the dating problem: the style can still reflect ideology rather than family structure, if people are copying a familiar local style that is understood to reflect status, and that need have nothing to do with Caracalla.

To answer the question of whether inscriptions from the Latin west are likely to provide an accurate guide to family structure, we need another kind of evidence altogether. In the case of family structure the necessary body of evidence comes from papyri. In 1994, Roger Bagnall and Bruce Frier published the results of their analysis of census returns from Roman Egypt (Bagnall and Frier 1994). On the basis of their analysis of the returns, Bagnall and Frier show that nuclear households make up a plurality rather than a majority of Egyptian households (Bagnall and Frier 1994: 60–2, 67). They further show that, while there is a bias in the evidence towards metropolitan households, which show a bare majority of nuclear families, these represent a far smaller proportion of the overall population. The advantage of the census returns is obvious. Although they present snapshots of a household at a given moment, they are not liable to reveal artificially permanent relationships in the same way that inscriptions might. Instead, what the returns reveal is that actual households alternate "erratically over generations between simpler and more complex forms" (Bagnall and Frier 1994: 64). For the historian using inscriptions, these conclusions show that the inclinations of Meyer and Woolf are more likely to be correct than those of Saller and Shaw, that even "private" texts are the result of a desire to publicize an ideologically defined state of affairs.

The equestrian career

In the introduction to this volume, Potter offered an account of the typical senatorial career. This is largely based upon inscriptions, with some admixture of textual evidence that has been used to create an image of the typical progression of an aspiring senator. Although there will remain some areas of debate – especially around the question of whether some men who were recognized as being particularly good soldiers gained an advantage over their peers – the picture is well enough established by the combination of evidentiary categories to be regarded as essentially secure. We are on somewhat different ground when it comes to the other major governmental institution, the equestrian bureaucracy, especially that which includes the fiscal administration of the empire.

In the early Julio-Claudian period there were three kinds of procurators, the praesidial (governors of minor provinces), fiscal (charged with the administration of various tax revenues and infrastructure), and personal (charged with tasks necessary for the maintenance of the emperor's *patrimonium*) (Brunt 1966: 461–5). Atop all of these were the "secretariats" in the palace and the great prefectures. The four great prefectures were Egypt, the *annona*, the *vigiles*, and the praetorian. The secretarial positions, in the second century, included the *a libellis*, in charge of legal appeals to the emperor, the *ab epistulis*, a post usually divided between officials charged with either Greek or Latin letters, and the *a rationibus*, the official in overall charge of the revenues of the imperial properties. In general terms the secretarial positions could be defined as equestrian assistants to the emperor in hearing legal cases, receiving and responding to the letters and decrees of cities and petitions of individuals, and in handling other matters connected with the administration of the empire (Dio 52.35.5, with Millar 1977: 105).

How did people move from one position to another and was there any sense of a prescribed sequence in an equestrian career? We know that there was a career that could be specifically chosen as early as the first century because, aside from the epigraphic evidence of equestrian officeholders, Tacitus tells us that men could chose between equestrian and senatorial careers – but he does not tell us more than that. In 1950 Pflaum attempted to fill in the missing information when he essayed to update Otto Hirschfeld's fundamental study of Roman administration (Hirschfeld 1905). Pflaum felt that Hirschfeld's book suffered from a number of faults, not the least being that "there was an absence of precise classification of the different posts in the procuratorial career, a task rendered impossible, Hirschfeld thought, by the fact that there was not a fixed hierarchy" (Pflaum 1950: 1). There was good reason for Hirschfeld to think as much. For one thing, there was no fixed order of promotion into the lower ranks of the procuratorial career – men could enter either of the two first levels (those with salaries set at 60,000 or 100,000 sesterces) from military commands such as the command of an auxiliary cohort, or service as a military tribune or chief centurion of a legion (*primus pilus*). If there was no fixed entry point, it might stand to reason that there would be a certain amount of fluidity in the system all the way along.

Even admitting that movement from the lower into the upper ranks of the procuratorial administration was fluid, Pflaum detected general patterns in the order that posts were held in the three main grades of procurator: the *sexagenarii*, *centenarii*, and *ducenarii* (men with salaries of 60,000, 100,000 and 200,000 sesterces). He noted, for instance, that most of the posts held by *sexagenarii* were as assistants to other officials (Pflaum 1950: 231), that *centenarii* never went from holding a provincial post to holding a position such as procurator *ad bona damnatorum*, or procurator in charge of the property of the condemned (that is to say property that was confiscated to the *fiscus*), and that people never went from higher salary grades to lower. He was also able to establish that the fixed ranking system of procurators was established under the Flavians, and that there was a steady increase in the number of procurators in the course of the second century CE, with 62 posts attested, as of when he was writing in 1950, under Domitian, 127 under Marcus Aurelius, and a massive upsurge under Septimius Severus, in whose reign 174 posts are attested (Pflaum 1950: 105).

Having established that people did hold certain posts after they had held other ones, Pflaum attempted to reduce the scheme of promotion within the different salary grades to a fixed pattern, especially for the *ducenarii*. The first post held was usually a minor provincial governorship, a provincial procuratorship (see Ando, this volume) or an urban post such as prefect of the inheritance tax. It is with the second and subsequent posts that Pflaum's analysis begins to falter amid the complexity of the evidence. There is no obvious difference between many of the second, third, and even fourth posts, and no obvious, or guaranteed, promotion from procuratorial posts to the imperial secretariat or the imperial prefectures. When too great regularity is sought, there is simply not enough evidence in the inscriptions to allow for answers to the questions that Pflaum asked.

Although part of Pflaum's project did not succeed, taken as a whole it nevertheless achieved important results. Pflaum's collection of the evidence remains splendidly valuable work, and the observation that the equestrian bureaucracy expanded in ways that the senatorial did not, is arguably a point of enormous significance.

Although Pflaum's question about promotion was thoroughly reasonable, his predisposition to find a positive answer led him to over-interpret the evidence. It also distracted attention away from other issues. The notion that there could be promotion from one position to another necessitated the view that there was a specific point at which officials were reviewed. If this were the case, and we know in fact that it was, then one might reasonably ask, What were the criteria for appointment, reappointment, or promotion? What was the relative balance between demonstrated ability and friendship with other important people? We simply do not know for certain, but there are some facts that are suggestive. One thing we know is that there was a specific point in each year at which the emperor evaluated people for equestrian jobs. Another is that letters Pliny sends in connection with equestrian promotion (see the Introduction to this volume) stress previous accomplishment, suggesting that there was a feeling that equestrians, like senators, were expected to build a track record of achievement. A third is that even senior administrative officials in Egypt tended to have little or no previous experience in the province (Brunt 1975: 141–2, and p. 164 below), but they all had track records in administration. What Brunt did not consider was the extent to which their appointments were always as the heads of the departments where long-serving officials did the bulk of the day-to-day work. It is notorious that managers learn how to handle situations rather than specific circumstances. Experience and training gives them the ability to manage (in theory) whatever situation they find themselves in, and to work with specialists in those areas. Without examining the evidence for the interaction between senior officials and the professionals who worked for them, we cannot really understand how the administrative system worked. At issue here is the central problem of finding an intersection between different forms of evidence. Inscriptions show us what a man wanted people to know about him: they reflect the status that he attained through the performance of his duties. The career inscriptions upon which our knowledge of the equestrian career are based cannot tell us how people carried out their jobs, and how the administration that they were part of actually functioned. If we want to see what equestrian officials actually did, we need to look instead at the papyri.

3 The Egyptian Question

The nature of the source material

Despite recent discoveries outside of Egypt, the most obvious fact about the study of papyrology is that the vast majority of surviving literary and documentary texts come from Egypt. The peculiar climatic conditions of Egypt have ensured the survival of tens of thousands of papyri, and even as more papyri, or similar documents, have come to light from elsewhere, it remains that we have nothing comparable in scope to the wealth of material that comes from Egypt. The concentration of the evidence in one part of the empire means that historians must decide what is primarily relevant to the particular conditions of Egypt, and what they should regard as being illustrative of the broader issues of social interaction within the empire as a whole. Although this discussion will be limited to actions in the official sphere, the same general rules hold true for interactions in the private sphere.

The survival pattern of papyri

The survival of papyri is uneven both in space and in time. For instance, with the exception of some notable finds of carbonized papyri in Thmouis and Boubastos, we have almost no papyri from Alexandria, the provincial capital, or the Delta, the most densely populated part of Egypt. What we know about this area comes from papyri that somehow found their way, mostly through the migration of government officials, into the *chora*, the Egyptian countryside. This anomaly is further complicated by the uneven pattern of survival within the *chora* itself. Documents that shed light on the administration are, for unknown reasons, thinly spread in the first century, but become much richer in the second and third centuries, up to the accession of Diocletian. Geographically, the distribution of the evidence, at least in its current state, is also problematic, because it comes from only two sources: firstly, the ruins and trash-piles of a handful of towns and villages in the Fayum, located on the fringes of the desert that literally dried up in the later Roman period; and secondly, from a few local centers of imperial administration such as Hermopolis, Antinoopolis, and most importantly Oxyrhynchus, as well as some, very limited, evidence from Upper Egypt or from the deserts to the east and west (Bagnall 1995: 26–9; Habermann 1998). Such an uneven pattern in the survival skews our understanding of Roman administration in Egypt: while there is rich documentation for the study of the local administration the evidence is very scarce at the central and regional levels.

Importance of the papyri: "archives," "dossiers," and individual documents

It is now some 30 years since Alan Bowman made a powerful case for the role of papyrology in understanding Roman history beyond the boundaries of Egypt, as well as within its confines (Bowman 1976, 2001). Since then historians of all sorts have increasingly come to realize the significance of papyri for the study of the Roman Empire at large, and have attempted to make the Egyptian evidence more pertinent to Roman historiography (Bagnall 1995), while, at the same time, refining our understanding of Roman institutions and administration in Egypt itself (J. D. Thomas 2001).

The first problem that both sorts of historians have had to face is the fact that the clandestine activities of Egyptian farmers and antiquities dealers removed ancient artifacts from their immediate physical, associative context, meaning that most papyri in modern collections are disembodied objects. Those discovered during scientific archaeological excavations that can be studied in their original context are, unfortunately, a minority. The result is that we have very few archives that were assembled by their original, ancient owner(s). In response, papyrologists have been struggling to cluster papyri temporally and spatially on the basis of internal information such as date, place of origin, and prosopography. In some cases they have succeeded in reconstructing modern "dossiers" that once may have belonged to a particular individual (on the issue of modern "dossier" versus ancient "archive," see A. Martin 1992; above, section 1). For convenience and accuracy, the term "dossier" will be used throughout this discussion, except for cases where the term "archive" can be used indisputably.

The most reliable historical information about the middle and lower levels of the Roman administration of Egypt comes from groups of closely interrelated documents, ranging in size from just a dozen to several hundred texts. (Montevecchi 1988: 248–61, 575–8, lists 135 so-called "archives," dating from the Ptolemaic to the Byzantine period, but most of them are in fact "dossiers.") Surviving "dossiers" regularly focus on an individual or a family, rarely on an office. As expected, no government or state "archive" from Alexandria has survived, but rather "dossiers" of middle and low ranking officials as well as wealthy individuals from communities of the countryside. This category of "dossiers" is important for the study of imperial administration because of its mixed nature, containing not only private documents (e.g. private correspondence), but also texts that show the individual and his family acting in the public sphere either with other private individuals (e.g. loans and leases) or with representatives of the government (e.g. petitions, applications). In fact, very often members of these upper crust families in the countryside were intricately involved in the local government. That said, the information of individual, "non-dossier" documents should not be undervalued.

These texts range from trivial lists of expenses or objects to prefectural decrees and imperial legislation. To a large degree, isolated documents provide much of what we know about the higher levels of the central administration (Bagnall 1995: 33–40).

State and local archives

Both the pharaohs and the Ptolemies maintained extensive archives. The Romans retained and enlarged this system of record-keeping. State archives existed on the local level (village or *toparchy*), the *nome* capital, and the main libraries in Alexandria (the *katalogeion* with its branches). Despite the fact that the only public record office that has survived archaeologically is from the capital Mendes-Thmouis in the Delta where only relatively few carbonized papyri were recovered (*P.Thmouis* I), it is clear that the quantity of archived documentation in Roman Egypt covered all aspects of civil and financial administration, from citizenship and taxation to ownership and inheritance of real estate. In addition, the Romans introduced a system that required that a document not written by a notary could only be used in a law-court if it was given publicity (*demosiosis*) by submitting two copies to the state registry offices in Alexandria. The result was that the amount of documentation was overwhelming for all the officials involved from the bottom up; it was one of the prefect's primary goals to ensure that the documents were kept in good condition and order throughout Egypt (Cockle 1984). Our best evidence for the difficulties caused by this requirement comes from an edict that was issued in 89 CE by the prefect Mettius Rufus (*Sel.Pap.* II 219), which likewise reveals the interest of the central authority in the way that records were kept and documentation secured on the local level. In sum, the edict is an excellent example of the micro-managerial style of the provincial administration, seeking to ensure control of people's business to maximize Rome's revenue. That said, the edict did not solve the problems of record-keeping. Two documents from the first quarter of the second century reveal an extraordinary disorder in the papers of the public record office and the registry of real property in the Heracleides division of the Arsinoite *nome* (*P.Fam.Tebt.* 15 and 24). One of these texts (no. 24) makes reference to Rufus' edict, which was clearly ignored, since it goes on to describe documents and texts in the local office archive as being in "bad condition," "mutilated," and "lost and damaged." The disarray led to investigations, and a dispute that lasted for several years.

The Roman interest in preserving records of every transaction is revealed clearly at the village level of administration. For instance, several surviving rolls from the village registry office of Tebtunis (the only local archive of which part has survived!), dating some 50 years before the edict of Mettius Rufus, show that his instructions about how summaries of transactions should be recorded in the local offices followed a standard Roman practice that was in use well before his time (*P.Mich.* II). The following brief excerpts are representative of the format of the abstracts and demonstrate that they fully conform to Rufus' instructions:

> To the good fortune. Register of the sixth year of Tiberius Claudius Caesar Augustus Germanicus Imperator, month Sebastos 8.
> [Agreement] of obligation to remain in service (*paramone*) for the sum of 24 drachmai, (made) by Herakleides to Stotoetis. (Fee:) 6 oboloi.

[On the 9th. Acknowledgment] of deposit of 248 drachmai, (made) by Ptolemaios and his wife to Herodion. (Fee:) 6 drachmai.

Acknowledgment of receipt of a maintenance, (made) by [- - -]onopis and her husband to Orseus. (Fee:) 4 drachmai.

[On the 10th. Acknowledgment] of receipt of rent and...of farming, (made) by Soueris to Kronion (Fee:) 10 obols.

[Agreement of sale of cattle], (made) by Kronion to Horion. (Fee:) 6 drachmai, of which 4 drachmai were paid.

[On the 12th. Acknowledgment (of receipt)] of a dowry of 32 drachmai, (made) by Papontos to Didyme. (Fee:) 6 obols.

[Acknowledgment (of receipt)] of a dowry of 28 drachmai, (made) by Phemnasis to Menemachos. (Fee:) 6 obols. (*P.Mich.* II, no. 123, Recto, col. II, first 8 entries)

The documents from the Tebtunis archive record 800 such summaries for the year 45/6 CE, covering a broad range of transactions: dowry contracts, leases, sales, loans, mortgages, apprenticeship agreements, etc. Clearly, the staff at this village was kept very busy. Overall, the Roman administration tried to document – and thus control – every aspect of economic life by recording in detail people, land, and livestock. Such an intricate bureaucratic system relied on a very complex system of administrators, to which we shall now turn.

4 The Imperial Administration of Roman Egypt: An Overview

Contacts between Egypt and Rome began as early as the second century BCE, when some of the Ptolemies sought help from Rome in moments of crisis and internal strife. Thus the Romans must have acquired some familiarity with the country and its administration before their arrival there. In annexing Egypt, Augustus retained several Ptolemaic administrative structures virtually unchanged, including the division of the country into some forty *nomes* (districts into which Egypt was divided for the purpose of regional government). This system was retained during the first century of Roman rule. However, the Romans maintained or introduced certain peculiarities in Egypt's administration, which lasted through the end of the third century CE, almost all caused by the perception that Egypt was a powerful – hence, dangerous – country for the emperor in Rome. More specifically:

A The prefect and the procurators, unlike those of the other provinces, were from the equestrian rather than the senatorial class;
B Roman senators and equestrians were not allowed to visit Egypt, except with permission from the emperor;
C The Romans, following Ptolemaic practice, retained a closed monetary system in Egypt until Diocletian abolished it in 296 CE (for early Roman Egypt, see Bowman 1996).

The degree of Egypt's "Romanization" has been much debated in the past, but it has been convincingly shown that although the Romans retained much of the Ptolemaic terminology, they introduced new institutions and adapted old ones (Lewis 1970). In particular, the Romans introduced several innovations in the areas of administration of metropolitan cities (councils), land tenure (widespread private ownership), public services (city- and village-level liturgies), and legislation (Roman law).

It is impossible to discuss the papyrological documentation for every level of Roman administration in Egypt. The system was too complex and changed constantly over time. Table 3.1 gives a somewhat idealized picture of the system, summarizing offices that existed nearly throughout the Roman period. Overall, Egypt had a three-tiered system of administration: at the top stood the emperor's representative, the prefect (= provincial governor), and his immediate subordinates (*iuridicus* = legal advisor; *archiereus* = administrator of temples; *dioiketes* = finance officer; *idios logos* = official in charge of the imperial "private account;" procurators = financial officials; military commanders; and *epistrategoi* = four regional officials). They were all of equestrian rank, had no experience with Egypt (only broad training in Roman administration), and held their positions for three to four years. Beneath them was the *strategos*, the key figure in the administration of the *nome* (perhaps also a salaried official). Originally (in the Ptolemaic period) an officer with mainly military duties, the *strategos* gradually became a civil official with mainly financial and judicial responsibilities whose power declined during the middle of the third century CE, before being replaced by the *exactor* in the first quarter of the fourth century. The *strategos* with his assistant, the *basilikos grammateus* (royal scribe = secretary of the *nome*) was the mediator between the central government and the lower levels of administration in the cities (the magistrates and town councilors, especially after the widespread introduction of the *boulai* under Septimius Severus in 200/1) and in the villages (the secretary and the elders). The system involved a wide range of liturgists (performing compulsory public services) at the local level (J. D. Thomas 2001: 1245–8).

In order to illustrate the structure and functionality of the Roman administration in Egypt, the remainder of this chapter will provide brief overviews of select officials at each tier. Starting with the emperor in Rome, the discussion will move all the way down to the village scribe and will highlight areas that are critical for our understanding of Roman innovations and the nature of imperial rule in Egypt. Some representative documents will be introduced as a means of illustrating each tier or office.

The emperor and his control of Egypt

The Roman emperors were absentee rulers, but they kept a close watch on Egypt because one-third of the annual grain supply of the city of Rome was derived from the Egyptian land tax, and the province was notoriously prone to unrest. In response to these problems, the emperors tried to manipulate the province in two ways:

A Some of the emperors or members of their families visited Egypt, most notably Germanicus (whose visit had not been approved by Tiberius: Tac. *Ann.* 2.59), Vespasian, Hadrian, Septimius Severus, Caracalla, Aurelian, and lastly Diocletian – the last two in response to usurpation and revolts;

B Most importantly, they produced edicts dealing specifically with Egypt, well attested in the papyrological and the literary record (see e.g. the *Sel.Pap.* II, nos. 211–17, and the list in Montevecchi 1988: 126–7).

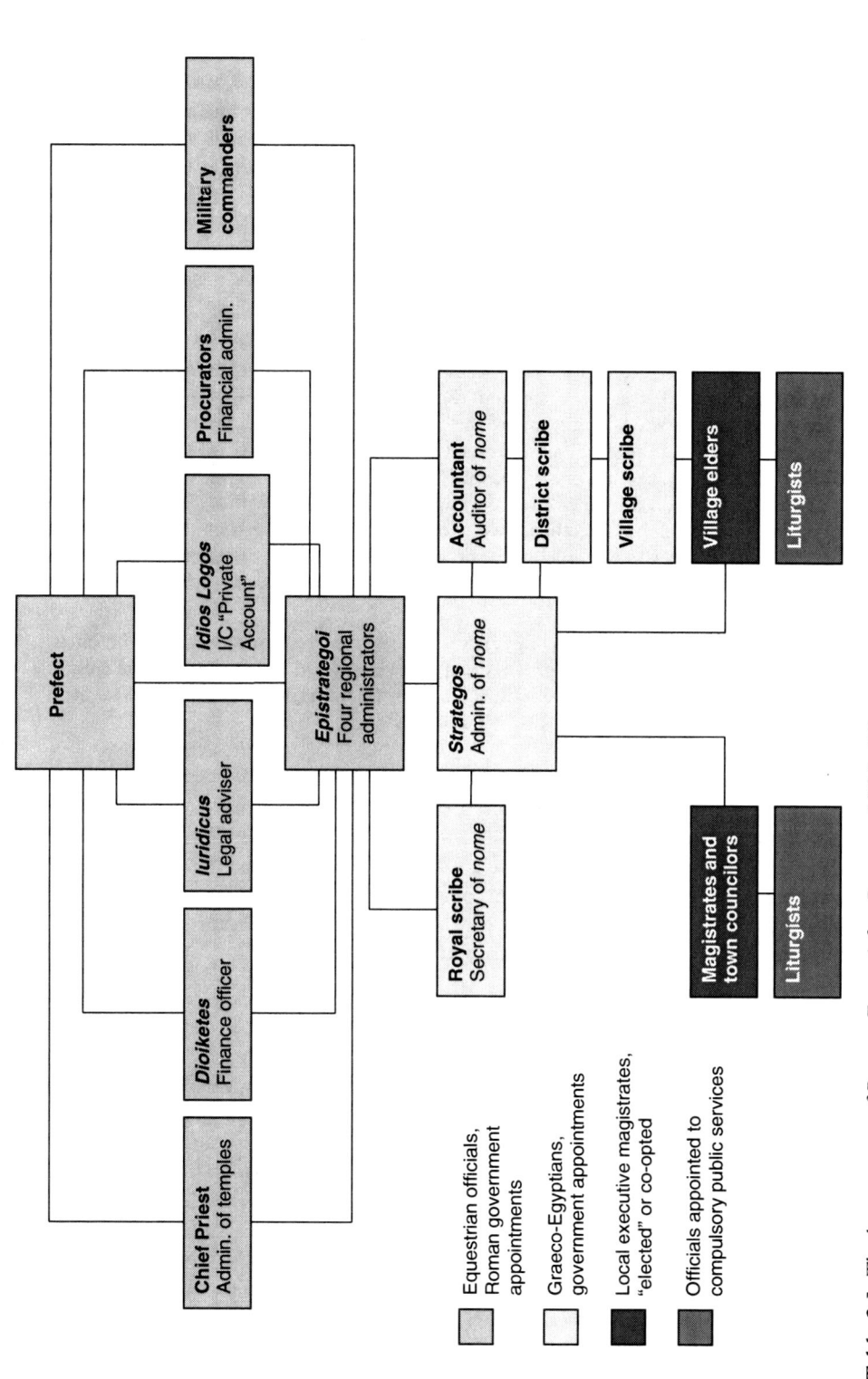

Table 3.1 The bureaucracy of Roman Egypt (after Bowman 1986: 67)

One of the best documented events is the visit of Caracalla in 215 CE, recorded by two contemporary historians (both hostile to the emperor), Cassius Dio and Herodian. Apparently, the Alexandrians offended Caracalla by connecting him with the murder of his brother Geta. In retaliation, Caracalla dismissed all "Egyptians" from Alexandria, except for the permanent residents, that is essentially everyone, except for Roman and Alexandrian citizens. He confiscated properties, removed the prefect from office, and turned his troops loose on the city for plunder and slaughter. After several days he called a halt of the violent acts and then issued several orders, such as the following:

> All Egyptians in Alexandria, especially country-folk, who have fled from other parts and can easily be detected, are by all means to be expelled, with the exception, however, of pig-dealers and river boatmen and the men who bring down reeds for heating the baths. But expel all others, as by the numbers of their kind and their uselessness they are disturbing the city. I am informed that at the festival of Sarapis and on certain other festal days Egyptians are accustomed to bring down bulls and other animals for sacrifice, or even on the other days; they are not prohibited for this. The persons who ought to be prohibited are those who flee from their own districts to escape rustic toil, not those, however, who congregate here with the object of viewing the glorious city of Alexandria or come down for the sake of enjoying a more civilized life or for incidental business.
>
> *A further extract*: For genuine Egyptians can easily be recognized among the linen-weavers by their speech, which proves them to have assumed the appearance and dress of another class; moreover in their mode of life, their far from civilized manners reveal them to be Egyptian country-folk (*P.Giss.* 40 ii = *Sel.Pap.* II 215).

In addition to recording these particular historical events, this document is perhaps even more significant for understanding the Roman perception of "Egyptians," and more broadly their construction of cultural differentiation. By this period the term "Egyptian" had no ethnic or cultural connotation, but referred broadly to the entire Graeco-Egyptian population of the countryside, which was trying to find refuge among the nameless masses of the city in an attempt to escape the hardships of countryside life and the burden of compulsory public services.

The prefect

The prefect was the supreme resident administrator and lawgiver. The entire population of Egypt, at least in theory, had the right to petition him, as it had the king or the queen in the Ptolemaic period. Hundreds such petitions and responses have survived, almost exclusively in the hands of the petitioners or the local offices. The prefect also communicated with the population through edicts and letters on a variety of issues. He held regular *conventus* (meetings with local officials and people) in a few designated population centers, carrying out inspections of public works, finances, etc. As in other provinces of the empire, the *conventus* in Egypt followed a fixed calendar: the prefect was in Pelusium in January (for the Eastern Delta) and in Memphis or Arsinoe from late January to mid April (for middle and upper Egypt); then he spent the rest of the year near Alexandria (Bowman 1976: 162–3, and J. D. Thomas 2001:

1244–5; for the *conventus* see Foti-Talamanca 1974 and Lewis 1981; for a list of edicts, rescripts and letters see Montevecchi 1988: 129–35 and 553–4).

The population was keen to express grievances during the annual *conventus*. The number of petitions that reached the prefect must have been overwhelming. One text (*P.Yale* I 61) informs us that during his visit to Arsinoe in 209 CE the prefect received 1,804 petitions in two and a half days, or about 700 to 750 per day (Lewis 1983: 189–90)!

Perhaps the most important responsibility for the prefect – and for the rest of the imperial administration – was land administration and tax collection. The Egyptian population was controlled through the fourteen-year cycle census and the land was registered in detailed cadastres, both of which provided the information for tax assessment on individuals as well as on the land and its products. The Romans instituted a vast array of taxes both in money and in kind through an intricate system that involved appointed officials working together with the *strategos* and a few private contractors. As the edict of Mettius Rufus (discussed earlier) demonstrates, upon acquisition of taxable – movable or immovable – property, all owners were required to file reports with the local record offices.

It is difficult to judge with certainty how burdensome this system was, but papyri show that farmers attempted to run away, and later that the government tried to bind them to their place of origin. Problems in the area of financial administration in Egypt appeared as early as the last years of Nero, when expenses increased in Rome and the state was almost bankrupt. Indeed, the edict of Tiberius Julius Alexander (68 CE), which deals with regulations on land administration and tax collection, stipulates penalties for officials evading rules, cancels immunities, and reveals extortion and corruption in the imperial administration in Egypt. Overall, the edict reflects the gloomy state of the Egyptian economy in that period and does not appear to be simply anti-Neronian propaganda (*OGIS* 669 = *SB* V 8444).

The procurators

The financial administration of Egypt was so important that, in addition to the prefect, several equestrian procurators were also involved. Just exactly what each official did is now somewhat difficult to determine because the responsibilities of the various officials overlapped, or we lack the vital information that would clarify the situation. That is why, despite recent studies of the *dioiketes*, the *epistrategos*, the *iuridicus*, and the *archidicastes*, we are still seeking more evidence (see J. D. Thomas 2001: 1246).

Here it will suffice to highlight one of these offices, the *idios logos*, whose regulations are known primarily through one long, yet fragmentary papyrus (the *Gnomon of the Idios Logos*), containing more than a hundred rules that were enforced by the "Privy Purse" whose administrator was appointed by the emperor himself (= *BGU* V 1210, after 149 CE; another shorter fragment, *P.Oxy.* XLII 3014, dates to the first century CE; while *P.Oxy.* XLIII 3133 shows that the office survived as late as 239 CE [Bowman 1976: 163–4; Swarney 1970 on the duties of this official]). Although the *Idios Logos* began in the Ptolemaic period as a special account that recorded income received from the sale of ownerless or confiscated land, the office had expanded by the middle of the second century CE, and until its possible abolition during the sweeping reforms of Philip the Arab in the middle of the third century, its holder assumed responsibility for virtually all aspects of administration (religious, civil, and financial) in Roman Egypt. The implications of the records of this official for our understanding of not only Egypt under Roman rule, but potentially for the Roman state as a whole, are far-reaching, since the picture that we get would tend to undermine the standard view that the Roman state was uninterested in local administration. As Naphtali Lewis has pointed out, "perusal of the stringent regulations [of the *Gnomon*] leaves no doubt that a prime objective set by Augustus and maintained by his successors for two hundred years was to impede social mobility and keep the several population strata as discrete and immutable as possible: *divide et impera*" (Lewis 1983: 32). The Romans defined class and status on the basis of descent and wealth. The following excerpts demonstrate the social, fiscal, and legal implications of the various class distinctions: Romans, Alexandrians, gymnasials (members of the Greek *gymnasium*), metropolites (the elite of the *nome metropoleis*), and villagers:

> 5. Property bequeathed by Alexandrians to persons not qualified is given to those who can legally inherit from them, if such there be and if they claim it at law.
> 8. If to a Roman will is added a clause saying "whatever bequests I make in Greek codicils shall be valid," it is not admissible, for a Roman is not permitted to write a Greek will.
> 14. A metropolite cannot bequeath to his freed slaves more than five hundred drachmae or an allowance of five drachmae a month.
> 18. Inheritances left in trust by Greeks and Romans or by Romans to Greeks were confiscated by the deified Vespasian; nevertheless those acknowledging their trust have received the half.
> 19. Bequests made to freedmen who have not yet acquired their emancipation are confiscated. It is legal emancipation if the person freed is over thirty years old.
> 23. Romans are not permitted to marry their sisters or their aunts, but marriage with their brother's daughters has been allowed. Pardalas, indeed, when a brother married a sister, confiscated the property.
> 38. Children of a metropolite mother and an Egyptian father remain Egyptian, but they can inherit from both parents.
> 39. Children of a Roman man or woman married to a metropolite or an Egyptian assume the lower status.
> 53. Egyptian women married to discharged soldiers are, if they formally style themselves Romans, subject to the article of nonconformity to status.
> 55. If an Egyptian serves in a legion without being detected, he returns after his discharge to the Egyptian status. Discharged oarsmen return likewise, except only those belonging to the fleet of Misenum. (translations taken from *Sel.Pap.* II 206 and Bowman 1986: 127–8)

5 Local Administration in Roman Egypt

The strategos: *chief administrator of the* nome

The key figure and crucial link between the higher and lower levels of Roman administration in Egypt was the *nome strategos*, who bridged the gap between the prefect and the procurators and the local government in the cities and villages (though *fasti* for this office have been kept up-to-date, there has been no modern, synthetic work; the articles in Hohlwein 1969 are reprints from 1924–35). Thus this office secured and reinforced the demands from the top and represented or ignored the concerns from the bottom of the administrative pyramid. Among his several duties, the *strategos* oversaw the land economy, administered the assessment and collection of taxes from cities and villages, had judicial and police power, and made most of the crucial decisions regarding the appointment of individuals to compulsory public services (liturgies). He was appointed from outside the *nome*, probably directly by the prefect (*P.Oxy.* 4114–16, introduction; Gagos and Sijpesteijn 1996; J. D. Thomas 2001: 1246–8).

The *strategos* was in constant communication not only with the top level of administration, but also especially with the magistrates and (after 200/1) the councilors of the *metropoleis* as well as the village administrators, primarily the village scribe and other officials connected with the administration of taxes. His office was probably flooded with complaints, petitions, reports, and letters, and he must have produced a matching amount of documentation.

Unfortunately, no complete archive of this office has survived. The most comprehensive modern "dossier" is that of Apollonios, *strategos* of the Apollonopolite *nome* in Upper Egypt (113–20 CE). At present count, some 225 documents have been connected with this official. These form a hodge-podge of Apollonios in private and official roles, provide information about his family, and at the same time link his term in office with the famous Jewish revolt of 115–17 (see Eliav, this volume).

Most of the surviving documents do not come from his headquarters, but rather from a private residence of the family either in the city of Hermopolis or from the nearby countryside, in middle Egypt. Other texts, where he appears in official capacity, have been connected with him on prosopographical grounds. The private documents demonstrate, as expected, that the family belonged to the upper levels of Graeco-Egyptian society and owned substantial property in Hermopolis, where his family was stationed for most of his service period (see *C.Pap.Jud.* 436–44 and Rowlandson 1998: 118–24).

The outbreak of the Jewish revolt around 115 CE seems to have separated the family, with most members staying in Hermopolis. The relevant documents are important for viewing the *strategos* not only as part of the campaigning forces – he apparently went as far north as Memphis – but also as an upper-class family man who wished to protect his kin and property in moments of crisis. The Jewish revolt began with the appearance of a "Messianic" figure and spread north to Cyprus and then southeast to Egypt where it eventually reached Hermopolis. By late autumn of 117 Apollonios had written twice to the prefect asking for a leave of 60 days to take care of his private affairs:

> ...For, not only have my affairs been completely neglected owing to my long absence, but also on account of the onslaught of the impious Jews practically everything I possess in the villages of the Hermopolite nome and my interests in the nome metropolis require restoration by me. If you accede to my request, after straightening out my affairs as best I can I will be able to turn to the duties of my office in better spirits. (P.Giss. 41 = *Sel.Pap.* II 298 = *C.Pap.Jud.* 443)

Administration and liturgies in metropoleis and villages: an overview

The local administration depended heavily on a combination of institutions of local government in the *metropoleis* and a widespread system of liturgies throughout the *nomes*. In fact, these two features are the hallmark of the Roman administration of Egypt; nothing of this sort or scale existed in the Ptolemaic period when the system depended primarily on paid government agents. The Roman model aimed at redirecting the burden of tax collection and internal administration of the local communities from the central government to the elites of the countryside, an arrangement that was typical of the empire as a whole (see Ando, this volume; Gleason, this volume).

The institution of both the *boulai* and the liturgies, along with much of the vocabulary and the honorary titles that came with the former (e.g. "gymnasiarch" = gymnasium director, "kosmêtês" = order master, etc.), and the concept of benefaction and wealth redistribution lying behind the latter, were modeled on Classical Athens.

Metropoleis *and* boulai

Before the introduction of the city councils (*boulai*) in 200 CE the *strategos* and his officials had administrative control over the entire *nome*, including the *nome* capitals, the *metropoleis*. The elites of these cities were styled "metropolites" and were the descendants of the Greek settlers of the Ptolemaic period; no descendants of mixed marriages were allowed in this class and males around the age of 14 had to undergo the process of *epikrisis* (verification of status). Among them there were other elite groups, perhaps with more privileges, called for example "the 6,475 colonists" in Arsinoe or "those of the gymnasium" in Hermopolis and Oxyrhynchus. Like other elite groups elsewhere in the empire, the Egyptian metropolites were involved in philanthropic projects for the community (e.g. erecting or refurbishing buildings such as baths and stoas), paying the expenses out of their own pockets. In return they received honorific titles, but these were mostly for decorum and did not represent real power. Groups of people with such titles did not represent more than committees overseeing certain community functions.

In 200 CE Septimius Severus introduced a *boule* (city council) in each *nome* capital (*metropolis*). The best documented *boule* is that of Oxyrhynchus. The papyri inform us that there were probably around 100 councilors, all of the Greek "gymnasial" class, with property qualifications as well as lifetime and hereditary membership. The council had a president (who had held other offices previously and performed the most important duties), a secretary, and a treasurer. The council met perhaps once a month, with extra meetings as required; the meetings were probably held at the theater. Although it could make recommendations to the assembly of the city, the *boule* had no real judicial power. The main goal was the collection of taxes in the entire *nome*. It also supervised and managed the finances of the city and public works and buildings. Though the *boule* had a certain degree of autonomy in matters of local governance, it was watched closely by the *strategos* when it came to its most important task, the collection of the *nome* taxes. Documentary evidence suggests that this system had already begun to slow down in the middle of the second century and often individuals were coerced to undertake the various tasks. By the middle of the following century, there was such a crisis that villagers were forced to undertake metropolitan services, against the rule of law, as the following very fragmentary papyrus, recording an interchange between lawyers and a prefect of Egypt, suggests:

> I read the law of the Emperor Severus to the effect that villagers must not be impressed into compulsory service in the metropolis... and after Severus all the prefects have judged thus. The laws are indeed to be esteemed and revered... What do you say to the law of Severus and the decision of the prefects? Severus promulgated his law in Egypt when the towns were still prosperous... the argument of prosperity, or rather decline in prosperity, is the same for the villages and the towns... the force of the law increases with the passage of time. (*SB* V 7696.82–6, 100–5 [250 CE]; translation from Bowman 1986: 66)

Much of what we know about the municipalization of Egypt and the sharp break with the Ptolemaic period is due to the works of Bowman (1971), Bowman and Rathbone (1992), and Lewis (1970 and 1984) respectively. Though it is almost certain that many of these magistracies existed in Alexandria in the early years of Roman rule, it is still uncertain when they were introduced into the *metropoleis* of the countryside and they may not have existed until the beginning of the second century (J. D. Thomas 2001: 1250–1).

The liturgies

Let us now have a cursory look at the compulsory public services (liturgies) (see also Gleason, this volume). The notion of liturgy is directly connected with the Roman concept of *munera*, which a citizen, depending on his wealth and income (*poros*), was supposed to undertake. Although some compulsory service existed in the Ptolemaic period, the elaborate liturgical system in Egypt as it evolved in the Roman period finds no exact parallel in the rest of the Mediterranean world, and there remain questions regarding the introduction of the system: some scholars have argued that the system was introduced as early as Augustus, while others do not see any evidence until Trajan (J. D. Thomas 2001: 1249). Whatever the date of its introduction, one thing is clear: the main goal of this system, which worked hand in hand with the city magistracies and the metropolitan *boulai*, was the effective supervision and collection of taxes.

The liturgical system, like the imperial administration, consisted of multiple tiers. At the very top were the elite metropolitans and (after 200 CE) the bouleutic class. Below them were villagers and the non-elite metropolitans who served as lower-ranking tax collectors and policemen. At the very bottom were the poorest who did not have the sufficient *poros*: most of these people were asked to use their bodies to fulfill their liturgical duties (J. D. Thomas 1983).

As with taxation, several groups were fully exempt or received temporary relief from liturgies: Roman citizens, Alexandrians and Antinoites, fathers of five children, members of the same household, women, veterans, physicians, priests, etc.; the list is indeed long (Lewis 1997: 89–96). But the majority of the population, depending on their *poros*, had to serve in some way. At present at least 100 separate liturgies are known whose terms ranged from one to three years, some being seasonal. The tax liturgists were not only responsible for defraying the expenses of the office, but they were individually and collectively responsible for turning in to the appropriate office the quota assigned to their designated area. The procedures of nomination are well attested in the papyrological record. Once a liturgical office was announced, there followed a process of nomination by the local (metropolitan or village) authorities with the ultimate appointment made by the *strategos* of the *nome* (Lewis 1997). On the village level, the key figures were the village scribes (*komogrammateis*) who were eventually replaced by the *dekaprotoi* (J. D. Thomas 1975).

The liturgical system was harsh on those who lived in the metropolitan centers. But, as papyrological evidence demonstrates, it was even harder on those living in the villages, for efforts to avoid, or protest against nomination to liturgies are plentiful at both levels.

Operation and communication

In closing, a few words are in order on how this huge system operated, more specifically how the prefect and the procurators (save for the *epistrategos* who was a regional officer) communicated with the middle and local levels of the administration. It is clear that the prefect met in person with the *strategoi* and other local officials during his *conventus* and other regular trips in the countryside. But for regular, written, communication there was a two-way system that allowed information to be transmitted both from the top and the bottom. Recent research has shown that the prefect communicated with the lower level administration of the *nome* through letters addressed commonly to a single or more rarely multiple *strategoi*. In all likelihood the letter carrier took several copies of the document with him, one for each *nome*, and then following a specific delivery route along the Nile handed the copies to the *strategoi* in a sequence from north to south, starting with the nearest. Evidence suggests that there was regular postal service for official correspondence, which allowed the delivery of reports and other documentation also from the *nome* level to Alexandria. Although villages may have had to submit some reports as regularly as every five days, it is unlikely that these were delivered directly to Alexandria, but rather to the office of the *strategos* (J. D. Thomas 1999).

Epilogue

The preceding can hardly do justice to the importance of papyri for our knowledge of the economy and Roman imperial administration of Egypt. Over the past century historians and papyrologists have been painstakingly producing monographs and articles on specific aspects of both topics. All modern work goes back ultimately to Wilcken's magnificent *Grundzüge und Chrestomathie* (1912) – it is amazing how slow the progress has been since then in many respects. Then, there is Oertel's early work on liturgies (1917), Wallace's on taxation (1938) and Jouguet's on administration (1911). Recent scholarship has also been prolific and we can only mention some examples here: Bonneau (e.g. 1972, 1993) on the administration of agricultural features, Kruse (2002) on the royal scribe (*basilikos grammateus*), Haensch on the *capita provinciarum* (1997) and on petitions (1994), an entire volume of *ANRW* (1988) dedicated to Egypt.

The content of the papyri, however, unlike inscriptions, move beyond the formal display of imperial power. They certainly allow an intimate look into the government in action, but at the same time provide the primary material for the exploration of issues such as literacy, the family, religion, gender relations, etc. In many respects, papyrologists can rightly be called voyeurs of the lives of people in Graeco-Roman Egypt.

6 Conclusion

As we stated at the beginning of this chapter, the greatest difference between the documentation offered by papyri and inscriptions stems from the fact that inscriptions largely reflect finished processes while papyri tend to reflect ongoing projects. The formal similarities between epigraphic and papyrological projects, the creation of corpora to enable the study of these documents, and the need for careful restoration that makes it possible to understand what a text once said cannot occlude the substantial differences between the nature of the evidence obtained from these two sources. The papyrological archives that have survived and "dossiers" that have been re-created give us a sense of just what is missing from the epigraphic record, the vast range of material that was potentially available but that was not inscribed. While epigraphy may, as we have suggested, allow us to reconstruct career patterns, it is the papyri that will provide the best evidence for the sorts of problems that people faced in their careers. More significantly, while inscriptions reflect processes that people wanted to have memorialized, they may give an entirely misleading impression of how government worked. Although papyri certainly reveal, for instance, the vast amount of work that the ancient system of petition and response could create, they also reveal a much more proactive imperial government than we tend to see in our inscriptions. Papyri reveal the deep penetration of imperial government into the daily lives of the average Egyptian. This in turn may shed light upon the development of monumental writing in the Roman Empire as an epiphenomenon of the documentation required of imperial administration. The imperial government, as we see it in Egypt, is dependent upon the collection of data that, in part, marks the status of individuals at all points in their lives. Is it surprising, then, that we should see a vastly increased desire to mark the passing of one's life in areas where the Roman state introduced a culture of administrative writing? Likewise the vastly greater pre-Roman epigraphy of the Greek world would seem, at least in part, to reflect the more widespread use of writing in civic life before the rise of Rome.

In concentrating on administrative behaviors, we have drawn upon well-developed areas of scholarship. Likewise, as suggested above, the combination of epigraphic and papyrological evidence has resulted in significant advances in our understanding of the nature of the ancient family, and suggests patterns of organization in economic life. As work continues on the ownership of documents in Egypt, literary as well as administrative, we can gain a better view of the extent of literary culture, and the ways in which elite culture spread outwards from the city into the countryside. At the same time we may also be able to gain greater insight into the limitations of that culture, and a sense of the points at which Greco-Roman cultural values ran up against those of indigenous peoples.

The technical demands of papyrology and epigraphy have tended in the past to dictate that the two disciplines follow parallel tracks. In the future, as studies that combine papyrological and epigraphic work expand, we expect that the dialogue between the two disciplines will enable a deeper understanding of the Roman world as a whole.

ACKNOWLEDGMENTS

The authors would like to express their thanks to David Thomas, Jim Keenan, and Alan Bowman for advice on sections of this chapter. The authors take responsibility for errors or eccentricities that remain.

CHAPTER FOUR

Art, Architecture, and Archaeology in the Roman Empire

Lea Stirling

Throughout the countryside, streets, and museums of the former Roman Empire are physical remains of that empire such as aqueducts, amphitheaters, portraits of emperors and anonymous citizens, and terracotta lamps. These ruins, art objects, artifacts, potsherd scatters, and even seeds and bones all testify to aspects of the ideology, beliefs, aspirations, social norms, and lifestyles of the inhabitants of that empire. Some of these material remains are studied as art objects, while others are considered archaeological, but they present the fullest picture of Roman life when taken together. Given the immensity of this body of information, I do not present a chronological survey, but rather a consideration of the chief genres of artistic monument and the leading avenues of archaeological research, grouped thematically instead of by method of investigation. Art cannot be understood independently of the society that produced it, and we find the power relationships, agendas, and anxieties of the Roman world embedded in its art. From this immense and unwieldy corpus of information, we may distil some major contexts: the emperor, the cityscape, the countryside, the home, and death. Looking at the Roman army provides a further example of how very different kinds of evidence can be integrated to contribute to a historical picture.

Before continuing, however, we must first raise the most fundamental questions in these disciplines. What is Roman art? What is Roman archaeology? These questions are not so redundant as they might at first appear, and scholars have continuously evaluated them (Brendel 1979; Kampen 2003; James 2003). "Roman" art and archaeology might reasonably refer to the material culture of the city of Rome only, of Roman citizens only (wherever they might live), or slightly more broadly, that of Rome and the Italian peninsula. It could refer to art, artifacts, and architecture that have Roman qualities, assuming that those qualities can be given a consistent definition. The most expansive answer to these questions, and the one I shall use here, is that Roman art and archaeology are the material culture of the city of Rome and the regions under its rule. This approach raises different complications, however, as it might appear to deny regional diversity, the continuation of indigenous traditions, or resistance to Roman practices. I will return to these questions in the final section of the chapter.

1 Representing Power: Art Used in the Service of Empire and Rulers

An important role for art in the Roman Empire was to convey the power and accomplishments of the emperor, both to his subjects in all walks of life and especially to possible rivals among powerful senators and generals. Triumphal arches, altars, and custom-designed fora spread outwards from Rome to major provincial cities as a way of asserting the emperor's presence at nodal points on the urban landscape, and signified a special relationship between a city that received them and the ruling power, while at Rome, imperial munificence extended to baths, amphitheaters, and the Circus Maximus as a way of linking the emperor with his subjects. Historical scenes, carved in relief, decorated many of the monuments dedicated overtly to the emperor's victories and accomplishments and celebrated the ideology of victory that helped sustain the imperial power. The emperor's portrait was disseminated throughout the empire, in stone for temples and other public places (and some houses), and also on the more accessible medium of the coinage. Let us consider some of these genres with more specific examples.

Whereas Greek and Hellenistic artists and patrons largely preferred to commemorate historical events through mythical, allegorical scenes, Roman patrons and artists often chose to depict real participants and aspects of actual historical events. Triumphal arches and columns are the most famous examples of "narrative historical relief." The column of Trajan (dedicated in 113 CE) portrays aspects of Trajan's two successful wars against the Dacians. While it is clear that the "narrative" is built out of stock scenes of life on campaign, such as soldiers constructing camps or fighting, and the emperor giving speeches or sacrificing, it is nevertheless "historical" in that the Romans and Dacians are represented as themselves, and one may recognize certain historical figures, such as Trajan, or specific events, including the suicide of the Dacian king Decebalus.

Triumphal arches were a major venue for commemorating military accomplishments. Several well-preserved arches with extensive sculptural decoration can still be seen in the Roman forum today, but it must not be forgotten that decorated arches were also erected in cities of the provinces. Depictions on coins and cuttings atop the arches themselves remind us that bronze statuary often stood atop these arches. Still more unsculpted but nevertheless imposing arches proclaimed imperial accomplishments through inscriptions. A heavily sculpted arch at Orange (France) is usually attributed to the emperor Tiberius and depicts Roman victories by land and sea over both Gauls and Germans. The emphasis on subjected Gauls must have carried different messages to Gallic inhabitants and to descendants of the Roman veterans who established a colony there in 36–35 BCE. A slightly earlier arch at nearby Glanum depicted bound Gauls, a theme echoed in the triumphal décor of the fountain in the forum (Bromwich 1993). Located at major intersections, arches relayed their messages to countless passers-by each day. Commemorative arches dedicated to Germanicus were placed in locations that marked the eastern and western boundaries of the empire. Inscriptional records of the deliberations of the Senate concerning these arches show the careful oversight that both Senate and emperor exercised over their placement (Potter 1987).

Julius Caesar and several emperors of the first century added custom-designed fora to the landscape of downtown Rome. With axial layouts, custom designs, and glamorous building materials, these plazas contrasted with the republican forum (the Forum Romanum), whose buildings and monuments had developed organically over centuries. Like earlier ones, the temples in the imperial fora held booty (both weapons and art objects) from defeated foes and acted as didactic museums or art galleries of Roman conquest. In the forum of Augustus, the temple of Mars Ultor (the Avenger) displayed Roman military standards that had been captured by the Parthians in 55 BCE, but were returned in 20 BCE through a negotiated settlement. By the time the temple was dedicated in 2 BCE Mars' epithet "the Avenger" referred to the restoration of the Parthian standards, but the older generation might remember that Augustus (then Octavian) first promised the temple to commemorate vengeance against Julius Caesar's assassins. The temple's pedimental sculpture displayed Mars with his consort Venus (the mythical founder of the Julian house), emphasizing how the lineage of Augustus and the identity of Rome itself were intertwined. Further repetition of this message came from the inscribed statues of Roman heroes (with Augustus' ancestors liberally represented) that lined the porticos. From the centers of the two side apses (*exhedrae*), Rome's original founders Aeneas and Romulus gazed at the statue of the new founder Augustus, placed in front of the temple. State matters of peace and war were conducted in this temple and forum, thereby both celebrating the emperor's ideology of victory and emphasizing the ensuing prosperity (Zanker 1988). The Forum of Trajan imitated the exhedrae and other features of Augustus' forum, but here the defeated enemy figured more prominently in the decoration, with ranks of submissive Dacians above the colonnade, relief panels of battle scenes, and the winding battle narrative of the column.

Portraits of the emperor and his family were an important medium for expressing imperial power and particular messages of accomplishment or dynasty. They appeared in public buildings and spaces of all sorts (including as "guests" in the temples of other gods), in temples of the imperial cult, and in some privately owned spaces as well. Stylistically these portraits do not follow a "linear" development (for instance, towards or away from naturalism). Concurrent traditions of veristic and idealized portraiture had been well established at Rome since republican times. Emperors variously preferred different styles and selected from an array of motifs and techniques to shape messages concerning power, dynastic links, philosophical leanings, and the like (Nodelman 1975; Kleiner 1992). There is thus far more than a "likeness" to consider when viewing Roman portraits, imperial or otherwise.

For an example of the careful crafting and choices that could enter into preparing a portrait and an image, we may turn to the empress Livia, wife of Octavian/Augustus (Bartman 1999). The restrained hairstyle and traditional Roman clothes (including the *stola*, a symbol of matronly virtue) on these portraits show Livia's support for

Augustus' espousal of traditional values and conservative moral legislation (Figure 4.1). They intentionally contrast with more elaborate Hellenistic fashions in hairstyles and garments that were also current in Rome at this time. Many statues evoke Livia's modesty and piety through the shawl pulled over her head (the garb of sacrifice), while wreaths on others call to mind the Augustan message of peace and prosperity. Even the hand gestures of these portraits are more authoritative than those of other female portraits of the day. Although the empress lived to the age of 87, all her portraits depict idealized and youthful beauty; the same idealism appears in the portraiture of Augustus and, indeed, of nearly all the Julio-Claudians. As the wife

Figure 4.1 Portrait of Livia, wife of Augustus. Her dress and hairstyle reflect her husband's traditionalist social ideals

of Augustus and the mother of his adopted heir Tiberius, Livia was a major link in Rome's first imperial succession. Thus, fresh portraits continued to circulate under Tiberius, as seen in a group of statues erected in a building in the forum of Béziers early in his reign. These included the ever-youthful Livia, Augustus (posthumous), Tiberius, his adopted son Germanicus, and other young members of the dynasty (Balty and Cazes 1995; Rose 1997: 126–8).

Livia's signature hairstyle, with a fluff of hair over the forehead, became popular in non-imperial portraits, which sometimes even imitated her facial features. In general, imperial hairstyles, particularly those of imperial women, were emulated in private portraits (and presumably fashions), thus providing an important dating criterion. Subsequent women of the Julio-Claudian dynasty developed distinctive hairstyles, while the men of the dynasty produced portraits that imitated both the hairstyle and facial features of Augustus (irrespective of their actual blood relationship). Later emperors (Trajan, Constantine) continued to evoke the hairstyle and idealism of Augustan portraiture to compare their rule to Augustus' golden age. All these careful choices demonstrate the many levels at which Romans read a portrait. A further expression of the power of portraits is the mutilation and destruction of images of emperors condemned after their death (Varner 2001).

2 Architecture and Archaeology in the City

Certain typical building structures such as fora, basilicas, baths, aqueducts, amphitheaters, and theaters (to name some of the most outstanding) existed in most cities above a certain size around the Roman Empire, and may often be taken as markers, at least in the west, of specifically Roman social ideals (MacDonald 1982, 1986; Edmondson, this volume). It is important to remember that these buildings functioned as status markers in addition to playing a functional role. Local patrons (and sometimes the emperor), always commemorated by an inscription, donated the buildings, supplied aspects of their décor, or underwrote repairs to them. Let us look more closely at fora, amphitheaters, baths, and aqueducts.

The forum was the administrative and commercial center of a city. The planned fora of the provincial cities were often axial and fairly symmetrical, surrounded by Roman-style buildings (for Mérida in Spain, see Edmondson, this volume). These buildings served as offices, shops, and venues for conducting the public business of the courts and city council (the role of broader public assemblies declined through the imperial period). One of the most important of these structures was the basilica, a building type that only came into use in the Roman period (Welch 2003). In its Roman sense, the term basilica refers to a building form with a wide central space flanked by one or more colonnaded aisles. An apse at the end could provide focus and proved to be well suited to representing hierarchical relationships. The basilica was a simple but effective design for providing fairly open interior spaces suitable to tribunals, meetings, civil administration, and the like. Its associations with power explain why aristocrats of late antiquity sometimes incorporated a large basilica-shaped hall into their most public suites (Ellis 1988). This building form, eminently suitable for indoor assemblies, and not directly associated with pagan religion, was later adopted for early churches.

The advent of Roman power often meant the addition of a capitolium, a temple to the tutelary deities of the city of Rome: Jupiter, Juno, and Minerva, as worshipped on the Capitoline hill. Provincial capitolia were modeled on the one in Rome, using an imposing podium to elevate the temple and emphasize its frontal aspect over all others. Three cult chambers or niches housed the three divinities. In the forum of Gorsium in Pannonia, created under Trajan, a head of Jupiter was found in the central chamber (Fitz and Fedak 1993).

In addition to supporting administrative functions, the insertion of a planned Roman forum into an existing native city also sent a political message. Even in the east, where the traditional forms of urban culture could more easily absorb Roman structures, the Roman forum was sometimes placed in a different location from the preceding agora, as at Athens. Carthage and Simitthu in North Africa provide striking examples of the erasure of indigenous structures as part of the advertisement of the connection to Rome.

In 29 BCE Octavian sent colonists to reoccupy Carthage, which had been largely unoccupied since its sacking in 146 BCE at the end of the Third Punic War. For the forum of the new Carthage, Roman town planners chose the citadel of the city, the Byrsa hill. Not content simply to build over the rubble of the Carthaginian buildings there, including the temple of Eschmoun, Roman town planners "bulldozed" an estimated 4–5 meters off the apex of the hill, pushing the earth over ruined buildings at the sides to create a new wider plateau at the top (with far-reaching archaeological implications: the buildings from the top of the hill were completely eradicated, but the redistribution of earth at the sides of the hill preserved aristocratic housing districts under sweeping strata of earth) (Lancel 1995: 151, 430). The Roman forum of Carthage, which soon became the capital of the province of Africa Proconsularis, rose atop this artificial mesa. Although the memory of particular buildings had probably diminished in the several generations that had passed between 146 and 29 BCE, the changed contour of the Byrsa hill would nonetheless have been visible as an announcement of Roman presence and power around the bay of Tunis.

Some 165 kilometers from Carthage, ancient Simitthu (modern Chimtou) was an important Numidian city, and a major landmark in its pre-Roman topography was a cluster of large aristocratic tombs (Figure 4.2). Two circular tombs in particular must once have stood to a considerable height. In the early Roman period these tombs were razed to foundation level and covered over by the pavement of the Roman forum (Rakob 1993: 5). In this case, sizable markers of the city's former power were completely obliterated, replaced by a symbol of the administrative power of the new regime.

The single most famous symbol of Rome is the Flavian amphitheater, better known by its colloquial later name, the Colosseum. Like most Roman buildings, the Flavian amphitheater functioned on many levels and illustrates a different kind of deliberate urban erasure of the preceding regime. At the time of its construction (72–80 CE) over the spot where Nero's much resented private park and artificial lake had been, it was a monumental symbol of the new regime's intent to restore the center of Rome to the use of Roman citizens, a public benefaction to offset Nero's selfish private grandeur. Its construction was bankrolled by the spoils of Vespasian's suppression of the revolt in Judaea (66–73 CE), a provincial rebellion that official sources preferred to call the Jewish War. The amphitheater format itself, linked to military culture

Figure 4.2 Roman forum at Chemtou, with foundations of Numidian tombs exposed at the center. These were paved over in Roman times. A basilica appears behind the tombs. Photo: L. M. Stirling, by permission

(Welch 1994), reflected Vespasian's gratitude to the armies who had supported him in the recent civil war. Gladiatorial games and beast hunts were themselves significant symbols of imperial lavishness and Roman rule over the distant lands that supplied the animals and slaves. Vespasian (69–79 CE) did not live to see the completion of this building, but his son Titus (79–81) held a hundred-day extravaganza of inauguration for it in 80 CE. Although the building seems not to have been fully finished at that point, Titus' decision may have stemmed from a wish to emphasize his connection to his father or expiate the memory of the disaster around Pompeii in August of 79.

The virtuosity and renown of the Colosseum rather than its absolute typicality make it a good example from which to discuss the amphitheater (Figure 4.3). Built from the quintessentially mouldable medium of concrete, the building was sheathed entirely in gleaming marble and decorated with statuary and engaged columns. Citizens entered the building through 76 numbered entrances, and were conducted to their appropriate seats with minimal contact between social ranks. From these seats, arrayed hierarchically, some 50,000 inhabitants of Rome could view both games and emperor. Fights and beast hunts took place in the arena, below which was a complex network of corridors, cages, and shafts for moving animals, people, and props around with speed and safety. The emperor Titus famously flooded the arena and held naval battles during the inauguration ceremonies, but these seem to have occurred before the substructures of the arena were complete. Nets, rollers, and other safeguards around the sides of the arena prevented animals from escaping into the ranks of spectators (Bomgardner 2000).

Figure 4.3 The Colosseum at Rome, constructed 72–80 CE. Sestertius of Titus (*RIC* Titus 438n ANS 1954.203.170). Photo courtesy of the American Numismatic Society

Although the Colosseum is the most famous Roman amphitheater, nearly 200 others survive archaeologically throughout the former Roman Empire, mostly in its western provinces (Golvin 1988). Factors of urban topography or available building materials create variations and regional groupings among surviving amphitheaters. Architects in Britain and other northern provinces used turf-and-timber construction – but this cheaper construction material did not lessen the building's status as a prestige project or a symbol of connection to Rome (Welch 1994). Specialized structures to control wild animals appear only in North Africa and sites on the shipping routes from North Africa to Rome, not in the rest of the empire. Thus, the amphitheaters at Capua and Pozzuoli (south of Rome) have extensive subterranean passages and other features for handling animals, while the equally luxurious amphitheaters at Arles and Nîmes do not (Bomgardner 2000: 73, 115). In the east, there was less need for purpose-built gladiatorial structures since preexisting theaters and stadia could be adapted to the same purpose. Once again, eastern and western provinces show different forms of adaptation to Roman rule.

Public baths were another form of indulgence provided by emperors and members of the elite in celebration of a political order that enabled even the common person to enjoy the pleasures of *otium* (Fagan, this volume). The baths were about more than getting clean – a basin of water and a cloth would suffice for basic hygiene. Rather, baths were a social institution that offered the inhabitants of a city the chance to network and socialize in a spacious environment that might well be considerably more opulent than their own. Every city possessed bath-houses on a multitude of scales: smaller, less sumptuous structures with irregular layout known as *balneae*, and much larger, axial structures referred to as *thermae* or imperial-style baths (see Fagan, this volume).

Given that baths represented an extension of aristocratic pleasure, it is not surprising that their decoration – marble veneers, mosaics, frescoes, and statues of all types – likewise involved a public display of opulence in which all might participate. By and large, statuary in baths emphasized divinities and other figures associated with health, fitness, and water; baths were also a venue for honorific statuary of local patrons, governors, or emperors. As an example, we may turn to a statuary collection built up over time at the civic *thermae* in Gerasa (Jordan). Portraits dedicated by prominent citizens stood just outside the entrance, while inside were two groups of mythological sculpture, one equestrian statue, and a colossal portrait of Caracalla (Friedland 2003). Such decorations would send many messages to the patrons of the bath. The donors of the portraits emphasized their identification with the ruling power by choosing togas rather than the Greek himation for their dress. Dedications inside the building were made by the city, and in one case, by a governor. With figures such as a satyr and a nude male portraying Apollo or Dionysus, the mythological statuary emphasized the leisure and cultural pursuits of the baths. The portrait of Caracalla reminds us that the imperial presence permeated public spaces. Indeed, some baths in Asia Minor housed an opulent chamber for the imperial cult (Yegül 1992), and other shrines or religious centers appeared within baths. Décor of baths could also reflect the perils of mass association, as we see from mosaics warning bathers to wear slippers on a hot floor or offering protection from demons and the evil eye (Dunbabin 1989).

Layout and decoration are not the only significant aspects of bathhouses. Refuse reveals much about the clientele and their habits. Hairpins and feminine jewellery found in the main drain at the baths inside the legionary fortress at Caerleon (Wales) make it evident that women and children (presumably the unofficial "wives" of the legionaries) also frequented the baths, their numbers (or at any rate, their loss of accessories) increasing over time (Zienkiewicz 1986). A few milk teeth were found in the later layers, possibly indicating not just the presence of children, but also of a dentist. A ceramic admission "ticket" also in the late layers may likewise indicate greater access to the public. Portable refreshments such as chicken joints, mutton chops, and shellfish left bones and shells in the drain. Over time these grew in size from finger foods to larger (but still portable) cuts of meat. The ceramics mainly comprised small dishes and cups, again items suited to small snacks. Drinking cups are a common find at Caerleon, as in baths everywhere.

A team of specialists built a small bathing structure at Sardis to evaluate aspects of fuel, firing, and heat circulation (Yegül and Couch 2003). They found, among other things, that the hollow tubes (*tubuli*) typically built into the walls of a bath building allowed the building to heat more efficiently, evenly, and safely to a high temperature and also reduced the rate of fuel consumption considerably.

Aqueducts were a related form of aquatic benefaction that served both utilitarian and prestige purposes (Adam 1992; Hodge 2002). These symbols of affluence and control of the natural environment served largely to supply baths and extravagantly decorated fountain-houses (*nymphaea*) within cities. They might also serve more practical purposes, such as supplying fountains, some wealthy homes, and occasionally industry or agriculture (A. Wilson 1999b), but these needs could be met through wells and cisterns, as they would have been in the decades or centuries prior to the city's attainment of the wealth and status needed to acquire an aqueduct. An aqueduct brought a continuous flow of water from a source that was higher than the city it served. The vast majority of aqueduct channels ran at ground level, where construction and maintenance were easiest and safest. The channels had to maintain a steady downward slope to keep the water moving; thus tall arcades maintained the height of the channel as it crossed valleys or approached a city across a long, level plain. An extreme example of the possible difficulties involved in maintaining a gradient is seen in the 50 kilometer-long aqueduct of Nîmes (which included the famous Pont du Gard). Over this distance, the change in height from the source of the water to the distribution tank it served in the city was only 17 meters, that is, a miniscule 34 cm/km.

The aqueduct-borne water supply ran day and night without cease (Hodge 2002). Thus, its recipients in the cities had to accommodate this steady flow. Public water fountains, often with a catchment basin below, ran steadily. It seems that the overflow from these may have sluiced the street surfaces and then the sewers (in cities that had them). Continuously flowing water must have cleaned out the networks of pools in baths overnight, as well as running beneath their multi-seater public latrines. The ceaseless flow of water enhanced the glamour of *nymphaea*, such as one at Miletos, whose three-storey aedicular façade resembled a theater, right down to the statuary decoration between the columns. Here the stream of water was a performance in itself. The enormous size of the civic cisterns of some North African cities suggests that they may have tried to store or manage some of this continuous flow, but these are exceptional in the empire as a whole.

Along with a good water supply, another urban feature that was both decorative and utilitarian was green space in the form of parks and gardens. Formal plantings added color and shade to Vespasian's Forum of Peace. At Pompeii, Wilhelmina Jashemski identified the cavities in the ground left by decayed roots by pouring plaster into them (Jashemski 1979). From this evidence, she was able to show that a considerable space within the walls of the city was under cultivation, including vineyards near the amphitheater, and that even formal gardens in peristyles usually contained herbs and plants for food alongside flowering plants (see also Ciarallo 2001; Jashemski and Meyer 2002).

3 Archaeology and the Countryside

Although many of the best-known archaeological sites are ancient cities and urbanism was a central feature of the Roman Empire, the majority of its occupants lived and worked in the countryside, or at the very least, owned property there (Kehoe, this volume). The spaces between cities variously housed farmland, country retreats, industrial complexes, sanctuaries, cemeteries, military zones, hunting terrain, and wilderness. Villas, forts, roads, bridges, aqueducts, and other visible or monumental structures in this landscape have been studied for some time through excavation and structural surveys (Percival 1976; Sitwell 1981; O'Connor 1993; Hodge 2002). Humbler sites and the landscape itself have not received as much attention, but farming and other kinds of rural production leave structural and environmental traces (MacKinnon 2004; for economic issues, see Mattingly, this volume).

Field survey, the study of surface artifacts and other remains of occupation over a broad area, has been one of the most important developments of the latter half of the twentieth century in Roman archaeology. Unlike excavation of a single site with its particular vicissitudes, field survey offers the opportunity to look at a broad region over a long time-span and evaluate (among other things) changes in types or locations of sites, agricultural usage, military occupation, or trade patterns over time (for the archaeology of production and trade, see Mattingly, this volume). The territory of an ancient city or a geographical feature such as a river valley may serve as the unit of investigation, often approached through a sampling strategy. Methods employed in survey have become increasingly systematic and multidisciplinary (Francovich et al. 2000). Survey has the advantage of being non-destructive and non-invasive. Also, it is usually less expensive than excavation.

The UNESCO Libyan Valleys survey investigated the pre-desert of Libya, where substantial farms and olive presses attested considerable productivity in ancient times in this highly arid zone that receives 35–75 millimeters of rain per year (Barker et al. 1996; D. J. Mattingly 1994). That the ancient climate was the same as today's is shown by the preserved seeds and pollens of naturally occurring species (weeds), which were all suited to this climatic regime, whereas the cultivated species were all ones that required considerably higher rainfall. Mapping sites, structural remains, and sherd scatters, archaeologists demonstrated how complex systems of retaining walls in the seasonal creek-beds (*wadis*) channeled runoff from the brief but intense rains into agricultural areas, where it sustained substantial production of olive oil, exported to the coastal region and beyond. The local population, so identified by (among other things) Libyan names on inscriptions, developed this system of floodwater farming under the pressure of Roman taxation. The gradual abandonment of this system of agriculture came about as part of a regional economic decline rather than through environmental change or warfare.

While the need for surplus to pay taxes stimulated agricultural intensification in Libya (and elsewhere), annexation into the Roman Empire seems to have had the opposite effect on Greece, the Roman province of Achaea (Alcock 1993). Here numerous different field surveys show both a drop in overall numbers of sites and the loss of the smallest sites in the countryside during the late Hellenistic and early Roman periods. Where it is possible to judge, it further appears that there was instability in occupation of sites, with long-occupied sites going out of use, and altogether new ones being developed. Contemporary literary sources, scant as they are on such a non-elite topic, create an image of instability followed by rural depopulation in Roman times, and modern scholars have sometimes taken this as an indication of extensive population decline in Greece in the Roman period. However, along with the disappearance of the little sites that archaeologists usually associate with independent, small-scale farmers comes an increase overall in the size of occupied sites and the appearance of some very wealthy sites (usually referred to as villas) in the landscape. These factors taken together indicate substantial change in the system of land ownership, with fewer, larger estates replacing a wider scatter of smaller farms. Rather than disappearing entirely, it is possible that some small farmers resided in nucleated settlements instead of on their property. In a few instances, surveys show that early imperial sites are clustered around urban centers, while more remote areas cease to have sites. Moreover, the continued prosperity and even expansion of Greek towns indicates a steady and substantial urban population base. Thus, archaeological data demonstrate that the apparent emptiness of the Greek landscape reflects not a straightforward and drastic population decline, but considerable change in patterns of land tenure, probably also coupled with some demographic attrition.

4 The Art and Archaeology of Living: Roman Houses

Countless homes excavated throughout the Roman Empire, differing in size, degree of wealth, and regional style, allow us to investigate the lifestyle within a Roman house. Current research on Roman houses attempts to understand them in their social context and integrate different forms of evidence (Allison 2001). Houses at Pompeii have perhaps received the most scrutiny and the most sophisticated efforts at interpretation (Wallace-Hadrill 1994). One of the most startling aspects of domestic life is the extent to which wealthy homes were open to the public. Customs of patronage on the one hand, and the expectation that the wealthy should show off their status on the other, created a house design with gradations of access. During a patron's "office hours," the entrance hallway and the atrium of a home were fully accessible to the public. Clients waiting in these handsomely decorated areas were afforded glimpses of further luxury and family life beyond. Privileged guests were invited further into the home and received in dining rooms and bedrooms of varying intimacy and luxury. Contemporary western notions of "public" and "private" do not find easy application in the Roman house. Wealthy homeowners used wall paintings, mosaic, statuary, and other forms of decoration to emphasize their wealth or allude to prestigious public service (Ling 1991; Dunbabin 1999; Gazda 1991).

As an example, portraits could be part of this display of status. Although wax masks for display in the atrium and during funeral processions were reserved for the holders of high office, portraits in other media (especially stone) exist in many houses (Flower 1996). These would depict both ancestors and current inhabitants. Individuals sometimes displayed imperial portraits, presumably as a message of loyalty, or to reflect their own high imperial service. Portraits of philosophers expressed particular philosophic allegiances to peers, and perhaps conveyed learning more broadly to those with less philosophic education (for a late-antique example, see R. R. R. Smith 1990). Occasionally portrait choices such as busts of Juba II in Roman houses at Cherchel in Mauretania reflected local identity or loyalties (Stirling 2005: 188). A house in Volubilis displayed a statue of a Hellenistic prince and one of Cato the Elder, the defender of Utica during Caesar's civil wars. The latter figure may have been chosen as a courageous Roman in an African context (Hales 2003: 205).

The Terrace Houses of Ephesus provide an illustration of how colorful artistic programs sent messages about status and society to their viewers. The last major redecoration of these houses (wall paintings, mosaics, and statuary) dates to the late second and early third centuries, prior to an earthquake of 262 CE, not the late fourth and early fifth centuries, as excavators initially proposed (Parrish 1999; Scherrer 2000; Krinzinger 2002; Lang-Auinger 2003). After the earthquake the houses were reoccupied into the seventh century. Wall paintings variously created faux marble paneling or light airy frameworks which sometimes contained masks or floating figures. In several of the "condos" within Terrace House 2, figures of muses and philosophers in the wall paintings illustrated the owners' commitment to intellectual pursuits and the culture of *paideia* (Gleason, this volume). Two small niches in one of these rooms may have held scrolls. A striding Artemis found in another room decorated with paintings of the muses must have fallen from a niche in that room (Figure 4.4). Flooring in coloured marble and geometric patterns complemented these figural decorations without competing with them.

Throughout the Terrace Houses, there was an extensive collection of statuary, both portraits and mythological figures (Aurenhammer 1995). Most of the statuary fragments were found in late layers of debris, but a few remained where they were displayed in the last period of occupation. Imperial portraits, including Tiberius, Livia, and Marcus Aurelius showed identification with the ruling power. Busts of Livia and Tiberius were found in a niche, in front of which was found a headless bronze coiled snake (7 meters long!). The snake surely represents Glycon, a version of Asklepios who became popular in the mid second century. It appears that the three statues stood together as a sort of shrine. Other statuettes showed Zeus, Marsyas, Aphrodite, and other divine or mythological figures. The astonishingly rich corpus of decoration in the Terrace Houses of Ephesos affords an unusually full examination of the colorful interiors of elite homes.

Whereas elites all across the empire favored houses based around a peristyle, humbler housing expressed more distinct regional styles, such as fortified farms in Africa and Spain, narrow "strip-housing" in the northwest provinces, or apartment blocks in Syrian villages (Ellis 2002). Some designs organize rooms along a central corridor, with perhaps a small court instead of the airy peristyle. Many non-elite dwellings make use of available space, however irregular, and they are often built in less durable materials. Even very modest homes often had a wash of color over their walls (Ellis 2002; Packer 1975). Working spaces and shops are often incorporated

Figure 4.4 Statue of Artemis at the Hunt next to a wall painting of a muse in apartment 4 of Terrace House 2, Ephesos. Photo: Österreichisches Archäologisches Institut

into these homes. Within wealthy homes, the lower status members of a household may not be very visible archaeologically (George 1997).

Archaeologists look to the contents of ancient houses and their middens of refuse to reconstruct basic facts of life in those houses. Such evidence must be interpreted with caution, however. In Pompeii, for instance, although the city was destroyed by an unexpected cataclysm in 79 CE, the contents of individual rooms have often seemed to jar with the function or status of the room as suggested by its decoration or location (Allison 1992, 2004). This difficulty probably arises from changes in the nature of houses after a devastating earthquake of 62 CE. Packing, salvage, hoarding, or looting during the actual event may have changed the "normal" appearance of the houses. Moreover, the findspots of tools, vessels, and other goods usually reflects their place of storage rather than their place of use (Berry 1997). Even so, patterns of discard have much to reveal.

Refuse at households in the Thames Valley in Britain provides insight into the ways in which life on these farms changed in the early Roman period (Meadows 1999). One farm did not seem to alter its habits of preparation and serving food, continuing to prepare meat by boiling and roasting on the bone and to use locally-made pottery. By contrast, at another farm, changes in consumption and architecture suggest that the inhabitants participated in aspects of a Roman way of life. The building was redesigned as a rectilinear structure with an enclosure wall and changed entrances. Roman styles of pottery appeared, including specialized serving wares, a phenomenon associated with Roman influence. Small cups, for instance, enter the assemblage at this point, evidently showing a change in the style of drinking away from sharing a large communal vessel. Meat-eating habits seem also to have changed. However, the continued use of pre-Roman pottery forms suggests that indigenous forms of dining persisted alongside Roman ones, presumably for different occasions.

Sometimes domestic finds reveal facts not only of physical life, but also of its spiritual or intellectual framework. Burnt deposits buried in the gardens of two Pompeian houses provide a glimpse of household worship. They contained fruits, nuts, pinecones, and parts of roosters, all offerings consistent with the painted depictions in household shrines (M. Robinson 2002). The nature of the offerings changed over time, apparently reflecting changes in domestic religion after the city became a Roman colony. In a house at Clermont-Ferrand in France, a group of statuettes was found on the floor of the vestibule (Provost and Mennessier-Jouannet 1994: 194–7). They included a *genius* and some Greco-Roman divinities as well as the Gallic gods Sucellus and Cernunnos. Many of the statuettes were heirlooms by the time of the destruction of the house in the third or fourth century.

5 The Art and Archaeology of Dying: Cemeteries and Funerary Art

Funerary practices from the Roman world have left rich material evidence in the form of cemeteries, monuments (including portraits), grave offerings, and actual skeletons (Pearce, Millett, and Struck 2001; Morris 1992). As disposal of human remains was forbidden inside cities, tombs clustered along the roads into a city, proclaiming the social hierarchy in death as in life, and seeking further commemoration through viewing and reading (usually aloud) by passers-by (Purcell 1987). In the countryside, tomb monuments variously set boundaries, controlled lines of view, and confirmed the authority of the owners of country estates. While it is clear that funerary monuments and finds have the potential to reveal much about Roman society, their interpretation is not straightforward. Different groups or social classes often have distinctive customs; conversely, conventions of austerity may blur social differences. Moreover, graves and funerary display depict how a person or his survivors wanted to be seen.

A great deal of funerary art survives from the monuments, tombstones, and sarcophagi of the Roman world. Commemorative portraits appeared as busts, statues, relief panels, or paintings (Kleiner 1992). As discussed above for imperial portraits, there are different elements involved in reading these images. Some were placed inside the tomb, to be seen by family members and mourners at subsequent funerals and religious occasions. An example is the soulful Fayum portraits painted in wax and placed over the faces of mummies. Likenesses placed on the outside of the tomb or stele proclaimed the accomplishments or stature of the deceased to a wider audience. The friezes showing the stages of industrial baking on the famous tomb of the baker Eurysaces outside the Porta Maggiore at Rome emphasized not only the success and scale of his enterprise, but also perhaps the work ethic that had made his business a success (Petersen 2003). A full-length togate portrait of the patron emphasizes his citizenship. This unique tomb is strategically placed at a convergence of two roads entering Rome, maximizing its visibility, and its sheer size rivals adjacent aristocratic ones.

Greco-Roman mythology provided another avenue of self-representation on tombs of the Roman period. This could be quite literal, as in the case of portraits depicting the deceased in the guise of divinities such as Venus or Hercules (Wrede 1981; Kleiner 1992). In the early empire, this format seems to have been most widely employed by slaves and freedmen and appears especially in reliefs on tombstones. In the second century, this practice seems to have spread more widely in society and appears in sculpture in the round and sarcophagi as well as reliefs. Such self-divinization likely imitates imperial identifications with different divinities. Another form of funerary art was the sarcophagus. Many sarcophagi were prepared with the heads on the major figure(s) left unfinished so that a portrait head could be added later for the patron. Some showed scenes of the deceased in significant activities such as reading scrolls, hunting, or fighting. Married couples represented the harmony of their union through clasping one another's right hand. Mythological scenes, many evidently distributed through pattern-books, represented allegories for death or rescue from it through mythologization.

Let us move from the monument to the grave within or below it. Funerary ritual, including such factors as the method of disposal (cremation or inhumation), the positioning of the body, its compass orientation, and the offerings left with it, has the potential to reveal the varying treatment of different groups in society (by age, sex, or class) or the ethnic affiliation of different groups in cemeteries (Figure 4.5). Infants and children are sometimes treated differently from adults or even buried in separate graveyards or inside homes. This differential treatment evidently reflects their liminal status in society and the family (Norman 2003). Infants generally seem under-represented in large cemeteries compared to the high infant mortality one might expect in a pre-industrial society. This too sharpens the suspicion that they could be buried in very different circumstances. Differential treatment of children leads to speculation about their standing in an era of high infant mortality and provides grist to debates about the extent of deliberate "exposure" of unwanted children.

Grave goods such as jewelry, ceramics, lamps, coins, or terracotta figurines can reveal aspects of religion or identity, although elements such as the images on lamps should not be over-interpreted. Shoes in graves may be gifts to aid the dead on their journey, but elaborate patterns on the soles seem to provide additional protective or cosmic symbolism (van Driel-Murray 1999). Food offerings for the dead were also more susceptible to influence from Roman or Mediterranean patterns in some regions than others (Stirling 2004). Graves in central France, for instance, show more continuity with Iron Age practices than do those of southern France (Bouby and Marinval 2004).

A final form of evidence in graves is, of course, the skeletons themselves. Aspects of how the corpses have been treated (such as orientation, or the choice of inhumation *vs.* cremation) reflect cultural choices at the time of death. Other data, both about living conditions and causes of death, remain in the bones themselves. A cluster of some 200 bodies excavated in the 1980s in the boathouses and beach of Herculaneum reveal important data about the population of the town and about the circumstances of individuals. Two separate studies of these bones have found somewhat different results (Bisel and Bisel 2002; Capasso 2001). These people ate a diet heavy

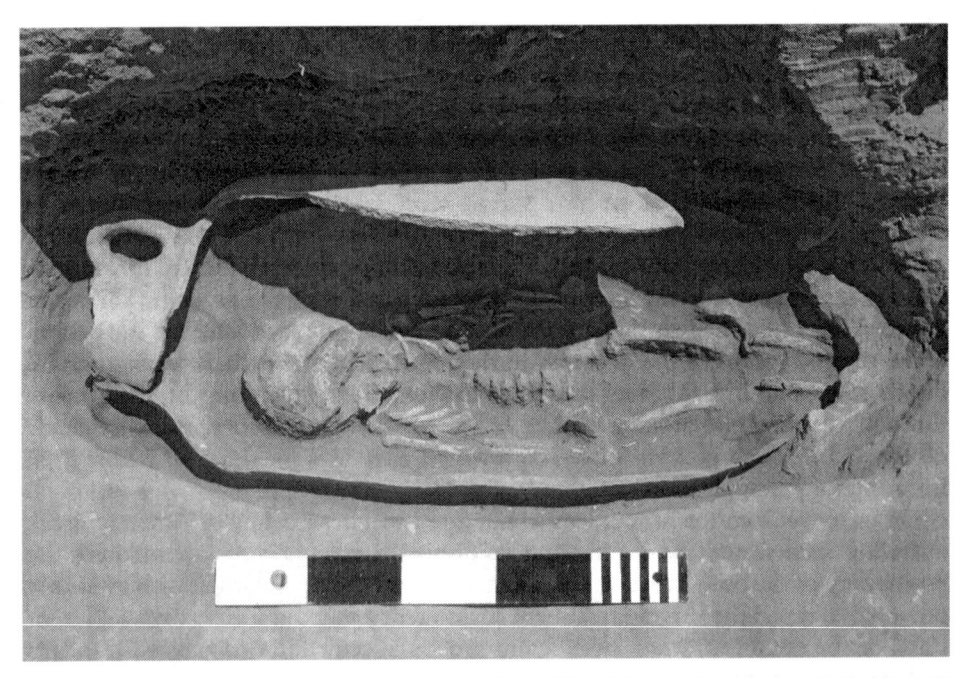

Figure 4.5 Infant buried in amphora at Leptiminus (Tunisia). Amphoras were divided in half to create coffins for the young. This burial comes from a cemetery containing children and adults. Photo: Leptiminus Archaeological Project, by permission

in vegetables and seafood and stressed their skeletons through physical labor beginning in childhood. Certain particular anomalies in the male skeletons of the group are associated with fishing activities, such as rowing a boat with one oar and holding nets in the teeth (Capasso 2001). Children as well showed stresses and anomalies indicative of physical labor. An oddity with the bodies from the Herculaneum boathouse, as with the skeletons recovered at Pompeii (admittedly collected and preserved somewhat haphazardly), is the small number of children within the group (Lazer 1997). Among victims of catastrophe we might expect to find children proportionally or even over-represented. As for causes of death, the different positioning and distribution of burned areas between the bodies on the beach as opposed to the boathouse shows that the bodies on the beach suffered much greater exposure to burning gases, while falling debris and inhalation of fine ash were more deadly for those in the boathouse (Capasso 2000).

6 Integrating Approaches: The Roman Army

Archaeology, with its many branches, provides multiple views on any subject. Let us consider the Roman army, a vast human machine that influenced in some fashion every aspect of Roman life. Art history, analysis of seeds and bones, landscape archaeology, and excavation all illuminate aspects of the Roman army.

Countless military tombstones across the empire record military careers and sometimes show the soldiers themselves. These inscriptions reveal aspects of the soldiers' self-image, especially when viewed within their particular context. In Mainz, for instance, tombstones of legionaries rarely have figural decoration; the vast majority of tombstones with portraits belonged to auxiliary cavalrymen. Whereas legionaries were Roman citizens, the auxiliary forces were recruited from non-citizen provincial populations and could attain citizenship on the completion of service. The choice of a heroic rider on the tombstones of these auxiliaries may reflect a desire to assert a higher social status and show themselves as the defenders of the Roman people (Hope 2000). Other Roman forts show a similar divide between plain legionary tombstones and decorated auxiliary ones. Interestingly, tombstones naming individual soldiers usually commemorate peacetime deaths, whereas the more anonymous but also more glamorous format of a trophy or other group memorial commemorated the wartime dead (Hope 2003).

Environmental archaeology provides a window into how the Roman army, through its mobilization of goods and people, did or did not influence local peoples. Animal bones and burned seeds from waste heaps, latrines, and other contexts at a wide variety of sites reflect the diet of soldiers, urbanites, and rural dwellers. In central Europe, study of seed remains indicates that numerous Mediterranean foods first arrived in the region in the Roman period (Bakels and Jacomet 2003). Many of these foods, especially fruits, were successfully introduced to cultivation in the area. Such foods appear first at large villas, but became standard at rural sites of all sizes after the mid-third century, and they remained part of the local diet ever afterwards. Other Mediterranean foods such as olives and dates could not be cultivated in northern climates; instead, these were imported, but on a limited basis. These appear earliest in the high-ranking parts of military compounds, and are later found in urban areas, especially those associated with the military, but never spread to rural sites or became common in the diet. Occasionally an imported food seems to pertain not so much to luxury diets as to religious needs. Pine nuts, the fruit of the stone-pine, appear in a number of religious sanctuaries and votive contexts such as a temple of Isis and the Magna Mater in Mainz, where they probably reflect offerings of pinecones (Zach 2002). Clearly some Mediterranean gods, like high-ranking army officers, expected a Mediterranean diet. In terms of meat supply, the Roman army seems largely to have adapted to prevailing local regimes. Thus, although pig was an important and high-status item in the diet of Rome and Italy, forts and other sites in Northern Europe and Britain show a heavy reliance on beef, in keeping with prevailing pre-Roman habits (Dobney 2001; A. King 1999).

Horse bones found at different types of sites in the Netherlands illustrate Roman regulation of stock for breeding larger horses (Lauwerier and Robeerst 2001). The average size of horses varies consistently by the type of site: the largest horse remains appear at military sites and villas within the Roman provinces of Germany, the shortest horse remains appear at sites outside the frontier of the Roman Empire (and at pre-Roman sites within it), and horse remains at native sites within the province are in-between. Evidently, Roman authorities carefully controlled the circulation of stock for breeding larger horses that could act as warhorses and were successful at keeping this stock inside the boundaries of the empire. The distinction in size between native and military or wealthy sites continued throughout the time of Roman power in the region. Cattle, on the other hand, gradually increased in size over time in the Netherlands and other regions of the Roman Empire. Thus, faunal evidence shows a distinctive handling of an animal that was a military resource.

Unusual settlement patterns in northwest Iberia may be related to practices of army recruitment. Field survey in the region has shown that in the Roman period, small hilltop fortresses remained an important focal point for settlement patterns. While overall numbers of rural sites increased in the Roman period, typically Roman features such as villas did not appear. Based on these patterns and epigraphic and comparative evidence, Martin Millett (2001) proposes that heavy recruitment for the auxiliary forces from this area, essentially as a form of taxation, may have inhibited economic and social development (whereas ancient taxes collected in cash are usually seen as stimulating the local economy by forcing the production of surplus).

All along the frontiers of the Roman Empire are physical remnants of the army's long-term presence: innumerable forts, of course, and also more unique structures such as Hadrian's Wall. Even traces of some of the army's less stationary activities occasionally survive in the archaeological record. The ditches around marching camps are visible in crop lines in Britain (Riley 1987; B. Jones 2000). The disturbance caused by the construction of these temporary structures changed the character of the surface soil, affecting the growth of plants above them. At dawn and dusk, especially in dry periods, differential plant growth is visible from the air as crop marks. Roman siege camps and an encircling wall survive in the desert around Masada, a hilltop fortress near the Dead Sea. More astonishing still is the colossal earth siege ramp built right to the top of the fortified hill (a height of 450 meters). These siege structures were built during the six-month siege of the site by Flavius Silva in 73–74 CE at the end of the Jewish revolt (a siege of that duration was admittedly a less temporary affair than the overnight camps in Britain).

Occasionally battles and their aftermath leave archaeological traces. A ten-kilometer long swathe of coins, weaponry, armor, and other Roman objects has helped identify the location of the battle of the Teutoberg forest (9 CE) as a narrow pass at Kalkriese near Osnabrück (Schlüter and Wiegels 1999). Ancient historians recount how German forces massacred three legions on the march under the incompetent legate Varus in a three-day debacle. Scholars have debated the location of the Varian disaster for a century, but the large concentration of military finds with a rather narrow date makes a very convincing case for Kalkriese. The dating of the Roman finds at Kalkriese is late Augustan. Many of the coins, moreover, are counter-marked with Varus' name, narrowing their date to his time as governor (7–9 CE), and not one is later than 9 CE. Earthen ramparts lining the pass were evidently part of the ambush. Scattered human bones in the region all belong to adult males; some had been deposited in pits after weathering on the surface for some time.

7 Regional Styles and Romanization: How Do We Cope with Diversity?

One of the most important features of Roman art, and perhaps the most challenging one to comprehend, is the multiplicity of styles that coexisted at any one time. Before we consider the issues connected with the interpretation of provincial art it should be emphasized that not only were there differences between the city of Rome and the distinctive regional styles of the provinces, but the art of Italian municipalities differed from that of the capital, and perhaps most strikingly of all, there were vastly different styles that coexisted within Rome itself, occasionally even on the same monument. These different metropolitan styles have variously been characterized through dichotomies such as Greek vs. Italic or patrician vs. plebeian, but many current scholars shy away from the restrictions imposed by binary interpretations. They attempt in particular to better distinguish the many diverse non-elite groups who seem to have selected "plebeian" art and evaluate the interaction between different artistic styles (Kampen 2003). Another important approach is to consider not just different patrons, but different viewers of art in different styles (Elsner 1995; Clarke 2003). What cannot be over-emphasized is that varying styles coexisted throughout the time of the Roman Empire; there is not a simplistic development from "good art" to "bad art" or *vice versa* (Brendel 1979; Kampen 2003).

Regional styles, expressed distinctively through medium, genre, style, and composition, are another aspect of this diversity in artistic production. Provincial art that does not resemble the Hellenizing tendencies of the senatorial elite at Rome has been variously characterized as incompetent imitations of central taste, as subversive, or as hybrid creations drawing on indigenous and Roman cultures (Scott and Webster 2003). A group of late third- or fourth-century tombs at Ghirza in the Libyan pre-desert provide an example of how regional styles and vocabulary can be read within their own context. Whereas the lively and non-classical friezes on these tombs were once assessed in stylistic terms alone and found wanting, David Mattingly focuses instead on the content of the scenes, showing how they emphasize the power and status of elite families whose names combine Latin and Libyan elements

(D. J. Mattingly 2003). To enhance this message, the patrons selectively chose Roman elements such as the imposing tower tomb format or decorative motifs such as bulls' heads that resonated in local religion. Read alongside the architecture of the tombs, these images depict the elite maintaining their authority through a strong ancestor cult that involved vast commemorative feasts and divination from dreams in tombs (incubation).

The existence of regional styles in art leads us to a major issue in Roman archaeology today: understanding the interactions between Romans and the many different cultures within the Roman Empire. These interactions and exchanges could take place in a host of areas, not just art, but also technology, language, nomenclature, political structure, house layout, diet, dress, and even funerary ritual. What were the processes by which symbols of Roman culture (such as the toga or the arena) appeared in the provinces (as they undoubtedly did)? And what were the ways in which non-Roman populations selected, resisted, subverted, or altered these elements? Such questions play a large role in current scholarship (Benabou 1976; M. Millett 1990; D. J. Mattingly 1997; Woolf 1998; Keay and Terrenato 2001). This process of change or acculturation is traditionally described as Romanization, but in a world where nations that were once empire-builders are now themselves multicultural, the intentionality, unidirectionality, and willing acceptance of Romanization by conquered peoples are all open to question. Even the word "Romanization" itself is now heavily contested (Hingley 2000; Webster and Cooper 1996). Jane Webster has proposed an alternative model of "creolization," the merging of two cultures to create a new one with elements of both (Webster 2001).

Clearly, there are many ways in which study of material remains can contribute to the debates around cultural interaction. I have already touched on topographically aggressive fora, changes in the countryside, households, and the diet of the living and the dead. In the west in particular, new urban forms symbolizing Rome were inserted into existing or new cities, sometimes rather violently. As a further example of the complicated relationships that could exist between local and Roman practices, let us consider the suburban cemeteries of Leptis Magna on the coast of Libya (Fontana 2001). With tower mausolea interspersed with groups of single tombs, these cemeteries resembled those of many other cities in Roman North Africa of the first century CE. However, many families, especially wealthier ones, retained the preexisting tradition of rock-cut tombs (*hypogaea*) containing cremation urns. Whereas Latin epigraphy, Roman building forms, and even some togate portraits were seen in the public spaces of the city from the Augustan period on, the arguably more private world of cemeteries presents a more conservative picture. Here Latin epigraphy arrived much later, on the exteriors of tombs in the second half of the first century, and on cremation urns inside them only in the early second century. Punic inscriptions or transliterated terms remained in use on the urns for some time. Indigenous names appear more frequently in the Latin funerary inscriptions of the exteriors than they do in inscriptions in public, official inscriptions, reflecting the importance of local lineage groups in the funerary context. Other aspects of the funerary ritual, such as burying the non-human elements from the pyre in a separate amphora, continue Punic burial practices.

Greek speakers in the eastern Mediterranean maintained a cultural identity through language, literature, philosophy, and rhetoric, mediated through an all-encompassing educational regime known as *paideia* (Gleason, this volume). Emphasis on Greek cultural arts and traditions provided a source of pride despite the reality of Roman rule. Modern scholars refer to this intellectual trend as the Second Sophistic. The emphasis on Greek identity manifests itself in many ways in the archaeological record. On Crete, for instance, cave cults enjoyed an unprecedented popularity (Alcock 2002). Worshippers evidently felt an important connection to the mythic past of the island here. Classicizing styles in sculpture remained popular. Through the first

Figure 4.6a Statuette of the weary Hercules discovering son Telephos, found in a late-antique suburban villa at Corinth. Photo courtesy of the American School of Classical Studies in Athens, Corinth Excavations

century CE the city of Corinth minted coins emphasizing its identity as a Roman colony (founded in 44 BCE, a century after its sack by Rome). Subsequent coinage, however, increasingly emphasized the Greek identity of the city (M. Walbank 2003).

One widely circulated statue type was the weary Herakles, shown in repose holding the apples of the Hesperides behind his back. The most famous surviving exemplar of this statue is the colossal Hercules Farnese found in the Baths of Caracalla (Figure 4.6a). Many versions of the statue from Roman Greece, however, omit the apples, and often Herakles is shown instead discovering his son Telephos in Pergamon (Figure 4.6b). One could attribute this iconographic variation to a preference for frontal display where details of the back of a statuette would be hidden in a niche.

Figure 4.6b Colossal statue of the Weary Hercules found in the Baths of Caracalla, Rome. Museo Archeologico Nazionale, Naples, Italy. Photo Alinari/Art Resource, NY

Alternatively, a Greek audience may have been pleased to see the quintessential Greek hero in a firmly eastern location with clear proof of his virility rather than bowed in exhaustion at the western edge of the world. Pergamene myths linked Telephos' descendants to the founders of Rome, thus placing Rome into a satisfactorily eastern context (Plut. *Rom.* 2). A bronze variant of this statue type found at Seleucia-on-the-Tigris raises questions of imperialism and identity in a different way. A bilingual inscription in Greek and Aramaic details how the Parthian king Vologaeses took the statuette as booty from the kingdom of Mesene on the Persian Gulf in 150 or 151 CE and set it up in a temple in his own capital. A late Hellenistic piece, the statuette was an heirloom by the time of its capture (Al-Salihi 1987; Potter 1991).

Epilogue

Difficult though it may be to define, Roman art offers an enticingly diverse panoply of monuments through which to glimpse Roman society. Archaeological research extends beyond the monumental or beautiful, to the mundane objects and non-elite or non-urban surroundings. Taken as a whole, material culture creates a valuable window on living, dying, ruling, and being ruled in the Roman Empire. It is clear that cultural interactions between Rome and the provinces were complicated and continually evolving, involving strategies of adaptation, selection, and resistance. As we have seen, evidence of these processes of change, however we choose to name them, may appear in many different types of material remains. It is no surprise that as modern societies cope with globalization, the question of how diverse peoples interacted with Rome's hegemonic power has come to the fore of scholarship.

CHAPTER FIVE

Interdisciplinary Approaches

James B. Rives

Much of what I have reported and shall report may perhaps seem trivial and trifling to record, as I am well aware. But no one should compare my annals with the writings of those who have composed histories of the Roman people in the old days. They could record great wars, the storming of cities, the rout and capture of kings, or if they turned attention to domestic matters, they could relate with unrestricted scope the conflicts of consuls with tribunes, agrarian and grain laws, the struggles of the plebs and the nobles. But my scope is narrow, my labor inglorious: peace entirely unbroken or but slightly disturbed, dismal deeds in the city, and an emperor unconcerned with extending the empire.

(Tac. *Ann.* 4.32)

Ancient historical studies have traditionally followed the literary sources in their preoccupation with wars and international relations, political events and institutions, and the careers and personalities of powerful and charismatic individuals. However, the first concern of the vast majority of the inhabitants of the Mediterranean in ancient times was not whether Alexander the Great would reach the Ocean that surrounded the inhabited world or whether Julius Caesar was justified in crossing the Rubicon, but food: how to feed themselves and their dependents.

(Garnsey 1988: ix)

1 Disciplines and Interdisciplinarity

The notion of "interdisciplinary approaches" necessarily presupposes that of disciplines. In order to discuss interdisciplinary approaches to the Roman Empire, therefore, we must first consider what we mean in this context by "disciplines" and what characterizes the particular "discipline" to which the study of the Roman Empire belongs. These questions are more difficult than they might seem at first glance. A good case could be made that the study of the Roman Empire does not constitute a discipline at all, but instead draws on a range of disciplines which individual scholars combine in various ways and to various degrees. Nevertheless, it is probably true that most people would regard the study of the Roman Empire as a part of "Roman history." It is furthermore true that the discipline of Roman history, together with ancient Greek history, has a distinctive genealogy that has endowed it with a distinct ive character. The historical study of the Greek and Roman worlds developed out of classical philology, the study of the Greek and Latin languages and literatures, and has traditionally been based largely on Greek and Latin literary sources, especially the works of ancient historians. As a result, as Peter Garnsey suggests, it has also tended to reflect the interests and orientations of the upper-class men who produced these texts. Where their interests lay is made quite clear by Tacitus: the activities of the economic and political elite, politics and war above all. Such topics have traditionally been the focus of Roman history, and I will suggest in my conclusion that in certain important respects they continue to be.

Over the last century or so, however, and especially over the last 30 years, scholars have become increasingly dissatisfied with the limitations that this traditional model of the discipline imposes on the study of the Roman Empire. As Garnsey also indicates, there are matters of fundamental importance that simply do not receive much attention in the literary sources. If Tacitus can dismiss as trivial (albeit with calculated effect) such matters as political trials and court intrigue, we may guess how he would have regarded the suggestion that a historian should write at length about issues of food production and distribution, particularly among rural peasants; surely, neither he nor any other Greek or Roman historian would have considered this a serious topic. There is in fact a whole range of important issues on which the literary sources are either totally silent or at best provide only incidental data. Historians interested in these issues must therefore make use of other types of evidence and employ other methodologies, and they often look to other disciplines for ideas. Similarly, a familiarity with other disciplines can in itself lead to an awareness of issues and problems other than those that emerge from the literary sources. In this respect, then, we might reasonably regard as interdisciplinary any approach that, by drawing ideas or techniques from other disciplines, seeks to move beyond the interests and orientations of the standard literary sources.

This brings us to the second of the questions with which I began: how do we define these other disciplines on which a Roman historian might draw? One way is to define them by the type of material on which they focus; so for example, the disciplines of epigraphy, papyrology, numismatics, and archaeology that have already been discussed in the previous chapters of this section. Although non-specialists might be tempted to see these simply as different fields within the general discipline of Roman history, there are two reasons why it is useful for the purposes of this chapter to regard them as distinct. Firstly, they require specialized knowledge and expertise that many Roman historians simply do not possess; archaeology above all, with its numerous and highly technical sub-disciplines, constitutes a broad field of its own, with distinctive orientations, controversies, and sets of methodologies. Secondly, as I have already suggested, the study of different types of evidence has led scholars to address concerns and develop analyses that go beyond those of the literary texts; as we shall see, these disciplines have played a crucial role in broadening and enriching the study of the Roman Empire.

A second way to define other disciplines is in terms of their characteristic orientations, questions, and methodologies. These are the things that tend to distinguish the major academic disciplines within the social sciences and humanities, for example, sociology, anthropology, geography, history, literature, and art history. Researchers in these disciplines have established areas of investigation and developed analytical tools very different from those that have traditionally defined Roman history; by drawing on them, Roman historians have been able to escape the dominance of the literary sources and to illuminate aspects of the Roman Empire that their authors either ignored or assumed as "natural." The influence of the social sciences and what is loosely called "critical theory" has been especially important, and it is perhaps this in particular that most people would think of in connection with the term "interdisciplinary."

Lastly, we can define disciplines in terms of cultural or linguistic traditions. Hence the study of the Roman Empire is generally a separate discipline from the study of other cultural areas, such as northern Europe or Persia. There are practical reasons for this separation, since the study of different regions and cultural traditions generally requires different sets of skills. The study of northern Europe, for example, depends largely on the techniques of prehistoric archaeology; historians of Persia, in contrast, have to master a different set of languages than historians of the Roman Empire. Yet the fact remains that these different cultural areas were contemporaneous and contiguous with the Roman Empire, and in some cases overlapped it: the empire incorporated many cultural areas with their own languages and traditions, and had significant interactions with surrounding regions. To study these overlaps and interactions necessarily requires an interdisciplinary approach. In this connection we may note in particular two disciplines that, again for genealogical reasons, are surprisingly separate from Roman history: Judaism and Christianity in the imperial period have tended to be studied on their own terms. Work that attempts to bridge this divide may also be regarded as interdisciplinary.

These then are some of the different ways that one might define "interdisciplinary approaches" to the study of the Roman Empire. In what follows, I offer a highly selective and idiosyncratic discussion of each of these in turn, and close by returning briefly to the problem of identifying the discipline itself.

2 Archaeology and the Study of Documentary Sources

With respect to the use of sources other than literary texts, the study of the Roman Empire has long been interdisciplinary. Just as Edward Gibbon was in many ways the first modern historian of the Roman Empire, so too was he one of the last who framed his work almost entirely in terms of the literary sources. This was not entirely the result of his own preferences: he clearly had an interest in coins and inscriptions, and at times drew on works that made use of them (e.g. Gibbon 1994: 1: 270 n. 76; 366 n. 28). But it was only after his death that scholars first began really to emphasize the importance of documentary evidence, and so to promote systematic efforts to collect and edit these materials. These developments particularly characterized the growth of professional, university-based historiography in Germany, and it was a German scholar who did most to incorporate the use of documentary sources, especially inscriptions, into the study of the empire.

Although Theodor Mommsen won the Nobel Prize for Literature for his narrative history of Rome, it was his work on inscriptions that had the greatest impact. Mommsen initiated the grand project of a comprehensive collection of all extant Latin inscriptions from antiquity, properly edited and arranged geographically according to Roman province. Most volumes of the *Corpus Inscriptionum Latinarum* appeared between 1870 and 1890, and although the issuing of updates and supplements had to begin almost immediately, its publication transformed the study of the empire by providing convenient access to the vast amount of data that these inscriptions contained (Gagos and Potter, this volume). Although many scholars used this material simply to further traditional lines of research, it encouraged others to investigate aspects of the Roman Empire that the literary sources did not cover. In particular, it became possible for the first time really to explore the history of the provinces, especially those in the western part of the empire, to which literary texts, with their focus on Rome and the imperial elite, refer only incidentally. Mommsen himself produced the first comprehensive study of the Roman provinces, and in so doing broke for the first time with the Rome-centered approach that had inevitably followed from a concentration on the literary sources (Mommsen 1885).

If the systematic study of documentary evidence had a great impact, that of archaeology was eventually even more profound. In the latter part of the nineteenth century the discipline of archaeology developed rapidly; among other changes, there arose a greater appreciation for the sorts of everyday, utilitarian material that had hitherto been largely ignored in the search for works of art. This new archaeological research accelerated the study of the Roman provinces that Mommsen's epigraphic work had initiated, by allowing researchers, for example, to trace the relative distribution of native and Roman material culture; it was in this context that scholars first developed some of the major analytical categories, such as Romanization, that still play a large if increasingly debated role in the study of the empire (see, e.g., Freeman 1997). Archaeological research also encouraged scholars to address a whole range of important social and economic issues on which the literary sources have little or nothing to say. This can perhaps best be seen in Michael Rostovtzeff's *Social and Economic History of the Roman Empire*, first published in 1926. Just as Mommsen had shifted attention from the capital to the provinces, Rostovtzeff placed his stress not on political and military events, but on the social and economic developments that (in his view) underlay them. Although Rostovtzeff's specific interpretation won little acceptance, his work remains a milestone in large part simply because it was the first comprehensive interpretation of the Roman Empire to give a central role to archaeological evidence (see Bowersock 1973).

3 The Social Sciences and Critical Theory

Although the importance of documentary and archaeological evidence for the study of the empire has long been widely recognized, in certain important respects it is only within the last 30 years or so that researchers have begun to exploit its full potential.

The main reason for this development lies in the increasing influence of the social sciences. The new fields of inquiry and the new methods of analysis that have been developed in the disciplines of geography, economics, sociology, and cultural anthropology have inspired scholars of the Roman Empire to treat documentary and archaeological evidence not merely as a supplement to the literary sources, but as the basis for completely new avenues of investigation. Like the disciplines noted above, the social sciences originated in the nineteenth century; their impact on Roman history, however, has been much more gradual. Indeed, Rostovtzeff's *Social and Economic History* was perhaps the first major work to show their influence, for all that his use of sociological and economic terminology was vague and problematic. For it was not merely Rostovtzeff's interest in the new archaeological research of his day that made his work so seminal, but even more his willingness to formulate hypotheses about historical development that neither depended on the evidence of the literary sources nor were defined by the issues on which they focused.

But despite Rostovtzeff, the influence of the social sciences was initially much stronger in other areas of history. This was particularly true in France, where Marc Bloch and Lucien Febvre, in the journal *Annales: économies, sociétés, civilisations*, which they founded in 1929, championed a historiography that stressed underlying environmental, economic, and social factors rather than the details of political and military developments. This *Annales* school of historiography, as it is called, emphasized issues of climate, geography, technology, agricultural practice, manufacturing, and trade, and made greater use of statistical analysis and quantification than had hitherto been the norm. It was also concerned with *mentalités*, the pervasive structures of religious and social belief that characterize different societies. In all these respects, *Annales* historiography applied the concerns and techniques of the social sciences to the study of past eras. The most famous work associated with this school was Fernand Braudel's *La Méditerranée et le monde méditerranéen à l'époque de Philippe II*, first published in 1949 (Braudel 1972-3). Braudel insisted on the primacy of what he called the *longue durée*, the long term effects of climate, geography, and technology on human life and social organization. Since the Second World War, and particularly in the last 30 years, the approach to historiography advocated by the *Annales* school has been increasingly applied to the study of the Roman Empire.

It is difficult to summarize or even survey the impact of the social sciences on the study of the Roman Empire (for a stimulating discussion of some particular aspects, see Phillips 1986: 2681-97). I shall instead make some selective observations on three general issues: environmental studies, the use of social scientific methodologies, and cultural/ideological analysis. Several of the studies that I shall mention, particularly in the first two areas, are not limited to the specific period of the Roman Empire. This fact is in itself significant, since one effect of much interdisciplinary work has been to question the convention of defining significant historical periods by political events (e.g., the battle of Actium in 31 BCE and the death of Constantine in 337 CE).

One of the most striking results of *Annaliste* influence has been a drive to expand historical analysis into the study of human interaction with the natural environment, to investigate both how the environment shapes human activities and how these in turn alter the environment. In this regard there has been a very fruitful interaction between *Annaliste* historiography and archaeology (see Bintliff 1991). Several recent archaeological projects have aimed to map out human interactions with the environment in fairly limited areas over long stretches of time. These projects typically rely heavily on the technique of survey archaeology, often supplemented with some limited excavation, and combined with scientific disciplines such as geomorphology, paleobotany, paleozoology, and paleoclimatology. For example, one of the most ambitious of such projects studied the Biferno valley in central Italy from Paleolithic times to the modern era. Its goals, in the words of the project director, were to examine how "the topography, climate, resources, and natural communications of the different parts of the valley offered different constraints and opportunities for settlement and land use," and to map out "the complex ways in which different kinds of societies have reacted to these from early prehistory to the present day" (Barker et al. 1995: 308). Intensive local studies of this sort over the last few decades have allowed for a more detailed exploration of the historical interaction of human society with its physical environment than was ever before possible.

Two major works of scholarship, both very recent although completely different in character, perhaps indicate that study of the physical environment will gradually become more widespread among ancient historians. The first is Peregrine Horden and Nicholas Purcell's massive study of the Mediterranean, *The Corrupting Sea* (2000). Horden and Purcell draw on a wide range of disciplines, especially environmental studies, archaeology, and anthropology, to build up a new global interpretation of Mediterranean civilization. Their overriding emphasis is on the distinctiveness of Mediterranean topography, which combines extreme fragmentation into a myriad of distinct geological and climatic zones, what the authors call microecologies, with the possibility of intensive small-scale movement by land and especially by sea, what they call connectivity. Within this framework, they argue, it is possible to achieve a better understanding not only of issues such as food production and trade, but also of religion and social structure. The appearance of such a grand synthesis is bound to stimulate further attention to and debate about the role of the environment in the study of the Roman world (see B. D. Shaw 2001).

The second work is the *Barrington Atlas of the Greek and Roman World* (Talbert 2000). Whereas most historical maps used in the study of the Roman Empire have tended to emphasize political over physical geography, the maps in the *Barrington Atlas* are based on the Operational Navigation Chart and the Tactical Pilotage chart, aeronautical series derived from satellite-generated data, which have been corrected so far as possible to show the physical conditions of antiquity. Their generous scale allows users easily to locate cities, roads, and other constructed features in relation to their physical surroundings. Naturally, the information provided on the maps is generalized and often highly selective; as a result it may even be misleading in certain respects (see, e.g., Alcock et al. 2001). But by combining up-do-date scientific mapping techniques with the results of recent geomorphological, archaeological, and epigraphic research and by presenting the whole in a readily accessible format, the *Atlas* makes it much easier than ever before for even the most casual student to have a greater appreciation for the physical aspect of the ancient Roman world.

As noted above, the adoption of social scientific methodologies has transformed the use of documentary and archaeological evidence. We may consider in particular three interrelated methodologies: quantitative analysis, the use of comparative data, and the formulation of interpretive models. An interest in quantification is in itself nothing new: even Gibbon was keen to compute the number of men under arms in the imperial forces (Gibbon 1994: 1: 47). But the development of mathematical statistics in the twentieth century led to a new use of quantitative data in sociology and economics, allowing researchers to measure, for example, the degree of causal connection between two variables. The application of these techniques to the study of the Roman Empire, however, runs up against a formidable obstacle: the available quantitative data are almost always woefully inadequate. Hence the importance of the second methodology, the use of comparative data, which can with due caution be used to fill at least some of the gaps. For example, specific information about crop yields in Roman antiquity is not available; such information does exist for other times and places, however, and can provide a point of departure. The same is true for comparative data about population trends, transportation, trade, and technology. Clearly, the use of such evidence involves potential dangers, and one must keep in mind possible variations in a whole range of conditions. What can in large measure provide an overarching framework for both these techniques is the formulation of interpretive models. An interpretive model may be defined as an abstraction, a hypothetical formulation that allows the researcher to step back from specific empirical data and to focus instead on the significant relationships that may underlie them. Such models provide a framework for both analysis and the use of comparative data, although they are themselves not without their pitfalls (see, e.g., the cautionary remarks of W. V. Harris 1999: 63–4). I will consider the role of these methodologies in one particular area of Roman history: demography.

Demography is a discipline that depends in large part on the availability of quantitative data, but one that can also make extremely effective use of comparative evidence and statistical models since, as one important scholar has pointed out, "in demographic history the number of probabilities is strictly finite" (Hopkins 1983a: xii). Although there do exist some quantitative data, they are generally hard to come by, especially for more complex demographic issues such as questions of age composition, marriage patterns, fertility, and mortality (see in general Parkin 1992, and the concise survey of Frier 1999). The most significant source of such data is the body of census returns preserved on papyri from Egypt; the returns typically include information about the sex, age, and relationships of individuals in households and survive for a period of about 250 years. Roger Bagnall and Bruce Frier, by analyzing this data in light of comparative evidence and model life tables, have been able to provide fairly reliable information about such matters as household structure, female life expectancy, patterns of male and female first marriage, and female fertility rates (Bagnall and Frier 1994: 170–3).

Investigation into such issues in other parts of the empire is inevitably hampered by the absence of adequate data sets. The evidence that does exist, however, can be used to examine more limited questions. For example, Keith Hopkins and Graham Burton applied statistical sampling techniques to the available information about Roman consuls and their family relationships in order to determine "how far Roman consuls were chosen from among the descendents of consuls or themselves had consular descendents" (Hopkins and Burton 1983: 127); this in turn provides a useful indication of the extent to which the imperial Senate constituted a hereditary aristocracy. Their conclusion that "during the first three centuries CE membership of the Roman Senate was to a large extent not hereditary" (Hopkins and Burton 1983: 194) runs counter to the impression created by the literary sources, and thus allows us to see the latter as expressive more of their authors' ideals than of reality. Another example: Brent Shaw has applied similar techniques to the corpus of Christian inscriptions from Rome and Italy in order to chart the seasonal variations in rates of mortality and marriage (Shaw 1996, 1997). He has shown that most marriages occur in the winter months and that this pattern can be correlated with the agrarian cycle. His conclusion overturns the long-standing belief that June was the most popular month for marriages, a belief based on certain passages of Ovid's *Fasti*. In this case as well, the use of sociological methodologies has not only corrected a misunderstanding, but has allowed us to see more clearly the ideological agenda of a literary source.

The last topic that I shall consider in connection with the impact of the social sciences is what may broadly be described as cultural and ideological analysis. Simply put, many current interdisciplinary approaches to the Roman Empire proceed from two of the fundamental insights of cultural anthropology and critical theory. Firstly, every element in a culture is in some way significant: the way people dress and eat, the way they structure their family, household, and social relations, the way they organize their days, their houses, and their communities, the way they conceive of and relate to the divine. All these things are meaningful and help us to characterize the underlying nature of that culture. Secondly, these meanings were not merely passive or neutral, but in many cases had the active function of producing and reinforcing certain social structures, especially relationships of class, status, gender, and ethnicity. As a result, most, if not all, aspects of a culture are susceptible of an ideological analysis. The impact of these two insights on the study of the Roman Empire, especially in the last 20 years, has been dramatic. On the one hand, scholars have begun to examine the ideological role of various aspects of high culture, such as art and literature, that were traditionally studied on a purely formal, aesthetic basis. On the other hand, they have started to analyze elements of Roman culture that were previously the province of antiquarianism, such as clothing, housing, and dining practices, or were dismissed as meaningless superstition, such as magic, astrology, and dream interpretation. I will discuss a few examples from each of these areas.

The study of Roman art has long been somewhat peripheral to the historical study of the empire, for all that the art itself was an enormously important part of Roman cultural life. There are again disciplinary reasons for this, since the study of Roman art typically falls under the discipline of "art history" rather than "Roman history," and the concerns of art history have traditionally centered on describing and ordering stylistic and formal developments within and between particular historical periods. Inevitably, then, there was in the past relatively little overlap between this field of study and traditional Roman history, with its focus on political and military developments. In recent decades, however, the influence of the social sciences and critical theory has transformed art history just as it has Roman history, so that there is an increasing interest in analyzing Roman art as a medium for communicating and constructing significant social meanings. R. R. R. Smith provides an excellent statement of this approach in his study of honorific portrait statues in the eastern Roman Empire. In his view, these statues "display a received and recognizable statue and portrait language to make and project plausible-looking statements about selected social, cultural, and political aspirations.... The statues, their inscribed bases, their portrait heads, and their architectural settings were all parts of quite complex statements, with a vocabulary and grammar to be read. The language of these monuments was understood unconsciously by an ancient viewer brought up amongst them. For the modern viewer some reconstructive interpretation is required" (Smith 1998: 92). Hence, we can analyze these statues not only in terms of their style and iconography, but also as elements in a broader discourse about cultural, political, and social status.

I will note here two examples of recent work along these lines, studies that focus respectively on the beginning and end of the Roman imperial period as traditionally defined. First, Paul Zanker's study of art in the age of Augustus brilliantly shows how the traditional concerns of art history and Roman history can in fact overlap in important ways. That Augustus transformed the Roman world politically and socially has been recognized since his own day; that there was in the same period a major stylistic change has also long been acknowledged. What Zanker did was to demonstrate a relationship between these two phenomena; he argues that Augustus' program "required a new visual language," so that there was in fact a "complex interrelationship" between "the establishment of monarchy, the transformation of society, and the creation of a whole new method of visual communication" (Zanker 1988: 3). In other words, the stylistic developments of the Augustan period were not merely coincidental with the political and social transformation, nor yet simply reflective of it, but were also instrumental in bringing it about. Second, Jas Elsner has revisited the old problem of the formal shift that took place in Roman art from the naturalistic style of the first two centuries CE to the abstract, hieratic style of the fifth and sixth centuries CE. His approach, however, is to focus not so much on the formal qualities of the two styles as on the process of viewing; he argues that the stylistic shift corresponds to an underlying cultural shift that provided "profoundly different *frames* for the ways viewers formulated their responses to images": "the naturalism or abstraction (that is, the style) of objects is dependent on a great many conceptual, sociological and essentially historical factors rooted in the way art is viewed at particular times" (Elsner 1995: 9, 13). By emphasizing the process of viewing, Elsner reminds us that what people saw in a given work of art depended in large part on the way they understood the world more generally, which was in turn necessarily bound up with a variety of social and cultural factors.

The study of literature provides an interesting parallel to the study of Roman art. Like the study of art, it has traditionally focused on issues of stylistic development and the analysis of individual works or genres, although for the reasons outlined at the beginning of the chapter the study of literature has had much closer ties to Roman history. And just as in the study of art, there is now a much greater concern with the ideological role of language and literature. Of course, there has long been interest in particular questions about particular works, often formulated in rather simplistic terms; for example, whether or not Vergil wrote the *Aeneid* as propaganda for Augustus. But in the last 20 or 30 years there has been increased sensitivity to the fact that all literature was produced in very precise social contexts and so inevitably reflects the circumstances of its production. Some scholars would now go further, asserting that it not only reflects social relationships but also helped construct them. Thomas Habinek has recently proposed that we regard Latin literature "as a medium through which competing sectors of Roman society sought to advance their interests over and against other sources of social and political authority;" in particular, he suggests that "many of the characteristics of Latin literature can be attributed to its production by and for an elite that sought to maintain and expand its dominance over other sectors of the population through reference to an authorizing past" (Habinek 1998: 3). This social and ideological function of literature extends even to the level of correct Latinity, i.e., the formulation of prescriptions about what constitutes "proper" Latin vocabulary, syntax, and style. Martin Bloomer has argued that "in approaching the construction of walls of decorum within and between literary texts, we must ask who is excluding whom, and why and by what means." Rules about acceptable usage in fact provided "a vehicle for anxieties about ethnicity, social order, social status, and gender" (Bloomer 1997: 6). In short, Latin literature, and Greek literature as well, was not simply a matter of aesthetics and style, but was part of the very social fabric; if we want to understand that society, we must understand the role of literature within it.

We may consider one example in a little more detail. As Bloomer notes, anxieties about gender were among the issues with which stylistic prescriptions were concerned. In the last ten years there has been considerable work on the relationship between rhetorical practice and masculinity. For years scholars tended to dismiss oratory in the imperial period as trivial, artificial, and insignificant. Nevertheless, rhetoric played a central role in education and elite culture during the imperial period; especially in the Greek-speaking parts of the empire, but elsewhere as well, virtuoso speakers attracted great crowds and wielded great influence. To understand this phenomenon adequately, we must reassess what we consider significant and adopt new tools that will allow for new analyses. As Maud Gleason has pointed out, "one reason that these [rhetorical] performances were so riveting was that the encounter between orator and audience was in many cases the anvil upon which the self-presentation of ambitious upper-class men was forged" (Gleason 1995: xx). We may put the accent here upon the word "men": oratory was an almost exclusively male activity, and one of the most effective charges one could bring against a rival was that he spoke like a woman. This was no accident: "because rhetorical skill was considered a definitive test of masculine excellence, issues of rhetorical style and self-presentation easily became gendered" (Gleason 1995: 160). Far from being trivial and unimportant, then, rhetoric in the imperial period turns out to have been a crucial forum for the construction of masculinity and the struggle for social and political power (see Richlin 1997c for a useful survey of the issues).

As I have noted, it is not only "high culture" that is currently providing the subjects of cultural and ideological analysis. I will end my consideration of this topic with two examples, one from the realm of everyday material culture, the other from the wide range of ancient disciplines that were until recently dismissed as mere superstition. Domestic architecture has long been an area of interest in the study of the Roman Empire, although less so than the monumental architecture of public buildings and temples. By and large, however, most work has been pragmatic and typological, concerned with identifying the functions of the various spaces within the house and with classifying the different kinds of structures. Since the mid-1980s, however, as the co-editor of one recent collection of papers has put it, "the study [has been] moving from questions of function to reveal new depths of understanding that stress the rôle of the house as an element of a society's social matrix, charged with the cultural ideology of its inhabitants" (Laurence 1997: 7). This more recent work again stresses that the organization of space in domestic architecture was not merely a passive reflection of social structures. "What we see in Roman domestic space, including the artifacts, is not evidence that can simply be 'read off,' but evidence for how Roman society reinforced the categories of male: female, free: unfree, married: unmarried, or adult: child, as well as a series of status hierarchies from élite to dispossessed"; in other words, "[domestic] space would appear to have played a rôle in the constitution of gender, slavery, and the transitional stages in the Roman life cycle" (Laurence 1997: 14).

Turning from material to intellectual culture, I will take as my final example the ancient practice of physiognomics, "the discipline that seeks to detect from individuals' exterior features their character, disposition, or destiny" (T. Barton 1994: 95). Traditionally, historians have paid little attention to physiognomics or to other "pseudo-sciences" such as astrology, alchemy, and dream interpretation; if they noted them at all, it was usually as evidence for the decline of rationality and the rise of superstition. More recent scholars have demonstrated that if we approach such material from a broadly anthropological perspective, we can derive from it considerable insights into the way that contemporaries viewed the world. Physiognomics employed as its chief principles of classification the dichotomies of male/female, Greek/barbarian, and human/animal, ideas that were deeply embedded in ancient culture; at the same time, it had the status of a technical discipline, like medicine or astrology, which it achieved through the systematic elaboration of analytical tools (see in general T. Barton 1994: 95–131). For example, Gleason has shown how the treatise on physiognomics by the celebrated second-century CE orator Polemo can serve "as a source for the 'body language' of his cultural milieu, particularly for the coercive way images of male deviance functioned in the semiotics of gender. Because gender categories were invoked as ordering principles for physiognomic data, the treatises of Polemo and his predecessors offer a unique source of insight into the way sex and gender categories could be used to sort human differences into readily comprehensible hierarchies and opposition" (Gleason 1995: xiii). Moreover, Polemo's mastery of physiognomics gave him a claim to authority that he could use against rivals in the struggle for imperial favor and political influence, notably against the eunuch Favorinus, whom Polemo attacked for effeminacy. Regardless of whether or not we regard it as superstitious, then, the study of ancient physiognomics and its use in society can provide us with valuable insight into ancient cultural attitudes.

4 Cultural and Linguistic Traditions

We may sum up the impact of the social sciences and critical theory as two-fold. On the one hand, scholars in recent decades have been much more willing to investigate a whole range of topics beyond the narrow field of political and military developments and have demonstrated that these topics are equally important for understanding the society and culture of the empire. On the other hand, in order to investigate these areas, they have deployed a wide range of analytical tools and methodologies that were originally developed in other disciplines. As I noted above, this two-fold impact is one of the reasons that documentary and archaeological evidence is playing an increasingly important role in the study of the Roman Empire. Both these developments are in turn important for the third and last of my categories of "interdisciplinary approaches," those that focus on the interactions between different cultural and linguistic traditions. I have already mentioned the key role played by archaeological and documentary evidence in the study of the Roman provinces. In addition, the social sciences and critical theory have provided crucial analytical tools for examining the relationship between Roman and/or Greek culture and the other traditions with which it interacted, both within and across the imperial borders. I will limit myself here to just a few observations.

As one example of interest in the interactions between the Roman Empire and areas beyond its borders, we may consider recent work on connections between Rome and northern Europe. As Barry Cunliffe has noted, "for far too long the study of the classical world of the Mediterranean and of the barbarian communities of temperate and northern Europe have remained very separate disciplines." But since the 1960s, he argues, two developments have led to increasing interactions between the two: firstly, "archaeologists have become more and more interested by the systems at work in society"; secondly, ancient historians have begun to study the ancient economy "in terms of model building, using a wide range of analogies and supporting their arguments with quantified data susceptible to statistical testing" (Cunliffe 1988: 1–2). In short, a convergence of interests and methodologies has created a common meeting ground for Roman historians and prehistoric archaeologists and so allowed for the interdisciplinary study of the economic and cultural interactions between the Roman Empire and northern Europe. Cunliffe himself, for example, has proposed a comprehensive interpretation of these interactions that treats the Mediterranean and Europe together as a complex but unified core–periphery economic system. Although other scholars have questioned the specific model proposed by Cunliffe, few would now take issue with his general conclusion that "barbarian Europe and the Mediterranean world must be studied together, since for much of the time their development was interdependent" (Cunliffe 1988: 201).

Roman interaction with other cultural and linguistic traditions was of course not restricted to the periphery of the empire: centuries of imperial expansion meant that a great many cultures had been absorbed into the Roman world. It is fair to say that in the last two decades there has been an explosion of interest in the interaction between Roman and local cultures within the empire. As I noted above, interest in this topic goes back at least to Mommsen in the nineteenth century; much early work, however, tended to be rather mechanistic in tracing the spread of Roman civilization and rather uncritical in evaluating its effects. More recent approaches, influenced especially by postcolonial theory, have tended to focus on the complexity of these interactions and particularly on the active role played in them by native peoples (for general discussion, see, e.g., D. J. Mattingly 1997 and Woolf 1998: 1–76). So, for example, the editor of a recent collection of papers argues that "we need to rethink our understanding of indigenous societies in contact with Rome. They were neither passive victims, nor enthusiastic participants, nor entirely free agents in those relations.... The first priority must be to locate indigenous people in the power networks and colonial discourse that bound them to Rome, and to seek to understand the prelude, processes and results of their complex negotiations (societal and personal) with the imperial power" (D. J. Mattingly 1997: 10). Similarly, Susan Alcock, in the conclusion to her study of Greece in the imperial period, says that its "primary advantage... lies in its attempt to recover some measure of response to imperial incorporation on the part of the population at large, to make them active participants in their own history" (Alcock 1993: 229).

Much recent work on this topic has been interdisciplinary in virtually all the ways that I have discussed so far: it employs social scientific methodologies and draws on critical theory, it is sensitive to environmental issues, and it is based largely on documentary and especially archaeological evidence. For example, Alcock uses the results of archaeological survey projects in order to compare the record of early imperial Greece with that of preceding and succeeding periods. Her organizing theme is that of landscape "as a *social* product, the consequence of a collective human transformation of the physical environment"; changes in settlement patterns or territorial boundaries, for example, provide evidence for "the restructuring of political authority or the redistribution of economic resources" (Alcock 1993: 6–7). To take another example, Greg Woolf (1998) employs a variety of indices to analyze some of the processes of change triggered by the incorporation of Gaul into the Roman Empire: the changing distribution of inscriptions, the creation and organization of cities, the transformation of the countryside through the spread of villas, shifting patterns of consumption as revealed in the distribution of ceramics, and changes in religious ideas and organization. By employing these sorts of interdisciplinary approaches, recent scholars have encouraged us to think more carefully about the complex social transformations and cultural interactions that result from the expansion of Roman power.

Although much research on these topics has been inspired by work on modern imperialism and colonialism, it often differs from it in relying more heavily on archaeological evidence. The reason for this is simple: unlike colonial populations in the modern period, very few local traditions and indigenous cultures within the Roman Empire have left any written sources that reflect their point of view. There are only three significant exceptions: the Greek tradition, whose relationship with Rome is extraordinarily complex, and the Egyptian and Jewish traditions. Although interesting work has been done in the last 20 years or so on all these traditions (see, e.g., Swain 1996 on Greek culture, Frankfurter 1998a on Egyptian), it is to the Jewish tradition that I wish to call attention here. Texts originating in the Israelite-Jewish tradition survive from almost all periods of antiquity, although admittedly in problematic forms: biblical texts, the "Old Testament pseudepigrapha," the Dead Sea Scrolls, and the rabbinic Mishnah, Talmuds, and Midrash. Given the possibilities that this literature presents for investigating the intellectual and cultural traditions of one particular ethnic/religious group that was absorbed into the Roman Empire, it is surprising how underutilized it is by Roman historians. Although this is no doubt partly because many of these texts are in languages and formats unfamiliar to most Roman specialists, the chief reason, as I noted earlier, is that Roman history and Jewish studies have long constituted separate disciplines: Jewish studies generally falls under the rubric of religious studies, which has an entirely different genealogy from that of Roman history. The same is true of early Christian studies. The extensive literary remains of early Christianity again constitute an invaluable source of evidence for the Roman historian, since many of these texts emanated from social strata outside the imperial elite. In this case there is not even a language barrier, since with very few exceptions Christian texts of the first three centuries are written in Greek or Latin.

The chief reason that they do not play a larger part in the study of the empire is again the disciplinary division between Roman history and religious studies.

It would be highly misleading to imply that there have been no attempts to bridge these gaps; on the contrary, there has over the years been a considerable amount of stimulating work done by important scholars on both sides of the divide. Nevertheless, the disciplinary boundary persists, noticeable particularly on the Roman side of things: Jewish and Christian sources remain more marginal to the study of the Roman Empire than they ought. To what extent this will change remains to be seen; I will here merely note one positive sign. It seems increasingly the norm for standard reference works in Classics and Graeco-Roman history to include coverage of Jewish and Christian topics. For example, the third edition of the *Oxford Classical Dictionary* (1996), has more extensive treatment of Christian material than the two earlier editions, with a lengthy entry on "Christianity" as well as entries on important Christian writers including St. Paul, Justin Martyr, Clement of Alexandria, Tertullian, and Origen. More strikingly, for the first time it includes Judaism, with entries not only on "Jews" and "religion, Jewish," but also, among others, "rabbis," "Dead Sea Scrolls," and "Mishnah." Another example is the massive, multi-volume and rather sprawling survey of the Roman Empire in the second part of *Aufstieg und Niedergang der römischen Welt*. Under the rubric "Religion," this collection contains extensive coverage of Judaism, both in Palestine and the Diaspora (volumes 19–21), and even more extensive coverage of Christianity (volumes 23–7). Whether or not students of the Roman Empire will consult this material is of course another question, but its availability in standard reference works will perhaps have the gradual effect of making it seem less alien.

5 Final Thoughts

In closing, we may return to our point of departure, and consider again the problem of identifying disciplines in the study of the Roman Empire. It should by now be clear that, as I suggested at the start, the study of the Roman Empire is almost by definition interdisciplinary, insofar as researchers must draw on a variety of sources and employ a wide range of methodologies in order to advance their work. Nevertheless, traditional disciplinary divisions continue to exert great influence. Two of these seem to me especially significant: that between archaeology and text-based approaches on the one hand, and that between "classical" studies and religious studies on the other. To some extent, there are strong practical reasons for these divisions: the demands of mastering the various skills that these disciplines require are such that no one could hope to achieve competence in them all. Nevertheless, it is vital that there be dialogue between specialists in these different areas; as I have indicated, such dialogue has begun and will if anything, I hope, increase.

It is also important to notice that the traditional model of Roman history still exerts a powerful influence. Written sources continue to be crucial, and the demands of mastering Latin and ancient Greek mean that language study remains an important element in the training of new historians; in turn, the time and effort people expend in acquiring these linguistic skills encourages them to privilege a text-based approach. One measure of the continued dominance of the literary sources is that standard accounts of the Roman Empire still tend to place the narrative of political and military events at the center, with accounts of society and economy, religion, literature and art relegated to interstitial "topical" chapters. Nevertheless, if the traditional model of Roman history continues to loom large in the study of the empire, its importance perhaps lies increasingly in serving as a foil against which scholars can elaborate newer interdisciplinary approaches. Certainly the variety of work noticed here suggests that we may be in the midst of a gradual sea-change in the study of the Roman Empire that will ultimately transform the discipline entirely.

PART II

Narrative

CHAPTER SIX

The Emergence of Monarchy: 44 BCE–96 CE

Greg Rowe

A recently-published Roman coin from 28 BCE symbolizes what the Roman imperial state would be (Rich and Williams 1999). One side of the coin shows young Caesar ("Octavian") wreathed in triumphal laurel under the legend, "Imperator Caesar, son of the Divine, consul for the sixth time." The state would be a monarchy. The other side shows young Caesar wearing a civilian toga, sitting on a Roman magistrate's bench, holding out a scroll from a scroll-case under the legend, "He revived the rights and laws of the Roman People" (Figure 6.1a). The state would preserve the legal framework of the republic. Over the last generation there have been profound changes in the way Roman political systems are viewed. The republic has come to be seen as a democracy, in which the Roman people (or the fraction attending assemblies at Rome) alone exercised all-important legislative power – and used it to give unprecedented military commands to Pompey, Julius Caesar, and young Caesar. The principate has come to be seen as a monarchy, in which the emperor was more than the sum of his formally-delegated powers. But fresh documents such as the coin remind us that the principate preserved the institutions of the republic – the Senate and the popular assemblies, the magistracies and the priesthoods – and the emperor's working relations with these institutions are now being seen to have given Roman monarchy its distinctive character.

1 Augustus

In the case of young Caesar, monarchic and republican elements had both been present from the beginning. The facts of young Caesar's rise to sole power are well-known: born C. Octavius in 63 BCE, named principal heir to his great-uncle Julius Caesar (44 BCE), defeated Caesar's murderers Brutus and Cassius (42 BCE), Pompey's son Sex. Pompeius (36 BCE), and Antony and Cleopatra (31–30 BCE). What is important is that during his rise young Caesar had consistently espoused two causes. One was avenging Julius Caesar by legal means (*RG* 2.1). As heir he shed "Octavius" and became "C. (Iulius) Caesar" – only his enemies called him "Octavianus." He implemented the Senate's divine honors to Julius Caesar (becoming "son of the Divine"), and he completed Julius Caesar's building projects – notably the Temple of Venus Genetrix, divine ancestress of the Iulii. But the other cause young Caesar professed was defending the republic. From 43 to 33 BCE he was, by popular statute, a "Triumvir for putting the Republic back in order" with formal power to appoint Roman magistrates and provincial governors. He called his rivals enemies of the republic: Brutus and Cassius, who "waged war against the Republic" (*RG* 2.1), the "pirate" Sex. Pompeius, who led "runaway slaves who had taken up arms against the Republic" (*RG* 25.1), and M. Antony, who led a "faction that oppressed the Republic" (*RG* 1.1). And from the beginning young Caesar's reign would be distinguished from Hellenistic monarchies by the presence of republican institutions. Both young Caesar and M. Antony chose as their closest associates "new men" who lacked senatorial ancestors. When Cleopatra rewarded M. Antony's general P. Canidius with tax privileges – "the annual exportation of 10,000 artabas of wheat and the annual importation of 5,000 Coan amphoras of wine without anyone exacting anything in taxes from him" – she did so by royal fiat, subscribing the order, "Let it be done" (van Minnen 2000). But when young Caesar's associate Vedius Pollio received similar privileges – tax immunity on Asian exports up to 10,000 denarii – it was by decree of the Roman Senate, communicated through an edict of the Roman consuls (*SEG* 39 no. 1180, 40). And when, in 12 BCE, Augustus eulogized his second-in-command M. Agrippa, he did so in terms of powers granted by the Senate and Roman people:

> you were granted the tribunician power by decree of the Senate... it had been sanctioned by law that your *imperium* was to be greater than anyone else's in whatever provinces the Republic of the Roman People summoned you. (EJ 366)

Once young Caesar had achieved sole power, there was no question of his dissolving the republic. Instead he made good on his promise to put the republic in order and began to establish a working relationship with it. As the recently-discovered coin shows, the process extended over several years. He began with domestic affairs, annulling acts of the triumvirs that were contrary to custom, restoring popular elections, and completing the first census of the Roman people in 42 years. The following year (27 BCE) he turned to provincial affairs. The Senate met as it formerly had done to decide which would be the provinces of the Roman people and what ranks of official would govern them; the Senate divided the empire into provinces of the Roman people (internal, pacified, with governors chosen by lot) and provinces of Caesar (frontier, garrisoned, with governors appointed by the emperor). Between the two there was little real difference: emperor and republic issued orders to both, and revenues from both went to the public treasury (Millar 1966). (In general, the emperor and the republic shared the task of governing; popular statutes, senatorial decrees, and imperial edicts seem to have been interchangeable in practice: aqueducts, for example, were regulated by decrees, statutes, and edicts [Fron. *Aq.* 2.100–29; EJ

282]; Greek-Roman relations in Cyrene, by edicts and a decree [EJ 311]; customs collection in Asia by consular edicts, a decree, and an imperial edict [*SEG* 29 no. 1180, 39–57]). More significant was the allotment of multi-provincial commands. With the defeat of Egypt, Roman domination of the Mediterranean was complete, so Augustus pushed inland, annexing the whole of the Iberian peninsula and the Alps and pushing the frontier beyond the Rhine and to the Danube. The superior commands were restricted to imperial family members: under Augustus, Augustus himself, his son-in-law Agrippa, or his stepsons Tiberius and the elder Drusus; under Tiberius, Tiberius' adopted son Germanicus and biological son the younger Drusus. Yet even these commands were formally bestowed by the Roman people and the commanders all seem to have had the republican title "proconsul." A recently-discovered imperial edict reveals that Augustus, when abroad, was formally a proconsul (Alföldy 2000), while a Tiberian senatorial decree shows that Germanicus, too, was a proconsul with powers bestowed by the Roman people:

> who had been sent out by our *princeps* at the instance of the Senate to put overseas affairs in order... a proconsul concerning whom a law had been brought before the People that in whatever province he entered, he was to have greater *imperium* than the person who was governing that province as proconsul. (*AE* 1996 no. 885, lines 30–6)

A monarchy was taking shape amid the republic – and the process was not always smooth. The emperor's position was partly defined by the powers the republic bestowed, but those powers evolved (after 23 BCE no annual consulship, special *imperium* for five-year terms, the newly-invented "tribunician power"), while the plebs urged Augustus to take on more (*RG* 5–6: dictator, curator of laws and morals). For most of the decade after Actium, senators and knights continued claiming recognition and authority that were no longer available: M. Licinius Crassus was denied the *spolia opima* for defeating a Macedonian king in single combat because he fought under the auspices of young Caesar (29–8 BCE); the first governor of Egypt Cornelius Gallus was convicted in the Senate for boasting of his victories (29–6 BCE); the Macedonian governor M. Primus was charged with waging unauthorized war (23–2 BCE); L. Cornelius Balbus became the last man from outside the imperial house to celebrate a triumph for a victory over the African Garamantes (19 BCE); and a popular aedile, M. Egnatius Rufus, had the temerity to stand for the consulship without imperial approval (19 BCE). Many such aristocrats were executed as conspirators, beginning with the triumvir's son M. Aemilius Lepidus, forced to commit suicide when accused of plotting to assassinate young Caesar (30 BCE).

And the monarchy would be dynastic. Like any Roman aristocrat, Augustus hoped to transmit his name, wealth, and public status to an heir. Even without formal rules, the Augustan succession had several recurring features. Because Augustus, like Caesar, had no sons, he had to obtain heirs through remarriage (in the form of stepsons), through the marriages of his daughter Julia, or by adoption. Women such as his wife Livia, sister Octavia, and daughter Julia achieved unprecedented public prominence, and the very idea of the family was expanded to include cognate as well as agnatic relations (Corbier 1994). Because these heirs were sent on military campaigns, they kept predeceasing Augustus, and Augustus had to keep reshuffling the dynasty. And, perhaps because they kept dying, Augustus brought up heirs in pairs, creating problems whenever an emperor died and left two potential successors (Tiberius and Agrippa Postumus, Gaius and Tiberius Gemellus, Nero and Britannicus). The dynastic principle – and the latest dynastic permutations – were readily grasped by provincial subjects, who swore loyalty to the present and future of the house. In the earliest-known provincial oath, from 6/5 BCE, the magistrates, Senate, and people of Conobaria in southern Spain specify the precise relationships of the princes' dynastic ties (son and grandson) and their republican titles (consul designate, pontifex maximus), vowing:

> for the sake of the welfare, honor, and victory of Imperator Caesar Divi f. Augustus, pontifex maximus, Gaius Caesar, leader of youth and consul designate, Lucius Caesar, son of Augustus, and M. Agrippa [Postumus], grandson of Augustus, to pursue by land and see unto extermination whoever will have done or said anything against them. (González 1988)

Just as significant as the precision with which they observe the status of the people involved is the fact that they conspicuously omit Augustus' stepson Tiberius, who had just retired to Rhodes in dudgeon over the rapid advancement of Gaius and Lucius.

But the regime's foundation was still military. On the Danube, the Pannonian revolt took three years to suppress (6–9 CE). Beyond the Rhine three Roman legions were defeated by Germanic armies. With these setbacks, the army ceased to be an instrument of consistent expansion and became the guardian in a "fortress Rome" posture that characterized the High Empire (Luttwak 1976). This was the last of a series of fundamental changes to the Roman army under Augustus. The civil war armies had been demobilized into veterans' colonies in Italy and overseas (Keppie 1983), in what may qualify as the greatest feat of governance in human terms in the ancient world. The legions, originally composed of citizen-soldiers mobilized anew each campaigning season, completed their transformation into a professional standing army paid by the republic (though Augustus contributed 170 million sesterces to found the soldiers' treasury in 6 CE: *RG* 17), but receiving bonuses and decorations from the imperial family (Maxfield 1981). The auxiliary cohorts – originally allied militias – were coordinated as a second corps of the Roman army, under Roman command and deployed around the empire. The overseas colonies, the legions and their decorations, the auxiliary units and their commanders, an emergency levy occasioned by a defeat, and above all the presence of the imperial family in soldiers' lives, all come together in a dedication from Alexandria Troas in Asia:

> To Gaius Fabricius Tuscus, son of Gaius, of the tribe Aniensis, duovir, augur, prefect of the cohort of Apulia and of the works that were accomplished in the colony by order of Augustus, tribune of the soldiers of Legion III Cyrenaica for eight years, tribune of the levy of freeborn men that Augustus and Tiberius Caesar held at Rome, prefect of engineers for four years, prefect of the cavalrymen of the praetorian wing for four years. He was awarded the unstained spear and gold crown by Germanicus Caesar, commander in the Germanic war. By decree of the decurions. (Brunt 1974a; EJ 368)

Technically the legions remained "the army of the Roman people," but materially and symbolically they were tied to the Caesars.

2 The Other Julio-Claudians

After Lucius and Gaius died (2 and 4 CE), Augustus adopted a rehabilitated Tiberius and by degrees brought him to a position of equal power (*imperium*, tribunician power). Yet, in his first meeting with the Senate after Augustus' death, Tiberius refused to acknowledge that he had "succeeded to his father's station" (Vell. Pat. 2.124.2), and senators took turns trying to get him to confess his supremacy. Three long senatorial decrees from the years 19–20 CE show how the Senate actually extended its competence under the emperors (Brunt 1984; Talbert 1984). One shows the Senate taking part in elections, senators casting the first votes for consuls and praetors (EJ 94a). Another shows the Senate upholding its dignity by condemning "those who contrary to the dignity of their order appeared on stage or at games or pledged themselves to fight as gladiators, as forbidden by senatorial decrees passed on the subject in previous years, employing fraudulent evasion to the detriment of the majesty of the Senate" (Levick 1983; *AE* 1991 no. 515; see Potter, this volume). The third decree shows the Senate sitting as a court, trying the Syrian governor Gnaeus Piso for insubordination, and directing soldiers' future loyalties:

> The Senate hopes that the soldiers will forever display the loyalty and devotion they displayed to the Augustan house, since they know that the safety of our empire reposes in the guardianship of that house. Greatest authority should belong to commanders who have with the most devoted loyalty worshipped the name of the Caesars, which protects this city and the empire of the Roman People. (*AE* 1996 no. 885, 163–5)

Above all, the Senate began decreeing honors to the imperial family, thus preserving a place for itself in the new order. In one of the decrees the Senate commissions memorials to Germanicus Caesar, including marble arches in Rome, on the Rhine, and in Syria, inscribed: "The Senate and Roman People dedicated this monument to the memory of Germanicus Caesar... he died serving the Republic" (*RS* 37, fr. i, lines 9–21).

Yet when Tiberius retired to Italy and Capri (25–6 CE), power in Rome devolved not on the Senate, but on the prefect of the praetorian guard (the urban garrison), Sejanus (Syme 1956), a man whose career in many respects resembles that of Agrippa, Augustus' chief lieutenant. Like Agrippa, Sejanus began his career a knight, one of the Roman aristocrats traditionally distinguished from senators by not holding public office, but now appointed to prefectures as powerful as any senatorial office (grain, Egypt, the praetorian guard). Again like Agrippa, Sejanus then received powers from the republic (*imperium*, the consulship, tribunician power). But unlike Agrippa, Sejanus never married into the imperial family. And when Tiberius told the Senate that Sejanus had been clearing a path to the imperial succession for himself by killing rivals, the Senate arrested Sejanus, tried him, and had him strangled. Typically, contemporary writers ascribe both his rise and his fall to the republic. In the beginning, Velleius Paterculus writes, "the Senate and the Roman People... were ready to summon for the preservation of its security the man they regarded as the most useful instrument" (Vell. Pat. 2.128.4). In the end, Valerius Maximus writes, "all crimes are surpassed by the thought of a single parricide.... He who essayed to subvert all,

Figure 6.1a–e The Julio-Claudian house: (a) Augustus (*RIC* Augustus 208; editor's collection, photo by Ivory Photo, Ann Arbor MI); (b) Tiberius (*RIC* 30; ANS 1935.117.357) (courtesy of the American Numismatic Society); (c) Caligula (*RIC* Gaius 33; courtesy of Yale University); (d) Claudius (*RIC* Claudius 116; editor's collection); (e) Nero (*RIC* Nero 47; editor's collection)

violating the bonds of friendship, was trampled down with all his race by the might of the Roman People" (Val. Max. 9.11, ext. 4).

Tiberius was succeeded by Germanicus' son Gaius (Caligula), who was 24 at his accession. Different emperors had different ruling styles. The older emperors of the period (Augustus, Tiberius, Vespasian) all partially retired, shared power with younger men, and died naturally; the younger emperors (Gaius, Nero, Domitian) tested the limits of autocracy, humiliated senators, and died early. Gaius, for example, murdered his co-heir Gemellus, built a palace stretching from the Capitol through the Roman Forum to the Palatine that used the Temple of Castor as an entrance, and tried to have his cult-image installed in the Temple in Jerusalem, setting off a Jewish revolt. But all emperors ruled in the context of the republic. This included participating in rites of the state religion. Thus, on May 29, 38 CE, "Gaius Caesar Augustus, president of the college of Arval Brothers, sacrificed in the company of the flamen Appius Silanus a fat ewe to dea Dia and gave the starting signal for the chariot-racers and acrobatic riders," according to recently-discovered portions of the Arval Brothers' Acts (Scheid 1998: no. 12). Yet the landscape and calendar in which the Arval Brothers operated were conspicuously imperial. The same year, the Arvals performed sacrifices on behalf of the Roman people at the emperor's home, the New Temple of Divus Augustus, the Theater of Marcellus before the statue of Divus Augustus, and the Ara Providentiae Augustae in the Campus Agrippae. They marked the birthdays of Julia Augusta, Antonia Augusta, Germanicus, and Gaius, and the days when Gaius entered Rome and was named *imperator* by the Senate and *pater patriae* by the Roman people. And on May 24, 38 CE, they co-opted a new Brother "in place of Tiberius Caesar, son of Drusus" – that is, Gemellus, Gaius' murdered co-heir.

But real power remained with the armies. A tribune of the praetorian guard assassinated Gaius and installed his uncle Claudius. Between the assassination and the installation was an interregnum during which the republic was briefly restored. According to the eyewitness Cluvius Rufus, as transmitted by Josephus, while the Senate was decreeing honors to the assassin, and the people were "proud to have regained their sovereignty," the soldiers seized the initiative. The guard considered whether a republic would be workable and in their interest, proclaimed Claudius, and conveyed their choice to the Senate and the people (Jos. *AJ* 19.157–89). Thus the principate continued on the military basis on which it had been founded, surrounded by the same republican apparatus.

Under Claudius Roman expansionism was renewed (Levick 1990: 137–61). Rome conquered Britain and annexed the two Mauretanias, Lycia, and Thrace, encircling the Mediterranean completely. The Roman Empire grew, Roman citizenship spread, yet Roman institutions – both old republican and new imperial ones – remained tied to the capital. One example was subsidized grain underwritten by the emperors, which seems to have been a privilege for all Roman citizens, not just the capital's denizens – at least that is the implication of an epitaph from Interpromium, across the Apennines from Rome, that links a Roman citizen residing locally with the Roman "corps of juniors" for distributing grain (*AE* 1992, no. 323). Another institution that remained tied to the capital was the courts, where four generations of Puteolan moneylenders, whose wooden-tablet records have been found near Pompeii, continued to settle disputes – although the praetor's tribunal had moved from its traditional place in the Forum Romanum to the Forum of Augustus, and although the moneylenders now swore oaths by Divus Augustus and the Genius of the living emperor in addition to Jupiter Optimus Maximus (Camodeca 1999: no. 68).

Under Claudius freed slaves of the emperor exercised their greatest power and both determined public policy and received public recognition. Pallas, the freedman in charge of Claudius' private accounts, drafted a revenue-enhancing senatorial decree and received senatorial recognition: an award of 15 million sesterces from the public treasury (which Pallas declined) and a statue with the inscription, "To him the Senate decreed this in return for his loyalty and devotion to his patrons," which still aroused the younger Pliny's indignation two generations later (Pliny *Ep.* 7.29; 8.6). But the administrators of the emperor's wealth, the *fiscus*, had already become a permanent second state alongside the republic.

The republic–emperor tandem reappears in an important document from the reign of Claudius' successor Nero, the 150-line customs law for the province of Asia (*SEG* 39 no. 1180). The core of the document is republican (an underlying law perhaps from the 120s BCE reconfirmed in 75 and 72 BCE), as is the core of the financial administration (revenue collection by private contractors, or *publicani*). But the legislative core is extended through imperial additions, and the financial administration also receives an imperial overlay: Augustus joins Senate, people, and plebs as legislative entities granting exemptions; Augustus apparently grants immunity to ships on their way to a festival of the imperial cult; and "the procurator of Nero Augustus who is in charge of the province," appearing in the document's last fragmentary lines, seems to assume jurisdiction over disputes between provincials and publicans (see Ando, this volume).

Nero was 16 years old at his accession and at first was reportedly guided by a regency comprising his mother Agrippina, the praetorian prefect Burrus, and the senator Seneca. Then Nero had his mother killed, built his Golden House on the ashes of the 64 CE fire, ruthlessly purged the Senate after the Pisonian conspiracy, and began singing on stage. Why did anyone put up with it? In part because imperial loyalists were abundantly rewarded by the republic. A nonagenarian timeserver who died under Nero, for example, received a public funeral and eight commemorative statues:

> To L. Volusius Saturninus... who died at age 93, the Senate decreed on the motion of Nero Claudius Germanicus, that he be buried in a public funeral, and that triumphal statues be set up to him in the Forum of Augustus, a bronze statue in the New Temple of Divus Augustus, two marble consular statues, one in the Temple of Divus Julius, a second on the Palatine in the Tripylum, a third in the Area of Apollo in view of the Senate-House, an augural statue in the Regia, an equestrian statue near the Rostra, and one sitting on a curule bench in the Pompeian Theatre in the Portico of the Lentuli. (EJ 367)

3 68–9 CE and the Flavians

Even when the Julio-Claudian dynasty fell, the imperial configuration remained: soldiers created emperors, emperors retained the republic. As Nero tottered, the provincial legions and the praetorian guard at Rome proclaimed successive emperors, beginning with the governor of Gaul, Iulius Vindex. Four of them made it to Rome to be recognized by the republic: Galba, Otho, Vitellius, and Vespasian. Yet even soldiers recognized that the imperial state would include the republic. When the Spanish legions acclaimed Galba in early April 68 CE, he "mounted a tribunal, on the front of which he had set up all the images he could find of those condemned and executed by Nero...and was declared *imperator* and *legatus* of the Senate and Roman People" (Suet. *Gal.* 10.1). Eight months later, on January 1, 69 CE, the Upper German legions revoked their oath to Galba and demanded a replacement, "allowing the power of choosing him to the Senate and Roman People" (Tac. *Hist.* 1.12). When the praetorians and the legions acclaimed Otho and Vitellius, the new emperors too received titles, powers, and priesthoods from the Roman people, a process we can follow in the Acts of the Arval Brothers for 69 CE (Scheid 1998: no. 40). On January 26, 69 CE, the Arvals sacrificed to celebrate Otho's election (*comitia*) to the consulship; on February 28, the tribunician power; on March 3, lesser priesthoods; on March 9, the pontificate. Then on March 14, the Arvals "pronounced vows for the health and return of Vitellius"; on April 30, they sacrificed to celebrate Vitellius' election to the tribunician power. Finally, on July 1, 69 CE, the eastern legions proclaimed Vespasian *imperator*, and Vespasian took the date as the start of his reign, although six more months would pass before he formally received power to make treaties, summon the Senate, and extend Rome's sacred boundary (*pomerium*) by popular statute (*ILS* 244). By the terms of the statute, Vespasian explicitly received the same powers as the "good" Julio-Claudians Augustus, Tiberius, and Claudius. Galba, Otho, Vitellius, and Vespasian each adopted the Julio-Claudian names *Imperator, Caesar, Augustus*. By the imperial right to ownerless property, each assumed the Julio-Claudian wealth. Each new emperor took his place in a developed monarchical system.

During the reigns of Vespasian and his sons Titus and Domitian the Roman Empire continued to grow. Vespasian and Titus had emerged from the suppression of the Jewish revolt against taxation and misrule (Goodman 1987). But the Roman Empire was not only a matter of military conquest and direct rule. As Polybius had recognized in the second century BCE, Roman power extended wherever "all had to harken to the Romans and obey their orders" (Polyb. 3.4.3) – to both tributary provinces and non-tributary "friendly kingdoms" (Millar 1996). Between the two the distinction was often fluid. Judea, for example, had gone from kingdom to province to kingdom to province. So did Commagene, on the upper Euphrates. Yet all the while Commagene preserved its ruling house, as an inscription cataloguing seven generations of the dynasty from 69 BCE to 72 CE now shows (Schmitz, Sahin, and Wagner 1988); the grandson of the last Commagenian king would become consul under Trajan.

As under the republic, the growth of the empire was projected onto the city of Rome. With spoils from the Jewish war, a fresh reading of the entrance inscriptions to the Colosseum reveals, Vespasian and Titus ordered the construction of their "New Amphitheater" (*CIL* 6^2, 8, 2, 40454a) (Figure 4.3). The tradition of returning generals using victory spoils to finance public monuments in Rome went back far into the republic. Pompey and Caesar raised the scale when they used spoils from the East and Gaul respectively to build the Theater of Pompey and the Forum Iulium with the Temple of Venus Genetrix. The tradition continued when Augustus used spoils from Egypt to build the Forum of Augustus with the Temple of Mars Ultor; the conquest of Britain allowed Claudius to extend the *pomerium*; and Domitian used spoils from Dacia to begin his forum, which Trajan completed in his own name (*LTUR s.v.* Forum Traiani). With this tradition must be contrasted the imperial innovation of the republic's erecting monuments for the emperor, his family, and his followers.

Domitian campaigned in person on the Rhine and Danube and raised legionary pay to 300 denarii a year in 84 CE – out of which a soldier at Carlisle took a 100-denarius advance already on November 7, 83 CE (Tomlin 1992). Domitian attended the Senate in triumphal dress instead of civilian toga, went everywhere surrounded by a dictatorial 24 lictors, and was eventually murdered in court intrigue. For all his overt militarism, Domitian's reign brought a new advance of republican government, as exemplified by the municipal code that ambassadors from Irni, in southern Spain, inscribed after meeting with Domitian in 91 CE (González 1986). Local "magistrates," the code provides, "should have in public the album of the person who holds the province and administer justice according to it" (sec. 85), the governor's album being based on the praetor's edict from Rome. "On whatever matter there is no explicit provision," the code continues, "the municipal citizens are to deal with each other in all these matters under the civil law under which Roman citizens deal or will deal with each other" (sec. 93). Domitian earned a posthumous reputation as a tyrant, though a re-reading of the inscribed career of one of that reputation's principal authors shows that the historian Tacitus had served in Domitian's republic as quaestor of Augustus, the emperor's spokesman in the Senate (*AE* 1995 no. 92). The Roman emperor ruled through republican forms.

124   *Greg Rowe*

a   b

Figure 6.2a and b The propaganda of the Galban revolution stressed continuity with the republican past. In this case, Galba's mint masters (6.2b) evidently reproduced the reverse of Brutus' celebration of the murder of Caesar (6.2a), while plainly observing the principle that the reverse legend continues the message of the obverse with *Libertas* on the obverse and *P(opuli) R(omani) Restituta* on the reverse. Figure 6.2a *RIC* 1 p. 205 n. 24 BMC 7 (photo courtesy of the British Museum). Figure 6.2b ANS 1944.100.4554

Figure 6.3a–c The Flavians: (a) Vespasian (*RIC* 50); (b) Titus (*RIC* Titus 94 ANS 1944.100.41797) (photo courtesy of the American Numismatic Society); (c) Domitian (author's collection)

CHAPTER SEVEN

Rome the Superpower: 96–235 CE

Michael Peachin

Introduction

> In the second century of the Christian era, the empire of Rome comprehended the fairest part of the earth, and the most civilized portion of mankind. The frontiers of that extensive monarchy were guarded by ancient renown and disciplined valor. The gentle, but powerful, influence of laws and manners had gradually cemented the union of the provinces. Their peaceful inhabitants enjoyed and abused the advantages of wealth and luxury. The image of a free constitution was preserved with decent reverence. The Roman senate appeared to possess the sovereign authority, and devolved on the emperors all the executive powers of government. During a happy period of more than fourscore years, the public administration was conducted by the virtue and abilities of Nerva, Trajan, Hadrian, and the two Antonines. It is the design of this and of the two succeeding chapters to describe the prosperous condition of their empire; and afterwards, from the death of Marcus Antoninus, to deduce the most important circumstances of its decline and fall: a revolution which will ever be remembered, and is still felt by the nations of the earth.
>
> (Gibbon 1994: 1: 31)

With these oft-quoted lines did Edward Gibbon introduce his splendid chronicle of the Roman Empire's collapse. And while this revolution, as Gibbon termed it, may no longer quite be felt by the nations of the earth, various of the points touched upon here are still crucial to any proper perception of that historical epoch, which inspired the following evaluation by him:

> If a man were called to fix the period in the history of the world during which the condition of the human race was most happy and prosperous, he would, without

hesitation, name that which elapsed from the death of Domitian to the accession of Commodus. (Gibbon 1994: 1: 103)

In this chapter, we shall not make any serious attempt to gauge the relative level of happiness or prosperity enjoyed by those living under Rome's sway. That task is undertaken, insofar as it altogether can be, elsewhere (see Ando, this volume). We will, on the other hand, consider other matters crucial to Gibbon's opening remarks. First, we shall ask what might seem to be a simple question: How did a person become emperor? That question is logically followed by a second: Once firmly seated upon the throne, how ought an emperor to rule? Or, to put this question another way: Why might the Romans, not to mention posterity, have judged Nerva, Trajan, Hadrian, and the two Antonines as able and virtuous also, on the canon of "good" emperors, which achieved fixed form by late antiquity (Syme 1971a: 89–112)?

1 Finding the First Man

Introduction

In the fall of 96 CE, the recently crowned emperor Nerva assigned a senator from southern Spain, Marcus Ulpius Traianus, to govern Upper Germany (Eck 1985: 45–6). A Roman did not set out on such a mission without having made the customary sacrificial offering to Rome's chief god, Jupiter Optimus Maximus. On the day appointed for Trajan to make that sacrifice, a crowd had gathered about the entrance to Jupiter's shrine, and Trajan barely forced his way through the crush. Then, as the temple doors finally opened, displaying the deity's statue within, the milling throng spontaneously roared, as if with one voice: *Imperator!* Only later would it be revealed that their acclamation was not, as they supposed, directed at the god Jupiter, but instead at the soon-to-be emperor, Trajan.

Another senator, Pliny the Younger, records this omen (*Pan.* 5.3–4). He also reminds us that Trajan had all along been selected by Jupiter to rule (*Pan.* 8). And a lucky thing it was, that the gods were willing to pick emperors; for the Romans themselves had never created a properly defined, official mechanism by which to accomplish this seemingly crucial governmental act.

A recent book has broadly characterized the period of the first emperor's reign as one of experimentation (Galinsky 1996; cf. also Wallace-Hadrill 1993: viii; Rowe, this volume). The experimental centerpiece was the creation of an imperial regime. However, since the very existence of monarchy could not be admitted it was impossible to construct anything that we would consider a proper constitution for the new imperial order. But aside from that, the Romans, a people fanatically loyal to tradition, traditionally had no written constitution. They were, from their very beginnings, accustomed to a government whose form evolved continually, and gradually, sometimes in written form, sometimes not (Lintott 1999: 1–2). Thus, insofar as constitutional matters generally are concerned, especially with regard to the transmission of imperial power, we are justified in perceiving the first three centuries CE as an epoch of continual experiment, or gradual development.

If we are to understand Rome as a superpower, which it surely was during the period here in question, we must admit that this particular superpower had at best a rudimentary system – and a rudimentary system in a state of constant flux – for picking the man about whom literally everything seemed to revolve. Moreover, the period treated in the present chapter is especially significant in this regard, since it may be that the second century witnessed an attempt to regularize, indeed, to create, what might be perceived as a nearly constitutional arrangement for imperial successions. But regardless of this, all the principal mechanisms that might come into play when the Romans made monarchs were already well formed when the last of the Flavian monarchs perished. By way of introduction to these mechanisms, let us briefly return to that moment.

It was mid-September 96 when the emperor Domitian succumbed to a conspiracy. Although the act itself was perpetrated by disaffected palace servants, the praetorian prefects (the commanders of the emperor's military bodyguard at Rome) may also have been involved; in any case, they approved the deed, once it was done. The empress, Domitia Longina, was likewise said to have been complicit (Suet. *Dom.* 14.1; Dio 67.15.2–4). And while it could not (and still cannot) be proved that any specific senator was privy to the plot, the reaction of the Senate, as a whole, was swift and unequivocal: its members raced to the Senate House, abused the now-dead prince in the most bitter terms, then pulled down and broke whatever images of him they straightaway could lay hold of. Having accomplished so much, they ordered Domitian's name erased from every inscription containing it, and proclaimed that all memory of him should be eradicated (Suet. *Dom.* 23; cf. also Pliny *Pan.* 52.4–5). Then, in the late afternoon of that same day, they proclaimed Marcus Cocceius Nerva, a distinguished senator, as their new emperor (Smallwood 1966: no. 15). Domitian's biographer puts the day's events in a nutshell: the plebs at Rome were indifferent, the soldiers were terribly upset, the senators were happy (Suet. *Dom.* 23.1).

Almost exactly a year later, Nerva found himself cornered by the praetorian guard. The guardsmen ordered him to surrender the murderers of Domitian, whom they immediately and viciously killed; Nerva was subsequently compelled to thank the guard for having destroyed such miscreants (Dio 68.3.3–4). Now, it is possible that this rebellion of the soldiers at Rome caused Nerva to seek a powerful ally in the military commander nearest the capital, namely, the very governor of Upper Germany, whom he had appointed a year before. It is equally conceivable, however, that that commander, in consort with other leaders of other provincial armies, had arranged for things to fall out as they did (Berriman and Todd 2001: 324–9, and especially Eck 2002; cf. also Fedeli 1989: 447–50). Be that as it may, in late October of 97 Nerva announced the adoption of Trajan, as both his son and successor. He did so standing beneath the very statue of Jupiter that just a year earlier had inspired a group of commoners unwittingly to acclaim Trajan *Imperator*. In these two transfers of power, we can observe those elements of Roman society which had played, and which would continue to play, a significant role in such matters: the members of the imperial household, the soldiers, the Senate, the populace at Rome.

In section 1 of this chapter, we shall examine the first two contingents (i.e., the imperial household and the soldiers) at some length as being the two groups most able, hence most likely, actually to make an emperor. On the other hand, both the people at Rome and the members of the Senate maintained firm opinions regarding the man who ruled; and their opinions, though much less likely to effect the actual crowning of a monarch, nonetheless mattered. Their tastes will therefore be considered in discussing the way in which emperors were expected to rule (below, section 2). But both in the first section and in that which follows, we shall keep an eye focused on the lack of system pervading this whole business, and thus on the continual jostling for say-so in the making of Roman emperors (for a brief, though excellent, and roughly parallel treatment of these matters, see Baharal 1996: 9–19).

The imperial household

One of the principles of monarchy established by Augustus (although, like most Augustan principles, it was never formulated expressly), held that rulers were to be raised from within the family, i.e. from what quickly came to be known as the "imperial household" (Corbier 1995; see further Lacey 1996: 190–209; Hurlet 1997: 365–538; Rowe 2002). Yet the Julio-Claudian and Flavian families had produced emperors who were, at least in senatorial eyes, absolute disasters. Much of the displeasure stemmed from the fact that women from the imperial family, as well as palace servants, had played too large a role in creating, and then in guiding, the first century's failed princes.

Against that background, it has long been tempting to suppose that Nerva was chosen not so much for his political distinctions, virtue, or abilities, but instead, because he was aged, in rather poor health, and without male descendants. He may have seemed the perfect candidate precisely because he would not found a dynasty (B. W. Jones 1992: 193–6; see, however, Berriman and Todd 2001: 312–14; and Eck 2002). It has even been suspected that in certain sectors of the elite an agreement was reached that princes would henceforth be carefully selected for their personal qualities and talents, and would not don the purple as a consequence of birth. This theme is raised more than once by Pliny in his *Panegyric* (e.g. 7.4–7, 89.1). Indeed, according to Pliny, the god Jupiter Optimus Maximus, knowing the greatness of Trajan, specifically told Nerva to adopt him (8.1, 94.4). Cassius Dio thought that Nerva, because he preferred outstanding qualities to family, chose Trajan (Dio 68.4.1–2). Hadrian himself is supposed to have delivered an oration from his death-bed, in which he praised adoption as opposed to inheritance (Dio 69.20.1–5). We might also note here the diatribe invented by the author of the *Historia Augusta* at the end of the fourth century CE. Claiming to address the emperor Diocletian (284–305 CE), the author of the *HA* avers that nothing good ever came of natural sons, and that the only decent imperial sons in all of Roman history were those who had been adopted (*HA Sev.* 20.4–21.8). But beyond all of this, a significantly less pronounced public role played by the women of the Trajanic and Hadrianic households has been thought to indicate a concerted effort to discourage dynastic aspirations (Boatwright 1991).

And yet, no matter how strong the desire for an adoptive system may have been, dynastic thinking hardly disappeared. Pliny himself prays to Jupiter that Trajan be granted a son, who could inherit the throne; failing that, the god is to select a suitable candidate (*Pan.* 94.5). Just to be sure, Marcus Aurelius wedded all of his daughters not to men of great families, but rather, to those whose virtue was great (Herod.

Table 7.1 Emperors, AD 96–235

For each emperor, the name by which he is commonly known and his regnal dates are given first. In the second line, his full given name comes first, followed by the nomenclature adopted by him upon being made emperor.

The Antonine emperors

Nerva, 96–8
  M. Cocceius Nerva → Imperator Nerva Caesar Augustus
Trajan, 98–117
  M. Ulpius Traianus → Imperator Caesar Nerva Traianus Augustus
Hadrian, 117–38
  P. Aelius Hadrianus → Imperator Caesar Traianus Hadrianus Augustus
Antoninus Pius, 138–61
  T. Aurelius Fulvus Boionius Arrius Antoninus → Imperator T. Aelius Caesar Hadrianus Antoninus Augustus Pius
Marcus Aurelius, 161–80
  M. Annius Verus → Imperator Caesar M. Aurelius Antoninus Augustus
Commodus, 180–192
  L. Aurelius Commodus → Imperator Caesar M. Aurelius Commodus Antoninus Augustus

The years of civil war, 192–3

Pertinax, 192–3
  P. Helvius Pertinax → Imperator Caesar P. Helvius Pertinax Augustus
Didius Julianus, 193
  M. Didius Severus Iulianus → Imperator Caesar M. Didius Severus Iulianus Augustus

The Severan emperors

Septimius Severus, 193–211
  L. Septimius Severus → Imperator Caesar L. Septimius Severus Pertinax Augustus
Caracalla, 211–7
  L. Septimius Bassianus → Imperator Caesar M. Aurelius Antoninus Augustus
Macrinus, 217–8
  M. Opellius Macrinus → Imperator Caesar M. Opellius Severus Macrinus Pius Felix Augustus
Elagabalus, 218–22
  Varius Avitus Bassianus → Imperator Caesar M. Aurelius Antoninus Pius Felix Augustus
Severus Alexander, 222–35
  Gessius Alexianus Bassianus → Imperator Caesar M. Aurelius Severus Alexander Pius Felix Augustus

1.2.2). Nor did the influence exerted by female members of the imperial family simply cease (Hekster 2001; Kunst 2000).

Hadrian, Trajan's cousin, once removed, and had married Trajan's great-niece, Vibia Sabina, by about 100 CE. Although some were therefore saying from early on that Hadrian would succeed Trajan, the latter died (August 7, 117) without having officially named a successor; it was Trajan's wife, Pompeia Plotina, who wrote to the Senate, announcing that Hadrian would now become emperor (Dio 68.69.1). Some even guessed the choice ultimately to have been hers, not Trajan's (Dio 69.1.1–4,

HA Had. 4.10, Aur. Vict. *Caes.* 13.13, cf. Birley 1997: 75–8). Nor should we neglect the fact that Salonia Matidia was also present and influential; she was both Trajan's niece and Hadrian's mother-in-law (Benario 1980: 81–2).

If there was a plan (orchestrated by the emperor and his close advisors) for adoption to become the official mode of imperial succession, then it looks as if the first transfer of power under the new "rules" was somewhat irregular. That is, there lurks the possibility that the final decision was taken not by Trajan in consultation with his friends and advisors during his lifetime, but by his wife, after his death, perhaps in concert with his niece, and perhaps, at least partly, against his will. In any event, the first adoptive emperor had not been able to ignore the members of his household in determining the succession.

Be that as it may, after nearly twenty years on the throne, it would come time for Hadrian to make a new prince, and in 136, he chose the distinguished Lucius Ceionius Commodus (see Table 7.2). It may be suspected, however, that Commodus was intended to function effectively as regent (advanced tuberculosis was already causing him to cough blood at the time of his adoption), and that Hadrian was aiming at the 15-year-old Marcus Annius Verus, who was already engaged to Commodus' daughter, Ceionia Fabia. Moreover, this Verus, like both Trajan and Hadrian, belonged to a family whose roots lay in Baetica in southern Spain, and was perhaps distantly related to Hadrian through his mother-in-law (see Table 7.3). In any case, Hadrian had taken a great liking to the boy from early on.

Regardless of whatever else he may have been planning, the choice of Commodus made it necessary for Hadrian to eliminate his own brother-in-law, Lucius Julius Ursus Servianus, as well as that man's grandson (also Hadrian's grand-nephew), Gnaeus Pedanius Fuscus Salinator (Birley 1997: 289–92; Champlin 1985). In other words, if Hadrian hoped to secure the fortunes of a new emperor, there were members of the old imperial family who needed to be removed.

These plans were jeopardized towards the end of 137 when Ceionius Commodus died of his tuberculosis. With Annius Verus too young to rule, and his own health failing seriously by early 138, Hadrian selected another man to take his place. He adopted Titus Aurelius Fulvus Boionius Arrius Antoninus, who was married to Annius' aunt (see Table 7.3). Antoninus was a respected senator, himself born in Italy, though his family hailed from Nîmes, in southern France. Another step was taken simultaneously. Hadrian ordered Antoninus to adopt two young men, to guarantee the imperial succession for yet another generation. One of the youths was Lucius Ceionius Commodus (as emperor: Lucius Verus); the son of the deceased (see Table 7.2). This Ceionius Commodus would later marry a daughter (Annia Aurelia Galeria Lucilla) of the second man adopted by Antoninus Pius at Hadrian's bequest: Marcus Annius Verus (again, as emperor: Marcus Aurelius). Of the two new heirs, Verus was clearly the favorite. Therefore, he was presently wed to Antoninus Pius' daughter, Annia Galeria Faustina, the earlier betrothal to Ceionia Fabia lapsed when her father died.

In the end, then, Marcus Aurelius was Antoninus Pius' nephew by marriage, adopted son, and son-in-law. Lucius Verus was, in turn, Antoninus' adopted son, and grandson by marriage. Consequently, the relationship between Marcus Aurelius and Lucius Verus, step-brothers by virtue of their common adoption, acquired a

Table 7.2 Nerva, Trajan, Hadrian, and Lucius Verus[i]

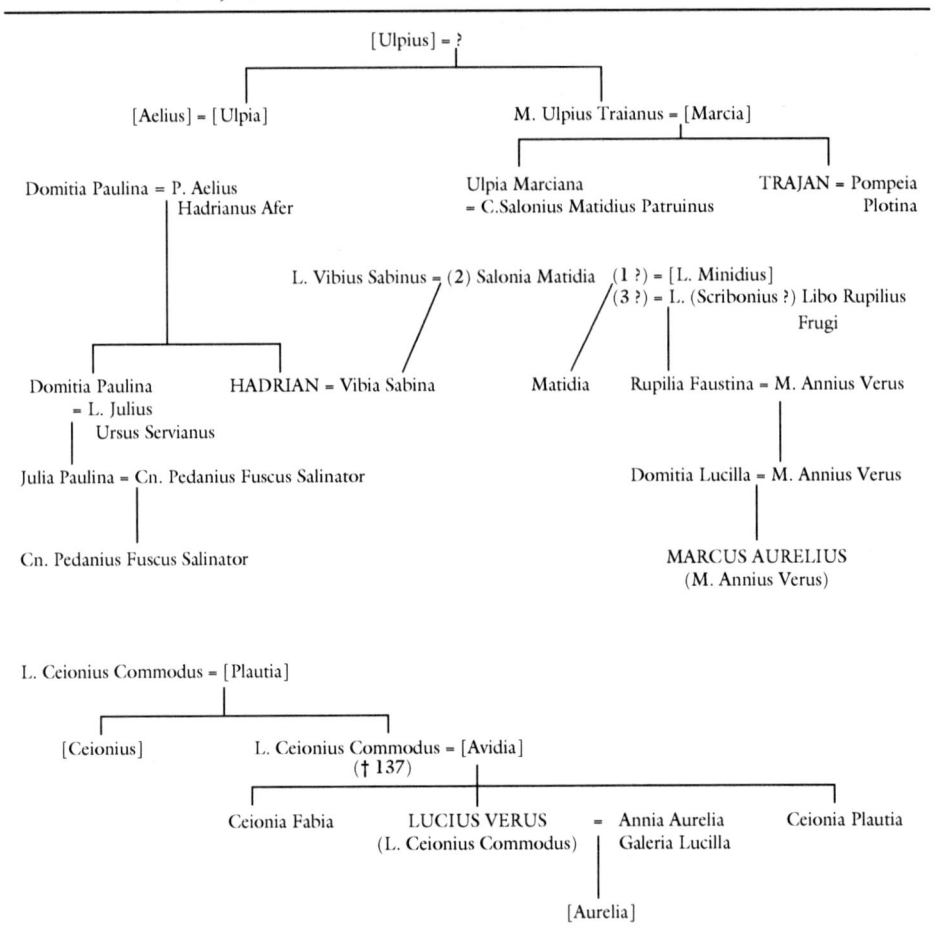

```
                              [Ulpius] = ?
            ┌──────────────────────┴──────────────────────┐
    [Aelius] = [Ulpia]                          M. Ulpius Traianus = [Marcia]
                                                 ┌───────────────┴──────────┐
  Domitia Paulina = P. Aelius              Ulpia Marciana             TRAJAN = Pompeia
                    Hadrianus Afer     = C.Salonius Matidius Patruinus          Plotina
                                                      │
              L. Vibius Sabinus = (2) Salonia Matidia  (1 ?) = [L. Minidius]
                                                       (3 ?) = L. (Scribonius ?) Libo Rupilius
                                                                                Frugi
   ┌─────────────┬──────────────────┬──────────────┐
 Domitia Paulina   HADRIAN = Vibia Sabina      Matidia     Rupilia Faustina = M. Annius Verus
  = L. Julius
    Ursus Servianus
        │                                                           │
 Julia Paulina = Cn. Pedanius Fuscus Salinator            Domitia Lucilla = M. Annius Verus
        │                                                           │
 Cn. Pedanius Fuscus Salinator                              MARCUS AURELIUS
                                                            (M. Annius Verus)


         L. Ceionius Commodus = [Plautia]
         ┌──────────────┴──────────────┐
   [Ceionius]              L. Ceionius Commodus = [Avidia]
                                 († 137)
                      ┌──────────────┼──────────────┐
               Ceionia Fabia     LUCIUS VERUS    = Annia Aurelia    Ceionia Plautia
                              (L. Ceionius Commodus) │ Galeria Lucilla
                                                     │
                                                 [Aurelia]
```

---

[i] For more on these emperors, and the family members, see Birley 1998: 308–10. On the Ceionii Commodi, hence, Luius Verus, see Birley 1987: 246–7.

father–son aspect as a result of the marriage of Verus to Marcus' daughter. Hadrian had ensured that all stayed in the family. Adoption, was at work, but dynastic thinking is just as prominently on display.

Things functioned smoothly for a number of years. When Hadrian died (July 10, 138), Antoninus Pius took up the purple. Upon his death (March 7, 161), Marcus Aurelius and Lucius Verus immediately became co-emperors. Their complex relationship might well have resulted in trouble, had not Verus died in the early days of 169. It was also a stroke of luck that his marriage to Annia Lucilla (again, Marcus'

Table 7.3 Antoninus Pius, Marcus Aurelius, Commodus[i]

```
Arria Fadilla = T. Aurelius Fulvus        Rupilia Faustina = M. Annius Verus
                     │                                   │
         ┌───────────┘         ┌─────────────────────────┼──────────────────────┐
ANTONINUS PIUS = Annia Galeria Faustina    M. Annius Libo    M. Annius Verus = Domitia Lucilla    [Annia] = C. Ummidius Quadratus
(T. Aurelius Fulvus                                                                                         Sertorius Severus
Boionius Arrius
Antoninus)
                             │
        ┌────────────────────┴───────────────────────────────────────────┐
        Annia Galeria Faustina = MARCUS AURELIUS              Annia Cornificia Faustina = C. Ummidius Quadratus
                                 (M. Annius Verus)                                            Annianus Verus
```

| 1. Domitia Faustina (147–151) | 2. T. Aurelius Antoninus | 3. T. Aelius Aurelius († 149) | 4. Annia Aurelia Galeria Lucilla (150–182) | 5. Annia Galeria Aurelia Faustina | 6. T. Aelius Antoninus (152–152) | 7. son (157–158) | 8. Fadilla | 9. Cornificia († 213) | 10. T. Aurelius Fulvus Antoninus († 165) | 11. COMMODUS (L. Aurelius Commodus) | 12. M. Annius Verus | 13. Hadrianus | 14. Vibia Aurelia Sabina |

[i] For the children of Marcus Aurelius and Faustina, I follow Birley 1987: 247–8.

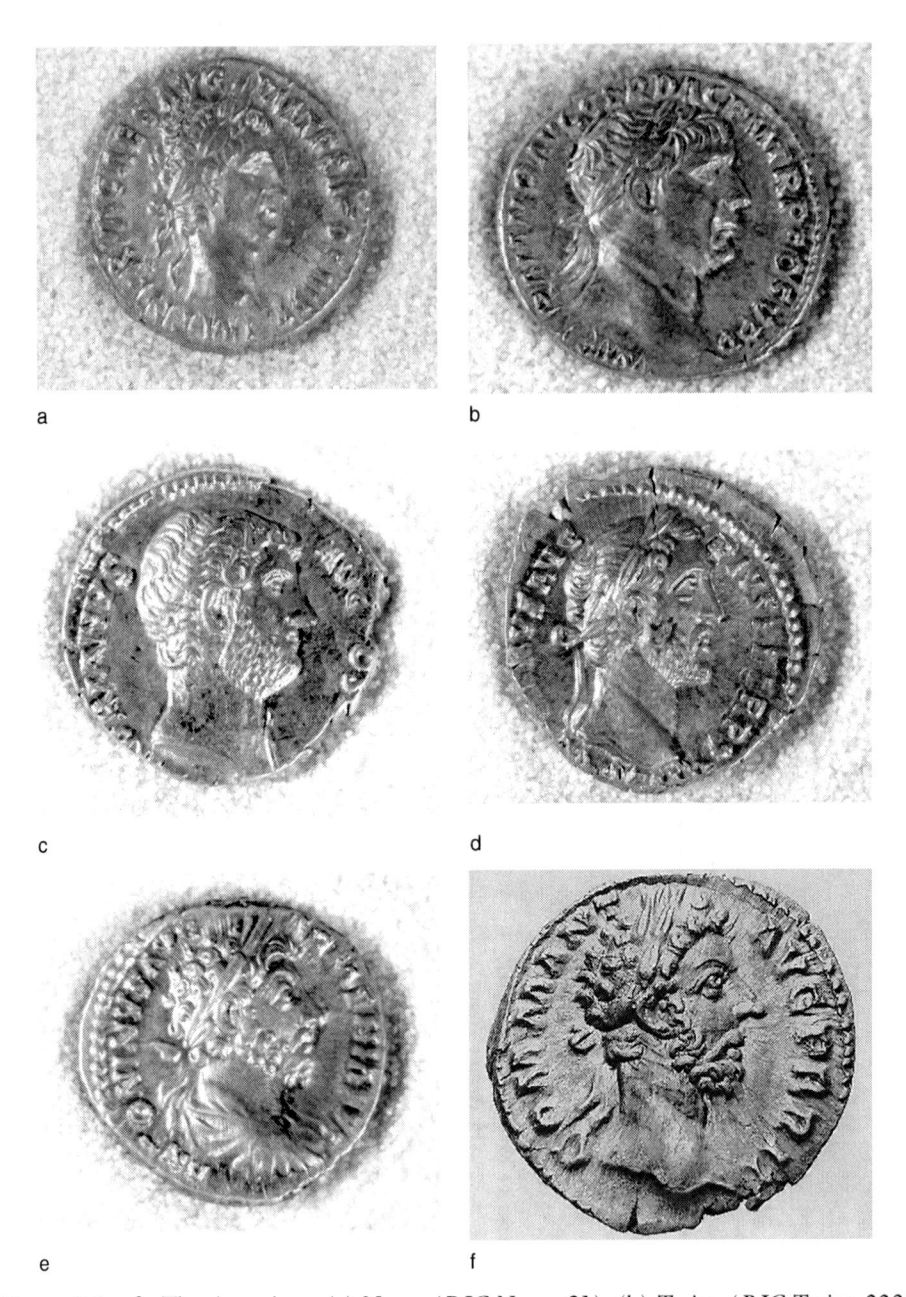

Figure 7.1a–f The Antonines: (a) Nerva (*RIC* Nerva 31); (b) Trajan (*RIC* Trajan 223); (c) Hadrian (*RIC* Hadrian 267); (d) Antoninus Pius (*RIC* Antoninus 229a); (e) Marcus Aurelius (*RIC* Marcus 82a); (f) Commodus (*RIC* Commodus 97) (all coins from the editor's collection)

daughter) had produced only a daughter. Marcus was left as sole emperor. But, who should, or would, follow him in the purple?

Marcus and his wife ultimately produced 14 children: six girls and eight boys (see Table 7.3). The majority of these children died young (something absolutely normal in the second century CE – see Frier 2000: 787–97). Indeed, as Marcus' life was rapidly drawing to a close in early 180, five of the girls still lived, but only one of the boys. When the emperor expired, on March 17, 180, that boy, Lucius Aurelius Commodus, became Rome's emperor. Cassius Dio, who had personal experience of both these monarchs, wrote that Marcus would have been thoroughly pleased with his own life, but for one thing: the son, whom he had raised with such great care, turned out to be his greatest disappointment. And so, with the accession of Commodus, a reign of gold gave way to one of rust and iron (71.36.4).

For the first time in a hundred years, the Roman Empire passed from father to biological son. Nerva, Trajan, Hadrian, and Antoninus Pius, none of whom had a son by blood, all adopted a successor. Yet Marcus did have a son, and he allowed that boy to become emperor. This has caused a problem for modern scholars. Despite the scraps of evidence that point to an orchestrated policy of adopting emperors, we must be willing to admit that perhaps there never was an official policy of selecting the best man for the job; perhaps necessity gave rise to choices that could be viewed *ex post facto* as policy (Herz 2000: 319). But wherever the truth may lie, it seems fair to say that the power of the father–son bond could hardly be overcome. Family, especially in this particular manifestation, was simply supreme.

Now, family members, as history had demonstrated, might pose a serious threat to reigning emperors; and this turned out to be the case early in Commodus' reign. We are told that the new ruler's various depravities – including drink, sex, and astonishing cruelty – caused one of his elder sisters, Annia Lucilla (Lucius Verus' widow), to despair, and to plot against him *(HA Comm.* 1–4.4). The result was her initial exile to Capri, and later her execution (probably in 182 cf. Raepsaet-Charlier 1987: 67). Other, more distant, family members were also supposedly involved, and eliminated.

Commodus himself, according to the reports we have, took little interest in governing, nor do we hear that he gave any thought to the question of succession. He had no children, banished and then executed his wife shortly before his own death (Raepsaet-Charlier 1987: 149–50), and apparently allowed palace servants and his mistress, Marcia, to run amok – indeed, largely to run the empire. In the end Marcia served him poisoned wine, and then sent his personal trainer to strangle him (December 31, 192).

Commodus was regarded by those who wrote about him as a "bad" emperor (though for some later, more favorable judgments, see Hekster 2002: 184–6). After his death, Commodus was loudly abused by the assembled Senate for having been "more savage than Domitian, more defiled than Nero" (*HA Com.* 19.2). In short, a son had followed his father, and had brought back all the evils of the first-century dynasties: the power of palace minions and women, executions of senators, disregard for the "proper" business of empire, personal excesses of various sorts. And finally, Commodus brought on the ultimate evil: civil war.

Despite any lessons that might have been taken from history, or perhaps because of these lessons, Septimius Severus, the African senator who emerged supreme from the bloody chaos that followed Commodus' death, chose the path of dynasty (see in detail Baharal 1996: 20–42; see also Table 7.4). What is more, he opted for dynasty looking both backward and forward in time. Two years after winning power, and apparently after an initial victory in a war against the Parthians, Severus adopted himself into the Antonine imperial family. Coins issued early in 195 label him as "Son of the divine Marcus Pius" (H. Mattingly 1950: xci, 136). As Cassius Dio remarks, this action also made Severus the brother of Commodus (Dio 76.7.4; also *ILS* 8805.3, where Severus is "brother of the divine Commodus," and is specifically brought into relation with each emperor all the way back to Nerva). At roughly the same moment, Severus' seven-year-old son, Lucius Septimius Bassianus, received a new name, becoming Marcus Aurelius Antoninus. The Antonines lived on, by virtue of posthumous adoption, as the Severans' ancestors!

The Severan house was not, however, altogether happy. Caracalla murdered his younger brother Geta shortly after their father's death, and would subsequently rule in a fashion that largely alienated the senators. He would himself be murdered in early April of 217.

The praetorian prefect, Marcus Opellius Macrinus, a man born to the equestrian rather than senatorial order, who eliminated Caracalla, retained the throne for only a year (see below). His rapidly diminishing popularity with the soldiers provided an opening for Septimius Severus' sister-in-law, Julia Maesa, who convinced part of the army in the East that her grandson, Varius Avitus Bassianus, was Caracalla's bastard son. Macrinus was soon dead, and another of the Severan boys (he was about 14 years old) took up the reins of empire. Membership in the family had made the difference.

When Elagabalus, as Bassianus came to be called, turned out not to be the kind of emperor envisioned by his grandmother, Maesa began to support another of her grandsons. In March of 222, Elagabalus was murdered by the soldiers at Rome, and the last of the Severans, his cousin Gessius Alexianus Bassianus, became emperor. Severus Alexander, as he was styled on the throne, was about 12 years of age, and so his mother, Julia Mamaea, saw to matters of state. The increased power and influence of the Severan women generally was the cause of not a little bitterness and resentment (Kettenhofen 1979).

Let us summarize briefly. It seems clear that age-old Roman notions about the importance of family in politics retained a firm grip on the selection of emperors throughout our period. There may have been a conscious attempt, given the disappointing experiences with the Julio-Claudian and Flavian families, to exclude blood from the making of monarchs. If there was such a planned effort, it was ultimately defeated, at least in part, by the force of tradition. Strong support could apparently always be found for a blood relative, especially a son, of the reigning emperor. And so, dynastic thinking lurks even in the context of adoptive succession. Indeed, new dynasts, like the Severans, might even suppose it wise to adopt themselves retrospectively into an extinct imperial family. A glance at the names taken by the men of our period when they became emperor (see Table 7.1) clearly demonstrates the importance of family ties. Moreover, the importance of family helped to lend the women of the imperial household great power. That was little appreciated by the men of the senatorial order. Nor, for that matter, were the slaves and freedmen who staffed the palace, and who also from time to time became influential, very well liked by that same group of luminaries.

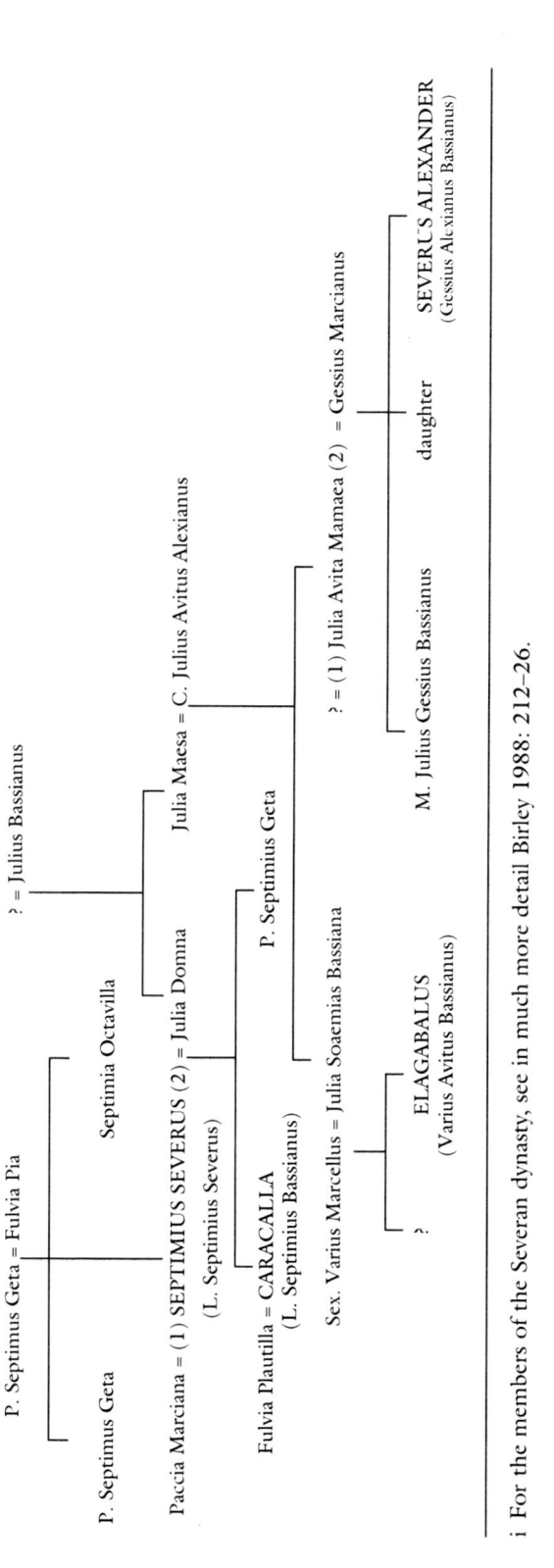

Table 7.4 The Severan Emperors[i]

```
P. Septimus Geta = Fulvia Pia                                    ? = Julius Bassianus
         |                                                                |
         |           Septimia Octavilla                                   |
         |                                                                |
P. Septimus Geta                                              ┌───────────┴───────────┐
                                                              |                       |
Paccia Marciana = (1) SEPTIMIUS SEVERUS (2) = Julia Domna     Julia Maesa = C. Julius Avitus Alexianus
                     (L. Septimius Severus)    |                          |
                                               |              ┌───────────┴───────────┐
                    Fulvia Plautilla = CARACALLA   P. Septimius Geta                   |
                                       (L. Septimius Bassianus)                         |
                                                                                        |
                              Sex. Varius Marcellus = Julia Soaemias Bassiana    ? = (1) Julia Avita Mamaea (2) = Gessius Marcianus
                                            |                                                     |
                              ┌─────────────┴──────┐                              ┌───────────────┴──────────┐
                              |                    |                              |                          |
                              ?              ELAGABALUS                    M. Julius Gessius Bassianus  daughter   SEVERUS ALEXANDER
                                        (Varius Avitus Bassianus)                                                (Gessius Alexianus Bassianus)
```

i For the members of the Severan dynasty, see in much more detail Birley 1988: 212–26.

Tradition, however, was not the only force that underlay the power of family. Clearly, the essential impetus came from the traditional importance of family ties, but that impetus found persons willing and capable of translating thought into action: the soldiers.

Soldiers

Theodor Mommsen said this of the selection of emperors:

> The assumption of the Principate, in its essential core, the Imperium, even if not an act of free self-determination on the part of the individual citizen, is nonetheless an act which, in purely legal terms, could depend either on a vote of the Senate, or on acclamation by some group of soldiers; and so, in fact, each and every man in arms had the right to make either himself, or any other, whom he chose, emperor. (Mommsen 1887/88: II.2 844)

Tacitus, on the other hand, claims that this prerogative of the military men was a "secret" of the imperial regime, first revealed during the civil war of 68/9 (*Hist.* 1.4.2). The Romans, at least in the surviving record, do not specify any possible "legal" role of the soldiers in such matters. Indeed, there seems to have been no fixed legal or constitutional principle in this regard. Nonetheless, there was at least a general understanding that it was not right for soldiers simply to make emperors, and that should they do so, the context was to be understood as revolt, or civil war. At the same time, as Tacitus implies, everyone seems to have admitted that the soldiers might, at any moment, put a man of their choice on the throne. Two groups of soldiers were relevant: the praetorians at Rome, and the legionary soldiers stationed on the frontiers of the empire (Campbell 1984: 365–414).

Over the course of the first century, both groups had made, or had helped to make, monarchs. And then, in the changes of 96–7, the praetorians were again involved: the prefects were apparently privy to Domitian's murder, and the guard, as a whole, forced (or helped to force) Nerva to adopt Trajan. And of course, one can wonder if Trajan was adopted precisely because he was commander of the military force nearest to Rome; there was a rumor, during Nerva's short reign, of a great commander in the East, who briefly toyed with the idea of military takeover (Alföldy and Halfmann 1973; with Brennan 1990 [2000]: 46; see now, Eck 2002).

Put bluntly, the more "constitutional" reigns of Nerva and Trajan did not witness the disappearance of the military as a powerful factor in selecting emperors. On the other hand, the conceivable "settlement" of the matter of the succession developed in this period might appear also to have affected the capacity of the soldiers to raise men to the purple. For on the whole, during the reigns of the "good" emperors, the troops were not much involved in politics.

Trajan died as he was being transported back to Rome from the eastern frontier, where he had been on campaign against the Parthians. Aside from his wife, Plotina, and his favorite niece, Salonia Matidia, the praetorian prefect, Acilius Attianus, was on the spot in Cilicia when the emperor passed away. It seems unlikely that Plotina would have sent her letter announcing Hadrian's assumption of the purple without having consulted the guard prefect (cf. Caballos Rufino 1984: 242). It would likewise seem that the allegiance of the troops, especially those in the East, must quickly have been sought. The fact that Hadrian immediately provided the eastern soldiers with a double bonus is suggestive *(HA Had.* 5.7). Still, the military appears neither directly, nor actively, to have influenced the choice.

Later, as Hadrian approached his end, and Antoninus Pius took up the reins of empire, the military was completely passive. The dying prince replaced his praetorian prefect with two new men, and provincial commands were awarded to those whose loyalty appeared certain (Birley 1997: 296). In other words, the conceivable threat of military takeover seems not to have been utterly ignored. There was, however, no overt involvement of any soldiers in this transfer of power.

Things went similarly with the next succession. In early March of 161, Antoninus Pius fell ill, and realized he was about to die. Announcing that he would entrust both the Roman state and his daughter to Marcus Aurelius, Antoninus asked that a statuette of the goddess Fortune be brought to him, and then peacefully went to sleep (*HA Ant. Pius* 12.5–6). This all transpired in the presence of the praetorian prefects. Otherwise, no soldiers were to be seen.

Fifteen years later, however, the provincial soldiery became suddenly more active. Gaius Avidius Cassius, who had been appointed in 170 to oversee a vast section of the eastern part of the empire (his official title was *rector Orientis*, i.e., "Supreme Commander of the Orient"), proclaimed himself emperor in April of 175. Initial support came from the Syrian troops, though Cassius claimed to be assuming the purple "because" the soldiers in Pannonia had "chosen" him (Dio 71.23.1). It may also be that Cassius was goaded on by Marcus' wife, Faustina, who feared that Marcus would die, leaving her and her children at the mercy of whatever person might then grab the purple. She supposedly preferred to put a man of her own choosing on the throne first *(HA Avid. Cass.* 7; Dio 71.22.3). In any case, several provincial governors in the East supported Cassius, thus providing a potentially large army; there might have been a harrowing civil war, had not a couple of soldiers summarily dispatched the would-be prince (Dio 71.27.2). The "reign" had lasted about three months; and soldiers had determined both the rise and the fall of Avidius Cassius.

When Marcus died, Commodus peacefully ascended the throne. During his reign, however, the threat of military takeover began to loom larger. Tigidius Perennis, an Italian, was the sole praetorian prefect from 182 until 185, during which time he largely ruled the empire (Howe 1942: 65–6; Absil 1997: 184–5). It is furthermore reported that Perennis planned to put himself on the throne, and that this scheme brought on his own end (Herod. 1.9). Perhaps the more immediate cause of his demise, though, was his attempt to stamp out the last embers of a military revolt, which began when the soldiers in Britain attempted to make their commander, Priscus, emperor (on this matter see Birley 1981: 260–1). Be that as it may, in the wake of Perennis' death, Commodus awarded himself the epithet *felix*, "happy, lucky" (*HA Comm.* 8.1; H. Mattingly 1940: clix). He also at some point took to keeping the children of provincial governors hostage in Rome, hoping thus to avoid usurpation by commanders on the frontiers (Herod. 3.2.4; see, however, Zimmermann 1999: 202). In short, Commodus trusted neither the praetorians in the capital, nor the legions on the frontiers.

With Perennis gone, one of the emperor's palace servants effectively took control of the government during the period from 185 until 189. This was Marcus Aurelius Cleander, a slave from Phrygia in Asia Minor, who had been freed by the emperor, and had risen to be Commodus' "Master of the Bedchamber." He, however, was executed after the city populace rioted over a food shortage, supposedly Cleander's doing (Garnsey 1988: 226). The significant point for us is that during his ascendancy (specifically in the years 187–9), Cleander held what appears to have been a unique position in the history of the imperial administration. He was known as the *a pugione*, literally the "Master of the Dagger," though this title ought probably to have implied something more like "Commander of the Imperial Bodyguard." Perhaps he was direct superior to the praetorian prefects (on his official position, see now Absil 1997: 226–31). In any case, he clearly had some kind of command of troops at Rome, and, on the basis of this position, managed to control the empire for roughly two years.

Cleander's death was followed by several rather chaotic years, culminating in Commodus' murder. One of the prime movers of the plot was the new praetorian prefect, Quintus Aemilius Laetus, who hailed from North Africa.. As soon as Commodus died, Laetus contacted Publius Helvius Pertinax, the prefect of Rome, suggesting that he should now be emperor. Pertinax, who may have been in on the plan, after assuring himself that Commodus was indeed gone, went to the praetorian camp, announced the emperor's death, offered a very large bonus, and was hailed as emperor (Birley 1988: 86–8).

The new reign was short (three months). Pertinax, who was much stricter with them than Commodus had been, made the praetorians uncomfortable, so that they were continually on the edge of revolt from the very beginning of his reign (Herod. 2.4.4–5). As March of 193 drew to a close, 300 guardsmen, supposedly at Laetus' behest, decided to rid themselves of the man they quickly had come to despise, and murdered Pertinax *(HA Pert.* 10.8–11). There was no plan for the sequel. When he learned of the guard's revolt, Pertinax had sent Flavius Sulpicianus, his father-in-law and the current urban prefect, to the praetorian camp to keep order. Upon the death of his son-in-law, Sulpicianus began to maneuver to have himself proclaimed emperor (Dio 74.11.1). Some of the praetorians, however, did not favor him, and sought the Senate House. There they found another candidate, Marcus Didius Julianus, whom they promptly brought forth. An auction of the empire ensued at the walls of the praetorian camp, and a final bid of 25,000 *sestertii* (the equivalent of five years' pay) per soldier bought Julianus the throne. He was in such a generous mood, that he ultimately decided to award each man 30,000 *sestertii* (*HA Did. Jul.* 2.4–3.2; it may be noted that Marcus Aurelius gave each praetorian about 20,000 *sestertii* upon his accession, and that this was done under no compulsion – Dio 74.8.4).

Although the praetorians had reasserted their power, it would do them little good. For they would only reap the ferocious wrath of the next man to sit securely upon the throne. Septimius Severus cashiered the auctioneers at sword-point, and ordered that they never approach within 100 miles of Rome, on pain of death, telling them that they deserved to die a thousand times, given the crimes they had committed (Herod. 2.13.5–9). Nor did the man to whom they sold Rome profit from his investment. Didius Julianus survived for only two months (March 28–June 1, 193), before one of the guard murdered him. The Senate had anyhow condemned him to death. In the end, it would seem that the use of force to make an emperor was, perhaps, not ideal, but could somehow be reconciled. The brazen use of money in such matters was simply intolerable.

With such things transpiring at Rome, there was turmoil on the frontiers. News of the sale at the praetorian camp traveled fast. In short order, three different groups of soldiers, in three different places, declared three different provincial governors to be emperor. The acclamations came in the first days of April. At Carnuntum, in the middle of the empire, Severus received the call to rule. It can only have been a few days later when, at Antioch, Lucius Pescennius Niger was awarded the purple by his legions. Severus quickly offered a position as junior emperor to the governor of Britain, Decimus Clodius Albinus, who also had been nominated by his troops. Initially, Albinus accepted. This all set the stage for a series of battles between Severus, Niger, and Albinus, and their respective soldiers. The fighting would not end until Albinus was defeated and killed by Severus in early 197.

In the events of 193–7, we can observe the convergence of several trends. On the one hand, when Commodus perished without either a son or other successor designate, the military strode into the vacuum. Those soldiers best positioned geographically were the praetorians, which is why they determined the length of Pertinax's tenure of the purple. Their subsequent auction of the throne to Julianus may have been the catalyst that brought the provincial legions once again into the fray. But jealousy may also have played a role. The praetorians who, until their dismissal by Severus, had been almost universally of Italian stock, were significantly better paid than the legionary soldiers, and enjoyed various privileges not held by the frontier troops. It may simply have been too much for the hardened legionaries to stand by and watch as a bunch of pampered slackers (in their view) profited from the abhorrent (in their view) sale of the throne. Nor, though, should the personal ambition of Septimius Severus, Clodius Albinus, or Pescennius Niger be ignored.

However all of this may be, we see that when family failed to produce the next prince, soldiers, in consort with their commanders, stepped quickly into the breach. The "secret," which Tacitus claimed to have been revealed by the events of 68/9, was laid bare again in 193. In short, whether or not the soldiers possessed some constitutional right to make emperors, they were a presence to be reckoned with. Nor does that lesson seem to have been lost on the creator of the Severan dynasty. Septimius' last words, spoken to his sons, Caracalla and Geta, were supposedly these: "Do not disagree between yourselves, give money to the soldiers, and despise everyone else" (Dio 76.17.4).

Giving money to the soldiers was one of the very first things Caracalla did, for he wanted them to proclaim him sole emperor. They, however, chose to force him to live, at least for the moment, with his brother Geta as co-emperor (Herod. 3.15.4–5). Once Geta was removed on December 19, 211, Caracalla could assiduously follow his father's advice. He increased the soldier's pay, and devoted himself principally to things military. He was nearly always on campaign, all the while living as did the legionaries themselves. And yet, he seems to have recognized the danger posed by armies to those who possessed the purple. For example, by the end of his reign, no province, hence, no provincial governor, held more than two legions (Birley 1988: 191). In other words, while his own inclinations brought him to follow his father's advice, he also seems to have taken precautions to restrain the potential power of those same troops.

Regardless, it was at the hands of military men that Caracalla would perish. In early April 217, Caracalla decided to offer sacrifice at a shrine near Carrhae in Syria. On the

Figure 7.2a–d The Severans: (a) Septimius Severus (*RIC* Severus n. 308); (b) Caracalla (*RIC* Caracalla 191); (c) Elagabalus (*RIC* Elagabalus 88); (d) Alexander (KM 1991.2.693) (7.2a–c from the editor's collection; 7.2d reproduced courtesy of the Kelsey Museum at the University of Michigan)

way back, he was supposedly murdered by one of the soldiers accompanying him, who was in turn immediately slain by the other soldiers in the small entourage. Two days later, one of the praetorian prefects (both were taking part in the expedition) was hailed emperor. Many supposed that he had provided for the murder. Thus did Macrinus, suddenly rise to the rank of emperor (April 11, 217).

The Severan house reasserted itself just over a year later, again with support from the army. On May 16, 218, the soldiers of the *legio III Gallica*, stationed near Emesa, proclaimed Varius Avitus Bassianus emperor. The whole thing was apparently managed by Julia Domna's sister, Julia Maesa. But the ultimate success of the revolt depended on the willingness of troops to follow the family instead of the interloper, whose own troops began to defect, so that in about a month, Macrinus was defeated and killed.

The new emperor's behavior rapidly enraged most every sector of Roman society. Antics such as nocturnal stints as a faux female prostitute did not go over well (Dio 79.13.2–4). There were thus various rumblings of military revolt – some even purportedly fomented by lowly private citizens, who thought themselves worthy of the purple (Dio 79.7.1–4). Julia Maesa thereupon chose another of her grandsons to favor. This boy, Gessius Alexianus Bassianus, was made junior emperor (*Caesar*) in the summer of 221. Over the course of the next year, animosity between Elagabalus and Bassianus grew, until the former attempted to have his cousin murdered. The soldiers in Rome were infuriated, and, in early March of 222, they slaughtered Elagabalus along with his mother. Their decapitated bodies were dragged through the city streets, the emperor's remains were cast into the Tiber, and his mother's corpse was dumped on a waste heap (Dio 79.20.2). Julia Maesa had again selected the emperor, and the praetorians saw to it that he came to rule. Imperator Caesar Marcus Aurelius Severus Alexander Pius Felix Augustus, as he was now styled, was 12 years old.

There was apparently one attempt at military takeover during Severus Alexander's reign. A man called Taurinus is said to have been proclaimed emperor, but then, out of fear, to have drowned himself in the Euphrates (*Epitome* 24.2). The rule of the last Severan came to a violent end. Alexander, along with his mother, had gone north to fend off attacks by the Germans. The imperial train was at Mogontiacum (modern Mainz), when Alexander decided to negotiate with the enemy, rather than to fight. This enraged the young recruits, who mutinied, murdered the emperor and his mother, and put their own commanding officer on the throne. Thus did Gaius Julius Verus Maximinus come to the throne.

But something new had now happened. Maximinus was not born to an aristocratic, senatorial family – indeed, he came not even from an equestrian family. Nor was he from one of the more civilized portions of the Empire. Rather, he is said to have been the son of peasants who resided in Thrace. He had worked his way up through the ranks of the army, largely by means of his great size and utter ferocity. In short, Maximinus the Thracian was not only made emperor by the army, he was himself an army man through and through. The soldiers had picked one of their own, and as a result of their choice, that man became simultaneously senator and emperor (Potter, ch. 8, this volume).

Conclusions

We might summarize the situation with regard to family, soldiers, and the creation of emperors as follows. When Nerva was raised to the purple in 96, one could look back over roughly a century of imperial rule. In doing so, it must have been painfully evident that emperors had not been chosen according to any fixed principle. It must have seemed pretty clear that Augustus wanted his successors to come from his close family. This is what happened over several generations. However, as things turned out, those who influenced the choice were frequently not the "right" people, and several of those who had gained the throne did not rule "properly." The machinations of family members and soldiers had too often resulted in bad emperors.

In any case, one result of this history may have been a planned, concerted effort at change. It is conceivable that, under Nerva and Trajan, a system was devised, whereby the selection and resultant adoption of a particularly suitable candidate by the reigning emperor would become the new method by which princes were created. On this scheme, family members were neither to make, nor to be made, the emperor. Nor, according to this plan, will the military have played a significant role in the process. In the end, the surviving evidence is insufficient to allow us to be certain whether all the talk of adoption was generated by necessity, since Nerva, Trajan, Hadrian, and Antoninus Pius all lacked a son, or whether it was the result of planning. Nonetheless, it is clear that, along with the influence exerted by family and the soldiers, for a period of time in the second century CE, ability, or suitability, played some role in the process of finding Rome's first man.

2 What's an Emperor to Do?

Introduction

By way of introducing this second section of the present chapter, let us return to the brief reign of Didius Julianus. Having purchased the throne from the praetorians, Julianus proceeded straightaway, accompanied by his new, heavily armed, retinue, to the Senate House. There, he received the official sanction of the conscript fathers, albeit under duress. On the following day, the senators all visited him to pay their respects. Since they both feared and hated their new prince, they feigned a happy mood in his presence. The urban populace, on the other hand, was vociferous in its displeasure, loudly branding Julianus a parricide and a thief. So he offered them money. When they responded that they desired no cash from him, that *they* could not be bought, Julianus' tolerance had been pushed too far. He set the soldiers on them, and a number of people were killed. The crowd then betook itself to the *circus maximus*, where a night and a day were spent shouting abuse of Julianus, and pleading that the legionary soldiers might come to Rome and rescue the people from the lout and his praetorians. In the end, the people gave up, and went home – though not at all happily. The general mood in Rome remained sullen (Dio 74.12–13). The events of these two or three days clearly demonstrate several things.

First, the Senate had little to say in the selection of emperors. On the other hand, it was essential that the Senate, once the emperor had been (by whatever process) proclaimed, "officially" grant him his position (Talbert 1984: 354–8). For this, in combination perhaps with a law passed by one of the popular assemblies, was the only available method of giving a new prince the sheen of legitimacy (note, however, that the last recorded act of a Roman popular assembly comes from 97 CE, just as our period starts – see Rotondi 1912: 471). But even more importantly, senatorial opinion was crucial for any emperor who hoped to die naturally, or to function decently; for these were the men upon whom he must rely in the actual running of the empire. And of course, the historical record was largely written by senators, so emperors who desired to be remembered well needed to please this group of potential authors.

As for the Roman populace, they could become very loud, and very annoying – even significantly dangerous. Nonetheless, while they could dislike, criticize, and generally make life difficult and unpleasant for the reigning emperor, they generally could not select him (by the late second century, however, this group had gained rather more power in this respect: see Sünskes Thompson 1993).

The traditional picture of the people's political activity holds that, during the republican period, the aristocracy pretty well controlled the common folk. A web of client–patron relationships, along with various "constitutional" arrangements, prevented the people, as a whole, from being able to exercise much real political muscle. Hence, when the republic was dissolved, they, unlike the aristocracy, lost rather little in any practical, political sense. They therefore wholeheartedly supported the monarchy, unlike the more elite members of society. The main concern of the *plebs urbana*, once basic needs (largely a steady supply of food and entertainments) had been met, came to be that emperors comport themselves in a fashion that the urban populace found appropriate (Yavetz 1969: esp. 130–40).

Recently, however, the very nature of the republican political system has been called into question. In particular, one school of thought now holds that the republic was much more democratic than many have been willing to admit, and that the common people really did have significant political clout (see Millar 1998; though for an argument more along the lines of the traditional picture, see now Mouritsen 2001). If this interpretation is correct (or if it be accepted), then we (or those who take this line) will have to think again about the position of the *plebs urbana* under the imperial regime. For if the Roman people did lose real liberties and real political standing with the advent of the principate, then their expectations of the new political order deserve some reconsideration. Although this problem cannot be settled here (indeed, it may never be settled absolutely), the debate should be kept in mind as we consider the political position of the urban populace.

Let us return to the main line of our argument. While neither the senators nor the urban plebs could realistically hope to make an emperor, either group could contribute significantly to a ruler's downfall. And for that reason, if we ask what an emperor was "supposed" to do, we must consider the wishes of these two groups – as well, of course, as the desires of the soldiers. For emperors who could please these three constituencies would surely be judged to have ruled well and be classed among the "good" emperors, while failure at this task was likely to be fatal, both to the emperor himself and to his memory in the annals of history.

We shall turn momentarily to an examination of what an emperor had to do to keep each of these groups content, thus to the constraints on his conduct as emperor. As we shall see, what made for a "good" emperor, in Roman eyes, was not necessarily what might occur first to a modern audience. But before considering such matters, it is worth asking, although briefly, (a) just what an emperor, at least in theory, was *allowed* to do, and (b) again, broadly speaking, what he was *supposed* to do.

What was the emperor "allowed" to do?

By the middle of the second century CE, at the very latest, the practice of magic had become a generally recognized capital offense (cf. Mommsen 1889: 639–43; Rives 2003). And yet, we hear that various of the emperors of our period (both "good" and "bad") either practiced magic themselves, or openly employed magicians. Hadrian's curiosity is said to have caused him to try all kinds of magic spells (Dio 79.11.3). An Egyptian magician named Arnouphis accompanied Marcus Aurelius during the Marcomannic wars, and worked a miracle which saved the Roman army (Dio 71.8.4). Caracalla was so taken with a magician named Sempronius Rufus that he recalled the man from the insular banishment to which Severus had condemned him (Dio 77.17.2). Indeed, Caracalla was supposedly altogether enthralled with magicians (Dio 77.18.4, Herod. 4.12.3–4); so too Elagabalus, who allegedly employed their arts on a daily basis (*HA Heliogab.* 8.2). The point of relating such information is this. An emperor, if he so chose, could apparently engage in an activity that otherwise was considered illegal, that for the rest of the population was perceived to be a capital offense. Was the *princeps* allowed to do, then, whatever he liked? And if so, in just what sense was such latitude granted him?

In fact, a number of ancient authors say precisely that an emperor could do whatever he pleased: he could determine that which was legally binding for everyone else, and, simultaneously, disregard any and every law, if he so wished. The process that had led to this freedom of maneuver began with Julius Caesar, who is supposed to have recommended that people accept all things decreed by him as legally binding (Suet. *Jul.* 77). By the early third century, the great jurist Ulpian flatly stated that whatever the emperor wanted would have the force of law (D. 1.4.1 pr.). Both Ulpian and Cassius Dio were furthermore of the opinion that the emperor stood above the law (D. 1.3.31; Dio 53.18.1). Dio, at one point in his history, illustrates the point. Septimius Severus' praetorian prefect, Plautianus, is supposed to have caused several hundred men and boys, some even of high social rank, to be castrated, so that these might provide an appropriate entourage for his daughter. According to Dio, this made Plautianus seem to have power nearly equal to that possessed by the emperor (Dio 75.14.4–6). Or, we might remember something supposedly said by Julia Domna to Caracalla. When he was having trouble controlling his sexual desire for her, she reminded him that he could do whatever he liked, "or do you not know that you are emperor, and that you make the laws rather than obey them?" (*HA Carac.* 10.2).

More significant than such privately held, or informally expressed opinions, is the record of the actual bestowal of imperial power on Vespasian. A fragmentary inscription preserves a unique document, the so-called *lex de imperio Vespasiani* ("Law Concerning the Imperial Power of Vespasian"). The extant portion of this law shows the new emperor was granted various specific powers, rights, or prerogatives – e.g., he may constitute treaties with whomever he likes, he is allowed to convene the Senate whenever he wants, etc. Toward the middle of these dispensations, however, comes the following clause:

> that whatever things he judges to be to the benefit of the state or befitting divine, human, public, or private affairs, to him shall there be the right and the power to carry out and to do these things, just as there was to the divine Augustus, and to Tiberius Julius Caesar Augustus, and to Tiberius Claudius Caesar Augustus Germanicus…
> (Crawford 1996: no. 39.17–21)

It seems difficult to imagine that this is anything other than an official, hence presumably "constitutionally" binding, proclamation of the informally-expressed sentiments listed above.

In short, while the position of emperor was, on the whole, not terribly well delineated or systematized by the Romans, the fact that an emperor had absolute, unfettered power was widely and well understood, and, at least in the case of the grant of imperial power to Vespasian, actually written into law. We are told that Septimius Severus and Caracalla frequently responded in the following manner to petitions: "It may be, indeed, that we are freed from the laws; nonetheless, we live according to them" (*Inst.* 2.17.8). Or, we can look back to the start of our period, when Pliny, with near astonishment, remarked that Trajan had decided to subordinate himself to the laws that were not meant to apply to an emperor. The reaction of Pliny, and his peers, was to desire to grant Trajan even more powers (*Pan.* 65.1).

At the core of such sentiments lies a very simple principle. Those emperors, who hoped to be understood as "good," had to come to grips with the fact that the vast freedom allowed the *princeps* was not a carte blanche. Freedom from the law entailed, at least ideally, an extremely heavy burden of responsibility. The "good" emperor had to understand just how and when to subject himself to the laws. He had to understand what was expected of him by his society, by his subjects.

Saint Paul, advising his followers in Corinth as to the kind of behavior they should exhibit so as to please a heavenly audience, put the matter in such a way as could perfectly well have applied to the emperor and his behavior: "Everything is allowable to me, but not everything is helpful" (*I Cor.* 6.12). Let us then turn to the kinds of imperial behavior that might have been classed, in broad terms, as helpful.

What was the emperor "supposed" to do?

Since there was never a proper constitution for the principate, we would be well advised to consider firstly how an emperor might learn what was expected of him. How did he identify something like a "job description" for his position? The *lex de imperio Vespasiani,* and any similar such statutes which may have existed, will have given him some information; these will not have been sufficient to enable a man to fall into the category of the "good" emperors. There was, on the other hand, one document which may have been more useful in this respect, and set the tone from the very beginning.

When he died, Augustus left a text to be inscribed on bronze tablets, and then affixed to his tomb. The same text was displayed publicly elsewhere around the empire. We now call this document the *Res Gestae Divi Augusti* (*Deeds of the Divine Augustus*). In the main, the tract describes what Augustus accomplished during the 40-odd years of his sole rule. The account of his actual deeds is prefaced by a fairly extensive list of the various honors, grants of power, and the like, that formed the basis of Augustus' "constitutional" position. Herein lies the political legitimization for all the actions that follow. In the course of this first part of the work, though, Augustus says something of great significance. Having reminded his audience that he restored many examples of ancestral customs, which were falling into desuetude (in Latin, *multa exempla maiorum exolescentia*), Augustus asserts "and I myself have left for those who come after me examples of many things, which should be imitated" (*RG* 8). In the remainder of his *Res Gestae,* Augustus presents these *exempla* which ought to be imitated. One is thus tempted to suppose the first emperor was attempting to leave, to the extent that he could, a job description for his successors (see Ramage 1987: 111–16). The emperor who wanted to know what he was "supposed" to do, might well try to emulate, as best he could, what Augustus (or other "good") emperors) had done.

Beyond Augustus and his *Res Gestae*, we have from the reign of Trajan a document that surely was meant to be understood as a kind of blueprint for the functioning of a "good" emperor: Pliny the Younger's *Panegyric*. This is the revised text of a speech given by Pliny in 100, thanking Trajan for having made Pliny consul. The speaker uses the occasion to praise his emperor, and in doing so, paints a plain picture of the manner in which an ideal ruler will comport himself. Indeed, Pliny says that Trajan, in becoming himself an *exemplum*, will show future emperors how to behave (*Pan.* 75.4–6).

Let us then briefly consider Augustus' *Res Gestae* and Pliny's *Panegyric*. It is possible to distill from these a prescription for proper imperial behavior. With this in mind, it will be easier to see how and why the emperors with whom we are here concerned might have been judged "good" or "bad." Or at least, we will be able better to analyze the kinds of activities attributed by our (again, largely senatorial) sources to emperors according to their classification of those princes as "good" or "bad."

The contents of the *Res Gestae* can be broken down into categories of activity. It is important to note, however, one theme that pervades the entire text, no matter whether an honor is being granted or an action described: the emperor is always modest, even self-effacing, never improperly (in Roman terms) boastful or overbearing. Having noted this extremely important fact, we might simply list the kinds of things to which Augustus devotes much care. The well-being and comfort of the populace at Rome are crucial. For them there are numerous donations of money and food, and the provision of entertainments of various sorts. The capital city was adorned with magnificent structures of every conceivable kind. Moving beyond Rome and its populace, any and all possible foreign threats were laid to rest. Even people from as far away as India, to whom only *talk* of Rome and Augustus had penetrated, sent ambassadors to Augustus, begging him for an amicable relationship.

In short, the emperor's job, in purely pragmatic terms, is effectively divided into two spheres by Augustus: (a) care for the city of Rome and its inhabitants, and (b) careful attention to the honor and safety of the empire vis-à-vis any external threats. It is also worth remarking that the tract ends with Augustus remembering that the Senate, the equestrian order, and the entire Roman people officially awarded him the epithet *pater patriae* ("father of the fatherland"). In other words, it appears that what he has become is somehow to be perceived in the light of his functioning as a father figure to all those living under Rome's sway. And like the father of a Roman nuclear family (on whom see Saller 1994: 102–53), while he has, in principle, the authority to annihilate any family member judged to deserve that punishment, such powers are better left unexercised.

It should therefore not be a great surprise to find that Pliny also accords the epithet *pater patriae* (or various periphrases of it based on the noun *parens*, i.e., "parent"), which was also granted to Trajan, a prominent position in his *Panegyric* (see 21.1, 67.1, 84.6, 87.1, 87.3, 94.4). And as in the *Res Gestae*, there is a constant concern for the kind of virtues listed right at the outset, namely, Trajan's *pietas* ("dutiful respect"), *abstinentia* ("restraint"), and *mansuetudo* ("mildness") (*Pan.* 2.6; for a fuller list and discussion see Fedeli 1989: 457–61). Beyond his virtues and demeanor, the actual activities engaged in by Trajan correspond closely to those highlighted by Augustus. The populace of Rome is attended to with food (*Pan.* 29–32) and money (*Pan.* 26–8). Public entertainments (*Pan.* 33) and public building (*Pan.* 51) also receive specific mention. Trajan inspires awe in Rome's enemies, is himself a willing and competent soldier, and so has won the allegiance and respect of the military (*Pan.* 12–17). All of this is perfectly in line with Augustus' picture of the princely position. Three matters, however, are added by Pliny. There is a fair amount of talk about finances, usually involving a contrast between the practices of Domitian and those of the new emperor. The upshot is that Trajan has significantly more respect for the property of the elite (*Pan.* 36–43). Beyond this, we are told that the provinces are now ruled well (*Pan.* 70); and we hear of the current emperor's minute attention to his duties as judge (*Pan.* 77, 80; cf. Millar 1977: 528).

Thus far, we have seen that an emperor could do whatever he wanted, but was (ideally) responsible for restraining himself. From Augustus' *Res Gestae* and Pliny's *Panegyric* it becomes apparent that an emperor's chief concerns were: (a) the care of Rome and her populace, (b) proper attention to the defense of the empire, and (c) careful cultivation of the proper imperial demeanor. We have also seen that the panel of judges (i.e., those imagined by our literary tradition) who rated a prince's behavior according to these categories, consisted primarily of the Senate (and equestrians), the soldiers, and the Roman plebs. We may now turn to each of these groups, and consider in slightly greater detail what things factored into their ranking of imperial performances.

Pleasing the Senate, the army, and the plebs

We shall now look more specifically at what a senator, a soldier, or (say) a tavern keeper in Rome may have wanted from his emperor. An initial caveat is, however, appropriate. Our record of such matters was not created by members of all these groups. It was only members of the senatorial and equestrian elite who created the record upon which our judgment must rest. Thus, we can detect the opinions of the soldiers or the Roman plebs only by gazing through the lenses provided by their social superiors. For present purposes, we shall simply assume that those are reasonably accurate.

Let us start at the top. Senators (and equestrians) expected their emperors to carry out the pragmatic essentials of the job as listed above. However, it would appear that in rating princes, the Roman elite tended to give most weight to matters of (what we would call) social conduct. The requirements had even, by the time of the Antonines, attained a nearly codified status. He who intended to be regarded as "good" had to behave in such a way as to display what could be summed up as "civility" (in Latin, *civilitas* – see Wallace-Hadrill 1982; and note Eutrop. 8.4.1, summarizing his praise for Trajan, thus: "He nonetheless surpassed his military glory with his civility and his moderation").

The path to a persuasive "civil" performance involved an intricate game of make-believe. Firstly, the "good" emperor had to pretend to refuse things: honors, special epithets, triumphs, etc. He might well, in the end, accept such offers; but he ought, in the first instance, to decline (cf. Herod. 2.3 on the elaborate game of refusal played by Pertinax when he was put up as emperor). Secondly, despite the fact that his rule was absolute, he was at least to feign subjection to the laws. Thirdly, the "good" emperor was routinely expected to display the qualities or virtues that Pliny sets out in his *Panegyric*: respect, restraint, mildness, and the like. In short, he who best pretended that something like the republic still existed, who best pretended that he was not an utterly supreme and absolute monarch, but instead, *primus inter pares*, was also he who would be recorded as a "good" emperor.

All of this can be perceived from a slightly different angle. The argument can be made that perhaps the single most essential thing underlying the Roman imperial form of government, and consequently the emperor's very position, was a system involving the constant exchange of honor and honors. Proper doses of this "honor-currency" administered in the proper ways and at the proper times, can be argued to have kept the wheels of empire spinning. And within this "honor-community," the emperor functioned both as chief dispenser and chief recipient. Thus, to be recognized as "good," a prince had to play the game of honoring, and being honored, with aplomb. It is perhaps easiest simply to quote Jon Lendon on this matter:

> Honor, whether used consciously or unconsciously, served to muffle the shouting of orders, the jingle of coins, and the screams of the tortured. Viewing the world in honor terms made ruling the empire easier and made living in it, and obeying it, more tolerable. An iron tyranny seemed to give way to a golden commonwealth of honorable persons and cities. Gilt, we think; but the mirage was connived in by rulers and ruled alike. (Lendon 1997: 270)

What is perhaps astonishing to a modern audience is the force potentially wielded by the emperor's perceived *civilitas*, or by honor, qualities which we might incline to view as part and parcel of a preposterous game of make-believe.

In any case, the sheer power of civility or honor among the Romans can be illustrated by taking into consideration another absolutely crucial matter for senators, namely, their personal security. We hear that all of the "good" emperors of our period promised never to kill a senator (or at least, not to do so without a proper trial). Emphasis is laid by our sources on such an oath having been taken by Nerva, Trajan, Hadrian, Antoninus Pius, Marcus Aurelius, Pertinax, and even Macrinus. On the other hand, Commodus, Septimius Severus, and Caracalla were excoriated for having killed many senators. Severus was even labeled the "murderer of so many and such illustrious men" (*HA Sev.* 13.8). Indeed, the manner in which that emperor supposedly swore not to kill senators is itself instructive. He is said to have forced the Senate to decree that he should not be allowed to murder members of that august body (Dio 75.2.1; cf. Herod. 2.14.3–4, *HA Sev.* 7.5). The whole matter of executing senators is perhaps nicely summed up in the question asked by Didius Julianus as he faced his own executioners: "But what have I done wrong? Whom (i.e., what senator) have I killed?" (Dio 74.17.5).

On the surface, then, the execution of senators might seem to be a more objective measure for judging emperors than trying to evaluate their virtues or "civility." And yet, appearances deceive. On the one hand, "good" emperors did put senators to death. We have observed Hadrian's actions with regard to L. Julius Ursus Servianus: he died when he got in the way of the emperor's aspirations for the succession (see above, p. 131). Moreover, Hadrian had several senators of consular rank murdered just at the start of his reign. There was criticism of this, but Hadrian survived it, to become one of the canonical "good" emperors (Birley 1997: 87–9). And what makes the whole business even more disturbing is the fact that upon closer inspection, the ancient outcry regarding senators put to death by (e.g.) Severus or Caracalla must be taken with a grain of salt (see respectively Alföldy 1968 and Sillar 2001).

In short, a "good" emperor, despite the fact that he executed senators, might remain "good," whereas a *princeps* judged on the same grounds to have been "bad," turns out perhaps to have been less bloodthirsty than he was portrayed by ancient authors. The seemingly rock-solid category for judgment of such matters begins to wobble, and we are cast back upon the mechanisms of "civility" and honor, in our search for that which made senators happy (or not) with emperors.

But what of soldiers? And what of the plebs? There is no doubt that both of these groups expected tangible benefits from emperors, and that when such emoluments were not forthcoming, there could be trouble. Nonetheless, for both soldiers and their civilian peers, matters of style carried much weight. Indeed, here, as in various other areas, we can observe the percolation of ideals held by the aristocracy down to the lower orders of society (Lendon 1997: 89–103).

Where the soldiers were concerned, an emperor needed to comprehend and take part in the ritual of being a soldier; to become, as it were, a "fellow-soldier." For example, by wearing clothing inappropriate to the military realm, an emperor might immediately and irrevocably alienate his troops (cf. Herod. 5.2.4–5). But beyond this, he had to appear as a particular kind of "fellow-soldier"; he had to don the mantle of a certain, proper kind of aristocratic military officer. Emperors who did not meet their soldiers' requirements in these more subtle fashions, ran the risk of being toppled – or relegated to categorization as "bad" (Campbell 1984: 417–27; Lendon 1997: 252–65).

As for the plebs, they too could be much impressed, or irritated, by the manner in which emperors ruled. For example, the *princeps* who did not appear at the games, or who, when he did appear, read correspondence, without glancing at the action, would find little favor. On the other hand, the emperor who presented himself stripped and ready to fight as a gladiator was a great embarrassment (Herod. 1.15.7). Especially important for us, however, is the fact that a significant development in the relationship between the plebs and the *princeps* appears to have occurred precisely in the reigns of Nerva and Trajan.

Nerva begins a pattern of courting the plebs that was trendsetting for the remainder of our period (Brennan 1990 [2000]). In addition to this, the denarii produced by the mint at Rome reveal a sudden, new interest in advertising the emperor's virtues (the most prominent are equity, piety, courage, generosity, foresight, and modesty). Indeed, the argument can now be made that it is possible "to see both the mint and Pliny (i.e., his *Panegyric*) as mirrors of some larger, discursive shift that took place around the beginning of the second century" (Noreña 2001: 156). This shift fits very well chronologically with the new importance of the emperor's *civilitas*. In other words, if we can assume that the coins minted in Rome were intended for an audience that went well beyond the limits of the senatorial and equestrian orders, then the dialogue about imperial virtues must be seen as a matter of import also for those who sat in the less prestigious theater seats (for a diagram of the socially determined seating in the theater, see B. D. Shaw 2000: 389) – and, for that matter, to those camped in the misty forests of Germany, or in the sands by the Euphrates.

To summarize: there were practical tasks that emperors were expected to see to. They had to care for the city of Rome. They were responsible for protecting the Roman Empire, both physically, and in terms of its honor. In doing this, the proper *princeps* would become, in a particular way, a soldier. Beyond these matters, the judge's seat had become, by the second century, a place where an emperor was expected frequently to be seen. So much for a "job description" of *princeps*. But hovering over and governing all of this was another set of expectations, and these were most influential in the final evaluation of the quality of any emperor's time on the throne. "Good" emperors were those who knew how to wrap themselves in *civilitas*, and to use the currency of honor in the appropriate ways. The man who failed at these tasks could only be perceived, hence recorded, as a "bad" emperor.

CHAPTER EIGHT

The Transformation of the Empire: 235–337 CE

David S. Potter

What are we to make of the 102 years that separate the death of Severus Alexander from that of Constantine? Are they a prelude to late antiquity? Are they a postlude to the classical era? Do they see the creation of a military dictatorship? Is the later Roman Empire a different beast from the early? Many of these problems are caused by the unusual nature of the second century. The extraordinary stability of the period from 96 to 180 CE was a condition from which one can only descend, a view taken by Cassius Dio and Herodian, who imply that the reign of Marcus was a high point, while the succeeding period, in which they grew to maturity, was much worse.

1 Succession and Security

It was the ambition of every man who took the throne to reenact Augustus' creation of a hereditary monarchy. Augustus and Livia, however, had had to rely on adoption when they failed to produce a male heir to the throne; likewise, since subsequent Roman emperors would remain formally monogamous, the chances of producing a biological heir who would survive to reach the throne were slim. Vespasian was the only emperor in the first century to be succeeded by biological children, something that would not happen again until Commodus succeeded Marcus Aurelius in 180. In the next century, Septimius Severus and Valerian – although by no means the only ones to have sons – were the only rulers to be succeeded by male children until Constantius I engineered the accession of his son, Constantine, in 306.

Adoption was a surer path to dynastic longevity than biology, for it had the coincidental benefit of ensuring that a competent adult would be in line for succession, while, at the same time, giving the reigning emperor room to negotiate with the governing class (for details, see Peachin, this volume). It is perhaps an accident of fortune that many of the men who took the throne between 235 and 253 either had male children, often rather young, or brothers. Shackled by the fact of their biological success, emperors lacked the ability to negotiate the succession within the governing class. The presence of male children may be seen as one of the genuinely unusual features of third-century history; one of the keys to Diocletian's success in breaking the cycle of instability and violence that had troubled the empire in the half century prior to his accession now becomes clear: Diocletian had a daughter.

The situation with respect to the frontiers was more complex. The sudden failure of the Roman state to hold the initiative in foreign affairs may be attributed above all else to stagnant military doctrine and related failures of imagination (Potter 2004: 125, 213). The tactical organization of the Roman army in 235 had not changed significantly since the end of the second century BCE (Pollard, this volume). The long wars waged by Marcus Aurelius against northern tribes should have served as a wake-up call since the fact that the emperor was forced to spend most of his reign on the frontiers suggests that the tribes had adapted themselves to the Roman style of war. So too should the successful Parthian invasion of Commagene and Syria in 161 have raised some question as to the fitness of the army. Although the Parthians were repulsed, and their capital at Ctesiphon laid waste in 165, the incursion of 161 was the most dangerous assault upon the Roman east since the forties BCE. Roman success in the war may be attributed to the ability to force the Parthians to defend fixed points, and the weakness of the Parthian military establishment. The emergence of the vastly more competent Sasanian regime in 225 CE changed the balance of power in the east just as tribes north of the frontier developed new ways of penetrating static Roman defensive lines along the northern borders.

2 Emperors, Rebels, and Barbarians

Opellius Macrinus (217–18 CE) and Gaius Verus Julius Maximinus (235–8 CE) are rarely seen as significant figures in Roman imperial history (but see Peachin, this volume). Yet the actions of both outsiders – they were the first men without senatorial antecedents to claim the throne – show us how strongly felt was the urge to dynastic succession. One of Macrinus' first acts was to proclaim his son Caesar, and when the revolt of Elagabalus began to gain momentum, he raised his son to the rank of Augustus. Macrinus felt that if he could prove that he was a likely founder of a dynasty, his soldiers would be more likely to remain loyal. He might even have been proved right about this if he had not lost his nerve at a crucial moment in the battle at Immae and deserted his men (Dio 78.38.4). As for Elagabalus, people claimed that he looked like Caracalla. This is possible, though it is doubtful that he looked as much like Caracalla as his mint masters made him appear when the regime began to unravel (Potter 2004: 155).

Maximinus was descended from colonists settled by Trajan in the Balkans, and he appears to have been a mid-grade officer charged with levying troops when he led his revolt against Alexander (Syme 1971a: 179–89). He succeeded, we are told, because the army regarded Alexander with contempt, seeing him as the creature of his mother (Herod. 6.9.6). Whether or not this is true, it is significant that the story should have been told. The assertion that the soldiers had called Alexander a "boy tied to his mother's apron," was not especially accurate. Alexander was then 25 years old, but he had produced no heir, and his regime had tried to reverse the very close relationship with the army that had been asserted under Caracalla and Severus (Campbell 1984: 196–7). There had been several military revolts against Alexander in the context of the failed campaign against the Persians, as well as complaints from the legions about at least one senior appointee – Cassius Dio (Dio 80.4.2–5.1) – and the murder of Ulpian by the praetorian guard. It appears that under Severus Alexander we see a shift in the nature of dynastic loyalty. In the Antonine age, when the throne was passed via adoption, the army had played little direct role in the proceedings. The shift had begun under Septimius Severus, as Michael Peachin shows in his chapter. The origins of the revolt of Elagabalus were largely attributable to Macrinus' effort to reverse what were seen as Severan gifts to the army in the form of pay increases, and the ability of Elagabalus' supporters to link his image with that of Caracalla, the "soldier's friend," by claiming that he was Caracalla's illegitimate son (Dio 78.31.3; Herod. 5.3.10). For the soldiers it appears that the Severan dynasty was seen as the guarantor of their privileges, and they were not prepared to continue to show the same loyalty to the regime if they felt that members of the dynasty were not living up to their end of the bargain (Campbell 1984: 411–13).

Maximinus appears to have understood the soldier's point of view. After his accession he paid a large donative (financial gift) to the army on the Rhine – though quite possibly not to other legions (Potter 1990: 25–6). His proclamation of his young son Maximus as Caesar may be seen as an assertion that a new dynasty had arisen that would understand the singular importance of the soldiers to the empire. Indeed, the civil war of 238 may be seen as a conflict between two visions of imperial authority, one being that it derived from the soldiers, the other that it derived from the consensus of the governing class. It is striking that the Senate opposed Maximinus by electing a board of twenty to administer the war, and selected two elderly officials as emperors. One of them, Pupienus, had a son of mature years, who was notably excluded from the imperial college (Dietz 1980: 133). This gave the new rulers room to negotiate. When the friends of the deceased Gordian I, whose failed revolt in North Africa was the opening phase of the civil war, asserted their continued importance by sparking a riot in which the crowd demanded that a blood relative of Gordian (his grandson) be added to the college, the new emperors were able to agree to his proclamation as Caesar (Herod. 7.10.5–9).

Maximinus and Maximus, who, like the young Macrinus, was raised to the rank of Augustus when the revolt broke out, fell victim to their soldiers outside of Aquileia (Herod. 8.3.8–9). We will never know what happened for certain, but it is not improbable that, expecting that he would be able to move rapidly on the capital, Maximinus had not prepared properly for a siege. Maximinus had prided himself on his image as a great warrior, but he was appearing anything but great at this point, and that may have contributed to the sudden change of heart on the part of at least some of his men.

The regime that emerged in the middle of 238 looks like yet another compromise. The soldiers murdered Pupienus and Balbinus, but allowed the young Gordian to live. Pupienus and Balbinus may have appeared as precisely the sort of officials whose authority the soldiers had resented under Alexander: they were elderly and they were not about to assert their devotion to the men (they had permitted the praetorian guard to be besieged by the mob at Rome in the course of the insurrection). Gordian was too young to do much of anything, and it is plain that those who took power in the new regime, chiefly equestrian officials who had made their careers in the service of the *patrimonium*, were primarily interested in reconciling the former supporters of Maximinus with those who had served the victorious side. One of the losers in all of this was the man who ought to have been considered the greatest hero of the new regime, Tullus Menophilus, an ex-consul and member of the board of twenty who had commanded at Aquileia during the decisive siege (Dietz 1980: 233–45). He was given the governorship of Lower Moesia, charged with treason, and, presumably, executed. P. Aelius Ammonius, the procurator of the province, replaced him as governor. Ammonius may be seen as a tool of the group of senior equestrian officials led by C. Furius Sabinus Aquila Timesitheus, who had played no part in the events of 238, but would now become praetorian prefect. The only member of the board of twenty whom we know to have continued a prominent career after 238 was an equestrian jurist named Rufinus, who stressed his equestrian dignity even after he had been adlected into the Senate (Millar 1999a: 90–108). Timesitheus' daughter became the wife of Gordian, so that if a question of dynastic succession should arise, it would be the family of Timesitheus that would play the crucial role. Timesitheus himself died in 243 after a successful campaign to drive the Persians from territory that they had seized under Maximinus.

There would be no Gordianic dynasty because Gordian was assassinated in the course of an unsuccessful invasion of the Persian Empire during 244. He was succeeded by the praetorian prefect, Julius Philippus, a man from the province of Arabia, who seems to have been elevated to the prefecture by his brother, Priscus, Timesitheus' colleague in office (Potter 1990: 215). Philip took the novel step of appointing two of his relatives, Priscus and a man named Severianus, to senior commands in the east and the Balkans respectively (Zos. 19.2). He also made his son Caesar. At the same time he ordered the massive reconstruction of his hometown of Chabha in modern Jordan as Philippopolis to make it an appropriate *patria* or home city for an imperial family (Millar 1993a: 156). In the course of this he arranged the deification of his father, Marinus. Philip's assertion of dynastic ambition recalls that of Septimius Severus, and seems to have marked a strong break with the style of collective government under Gordian. It also appears to have been unpalatable. He was killed in a military uprising led by a senior senator named Decius in 249. Decius too had dynastic ambitions, for he had two sons, one of whom appears to have been in his early twenties. This older son, Herennius Etruscus, was raised first to the rank of Caesar, and then to the rank of Augustus following a catastrophic defeat that his father suffered at the hands of the Goths. Decius followed up this defeat by launching an ill-advised attack on the Goths at Abitus (Birley 1998: 77; Potter 1990: 278–82). He was killed, and power passed to Trebonianus Gallus, who briefly associated Decius' surviving son with himself and his own son, Volusianus, in power. This too proved a failure; Gallus was killed in a military uprising during 253. Aemilianus, the leader of the revolt against Gallus, was killed a few months later by Valerian, who had supported Gallus (Christol 1980: 73).

Valerian followed in the footsteps of his immediate predecessors, attempting to solidify his power by asserting dynastic ambitions. In this he was aided by the fact that he had an adult son, Gallienus, who was father to several sons, some of whom appear also to have reached maturity (Christol 1975). If he had been a better general, or simply a luckier man, Valerian might have succeeded. The fact that Gallienus was able to act as a fully functional colleague made it possible for Valerian to bring unprecedented security to the imperial office: there were no revolts during the seven years that he survived as emperor. Had Valerian not fallen victim to Sapor of Persia, who took him prisoner in 260, the course of subsequent Roman history might have been different, for his career suggests that it was still possible to maintain the Antonine model of government that Peachin has described in his chapter. The feasibility of that model was destroyed when Valerian was taken off to finish his days building bridges in Iran (Potter 2004: 256).

3 The Sasanians

For centuries after the reign of Augustus, the eastern frontier of the Roman Empire south of the Taurus Mountains had rested upon the western bank of the Euphrates River. North of the Taurus, the kingdom of Armenia had been Rome's neighbor. Control of that realm had been negotiated with the Arsacid kings of Parthia so that their nominee to the throne had to be approved by the Roman emperor. The province of Syria had more than once been home to pretenders to the Arsacid throne in Ctesiphon. The arrangement with Parthia had enabled Rome to maintain control of the east with an army of six legions in the time of Marcus Aurelius. Three of these legions were concentrated in Syria, where the main threat could be expected; one was relatively isolated at Melitene in Commagene, while the other two formed the garrison of Arabia, with responsibility for patrolling the desert as well as supporting the garrison of Syria. Rome counted on having ample advance warning of Parthian maneuvers, and might reasonably have expected that no Parthian army could have been larger than the roughly 30,000 men who could be supplied on campaign. The successful invasion of the Parthian kingdom that Trajan carried out in the last years of his life may also have suggested that the balance of power had shifted irretrievably in favor of Rome.

Parthian armies appear to have consisted largely of horse archers and heavy cavalry, and to have been raised with difficulty. The Parthian empire was divided into a number of subsidiary kingdoms whose rulers were ordinarily relatives of the king (Frye 1984: 217–33). It appears that the king depended upon these subsidiary rulers to provide troops when he needed them. Often they seem to have been fractious and disloyal. When content and properly commanded, however, they were not inconsequential.

Seven years after the war with Macrinus, the Parthian regime was swept away by a new dynasty from the province of Fars in southern Iran. Fars was the ancestral home of the ancient Achaemenid kings, and seems to have remained a center for the cult of Ahura Mazda and the Zoroastrian priesthood. The regime that replaced the Arsacids, founded by Ardashir, proved to be vastly more effective in mobilizing its forces, and driven by religious zealotry. Ardashir saw himself as the servant of Ahura Mazda, and his foes as the servants of Ahriman, the embodiment of evil.

The Roman response to the rise of Ardashir was marked by incomprehension and fantasy. Both Cassius Dio and Herodian write of Ardashir as a man who was motivated by the desire to regain the ancient empire of the Achaemenids, a view that is utterly without support in third-century Sasanian texts (Kettenhoffen 1984: 177–90;

Potter 1990: 370–80). At best, the advisors of Severus Alexander may have seen the Sasanian revolution as just one more manifestation of the endemic instability of the Parthian kingdom. As a result they opened the door to refugees from the old regime, supported the Arsacid king of Armenia as a client, and received the Arab city of Hatra as a protectorate. Although Ardashir's primary interest appears to have been to solidify the position of his own extended family as the royal family in the empire – members of the Sasanian clan replaced Arsacids wherever Ardashir could arrange it – Alexander's advisors could not see that by supporting Arsacid survivors they were inviting conflict.

Ardashir began to raid Roman territory almost immediately after he had taken power at Ctesiphon, making Roman armies look plodding and inept. When Alexander launched a massive invasion of his territory in the early 230s, Ardashir drove it back, inflicting heavy casualties. In 235 he captured the cities of Nisibis and Carrhae, giving him control of the easiest invasion route across northern Mesopotamia and effectively ruining the frontier arrangements established by Septimius Severus, who had created a Roman province that extended across northern Mesopotamia to the Tigris (Kettenhoffen 1995: 159–77). In 241, Ardashir destroyed the city of Hatra, and turned over the throne (we do not know whether he died or abdicated) to his son, Sapor I (Potter 1990: 190).

It had been centuries since the Roman state confronted an enemy as deadly and determined as Sapor proved to be. It is arguable that he was a general whose skill was comparable to that of Hannibal, for like Hannibal he seems to have proceeded from a careful study of the Roman way of war, and the disasters that he inflicted on Roman armies were on a par with some of the great catastrophes suffered at the beginning of the Second Punic War. His armies, like those of his father, also possessed a skill at siege warfare that appears to have been absent from the armies of the Parthian kingdom. The record of Sasanian success against places like Hatra (which had withstood a siege by Septimius Severus), Carrhae, and Nisibis is impressive enough; archaeological evidence from Dura Europus reveals that the Sasanians had engineers capable of sophisticated operations including tunneling beneath the walls of cities. This was combined with an ability to move armies with a speed that Roman generals found bewildering. In 244, Sapor, although beaten a year before at Resaina in northern Mesopotamia, managed to defeat the army of Gordian when it advanced down the Euphrates; in 252, aided by a Roman deserter named Mariades, he fell upon a Roman army and destroyed it (Potter 1990: 267–77, 297–8, 300–3). He followed up this victory with a summer-long tour of destruction throughout Syria. In 260 he outmaneuvered Valerian in the vicinity of Edessa (Potter 1990: 331–7). This victory was followed up by another long raiding expedition.

Although the Sasanian kingdom fell into a period of disarray for several decades after Sapor died (Frye 1984: 303–5), it is plain that the new power was categorically different from the one that had preceded it. Rome now had an enemy that it could not ignore. The Sasanians were capable of taking the initiative in their dealings with the empire, and would often be able to dispose more powerful forces. It was not since the early years of the republic that any Roman state had been confronted with an adversary of such power, and it broke the mould in which standard Roman behaviors in dealing with foreign peoples had been formed. Arab traditions reveal that Ardashir and Sapor both took an interest in the tribes of northern Arabia, seeking to bring

Figures 8.1a–j Sapor and his enemies. One of the most obvious differences between Persia and Rome in the mid-third century was the stability of Sapor's regime as compared with the situation in the Roman Empire. This plate depicts Sapor and the emperors of the central government who held power between 241 and 272. (a) Sapor I (Gobl); (b) Gordian III (*RIC* Gordian III n.5); (c) Philip I (*RIC* Philip 44b); (d) Decius (*RIC* Decius 29c); (e) Trebonianus Gallus (*RIC* Gallus 69); (f) Aemilianus (*RIC* Aemilianus 6); (g) Valerian (*RIC* Valerian 46); (h) Gallienus (*RIC* Gallienus 192a); (i) Claudius II (*RIC* Claudius II n. 32); (j) Aurelian (*RIC* Aurelian 381). (Figure 8.1a courtesy of CNG; all other coins from the editor's collection)

them within the Sasanian orbit (Bowersock 1983: 132). We do not know how significant an innovation this was, but the evidence for Palmyrene trade through the Persian Gulf state of Mesene (usually a part of the Parthian kingdom) suggests that the Palmyrenes had built up a substantial military force of their own to control these tribes, and that this dominance was challenged by the new regime. Likewise, the establishment of a member of the Sasanian royal family (a far more close-knit group, at least in the early period, than the Arsacid clan had been) in Mesene brought that region much more closely under the control of Ctesiphon. There is some reason to think that, in the course of the 250s, after Sapor's victory and subsequent sack of Antioch, the shift in the balance of power in the desert began to have a very negative impact on Palmyra. Such a shift might explain why the power of Palmyra, invisible at the time of Sapor's first invasion in 252, became a significant factor during the immediate aftermath of the campaign of 260 (Hartmann 2001: 76–86).

In addition to changing the military and diplomatic balance of power, the Sasanian dynasty had a significant impact on the flow of ideas. Sapor appears to have been something of a proselyte for the wisdom of Zoroaster. It was under Ardashir that an official edition of the ancient *Gathas* of Zoroaster was assembled, and we know that Sapor actively promoted the cult in the lands that he conquered. It was under Sapor that the career of Kartīr, who occupied a preeminent position in the religious structure of the state after Sapor's death, got its start.

Devoted though they were to the wisdom of Zoroaster, neither Ardashir nor Sapor appear to have been religious bigots. It was in the time of Ardashir that one of the most remarkable religious movements of the third century began. This was the faith founded by the prophet Mani, whose revelation combined various forms of indigenous eastern thought with a peculiar brand of Christianity. Although he was executed as a result of the machinations of Kartīr in the reign of Bahram II, Mani had been received by Sapor, and made extensive contacts in the Sasanian court.

Mani traveled widely throughout the Persian Empire, and once visited India, but he does not seem to have visited the territory of Rome himself. His missionaries did, possibly following the trade routes between India and the west. There is a tradition that Zenobia received them at Palmyra, and they seem to have reached Egypt in the course of the 260s (Gardiner and Lieu 1996: 153). They were to have a significant impact during later centuries both on the intellectual life of the Roman world and in central Asia. Another sign of the increasing importance of traditions that emerged in the Persian Empire might also be the peculiar decoration of a late-third- or early fourth-century Mithraeum, found near Apamaea in Syria, which, by way of contrast with Mithraea in the west, is decorated in a distinctively Persian style (Gawlikowsky 2000). Yet another result of the diffusion of ideas from the Persian Empire westward would be an increasing tendency as the third century turned into the fourth to regard such wisdom as dangerous to "true" Roman thought. Diocletian would order the burning of Manichaean books, and Constantine would later attempt to preach the virtues of Christian doctrine to Sapor II (Corcoran 2000: 135–6; T. D. Barnes 1985: 130–2). In the course of the fourth century, with the rise of Christianity within the Roman Empire, the struggle between the two powers would include a definite undercurrent of religious hostility. This need not be seen simply as a result of the exclusivity of Christian doctrine (well matched by that of Zoroastrianism). It may also be seen as a sign that, while the Roman state might not be bothered by views emanating from peoples thought to be weaker, it was less welcoming once those peoples were seen to be its political equals.

4 Alternatives to Rome

If the dynastic principle was central to the conception of power in the empire, the persistent failure of emperors to establish dynasties, taken with the root cause of that failure – the instability of power and the inability to control the frontiers – undermined the imperial ideal (see the discussion in Peachin's chapter). For centuries Roman provincial government had been based on the notion that each city within a province would negotiate its status individually with the ruling power, with the result that each province was a sort of administrative quilt (Ando, this volume). If anything, this process was accelerated in the course of the third century as the rapid turnover of emperors gave cities a chance to negotiate favors for themselves at the expense of their rivals (Ziegler 1985). The value of the rewards gained under one emperor was called into question if he did not last; links established with a dynasty that passed away were no links at all. So too might military failure undermine any favors that Rome had provided. It did a city like Palmyra little good to have been recognized as a *colonia* by Septimius Severus if the Roman state could not help it maintain its control of the desert. Cologne could, perhaps, still celebrate its foundation as a *colonia* in honor of Nero's mother, but that did it little good if the reigning emperor could not prevent the Alamanni from crossing the Rhine and ravaging its territories. In the middle of the third century we suddenly begin to see efforts at self-help. A provincial militia is mentioned on an inscription from Augsburg. At Emesa in 253 a local aristocrat named Uranius Antoninus had repulsed some Persian raiders; we do not know if he is the same person as the unnamed "hero" who called upon a local god to repel the enemy at a place called Qal'at al-Halwys in the same period (*AÉ* 1993 no. 1231; *IGLS* 1799, with Baldus 1971: 250–2). In 268 we are told that the cities of Greece assembled an army to repel Gothic invaders from the sea who sacked Athens despite the best efforts of its citizens (who evidently rallied in the countryside and inflicted some sort of reverse on their enemies). The efforts of the larger Greek contingent are reflected in an inscription honoring a man from Gytheion in Laconia saying, "they fought in the front rank of the Greeks, they repulsed the enemies of the Athenians with our ships and our infantry, we died at sea under the swords of the barbarians. My brother prepared this tomb for me. I am Epaphrys, I lived twice ten years and twice six years" (*IG* 5.1 n. 1188). In cities where walls had not been maintained, they were repaired, and we are told that in the absence of Roman garrisons, the citizens were forced to defend themselves (Mitchell 1993: 1: 235–6).

The principal benefits of Roman rule were political stability and peace; when Rome could no longer guarantee either, it was up to the inhabitants of the provinces to defend themselves. There was a series of revolts against the power of the central government in the immediate aftermath of Valerian's debacle, and there had been quite a few in the decade before he had taken the throne. Few of these revolts involved direct threats to the emperor – to have such ambitions one needed to be a member of the establishment. Many of these revolts seem to be protests against imperial inefficiency, against the failure of emperors to maintain the implicit contract that they had with their subjects. The local governing classes of the empire would return loyalty for security.

In the wake of the first Persian raids into Mesopotamia under Ardashir, we hear that the garrison of Mesopotamia murdered its governor, and at least one more mutiny occurred when Alexander came east (Dio 80.3.4; Herod. 6.4.7). His movements were slow, and it may well be that the troops felt that they had been needlessly exposed to danger – a view that was evidently current amongst the troops brought east from the northern frontiers, who felt that their families were imperiled by their service in the east. In addition to the mutinies, there is also record of two "usurpers" in the east who are unconnected with the legions (Potter 1990: 20 n. 55). They may be seen as local notables undertaking local defense. This model certainly fits the case of Uranius Antoninus of Emesa, mentioned above, as well as the Palmyrene response to Sapor's invasion in 260. In addition to these people, we know, albeit only from coins, of two men with Celtic names in the west, and of two more men in the east, Jotopianus and Mariades, who led insurrections in Syria under Philip and Decius. Jotopianus may have been engaging in some sort of protest (Potter 1990: 39–40). Mariades seems to have been a highly successful brigand with connections in the ruling class of Syria. He is said to have had supporters who betrayed Antioch to Sapor in 252 (*FHG* 4.192 F. 1). Breakdowns in imperial control of this sort would continue into the 270s: we have evidence, both from literary and archaeological sources, of a revolt in Cilicia, as well as record of a civil war in Lower Egypt, in which one group in the province called in the Blemmyes, a Nubian tribe, to attack Coptos (Mitchell 1995: 177–217; Zos. 1.69.1–71.1).

The less well attested disorders of the period provide a background for the two most serious insurrections of the 260s and 270s, those of the so-called *imperium Galliarum* and of Palmyra. The Palmyrene insurrection needs to be seen as a two-phase operation. In the first phase, Odaenathus, the leading man of Palmyra, and commander of the local army, allied with two rebels from within the imperial command structure, Macrianus and Callistus, who had rallied the remnants of imperial forces after the capture of Valerian. Odaenathus joined with these men in their resistance to Sapor, but, when they failed in an attempt to overthrow Gallienus, Odaenathus betrayed his former allies. Gallienus then brought Odaenathus within the imperial command structure in the east by awarding him the title of *corrector totius orientis*, which gave him the right to command Roman troops (Potter 1996a). Gallienus retained the authority to appoint governors to the eastern provinces, a reasonable solution from the Palmyrene point of view, as there is no reason to think that Palmyra possessed the people with the experience necessary to take up these responsibilities. The stability of this arrangement is reflected by the fact that Odaenathus chose Antioch as the site for the celebration of his subsequent victories over Sapor and the elevation of his eldest son to the position of King of Kings, a title that Odaenathus also claimed for himself (Schlumberger 1942–3: 36–50). An extraordinary lead token discovered at Antioch depicts Odaenathus' son wearing a crown modeled on that of an Arsacid king (Seyrig 1963: 159–72). The combination of the title and the physical representation reveal that Odaenathus perceived himself as the defender of the region against the Sasanians, and as the rival of Sapor. He felt that there was no contradiction between his title and his position within the government. Odaenathus' desire was evidently to control the border region, and, possibly, to reverse the Sasanian control over the desert tribes. He was a figure deeply embedded in the power politics of his region in which Rome was but one of a number of players.

Events in the west during the 260s had numerous parallels to those in the east. The revolt of Postumus, who would establish the *imperium Galliarum*, seems to have broken out as a result of a dispute over property recaptured from the Alamanni. Gallienus' personal representatives in the region, his young son Saloninus and the praetorian prefect who was "advising" him, demanded full restitution of booty to the provincials (Zos. 1.38.2). This Postumus, possibly driven by the interests of his troops, refused to do. Instead he attacked Cologne, where Saloninus and the prefect resided, killing both. In the summer of 260, when these events took place, it must have appeared likely that Gallienus himself had little time left (König 1981: 43–57; Christol and Loriot 1997: 223–7). The authority of his regime had been shattered by the capture of his father, and he was faced not only with the emergent regime of Macrianus in the east, but also with a pair of revolts in the Balkans. That he survived these challenges is a reflection of the self-interest of the officer corps that supported him.

The murder of Saloninus made it impossible for Gallienus to make any arrangement with Postumus, whose revolt could not be ameliorated as had the earlier rebellion of Odaenathus by any signal service. Still, although he won the support of the garrisons of Spain and Britain, Postumus would make no serious effort to invade Italy. Instead, he built a regime that appears to have been largely based upon the loyalty of the Gallic aristocracy (König 1981: 102–11). He secured the support of that group by concentrating his efforts on protecting the Rhine frontier. An invasion by Gallienus failed when Gallienus was wounded, and a rough equilibrium set in. Postumus ruled his part of the empire, while Gallienus maintained direct control over Italy, Africa, Egypt, the Balkans, and Asia Minor, keeping the peace on the eastern frontier through the agency of Odaenathus. In theory, the combined power of the eastern and central provinces should have been sufficient to crush the *imperium Galliarum*. This would not be the case, however; Gallienus had to allow Odaenathus to look after his own interests. Instead of sending troops west, Odaenathus conducted a series of successful actions against the Persians. At this point it is no longer reasonable to think of a single Roman Empire. It is preferable to see the administration of territory that had once formed the unified empire as having broken down into three parts, each one defined by the need to counter specific threats with its own local power structure: the Gallic empire controlled the Rhine frontier; the regime of Claudius II, who succeeded Gallienus in 268, had the Danube as its primary area of interest; and that of Palmyra held the east. These geopolitical facts might be disguised by later regime changes, but they remain at the heart of later restructurings of imperial power into the fifth century. The Roman Empire could no longer control the frontiers with a unified administrative structure based at Rome.

5 Emperors from the Danubian Provinces

It would be hard to overemphasize the importance of the division of the empire in the 260s for the course of later Roman dynastic history. While it was by no means obvious that the regime that would succeed in reuniting the disparate parts of the empire would emerge from the staff of Gallienus, the fact of the matter was that it did. In early 268 there was every reason to think that Gallienus' empire was on the verge of collapse. Aureolus, his most successful general, based at Milan, suddenly declared his allegiance to Postumus. In the summer of the same year, large raiding parties from north of the Danube once again began to penetrate the frontiers of the empire. In the early 250s they had discovered that Rome's naval defenses were weak; large fleets had ravaged the coast of Asia Minor in 252 and 258. A new fleet was assembled in the course of 268, while, at the same time, other forces crossed the Danube (Potter 2004: 263–4). In the east, Odaenathus was murdered during the spring of 268, and his widow, Zenobia, claimed his position for her son, Vaballathus (the elder son of Odaenathus who had shared his title had either predeceased his father or been killed with him) (Potter 2004: 263).

It was then that fortune intervened, albeit briefly, on the side of Gallienus. Postumus was murdered at Cologne, and the *imperium Galliarum* plunged into chaos for the rest of the year (Drinkwater 1987: 33–4; König 1981: 132–40). Freed from the threat of an invasion from the north, and abandoning the Danubian provinces to their fate, Gallienus concentrated his efforts on Aureolus, only to fall victim himself to a military conspiracy in August. The general staff arrogated to itself the power to make an emperor, arranging the proclamation of Marcus Aurelius Claudius. Claudius defeated Aureolus, and, in the course of the next year, succeeded in defeating the raiders in the Balkans at a battle fought at Naissus, the modern city of Niš in Serbia. He was less successful in his other endeavors, failing to support the city of Autun, which had revolted against Victorinus, who emerged as the new Gallic emperor by the end of 268, and provoking war with Zenobia. The Palmyrenes defeated an army sent from the west, while also invading the provinces of Arabia and Egypt. Despite the open conflict, the Palmyrenes still seem to have hoped for an ultimate resolution to their dispute with the central government that would be peaceful. Papyri reveal that senior officials of Claudius retained their jobs, a continuation of Palmyrene reliance upon experienced administrators for provincial administration (Potter 2004: 270–1). Hopes for peace may have been enhanced by the fact that Claudius died on campaign in the Balkans very shortly after the Palmyrene offensive, and his successor, Aurelian, was beset by dangerous invasions of Italy as well as a serious revolt in Rome itself.

When Claudius died in the course of 270, the general staff ignored his evident wish to be succeeded by his brother, Quintillus, and selected Marcus Aurelius Aurelianus as its emperor. Surviving serious threats to his own security in the course of the 270, Aurelianus, or Aurelian as he is commonly known, set about forging an alliance between the Balkan generals who dominated the high command and the traditional Italian aristocracy. There is a story, reported by the late fourth-century historian, Aurelius Victor, that Gallienus had issued an edict banning senators from military commands (Christol 1986: 45–54). The story is false, but it does reflect an important development. Men of equestrian background had been replacing senators in many major military and provincial commands, had dominated the government in the 240s, and, as the careers of Macrinus, Maximinus, and Philip show, had been able to take the throne themselves. What the story about the so-called reform of Gallienus reflects is that after Gallienus, only one man rose from the Senate to the palace. That men from the Balkans dominated military commands in the 270s is simply a result of the fact that the bulk of the army under Gallienus was from the Balkans, and these men carried through important reforms in the structure of the army: the creation of a central cavalry reserve (initially commanded by Aureolus), and the evident regularization of staff positions reflected in the newly significant title of *protector* (Christol 1977: 393–404). The cavalry corps may have been joined by some infantry formations to form the *comitatus*, which would accompany the emperor on campaign. The creation of the *comitatus* is important because it represents a clean break with the old legionary organization of the army, and, while units called legions would remain, they would be much reduced in size. This reform would seem to have made it easier to integrate different tactical units on the battlefield. The army of the later third and early fourth centuries would be a more effective force than the army of the age of Severus.

After ensuring the security of Italy in 270, Aurelian set about the reunification of the empire, bringing first Palmyra, and then the *imperium Galliarum* under his control. Despite the later tradition that he was a harsh man, given to acts of extreme brutality, it appears that Aurelian was in fact a remarkably diplomatic and mild conqueror. Officials who had served under the Palmyrenes in Egypt are known to have retained their positions, which may explain why the initial reconquest of that province appears to have passed without bloodshed (*P.Oxy.* 2612). Elsewhere we know of at least one official of the *imperium Galliarum* who continued his career, while the last emperor of that regime, Tetricus, who surrendered, also received an official position (König 1981: 181). Zenobia of Palmyra, who appears still to have been a young woman at the time that she was captured, was taken to Rome where she remarried (Milik 1972: 320). Her descendants are attested at Rome in the late fourth century. A contemporary historian, Dexippus, who wrote a history of the wars with the northern tribes (as well as at least two other historical works), appears as well to have stressed Aurelian's diplomatic abilities (*FGrH* 100 F. 6–7). One other notable feature of the reconquest was the decision, early on, to abandon the province of Dacia as indefensible (Tausend 1999: 126–7).

Aurelian failed, however, to address many structural problems, and his decision in 274 to reform the imperial silver coinage was a disaster (Howgego 1995: 126; Harl 1996: 145–8). Despite the well documented decline in the silver content of the imperial coinage throughout the third century, the notional relationship of the silver and gold coinage had been preserved, preventing significant inflation. Aurelian's decision to issue a new style of coinage, changing the relationship, caused immediate and rampant inflation. The coinage reform was followed – though we have no evidence that there was a connection – by the formation of a conspiracy against Aurelian in the general staff. He was murdered early in 275 near Perinthus.

Aurelian had made no dynastic provision, and it appears that the general staff was deeply divided over the question of both the succession and the fate of the conspirators, who were allowed to escape. After some delay (though not the six-month interregnum created by later historians) an elderly senator named Marcus Aurelius Tacitus was proclaimed emperor (Syme 1971a: 243). Unable to heal the rifts in the general staff, he was assassinated within a year by the same group that was responsible for the assassination of Aurelian. After a brief civil war in which Tacitus' brother, Florian, was incapable of holding the throne against the challenge of Marcus Aurelius Probus, some order was restored when Probus took stern action against the party of the assassins – it is said that he summoned them to a banquet and had them killed (Zos. 1.65.1–2; Sauer 1998).

Although he had reunited the empire, Aurelian had not found a way to ensure the loyalty of either provincial officials or provincial aristocracies to the regime; these problems may have been exacerbated by the chaos that followed his death. The reign of Probus (276–82) is largely a tale of revolts by officials (there were at least four uprisings prior to the successful revolt led by the praetorian prefect, Carus, which ended Probus' reign) and major unrest in the provinces. Despite his ability to suppress these revolts, Probus failed to respond proactively to the root causes of unrest. This would be the accomplishment of yet another man from the Danubian provinces, the emperor Diocletian, who took power from Carus' son, Carinus, in 285.

6 The Tetrarchy

Succession and security remained the principal factors governing imperial policy under Diocletian and his successors. Once Diocletian determined that he could only survive by establishing regimes loyal to himself in different parts of the empire, the empire for most intents and purposes ceased to be a single entity. There would be a sole emperor for only 13 years between 285, when Diocletian appointed Maximian, a man related to him by neither blood nor marriage, as his deputy emperor, or Caesar, and the death of Constantine in 337: this was the sole reign of Constantine after 324. After Constantine, there were brief periods when there were not multiple holders of the title Augustus: the sole reigns of Constantius II from 353 to 360 (ending when Julian, his nephew and Caesar, rebelled), the reigns of Julian and Jovian from 361 to 364, and the last months of Theodosius in 395. Even this is deceptive, for Constantius appointed Julian as his Caesar in 354 precisely because he felt that he needed a family member to carry the banner of his regime in Gaul while he was busy elsewhere; and Constantine had elevated his sons to the rank of Caesar well before 324, giving them ever more responsibility as time passed. Indeed in the years immediately prior to his death, Constantine appears to have envisioned a sort of return to the Diocletianic system, with no fewer than five Augusti ruling concurrently once he died. In 334 he elevated his nephew Dalmatius to the rank of Caesar with responsibility for the Balkans, while of his sons, Constantine II administered Western Europe, Constans took Italy, some portion of the Balkans and Africa, and Constantius II held the east. Another nephew, Hannibalianus, was designated King of Armenia with the view that he would rule whatever portion of the Persian Empire Constantine could conquer in the war that he planned in the last years of his life (T. D. Barnes 1985: 132).

What is perhaps most interesting about Constantine's plan is that it was biologically unnecessary. With three sons, he could simply have divided the empire three ways. He seems, however, to have felt that it would be better not to do this, and the best explanation is that he felt that a tripartite division of power would not be successful (in this view he was proved correct).

What differentiated Constantine's plan from that of Diocletian is that Constantine decided that blood relationship was a prerequisite for membership in the imperial college; Diocletian, at least initially, had decided that proven ability should govern membership in the college, though it would appear that he changed his mind on this point on more than one occasion. His system of government was very much the work of trial and error (for details, see Elton, this volume). There is no reason to think that when he appointed Maximian Caesar, he envisioned that he would soon make him Augustus. But the situation in the west was complicated – there would be a revolt in Gaul soon after he left Maximian in Italy, and it is likely that he felt that Maximian needed the authority conferred by the title Augustus to deal with his subordinates. When he raised Maximian to the rank of Augustus he also took the title Jovius for himself, giving Maximian the title Herculius (Nixon and Rodgers 1994: 44–5). The divine names were selected to make clear the ranking of the two men: Diocletian was senior, Maximian was junior.

In the early 290s it may have become clear that two emperors were insufficient. In 286 a general on the Rhine, Carausius, had rebelled against Maximian, and Maximian was having grave difficulties bringing the revolt to an end (Casey 1994: 42–3). At the same time Diocletian appears to have been devoting himself to the Danubian frontier. He journeyed only once to the east, and he may have sensed that here, too, the imperial authority was under-represented. In late 290 or early 291, after what appears to have been a catastrophic failure on the part of Maximian in the war with Carausius, Diocletian met with his colleague at Milan (T. D. Barnes 1982: 52). It may have been then that they decided that they would appoint two Caesars, when circumstances made it possible. In 293, Maximian scored a major triumph over Carausius, driving him from the mainland. The man responsible for this victory was his son-in-law, Constantius. On March 1, 293 Constantius was made Caesar; either on the same day, or in May, Diocletian proclaimed Maximianus Galerius, who married his daughter, Valeria, Caesar as well (T. D. Barnes 1982: 62 n. 73; Kolb 1987: 73).

There were many idioms through which the new college of emperors could be presented to their subjects. On the remodeled coinage that was introduced as they were in 293, they tend to look rather alike, men with beards and close-cropped hair. On the famous porphyry statue group built into the Cathedral of St. Mark at Venice, the two Caesars are distinguishable from the two Augusti because they have less full beards, suggestive of their "youth" (neither was a young man). Most spectacularly, we now have a group of mosaics from the palace that Galerius constructed as his retirement home at Romuliana in what is now Serbia. Here is perhaps the most nuanced view, as befits one who had a stake in the system. Each of the tetrarchs has a distinctive appearance (Srejović 1994: 143–52).

The wisdom of Diocletian's action was revealed a few years later. A poet who most likely wrote in Egypt at the end of the decade offers a very interesting picture of the tetrarchic regime. The event that inspired his poem was Galerius' victory over the Persian king, Narses, in 297. In describing the outbreak of the war he says:

> Other kings would have rushed to his aid from Italy, if Iberian Ares had not restrained one, and the din of battle on the island of Britain had not flared up around another. Just as one god comes from Crete, another from sea-girt Delos – they are Zeus over Mount Othrys and Apollo to Pangaion – the throng of Giants trembles as they put on their armor: so did the elder king, bringing an army of Ausonians come east together with the younger king. (*Sel. Pap.* 135)

Aside from the war with Persia the events mentioned here are Constantius' victorious campaign in Britain, which ended the revolt of Carausius (who was murdered by his own men just before the end and replaced by a man named Allectus), and a revolt in Spain, for which this text is our sole evidence. Diocletian in fact played no direct role in the Persian war, leaving the command to Galerius, who suffered a serious defeat near Carrhae in 296 before advancing through Armenia in the following year to win a decisive victory. Even as Galerius advanced, Diocletian was called away to Egypt to suppress a revolt. The series of victories won by the four members of the college finally solidified the control of the empire, and, for a time at least, of the eastern frontier. According to the terms of the treaty imposed upon the Persians, five provinces were added to the empire in the east that enabled Rome to control potential invasion routes through Northern Mesopotamia and Armenia (Winter 1988: 171–82). In Egypt, Diocletian followed up his victory with a campaign into the Sudan against the Blemmyes. Constantius returned from Britain to Trier, which, in effect, became his capital. Maximian moved on from suppressing the revolt in Spain to campaign against nomadic tribes in North Africa from 297 to 298. After a brief stop at Rome in 299, it appears that he intended to make Milan his capital. Diocletian's principal palace would be at Nicomedia in Bithynia, and Galerius would establish himself at Sirmium, close to the Danube frontier.

In the wake of the great successes won by himself and his colleagues, Diocletian would increasingly turn his attention to the reorganization of the empire. His policies included re-tariffing the new coinage that he had introduced in 293, an effort to regulate prices throughout the empire, and a persecution of the Christians. These followed a series of earlier reforms: in addition to the aforementioned reform of the coinage, there was a regularization of the tax system of the empire, probably in 296 (and quite possibly the cause of the revolts that broke out at that time), and an effort to codify Roman law (Corcoran 2000: 25–42). Diocletian also appears to have supported a scheme for the continuation of the collegial system that would involve his retirement, along, ultimately, with that of Maximian, the promotion of the Caesars to the rank of Augustus, and their replacement by two new Caesars: Constantius' eldest son, Constantine, who had served on Diocletian's staff in the 290s, and Maximian's son, Maxentius, who married Galerius' daughter.

Shortly after 300 something seems to have changed. The image of the tetrarchy that Galerius portrayed in his palace had perhaps some unfortunate consequences for himself. If the Augusti retired in the order in which they had entered power, he would be left as Caesar, while Constantius would become the colleague of Maximian. It does not appear to have been until 303 that Diocletian decided that this could not happen, for in that year he went to Rome for perhaps only the second time in his life, to celebrate the twentieth anniversary of his joint accession with Maximian: the count of Maximian's regnal years was suddenly changed to make it equal with that of Diocletian's (Chastagnol 1967). Maximian, willingly or no, swore an oath to Diocletian that he would step down at the exact same time as his colleague. Diocletian's decision that it was time to retire may have been inspired by a serious illness that began while he was in Rome. It may also have been at this same time that he decided that Constantine and Maxentius would not succeed to the position of Caesar. Sources hostile to Galerius (none have survived that would tell his side of the story) assert that he forced Diocletian to make these decisions. We will never know the truth; the one thing that does seem true is that, although Diocletian had long since decided upon abdication, and had had a retirement palace built for himself at Split (in modern Croatia), he put off a final decision as to whether to endorse the notion of biological succession to the very end. His decision against it would ruin the system of government that he tried to introduce. The two new Caesars, Severus and Maximinus Daia, were seen as too closely aligned with Galerius.

The retirement of Diocletian and Maximian on May 1, 305 precipitated a crisis. Constantius demanded that Galerius send him Constantine, who was serving under Galerius in the Balkans, while Maxentius took up residence outside of Rome (we have no way of knowing when he did this). Constantius may have sensed that his own health was failing, and he was determined that his own son would succeed him. In the summer of 306, if not before, Constantine joined his father for a campaign in Britain. When Constantius died on July 25 at York, the stage was set for the proclamation of Constantine as Caesar. Galerius, who may well have expected the move, acquiesced (Potter 2004: 346). What he could not tolerate was the revolt at Rome in October, by which Maxentius, with the aid of his father Maximian, proclaimed Augustus once again, claimed a place in the imperial college for himself as a *princeps*.

Maximian remained a powerful figure, and his own discontent with the settlement imposed by Diocletian is manifest in his subsequent conduct. He appears to have been popular with the army that he had led for many years, so that when Severus attempted to lead it against Rome, it deserted. Severus was taken captive and placed under house arrest. Maximian then traveled to Gaul in the company of his very young daughter, Fausta, whom he would marry to Constantine, whose wife, Minervina, had died after bearing him a son (T. D. Barnes 1982: 42–3). Maximian stood as a champion of biological succession against the collegial model promoted by Galerius and Diocletian. What is perhaps most interesting about this is that, after realizing that he lacked the military force to overthrow Maximian and Maxentius in 307, Galerius was willing to negotiate. Indeed, throughout the rest of his reign, Galerius appears to have tried his best to keep the peace. Although he would not recognize Maxentius, and could not after Maxentius murdered Severus and styled himself Augustus, he was willing to negotiate with both Constantine and Maximian. In 308, after Maxentius quarreled with Maximian and forced him to flee Italy, Galerius hosted a meeting, which included Diocletian, who had assumed the consulship, at Carnuntum. Maximian agreed to retire once more, going to live with Constantine in Gaul, while Galerius elevated Licinius, said to be a close friend, to the rank of Augustus to replace Severus. Constantine and Maximin Daia remained Caesars. Maxentius was not accorded recognition in the imperial college.

The settlement of Carnuntum assured the peace of the empire until Galerius' death in 311. As Maximian had either been killed or committed suicide after a failed revolt against Constantine in 310, the old generation had now passed away. The new generation was not interested in peace; each of the emperors now wished to rule at least half of the empire himself. The man with the most obvious difficulty in reaching this goal was Licinius, who found himself between two hostile powers, Maximin and Maxentius. He sought an alliance with Constantine, who could scarcely refuse, since the failure of Licinius would result in his having to face an overwhelming force in the aftermath. In the end it would be Constantine who struck first.

Constantine's campaign in 312 is a moment of world historical significance. Constantine would have been only too aware that both Severus and Galerius had failed dismally in their attempts on Rome. In each case failure ensued when the campaign bogged down in siege operations or their prospect – Severus' army had deserted on the way to Rome, and Galerius had not even attempted to besiege the city. Constantine, who seems to have had a strong sense that a god was helping him, even if he was not sure which one, appears in the period leading up to the campaign to have decided that the Christian God would be the one who could help him. No rational political calculation could have influenced Constantine. He had previously claimed a special relationship with Apollo in his guise as a sun god, and he would continue to advertise that connection long after he was identifying himself as Christian to Christians. Indeed, it seems to have taken him some time to move from a henotheistic understanding of the Christian God as the "highest God," to the monotheistic understanding that is enshrined in the best-known religious document of the period, the Nicene Creed of 325. We will probably never know why he decided that the Christian God, whom he plainly did not understand very well at this point in his life, would be his protector. The fact, however, that he did take this position would result in the transformation of the Christian Church from a fringe group within the empire to a religion that would shape human understanding, for good or ill, in the centuries to come.

Once he had decided upon his protector, Constantine moved his army with exemplary speed, drawing a series of armies that had been sent by Maxentius to northern Italy into open battle. He was able to destroy them, and captured cities that resisted by storm. He reached Rome by October, and it is quite possible that his success had so demoralized the opposition that Maxentius felt that he had to risk an open battle, even under deeply unfavorable conditions (with the river Tiber at his back). The destruction of Maxentius' last army, and the death of Maxentius himself in battle, made Constantine ruler of half the empire. In February, 313, he met Licinius at Milan; the alliance between the two was there strengthened by Licinius' marriage to Constantine's half-sister, Constantia.

In the spring of 313, Maximinus invaded the territory of Licinius. The result was spectacular military failure: Maximinus committed suicide at Tarsus in July. Peace between Constantine and Licinius did not, however, last long. They were at war in 316–17, with Constantine winning a limited strategic victory to back up further spectacular successes on the battlefield by the spring. Although Licinius retained most of his portion of the empire, Constantine gained a solid foothold in the Balkans as a result of the peace treaty. In 324, he exploited his advanced positions by launching another invasion of Licinius' territory. Heavily defeated, Licinius retreated to Nicomedia, where he surrendered to Constantine in the autumn. Licinius was allowed to retire to Thessalonica, where Constantine had him murdered on what may have been bogus charges of conspiracy less than a year later.

7 Constantine

Aside from the ongoing establishment of Christianity as a favored religion in the empire, a process which had begun with an edict of restoration issued in 313 by Constantine and Licinius at their meeting in Milan, the most important development of the reign of Constantine was the foundation of a new imperial capital at the ancient site of Byzantium. This decision, taken very shortly after the defeat of Licinius, was one feature of a period of intense activity that included the integration of Licinius' government within the structure of Constantine's (the process is partially reflected in a series of legal texts) that may be seen as paralleling Constantine's effort to integrate the eastern and western churches.

Constantine had reason to be worried about the unity of the church, and his first effort at resolving controversy within the church – connected with a serious division in the North African provinces – had not been a success (Elton, this volume). Nevertheless, he still seems to have believed that his preferred method of dealing with controversy through church councils was the right one (Drake 2000: 225–7). When one faction, taking its name from the schismatic bishop Donatus of Carthage, refused to accede to the orders of repeated councils, Constantine had briefly issued a persecution edict. He soon thought better of it, and abandoned direct intervention in North African affairs. In the east, he soon learned that there was a serious dispute about the nature of the Trinity. The essence of the dispute was whether the Son was a creation of the Father or not. The view that the Son was in some way subordinate seems to have been the majority view, and even seems to have been in accord with Constantine's own thinking prior to the council that he summoned at Nicaea in 325. There, for reasons that will ever remain obscure, he brokered a deal by which the council agreed to a formulation, the famous Nicene Creed, which declared the equality of Father and Son (Kelly 1977: 231–7). Since Constantine seems at this point to have viewed the Christian God as a sort of divine equivalent of the Roman emperor, it is a remarkable development, and one at odds with the subordinationist theology he had previously espoused when he had claimed that Licinius was a disobedient junior Augustus who deserved to be chastised (Corcoran 1993: 99). In some sense Constantine's change of heart may best be explained by the arrangements that he appears to have set in motion with respect to the succession, for he would place all the Caesars on an equal level with each other. Collegial government on earth was perhaps easier to envision if there was also to be collegial government in heaven.

The foundation of Constantinople, and the shift of the center of power from west to east, was complicated, and perhaps enhanced, by a domestic tragedy. In 326, Constantine suddenly ordered the execution of his eldest son, Crispus, who had been based at Trier for most of the preceding decade. Crispus had returned to the west after the victory, and we simply do not know what went wrong. A later account, deeply hostile to Constantine, reports that his wife, Fausta, claimed that Crispus had made sexual advances to her. When his mother, Helena, revealed Fausta's deception, Constantine is then said to have ordered that Fausta be smothered in an overheated bathhouse (Zos. 2.29.1–3). There is no reason to believe any of this: other sources separate the demise of Crispus from that of Fausta, and one tradition places the death of Fausta several years after that of Crispus (Jer. *Chron. s.a.* 328; Potter 2004: 380–1). In the wake of Crispus' death and what is probably best seen as the enforced retirement of Fausta, there could now be only one center of power, and that would be wherever Constantine chose to reside (for details see Elton's chapter in this volume).

In the end, Constantine's dynastic policy, as we have seen, looks very much like a reprise of Diocletian's model of succession. In terms of his administration of the

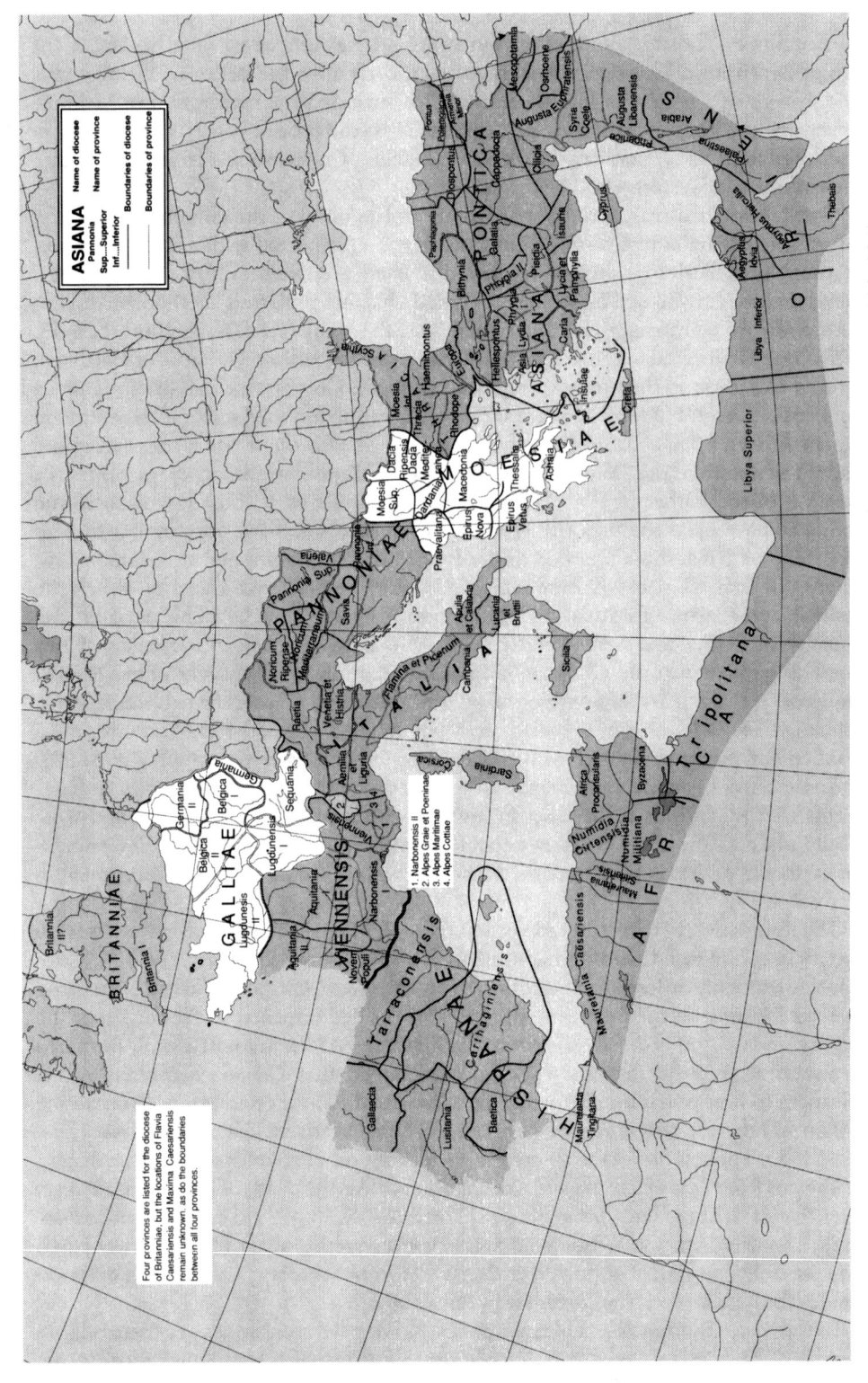

Map 2 Dioceses and provinces of the Roman Empire according to the Verona List (c. AD 303–324)

empire, as Hugh Elton shows in his chapter, it is probably best to see the whole period from 285 to 337 as a unity, with one major change being the role of Christianity, although Constantine did not compel subjects who were disinclined to convert to do so. In terms of dealings with foreign peoples, the early fourth century offers a superficial parallel to the late second in that the empire was again able to dominate the frontiers. Events in the rest of the century would reveal that this was not really the case – both Diocletian and Constantine benefited from the temporary weakness of the Sasanian dynasty. What is perhaps most significant, broadly speaking, is that the aims of the Roman state remain very little changed at the end of the period in question. Beneath the surface, however, as would become clear in the course of the next hundred years, these aims became impossible to maintain.

PART III

Administration

CHAPTER NINE

The Administration of the Provinces

Clifford Ando

1 Introduction

The forty-fifth book of Livy's *History* narrates the collapse of the Hellenistic kingdoms as autonomous powers. One sequence of events has particular relevance here. In 179 BCE, Perseus of Macedon came to power. He was the elder son of Philip V, who had sought unsuccessfully throughout his reign to thwart Rome's growing influence and increasing interference in peninsular Greece. Perseus himself accepted war with Rome as the price of his independence in 171 and lost it by 168 BCE (Derow 1989: 303–19). The Roman Senate dispatched ten commissioners to advise Lucius Aemilius Paullus, the victor over Perseus, on the organization of Macedonia. Paullus invited ten citizens of each city in Macedon to present themselves at Amphipolis to hear the results of his deliberations. A herald ordered those assembled to be silent. Paullus, who was completely bilingual, then delivered his judgment in Latin while seated in his curule chair, his lictors and attendants in array before him; the praetor Gnaeus Octavius translated his pronouncements into Greek.

Paullus and the Roman Senate ordered the Macedonians to be free, to keep their cities and territories, to use their own laws and elect their own magistrates. They were, however, henceforth to pay a tax to Rome. Macedonia was to be divided into four districts; the boundaries of these districts deliberately cut across natural boundaries formed by rivers and mountains. Four cities were designated capitals of these districts; there each district was ordered to organize a council. Intermarriage and transactions in real estate between districts were forbidden; gold and silver mines were not to be worked; the Macedonians were not to cut timber for ships or import salt. Cities whose borders were threatened by barbarians were permitted to retain armed guards; presumably, all other cities were disarmed (Livy 45.29). Paullus followed the recitation of this *formula Macedoniae*, or "schedule" for Macedonia, by delivering *leges*, laws: but what Livy in fact narrates is an extraordinary series of decisions by which the governance of individual cities and the regional councils was handed over to pro-Roman forces, while anti-Roman aristocrats were ordered to take themselves and their sons to Italy, there to dwell in exile (Livy 45.31–2). The Macedonians accepted their freedom with mixed feelings: to those whose business dealings were disrupted it seemed as though Macedonia had been torn asunder, "like an animal being dismembered limb by limb." "To such an extent were even the Macedonians ignorant how great Macedonia was, how easily it might be divided, and how self-sufficient each part could be" (Livy 45.30.1–2).

The paradoxical freedom of the Macedonians came to an end in 146 BCE. It would be nice to know more about Macedonian perceptions of their autonomy before and after Macedonia's organization as a province in that year (Derow 1989: 319–23). Yet even without that information, Livy's exceptional narrative can serve as a point of departure, for the tensions visible at every level of society, government, and commerce in Macedonia were replicated across the length and breadth of the Roman Empire. It is on the management of an empire thus created that we focus our attention in this chapter.

2 Structures, Principles, and Structural Problems

The study of Roman government is bedeviled by methodological difficulties; most intractable among these are the rules of evidence. We possess no synoptic diagram of the Roman bureaucracy, no handbook of the empire's taxes. Even for the first two centuries of the common era, the period with which this chapter is centrally concerned, the significance of such evidence as we do possess is heatedly debated (Eck 1999). I cite two disparate examples: we know that governors of provinces issued edicts setting forth the principles and regulations of their administrations – Cicero's for Cilicia in 51–50 BCE is perhaps the best attested, but merely through allusions in his letters (Pliny *Ep.* 10.96.7 and Ulpian *D.* 1.16.4.4–5 on publication of edicts; see also Marshall 1964; Galsterer 1986: 16–17). In the mid-second century CE the lawyer Gaius wrote a commentary on *the* "Provincial Edict" in 32 books, of which some 335 fragments survive (Lenel 1889: 1: 189–237). We simply do not know whether by his day some emperor had ordered the production and use of a standard edict for all provinces. The absence of later commentaries by the better-preserved Severan jurists is not decisive: Caracalla's grant of citizenship to all freeborn residents of the empire in 212 CE will have dramatically altered the legal landscape: any and all earlier "provincial edicts" will have had to be entirely rewritten. (Hence Ulpian, writing after Caracalla's edict, produced ten books "On the Duties of a Proconsul" and one "On the Duties of Imperial Administrators of Cities" [Lenel 1889: 2: 958–9 and 966–91], and none, so far as we know, on the classic topic of provincial edicts, namely, the governance of non-citizens.)

Again, many bureaucratic protocols and administrative procedures of Roman government were long best, and sometimes exclusively, attested on Egyptian papyri: these include the registration of births and deaths (birth registrations: Ando 2000: 355–6; death registrations: Virlouvet 1997), the recording of real estate transactions (A. E. Hanson 1994; Wörrle 1975), systems of taxation (Rathbone 1993), and the mechanics of judicial hearings (Haensch 1992, 1997). There was a time when scholars dogmatically insisted that Roman Egypt was unique and therefore excluded its evidence from attempts to reconstruct practice elsewhere. Epigraphic and papyrological discoveries of the last two decades have dramatically shifted consensus on this question (Feissel and Gascou 1995: 66; Lewis 1995: 138–49, 298–305; Eck 1999: 13–14). A major cause of this problem is the systematically asymmetrical nature of our evidence: from Egypt survive many documents originating with the imperial government, testifying to its interest and procedures; from almost every other region of the empire survive only texts that private individuals or local collectivites saw fit to inscribe on stone or bronze, and their commitment to reproducing the protocols and language of official texts varied widely (Ando 2000: 80–90; and Gagos/Potter, this volume). One important recent trend, spurred in part by the discovery and publication of the wooden writing tablets from Vindolanda near Hadrian's Wall in Britain, has been an increasing awareness of the range of media on which the Roman government published and stored information. If we cannot now recover them and their contents, we can at least remain cognizant of their utility and extent (Eck 1998; Ando 2000: 97, 102–3, 110–11, 356–7; Salway 2000: 120–3; E. Meyer 2004).

Officials and their staff

In the first two centuries of this era, the central government dispatched in any given year around 160 elite officials to govern its 55 million subjects. These officials fall roughly into two groups: holders of *imperium* ("right of command"), formally, at least, properly elected magistrates exercising power within an assigned domain; and supervisors of the government's finances (on the geographical limits placed on magisterial authority see Ulpian, *D*. 1.16.1, "A proconsul holds his proconsular insignia as soon as he leaves the City, but he exercises power only in the province that is assigned to him" [cf. Paul *D*. 1.18.3]; on financial agents see A. H. M. Jones 1960: 117–25). In theory, governors of provinces under the empire fell into two categories: magistrates elected at Rome and later assigned to provinces notionally under control of the Roman people, and officials acting on the emperor's behalf, holding *imperium* delegated by him, and assigned to provinces subordinated to the emperor's long-term control by legislative act. In practice, emperors and Senate often worked together: each received embassies from individuals as well as provincial communities, and they consulted each other in formulating and enacting responses and policies. More importantly, provincials looking in do not seem to have noticed such niceties of Roman constitutional law: they implicitly understood monarchy, and it was the emperor who instructed them to honor the Senate (Millar 2002: 271–320; cf. Ando 2000: 152–74).

The separation of fiscal authority from other juridical and administrative responsibilities, on the other hand, represents one of the most significant changes in Roman government between republic and principate: under the republic, the formal subordination of quaestorian accountants to praetorian and consular magistrates on the one hand, and the political influence of the private tax-collecting corporations on the other, had granted enormous scope for abuse of provincial populations, which was in principle largely removed in the early empire (cf. Brunt 1990: 53–95, 487–506).

When speaking of "the government's finances," furthermore, we must remember that Rome recognized a distinction between the emperor's personal property and the property of the state, although the nature of that distinction and its development remain highly controversial (Millar 1977: 175–201; Brunt 1990: 134–62). Among their holdings, emperors owned vast estates in the provinces, and the number and size of these grew rapidly over time (Millar 1977: 175–89; Kehoe, this volume). The effects of this growth were not simply economic; the emperor's personal financial interests were managed by procurators who came to exercise great extra-judicial and extra-constitutional influence (although much about the legal framework that structured their relations with provincial governors remains under debate: see Millar 1964b and 1965; Brunt 1990: 163–87).

In theory, the scope of an elected magistrate's power was broad, and this was particularly true of his authority over non-citizens (cf. A. J. Toynbee 1965: 2: 148). In the words of the early third-century jurist Ulpian, "since a proconsul has the fullest judicial authority [sc. in his assigned province], he possesses there the powers of all those who preside over courts at Rome, whether magistrates or extraordinary commissions; there is, therefore, no matter in his province that cannot be admitted to judicial examination on his authority" ("On the Duties of the Proconsul" bk. 2 = D. 1.16.7.1 and 9.pr.; see also Ulpian D. 1.18.6; Cic. Q. fr. 1.1.22 for a similar formulation in the first century BCE). Governors were, moreover, required to travel a regular, publicized circuit around their provinces, making themselves accessible to those they governed (section 4 below). What is more, governors could and routinely did delegate jurisdictional and administrative authority of many kinds (cf. Ulpian, "On the Duties of the Proconsul" bk. 1 = D. 1.16.4.6 and 1.16.6.pr.–1). All this might seem to allow for the wide and frequent exercise of authority by Roman magistrates throughout the provinces of their empire.

And yet, the size of governors' staffs was surprisingly small: beyond attendants – lictors, heralds, messengers, scribes, and a bodyguard (Oliver 1966) – those accompanying a governor into his province included a very limited number of official and unofficial assistants (cf. Cic. Q. fr. 1.1.1.10–14; Brunt 1990: 271; Nelis-Clément 2000). The former were normally of equestrian rank and formally separable into civil and military grades, both of whom were called *legati*, "legates," a term widely used to designate someone exercising delegated or derivative *imperium*. In practice, to the provincial seeking a representative of the government, these distinctions in rank and authority seem to have mattered little: provincials are attested accosting centurions without any jurisdictional capacity whatsoever, importuning them to adjudicate disputes. Procurators supervising imperial estates in particular seem to have multiplied in number and grown vastly in their influence, often extra-constitutionally (cf. Gascou 1999). What is more, Roman law recognized the importance of its officials making themselves available even in transit to and from their provinces (*Lex de Provinciis Praetoriis* = RS 12, Cnidos copy, col. IV, ll. 31–9; cf. Cic. *Fam.* 1.9.25); this haphazard system largely came to an end in the notionally more ordered world of the empire (Paul D. 1.18.3; cf. Peachin 1996).

A governor's unofficial staff consisted of his *amici*, his "friends"; the orator Fronto wrote to Antoninus Pius that "he diligently requested the aid of friends in all matters that related to the ordering of his province" (*Ant.* 8.1). Such men typically ranged widely in age and experience, from those who might offer genuinely well-informed advice on matters of politics and law to friends and relatives seeking experience and patronage at the start of their careers.

In practice, then, Roman government was extraordinarily circumscribed (Hopkins 1980: 120–1). Given its limited investment in personnel, it could scarcely be otherwise. Its extraordinary efficiency, both mechanical, in its construction and exploitation of roads and networks of communication, and human, in the dedication of its officials, aided its cause. But in the end, for the maintenance of order, collection of information, and extraction of revenue, Rome must have relied heavily on the institutions of government in the cities and territories it ruled (Hopkins 1980: 121; Galsterer 1986). It is to them and their relations with Rome that I now turn.

Cities and their aristocracies

As the Macedonians learned swiftly and brutally in 168 BCE, freedom from Roman interference, even in the absence of annexation, was a precarious condition (Bernhardt 1971, 1985 and esp. Derow 1989). If the Romans required the assistance of local governments to maintain order, on the one hand, and required order to facilitate the extraction of wealth, on the other, they could not afford to leave much to the whim of local elites. The politics and dynamics of cities' internal self-governance lie outside the scope of this chapter. Here we need only to examine the most salient of the systematic, structural changes imposed by Rome on the cities through which it governed.

The paradigm outlined for Macedonia, that of placing the governance of cities in the hands of upper-class individuals whose self-interest aligned them with Rome, held good throughout the empire. The underlying attitudes to class and quality that shaped this practice are revealed with particular clarity in Pliny the Younger's commendation of Calestrius Tiro who, Pliny wrote, had befriended every honest man and obtained the admiration of the low without losing the respect of the high. Pliny congratulated Tiro above all on the way in which he preserved *discrimina ordinum dignitatumque* (distinctions of rank and status), "for if these are confused, upended and destroyed, nothing is more unequal than the resulting equality" (*Ep.* 9.5; on the social performance of *discrimina ordinum*, concentrating on the theater, see E. Rawson 1991: 508–45). In the urbanized east, Rome encouraged the development of *de facto* oligarchies by ensuring that "communities were governed by the designs of their best citizens" (Cic. *Q. fr.* 1.1.25). Thus in peninsular Greece in 146 BCE, Lucius Mummius and his ten senatorial commissioners "put an end to democracies and established magistracies on the basis of property qualifications" (Paus. 7.16.9). This policy was well calculated, not least because it left the task of accommodating Greeks to their new "constitution and laws" in the hands of Rome's Greek apologists (Polyb. 39.5.1–2, with Walbank 1979: 734–5; cf. *RDGE* 43, ll. 9–10, from Dyme in 115 BCE, referring back to 146), who in turn rewarded Mummius and the senatorial commissioners with statues at Olympia (e.g. *SIG* 676; cf. Polyb. 39.6, with Walbank 1979: 735–7). Similar patterns – and occasional evidence of direct Roman involvement – can be detected throughout the east, not least in the spread of similarly-designed *curiae*, meeting-houses for city councils (Mitchell 1990: 188, on electoral processes at Oenoanda in Lycia; Mitchell 1993: 1: 88, on Pompey's organization of Cilicia, Bithynia, and Pontus; Balty 1992 on imperial *curiae*; and in general Millar 1993b: 241).

Whether the Romans should be held accountable for the end of "democracy" as such is rather less clear (de Ste. Croix 1981: 306–26, 518–37). On the one hand, we occasionally hear of "election" to city magistracies by the city council rather than its assembly (Chaniotis 1985). Yet assemblies continued to meet, and some flourished, under Roman rule: Plutarch wrote a manual for young politicians that contained advice on managing the passions of the populace in assemblies (*Mor.* 799c–f, 814a–b, 815a–c); and we know from Dio that a disturbance at Prusa caused that city temporarily to lose the right for its assembly to meet (*Oration* 48). Even in the late third century, when the city of Tymandus in Pisidia petitioned for the "rank and status of a city," it both claimed sufficient men to fill its council and sought the right to pass decrees and elect its own magistrates (*ILS* 6090 = *MAMA* 4, 236). It is, furthermore, clear that cities were expected largely to run themselves. According to Plutarch, it was discord between factions within cities that led to the loss of self-governance: one side would stir up the assembly, the other would needlessly and sycophantically submit local matters to the scrutiny of their Roman overlords. Better to reflect on "the boots of the Roman soldiers poised over one's head" and simultaneously to recall "the Romans' great eagerness to promote the political interests of their friends" (Plut. *Mor.* 813e and 814c, with C. P. Jones 1971: 110–30; 1978: 95–103).

In the west, Roman policy adapted to local circumstances. Since the Romans continued to use local aristocracies and regional dynasts as *instrumenta servitutis* ("tools of enslavement": Tac. *Agr.* 14.2), they often had to encourage such people to dwell in cities, laid out along Roman lines. When in 77 CE the Spanish city of Sabora asked Vespasian's permission to relocate to level ground, they were merely late in responding to an initiative that began in the reign of Augustus (*ILS* 6092; Florus 2.33.59–60; Dio 54.11.5; on urbanization in the western provinces see W. S. Hanson 1988 and Ando forthcoming). The complex processes of materially and politically cultivating a local aristocracy, encouraging their acculturation, and gradually co-opting them into the governing class of the empire itself, require great ingenuity to reconstruct in any detail, but their efficacy in producing quietude and engendering loyalty is beyond doubt (Syme 1977 constitutes one remarkable case study; see also Syme 1999: 3–126, esp. 53–89; Syme 1958a: 585–624; and Jacques 1984).

The political climate produced by these policies has been described as a culture of loyalism (Rowe 2002). On the one hand, through fear, confusion, flattery, or internal strife, cities ceded more and more decision-making authority to Roman officials (Millar 1977: 363–463), and competed not for transcendent preeminence or military power, but for esteem within the Roman order. Thus Ephesus complained to Antoninus Pius because Smyrna had not addressed it with sufficient deference; the same city demanded and won the privilege that the governor of Asia proceed to his province by sea and disembark first in Ephesus, "first of all *metropoleis*" (*SIG* 849; Ulpian "On the Duties of the Proconsul" bk. 1 = *D.* 1.16.4.5; Robert 1977; Ando 2000: 131–74). At the same time, the Mediterranean flourished materially and culturally as never before; if one consequence of Roman rule was a decline in civic autonomy, another was a profound reorientation in self-conceptions of political identity and in political theory, and a remarkable efflorescence of cultural and municipal institutions designed for public consumption and devoted to the common weal (Millar 1993b; Ando 1999, 2000).

The organization of the landscape

Roman imperialism developed its most characteristic technologies to satisfy a passion for inventory (Nicolet 1996). In the conquest and settlement of new territory – a process that the Romans called reducing it *in formam provinciae*, "into the form or configuration of a province" – this passion found expression in three, interrelated processes: an inventory of cities, a census of the population, and a survey of the land. The results were documented in several ways, but especially through *formulae* (registers of people and land) and *formae* (maps) (Nicolet 1991).

While it is true that Rome tended to *assess* taxes on individuals and their land, it tended to *collect* taxes through cities. Rome needed, therefore, to account for all the land and communities in its provinces (Nicolet 1996). To that end, the Romans established in each province centers of jurisdiction, then assigned to those centers contiguous territories and subordinated all settlements in those territories to the *conventus*, the assize-city at its center (Fron. 2.12–15 Campbell; Mitchell 1993: 1: 32 and 88; on legal aspects of subordination see Laffi 1966). The *formula* of the province listed first those cities designated to hold an assize, and then the communities subordinate to them: these were themselves distinguished by their legal status and then listed alphabetically (Robert 1949; Habicht 1975; B. D. Shaw 1981b; Christol 1994; Nicolet 1996: 10–14; Ando 2000: 150–2).

Rome relied principally on three mechanisms to integrate the countryside into its network of cities (Ando forthcoming). First, it littered the provinces with boundary stones: the borders between cities, assize districts, and communal, private, and tax-exempt land (almost always belonging to religious foundations) were delimited and emblazoned on the landscape (see, e.g., Hyginus *On Establishing Boundaries* 156.18–24 Campbell; *MAMA* 9, pp. xxxvi–xliii; Burton 2000). Second, it surveyed huge stretches of provincial land, especially such arable land as was already farmed, and redistributed it according to Roman principles, in massive grids of rectilinear plots covering thousands of acres: the centuriation of Africa probably began contemporaneously with the organization of the province in 146 BCE by Scipio Aemilianus and his ten senatorial commissioners (Chevallier 1958: 64–78; cf. Clavel-Lévêque 1983). Third, Rome united those cities it favored, facilitated the suppression of those who resisted, and overawed many with its dominance of nature, through its digging of harbors, tunneling through mountains, construction of aqueducts, and laying of roads (see, e.g., *ILS* 5795 and 5863; cf. Purcell 1990; Ando 2000: 322–3). The scarring of the landscape had its administrative analog in Rome's production, storage, and display of maps, whose forms and taxonomic orientation mirrored the legal and juridical concerns of Roman geographic thought (Moatti 1993).

The effects of this activity, both within and between communities, as people were tied to parcels of land and land to people, must have been profound. The Augustan geographer Strabo, for example, allowed that it had been hard enough to distinguish Phrygian, Carian, Lydian, and Mysian elements in central Asia Minor before the Romans came, but they had made the situation more complicated by dividing the region into assize districts not according to race but on some other rationale (13.4.12). Forcibly deprived of contact and connection with the social fabric that had constituted and nurtured their identities, provincials found themselves reassigned to new and different places in the social and geographic reality of the Roman Empire.

Conservatism and change

The processes through which Rome acquired and settled territory generated provinces that resembled complex mosaics: Roman commanders routinely rewarded allied communities with legal privileges, most notably the freedom to use their own laws and impose their own taxes and, very exceptionally, freedom from Roman taxation (see, e.g., *RS* 19, esp. ll. 31–6; on local rights of taxation see Millar 1977: 425–8; on the hierarchy of cities in general see J. Reynolds 1988: 23–5, and Millar 1999b). The *formula* of a province will, therefore, have recorded the fact that some cities were "exempt from the schedule of the province" (J. Reynolds 1982, no. 14 l. 3 and no. 15 l. 12–14; cf. Robert and Robert 1989, Ménippos col. 1, ll. 39–40, and *RS* 19, ll. 18–30). Privileged communities subsequently devoted enormous effort to retaining their status, sending embassies to each new emperor seeking to confirm privileges granted long ago: early in the third century CE, the Thudedenses, the inhabitants of what the Romans considered a proto-urban settlement near Tipasa in Mauretania, asked Caracalla to confirm the territorial boundaries and tax-immunity granted them by Juba II and confirmed by Augustus two centuries before (*AÉ* 1985, 972; see also Plin. *Nat.* 5.25; on embassies from cities to the imperial court see Millar 1977: 394–447; on the storage and display of the documents these embassies generated see Ando 2000: 90–6).

The citation of treaties and imperial letters constituted one important check on innovation in imperial administration: having issued official documents, Rome then had to adhere to their stipulations (Ando 2000: 36–40, 351–82). Another African text, the Tabula Banasitana, reproduces a letter from an imperial freedman in the reign of Commodus, certifying through the quotation of documentary evidence the possession of Roman citizenship by one Julianus of the Zagrenses and his immediate family. The freedman copied the document from, and checked it against, "the record of those granted citizenship by the divine Augustus and Tiberius Caesar Augustus and Gaius Caesar and the divine Claudius and Nero and Galba and the divine Augusti Vespasian and Titus and Domitian Caesar and the divine Augusti Nerva and Trajan Parthicus and Trajan Hadrian and Hadrian Antoninus Pius and Verus...." (*IAM* 94). The enormous respect for bureaucratic rationality evinced in the Tabula Banasitana is perhaps most remarkably attested in a Neronian law on the customs of Asia, issued in 62 CE and discovered at Ephesus: the law, consisting of more than 155 long lines, summarizes the regulations for Asian customs established in an initial law of 122 BCE; it then cites all subsequent modifications to that law, from 72, 17, 12, and 2 BCE, as well as those passed in 5, 8, 37, and 62 CE (*SEG* 39 no. 1180, on which see Nicolet 2000: 335–84).

At the same time, powerful forces promoted a gradual coalescence in administration, in matters of both procedure and substance. First, Roman officials could not but actualize their respect for *mos regionis*, "local custom," in ways informed by deep-seated habits of mind (cf. Ulpian *D.* 25.4.1.15). In one famous case, the city of Contrebia in Spain sought the aid of C. Valerius Flaccus to settle a dispute between two communities in its territory. Flaccus responded by providing a legal framework through which Contrebia could settle the matter itself: although he urged the use of Celtiberian law, Flaccus understood the case to concern *ager publicus* and *ager privatus*, communal and private land, and suggested that the decision be reached through the *fictio*, the legal fiction, that the rules of one community applied to both. In other words, Flaccus urged Contrebia and its communities to accommodate their laws to the categories and modes of argument of Roman law (Galsterer 1986: 22; Ando 2000: 342). The law of the municipality of Irni, in Spain, issued under Domitian, likewise provided that all matters not explicitly covered by its clauses should be resolved as though their case concerned Roman citizens and was being heard in Rome by a praetor of the Roman people (*Lex Irnitana* 93 and cf. 85, 91; Gardner 2001).

Second, both individuals and communities increasingly had recourse to Roman officials to settle their disputes with each other, even in the Greek east, where there existed in the Hellenistic period widely-attested practices of third-party arbitration (Mitteis 1891; Marshall 1980; Ager 1996). At the communal level, the change is most visible in disputes over territory, where the trend was rapid and overwhelming (Rousset 1994: 100, 103, 108; Burton 2000).

Finally, the rulers of Rome continuously made new law. Ancient and modern scholars tend to distinguish legal rulings intended by their authors to settle individual cases from those designed for broader application; in practice, judges routinely accepted the value of imperial legal rulings as precedent, regardless of their genre (Ando 2000: 373–82). Such law-making, whatever its intent, had particular ramifications for the autonomy of cities when it addressed the status of individuals, not least in their liability for civic liturgies (Millar 1983). The Christian polemicist Tertullian spoke to a cultural, political, and legal phenomenon of the first importance when he proclaimed that the world of the late second century CE was manifestly better cultivated and better arranged than it had been formerly: "everywhere there are houses, everywhere people, everywhere the *res publica*, the commonwealth, everywhere life" (*An.* 30; Mócsy 1962; Ando 2000: 1–15).

3 Citizens, Aliens, and Their Money

The empire interfered most obviously and regularly in provincial life through mechanisms designed to facilitate the extraction of revenue. The Roman government imposed a bewildering array of direct and indirect taxes in cash and kind, some of which were temporary or specific to particular provinces or both. Here we can do no more than sketch the most regular features of the system (A. H. M. Jones 1974: 151–85; B. D. Shaw 1988; Brunt 1990: 324–46; 531–40; Rathbone 1996; and Eck 2000).

The principal incidence of Roman taxation fell on individuals and their property. Its primary ideological justification was support of the army: hence Roman citizens were, supposedly, first subjected to taxation in order to pay the wages of soldiers fighting Rome's first sustained military campaign (Livy 4.59.11–60.8) and income from booty occasionally led to refunds (Livy 39.7.5). Roman citizens were exempted from direct taxation after the Third Macedonian War; that only provincials paid thereafter was not a punishment: they paid for *pacem sempiternam...atque otium*, "eternal peace and leisure" (Cic. *Q. fr.* 1.1.34; cf. Ando 2000: 175–90).

In light of this emphasis on militarism and its costs, it is salutary to recall that most of the cultural appurtenances popularly associated with imperial culture – public cult and its games and civic banquets, competitions for artists, speakers, and athletes, as well as the funding of the great majority of public buildings and public display of art – were financed by private individuals, whose expenditures in this regard helped to justify their economic power and legal and political privileges (Veyne 1976; Duncan-Jones 1982: 63–119; 1990: 174–84; Lendon 1997).

The collection of data

Rome's primary vehicle for collecting data on populations and property was the census (on the republican census see Nicolet 1980: 49–88; for the imperial period see Brunt 1990: 345–6; for its role in the financial system, see Lo Cascio 1999; on its ideological import see Ando 2000: 350–62). Many states around the Mediterranean had kept rolls of their citizens and those records had often served both ideological and financial purposes. In virtue of its examination of the juridical status and consequent tax liability, the census had enormous social importance, and it is clear that census returns, especially those recording citizenship and tax exemptions, were among individuals' most cherished possessions (Ando 2000: 353–8).

The conduct of the census required heads of household to present themselves to supervising magistrates and supply information about themselves, the members of their household, and the habitable and arable property in their possession (Ulpian "On the Census" bk. 3 = *D.* 50.15.4.*pr.*). It is possible that the *forma censualis*, the "form of the census," sought different information in different provinces according to local needs: certainly Egyptian farmers were required to file supplementary declarations registering such fields as went uninundated by the Nile and which would therefore lie fallow for that year (e.g. *P.Mich.* 6.366–9; cf. *Sel. Pap.* 321–2); they also declared the size of their flocks and any variations in them (*P.Amh.* 2.73). Only some areas will have had properties with fish ponds, salt pans, and harbors generating income (Ulpian "On the Census" bk. 3 = *D.* 50.15.4.6–7); and republican censuses asked individuals to compute their liquidity, by subtracting outstanding debts from present assets, and to list their durable goods, particularly their agricultural implements (Pompeius Festus s.v. *rudus*; Gel. 6.11.9; Livy 6.27.5; A. H. M. Jones 1974: 164; Brunt 1990: 329–36; Ando 2000: 357–8).

Data are insufficient to speak with any certainty about provincial censuses in the late republic: Rome acquired so much territory so quickly, amidst such political instability, that it may have been impossible to conduct an adequate census of it. Yet the acquisition and use of statistical abstracts is well-attested as an ideal even then (Nicolet 1996). Augustus seems to have conducted censuses throughout the empire (although not all at once, *pace* Lk. 2:1–3), and thereafter evidence confirms a census in virtually all provinces soon after their acquisition and periodically after that, though we cannot now determine if there was a regular cycle in every province, or if subsequent censuses were supervised by Roman or local officials (Brunt 1990: 345–6; Lo Cascio 1999 on supervision of censuses after the first).

Direct taxes

The systematic use of the census under the principate permitted a large-scale transformation in Roman taxation. No longer did Rome regularly rely exclusively on private corporations of tax collectors, whose desire to make a profit on their investment led to rampant abuses, both of the system by which they won their contracts and particularly of provincial populations (Badian 1972, with Brunt in A. H. M. Jones 1974: 180–3; Brunt 1990: 354–432 for the continued use of corporations under the principate). Rather, in theory provincials now paid two direct taxes: a poll-tax and a tax on land (the *tributum capitis* and *tributum soli*), where the tax on land was, notionally, a tax on its produce or productive capacity (Ulpian "On the Census" bk. 3 = *D.* 50.15.4.1). Census data allowed Roman officials to assess liability as a fixed proportion of a province's aggregate assessed property and total population: the burden was certainly computed province by province (Suet. *Ves.* 16.1; Appian *pr.* 61; Hyginus *On Establishing Boundaries* 160.27–162.2 Campbell), assize by assize (*I. Ephesus* 13), and city by city (Ulpian "On the Census" bk. 3 = *D.* 50.15.4.2). Primary responsibility for its collection seems to have devolved on civic magistrates who possessed considerable latitude in performing this duty (see esp. *IG* 5.1, 1432), and who are occasionally attested visiting their city's subordinate villages to collect their share (Jos. *BJ* 17.405; Rostovtzeff 1957: 388–92, as well as Millar 1977: 426, on *SIG* 837; A. H. M. Jones 1974: 165–6; and Corbier 1991b. On Egypt see Sharp 1999; on the function of the *conventus* of Asia in organizing the finances of the imperial cult, on analogy, presumably, with its role in collecting taxes, see Habicht 1975).

Indirect taxes

Rome also levied a series of taxes on trade and property transfers, some of which generated large revenues. Foremost among these were *portoria*, or customs and tolls (Cic. *Rull.* 2.80; De Laet 1949): these were levied on goods entering or leaving the empire, whether through Egypt or Palmyra to and from the east (Strabo 17.1.13; *CIS* 2.3, 3913, with Matthews 1984), or through Gaul to and from Britain (Cic. *Font.* 19; Strabo 4.5.3), as well as between and within provinces. Their rates were usually between two and five percent. The regulations governing these could be enormously complicated. Those for Palmyra, for example, specify the duties owed on long lists of specific products and often require higher duties on exported than on identical imported goods. The *portoria* of Palmyra were administered locally, although, like all local taxes they were approved by Rome. In Palmyra as elsewhere, the collection of indirect taxes was the responsibility of local officials; the revenues themselves flowed into the coffers of the central government (E. G. Turner 1936). Imperial customs duties outside Palmyra, it should be noted, remained in most provinces the most prominent source of revenue under the control of the publicans.

The slave trade attracted special taxes. Late in life, Augustus instituted a four percent tax on the sale of slaves (Dio 55.31.4); Tacitus informs us that Nero shifted responsibility for this tax from the purchaser to the dealer, and that dealers raised their prices accordingly (*Ann.* 13.31.2). It is entirely typical of the state of extant evidence that we know nothing of the mechanism through which this tax was collected, particularly before Nero's innovation. Owners also paid the *vicesima libertatis*, "the twentieth for freedom," a five percent tax on the value of slaves, due at their manumission.

Finally, in 6 CE, in order to establish a pension fund for veterans (the *aerarium militare*, the military treasury), Augustus imposed a *vicesima hereditatum*, a five percent estate tax, on middle- and upper-class Roman citizens, on such property as they left to any but their immediate family; this treasury also received the income from a one percent tax on auctions, instituted "after the civil wars" (Suet. *Aug.* 49.2; Tac. *Ann.* 1.78.2; Dio 55.25.5).

Taxes in kind and transportation services

Many provinces paid at least part of their direct taxes in kind (Duncan-Jones 1990: 187–93), and many communities, not least those near permanent army camps, were subject to further demands. Such payments were overwhelmingly made in grain: the most famous exceptions – the German Frisii paid in hides "because of the poverty of their means" (Tac. *Ann.* 4.72.1), and the Batavians sent recruits (Tac. *Hist.* 5.25.1–2) – proving the rule. Payment in kind may have been necessary or desirable in less monetized regions, but Roman administrators seem to have regularly abused those from whom they demanded grain. Most notoriously, a Roman official would specify a delivery point far from the payer and graciously accept a bribe or an inflated payment in cash instead (Cic., *Ver.* 2.3.191; Tac. *Agr.* 19.4).

Finally, the extraordinary network of roads with which Rome united its empire will have brought costs as well as benefits to the communities it touched. It would, of course, be impossible to overstate its usefulness: when the city of Orcistus in Phrygia petitioned the emperor Constantine for city-status, it cited its location at the intersection of four roads, "which made it a convenient and suitable resting-place for public officials and, indeed, the public at large," as a guarantee of its future economic viability (*ILS* 6091 = *MAMA* 7, 305). But to make the roads useful for administration and not simply trade, the government needed a vast array of personnel and material at the ready. Literary sources tell us that Augustus established what later writers called the *cursus publicus*, the state mail and transport service (Suet. *Aug.* 49.3; Pflaum 1940); what we learn from epigraphic evidence, most particularly a letter to Sagalassus in Pisidia, written by one Sextus Sotidius Strabo Libuscidianus early in the reign of Tiberius, is that local communities were responsible for supplying the wagons and mules that made the system work. Strabo gave Sagalassus a *formula* or schedule, listing its obligations: these the village had to meet only, but exactly, from the point on the road where its borders met those of its neighboring municipalities, Cormasa and Conana; it could pay another village to fulfill these obligations; and it had to meet them only at the request of those on official business: imperial procurators, senators, *equites* in the service of the emperors, ranking military officers, and those carrying appropriate *diplomata*, letters of transit. It is quite possible that these communities were also called upon to transport goods for the military, and it goes without saying that this system was open to abuse. Indeed, the vast dossier of epigraphic evidence for it consists almost entirely of texts issued to control abuse, inscribed on stone and displayed for public consumption by communities seeking to protect themselves from excessive exactions (Mitchell 1976; cf. Frend 1956).

4 Maintaining Order

Ulpian may have urged that "it befits a good and wise governor to take care that the province he rules be peaceful and orderly" ("On the Duties of the Proconsul" bk. 7 = D. 1.18.13.*pr.*), but the mechanisms available to a governor for achieving quietude were rudimentary at best. The astonishing popularity of Roman means for settling disputes is, therefore, an historical problem of the first rank (but cf. Galsterer 1986: 18, asserting the importance of municipal codes and municipal courts, and Millar 1981: 68–72: the world of the *Golden Ass* is "one wholly without policing by any Imperial forces").

The history of this problem was shaped by two, interrelated forces. First, Roman law had long established two parallel systems of adjudication, one for disputes between citizens and another for those between citizens and aliens. Second, demographic changes in the formative period of the empire necessarily brought Roman scrutiny to the conduct of local courts: the late republic brought a staggering increase in Roman emigration to the provinces, particularly those in the east (Errington 1988); the civil wars created large numbers of veterans, whom Roman dynasts settled in colonies throughout the empire (Brunt 1987: 589–601); and the emperors of the early principate routinely – and sometimes systematically – granted citizenship to individuals in provincial cities (Millar 1977: 479–83; Sherwin-White 1973: 221–87). The presence of Roman citizens in such numbers in communities of varying status created enormous pressure on local magistrates and Roman governors alike (cf. B. D. Shaw 2000: 362–73). The former sometimes responded by accommodating local systems of government to Roman ideals, as they were locally understood; the latter often responded by adjudging according to Roman ideals, as they understood them.

The law and knowledge of law

In suggesting that cases not covered by its clauses should be adjudicated according to Roman law, the municipal code of Irni raises a number of problems as fascinating as their solutions are enigmatic (Ando 2000: 73–80, 373–85; Galsterer 1986 and M. H. Crawford 1988 are useful but remain handicapped by narrowly legalistic approaches; for questions raised by the *Lex Irnitana* see González 1986: 148–50 and Galsterer 1988). I single out two. In the first place, the law required that the city's magistrates display for the better part of each day in legible writing the jurisdictional clauses of the provincial governor's edict, and that judges rule according to them (*Lex Irnitana* 85). On the one hand, this requirement echoes a widespread anxiety in Roman law that legal texts be accessible to those bound by them; and yet, in an era of low literacy, this seemingly admirable regard raises as many concerns as it allays (Ando 2000: 96–108).

Second, cities of municipal status were entitled to "use their own laws," and the emperor Hadrian, at least, thought this level of autonomy desirable: it should have fostered local patriotism (Gel. 16.13.8–9). But the inhabitants of such cities inevitably had a range of legal statuses: quite apart from the legal import of the "Latin" citizenship held by the city's "citizens," such a city's magistrates will have gained

Roman citizenship upon completing their tenure of local office (Burton 2001), and many other individuals will have resided in them who did not hold local citizenship. Under these conditions, it is perhaps not surprising that even local magistrates might turn to the empire's one overarching body of law as a paradigm or source (Gardner 2001; Stolte 2001): the extraordinary, fragmentary Tablet of Heraclea is but one famous, early example of a city's refashioning its internal self-governance in response to the political and juridical realities of the Roman Empire (*RS* 24).

Insofar as the Flavian municipal law was drafted at Rome (Frederiksen 1965; Galsterer 1988: 89), it must be seen within a long tradition by which Roman magistrates assimilated local conditions to Roman habits of thought (cf. Gardner 2001). At Contrebia, this took place under the explicit provision that the disputants resolve their conflict using local laws; elsewhere, Rome gradually expanded the range of cases that magistrates in particular regions should cede to Roman courts (e.g. *RS* 16, 28, 29–30). All this legislation sits alongside the famous and imperfectly understood right to appeal of Roman citizens who found themselves on trial in the provinces (*SEG* 9 no. 4; *D.* 48.6.7, 8; A. H. M. Jones 1960: 51–65, and Oliver 1979).

The assize system

Roman governors were required to make themselves available to their provinces to settle disputes and receive petitions on matters great and small (Marshall 1966 for the republic; on the empire see in general Burton 1975 and Haensch 1997: 334–42, and Meyer-Zwiffelhoffer 2002; for Egypt see Lewis 1981 and Ando 2000: 375–7, with Haensch 1994 and 1997; for Asia see Robert 1949 and Habicht 1975). Cities within each province were designated to hold a *conventus* or assize, and a schedule of the governor's circuit and the regulations for his court must have circulated widely within each province (*P.Oxy.* 2754; Haensch 1997: 329–32; Ando 2000: 375–6). The popularity of the governor's court is variously attested, by literary sources which praise the economic benefits that accrued from the trade in tourism it brought (D.Chr. 35.15–16, 38.26, and 40.33), by the efforts cities undertook to win a place on the governor's circuit (e.g. *SEG* 28 no. 1566, ll. 69–77), and by the legal petitions and rescripts that cite their place in the record-books of any given *conventus* (Ando 2000: 376–7).

A Roman judge in the provinces could conduct any given case in one of two ways. First, he could use Roman formulary procedure, either by explicit quotation of or reference to the *formulae* published by the praetors at Rome: this was Cicero's practice in Cilicia, and it was probably customary under the republic (*Att.* 6.1.15 with Galsterer 1986: 17, and 1996: 397–403). Even then, Cicero and others left themselves latitude for maneuver: Cicero did so by paradoxically leaving many things "unwritten" in his provincial edict, while promising that he would approximate his rulings to the praetor's edict (*Att.* 6.1.15), while Verres in Sicily had justified the omission of a law on legacies from his provincial edict by allowing that he would act in accordance with the "urban edict" regarding "any matter that arose unexpectedly (*ex improviso*)" (*Ver.* 2.1.112).

Second, a judge was free to inquire into the facts of any given case himself, through a procedure called *cognitio extra ordinem* or *cognitio extraordinaria*, meaning simply a non-formulary judicial inquiry. This left plaintiffs greater scope to debate finer points of law and the judge and his advisors correspondingly greater scope in crafting their decision. Extant evidence suggests that this became far the most common procedure in the provinces under the principate: after all, provincials who knew Roman legal *formulae* were free to cite them in *cognitiones* – as Babatha cited the praetorian *actio tutelae*, a *formula* for suits regarding guardianship, only 19 years after the annexation of Arabia (*P.Yadin* 28–30) – and judges were likewise free, in such a hearing, to interpret praetorian *formulae* as expressions of substantive law (Stolte 2001: 176; see also Ando 2000: 378). Such was the fluid state of the law and legal theory in the provinces of the empire (Millar 1981: 71; for formal arguments see Peachin 2001 and Sirks 2001).

Policing

Ulpian followed his exhortation to governors to maintain the peace with some instructions:

> This he will easily obtain if he zealously sees to it that his province lacks wicked men, by himself seeking them out. For a governor ought to seek out blasphemers, bandits, swindlers and thieves and punish them in proportion to their crimes, and bring compulsion to bear upon those who aid and abet such men, as without aid a bandit cannot remain hidden for long. ("On the Duties of the Proconsul" bk. 8 = D. 1.18.13.*pr.*)

The ability of Roman governors to act on such admonitions was probably even more limited than their desire to do so. Such criminals as dwelt outside the urban fabric could easily escape the rudimentary institutional mechanisms of Roman rule (B. D. Shaw 1984a and 2000). When preparing for his ultimately abortive governorship of the heavily urbanized province of Asia in 153/4 CE, the orator Fronto asked a friend, one Julius Senex, to join his staff "not simply for his loyalty and diligence, but also for his military zeal in the hunting and suppressing of bandits" (*Ant.* 8.1). We may doubt whether Senex would have achieved much. High-ranking Romans were known to disappear during journeys even within the Italian peninsula (Pliny *Ep.* 6.25); in the early third century, the famed bandit Bulla Felix and his band of hundreds apparently eluded capture within Italy for two years, during a period when the emperor Septimius Severus not only lived there but had recently sent heralds "throughout Rome and Italy" to invite the populace to attend his Secular Games (Herod. 3.8.10). If Bulla really was caught, asleep in a cave, on information extracted from his lover, his case will highlight all the more the limitations of Roman policing (Dio 76.10).

Governors could, of course, summon the army to their aid. In some areas, locally garrisoned soldiers clearly performed a policing function, but as a tool the army was as powerful as it was imprecise. Without a doubt, the vast majority of policing was performed by local authorities (Sperber 1970). Of course, Roman authorities gradually insinuated their own ideals and practices into the codes of conduct that governed such local "keepers of the peace," and in Egypt may have done a great deal to organize them (Bagnall 1977). So, for example, Antoninus Pius as governor of the province of Asia ordered local policemen to interrogate criminals only in the presence of a stenographer and to forward a transcript, together with the prisoner, to the magistrate who would try the criminal (Marcian "On Criminal Proceedings" bk. 2 = D. 48.3.6.1); the abundant juristic literature on this topic can be set alongside evidence supplied by martyr acts, in which Christians occasionally force civic magistrates to adhere to the regulations of their Roman overlords (*Acts of Pionius* 15.1–5; but cf. Lopuszanksi 1951).

5 The Ambitions of Government

A number of scholarly trends have converged in recent years, urging us to view Roman government as minimalist in both its aims and achievement. Essentially reactive, it possessed neither the interest nor the ability to formulate policy, particularly concerning processes as complex as urbanization or acculturation. Advocates of this view understand, of course, that the empire was an extraordinarily complex collectivity, and that furthering understanding of it requires enormous efforts at collecting and analyzing data; indeed, they make a disproportionate number of distinguished contributions of this kind (Eck and Müller-Luckner 1999; de Blois 2001). Yet work along these lines has often promoted such particularism in the treatment of data as to subscribe, consciously or unconsciously, to a number of related epistemological fallacies: every text is so firmly and precisely situated in a context (about which we in fact know extremely little) that it becomes "unique," rendering comparison impossible and disinclining scholars to study data in aggregate; likewise, only such actions and beliefs as are attested by surviving evidence are admitted to have been thought or performed, rendering the construction and use of models impossible.

Where Roman government is concerned, we might ask how or whether our data, which concentrate so heavily on matters of law and finance, can be made to harmonize with that strand of Roman imperial propaganda that justified the empire by summoning Romans "to inculcate the habits of peacetime" (Verg. *Aen.* 6.852; cf. Woolf 1998: 54–67; Ando 2000: 49–70, 336–51). One view, widely shared in the Roman world, held the primary tool of any such program to be the law: not for nothing did the late Roman scholar Servius gloss Vergil's *paci...morem* with *leges pacis*, "the laws of peace." This view was itself predicated upon a particular understanding of civil society and the bonds that held it together (Ando 2000: 9–11, 406–12); nor would anyone in the ancient world have questioned that the arts of civilization could only be cultivated in a city properly designed, ordered, and adorned (B. D. Shaw 2000).

Further work on Roman government should perhaps look first to the Euphrates. An extraordinary cache of papyri, first announced in 1989 and systematically published between 1995 and 2000, illuminates the organization of the eastern regions of Coele Syria in tantalizing detail. Having acquired a land of villages, the Romans selected one, Appadana, to become its primary instrument of governance. Appadana becomes a city, is granted a Greek name, Neapolis, and acquires the political and social structures of a late-Roman Greek city: a council, whose members have Roman citizenship and Roman names, and residents interested in the actions available to them in the legal regime that henceforth would order their world (*P.Euphr.* 1 and 4; *P.Bostra* 1).

CHAPTER TEN

The Transformation of Government under Diocletian and Constantine

Hugh Elton

The half-century of Diocletian and Constantine (284–337 CE) is often presented as a period of revolution when a new empire was fashioned. During this period there was a complex series of reforms of the whole mechanism of government, but despite the undoubted importance of Diocletian and Constantine, not all developments in the third and fourth centuries should be attributed to them. Focusing on these rulers obscures the contributions of other emperors during this period. The reality of the new empire of Diocletian and Constantine was a generalized groping towards a formalization of existing practices carried out in a sporadic fashion. Understanding the changes is difficult because of the challenges presented by the sources. The source material from the mid-third century is weak and there is no connected narrative for the reign of Diocletian. This means that first attestations can easily occur some time after changes had first been introduced. A good example of this is the formation of regiments of *lanciarii*, sometimes attributed to Diocletian (van Berchem 1952: 107). As a result of recent archaeological work at Apamea in Syria, we now know that *lanciarii* existed in the early third century (Balty 1988; *AE* 1993 nos.1574–5). After the reign of Diocletian, the source material increases in volume, but its interpretation remains difficult thanks to Constantine's status as first Christian emperor and victor in a series of civil wars, which affected the way in which he was described by both contemporaries and later writers (Lieu and Montserrat 1996).

On May 23, 326 Acilius Severus, the Prefect of Rome, received a law from Constantine. The emperor was in either Aquileia or Milan or on the road between the two cities. The law concerned the *peculia* of the *palatini* "who follow our standards, who always assist our actions, who, bent on their clerical duties, are exposed to lengthy journeys and difficult marches, are no strangers to the dust and toil of the camp" (*CTh.* 6.36.1). Both emperors and government were itinerant and their travels covered most of the empire. Maximian, for example, was in Aquileia in March 296, spent the summer on the Rhine, the autumn in Spain, and then crossed over to Africa where he was on campaign by the following March, if not earlier. It would be easy to confuse emperors with generals, were it not for the fact that imperial movements can often be tracked by the laws issued as the emperors moved. Late third- and fourth-century government centered on the emperor, so any analysis of the state should start there.

In theory at least, emperors existed to provide law, order, and justice for their people. While there are many different ways of thinking about the emperor, this section follows Millar's concept of "the emperor was what the emperor did" (Millar 1977: 6). Regardless of the perquisites of office, being Roman emperor was a demanding and often dangerous job – Maximian's travels show the constant military pressure on the state. But ruling involved other tasks as well: hearing appeals, public appearances, etc. From Diocletian onwards, the empire was almost always run by multiple emperors, a recognition that the state was too unwieldy to be run by one man. Only a year after his accession, Diocletian began to share power with Maximian in 285 (Leadbetter 1998). From 293 he expanded the arrangement to include Constantius and Galerius in a college of four emperors known as the tetrarchy. The unity of the tetrarchy, its *indivisum patrimonium* (*Pan.* 3[11].6.3), was constantly stressed: the acts of one emperor were the acts of all four. Since the tetrarchs met only rarely (and the first tetrarchy never met as four men in the same city), this was especially important. Thus the ninth milestone from Verona was erected in the name of "Imperator Caesar C. Valerius Diocletianus Pius Felix Invictus Augustus and Imperator Caesar Marcus Aurelius Valerius Maximianus Pius Felix Invictus Augustus and Flavius Valerius Constantius and Galerius Valerius Maximianus, most noble Caesars" (*ILS* 636). There developed a distinctive iconography by which all four emperors were shown together, seen in e.g. the Venice Tetrarchs, the Arch of Galerius, and in the Temple of Ammon at Luxor (Rees 1993). Constantine carried out the same practice. An inscription from Cirta in the North African province of Numidia was dedicated by the provincial governor to "the perpetual victory of our lords Constantine Maximus, triumphator, always Augustus, and to Constantine and Constantius and Constans, most noble and flourishing Caesars" (*ILS* 715). On Diocletian's retirement in 305, the first tetrarchy was replaced with a second tetrarchy of Constantius, Galerius, Maximinus, and Severus, though this soon fell to pieces in a series of civil wars. When the fighting was over and Constantine was dominant as sole ruler, a system of multiple rulers was re-instituted, with Constantine appointing his sons and a nephew as Caesars. The final version of this new tetrarchy involved Constantine II based in Gaul, Constantius II on the eastern frontier, Constans in Italy, Africa, and the western Balkans, and the nephew Dalmatius in the eastern Balkans. Although these large imperial colleges, confusing to both modern scholars and contemporaries, were an innovation, the idea of multiple rulers was not. The same advantages (stability of succession, ability to deploy imperially-led forces on more than one front) had been appreciated by emperors since the Flavians in the first century CE, if not before. During the third century, there were several periods of multiple emperors, whether jointly appointed (Balbinus and Pupienus), father and son (Valerian and Gallienus, or Carus, Carinus, and Numerianus), or coexisting (the central empire of Valerian and Gallienus or Aurelian, with subsidiary states in Palmyra

Figures 10.1a–d The tetrarchs: (a) Diocletian (*RIC* 79a); (b) Maximian (KM 1991 2.816); (c) Constantius I (*RIC* Constantius I n. 32a); (d) Galerius (*RIC* Galerius 24b) (Figures 10.1a, b, and d from the editor's collection)

and the Gallic Empire). Diocletian's measures were thus a rationalization of existing practices. The precise relationship of *Augusti* to Caesars is not well understood. All were emperors, but *Augusti* were clearly superior to Caesars. The 305 retirement settlement of Diocletian was the result of diktat, not negotiation, and later senior *Augusti* were less able to be autocratic. It seems that Caesars in the tetrarchy did not have their own administrations, but rather shared those of the *Augusti*. However, they did have their own courts, armies, and powers to issue laws (Corcoran 2000: 266–74). Though the cooperation of the tetrarchs and thus the success of the tetrarchic system depended on Diocletian's will, and so disintegrated on his retirement, in the short term it provided enough stability to allow other changes to occur. Imperial deployment in 298 showed the strengths of the new system, with the tetrarchs dealing simultaneously with problems on four fronts. Constantius held the Rhine against the Franks while Maximian was still in Africa, probably fighting the Laguatan. In Syria, Galerius invaded Persia while Diocletian was in Egypt (Zuckerman 1994). Similar flexibility was provided by Constantine's reliance on his family, recognized by Eusebius, who described Constantine's illumination of the world through his Caesars (Euseb. *LC* 3.4).

The intense military pressures of the third century meant that emperors and their retinues spent most of their reigns on the frontiers, or marching along well-worn routes linking border regions. These imperial retinues, known as the *comitatus* (more graphically as *stratopedon* in Greek: literally "the camp"), included the emperor's household, personal attendants, cooks, barbers, etc. Many of these men were attended by their slaves. When at war, a substantial military contingent accompanied the emperor, but even when not on campaign, there were thousands of guard troops in attendance. The whole administrative machine of the empire also accompanied the emperor, allowing him to issue laws, collect taxes, hold trials, and hear appeals. Files could be consulted since court records were sent to the emperor (*CTh*. 1.16.3 [319]). There was also the traffic of ambassadors and messengers who were constantly arriving. The staff all needed to be fed; many of them needed their own horses or mules, and these needed to be fed too. A single receipt from Egypt for part of one unit in February 295 shows the scale of the system: "Valens, *optio* of Legio VII Claudia under Julianus *praepositus*, I have received 1740 lbs of fodder in three days from Sarmates and Didymus, *curatores* of the Oxyrhynchite nome" (*P.Oxy.* 43 col. 5). These supplies kept coming in an unending stream. The system allowed the emperor, when necessary, to move in winter, though the cost could be high. In 313 Maximinus "moved his army out of Syria when winter was at its most savage and with double marches rushed into Bithynia with an injured force; for the baggage animals of all sorts were lost to rain and snow, to mud, cold and exhaustion and their wretched carcasses in the road announced now to the soldiers the result of the future war and a similar slaughter" (Lact. *DMP* 45.2–3).

As the emperor and his entourage moved, he kept on entering cities. There was a ceremonial process, known as *adventus* ("arrival") that regulated the way in which the emperor interacted with his cities (MacCormack 1981). Outside the city gate, the town councilors assembled to honor the emperor, along with other important local figures, priests, and musicians. When Constantine arrived at Autun in 311, an orator claimed that "we decorated the roads by which he might come into the palace, with modest ornamentation, but with the standards of all our collegia, the statues of all our gods and a very small number of loud Instruments which, in short bursts, we brought round to you often, by running" (*Pan.* 8 [5].8.4). Some cities were rarely visited (Autun's only other known visit in this period was by Constantius I in 295), but others saw the emperor on many occasions, especially those on major communication routes like Trier, Milan, Serdica, Sirmium, Nicaea, Nicomedia, and Antioch. The late third century saw a series of new constructions in these cities to support emperors and their retinues. Typical features were a palace (for audiences), a hippodrome (for races and public appearances) – these two buildings were often linked – a treasury, and vast numbers of warehouses. In 310, a panegyrist described Trier: "I see a Circus Maximus, the rival I believe of that in Rome, I see basilicas and a forum, royal works, and a seat of justice are being raised to such a height that they promise to be worthy neighbours of the stars and the sky" (*Pan.* 7 [6].22.5). Troops and retinues were scattered throughout the city, often billeted on private individuals.

With emperors spending much of their time in new places or in or between frontier regions, the city of Rome continued to be marginalized. Diocletian went there only for his *vicennalia* in 303, but didn't like the city. He was especially fond of Nicomedia. Its attractions were similar to those of Byzantium, where Constantine founded his new city of Constantinople in 324. Both had good communications, lying on the main military route between the eastern and Danubian fronts, with good sea access. Constantine too was rarely in Rome – only three visits are recorded: in 312 to defeat Maxentius, in 315 for his *decennalia* and in 326 to celebrate his *vicennalia* (after celebrating it in 324 at Nicomedia). His *tricennalia* in 335, however, was celebrated in Constantinople. Although Constantinople went on to become a "second Rome," it was not intended as such. It had no Senate initially, though its preferred status was shown by the establishment of a corn dole in 332 and the early existence of a *praetor* (*Chron. Pasch. s.a.* 332).

Constantinople also benefited from its imperial foundation by plundering other cities for suitable decoration. Churches were built there rapidly, but existing temples were left intact. It was impossible within Roman minds, pagan or Christian, to separate religion and the state. Peace on earth and even the harvest depended on treating the god or gods correctly. As Maximinus wrote in 312, "who can be so senseless or bereft of all intelligence as not to perceive that it is by the benevolent care of the gods that the earth does not refuse the seeds committed to it" (Euseb. *Eccl. Hist.* 9.7–8). Failure to do this had negative consequences. The emperor was the chief priest of Rome, the *Pontifex Maximus*, a post held by both *Augusti* under the tetrarchy (*ILS* 639). The Diocletianic persecutions of 303 began because sacrifices were turning out poorly on account of Christians being present. From 305, the civil wars following Diocletian's retirement meant that imperial treatment of Christianity became politicized. Romans wanted to know whether the continuing problems were the result of allowing Christians freedom or because freedom had been denied to them. Galerius' persecutions meant that support of Christianity could bring political benefits to his rivals. In the west, Constantine was tolerant from 306 and Maxentius did not persecute and even returned some property to Christians. In the east, Galerius cancelled his persecution in 311, in part due to a painful disease which he attributed to the Christian god. Maximinus, however, continued the persecution, and cities under his control, including Nicomedia and Antioch, banned Christians from meeting in their territory. This persecution was relaxed in winter 312, then cancelled in spring 313 immediately before his defeat (Mitchell 1988). Thus Licinius' and Constantine's toleration from June 313 (proclaimed in the Edict of Milan) was a late development. Its motivation too was typical, in that Licinius and Constantine explained that, having "discussed everything relevant to the public advantage and safety, we considered that, among those things which we saw would be relevant to many people, priority should be given to setting in order those matters involving reverence for the divinity, in order that we might give both to Christians and to everyone the freedom to follow whatever religion they wish, so that whatever divinity resides in the heavens might be well-disposed and favorable towards us and all who have been placed under our authority" (Lact. *DMP* 48.2). The same issue of concern for imperial unity can be seen in Constantine's handling of the Arian controversy. Bishop Eusebius of Nicomedia, Licinius' main residence, was at odds with bishop Alexander of Alexandria, and was supporting Arius against him. After the defeat of

Licinius in 324, Constantine became involved, in part because the issues were already discussed at Nicomedia. He dismissed the theological question (centering on the nature of the relationship of God the Father to God the Son) in favor of church unity, and wrote to both Arius and Alexander, asking whether they could agree to differ (Euseb. *VC* 2.64–72). When this proved impossible, he attempted to resolve the problem by summoning a council of bishops, i.e. a convocation of the entire church, representing both East and West. Constantine fixed the time, place, and agenda, attended and played an active part in the meeting at Nicaea in May 325. By the end of the council, only three of the delegates, Arius, Eusebius of Nicomedia, and Theognis of Nicaea, refused to sign anathemas against Arius and so were exiled. According to the emperor, "the decision of 300 bishops must be considered no other than the judgement of God" (Socr. *Hist. Eccl.* 1.9). Constantine then worked hard to persuade Arius to accept the council's judgment. The Council of Jerusalem in 335, once reassured that Arius had been personally examined by Constantine and ascertained to be orthodox, re-admitted Arius to the church. Constantine's concerns seem hardly theological. Edicts against heretics were issued in the same spirit of imperial unity rather than theological correctness (*CTh.* 16.5.2 [326]).

Emperors had a clear relationship with the divine powers. In the 270s and 280s, Aurelian and Carus had already described themselves as *dominus et deus* ("lord and god") (Peachin 1990). This relationship continued in traditional fashion and was hardly affected by Christianity. Thus the emperor continued to hold the office of Pontifex Maximus and was given divine honors through the imperial cult, even if Christians did not always participate. An inscription from Arycanda in Lycia in 312, after quoting Maximinus' statement on the care of the gods, asked Maximinus and Licinius that "injunctions be given for all to devote themselves steadfastly to the worship of the gods" (*CIL* 3.12132). The imperial cult continued to be celebrated by Christian emperors. In 333/5, Constantine allowed the construction of a temple dedicated to his family at Hispellum in Italy, provided that no sacrifices took place (*ILS* 705), although other priests still erected inscriptions showing that they had performed all "public services" (*leitourgeian*), which presumably did include sacrifices (*SEG* 41.1390). And on the death of an emperor, he was often deified by the Senate, as happened to Diocletian, Constantius, and Constantine, for example. Imperial propaganda stressed the special status of emperors, making clear the divine sponsorship of their actions. An inscription from Dyrrachium mentioned "our lords Diocletian and Maximian, unconquered Augusti, born of gods and creators of gods" (*ILS* 629). This aspect was modified by Diocletian who devised new titles by which he associated himself with Jupiter and Maximian with Hercules. As with tetrarchic unity, this theme was disseminated widely. New legions were created, named Ioviani and Herculiani after these deities. When the theater of Pompey in Rome was restored by L. Aelius Helvius Dionysius, probably in 301–2, its new gates were named the *porticus Iovia* and *porticus Herculia* (*ILS* 621–2). Coins reinforced these associations, with IOVI CONSERVATORI on the reverse of many of Diocletian's issues, HERCULI CONSERVATORI on Maximian's reverses. This relationship with Jupiter and Hercules continued under the second tetrarchy (*ILS* 658–9, 681), with Licinius describing himself as IOVI CONSERVATORI into the 320s (*RIC* 7.676–82). Non-Christian, though traditional, epithets, like SOL INVICTUS, were found on some of Constantine's coins as late as 324.

Another tetrarchic change was the introduction of increasingly elaborate court ceremonial, by which court protocol was remodeled on Oriental principles. New officials, often eunuchs, are now attested as playing an important role in controlling access to the emperor. The *praepositus sacri cubiculi* ("officer in charge of the sacred bedchamber") is first attested in 326, and the *primicerius sacri cubiculi* (there is little difference in these two titles) perhaps in 312, definitely in 326. Despised by contemporaries, their considerable power depended on the emperor's favor (Hopkins 1978a). Once past the eunuchs, approaching an emperor involved a formal process of *adoratio*, kneeling and kissing the corner of the imperial robe, a practice apparently introduced by Diocletian (H. Stern 1954). The court was a difficult world, even if one could reach the emperor's ear. Promotion was dependent on the emperor, who always played a role in appointing senior officials and could be swayed by personal factors. Constantine, for example, gave some preference to Christians. The most famous was Ablabius, who was *vicarius* of Asiana in 324/26, praetorian prefect in 329–37 and consul in 331. But Constantine also appointed Sopater, a pagan sophist from Syria, as an assessor at court because he was "captivated" by him. Sopater was later executed through a plot laid by Ablabius (Eun. *VS* 462). Politics affected cities as well as individuals. The Phrygian town of Orcistus, in appealing for an upgrade of its civic status to city, mentioned that all of its population were "followers of the most holy religion." Since the petition was supported by Ablabius and favorably received by Constantine, they were probably Christians (*MAMA* 7.305).

Ruling the empire or even finding out what was happening required the emperor to exert his will. His voice could be heard directly and imperial visits were an effective way of reminding the empire of his existence. The imperial voice could be heard at a distance in many ways. Images of the emperor were everywhere, in government offices and on coins. All official documents contained references to his existence. Laws were posted which issued his commands (Matthews 1998). Judges enacted his law. Governors collected his taxes. And everywhere troops were present as a reminder of the consequences of disobeying the emperor's will. The machinery functioned on a combination of fear and faith. Fear was guaranteed by the existence and use of a powerful army, intended to allow the emperor to defend himself and to protect the state. Without this support, imperial decisions could not be carried out – hence the harsh treatment of dissidents who denied the authority of the Roman emperor, especially in the army. The frequent military sacrifices on behalf of the emperor could be interpreted as idolatry by Christians, though many served as soldiers. When interrogating the reluctant conscript Maximilianus in 295, Cassius Dio, the proconsul of Africa, observed that "there are Christian soldiers in the sacred *comitatus* of our lords Diocletian, Maximian, Constantius and Galerius and they serve" (*acta Maximiliani* 2.9). These included men like Aurelius Gaius, buried at Cotyaeum in Phrygia in the early fourth century. After serving throughout the empire, Aurelius left the army (perhaps because of the 303 persecutions) and "in tribute to Julia Arescusa my own wife most dear I have erected this stele from [the fruits of] my own labors as a memorial until the Resurrection" (Sartre 1983; *SEG* 31.1116). With the acceptance of Christianity, Christians had to serve as soldiers. The Biblical commandment that "thou shalt not kill" was no bar to service and at one of Constantine's first church councils, at Arles in August 314, the assembled bishops agreed to excommunicate soldiers who put down their arms in peacetime; military service was clearly a necessity (Opt. App. 4, canon 3). However, even under Christian emperors, most troops remained pagan, drawn from the countryside where the majority were non-Christian until at least the end of the fourth century. Some veterans greeted the emperor in 320 (or 326): "when he had entered the headquarters (*principia*) and had been saluted by prefects and tribunes and by the *viri eminentissimi*, he was acclaimed, 'Augustus Constantine, May the gods preserve you for us. Your safety is our safety'" (*CTh.* 7.20.2). The elite regiments of the Ioviani and Herculiani, created by Diocletian, still occupied the most privileged positions in the army at the end of the fourth century. But throughout the period, the army remained an instrument of the state, whether used by Galerius to destroy churches or to persecute Christians and Manicheans or by Constantine to destroy pagan temples and to enforce persecution of Donatists.

As with separating secular and religious, distinguishing civil from military is difficult. All arms of government service were described as *militia*, though this could be qualified as *militia armata* and *militia officialis*. The persecutions of Christians in Caesarea in Palaestina Prima were carried out by the governor's office sending troops to investigate, using census lists created for taxation purposes. The overlap is exemplified by the office of praetorian prefect, usually held by two equestrians. Their backgrounds varied, though some were lawyers, like Hermogenianus under Diocletian (Corcoran 2000: 85–90). On occasion, prefects commanded the *comitatus*, as when Volusianus led an army of Maxentius against Alexander in Africa in 309, though most did not have extensive military backgrounds (Zos. 2.14.2). More usual were their other military duties, including recruiting and provision of supplies for the army, *comitatus*, and government officials, as well as feeding Rome (and from 332 Constantinople). Prefects also acted as judges. Constantine in 331 stated that "we do not permit appeals to be made from the praetorian prefects who alone should be described as judging in the divine stead (*vice sacra*) lest the veneration due to us should be seen as impugned" (*CTh.* 11.30.16). They also acted as the emperor's chief of staff and were responsible for public works, roads, and the imperial post. After Constantine defeated Maxentius in 312 and Licinius in 324, the praetorian guards were disbanded and prefects ceased to have a military command role. Their numbers varied, since each emperor had his own prefect. Like emperors, they acted collegially (Feissel 1985 = *SEG* 35.1484; Feissel 1991).

Although one of the most powerful officials, praetorian prefects were only part of the machine of government. In the late third century, most other aspects of the rest of the empire were run from the *comitatus* by the several *scrinia* (departments), the principals of which were the *magister libellorum* (in charge of judicial petitions), the *magister epistularum* (imperial correspondence), and the *magister memoriae* (memoranda). This system had been completely reformed by the 330s. The office of prefect, perhaps over-powerful (in the third century, prefects had murdered and replaced emperors on more than occasion), and certainly demanding, with its financial, administrative, judicial, and military responsibilities, underwent restructuring. Late in Constantine's reign, the military role of prefects was taken by new officers, the *magister peditum* and *magister equitum* (Zos. 2.33). The office of *magister officiorum* had appeared by 320 to oversee the various *magistri scriniarum*, as well as the *agentes in rebus*, imperial investigators. Constantine created the office of *quaestor sacri palatii* to draft imperial constitutions in place of the *magister libellorum* (Harries 1988). He also created a new rank between *duces* and prefects, that of *comes*, a companion of the emperor. In the third century, this was a description of a relationship to the emperor, but Constantine formalized this title as both an honor and a rank. As an honor it was attached to positions close to the emperor such as *comes et magister militum*. As a rank, it was usually given to senators, though subdivided into several grades (Mann 1977). Many of these officials met in the consistory, the advisory imperial council that included most of the senior officers of the *comitatus*, both civilian and military.

The way in which provinces were administered changed, too. Before Diocletian's reign, the civil and military aspects of provinces were administered by the governor (usually a senatorial *legatus*, though there were already some equestrian governors: Pflaum 1976), the financial aspects by an equestrian procurator. By the end of Constantine's reign, a province's military aspects were administered by a *dux*, the civil and financial by the governor (*praeses, corrector, consularis*) (Mann 1977). The new military frontier commands often covered more than one civil province, producing officers such as the *dux Pannoniae Primae et Norici Ripensis* or the *dux Aegypti Thebaidos utrarumque Libyarum* (*AE* 1934.7; *ILS* 701). These *duces* themselves were not new, though they became far more common than they had been in the third century. *Duces* could still carry out civic duties: e.g. in Scythica, Aurelius Firminianus built a city gate at Tomi under Diocletian and Maximian (286/93) (*ILS* 4103), and late in his reign Constantine wrote to Ursinus, the *dux* of Mesopotamia, banning castration (*CJust.* 4.42.1). However, some governors may have retained military functions into Constantine's reign, as suggested by a dedication from the tribune Successus to Arrius Maximus, *consularis* of Syria Coele (*AE* 1940 no. 168).

The separation of civil and military hierarchies had other consequences. Beginning in the early third century, many senatorial families ceased to compete for or hold government positions, and by the end of the century these families usually only held office as provincial governors (*correctores*) in Italy or as the *proconsul* of Asia, Achaea, or Africa. Even these commands were much smaller than they had been, Africa for example having been subdivided into three provinces. The urban prefecture of Rome was also a prestigious office, and one that did not require travel outside Italy. At the same time, other families, for the most part *equites*, concentrated on military positions. With no need to hold civic offices, often in Rome, Roman officers could now be career officers, rather than aristocrats with military responsibilities. There was thus the beginning of an imperial aristocracy based on holding offices rather than land. These changes also allowed the promotion of non-Romans into higher ranks, a process often described as "barbarization." This was not a deliberate policy change, but an unintended consequence of the changes in command structures. Thus the Frank Bonitus fought for Constantine against Licinius and had a Roman wife, while Crocus, the Alamannic king present at Constantine's accession in 306 was probably in command of troops (Amm. Marc. 15.5.33; Aur. Vict. *Caes.* 3). The promotion of many equestrians into the senatorial order also started to blur the distinctions between the two. Constantine did create a new senatorial rank of *consularis* for governors of some provinces, especially in Italy, but some of the holders had recent equestrian antecedents.

More emperors meant more soldiers, palaces, and administrators. In the words of Lactantius, "the provinces were divided into minute portions, and many *praesides* and a multitude of inferior officers lay heavy on each territory, and almost on each city.

There were also many *rationales* and *magistri* and *vicarii* of prefects" (*DMP* 7.4). The government of the late empire is often described as bigger than that of the early empire (Heather 1994; Garnsey and Humfress 2001: 36–8), although calculations of the small size of the early imperial administration perhaps underestimate the role played by governor's households in running the state. The number of provinces was increased in Diocletian's reign, as they were, in Lactantius' phrase, "chopped into slices" (*DMP* 7.4); an early-fourth-century document, the Verona List, lists almost 100 provinces (T. D. Barnes 1982: 195–225). The increase in numbers took place gradually and there was no single edict changing the structure of all the empire's provinces in one fell swoop. Nor was this a new practice. In Anatolia, Isauria had been carved out of Cilicia by the reign of Gordian III, if not earlier (*CIL* 3.6783), and Caria and Phrygia was split off as a province from Asia in the 250s, before being split again into separate provinces in 301/5 (Roueché 1989). Under the tetrarchy, many provinces were split into smaller parts: Asiana, for example, went from being one province to seven. At the same time, eight provinces were carved out of Italy. Many small provinces, however, continued unchanged. The process of splitting provinces continued after Diocletian. Licinius created Aegyptus Iovia, Aegyptus Herculia, and Arabia Nova out of Aegyptus in 314/15, although he reassembled them by 324.

The increase in the number of provinces and officials led to the development by Diocletian of a new level of administration above provincial governors, that of *vicarius*, technically deputies of the praetorian prefects (*vicarii agens vices praefectorum praetorio*) (Barnes 1982: 141–7). There were 12 *vicarii*, equally divided between east and west, who were responsible for dioceses, groups of between six and 18 provinces. Most of their duties were judicial and financial. The diocesan structure was used to organize mints and by the end of Diocletian's reign a mint had been established in most dioceses, usually at cities frequented by emperors, such as Nicomedia or Trier. This was a gradual process; Spain never had a mint, perhaps because of its lack of garrison, and one was not established in Viennensis until 313. It was not a rule, however: the only mint in north Africa, at Carthage, was moved to Ostia c.307. When Domitius Alexander revolted in Africa a few years later, his coinage was of noticeably poor quality (Hendy 1972, 1985).

Reducing the load on provincial officials made the empire more efficient, since governors were now responsible for a much smaller number of cities. Their main responsibilities were to collect taxes, hear legal cases, and enforce the imperial will. The governor's role in tax collection changed as a result of Diocletian's reforms of the taxation system. Managing imperial income was complicated. The income from the substantial imperial estates (in cash or kind), many of which were rented out, was handled by the *res privata*. Cash payments from the rest of the empire were handled by the *res summa*, which became the *sacrae largitiones* from Constantine's reign. The *res summa* collected taxes levied in cash, as well as the *aurum coronarium* (and the *chrysargyron*, first attested in 325), and paid out donatives. Its role became more important with the increasing emphasis on cash income in the fourth century. A third stream of income came from goods levied in kind by the praetorian prefect to support the army and comitatus. In 297, Diocletian regularized this process as the *annona militaris*. Rates were not fixed, but based on state needs. The levy was based on land units (*iugera*) and head counts (*capita*), assessed for every farm, village, and city (many of which had previously been exempt) following extensive local surveys (Millar

1993a: 535–44). Although the way in which these were calculated varied regionally, this did not affect the calculations of the prefect. When the system was introduced, censuses were made, but these were rarely adjusted. It was possible, though, to adjust taxation rates. They usually went up, though in the late 350s, the Caesar Julian was famously able to lower assessments in Gaul from 25 *solidi* per *caput* to seven (Amm. Marc. 16.5.14). The goods were collected by tax collectors, who were personally responsible for taxes; any shortfall then fell on the local council which appointed them. Tax collection could be popular with collectors, as it gave an opportunity to make money if more was collected than required. Italy had always been subject to collections for the *annona*, so with the main state demands now coming in this form, it now paid more. However, when Severus attempted to impose the *capitatio* on urban populations Italy in 306 it was unpopular, enabling Maxentius' seizure of power (Lact. *DMP* 26.2). Assessing the burden of the taxation system is difficult, though Diocletian's work probably increased the efficiency of collection, especially of the *annona*. Lactantius said that the beneficiaries of taxation exceeded the tax-payers, though Aurelius Victor thought that taxes were much more tolerable at this period than they were two generations later (Lact. *DMP* 7.3; Aur. Vict. *Caes.* 39.32).

With much of the taxation collected in kind, the state was able to insulate itself from some of the inflationary problems of the period. Coins were minted in gold, silver, and bronze. The traditional silver coinage, the denarius, suffered particularly from debasement, though this did not affect gold coinage, since the exchange rate was based on metal content, not face value. The relationship between the bronze and silver coinages fluctuated continually. Although bronze was minted for military pay and for small change, it was not withdrawn through tax collection. Continued minting thus increased the money supply and fueled inflation. Coinage reforms had already been attempted by Aurelian. Diocletian in 286 struck gold at 60 to the pound and created a new silver coin, the *argenteus*, struck at 96 to the pound from pure silver in 294. Another response to the crisis was the Price Edict of 301, which was intended primarily to regulate government purchases and to protect soldiers' income. This set a maximum price for a *modius* of wheat at 100 denarii, but by 335 a *modius* cost c.6,000 denarii (*P.Lond.* 1914), i.e. 60 times as much (Corcoran 2000: 205–33). Changing the coins in circulation and fixing prices was not enough. It was not until Constantine's creation of gold *solidi* (struck at 72 to the pound) from 309 that some long-term stability was brought to the currency. This coinage could only be spread as Constantine conquered territory, so it was not until 324 that gold *solidi* were a universal currency. Constantine benefited from his capture of the treasuries of his civil war rivals and from his confiscation of temple treasures (emulating Maximinus in the 230s: Herod. 7.3.5), both of which allowed large amounts of the new coinage to be introduced at once. A renewed emphasis on taxes in precious metals (and commutation) and the introduction of new taxes (the *chrysargyron*) allowed the government to keep the coinage stable (Hendy 1985: 284–5).

Governors also heard legal cases, ideally in public (*CTh.* 1.16.6 [331]). Although many governors had some legal experience, this was not a requirement for appointment. Resolving cases was made somewhat easier for judges by two collections of law in Diocletian's reign, the *Codex Gregorianus* (first edition c.292) and the *Codex Hermogenianus* (first edition 295). These collections were composed mostly of rescripts (imperial replies to private petitions), while most of the Constantinian laws preserved (generally in the *Codex Theodosianus*) are edicts (imperial pronouncements). These different focuses reflect different collection strategies, rather than any change in imperial practice (Corcoran 2000). Governors did not always use such aids, however, but often returned appeals to lower officials. In 318, Valerius Ziper, *praeses* of Aegyptus Herculia, replied to a petition from Aurelius Isidorus concerning his dispute with a fellow-villager over a debt, "the *praepositus pagi* [a local official], after having decided between you, will provide the appropriate assistance in the matter of the debt owed you" (*P.Cair. Isid.* 76). The private petitions preserved show that individuals of low status, including women and slaves, could transmit petitions to the emperor and receive a response. Some even managed this twice, like Calpurnia Aristaeneta at Maximian's court in Milan in 286 (*FV* 282). Governors did not have a monopoly on jurisdiction; military courts existed as well and Constantine empowered bishops to hear civil suits in certain circumstances (Harries 1999: 191–203). By 333 he ruled that any party in a legal case before the verdict was passed could appeal to a bishop's jurisdiction, the bishop's judgment was not subject to appeal, and had to be executed by the state. When his Christian praetorian prefect Ablabius questioned this, it was explicitly reaffirmed by Constantine (*Sirm.* 1 [333]).

Governors were also responsible for many enactments of the imperial will, either in response to an edict or as a result of a direct order delivered by letter. Some were simple, as when Diocletian wrote to Aurelius Isidorus, the procurator of the Thebaid, in 299, giving him instructions about the transportation of columns of granite from Syene to Alexandria (*P.Panop.Beatty* 2.50). Others were more complicated. A dispute between two Christian factions (orthodox and Donatist) in Carthage led to Constantine's intervention in several ways, including by means of letters to the governor. Once Constantine had defeated Maxentius in 312, he wrote two letters to Anullinus, proconsul of Africa, which showed clear and pointed support for the Catholics. Although this was a religious dispute, Constantine was using both secular and ecclesiastical channels. The Donatists proceeded to appeal to Constantine three times over the next three years. Constantine responded by calling councils at Rome in 313 and Arles in 314, summoning ecclesiastical officials in his capacity as secular ruler. Constantine, who was present, called the judgment of Arles on the Donatists in 314 a "Judgment of Christ: for I say – and it is the truth – that the judgment of priests ought to be regarded as if the Lord himself sat in judgment" (Opt. App. 5). A final resolution of the dispute was delayed in 316 because of the war against Licinius, but in spring 317 Constantine began exiling the Donatist leaders and confiscating their property. However, imperial persecution of Christians and creation of martyrs was a hard concept to defend or implement and persecution tailed off rapidly. By 321, the Donatist exiles had been recalled, and Constantine wrote to the Catholic bishops, saying that revenge would be left to God. For Constantine, this appears to have been as much about imperial unity as it was about religion; there were no theological issues involved. It was difficult for imperial officials to enforce imperial commands while living in a community among their peers and many must have been grateful that their terms of office were short.

The half-century between Diocletian's accession and Constantine's death was a period of significant change and development in the Roman state. It is important to remember that change occurred both before and after this period. Most measures were not new, but were institutionalizations of existing practices. Too much emphasis can easily be placed on Diocletian and Constantine personally and not enough on their imperial colleagues. The most significant change was in the restructuring of administrative hierarchies, with the state now run by imperial officials rather than by equestrian and senatorial aristocrats. There was more government in the fourth century than there had been earlier, though it remains unclear how heavy the demands were or whether the state actually strangled efficiency. Thus the demands of supporting multiple emperors and their courts as well as new provincial governors, *vicarii* and *duces*, need to be set against more efficient collection of taxation and judicial process. There was also a secession of part of the world from imperial control with the creation of a Christian church, though the problem of who was its master – emperor or God – was still unresolved when Constantine died. Lastly, though the framework of the empire itself may have been more efficient, government itself, as always, depended on the people involved – exemptions and contradictions in policy and enforcement were frequent.

CHAPTER ELEVEN

The Roman Army

Nigel Pollard

In his book on relations between soldiers and civilians in Roman Egypt, Richard Alston (1995: 3–4) bemoaned a tendency in past decades for the study of the Roman army to be treated as "almost a sub-discipline of ancient history" (and, one might add, of archaeology), with inward-looking preoccupations and obsessions, emphasizing the study of organization, rank, deployment, and the typologies of military installations. This approach has, quite rightly, put off many students and scholars. However, the study of the Roman army is important and interesting, but only if we re-integrate it into the wider context of Roman history as a whole. This is easy to do, since one or another aspect of the Roman army is relevant to just about every major sub-discipline of, and approach to, Roman imperial history – including politics, provincial administration, social and economic history, and the study of local cultures within the empire. The Roman army was a crucial source of imperial power and its support made and broke emperors (see Peachin, this volume). Its members were the most numerous representatives of the Roman state and performed many of the basic tasks required to run the empire. It was the state's greatest financial burden, present in each and every province. It was composed of individuals from all groups of Roman society and acted as a means of social mobility for some. Its members formed a distinctive institutional group within Roman society but, as representatives of Roman power and culture, interacted daily with members of each and every local culture in the empire. For all these reasons, some knowledge of the Roman army is crucial to an understanding of the Roman Empire. This chapter is intended to provide a sketch of the history and character of the Roman army as an institution and then to explore its role in the wider study of Roman imperial history.

1 The Augustan Army

Augustus standardized the pay and allowances of the entire Army – at the same time fixing the period of service and the bounty due on its completion – according to military rank; this would discourage them from revolting, when back in civil life, on the excuse that they were either too old or had insufficient capital to earn an honest living. (Suet. *Aug.* 49, tr. M. Grant)

On gaining sole control of the Roman world in 31 BCE, Octavian faced a number of problems. These included the need to demobilize the inflated armies of the civil wars without causing excessive unrest, the need to focus the loyalty of the remaining forces on the state (or rather, on himself, as the leader of the state), and to prevent other ambitious individuals from winning soldiers' loyalties as he had done himself in his rise to power. Octavian came to power in the same way as the republican potentates (Marius, Sulla, Pompey, and Caesar) who preceded him – namely by securing the support of troops who were loyal to him rather than to the republic or any other general – and by success in battle, ultimately the naval defeat of Antony at Actium. Ancient and modern writers have expressed doubts about Octavian's personal bravery and military ability (see Antony's slander in Suet. *Aug.* 16), but his genius lay not in winning battles but in reforming the Roman army in a manner that ensured that he was not replaced in the same way he had come to power (for a useful general survey see Keppie 1984: 145–71).

Augustus reduced the size of the bloated civil war armies, professionalized the remaining force and focused its loyalty on the emperor. As republican Rome had conquered the Mediterranean basin, the military requirements of conquering and garrisoning an empire with what had originally been a local militia had caused enormous strains, social, political, and economic. Augustus' reforms also provided the Roman Empire with an effective standing force to garrison a huge empire. The essence of these reforms endured to provide the structural framework of the army well into the third century CE. However, the Augustan reforms also sowed the seeds of future problems, notably political and economic.

Resettlement of veterans

At the end of the war between Octavian and Antony, their combined armies totaled some 60 legions (about 300,000 men, estimated on the basis of *RG* 3.3). Augustus reduced this to 28 legions. This entailed both risks and opportunities. He might create a mass of discontented ex-soldiers to provide military support for a future challenger for power. He might lose the support of Italian towns by expropriating land to resettle veterans. On the other hand if he rewarded the veterans appropriately, their future loyalty would lie with him and thus secure his position.

Augustus advertised prominently in the *Res Gestae* his foundation of provincial veteran colonies as well as Italian settlements and the discharge of 300,000 veterans to those colonies or to their homes, each rewarded with money or land (*RG* 28; 3.3). He boasted that he had given 600 million sesterces (150 million denarii) to pay for land for veterans settled in Italy and 260 million denarii to buy provincial land (*RG* 16.1). Payment rather than confiscation may have reduced the tensions caused by Octavian's earlier resettlements of veterans (see, for example, Verg. *Ecl.* 1 and Suet. *Aug.* 13). His major colonial settlements took place in 30 and 14 BCE, but subsequently he rewarded veterans primarily with cash *praemia* rather than land. From 6

CE these were drawn from the *aerarium militare*, a new military treasury primed with 170 million sesterces of Augustus' own money (Dio 55.25.1–3; *RG* 17.2), another largess by the emperor to secure the veterans' loyalty. Thereafter this treasury drew funds from new taxes on inheritance and auction sales (Dio 55.25.5–6; 56.28.4; Tac. *Ann*. 1.78). The provision of a regular structure for the retirement of veterans focused their loyalty on the emperor and the state and avoided some of the problems of the republican period, when soldiers looked to individual commanders to provide for their retirement from booty and confiscated land.

The Augustan regular army

In 13 BCE the length of military service was set at 16 years for legionaries and 12 for praetorians, and in 5 CE these terms were changed to 20 and 16 years respectively (Dio 54.25.6; 55.23). In theory the 20-year term for legionaries remained through the principate (confirmed by Tiberius in Tac. *Ann*. 1.78), although in practice many soldiers seem to have served longer. The troops who mutinied in Pannonia in 14 CE complained that some had served for 30 to 40 years (Tac. *Ann*. 1.17), and a study of epigraphic evidence for the service of men of *legio III Augusta* in Africa suggests c.23–6 years was typical in the second century CE (Le Bohec 2000: 64). These terms of service meant that the army became a career in a formal sense for most soldiers.

The post-Augustan army often is characterized as a volunteer army, and, given a smaller army and attractive conditions of service, that may well have been true to a much greater extent than in the civil wars of the first century BCE. The instances of conscription attested in the reign of Augustus happened in exceptional circumstances – the Pannonian revolt of 6 CE and Varus' defeat in Germany in 9 CE (Suet. *Aug*. 25.2; Dio 55.31.1; 56.23.2–3), and perhaps imply that conscription itself (at least in Rome and Italy) was unusual. Nevertheless, there are a number of references to *dilectus* (levies of conscripts) during the principate, both in Italy and the provinces, and it is likely that conscription remained important as a source of at least some of Rome's manpower (Tac. *Ann*. 4.4 [23 CE]; 16.13 [65 CE, in Gallia Narbonensis, Africa, and Asia], with Brunt 1990).

Demobilization of the civil war armies left a standing force of 28 legions, reduced to 25 after Varus' defeat in Germany in 9 CE (Tac. *Ann*. 4.5; Dio 55.23.2). They were supplemented by roughly equal numbers of auxiliary and allied troops (implied by Tac. *Ann*. 4.5). Given that Augustus regularized the terms of service of the legions, it is likely that he began integration of the auxiliary forces (previously a mix of allied, subject, and mercenary troops) into the structure of the new professional army (Keppie 1984: 150–2). However, this process (discussed below) clearly was a gradual one that continued at least through the Julio-Claudian period. Augustus also regularized the status, service, and deployment of the Roman navy, with the establishment of major bases at Misenum and Ravenna (Suet. *Aug*. 49; Tac. *Ann*. 4.5).

The praetorian guard

The establishment of a regular central praetorian guard, derived from the ad hoc bodies of picked troops who guarded republican officials, was another Augustan innovation. Cassius Dio notes that Augustus arranged for his bodyguard to be paid more than other soldiers in 27 BCE (53.11), and subsequently he confirmed their preferential conditions with shorter terms of service too (discussed below). Initially there were nine cohorts of praetorian guards (Tac. *Ann.* 4.5; Dio 55.24.6, stating ten, is anachronistic). In breach of republican prohibitions on the regular presence of troops in the city, three praetorian cohorts were kept in Rome (along with the three urban cohorts, essentially a paramilitary policing force and another Augustan innovation: Dio 55.24.6, again probably wrong on the number of cohorts). The rest were stationed in towns around Rome (Suet. *Aug.* 49). Like other Julio-Claudian emperors, Augustus also maintained a personal bodyguard of German (typically Batavian) mercenaries, probably because they were less likely to be drawn into political intrigue than the Italian praetorians (Dio 55.24.7; Suet. *Aug.* 49). They were disbanded by Galba (Suet. *Gal.* 12).

2 The Army of the Principate

The legions

The number of legions in the empire (each composed of c.5–6,000 men) stayed much the same until well into the third century CE. However, a comparison of Tacitus' account of their deployment in 23 CE (*Ann.* 4.5), and Dio's (55.23.2–7; 24.2–4) description of the situation in his own day (early third century CE) reveals that their deployment changed over time. The increased emphasis on the Balkan provinces (such as Pannonia and Moesia), and a consequent shift away from the Rhine, is noteworthy, as is the relative size of the British garrison (Table 11.1). Marcus Aurelius raised two new legions (*II* and *III Italica*) for service in the Balkan provinces as pressure on that frontier mounted in the later second century CE, but the largest increase was Septimius Severus' creation of three new legions with the title *Parthica*. Two garrisoned the new province of Mesopotamia. *II Parthica* was normally based at Albanum, just south of Rome, the first legion to be based in Italy for over two centuries. However, epigraphic evidence from Apamea in Syria shows that the legion was redeployed there regularly for imperial campaigns through the first half of the third century CE, suggesting it served as a central reserve (Balty 1988; Balty and van Rengen 1993; van Rengen 2000; Some of the inscriptions are reprinted in *AE*, esp. 1993 nos. 1571–91).

Through the second century CE, the frontiers of the empire became more settled and formalized in many regions. An obvious but clichéd illustration of this is Hadrian's Wall in the north of Britain, but the physical form of Roman frontiers varied from region to region. Even the development of walls and fortifications did not imply limits to Roman power or a defensive strategy. These fortifications were used as bases for offensive action and Roman power was maintained beyond them by both diplomatic and military means (Whittaker 1994; Elton 1996a). As part of this process, legions tended to settle down into long-term quarters in fortresses such as Eboracum (York), Ara Ubiorum/Colonia Agrippinensis (Cologne), Mogontiacum (Mainz), Vindobona (Vienna), Aquincum (Budapest), and Singidunum (Belgrade). Often they served as the nucleus of a developing civilian settlement, initially a dependent settlement with the status of *canabae*, but many (including some of the above, and Carnuntum in Upper Pannonia) evolved into proper cities with the status

Table 11.1 The deployment of the legions in the principate

Province/region	Tac. Ann. 4.5 (AD 23)	Dio 55.23-4[i] (e. Severan)	ILS 2288[ii] (Antonine and later Severan)
Rhine/Germanies	8	4	4
Britain	N[iii]	3	3
Spain	3	1	1
Africa/Numidia	2	1	1
Egypt	2	1	1
Arabia	N	1	1
Judaea	(with Syria)	2	2
Syria	4	3	3
Mesopotamia	N	N	2
Cappadocia	N	2	2
Dacia	N	2	1
Pannonia	2	4	4
Moesia	2	4	5
Dalmatia/Illyricum	2	0	0
Noricum	0	1	1
Raetia	0	1	1
Italy	0	0	1
Total legions	**25**	**30**	**33**

Numbers are the number of legions attested in the province or region by that source

i Dio 55.23–4 reflects the situation before Septimius Severus' creation of the three legions *Parthicae*, deployed in his new province of Mesopotamia (2) and in Italy (1).

ii *ILS* 2288 (*CIL* VI.3492) is a column base from Rome originally inscribed with the locations of the legions in the reign of Marcus Aurelius, with the three new Severan legions added subsequently.

iii "N" indicates that that province was not part of the empire (or was a client-kingdom) at that time.

of *municipium* or *colonia*. On the eastern frontier legions often were based in or near existing cities, such as Zeugma in Syria and Jerusalem (Isaac 1992; Pollard 2000).

Instead of moving whole legions around the empire, it became a common practice to deploy detachments termed vexillations (after the *vexillum* standard they used). We certainly see substantial bodies of legionaries serving away from their parent legions by the later first century CE (Jos. *BJ* 2.499; 5.43–4) and it was a common practice by the Antonine period. For example, an inscription shows that a senior centurion, T. Pontius Sabinus, led (as *praepositus*) thousand-man detachments from three German legions to campaign in Britain (*ILS* 2726). Vexillations might include attached auxiliary units or even consist entirely of them, as in the inscription *CIL* III.600, which lists six cavalry units (*alae*) and 15 auxiliary infantry cohorts led by a *praepositus* in Mesopotamia.

While, as Table 11.1 shows, most of the legions were based in frontier provinces, even the governors of traditionally "unarmed" provinces like Asia had detachments of legionaries (often commanded by centurions) and auxiliary units for administrative and internal security duties. There are numerous references to small groups of soldiers used for policing, as prison guards and under the command of other officials such as the procurator in the younger Pliny's letters from Bithynia-Pontus (Pliny *Ep.* 10.17b–18, 19–20, 21–2, 27–8, 77–8).

The auxiliary forces

The auxiliary forces provided the Roman imperial army with most of its cavalry, along with infantry units, including some specialists like archers, of lower status than the legions. Most auxiliaries were recruited from *peregrini*, free non-citizen inhabitants of the empire, who received citizenship on their retirement, in contrast to the largely citizen legionaries. However, individual Roman citizens joined auxiliary units too, and (as unit titles show) some units were raised from Roman citizens or rewarded with citizenship during their service. The distinction may have grown increasingly blurred, and the *Constitutio Antoniniana* made it meaningless.

Auxiliary infantry were organized in cohorts, most, notionally, 500 strong (*quingenaria*/quingenary), but in practice rather smaller. From the later first century CE onwards we also know of larger cohorts, notionally of 1,000 men (*milliaria*/milliary). There were also cohorts described as *equitatae* (mounted), composed mostly of infantry, but with a detachment of cavalry. One such unit was the 20th cohort of Palmyrenes, based at Dura-Europos in Syria. An early third century papyrus document (*P. Dura* 82 = Fink 1971: no. 47) shows that on one particular day the strength of this milliary cohort was 923 troops, including 223 cavalry and 34 camel riders. Auxiliary cavalry was organized in units called *alae* (wings), also quingenary or milliary (Le Bohec 1989b; Holder 1980; Cheesman 1914).

By the end of the first century CE most auxiliaries were part of the regular, professional Roman army, with individuals serving under Roman officers. As mentioned above, this regularization may have begun under Augustus, but apparently it developed through the century. At first, some auxiliary troops were still irregular levies serving under their own leaders. Batavians of the Lower Rhine, who were excused direct taxation because of their importance as soldiers (Tac. *Hist.* 4.12; *Germ.* 29), probably were among the "hurriedly raised bands of Germans" contrasted with regular auxiliaries in the army of Germanicus in 15 CE (Tac. *Ann.* 1.56). By the middle of the first century CE, Batavians were serving in regular cohorts in Britain, but still under their own leaders (Tac. *Hist.* 4.12). Civilis, a Batavian tribal leader and former Roman auxiliary officer, led a revolt in 69 CE (Tac. *Hist.* 4.32). In 68 CE, some of the auxiliaries in Vitellius' army (largely drawn from the Rhine frontier) were recognizable by their ethnic names and native weapons (Tac. *Hist.* 2.89).

As mentioned above, Tacitus implies that the total number of legionaries in the empire was roughly the same as the number of auxiliaries (*Ann.* 4.5). This should be taken only as a rough estimate, with significant variation from region to region and over time. For example, it is estimated that the Hadrianic auxiliary garrison of Britain consisted of 14 *alae* and 47 cohorts (seven of them milliary), almost double the number of men in its three legions (Holder 1982: 17). To establish which auxiliary units were based in each province, we use epigraphic evidence, including military diplomas, discharge documents inscribed on bronze tablets to certify the status of retired auxiliary troops (as well as praetorians and sailors). These useful documents (collected in *CIL* XVI and a series of volumes edited by Margaret Roxan 1978, 1985, and 1994; Roxan and Holder 2003), when intact, provide a date, the name of the individual discharged, his place of origin, the province he served in, and the name of his unit. The names of auxiliary units typically include an ethnic title, usually denoting where the unit originally was recruited. For example, *ala III Augusta Thracum* was a cavalry unit originally raised in Thrace, *cohors IV Gallorum* an infantry unit raised in Gaul, and *cohors I Hamiorum sagittaria* was a cohort of archers raised at Hama in Syria. Most auxiliary units moved away from the province in which they were first recruited. For example, Gemellus, son of Breucus, a Pannonian, served in the first *ala* Tampiana of Pannonians stationed in Britain. He was discharged in 122 CE, and apparently retired back to Pannonia, as his diploma (*CIL* XVI.69) was found in modern Hungary.

Military diplomas also list other units in the province that discharged veterans at the same time as the bearer of the diploma. An individual diploma rarely provides us with the identities of all the auxiliary units in a given province, but often they can be patched together to give a likely total. For example, the eight cavalry *alae* and 18 infantry cohorts listed in Syria in two texts issued on the same day in 88 CE (*CIL* XVI.35; Roxan 1978: no. 3) perhaps represent the complete auxiliary garrison of the province, which also had three legions.

As the Roman army defended increasingly well-defined frontiers through the second century, we see evidence of auxiliaries deployed in a dispersed manner in the frontier zones, engaged in patrolling, policing, and other duties. For example, a (90s CE) unit strength report of the first cohort of Tungrians, preserved on a writing tablet from the fort of Vindolanda in Britain (*Tab. Vindol.* II 154 = Campbell 1994: no. 182), records that this milliary unit had an actual strength of 752 men. However, only 296 of these were present (and only 265 healthy) at the fort. A further 337 were at Coria (Corbridge), 46 are described as *singulares* (probably detached to the governor's guard in London), and the rest were at six other locations. Early third century papyrus duty rosters from Dura-Europos present a similar picture. *P.Dura* 100 (= Fink 1971: no. 1) lists men of the 20th cohort of Palmyrenes at no fewer than six locations besides Dura itself as well as on the governor's staff, escorting the emperor and (perhaps) hunting lions.

While auxiliary troops often were dispersed throughout the frontier zone, legions were perhaps more concentrated, sometimes based a little to the rear, in reserve (Luttwak 1976: fig. 2.2; 2.4 for an abstract depiction of such a frontier scheme). For example, in Britain Hadrian's Wall was mostly manned by auxiliaries while the three legionary bases were further south, at York, Chester, and Wroxeter. However, the traditional view of separate deployment and basing has been undermined, for example, by finds of apparently legionary equipment in supposedly auxiliary forts (Bishop and Coulston 1993: 209), and there is certainly epigraphic evidence for legionary vexillations serving alongside auxiliaries in frontier areas of Britain.

In addition to regular auxiliary troops, there were also forces provided by client kings, particularly in the eastern provinces in the first century CE. For example, at the start of the First Jewish Revolt, Cestius Gallus, the governor of Syria, had 14,000 men (mostly archers and cavalry) provided by three local rulers in addition to a full Roman legion, three legionary vexillations of 2,000 men each, six auxiliary cohorts, and four *alae* (Jos. *BJ* 2.500–1). Subsequently, we see ethnic units (often called *numeri* –

misleadingly, since this term is applied much more widely) serving alongside regular Roman legionaries and auxiliaries (M. P. Speidel 1975). These troops fighting, initially at least under their own leaders in their native manner, included the Moors who fought under Lusius Quietus for Trajan (*HA Had.* 5.8) and subsequent Roman armies into the third century CE (Herod. 3.3.4–5; 6.7.8; Dio 78.32), and the Palmyrenes who served over much of the empire in the same period.

The army command structure

From the reign of Augustus, major military forces typically were commanded by imperial legates (mostly provincial governors, and thus combining civil and military duties) ultimately responsible to the emperor himself. The province of Africa was an exception in that its senatorial governor commanded its legionary garrison, but only until 37 CE, when Gaius transferred its command to a separate *legatus Augusti* (Tac. *Ann.* 4.48). Egypt, of course, was governed by an equestrian prefect who commanded the legions there (as was the case in the Severan province of Mesopotamia).

Individual legions typically were commanded by senatorial officers also known as legates, except for the legions of Egypt and Mesopotamia which were under equestrian *praefecti*. Commanders of auxiliary *alae* and cohorts, known as *praefecti* too, also typically were drawn from the equestrian order and, in contrast to the senatorial officers, might be career soldiers (see Campbell 1994: nos. 102–9 for examples of their careers). Five of the six tribunes, subordinates of the legate in each legion, came from the equestrian order, the sixth being a junior senator.

About 60 centurions of different grades served within each legion (see Campbell 1994: nos. 85–97 for examples of centurions' careers). They maintained discipline, provided low level command in battle, and commanded detachments away from the main body of the legion. The stereotype of the Roman centurion is of an experienced soldier promoted from the ranks, and certainly a proportion of them came from such backgrounds. However, some were recruited straight into the legionary centurionate from the praetorian guard, and many were recruited directly from wealthier groups in society, including *equites* (Le Bohec 2000: 76–8, based on his study of *legio III Augusta* in Africa; Dio 52.25.7 implies that centurions of equestrian origin were not unusual).

Below the rank of centurion were individuals often termed *principales* (junior officers within the century with the title *optio*, *tesserarius*, or *signifer*, and some administrative specialists in the legion's headquarters), who typically received one-and-a-half times normal pay (*sesquiplicarii*), or double pay (*duplicarii*). There was also a vast array of technical and clerical specialists within the legion, including surveyors, blacksmiths, weapon makers, and medical orderlies who were known as *immunes*, because they were exempt from certain fatigue duties (*D.* 50.6.7 = Campbell 1994: no. 35; in general see Davies 1974).

The imperial army in battle

The legions of the imperial army were composed largely of close order heavy infantry, the main strength of Roman armies for much of its history (although they included a small detachment of cavalry). Legionary infantry wore helmet and armor, sometimes the *lorica segmentata* of metal strips, familiar from Trajan's Column, otherwise chain mail or scale (for weapons and armor in general see Bishop and Coulston 1993). They carried a curved shield (often the rectangular variety depicted on Trajan's Column), a short stabbing sword (often referred to as *gladius*), and *pila*, short-ranged heavy javelins.

As mentioned above, auxiliary troops typically may have fought with indigenous weapons and equipment at first, but as their service became regularized, so did their equipment. While a number of ancient sources characterize auxiliary infantry as lighter than legionaries (see below), helmets and armor (mail or scale rather than segmented) often were worn, and flat shields carried. Lighter javelins and a longer sword termed *spatha* were typical offensive weapons, and specialist units used bows. Trajan's Column shows two differently equipped types of Roman infantry, long assumed to be legionaries and auxiliaries, the latter apparently wearing chain mail in contrast with the legionary *lorica segmentata*. They also have different shields. The assumption that legionaries and auxiliaries were always differently equipped has been challenged on the basis of archaeological finds (Maxfield 1986), but Bishop and Coulston (1993: 206–9) have upheld the distinction on the basis of inscribed tombstones that invariably show men labeled as legionaries with curved shield and *pilum* and those named as auxiliaries with flat shield and javelins.

Auxiliary cavalry (Dixon and Southern 1992) typically were armored and used the *spatha*, and short spears both for throwing and thrusting. An inscription of 128 CE from Lambaesis in Africa preserves a speech of Hadrian praising troops for their performance in exercises, and he specifically refers to the skill of men of *ala I Pannoniorum* (as well as legionary cavalry and those of a *cohors equitata*) for their ability in throwing javelins (*ILS* 2487 + 9133–5 = Campbell 1994: no. 17). On the other hand, cavalrymen's tombstones (for example that of S. Valerius Genialis of an *ala Thracum*, from Cirencester, *RIB* 109) often show them using a spear to thrust overhand. *Contarii*, cavalry equipped with long lances, certainly existed in small numbers by the reign of Trajan, and *cataphractarii*, very heavily armored cavalry, probably based on Parthian equivalents, by the reign of Hadrian. There were also specialized lighter cavalry by the second century, including the Moors already mentioned. However, these broad observations on weapons and equipment must be qualified by the observation that Roman weapons and equipment probably were never as standardized and homogeneous as suggested by sculpture and modern re-enactment societies.

We have relatively little evidence for the detailed functioning of Roman armies in battle, although this is perhaps not so surprising given the amount of time they spent in peacetime routine rather than in open warfare. However, the Roman army at war is a topic that has been discussed at considerable and effective length recently by Goldsworthy (1996), applying to Roman warfare an approach used by Keegan (1976) to study later periods. Ancient military manuals such as that of Vegetius are problematic as source materials as they are often academic, theoretical, and abstract rather than practical and contemporary in content. The most useful and detailed historical accounts of battles (or, in the case of Arrian, a planned battle) include Tacitus' description of the battle of Mons Graupius in Scotland in 83 CE (*Agr.* 35–7), Josephus' account of a battle between Romans and Jewish rebels in 66 CE (*BJ* 2.542–55 = Campbell 1994: no. 157), and Arrian's account of the tactics he intended to employ if he encountered the nomad Alans in Cappadocia in 135 CE (*Alan.* 11–21 = Campbell 1994: no. 159).

These show a number of important and recurring themes: the deployment of auxiliary infantry on the flanks or in a line in front of the legionaries; the stationing of cavalry on the flanks; and the emphasis placed on flexible use of reserves, a hallmark of Roman armies since at least the Punic Wars. While auxiliary infantry certainly could be effective at close quarters (Tac. *Agr.* 36; *Ann.* 14.37), a number of passages demonstrate their flexibility as skirmishers too, bearing out the equipment differences noted above. Tacitus, describing a battle in Britain, contrasts the *gladius* and *pilum* of the legionary with the *spatha* and *hasta* (a rather general term for a spear or javelin) of the lighter troops, and the close-order advance of the former with the latter's use of missile weapons (*Ann.* 12.3.5). Discipline and training gave the Romans a powerful advantage over many of their enemies, the latter giving rise to Josephus' famous tag (*BJ* 3.76) that Roman exercises were bloodless battles and Roman battles bloody exercises.

Construction and engineering activities had been another important feature of Roman armies since the republican period – Polybius' account of the layout of a Roman marching camp is an early manifestation of this (Polyb. 6.40–2) – and continued to be through the imperial period, as shown by sources as diverse as the scenes of river crossing and building on Trajan's Column and the archaeological evidence of the short-lived legionary fortress at Inchtuthil in Scotland. Roman prowess in siege warfare is demonstrated, for example, by the siege works at Masada as well as Josephus' account of that siege (*BJ* 7.304–20 = Campbell 1994: no. 162). Roman armies made extensive use of artillery (bolt-shooters like large crossbows as well as stone throwers), mostly in sieges but sometimes in the field too (in general see Marsden 1969, 1971).

3 The Roman Army in Politics

The Roman army played an important role in imperial politics and, equally, the demands of domestic politics generated conquest and sustained an ideology of imperial expansion. Just as elite political competition in the republic had driven powerful individuals to seek military glory by expanding the empire, so military success was one important characteristic of a successful emperor. Furthermore, the army was important in installing, maintaining, and overthrowing emperors. The praetorian guard, with its proximity to the *princeps* at the center of imperial power, was of obvious importance, but ultimately it was the major groupings of frontier legions (especially those based in the Balkan provinces) that proved decisive. It was their repeated interventions in politics at the center that gave rise to some of the structural stresses experienced by the empire in the third century CE (see Campbell 1984, esp. 1–156, 365–414; Peachin, this volume; Potter, this volume).

While a Roman emperor (of the principate, at least) was not primarily a warrior, the themes of emperor as soldier, commander, and conqueror were repeated constantly in art, on coins, in rhetoric, and in historiography. Triumphal arches and columns advertised the imperial virtues associated with military conquest. Coins depict emperors addressing the army and historical reliefs (e.g. the Cancellaria reliefs and the Marcus Aurelius panel reliefs) show them celebrating triumphs (largely restricted to the emperor and his family) and portray ceremonial set-pieces associated with campaigning, such as the emperor's departure for, and return from, war. Inscriptions record emperors' victory titles, such as *Germanicus* ("Victor over the Germans"), *Dacicus, Parthicus,* and others, while *imperator,* the republican salutation of a successful general, became one of the *princeps'* regular titles (Campbell 1984: 122–33). The various military manifestations of the emperor (as fellow-soldier, military disciplinarian, and successful conqueror – but also lover of peace) were standard themes of imperial panegyric (see Pliny *Pan.* 12–18, Men. Rh. 2.373–4 [Russell and Wilson 1981: 84–9]). Suetonius typically devotes a thematic section of his imperial biographies to military activities even in the case of unmilitary emperors (compare *Cal.* 43–8 with *Tib.* 16–20), and military matters continue to occupy an important place in works of history (such as those of Tacitus and Dio) increasingly dominated by court personalities and intrigue.

The need for an emperor to present himself in the tradition of military commander and conqueror to a domestic audience might lead to expansion that in purely practical terms was of dubious value. Suetonius is scathing about the true value of Claudius' conquest of Britain, but ascribes it to Claudius' desire to win a proper triumph (*Claud.* 17). Trajan was honored for his conquests even though some attributed them to his love of war and a desire to emulate Alexander the Great rather than any rational imperial strategy (Dio 68.7.5, 29.1, 30.1). In contrast, some later writers (Fronto *Prin. hist.* 11; *HA Had.* 9) criticized Hadrian for consolidating rather than conquering, despite his impeccable military background (*ILS* 308; Dio 69.5.2, 9.1–5). The bizarre pseudo-military activities of emperors such as Gaius (see Suet. *Cal.* 44–6 for his "invasion" of Britain and faked skirmishes in Germany), and Nero (see Dio 63.8–11, 20; Suet. *Nero* 44) must reflect either the emperors' own desire to present themselves as military figures (Gaius was the first to be depicted addressing the army – in *adlocutio* – on coins), or, at the very least, the writers' perception of, and desire to subvert, the stereotype.

The praetorian cohorts

It is hardly unexpected that the praetorian guard, in immediate proximity to the emperor at the heart of imperial power, played an important role in bringing emperors to power and overthrowing them. However, it often proved less successful in maintaining them in the face of opposition from other elements of the army.

The whole force was concentrated in a single camp in Rome in 23 CE, by Aelius Sejanus, Tiberius' praetorian prefect (Tac. *Ann.* 4.2), whose career provides a case study in the power an ambitious commander might wield. Similar, later, figures include Tigellinus under Nero and Septimius Severus' praetorian prefect, Plautianus. However, for present purposes we should distinguish between the actions of individual commanders and those of the praetorians collectively.

Initially the praetorians were recruited directly from the civilian population of Rome itself and central Italy (Tac. *Ann.* 4.5). Dio indicates that until the reign of Septimius Severus most came from Italy, Spain, Macedonia, and Noricum (74.2.4–5). Septimius disbanded the existing guard (which had opposed him) and replaced its members with former legionaries, most of them from the Balkan legions that supported him (Peachin, this volume). A second body of guards, the cavalry *equites singulares*, was established probably by Trajan and coexisted with the praetorians (M. P. Speidel 1994). The latter were finally disbanded altogether by Constantine in 312 CE, because they had supported his rival, Maxentius (Zos. 2.9.3; 7.2).

We see the initial political power of the guard in the accession of Claudius (Suet. *Claud.* 10; Dio 60.1.1), allegedly found hiding in the palace by a guardsman on the death of Gaius, carried off to the praetorian camp, and acclaimed emperor. This acclamation was reinforced by Claudius' payment of a 15,000 sesterces (3,750 denarii) donative, making him, according to Suetonius, the first emperor to buy the loyalty of his troops. The relationship of Claudius and the guard is strikingly portrayed in a series of gold and silver coins (*RIC* I, 122–3, pl. 15, nos. 20, 23) depicting the *receptus* (acceptance) not only of Claudius by the guard but also of the guard by Claudius. The guard played a crucial role in the accession of Otho (Suet. *Otho* 4–8) and famously succumbed to the bidding of Didius Julianus in the "auction" of empire conducted at the praetorians' camp in 193 CE after their overthrow of Pertinax (Dio 73.11; cf. Herod. 2.6; Peachin, this volume). Even when an emperor was not directly chosen by the praetorians, their participation was important in consolidating and retaining power. Tacitus describes how Nero emerged from the palace on his accession, was carried by the duty cohort to the praetorian camp on a litter, offered a donative, and was hailed emperor (*Ann.* 12.66).

Likewise the praetorians might exercise an influence on internal politics to the advantage or detriment of the reigning emperor. While Tiberius showed senators the praetorians at drill, according to Dio, to intimidate them, in 97 CE they forced the ruling emperor Nerva to execute individuals implicated in the death of Domitian (Dio 57.24; 68.3.3–4; Peachin, this volume). In the reign of Severus Alexander, the praetorians murdered Ulpian, the praetorian prefect, and fought running battles with the civilian population of Rome for three days (Dio 80.2.2–4).

However, the praetorians often proved less effective in maintaining their chosen emperors in power. The guards who brought Otho to power do not seem to have been very effective in fighting for him against Vitellius' Rhine legions, and Tacitus (*Hist.* 2.18–19) notes their indiscipline and inexperience. Likewise Didius Julianus' praetorians were ineffective against Septimius Severus, allegedly because they had "learned to live luxuriously" (Dio 73.16.3). Similarly Maxentius' infantry (presumably including the praetorians) seems to have been less enthusiastic than his cavalry when fighting for him against Constantine (Zos. 2.16.3–4).

The praetorian guards also put an end to the reigns of several emperors. Although Pertinax had promised them a donative of 3,000 denarii on his accession, nevertheless they killed him within a few months (Dio 73.1.2, 8.1–10.2; *HA Pert.* 4.6; Herod. 2.4.4–5). Likewise Elagabalus was murdered by praetorians in 222 CE (Dio 79.20; Herod. 5.8.5–9), and Pupienus and Balbinus in 238 CE (Herod. 8.8.4–7).

The frontier legions as a political force

Ultimately the praetorian guards' political power was overshadowed by that of the major groupings of frontier legions. Tacitus famously stated that the events of 68–9 CE meant that "a well-hidden secret of the principate had been revealed. It was possible, it seemed, for an emperor to be chosen outside Rome" (*Hist.* 1.4, tr.

Wellesley). Galba initially had the backing of troops from Spain, but lost military support allegedly because of his stinginess and authoritarian character (Dio 64.3.3, 4.1; Suet. *Gal.* 16). Subsequently Otho was backed, unsuccessfully, by the praetorians. Vitellius owed his brief rule to the backing of the legions of the Rhine frontier (Suet. *Vit.* 8.2), and Vespasian his much longer grip on power to support from the eastern legions who proclaimed him emperor and, crucially, the legions of the Balkan provinces under Antonius Primus who actually defeated Vitellius' army for him (Tac. *Hist.* 2.85–6). The fourth-century writer Aurelius Victor, writing with nearly three centuries of hindsight of similar civil wars, claimed:

> [Vespasian], because envoys from the Moesian and Pannonian armies had arrived.... seized the imperial power. For the soldiers mentioned above, after they had discovered that Otho had been made emperor by the praetorians and Vitellius by the German legions, in rivalry, as is their custom, so they should not seem different, urged on Vespasian, upon whom the Syrian cohorts had already agreed. (*Caes.* 8.2–3, tr. Bird)

This is an interesting reflection on the spirit of competition between the different regional army groupings. As the first emperor from outside the Julio-Claudian aristocracy of Rome, Vespasian only won power by the sword, and his military ability and popularity with elements of the army were the only real qualifications he had to be *princeps*.

Through much of the second century CE, the adoption of intended successors ensured that imperial accessions were largely peaceful (Peachin, this volume). However, Trajan's support from the German legions was important in ensuring his adoption by Nerva and his subsequent accession, as they provided an important counter to the power of the praetorians who opposed Nerva. Indeed, one ancient writer (the author of the fourth-century *Epitome on the Emperors*) hints that Trajan's succession may have been more of a military coup than the orderly adoption depicted in the official version (*Epitome* 12.8–9). The aftermath of the death of Commodus saw a situation not unlike that of 68–9 CE, with Pescennius Niger supported by the eastern legions, Clodius Albinus' support in the garrison of Britain, and Septimius Severus drawing on the Danubian legions to achieve ultimate power against the praetorians in Rome as well as his two rivals (see Dio 73.14.3 for the contenders and their support).

Severan reforms and the third century

While the army of the Severan period remained broadly similar to that of previous centuries in terms of its organization and equipment, the perception conveyed by many of our sources for that period and for the third century in general is that the army became much more important than before in a number of different areas of Roman life, political, social, and economic.

The famous dying words of Septimius Severus to his sons, as reported by Dio – "Be harmonious, enrich the soldiers and scorn all other men" (Dio 76.15.2–3, tr. Cary) – may be too epigrammatic to be true, and the negative portrayal of the army at this period by Dio and others may be the result of upper-class and metropolitan prejudices. Nevertheless, these views reflect some important consequences of the Severan coup. As Campbell (2002: 119) states, "the inevitable consequence of the first capture of Rome with an army for 124 years was a closer relationship between emperor and army, which made it difficult to conceal the reality of an autocracy backed by military force." Likewise the overwhelming importance of the army and of the emperor as military commander in facing the frontier crises of the third century made it inevitable that it would become more prominent in all aspects of Roman life.

As already mentioned, under Septimius there was a substantial increase in the number of legions, and a corresponding increase in auxiliaries. There were also pay rises under Septimius and Caracalla, leading to at least a perception that the empire was being bled dry to pay for the army (Dio 77.9.1; 77.10.1 on Caracalla), although much of it was paid for by debasement of the coinage (Crawford 1975: 562–3). Soldiers were also given new privileges, such as the right to contract legal marriages (previously forbidden) and the right to wear gold rings (Herod. 3.8.4). Dio claimed (74.2.3, although the general applicability of the statement is debatable) that the army was becoming more politically important to the emperor than it should, and even (74.2.6, a reflection on Septimius' Balkan support) that it was becoming increasingly strange and foreign.

The rise and early successes of the Sasanian dynasty on the eastern frontier, combined with existing frontier pressures in the Balkans, meant that the military functions of the emperor and the political influence of the armies had become paramount by the end of the reign of the last Severan, Alexander. His successor, Maximinus, was the first of a series of emperors (including Decius, Gallienus, Aurelian, and, ultimately, Diocletian) from military backgrounds, mostly from the Balkans and mostly brought to power by the armies of the Danube frontier. Maximinus was the first Roman leader who might be characterized as a soldier-emperor (Campbell 1984: 55–6; Potter, this volume). The focus of his reign was warfare, and he never even visited Rome, instead sending dispatches from the front emphasizing his own personal military leadership and ordering paintings of his heroic deeds to be set up in front of the Senate House (Herod. 7.2).

4 The Army and the Imperial Economy

The Roman army was also a significant element in the Roman economy, as payment and supply of the armed forces were almost certainly the state's greatest expense. Consequently, some scholars have depicted the army as performing a crucial structural role in the operation of the imperial economy. For example, Hopkins' well-known model (first published 1980) emphasizes the cycling of cash taxes and army pay between the center of the empire and frontier provinces as fundamental in stimulating production and exchange. It is also likely that payment and supply of the army was an important factor motivating and determining production and circulation of coinage in the Roman world (see, for example, Crawford 1975).

The cost of the army

Individual legionary soldiers were paid 225 denarii a year (calculated from the "ten asses a day" of Tac. *Ann.* 1.17) from the reign of Augustus to Domitian. In 83 CE the latter increased this to 300 denarii (Suet. *Dom.* 7.3; Dio 67.3.5). The next pay rise came under Septimius Severus (Herodian 3.8.4; *HA Sev.* 12.2), although its magnitude is unclear. The evidence is set out by M. Alexander Speidel (1992: 88) and Alston (1994: 113–15), who argue for a one hundred percent rise (to 600 denarii) and 50 percent rise (to 450 denarii) respectively. Herodian states that Caracalla gave a 50 percent rise to the praetorians in 212 CE, and Dio implies that all the troops received this rise (Herod. 4.4.7; Dio 78.36.3–4). That would produce an annual legionary salary of 675 or 900 denarii, depending on the size of Septimius' increase. This level was in turn doubled by Maximinus in 235 CE (Herod. 6.8.8).

The relationship of auxiliary pay to legionary pay has been the subject of recent debate. M. Alexander Speidel (1992, following an argument advanced by M. P. Speidel 1973) has interpreted a document from Vindonissa to suggest that basic annual pay for an ordinary auxiliary soldier was five-sixths of that of a legionary ranker. While this has met with wide acceptance, Alston (1994: 122) questioned and rejected Speidel's interpretation and instead made the radical suggestion (advancing no positive evidence) that auxiliary pay may have been at the same basic rates as legionary pay. He argues that the Roman army was less status-differentiated than modern colonial armies; hence scholars' assumption that it would differentiate in terms of pay is unjustified. One might object that while there is little explicit evidence of legionary–auxiliary differentiation in terms of service, the Roman army and Roman society in general were so hierarchical and differentiated that such uniformity is implausible. MacMullen (1984b) has advanced a rough formula for calculating the overall cost of army pay. Using this for an army of 28 legions paid at the post-Domitianic rate, with a comparable number of auxiliaries paid (very roughly) at five-sixths that rate, the total comes to just over 100 million denarii a year.

Other expenditure on the army included the *praemia* paid to veterans on retirement and donatives paid on imperial accessions and anniversaries. Veterans received 3,000 denarii per man (5,000 for praetorians) from the reign of Augustus and 5,000 per ordinary soldier under Caracalla (Dio 55.23.1; 77.24.1; the figure given for praetorians in the text is garbled). However, some veterans still received land to colonize in lieu of cash payments. There was little settlement of veterans on Italian land after Augustus (but see Tac. *Ann.* 13.31; 14.27), but overseas veteran colonies remained important to the reign of Hadrian, and veterans continued to receive land in frontier areas in later centuries (Mann 1983: 65–8).

On the death of Augustus (and hence the accession of Tiberius), each legionary received a donative of 300 sesterces (75 denarii), with 1,000 going to the praetorians and 500 to the urban cohorts in accordance with the deceased emperor's final testament (Suet. *Aug.* 101.2). As noted earlier, Claudius gave the praetorians 15,000 sesterces (3,750 denarii) on his accession, and Josephus says that he promised donatives to the rest of the army too (*AJ* 19.247), though it is possible that non-citizen troops, mostly auxiliaries, were excluded, as they were from the donative offered by Gaius upon his accession in 37 CE (Dio 59.2.3). It seems probable that the legions were included in these gifts even though most subsequent references only specify praetorians, as in the case of the 5,000 denarii given by Marcus Aurelius upon his accession (*HA Marc.* 7.9; Dio 73.8.4). It is possible that the proportions in the will of Augustus became standard (Campbell 1984: 167–8). The exclusion of non-citizen troops from these donatives, at least initially, suggests that in some sense they reflected the special relationship between the emperor and the Roman people.

Smaller donatives were paid on imperial anniversaries, such as the 25 denarii given by Claudius to the praetorians on the anniversary of his accession (Dio 60.12.4), and the 250 given to them by Septimius on the tenth anniversary of his, a sum that may be explained by the fact that this was the sum that he had paid when strapped for cash at the time of his proclamation in 193 CE – resisting a demand from the troops for ten times that amount (Dio 76.1.1; Herod. 2.14.5; *HA Sev.* 7.6, cf. Dio 46.46).

The army and the civilian economy

However much individual soldiers earned, it is clear that some pay was withheld for expenses and in savings. A number of papyri list these deductions, and one well-known example (*P. Gen. Lat.* I, recto 1 = Fink 1971: no. 68 = Campbell 1994: no. 24) shows sums withheld for food, boots, socks, clothing, and the camp Saturnalia, as well as sums kept on deposit. Even if supplies were provided to individuals by the army, they had to be acquired from somewhere. Some things were produced by the army itself, in productive facilities owned by the state, such as the large military brick, tile, and pottery factory at Holt near Chester in Britain (Peacock 1982: 136–50 provides a summary). Some items were requisitioned or otherwise acquired from resources owned by the state. *P. Dura* 64 (= Fink 1971: no. 91) shows the transfer of barley to soldiers from an imperial estate, probably rents taken in kind from tenants by imperial officials, and there are a number of ancient references to (perhaps exceptional and abusive) requisition by the army (Pliny *Pan.* 29; Dio 77.9.3).

However, the majority of military supply needs were probably met from civilian sources and most (at least in the early and middle empire) in return for cash payment, leading to the transfer of coinage envisaged by Hopkins and others. A few documents that survive, mostly by chance, show this process. A papyrus of 138 CE (*BGU* 1564 = Campbell 1994: no. 239) shows an advance payment being made to civilian weavers in Philadelphia (Egypt) on a contract for clothing and blankets for the army in Cappadocia. Recently discovered writing tablets from Vindolanda (Britain) appear to show commercial acquisition of a very wide variety of goods (food of many varieties, clothing and textiles, hides, and wooden cart parts) by the army from civilians, although in most cases the exact status of those involved and the nature of the transaction is open to some doubt (see *Tab. Vindol.* II 180, 182, 184, 186, 192, 207, 302, 309, 343, with editors' notes).

In addition to being an expense for the state's resources, the Roman army was directly responsible for some of its income. Besides the general acquisition of booty from war, the army oversaw the extraction of resources such as precious metals for the state from the provinces. The importance of exploitation, both official and unofficial (see below) by the army as an agent of Roman imperialism has sometimes been overlooked in favor of models that emphasized economic development and stimulation. In some cases this may reflect scholarship originally shaped in an environment of more recent, western imperialism.

5 The Army and Roman Society and Culture

The Roman army sometimes has been seen as, in some senses, a mediator between the central power of the empire and provincial populations. Besides the economic aspects discussed above, soldiers, as the most numerous representatives of the Roman state in the provinces, have often been considered important in transmitting "Roman-ness" to its subject populations, whether in the form of citizenship or aspects of culture as diverse as language and urbanization. This process is often termed "Romanization" (see Webster 2001 for a summary of its historiography and a critique; and M. Millett 1990 for a recent view of the process in Britain, including the role of the army).

Soldiers' origins: legionaries

In many ways, the composition of the Roman army reflected the range of cultural, legal, and social statuses found in the wider Roman world. Legionaries were, for the most part, recruited initially from the most culturally and legally Roman section of the population, namely Roman citizens. However, their origins changed over time, just as, for example, the origins of senators changed over time. At first (in the west, at least), most were from Italy, but through the reigns of Claudius and Nero, roughly half were provincial Roman citizens (typically from the more Roman, often colonial, populations of provinces like Gallia Narbonensis, and Baetica and Tarraconensis in Spain). By Trajan's reign, legionaries of provincial origin outnumbered Italians by roughly four or five to one (Le Bohec 2000: 78–87; Forni 1953: 66). Subsequently, local recruitment (sometimes from veteran colonies) and recruitment of individuals born *castris* ("in the camp," soldiers' sons living around legionary encampments) became common in most parts of the empire. For example, Wilkes' (1999: 99) study of an inscription of *legio VII Claudia* (195 CE), based in Moesia Superior, shows the discharge of 142 men whose origins are preserved. At least 102 of them were recruited within the same province, six or seven born *castris*, 97 from the two veteran colonies in the province. A similar inscription from Alexandria (*ILS* 2304 = *CIL* III.6580 = Campbell 1994: no. 249 [194 CE]) shows 41 men whose origins are legible, 32 from Egypt, 24 of them born *castris*. Le Bohec's study (1989a: 491–530) of similar evidence for men of *legio III Augusta* in Numidia shows about 25 percent of recruits born *castris* in the Antonine period and nearly 40 percent in the Severan period.

Legionary recruitment also reflected the Latin–Greek cultural distinction between the eastern and western halves of the empire, with legionaries serving in the eastern provinces mostly recruited from culturally Greek provinces and those deployed in the west mostly from culturally Latin areas in the center and west of the empire (Forni 1953: 83–5). As noted above, even status divisions within the Roman citizen body were recognized in recruitment, with individuals from the Romanized gentry of some parts of the empire drafted straight into the centurionate.

Soldiers' origins: auxiliaries

As already stated, typically auxiliary troops were recruited from peregrine (free non-citizen) peoples, although some recruitment of men from beyond imperial boundaries was a recurring feature of Roman armies throughout history. Units were raised in all parts of the empire, as unit titles on military diplomas show, but certain traditionally warlike (and less Romanized) provinces such as Gallia Belgica and Lugdunensis and Thrace were of particular importance early on. The degree to which units might continue to recruit from their native province seems to have varied over time and from region to region of the empire, but within a few decades of moving from their place of origin most existing units seem to have raised replacement recruits from the province in which they were based and from other nearby provinces (for a general summary see Haynes 1999: 166, and Holder 1982: 52–3 on this process in Britain).

While this distinction between recruitment of citizens into legions and peregrines into *auxilia* served to emphasize and perpetuate existing legal and social distinctions within the empire, army recruitment was also a mechanism for social mobility. The diplomas of auxiliary veterans show that they received Roman citizenship on retirement. Moreover, citizenship was also granted to their wives and children. Ordinary serving Roman soldiers could not contract legally valid marriages from at least the reign of Claudius (Dio 60.24.3) to that of Septimius Severus (Herod. 3.8.4; see Campbell 1978 and Phang 2001: 115–33). However, the formula on the diplomas makes it clear that military authorities accepted that informal relationships did exist and that they recognized them on soldiers' retirement.

The degree to which soldiers formed family relationships with local populations may have varied a great deal from province to province and even unit to unit (see, for example, Alston 1995: 54–6, 58–9; Pollard 2000: 152–9). At Dura-Europos in Syria, for example, one document (*P. Dura* 32 [254 CE], hence after the *Constitutio Antoniniana*) shows intermarriage of a legionary and of a local civilian, suggesting a degree of integration between soldier and civilian population. Conversely another (*P. Dura* 30) shows a woman who is probably the sister and widow of soldiers marrying another auxiliary soldier in his unit's winter quarters, witnessed by soldiers. Such "institutional endogamy," within the confines of families already associated with the army, may have been particularly important where *castris* recruitment was common and probably tended to separate the army from local civilians.

Soldier and civilian

The general question of the nature of social, cultural, and legal relationships between soldiers and civilians is one that has been debated at some length in recent decades (Campbell 1984: 246–63; Alston 1995, 1999; Pollard 1996, 2000). While some scholars have argued for integration, and others for separation, these extremes are more useful as starting points for discussion than as depictions of reality. Undoubtedly both integration and separation coexisted, perhaps in different degrees from province to province and individual to individual, and different kinds of evidence (private letters, official petitions and contracts, upper-class literary commentary on the army) tend to present different perspectives.

Particularly given tendencies to local recruitment, soldiers often lived and worked among the population from which they were drawn, and one might expect to find evidence of continuing social relations between the two groups. Intermarriage might strengthen such relationships. As we have seen, it is likely that there were also economic relationships between soldiers and civilians. On the basis of a wealth of detailed information from papyri from Egyptian sites such as Karanis, Alston (1995, 1999) concluded that such strong social relationships did exist among army veterans and local civilians, and that district centurions, on detached policing duties in the villages, fitted in well to existing structures of power and patronage, acting as arbitrators in local disputes. There is good evidence from other provinces of veterans integrating into local civilian communities, albeit sometimes with enhanced status and wealth due to their military service (for example, see MacAdam 1983: 113–14 on the villages of southern Syria and Arabia).

On the other hand, soldiers often were used as the lowest level of administration of an empire that did not have many civilian administrators, and they engaged in policing, tax collecting, and low level juridical activity among other things (Davies 1974 still provides a useful survey; see also Isaac 1992: 115–18; Alston 1995: 81–96; Pollard 2000: 85–104). They could legally demand accommodation in the homes of private individuals (*hospitium*) and requisition animals, vehicles, and labor for official transport duties (*angaria*) (Isaac 1992: 291–7; Pollard 2000: 104–9). Even the proper conduct of such duties might lead to tensions with the subject population, but there is considerable evidence of abuse of authority, status, and privilege (Campbell 1984: 246–54; Isaac 1992: 269–310; see also Campbell 1994: nos. 286–301 for examples of both duties and abuses). Apuleius' much-repeated story (*Met.* 9.39–42 = Campbell 1994: no. 291) of how a legionary robbed and beat a civilian on the pretext of requisitioning his ass is a fictional and humorous one. However, legal scholars (*D.* 1.18.6.57 [Ulpian] = Campbell 1994: no. 292), Roman officials (an edict of the prefect of Egypt, *PSI* 446 = *SP* 221 = Campbell 1994: no. 293), and local communities (the village of Phaena in Syria [*IGRR* 3.1119 = Campbell 1994: no. 296]) all refer to abuse of *hospitium* and *angaria*. Likewise documents from Egypt (e.g. *SB* 9207 = Campbell 1994: no. 297) record extortion by soldiers, while a writing tablet from Britain (*Tab. Vindol.* II.344) records an appeal against violent ill-treatment of (probably) a trader by soldiers.

Soldiers also had legal privileges that may have set them apart from civilians. While Juvenal's complaints on this subject (*Sat.* 16) undoubtedly were exaggerated for humorous effect, jurists and other legal sources (*D.* 49.16.4.8 = Campbell 1994: no. 176, for example) envision that a man might join the army to gain an advantage in a forthcoming lawsuit. Likewise veterans had privileges (besides perhaps being relatively wealthy due to their savings and *praemia*) that might be resented by some civilians. For example, they were exempt from some taxes (as set out in Domitian's edict of 94 CE, *ILS* 9059 = Campbell 1994: no. 341) and some degrading forms of punishment, such as beating with rods and being thrown to the beasts (*D.* 49.18.1–5 = Campbell 1994: no. 336).

Some scholars (B. D. Shaw 1983; MacMullen 1984c; Pollard 1996; see also papers in Goldsworthy and Haynes 1999) have suggested that the separation of soldiers from civilians was further enhanced by the social exclusivity of the army as a whole and of individual army units. Such exclusivity may have been promoted by common values, links of family, rank, and comradeship as well as shared cultural bonds such as those of religion. At Dura-Europos, for example, soldiers participated together in official unit-level religious ceremonies paying cult to the emperor and a range of other deities, as shown by a papyrus calendar of festivals (the *Feriale Duranum*) of the 20th cohort of Palmyrenes and a vivid mural of one such ceremony (*P. Dura* 54 = Fink 1971: no. 117; Cumont 1926: 89–114, pls. xlix–li; Pollard 1996: 221). Soldiers at Dura (and elsewhere) also gathered and worshipped together in private cults such as that of Mithras and Jupiter Dolichenus (Pollard 1996: 221–2), enhancing military solidarity on a private as well as official level. If such an "inward looking ethos and customary behavior" (B. D. Shaw 1983: 151) did dominate the social and cultural relationships of individual soldiers, then it may have made it easier for Roman officials to use the army for oppressive purposes against provincial civilians, and even turn it against a ruling emperor. However, Alston (1999, providing evidence from Egypt) has warned against assuming that the institutional characteristics of the army necessarily superseded individual soldiers' other social and cultural networks.

Thus there is plenty of evidence for things that might set soldiers and civilians apart. Whether we should take such often anecdotal material as typical is a difficult question. However, Roman soldiers were representatives of an often violent and rapacious imperial state, and we should not assume that the empire was universally popular among its subjects.

6 The Later Imperial Army

While the Roman army of the Severan period was not unlike that of Augustus in many respects, the Roman army of Constantine was quite different. Many of the changes are conventionally attributed to Diocletian and his tetrarchic successors (including Constantine himself), but given the relative scarcity and often problematic character of the evidence from the third and early fourth centuries, it is not always easy to establish when such changes came about. Many of the important sources for the later Roman army, such as the *Notitia Dignitatum* (a late fourth–early fifth-century document listing units of the army and where they were deployed), Vegetius' military manual, and Ammianus Marcellinus' histories, post-date Constantine's reign.

It is hardly surprising, given the external threats to the empire through the third century CE, that the Roman army had expanded by the reign of Diocletian. It is more difficult to be certain of the magnitude of this growth. The comment of Lactantius, a bitterly hostile Christian writer, that Diocletian's institution of the tetrarchy had led him to increase the size of the army fourfold (*DMP* 7.2) should be treated with a good deal of skepticism, but certainly one gets the impression from post-tetrarchic sources (many of them legal) that the army of the later empire was larger and perhaps sometimes struggling to recruit sufficient troops. Conscription (often replaced by substitution or commutation to cash) was normal by the fourth century. However, large scale "barbarization" of the army, if it ever happened at all (Elton 1996b: 136–54), was a phenomenon that occurred after the reign of Constantine. The Roman army had always drawn individual recruits from beyond the frontiers, as well as complete "ethnic" units, and certainly Germans, Goths, and others served in these capacities in the tetrarchic armies.

It is clear that many new units were raised in the tetrarchic period. A. H. M. Jones (1964: 1: 59) suggests the number of legions was approximately doubled. At the same time there is also considerable evidence, both from examination of fortress sizes and from papyrus documents, that some or all units were considerably smaller than they had been in the early and high empire (Duncan-Jones 1990: 110–17, 214–21; Southern and Dixon 1996: 30–3 provide a useful summary), with some legions perhaps of 1,000 men and some *alae* and cohorts with less than 200.

The infantry of the late imperial armies certainly looked different from their predecessors, although on a technological level they were not very different. They wore armor (mostly mail: Bishop and Coulston 1993: 141–5, 167; Elton 1996b: 110–14) and helmets, and carried shields. Their offensive weapons included a mix of thrusting spears, light and heavy javelins with names such as *spiculum*, *verutum*, and *lancea*, and the longer *spatha* sword (Bishop and Coulston 1993: 123–6, 160–2; Elton 1996b: 108–10; Veg. 2.15). Vegetius implies that the lead-weighted darts he calls *mattiobarbuli* and *plumbatae* were introduced in the reign of Diocletian (*Mil.* 1.17). He also calls for archery training for a high proportion of recruits (1.15; 3.14), some of whom were to fight in mixed units with the heavy infantry, a practice not attested in earlier imperial armies.

A high proportion of the units listed in the *Notitia Dignitatum* are cavalry units, many of them *vexillationes equitum* rather than traditional *alae*. Legal documents (*CJust.* 7.64.9; 10.55.3 = Campbell 1994: nos. 387–8) imply that their members had status and privileges equal to those of the legions. This increase in status and prominence (and perhaps, to some degree at least, of relative numbers; but see Elton 1996b: 105–6) of cavalry may reflect a need for greater mobility to meet frontier threats. In this respect Diocletian and Constantine may have been the partial inheritors of a process begun by Gallienus, who by 268 CE had concentrated a large force of cavalry under a single commander at Milan, a convenient location for dealing with threats to Gaul (Zos. 1.40.1). The titles of some late Roman cavalry units in the *Notitia Dignitatum* suggest a titular link (but probably no more) with those of Gallienus, as they include *equites Mauri* and *equites Dalmatae*, and we know that Gallienus used Dalmatian cavalry, while Aurelian employed Dalmatian and Moorish cavalry (Zos. 1.40.2, 52.3–4). Other cavalry unit titles in the *Notitia Dignitatum* include *equites sagittarii* (horse archers, especially on the eastern frontier), and more heavily armored units known as *clibanarii* and *cataphractarii*. Despite this apparent emphasis on cavalry, infantry remained the core of Roman armies.

The army of the *Notitia Dignitatum* is divided into *limitanei*, or frontier troops, typically commanded by officials known as *duces* and *comitatenses*, members of field armies at regional and empire levels, serving under *magistri militum*. It is not clear exactly when this division of the army occurred. In some sense the field army (*comitatus*) may go back as far as Gallienus' cavalry force. Some documents suggest that it existed in some form by the reign of Diocletian (Southern and Dixon 1996: 15–17, 35–7 provide a useful summary). Certainly it existed by 325 CE (*CTh.* 7.20.4 = Campbell 1994: no. 394), since a letter of Constantine distinguishes between *comitatenses* and frontier troops (*ripenses* and others). However, there is no reason to assume that the complex structure depicted by the *Notitia Dignitatum* existed this early. Zosimus' pagan and thus anti-Constantinian complaint that Constantine weakened Diocletian's frontier defenses by withdrawing troops to garrison cities in the interior may be a garbled reflection of an increase in the numbers of *comitatenses* undertaken by the former (Zos. 2.34 = Campbell 1994: no. 382).

The reasons for this division and dispersal (smaller unit sizes, more fragmentation) of the army may be military, political, economic or a mixture of all three. Militarily it may be seen as an attempt (albeit a gradual one) to create a form of "layered" defense to slow down and deal with penetrations of the frontier (Luttwak 1976: 127–90 for a model of "defense-in-depth"); politically it may be viewed as a way of preventing the concentration of too much military power under the command of any one individual; economically as a result of the increased difficulty of supplying large concentrations of troops in a system that increasingly relied on supply in kind and hence the transport of bulky goods such as grain.

The structural role of the later Roman army in the imperial economy was significantly different from that of earlier centuries. While soldiers continued to receive annual cash *stipendia* and, perhaps more importantly, regular imperial donatives (see Duncan-Jones 1990: 105–17), the emphasis of the supply and payment system was on provision of *annona* in kind (albeit regularly commuted to cash). Likewise at least some of the army's equipment and clothing were produced in imperial workshops, listed in the *Notitia Dignitatum*. Reluctance to move bulk goods over long distances may have been one factor in determining the structure and deployment of the later Roman army.

CHAPTER TWELVE

Greek Cities Under Roman Rule

Maud W. Gleason

1 Preamble: Being Roman and Being Greek

Romans, broadly speaking, thought that being Roman was a matter of both mores and material culture (Woolf 1994). They saw "Romans" sharing, not a kinship group, but a value-system, one that was conservative, respectful of social hierarchy, and scrupulous in the observation of religious taboos. "Romans" were people whose own self-discipline, combined with their power to mobilize the labor of others, imposed a rational order over much of the known world. This rationalization of space involved a network of centuriated farmland, roads, and aqueducts whose critical nodes were cities, each of which replicated, on a grand or humble scale, the basic infrastructure of the capital city itself: fora, temples, porticos, and baths.

Greeks saw their world differently. They imagined themselves more as a kinship group, speaking a common language, descended from common ancestors (both historical and mythological), and worshipping a common pantheon, whose Olympian universality was balanced by deliberately distinctive forms of local cult. A Greek's first loyalty was always to his city, but the Greeks' prickly civic particularism was to some extent balanced by a tradition of joint activities in leagues.

To a Roman eye, the Greeks were poised somewhere between civilization and decadence, their intellectual and artistic achievements not matched by military might or sobriety of morals. But Greeks did live in cities, and so as long as they paid their taxes, let the better sort of people run local politics, and expressed appropriate respect for the emperor and his deputies, they were Romanized enough.

Did Greeks consider themselves Romanized? Many aristocrats had Roman citizenship and used the family name of the Roman emperor or general who had first granted citizenship to their family. After the emperor Aurelius Caracalla extended Roman citizenship in 212 CE, any free person could style himself "Aurelius," and many did. Yet Greeks with Roman names did not stop considering themselves Greek. And since material culture was not a determining component of Greek identity,

Greeks felt no less Greek when they adorned their cities with Roman amenities and integrated the emperor's effigy into the ceremonies of their civic life. Scholars still debate the extent to which the intellectual productions of Greek aristocrats show signs of resentment, assimilation, or regret (Bowie 1970; Swain 1996), but the public face of city life combined cultural loyalty to the idea of being Greek with highly demonstrative loyalty to the hegemony of Rome (Smith, this volume).

In some ways Roman hegemony actually fostered their subjects' self-identification as Greeks. In Egypt, and elsewhere in the east, Roman rule involved a partnership with the local aristocracy, usually a hereditary caste of land-owning families. When Cicero wrote to his brother about "the Greeks of Asia" he meant the propertied and educated elite of the province that his brother was governing at the time (*Q. fr.* 1. 1). Previously, such persons might have identified themselves more parochially as Lydians or Mysians (Mitchell 2000: 124), but they were quick to present themselves as "Greeks" to Romans who guaranteed their position of local privilege in exchange for their loyalty to Rome.

2 Defining the Greek City: Language, Ancestors, Gods, and Buildings

Even though cultivated men sometimes romanticized rusticity, deep down everybody knew that civilized life was a performance that *needed* an audience. Greek athletic and cultural activities required an urban setting. So to be fully Greek was to live in a city. But what made a city Greek? Above all, Greek cities felt connected to each other and to the past through language. Educated men conversed in Greek from southern Gaul to Syria and from Thebes in southern Egypt to the Bosporan kingdoms north of the Black Sea. Indigenous languages were still used in Cappadocia, Galatia, and rural Phrygia in Augustus' time. In Western Asia, however, indigenous languages had mostly died out, a process Strabo saw as connected with the advent of Roman rule, whose administrative boundaries did not correspond with those of pre-existing ethnic groups (Strabo 12.4.6; Mitchell 2000: 120–1). It can be difficult to know what language ordinary people spoke, though we do have evidence of what they wrote. In Jerusalem and Galilee, Hebrew, Greek, and Aramaic were all in current use before the destruction of the Temple in 70 CE (Millar 1993a: 352); Greek was the public language of the cities of northern Syria, though Syriac was used along the Euphrates (Millar 1993a: 241–2). In Egypt, peasants spoke demotic, but Greek was the official language of administration (Lewis 1983: 187). In Naples, people used Latin in their epitaphs, but Greek for honorific decrees (Lomas 1993: 176). In general, in cities where the elites had pretensions to Greek culture, Greek was the language of city government and public inscriptions, of rhetorical and literary performance. Greek was also the language in which the city and its representatives communicated with the emperor and his representatives. And Greek was the language in which the emperor addressed his communications in return (Millar 1977). Romans might boast of being bilingual; Greeks did not (Dihle 1994: 45–6; Swain 1996: 40–2).

In addition, a Greek city had certain characteristic ways of locating itself in space and time. Greeks' sense of a common identity as a kinship group informed the practice of tracing a city's origin back to colonization by a mother-city in Classical

Greece or to foundation by a god or hero from Greek mythology. It was important to be "on the map" of the Greek past, historical or mythical. A city that claimed to have been founded by Perseus, for example, would celebrate that connection in oratory, allude to it in diplomatic dealings, and commemorate it in coinage and in cult (C. P. Jones 1999: 115; Robert 1987: 74–86). The people of Aphrodisias did not hesitate to remind the Romans that their city had been founded by Aphrodite, the divine ancestor of Julius Caesar and Augustus (Tac. *Ann.* 3.62; J. Reynolds 1982 no. 32). This diplomatic game was played competitively. For example, in the reign of Tiberius, 11 cities claimed to be the most suitable spot for Asia's new temple of the emperor. Eleven diplomatic teams converged on the capital to claim the honor, variously citing antiquity of origin, grandeur of setting, and previous services to Rome. Sardis alleged a common ancestry with the Etruscans, and hence with the Romans; Smyrna somewhat absurdly claimed title to the honor on the grounds of three incompatible genealogies (descent from Tantalus, Theseus, or perhaps an Amazon), but had the best record of service to the Roman state and for this reason (in Tacitus' opinion) won the day (*Ann.* 4.55–6; Strubbe 1984–6). Again we see that the exigencies of dealing with Rome accentuated claims to Greekness.

Religion was also an important part of Greek identity, and a prominent part of city life. Greek cities worshipped more or less the same gods in more or less the same ways. Processions, sacrifices, hymns, and feasts provided a common format that allowed for infinite local variations in ritual details. The gods themselves varied regionally in their titles and attributes. Our Artemis would not look exactly like your Artemis, perhaps because she had evolved out of syncretism with a different local goddess, or perhaps because her cult statue had different features. However, our statue of Hadrian would look pretty much like your statue of Hadrian, because emperors seem to have found ways to propagate fairly consistent visual images of themselves (Potter 1994: 128). Our Hadrian might reside as a guest in the temple of Apollo, while yours might adorn a gymnasium, a complex of public fountains or even, by imperial permission, have a special temple of his own.

Worship of the gods was only one of the features of urban life that required an architectural setting (Mitchell 1993: 1: 80–1). A Greek city had a fairly standard set of architectural components, some of which definitely show Roman influence (Macready and Thompson 1987; MacDonald 1986). Commerce required public structures: a harbor, an agora, arcades with shops, aqueducts, and sometimes less glamorous structures like channels for industrial waste (van Nijf 1997: 89–90; Pliny *Ep.* 10.98). Many commercial activities required water, as did the ancient city's leisurely habits of personal hygiene. Fountains and public baths were a delightful by-product of the Roman peace, since the aqueducts required to fill them could not be constructed across hostile territory (Coulton 1987). Greek gymnasia, elaborated by the zeal of local benefactors, evolved into bath-gymnasium complexes. The gymnasium was often simple, of classical Greek design, but the baths right next to it were more elaborate structures inspired by Roman habits of monumental architecture and incorporating the Roman idea of taking the waters in a sequence of different temperatures (Fagan 1999a; Yegül 1992). These complexes often contained a room devoted to imperial statuary. The statues of local benefactors, living and dead, adorned the site of their benefactions – indeed all the public places of the city. Structures of commemoration were a basic ingredient of urban space.

Gatherings devoted to politics and entertainment, which drew large crowds, often used the same venue. The assembly often met in the theater for routine business. Criminal justice was often handled in the marketplace, but the interrogation of a celebrated criminal might be transferred to the theater by popular demand when the marketplace overflowed (*A. Pion.* 7). Traditional Greek theaters were often modified to accommodate wild beast hunts or gladiatorial combats, and of course regularly played host to less sanguinary diversions: performances or competitions in rhetoric, music, drama, and mime. A Greek fable conned by schoolboys shows how closely connected urban living, politics, and entertainment were in people's minds. In this fable the monkeys decide to build a city for themselves like the cities of men:

> Look how happy men are because they have cities: they have each their own house, and go up all together into the assembly and into the theater and delight themselves with all kinds of sights and sounds. (Hermog. *Prog. p.* 3 Rabe)

Men did indeed take pride in the architectural amenities of their native cities, and both public funds and the philanthropy of leading citizens were devoted (sometimes unwisely) to improving them. One could hold one's head up higher visiting another city if one's native city were known for its fine public buildings; it was painful to blush for ramshackle shops and dilapidated bathhouses when the governor came to town (D.Chr. 40.9).

3 Different Kinds of Cities

"Well you know," said Dio, haranguing his native city in Bithynia, "that it is natural for a city's pride, its people's dignity, and its reputation with visitors and governors to be enhanced by its buildings, by its festivals, and by the fact that its citizens are immune from judicial scrutiny by outsiders and are not bunched together in the official reckoning like some *village*..." (D.Chr. 40.10). In order to be more than a village, a city had to qualify in terms of size. The largest Greek city was Alexandria, half the size of Rome, with a population at its peak of about half a million. Then came Antioch, Apamea, and Palmyra, with perhaps 200,000, and Ephesus with 150,000. A small city might have only 50 people in its council, and a population of a few thousand. A city also needed enough men of means to serve as councilors. It needed architectural amenities. And it needed imperial initiative or permission to change its status (on these requirements see the reasoning of Constantine in response to an upgrade petition from Orcistus: Mitchell 1993: 1: 179).

There was in fact a patchwork of city statuses. Some cities were Roman *coloniae* (Corinth, Berytus), which were free of direct taxation. A pre-existing Greek city could be upgraded to the rank of *colonia* by imperial permission and given a Latin name referring to the imperial family like "Caesarea" or "Hadrianopolis" (A. H. M. Jones 1971; Millar 1993b: 238). These cities would technically also be *coloniae*, but without any Roman settlers and usually not free of direct taxes. Some cities were "free and autonomous" in the sense that they could use their own laws and were exempt from the governor's visits and judicial supervision; some enjoyed various degrees of tax-free status (*ateleia, immunitas*), usually temporary or removing indirect taxes only (Pliny *Ep.* 10.47; Millar 1977: 430–1).

Some cities functioned as the provincial capital, serving as the governor's seat and proudly claiming the title of "Metropolis" or "first city of Bithynia." (It could be a point of pride for a smaller place to style itself "seventh city" of its province.) The governor would also visit other important cities on his judicial rounds; an assize-center was a busy and important place.

Some cities were distinguished by an imperial temple (Friesen 1993); others were famed for their ties to ancient religious shrines. Ephesus had a famous temple of Artemis; Delphi and Claros near Colophon had oracles of Apollo. Delegations from distant cities came there to consult the god, often accompanied by children's choirs and, presumably, substantial support personnel. Over 300 inscriptions from the second century record the presence of these visitors at Claros (Lane Fox 1986: 171–81, with Robert and Robert 1989 and Robert 1992).

A Greek city might be a member of a *koinon* or league (Deininger 1965). The Lycian league took charge of common festivals and the local administration of justice. It had a distinctive system of proportional representation amongst its member cities (Strabo 14.3.3). The Galatian league likewise seems to have its roots in a sense of tribal identity (Mitchell 2000: 122–5). But each province (and sometimes discrete regions within a province) had a league of its own. These provincial *koina* were more generally "Hellenic" in their identity; their activities centered around the imperial cult. Each league had a sort of president. The "Macedoniarch," for example, was the official in charge of the *koinon* of Macedonia; he was sometimes, but not always, high priest of the imperial cult at the provincial level (Sartre 1991: 113–16, 263). Athens was the seat of the Panhellenion, a league founded by Hadrian whose members, culled from five provinces, had to be able to prove descent from one of the mother-cities of Old Greece (Spawforth and Walker 1985, 1986; C. P. Jones 1996). Competition for membership could exacerbate local rivalries: Cyrene, a member-city in North Africa, apparently tried to blackball the membership application of an upstart provincial neighbor that was, though technically a Greek city, no match for Cyrene's ancient pedigree (Oliver and Clinton 1989: 274–8; C. P. Jones 1996).

4 Components of the Social Order

Just as there was variety in the size and status of the cities themselves, so there was great variety in the wealth and status of their citizens. It was possible for a city to vault over its neighbors to a higher status by a well-executed petition to the emperor, but it was unusual for an individual citizen to experience a radical re-ordering of his social position. Some aristocrats did win individual grants of Roman citizenship before Caracalla made it universal. But this privilege was usually bestowed in recognition of the wealth and social position they already had.

We can observe some of the social striations of a Greek city in the protocols of a second-century aristocrat's benefactions to certain categories of her fellow-citizens. Menodora, from the otherwise unknown city of Sillyon, distributed cash awards to commemorate the successive service of herself, her son, and her daughter in the prestigious municipal office of *gymnasiarch* (gymnasium-director):

85 denarii for each member of the *boule*
80 for each member of the *gerousia*
77 for each member of the assembly
 3 for each of the assembly-members' wives
 9 for each citizen
 3 for each *vindicatus*, freedman, and *paroikos* (*IGRR* 3.801)

Clearly, the members of the *boule* (Council) were on top. These were ex-magistrates and men of hereditary wealth who, upon reaching majority, paid an honorarium to enter their city's governing council. The *gerousia* was a social and religious organization of the city's older men. Many cities had groups of young men (*neoi*), adolescents (*ephebes*), and boys (*paides*); perhaps these groups were not included here because Menodora's tenure of the gymnasiarchy had already benefited them in other ways. In this city the members of the assembly (*ecclesiasts*) were clearly a privileged group, not co-extensive with the citizenry as a whole. The *ecclesiasts*' wives were also a privileged category: these were the only women singled out for special mention, though marked as inferior in status to their husbands. Finally came three groups of persons who were not of full citizen status: both *vindicati* and freedmen were probably ex-slaves who had attained freedom in different ways, while *paroikoi* were "neighbors," perhaps city-dwellers who had been born in local villages or more distant cities.

Menodora herself had held all sorts of posts. As *gymnasiarch*, she would have been responsible for the city's gymnasium, using her own funds to supplement what the city had allocated to purchase anointing oil and fuel for heating the baths. She had given her name to her year as eponymous magistrate, like her father before her. She was Priestess of All the Gods, Priestess of Demeter, Hierophant-for-life, and Chief Priestess of the Imperial Cult (*IGRR* 3.802). She had been, like her father, one of the *dekaprôtoi*, a group of ten wealthy citizens who took responsibility to see that the city's tax liability was met (Sartre 1991: 86). In addition she set up a foundation for the feeding of her city's indigent children. Menodora was evidently the last of her line. Probably this is why she was elected to so many of the offices held by her male ancestors (van Bremen 1994; 1996: 108–13). When her son died she set up a temple to the goddess Tyche in his memory (*IGRR* 3.800). All these benefactions were recorded on stone by the Council, the *gerousia*, and the people of her grateful city.

Menodora's social categories were defined by age and gender, citizenship status, and political role. Occupational groups were beneath her notice, but these organizations were very important to their members. Occupational groups honored their benefactors and recorded some of their own activities on stone or papyrus, offering us a rare glimpse past the elite into the world of working people. There are attested associations of actors, athletes, builders, butchers, carpenters, dyers, fullers, gardeners, goldsmiths, linen-weavers, porters, ship owners, shoemakers, traders, wool-weavers, and many more (van Nijf 1997). Members of these associations worked together and were often buried together. They dined together, buying wine and garlands with funds left by their departed colleagues, whose endowments mimicked on a small scale the grand commemorative strategies of the elite. Association members collectively endeavored to improve relations with the relevant authorities. The ferrymen might put up an effusive inscription honoring the harbormaster for his "virtue" (van Nijf 1997: 92–3). Associations sought favorable conditions for trade. The salt-dealers of Tebtunis, for example, appointed fines for members who set their prices too low or developed an exclusive relationship with big customers. To enlist the enforcement support of local authorities, these fines were to be split between the association's own coffers and the public treasury. To enhance the association's solidarity, members were required to ingest a specified quantity of beer on the twenty-fifth of each month (van Nijf 1997: 13–14). Members of occupational groups were probably a significant component of any city's assembly. Cicero speaks scornfully of the assemblies of the cities of Asia: they are full of men who are "needy and light-weight:...craftsmen, shopkeepers, makers of belts and shoes" (*Flac.* 17–19, 52–61).

Little-mentioned, slaves labored in many workshops and private homes. Public slaves, sometimes ex-criminals, received a salary for low-level civic tasks like cleaning sewers and public baths, or repairing roads – one governor found ex-cons working as prison wardens! (Pliny *Ep.* 10.31–2).

5 City Government

Greek traditions of self-government were reflected in the fact that Greek cities under Roman rule formally resembled the democracies of the classical period, with assembly, council, and eponymous magistrate. The balance of power, however, was now quite different (de Ste. Croix 1981: 518–37). Though formal decrees always began, "It seemed best to the Council and the People...," in the Roman period the assembly of the people lost the power to initiate legislation. And membership in the assembly, as we have seen in Menodora's city, was not automatically available to every citizen. Membership in the council became a permanent privilege based on a property qualification, rather than an annual office determined by lot. In Greece this shift towards a more oligarchic government had been going on since at least 146 BCE, when the Roman general who crushed the revolt of the Achaean League "put a stop to democracy and set up governments based on property qualifications" (Paus. 7.16.9). At Athens, the assembly kept on meeting for almost another 300 years, though it seems to have spent more time voting honorific decrees than formulating substantive policy. The mass of citizens was not entirely without political influence, however. Though formally deprived of political initiative, they could express their views via various forms of disorderly conduct. Dio, whose career as a Bithynian politician had its share of ups and downs, contrasts the decorous praise a politician hoped to receive in the assembly with the disrespectful treatment he might encounter in the marketplace (D.Chr. 51.2).

In some cities, participation in the elite Hellenic youth organization of the *ephebeia* was a prerequisite for entry into the Council. Since only youths of wealth and leisure could join the *ephebeia*, it may not have always been necessary to fix a specific property qualification for entry into the Council. In many places, being a magistrate was a prerequisite for joining, but since magistrates might have to provide expensive municipal services out of their own pockets, people of modest means were in effect disqualified.

6 The Duties of the Well-To-Do

Greek cities characteristically harnessed the energy and assets of their wealthiest citizens to provide public services. This was necessary because Greek cities under Roman rule lacked direct powers of taxation (Sartre 1991: 133). A city could collect rents from municipal real estate, fines for various infractions, and perhaps some customs duties, but the architectural amenities and communal activities that made urban life worth living required deep pockets. The general term for the practice of wealthy citizens providing funds for civic purposes is euergetism, the "doing of good deeds." The donor of funds was known as a euergetist. This practice had a long history in the ancient world (Veyne 1976). But it reached its apogee in the Greek cities of the Roman Empire, leaving behind an enormous architectural and epigraphic legacy that scholars are still working hard to absorb.

A euergetist might exercise his or her beneficence while serving as a magistrate or performing a liturgy. Strictly speaking, a magistracy was an elected office with executive responsibility, while a liturgy was a quasi-voluntary financial obligation. But because municipal revenues were perennially inadequate to meet the expectations of the citizens, magistrates were often, like liturgists, expected to meet the expenses of office out of their own private wealth (see also Gagos and Potter, this volume).

The well-to-do provided the following public services for their fellow-citizens: superintending the deliberations of city government, financing the baths and gymnasia, supervising markets and the food supply, and funding festivals. The eponymous magistrate lent his name to the calendar year (each city had its own name for this official); the Secretary of the Council would superintend political business. We have already encountered the generosity of Menodora the *gymnasiarch*. The *agoranomos*, an official in charge of markets, had to see to the upkeep of his city's harbor facilities and commercial district. What is more, he was expected to keep grain prices stable. This might require a personal subvention (Sartre 1991: 139). Some wealthy citizens served in more than one capacity: one superstar euergetist from Apamea performed the duties of both *gymnasiarch* and *agoranomos* during the assize season, when the city was crowded with visitors who drove up the cost of provisions in the market and used up all the oil at the baths. Furthermore, he promised that he would himself cover the city's usual contribution of 15,000 denarii during his son's gymnasiarchy, and buy all the oil needed for the gymnasium during the assize (*IGRR* 4.788). Priests, who were not professional clergy, but wealthy citizens, often helped to finance public worship and celebrations in honor of the divinity they served. The *agonothetes* had the general responsibility of organizing and provisioning festivals and games. He had to manage the city's entertainment funds, including various private endowments, and contribute out of his own resources as well. Beasts had to be bought for the preliminary sacrifices, cash prizes had to be put up for the competitions, and banquets prepared to celebrate afterwards. Banquets required entertainers as well as food: perhaps a pantomime star, or the latest crooner with his cithara (Dio deplores the ruinous practice of courting popularity with extravagant public entertainments in *Oration* 66).

Besides giving public entertainments, wealthy citizens competed for reputation by funding new public buildings. Construction projects were a grand way to leave one's

Figure 12.1a The entrance to the agora at Ephesus, modeled on a Roman triumphal arch, was erected by Mazaeus and Mithridates, two freedmen of Augustus

Figure 12.1b The marble street at Ephesus. Along the western edge was a gallery of columns, constructed between 54 and 59 CE, supporting a Doric style ceiling. There was also a columned portico on the eastern side. It was an admirable area to place inscriptions honoring civic benefactors

mark, but could become quagmires of mismanagement. Pliny complained to Trajan that Nicaea was trying to build a theater on soggy ground: 10 million spent and the whole thing sinking. Dio tried to beautify his native city by tearing down some dilapidated commercial buildings and replacing them with a fancy marble portico. To begin with, he obtained a letter of endorsement and some funds from the emperor. Dio also promised to contribute a substantial sum himself. Other subscribers signed on, but never paid up. Convinced that the project was being delayed by peculation, the people began to protest and became so riotous that the assembly was shut down by the proconsul (D.Chr. 40, 47, 48; C. P. Jones 1978: 111–14). The paper trail resumes when we find Dio arraigned before the next proconsul by a rival professor of philosophy. It was alleged that he had erected a statue of the emperor inside a mausoleum (thus committing sacrilege), and was, furthermore, in arrears in the auditing of his portico accounts (Pliny *Ep.* 10.81 and 58–60). We do not know how this mess was resolved, but we can guess: Dio was a cultivated person who had connections with the emperor, while his rival, though locally popular, was a convicted forger in the governor's bad books.

7 The Donors: Motives, Rewards, and Evasions

We have seen that public benefaction could cost a lot of time and trouble as well as money. It is natural to wonder, what was in it for the donor? Why did these wealthy citizens choose to adorn their cities more lavishly than their private villas? A crucial factor was their sense of an audience. A few dozen dinner guests was not audience enough. Well into the Roman period, Greeks clung stubbornly to the belief that the proper audience for an aristocrat's identity-performance was the city. Wealth came from inherited land and the exploitation of rural labor, but one *performed* one's entitlement to that inheritance in the city. Time and again euergetists were acclaimed in the theater as "Aristocrats, Olympians, Saviors, Nourishers" (D.Chr. 48.10). These moments of glorious recognition served both to establish social distance between the benefactor and his public, and to confirm the public's exclusive right to validate that distance. One might say that the euergetist invested some of his wealth in envy-reduction. As Plutarch advised a wealthy citizen of Sardis, "the people think worse of a rich man who does not share his money with them than they do of a poor man who steals from common funds, for they think that a rich man [who does not perform liturgies] looks down on them and despises them..." (*Mor.* 822a). Of course the envy that a rich man reduced in his inferiors might recrudesce in his peers, but from the people's point of view, competition between benefactors was all to the good. Aristocrats certainly could be pressured by unfavorable comparisons with their political rivals; a crowd that could chant "Olympian!" could also scream "Cheapskate!" Aristocrats were also under pressure to live up to the munificence of their own parents and ancestors. Honorific decrees insistently note how the honorand renews the generosity of his or her forebears. Dio's ancestors had been honored with statues and decrees, his mother even with a shrine (D.Chr. 44.3).

The most common forms of material recognition awarded to euergetists were statues and honorific decrees. These decrees were not intended to adorn the walls of the honorand's private office. Rather, they were inscribed on stone walls and statue

Figure 12.2a The theater at Ephesus. Originally constructed in the time of King Lysimachus, the theater was frequently embellished by local benefactors. The typical imperial alteration, whereby the lower courses of seats were removed to facilitate beast hunts and gladiatorial combat is evident in this photo. The theater also offered a venue for citizens to protest, as in the story in the Gospel of Luke about the complaints of the silversmiths against the activities of Paul (photo courtesy of Sarah Levin-Richardson)

Figure 12.2b Tetrapylon at Aphrodisias. A tourist attraction in both ancient and modern times, the Tetrapylon, framing the approach to the temple of Aphrodite, was repeatedly rebuilt. The original civic building is a splendid example of second-century civic pride expressed in public architecture. Interestingly, the building was rebuilt in the fourth century, when the temple of Aphrodite was presumably less of an attraction than it was in the second century (photo courtesy of Sarah Levin-Richardson)

bases in all the city's most important public spaces. Indeed, the entire landscape of the city served as a mnemonic device. One could not move through the agora, the gymnasium, or the colonnaded streets without being reminded of the generosity and achievements of the city's elite, extending back for generations. The wording and placement of these honors were the result of extensive negotiation and discussion in the council and assembly: "It seemed best to the Council and the people... to crown Diodoros with a gold crown and to construct for him an exhedra in the new gymnasium, between the solarium and the portico... in which a marble statue of him is to be erected..." (*IGRR* 4.293). Presumably the Council had more say in these details than the assembly, but even members of an occupational association might ask for permission to put up an inscription honoring a prominent citizen, and so get themselves on the map, as it were, of the city's commemorative system (van Nijf 2000).

Now it must be confessed that the public image presented by a Greek city's official inscriptions – a harmonious sodality of gracious benefactors and grateful beneficiaries – is somewhat misleading. Not everyone was willing to spend who should have been, and some categories of persons had official exemptions. Educators and physicians performed a public service by exercising their professions. Therefore Hadrian "wrote that philosophers, rhetoricians, grammarians, physicians were immune from the offices of *gymnasiarch*, *agoranomos*, priesthoods, from the provision of lodging (to servants of the imperial government), service as buyers of grain or oil, that they were not to be jurors, ambassadors, or to be enrolled either in the army against their will or to be compelled into any provincial or other service" (*D.* 27.1.6.8 = Oliver and Clinton 1989: App. 9). Hadrian's successor had to limit the number of such exemptions allowed in any one city:

> The smallest cities may keep five physicians, three sophists, and the same number of grammarians free of liturgical duties. The bigger cities [where assizes are held] may have seven healers and four teachers of each type. The biggest cities [*metropoleis*] may have immunity for ten doctors and five rhetors and five grammarians.... There is no set number for philosophers, since philosophers are so rare. But I think that those who are extremely wealthy will offer the benefit of their wealth voluntarily to their hometown. For a person who quibbles about money shows himself no philosopher. (*D.* 27.1.6.2, 7, 8 = Oliver and Clinton 1989: App. 8)

Aelius Aristides quibbled. A rhetorician born in the insignificant city of Hadrianotherae, he made his home at Smyrna, when not taking the cure at Pergamum's sanctuary of Asclepius. Because he was a man of considerable wealth, he was pestered from all sides by demands that he perform liturgies. He resisted with energy remarkable in an invalid. First Smyrna tried to elect him high priest of the Imperial Cult. Then they nominated him tax collector. Clearly, Smyrna was not willing to count him as one of their liturgically-immune teachers of rhetoric. They had a point: he didn't teach. But on the strength of his reputation as a "star" of Hellenism, Aristides appealed to the emperor, from whom he was eventually able to present letters affirming his immunity. Until these arrived, he trailed after the governor from one assize-city to the next awaiting various hearings. During this period his native city hopefully nominated him to the governor as a candidate for Chief of Police (here we can see in miniature how reluctance at the local level promoted Roman intervention in municipal affairs). In Pergamum, while waiting for his case to be called, Aristides received another summons, this time from Smyrna, appointing him *prytanis* (chair of a standing committee of the Council). When called before the governor, he delivered an oration that consumed five measures of the water clock. ("More like a display performance than a lawsuit," he noted with satisfaction in his diary.) The opposing advocate from Smyrna was stunned; he could muster only a few words. The governor sent him back to Smyrna with an order that Aristides' immunity be confirmed (Aristid. *Or.* 50.68–103).

Clearly, too many such grants of immunity would weaken the system. Athletes, performing artists, and victors in the sacred games often were granted immunity; poets and surveyors sought it in vain (*D.* 27.1.6.13; 50.4.11.4; Millar 1977: 456–63 on athletes and performers). But the key change came in the fourth century when emperors began to reward those who held posts in the imperial civil service, along with the Christian clergy, with immunity from Council membership and the other liturgical obligations of their native cities. This change had the intended effect of shifting the focus of elite ambition away from the cities and towards the imperial court. The unintended effect of this change was to hamstring the fiscal system of the Greek cities.

8 Relations With Governors

To an extent that seems incredible nowadays, Rome practiced government with minimal bureaucracy. There was only one governor per province (though provinces were subdivided in the later empire and thus the number of officials increased). The emperor also sent out agents (*procuratores*) to administer his own land-holdings and assist in the collection of special taxes. These individuals operated independently of the governor, as did the special commissioners appointed by the emperor to take charge of the finances of individual cities when municipal mismanagement had produced a crisis (see Ando, this volume). In Ephesus, for example, in the second century, an imperial commissioner was authorized to audit the accounts of municipal officials going back 20 years and render decisions that were beyond appeal (Eck 2000: 280). Sometimes the cities of an entire province or region – even nominally "free" cities – might be subjected to the financial supervision of a senatorial commissioner responsible only to the emperor. Such interventions may have been designed to save the cities' pride in that they obviated intervention by the governor, but they must in practice have subjected local aristocrats to a painful degree of arbitrary decision-making.

In some provinces, the governor was chosen by the emperor (*legatus Augusti*); in others he was an ex-magistrate (*proconsul*) chosen from the Senate. There were relatively few legions in the eastern provinces, except during wars with Parthia and rebellions in Judea. In provinces with only one legion, the governor might command it; otherwise there was a separate commander (*legatus legionis*). The governor went out to his province with a group of unofficial advisors, mostly his friends, and with a staff of quaestors and legates to whom he could delegate financial and judicial authority. (These junior officials were usually senatorial or equestrian Romans learning the ropes of imperial administration). From his friends and local resident Romans he would constitute his *consilium*, an advisory panel. It was important for provincials to gain access and influence through these semi-official channels since the governor's decisions could not be legally challenged during his period of office, and only with difficulty after that.

The governor took up residence in the chief city of his province, but from there he traveled to hold judicial sessions in the cities on his official assizes circuit (Burton 1975). People from all walks of life, not just wealthy litigants like Aristides, would flock to town when the assizes were being held: "an innumerable crowd of plaintiffs, jurors, lawyers, officials, underlings, slaves, pimps, mule-drivers, peddlers, prostitutes, and laborers..." (D.Chr. 35. 15). People who lived in smaller cities or the countryside might never see the governor, unless they had the misfortune to be embroiled in a lawsuit or to live along one of the province's main roads, where they could be forced to provide food, fodder, or transport for the governor's retinue as he passed by (Mitchell 1976).

How did the governor regard those he governed? Cicero, former governor of Cilicia, wrote a letter of advice to his younger brother Quintus who was then governor of Asia (*Q. fr.* 1.1). It reveals the complexity of a governor's attitudes to those he governed. Quintus is to be commended for passing up so many opportunities to help himself to the abundance of artwork, luxury goods, and financial opportunities in his province (8). He is to beware of resident Romans in his *consilium* who may abuse his trust: such individuals have, "unlike us," left Italy out of a lust to make money abroad (15). Friendships with the Greek elite call for caution too: most of these persons are not worthy of Ancient Greece. They are "deceptive, inconstant, and schooled by long servitude to ingratiating ways" (16). Quintus has nonetheless taken pains to see that city government is in the hands of the "best people" – that is, the wealthy (25). Of course, Cicero says, governors are always obliged to seek the welfare of the governed, and the Greeks of Asia are not, after all, like the barbarians of Africa, Spain, or Gaul, but a civilized race – the race, in fact, from which civilization (*humanitas*) has spread to others. Therefore it behooves Romans to return the gift in kind (27).

In another letter, presumably not meant for wider circulation, Cicero enumerates a whole catalogue of Greeks who have come to Rome with complaints about Quintus. Cicero says he has tried to neutralize them by feigning friendly overtures. The group from Dionysopolis, initially quite hostile, he has softened up by treating their leader like an intimate friend. "Megaristus of Antandros – that incredible lightweight, Nicias of Smyrna, and those total non-entities – even Nympho of Colophon, I have embraced these people with all my cordiality. I did all this [for your sake and] not because I like these individuals or their tribe in general. I'm sick of their triviality and obsequiousness, of how they're always keeping an eye on the main chance rather than on their duty" (*Q. fr.* 1. 2. 4). In fact, the ingratiating hypocrisy that Cicero deplores in the Greeks seems not much different from the sham friendliness that he feels constrained to exhibit himself. Yet he would have been very offended by the insolence of any provincial who *failed* to be obsequious, spoke to him too frankly, or presumed to question his own sincerity.

Mutual suspicion and the power imbalance tended to poison relations between the governors and the governed, even the local elites whose supremacy in the cities the

Romans supported. Unlike Cicero, however, most governors did not leave a corpus of private letters. So in most cases we can only infer a governor's attitudes from his behavior, and often we only hear about a governor's behavior when it became so oppressive that the afflicted provincials ventured to send a delegation to Rome. It was possible in principle to file a criminal indictment against a former governor for extortion (*res repetundae*), and such prosecutions, if successful, could deprive the offending governor of his civil rights (*infamia*), and force him to disgorge his ill-gotten gains (Brunt 1990). But success was uncertain, not least because senators on the juries tended to sympathize with the accused, who were their social equals.

When his friend Flaccus was indicted for maladministration in Asia, Cicero spoke in his defense. Flaccus had assessed a special tax to build a fleet to defend his province from pirates, but it seems no ships were ever built. He was also accused of appropriating for himself monies that the cities had contributed to fund games in honor of his own father, who had been governor a generation before (*Flac.* 55). Furthermore, Flaccus failed to send the poll tax collected by the Jews to Jerusalem (67). Cicero plays upon the prejudices of his audience as he attacks the character of the provincial witnesses. He sets up a contrast between good Greeks, who are honorable, educated, and self-controlled, and the bad Greeks (shameless, uneducated, and shifty) who are trying to incriminate his client (9). He concedes to Greeks in general their literature and learning, but reserves for Romans the moral qualities of *fides*, *mores*, and *disciplina* (9, 11). Asiatic Greeks (as opposed to the Greeks from Old Greece whom Cicero introduces as character witnesses for the defense) are characterized in general by *levitas, inconstantia*, and *cupiditas*: unreliability, inconstancy, and greed (66). Some witnesses, present in the courtroom, are attacked by name, like Menandrius of Tralles: "impecunious, squalid, without rank, reputation, or property" (52). Thus provincials who took their city's case to the Roman Senate risked personal humiliation as well as the failure of their suit. They might also be undercut by rival embassies appearing in the governor's support (100). Since a Roman trial was more of a contest between reputations than an investigation into facts, it did not matter that the Greeks who testified in support of Flaccus did not actually come from the province he governed.

9 Relations With the Emperor

It might sometimes be necessary to appeal to the emperor. A freedman of the emperor Claudius had managed to set up an extortion racket in Cibyra that brought him 3,000 denarii a year. But Cibyra had a distinguished citizen, extremely wealthy and already possessed of Roman citizenship, who was able to go to Rome and persuade Claudius to recall his corrupt agent (*IGRR* 4.914). In provinces like Egypt where the emperor, not the Senate, selected the governor, appeals against maladministration had to go to the emperor himself. When Philo led a delegation representing the Jews of Alexandria to the emperor Gaius in 40 CE, the Greeks of that city sent a counter-delegation. This delegation suborned the emperor's valet, an Alexandrian ex-slave, to poison his mind against the Jews by ridiculing their customs at every opportunity (Philo *Leg.* 166–78). The Jewish delegation tried without success to neutralize this informal channel of disinformation. When they found Gaius in his mother's garden on the banks of the Tiber, he seemed at first to be well-disposed, and sent them to schedule an official hearing with his secretary (181). However, the secretary stonewalled, and no official invitation materialized.

The Jewish delegation followed the emperor in his pleasure-seeking peregrinations down to the Bay of Naples, where they received the disastrous news that Gaius had ordered a cult statue of himself set up in the Temple in Jerusalem (188). When at last Gaius gave them an audience, he was back in Rome supervising various improvements in his gardens. Things began badly: he addressed the Jews as haters of God, inasmuch as they denied his divinity. At this, the Greek delegation jumped for joy and pointedly acclaimed his Divine Majesty (354). Things got worse: Gaius began to stroll through his construction projects intermittently giving orders about interior decoration and catechizing the Jews about their beliefs ("Why don't you eat pork?"). He made no attempt to restrain the Greek ambassadors, who became increasingly jubilant and disrespectful, and finally dismissed the delegations without a definite answer. The despair of the five Jewish ambassadors, who had been hoping for a clear-cut exemption from the demands of imperial cult, was compounded by the fact that certain individuals in the palace who had hitherto seemed supportive gave clear indications now that they had run out of enthusiasm (372).

Not every embassy ended in humiliation and disaster, but this episode with Gaius gives us a rare glimpse of how bad they could get. In fact, most of what we know about embassies comes from the epigraphic record, and the epigraphic record is thoroughly biased in favor of success. When ambassadors returned with a favorable answer, their cities inscribed the emperor's letter on the side of a public building or on a specially dedicated wall (Potter 1994: 117–20). The successful ambassador would be voted a package of honors: a public crowning, a front-row seat in the theater, and perhaps a statue, on whose base a list of his accomplishments on behalf of the city would be incised.

At the emperor's accession, embassies of congratulation would come from cities all over the Greek world, bringing him gold crowns and often a petition that he confirm their previous privileges (on embassies and requests made to the emperor see Millar 1977: 228–40; 385–447). To these requests it cost him nothing to say yes. In the later empire, this congratulatory practice of "crown gold" evolved into something much more like a tax (Millar 1977: 140–4). If an embassy requested new privileges, the emperor often had to adjudicate between rival claimants and assess the impact on the treasury. When he could afford it, he might bestow significant largess on a city suffering from earthquake damage, or award a temporary remission of taxes to a region troubled by crop failure. He might give money for building projects (perhaps thinking privately to himself, as Trajan wrote to Pliny, "these Greeklings must have their gymnasia"; Pliny *Ep.* 10. 40). Imperial windfalls were not automatic: asking for them was a little like playing a slot machine. But one could decrease the chances of ridicule and increase the odds of success by sending an ambassador whose wealth, social connections, and education would command respect in Rome.

10 Education: the Culture of *Paideia*

An ambassador's education mattered because education (*paideia*) meant something grander than just the training of the young. It was a term that encompassed the whole

Greek claim to cultural supremacy. In inscriptions honoring the achievements of successful adults, as well as in the poignant epitaphs of those who died young, one often finds skill with words praised in tandem with virtues of character (Marrou 1964; Schmitz 1997: 136–46). The chief goal of educational training, as practiced by the elite, was extempore eloquence in an archaizing dialect of Attic Greek. The eloquence obtained through *paideia* was assumed to entail both personal virtue and political success (unscrupulous persons who could sway a crowd were deemed to be using illegitimate techniques). Training in eloquence was training in the deportment and self-assurance necessary to perform the part of aristocratic manhood (Gleason 1995). To be successful in a legal contest or in a hearing before the emperor, one had to be able to impose one's own interpretation of a situation on one's audience in the face of competing claims to equity and truth. It was important to be logical; it was important to speak fluently; it was important to demonstrate that one had the self-discipline to master Attic Greek. But it was also important not to be intimidated by the opposition. In meeting the emperor or a Roman governor, one had to strike the right note of self-assurance, without being rude (a sophist from Seleucia once barked "Listen up!" to an inattentive emperor). One also had to avoid drying up altogether, as Aristides was prone to do.

Paideia helped an ambassador because its arduous training procedures prepared an elite man for successful self-assertion; and a governor could accede to a request made elegant by eloquence without losing face: he would look like a connoisseur of culture, not like someone yielding out of weakness. Most ambassadors were cultivated men who were politically active in their city of origin. Sophists, rhetorical stars who practiced competitive *paideia* as full-time teachers and performers, also undertook embassies – sometimes to spectacular effect. Dio won his native city the right to add 100 new members to the Council, their entry fees filling the city's coffers (D.Chr. 45.3–7; 48.11). He also got his city promoted to the governor's assize circuit (40.13, 33). And Polemo helped Smyrna beat out Ephesus in the race for a second imperial temple. He appeared before Hadrian (a soft touch, as a self-conscious philhellene) and persuaded him to contribute one and a half million drachmas towards the foundation of new imperial games (*IGRR* 4.1431). Sophists often came from the best families (Bowersock 1969; Bowie 1982), and legitimated the dominance of the land-owning class by embodying eloquence as if it were a product of their "natural" superiority (Schmitz 1997).

"The root of *paideia* is bitter, but its fruits are sweet." Students at the elementary levels would have to expand upon such platitudes. They would take a phrase through various changes of case and tense, then work their way up to telling fables, such as the one about monkeys founding a city, in direct and indirect speech. Older boys would learn to ring the changes of imaginary court cases. "A man found his son was in love with a prostitute and tied him up. The prostitute, in full revel, burst in on him. The son broke his bonds and hung himself. The father accuses the prostitute of murder" (Sopater 365). One would have to take up in turn the cause of plaintiff and accused, finding plausible motives and justifications for each. Or one might have to impersonate Demosthenes deciding whether to beg pardon of Philip of Macedon.

What was the effect of this training on the boy who practiced it? He would have to be patient, dutiful, and ambitious to assimilate the required canon of classical texts.

He would be expected to make allusion to these (in old-time Attic) for the rest of his life. He would learn to be competitive: every rhetorical performance was a competition, whether the performers were beginners in the schoolroom or professionals in a public place. He would experience himself as part of an endless continuum of classical Greek culture as he improvised in traditional language on traditional themes (Webb 2001). He would learn to frame his case in terms of social status and general considerations of equity, as he might in a future courtroom (Winterbottom 1982). He would learn to fear humiliation in front of his peers if he made any errors as defined by the norms and rules of grammarians. But he would also learn that those norms and rules were to some extent arbitrary, and could be ignored with impunity by authors of high status – good preparation for an adult life that would be governed both by norms and rules, and by arbitrary authorities above those norms and rules (Atherton 1998).

The praises left on marble and in the pages of Philostratus give to lives of outstanding rhetorical accomplishment a triumphant sheen that seems almost designed to distract our attention from questions about what cultural forces were at work beneath the surface. First of all, we might wonder: what is the real meaning of archaism of content? Why did Greeks under Roman rule elaborate in their rhetorical exercises topics either from a fantasy world of soap-opera themes or from the classical Greek past? Bowie (1970) initiated an ongoing discussion of how aristocrats of this period coped with the restricted scope of their political activity in the present by focusing their cultural productions on the past.

We might also wonder, what was the point of archaism of style? The Greeks who claimed *paideia* spoke neither the Latin of their rulers nor the common Greek of their own city's streets. To modern readers accustomed to the rhetoric of social equality, there is something surreal about this situation. But the ancients practiced a rhetoric of social differentiation. Choosing to display one's knowledge of a rarefied literary dialect was a way of making a statement about one's identity (Swain 1996). Elite identity was not monolithic, however. Portrait sculptures show that there was a range of stylized identities available to elites of the Greek east (R. R. R. Smith 1998), and some aristocratic families emphasized athletic rather than rhetorical success (van Nijf 2001).

Scholars speculate about what might be the political implications of this educational system. Some suggest that the highly textured allusiveness of sophistic literary production made it possible to create texts that could be read – if one were sophisticated enough – on multiple levels, not all of them favorable to Rome (Whitmarsh 1998b). Others wonder about the incongruity of using exempla from the Athenian democratic past to inculcate proper deportment in a decidedly undemocratic elite (Connolly 2001). One of the perquisites of elite citizens under Roman rule was immunity from corporal punishment. What were the social and psychological consequences of an educational system that relied on corporal punishment of elite children even as it prepared them for privileged status as adults (Atherton 1998; Gleason 1999b: 300–2)? Finally, were Greek claims to cultural hegemony so insistent because some of their Roman rulers were insufficiently impressed? When Cicero wrote his brother that the Greeks were the original discoverers of *humanitas*, and that it was time for Romans to return the favor, he seems to be implying that Greeks were in decline and civilization was now for Romans to bestow.

11   Discord: Feud and Faction

One of the reasons Romans felt entitled to rule Greeks was the Greeks' proclivity to quarrel amongst themselves. The competitive spirit that infused the performances of rival sophists also informed relations between rival cities (Sartre 1991: 190–8). There were rivalries of long standing between Ephesus and Pergamum and Ephesus and Smyrna, between Prusa and Apameia, Tyre and Sidon, Nicaea and Nicomedia. Nicomedia was the Metropolis of Bithynia, and wanted to be the only city claiming the title of "First City of Bithynia," which Nicaea, a city of more ancient foundation, also claimed (Robert 1977). These titles affected how one city was regarded by others, since they constituted a ranking system that determined the order in which delegations from various cities were seated at games and the place they took in processions at sacred festivals. Three cities claimed the title "First City of Asia." One of these, Ephesus, entitled itself, "First and Greatest Metropolis of Asia, Warden of Two Temples of the Emperor by decree of the Sacred Senate, Temple-Warden of Artemis, Friend of Augustus, the City of the Ephesians," while Smyrna claimed to be "First in Asia in Beauty and Size, The Most Famous, the Metropolis, Warden of Three Temples of the Emperor by decree of the Sacred Senate, Ornament of Ionia, the City of the Smyrnians" (Sartre 1991: 196). It was the emperor who ultimately had the authority to bestow or remove these titles, and as the Greek cities competed for them, they structured themselves into a hierarchy.

These inter-city rivalries had consequences: they could affect how cities were treated by Rome. Dio warned the Nicomedians that their passion for elaborate civic titles was mocked in Rome as the "Hellenic handicap." He was acutely aware of how bad governors could play rival cities off against one another to ensure that they were never called to account for their wrong-doing (D.Chr. 38.36–8). And if civic rivalry expressed itself in grandiose building plans, it made it all the easier for Romans to send in a *corrector* to reorganize city finance. Sometimes rivalries became violent. During the civil war of 193–4 CE between Severus and Niger, Nicaea, "out of hatred of Nicomedia," took the opposite side – which lost – and Nicaea, among other punishments, lost the title of "First City of Bithynia" (Herod. 3.2.9; Robert 1977). In Syria, Laodicea and Antioch took civil war as an opportunity to spite each other, as did Berytus and Tyre, with similarly disastrous consequences for the losing side. One can well see how the Romans might feel that the Greek cities would ruin themselves if left to their own devices (Dio 52.37.10).

Thus whenever we see coinage celebrating "concord" between two cities, with Asclepius of Pergamum, for example, depicted exchanging harmonious glances with Cybele of Smyrna, it is worth asking why that statement was needed (examples in Mitchell 1993: 1: 204–6). Although epigraphic decorum did not permit unpleasant matters to be mentioned directly, the proud titles cities gave themselves, along with the slogans and images they put on their coins can, if read carefully, reveal discordant social undercurrents. Sophist-statesmen would sometimes try to tackle these problems in their speechmaking (C. P. Jones 1978: 83–94), and it is perhaps their efforts that should be credited with seasons of "concord," however fleeting.

There were rivalries within individual cities as well. We see the flour-sifters' and dough-kneaders' associations in Side making a joint dedication to "concord," presumably an attempt to make peace after some fracas, in imitation of the gestures practiced by their social superiors in the pursuit of high diplomacy (van Nijf 1997: 15 n. 25). The price of bread was a key ingredient in social stability, and riots and lynchings might be the consequence of a shortage. Landowners might be tempted to withhold their stocks from the market in hopes of higher prices; as a result, the situation would further deteriorate. There were bad harvests in Syria during the years 382–4 CE, when Libanius was active as a sophist in Antioch. The populace at first blamed the Council (landowners all), and the governor summoned supplementary supplies, but bread prices kept rising. Then the emperor's Supreme Representative in the East (an administrative innovation of the late empire) tried to urge the bakers' corporation to adopt more reasonable prices voluntarily. He was reluctant to use force lest they simply leave town. But this moderate approach earned him accusations that he was taking bribes, so the Supreme Representative switched to more coercive tactics. He had the bakers arrested and strung up on the rack in the agora. He had already flogged six of them, and was starting in on the seventh, asking with every stroke to whom had they given bribes to be able to charge such high prices for their bread, when Libanius arrived on the scene, parted the gaping mob with his hands, and launched into a long reproachful speech about the injustice and folly of these tactics. A riot was just around the corner (Lib. *Or.* 1.205–8). Here we see the coercive force of the Roman rulers brought into play by the failure of local efforts to control a crisis. This is just the sort of intervention that the secretary of the *boule* at Ephesus tried to head off when he told the silversmiths protesting Paul's preaching to disperse from the theater. "For we are in danger of being charged with rioting today..." (Acts 19:23–41, cf. Plut. *Mor.* 814B–815B).

In these episodes we see elite individuals using a combination of rhetorical skill and physical courage to check a violent official and control a violent crowd. The ability to exert control over self and others in this way was one of the fruits of *paideia* training. Crowds that lacked education were deemed to lack self-control. Hence we see Dio attempting a persuasive redefinition when he urges the citizens of Prusa to "render your city *truly Hellenic* and free from rioting.... For there is, friends, a kind of *paideia even of the people*, and a civic character that is fond of wisdom and reasonable" (D.Chr. 44.10–11).

12 Concord and Festivity: Processions, Games, Sacrifices, and Feasts

Greek cities were at their best in times of festivity, when wealthy citizens achieved the recognition and pre-eminence they craved by funding celebrations for the whole community. There was little to celebrate in Boeotia in the year 37 CE, when it looked for a moment as if its economically depressed cities would have to drop out of the Achaean League. It was time to congratulate the emperor on his accession, but no one had volunteered to join the league's embassy. A wealthy benefactor named Epaminondas stepped forward to save the honor of Boeotia, and when his home city later elected him Festival Supervisor (*agonothetes*), he did not disappoint.

Epaminondas revived the games in honor of Apollo Ptoos, which had been in abeyance for 30 years, re-founding them as "The Great Games of the Ptoia and the

Caesars." The games themselves happened only once every four years, but it is simply astonishing how much good eating Epaminondas was able to cram into this period. He feasted the magistrates and the Council annually, and treated the whole town to breakfast every four years. In the year of the actual festival, he gave every male – citizens, neighbors, and non-citizen property-owners – a measure of grain and half a jug of wine for the impending festivities. He marshaled the Great Procession and piously served as impresario for the Ancestral Dance of the Trailing Veils. He sacrificed a bull to the gods and Caesars and continuously distributed meat, breakfasts, sweet wine, and complete meals. During a ten-day period he invited the citizens to breakfast in groups, including their sons and male slaves that were of age, while his wife Kotila hosted the citizen wives, unmarried daughters, and female slaves. He even invited the booth-holders who had come for the fair and the show crews to a private breakfast. In the theater during the dramatic and musical competitions he treated all present, including guests from other cities, to sweet wine, and tossed party favors into the audience (Oliver 1971; Robert 1969b: 34–9).

Typical here is the fusion of activities honoring the traditional Greek gods and the Roman emperor to maintain the city in harmonious relationship with the superordinate principles that guaranteed cosmic order and prosperity. Also typical is the integration of religious activity with athletic and musical entertainment. What is not typical is the broad social range covered in Epaminondas' benefactions and the lack of discrimination between status-groups in the quality and quantity of gifts provided. At Ephesus, in contrast, certain groups, particularly the ephebes, received bigger distributions than others according to the records of a processional foundation (Rogers 1991a: 44–72). In most cities, festivals began with a procession that articulated the cosmic and social order.

We have detailed records documenting the foundation of a new festival at Oenoanda that show how much the proper composition of this procession mattered. The founder's original idea had been to commemorate himself, Demosthenes, in a festival of musical competitions. His original proposal incorporated two sacrifices to ancestral Apollo, but included no special instructions about the pre-sacrificial procession (Wörrle 1988; Mitchell 1990). Imperial permission was promptly secured, but it took a year of negotiations involving the city's Council, the assembly, and the surrounding villages, before the festival plan took final form (Rogers 1991b). What these negotiations added to the program was a procession that included all the local leaders and represented both the emperor and the city's patron god as images to be worn on the head of the festival's founder in the form of an expensive ceremonial crown. On the first day of the Demostheneia, which took place every fourth year, the founder or his representative, in crown and purple robe, was to lead the procession with a sacrificial bull. The city's priest and priestess of the emperor were to come next with another sacrificial bull. Then, with varying numbers of bulls, came the three Festival Supervisors, the Secretary of the Council, the five rotating Presidents of the Council, the Market Supervisors, the Gymnasiarchs, the City Treasurers, the Chiefs of the Rural Constabulary, the Supervisor of the Ephebes, the Supervisor of Boys, the Superintendent of Public Works, and headmen representing about 35 outlying villages and farmsteads (grouped by pre-arrangement into clusters for the provision of bulls). Non-complying individuals were to be humiliated by public proclamation.

Why did the Council and people of Oenoanda insist on adding a festival procession that incorporated civic and village officials as well as homage to the emperor into Demosthenes' foundation? The original proposal, however elaborated its musical prizes, was definitely lacking a gastronomic component, a defect which the revised program would rectify with an abundance of sacrificial meat. The officials who were to provide the sacrificial animals were to receive in exchange a chance to process in a living tableau of the civic hierarchy that included recognition of the economic contribution of outlying rural communities. Apollo was presumably still to be honored on the twelfth and the fifteenth day according to the original plan, but somehow it seemed appropriate to people that a parade of officials initiating a Greek competition should require the authorizing and controlling presence of the Roman imperial image.

13 Epilogue

The focus of this chapter has been the early and high empire – a period in which Roman control over the Greek world was a dynamic process, not a static state, and the Greeks themselves contributed not a little to the forms it took. In Late Antiquity, Roman fiscal control tightened as units of government became smaller and government officials multiplied. Local elites began to focus on the imperial court as their arena of achievement, and the liturgical duties of some – especially the collection of taxes – became more onerous as immunities multiplied for others. Eventually, local bishops, generally from wealthy families, took over the production of urban ceremonial events and redistributed wealth according to new criteria. The preeminence of Greek *paideia* was challenged, then to a large degree reabsorbed into the culture of the Christian elite, but political culture, civic finance, and communal celebration were permanently transformed.

CHAPTER THIRTEEN

Cities and Urban Life in the Western Provinces of the Roman Empire, 30 BCE–250 CE

Jonathan Edmondson

1 Introduction

In the opening book of Vergil's *Aeneid* the Trojan prince Aeneas, fleeing the ruins of his native city, arrives on the shores of North Africa to find another group of fugitives, Phoenicians from Tyre, establishing a new settlement on the site that will become Carthage. On a reconnaissance mission he and his companion Achates catch their first sight of the new city and its leader, Dido.

> They now started to climb the hill which loomed large over the city and looked down over the citadel opposite. Aeneas was amazed at the massive structures, where once there had been simply huts; he was amazed at the gates, the din of activity and the paved streets. The Tyrians were hurrying about busily, some tracing a line for the walls and manhandling stones up the slopes as they strained to build their citadel, others choosing the best site for a building and marking its outline by ploughing a furrow. They were establishing their laws and selecting their magistrates and respected senate. At one spot some were excavating the harbor, and at another a group of men were laying out an area for the deep foundations of a theater. They were also extracting from quarries mighty pillars to stand tall and handsome on the stage which was still to be built.... In the center of the city there was a grove of trees that provided a wealth of shade.... Here Dido the Sidonian was in the process of building a huge temple for Juno; already the offerings dedicated there made it opulent and the goddess's powerful presence could be felt. Its threshold was made of bronze, raised high upon steps; bronze-plated were its beams, bronze were its doors that hung on creaking hinges.... Then alongside the folding doors that led to the goddess's inner sanctum Dido took her seat beneath the temple's dome upon her raised-up throne, surrounded by armed guards. She was already giving her people new laws and statutes and deciding by her own balanced judgment, or by lot, a fair division of the toil required of them. (Vergil, *Aen.* 1. 419–29, 441, 446–9, 505–9)

Dido is here depicted as the very model of a Roman leader. She is busy framing laws, making important political decisions and, not least, supervising the construction of a monumental urban center on a site that had previously been occupied by just a few simple huts. The paved streets, the wall-circuit and its gates, the citadel, harbor, theater and large sumptuous temple of Juno all gave this new community a striking visible presence on the landscape and announced that a civic community worthy of that name was being founded. Not least Aeneas witnessed the ploughing of the sacred furrow (the *sulcus primigenius*) around a building, a ritual that the Romans would come to deploy for marking the outer limits (*pomerium*) of a city; consequently, this act, more than any other, came to symbolize the foundation of a new city.

As Vergil was writing these lines in the 20s BCE, the Punic city of Carthage, in ruins since its destruction by the army of Scipio Aemilianus in 146 BCE, was being refounded as a Roman colony, the Colonia Concordia Iulia. A massive urban grid encompassing 300 hectares was being laid out and a large forum, 190 meters long by 165 meters wide, was under construction on artificial terracing on the Byrsa hill (Gros 1990a; Rakob 2000). Vergil's words thus had plenty of contemporary resonance. But they also encapsulate the Roman belief that a city, that is, an autonomous civic community that controlled a clearly defined territory, needed to be equipped with a monumental center just as much as it required laws, a constitution, local magistrates, and a local senate. Any city worthy of its name had to have a built environment for the proper functioning of its political, religious, and social life.

Julius Caesar had made much the same connection, if more laconically, when he mentioned how in 49 BCE his legate T. Labienus "had given a constitution to and provided at his own expense a monumental center for" the new municipality of Cingulum in the hitherto under-urbanized region of Picenum in central-eastern Italy (*BC* 1.15.2). Thus it is not surprising that when Roman artists came to represent a city in visual form, they stressed its monumentality. A fresco from a Flavian-period building on the Oppian hill in Rome shows a city ringed with a set of walls crowned with circular towers (La Rocca 2000; Caruso and Volpe 2000). It has a fortified harbor with two protective moles, while a river or canal flows into its urban center through an arched entrance flanked with towers. Visible inside the city are a theater with a portico behind its stage-building (a *porticus post scaenam*), several temples, and a large square forum with surrounding colonnade and impressive entrance arch. The city is laid out on a regular grid with the main cross-streets, the *kardo* and *decumanus*, clearly delineated. A fragmentary relief from Avezzano (now in the Museo Nazionale at Chieti) emphasizes many of the same ideals (Gros 2001: 21). It shows a city once again proudly equipped with ashlar masonry walls and a gate, its houses neatly organized within a rectilinear grid (Figure 13.1a). Another fragment has a public building adorned with statues (Figure 13.1b). On the first fragment, immediately outside the walls we can glimpse the surrounding countryside with its fields, trees, villas, and tombs. The clear implication is that a city's territory was perceived as being an integral part of any civic community.

There can be little doubt that in their conceptualization of cities the Romans required them to have a monumental center in order to qualify for civic status. This idea was not unique to the Romans. The Greeks had long since held it and continued to expound it now that they found themselves under Roman rule. Pausanias, for example, writing in the mid- to later second century CE, questioned whether

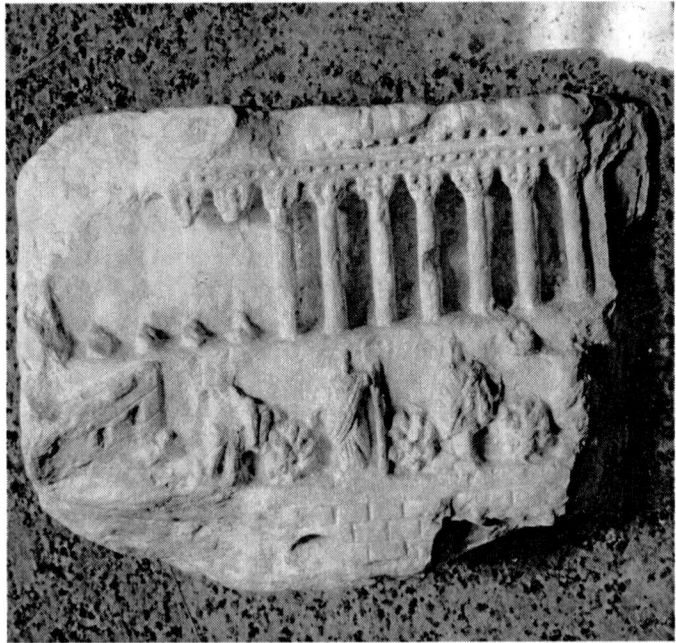

Figure 13.1a and b Relief from Avezzano, Italy, showing city and surrounding countryside (DAI, Rome, Inst. Neg. 79–2757 and 79–2755)

Panopaeus in Phocis in central Greece deserved the title of "city" "when it has no public buildings, no palaestra, no theater, no market-place, when it has no running water linked to a fountain and its inhabitants live on the edge of a ravine in hovels like mountain huts" (10.4.1; cf. Finley 1977). Vergil's Dido, we will recall, had demolished African huts (*magalia*: *Aen.* 1.421) to build her new city. Huts and hovels were simply not commensurate with urban civilization.

But cities were more than just monumental spaces; they also helped to spread the political and cultural ideals of Rome in areas brought under Roman control. Strabo, who wrote a geography of the known world during the reigns of Augustus and Tiberius, emphasized this repeatedly in his discussion of Rome's western provinces. Cities allowed the Romans to settle in a fixed location previously mobile, and hence dangerous, peoples, who could then be expected to turn to the civilized practice of agriculture in the territory of that city. This occurred, for example, in the area to the north of Massilia (modern Marseilles):

> The barbarians who are situated beyond the Massiliotes were already becoming more subdued and instead of brigandage they had already turned towards civic life (*politeia*) and settled farming (*georgia*) because of the sovereignty of the Romans. (4.1.5; cf. 4.1.11 and 4.1.14 for similar sentiments about the Allobroges and people around Tolosa respectively)

Strabo spells out the benefits of an urban lifestyle in even clearer terms in discussing the region of southern Spain known as Turdetania, which formed much of the Roman province of Baetica:

> Together with the fertility of the land, civilization and an urban lifestyle have developed among the Turdetanians.... The Turdetanians, especially those who live along the (river) Baetis (modern Guadalquivir), have completely changed over to the Roman way of life, not even remembering their native language any longer. The majority have become Latins and they have received Romans as colonists, with the result that they are now very close to becoming completely Roman. (3.2.15, C151)

For Strabo, therefore, the growth of cities and civic life were central to the process of becoming Roman. Cities facilitated cultural transformation as centers of Roman-style education, but they also allowed Roman models of law and local government to spread into areas that had not previously experienced strong centrifocal control. It is the importance of cities for the administrative and cultural history of the western provinces under Roman rule and the social milieu of these cities that will be the focus of this chapter.

2 Cities and the Framework of Roman Provincial Administration in the West

For the administration of Rome's provinces, cities were the crucial organizing principle without which the system could not have worked. The situation in the late republic is far from clear. Literary sources allow us to gain a very patchy image of urban life, while archaeological exploration has all too rarely extended to the republican levels of the cities that have been excavated. But even given the limited state of our knowledge, we can still glimpse the importance of emerging urban centers for

Roman control and taxation of the western provinces. In the Iberian peninsula for instance, Tarraco (Tarragona), Emporiae (Ampurias/Empúries), Carthago Nova (Cartagena), Corduba (Córdoba), Hispalis (Seville), Gades (Cádiz), and Olisipo (Lisbon) are all attested as Roman military and administrative bases during the later second and first centuries BCE (Ramallo Asensio 2003; Roddaz 2003; Edmondson 1996a), while in Transalpine Gaul the colony of Narbo Martius (Narbonne), established in 121 BCE, played a similarly important role (Ebel 1973; Hermon 1993). Many of the features we associate with civic life in the imperial period had already developed at Gades, for example, by 43 BCE, when Asinius Pollio reported to Cicero – with no little disgust – the shameful acts of the local notable, supporter of Caesar and now Roman senator, the younger L. Cornelius Balbus (*Fam.* 10.32). As in the city of Rome, the theater at Gades already had its first 14 rows reserved for Roman equestrians, of which there was a sizeable number in this flourishing port-city by the end of the republic (Strabo 3.5.3). It was here during a festival (*ludi*) that Balbus staged a play (a *fabula praetexta*) which took as its theme some of his own exploits during the civil wars. Moreover, at gladiatorial spectacles he allegedly had Roman citizens thrown to the wild beasts, while he also condemned a soldier loyal to Pompey to a local gladiatorial training-school, where, disregarding the soldier's status as a Roman citizen, he had him burned alive.

However, it was the reorganization of the provinces begun by Augustus after his victory in the civil wars that triggered considerable urban development throughout the Roman west. Each province came to comprise a mosaic of self-governing civic communities (*civitates*), each of which consisted of a clearly defined rural territory (*ager* or *territorium*) and a built-up urban center (*oppidum* or *urbs*). Rural villages (*vici*) and smaller nucleated communities – *castella*, for instance – were politically subordinated to the *civitas* capital in whose territory they lay. Sometimes the territory of a *civitas* could include rural subdivisions known as *pagi*, as occurred, for instance, in the large territories of Carthage and Cirta in Africa (Gascou 1983), or in Gallia Narbonensis, where *pagi* of the territories of Arelate (Arles), Narbo (Narbonne), and Carcaso (Carcassonne) are attested in inscriptions (*ILS* 6988, 5421; *AE* 1969–70, no. 388 respectively; on *vici* and *pagi*, Tarpin 2002). Each city possessed its own revenues, including local taxes and land that it leased out for rent, but these resources were insufficient to support all aspects of its civic life and so had to be supplemented, as we shall see (below, section 5), by financial contributions made by the local elite. Occasionally cities also controlled land far beyond the boundaries of their immediate territory, often renting it out and hence gaining revenue from it. Thus in 103 CE 12 percent of the territory of Veleia in northern Italy was owned by the city of Luca, located 130 kilometers to the south (*CIL* XI 1147 = *ILS* 6675, with Duncan-Jones 1976: 8 = 1990: 123).

This network of cities was central to Roman governance in several ways. First, cities served as focal points for the collection of taxes and the administration of justice. The direct taxes owed to Rome by each province were assessed community by community and the local civic elites were responsible for collecting and transferring them to the Roman official responsible for the province's finances (a procurator or quaestor). Occasionally after crop failures or other problems a member of the local elite might shoulder a disproportionately large share of his city's taxation burden, as occurred, for example, at Ebusus (Ibiza), where a man bequeathed 90,000 sesterces to the *r(es) p(ublica) Ebusi[t(ana)]* to help pay his community's annual tax (*tributum*) to Rome (*CIL* II 3664 = *ILS* 6960). For the purposes of jurisdiction, the communities of each province were grouped into assize districts (*conventus*), each with a single city named as assize center. Hence, for instance, the province of Baetica had four juridical *conventus*, centered at Corduba, Astigi, Gades, and Hispalis; Hispania Tarraconensis had seven, centered at Tarraco, Caesaraugusta, Carthago Nova, Clunia, Asturica, Lucus Augusti, and Bracara, while Lusitania had just three, centered at Emerita, Pax Iulia, and Scallabis (Plin. *Nat.* 3.7, 18; 4.117 respectively). Similarly, the province of Dalmatia was divided into three *conventus* centered at Salona, Narona, and Scardona (Plin. *Nat.* 3.139, 142). The Roman provincial governor would visit each of the *conventus* centers on his annual judicial tour of duty to hear lawsuits, listen to petitions, and settle disputes. In some parts of the Roman west these districts came to play a role in the organization of imperial cult activities (Étienne 1958: 177–95). Thus at Tarraco, capital of the province of Hispania Tarraconensis, statues were set up to honor priests (*sacerdotes*) of Rome and Augustus of the *conventus* centered at Asturica and Bracara respectively (*CIL* II 6094, 4215 = *RIT* 275–6) and dedications have been discovered honoring the Genius (i.e., protecting spirit) of the *conventus* centered at Asturica, Clunia, Caesaraugusta, and Tarraco, as well as another where the name of the *conventus* is lost on the inscription (*CIL* II 4072–4; *RIT* 24–7; López Vilar and Currula Ferré 2001).

In addition, cities were responsible for the upkeep of the roads that ran through their territory and for providing transport for Roman officials traveling on state business. They also had to provide hospitality for visiting Roman dignitaries and in emergencies had to muster any supplies that the Roman state demanded. At the colony of Urso (Osuna) in southern Spain all colonists between the ages of 14 and 60 had to contribute five days of corvée labor per annum, some of which was used towards maintaining the roads (*Lex Ursonensis* 98; cf. *Lex Irnitana* 83), while at Ercavica in central Spain a local notable bequeathed a sum of money to the city so that it could use the interest to fund an eight-mile stretch (c.12 km) of the road to Caesaraugusta (Zaragoza) (*CIL* II 3167, with Alföldy 1987: 73). As for requisitioning, when the Roman army early in Claudius' reign was mopping up after a revolt in Mauretania, the cities of Baetica across the Straits of Gibraltar were required to provide grain to feed the Roman troops (Dio 60.24.5).

Finally, the growth of many autonomous civic communities across the Roman west allowed for the formation and consolidation of a stable local elite, who played a crucial intermediary role in the maintenance of Roman control. The political constitutions of these cities required the elite to serve as local councilors (*decuriones*) and to hold a sequence of magistracies and priesthoods that obliged them on a regular basis to exercise their political, judicial, and religious authority (see below, section 5). In short, cities provided the elite with the ideal stage on which to maintain their social distinction vis-à-vis their fellow citizens and to advertise their loyalty towards Rome. In return for their services, members of this local elite were often rewarded with enhanced personal status. Many gained Roman citizenship, some Roman equestrian or even senatorial status. But it was their local civic environment that allowed their social power to become entrenched. Hence it is no exaggeration to assert that Roman provincial administration could not have functioned effectively without such cities and without the social order that developed in each of them.

3 The Varying Status of Cities

Not every city within each province, however, was identical in terms of its juridical status; rather a hierarchy of different types of community developed. Furthermore, this hierarchy did not remain static, since communities could and did appeal to the emperor to be upgraded in status, as we shall see. As a result, there was often a distinct rivalry between neighboring cities, as each competed to outdo its neighbor in terms of status and prestige.

Civitates stipendiariae

The majority of communities in the western provinces at the time of Augustus were *civitates stipendiariae*, "tribute-paying communities." For the most part the inhabitants of these *civitates* were non-citizens (*peregrini*, in Roman legal terms), although some members of the local elite on an individual basis gained Roman citizenship as a reward for their loyalty and good services to Rome. This is clear, for example, at Ammaia (São Salvador de Aramenha near Portalegre in Portugal), where a statue was set up during the reign of Nero to honor Publius Cornelius Macer, a local magistrate who had been granted Roman citizenship by the emperor Claudius in the years before the community became a *municipium* (*CIL* II 159 = *ILS* 1978). In the interior of Gaul, Spain, and Britain and in the Danubian provinces, these *civitates* were often somewhat artificial creations, especially where the Roman provincial governor had amalgamated various peoples to form a new civic community. In remoter regions, such as northern Lusitania or the interior of Dalmatia, Rome seems to have allowed native leaders (*principes*) to retain authority over their own *populus* for 50 years or more, since the process of creating the *civitates* could not be completed overnight (Alarcão 1988: 29–32; Wilkes 2003: 235). Tacitus mentions the tireless work that Cn. Domitius Corbulo put in as legate of Germania Inferior under Claudius in organizing the Frisii into *civitates*: he had to establish a local senate, magistrates, laws, and a territory for each new community (*Ann.* 11.19). Inscribed boundary markers provide a few glimpses of this carving out of new territories (*ILS* 5948–81; Campbell 2000: 454–67). A typical example, dated to 5/6 CE by Augustus' titles, was found at Ledesma near Salamanca in north-eastern Lusitania:

> Imperator Caesar Augustus, pontifex maximus, with tribunician power for the twenty-eighth time, consul for the thirteenth time, father of the fatherland: Augustan boundary-stone (*terminus Augustal(is)*) between Bletisa, Mirobr(iga) and Salm(antica). (*CIL* II 859 = *ILS* 5970)

Disputes arose between communities over boundaries and these often required the intervention of the Roman provincial governor. Such occurred, for example, in Dalmatia under Caligula, where the decision reached by the centurion delegated by the governor to settle the dispute was inscribed on a rock-face near Vaganj in Bosnia, presumably where the boundary was established:

> Lucius Arruntius Camillus Scribonianus, legate with propraetorian power of Gaius Caesar Augustus Germanicus, provided Manius Coelius, centurion of the Legion VII,

as an adjudicator between the Sapuates and the Lamatini. He was charged to define their territories and place boundary-stones. (*CIL* III 9864a = *ILS* 5950)

Provincial governors sometimes established a *civitas* capital at a site that had already been occupied in the later Iron Age; alternatively, a new center was created some distance from the Iron-Age site and often in a more accessible location. Thus in Gallia Lugdunensis the *oppidum* of Bibracte (Mont Beuvray) in the territory of the Aedui had already developed a number of urban features by the time Augustus began to reorganize the provincial landscape in this area. However, the decision was taken to abandon Bibracte in favor of a lowland site some 20 kilometers away, where the new *civitas* capital of Augustodunum (Autun) was established (Goudineau and Peyre 1993; Woolf 1998: 7–10). Since many of the names of these new communities were artificial coinages, the name of the people (*populus*) who occupied the region was often retained – at least in the early imperial period. Thus in his list of communities of the Gallic provinces the elder Pliny gives both the urban toponym and the more traditional ethnic for several cities: for example, Aquae Sextiae of the Salluvii, Avennio of the Cavares, Apta Iulia of the Vulgientes, Alebaece of the Reii Apollinares, Alba of the Helvii (*Nat.* 3.36). In some areas the ethnonym was never forgotten and re-emerged in late antiquity. So the city of "Paris" preferred to recall its origins as the *civitas* capital of the Parisii rather than retain its Roman toponym, Lutetia, as did Tours, *civitas* capital of the Turones, which had been given the name Caesarodunum. Indeed the historian Ammianus Marcellinus reveals (15.11.12) that Caesarodunum had already reverted to being called the *civitas Turonum* by the fourth century CE.

Municipia

Some indigenous communities were deemed politically and culturally more advanced than others and as a result were granted the "Latin rights" of citizenship (the *ius Latii*, *Latium*, or *Latinitas*), and occasionally municipal status. (In some cases it provided Augustus with a means of rewarding a community that had remained loyal to him during the civil wars.) Some scholars have argued that the grant of the Latin rights brought with it automatic promotion to municipal status, but a more nuanced reading of the sources suggests that communities that were not *municipia* could still hold the *ius Latii* (Sherwin-White 1973: 360–79; Le Roux 1986). A community's promotion to the status of a "municipality of the Latin rights" (*municipium iuris Latii* or *iuris Latini*) was confirmed by means of a formal statute of the Roman people (a *lex populi Romani*), which resulted in its citizens becoming "Latin citizens" (*cives Latini*). This is the natural implication of the reference to *Latini* in two clauses of the municipal charter granted to Irni under Domitian (*Lex Irnitana* 28 and 72), which in retrospect excludes Fergus Millar's self-admittedly heretical suggestion that the category of *cives Latini* never existed (Millar 1977: 630–5; cf. 2004: 342, n. 13). Occasionally a community contained enough Roman citizens to merit the status of a "municipality of Roman citizens" (*municipium civium Romanorum*), as occurred at Olisipo (Lisbon) by the Augustan period (Plin. *Nat.* 4.117), and at Volubilis in Mauretania Tingitana, which gained this status from Claudius after the city had provided troops in 40–41 CE to help put down the revolt of Aedemon, freedman of the recently deceased King Ptolemy of Mauretania (*ILAfr* 634 = *FIRA* I 70, tr. Sherk 1988 no. 50).

The promotion of native communities to the Latin rights and then to municipal status was an ongoing process, occurring at different moments in different regions of the Roman west. A few communities in southern Spain and Gallia Narbonensis had already been promoted by Julius Caesar. Many more were promoted by Augustus (Sherwin-White 1973: 225–36; Brunt 1987: 602–7). Claudius extended these grants in central Gaul, Noricum, northern Dalmatia, and Mauretania, for instance, but it was under the Flavian emperors that the process gained particular momentum. During his censorship in 73/4 Vespasian granted Latin rights to "the whole of Hispania" (Plin. *Nat.* 3.30), a blanket grant which (in my view) is best interpreted to mean that it allowed individual communities then to petition for formal bestowal of these rights and possibly also municipal status (Richardson 1996: 179–230). The bronze plaques that survive from Salpensa, Malaca, and, most fully, from Irni in Baetica with the texts of the statute of the Roman people (*lex populi Romani*) granting their municipal status were the products of the successful application of each of these communities for promotion. In north Africa the Flavian period also saw some promotions in status of communities – this was when Lepcis Magna, for instance, gained the *ius Latii* – but the largest number of grants of municipal status occurred during the second and early third centuries CE (Jacques 1972; for Hadrian's contribution, see Boatwright 2000: 36–56).

Such promotions required an influential member of the local elite to lobby the Roman emperor. During the reign of Antoninus Pius, the city of Gigthis (Bou Ghara) in the eastern part of Africa Proconsularis known as Tripolitania (D. J. Mattingly 1994: 128–31) successfully petitioned the emperor for the status of a *municipium Latii maioris* (i.e., the much rarer form of Latin rights whereby not just the magistrates but the entire local senate received Roman citizenship). As a result, the local senate honored the city's envoy, a Roman citizen who had held the senior magistracy and a priesthood in the community, with a statue to commemorate the hard work he had put in and the financial contribution he had made in funding his embassies, as the inscription on the statue-base made clear:

> In honour of Marcus Servilius Draco Albucianus, son of Publius, of the (Roman voting tribe) Quirina, duovir, flamen in perpetuity, because in addition to his numerous good deeds towards the community and his very expansive zeal for munificence he undertook at his own expense two embassies to the city of Rome to petition for the major Latin rights (*Latium maius*). When at last he reported on the success of his mission, the order (i.e., local senate) voted to erect (this statue) in his honour at public expense. And when he, pleased with the honour, returned the money to the community, the local citizen body (*populus*) set it up on its own initiative. (*ILS* 6780)

Colonies

Quite distinct from the *civitates stipendiariae* and *municipia* were the Roman colonies implanted on the provincial landscape by Julius Caesar, the triumvirs and, most of all, by Augustus in the period from 30 to 13 BCE, with occasional foundations in subsequent years (Vittinghoff 1951; Brunt 1987: 589–601). While *municipia* were in theory governed according to local law and political traditions (although they were often strongly influenced by Roman practice), colonies used Roman law and had their constitutions directly modeled on that of Rome. In his work *Attic Nights*, composed in the mid-second century CE, Aulus Gellius underlined the key differences as follows:

> Colonies do not come into the Roman state from outside nor grow from their own roots, but they are, as it were, propagated from the Roman state and have all the laws and institutions of the Roman people, not those of their own choosing. This condition, even though it is more exposed to control and is less free, is nonetheless thought to be preferable and more prestigious because of the greatness and majesty of the Roman people, of which these colonies seem to be almost small scale images and reflections. (Gel. 16.13.8–9)

The initial settlers in most colonies were veteran soldiers, large numbers of whom had to be demobilized after the civil wars of the 40s and 30s BCE. Some colonies included members of the urban poor, siphoned out of the city of Rome in an attempt to alleviate some of the social, economic, and political problems that beset the city as its population rose steeply to almost one million by the mid-first century BCE. Occasionally a number of local provincials were integrated within their initial citizen bodies (Suet. *Jul.* 42.1; Brunt 1987: 246–59). Since most colonies possessed full Roman status, all citizens of colonies as a result also held Roman citizenship. In some areas, as at Nemausus (Nîmes) in southern Gaul, colonies with the Latin rights of citizenship were established, whereby as in municipalities the local magistrates were automatically granted full Roman citizenship after holding local office.

In some of the remoter provinces – Britain, for instance, or the military zones of the Rhineland – colonies were established on or near sites that had previously served as legionary camps. Camulodunum (Colchester) was founded in 49 CE on the site of the camp of the Legio XX, while in the 80s a colony was settled at Lindum (Lincoln), which from the 60s onwards had been the base of the Legio IX and then Legio II Adiutrix (Hurst 1999, 2000). In both cases the former military facilities were reused for the new civilian settlements, with barrack-blocks, for instance, simply converted into civilian housing. Similarly in the new province of Dacia Trajan founded the Colonia Ulpia Traiana Sarmizegetusa in 108 on the site of the former encampment of the Legio IV Flavia. In Germania Inferior, the Colonia Claudia Ara Agrippinensium (Cologne) and the Colonia Ulpia Traiana at Xanten were established as colonies in 50 and 98 respectively, but in the vicinity of, rather than on the site of, Roman military bases (Galsterer 1999).

During the second century colonial status was granted to certain *municipia* in response to the familiar routine of an embassy sent with a petition to the emperor. Lepcis Magna (Lebda in modern Libya), for example, which had become a *municipium* with the Latin rights under Vespasian, was granted colonial status by Trajan in 109 without a *deductio* of new settlers (D. J. Mattingly 1994: 116–22). Trajan's generosity was commemorated on a monumental arch erected in 110 by the senate and citizen body of Lepcis:

> To Imperator Caesar Nerva Traianus Augustus, son of the deified Nerva, Germanicus, Dacicus, pontifex maximus, with tribunician power for the fourteenth time, saluted six times as *imperator*, consul for the fifth time, father of the fatherland. The senate and people of the Colonia Ulpia Traiana Fidelis Lepcis Magna erected this arch with its decoration by unanimous consent at public expense. (*IRT* 353)

As we shall see (below, section 4), promotions in status such as this often led to significant expansion and development of urban centers. A further privilege that was occasionally granted to colonies was the "Italic rights" (*ius Italicum*), whereby they were assimilated to the communities of Italy and so were no longer liable to taxation by Rome (*D.* 50.15.1, 6–8). Septimius Severus, for example, bestowed this privilege in c.203 upon his native city of Lepcis Magna, a point to which we shall return.

4 Monumental City Centers

We have already noted (above, section 1) that in Roman ideology there was an expectation that the bestowal of a political constitution upon a city should be marked by the construction of a monumental center. Archaeological evidence from cities confirms this general picture, but suggests that the process did not occur at the same pace or with the same intensity in all regions of the Roman west. Roman colonies, as we have seen, were implanted from the center of power. The Senate and people of Rome appointed a *deductor* to oversee the foundation, a responsibility that Lucius Munatius Plancus, consul in 42 BCE, felt important enough to have inscribed on his epitaph on his mausoleum near Caieta (Gaeta) in Campania (*ILS* 886: ... *in Gallia colonias deduxit Lugudunum et Rauricam*). The *deductor* was responsible for the initial planning of the urban center, for the apportionment by lot of land in the colony's territory and for the selection of the first local council (*ordo decurionum*), thereby creating the colony's initial elite. Not surprisingly, this official sent out from Rome had distinctly Roman notions of what a city should look like. Hence colonies came to be seen as "small-scale images and reflections" of the "greatness and majesty of the Roman people," to quote Aulus Gellius once again (16.13.9). The peculiar topography of the city of Rome and its lengthy evolution meant that it was by no means the best model for a colonial foundation. And so it was the colonies sent out by Rome to defend coastal Italy in the fourth and third centuries BCE and those established in the Po valley and Cisalpine Gaul in places like Placentia (Piacenza), Luna (Luni), and Comum (Como), founded in 218, 177, and 89 BCE respectively, that provided the blueprints that were exported to the western provinces in the early imperial period (Ward-Perkins 1970; Zanker 2000).

A good example of how a Roman colony reflected the "greatness and majesty of the Roman people" is provided by the Colonia Augusta Emerita (Mérida in southwest Spain) (Figure 13.2a; for up-to-date syntheses, see Mateos Cruz 2001; Dupré Raventós 2004). The colony was founded in 25 BCE for the veterans of the Legions V Alaudae and X Gemina, which had taken part in the first phase of Augustus' wars in Cantabria and Asturia in the far north and northwest of Spain (Dio 53.26.1). While there is some scattered archaeological evidence for previous occupation, it was clearly not a major settlement when Augustus chose it as the site for this new colony. Situated on the river Anas (modern Guadiana), it soon came to play a major role in the communications network of the western half of the Iberian peninsula, controlling the point where the major north–south road from Asturica (Astorga) to Hispalis (Seville) crossed the river and intersected with the major east–west road that led from Toletum (Toledo) in central Spain to Olisipo (Lisbon) on the Atlantic coast. The monumental bridge across the Anas with its 56 arches was one of the earliest of the colony's building projects, emphasizing Emerita's importance as a key node in the communications network of Hispania (Álvarez Martínez 1983).

An urban grid was immediately laid out and many traces of its cross-streets (*decumani* and *kardines*) have come to light, as have some of the sewers that underlay them. The colony was provided with an impressive perimeter wall with gates and towers from the start, and not surprisingly this was one of the main images that featured on the coins minted there under Augustus and Tiberius (Burnett and Amandry 1992: 69–73, nos. 12, 20–7, 30–3, 38, 41–4). Six blocks (*insulae*) of the urban grid were left open at the intersection of the *kardo maximus* and *decumanus maximus* for the colony's forum, which had as its focal point a temple, initially constructed of local granite and decorated with stucco, raised upon a high podium. Long known incorrectly as the "temple of Diana," it was almost certainly a temple dedicated to the cult of the emperors (Álvarez Martínez and Nogales Basarrate 2003). Within ten years of the colony's foundation, M. Agrippa, now Augustus' son-in-law, had provided the funds for a theater, dedicated in 16 BCE (*CIL* II 474 = *ILS* 130), perhaps to coincide with the elevation of Emerita to be capital of the new province of Lusitania. Not to be outdone, Augustus followed suit in funding an amphitheater, dedicated in 8 BCE directly alongside the theater (*HAE* 1479, with Ramírez Sádaba 1994). At least one of the colony's aqueducts may trace its origins back to the foundation period: the "Aqua Augusta," as a monumental inscription describes it (*AE* 1984, no. 493), which brought water some 15 kilometers to the urban center from the still preserved "Cornalvo" reservoir. By the mid-first century CE it had been supplemented by two further aqueducts, one of which, the so-called "Los Milagros" aqueduct, was connected to another surviving reservoir, the "Proserpina," located 7 kilometers northwest of the colony (Grewe 1993: 246–55; Mateos Cruz et al. 2002).

The Julio-Claudian period saw considerable development in the city. Another forum, with impressive marble decoration, was added alongside the original forum (Figure 13.2b), and this *forum adiectum* was decorated in exactly the same manner as the Forum of Augustus in Rome (Trillmich 1995). The upper attic of its portico featured Karyatids and shield-roundels (*clipei*), some with the head of Jupiter Ammon, others with that of Medusa (Figure 13.3a–b). Its back wall had niches for statues, which included a group depicting Aeneas fleeing the city of Troy with Anchises on his shoulder and leading his son Ascanius by the hand (Figure 13.4), as well as a possible Romulus, some of the kings of Alba Longa, and a group of togate *summi viri*. The identification of the Aeneas-group has been confirmed by two fragments of an inscribed *elogium* of Aeneas, a copy of the original in the Forum of Augustus in Rome, which matches the version long since known from Pompeii (de la Barrera and Trillmich 1996; cf. *Inscr. It.* XIII.3, no. 85). In addition, a series of marble reliefs has been shown to belong to this public space; the depiction of Agrippa in the act of sacrifice may once have graced a large altar, it has been suggested, possibly even the Ara Providentiae that was featured on one of the colony's coin types (Nogales Basarrate 2000).

In the Julio-Claudian period four *insulae* to the north of the *decumanus maximus* were cleared of private housing to make way for another large porticoed forum, with the misnamed "Arch of Trajan" its monumental entrance-gate. At its center stood a large temple, modeled, it appears, on the Temple of Concord in Rome. This complex may have served as the center for the imperial cult activities of the province of Lusitania, but while this is possible, we still await definitive proof (Mateos Cruz 2001: 196–8). The colony could also boast a large circus, monumentalized in the Julio-Claudian period (Sánchez Palencia et al. 2002). At the same time its domestic architecture, whether the intramural houses or the much larger extramural suburban houses with mosaics and painted wall-decoration, took the form of typical Roman houses of the mid-first century CE (Alba Calzado 2004).

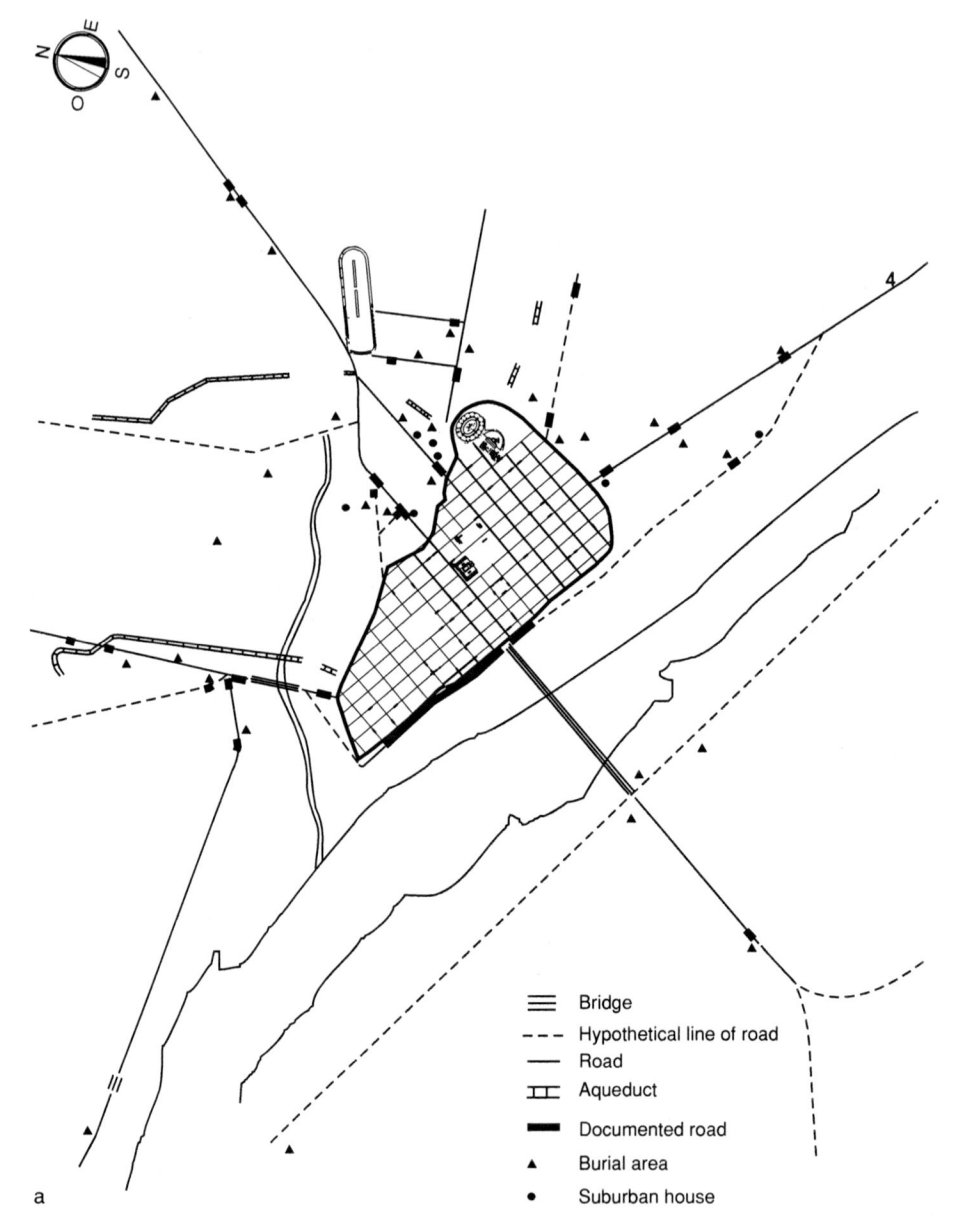

Figure 13.2a Colonia Augusta Emerita (Mérida, Spain): (a) plan of the city and environs (P. Mateos Cruz, courtesy of Consorcio Ciudad Monumental de Mérida)

Emerita's impressive public buildings, graced with marble sculptural decoration that would not have looked out of place in the city of Rome, gave the colony the look and feel of an imperial center. Its monuments allowed Roman provincial officials and local civic magistrates to conduct their public business on a distinctly Roman stage. The statues of members of the imperial family that peopled the stage (*scaenae frons*) of the theater and the portico behind the *scaena* or the visual tutorial in Roman myth

Figure 13.2b Colonia Augusta Emerita (Mérida, Spain): (b) reconstruction of the monumental center, showing the original forum and "*forum adiectum*" (right) and so-called "provincial" forum (left), as reconstructed by J.-C. Golvin, J. M. Álvarez Martínez, and T. Nogales Basarrate (courtesy of Museo Nacional de Arte Romano, Mérida)

and history provided in the marble *forum adiectum* all helped invest the colony's urban landscape with memorable images of Roman power. Those Lusitanians who traveled to the city to press legal cases before the governor's tribunal or to enjoy the spectacles that formed part of the colony's religious festivals would have returned home with vivid mental impressions of what a proper Roman city should look like.

Similar iconographic schemes have been discovered at other colonies in the Roman west – at Arelate (Arles) in Gallia Narbonensis (Gros 1987), and at Tarraco (Tarragona) in Hispania Tarraconensis, for instance – and the link with imperial cult activities became ever stronger as the first century CE progressed. This is particularly evident at Tarraco, where the entire upper part of the city was transformed in the Flavian period by the creation of a tiered complex for the province's imperial cult celebrations (Figure 13.5). A temple stood at the center of a porticoed square dominating the town just as the cathedral that occupies the site still does today. Below it was a vast forum, constructed on artificial terracing, 175 meters wide by 318 meters long, with its surrounding portico a staggering 14 meters wide. This terrace in turn looked down upon a circus, unusually set in the heart of the city. The decoration of this forum was again modeled on the Forum of Augustus in Rome (TED'A 1989; Mar 1993). At the colony of Nemausus (Nîmes) a pre-existing Gallic sanctuary around a sacred spring was developed into a monumental *Augusteum* with temples, a central altar, U-shaped portico, and theater from the early first century CE onwards (Gros 1984).

However, it was not just colonies that came to be adorned with images and architecture redolent of Roman power; indigenous communities were transformed too. Statues of, and dedications to, members of the imperial house filled the public buildings of many western cities: not just the temples dedicated to the cults of the *domus Augusta*, but also the forums, basilicas, curias, monumental arches, theaters,

Figure 13.3a *Forum adiectum*, Emerita: (a) general view

amphitheaters, and baths (Gros 1990b on Gaul and Spain; Hurlet 2001 on Africa). The most dramatic transformations often followed a promotion to municipal status, as the local elites, many now Roman citizens, funded new monumental centers that announced their loyalty to Rome. The small settlement at Glanum (near Saint-Rémy-de-Provence) within the cultural orbit of the Greek colony at Massilia (Marseilles) could boast by the beginning of the first century BCE an impressive set of public buildings in Hellenistic style: a Tuscan temple with trapezoidal building nearby, an agora with Doric porticoes, and a *bouleuterion* and various smaller buildings in the immediate vicinity of a sacred spring. In about 40 BCE, when Glanum was granted the *ius Latii*, the Hellenistic *bouleuterion* was overlaid with twin temples in Roman style, later surrounded by a U-shaped portico. The Tuscan temple and trapezoidal building below it were removed to make way for a new forum, which was closed off at its north

Figure 13.3b *Forum adiectum*, Emerita: (b) reconstruction of R. Mesa (courtesy of Museo Nacional de Arte Romano)

end by a large basilica and behind that by a series of administrative buildings, including a possible *curia* for the local decurions (Figure 13.6). This forum–basilica–curia complex, raised up on artificial terracing, dominated the houses and streets below. It very strikingly emphasized the political dominance of Rome in this previously Hellenized town (Roth-Congès 1992, 2000; Gros 1991: 31–4; 1996: 221–2).

Similarly in northern Lusitania the Iron-Age settlement at Condeixa-a-Velha near Coimbra was chosen to be one of the new *civitates stipendiariae* in the Augustan reorganization of the region. It was given the name Conimbriga. In the Augustan period an impressive perimeter wall was built and in the center of the city a forum with temple, basilica, curia, and shops laid out on a perfectly Roman model (Figure 13.7a). Atrium-style houses started to appear, while a public bath complex attested to the fairly rapid spread of Roman culture to this outlying region of the west. In the Flavian period the urban center was completely remodeled, with the Augustan forum dis-

Figure 13.4 Reconstruction of statue-group of Aeneas (center), Ascanius (left), and Anchises (right) from the *forum adiectum*, Emerita. Photo: courtesy of Museo Nacional de Arte Romano, Mérida, based on drawing of W. Trillmich, U. Städtler, and T. Nogales Basarrate

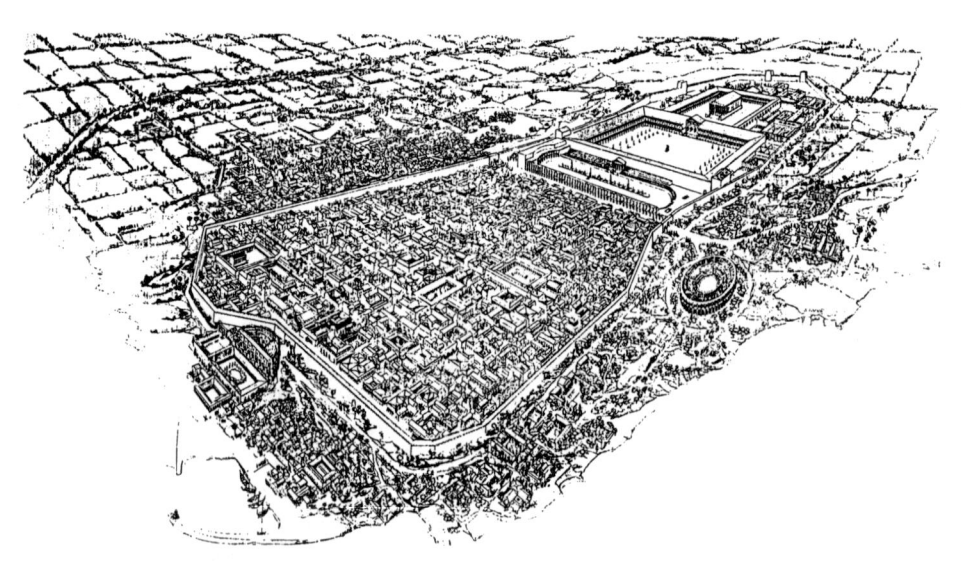

Figure 13.5 Colonia Iulia Urbs Triumphalis Tarraco. Reconstuction of F. Tarrats. After P. Gros, *L'Architecture romaine. I. Les monuments publics*, Paris, 1996, p. 353, fig. 410

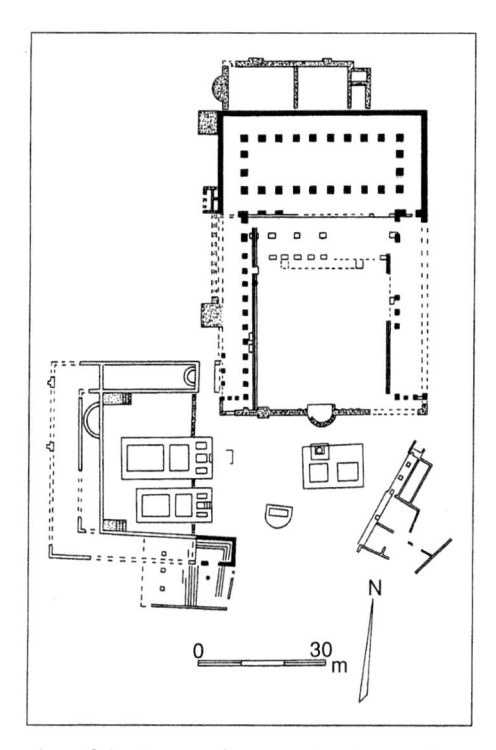

Figure 13.6 Glanum: plan of the Roman forum and twin temples, surrounded by U-shaped portico. After P. Gros, *L'Architecture romaine. I. Les monuments publics*, Paris, 1996, p. 224, fig. 269

mantled and replaced with a much larger one given over totally to a temple and surrounding portico with cryptoporticus beneath (Figure 13.7b). This new forum was dedicated to the imperial cult (J. Alarcão and Étienne 1977; A. Alarcão et al. 1997). This dramatic change to the urban topography must be connected to Vespasian's grant of Latin status to the whole of Hispania. The city took on the title "Flavia," as an altar dedicated to *Fl(avia) Conimbrica* and its *Lares* reveals (*AE* 1969–70, no. 245 = *Fouilles de Conimbriga* II, no. 10). It may also at this time have been promoted to municipal status, but there is as yet no definitive proof of this. It was the local elite who would henceforth gain Roman citizenship by holding local magistracies at Conimbriga and it was doubtless they who decided to remodel the urban center at this crucial moment in their city's history.

The examples of Glanum and Conimbriga suggest that the creation and remodeling of monumental centers often stemmed from the initiative of the local elite. This is in contrast to what normally occurred in colonies, where much of the impetus came from Rome and even from members of the imperial family. Another occasion when the impulse came from the center was when Roman emperors intervened to embellish their ancestral cities. The families of Trajan and Hadrian both hailed from Italica (Santiponce) in Baetica, a small *municipium* 12 kilometers north of the much more important and thriving port-city of Hispalis (Seville) on the river Baetis (modern Guadalquivir). During the reign of Hadrian, the *municipium* appealed to

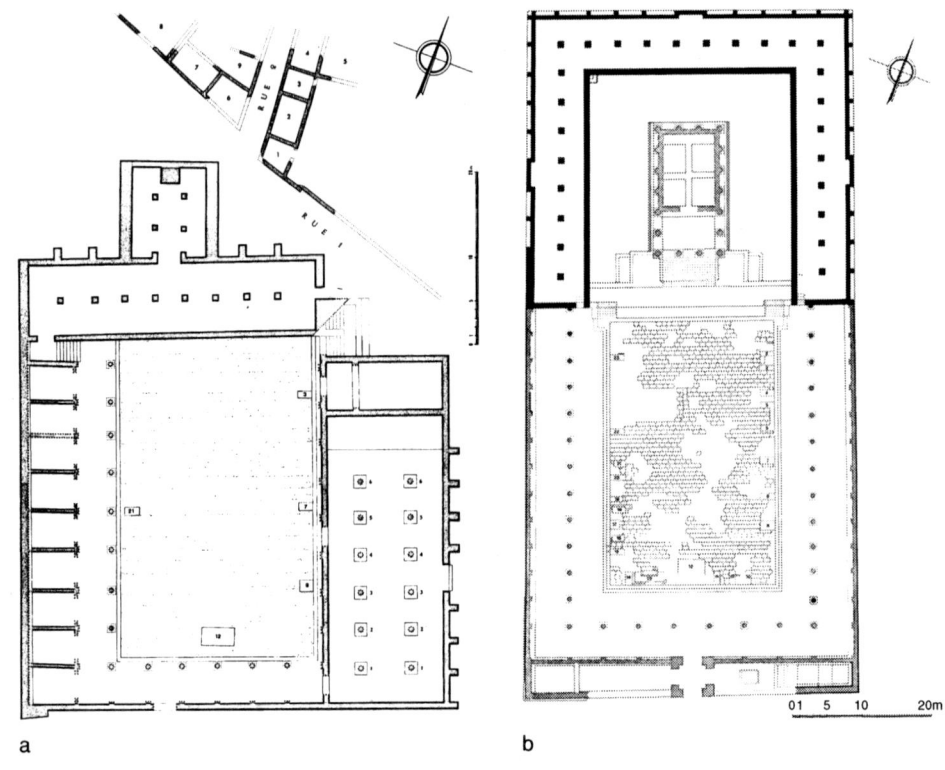

Figure 13.7a and b Conimbriga: Forum (a) in Augustan period and (b) as later remodeled after Flavian grant of the *ius Latii*. After A. Alarcão, R. Étienne, and J.-C. Golvin, in R. Étienne and F. Mayet (ed.), *Itinéraires lusitaniens. Trente années de collaboration archéologique luso-française*, Paris, 1997, pp. 50–1, figs. 20–1

the emperor to be raised to the status of a colony. Even though this request allegedly puzzled him, Hadrian granted it and then helped to fund a massive expansion of the city (Dio 69.10.1). The city had previously occupied just 13.5 hectares; under Hadrian it more than doubled in area to 38 hectares (Figure 13.8a). A large amphitheater, a new public bath complex with associated palaestra, meeting-halls for at least two urban associations (*collegia*), along with wide colonnaded streets and spacious town-houses have all now been revealed by excavation and geophysical resistivity survey. The focal point of the new part of the city was an enormous shrine to Hadrian's adoptive father, the now deified Trajan. The temple itself measured 30 meters across its façade and 48 meters down its side, while the whole complex of this so-called "Traianeum" occupied two *insulae* of the new urban grid (Caballos Rufino and León Alonso 1997; Rodríguez Hidalgo et al. 1999; Boatwright 2000: 162–7; for the Traianeum, León Alonso 1988).

Similarly, the topography of Lepcis Magna in north Africa was radically altered by the rise to power of one of its citizens, Septimius Severus, in 193. Originally Punic, the city had been allied to Rome as a *civitas foederata* from the second century BCE. It became a *municipium* with Latin rights under Vespasian and then successfully petitioned Trajan to be promoted to colonial status, as we have seen (above, section

3). The local elite had initiated an extensive program of monumentalization under Augustus. Annobal Tapapius Rufus, a local magistrate who still bore the Punic title of *sufet*, as well as a partially Punic name, dedicated a market building (*macellum*) in 2 BCE (*IRT* 319); another *sufet* funded a theater (*IRT* 321), while a *chalcidicum* (in this case probably a commercial rather than administrative building) was also dedicated to the Divine Spirit (*numen*) of Augustus in 11/12 CE (*IRT* 324). Between 14 and 19 CE an earlier sanctuary of Liber Pater and Hercules was destroyed to make room for a temple of Rome and Augustus. But none of these buildings could compare with the gigantic scale and unified nature of the Severan building program: baths, new port installations, a long colonnaded street, and new forum known from inscriptions as the Forum Severianum or Forum Novum Severianum (*IRT* 562, 566). The latter was dominated by a temple constructed on an imposing podium; abutting this forum to the east was a long basilica, similar in design to that of Trajan in the forum at Rome that bore his name (Figure 13.8b) (Ward-Perkins 1993; Gros and Torelli 1988: 294–9).

How Rome's provincial subjects below the elite viewed these monuments for the most part remains obscure to us. The case of the colony at Camulodunum (modern Colchester) in Neronian Britain might suggest that provincials were not always eager recipients of these new and somewhat overpowering complexes. Tacitus claims that the temple set up there to the deified Claudius was viewed by the locals as "a citadel of everlasting domination" (*arx aeternae dominationis*), and the fact that provincials were chosen to be the *flamines* of the cult was seen as a cynical mechanism designed by the Romans to force the local elite to "pour out their whole fortunes under the pretext of religious devotion" (Tac. *Ann.* 14.31; Fishwick 1995). Although there may well have been some opposition to these building programs, it is important to remember the context of Tacitus' remarks and not to extrapolate too glibly from them. In 61 the Britons under Boudicca were about to revolt against Rome and Tacitus seems to be conveying some of the hostile anti-Roman rhetoric used to justify that revolt. On the whole, the practical amenities and visual splendor of the larger urban centers seem to have won over any lingering disaffection.

Clearly the local elite were in favor of these building projects, since they sponsored so many of them and won praise for their efforts from visiting Roman officials and from emperors further afield. Such monuments provided the elite with an impressive stage on which to conduct their public activities and fashion their identity, most of all in relation to the ruling power, Rome. The temples were, in most cities, the most prominent buildings, emphasizing the civic importance of cultivating the favor of the gods. Cults to the imperial house, both local and provincial, as we have seen, increasingly came to dominate the physical landscape of the cities, as such cults loomed larger in the consciousness of their inhabitants (Beard, North, and Price 1998: 1: 313–63). The forums, council chambers, and basilicas allowed Roman-style political and judicial business to be conducted in appropriately authoritative settings. Baths and gymnasia, since they were centers for intellectual as well as physical exercise, emphasized that maintenance of the body and cultivation of the mind were key elements of a civilized lifestyle. Theaters, amphitheaters, and circuses allowed Roman-style entertainments, often played out in the context of religious ritual and imperial cult activities, to spread to many cities

270 *Jonathan Edmondson*

a

☐ Old city

☐ Hadrianic extension

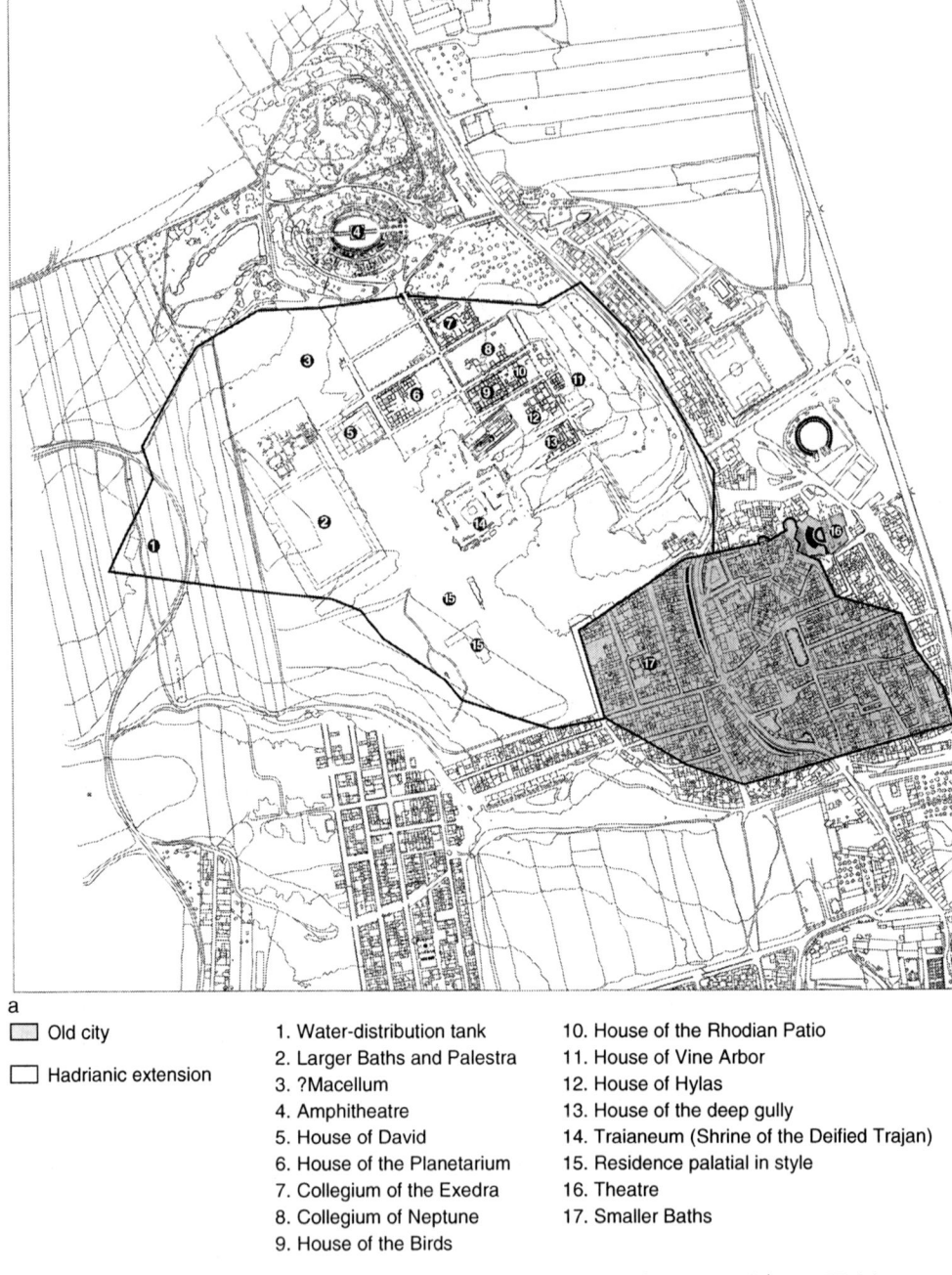

1. Water-distribution tank
2. Larger Baths and Palestra
3. ?Macellum
4. Amphitheatre
5. House of David
6. House of the Planetarium
7. Collegium of the Exedra
8. Collegium of Neptune
9. House of the Birds
10. House of the Rhodian Patio
11. House of Vine Arbor
12. House of Hylas
13. House of the deep gully
14. Traianeum (Shrine of the Deified Trajan)
15. Residence palatial in style
16. Theatre
17. Smaller Baths

Figure 13.8a Cities remodeled by emperors: (a) Italica: plan of J. M. Rodríguez Hidalgo, showing old city (shaded) and Hadrianic extension. After *Itálica MMCC: Actas de las jornadas del 2.200 aniversario de la fundación de Itálica*, Seville, 1997, p. 116, fig. 1

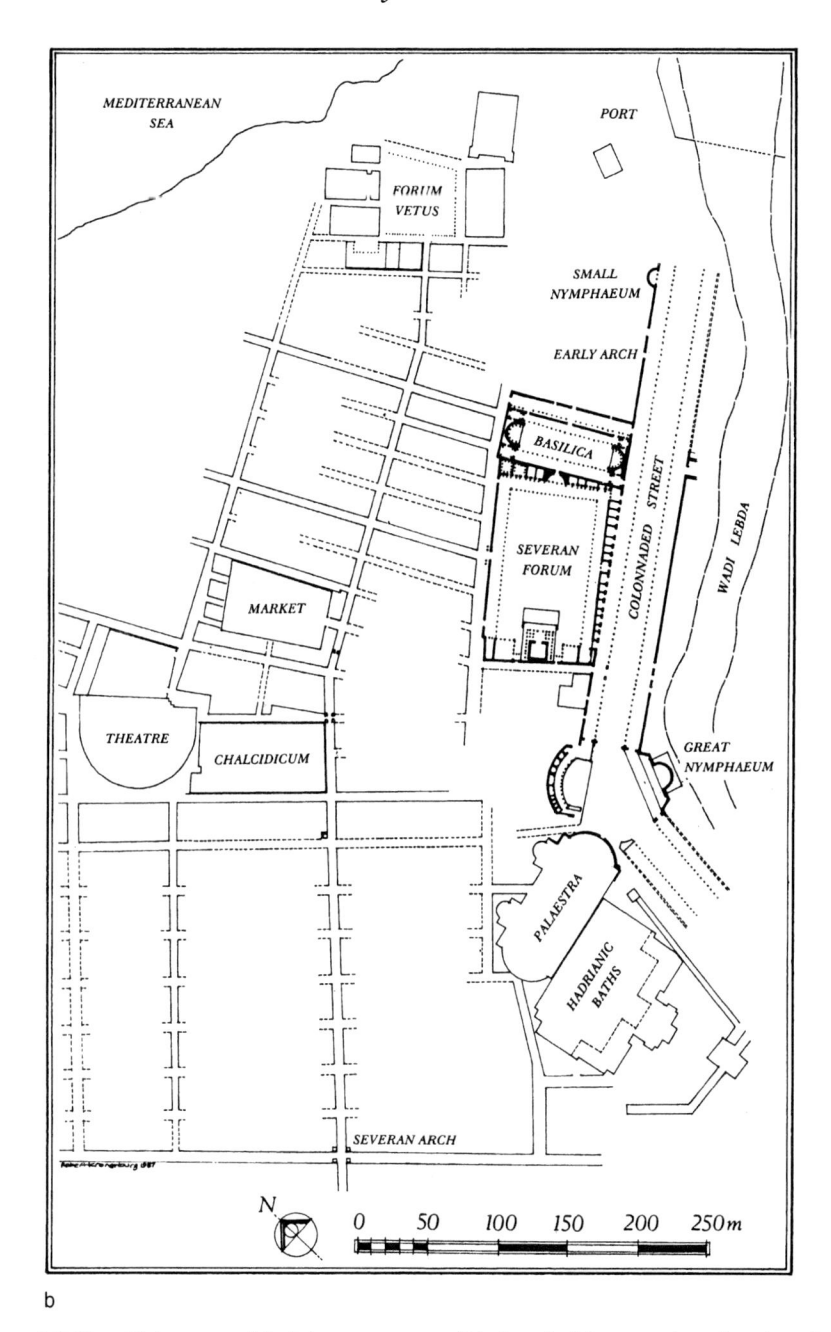

Cities and Urban Life in the Western Provinces 271

Figure 13.8b Cities remodeled by emperors: (b) Lepcis Magna: plan showing Severan additions to monumental center. After J. B. Ward-Perkins, *The Severan Buildings of Lepcis Magna*, London, 1993, p. 6, fig. 3

of the Roman west, creating some degree of shared experience between center and periphery. In short, the built environment of these western provincial cities allowed a particularly Roman kind of civic life to develop. It is to the social fabric of these cities that we must now turn.

5 Urban Society

As we have already noted, it was the local elite who constituted the crucial link between provincial communities and the Roman authorities, both the provincial governor and the Roman emperor. We are much better informed of how the elite operated in colonies and municipalities, but *civitates stipendiariae* also had their own councils and magistrates – sometimes *II viri* on the model of communities of Roman status, but more often *magistri*, although on occasion indigenous titles persisted such as the *sufetes* of Punic North Africa (*ILAfr* 634, tr. Sherk 1988, no. 50, Volubilis) or the *vergobreti* of the three Gauls (*ILS* 7040 = *ILA Santons* 20, Mediolanum Santonum). Everywhere the local elite was composed mainly of members of the local council (*ordo decurionum*). Membership in the *ordo* brought dignity and rank not just upon those who served as decurions themselves, but upon their families as well (Langhammer 1973; Jacques 1984). This was the group to which emperors turned when they needed to replenish the Roman equestrian and senatorial orders: the "flower of the colonies and municipalities, good men and rich men too" (*flos coloniarum municipiorumque, bonorum scilicet virorum et locupletium*), to quote the words that Claudius used in 48 CE to justify the recruitment of the local notables of "long-haired Gaul" (Gallia Comata) into the Roman senate (*ILS* 212, col. II, lines 3–4; cf. Tac. *Ann*. 11.23–5). Such advancement was expedited when the local notables had social links to members of the Roman ruling class. These were forged through contact with Roman senators or equestrians who served as provincial administrators or when members of the local elite went on embassies to the city of Rome or because many local councils invited prominent senators and equestrians to become patrons of their city (cf. *Lex Ursonensis* 97, 130; *Lex Irnitana* 61; Saller 1982). Not surprisingly the *ordo decurionum* came to form the third broad status group (*ordo*) in the Roman social hierarchy beneath the senatorial and equestrian orders.

The size of each local council varied according to the city's population. One hundred appears to have been the standard number, but smaller councils are known, such as that at Irni (El Saucejo, 90 km southeast of Seville), which had just 63 members (*Lex Irnitana* 31). Membership was to a large degree hereditary, as the richer families felt it their right and duty to provide at least one member of this body per generation, but this does not mean that new families never succeeded in breaking into the local ruling class (Garnsey 1974; cf. Jacques 1984: esp. 570). Decurions paid a fee, the *summa honoraria*, to join the council, as did those elected to local magistracies (Garnsey 1971; Duncan-Jones 1982: 147–55; Briand-Ponsart 1999). Once admitted to the council, decurions remained there for life, providing they were not challenged and removed for unfitting behavior (*Lex Ursonensis* 105, 123–4). In return, they got to control all aspects of local civic life in the urban center and its dependent territory.

It was usually from among members of the *ordo decurionum* that the local magistrates were elected to serve for a term of 12 months, although iteration in office was permitted. The senior college of magistrates were the *II viri iure dicundo* (the "two men in charge of jurisdiction") and every fifth year they assumed the function of censors, with *quinquennalis* added to their title to reflect their enhanced powers. The *II viri* were responsible for the political leadership of the community, for administering law and order, overseeing the city's revenues and finances, establishing the religious calendar for the year, and making sure that the religious rites were carried out. They would also intervene on behalf of their city with neighboring communities or with the Roman provincial governor or procurator as the need arose. Below them in rank were the *aediles*, the two junior magistrates responsible for supervising the local grain supply and market, and for the upkeep of the city's temples and urban infrastructure (streets and drains), as well as for local policing. The larger cities often also had a college of quaestors, responsible for financial matters; the *II viri* looked after this in smaller communities. Many of these same individuals also served as the city's major priests: *pontifices, augures* and – of increasing importance – the *flamines* responsible for the local imperial cult.

Such magistrates and councilors dominated the public life of the cities. Rank was crucial to their dignity, and it is no surprise to find lists of decurions arranged in minutely hierarchical fashion. The best evidence for this is the album of the council of Canusium (Canosa) in southern Italy (*CIL* IX 338), dated to 223 CE, but the same preoccupation with rank was widespread. It made a difference whether one was of quinquennial (i.e., local censorial) rank or duoviral, aedilician, or quaestorian, while the highest-ranking members of local society were those who had gained Roman equestrian or – still better, if more rarely – senatorial rank.

Below the *ordo decurionum* a secondary *ordo* developed in many cities that was composed of current and former *Augustales* or *VI viri Augustales*, who were for the most part upwardly mobile freedmen (Abramenko 1993 is crucial for Italy, but many of his insights extend to the provinces, on which see Duthoy 1974, 1978; Le Glay 1990a). As a college, they played a central role in local imperial cult activities, and the institution allowed these rich individuals, whose servile origins usually debarred them from serving on the council, to play a prominent and dignified role in the public life of their city. Like local magistrates, they contributed some of their wealth to support civic projects, as we shall see, and in return their freeborn (and hence more respectable) sons were often recruited into the *ordo decurionum*. Another intermediate group, often neglected by scholars, were the local *apparitores*, who served as secretaries, lictors (that is, ceremonial attendants), messengers, and assistants to the magistrates. Their importance is clear from their various privileges and duties laid down in the civic charters from Spain (e.g. *Lex Ursonensis* 62, 81; *Lex Irnitana* 73). As with their equivalents at the level of the Roman state, they represented a liminal group, occupying a position on the social boundary between the elite and non-elite (Purcell 1983).

Much more numerous than any so far mentioned were the members of the local *plebs*, the freeborn citizens who formed the bulk of the local population, but who are much less visible in our sources, which have an inherent bias in their focus upon the elite. One group within the local *plebs* that is more noticeable are freedmen, overrepresented in the epigraphic record since they were often anxious to leave their mark on the local landscape with an eye-catching funerary monument, just like the fictional freedman Trimalchio in Petronius' *Satyricon* (esp. *Sat.* 71). Alongside the local citizens (*cives*), who comprised the civic body (*populus*), were the residents (*incolae*), who had decided to establish their domicile in a new community, but who retained citizenship in the city of their birth. While they were usually excluded from local office-holding, some played a prominent role in local civic life, often joining the *cives* in setting up honorific statues for local worthies, as we shall see at the end of this chapter. At the juridical base were the slaves, by whose labor many of these cities were built and much of the wealth of the local elite created or enhanced. Cities owned public slaves too, who assisted the local magistrates in their various administrative tasks (cf. *Lex Irnitana* 78; cf. 19, 72).

Local society was thus highly stratified, but the various clubs (*collegia*) that flourished in many cities of the west helped to elide some of these sharp juridical distinctions. Associations of bakers and bargemen, wine-merchants and goldsmiths, and, most of all, craftsmen (*fabri*) brought together in a convivial setting many freeborn citizens of middling rank, successful freedmen, and even slaves (*ILS* 7211–331; Waltzing 1895–1900; for archaeological evidence for club headquarters, see Bollmann 1998; Bouet 2001). *Collegia* of craftsmen were already established in Britain, for example, by the Neronian period at Camulodunum (*RIB* 91), and examples have been found as far afield as at Salona in Dalmatia, Aquincum and Emona in Pannonia, and Apulum in Dacia (*ILS* 7236, 7230, 7235a, 7229, respectively). Distinctly Roman models of civic organization influenced how these *collegia* were administered. For each was structured like a miniature Roman city: each was established by means of a charter (*lex*) (*ILS* 7212–13, Lanuvium, Rome); each had its own patrons, decurions, and magistrates (usually *magistri*, but we also hear about *quinquennales* and quaestors); just like the *ordo decurionum*, their members were divided into boards (*decuriae*) (cf. *Lex Irnitana* F); and each could pass its own resolutions (*ILS* 7214–15).

Women were not strictly speaking members of the local civic body (*populus*), but this did not stop the mothers, wives, daughters, and sisters of the elite from playing a prominent role in the public life of their communities. They, like their male relatives, funded a number of building projects and sponsored various public spectacles and civic events. As a result, statues in their honor were set up amidst the forests of statues that came to occupy many of the public spaces of the cities of the west. In Roman colonies, which operated according to Roman civil law, women could own property of their own, distinct from that of their husbands, and those who had given birth to three children were free to manage such property without the intervention of a male tutor by the process known as the "right of three children" (the *ius trium liberorum*). Since Roman law came to influence the normative practices of many provincial cities that were not strictly required to use Roman civil law (Galsterer 1986), some women, we may assume, came to be significantly wealthy in their own right and thus able to make an independent contribution to the welfare of their communities. But even so, many female benefactors clearly hoped that their munificence would help further the careers of male members of their family; their husbands, sons, or brothers were often named on the monuments that honored such women for their generosity (Navarro Caballero 2001, focusing on Hispania).

The growth of cults to the imperial house throughout the Roman west gave elite women further opportunities to play prominent roles at the civic and even provincial levels. Every colony and municipality and many *civitates stipendiariae* developed their own local cults to the *domus Augusta*, with a male *flamen* and female *flaminica* responsible for overseeing the community's devotional acts. Tarraco set the precedent in 15 CE when its ambassadors gained permission from Tiberius to build a temple to the recently deified Augustus in their city (Tac. *Ann.* 1.78). As the first century progressed, provinces too started to organize province-wide cults, for which a male *flamen* and a female *flaminica* were appointed for a year's term by a council of delegates of all the communities of the province (the *concilium provinciae*). It was the responsibility of the *flamen provinciae* to look after the *sacra* in honor of the deified male members of the *domus Augusta*, while the *flaminica* tended to the cult of the deified women, or *divae* (Fishwick 2002). These religious institutions came to provide the most exalted stage of a public career in the Roman west for ambitious men and women, thus emphasizing the importance of loyalty to the imperial house for social advancement. As a result, a number of *flaminicae* (both local and provincial) made contributions to their home community to mark their holding of this prestigious position. At Thugga, for example, in the mid-second century Iulia Paula Laenatiana, *flaminica perpetua* (i.e., someone who had been granted the honors of a *flaminica* in perpetuity probably after an impressive year as *flaminica*), erected a temple to Minerva out of her own funds (*CIL* VIII 1472 = 26490). Twenty years or so later, another *flaminica perpetua*, Nahania Victoria, joined her husband in funding a temple of Mercury (*CIL* VIII 26482–5). In these acts of generosity, Iulia Paula and Nahania Victoria fit perfectly into a pattern whereby priests and priestesses of the imperial cult at Thugga regularly funded buildings, especially temples, in this colony (Le Glay 1990b; cf. Pavis d'Escurac 1980 for Timgad). The considerable wealth of such women is well illustrated by a dedication made in the early third century at the Traianeum in Italica in Baetica. To mark her second holding of the local flaminicate, Vibia Modesta dedicated a silver statue weighing 132 lbs 2½ ozs to Augustan Victory (*Victoria Augusta*), an appropriate divinity to honor at this shrine to the deified Trajan. The statue was bedecked with jewels: earrings with three clusters of ten pearls, 40 gemstones, eight beryls, and a gem-encrusted gold wreath. Inside the temple she dedicated her own *flaminica*'s gold wreath together with gold busts of Isis, Ceres, and Juno Regina (*AE* 1983, no. 521).

The social predominance of the *ordo decurionum* was frequently underlined on civic occasions. At public spectacles in the theater, amphitheater, or circus decurions were given privileged front-row seating (*Lex Ursonensis* 125–7). They were also treated to banquets and dinners at public expense (*epula publica* and *cenae publicae*), to the exclusion of other groups in local society (*Lex Irnitana* 77, 79), who, it seems, often proved eager spectators at such glittering scenes (cf. D'Arms 1999). Decurions could vote to allow someone of lower rank to join them in their front seats or at such feasts as occurred, for example, at Epora in Baetica, when a freedman *Augustalis* was rewarded for dedicating a statue of the Roman she-wolf (*lupa Romana*) by being invited to join the decurions at their public dinners (*CIL* II 2156 = II²/7139 = *ILS* 6913). Monuments that propagated the mythical history of Rome, thus loyally inscribing consciousness of *urbs Roma* in the minds of provincials, were seen to bring tangible rewards. (For statues of the she-wolf, cf. *CIL* VIII 958 = *ILS* 6819; *CIL* II 4603; she-wolf with Romulus and Remus, note *CIL* VIII 12220 = *ILS* 6820; *CIL* II 5063 = II²/5 772; León Alonso 1995: 164, no. 55; note also the statue group of a sow with 30 piglets, as encountered by Aeneas at Lavinium, dedicated at Obulco in Baetica: *CIL* II 2126 = II²/7 93 = *ILS* 6911.)

But it was in contributing their own funds to enhance civic life that the local elite made their greatest mark on their cities and won the support of the lower-ranking members of their community. As we have seen, they were expected to contribute funds to mark their entry to the council and for serving as magistrates. In addition, local magistrates were required to fund at least in part the main religious festivals that took place during their term of office: at Urso the *II viri* had to provide four days of gladiatorial presentations (*munera*) or theatrical shows (*ludi scaenici*) in honor of Jupiter, Juno, and Minerva, while the *aediles* had to put on three days of similar spectacles to honor the same gods as well as one day of spectacles either in the circus or the forum in honor of Venus Genetrix, the patron divinity of this Caesarian colony (*Lex Ursonensis* 70–1). But many magistrates often went well beyond what was statutorily required of them.

Typical are the contributions made at Giufi (modern Henschir Mscherga) in Africa Proconsularis by Decimus Fundanius Primianus. To mark his holding of the aedileship, he set up a statue to Apollo Augustus, just as his father had done before him, and on its base he outlined just how much his *summa honoraria* had amounted to: 8,000 sesterces. But as so often, this was not the end of his contribution. To mark the dedication of the statue, he with his fellow *aedile* put on *ludi scaenici* and provided free oil and access to the gymnasium for the *populus* and banquets for the decurions (*CIL* VIII 858 = *ILS* 5073). He thus permanently enhanced the urban environment at Giufi and also provided *voluptates* for the people. By restricting the banquet to the decurions, he publicly reinforced the exclusivity and hence prestige of the local elite. Lineage and rank meant a lot in small communities such as Giufi, and Fundanius took pains to describe himself as the son of Fundanius Felix "of aedilician rank" and grandson of Fundanius Primus, "*flamen perpetuus*."

Many of the aspects of local civic life that we have been discussing are encapsulated in a particularly eloquent case from Singili(a) Barba (Cerro del Castillo near Antequera) in southern Spain. Here a local *II vir*, Marcus Valerius Proculinus, was honored with a bronze statue after a memorable year in office in 109 CE. On its imposing base (no less than 1.75 meters tall), his achievements were recalled as follows:

> To Marcus Valerius Proculinus, son of Marcus, grandson of Marcus, great-grandson of Gaius, (enrolled in the Roman voting tribe) Quirina, *II vir* of the *municipes* of the free municipality of Sing(ilia). The citizens and residents (set this up) from money they had collected. This man in his duovirate gave public games and the same number of private games; he summoned the entire citizen body who were living in the *municipium* and the residents as well and gave them oil and free access to the baths. The same man, on the day that he gave games of the youth in the theater, provided (entry to) the gymnasium and baths free of charge for men and for women. The citizens and the residents on the day before the Kalends of January (i.e., 31 December) as he was stepping down from his duovirate publicly paid him thanks in the forum for having administered the community well in the opinion of everyone. From the funds raised they provided victims to be sacrificed and this statue. The council passed a decree allowing him to choose a place for the statue to be erected. He was *II vir* during the consulship (at Rome) of A. Cornelius Palma Frontonianus for the second time and P. Calvisius Tullius. (*CIL* II^2/5 789)

His multiple acts of generosity had clearly impressed the people of Singili(a) Barba – citizens and residents alike – and helped to bind them together. He had gone well beyond the expected levels of generosity by providing "private games" (*ludi privati*), an unparalleled expression, but one that appears to mean that he had provided extra days of games beyond the number required of a magistrate, and by sponsoring displays in the theater by the local elite youth (the *iuvenes*). Many of these *iuvenes* would take their place as the next generation of decurions and so Proculinus had given them a public stage, as it were, for them to display their merits. Furthermore, he had provided free entry to the baths and gymnasium for all groups in Singili(a) – men and women, citizens and non-citizens – giving them free olive oil with which to anoint themselves and presumably providing the fuel that heated the baths. In so doing, he had created a sense of community that cut across the hierarchical strata of local society, helping to integrate those groups that did not, juridically speaking, form part of the local *populus*: the women and temporary residents (*incolae*). In a gesture of reciprocity, citizens and residents jointly decided to collect money to pay for a statue and the appurtenances necessary for a ceremony to thank Proculinus publicly for his achievements. We can vividly imagine the scene on December 31, 109 when the forum at Singili(a) Barba would have been packed to capacity as sacrifices and prayers accompanied the formal vote of thanks offered to this distinguished local worthy. His prestige, and that of his family, can only have been enhanced by this memorable occasion. And he was proud of his distinguished birth, tracing his lineage back three generations as part of his name.

Thousands of similar acts took place on a regular basis in many parts of the Roman west, as the elite provided for the less fortunate and the less fortunate expressed their gratitude in public acts such as this. Such rituals of reciprocity on the surface at least bound the heavily stratified layers of local society together into a consensual whole. The lower orders, it appears, were content to accept their inferior social position so long as the elite provided for them not just the necessities of life, but some of the pleasures of urban living too: the delights (*voluptates*) and good cheer (*hilaritas*) that festivals, games, baths, and the gymnasium all combined to produce. And it was cities that made these *voluptates* possible, as the jurist Ulpian emphasized in the early third century when he explained the legal rules on how to determine a person's domicile:

> If a man always does his business not in his own colony (i.e., the colony of his birth) but in a particular municipality, if he sells, buys and makes contracts there, if he uses the forum, the baths and enjoys the spectacles in that place, if he celebrates festal days there and enjoys all the advantages (*commoda*) of the municipality but none of those of colonies, then this is where he is regarded as having his domicile rather than in the place where he goes in order to cultivate the land. (*D.* 50.1.27.1)

But on occasion tensions arose and personal politics fomented rivalries within the local elite. In the later second century, for example, the centurion Lucius Caecilius Optatus retired from the army and rose to hold the aedileship and then the duovirate three times at Barcino (Barcelona), where he also served a term as *flamen* of Rome, the deified emperors, and the Augusti (*flamen Romae divorum et Augustorum*). He then set up a legacy to fund an annual boxing match and free oil at the baths for the people of Barcino, but added a powerful rider: the bequest would only remain valid so long as the community excused any of his freedmen or his freedmen's freedmen who might become a *VI vir Augustalis* from the obligations (*munera*) that this position entailed. If the decurions of Barcino were unwilling to uphold that condition, Optatus would transfer his bequest to the colony of Tarraco, 80 kilometers to the south (*CIL* II 4514

= *ILS* 6957 = *IRC* IV 45, tr. LR[3] II, p. 260). Clearly members of the local elite could sometimes use the promise of a benefaction to negotiate favors for themselves or their household from their local council. Optatus' threat to take his bequest to Tarraco suggests that he sensed a certain resentment towards him among his fellow decurions. What is more, it shows that a strong rivalry existed between the colonies of Barcino and Tarraco, as was often the case between neighboring cities in many parts of the Roman west (Syme 1981). In the late 60s, for example, the rivalry between the north African cities of Oea and Lepcis Magna became so intense that the former invited the Garamantians to pillage the territory of the latter, which required the intervention of Roman auxiliary troops to expel the nomadic tribesmen from Roman territory (Tac *Hist.* 4.50). Emulation (*aemulatio*) was something the Roman authorities encouraged; it often brought beneficial results, but it could also cause tension. So although there was generally solidarity and consensus within the local elite, we should remain alert to occasional dissonances and disputes among individual members.

6 The Limits of Local Autonomy

While each civic community in the Roman west was in theory autonomous, this autonomy was compromised by the reality that all these cities were politically subject to Rome, even those *municipia libera* like Singili(a) Barba whose titles suggested they were "independent." Plutarch, in discussing how best the Greeks might conduct themselves under Roman rule, talked about the senatorial shoes (*calcei*) of the proconsul of Asia "looming over the heads of the Greeks" (*Mor.* 813e). Even if this emotive image is somewhat exaggerated for the Greek east and *mutatis mutandis* for the Roman west too, the potential of Rome to intrude can never have been too far from the minds of its provincial subjects. Firstly, jurisdiction: the municipal charter from Irni makes it clear that the scope of local jurisdiction was quite limited. When a case involved property worth more than 1,000 sesterces, it lay beyond the jurisdictional powers of the local *II viri* and had to be referred to the Roman provincial governor for settlement (*Lex Irnitana* 84). Furthermore, the governor, as part of the provincial edict that he published on taking up his post, had the right to determine his own rules regarding the functioning of local jurisdiction (*Lex Irnitana* 85). Any Roman citizen (and hence certain members of the local elite) could choose to bypass a local court and take any lawsuit directly to the governor's tribunal. How practical this was, however, given that the governor held assizes only periodically and in a limited number of cities in his province, must remain an open question. Social ties with the governor, however, would improve an individual's chances of gaining a hearing.

Secondly, it was a Roman governor's duty to step in when he felt that local finances were not being handled judiciously by a city's magistrates. The limited administrative staff at his disposal and often large number of cities for which he was responsible meant that it was difficult to perform this function thoroughly and effectively, but he still had the power, and responsibility, to intervene. Some rules were established centrally to govern the expenditure of local elites. In 58, for example, the Sicilian city of Syracuse petitioned the Roman Senate to exempt it from the rules limiting the number of gladiators that could be put on at local presentations (*munera*) (Tac. *Ann.*

13.49). Although in this case the exemption was granted, there was clearly a sense, even under Nero, that excessive spending by local elites could threaten the economic viability of provincial cities. This was indeed prescient, for from the later first century onwards the emperor had to send out from Rome officials of senatorial or equestrian rank known as *curatores rei publicae* to deal with the financial problems of a number of provincial cities. Especially revealing is the mission of the younger Pliny, dispatched by Trajan to Bithynia as provincial governor to scrutinize the financial affairs of all the cities of that province. His letters sent back to the emperor between 109 and 111 (or perhaps 110 and 112) reveal a chaotic picture of maladministration (Pliny *Ep.* 10.15–121, with Millar 2000). Although we lack such vivid testimony for the Roman west, a number of *curatores* are attested epigraphically for various cities and were clearly dealing with many of the same problems. The patchy nature of our evidence, however, makes it difficult to gauge how frequent and widespread were the interventions of such officials (Burton 1979; Jacques 1984).

Individual provincials could appeal to the provincial governor or even the Roman emperor against the authorities of their cities if they felt they had a valid grievance. This occurred, for example, in Baetica in the late 70s in the case of one Servilius Pollio, who had leased the right to collect some of the local revenues (*vectigalia*) of the *municipium* of Munigua (Mulva, 30 km northeast of Seville). Left out of pocket by the refusal of the city to pay him what he was owed, he had appealed to the proconsul of Baetica, who adjudged in his favor. The magistrates and decurions of Munigua in turn felt aggrieved and sent an embassy to the emperor Titus to appeal the proconsul's decision. On September 7, 79 Titus dismissed their appeal, admonishing the ambassadors and pointing out that their city should have been fined for its improper appeal. However, preferring to demonstrate his "customary indulgence" (*indulgentia*), he provided the city with 50,000 sesterces to help them pay off Pollio (*AE* 1962, no. 288, tr. Sherk 1988, no. 92 = LR³ II, p. 242).

Finally, members of the local elite, as we have seen, were expected to provide services and funding (*munera*) to sustain the sort of civic activities that a city's limited revenues could never support unaided. However, individuals could, and increasingly did, appeal to the emperor for exemptions from such *munera*. In addition, rules of exemption for certain categories of individuals gradually evolved during the second century (Millar 1983). Such appeals and the evolution of rules of exemption, determined centrally but applicable across all cities of the empire, also led to the erosion of local autonomy. They reduced the ability of cities to put social pressure on their elites to undertake these much needed civic contributions.

7 Conclusion

In his account of his father-in-law's career under Domitian as provincial governor in Britain, Tacitus underlines the role that Cn. Iulius Agricola played in the urbanization of that province:

> To ensure that men who were scattered and uncivilized and for this reason naturally inclined to war might become accustomed to peace and quiet through pleasures (*voluptates*), Agricola encouraged individuals and assisted communities to build temples, forums

and town houses by praising those who were eager and reprimanding those who were dilatory. Thus competition for honor (*honoris aemulatio*) took the place of compulsion. Furthermore he educated the sons of the local aristocracy in the liberal arts and ranked the natural talent of the Britons superior to the trained skills of the Gauls. As a result, those who had just recently been rejecting the Roman language now conceived a desire for eloquence. Then even our style of dress came to be favored, the toga was to be seen everywhere. Gradually people started to give in to the attractions of vice: porticoes, baths and the elegance of banquets. And this was called "civilization" (*humanitas*) by people who did not know any better, although it was in fact part of their enslavement. (Tac. *Agr.* 21)

These remarks develop some of the ideas articulated by Strabo in the passages discussed at the start of this chapter. The Romans were keen to reorganize peoples with scattered settlement patterns into communities with fixed limits and a clearly identifiable administrative center. A crucial element of each new *civitas* capital was a monumental urban center, adorned with buildings familiar from the urban landscapes of Rome and Italy. Significantly, Tacitus begins his list of such buildings with temples and, as we have seen, temples provided the focal point of most cities, reminding the local inhabitants of the importance of placating the gods to ensure the continuation of the Roman peace. Tacitus also emphasizes how crucial the local elites were to this civilizing process. It was often their personal interaction with an imperial administrator such as Agricola that sparked such building programs. Once the idea of the city had been planted in the minds of the local elite, it was fostered by their growing familiarity with central Roman concepts such as *humanitas*, gleaned from their reading of key Roman texts (not least Vergil's *Aeneid*). But most of all it was their ambition to enhance their own status and outdo their counterparts in neighboring communities (*honoris aemulatio*, in Tacitus' words) that provided the fuel to carry these projects through to fruition.

Tacitus' words, however, obscure the fact that this was often a slow and gradual process. The *civitas* capitals of Britain could not suddenly boast a full panoply of Roman-style public buildings; it took time for their monumental centers to develop, and often ambitious schemes, clear from the initial grid-plans laid out on the landscape, were never fully realized. While most of the cities of Baetica and Gallia Narbonensis had fully-fledged monumental centers by the Flavian period, Britain, the Danubian provinces, and even Africa had to wait until the mid-second century or sometimes later still for these urban programs to be completed. In some areas monumental cities remained thin on the ground: settlements were designated as *civitas* capitals of a given territory and used by the Romans for the purposes of administration, but never developed the full physical fabric of a proper Roman city. In the interior of Gaul, for example, many continued to live in rural villages, only visiting the major centers once or twice a year at the very most (Woolf 1998: 135–41; for the smaller towns of Britain, see Burnham and Wacher 1990). So while it is generally true that urbanization was one of the most important consequences of Roman rule in the west, by no means was it experienced with equal intensity across the entire region. There were some clear similarities, to be sure, in the architecture to be found in urban centers as far afield as southern Spain and the interior of Gaul or Britain, but the texture of urban life was by no means identical. Much depended upon the local context and upon the needs of the local elite as they continued to negotiate a social and political relationship with the representatives of Rome sent to administer their province and, not least, with the Roman emperor himself.

PART IV

Social and Economic Life

CHAPTER FOURTEEN

The Imperial Economy

David Mattingly

1 Introduction: Theory and Evidence

The Roman economy is often presented as underdeveloped and underachieving (Garnsey and Saller 1987: 43–7). Such views are the legacy of the huge intellectual contribution of Moses Finley (1985) to the debate on the ancient economy. Key elements of what I shall term the Finleyite primitivist (minimalist) vision of the Roman economy are: an emphasis on subsistence agriculture; the role of towns as centers of consumption, rather than of trade and industry; the low social status of craft workers; retarded technological diffusion; and a lack of economic rationality, illustrated *inter alia* by the low level of non-agrarian capital investment (Finley 1985; de Blois et al. 2002; Duncan-Jones 1982: 1; Hopkins 1983a: x–xiv). Such views are not unchallenged, however, and there is also strong support for a vision of a more evolved and complex economy than Finley was prepared to admit (K. Greene 1986; W. V. Harris 1993b). Strong evidence has been adduced in favor of more rational economic accounting on Egyptian estates in the Fayum (Rathbone 1991). Rather more surprising perhaps is the fact that similarly sophisticated accounting systems are to be found even in the remote oasis communities of the Egyptian desert (Bagnall 1997). In several recent discussions an emerging strand is that the Roman economy contained elements of both achievement and underdevelopment (de Blois et al. 2002: xiii–xviii; Jongman 2002: 43–7; Mattingly and Salmon 2001b: 8–11). In this chapter, I shall briefly review some of the key points of theoretical debate and then comment on a series of different areas of economic activity that I think illustrate both the controversies and the potential of the evidence now available on the Roman economy.

The contributions of Hopkins to the debate have been important in introducing a series of modifications and qualifications to the primitivist view (Hopkins 1978c and d, 1980, 1983a and b, 1995/6; K. Greene 1986: 9–16 for a useful summary). He has argued that between 200 BCE and 200 CE overall agricultural production and the amount of land in cultivation rose, accompanied by an increase in both population and per capita production; a higher proportion of the population in this period was engaged in non-agrarian production and service industries; inter-regional trade in manufactured and staple commodities reached a peak; taxation in the Roman world may have been a stimulus to trade. It is on this early "imperial" period of Rome's history that I shall focus, though important studies exist on the Late Roman Empire and its changing economy (de Blois and Rich 2002; Garnsey and Whittaker 1998; A. H. M. Jones 1964, 1974; Wickham 1988; Whittaker and Garnsey 1998). In late antiquity, the nature of the Roman economy changed considerably, with inter-regional trade shrinking in the west, but initially expanding in the east after the foundation of Constantinople (Kingsley and Decker 2001). Overall, the transition to the Dark Ages was slower than was once believed, but the break-up of the empire had undoubted repercussions on its economy (Liebeschuetz 2002).

The nature of the evidence relating to the Roman economy is very uneven. Literary sources are few, reflecting the social mores of the time as much as reality (note that upper-class Romans professed that "of all pursuits by which men gain their livelihood none is better than agriculture... none more fitting for a free man," Cic. *Off.* 1.152). Documentary evidence in the form of papyri and writing tablets is limited to a few locations, most notably Egypt, and its typicality has been much debated. There is a dearth of ancient quantitative data on the Roman economy and our views on ancient attitudes are heavily colored by the disparaging remarks of Roman aristocrats regarding trade. Socially speaking, farming and land-ownership were the most respectable sources of wealth; manufacturing and commerce were looked down on. But there is ample evidence to suggest that even senators were loath to overlook non-agrarian money-making possibilities altogether, getting round the social stigma by using slaves and freedmen to look after their interests in such ventures, or advancing loans (D'Arms 1981). Elite involvement may have been even higher outside Italy, as there is still less evidence regarding the attitudes of the provincial curial class to manufacturing and commerce.

Archaeological evidence is increasingly abundant, but is also biased by factors of preservation. Organic commodities, such as foodstuffs, animal products, wooden artifacts, and textiles, are poorly conserved in most archaeological deposits, but are demonstrably key components of trade in any age in the past. This is especially the case with textiles – their primacy in Diocletian's Price Edict is striking – though the archaeological evidence is elusive (Drinkwater 2001, 2002; A. Wilson 2001). Certain other valuable items, such as glass and metal items, could be recycled and are disproportionately under-represented in rubbish deposits. The most abundant archaeological materials are ceramics, their numbers reflecting their essential fragility more than their economic value. Yet pottery vessels were often containers for other commodities, such as olive oil, fish sauces, or wine, or were traded alongside now-perished commodities, and thus may stand in as proxies for trade in those other goods. Some of the best archaeological evidence for ancient commerce has come from shipwrecks, where the composition and quantification of near-intact cargoes can sometimes be calculated (A. J. Parker 1992).

It is generally accepted that the Roman economy was predominantly based on farming, essentially agriculture, much of it at or close to subsistence levels. Yet in many regions of the Roman Empire, there were significant changes in rural settlement and output following the incorporation of land within the empire (Barker and

Lloyd 1991; Carlsen et al. 1994; Garnsey 2000; K. Greene 1986: 67–141; Rich and Wallace-Hadrill 1991). The conquest of huge territories gave unparalleled opportunities for the reorganization of landholding arrangements. The imposition of the Roman taxation system may also have had an impact, but above all it was the organization of labor and production by the local elites operating within the new framework that meant that significant surpluses could be generated from unprecedented crop specialization at the regional level. The clearest evidence of such changes can be traced in areas like North Africa, where several regions developed a clear specialization in olive oil production, with a significant capacity for export (D. J. Mattingly 1988a).

It is also increasingly recognized that the non-agricultural sector of the Roman economy was of considerable importance at the regional level and that some cities show a degree of specialization in their commercial and/or manufacturing activity (Mattingly and Salmon 2001a). The scale and significance of the construction industry at major cities can now be better evaluated (DeLaine 1997, 2000, 2001), along with the infrastructure of other service industries in towns. The image that most cities were passive consumers of localized rural production is no longer sustainable.

One of the major brakes on the development of the Roman economy was the relative difficulty of the empire's communications and the constraints of its transport systems. It has been suggested that it was cheaper to transport grain from one end of the Mediterranean to the other by ship than to move it 75 miles overland (Jones 1964: 841–2). This pessimistic view of land transport is reinforced by studies of the costs of sea:river:overland transport in the Roman world, which can be expressed in the ratio 1:4.9:28 (K. Greene 1986: 39–40). However, such deterministic views take no account of other factors that may have contributed to patterns of transport, such as risk, seasonality, or lack of alternatives. In practice, detailed studies of Roman roads, river transport, and maritime traffic support the view that the first two centuries CE in particular saw substantial growth in the scale and volume of transportation in all these areas (K. Greene 1986: 17–44; Laurence 1998; A. J. Parker 1992: 16–30; Rougé 1981).

It is clear that the Roman economy was not a homogeneous entity, but that there were important infrastructural and regional differences at play across the empire. The degree of "connectivity" within and between regions remains uncertain (Horden and Purcell 2000). However, lack of uniformity should not occasion surprise in an empire that spanned an area of over 3.5 million square kilometers (the same area today is broken up into more than 30 nation-states), with a population of over 50 million people. What is perhaps most striking is the degree of interconnectedness and integration achieved in a territory of this size (Fulford 1987; Woolf 1992).

At the heart of the empire lay an exceptionally large and atypical city (Morley 1996; Pleket 1993a). A key ingredient of the Roman economy was the element of state control occasioned by the elaborate arrangements, known as the *annona* system, set in place to ensure the food supply of the city of Rome and of the army (Aldrete and Mattingly 1999; Garnsey 1988; Sirks 1991; Whittaker 1994: 98–130). In the early principate, there was no state merchant fleet, so the carriage of cargoes to Rome was regulated by payments of subsidies (*vecturae*) and other inducements to private shippers.

These state redistributive mechanisms of trade were no doubt most influential in certain localities at certain times, rather than generally or evenly across space and time, but nonetheless functioned as a mechanism for integrating regional economies (Remesal Rodriguez 2002; Woolf 1992). It is clear that market trade developed alongside the redistributive system and, on some trade routes, was indivisible from it (K. Greene 1986: 45–8; W. V. Harris 1993b: 14–20).

Other mechanisms of exchange such as individual gift exchange, elites' redistribution of the products of their own estates to their urban houses or other properties, and barter are likely to have persisted and played a role at all times (Whittaker 1985). In sum we can discern regional differences in economic activity and success, suggesting that there was not a single integrated economy, but rather a series of interlocking regional ones.

2 Growth and Scale

There is considerable debate about whether the Roman economy experienced "growth" as that concept is understood in modern economics (Hopkins 1978d; P. Millett 2001; Saller 2002). Growth is normally defined, in modern textbooks, as the process whereby a community increases its wealth in a manner that is sustained through time and that is generally linked to a per capita rise in production of goods and services (L. G. Reynolds 1986). Aggregate increase in production is not true economic growth if it is simply the product of a commensurate increase in population, with per capita productivity remaining the same. The non-survival of detailed census records and historical documents on productivity from antiquity constrains our ability to answer the question conclusively. Nonetheless, for the Roman world, the evidence seems far stronger for the very end of the republic and the early principate (100 BCE–200 CE), for which there is strong archaeological evidence for growth in sectors of the rural economy (Hitchner 1993) and a rise in Mediterranean shipping, urban manufacturing, and the non-agricultural sector of the economy (P. Millett 2001: 31–5).

Although it was very large in scale and advanced in some respects by the standards of other pre-industrial societies, the Roman economy was unlike the sophisticated capitalist systems of modern times. Indeed, it has been argued that Rome practiced a form of "political capitalism," rather than "mercantile or rational capitalism" (Love 1991). In contrast, Rostovtzeff's classic study (1957) was typical of a simplistic tendency at one time to equate the Roman economy with modern economic behavior, which led to Finley's scholarly reaction. The issues are still much debated, but the current consensus is now shifting somewhat away from the extreme position taken by Finley, with an increasing recognition that economic growth was achieved in some regions of the Roman Empire and that the overall scale of economic activity, increasingly demonstrable by archaeological data, was significantly higher than that achieved in most pre-industrial societies (P. Millett 2001: 31). Whilst Roman economic concepts and structures were different from modern ones, that does not necessarily justify characterizing them as primitive or underdeveloped. By the standards of pre-industrial societies, the Roman economy was vast in scale and surprisingly sophisticated in many of its practices. There are indications in papyri, for instance, that economic rationalism underlay some complex accounting processes (Kehoe 1992; Rathbone 1991). Impressive levels of management can also be traced in areas of craft production (Aubert 1994; see also various studies in Harris 1993a). The Roman economy involved the interplay of rural and urban production, the exploitation of labor (including a significant level of slavery within Italy), and the infrastructures of exchange.

Some measure of the scale of the Roman economy can be gauged from estimates of the cost of running the empire. In the mid-second century CE, Duncan-Jones (1994: 33–46, esp. table 3.7) estimates this at between 832–983 million sesterces (roughly 1,000 times the minimum senatorial census requirement). According to Duncan-Jones, 72–77 percent went to the army, though he probably underestimates the costs of ornamenting and feeding the city of Rome. The ultimate success of the Roman economy was that the state did not have to bleed the provinces dry to meet this level of expenditure (on taxation, Duncan-Jones 1990: 187–210). The development of cities, consumption of manufactured and imported goods, and the rise of regional elites into positions of power in the imperial service all attest to the generation of local wealth in many provinces. The effects were uneven and we can track a shift in economic power over time – for instance, to Africa by the late second century CE (Mattingly and Hitchner 1995: 198–204).

Another approach to the scale of the economy is to take the astonishing figure of 50–100 million sesterces given by Pliny for the annual cost of imports into the empire from Arabia, India, and China (*Nat.* 6.101; 12.84). Research in India and on the Red Sea coast is offering support for the strength of these trade links (de Romanis and Tchernia 1997).

3 Technology and the Economy

Finley's view of the economic and technological stagnation of the Roman world (1965) has been challenged from a number of standpoints (K. Greene 2000a, b). First, it is not true to say that there was no technological development and no evidence of the diffusion of new or developing technologies (K. D. White 1984). The poor development and distribution of water mills, for instance, has long been held up as an example of the technological failings of the Roman Empire, but recent archaeological discoveries have made it clear that the technology was far more widely adopted (even in the arid south and east Mediterranean lands) than has previously been appreciated (A. Wilson 2002a: 9–17). Water power was also used for much more than milling grain, as finds of stone anvils eroded by the action of trip hammers from mining districts in Spain and Britain demonstrate. It is also clear that a key characteristic of the Roman economy was the application of technology on a new scale, whether in terms of the size of Roman opencast mines, the impact of global pollution at the ice caps, or the scale of Roman olive presses (see below).

A key measure of Roman technological progress is to compare the pre-Roman application of technology with that achieved under Rome. In many areas of life we can point to an increased use of existing technology, often developed on a larger scale of operation than theretofore – again olive press technology may serve as a good example (D. J. Mattingly 1996b; Mattingly and Hitchner 1993). Other areas are equally indicative: glass making became increasingly widespread, but with a separation between producers of raw glass and manufacturers of glass vessels (E. M. Stern

1999); kiln technology for pottery and brick production became widely diffused, with increasing scale and technical specialization (Peacock 1982); specialized malting ovens for beer production and grain drying are widespread on Romano-British sites, but absent in the Iron Age (Jones and Mattingly 2002: 228–30); large-scale rotary mills (variously powered by human labor, animals, and water) served a variety of functions in towns and country (A. Wilson 2002a).

Another approach to technology is to assess the extent to which it was appropriate to different communities and regions. The concept of a "technology shelf" from which communities selected what was most appropriate to themselves, rather than an invention-led model of technological diffusion has much to recommend it (K. Greene 1994).

4 Agriculture

The Roman conquest of empire carried with it huge economic implications, not least in terms of the disposal of the acquired territory (Fulford 1992; D. J. Mattingly 1997: 18–19, 117–35). Land was both a key motor of military conquest and underpinned economic activity throughout the empire. In Egypt, for example, taxes on land and the products of farming are estimated to have contributed over 60 percent of state revenues (Duncan-Jones 1994: 53). The reallocation of land to subject peoples was a key stage in the transfer from military control to civil rule and was often accompanied by land survey. Where land was taken for the creation of colonies, these lands were normally surveyed and partitioned in detail on an imposed grid system (centuriation). The feats of the Roman land surveyors (*agrimensores*) can be appreciated both from extant writings (Campbell 2000) and from the physical evidence of such systems in the landscape (Dilke 1971).

For the Mediterranean region, the basics of Roman agriculture were the "triad" of cereals (Spurr 1986), grape vine (Fleming 2001; Purcell 1985; Tchernia and Brun 1999), and olive (D. J. Mattingly 1996a). In most areas agriculture outweighed pastoralism, though even in Italy there were regions that were known for stock raising, such as the Apennine valleys (Whittaker 1988). The relatively arid Mediterranean climate, mainly simple technology, and variable soils imposed constraints on the productivity of Roman farming, but the overall extent of cultivated land during the Roman period was probably not again surpassed until recent centuries.

There was a well-developed tradition of writing agricultural manuals, though in truth these were more works on estate management than on the practical details of farming methods. The most influential surviving works were by the Roman aristocrats M. Porcius Cato and M. Terentius Varro and the Spaniard Columella (K. D. White 1977). These sources dealt unequally with the various components of farming: viticulture is generally given first place in terms of length of exposition (reflecting an age-old aristocratic interest in the production of wine), then cereals, then olives. In Varro's account stock raising features prominently, as does market gardening, and in general terms the "ideal" Roman agricultural estate seems to have been conceived as a self-sufficient mixed-farming unit. All the writers also describe the management of slave labor (showing the Italian context of their experience – rural slaves were far less common in the provinces), and the construction of estate buildings (villas). The most spectacular archaeological example of one of these Italian aristocratic estates is the Settefinestre villa near Cosa (Carandini et al.1984).

From other Roman sources, we know that one result of Roman expansion was the creation of large numbers of smallholders, in part through land allocations to time-expired soldiers. However, they do not feature in the works of the agronomists and archaeological evidence suggests that in many areas there was a tendency towards the consolidation of larger estates (described as *latifundia* in Italy) out of the early smaller distributions. Many farmers ended up serving as tenants rather than as freeholders and, particularly outside Italy, the importance of this sort of dependent labor in supporting large estates cannot be overemphasized (Garnsey 1980; Kehoe, this volume).

The reality of Roman farming in the provinces was in many respects rather different from the picture that we derive from the literary sources of its practice in Italy. Although we can detect the formation of large estates in many regions, coupled with the emergence of a "villa economy," there are several clear instances of crop specialization. Papyrological evidence from the Heroninos archive, relating to an estate in the Egyptian Fayum, reveals a complex infrastructure linking several production units. Although producing a variety of crops, the main cash crop was wine, which was produced and traded on quite a large scale (Rathbone 1991). Similar regional specializations in olive oil production can be detected in southern Spain and several regions in North Africa (D. J. Mattingly 1988a), and in wine in southern Gaul (Tchernia and Brun 1999). These economic success stories are also matched by regions such as Greece, where the early Roman period appears to have been one of contraction and underdevelopment, in contrast to renewed development in late Roman times (Alcock 1993).

Outside the Mediterranean zone in temperate Europe, the existence of heavier soils was offset by more reliable and abundant rainfall. Cereal cultivation became well developed, and viticulture gradually extended far to the north of its previous limits, even reaching Britain and Germany. The olive, on the other hand, remained restricted to the Mediterranean climatic zone, due to its vulnerability to cold. Stock raising for meat and secondary products was in general a more important element in north-western Europe, exploiting the abundant pasture lands (A. King 2001). Beer, produced from barley malt, and the use of animal fats in cooking and for lighting remained key cultural markers of the north, despite the partial inroads by winemakers and the imports of olive oil.

In North Africa, two regions were crucial for the production of cereals needed to feed the city of Rome: the Nile delta in Egypt and northern Tunisia. The existence may be noted in both regions of large imperial estates and a complex infrastructure for gathering the *annona* grain from other producers (D. Crawford 1976; Kehoe 1988a; Rickman 1980). Less suitable cereal lands in Africa were strongly developed for other crops, notably the olive, making North Africa a far more dynamic region economically than its modern agriculture would suggest (D. J. Mattingly 1988a).

There is a large literature on the management and organization of Roman rural production (see Kehoe, this volume). The Roman provincial economies may have been built on the labor of lots of peasants, but they were dominated by the output of the bigger players, and major estates were a feature of most provinces of the Roman world. The key conclusion to be drawn from the archaeological and documentary evidence relating to these major estates is that they could be extremely large in scale, and rationally organized so that profitability and costs could be assessed adequately and tied into wider commercial networks for disposing of their often considerable surpluses. The Appianus estate in the Fayum, for example, comprised several units of production, based on villages each under the financial control of a *phrontistês*, with a very sophisticated system of monthly accounts that could take account of internal paper transfers due for the loan of animals and labor between different units (Rathbone 1991). Archaeological evidence supports the view that such estates could have generated huge surpluses – as demonstrable in the case of wine production at sites in Italy and southern France, which possessed three–four presses and wine fermenting cellars capable of producing and storing several 100,000 liters (Amouretti and Brun 1993; Carandini et al. 1984). In Libya, the largest olive oil factory (oilery) yet discovered contained a massive 17 olive presses, capable of processing in a peak year well over 100,000 liters of olive oil (D. J. Mattingly 1988b).

5 Towns and the Roman Economy

The consumer city is a model that has been used to characterize the ancient city. It was originally developed by Max Weber, expanding on the work of Sombart, as one in a series of ideal types of city, and subsequently enlarged on by Moses Finley (Cité 1989; Finley 1977; Jongman 1988, 2002; Whittaker 1990, 1993). A "consumer city" is one where the major income of urban consumers comes from rural rents, where the products of local rural labor supply the subsistence needs of the urban population, and where manufacturing and inter-regional commerce are "essentially petty." Many ancient historians have found the model very attractive in that it seems to fit well with literary testimony of the ruling classes on their economic outlook and urban-centered lifestyle. Finley, in particular, argued that the parasitical relationship between consumer city and its rural hinterland operated in favor of highly localized and small-scale economies and against economic development, urban manufacturing, and inter-regional trade (1977). In recent times, opposition to the model has increased, in part because Weber's ideal types were essentially designed to model the *economic* characteristics of pre-industrial cities (Weber 1958), whereas the "consumer city" has become a leitmotif for the ancient city as a political and social center (Erdkamp 2001; Parkins 1997b). In addition, the growth in archaeological evidence has shown that the urban economy was far less uniform than is sometimes assumed and that some towns, notably harbor cities, had a much greater engagement with manufacturing and commerce (A. Wilson 2002b).

The scale of manufacturing in the ancient world has been much debated. There was a significant level of production that was little more than domestic. At the other extreme, it is generally admitted that the term "factory" is inappropriate and that the largest level of production may be characterized as a manufactory, perhaps employing up to 30 people and with some job specialization (Peacock 1982: esp. 1–11, 90–128; cf. Fulle 1997). However, recent work on Pompeii has emphasized the *aggregate* significance of numerous small workshops (Laurence 1994; D. J. Mattingly 1990; Parkins 1997b), and similar studies of textile production/fulling at Timgad in Algeria or of fish products at Sabratha in Libya show the potential for this sort of analysis elsewhere (A. Wilson 1999a, 2001, 2002b). At the Tunisian port city of Leptiminus, extensive surface survey of the city and its suburbs has revealed that these heavily developed suburbs covered an area as large as the urban core. The production of amphorae for the overseas transport of olive oil and fish sauces was the major component here (Mattingly et al. 2001; Stirling et al. 2001: 215–19). This sort of evidence is compatible with the long-known epigraphic dossiers of craft workers from Rome, Pompeii, and other epigraphically-rich centers (Brewster 1917; Burford 1972; Loane 1938).

Although there is now more evidence for manufacturing activity at major urban centers, not all industry was located in towns. Some major craft activities have a much more rural distribution. Pottery manufacture is dependent on the location of the raw materials (clay, sand, water) and fuel for firing. The markets for potters also varied and included the military and estate owners with liquid commodities to shift to market. Many landowners with access to raw materials evidently tried to develop them *in situ*.

6 Extractive Industries: Mining, Metallurgy, and Quarrying

The principal natural resources of the earth were regarded by the Roman state as amongst the main spoils of victory (*pretium victoriae*). The Roman world was a huge consumer of metals of almost every type, with the coinage alone dependent on gold, silver, copper, and tin (K. Greene 2000a: 747–52). Because of an outflow of specie beyond the frontiers of the empire and the recurrent removal of material from circulation into savings hoards, the recycling of the existing coin supply was not sufficient to satisfy demand and mining activity was a vital element of the economy under state regulation. Sometimes exploitation was carried out under direct state control, though more commonly the state operated in partnership with private entrepreneurs who bid for contracts. The Roman procurators in charge of mining districts had a wide range of concessions to lease out – everything from mine workings (run on a share of production basis) to shoe making or running the bath houses in the mining villages (Ørsted 1985: 203).

There are indications in some provinces, notably Spain, that mining activity reached an unprecedented scale for a pre-industrial society (D. G. Bird 1972; Domergue 1990; Woods 1987). The most extraordinary site is known today as Las Medulas after the modern village that sits in the center of a vast opencast area (over 2 km in diameter and several hundred meters deep). This remarkable manmade crater was produced through the use of sophisticated hydraulic mining techniques, using water power to undermine the edges of the growing opencast and to wash c.17 million cubic meters of debris further down the mountain. The total opencast area of the mine occupies c.5.4 square kilometers and the outwash from it deeply buried a further 5.7 square kilometers of land (Sanchez-Palencia 2000: 225). Las Medulas is the largest of c.230 gold mines in northwestern Spain, with a combined output peaking at 20,000 pounds of gold a year in the first century CE (Plin. *Nat.* 33.4.78). The figure seems less implausible once you have peered over the edge of the opencast at Las Medulas!

Another way to approach the question of the scale of Roman mining activity is to look at the emerging picture of global pollution registered in the Greenland ice-cores. Analysis of the ice-cores has revealed that fresh layers of ice are formed each year and that by counting back, the ice can be accurately dated, rather like tree rings. The chemical analysis of ice across time has now demonstrated that the major pre-Industrial Revolution peak in hemispheric pollution occurred in the Roman period, with notable peaks of both copper and lead (Hong et al. 1994, 1996a, b; Rosman et al. 1997). What this translates to at a local level is best illustrated by recent work in Wadi Faynan, Jordan, where a major Roman copper mine and smelting operation were evidently responsible for a hugely toxic environment, with dangerous levels of a cocktail of poisons traceable even today in vegetation and the animals that graze on it (Barker et al. 2000: 44–6).

The use of marble in Roman construction increased in scale and extent from the reign of Augustus, and Tiberius appears to have made decorative stones an imperial monopoly alongside metals (Dodge 1988, 1991; Dodge and Ward-Perkins 1992; Fant 1988, 1989, 1993). The Romans were particularly interested in the exploitation of colored stones and recent work in the Eastern Egyptian desert has revealed much about the nature of imperial operations there. Two major quarry locations have been surveyed: Mons Claudianus, producing a grey granite, and Mons Porphyrites, producing the much-prized purple porphyry (Maxfield and Peacock 2001; Peacock and Maxfield 1997). It is clear from the wealth of epigraphic documents from these sites that the labor force was predominantly salaried and free, rather than slave–conscript. The same appears to be broadly true of ancient mining enterprises – though it is equally certain that some penal labor was involved – and the implication is that these extractive industries attracted specialist workers with above average wages. Detailed studies of the diet at these quarrying sites has revealed a surprisingly luxurious range of foodstuffs in the peak periods of operation, much of it imported from the Nile valley (van der Veen 1998). The logistical implications are considerable (Adams 2001; Maxfield 2001).

7 Coinage, Coin Use, and Markets

Money is synonymous with modern understanding of markets. Study of Roman coinage systems has a distinguished pedigree and has made major contributions to our understanding of the Roman economy (Duncan-Jones 1994; K. Greene 1986: 48–66; Howgego 1995; Kent 1987; King and Wigg 1996). Although there were times and places where the money supply seriously lagged behind, the most striking feature is the level of monetization and integration achieved (Howgego 1992, 1994). The eventual evolution of a coinage system fitted to serve small market transactions is one of the clearest indicators of a market economy, though even more striking is evidence to show that non-cash transactions were often accounted in cash terms to create simple credit systems (Rathbone 1991: 318–30). Although ancient banking was relatively local in operation (Andreau 1999, 2000), there are instances of loans being taken out in one sea-port and repaid in another after sale of cargo (*D.* 45.1.122.1).

The existence of markets in the ancient world – in the sense that they are understood by modern economists – has been much debated (Polanyi et al. 1957; Temin 2001). If abstract markets remain elusive, the evidence for "institutional markets" is more concrete. The development of physical market locations parallels the evolution of the coinage (de Ligt 1993; Frayn 1993). Many Roman markets were periodic ones, held on a regular cycle, originally based on an eight day week, making markets every nine days reckoned inclusively – hence their term, *nundinae* (de Ligt 1993; MacMullen 1970; B. D. Shaw 1981a). The Roman state maintained strong controls over markets; it was necessary to seek approval from the Roman Senate or emperor to establish a new market (*CIL* VIII 11,451, 23,246).

8 The Inscribed Economy

Instrumentum domesticum is the modern Latin term used to describe a range of inscriptions incised, stamped, or painted on a range of portable artifacts from the ancient world (W. V. Harris 1993a). Examples include: stamps and/or molded marks on pottery vessels and amphorae, glass, bricks and tiles, lead pipes, wooden barrels, etc.; control stamps on metal ingots and quarried stone; metal tags and lead seals used in the transport of goods; and graffiti (often denoting ownership of personal artifacts). The definition normally excludes portable documents such as coins, papyri, *ostraca*, or writing tablets, as well as all inscriptions on stone. Although much of the material simply provides evidence of the ability of people to write their own names on their possessions (though this is not without interest in itself), some of these inscriptions can be quite detailed and highly informative about the operation of ancient society and institutions. A good example is provided by the sets of painted inscriptions (*tituli picti*) on an olive-oil amphora from southern Spain, generally known as the Dressel 20 type (Keay 1988: 98–104). This globular jar, with average volume of c.70 liters, reveals Roman procedures governing the bottling of olive oil at port sites along the navigable Guadalquivir river, and was evidently designed to rigorously control trade and minimize fraud. The amphorae were first weighed empty and this figure was marked on the vessel; next came the name of the merchant who was to transport the oil overseas; in a third line the weight of oil contained in the amphora was added (after reweighing and deducting the empty amphora); and a fourth set of notations reveals the names and signatures of those responsible for carrying out and monitoring the weighing, as well as an indication of the actual farm from where the oil originated. The whole process of trade in Spanish olive oil appears to have been highly regulated from the farm to the mass disposal of amphorae on Monte Testaccio, a 50 meter-high and 1 kilometer-circumference mountain of potsherds in the commercial area of Rome (Rodriguez Almeida 1984; Blasquez Martinez and Remesal Rodriguez 1999/2003). A series of late Roman *ostraca* from the harbor area at Carthage attest to the existence of a similarly sophisticated system for weighing and stock-taking controls of olive oil passing through imperial warehouses there (Peña 1998). In both cases, the detailed nature of the recording systems put in place suggests a connection with the *annona* and may be thought characteristic of the sort of economic controls governing its operation.

9 Shipwreck Archaeology

Over the last 50 years, following the development of the aqualung, more than 900 shipwrecks have been recorded in the Mediterranean – representing an extraordinary growth in this form of evidence (A. J. Parker 1992; Throckmorton 1987). The overwhelming majority of these wrecks lie in shallow coastal waters and their reporting shows a distinct distributional bias to the areas where recreational diving is most practiced (what one may term the "Riviera" effect). We must be cautious, therefore, until more diving has been carried out along the North African coastline, in the Levant, and along the Turkish coast, and the results published, about the conclusions we draw from the apparently very uneven distribution of wrecks. Moreover, new research is revealing large numbers of deep-water wrecks, which are much less susceptible to ancient salvage and modern disturbance (McCann and Freed 1994).

Wreck sites provide us with vital evidence relating to ship size, cargo capacity, marine technology, cargo composition and lading, and patterns of trade. The description of the ancient equivalent of a "super-tanker" (Luc. *Nav.* 5) can now be compared with the archaeological evidence of actual ships. These suggest that the most common category of sea-going vessel was of small size, up to 75 tonnes capacity (c.1500 amphorae), probably designed for coastal transport. There was a medium size of between 75–200 tonnes (2–3,000 amphorae), and a large-size group of around 250–300 tonnes (6,000 amphorae), and upward of 30–40 meters in length by up to 10 meters beam. Notwithstanding the fact that these ships are small by modern standards, there were few vessels larger than the top group before the early modern period.

The Madrague des Giens wreck off the southern French coast near Toulon is an interesting example of the larger class of Roman merchant ship. When it sank in 60–50 BCE, it was carrying a large cargo of Italian wine from southern Latium (estimated at 6,000–8,000 amphorae, equivalent to c.150–200,000 liters). The amphorae were tightly stacked in the hold in three or four layers and packed around with pine branches. Other elements of cargo included several hundred black gloss fineware vessels and hundreds of coarseware plates, jars, and pitchers, along with a consignment of pinecones (A. J. Parker 1992: 249–50).

Another interesting wreck site, known as Port Vendres II, provides evidence of trade originating in southern Spain in the 40s CE (K. Greene 1986: 162–3; A. J. Parker 1992: 330–1). The ship went down close to the Franco-Spanish border and may have been heading for either the mouth of the Rhone or for Italy. The mixed cargo (evidently put on board for at least 11 separate merchants) comprised amphorae – primarily the Dressel 20 type for transport of olive oil, but also wine, *defrutum* (sweet must), and fish sauce – fine pottery, glass, and metal ingots (tin, copper, and lead). The location of the wreck in only 7 meters of water close to the mouth of an ancient harbor made it very accessible for ancient salvage efforts and it is possible that the original cargo contained a larger number of ingots than the 23 recovered in the modern excavations, as these would have been a prime target of ancient salvage divers. The Port Vendres ship is illustrative of the close links between trade in a range of different products from a single region, where the most valuable commodity (here metals) may have served to underwrite or subsidize the transport costs of other elements. The economy of Baetica (S. Spain) was heavily dependent on mining activity in the Sierra Morena region, north of the River Guadalquivir, which was navigable by river craft and became the focus of the trade in olive oil produced on a very large scale in this region. There was some wine production also, and fish sauce production was widely developed along the coastal strip on both sides of the Straits of Hercules (Curtis 1991b) and was fed into the trade pattern at major harbors such as Gades (Cádiz). The distribution of finewares produced in southern Spain in Gaul and Italy appears to be entirely due to their traveling in piggy-back fashion with the major cargoes from this region.

10 Trade and Commerce I: Pots As Evidence for Trade

"Pottery can be represented as a sort of spy, or a symptom of a much more complex reality" (Pucci 1983: 106). Pottery is overwhelmingly the most abundant manufactured material surviving from antiquity. This gives it a peculiar importance in archaeological studies of the ancient economy, and one that is out of all proportion to its actual economic value in Roman society (Carandini 1983; K. Greene 1992; Peacock 1982). With the help of improved characterization studies, the origins of many distinctive forms of pottery are now known and their distributions can be traced and their local occurrence assessed quantitatively (W. V. Harris 1993a). It is less certain what we can prove from distribution patterns alone, especially where it is suspected that the pottery has been traded "piggy-back" alongside archaeologically less-visible commodities.

The study of amphorae offers the greatest potential for understanding Roman trade, since the containers are representative of commerce in their contents (Amphores 1989; Peacock and Williams 1986). In many instances a particular commodity can be ascribed to a distinctive form of amphora (olive oil for the Dressel 20, wine for the Dressel 1, and so on). Studies of regional pottery supply patterns are also starting to demonstrate the local and long-range connections of a number of sites and how these fluctuated over time (Fulford 1989; P. Reynolds 1995). The quantities of amphorae known to have been shipped are impressive. Monte Testaccio, for instance, is conservatively estimated to represent c.60–80 million oil amphorae. Several large deposits of Italian wine amphorae dredged from the bed of the Rhone in the nineteenth century are reckoned to have totaled more than 100,000 vessels (Tchernia 1983). Recent research has also emphasized a massive increase during the Roman period in production and trade in fish products, including the celebrated rotted fish sauces (Ben Lazreg et al. 1995; Curtis 1991a, b).

The overall volume of manufactures and their distribution patterns are extremely impressive. Above all, one is struck by evidence of large-scale activities, well above the subsistence needs of individuals or inward-looking communities. First-century CE kilns at La Graufesenque in southwest France could apparently accommodate up to 30,000 high-quality pots in a single firing and millions of these vessels were evidently distributed across the western empire during the operational period of the site (Peacock 1982: 114–28). A pottery workshop lease in Egypt specifies the annual production by the potter for the estate owner of 15,000 amphorae with a total capacity of c.100,000 liters of wine (Cockle 1981).

11 Trade and Commerce II: Mechanisms

The geographical, political, and social imperatives of the Roman Empire contributed a number of peculiarities to its economy. We might conceptualize this in terms of a political economy that operated alongside a social economy that was in turn interleaved with a true market economy. The political economy was primarily the product of the need to extract surplus from the empire to support the mechanisms of state.

These included securing the food supply for the city of Rome and for the army (the *annona*), exploiting mineral resources to sustain the coinage system, and obtaining and transporting the raw materials to embellish the capital – notably from widespread imperial quarries for a range of decorative stones. Although Rome claimed a monopoly over significant mineral resources and sources of marble and decorative granites, and had access to substantial volumes of foodstuffs from state lands and imperial estates or as tax in kind, the expense of exploiting these resources and of transporting the commodities huge distances to their chosen destination would have defied normal economic logic. This was a redistributive exchange system operating on a grand scale (Aldrete and Mattingly 1999). For example, monolithic columns of granite weighing up to 200 tonnes were quarried at Mons Claudianus in the eastern Egyptian desert and then transported more than 120 kilometers overland to the Nile and then onwards to Rome (Maxfield 2001). The infrastructure to support this extraordinary operation, involving permanent settlements at the quarries, the requisition of huge numbers of draught animals, and construction of special boats, etc., could only have been undertaken by a state such as Rome (Adams 2001). The operation of the political economy of the *annona* and of the extraction and transport of metals and stone thus represents a huge anomaly in the Roman economy. It is clear that some of the archaeological evidence of long-distance movement of goods around the Roman world can be related to this political economy, which subsidized or underwrote transport costs (A. Kolb 2002).

The Roman army was another institution with a distinctive mode of economic operation that set it apart from the rest of provincial society (Erdkamp 2002). The army had complex networks of supply contracts, often operating across provincial boundaries (Carreras Montfort 2002; Whittaker 1994: 98–131). Evidence on preserved writing tablets from the late first-century CE fort of Vindolanda in northern Britain provides many insights into the operations of the military quartermasters and supply specialists – the *beneficiarii* (Bowman 1994; Carreras Montfort 2002: 77–9, 82–7; Remesal Rodriguez 2002). In one tablet, a certain Octavius writes to Candidus concerning a range of deals he is brokering – concerning grain, animal hides, and leather ware (*Tab. Vindol.* II. 343). The military was a cash purchaser on a large scale and contracts were filled at three levels: in the immediate locality of a fort, within the province, and from extra-provincial sources. Long-distance movement of goods was perhaps more common than might be imagined, since traffic in goods under military contracts was not liable to the normal customs dues on inter-provincial trade (though the state evidently had to guard closely against sharp practice by merchants who claimed exemptions also for additional cargo). The similarity of materials being transported to Rome and to the army garrisons and the close correlation of administrative controls (insofar as they can be discerned) suggest plausibly that military supply was also under the overall supervision of the *praefectura annonae* from an early date (Remesal Rodriguez 2002). The potential impact of the military supply network on economic patterns and development in frontier provinces such as Britain is increasingly recognized, despite the limitations of the evidence (Fulford 2004).

However, it is also apparent that free market trade flourished alongside the imperial economy, especially in the core provinces of the empire. This can be seen in part in the long-distance transport and wide distribution of many goods to centers other than the city of Rome and the main military frontiers. This was a widespread trading economy, sustained by the purchasing power represented in many Roman cities. Mercantile relations extended well beyond the imperial frontiers, for instance, towards India and China in the east and sub-Saharan Africa in the south.

It has sometimes been asserted that long-distance Roman trade was above all about luxuries and that staple foodstuffs and articles of low intrinsic value would rarely circulate beyond a 50-mile range from where they were produced. However, there is a wealth of archaeological evidence to contradict this assumption about transport costs in the Roman world. The regular occurrence on shipwrecks of large quantities of low value coarseware pottery vessels is a case in point (Pucci 1983: 110–11). There are two possible explanations and both of them may have contributed to the observed pattern. First, the *annona* system did not have to conform to normal rules of economic rationality and could implement mass transfer of grain from Egypt to Rome or olive oil from southern Spain to Britain (Carreras Montfort 2002). The second possibility is that the existence of a core of "tied" trade under state contracts had a far more widespread effect of cross-subsidizing the transport of other commodities and of stimulating demand in civil markets. The distribution patterns for many products extend well beyond the major supply routes leading to the city of Rome or the main military markets.

Who were the merchants and shippers of the ancient world? We have already noted the social distance that Roman senators established between themselves and such activity, but there is evidence to show that fortunes were made in trade and that in the provinces at any rate some merchants were prominent individuals (Giardina 1993b; W. V. Harris 2000; Paterson 1998). Not all were the archetypal "wealthy freedman" made infamous in the *Satyricon* of Petronius. Even if the literary sources are relatively silent about merchants, evidence survives in the form of public inscriptions and in painted notations (*tituli picti*) on trade goods. For instance, the *collegium* of Augustales at Misenum numbered over 100 members, indicating the importance of wealthy freedmen traders in that harbor town (D'Arms 2000).

My overall judgment of the Roman imperial economy is that it was extraordinary by the standards of a pre-industrial world, most notably in terms of its scale. However, it was a very imperfect and heterogeneous institution (and many of the points made by the primitivists are accurate to this extent). Yet it did achieve growth and it created a level of regional integration, or at least interconnectedness, that marks it out from other ancient economies. The role of state regulation was of high importance in many areas, but since the Romans tended to operate through the use of private individuals and companies (as estate and mine lessees, shippers, and contractors), the resulting pattern is a colorful mosaic of tied and free market activity.

CHAPTER FIFTEEN

Landlords and Tenants

Dennis P. Kehoe

1 Introduction

Agricultural wealth played a crucial role in the social and political structure of the Roman Empire. The elite classes that ruled the empire, including the emperor and the imperial family, the senatorial and equestrian orders, and the curial classes in the empire's many cities, depended on the production of their estates for the revenues that maintained their social and political privileges. The elite's share of the Roman agrarian economy was considerable, and it is likely that it only increased during the first three centuries CE as the aristocracy was increasingly recruited from across the empire as a whole instead of exclusively from Italy (Duncan-Jones 1990: 121–42; Hopkins 1995/6). We can appreciate the enormous disparities in agricultural wealth by comparing the fortunes of the empire's wealthier landowners with those of more modest landowners. The Roman senator Pliny the Younger (c.61–113), whose published correspondence includes a great deal of information about the financial concerns of upper-class Romans, owned estates worth perhaps 15–17 million sesterces (Duncan-Jones 1982: 17–32). This figure represents a multiple of the minimum property qualifications for senators and equestrians set by Augustus, which were one million and 400,000 sesterces, respectively. The minimum census requirement for members of the councils in many cities in Italy and the provinces was 100,000 sesterces. At the same time, Pliny's fortune was dwarfed by those of the very wealthiest members of the Roman elite, which were measured in hundreds of millions of sesterces. To put these levels of wealth in perspective, the census qualification for Egyptian villagers in the early empire on whom the duty to perform public liturgies fell might be at most the equivalent of a few thousand sesterces. The annual pay of a legionary soldier at the time of Augustus was 900 sesterces.

As great as the fortunes of wealthy private individuals were, the state was by far the largest landowner in the Roman Empire. The imperial government derived substantial revenues from state-owned land, or imperial estates, which were to be found in

Italy and in all the provinces. These estates came into imperial ownership from a variety of sources, including bequests to the emperor by grateful senators, the defaulting of property to the state when people died without heirs, and the confiscation of property of those unfortunate enough to be condemned for capital crimes or for tax arrears. The revenues from imperial estates played a crucial role in the public programs supported by the Roman government, and they supplemented the revenues that the state gained from taxes imposed on privately held land. Thus revenues from imperial estates in North Africa provided wheat and later olive oil to the programs in Rome that distributed these products to the urban populace. In Egypt, the state arranged for the shipment of grain collected as taxes from private land and as rents from state-owned land down the Nile to Alexandria, from where it was shipped to Rome or to other cities in the east. Other social programs sponsored by the imperial government and private benefactors also revolved around agricultural production. For example, to fund alimentary foundations in Italian cities, the state lent sums of money to participating landowners based on the size of their holdings. The interest paid by these landowners provided funds to support the raising of children.

The substantial stratification of wealth and the social and political privileges that the elite enjoyed raise a basic question about the nature of the Roman agrarian economy. Was this economy completely dominated by a landowning elite, with the vast majority of the empire's wealth subject to the control of powerful landowners, or did the Roman economy also provide opportunities to a broader range of people to prosper from agriculture? The development of the imperial peace created enormous opportunities for Roman estate owners to make profits by supplying agricultural products to the growing urban population in the empire. Indeed, the archaeological evidence for olive and wine presses indicates that landowners in many parts of the empire, in particular in Spain and Africa, invested heavily in the production of wine and olive oil, which could be sold as a cash crop to supply not just Rome but cities in the provinces as well (Peacock and Williams 1986: 54–66; D. J. Mattingly 1988c). At the same time, we should not overestimate the economic power of the Roman elite. In a largely agrarian economy, elite Roman landowners lacked the freedom of choice in investing their wealth that we might associate with a modern, market economy. Investment in agriculture represented the preeminent form of financial security for upper-class Romans, a source of income that could be expected to be stable over the long term and that also carried social prestige (Veyne 1979). In light of this fact, the strategies that Roman landowners adopted in managing their agricultural wealth are likely to have been very conservative, aimed at preserving wealth and maintaining their social privileges. Such a conservative strategy had important implications for the relationships between Roman landowners and other small farmers – in particular, the tenants who cultivated much of their land. Many upper-class landowners, then, sought to avoid risk and contented themselves with an income generated from the production of their tenants. The incomes of such landowners depended not so much on their ability to adjust their investment strategies to changing market conditions as on their ability to capture some of the surplus production of their tenants (Horden and Purcell 2000: 231–97, esp. 245).

Environmental and technological constraints limited the productivity of Roman agriculture. Agriculture in the Roman Empire tended to be extensive, since farmers had little capacity to apply fertilizer or other inputs to raise the productivity of the land. In many parts of the Roman world, farmers used the two-field system, often called "dry-farming," to cultivate wheat. Adapting to the hot and dry summers and rainy winters of the Mediterranean climate, farmers would repeatedly plow the land to preserve moisture, sowing the crop in the fall, and after harvesting it in the spring, letting the land lie fallow for one year (Grigg 1974: 123–51). Yields under such conditions are likely to have been modest, on the order of about 500 kg/ha, a figure that would be on the low end of yields attested in medieval Italy (Spurr 1986: 82–8). To increase the production of their land, farmers could engage in polyculture, which involved the cultivation of grain in combination with tree crops such as vines or olives (Horden and Purcell 2000: 209–20; Sallares 1991: 304–9). Many farmers supplemented their incomes by raising livestock, especially sheep for wool and also for meat (Horden and Purcell 2000: 197–200). But the shortage of pasture often meant that livestock had to be kept away from the cultivated area, which deprived farmers of the use of their livestock's dung, which was the most common source of fertilizer. In areas without annual precipitation of 300–400 millimeters, irrigation would be required to cultivate wheat and other crops (Horden and Purcell 2000: 237–57). In arid regions of Africa, for example, irrigation involved capturing the water from occasional violent rainfall to cultivate crops in terraces dug out of hillsides, or tapping springs to water olive trees (B. D. Shaw 1982, 1984b).

2 The Organization of Estates

The strategies that Roman landowners followed in managing their wealth had to be adapted both to the geographical conditions affecting agricultural production and the overall climate for investment in agriculture in the Roman Empire. Perhaps the greatest boom in agriculture, in Italy at least, occurred during the last two centuries of the republic and the first century CE, when an increasingly wealthy upper class invested its wealth in land and was able to make great profits by supplying agricultural products to the growing urban population in Rome and other Italian cities. These landowners developed the so-called villa system of agriculture, characterized by intensively cultivated estates that produced wine and other cash crops. This type of agriculture was associated especially with coastal regions of Italy, which provided easy communications by sea with urban markets (Morley 1996: 129–38). The labor force on these estates consisted primarily of slaves, under the supervision of a bailiff, or *vilicus*, who was often also a slave. These estates were compact in size, comprising at most several hundred hectares. The wealthiest landowners might possess numerous compact estates, often located in diverse regions within Italy. This pattern of ownership lessened the landowners' exposure to the substantial risk posed by the irregularity of rainfall in Roman agriculture. Estates like the Villa Settefinestre at Cosa in Etruria, the most carefully excavated Roman estate, typically included a residence, the *pars urbana*, that served to accommodate the owner during visits to the estate (Carandini 1989). These *villae* became increasingly luxurious over the course of the late republic and the first century, and the lines between the economic and social function of an estate could become blurred. The *pars rustica* of such an estate would commonly include pressing facilities and buildings that could accommodate a substantial labor force of slaves.

The landowner's profit from this type of estate depended on concentrating the efforts of the slave staff on the cultivation of cash crops, especially wine and olive oil. At the same time, the slaves could be kept fully occupied throughout the agricultural year by producing most if not all of the food that the estate consumed; in this way the estate remained largely autonomous. Because of the seasonal nature of agricultural labor, it was not economical to maintain a slave staff that could perform all of the labor on the estate throughout the year. Instead of carrying the expense of keeping slaves who would not be fully employed, landowners would recruit additional labor at the harvest and other busy seasons from nearby small landowners or even tenants. Thus in coastal Italy, at least, an area with probably the largest concentration of estates owned by the upper classes, small-scale peasant agriculture remained a basic feature of the economy throughout the early imperial period (Rathbone 1981).

Slaves were often maintained under conditions that were extraordinarily cruel by modern standards. Many agricultural slaves, called *vincti*, were kept in chains and housed in slave-barracks, or rather jails, called *ergastula*. These were dimly lit buildings that provided slaves with basic shelter and few comforts, if any. At the same time, slaves were subject to violent punishment if they shirked their labor (Bradley 1994). Because the profit of the villa depended on maximizing the effort extracted from the slaves, estate owners were concerned to keep their slaves busy throughout the year. The Roman agriculture writer Cato, a senator writing in the second century BCE, exemplifies this attitude in his prescriptions for the estate owner's correct management of his slave labor force. In Cato's view, when rainy weather or storms made it impossible to undertake normal agricultural duties, the slaves were to be kept busy by working indoors on such tasks as cleaning storage jars, sweeping out the villa, moving grain, carrying dung out to the dung heap, cleaning the seed, repairing ropes, and mending clothing. Even on holidays, the slaves were to be kept busy by cleaning ditches, repairing roads, and cleaning up the gardens and other farmland. When the slaves were sick, they were not to be given their normal food ration. The point is that slaves represented a commodity, one that entailed a fixed cost to the landowner (*Agr.* 2.3–5). Some slaves kept under these conditions might be worked to death.

In the empire, it seems likely that the exploitation of slaves was modified somewhat as they became more expensive. The end of the republican wars of conquest reduced the importation of large numbers of slaves into Italy. As a consequence, agricultural slaves were increasingly bred on Roman estates. However, it remains a hotly debated topic to what extent slave breeding met the Roman Empire's demand for slaves. Some of the demand for slaves was met by imports from outside the empire. Within the empire, exposed children might be raised as slaves, and others might be sold into slavery (Scheidel 1997; cf. W. V. Harris 1999). The agronomist Columella, writing in the first century CE, offered special incentives to female slaves who produced offspring (*Rust.* 1.8.19); Columella may have been imitating the emperor Augustus' marriage legislation, which offered privileges to women who produced three children. But we should not exaggerate the improvement in the situation of slaves. Pliny the Younger, as we will see, did not maintain chained slaves, but he was aware that this practice was still common in Italy (*Ep.* 3.19.7).

In his recommendations about the proper treatment of slaves, Columella indicates that the relationship between landowner and slave was in essence one of exploitation, no matter how kind the landowner might seem. Columella exhibits a seemingly more humane attitude towards slaves than Cato, but at the same time his concern is still to maximize the effort that could be obtained from them:

> As regards other slaves these precepts are generally to be preserved, and I do not regret maintaining them, namely, that I speak on rather familiar terms more often to the country slaves than to the household slaves, as long as they have not comported themselves badly, and, since I understand that because of this friendliness on the owner's part their perpetual labor is lightened, I might sometimes joke with them and permit them to joke more. I now often follow this practice, that I deliberate about some new tasks with them as if they were more experienced, and through this I learn the nature of each one's mind and how intelligent it is. Then I see them more willingly approach a task that they think they have been consulted about and that they think has been undertaken on their recommendation. (*Rust.* 1.8.15)

Columella's seeming friendliness towards his slaves was all part of a general policy to manage slaves with a system of rewards and punishments. He still kept slaves in chains, and fair treatment of slaves was recommended only in order to avoid making his labor force intractable through the excessive cruelty of their overseers (*Rust.* 1.8.16–19).

Since the villa system generated enormous wealth for some landowners, it is noteworthy that it was not exported to the provinces in the early empire. In fact, the villa system in Italy declined rather precipitously beginning in the late first century CE. To be sure, the success of the classical villa system seems to have been the product of a particular set of circumstances: an increasingly wealthy group of landowners, rapid expansion of the urban population in Rome, and the creation of new markets, most notably in Gaul. These particularly favorable circumstances could not endure indefinitely. In the late first and second centuries, the villa system underwent a substantial transformation, with the compact villas in many locations giving way to larger estates cultivated less intensively. This transformation has been interpreted as a sign of a major crisis in Italian agriculture, for which several explanations have been offered. One explanation is that it was no longer profitable for landowners to maintain large numbers of slaves in the face of competition from provincial landowners, especially in Gaul and Spain. Indeed, imports of wine into Rome from Gaul and Spain increased in the early empire, while Spain also became one of the empire's leading suppliers of olive oil. At the same time, we should not overstate the nature of the crisis, especially the extent to which the transformation of the villa system impinged on the fortunes of upper-class landowners (Morley 1996: 135–42). In the early empire, the rapid growth of Rome as a consumer city ended, while the class of elite landowners spread outward from Italy to the western and then to the eastern provinces.

The emerging class of elite provincial landowners derived its income by supplying what was by the second century CE a more stable but still considerable urban market for the same agricultural products that their Italian counterparts had produced through the villa system in the late republic. Often it was small-scale tenants cultivating farms within larger estates who produced these cash crops. The estates of upper-class landowners in the Roman Empire varied considerably from region to region in their composition and organization. Italy in the early imperial period is famous for its extensive estates, or *latifundia*. In fact, estates that we might characterize as *latifundia* consisted of numerous much smaller farms, or *fundi*, that might not even be contiguous. Such estates grew over time as their owners purchased or inherited individual small farms. This is the pattern of landownership revealed by the famous alimentary table from Veleia in northern Italy, which records the properties pledged by landowners in the town to support a program to provide food for children (De Neeve 1984: 224–30).

The case of Pliny the Younger sheds light on the patterns of upper-class land ownership in Italy. Pliny derived his income from estates in two locations, his home town of Comum in northern Italy, and the Umbrian town of Tifernum Tiberinum. At the latter location, Pliny's estate consisted of a number of individual farms that he describes as scattered among parcels belonging to an adjacent estate whose purchase he was considering (*Ep.* 3.19.1; De Neeve 1990: 373). These estates were under the management of employees called *actores*, who were probably either slaves or freedmen of Pliny. These *actores*, in turn, reported to Pliny's business managers, or procurators. A slave-labor force under the supervision of the *vilici* may have worked some of the land on Pliny's estate, but the bulk of Pliny's land was leased out to tenants, who cultivated the individual *fundi*.

The juxtaposition of large estates and a small-scale peasant agricultural economy is even more likely to have characterized other regions of Italy and the provinces. During the early imperial period the western provinces, especially Spain, southern Gaul, and Africa provided fertile recruiting grounds for the Roman elite, contributing large numbers of families to both the senatorial and equestrian orders. This development was surely a product of the development of the agricultural economy in these provinces, with a class of large landowners exercising an increasing dominance in the rural economy. Early imperial Gaul saw a distinct transformation in the countryside, as numerous dispersed villas gradually supplanted nucleated hilltop settlements. These villas were decorated on a scale not seen before in Gaul, and they indicate that the wealthier landowners in Gaul were adopting a basic Roman cultural form. The Gallic villas, however, were often modest in size, in some regions ranging from 50 to 100 hectares (Woolf 1998: 142–68). The evidence for these villas is largely archaeological, and we have very little information as to how they were cultivated, whether by slaves, tenants, day-laborers, or some combination of all three. Recent archaeological work in Africa confirms the impression offered by inscriptions and literary evidence that this region of the Roman Empire also saw the growth of substantial estates, often devoted to the cultivation of olives as a cash crop (D. J. Mattingly 1988c; M. De Vos 2001: 21–9).

Some parts of the empire saw the development of large private estates comparatively late, as in Egypt, where such estates began to appear in the second and third centuries (Rathbone 1991), or Palestine, where large estates apparently only formed in the third and fourth centuries (Z. Safrai 1994: 322–64). In these areas, the absence of large landowners could mean that other institutions played a significant role in setting the conditions under which agriculture was practiced. In Egypt, agricultural land in the Nile valley and Fayum was often divided into relatively small parcels, separated by embankments that were designed to capture the Nile flood. Grain was the usual crop in such land. Land not reached by the Nile flood needed to be irrigated artificially. Often irrigated land was devoted to orchards and vineyards. Much of the land was privately owned, but the state also maintained control over a great deal of land in most if not all *nomes* (administrative divisions). This circumstance, in all likelihood, promoted greater equality of land distribution, since state land in Egypt was customarily leased out in small plots to individual cultivators, who enjoyed security of tenure and could often pass their cultivation rights on to their heirs (Rowlandson 1996: 70–101). Egyptian agriculture required the continued maintenance of irrigation dikes and drainage canals to make sure that the flood reached all the land that had to be irrigated and also that the water could be drained to allow the sowing of the crop. This work was organized communally at the village level, and under Roman rule the state imposed the task of maintaining the irrigation facilities on the farming population as a liturgy. Thus most male peasants in Roman Egypt were required to provide five days of labor each year working on the dikes and canals (Lewis 1983: 107–33). In the more intensive agriculture of Egypt, wheat yields were substantially higher than elsewhere in the empire, on the order of perhaps 1,000 kg/ ha (Rathbone 1991: 242–4, 465).

On occasion, documentary papyri make it possible to examine the pattern of landownership to a degree of detail not possible elsewhere in the Roman Empire. In an analysis of landholding in the Hermopolite *nome* in the fourth century, for example, Roger Bagnall concludes that the majority of landowners owned plots of land between ten and 50 *arouras* in size (10 *arouras* is approximately 2.5 hectares, an amount of land probably sufficient to support an individual family). Only a few villagers might own land in excess of this amount, but the wealthiest landowners in the village were probably residents of the *nome metropoleis*. These landowners did not own land in the village on a larger scale than the largest landowners among the villagers, but in all likelihood such landowners had holdings in many villages at the same time, so that their level of wealth probably exceeded that of even the very wealthiest villagers (Bagnall 1992). This pattern of landownership seems to have been approximated in other areas in Egypt. One location that has been subject to recent study is the city and surrounding territory of Oxyrhynchus (Rowlandson 1996: 102–38). The Oxyrhynchite *nome* had a population on the order of 100,000– 120,000. There too, the vast majority of landowners had relatively modest holdings of 5–50 *arouras*, while a much smaller number of landowners had 500 *arouras* or more of land (c.125 hectares).

The village also provided the organizational framework for larger estates in Roman Egypt. The private estates that developed typically consisted of a variety of individual parcels scattered among other lands in a village. There is little evidence for the use of slaves in agriculture in Egypt, certainly not in the way in which slaves were employed in Italy. Often tenancy provided the means for the owners of scattered parcels, like the urban landowners at Oxyrhynchus, to generate an income from such lands. But as the largest landowners gained control of increasingly large holdings, they began to realize some economies of scale. In the second and third centuries, some estates had a central facility, or *epoikion*, that housed workers on the estate and might also include facilities for pressing grapes and olives (cf. Banaji 2001: 174–6 for *epoikia* in late antique Egypt). The best attested of these estates is the one belonging to Aurelius Appianus, a third-century landowning magnate from Alexandria. The organization of this estate is attested in great detail by the Heroninos archive, a collection of some 450 documents, including drafts of monthly accounts and correspondence associated with the working of the estate. The Heroninos archive takes its name from the manager of the division, or *phrontis*, of the estate located at the village of Theadelphia (Rathbone 1991). These divisions consisted of numerous individual parcels cultivated with wheat, fodder crops, and vines. At the level of the village divisions, the labor on the individual parcels was supplied by a small number of permanent workers, supplemented by numerous workers hired from the village on a daily basis. Presumably these workers were recruited from smaller landowners and tenants working in the village, as well as from the landless rural population. Some parcels whose cultivation could not be integrated into the village division were leased out to tenants. The central management of the estate, to which the individual managers reported, maintained control over key resources, such as draft animals, and it supervised the workers who managed these resources. This system of centralized management made it possible to keep the costs of production in the individual divisions under control by sharing centrally-maintained resources that the individual divisions would otherwise have to duplicate.

3 Farm Tenancy

The economies of scale achieved on the estate of Appianus depended on the careful oversight of a centralized administration that could monitor on a regular basis the efforts of individual managers. Landowners who were not able to maintain such a level of supervision turned to alternative methods of managing their estates. One solution was to lease estates out to large-scale tenants, who took upon themselves the problem of organizing the labor needed to cultivate the land and market the crops. Sometimes the tenant was a slave of the landowner. Leasing to a slave-tenant, or a *servus quasi colonus*, provided the landowner with important advantages. The lease arrangement gave the *servus quasi colonus* an incentive to manage the property well, since he could keep a share of the profits and use this to purchase his freedom. At the same time, the landowner exercised greater control over a slave-tenant than would be possible with a tenant of free status (Scheidel 1994: 131–49).

Large-scale leasing suggests how farm tenancy could contribute to solving managerial problems. But large-scale tenants represented a small minority of farm tenants; the vast majority of farm tenants were engaged in the more basic task of working the land. One of the questions surrounding farm tenancy in the Roman Empire is whether the provision of labor was the chief contribution of farm tenancy (Rowlandson 1996: 213–36), or whether landowners also relied on their tenants to invest their own resources in the cultivation of the land. In the latter case, the relationship between landowners and tenants would have been a kind of "partnership." The contribution of the landowner was to cover the substantial costs of pressing facilities and other equipment, while the tenant provided equipment, animals, and slaves. This at least is the allocation of resources envisioned in conventional Roman lease law (Frier 1979). This sort of arrangement made it possible for the tenant to cultivate crops such as vines, for which the expenses might be prohibitive if the tenant had to bear the costs alone. The landowner gained from this, since the tenant had an incentive to keep the farm in good working order by investing his own resources in its upkeep. Whether the relationship between landowner and tenant was more akin to partnership or to exploitation depended to a large degree on the bargaining power of the tenant.

To be sure, there was a great deal of stratification in the ranks of tenants in the Roman Empire, with tenants ranging from wealthy members of the elite who took over the task of managing large estates to small-scale tenants, with few resources of their own, who were in effect laborers. One of the key factors determining the economic independence of small farmers working as tenants was their access to draft animals: tenants who provided their own plow oxen were likely to exercise far greater bargaining power than their counterparts who depended on their landowners for the provision of draft animals and other important resources (Foxhall 1990). In addition, the lines between landowners and tenants might be blurred, with small-scale landowners supplementing their incomes by leasing in additional land. This pattern of combining land ownership with leasing can be traced in the rich documentation of Roman Egypt (Kehoe 1992: 140–65).

We can appreciate the contribution that farm tenants might make to the financial interests of upper-class landowners by considering again the situation of Pliny the Younger. Pliny relied upon his tenants to invest their resources in the production of the cash crops, including wine, on which his income depended. Pliny's tenants occupied their farms under leases that were formulated in terms of conventional Roman private law. They paid cash rents (at least before he instituted sharecropping on his Tuscan estates: *Ep.* 9.37). Likewise, the leases of the tenants were short-term, since Pliny discusses the need to renegotiate the leases on several occasions (*Ep.* 7.30.3; 9.37; 10.8.5). It is also likely that Pliny's tenants contributed substantial resources of their own. When discussing the possible purchase of the estate adjacent to his own property at Tifernum Tiberinum, Pliny mentions the need to reequip the now impoverished tenants on that estate with slaves. Apparently, these tenants had previously provided their own slaves, but when they had fallen behind in their rent, the previous owner of the estate confiscated them, presumably with other property pledged as security:

> But this fertility of the land is worn out by the feeble cultivators. For the previous owner too often sold their pledges, and while he reduced the tenants' arrears of rent for the time being, he exhausted their resources for the long term, as a result of the loss of which their arrears have grown again. They (sc. the tenants) must be equipped with slaves, which will be all the more expensive a proposition because the slaves are honest (*frugi*); for I myself do not have chained slaves anywhere nor does anyone there. (*Ep.* 3.19.6–7)

The troubles that Pliny encountered notwithstanding, this form of tenancy seems well designed to serve the interests of upper-class landowners seeking stable incomes from their farms. Pliny's tenants cultivated substantial farms, covered many of the costs of farming from their own resources, produced crops that could be sold on the market, and paid Pliny a regular, fixed rent out of the proceeds. Since they paid a rent in cash, they took upon themselves the task of marketing the crops and bore the risk for the size of the harvest and for the market price of the crops.

The long-term productivity of small-scale tenants was crucial to the Roman estate economy, as we can see in the land tenure system that the Roman government maintained on its imperial estates in North Africa. The evidence for how the North African imperial estates were cultivated comes from a series of inscriptions, dating to the second and early third centuries (Flach 1978; Kehoe 1988a; Kolendo 1991;

De Ligt 1998–9; M. De Vos 2001), from the fertile Medjerda (ancient Bagradas) valley in northern Tunisia. The interpretation of these complex inscriptions remains a matter of continuing scholarly debate, but it is possible to sketch in broad outline how the estates were cultivated. The state largely relied on small-scale farmers, or *coloni*, who held lands on the imperial estates under perpetual leaseholds based on a regulation called the *lex Manciana*. Although this point is not certain, the law was probably a lease regulation originally adopted on private land. Then, after the private estates on which it was used passed into imperial ownership, it became a general regulation defining land tenure on African imperial estates. The *coloni* were share-croppers, generally paying one-third of their crops as rent. They could maintain their rights to their land as long as they continued to cultivate it, and they could pledge these rights as security in loans and pass them on to their heirs.

The Roman government sought to establish the *coloni* as permanent cultivators by giving them incentives to make the substantial long-term investment required by olive culture. These incentives first involved ad hoc efforts to extend the application of the *lex Manciana*. Under Hadrian, these efforts were superseded by a more general regulation, called the *lex Hadriana de rudibus agris*, or the "law of Hadrian concerning unused lands." This law granted *coloni* bringing unused lands on imperial estates under cultivation perpetual lease rights and also offered them incentives to cultivate olives by exempting them from the obligation to pay rent for ten years. Imperial procurators announced the law of Hadrian with great fanfare as they implemented it on a particular group of estates:

> Speech of the procurators of the emperor Caesar Hadrian Augustus: because our Caesar [in keeping with] his tireless care, because of which he is assiduously vigilant for the interests of humankind, orders all parts of the fields that are suited for both olives or vines as well as cereals to be brought under cultivation; therefore by the permission of his providence the authority accrues to everyone to occupy even those parts which are in the leased out centuries of the estate of Blandus and Udens and in those parts which have been joined to the Tuzritan estate from the Lamian and Domitian estate, and are not being worked by the lessees; to those who have occupied them that right of possession and enjoyment and bequest to one's heir is given, which is included in the law of Hadrian concerning vacant lands and those which have not been cultivated for ten consecutive years..." (*CIL* VIII 25943, 26416)

This program, begun under Hadrian, continued at least until the reign of Septimius Severus, as the republication at that time of the incentives in the *lex Hadriana* indicates. Indeed, there are signs that the small-scale approach to fostering olive culture and more intensive agriculture had a lasting impact on the North African landscape. Thus in the Vandal period, the Albertini tablets, deeds of sale from a private estate at a location far inland from the Medjerda valley, indicate that land was cultivated on this estate under terms of tenure based on the *lex Manciana* (D. J. Mattingly 1989; Weael 2003). The process by which a program probably designed for imperial estates affected the land tenure systems on private estates in a much later period, however, remains unknown.

The efforts of the Roman government to exploit its estates did not come without conflict, however. To enforce the obligations of the *coloni*, the Roman administration appointed middlemen, or *conductores* (the lessees in the document quoted above).

These were large-scale lessees who leased from the Fiscus the right to collect the share rents from the *coloni*. In addition, the *conductores* cultivated certain lands not occupied by the *coloni*, and the *coloni* had to provide labor on this land, generally six days each year, as well as the use of their draft animals. There were apparently frequent conflicts between the *coloni* and the *conductores* over the former group's obligations. Indeed, in a petition to the emperor Commodus (181 CE), *coloni* from an imperial estate called the *saltus Burunitanus* complained bitterly of the treatment that they were accorded by one *conductor* in particular, named Allius Maximus, who, according to the description of the *coloni*, had repeatedly bribed the imperial procurators to allow him to raise the share rent of the *coloni* and to exact additional labor services. The *coloni* offered a rather desperate description of their situation in their appeal to the emperor:

> Please come to our aid, and since, as poor rustic people tolerating a livelihood gained from the work of our own hands, we are unfairly matched with a lessee most influential among your procurators because of his lavish gifts, to whom he is known through the changes of succession by the circumstances of his lease, take pity on us and deign to instruct by your rescript that we not furnish more than we are obliged to in accordance with the law of Hadrian and the letters of your procurators, that is two days of labor three times, so that by the benefit of your majesty we rustics, your servants and children of your estates, should no longer be disturbed by the lessees of fiscal farmland. (*CIL* VIII 10570, 14464)

The conflicts evident on imperial estates in Africa were not an isolated phenomenon; they seem to have arisen on imperial estates in other areas of the Roman Empire as representatives of the Roman government, perhaps reacting to fiscal pressure, sought to exact greater revenues from the farmers cultivating the land. Thus tenants on an imperial estate at a site called Aga Bey in Phrygia (Asia Minor) complained bitterly to the emperor (probably Philip the Arab, c.245 CE) about abuses that they were suffering at the hands of imperial tax officials called *kolletiones*. These tenants threatened to abandon the estate and take up residence on private land:

> It is necessary for us who have been forsaken, not tolerating the outrages of the *kolletiones* and of our opponents for the reasons we have said, to abandon both our fathers' hearths and our ancestors' tombs and to migrate to private land to be saved – for those living the evil life spare people living there more than your own farmers – and become fugitives from the imperial estates, in which we were born and raised and where, abiding as farmers from the time of our ancestors, we maintain our obligations to the imperial treasury. (Hauken 1998: no. 3, lines 43–54)

The complaints by the imperial tenants have to be seen in perspective, however. The publication of the two inscriptions quoted here as well as of numerous others surely indicates that the imperial tenants achieved some success in asserting their claims. Thus on the African imperial estates, although the *conductores* were far wealthier than the *coloni*, the *coloni* were the farmers permanently resident on the estate and the ones on whom the production of the estate ultimately depended. Thus when actions by *conductores*, or, in Asia Minor, imperial tax officials, threatened the welfare of these farmers, the imperial government had little choice but to intervene on the side of its farmers.

The situation of the *coloni* on the North African imperial estates sheds light on one of the questions raised at the outset of this chapter, namely, whether the Roman agrarian economy was completely dominated by the interests of large landowners, or whether it also created opportunities for other farmers to prosper. Certainly the maintenance of an extensive system of imperial estates, with substantial tracts of fertile farmland essentially withdrawn from the private economy, provided favorable tenure rights to many small farmers and also offered them protection against powerful landowners. Did tenants on private land share in any of the benefits that their imperial counterparts enjoyed?

This is a difficult question to answer, but it does seem likely that private landowners had to be flexible with the terms of tenure for their tenants, since they were subject to the same constraints in managing their lands as the imperial government. We can appreciate some of the difficulties that landowners faced if we consider the question of risk. Agriculture in the Mediterranean world was subject to frequent droughts (Horden and Purcell 2000: 178–9), which would leave landowners and tenants with the difficult task of sorting out who would cover the costs of diminished harvests and lost income. The classical Italian farm lease imposed the bulk of the risk on the tenant, who, because he paid a fixed rent in kind, bore the risk not only for the harvest, but also for the market prices that his crops would obtain. Roman law did grant the tenant some relief for an unforeseeable disaster, or *vis maior*, such as an earthquake, flood, an infestation by locusts or birds, or an invading army. But Roman law offered the tenant no relief for the foreseeable risks from agriculture, termed *vitia ex re* (Frier 1989–90). The problem was that this regime created a somewhat artificial distinction between an unforeseeable disaster and a supposedly foreseeable risk, such as a drought, that would make it equally impossible for the tenant to fulfil his obligations.

It is likely that many landowners had to be just as flexible as Pliny was when dealing with his tenants. Continuing poor crops created problems for Pliny's tenants, who were constantly behind on their rent. Even so, Pliny never contemplated dismissing them. Instead, he endeavored to modify their lease terms so that they could remain on his estate, cultivating the land productively. First, Pliny remitted their rent, and then, when this measure did not solve the problem, he replaced the traditional system of leasing with sharecropping. This was a measure that reduced the tenants' risk, but at the same time imposed many additional costs on Pliny, including the increased oversight that sharecropping requires, and the costs associated with marketing the crops. Pliny adopted this measure precisely because he wanted to preserve what was most advantageous in his relationship with his tenants, namely, their continued productive cultivation of his land:

> For in the prior lease period, their arrears grew, although after substantial remissions; as a result many no longer have any concern to reduce their debt, which they despair of being able to pay off in full. They even seize and consume the produce, no longer believing that their efforts at thrift are beneficial to themselves. One must therefore meet the growing problems and cure them. There is one means of curing them: if I should lease not for cash but for shares of the harvest and then appoint from my own people some collectors, as guardians of the produce. And indeed there is no more just type of return than what the land, the weather, and the year bring. But this demands great trust, sharp eyes, and numerous hands. Still, one must experiment and, as with a long-standing disease, try every change of remedy. (*Ep.* 9.37.2–3)

The Roman government was drawn into this issue because it frequently had to adjudicate tenants' claims for remissions of rent. In dealing with this issue, the Roman government recognized that social concerns might force landowners to adopt the same policy as Pliny followed in dealing with his tenants and be more accommodating than would be required under a strict interpretation of Roman law. In this circumstance, the concern of the Roman legal authorities was not to privilege the interests of either landowners or tenants over those of the other group. Rather, it sought to sort out the rights and obligations created for both groups when landowners granted remissions of rent. The consistent principle that the Roman government followed in this effort was to make sure, if possible, that remissions of rent granted beyond the strict requirements of Roman lease law would not result in the termination of the contractual relationship between landowners and tenants (Kehoe 1997: 221–34). In addressing tenants' requests for remissions of rent, the Roman government often dealt with lease arrangements that were based not on the conventions of traditional Roman private law, but on local customary arrangements. The Roman government consistently tried to respect local arrangements and recognize them as legally binding in terms of Roman law. This was the approach that the emperor Diocletian used in responding to a petition concerning a remission of rent:

> Concerning leases the faith of the contract is especially to be observed, if nothing specific should be expressed against the custom of the region. But if some landowners have remitted rent payments in contravention of the terms of the contract and the custom of the region, this should not be able to prejudice the claims of other landowners. (*CJust.* 4.65.19, 293 CE [Diocletian])

The Roman legal authorities displayed this same flexibility in adapting other areas of the law to the realities of the Roman economy, such as in their interpretation of the tenant's security of tenure. In classical Roman law, tenants did not enjoy possession of the land held under lease, so that they could be evicted from the land every time it changed hands. But the example of Pliny suggests that Roman landowners found ways to be more flexible in assuring tenants greater security of tenure. As in its treatment of risk, the Roman government occasionally recognized as legally binding traditional tenure arrangements offering the tenant greater security of tenure (Kehoe 1997: 181–236). This approach to land tenure explains a rescript from the emperor Alexander Severus to a tenant who had lost his lease when the farm that he was cultivating was sold. In this rescript, the emperor recognized that landowners and tenants might make agreements that offered the tenant much greater security of tenure than that implicit in conventional Roman lease law:

> It is not necessary for the purchaser to allow the tenant to whom the previous owner had leased to remain, unless he purchases under this condition. But if it should be proved that he had consented in some type of agreement that the tenant remain in the same lease, even if the agreement is not written, he is compelled in a judgment of good faith to comply with what has been agreed upon. (*CJust.* 4.65.9, 234 CE)

This survey of the evidence allows us to identify some of the basic relationships that defined the Roman agrarian economy. Even though the situation of the landowning elite was quite enviable, we must also recognize the limitations on their ability to make profits from agriculture. The revenues that the state and the landowning elite derived from agriculture helped to sustain the magnificent urban culture of the Roman Empire, but these revenues depended on extracting surplus production from numerous small-scale tenants. This system of agriculture tended to become fossilized, with landowners having little capacity or inclination to invest heavily in technology that might make agriculture more productive. Such growth in the economy as did occur was more likely to have been the result of population pressure rather than from the increasing productivity of labor. Under these conditions, landowners seeking stability sought to preserve what was most advantageous to them, which was securing the services of tenants. This effort to preserve stability came to its logical conclusion in the third and fourth centuries, when the Roman government, to maintain its tax revenues, assigned landowners increasing responsibilities in collecting taxes and, to make sure that these landowners could meet their fiscal obligations, bound certain types of tenants, or *coloni*, to the land that they were cultivating. Even if the bound colonate in the later empire resulted from the fiscal concerns of the Roman government rather than from economic policy, the origins of this development lie in the institution of farm tenancy as it was practiced in the early empire.

CHAPTER SIXTEEN

The Family

Judith Evans Grubbs

A comprehensive study of the family in the Roman Empire would have to take into account the vast extent of the empire and the diversity of ethnic and linguistic groups, religions, and social systems under which its inhabitants lived. The life experiences and family relationships of a member of the senatorial elite of Italy, part of a large network of kinship and patronage ties, with a household of perhaps several hundred slaves, would have little in common with those of an Egyptian villager living barely above subsistence level, sharing a tiny house with four or five other relatives, including, perhaps, his sister-wife (Bagnall and Frier 1994: 66–71 on household size; 127–34 on brother–sister marriage). Marriage and family life on the Roman frontiers – along Hadrian's Wall in Britain, or at Dura Europos on the Euphrates – would be subject to conditions unknown to the prosperous local elites of the cities of Asia Minor or North Africa, with their theaters, temples, and bath complexes all funded by the generous benefactions of wealthy families. For a full understanding of the multifarious household configurations and lifestyles of families throughout the empire, we would need to draw not only on Latin and Greek literature (especially novels and biography) but on legal and medical writings, funerary inscriptions (of which tens of thousands survive), documents preserved on papyrus from Egypt and elsewhere in the Middle East, and archaeological remains.

Such a study has never been done – and could never satisfactorily be done, given the paucity of evidence for the lives of most of the empire's population. Our knowledge of the family in the empire is fragmented, with small brightly lit areas where enough evidence has survived to provide a sense of lived reality in an otherwise vast darkness. Rather than make broad generalizations on "Roman family life" that inevitably would be inapplicable to much of the population, this chapter will focus on three of those brightly lit areas, the experiences of individuals who have left a first-hand account of their familial or marital relationships. These three are admittedly not typical of the vast majority of imperial subjects (who were illiterate and so have not left their own accounts), but represent instead the senatorial and municipal elite of Rome and the Latin west.

1 Eulogy for a Loyal Wife: The "Laudatio Turiae"

Sometime during the reign of Augustus, a wealthy Roman buried his wife of many years. At the funeral, he gave a long and moving eulogy (*laudatio*), which he then had inscribed on her gravestone. They belonged to the Roman elite, and had survived the harrowing years of the civil wars together. In his eulogy, the speaker tells not of his wife's ancestors and their deeds, as would be usual in a funeral oration (Horsfall 1983: 91), but of *her* courage and her devotion to him, and his to her.

About half of the entire speech is lost, including the name of the deceased herself. She has often been identified with a woman named Turia, wife of Q. Lucretius Vespillo (consul in 19 BCE), known to us from literary sources, because like Vespillo's wife, she saved her husband's life when he was proscribed during the civil wars. But the identification is doubtful; for convenience she is referred to here as "Turia," although this is very unlikely to have been her name.

The beginning of the inscription is lost; what we have starts thus:

> ...You were suddenly orphaned before our wedding day, when both of your parents were killed together in the deserted countryside. Through you most of all, since I was away in Macedonia and your sister's husband Cluvius was in the province of Africa, your parents' death did not remain unavenged. You performed this act of family devotion (*munus pietatis*) with such industry, ceaselessly opportuning [the authorities] and demanding punishment, that we men would not have achieved more if we had been on the spot. But you have these [accomplishments] in common with that purest of women, your sister. (*Laudatio* col. 1.2–8)

Even as a young unmarried woman, Turia had shown courage and perseverance beyond what was expected of women. Normally, avenging a family member's murder was a man's job (Evans Grubbs 2002: 60–70). But in the absence of any men-folk, the sisters took action. Not long afterwards, Turia was again forced to act for herself legally when an attempt was made by her father's relatives to break his will (which had made Turia and her husband and sister heirs) by claiming guardianship over the property and over Turia herself. The relatives claimed that Turia's parents had married by *coemptio*, an old form of marriage which entailed the wife coming under her husband's legal power (*manus*), while her sister had entered a marriage with *manus*, and thus had no claim on her father's estate without a will. Turia's defense of her father's will again displayed family duty (*pietas*) towards her sister and loyalty (*fides*) towards her husband.

Pietas is the ideal of any family relationship (Saller 1994: 105–14). The Latin word can be loosely but awkwardly translated as "sense of duty," "dutiful respect," or "devotion to family." Children were to observe *pietas* towards their parents: it is more than anything else the devotion of Vergil's Aeneas to his father Anchises that earns him the epithet *pius*. But *pietas* was a two-way street: parents (both fathers and mothers) had a duty to their children, too, and Turia and her sister displayed *pietas* not only to their parents but to other family members. They brought up deserving female relatives and provided them with appropriate dowries; Turia's husband is careful to mention, however, that he and his brother-in-law actually substituted their own funds so that the sisters' patrimony would not be diminished (*Laudatio* col. 1.44–9).

Married women of the elite usually had their own property, unless they were still under their father's legal power (*potestas*) or had come under their husband's authority (*manus*) as had Turia's sister. Roman law required that a wife's property be kept separate from her husband's, except for her dowry, which belonged to the husband during marriage but which she could reclaim upon divorce (Evans Grubbs 2002: 95–102; Treggiari 1991a: 323–96). Turia and her husband, however, seem to have administered their property jointly:

> We preserved all your patrimony received from your parents with shared diligence; for you had no concern for acquiring what you handed over completely to me. We divided our duties so that I bore the guardianship of your fortune, and you sustained the care of mine. (*Laudatio* col. 1.37–9)

The couple's trust in each other's financial management illustrates the Roman ideal of marital *concordia* (see Dixon 1991; Treggiari 1991a: 249–53):

> Why should I recall your domestic qualities – your chastity, obedience, graciousness, amiability, zeal in wool-working, piety without superstition, your unostentatious dress, your modest adornment? Why should I speak of your affection, your duty to family (*pietas familiae*), since you devoted yourself just as much to my mother as to your own parents and you cultivated the same tranquility with her as with them – and the other innumerable qualities which you had in common with all matrons who enjoy a worthy reputation? (*Laudatio* col. 1.30–4)

These are indeed the qualities so often lauded on other (much shorter) epitaphs of Roman women – the canonical virtues of a wife (Treggiari 1991a: 229–53). Where Turia differed, her husband continues, was in the extraordinary courage and resourcefulness she displayed during the civil wars. She helped her husband, who had supported Julius Caesar's rival Pompey, by surreptitiously sending him her own money and jewelry while he was in exile after Caesar's defeat of Pompey at Pharsalus in 48 BCE. She also physically defended his house in Rome from men sent by the former owner, Milo. Through her entreaties, he was able to obtain clemency from Caesar, only to be proscribed by the triumvirs after Caesar's death. Again, her efforts led to a pardon from Octavian (the future Augustus), but she endured humiliation and even physical abuse at the hands of the triumvir Lepidus when she showed him Octavian's edict recalling her husband, "prostrate on the ground at his feet, you not only were not raised up, but you were dragged and seized like a slave, your body filled with bruises" (*Laudatio* col. 2.14–15).

"Marriages of so long a duration are rare, ended by death, not cut short by divorce: for ours happened to endure into its forty-first year without offense" (*Laudatio* col. 1.27). This was indeed a long-lasting union. Although the divorce rate in Augustan Rome was not as high as in the United States today, divorce was a fact of life for upper-class Romans (not enough is known about the marriages of the lower classes, but lack of economic resources may have discouraged divorce, especially by women).

In the early empire divorce was, like modern "no fault" divorce, easy and accessible for both men and women (Treggiari 1991b). As even in the most successful marriages, the possibility of divorce arose between Turia and her husband. For the couple had never been able to have children, and so had not fulfilled the primary purpose of Roman marriage: the procreation of legitimate heirs. During the early years of their marriage, the stress of the civil wars and the separation it entailed had made having children difficult. By the time peace came, Turia was probably well into her thirties, and her chances of conceiving greatly diminished:

> Distrusting your fertility and grieving about my childlessness, afraid that by being married to you I was giving up hope of having children and would be unhappy for that reason, you spoke openly about divorce. You said that you would hand over our empty home to another woman's fertility, with no other intention except that, with our well-known marital harmony (*concordia*), you yourself would seek out and procure for me a worthy and suitable marriage match, and you would promise to consider my future children as held in common with you and as if they were yours. Nor would you make a separation of our property, which up to then had been held by us in common, but it would continue to be under my authority and, if I wished, under your stewardship. You would have nothing divided, nothing separated, and you would thereafter exhibit to me the services and sense of duty (*pietas*) of a sister and a mother-in-law. I must confess that I became so inflamed, I almost went out of my mind; I was so horrified at your efforts that I scarcely regained control. For the possibility of a divorce between us to be considered before the law had been spoken by fate – that you were able to conceive in your mind some situation whereby you would cease to be my wife while I was still alive, when you had remained most faithful to me when I was an exile almost from life! What desire or need of having children would be so important to me, that I would for that reason cast off my faithfulness (*fides*) and exchange sure things for unsure? – But why should I say more? You remained my wife with me; for I was not able to yield to you without my own dishonor and our mutual unhappiness. (*Laudatio* col. 2. 31–47)

Readers are often struck by the unusual offer Turia made – not simply offering an amicable divorce (sterility had from earliest times been considered an appropriate motive for divorce), but proposing to stay on in the household as a "sister" or mother-in-law! Presumably the new wife would be considerably younger (as was Pliny's wife Calpurnia, see below), and Turia's role would be one of older, experienced woman to young teenage bride. Even more extraordinary, however, is that her husband saw fit not only to mention her offer in the *laudatio*, but to inscribe it permanently on stone for all to read, along with his shocked reaction. There is more to this than memorializing a very private scene from a marriage: evidently the narrator thought that describing this event enhanced not only Turia's reputation, but his own. To understand the full import of his words we must look at the legal and social policies of the new emperor Augustus.

In 18 BCE Augustus enacted the *lex Julia de maritandis ordinibus* ("Julian law on the marrying of the social orders"), mandating marriage and child-bearing for men between the ages of 25 and 60 and women between 20 and 50. Those who were not married could not receive inheritances or legacies except from relatives within six degrees of kinship (a group that included parents, grandparents, great-grandparents, children, grandchildren, great-grandchildren; uncles, aunts, great-uncles and great-aunts, cousins and second cousins). Married couples who did not have children were not allowed to leave more than ten percent of their property to each other by will. Those who did have children received certain privileges: men were given preferment in government office, and freeborn women who had borne at least three children (and freedwomen who had borne four) were released from the need for a *tutor mulierum*, a "guardian" whose authorization was normally required when a woman wished to undertake certain legal or financial transactions (Evans Grubbs 2002: 23–43). The law also banned marriage between senators (and their children and grandchildren) and former slaves. Another law, also probably of 18 BCE, the *lex Julia de adulteriis* ("Julian law on adulteries") made adultery (defined as extramarital sexual relations by or with a married woman) a public crime, punishable by relegation and loss of property. Subsequent legislation of 9 CE (the *lex Papia Poppaea*) tightened up loopholes in the marriage law and at the same time mitigated some of its provisions (Evans Grubbs 2002: 83–7; Parkin 2001; Treggiari 1991a: 60–80).

These laws applied to all Roman citizens, but were primarily directed at the senatorial and equestrian elite, who were most likely to give and receive legacies from non-kin (Hopkins 1983d: 235–47; Wallace-Hadrill 1981). Augustus believed that the upper classes were not doing their duty by marrying and procreating legitimate children, and that families were not adequately policing the sexual behavior of their women. His legislation made a political statement stressing the emperor's dedication to "family values" and his right to regulate the most private aspects of his people's lives. Not surprisingly, there were protests from the elite (Suet. *Aug.* 34; Dio 54.16.1–2).

We do not know if Turia and her husband were directly affected by the Augustan marriage law. In 18 BCE, they may have been beyond the age limits of the law and so exempted from its provisions (Horsfall 1983: 93–4; Parkin 2001). In any case, Turia's distress over her inability to bear children would only have been exacerbated by Augustus' promotion of marital fertility. Hence her husband's emphatic insistence that his wife really did want children, and that she was willing to divorce him so that he at least could achieve that goal. But by inscribing for posterity (and for Augustus) his own passionate refusal to give up the woman he loved in order to fulfill the imperial mandate, he was explicitly privileging the marital bond over a Roman male's duty to produce heirs to his name and property. He, too, could show *fides* and *pietas*.

2 A Roman Gentleman: Pliny the Younger

One of our best sources for family life among the Italian elite in the early empire is the correspondence of Pliny the Younger, a wealthy, cultured upper-class Roman from the north Italian town of Comum (modern Como), who lived from about 61 to about 112 CE. Pliny began a legal career at the age of 18, and embarked upon the senatorial career track (*cursus honorum*), eventually attaining the position of suffect consul late in the year 100. He served under both the hated emperor Domitian and his successor, the beloved Trajan.

Pliny wrote many letters to friends, family, and political acquaintances, and had nine books of his private correspondence (comprising 247 letters) published during his lifetime. This means that the letters were not only chosen with a view to the impression they would make on readers, but were also subject to revision – or even rewriting – after they were first sent (Hoffer 1999: 9–10). The letters, then, are not exclusively private documents, but are intended to project a persona of Pliny as a cultivated, humane gentleman with all the proper feelings. Nevertheless, they provide valuable evidence for the life and ideals of elite Romans of the early empire – their interest in marriage as a union of compatible people who would promote family interests and pass down the family name and wealth, their feelings towards wives and children, and their role models (Bradley 1993: 247–50; A. E. Hanson 1999a).

Here we will look at Pliny's own family experiences, which were not unrepresentative of his class and time. He was born Publius Caecilius Secundus, the son of a local magistrate of Comum. His father died when Pliny was still a child, so he had a *tutor impuberum*, a guardian appointed for males under 14 and females under 12 who had no living *paterfamilias* (male head of household, a father or paternal grandfather). It was not at all unusual for a Roman to lose his (or her) father before puberty, and consequently *tutores* played an important role in Roman society (Saller 1994: 181–203). A *tutor* was not a parent-substitute as guardians are today; he did not live with his ward (*pupillus/pupilla*) but rather was a watchdog of the ward's financial and legal interests. Pliny was brought up by his mother, of whom he speaks fondly in the letters. On the other hand, he says nothing whatever about his father; perhaps there is a note of wistfulness in a letter to a certain young man, Genialis, who had been reading Pliny's speeches with his father:

> Lucky you, who happened to have both the best and most closely related role model (*exemplar*)! Indeed the man you have as most suitable to be imitated is the one whom nature wished you most to resemble. (*Ep.* 8.13)

Not that Pliny himself lacked for role models: his *tutor* was the war hero Verginius Rufus, who had twice turned down the chance to be emperor during the civil wars of 68–9. Verginius continued to serve as political mentor to Pliny long after he reached adulthood (*Ep.* 2.1; 6.10; 9.19). Perhaps more influential, however, was Pliny's maternal uncle, Gaius Plinius Secundus (Pliny the Elder), the famous scholar and commander of the imperial fleet at Misenum on the Bay of Naples, who died in 79 CE while rescuing those in the path of the erupting Mt. Vesuvius. In his will, the elder Pliny made his nephew heir on condition that he take his name; Publius Caecilius Secundus then became Gaius Plinius Caecilius Secundus. This practice, though known today as "testamentary adoption," was not adoption in the Roman legal sense, though it had a similar purpose: to secure an heir to whom the testator's family name (*nomen*) and property could be passed on (Corbier 1991a; Gardner 1998: 128–30). The elder Pliny can be considered a sort of "father-substitute" for his nephew; he was living with his sister and her son at the time of his death, and Pliny speaks of him with admiration (*Ep.* 3.5; 5.8; 6.16).

Pliny's mother may have died not long after her brother; there are no letters to her, and Pliny mentions among his possessions *praedia materna*, property inherited from his mother (*Ep.* 2.15). Like most Roman aristocrats, Pliny had substantial holdings in different parts of Italy, with at least six villas in all, including several at Comum as well as in Umbria, a house on the Esquiline in Rome and a villa outside Rome near Ostia (Duncan-Jones 1982: 22–4).

Pliny married at least twice; some scholars posit three wives, though the letters mention only two (Hoffer 1999: 232–3). Only the last one, Calpurnia, receives letters; Pliny married her sometime after his previous wife's death in 97 CE. Even after his remarriage, he remained on excellent terms with his former mother-in-law, Pompeia Celerina, who was very rich and encouraged Pliny to treat her house and wealth as his own (*Ep.* 3.19). Indeed, he joked that her slaves gave him better service than his did (*Ep.* 1.4).

Like Pliny, Calpurnia was from Comum. Both her parents were dead, so she was raised by her paternal grandfather (who, as the oldest male ascendant, was her *paterfamilias*) and her father's sister, Calpurnia Hispulla. The families evidently had known each other a long time; Pliny says that Hispulla, whom he calls a "model of family devotion" (*pietatis exemplum*) had revered his own mother as a daughter would. Moreover, Hispulla apparently took an active role in arranging the marriage; as Pliny says, "we vie with each other in thanking you: I because you gave her to me, she because you gave me to her, as if you chose us for each other" (*Ep.* 4.20). Pliny's relationship with his grandfather-in-law was less relaxed than with Hispulla; Calpurnius seems to have been a rather irascible old man, and the letters to him have a nervous and apologetic tone.

Generally, women married for the first time around 20 and men around 30 (Saller 1994: 25–41; Treggiari 1991a: 398–403). Among the senatorial elite, both sexes tended to marry about five years earlier; we might recall that the Augustan marriage laws expected men to be married by 25 and women by 20. Thus a husband in a Roman marriage was usually about ten years older than his wife. In Pliny's case, the discrepancy was much greater, since he had been married before: he was around 40, whereas Calpurnia was about 15. This huge difference in age must have affected the dynamic of their marriage significantly. Indeed, Pliny's letters to and about Calpurnia evince a mixture of romantic love and avuncular solicitude.

We have three letters written by Pliny to Calpurnia when he was in Rome on business (as a public figure and practicing lawyer, he had to spend a lot of time in the city) and she was in Campania, recovering her health. They are noteworthy for their avowals of romantic passion, previously found in Latin literature only in elegiac poetry for real or imagined mistresses. It has been said that these letters "blend together, for the first time in European literature, the role of husband and lover" (Sherwin-White 1966: 407).

> Never have I complained more about my preoccupation with affairs, which did not allow me to escort you to Campania for health reasons or to follow your footsteps.... Indeed, I would long for you with concern even if you were strong, for to hear nothing for a while about a person one most ardently loves brings distress and anxiety.... I fear everything, I imagine everything, and as is the nature of those who fear, I most conjure up what I most dread. All the more intemperately do I beg you to give thought to my fears with one or even two letters every day. For I will be more secure while I am reading, and as soon as I have read, I will start to fear again. Farewell. (*Ep.* 6.4)

This highly stylized plea had its desired effect, for soon after Pliny responds to Calpurnia's letter (which, unfortunately, we do not have):

> You write that you are strongly affected by my absence and that you have this one comfort, that you can hold my little books instead of me and often even place them in my stead. It is pleasing that you miss us [sic; Pliny uses the authorial "we"], pleasing that you find relief in these remedies; I in turn read your letters repeatedly and take them again and again into my hands as if they were new. But all the more am I inflamed with longing for you: for if someone's letters are so pleasant, how much sweeter are her conversations! But write as often as possible, although this causes torture as well as delight. Farewell. (*Ep.* 6.7)

Pliny even plays the *exclusus amator*, the lover shut out by his mistress, who moons around outside her door:

> It is incredible how much I long for you. Love first of all is the reason, and then also the fact that we are not accustomed to be apart. Thus I keep awake a large part of the night imagining you; thus it is that in the daytime, during those times when I used to call upon you, my feet themselves lead me (as it is most aptly put) to your chamber, and finally I depart, sick and saddened, like one shut out upon an empty threshold.... (*Ep.* 7.6)

It is difficult to get a sense of the young woman to whom these letters were addressed. Apparently Calpurnia was intellectually inclined: in addition to holding Pliny's books when she couldn't hold him, she also (according to Pliny's letter to Hispulla, cited above) sang poems he had written and set them to music, took an anxious interest in the outcome of his law cases, and even hid discreetly behind a curtain when he gave public recitals (*Ep.* 4.19). She was not the robust type; it is hard to imagine her running the sort of risks Turia had in shielding her husband from his enemies. But both Calpurnia and Turia faced the same difficulty: inability to bear children. We learn of this from a remarkable pair of letters, the first to Calpurnia's grandfather, Calpurnius Fabatus, the second to her aunt Hispulla:

> [to Fabatus] The more eager you are to see great-grandchildren from us, the sadder you will be to hear that your granddaughter has had a miscarriage. Since, in her girlish way, she did not know she was pregnant, she disregarded certain things that pregnant women ought to be careful about and did things she ought to have disregarded. She has paid for this error with a great lesson, as she was led to the brink of death. Thus, though you have to accept reluctantly that your old age has been deprived of, so to speak, a posterity already underway, you ought also to thank the gods that while they denied you great-grandchildren for the time being, they preserved your granddaughter... For you do not wish for great-grandchildren more ardently than I wish for children... May they only be born and change this sorrow of ours to joy. Farewell. (*Ep.* 8.10)
>
> [to Hispulla] Since I consider that your feeling toward your brother's daughter is even more tender than a mother's indulgence, I know I should announce to you first the final outcome, so that gladness, coming first, will not leave room for uneasiness.... Now she is joyful, now, already restored to herself and to me, she begins to revive and to ascertain the crisis through which she passed. All the same, she was in the greatest danger (it can now be safely said). It was not her fault, but to a certain extent the fault of her youth. Thus her miscarriage and the sad proof of a pregnancy she did not know about. So although your longing for the brother you lost was not granted comfort by a nephew or niece, remember that this has been deferred rather than denied, since she is safe and it

can still be hoped for. At the same time, explain to your father this misfortune, which is more readily excused by women. Farewell. (*Ep.* 8.11)

Pliny published these two accounts of his wife's miscarriage in a book of letters mostly concerned with elite gossip and literary matters. As with the funeral oration by Turia's husband, subsequently carved in stone, the modern reader is taken aback by the willingness of a Roman husband to make public his wife's (and his) fertility problems. The explanation must lie in the pressures placed upon men and women of the Roman elite to reproduce themselves, both in the service of the state and for the perpetuation of family lines and properties. In Pliny's case, the pressure seems to have come primarily from his grandfather-in-law. A very old man whose own son was dead and whose daughter was childless, Calpurnius was anxious to see an heir from his granddaughter before he died. As it happened, Pliny did not need to worry about the inheritance penalties that childlessness brought under the Augustan law, for Trajan had granted him the *ius liberorum*, the "right of children" which gave the recipient the same rights as a person with three children (Evans Grubbs 2002: 37–9). In thanking the emperor for the grant, Pliny declared that with Trajan on the throne, "all the more do I desire children, whom I wished to have even in that very sad time [the reign of Domitian], as you can well believe from my two marriages" (*Ep.* 10.2).

Pliny was right to emphasize Calpurnia's narrow escape from death. Elsewhere, he refers to the tragic deaths of two daughters of Helvidius Priscus, who both died giving birth to girls, "it seems so sad to me that well-born girls in the flower of their youth were destroyed by their fertility" (*Ep.* 4.21). Ironically, Augustus' legislation, which required that women be married by age 20, may have increased the risk of miscarriage and death in childbirth from teen pregnancies. It is often assumed that the Roman elite practiced some sort of family limitation, perhaps through abortion (though this was dangerous for the mother) or contraception (though this was often unreliable) (Dixon 1992: 119–22; Frier 1999: 94–100; Hoffer 1999: 228–33). There were reasons for even the wealthier classes to want to limit the number of children, in particular, to avoid fragmentation of family properties; the Romans did not have primogeniture, and all legitimate children, male and female, would inherit from their father. Pliny himself, when explaining why he established an alimentary scheme at Comum to support local children (on the model of Trajan's *alimenta*, meant to encourage Italian families to have children; see B. Rawson 2001), refers to the "tedium and hard work of rearing" (*Ep.* 1.8). But his letters also provide plenty of evidence for the Romans' desire for offspring and their sorrow at the loss of children, particularly those who had passed early childhood and were approaching adulthood (*Ep.* 2.7; 4.2 and 7; 5.16).

Pliny and Calpurnia do not appear to have ever had children. In about 110 CE, Pliny was appointed by Trajan to go out to the province of Bithynia and Pontus (northern Turkey) as governor, where among the problems he encountered were recalcitrant members of a new religious cult, Christianity (*Ep.* 10.95–6, with Sherwin-White 1966: 772–87). Calpurnia went with him; the last letter we have of Pliny, sent from Bithynia, informs Trajan that he has allowed Calpurnia to use the imperial post to return to Italy upon her grandfather's death in order to be with her aunt [*Ep.* 10.120]. Pliny himself probably died around 112 while still in Bithynia.

3 Faith over Family: Vibia Perpetua

About a century after Pliny published his correspondence, a young woman in Roman North Africa wrote down a quite different account of herself and her family. Vibia Perpetua was a Roman citizen and member of the local elite of Thuburbo Minus (a town not far from Carthage), bilingual in Latin and Greek (and probably Punic too), and literate – not, of course, the product of the sort of rhetorical and literary training that Pliny had enjoyed, but unusually well-educated for a woman of her time. But any resemblance between the two stops there. For whereas Pliny had punished Christians as criminals, Perpetua actually converted to that disreputable and illegal religion.

Perpetua was one of a group of catechumens (converts who were not yet baptized) arrested in 203 and executed in the arena at Carthage. The story of their martyrdom, with particular attention to the deaths of Perpetua and of another young woman, the slave Felicitas, was written down by a member of the local Christian community who had witnessed the events. The *Passion of Perpetua and Felicitas* is particularly compelling, however, because its editor also included what has been called Perpetua's "prison diary," her own account of her confinement and trial before the governor. This is one of a tiny number of writings by a woman to survive from the Roman period, and is unique for the direct and intimate style in which Perpetua narrates her experiences. The focus of her account is firmly on her own family relationships, especially her conflicts with her pagan father, who was distraught over his daughter's refusal to save her life and her family's reputation by denying her new-found faith. Even Perpetua's visions – an important part of her account – involve another family member, her long-dead younger brother (Bremmer 2002: 88–93; Bradley 2003).

The editor of the *Passion of Perpetua* explicitly tells us that Perpetua was "honorably born, well-educated, properly married" (*honeste nata, liberaliter instituta, matronaliter nupta*), that she was about 22 years old, had a father and mother and two (living) brothers, one of whom was also a catechumen (though not arrested with her), and an infant son "at the breast" (*P. Perp.* 2). Her status and educational level are evident from the story she tells; her nomenclature indicates that she was a Roman citizen, and her family was probably of curial (municipal elite) status. Her father had a position to maintain in the community – a position severely jeopardized, indeed ruined, by his daughter's arrest and execution as a Christian. Perpetua's marital status is much less clear: we hear nothing about a husband apart from the enigmatic phrase *matronaliter nupta* (which presumably signifies legitimate marriage, *iustum matrimonium*, though *matronaliter* is not a term found in the legal sources). If she had been widowed, one would expect the editor of her account to mention this; on the other hand, if she were divorced, he might well prefer to leave this fact unmentioned, given Christian disapproval of divorce (Evans Grubbs 1995: 242–53). More puzzling – and revealing – is the fact that Perpetua herself never mentions her husband, either in relation to herself or her baby, a point so odd to a Roman reader that the author of the fourth-century *Acta* "normalizes" Perpetua's story by stating that her husband was at the trial (B. D. Shaw 1993: 33–6). Unlike her father and her brother, he does not visit her in prison or appear at her trial. He may have abandoned her after her arrest and subsequent notoriety as a Christian.

It is odd also that neither her husband nor his family are interested in the baby; under Roman law, children conceived in a legitimate marriage belonged to the father (or to his *paterfamilias*, if the father had died). Although Perpetua kept her baby with her until he was weaned (as he was, of necessity, shortly before her execution), we would still expect the baby's paternal relatives to claim him after her death. Yet it appears that Perpetua's father took the baby after her trial and that he was reared by her family. Perhaps the stigma of a condemned Christian wife and mother was too much for the (ex?)husband and his kin, and they did not want responsibility for the child. (Similarly, another member of the Christian community took the newborn infant of the slave Felicitas, who had given birth in prison; legally, it belonged to Felicitas' owner, who evidently preferred not to assert his or her rights.) Perpetua several times refers to her anxiety about nursing her baby, whom she was allowed to have with her for part of her time in prison. It is significant that she *does* breast-feed him; the use of wet-nurses, though criticized by ancient moralists, was evidently quite common, particularly among the elite but also at lower levels of society (Bradley 1991: 13–36; Dixon 1988: 120–9). The baby was probably at least a year old when Perpetua was arrested, since he was apparently weaned without difficulty when she at last had to give him up; he could have been two or older, and the father long gone.

Perpetua's own account begins with a confrontation with her father, one of four such encounters she records:

> When we were still with the official attendants [in prison] and my father wanted to overturn me with words and persisted in casting me down on account of his love for me, I said, "Father, do you see, for example, this vase lying here, or water pitcher, or whatever?"
> And he said, "I see it."
> And I said to him, "It can't be called by any other name than what it is, can it?"
> And he said, "No."
> "So I also cannot call myself anything other than what I am, a Christian." Then my father, moved by this word ["Christian"], threw himself toward me in order to pluck out my eyes, but he only annoyed me and he left defeated, along with the devil's arguments.
> Then for a few days, because I was free from my father, I gave thanks to the Lord and was refreshed by his absence. (*P. Perp.* 3)

She insists on seeing her father as an adversary; repeatedly she describes him as trying to "cast me down" with diabolical (because tempting?) arguments. Later she is visited by her mother and brother, to whom she entrusts her child. "And so I was pining away because I saw that they were pining away because of me." Both appear to be Christian sympathizers; elsewhere Perpetua says that her father alone of all her family did not rejoice at her impending martyrdom – this does not mean that they were glad she was going to die, but that, like all Christians, they believed that martyrdom was a great privilege and ensured eternal life for the martyr. When she obtains the right to have her baby with her in prison, "immediately I gained strength and was relieved from my distress and anxiety for my baby, and suddenly the prison became for me a governor's mansion, so that I preferred to be there rather than anywhere else."

> After a few days a rumor went the rounds that we would be heard [in court]. Moreover, my father also came up from the city, consumed with weariness, and he approached me in order to cast me down, saying, "Have pity, daughter, on my gray hairs, have pity on your father, if I deserve to be called father by you; if I brought you forth with these hands to the flower of your youth, if I put you first before all your brothers: don't hand me over to the dishonor of men. Consider your brothers, consider your mother and your aunt, consider your own son who will not be able to live without you. Put down your pride, don't destroy all of us. For no one of us will be able speak freely, if you have suffered anything."
> He was saying these things like a father out of affectionate duty (*pietas*), kissing my hands and throwing himself at my feet; and weeping, he no longer called me daughter but lady (*domina*). And I grieved for the misfortune of my father, because he alone from my whole family would not rejoice about my suffering (*passio*). And I comforted him, saying, "It will happen on the [prisoners'] platform as God wants. For know that we have not been put in our own power, but in God's." And he departed from me very saddened. (*P. Perp.* 5)

When the Christians went on trial before the acting governor, Hilarianus (on whom see Rives 1996), Perpetua's father again appears:

> We went up onto the platform. The others, when asked, confessed [that they were Christians]. Then it happened also to me. And my father appeared right there with my son, and he dragged me from the step, saying, "Worship the gods. Have pity on your baby!"
> And Hilarianus the governor... said, "Spare your father's gray hairs, spare your infant boy. Make a sacrifice for the safety of the emperors."
> And I replied, "I will not do it."
> And Hilarianus said, "Are you a Christian?"
> And I replied, "I am a Christian."
> And when my father stood up in order to cast me down, he was ordered by Hilarianus to be thrown to the ground and he was struck with a rod. And my father's misfortune grieved me as if I had been struck; I grieved so for his wretched old age.
> Then (Hilarianus) announced sentence on us all and condemned us to the beasts, and we went down joyfully to prison. Then because my baby had become accustomed to being breast-fed and to remaining in prison with me, immediately I sent the deacon Pomponius to my father, asking for my baby. But my father refused to give him over. And just as God wanted, he did not long for my breasts anymore nor were they inflamed, so that I was not tormented by anxiety for my baby or pain in my breasts. (*P. Perp.* 6)

Presenting the defendant's young child in court in a bid for sympathy was a centuries-old practice. In this case, however, it is not the judge who needs convincing, but the accused herself, who remains unmoved. Her father's obstreperousness in court earns him a humiliating punishment, beating with a rod – a penalty from which those of his class would normally have been immune (the Vibii were presumably *honestiores* ["more honorable," on which see Garnsey 1970]). Perpetua's father makes one more appearance, as the day of the spectacle in which she will be killed draws near:

> My father came to me, consumed with weariness, and he began to pluck out his beard and to throw it on the ground, and to lie prostrate on his face and to cast reproach on his years, and to say such words as would move all creation. And I grieved for his unhappy old age. (*P. Perp.* 9)

But even as Perpetua distances herself from her father and her baby, forsaking the family responsibilities of this world for reward in the next, she creates for herself another family – in which she plays the same roles of mother and daughter – through a series of self-induced dreams (Salisbury 1997: 92–115; Bremmer 2002: 95–119; Bradley 2003). In her first dream, after her father's first visit and when she has been allowed to have her baby with her, Perpetua climbs a long ladder, avoiding weapons and implements of torture, and treading on the head of a diabolical serpent on her way to the top. There she finds a gray-haired man, a shepherd milking his sheep, "and he raised his head and looked at me and said to me, 'Welcome, child' (*teknon*, the Greek word). And he called to me and gave me some of the cheese which he was milking...". It is her father, transformed into a Christ-figure, who nurtures her as she nurtured her child in prison. Her second dream, after her trial and final separation from her baby, is even more revealing. Suddenly, in prayer, she speaks the name of her long-dead brother, who had died at age seven from a cancer on his face: "I see Dinocrates, coming out of a shadowy place where there were many others, and he was really burning hot and thirsty, with dirty clothing and a pale coloring, and there was on his face the wound which he had when he died." In her vision, Dinocrates was trying in vain to drink from a pool full of water, whose rim he could not reach. "And I awoke, and I knew that my brother was afflicted. But I had faith that I would be of help to him in his affliction" (*P. Perp.* 7). She prays, and receives a follow-up vision:

> I saw that place which I had seen before, and Dinocrates, with a clean body, well-dressed, taking refreshment, and where there had been a wound I saw a scar. And I saw that pool, which I had seen before, with its rim lowered down to the boy's navel (*umbilicus*), and he was drawing water from it without ceasing. And above the rim was a golden dish full of water. And Dinocrates began to drink from it, but the dish did not lessen. And, satiated, he started to play in the water as babies (*infantes*) do, rejoicing. And I woke up, and I understood that he had been removed from his punishment. (*P. Perp.* 8)

Perpetua had to give up the baby to whom she had given life, and could no longer nurse him; but by her prayers, she has given new life to her little brother, and has assuaged his thirst. As she removes herself from her family roles in this world, she re-creates them in the next (see Salisbury 1997: 105). But her fourth and final vision, on the eve of her martyrdom, is quite different: she *becomes a man* in order to do combat against "the Egyptian" (Satan). Knowing that she is about to die in the most public, "masculine" way possible (as a wild-beast fighter), Perpetua sheds all her private, "feminine" roles, whether real or dreamt.

On March 7, Perpetua and her companions went gladly to their deaths in the arena, as a special spectacle celebrating the birthday of the emperor's son Geta. Perpetua and the slave Felicitas were exposed to an enraged cow (intended to be humorously appropriate to their female sex). Perpetua did not die from the encounter; she had to be executed afterwards by the sword – a fitting end for one of her status.

"If anyone comes to me and does not hate his own father and mother and wife and children and brothers and sisters, and even his own life, he is not able to be my disciple" (Lk 14:26, cf. Mk 10:29). The full impact of Jesus' words is made clear by Perpetua's account: conversion to Christianity entailed rejection of the world, including, especially, one's own family. Perpetua's father did not exaggerate when he said that after her death in the arena, no one of her relatives would be able to speak freely; they would all be under suspicion, whether or not they were Christians too. In twenty-first-century America, when political rhetoric often associates religion (primarily Christianity) with "family values," it is salutary to remember that early Christianity was far from "pro-family." Eventually, when the persecutions ended (110 years after Perpetua's death) and Roman emperors took up Christianity, the stark contrast between dedication to God and devotion to family was softened (Arjava 1996; Nathan 2000). The family legislation of the first Christian emperor, Constantine, for the most part followed the policies set by his predecessors, with two major changes: unilateral divorce became harder to obtain (especially for women) and the Augustan penalties on the unmarried were abolished. The first was probably prompted at least in part by Christian influence; the second was more likely a response to senatorial unhappiness with Augustus' laws than to the Christian admiration for celibacy (Evans Grubbs 1995). Ascetic renunciation replaced martyrdom as the manifestation of Christian rejection of the world, and monasticism offered an alternative to traditional family structures. But *patria potestas* continued to be a living legal and social concept in late antiquity (Arjava 1998), while marriage practices and parent–child relations continued along traditional lines up to the end of antiquity. Perpetua's experience reminds us how radical and inimical to the Roman concept of family Christianity could be.

4 Conclusion

The three accounts discussed here span more than two centuries and have come down to us in different ways: a funerary epitaph engraved on stone; a collection of letters published by a well-known literary figure during his lifetime and known to us via a (now lost) sixth-century manuscript (Radice 1969: xxvi); and a prison narrative preserved by the Christian community of Carthage, where it was read out in church each year on the anniversary of the author's death (and in the process reinterpreted by late antique church authorities) (B. D. Shaw 1993; Salisbury 1997: 166–79). Though the circumstances of their composition and preservation differ significantly, all three narratives share a common trait: despite their (to us) highly personal nature, all were consciously composed with an audience in mind, and all are in a sense *apologiae*, explanations of the authors' motivations and actions. The anonymous husband who commemorated his wife did so in a speech given at her funeral, which he then memorialized permanently for all to see; Pliny clearly chose for dissemination those letters which he believed revealed him in an understandable and attractive light; and Perpetua knew that her status as a martyr gave her account (and especially her visions) great authority in the eyes of other Christians, present and future. Intimate though these documents are, they are not "private" in the sense that they were meant only for the author and perhaps a few close companions. They tell us only what their authors want us to know. But that does not detract from their value as historical evidence, for these deliberately composed accounts tell us much about the values of the individual and his or her society, and demonstrate how social, religious, and political ideals could come into conflict with the desires and needs of real men and women. Pliny and Turia's husband feel compelled to tell the world (and the emperor) that they really do want children, but that they love and esteem their wives as much as if not more than any potential offspring. Perpetua shows her fellow Christians that she is willing to sacrifice her own and her family's well-being and happiness for her faith, but she also lets them know how painful and traumatic that sacrifice is.

The social and political pressures placed on Romans like Pliny, Perpetua, and Turia's husband were quite different from those faced by Americans and Europeans today: imperial demands that citizens marry and produce children, and the harsh repression of a non-conformist religious cult by means of degrading public execution. But however unfamiliar the circumstances in which they wrote may seem to us, the emotions they (intentionally) reveal are instantly recognizable: grief at the death of a beloved long-time partner; awkwardness in explaining a wife's miscarriage to her family; conflict between a determined daughter and an elderly father devastated at the loss of his favorite child in the most horrible way imaginable. It is through these narratives of family relationships, very private but at the same time very public, that we come closest to the Romans as human beings.

CHAPTER SEVENTEEN

Sexuality in the Roman Empire

Amy Richlin

The Roman Empire: vast in space, long in time. How can we imagine something as elusive as sexuality over that wide expanse? Since the 1970s, classical scholars have been thinking about sexuality in the ancient Mediterranean, but most have focused on Greeks from Athens and Romans from Rome. Thanks to the interest taken in the subject by Michel Foucault in his last work, discussion has often revolved around questions Foucault found important, especially pederasty and sexual identity (Foucault 1988; for overviews, see Edwards 1993; Larmour et al. 1998; Skinner 1996). But in order to get an idea of sexuality as a whole in the Roman Empire as a whole, we need to dolly back.

Let me propose a thought experiment: the Kinsey II Expedition to the Roman Empire. Afire with the possibilities opened up by the invention of a reliable time machine, Kinsey II and his crew of lab-coated assistants have grabbed their clipboards and questionnaires and are about to set out on an immense project. They will fan out to all parts of the Roman Empire, starting in the year 14 CE and returning to antiquity at 70-year intervals: 84, 154, 224, 294, 364, 434. Much as they wish they could carry on to the fall of Byzantium, they have decided to take the end of the empire in the West as a stopping point.

They have devised a simple questionnaire: 20 questions. Imagine their findings on an enormous grid, with the 20 questions down the left-hand margin, and across the page the responses from people from all walks of life, in all parts of the empire; seven groups per question, each a long lifetime apart, each subdivided per social group and per location. This is a period of history in which many people were slaves, and a large proportion of the population lived in the country, and, as always, half the people (selective infanticide aside) were female; the Kinsey II group is careful to make selections for interviewees proportionate to the current demographics (on selective infanticide, see Boswell 1988: 40–3, with bibliography). Moreover, they have with them another new invention, a simultaneous translator that allows them to talk to people in any of the hundred languages spoken in the empire, from the

Armenians and Babylonians in the east to the Spanish tribes in the far west, from the desert nomads in the south to the Celts and Germans in the far north, so they go to all these places and ask their questions. Through tact and luck they manage to avoid being crucified or eaten or stoned to death; thanks to antibiotics and rubber gloves they avoid malaria and various plagues. The crew for Pompeii goes in six years early, thus avoiding being blown up with Vesuvius. They complete their collection of data. Their statistical model allows for the fact that people lie about sex.

Now imagine that over this enormous grid we could put a clear plastic overlay showing where we do have statements from people about sexuality, with every one colored in. We would see huge clear spaces on the overlay: where Kinsey II spoke with women, we would have almost nothing; where they spoke with slaves, even with workers of any kind, almost nothing; where they journeyed into the country, nothing; where they spoke languages other than Latin, Greek, Hebrew, Aramaic, and a little Egyptian, nothing; whole huge areas of the empire are just clear plastic on our chart, and long stretches of time in the third century CE. But not to worry, because beneath the overlay would be all the words painstakingly collected by Kinsey II, which cover all times and all places and all people equally.

In fact, of course, all we have is the overlay sheet, and what Kinsey II might write is wholly invisible to us. We can look for what the people we do have say about the people we have no access to, but since we hardly expect them to give an accurate account of themselves, we have low expectations of the truth value in what they say about others. We might still make up some kind of narrative out of it.

To put this narrative in perspective, a few things about Kinsey I – Alfred C. Kinsey, Professor of Zoology at Indiana University. In *Sexual Behavior in the Human Male* (Kinsey et al. 1948), Kinsey says that: 12,000 people were interviewed for the report, but he hoped to interview 88,000 more (dedication); his questionnaire included 521 items, though an interview was likely to deal with only 300 or so of these (63); he undertook his study of human sexual behavior because, "as a taxonomist, [he] was struck with the inadequacy of the samples on which such studies were being based" (9). He had previously worked with insects, where, he says, "we had had 150,000 individuals available for the study of a single species" (9).

His Figure 1, a map of the United States (Kinsey et al. 1948: 5), shows "Sources of histories"; there is a pronounced skew towards the northeast, with many of the western states having only 50 interviews apiece. (If we mapped what we have from the Roman Empire, many of its provinces would have zero.) He used a twelve-way breakdown to aim for thorough coverage of social groups (63–82), including "Rural-Urban Background" (79), which is further broken down into five subgroups. One list of the kinds of persons who were interviewed includes: "Bootleggers, **Clergymen**, Clerks, **College professors**, Farmers, Female prostitutes, Gamblers, Housewives, **Lawyers**, Male prostitutes, **Marriage counselors**, Ne'er-do-wells, **Persons in the Social Register, Physicians**, Pimps, Police court officials, Prison inmates, Professional women, Thieves and hold-up men, Women's Club leaders" (39). I have boldfaced the categories on this list that can be represented from ancient sources as a sort of miniature version of the thought experiment with the grid and the overlay. It is customary these days to look down on Kinsey; we must think first of how little we are able to do in comparison with him. His example is helpful in constructing a narrative that knows where its holes are.

1 Timeline

The expedition would have to take into account at least the following historical shifts and events:

by 14 CE: Rome: the Julian Laws promoting marriage and childbearing and criminalizing adultery have just been passed. Now a "world-city," Rome has become a place where writers, as Juvenal would later say, stand at the crossroads with a notebook (*Sat.* 1.63–4; see Habinek 1997).

by 84 CE: Pompeii is buried (79 CE); the Temple in Jerusalem is destroyed by the emperor Titus (70 CE), while the Jewish diaspora has been well under way for some time, with some efforts at resistance. Paul has been an active organizer of the nascent Christian sect after the death of Jesus of Nazareth. Rome has invaded Britain and put down Boudicca's rebellion.

by 154 CE: The emperor Domitian tightens up the enforcement of the punishment of sexual misconduct with legal disabilities (85–90 CE), and makes the castration of infant slaves illegal (McGinn 1998: 106–16; Mart. 9.6, 9.8); some Greek and Roman pundits write serious tracts on marriage, others stage debates on the relative merits of sex with women and with boys. Alexandria and Antioch are major cultural centers. There is a boom in texts about sex in Greek and Latin; romance novels grow in visibility (Elsom 1992; Goldhill 1995; Konstan 1994; Reardon 1989). Some Rabbis critique Roman mores. Rome invades Dacia, Armenia, and Mesopotamia; Palestine rebels under Bar Kochba (131–35).

by 224 CE: Christian pundits, as the church now begins to be institutionalized, debate the relative merits of procreative sex within marriage vs. celibacy (notably Tertullian and Clement of Alexandria). Roman jurists collect and codify Roman law; the Rabbis collect the Mishnah. Along with novels, apocalyptic texts are popular (see Himmelfarb 1983 on tours of Hell). The law has begun to draw sharp divisions between *honestiores* and *humiliores* in assigning punishments to crimes (Garnsey 1970). Rome faces attacks along the Danube frontier; Rome annexes Osrhoene and Mesopotamia.

by 294 CE: Persecutions of Christians produce a boom in martyr texts, many with erotic elements. Rabbis who have fled Palestine for Babylonia begin to develop norms for Judaism that differ from the Greek-influenced norms of Palestine; the stricter Babylonian norms will prevail. Secular erotic writing has become scarce; pederastic literature is disappearing. Rome has abandoned Dacia, and Germans and Persians invade across the northern and eastern frontiers. The western provinces and Palmyra briefly break away from the empire.

by 364 CE: Constantine begins to halt persecutions of Christians in 306 CE, and imperial favor is increasingly shown to the church. Despite an interruption during the reign of Julian (360–63 CE), this trend continues. Monasticism is now flourishing; eunuchs have become important presences at the imperial court. Erotic writing blooms again in Gaul with Ausonius, but without pederasty. Goths move into the empire.

by 434 CE: State support for pagan cults has been withdrawn. Monasticism continues. Women go in for religious tourism in Egypt and the Near East; Olympias founds a women's religious community in Constantinople, Paula founds one in Judaea. The *Theodosian Code* appears in 438 CE, collecting laws since 313, some imposing extremely violent punishments for acts defined as sex crimes. Saints' lives become popular, often much resembling novels in structure. The redaction of the Babylonian and Palestinian Talmuds begins. Rome is sacked by the Goths (410 CE); the western empire is invaded by Germanic peoples.

Overall: In 203 CE, Perpetua writes in her prison journal that she had a dream about her brother Dinocrates in which "there was a great abyss between us: neither could approach the other" (Kraemer 1988: 100). This brother had died a pagan at the age of seven. The abyss between Christian sister and pagan brother could well stand as a figure for the sexual life of the empire before Perpetua, in the reign of Septimius Severus, and after her: a great change is in progress, and women will finally join the conversation. Phyllis Culham (1997), asking "Did Roman women have an empire?", concludes that elite women did, at least in that they gained access to the public sphere through benefaction. It might be said of the late empire that women were able to *give up* sex publicly on an almost equal footing with men. But for the poor, at risk of slavery and prostitution, not much ever changed.

2 Sources

What *do* we have? Most of what we have is textual and comes from elite males, a problem familiar from all areas of ancient history but especially serious for sexuality. Luckily we have some collections of published letters, but we have no diaries and none of the personal letters now available in archives for later periods of history. The letters of ordinary people that we do have on papyrus from Greco-Roman Egypt rarely discuss anything sexual at all (Montserrat 1996: 5–15). We are forced to fall back upon art (Clarke 1998; Elsner 1996; Fredrick 1995; Johns 1982; articles by Bergmann, D'Ambra, Elsner, Kampen, and Kellum in Kampen 1996; Montserrat 1996; Satlow 1997).

Since sex, then as now, was considered a low subject, as a general rule, the lower the art form the more it has to say about sex: comedy, joke books, satire, invective, erotic poetry, graffiti, magic spells and curses, inscriptions, tchotchkes and amulets, interior decoration. But rhetoric, history, and life writing all have a sex department, as do the technical writers (on agriculture, architecture, astrology, geography, interpretation of dreams, medicine, natural science, physiognomy). Most of all, moral philosophy and religion express strong opinions on sexuality, and laws lay down the law.

All of these cultural forms are enforcers of behavior: a joke tells people how to behave as much as a law. And these forms often conflict, even within a single culture of the Roman Empire, even before 200 CE. What happens to a Roman man who has sex with another man's wife? Depends who you ask (Richlin 1981a): a criminal prosecution (Augustus), exile and a fine (Paulus the jurist), flogging, castration, rape, or death (Horace, Valerius Maximus), he gets his ears and nose cut off, or has to fellate the husband (Martial), a dead fish up the anus (Juvenal), anal rape (Apuleius), not much (gossip from all periods). *A fortiori*, although the cultures that lived side by side in the Roman Empire had a lot in common, by no means were their sexual mores identical; sometimes they express their amazement at each other, and quite often they define the otherness of others by attributing to them amazing sexual practices (the National Geographic approach; see Evans 1999: 61; Satlow 1995: 67–8). Thus Philo says the Persians, Greeks, and Egyptians commit incest (*Spec. Leg.* 3.13, 15, 23); the geographer Mela describes communal marriage and ritual prostitution amongst African tribes (1.45, 46); the natural historian Pliny describes tattooing and naked display amongst the barbarians (Plin. *Nat.* 22.2); the historian Ammianus Marcellinus explains that the Persians are oversexed but do not practice pederasty (Amm. Marc. 23.6.76).

It is easy to be misled by the self-assurance of legal writers, though we all know that some laws are more enforceable than others and that a large proportion of any citizen body may habitually subvert a given law. As various scholars have pointed out, laws may best indicate what lawmakers were worried about; Paul would not have needed to insist that women should not speak in church if women were not doing so, and Philo, fulminating against perverts, says you can see them downtown any day. And law has its own geography; as Ross Kraemer in particular has pointed out, it is a big mistake to define "Judaism" in antiquity as "what the Rabbis say," since Rabbis were highly localized in Palestine and Babylon and plenty of Jews in the empire lived elsewhere (Kraemer 1991: 44; Eliav, this volume). Rabbinic rules were not even hegemonic locally before 200 CE, or perhaps in antiquity at all (Boyarin 1993: 231; Peskowitz 1997: 132–3; Satlow 1996; Eliav, this volume). *Infamia* – loss of civil rights due to misbehavior of various sorts, including sexual – is a key legal concept in Roman law, and must have much affected people classified as *infames* in the city of Rome, and probably in Italy (Edwards 1997; Richlin 1993): Did it matter in Asia Minor? In Gaul? In Britain? In North Africa? Hard to say, and it is dangerous to generalize from the evidence of later periods to earlier centuries (Harries 1999: 77–98; Ando, this volume).

Moreover, while a joke tells people how to behave as much as a law, we don't have everyone's jokes; extant Jewish and Christian sources tend to be serious. A lot of Greeks and Romans thought oral sex both disgusting and funny; Ausonius did, too; any Jews? We don't know.

In the past 30 years, the number of publications on sex and gender in antiquity has grown from very small to very large. This knowledge is usually compartmentalized, with most historians focusing on one culture apiece: "Rome," for example, is "what canonical writers in Latin (and some Greek) say." But Jews and Christians *were* Greeks and Romans; indeed, it was possible to be a Greek-speaking person whose birth language was Aramaic, practicing a Jewish/Christian religion and paying taxes to Rome. The few scholars to take an integrated or synoptic approach are not classicists but historians of religion, and I would single out for special mention Ross Kraemer (1988, 1992) and Bernadette Brooten (1996), whose work deals thoroughly with four cultures, and who both have brought once obscure texts into the spotlight. Scholars who deal with Jewish or Christian culture or with the Roman Empire after 200 CE generally have had to take an integrated approach due to the nature of their sources: much less centered on a vague "Rome" or some putative monolithic "Greece," much less overwhelmingly elite/urban and indeed often marginal (the gospels, the Gnostic texts, and in some ways, rabbinic writing).

Time as well as space poses problems: Greeks, Romans, and Rabbis were all fond of looking backward, and often use the past to talk about the present. The Romans were not only ancestor-worshipers but nervous about naming names. This is why many of the sexual stories in Latin are either apocryphal, or attributed to characters carefully labeled as fictitious, or transmitted by writers living decades, sometimes centuries, after the death of the people they name. The problem is acute, for example, in the case of the *Historia Augusta*, which is almost the only source we have for long stretches of the late second and third centuries, including the scandalous lives of the emperors Commodus and Elagabalus. It is now thought to have been written around 400 CE and to be not very trustworthy. Lucian writes in a world that seems to be half his, half classical Athens; Ausonius replicates Martial, translates the *Greek Anthology*, and makes his most obscene poem out of bits of Vergil; Macrobius rattles off the jokes of Cicero and Julia; and the blood-soaked pages of Ammianus Marcellinus refer casually to Verres and Cato the Censor as if they were neighbors, and, while dismissing Juvenal as a popular writer, attack the denizens of Rome in terms borrowed from him. It is never easy to tell whether writers like these are really talking about their own time when they say they are talking about a time long ago. The same is true of Livy, after all (see Smith, this volume).

This problem in reverse: some texts were popular over centuries, especially novels and saints' lives, which preserve norms whose relevance to the current locale and culture we often cannot know. (We still read Jane Austen, but do not live like Fanny Price.) Thus novels including debates over the pros and cons of boys vs. women as sex objects seem to have continued to be read in cultures from which pederastic love poetry had all but disappeared. Did they seem quaint? Frank? Risqué? Pornographic? The saints' lives, and some novels, were translated into multiple languages in antiquity; their circulation must have been healthy.

And then there are the Rabbis, among them the only substantial critics of Roman hegemony left to us; in the Mishnah (compiled around 200 CE; Eliav, this volume) and the two Talmuds (compiled over the next 400 years, in Palestine and Babylon) are preserved discussions going back to the first century CE, oddly reminiscent of the elder Seneca's patchwork memoirs of the rhetorical schools of his youth in the reign of Augustus. The difference is that these debates spin on for centuries. It is hard to know when anything in the Talmud was actually said, though there are clues; it is also clear that, over time, and between Jerusalem and Babylon, stories morphed like folk tales into whatever suited local needs.

Daniel Boyarin comments on rabbinic texts, "it is the failure of the narrative to totalize that is significant, not its success" (1993: 166). Chapters in tractates are polyvocal: a dozen points of view are expressed by various speakers, or by the redactor, and no conclusions are drawn. The whole point is that the reader is supposed to be joining in the debate. So on marital sex:

> Rabbi Shimeon bar-Yoḥai, [Palestine, 130s CE]: There are four things that the Holy, Blessed One hates, and I do not like them either: . . . [including] one who has intercourse while any living creature is watching.

Rav Yehuda, to Rabbi Shmuel, [Persia, 250s CE]: Even in front of mice.
Rabbi Shmuel, in reply: Wise-guy. No, it refers to those like the household of John Doe [= Romans] who have intercourse in front of their male and female slaves. (*bNiddah* 16b–17a, trans. Boyarin 1993: 125, with lively discussion)

The first speaker, Rabbi Shimeon bar-Yohḥai, lived (according to a legendary story) under Hadrian as a fugitive for 13 years because he was wanted by the Romans for subversive behavior (see *bSabbath* 33b, which includes his sexual critique of Roman imperialism). The second pair are Rav Yehuda (d. 299) and his teacher R. Shmuel (d. 254), founder of one of the great Babylonian schools. Boyarin interprets Shmuel's answer as an attack on a well-known Roman practice (1993: 126).

When we write narrative histories of the ancient world, we start with a list of texts scattered over time, much like a tractate, which we then smooth out. Our fragmentary Kinsey II Report would instead present 20 tractates, in which Rabbis, bishops, jurists, poets, historians, biographers, lovers, slaves, monks, and many more – even a few women – have their say.

3 Questionnaire of the Kinsey II Expedition

Whereas the Kinsey Report focused on experience, the nature of the sources for the Roman Empire forces researchers to focus on attitudes instead, though experience is attested in some responses. The content and order of the questions here are determined by preliminary research; the questions are listed roughly from those with the largest number of extant responses to those with the smallest.

What is your attitude towards...

(1) sex between men and boys?
(2) sex between adult males?
(3) sex for men with women outside marriage?
(4) sex for women with men outside marriage?
(5) what should happen to a man and woman who commit adultery?
(6) oral sex?
(7) sex between husband and wife?
(8) prostitution?
(9) abstinence?
(10) rape?
(11) contraception?
(12) abortion?
(13) sex between women?
(14) masturbation?
(15) circumcision?
(16) castration?
(17) sex with children below the age of puberty?
(18) incest?
(19) clitoridectomy?
(20) infibulation?

Four fragmentary surveys:

Even a sampling of the responses for all 20 of these questions would exceed the space available. Here are four that would have affected most adults.

What is your attitude towards...

(1) sex between men and boys?

14 CE: Horace, poet, freedman's son from southern Italy, Rome, 30s BCE:

> When your groin swells, if a slave girl or homegrown slave boy is near, that you could jump right away, would you rather burst with a hard-on? Believe me, I like sex that's easy and ready. (Hor. *Sat.* 1.2.116–18; on Horace's sexual satires, see Richlin 1992a: 174–85)

Ovid, poet, equestrian from central Italy, Rome, c.1 BCE:

> I hate sex that doesn't get both partners off; this is why I'm less moved by love with boys. (Ov. *Ars* 2.683–4; on sexuality in Ovid, see Richlin 1992a: 156–61; 1992c)

84 CE: Philo, writer and community leader, Jew, Alexandria, 30s CE:

> [A]nother evil... has ramped its way into the cities, namely pederasty (*to paiderastein*). In former days the very mention of it was a great disgrace, but now it's a matter of boasting not only to the active but to the passive partners who habituate themselves to endure the disease of effeminization... These persons are rightly judged worthy of death by those who obey the law, which ordains that the man–woman who debases the sterling coin of nature should perish unavenged... and the lover of such may be assured that he is subject to the same penalty... Certainly you may see these hybrids of man and woman continually strutting about through the thick of the market.... (*Spec.Leg.* 3.37–42, passim, trans. Colson 1935)

This is only an excerpt from a lengthy section on what are supposedly Jewish laws on sexuality, including strictures against sex during menstruation on the grounds that "the generative seeds should not be wasted" (32). At *Spec.Leg.* 1.325 Philo says that "the men who belie their sex" should be debarred from congregations, along with whores and the children of whores (326). At *Vit.Cont.* 59–62 he critiques Plato's *Symposium* and pederasty in general; at *Abr.* 133–41 he recounts the edifying story of the Cities of the Plain and how God punished the Sodomites. Throughout, Philo merges pederasty with the making of eunuchs and sex between adult males, which he sees as a continuum of practices (see Satlow 1995: 216). Philo also says of women who get into brawls in the marketplace and actually grab their male opponents by the genitals, "the hand shall be cut off which has touched what decency forbids it to touch" (*Spec.Leg.* 3.169–75, trans. Colson 1935).

Petronius, novelist, courtier, Rome, ?60s CE [unsuccessful poet, Eumolpus, character in novel, speaks]:

> When I was out in Asia serving with the quaestor, I had lodgings in Pergamum. And I was happy to be there... because of my host's very good-looking son, so I cooked up a plan

how I could not be suspected by the father. Whenever anybody said anything at dinner about the use of handsome [boys], I blushed so much, I expressed so severe a displeasure that my ears should be violated by obscene speech, that the mother totally started looking at me like I was some philosopher. So now I start taking the boy to the gym, I'm organizing his studies... (Petron. *Sat.* 85.1–3)

Petronius [freed slave, Trimalchio, character in novel, speaks]:

I was my master's sex toy (*ad delicias*) for fourteen years. What the master orders is not shameful. I also serviced the mistress. (Petron. *Sat.* 75.11)

154 CE: Martial, epigrammatist, originally from Spain, Rome, 90s CE:

The sulks and pride of these boys and their petulant quarrels... I prefer to a dowry of a million sesterces. (Mart. *Ep.* 12.75.6–8; on Martial's pederastic epigrams, see Richlin 1992a: 34–44, 55–6)

Dio Chrysostom, rhetorician, from Bithynia, performing in Rome, Greece, and Asia Minor, c.100 CE:

Indeed a man who is insatiable in desires of this sort [= seducing women], when he finds nothing scarce or resistant in that gender, scorning what is easy and having no respect for sex with women as something ready to hand and actually completely feminine itself, will go over to the men's quarters, lusting to dishonor those who will very soon be rulers and judges and generals, as if he would find there some difficult and hard-to-get kind of pleasure... (D.Chr. 7.151–2; note the slippery-slope argument. For discussion, see Houser 1998)

Juvenal, satirist, Italian, Rome, 110s CE:

... taking a wife? Don't you think it's better to have a boy sleep with you? (Juv. *Sat.* 6.28, 34; on Juvenal's sexual satires, see Richlin 1992a: 195–209)

Tacitus, senator and historian, Rome, 110s CE

A slave of the city prefect Pedanius Secundus killed him, whether because he had refused to free him though he had settled on a price or whether he was fired up with love for an *exoletus* and could not tolerate his master as a rival. (Tac. *Ann.* 14.42.1)

An *exoletus* is literally a "grown-up male," a "ripe male"; the word often seems to refer to male prostitutes, or to boys who are past adolescence but still attractive to older men.

Strato, poet, Sardis, 120s–30s CE:

I delight in the bloom of a twelve-year-old, but one of thirteen's much more desirable than he. One hitting twice seven is a sweeter flower of the Loves, and one who is beginning his third pentad is even more delightful. But the sixteenth year is that of the gods, and the seven-and-tenth is not mine to seek, but Zeus'. But whoever has a desire for those still older, he's no longer kidding around, but is on the lookout for "do so to me also." (*AP* 12.4)

The last words of the translation aim for a biblical equivalent to the poem's Homeric *ton d' apameibomenos*, "then answering him in reply."

Marcus Aurelius, son of the emperor, age 18, Rome, 139 CE, to his teacher Fronto:

> I am dying so for love of you...and...I still will love you while I live and breathe... (Fronto, *Ep. Add.* 7.1, trans. Haines adapted)

Cornelius Fronto, professor of rhetoric, Libyan, Rome, to M. Aurelius, 143 CE:

> Do you think that my consulship brought me as much joy as the proofs of your love you packed into that one letter?...nobody could ever have struck such a flame into a lover by potion or love-charm as you have made me dazed and love-struck both by your deeds and your burning love. (Fronto, *Aur.* 1.7.2)

Lucian, satirist, Greek, after 140 CE [three characters in a debate speak]:

> Charicles: But if anyone tries it on a boy of twenty, he seems to me to want to have it done *to* him, chasing after a double-pointed kind of sex. For, as they turn into men, the bulk of their limbs is hard, and the cheek previously soft is rough and covered thickly with fuzz, while the well-grown thighs are practically filthy with hair; and what's less visible than these parts, I leave to you who have tried it to know....[and as for sex with boys,] the one who's in charge, in his view, goes away having taken a choice pleasure, but for the one outraged there are first pain and tears, and then, as the pain loosens a little over time, you won't hurt him any more, so they say, but there's no pleasure whatsoever.
> Callicratidas: But for men [as opposed to animals, previously adduced by Charicles as evidence that male–male sex is unnatural], practical wisdom combined with knowledge based on frequent experiments, grasping what is best, has judged males the most steadfast of loves.
> Lycinus: And so everybody should marry, but the love of boys should be permitted only to the wise, for complete virtue grows least of all among women. (Luc. *Amatores* 26, 27, 36, 51; see discussion in Halperin 1992)

This debate on the relative merits of boys and women presents lengthy arguments on both sides; see especially also section 53, where another participant rejects Platonic love and describes an explicit "ladder" of sexual experience with boys. For other debates, see Plutarch *Amatorius* (*Mor.* 748f–71e); Ach. Tat. 2.35–7 (below), discussed in Konstan 1994: 28.

224 CE: Achilles Tatius, novelist, Alexandria, c.150–75 CE:

> It does look as if male-directed love is becoming the norm....Young men are more open and frank than women, and their handsome bodies offer a sharper stimulus to pleasure. (Ach. Tat. 2.35, trans. Winkler, in Reardon 1989: 205)

This Greek novel may date to 150–175 CE, and was very popular in Egypt, continuing to be read well into the Byzantine period (Winkler in Reardon 1989: 170–5). The lines quoted here are the beginning of a debate on the relative merits of pederasty and sex with women; it is a short version of the extended debates in Plutarch's *Amatorius* and Lucian's *Amatores*.

Paul, lawyer, Rome, c.220 CE:

> A man who shall have led a boy into illicit sex (*stuprum*) after abducting him or bribing his chaperon, or shall have accosted a woman or girl or done anything for the sake of unchastity... if he has carried out the crime, he is punished capitally; if he has not carried it out, he is deported to an island; the bribed chaperons are visited with the supreme punishment. (D. 47.11.1.2)

294 CE: Athenaeus, writer on parties, from Naucratis in Egypt, at Rome, c.228 CE:

> So you watch out, you [Stoic] philosophers, who have sex contrary to nature and sin against the goddess [of love], that you don't come to ruin the same way. For boys are beautiful (as the courtesan Glykera said) at the time when they look like a woman... (Ath. *Deip.* 605d)

The "ruin" here alludes to a story of a dancing girl torn to bits by a crowd as punishment for sacrilege. At 563d–e the speaker has stated that the charge against the Stoics is that they keep boys up to the age of 28. Compare 654f (the Stoics take boys around with them who already need a shave), 565d–f (if the Stoics want to call others *kinaidoi*, they shouldn't have boyfriends who shave their cheeks and rear ends). Contrast Cynic sexuality, known for crudity and public display (Krueger 1996).

Philostratus, sophist, Athens and Rome, 200–240s CE:

> Why, boy, do you point to your chin? You are not ceasing to be beautiful but beginning ... Homer, too, says that the bearded one is the loveliest, and he was a poet who knew how to see beauty as well as how to make it; he would never have said so if he himself had not first held and kissed the chin of his beloved. (Philostr. *Ep.* 15 [63])

As in the excerpt from Lucian above, the advent of body hair forms a conventional part of the poet's argument to the boy, warning of the end of his attractiveness; the attribution of pederastic desire to Homer is a sly extrapolation from the post-Homeric idea of pairs of male lovers in the *Iliad*. The identity of this author is somewhat confused, but he seems to be the same Philostratus who wrote the *Lives of the Sophists*; the *Erotic Letters* are prose poems, much resembling in theme the erotic epigrams written by Martial and the Greek epigrammatists, and likewise addressing boys as well as women. Especially notable is *Letter* 7 [44], a lengthy word-painting of the social behavior of boys and lovers.

Nemesianus, poet, from Carthage, Rome, c.280 CE:

> Whoever loves boys, let him harden his heart with steel, let him be in no hurry, and learn to love patiently for a long time, and not scorn a prudent spirit in tender youth, but even put up with sulks. Thus, someday, he will get his joy... (*Eclogue* 4.56–9)

This is to my knowledge the latest extant pederastic text in Latin.

364 CE: Isaac of Kellia, monastic, Egypt, 300s CE:

> Don't allow the boys to remain here in this way, for four churches at Scetis have become deserted because of boys. (Isaac of Kellia 5 [*PG* 65 225 A–B]; trans. and disc. in Masterson 2001: 109–10)

Athanasius, exiled bishop of Alexandria, 356–62 CE:

> Finally therefore, as the serpent was not able to take Antony in this way [i.e. in the form of a woman], but rather saw himself thrust from his [Antony's] heart, ... so as a black boy did he subsequently appear to him in a vision [as] the spirit of fornication. (Ath. *V. Ant.* 6.1, trans. and disc. in Masterson 2001: 123–4)

434 CE: John Chrysostom, preacher, Antioch, 380s CE:

> A certain strange and illicit sort of love has burst into our time: a disease has befallen us, very serious and incurable, a plague that is the foulest of all plagues.... Not just the written laws, but the laws of nature are being overturned.... Thus in the middle of the cities, as if in a vast desert, males practice indecency on males.... Moreover the fathers of the corrupted boys bear this in silence. (Jo.Chr. *Against the Opponents of the Monastic Life* 3 [*PG* 47: 360–2]; see Boswell 1980: 131–2, 362–3)

Ausonius, rhetorician and courtier, Bordeaux, 380s CE:

> "Which Marcus?" The one recently called the cat that goes for the chickens – [the one] who corrupted the entire boyish sex, a digger at the backdoor wound of perverse Venus, the poet Lucilius' "stealthy boy-screwer." (Auson. *Ep.* 77.5–8; modified trans. Masterson 2001: 62–4, with disc.)

This is the only piece by Ausonius that deals with pederasty, and not from the enthusiastic standpoint of Martial (otherwise a model for Ausonius), or Strato (though Ausonius translates about a dozen epigrams directly from the *Palatine Anthology*). The juxtaposition of "recently" (*nuper*) with Lucilius, and Ausonius' choice of interlocutor for the poem's frame – Pythagoras – puts a sort of unreality frosting on what is otherwise a lively and original epigram. And a lonely one. Ausonius does have one epitaph for a boy dying at the age of 16 and just losing his gender ambiguity (62), and a series on cute boys of mythology (97–103), but where an earlier epigrammatist would have made the boys explicitly sexy, Ausonius stops short of it, with a kind of emphatic ellipsis.

Shenute, abbot, White Monastery, Egypt, c.400 CE:

> Cursed is he who will kiss his neighbor or a boy with lustful passion. (Shenute, *Concerning the life of Monks* 25; trans. Foat in Brooten 1996: 350 n. 201, with disc. 348–50)

(2) sex between adult males?

14 CE: Phaedrus, fable-writer, freedman of Augustus, from Thrace, 10s CE:

> what ... produced lesbians (*tribades*) and soft (*molles*) males? ... [Prometheus] fitted a girl thing on the masculine type and put the masculine member on the women. So now lust enjoys a deformed pleasure. (Phaedr. 4.12.1–2, 12–14)

Here, as elsewhere, *tribades* seems to mean roughly "lesbians;" *molles*, literally "soft," refers to effeminate men who like to be penetrated anally. For discussion see Hallett 1989; Brooten 1996: 45–6.

Q. Haterius, lawyer, senator, Rome, c.10s CE:

> Unchastity (*impudicitia* = allowing anal penetration) is a source of accusation for a freeborn (male), a necessity for a slave, and a duty for a freed slave. (Haterius, as recalled in Sen. *Con.* 4. pr.10. For discussion, see Richlin 1993: 535–6)

"Phokylides," writer, Alexandria, c.10s CE:

> Transgress not for unlawful sex the natural limits of sexuality. For even animals are not pleased by the intercourse of male with male. And let not women imitate the sexual role of men. ([Phoc.] *Sent.* 190–2. Trans. van der Horst and disc. Satlow 1995: 215; cf. Brooten 1996: 63)

84 CE: Paul, Christian organizer and theologian, from Tarsus, at Ephesus, 57 CE:

> Know ye not that the unrighteous shall not inherit the kingdom of God? Be not deceived; neither prostitutes, nor idolaters, nor adulterers, nor effeminates, nor those who have sex with men ... shall inherit the kingdom of God. (1 Cor 6:9–10. See Brooten 1996: 260–1, and cf. *Rom.* 1:18–32, with Brooten's whole discussion, 1996: 215–302; Moore 2001: 133–72)

Anonymous inscription, Pompeii, before 79 CE :

> Equitias' slave Cosmus is a big queer and a cocksucker with his legs wide open. (Diehl 648 = *CIL* 4.1825)

The spelling in the Latin original probably indicates a person without advanced education. On Roman sexual graffiti, see Richlin 1992a: 81–3, 277–8; Milnor 2000.

154 CE: Suetonius, civil servant and biographer, from North Africa, Rome, 110s CE, writing about events between 85–90 CE:

> [the emperor Domitian] condemned certain men from either order under the *lex Scantinia*. (Suet. *Dom.* 8.3)

The *lex Scantinia* seems to have penalized sex between adult males, but its date (c.149 BCE) and content are vexed questions; see bibliography at McGinn 1998: 140–1; Richlin 1993: 569–71.

Tacitus, senator and historian, Rome, 98 CE:

> [The Germans] make the punishment fit the crime: they hang traitors and turncoats from trees, while cowards and the unwarlike and those who are *infamis* with respect to their body they drown in muddy bogs, pressing a wicker framework on top of them.

The distinction in punishments has this meaning: that crimes should be made public while they are being punished, but sins should be hidden. (Tac. *Germ.* 12.1–2; see Richlin 1993: 555)

Juvenal, satirist, Italian, Rome, 110s CE:

What neighborhood isn't full of moralizing perverts? Better a guy who announces his disease by his expression and his walk – he acts more honestly, more like a gent; I chalk it up to destiny. (Juv. *Sat.* 2.8–10, 15–17)

Juvenal's second satire concerns men who are secretly *molles* but dress like macho Stoic philosophers; this theme recurs in Martial and Lucian. For discussion see Richlin 1992a: 201–2; 1993: 548–54.

Rabbi Akiva, Palestine, 110s CE:

[Scripture says, "Do not lie with a male as one lies with a female." I only have (here) a warning for the penetrator...where is there a warning for the one penetrated...?] "'Do not lie with a male as one lies with a female,' read it: 'Do not be laid...'." (*Sifra Qod.* 9:14 [Weiss, 92b], on *Leviticus* 18:22, trans. in Satlow 1995: 195, with disc.)

See also Peskowitz 1997: 52–62. The *Sifra*, a legal midrash on *Leviticus*, was compiled in the late fifth or early sixth century CE; the attribution to Akiva may be fictional.

Julian redaction of the praetor's edict, under Hadrian, 120s CE:

Persons infamable on account of foulness [include] a man who has undergone womanish things in his body.... But whatever man has been raped by the force of robbers or the enemy ought not to be marked [as *infamis*]. (D. 3.1.1.5, 6; cf. Richlin 1993: 558–9)

Lucian, satirist, Greek, after 140 CE:

to get together with Rhetoric, you need not a masculine teacher, but] some wholly wise and wholly beautiful guy, with a wiggling walk and a lolling neck, a womanish look and a honeyish voice, reeking of perfume, scratching his head with the tip of his finger, primping his hair (now thin, but fleecy and hyacinth-hued), a delicate Sardanapalus or Kinyras, a very Agathon.... (Luc. *Rh. Pr.*11)

For the stereotype, see Richlin 1992a: 221, 258 n. 3, 285–6; 1993: 542; Gleason 1995; for the casual conflation of the Orient with effeminacy, see Richlin 1995: 201–15; and in the context of oratory, Richlin 1997c.

224 CE: Artemidorus, dream analyst, Daldis (Asia Minor), c.170 CE:

[to dream of having] sex with one's own female slave or male slave is good, for slaves are the dreamer's possession; therefore taking pleasure in them signifies the dreamer's being pleased with his own possessions.... To be penetrated by one's house slave is not good. This signifies being despised or injured by the slave. The same applies to being penetrated by one's brother...or a fortiori by one's enemy. (Artem. p. 88.5–12 Pack, trans. MacAlister 1992: 149, with discussion and bibliography)

Clement, Christian teacher, Alexandria, c.190–92 CE:

> He who denies his masculinity in broad daylight will certainly prove himself a woman at night. (Clement of Alexandria *Paed.* 3.3.20.3, trans. in Brooten 1996: 322 n. 76, 323, discussed 320–32)

"Paul," Greek-speaking ascetic, early 200s CE:

> [Paul sees in Hell] men and women covered in dust, and their faces were like blood, and they were in a pit of tar and brimstone, and they were running in a river of fire.... They are those who have committed the iniquity of Sodom and Gomorrah, men with men. (*Apocalypse of Paul* 39, trans. in Brooten 1996: 313, discussed 313–14)

For the date, see Himmelfarb 1983: 16–18: Origen seems to be familiar with the text, and the author probably wrote before institutionalized monasticism. Tours of Hell were popular beginning in the second century CE; these texts seem to be aimed at a general audience rather than a literary elite. Himmelfarb argues that the format reflects a mixed Greek and Jewish tradition. The texts often include a view of sexual deviants among the damned; homosexuality is punished as a sin in seven of the 17 tours she charts (1983: 70; cf. discussion of sins and punishments, 69–126). Compare the tenth-century Coptic church murals in Wilfong 1998.

Paul, lawyer, Rome, c.220 CE:

> A man who shall have raped a free male against his will is punished capitally. A man who of his own free will suffers illicit sex (*stuprum*) or impure outrage is fined of the half part of his goods; neither is he permitted to make testamentary disposition of the remaining part. (Paul *Sent.* 2.26.12–13)

This collection of opinions is thought by some to be spurious, though it was accepted as genuine in the fourth century CE; the penalty listed here is so much more lenient than those allotted in the later empire that it seems unlikely to be late. See Richlin 1993: 567.

Diogenes Laertius, biographer, before 250 CE:

> While [Cleanthes] was saying that, according to Zeno [both c.300 BCE], character is graspable from appearance, some lively young men brought before him a queer (*kinaidos*) who had become hardened from outdoor work, and asked him to show the man's character by reasoning. Flummoxed, he ordered the man to go away, but as the man did so he sneezed. "I have him," said Cleanthes, "he's swishy [*malakos*]." (D.L. 7.173)

Nothing is known of the life of Diogenes Laertius except that he lived in the early third century. This story, popular earlier, was recirculated by others as well; see discussion in Gleason 1995: 77, and Masterson 2001: 9.

294 CE: "Thomas," Syria, c.200–250 CE:

> And I saw the first pit, and as it were fire was blazing in its midst... "Into this torment are destined to come those souls which transgress the law, which change the union of

intercourse that has been appointed by God." (*Acts of Thomas* 6.55, trans. in Brooten 1996: 310, discussed 309–13; Himmelfarb 1983: 11–13)

Rabbi Ḥiyya bar Abbah, Galilee, 290s CE:

Is it not enough that we are subjugated to the seventy nations, but even to this one [i.e. Rome], who is penetrated like women? (*GenR* 63: 10 [Theodor and Albeck, p. 693], trans. and disc. in Satlow 1995: 213)

The text is ostensibly about Esau, who is, however, routinely identified with Rome. These sentiments are not restricted to Jewish circles: Romans say similar things about eastern peoples, and it is much like what Cassius Dio has Boudicca say about the Romans under Nero (62.6.2–5).

364 CE: Firmicus Maternus, astrologer, from Syracuse, 334–37 CE:

If Venus should be discovered located at the setting of the natal star, and Mars likewise should be found in a feminine sign, and the Sun and Moon too should be possessing feminine signs, that natal star points out a *cinaedus*-man to you. (Firmicus Maternus *Mathesis* 6.31.4, trans. Masterson 2001: 65, with disc.)

Constans, emperor, Milan, December 4, 342 CE:

When a man marries as a woman who would offer herself to men, what should he want when sex has lost its place? When the crime is the one which it does no good to know: when Venus is changed to another form: when love is sought, but is not seen; we order the laws to rise up and the statutes be armed with the avenging sword, so that (these) *infames* may be laid low with exquisite punishments, those who are or will be defendants. (*CJ* 9.7.6, trans. Masterson 2001: 48–9, with disc. through 52)

The translation of the first sentence is much vexed; see Masterson 2001: 47–8, with bibliography; Boswell 1980: 123. "Exquisite punishments" means death by torture; this law marks a watershed in the legal treatment of *cinaedi*.

434 CE: Ausonius, rhetorician and courtier, Bordeaux, 380s CE:

To a certain man who was making his groin smooth: [... But why depilate your buttocks?] Unless because the desire to be penetrated (*patientia*) craves the two-man disease, and you're a man in front but a woman in the rear. (Aus. *Ep.* 93.3, 5–6)

See also *Epigrams* 92 and 94, both addressed to men identified as *semivir* who have married adulterous wives; both are treated as men who desire to be penetrated anally. On *patientia*, see section 4 below.

Valentinian, Theodosius, and Arcadius, emperors, Rome, August 6, 390 CE:

All who have made a practice of sin by condemning their manly body in the guise of a woman to the passive nature of a sex not their own (for they seem to have nothing different from women) will expiate a crime of this nature in the avenging flames as the populace looks on. (*CJ* 9.7.6, trans. Masterson 2001: 48–9, with disc. through 52)

This law appears in a fuller version in the *Comparison of the Laws of Moses and the Romans*, which specifies that both partners are to die (5.1.1) and attaches the legislation to a prohibition of male prostitution (5.3.1–2); cf. Masterson: "this section of the *Collatio* is surely one of the markers of the end of the 'romance,' such as it had been, between 'normal' men and a class of their objects, the *cinaedi*" (2001: 52). Mommsen's comment in his edition of the *CJ*: *Haec lex interpretatione non indiget* ("This law requires no interpretation.").

Salvian, bishop of Marseilles, from Trier, c.439–50 CE:

[contrasting the Vandals with the Roman peoples of Africa] In such affluence and luxury did not a one of them become effeminate (*mollis*)?... Certainly Roman nobles became so all the time.... Certainly for a long time now among the Romans... those men believed themselves to be of a more manly strength who had most broken men to the disgracefulness of womanish usage. And so it came about that, when boy groupies were following the armies around, they were distributed as retirement benefits to veterans with a deserving record – as if, because they were brave men, they might change men into women. What a sin!... more like Greeks than Romans... The Roman state is now undergoing (*patitur*) what it has long deserved.– And this impurity began to be among the Romans even before the mission of Christ.... (Salvian, *De gub. Dei* 20–1 [= *PL* 53 167–8])

This work of Salvian is a bit past the Kinsey II deadline, but he and his text are of interest for several reasons: his home town was overrun by invaders four times in his lifetime; he repeats the noble-savage critique of Rome (see especially Tacitus, quoted above under 154 CE), but this time from the perspective of a native of Gaul using North Africa as an example of Roman-ness; and he brings in the issue of sex and the army, on which see Phang 2001: 229–95; Walters 1997a and b. Thanks to Sara Phang for this reference.

(3) sex between husband and wife?

14 CE: Julia, daughter of Augustus, mother of five, Rome, c.21–12 BCE:

[When those who knew of her sins used to marvel at how she gave birth to sons resembling (her husband) Agrippa, when she made such public property of her body, she said,] "Why, I never take on a passenger unless the ship is full." (recounted in Macrob. *Sat.* 2.5.9 [early 430s CE]; see Richlin 1992b)

Ovid, poet, equestrian, Rome, c.1 BCE:

But don't you fail your lady, hoisting bigger sails, and don't let her get ahead of you on the track either; race to the finish together: that's when pleasure is full, when man and woman lie there, equally vanquished. (Ov. *Ars* 2.725–8)

This poem is explicitly not directed at married women, and certainly not at married couples, but the narrator's philosophy of male/female sex is an important attestation of the sort of connubial values commonly associated with the second century CE and clearly present earlier.

84 CE: Sulpicia, satirist, Rome, 60s CE:

> If... should show me naked, having sex with [my husband], after the bedsprings have been [broken and] fixed again.... (Sulpicia the satirist, fragment; see Hallett 1992; H. Parker 1992b; Richlin 1992d)

Rabbi Eliezer, Palestine, c.80 CE:

> The obligation which is stated in the Torah: *Tayalin* [students? the unemployed?], every day. Workers, twice a week. Donkey drivers, once a week. Camel drivers, once every thirty days. Sailors, once every six months. (*mKetubot* 5: 6; trans. in Satlow 1995: 268)

This is one of many comments on the famous rule that among the duties of husband towards wife was the duty to have sex with her on a regular basis; see discussion in Satlow 1995: 268–82; Boyarin 1993: 107–66.

Musonius Rufus, Stoic philosopher, equestrian, from Volsinii in Etruria, latter half of the first century CE:

> For what purpose, after all, did the craftsman of the human species in the beginning cut our kind into two, and then make two types of genitals, the one female and the other male, and then make in each a strong desire for the other, for association and partnership, and mix into both a strong longing for one another, in the male for the female and in the female for the male? Isn't it clear that he wanted them to be together and to live together and to devise together things for one another's livelihood, and to engage together in the reproduction and rearing of children, so that our species will be eternal? (Musonius Rufus, from "Whether Marriage Is an Impediment to Doing Philosophy," trans. Nussbaum; in Nussbaum 2002: 320)

154 CE: Martial, epigrammatist, 90s CE:

> Wife, get out of my house or conform to my preferences... You won't let me bugger you: Cornelia allowed this to Gracchus, Julia to Pompey, Portia to Brutus; when the Trojan cupbearer was not yet mixing the wine, Juno served Jupiter in place of Ganymede. If you like to be serious, you can be Lucretia all day long; I want Lais at night. (Mart. *Ep.* 11.104.1, 17–22; Lais was a famous prostitute, see Richlin 1992a: 41, 159–60)

Plutarch, moral philosopher, Boeotia, c.100–120 CE:

> This is the way, I think, for the lady of the house: not to run away, nor to bear such things with bad grace when her husband begins, but not to initiate it herself, either. The latter is prostitute-like and hasty, the former is arrogant and lacking in affection. (Plut. *Coniugalia praecepta* 18 [*Mor.* 140c]; see Richlin 1998: 158–9)

Rabbi Akiva, Palestine, 110s CE:

> [A menstruating woman] imparts uncleanness to him who has sexual relations with her. (*mNiddah* 2:3 G, trans. Kraemer 1988: 47)

The tractate *Niddah* concerns ritual uncleanness due to menstruation; see Satlow 1995: 296–8. For comparison with Christian attitudes, see S. Cohen 1991; for Roman ideas on menstruation, Richlin 1997d.

224 CE: Clement, Christian teacher, Alexandria, c.190–92 CE:

> So it is altogether necessary to marry, both for the sake of the fatherland and of the succession of children and of the debt we owe to the universe as best we can. And so the poets pity a marriage "half-finished" and childless.... (Clement of Alexandria *Stromata* 2.23.140.1)

Clement wanted all sex to be procreative; see Brooten 1996: 325; Brown 1988: 132–6; E. Clark 1989: 90–1; Satlow 1995: 261.

Rabbi [Yehudah the Patriarch], Palestine, before 217 CE:

> [A certain woman came before Rabbi. She said to him: Rabbi, I set him the table, and he turned it over. He said:] "How is the case different from fish?" (*bNedarim* 20a–b, trans. Boyarin 1993: 110, with disc. at 109–13; cf. Satlow 1995: 239–41; 1996)

This passage concerns the Rabbis' attitude towards non-procreative sexual techniques, which they treat as a matter of choice (for the husband), like cuisine.

Heliodorus, novelist, Phoenician, Emesa (Syria), 200–250 CE (the speaker is Persinna, Queen of Ethiopia):

> Those who ... came to build the royal palace ... made use of the romance of Perseus and Andromeda to adorn the bedchambers. It was there one day that your father and I happened to be taking a siesta in the drowsy heat of summer.... that day your father made love to me, swearing that he was commanded to do so by a dream, and I knew instantly that the act of love had left me pregnant. (Heliod. 4.8, trans. J. R. Morgan [in Reardon 1989])

294 CE: Domitiana, Egypt [date uncertain]:

> Urbanus, whom Urbana bore, Domitiana, whom Candida bore, bring him to her, full of love, raging with jealousy and without sleep over his love and passion for her, and make him ask her to return to his house as [his wife]...Yoke them in marriage and [make them] live together in love for the rest of their lives. Make him her obedient slave, desiring no other woman or maiden, but Domitiana alone.... (*Ant. Fluch.* 5, trans. in Kraemer 1988: 108–9)

Kraemer notes the relation of the language in this magical papyrus to the Septuagint, but I would also draw attention to Domitia's investment in the values of the Greek romance.

Rabbi Abba bar Ayvo (also known as Rav), the founder and leading scholar of the rabbinic academy in Sura, Persia (in the mid third century CE):

> "She eats with him every Friday night." This is euphemistic. (Rav at *yKetubot* 5.8 30a–b; trans. and disc. in Satlow 1995: 270)

This famous dictum suggests that a husband's duty be performed every Friday night.

364 CE: Rabbi Avin, Palestine, 360s CE:

> The Holy One loves procreation more than the Temple. (*bNiddah* 16b–17a, trans. Boyarin 1993: 125, with lively discussion)

434 CE: Ausonius, rhetorician and courtier, Bordeaux, 380s CE:

> Eunus, because you lick the putrid genitals of your pregnant wife, you're in a rush to put your tongue to the buttocks of your unborn sons. (Auson. *Ep.* 86)

This is one of a string of epigrams on the repulsiveness of oral sex, especially cunnilingus (78, 79, 82–7), six of which are addressed to this Eunus, who is identified as a Syrian and a schoolteacher. Several of the epigrams involve elaborate word games based on elementary education, and 86 involves a double pun on *glossas* "tongues/explanations" and *natis* "buttocks/sons." Like 94, addressed to a *semivir* called Zoilus, all these poems are strongly reminiscent of Martial.

(4) sex between women?

14 CE: Hybreas, rhetorician, Mylasa (Asia Minor), 30s–20s BCE:

> [When he was speaking on the practice case about the man who caught the *tribades* and killed them, he began to describe the feelings of the husband...]: I looked first at the "man," [to see if] he was born like that or something had been stitched on.

Grandaus, rhetorician, ? Asia Minor, ? before 14 CE:

> They wouldn't allow male adulterers to be killed for such a cause; ... but if they caught a pretend-male adulterer...

The words of these Greek speakers are recalled by the elder Seneca, *Controversiae* 1.2.23 (published c.30s CE). Hybreas was famous; Grandaus is otherwise unknown, and this name may be corrupt. For discussion, see Hallett 1989. For the idea that lesbians wore strap-ons, see ps.-Lucian *Erotes* 28 (2nd c. CE), a *reductio ad absurdum* arguing that if men can have sex with men, women should be able to have sex with women. The speaker calls this *tes tribakes aselgeias*, "the rubbed licentiousness," saying he is using a word seldom heard and one he is ashamed to say.

Ovid, poet, equestrian, Rome, c.8 CE:

> a desire known to no one, freakish, novel... among all animals no female is seized by desire for female. (Ov. *Met.* 9.727, 733–4; see Pintabone 2002)

84 CE: anonymous graffito, Pompeii, before 79 CE:

> I wish I [fem.] could hold to my neck and embrace the little arms, and bear kisses on the tender lips. Go on, doll, and trust your joys to the winds; believe me, light is the nature of men.... (*CIL* 4.5296; arguments that this poem scratched onto a wall in Pompeii is from one woman to another were presented in Milnor 2000)

154 CE: Martial, epigrammatist, Rome, 90s CE:

> The lesbian Philaenis buggers boys, and, rougher than the hard-on of a husband, she bangs eleven girls a day. (Mart. *Ep.* 7.67; cf. Hallett 1989)

Herais, Hawara, Egypt, 100s CE:

> I adjure you, Evangelos, by Anubis and Hermes and all the rest down below; attract and bind Sarapias whom Helen bore, to this H., whom Thermoutherin bore, now; quickly, quickly. By her soul and heat attract Sarapias herself.... (*PGM* 32.1–19; trans. in Kraemer 1988: 95; cf. discussion in Brooten 1996: 78)

"Peter," ? Egypt, c.100–150 CE:

> But men and women [there in Hell have to jump repeatedly off] a high cliff... These were those men who defile their bodies, behaving like women, and those women who have sex with one another as a man (does) with a woman. (*Apocalypse of Peter* 17; trans. and disc. Brooten 1996: 306)

For the date, see Himmelfarb 1983: 8–11; this text was cited by Clement of Alexandria as scripture, and exists in Greek and Ethiopic.

Lucian, satirist, Greek, after 140 CE [one prostitute quizzes another who has a female customer]:

> ...they say there are women like that in Lesbos, masculine-looking, but they don't want to give it up for men. Instead, they consort with women, just like men.... How did she do it? That's what I most want you to tell me. (*Dialogues of the Courtesans* 5)

224 CE: Clement, Christian teacher, Alexandria, c.190–92 CE:

> [luxury] confounds nature; men... suffer the things of women, and women behave like men in that women, contrary to nature, are given in marriage and marry (other women). (*Paidagogos* 3.3.21.3, translated and discussed in Brooten 1996: 322 n. 76)

Tertullian, Christian theologian, Carthage, c.208–12 CE:

> Look at the whores, the marketplaces of public lust, and at the very rubsters [*frictrices* – literal Latin translation of *tribades*], and if you can wrench your eyes away from these disgraces of chastity publicly done away with, just look up, and you'll see they're the wives of citizens. (*De Pallio* 4.9; discussed in Brooten 1996: 317–18; McKechnie 1992)

Note that Tertullian seems to assume the spectator will be distracted by the bodies of these women from some sign in their faces that they are *matronae*.

294 CE: Rav Hunah, Persia, 290s CE:

> Women who "rub" with each other are ineligible to marry a priest. (*bYevamot.* 76a, A, trans. Satlow 1995: 190)

Rabbinic texts discuss sex between women rarely and briefly; this opinion of Rav Hunah is qualified by an unattributed (= consensus) opinion that seems to take such sex acts less seriously. Compare an unattributed opinion from the Palestinian Talmud (*yGittin* 8:10, 49 C) that says there are two schools of thought on this; discussion in Satlow 1995: 189–90, with fuller explanation in Brooten 1996: 64–70.

364 CE: Sophia, Hermoupolis Magna, Egypt, fourth century CE (?):

> By means of this corpse-daemon inflame the heart, the liver, the spirit of Gorgonia, whom Nilogenia bore, with love and affection for Sophia, whom Isara bore. (*Suppl. Mag.* 1.42 [trans. Daniel and Maltomini 1990: 138] with Brooten 1996: 81–90)

434 CE: John Chrysostom, Christian preacher, Antioch, 380s CE:

> [men who have sex with men] are excluded from any pardon, since they have outraged nature herself. And it is even more shameful that the women should seek this type of intercourse, since they ought to have more modesty than men. (John Chrysostom, *Commentary on Romans*, Homily 4 [*PG* 60: 417–22]; trans. in Boswell 1980: 360; see also Brooten 1996: 344–8)

Jerome, Christian scholar and monastic, Bethlehem, 412 CE:

> I have heard that you at once took my place in clinging to her companionship and never left her by so much as even a fingernail's breadth, as they say – living in the same house, the same bedroom, the same bed – so that to all in the city [= Rome] it became very well known that you had found a mother and she a daughter. A farm outside the city served you as convent and the country was chosen because of its solitude. And you lived there thus for a long time, so that because of the copying of you and the conversion of many women I rejoiced that Rome was made Jerusalem. Convents of virgins [were] everywhere .... (Jer. *Ep.* 127.8, with J. M. Bennett 2000 on recognizing "lesbian-like" behavior in pre-modern history)

Caelius Aurelianus, physician, Numidia, mid-400s CE:

> For [the effeminate men] are just like the women who are called *tribades*, because they practice both kinds of love, rush to have sex with women more than with men and pursue women with an almost masculine jealousy. (Caelius Aurelianus *On Chronic Diseases* 4.9, trans. in Brooten 1996: 150, with disc. at 147–62)

This text is a translation into Latin from the Greek of Soranus, so the idea seems to go back to the second c. CE but still to be current.

[Unattributed rabbinic opinion], Palestine, post-400 CE:

> You shall not copy the practices of the land of Egypt ... or the land of Canaan [Lev. 18: 3] ... And what would they do? A man would marry a man; and a woman [would marry a] woman. (*Sifra Aḥare* 9: 8 [Weiss, 85c–d]; trans. in Satlow 1995: 188, with discussion)

4 General Observations

(a) The institution of slavery underlies all responses. Despite ethical pangs, Christians and Jews kept slaves, and indeed for the Rabbis slavery carried an extra stigma (Hezser 2002). Widespread poverty and the concomitant practice of the abandonment or sale of infants meant that for many people sex was not a choice but an obligation, forced sex being a primary element in the degradation of slavery (Joshel 1992: 30–1). Many of those enslaved would have come from peripheral cultures, whose (now unknown) sex/gender systems may well have differed from their captors'. And colonized cultures themselves also took slaves (cf. Hezser 2002 on the Jews' circumcision of male captives).

(b) Sexual practices generally elicit evaluative reactions, both enthusiastically for and violently against. These often coexist, though there are definitely local differences in the mix. The same wording sometimes repeats over centuries, e.g. in condemnations of pederasty, but conflicts also persist.

(c) Urban Greeks and Romans during this period commonly constructed the sexual body as a set of plugs and sockets, receptacles for the phallus or tongue (so Hallett 1977; H. Parker 1997; Richlin 1981b, 1992a; Skinner 1979; Halperin 1990; a model rejected for classical Athens by Davidson 2001 and Hubbard 2003). Classes of individuals are then defined by their "activity," their plugness or their socketness: they penetrate or are penetrated. But socketness is often felt to be intrinsically female, and vice versa, as in the younger Seneca's description of women as *pati natae*, "born to undergo" (*Ep.* 95.21; On *patior*, see Richlin 1993: 531; Walters 1997b: 30–1). This view is in keeping with the understanding of the female body in this period (P. Clark 1998; Fredrick 1997; M. M. Levine 1995; Richlin 1984, 1995, 1997a, 1997d; Wyke 1994). "Socketness" in males is thus acceptable in adolescence, which is perceived as an epicene state, but not in adulthood. For some writers from other cultures this model seems to be alien and somewhat upsetting. It was perhaps the case that sexual subcultures flourished mainly in the *metropoleis*.

5 Very Frequently Attested Cultural Issues

Pederasty: Attitudes towards sex between adult males and boys between the ages of 12 and 18 vary among cultures and over time, from highly positive even for citizens (many Greek urban cultures, including Egyptians within this milieu), to generally positive though not for citizen boys (Roman urban cultures), to regretfully negative (various asceticisms), to strongly negative (Philo, rabbinic Judaism, monasticism). Noteworthy is the virtual disappearance of pederastic love literature in the late 200s CE, with Nemesianus a lone voice – though Philostratus' pederastic assembly line suggests a world of sophists churning it out in bulk. Pederasty remains a major cultural preoccupation to the end of our period and beyond, even if attested solely by diatribes.

Sex between adult males: All cultures of the empire express negative attitudes towards sex between adult males, with adulthood being considered to start around age 20. Writers who identify as outsiders to the *metropoleis* sometimes merge pederasty together with sex between adult males in their critiques, and critics often speak of sex between women and between men as comparable evils.

Sex for men with women and women with men outside marriage: Mediterranean cultures generally expect all citizens to marry, and girls might marry soon after puberty. All cultures define adultery as involving a married woman and a person not her husband. Sex outside marriage for husbands is often not considered intrinsically problematic, and indeed underpins many erotic texts. Sex for women outside marriage is considered bad, even for women for whom this constitutes their identity (prostitutes) or a major part of it (slaves), and women are obsessively claimed to be promiscuous. Having sex with women outside marriage is the third great cultural concern for male writers; for the few extant women writers sex outside marriage also looms large. Respectable women's self-definition seems to have depended on sexual self-differentiation from slave women. (On Roman women and adultery see Richlin 1981a, 1992b; on Jewish women and the ceremony of Sotah, see Peskowitz 1997: 131–53; Satlow 1996. On slave women, see Richlin 1997a; P. Clark 1998. On the sexuality expressed by the elegist Sulpicia, see Keith 1997.)

6 Frequently Attested Cultural Issues

Oral sex: Romans and some Greek writers under the empire repeatedly express negative attitudes towards oral sex, especially in invective and jokes; others take less notice (Richlin 1992a: 26–9; H. Parker 1997).

Sex between husband and wife: This is, by comparison, a less-discussed concern except for rabbinic writers, for whom marital sex is important and positive, and for some Christian writers, for whom it is important and of debatable value (Boyarin 1993; Satlow 1998b; Brown 1988). For historicization of marital affection in the empire, see Cohen and Saller 1994: 44–55, correcting Foucault 1988.

Prostitution: Prostitution was legal everywhere in the empire at all times (see McGinn 1998: 343–5), although efforts were sometimes made to outlaw male prostitution and to curb the practice of castrating enslaved babies to make eunuchs. The sex objects in many erotic texts are probably imagined as prostitutes even where this is not specified, and prostitutes figure as well in texts and art of all kinds (Henry 1992; H. Parker 1992a; McGinn 1989; 1998). Sacred prostitution has been shown to be fictional (Beard and Henderson 1997).

Abstinence: A positive attitude towards abstinence from sex is present from the first century CE onwards and is by no means exclusively Christian, being an element in Stoic philosophy as well as in some medical systems (see Pinault 1992; Foucault 1988). Rabbinic Judaism, however, values sex between husband and wife so highly that it is not comfortable with the idea of abstinence (Boyarin 1993: 134–66). Moral texts generally stress self-control, but this should be taken in the context of immoral texts. The whole issue grows in importance from about 200 CE onwards.

Rape: Rape was a crime throughout the period, but victims were often blamed, and Roman law is clear that there are those with whom rape "is not committed," i.e. persons who could never press charges – not only prostitutes but waitresses and others in certain labor categories (Edwards 1997; Fantham 1991; Richlin 1993). The rape of slaves was treated as property damage. Yet the rape of women is a popular plotline in Greek and Latin literature (Richlin 1992c). For rabbinic attitudes towards rape, see Wegner 1988: 23–7, 300–1; Satlow 1995: 132–5.

7 Sparsely Attested Cultural Issues

Contraception and abortion: Most cultures of the empire practiced both contraception and abortion, though most simultaneously placed a highly positive value on motherhood and babies. Attitudes towards contraception and abortion thus often manifest ambivalence; outside Christianity, only gynecological texts devote major attention to these issues (see Richlin 1997d: 208–10, with bibliography). Abortion and infanticide do appear in tours of Hell (Himmelfarb 1983; cf. Boswell 1988: 41–5). For rabbinic attitudes, see Satlow 1995: 232–6.

Sex between women: No one pays much attention to sex between women, but male-authored sources that do notice it or make up stories about it take a negative attitude. Evidence from women themselves is rare but not unattested – no more Sappho, just graffiti and love-charms (Brooten 1996; A. Cameron 1998; P. Gordon 1997; Hallett 1989; Milnor 2000).

Masturbation: Masturbation holds its usual humble place: the subject of low poetry, and associated with slaves; frowned upon by Rabbis and churchmen (Satlow 1995: 246–64 on rabbinic attitudes). Martial makes masturbation a substitute for a boy he cannot afford (Richlin 1992a: 135–6), and pictures slaves "masturbating behind the door" as they watch Hector and Andromache having sex (11.104.13–14; cf. Clarke 1998: 88 on voyeur figures in Roman erotic art). The dildo, a popular comic item in classical Greek text and art (Jeffrey Henderson 1992: 221–2), is all but unmentioned, if not extinct; it reappears briefly but spectacularly in ps.-Lucian *Erotes* (28) as a "monstrous enigma without seed."

Circumcision: Male circumcision constitutes a big marker of the division between Jews and non-Jews, though it was also practiced by other cultures at the time (see S. Cohen 1997; Montserrat 1996: 36–7). In non-Jews it is often associated with general anti-Semitic statements (Richlin 1997b: 32–3); here is Rutilius Namatianus, city prefect of Rome, in his famous poem on his return to Gaul in 417:

> A complaining Jew was in charge of the place, an animal alien to human food; he put his bruised bushes and dented seaweed on our bill, and cried out over the great cost of the water we poured. We gave back to him the insults owed to that obscene race, that shamefully snips off the genital head; root of stupidity, with its frigid sabbath in its heart, but a heart more frigid than its own religion. (*De Reditu Suo* 1.383–90)

For Christians circumcision posed problems; see Boyarin 1993: 7–8, 233; Brown 1988: 59.

Castration: Eunuchs and castration have no fans, though some individual eunuchs rose to positions of power (Hopkins 1978a; Kuefler 2001; Masterson 2001: 143–209; Roller 1997; and especially Butler 1998, on self-castration and slave identity). Origen's reputed voluntary castration may represent a trend in third-century Christian asceticism (Brown 1988: 168–9).

Sex with children below the age of puberty: What is now thought of as "pedophilia" is rarely mentioned, and comes up only in the context of prostitution, slavery, or a few salacious tales. The concept of "child molesting" does not exist, or of child pornography as a genre. Yet the Rabbis posit that female slaves might be used sexually after the age of three; the Romans had a law against sex with prepubescent girls, so maybe this was not just hypothetical (Roman law on *nondum viripotentes virgines*, Paul at *D.* 48.19.38.3; rabbinic rules on the virgin status of slaves past the age of three, *yMoed-Katan* 1:2, 1:4, cf. 3:1, 3:2 (with thanks to Catherine Hezser; see also Satlow 1996: 284)).

Incest: Similarly, incest, though forbidden in Roman law, receives very little attention, and is usually treated as an aberrant form of marriage rather than as akin to rape (Gardner 1986: 125–7). The exception is Egyptian brother–sister marriage, a remarked-upon anomaly (Montserrat 1996: 89–91).

Clitoridectomy: Clitoridectomy is attested as a *rite de passage*, though only in Egypt and rarely; elsewhere it is a medical procedure for the correction of improper (lesbian) desire (Montserrat 1996: 41–6; Brooten 1996: 162–71).

Infibulation: This practice (piercing and clamping the foreskin) shows up only in Roman jokes (Richlin 1997b: 32).

8 Mapping the Sexuality of the Roman Empire

If we could map all the Kinsey II responses, we would expect to see marked differences between rural and urban attitudes. For certain practices we might also be able to draw isobars: circumcision would be located in Egypt–Ethiopia–Arabia – Palestine–Phoenicia–Syria; iconography featuring male genitalia is mostly Italian; eunuchs seem to have begun in Asia Minor. Gender-marked clothing varies from place to place, though Greek dress is already popular in Italy by the late republican period. Women were supposedly more secluded in the East, but see Philo (section 3(1) above, under 84 CE) on women who brawl in the marketplace in Alexandria.

The Romans were the only culture in the empire to deck the walls with rows of phalli (W. Parker 1988 and Richlin 1992a on the ithyphallic god Priapus; on representations in art, Clarke 1998; Johns 1982: 61–75). Festooned with phallic amulets, even trimming their horses' tack with phalli, they must have seemed odd sexually to many of their neighbors; we do hear something about this from the Rabbis

(Cf. Satlow 1997: 435, "There can be little doubt that the rabbis would have seen the statues of Hermes and Priapus as ridiculous"). To be penetrated, for a Roman, was degrading both in a physical sense of invasion, rupture, and contamination, and in a class sense: the penetrated person's body was likened to the body of a slave. This experience of the individual is understood also on the state level, as war is associated with rape, both literally in the rape of the women and boys of the defeated enemy (Richlin 1992a: 98; cf. 1993: 553) – the alleged cause of Boudicca's rebellion – and figuratively, for example in the images of the emperor battering female embodiments of conquered peoples in the Sebasteion at Aphrodisias (Ferris 2000: 55–60); compare the Hebrew image of the rape of the daughter of Zion (Gordon and Washington 1995). Slavery would have introduced conquered peoples to the Roman sex/gender system at the lowest level. For those not enslaved, Roman occupation would have disrupted major centers of cultural production: for example, the destruction of the Temple meant that the ceremony of Sotah could no longer be carried out, nor did this stem from a Roman desire to liberate Jewish women (see Hill 1997 on conquest and the body; Ando, this volume on landscape).

Though Greek and Roman ethnographies cannot be taken as true, and though all ancient ethnographies assign sexual and gender weirdness to places they consider marginal, it seems possible that the Celtic and Germanic tribes were more gender-egalitarian than the Mediterranean cultures, which consistently emphasize the visibility of women in the northern cultures. But an epistemological paradox besets efforts to know about the hinterlands of the empire: we know them mainly post-conquest.

When this companion to the Roman Empire is redone in fifty years, it is my hope that my successor will be surprised that I could have omitted the Persians and Armenians, the tribes of Africa, Asia Minor, and the Balkans, and the Iron Age peoples of western Europe; that the necessary evidence will be available; and that archaeologists will have figured out how to do an archaeology of sexuality. Then maybe there will really be an overview of sexuality in the Roman Empire; meanwhile, these fragments.

ACKNOWLEDGMENTS

This chapter is written in fond memory of Jack Winkler, whose imagination, taste for the noncanonical, and penchant for thought experiments continue to inspire the study of sexuality in antiquity. Thanks to Clifford Ando, Mark Masterson, Sara Phang, Michael Satlow, Martha Vinson, Greg Woolf, and many friends in Jewish and Christian studies for their unfailingly generous help.

Translations throughout are my own unless otherwise stated. Some dates here are debated, for which see the cited bibliography.

CHAPTER EIGHTEEN

On Food and the Body

Veronika E. Grimm

"The beginning and root of all good, is the pleasure of the stomach!" The wisdom of this saying, which was attributed to the ancient Greek philosopher Epicurus, is the first lesson that a human infant learns. Food, the only source of energy for the sustenance of life, also provides one of the basic pleasures life offers. Food is at the heart of family and social life. Food sharing has always meant inclusion and acceptance in the group; while accusations of disgusting eating habits, often together with those of unacceptable sexual habits, are a well-tried means of social exclusion, employed quite profitably by the morally superior or gossipmongers for shaming and ridiculing their victims.

In the ancient Mediterranean world, feasting was as central to religious life as it was part of family and social life. The awesome rite of religious sacrifice culminated in a banquet; the ritual sharing and eating of sacrificial meat was an integral part of polytheistic cult. The gods honored in this fashion, including the god of the ancient Jews, shared with their worshippers a preference for the meat of domesticated animals. But unlike the god of the Jews, the gods of the Greeks and Romans did not prescribe special diets, and rarely required abstinence of their followers. In the absence of God-given moral injunctions, human legislation oversaw important aspects of public conduct, while philosophers and other guardians of morality worried about how one should live an ethical life, and ancient "healthcare professionals," doctors and athletic trainers, gave advice about health (Grimm 1996: 43–59). Food was a central concern for both moral and physical well-being.

Despite the wealth of references to food in its literature, the question of who ate what in the Roman world still remains quite contested. In the extant literary works, all written by men of the upper classes or by those who would have liked to belong to the upper classes, eating and drinking are used for a great variety of purposes, ranging from moral metaphors to character description or, more often, for character assassination, having little in the way of trustworthy objectivity.

The ancient empire of the Romans, which sustained itself for centuries, covered the lands around the Mediterranean sea and, at its zenith, extended further into areas of Northern and Western Europe and Asia that were increasingly removed in terms of climate, population, and culture from the Mediterranean core, which itself was quite a varied patchwork of climates, lands, languages, and traditions (Patterson 1987).

The question "who ate what" in this far-flung empire is not a trivial one; reliable answers for it would take us a long way in understanding an ancient culture that was crucially important in the formation of European civilization. Research devoted to answering this question has increased, and there are now a number of excellent scholarly books (e.g. Garnsey 1988, 1998, 1999; Curtis 2001; Sirks 1991; Morley 1996). Unfortunately there are no ancient statistical studies and no surveys of food consumption from antiquity to aid the investigator in this quest. The question, "who ate what," has to be approached by collating and critically evaluating more or less indirect evidence, each with its own specific problems.

Perusing uncritically some of the rich and vivid remnants of ancient literature, a consensus has long held that the Romans went with hardly a pause from being frugal, upright vegetarians – "pulse-eaters" – into decadence and unimaginable gluttony, eating and regurgitating the most diverse products of the known world all mixed together and moistened with rotten fish-sauce (Pray Bober 1999: 146–56)! Since only the "elite" could afford to devour the riches of land and sea, the same opinion has generally held that the "non-elite" or nine-tenths of the population of the empire lived on bread and water, on a "starkly vegetarian" diet (Sirks 1991: 362; Garnsey 1999: 16–17). These opinions, as I shall argue, need to be seriously modified.

References to food and eating are ubiquitous in Roman literature. They appear in the works of poets, orators, historians, biographers, and medical writers. Advice concerning food and eating forms a significant part of the teaching of various philosophical schools. All use food and eating for their own varied purposes of persuasion, each with its own "axe to grind." Consequently, as we shall see, none of these sources provide reliable information relevant for the actual diet of the wider population or even segments of it. On the other hand all of these writings are very strong on attitude, that is to say, on strongly held and highly emotion-laden opinion, and a failure to recognize this leads to their misuse and misinterpretation.

Many ancient writers regarded food in itself as a trivial necessity, not a worthy subject for their art; on the other hand many realized that food and eating habits could be used profitably for purposes of moral judgment, for embarrassing and ridiculing one's opponents and social targets. Knowing that food has a wealth of sensuous associations, that it can conjure up a rich variety of sights, smells, and textures, both enticing and disgusting, Roman writers became masters of its use as vivid metaphors for real or imagined excesses of the many-faceted society they saw around them. Emily Gowers, in her book *The Loaded Table* (1993), inspects the feast of verbal food that Roman writers and poets "cooked up" and gives a perceptive analysis of the way this "verbal food" expressed the writers' concerns with Rome and its empire, with the growth and increasing complexity of its society and their own place in it. The verbal feast served up by the poets was not, and was not even meant to be, a record of what people ate.

In the steeply hierarchical society of the Roman Empire the ruling classes held to an age-old set of beliefs and principles developed to underpin their own privileges. A

Roman aristocrat was expected to rule over his family, which included not only wife and children but also slaves and clients, dependants of various ranks. All of these he was to protect, and all of them owed him allegiance and service. An aristocrat was born to rule and to take part in the rule of the empire. This idea was strongly maintained even when the rule of the empire was concentrated in one man's hands. A man was considered fit to rule others only if he first proved that he could rule himself. Ruling himself, *encrateia*, was defined for him by the Stoic philosophers as the need to control his passions, as Shakespeare echoes it centuries later: "give me that man that is not passion's slave." The philosophers argued primarily against inordinate anger, fear, greed and grief, but the list of passions could be extended, or reduced on the other hand to a minimum of two, passion for food and sex. These two "passions" would then serve as a graphic marker for a multitude of other sins. Stoic teaching fitted well with the Roman ideal of *gravitas*, meaning seriousness, restraint, frugality in conduct. It followed from both that any concern with the comforts or pleasures of the body would be morally suspect and below the dignity of a high-born man. The true man, according to the Stoic view, concerned himself with matters of the mind:

> It is a sign of a stupid man to spend a great deal of time on the concerns of his body – exercise, eating, drinking, evacuating his bowels and copulating. These things should be done in passing; you should devote your whole attention to the mind. (Epict. *Ench.* 41)

This ideology went hand in hand with rules and expectations concerning proper masculine comportment (Gleason 1995). The well-born man had to present himself as one who unquestionably deserved his social position. This required, in addition to the already mentioned *gravitas* and self-control, also *philanthropia*, generosity towards his city and his dependants. "The Roman people hated private luxury but delighted in munificence extended to the public!" observed Cicero (*Mur.* 76), and many ancient writers seem to prove him right. Accusations of ostentatious luxury echo through Roman literature, coupled often with the hurt feelings of the writer who was left out of it. The poet takes cruel vengeance for the dinner party where he felt short-changed by memorializing the host in a poem for eternal shame. Millennia later we are still witness to his stinginess.

How should one read these complaints? Roman grandees used the evening meal, the *cena*, for various social purposes. When dining with intimate friends and social equals, the number of participants was small, usually not exceeding nine people. It was believed that beyond this number the occasion would become loud and unruly; instead of *convivium*, or "life-sharing," it would become *convitium*, "vice-sharing." A rich Roman was also expected to maintain a large network of social connections, to take care of his clients, entertain visitors to the city who came with recommendation from friends, and so on. The *philanthropia* expected of him required, amongst other things, the feeding and entertaining of a large crowd of people. The grand dinner party served this purpose. Following the work of John D'Arms (1984), many writers have elaborated the social inequality and hierarchical arrangement of the Roman dinner. But is this so surprising? Anyone who has ever attended large, modern banquets, wedding parties, fund-raising occasions, etc., knows that not everyone sits at high-table, that the farther one is seated from the place of honor, the colder the food he is served.

When Ammianus Marcellinus, the last great Latin historian, a Greek from the east, expresses his disappointment with the Roman aristocracy (14.6.7–24) we hear again the same complaints: luxury, ostentation, lack of true refinement, and gluttonous dinners. But on a more critical reading one may suspect that what hurt Ammianus most was not receiving the attention he felt was due to him and not being invited back next time. To understand the picture that he, and other newcomers like Galen, in the *Concerning Foresight* (*de praecognitione*), and Lucian, in the *Nigrinus*, paint of Rome one has to keep in mind that they came as provincials to the greatest city of the world, intent on fame and success. Rome must have appeared a bewilderingly large and threatening place in comparison with their home city which they knew well, and in which they were part of a familiar social network. The well worn clichés these writers use to describe the Romans reminds one of refugee intellectuals arriving in New York and complain that the city "has no culture!"

If food, in and of itself, was considered trivial by ancient writers, appetite was most certainly not. Hunger is a fact of life; all men hunger if deprived of food. Appetite, on the other hand, is a sinister and suspect attribute. It is individual, unpredictable, and uncontrollable, and therefore highly dangerous. Appetite, for food or sex, and most often for both, provided rich material for the gossipmongers. People have always worried about their fellow humans having more access than themselves to these basic commodities. In Roman thought, appetite, the source of passions, fits neither with *gravitas* nor with self-control, which explains its easy use as a weapon for character assassination in the hand of righteous or self-righteous critics.

There is a discernible conflict in even the best of the ancient historians, between the urge to tell it as it was and their equally strong need to teach a moral lesson or tell an intriguing tale of gossip, innuendo, and speculation. The requirement of the moral lesson is that the hero who fails must have a flaw in his character which makes him fail and justifies his sorry end. Gluttony is dragged in as an easy, almost mechanical device to substitute for careful analysis of what often was a very complex set of causes.

Of the many examples of the use of appetite to besmirch character in the hands of ancient historians, I will present here the fall of Vitellius, because in his case the historians' characterization is generally unquestioned, and he is often held up as an example and personification of Roman gustatory vice (see also Pray Bober 1999: 356, who suggests that modern notions that the Romans habitually indulged in gorging and vomiting were picked up from the biography of the "despicable Emperor Vitellius" written by Suetonius).

The following is a brief summary of his story: after the fall of Nero, Galba becomes emperor and Vitellius is sent to the legions in Germany. These legions, restless in the wake of the revolt of Vindex in Gaul, make Vitellius emperor, while in the center of the empire the praetorians kill Galba and make Otho emperor. A large extant part of Tacitus' *Histories* treats the ensuing civil war, from which the Vitellian forces emerge the winners for a time, while a well-organized conspiracy is being forged under Vespasian in the east, involving the Roman forces in Judea, Syria, and Egypt.

The war was fought with enormous investment on both sides. Vitellius does not appear to have been an unpopular emperor while he lived. Tacitus says that the common people of Rome and even slaves armed themselves to fight on his side.

But he failed. Tacitus criticizes him for not being able to restrain his forces, for not being eager to fight, for not believing the rumors about the Flavian conspiracy. The fact is that Vitellius failed, therefore there must have been moral turpitude involved. Since Vitellius seems to have been devoted to his wife and family and gave little scope in these quarters, the turpitude chosen is gluttony: indolent luxury and extravagant dinners; "at midday he was tipsy and was gorged with food," says Tacitus (*Hist.* 1.62). In summing up, the historian admits, somewhat inconsistently, that "his nature was marked by simplicity and liberality" then, in typical Tacitean fashion, he adds "qualities which if unchecked, prove the ruin of their possessor." In hindsight the historian decided that "undoubtedly it was to the advantage of the state that Vitellius be defeated" (*Hist.* 3.86). The interest of the victors demanded that his memory be blackened. The fact that he was a rather fat man, who may have liked good food, is a rather poor explanation of a complex series of events.

Other writers embellish the topic. The historian Cassius Dio dealt with Vitellius in book 64 of his work, first describing Vitellius' moral failures, then, to be fair, cataloguing his "good deeds." I shall reverse the order here. The list of good deeds first: Vitellius retained the coinage minted under his predecessors, Nero, Galba, and Otho, evincing no displeasure at their likenesses, and any gifts that they had bestowed upon any persons he held to be valid, and deprived no one of any such possession. He did not collect any sums still owing of former levies, and he confiscated no one's property. He put to death but a very few of those who had sided with Otho, and did not withhold the property of these from their relatives. Upon the kinsmen of those previously executed he bestowed all their funds that were still to be found in the public treasury. He did not even find fault with the wills of those who had fought against him and had fallen in battle. And so on. He won the attachment of the populace, but Dio, with characteristic disdain of the common people, attributes this to his constant attendance at the theater. He ate with the most influential men on free and easy terms, and this gained their favor to an even greater degree. He honored his friends and old companions.

Compare this picture to the catalogue of his flaws, compiled by the same author: He was insatiate in gorging himself and was constantly vomiting up what he ate, being nourished by the mere passage of the food. All the most costly viands were brought from as far as the ocean, not to say farther, drawn from both land and sea, and were prepared in so costly a fashion that even now certain cakes and other dishes are named Vitellian, after him. It is admitted by all alike, claims the writer, that during his reign he expended 900 million sesterces on dinners (giving the same sum, Tacitus only says "it is believed"). Then there is the story of the enormous dish that he filled with the tongues and brains of peacocks. This dish appears also in Suetonius, now wearing the name "the Shield of Minerva." The latter writer goes to extremes in using gluttony for character assassination: on this platter, he writes, Vitellius mingled the livers of pike, the brains of pheasants and peacocks, the tongues of flamingos and the milt of lampreys, brought by his captains and triremes from the whole empire, from Parthia to the Spanish strait (*Vit.* 13).

It becomes obvious to anyone who tries to put together all these contrasting characterizations that the good sides and the bad do not fit into a coherent, plausible picture. Even the famous Vitellian delicacies turn out on inspection not to be so outlandish. In Apicius' cookbook, a late antique compilation of recipes from assorted earlier works on cookery, there are, indeed, three recipes with the name of Vitellius attached, but none of them stands out for its particular extravagance (*Apicius* 5.3.5, 9, 8.7.7; the first two are recipes for beans, the last one is for roast pork). Interestingly, in the whole collection one cannot find any reference to peacock brains, flamingo tongues, and the like. There are instructions for roasting these birds, and for preparing sauces for them, and there is one recipe for meatballs made from peacocks, but no mention of brains. Romans bred peafowl both for its beauty and for the table (Varro *Rust.* 3.6–7). They enjoyed peacocks for the beauty of the males; females were eaten if not used for breeding. As these were fattened, and were expensive, they were associated with luxury. Varro mentions that a fattened bird in his days would fetch 50 denarii. Now to use only the smallest piece, the brain or the tongue of such an expensive bird, is a clever writer's ploy to give a sense of the absolute peak of insane luxury.

Two more examples from Roman literature have to be mentioned here, for the reason that they are often used as evidence for the Roman diet (see e.g. MacMullen 1974; C. P. Jones 1991; Garnsey 1998, 1999; Pray Bober 1999). One is Trimalchio's famous, or rather infamous, feast, on the extravagant and disgusting side; the other is the poem known as the *Moretum*, on the moral, vegetarian, and bare subsistence side of the argument. Both, we should remind ourselves at the outset, are works of fiction.

The author and inventor of the fabulously rich and even more fabulously crude freedman, Trimalchio, is generally believed to be Petronius, an aristocratic aesthete and courtier of Nero. Trimalchio appears in the longest complete episode in an otherwise fragmentary adventure novel, the *Satyricon*, that is set in a predominantly Greek atmosphere, somewhere around the Bay of Naples (see Myers, this volume). Trimalchio's feast is a clever and cruel satirical attack on the nouveau-riche ex-slave, who managed to enrich himself by trade and money lending, enterprises that were considered below the dignity of aristocrats, and who in the process of acquiring wealth, also acquired pretensions to refinement and culture, which were, of course, the natural preserve of the upper classes alone (Pray Bober 1999: 163). The author relentlessly ridicules Trimalchio's lack of taste and sophistication in matters of food and wine by emphasizing the contrast between the enormous wealth spent on the dinner and the disgusting, ridiculous, and insipid results. He plays up the crudeness and vulgarity of the conversation, the main concern of which is to brag of the host's wealth. Some modern writers discard the rest of the *Satyricon* and use the Trimalchio episode, out of its context, as if it were a realistic document of social history (C. P. Jones 1991: 185). Trimalchio's feast, if read in its context of a novel of adventures in low-life, becomes questionable evidence for social history. The rather heavy-handed satire is interesting not because it teaches us anything about actual Roman eating habits but because it is a forerunner of a long-lived literary-intellectual conceit, the aristocratic disdain for the middle classes, the first great "put-down" of the bourgeoisie. And in that genre it is exquisite.

Just as the dinner of Trimalchio is thought by some to exemplify the life of the wealthy, on the side of poverty the often cited literary evidence is the *Moretum*, a first century CE poem of unknown authorship, once attributed to Vergil. The poem describes in epic form and minute detail how, early in the morning, a frugal and hard-working farmer prepares his bread and a kind of herb and garlic laden cheese spread, the "moretum."

"Simulus," our farmer, has only one slave woman to help him, an African, described again with careful but unflattering detail. His farm, the poet tells us, costs him nothing but his hard work. He owns a fertile vegetable garden which he tends with skill and diligence. The produce of it, however, is not for his consumption, but for the public. Every so often he carries it to the town market from where he comes back "enriched" with money. When not engaged in his garden he ploughs his field with a pair of bullocks. The reader is assured that Simulus has no meat in his larder, that he slakes his hunger with bread and uses onions, chives, and watercress as relish.

While it is sometimes admitted that this is not exactly a slice-of-life portrait of the Italian peasant, and that the poet had his own literary purposes of moralizing or poking fun at a nostalgic bucolic genre, popular amongst the rich (Kenney 1984), the poem, it is claimed, does manage to convey something of the flavor of rural life (Garnsey 1999: 114). The question is, what flavor? It certainly does describe how rotary hand mills were operated, many examples of which were found in Roman military forts in Britain and elsewhere (Curtis 2001: 338); it lists the vegetables one might find in an Italian kitchen garden; it attests to the existence of local markets and market days (*nundinae*), and shows how the produce reached the market of nearby towns to be exchanged for money. Some farmers, like our fictional "Simulus," were undoubtedly very poor. This poem, however, is often made to carry a much larger burden, for it lurks in the background of many general assertions that the popular diet in the empire was mostly vegetarian (Wilkins et al. 1995: 2; Curtis 2001: 395), that meat was considered a luxury, and that only the wealthy could afford it. This view is often elaborated further with claims that only pigs were bred for consumption by the rich and that cattle were only slaughtered when old and could no longer be of any service (Sirks 1991: 362; Pray Bober 1999: 181), that sheep and goats were kept for wool, milk, and cheese, and that fish was a luxury food (Garnsey 1999: 16), notwithstanding the ubiquity of the sea and the rivers running into it! Other sources of animal food, chicken and other fowl, or field fare are never considered by those committed to the vegetarian argument (Frost 1999).

Telling others how to live seems to have been just as popular in the ancient world as it is today. In the Roman Empire physicians vied with other experts, philosophers, orators, apparently even athletic trainers in giving dietary advice. Can we expect to gain more reliable information concerning food habits from those who guarded health and well-being?

Health care was firmly based on diet. Food and drink were used to combat diseases and it was firmly believed that they were of general assistance in preserving health as well. Physicians claimed to be experts on the "nature" of foodstuffs, which had to be carefully fitted to the "temperament" or "constitution" of each individual. Health, according to the prevailing views in ancient medicine, consisted of an equilibrium between the four bodily humors, blood, phlegm, black and yellow bile, with their corresponding qualities of hot, cold, wet, and dry. Food, exercise, and climate were crucial in maintaining this equilibrium. Foods were categorized according to their nature as heating or cooling, moistening or drying. At the same time they were either strong, medium, or weak. Strong foods were believed to be most nourishing but hard to digest, weak foods least nourishing but easy to digest. With the aid of this list made up on the basis of Celsus' *Concerning Medicine* and Hippocrates' *Regimen in Health*, we may reconstruct the ideal "balanced" diet. Among the "strong" foods were generally counted beef and the meat of other large domesticated quadrupeds; all large game such as the wild goat, deer, wild boar, wild ass; all large birds, such as the goose, the peacock, and the crane; all "sea monsters," such as the whale and the like; all pulses and bread-stuffs made of grain, honey, and cheese. Among foods belonging to the class of medium strength were counted: the hare, birds of all kinds from the smallest up to the flamingo, fish, and root and bulb vegetables. Finally, to the weakest class were thought to belong snails and shellfish, all vegetable stalks, gourds, cucumbers and capers, olives, and all orchard fruits. Strong foods were "heating" foods; in addition to being most nutritious they were also thought to be aphrodisiacs. The more "heating" the food, the more it was supposed to increase sexual potency, or at least sexual appetite.

In thinking that relied heavily on analogy, "strong" and "weak" were loaded with meaning which, while having nothing to do with nutrition, became attached to food and drink. Thus "strong" food, roast beef, is also masculine food, food fit for a free man, as opposed to complicated rich sauces which are "effeminate" food.

Amongst the voluminous writings of Galen, a famous physician who practiced medicine in Rome in the age of the Antonines, there is an abundance of references to food and a number of treatises devoted explicitly to the nature of foods. Galen, who had an extremely high opinion of his own expertise, cautions against doctors who give general advice as to whether a given food is beneficial or not; some foods may be beneficial or harmful for all, but in most cases the effect of any food depends on the particular condition of the patient. In his three books on food Galen lists an extensive range of foodstuffs edible for humans, including grains, vegetables, meat, and fish, together with all their possible effects on temperament, health, and digestion. Galen's list of animal foods is amazing in its rich variety: in addition to the domestic quadrupeds generally used for food, i.e. pigs, cattle, sheep, and goats, he discusses meat from horses, wild and domestic donkeys, camels, dogs, bears, "even though they are worse than lions and leopards." "Not a few people eat panthers... some doctors even recommend them... in the autumn hunters serve fox because they are fattened by the grapes" (Mark Grant 2000: 155–6). Next comes his list of edible birds, which is again staggering: from chickens to ostriches, peacocks to sparrows, even bustards – the good doctor knows the nature of the flesh of all feathered creatures and their effects on digestion. Similarly with the denizens of rivers and seas.

Reading Galen on food one sees a human population that, instead of being "starkly vegetarian," would eat just about anything that moved! But how reliable are his lists? Again, Galen's work has to be considered in its proper social setting. The ancient physician, descendent of Hippocrates, saw his task as a dual one: to cure the sick and also to keep the healthy from getting sick. Diet meant not just food, but a whole system of regulated life, in which food, exercise, sexual activity, sleep, and so on, had to be fitted to the climate and the seasons, all in order to keep the body healthy. Galen considered himself the heir and most accurate interpreter of Hippocrates. He was, however, more than just a doctor of the kind whose main concern was curing his patients. Galen had higher personal ambitions; he wanted to be known also as a philosopher. His own writings, which constitute almost all that we know about him, are evidence that he was a vigorous and vociferous representative of the competitive rhetorical culture of the high empire, in which knowledge and expertise could lead to fame, wealth, and power. Winning fame in such fierce competition required proof of expertise; and expertise, acquired in long and arduous training, was displayed publicly by the ability to make finer and finer discriminations. The knowledge that could be attained by only a very few was highly valued (T. Barton 1994). Galen claimed that he could distinguish 32 different kinds of pulse beats in his patients, a skill indeed that few could ever match! Should we believe his extensive experience with all the exotic foodstuffs, or should we take his knowledge of the flesh of bustards and panthers as part of his claim to omniscient expertise?

How to keep a healthy man healthy and well concerned not only the doctors but also the philosophers, who extended the notion of health to include also that of the mind and soul as well. Vegetarianism as a choice arose first, as we will see, in philosophical discussions. The ideas that combined to give rise to philosophic views concerning diet go back to classical Greece; the "philosophic diet," however, achieved its true flowering during the affluent centuries of the Pax Romana, when the slogans of the Stoic ethic were incorporated into a Platonic theology. Before taking the "philosophic diet" as any indication of ancient food practices or even widespread attitudes, one has to consider the fact that these ethical writings were copied and transmitted to us mostly because a later age found them useful and uplifting. In their own time they may not have been always so highly regarded. The preacher of self-control, with his claim of superiority to the desires of ordinary people, with his reforming zeal aimed at curbing culinary and sexual indulgence, may have been admired by some, but was made the object of satire and the butt of jokes by others.

By the time of the empire most of the philosophic schools understood their task to be the teaching of how to live the "good life." Looking back to a "golden age" of simplicity from the wealth and complexity of a huge empire, each school or teacher proposed to inculcate in the follower a way of life that would lead to true happiness, that would make him or her immune to the frustrations of life and enable the follower to rise above the common crowd – to attain an aristocracy, not of birth, money, or political power, but of virtue (Habinek 1992).

It was the Stoic school that provided the clearest elaboration of ethical principles, which were more or less taken on by the other schools. According to the uncompromising view of the Stoics, the "good life" is one which is lived "in accordance with nature." Virtue is sufficient for happiness; virtue is the only good, all emotion is bad. The cardinal virtues to which one should aspire were prudence, temperance, justice, and courage. All are born with a capacity for virtue, but from the influences of their surroundings most have become morally ill. Only philosophy can teach the way to virtue. Through the virtue of temperance a person will so toughen his body and discipline his mind that he will achieve mastery of himself. Understanding and self-control will lead to true happiness, which according to the Stoics entailed *apatheia* – lack of passion, lack of anger, greed, fear, and desire. *Askesis*, that is the training of the mind and body for endurance would, they thought, lead to the achievement of the Stoic virtues. As one of the first steps in this training, one's attitude to food had to be re-educated, for the Stoics believed that the beginning and foundation of temperance lay in self-control in eating and drinking (Lutz 1947: 27–30).

The anxieties aroused by human omnivorous tendencies in a philosopher who believed that man should live "according to nature" are well illustrated by the views of a Roman Stoic of Nero's time, Musonius Rufus. Musonius deplores the corruption of an age which contrives all kinds of devices to increase the pleasure of eating, where some people have come to such a depth of decadence to have even written books about cooking, as the learned write about music or medicine! He warns his listeners about the multitude of vices that are connected with eating, and how they must try to free themselves from these:

> One should by constant practice accustom oneself to choosing food not for enjoyment, but for nourishment, not to tickle the palate but to strengthen the body. Certainly no reasonable being...will think it desirable to be like the majority who live to eat, and like them, to spend his life in the chase after pleasure derived from food.

Frugality being a virtue, one should prefer inexpensive food to expensive, what is abundant to what is scarce, but Musonius was especially concerned that one should only eat what is "natural" for humans and avoid what is "unnatural":

> food from plants of the earth is natural to us...and some products of domesticated animals, like cheese, but not meat.

He urged that "the most useful foods are those which can be used at once without cooking." Musonius argued that meat was a less civilized kind of food and more appropriate for wild animals, and, more importantly, that it was heavy food and an obstacle to thinking and reasoning, since "the exhalations rising from it, being turbid, darken the soul." People who use meat for food "seem slower in intellect" (Muson. XVIII).

With his vegetarian views Musonius was somewhat unique among the Stoics, who saw that all living creatures fed on other living creatures in nature, and consequently, were not against meat eating. They, like the writers of the Jewish Bible, regarded animals as having been created for the good of mankind, and believed that meat was "natural food" for us. Eating meat was not a vice for most of them; the vice was giving in to pleasure.

Preaching endlessly against pleasure was not limited to the Stoic school alone. No ancient moralizer would trust his fellow human beings to be able to maintain the golden mean, a reasonable equilibrium in their lives. Pleasure, they feared, had such power that once tasted, the individual would tumble headlong into the deepest morass of debauchery. Musonius' reason for advising against meat eating stems not from a rejection of the body or its sexual nature, but rather from his fear that stuffing the body with heavy food might block the spirit and interfere with thinking and reasoning.

Were people truly interested in following the advice of Stoic teachers? Did they practice dietary self-restrictions? Ancient literature seems to attest to the fact that some among the high-living wealthy liked to discuss frugality, and that some found gestures of asceticism flattering to their self-image. There can be no doubt that the Stoic ethic of self-control was viewed generally as a lofty aim; it agreed closely with Roman moral conservative principles. Seneca, Nero's teacher and advisor, a self-styled Stoic, and one of the richest men of his time, tells us about the influence the lectures of another Stoic philosopher, Attalus, had over him:

> ...when he began extolling to us the virtues of poverty and showing us how everything which went beyond our actual needs was just so much unnecessary weight, a burden to the man who had to carry it, I often had a longing to walk out of that lecture hall a poor man. When he started exposing our pleasures and commending to us, along with moderation in our diet, physical purity and a mind uncontaminated, not only by illicit pleasures but by unnecessary ones as well, I would become enthusiastic about keeping the appetite for food and drink firmly in place. (*Ep.* 108)

Seneca's longing for poverty was never, as far as we know, translated into action, but he writes that he actually became a vegetarian following the philosopher's teaching that "variety of diet was incompatible with our physical make-up and inimical to health." He gave up the practice after a year, in obedience to his father who objected to it, or so he claims. He assures his readers that he did learn a life-long lesson – he gave up mushrooms and oysters forever because these are luxurious foods that only increase the appetite. (They also may have been the most likely to be poisonous, a serious consideration in upper-class circles of the Neronian era!)

Despite the rousing lectures and the hypocritical posturing of the likes of Seneca, neither dietary self-restraint nor even simple vegetarianism was received with favor, even by most philosophers. Porphyry of Tyre, writing in the third century CE, paradoxically provides the best evidence for this in his treatise, *On Abstention from Animal Food*. Porphyry was an eloquent advocate of vegetarianism. He wrote this treatise for an aspiring student of philosophy, who, after trying vegetarianism, as Seneca had, returned to meat eating. Porphyry pleads with his young friend to reconsider his decision and lays out the arguments against the eating of meat in order to persuade him.

Porphyry writes that he is well aware of the fact that the common folk eat meat because they believe that it is healthy, and that the physicians share this view, for they even use meat to treat disease. He also knows that most of the philosophers belonging to the Peripatetic, Stoic, or Epicurean persuasions eat meat. He acknowledges that meat eating is appropriate for those engaged in heavy work, also for soldiers, athletes, or people recovering from illness; he recommends abstention from meat *only for contemplative philosophers, who lead a sedentary life and need no strength* (*Abst.* 1.1–27, 2.4).

There were three lines of arguments against meat eating in Greco-Roman antiquity: the religious one based on belief in the transmigration of souls, held by Empedocles and Pythagoras; the moral one, based on the conviction that animals as rational beings deserve justice, and that it is unjust to kill them for food, held by Plato; and finally the argument that a meat diet is unhealthy or expensive or both. Adding to these, Porphyry argues for the philosopher's need for tranquility of the soul which, he asserts, is hindered by overloading the stomach with rich food.

In arguments urging a meatless diet on a wider audience, these lofty ideas about tranquility of the mind and justice and fairness to animals lost ground to the increasingly more lurid views gaining favor among various self-appointed guardians of morality who saw food as intimately linked with sex, and who feared that pleasure arising from strong, heating foods would inevitably lead to sexual lust. From Porphyry's concern with justice and tranquility and Stoic anxieties about what food would fit "life according to nature," we turn now to a Platonist's view of the "good life" and its sustenance.

Plato left amongst his legacy to posterity the notion of the duality of spirit and matter. According to this, man was composed of a divine soul, which, descending from the spiritual realm, was captured by the material body. The aim of the soul is to return to its divine spiritual height.

By the time of the Roman Empire Plato was regarded as a cult figure and the founder of a philosophic sect that was characterized by a belief in the transcendence of god, the existence of immaterial spirit, and the immortality of the soul, all leading to an ascetic, world-negating tendency, which takes "likeness to god" as its slogan, rather than the Stoic "conformity with Nature" (Dillon 1982: 60–75).

The extreme attitudes to food that these ideas could engender are best illustrated by the writings of Philo of Alexandria, a first century CE Greek-speaking Jewish Platonist, whose fervently pursued aim in life was to combine Platonic philosophy and Jewish religion into a happy union. His aim was lost on the Jews, but was enthusiastically endorsed by early Christians, some of whom by the early fourth century thought him a Christian.

Philo's ethical writings are steeped in a radically dualistic, Platonic conception of the universe, according to which the "flesh" is a hindrance to the spirit (*Gig.* 29–33), the soul dwells in the body as in a tomb, and the body is "the dwelling place of endless calamities" (*Quis Her.* 68, 85, 273; *Som.* 1.139; *Deus* 111–15; *Ebr.* 101; *Abr.* 9; *Conf. Ling.* 177).

Control of the "passions" and disdain for the pleasures of the flesh were moralizing commonplaces shared, as we have seen, by Cynics, Stoics, Platonists, and other sundry moralizers in the Greco-Roman world. In Philo's religious piety, however, the "passions" were not only to be kept under control but were to be eliminated and the body rejected. The chief amongst the "passions" against which he struggled most were not the anger, or fear, or grief of the Stoics, but "*the pleasures of the belly and what is underneath it.*" The amount of emphasis that the dangers of gluttony receive in Philo's work reveals an obsessive fear of overeating and sex which is remarkable and rare in ancient Greek, Roman, or Jewish sources (*Spec.Leg.* 1.148, 2.50, 193–6, 3.9–11; *Op.* 158–9; *Det.* 101–3, 135–7, 156–9; *Vit.Cont.* 74, and countless other places).

The diet for those who pursue the philosophic life is best described in Philo's treatise *On the Contemplative Life*, which purports to describe an actual group of people who lived near Alexandria in Egypt and devoted themselves totally to "philosophy." They study for six days, each in solitude; only on the seventh does the group come together for a shared festive meal:

> None of them would put food or drink to his lips before sunset since they hold that philosophy finds its right place in the light, the needs of the body in the darkness... they assign the day to one and some small part of the night to the other. Some, in whom the desire for studying wisdom is more deeply implanted even only after three days remember to take food. Others so luxuriate and delight in the banquet of truths which wisdom richly and lavishly supplies that they hold out for twice that time and only after six days do they bring themselves to taste such sustenance as is absolutely necessary...

When on the seventh day they come together for a feast:

> they eat nothing costly, only common bread with salt for a relish and their drink is spring water. (*Vit.Cont.* 4. 34–7)

This sublime spiritual existence is, of course, a figment of the imagination. The human digestive system is simply not able to deal with the amount of bread and water at one sitting that would make up the loss of food intake in six or even three days. Adequate nutrition, the regular daily intake of basic nutrients, is essential to life, as most people would realize. Only those who never had to go without food would think it an ennobling experience to do so. But this fantasy became an increasingly popular literary device to single out individuals for philosophic sainthood among pagans; it had an even longer and more gruesome history among Christians. In the fourth century, the church historian Eusebius was so impressed by Philo's otherworldly lovers of wisdom that he borrowed their eating habits for his own description of Procopius, an early Christian martyr, who

> dedicated his life to philosophy and from childhood embraced chastity of conduct and a most rigorous mode of living... he lived on bread and water, ate only every two or three days and often passed even a whole week without food. (*Mart. Pal.* 1)

Despite the fact that few could adopt this way of life and remain alive, the image of the "divine man," a most popular literary figure of late antiquity, inevitably included descriptions of his miraculously meager diet. Dry bread, uncooked roots and herbs, no wine, no sex, no baths, sleeping on the ground, became the salient characteristics of the holy philosopher, pagan or Christian. Thus the concept of *askesis*, by which the Stoics meant a training of body and mind to be able to endure the "the slings and arrows of outrageous fortune" and to live one's life with dignity, acquired a totally different meaning. Influenced by the Platonists like Philo, Christians too longed for an unchangeable "eternal life." The contemplation of eternity brought with it disdain for everyday life. The neo-Platonist ideal of the soul's rising to the divine through detachment from the material world and freedom from passions was incorporated into an increasingly fervent ascetic propaganda, which devalued life on earth by promising another one after death; the body in the present life was unimportant, or even a hindrance to the glories awaiting in the next. As time went on, that glorious life in Heaven was promised only to those who mortified their flesh on Earth, while burning tortures of eternity in Hell were the rewards for pleasure lovers. Exhortations to vegetarianism in Christian literature had little to do with justice and fairness to animals, but a lot to do with the danger of sex. Fasting was urged as the only means of keeping one's chastity (Grimm 1996: 191–7).

Roman literature, as we have seen, used innuendo and gossip, ridicule and shame to control or censure those who had taken more of the good things of life than was their due. Shame and ridicule are always effective social weapons; they were even more so in a face-to-face society where a man's image formed a large part of his authority and where men intently scrutinized each other for any sign of weakness, "effeminacy," luxury, or other undesirable qualities that could undermine it.

The effectiveness of shame and ridicule as weapons may pale, however, in comparison with that of fear and guilt. The great innovation of Christian ascetic propaganda in the late empire was the production of a literature which aimed to instil in the faithful the fear of an ever-watchful god in whose eyes the pleasure accompanying the satisfaction of the most basic human needs was sin.

The literary phenomenon of the Christian self-mortifying holy men, who would easily outdo even Philo's frugal philosophers, is amazing indeed. In the mid-fourth century the exiled bishop of Alexandria offered to Christians in Rome his story of the life of Antony, an illiterate Egyptian peasant who spent decades in the desert fasting and fighting with "demons," who was so edified by his experiences that, upon returning to human company, he could defeat in arguments the best of Greek philosophers, and whose life offered a new model for sainthood. Perhaps all the more for its patently fictional character, this literary genre was a success, and it was widely imitated. The public could read about holy men who lived for years on nothing but five dates a day and muddy water; others lived on grass, others again stood motionless, without support or sustenance, on the top of columns. There were female ascetics too, according to John Chrysostom:

> who even at a tender age go without food, sleep and drink, mortifying their bodies, crucifying their flesh, sleeping on the ground, wearing sackcloth, locked in narrow cells sprinkling themselves with ashes and wearing chains. (*De studio praesentium* 3 = PG 63.488)

How terrified should the common folk be if all these innocents who left the world with its temptations still lived in fear. "If it were possible that one should die of fear, the whole world would die of terror," teach the Desert Fathers; "what a sight, to see the heavens open and God revealed in anger and wrath...We must weep without ceasing..." (*Apophth. Patr.* 4, 9).

What could have motivated the literature of this dire self-abuse and privation? The stories of ascetics and desert heroes were most likely created for the wealthy Christians in the cities who read books. To hold up an image of the desert-dwelling solitary who had no needs, not even for the most basic sustenance, was the new Christian way to warn against private greed and avarice. Jerome addresses his reader whom he expects to be a wealthy person:

> Let me ask those...who clothe their homes with marble, who string on a single thread the cost of villas, what did this destitute old man ever lack?...But paradise awaits that poor wretch, while hell will seize as its own you golden people. (*V.Paul* 17)

But the intention was more than just to embarrass the rich, the aim was to instil guilt and fear of damnation in a Christian flock who, according to John Chrysostom, were often unwilling to keep even the fasts ordered by the church.

Human beings evolved as omnivores, a fact that contributed to the survival of our species. Our ability and, indeed, our need to sustain ourselves on a wide variety of organic matter, has always aroused anxieties. These anxieties were, and still are reflected in debates concerning whose choice of diet is right, who gets more, and why, what is healthy, what is "natural," what is edible, what is disgusting, and so on. Ancient Roman literature is full of food, bread, wine, olive oil, vegetables, fruit, and meat, a lot of it. Food appears in controversies, arguments, advice, and strongly held, highly emotion-laden opinions and attitudes. Those who hold today that the ancient Mediterranean diet was "starkly vegetarian" or "mostly vegetarian," where only the rich ate meat and the great majority made do with bread and vegetables, have to explain the evidence to the contrary. It may be granted that a large part of this may reflect the life of the rich, but certainly not all. In addition to what was discussed above, consider the dietary laws of one ancient Mediterranean people, the Jews. These laws, binding on all the people of Israel, concern restrictions on what kind of meat could be eaten; there is not one law concerning vegetables. When the first Christians turned to converting the Gentiles, they relaxed the dietary requirements; a new convert could eat any meat except "animals that were strangled, had blood in them, or were sacrificed to idols" (Acts 15:19–20). When some of Paul's converts worried about their diet, the apostle advised them to eat any meat that they could buy in the market (1 Cor 10:25). Paul's converts in the first century may not have been the destitute poor but it is most unlikely that they were the idle rich. If the common diet was mostly vegetarian, the question would not have arisen. Church history indicates the difficulties encountered in imposing meatless fast days on the flock.

Analysis of food remains from around human habitations in recent archaeology seems also to contradict the vegetarian argument. Reports of the excavation in Rome, at the *Schola Praeconum*, indicate the systematic production of animals of standard age – young animals – for the Roman market, suggesting that the main meat consumed by the urban population was pork, followed by beef and lamb. The bone sample found that all parts of the body were represented for all three species. The authors write: "the inference is that some at least of the urban population whose food refuse was dumped in the *Schola Praeconum* had purchased even the poorest cuts of meat" (Whitehouse et al. 1982: 87–9).

A. King's study (1999) of regional comparison of mammal bones in the Roman world further showed that domestic quadrupeds were butchered for food all around the Roman world; the ranking of preference for the meat of these animals varied across different regions of the empire. In light of the literary evidence supported by these studies the vegetarian argument is hard to maintain.

This short review of ancient arguments concerning food has not resolved the problem of "who ate what" in the Roman world. The whole point is this: the question cannot be answered from a literature the aim of which was not the objective survey of facts and which may have been almost completely blind to the actual lives of the majority of the population. To conclude from this blindness that the majority lived in abject poverty is just as unjustified as would be its optimistic opposite. What Roman literature richly indicates is that concern with food and eating habits often expresses larger anxieties, about health, the body and sexuality, social position, and power relations in society.

CHAPTER NINETEEN

Leisure

Garrett G. Fagan

For it is by a man's pleasures – his pleasures indeed – that his sense of dignity, integrity and moderation can best be judged. For who is so dissolute that no trace of seriousness is to be found in his pastimes? Our leisure gives us away. (Pliny *Pan.* 82.8–9)

Hunting, bathing, gambling, laughing – that's living! (Gaming board inscription from Timgad, Numidia; *CIL* VIII 17938 = *ILS* 8626f)

1 Introduction: The Elite Concept of *Otium*

Leisure is not easily defined. In the industrial and post-industrial world, it is primarily a temporal concept: one is at leisure when one is not at work. But for many, leisure is also defined in terms of activity: one is at leisure when engaged in certain types of pursuit (golfing, for instance). Thus within the broad concept "leisure" lurk many gray areas. Golf is a leisure activity for most, but not for the professional golfer. And when an office-worker accepts the boss's invitation to join a weekend golf game, is it truly a leisure activity for the worker? When the Roman gentleman Pliny the Younger, whose letters provide an invaluable insight into elite attitudes during the high empire, whines about his toils (*labores*), few of them strike the modern reader as constituting work: attending a coming-of-age ceremony, a betrothal, or a wedding; giving evidence in a court case; witnessing a will; or acting as someone's legal representative (Pliny *Ep.* 1.9.1–3). Pliny's attitude demonstrates that leisure is in no small measure defined by what one considers "work." So for Pliny, it was the obligatory nature of his rounds, not the activities themselves, that made them *labores*. Work can therefore be considered whatever one does under a sense of obligation, and leisure as its opposite. A recent study of Roman leisure offers the following general definition: "Leisure is a system of symbols which acts to establish a feeling of freedom and pleasure by formulating a sense of choice and desire" (Toner 1995: 1–21, quote at 17). The definition is certainly workable but also notably vague, as it must be to encompass such a complex notion while maintaining its applicability in different cultures that will define leisure in a way specific to themselves. In the end, for most people, what constitutes leisure is self-evident – it is whatever their culture tells them is not work. This situation is directly reflected in the vocabulary of classical Latin, where *otium* expresses the notion of "leisure," and "work" was often designated with the word *negotium* or, more properly, "not-*otium*." To the Roman mind *otium* was the primary concept, and work ("not-leisure") was defined as its antonym.

Before commencing a review of Roman leisure activities, it is worthwhile to contemplate more closely the concept of *otium*. For the Roman elite (whose attitudes are preserved in the surviving literature), *otium* could indeed be a temporal designation (Hor. *Sat.* 1.1.31; Pliny *Ep.* 1.3.3; Gel. 11.3.1). It was also used in political contexts to denote a desirable state of security and tranquility that went hand-in-hand with *pax* and *concordia* (Cic. *Rep.* 2.54; Boyancé 1941; Hellegouarc'h 1972: 271, 410, 538). But *otium* was also very much a qualitative and moral concept (André 1966). What one did with one's *otium* was a reflection of one's moral character, as Pliny the Younger states unequivocally in his *Panegyric* to Trajan, quoted at the head of this chapter. To be *otiosus* could mean to be "at rest," in a pleasing or neutral sense (Pliny *Ep.* 1.9.8; 9.32), or to be "idle, lazy," in a negative sense (Pliny *Ep.* 1.13; *CIL* IV 813). In educated thinking, quality *otium* was spent in edifying pursuits, primarily reading and writing (see below) or thinking and discussing matters of merit (Gel. 11.3.1). Hunting too was considered decent, if not to the liking of all (Pliny *Ep.* 1.6). In contrast, idle *otium* was the mark of the indolent and so especially of the faceless masses, who lounged around in their taverns or sat thoughtlessly through their chariot races and other mass entertainments (Amm. Marc. 14.6.25; Pliny *Ep.* 9.6). Even today the board games of the feckless can be seen carved into the stone steps or porticoes of the public spaces of Roman cities around the Mediterranean (Ihm 1891; see also Purcell 1995). This sort of negative *otium*, spent in idleness or the indulgence of purely corporeal pleasure, was seen as actively corrupting, especially to the young mind (Pliny *Ep.* 7.24) or to the discipline of soldiers (Sall. *Cat.* 11.5; Fron. *Str.* 4.1.15). On the basis of this sort of thinking, the moral topography of Roman townscapes could be charted according to the probity (or not) of its various facilities (Sen. *Dial.* 7.7.3; Wallace-Hadrill 1995).

When it came to public leisure, there was no doubt as to its function or who was to manage it. "It is essential for those who are looking after the state that the people be very happy and devoid of all concern and contemplation, having handed their leisure over to others (*aliis permisso otio suo*) who must look after it and who must not make the mistake of having the people think that their leaders are neglecting their comforts (*commoda*)" (Cic. *Rep.* 1.52). This principle was put into effect by the emperors, as evidenced by the lengthy expenditures on public entertainments listed by Augustus in his *Res Gestae* (15.22–3) or the report that M. Aurelius, when absent from Rome, ensured that the richest citizens saw to the people's pleasures (*voluptates*), since rumor had it the emperor was trying to drive them to the study of philosophy (*HA Marc.* 24.5). Thus the elite was expected to provide *commoda* for the masses as a way of keeping them docile, even as those *commoda* were seen as generally corrupting and even ruinous to good moral character (e.g., Cic. *Tusc.* 5.78). Presumably, as long as the people who mattered (which included rank-and-file soldiers) were not corrupted by such low-grade *otium*, the moral welfare of the masses was of little concern. Yet Cicero also appreciated that the attraction of popular diversions for the elite was not to be underestimated: "But if we ourselves who are kept by our business from public pleasure and are able to find many other pleasures in the work itself, if we nevertheless are delighted and attracted to games, why are you amazed at the ignorant masses?" (Cic. *Mur.* 39). Cicero's *a fortiori* argument is self-serving, but it does raise the interesting scenario of the elite providing what they considered worthless leisure for the masses even as they themselves are being entertained by it, presumably to their moral detriment. As a moral sword, then, *otium* cut both ways.

2 Literary Leisure

"Leisure without literature is death, a tomb for the living man," writes Seneca (*Ep.* 82.3). There could be no clearer statement of how good *otium* was to be spent in the worthy pursuits of reading and writing. Pliny the Younger urges his friend Caninius Rufus to free himself from his petty concerns (*humiles et sordidas curas*) and devote himself to studies (*studiis*) in his leisure time: "Let this be your work and your leisure (*hoc sit negotium tuum hoc otium*), this your rest and toil, in these pursuits would you wake and sleep" (Pliny *Ep.* 1.3.3–4). The products of such studies made the rounds, so that members of the upper orders could quote each other's verses to one another (Sen. *Ep.* 24.19). An integral element of this literary culture involved producing works in the style of famous authors, so that when Pliny expresses concern for the health of one Passenus Paulus, he comments that Paulus used to write poems modeled on the Augustan poets Propertius (from whom Paulus claimed descent) and Horace (Pliny *Ep.* 9.22; cf. 6.15). While today such endeavors would be regarded as empty imitation, in ancient Rome it was seen as a worthwhile pursuit; even Pliny himself declares without a trace of embarrassment that he composes his works in conscious stylistic imitation of select predecessors (Pliny *Ep.* 1.2; 5.3). Leisure time spent amongst one's books studying and imitating the canonized *exempla* was the quintessence of quality *otium*.

Ancient books were meant to be read aloud. Even when alone, reading aloud was the norm (Knox 1968). When this consideration is added to the expressed centrality of literature in elite *otium* and the difficulties of mass publication and distribution, it seems inevitable that a culture of public reading should arise among the Hellenized Roman aristocracy of the late republic and early empire (Fantham 1996; Funaioli 1920; E. Rawson 1985). The habit was not unique to Rome: inscriptions reveal the existence of itinerant poets who moved through the towns of the Hellenistic world reciting their work (Guarducci 1924). From the late first century BCE onwards, the Roman literary sources are littered with references and allusions to public or quasi-public readings of literature, which could vary from small-scale events that rotated through private houses to full public performances staged in theaters by professional actors and dancers (Quinn 1982: 140–65). C. Asinius Pollio (consul in 40 BCE) is credited with staging the first *recitationes*, in which an author read from his own works, often at his home, to anyone who was interested (Sen. *Con.* 4 *pr.* 2; Dalzell 1955). In subsequent years, the recitation became such a prevalent form of literary leisure that *odea* were built to house them (Coleman 2000b: 243–5), notably the Hadrianic Athenaeum in Rome (*LTUR* 1.131–2 [Coarelli]).

The elite dinner party, with its relaxed and cultured atmosphere (see below), was a natural setting for literary activity, whether it was an (impromptu) performance by an attendee (Tac. *Ann.* 13.15.2–3) or the recital of a more polished piece written by third parties and read by a domestic slave or a hired voice (Nep. *Att.* 14; Pliny *Ep.* 1.15; 9.17). For those poets whose livelihoods depended on their art, the formal *recitatio* was a primary means of acquiring a reputation (Tac. *Dia.* 10.1–2; Stat. *Silv.* 5.3.215–16). The dinner parties of patrons would have been ideal places for poets to extend their circle of acquaintances and so meet possible commissioners of new work. Two of Martial's early books of poems were called the *Xenia* and *Apophoreta*, or "Take-Away Gifts," an allusion both to the nature of the short (snack-like) poems and to the likely gastronomic context of their performance (the *Xenia*, in fact, all refer to types of food served at dinner parties). The mythological subject matter of much dining-room decoration at Pompeii and elsewhere seems to have been deliberately chosen to resonate with the literary tastes of sophisticated banqueters, perhaps even in allusion to specific poems recited in the dining room (Ling 1995: 249).

It is important to recognize that these types of literary activities represented the elite ideal of how one should occupy one's leisure time. It was not to everyone's taste. A recitation could be terribly boring, especially if the writer/reciter lacked talent but did not have the sensitivity to recognize that fact. Pliny huffs and puffs at the disrespect shown even to good poets by their audience:

> This year has raised a fine crop of poets; there was scarcely a day throughout the month of April when someone was not giving a public reading. I am glad to see that literature flourishes and there is a show of budding talent, in spite of the fact that people are slow to form an audience. Most of them sit about in public places, gossiping and wasting time when they could be giving their attention, and give orders that they are told at intervals whether the reader has come in and has read the preface, or is coming to the end of the book. It is not until that moment – and even then very reluctantly – that they come dawdling in. Nor do they stay very long, but leave before the end, some of them trying to slip away unobserved and others marching boldly out. (Pliny *Ep.* 1.13.1–3, tr. B. Radice; cf. *Ep.* 6.15, 17)

The density of daily poetry readings over an entire month surely makes the audience's attitude understandable. Pliny himself could keep his guests for two days at a single reading (*Ep.* 8.21), and he refers to another reciter who kept his audience for three (*Ep.* 4.27). An aphorism about "too much of a good thing" comes to mind. The insistent reciter is a common target for the vitriol of satirists, such as the execrable Ligurinus who followed Martial everywhere, even into the toilet – "You read to me as I stand, you read to me as I sit; you read to me as I run, you read to me as I shit" (Mart. 3.44) – or the poet whom Petronius portrays as harassing the customers in a public bath so much that they almost beat him up (*Sat.* 91–2). As early as the late Augustan era, Horace could rant against the "pitiless reciter" (*recitator acerbus*), whose lack of talent was matched only by his resistance to criticism and who treated his audience as would a bear broken out of its cage (*Ars* 474–6).

The literary recitation, although publicly valued by the erudite guardians of quality *otium*, was hardly on a par with drinking, gambling, and bathing, let alone the mass entertainments of the circus or arena as a feature of Roman public leisure (see further White 1993: 59–63). Nevertheless recitations *were* put on as public events and were thus accessible to the masses, even if we have no means of gauging the frequency or the density of their attendance. (Petronius' comment that being identified as a poet in the wrong part of town could be dangerous [*Sat.* 93] suggests that the commoner was not well disposed towards the sort of literary pretension that gave rise to the public recitation.) The elite assessment of this situation is entirely predictable: although physically present, the ignorant mob lacked the mental acuity to appreciate what it was hearing (Cic. *Orat.* 173). The quality of literary leisure was quite simply wasted on them. But the Roman commoners do not seem to have minded too much – they had their own diversions.

3 Drinking, Gambling, and Hired Sex: Fun at the Roman Tavern

> Do you remember, you scum, when I came to you at almost the fifth hour with C. Piso, that you were coming out of some sort of dive (*gurgustium*), head covered, in your slippers? And when you breathed that repulsive bar (*taeterrimam popinam*) over us with that fetid mouth of yours, that you used the excuse of your health, saying that you usually looked after it with certain potions that tasted like wine? (Cic. *Pis.* 13)

That accusations of covert drinking in urban dives is a feature of political invective makes it plain that such places were considered unsuitable haunts for the upper classes (Cic. *Phil.* 2.77; Suet. *Nero* 26.1; Tac. *Ann.* 13.25.1–2). In fact, the elite sources are strident in their condemnation of urban bars and taverns, though not necessarily of drunkenness (D'Arms 1995). As far as they were concerned, bars were havens for the dregs of humanity – criminals, slaves, and the other loungers who made up the anonymous *vulgus* (Juv. 8.171–82). Members of the elite who frequented taverns risked the ruin of their reputations, as well as their moral fiber (Apul. *Met.* 8.1). Seneca sums it up plainly (*Ep.* 51.4): "I don't care to live among bars." The location of identifiable bars in the cityscape of Pompeii has been seen to support Seneca's assertion, in that they cluster at the gates or on the main thoroughfares, usually at a remove from the elite houses (Laurence 1994: 75–87; *contra* De Felice 2001: 129–56). Since drinking (and other activities) would continue into the night, bars were probably loud as well as unsavory places in Roman cities. Customers would drink too much, gamble, gossip, and fight (*D.* 48.19.11.2; Petr. *Sat.* 95–6). This, by the way, was in marked contrast to the traditional country inn, which was a perfectly respectable alternative to staying with friends or acquaintances as one traveled about (Hor. *Sat.* 1.5).

Latin has numerous words for "bar," but as with so much ancient daily terminology, it is not always clear what (if anything) differentiated one type of establishment from another. Cicero refers to the bar Cn. Piso emerged from as a *gurgustium*

Figure 19.1a and b Ostia, tavern on the Via di Diana, exterior view. Note street-front bar and benches out front. The open nature of the place suggests the vibrancy of street life in Roman towns (b) Ostia, tavern on the Via di Diana, interior view. Note the painting on the wall advertising food available for sale. The shelving below probably displayed fresh items, as in modern Italian restaurants

(a generic word designating a hovel or dive of any sort) and a *popina*. The latter appears very frequently in connection with bars, apparently denoting a bar-cum-snack shop that sold food and drink but did not offer accommodations. We also hear of the *caupona* (similar to a *popina* but which seems to have offered accommodation); the *stabulum*, *hospitium*, and *deversorium* (where accommodation was the paramount attraction); the *ganea* (an eating house); and the *taberna* (a generic term that appears to have covered most of the above, as well as shops in general). To this list Plautus adds *thermopolium*, a place that served heated wine. This rare word – it appears only four times – has often been used in modern sources to designate the Roman city bar (Plaut. *Rud.* 527–30; Kleberg 1957: 1–73). No doubt the usage of all these terms in ancient times was fluid and imprecise (compare the *ristorante*, *trattoria*, and *hostaria* in the cities of modern Italy). Attempting to draw hard-and-fast distinctions between, say, a *popina* and a *ganea* for the length and breadth of the empire that remain valid for its entire duration is probably a waste of time, since exceptions will quickly manifest themselves in our patchy and localized sources (Dosi and Schnell 1984: 73–98; Hermansen 1981: 185–205). But the very variety of terms applied to bars attests to the vibrancy of "pub culture" among the lower-class Romans, for whom they constituted an important vehicle of sociability and conviviality (Toner 1995: 65–88).

Fortunately we are not reliant solely on the elite's scornful vignettes to get an idea of Roman pub life, since it enjoys direct attestation. Physical remains of taverns and bars are found in well-preserved Roman cities. About 120 have been identified at Pompeii, though not without a suspicion that many non-taverns have been misclassified due to taxonomic ambiguity (Wallace-Hadrill 1995: 46). The taverns are often identified solely on the basis of counters with storage jars (*dolia*) set into them (Kleberg 1957: 33–43), but such fixtures are found also in ordinary shops. Thus only when other finds clearly suggest that food and drink was catered (such as inscriptions, decorative motifs, cooking vessels or facilities, wine amphora, etc.) can an establishment be securely identified as a *popina* or a *caupona* (Packer 1978: 43–51;

Dosi and Schnell 1984: 91–5; De Felice 2001: 176–306). At Ostia, only 38 bars can be safely determined, which further undermines the apparently inflated Pompeian total (Hermansen 1981: 125–83). The famous *thermopolium* on the Via di Diana in Ostia (Hermansen 1981: fig. 1.2.5) is a pleasant-looking place to modern eyes and features a counter fronting the street with benches set into the alcove in front of it, a large kitchen, a spacious two-room interior that could have accommodated many tables and chairs, and a *Biergarten* out back (Hermansen 1981: 130–2 [no. 3]). It was a further indication of lack of class that food and drink was often served to seated customers in these establishments, rather than to people reclining on couches (in *triclinia*) in the aristocratic fashion (Mart. 5.70.3). This is perhaps why some taverns advertised the availability of genuine *triclinia* to herald the exclusivity of their appointments (*ILS* 6036).

As surviving signs reveal, Roman taverns could carry strikingly modern-sounding names ("The Elephant," "The Cock," or "The Camel") as well as clearly ancient ones ("The Sword" or "The Mercury and Apollo") (Friedländer 1922: 1: 349). Graffiti offer glimpses into the goings-on in such places. "Ampliatus was here with his mates" reads one banal scrawl from a bar in Pompeii (*CIL* IV 3941). Another depicts a barmaid (*vinaria*) named Hedone reeling off a price list to her customers (*CIL* IV 1679): "Drinks served for an *as*. If you pay double, you'll drink better. If you pay quadruple, you'll drink Falernian" (Falernian was a highly prized Roman wine). A disgruntled customer wrote on one bar's wall, "If only such deceit cheated *you*, bartender: you sell water and yourself drink neat wine" (*CIL* IV 3948). The hard-drinking culture is further attested on inscribed "talking" wine goblets bearing commands like "Fill me up with wine, bartender," "Another one!" and "Spare me the pitchy wine – give me Aminaean!" (*CIL* XIII 10018. 103; 105; 135). One series of painted images with attendant dialogue from a bar in Pompeii charts the progress of a dispute over a board game. Two figures are shown seated at a gaming table. "I'm out," says one gamer. "No, it's three two's!" comes the reply. In the next scene the two are shown fighting and cursing each other as the bartender approaches, "You're going outside; enough ruckus" (*CIL* IV 3494; Casson 1974: 197–218).

As this last exchange makes clear, gambling was a standard accompaniment to drinking in the Roman tavern: "Give him wine and the dice," commands Syrisca the innkeeper in the poem "The Proprietress," ascribed to Vergil (*Copa* 37). The games varied in nature from simple dice games to more complex chess-like board games, or a combination of board games played with dice (Balsdon 1969: 154–9; Marquardt 1886: 2: 847–61). Although a part of Roman tavern culture, gambling was no more restricted to the lower orders than was inebriation. Senators, *equites*, and emperors could play and enjoy games of chance as well (Juv. 8.9–12; Suet. *Aug.* 71; *Claud.* 33.2; Purcell 1995). Of course, spectacles such as chariot races or gladiatorial bouts would naturally attract betting (Tert. *Spec.* 16). But gambling was not sanctioned by the Roman authorities. As early as 204 BCE there is mention of a *lex alearia* (Plaut. *Mil.* 164), and dicing and other games continued to be seen as a problem throughout the republic and empire (*D.* 11.5). The legal attitude was linked to moralizing objections to gambling, and indeed probably stemmed from them. Reckless gambling was symptomatic of a weak moral disposition, it led to loss of control and dignity, it privileged fortune over planning, and through it one gave into greed and thus faced ruination (Cic. *Div.* 2.85; Philostr. *VA* 5.36). The essential unity of these legal and moral outlooks is expressed in the wording of decrees that banned betting except at contests involving *virtus* (*D*. 11.5.2–3). Gambling, then, was only acceptable when conducted in a certain manner under certain conditions. That the taverns housed uncontrolled gambling was one more strike against them in the eyes of the morally pure (for a full consideration, see Toner 1995: 89–101).

While brothels (*lupanaria*) and individual prostitutes' cells (*cellae meretriciae*) existed to sate the sexual impulses of the general population, it is clear that taverns and inns could also serve the same purpose (McGinn 1998, 2004; De Felice 2001). A bar at Pompeii is decorated with erotic paintings (De Vos and De Vos 1982: 52), and in another, customers boast about their sexual antics: "Primegenius was here with a whore" (*CIL* IV 3500), or "Ampliatus Afer fucked here with his mates" (*CIL* IV 3942). (In the latter notice, it is not immediately obvious whether the action took place between Ampliatus and his *sodales* or whether they shared it with some unnamed partner[s].) That such bar-wall scribblings are not entirely the products of prurient imaginations is suggested by the cold legal language of the *Digest*, which identifies as a prostitute any woman who practices prostitution openly "not just where she does so in brothels but also where she is used to showing she has no shame in taverns or other places"; similarly, the law declares that "where one woman keeps an inn and employs others as prostitutes (as many often do on the pretext that they are servants), she must be classed as a procuress" (*D*. 23.2.43.1, 9; cp. *D*. 3.2.4.2; *CTh*. 9.7.1). The chronological spread of these data – from the first to the fourth centuries CE – suggests continuity in some aspects of Roman tavern life and adds hired sex to the list of the bar's corrupting attractions.

Given the wide variety of questionable activities associated with taverns, and the Roman authorities' standing suspicion of unsupervised public gatherings, it comes as no surprise that attempts were made to clamp down on them. Taverns, often associated in the authorities' outlook with the potentially subversive associations (*collegia*), faced restrictions and even outright bans under some emperors (Suet. *Tib*. 34.1, *Claud*. 38.2; Dio 60.6.6–7; Amm. Marc. 28.4.4). The fact that these regulations required repeated enactment reveals their ineffectiveness, but their function was as much symbolic as pragmatic, in that they staked out the elite's position on issues of morality and public display in opposition to a perceived plebeian culture centered on the taverns and cook-shops that stood outside elite norms (Toner 1995: 79–83). If Roman legislators could not actually do anything about what went on in taverns, they could at least be seen to be trying.

4 Banquets

Food consumption is both a functional and a symbolic act (Gowers 1993: 1–49, Grimm, this volume). Who has food, who does not, what one eats and under what circumstances can say much about wealth, social status, and even political power in any society, but especially in one where food is produced and distributed unequally, as it was in ancient Rome. In such conditions, those who control food resources wield power in a very real sense, and the social and political features inherent in the sharing of food are made all the more obvious. As a guest at Trimalchio's dinner party sardonically puts it, "the little people struggle, while for the big mouths it's always holiday feasting!" (Petron. *Sat.* 44). Whether shared among members of a family, invited guests, fellow club members, soldiers in a military mess, or the community at large, commensality was a reproducer of social and political relationships (Fisher 1988). In the Roman world, displays of conspicuous consumption at private dinner parties were mirrored by public banquets or food hand-outs presented as voluntary benefactions to the urban mob by elite benefactors. In thus displaying its generosity and advertising its concern for the common populace, the Roman elite was also reiterating its claim to social and political dominance over that populace through the medium of food. Analogous power dynamics were at play in the private dinner party. The Roman banquet, whether private or public, was the quintessential "power" meal (Garnsey 1999).

Recent analysis has identified "public" and "private" spheres in the elite Roman house, where the hall-study (*atrium-tablinum*) was the most public area and the bedroom (*cubiculum*) the most private (Laurence and Wallace-Hadrill 1997; Wallace-Hadrill 1994). The situation is not absolutely clear-cut, but in general the *atrium* was open to the street and therefore accessible to the public. While "public" business could be transacted in the *cubiculum*, access to it would normally be reserved for the tried and trusted, so that entrance required a specific invitation (Riggsby 1997). Intermediate areas in the house were the garden (*peristyle*) and dining-room (*triclinium*), places that served a more overtly public function than the bedroom but nevertheless required an invitation to enter. The importance of the dining room as a symbol of status is suggested by its luxurious decoration and the effort invested in locating it in the house to afford pleasing views of gardens, statuary, and fountains (Bek 1983; Ellis 1997; Ling 1995). It seems that in this space the host attempted to show off his wealth and status most pointedly to his guests (Drerup 1959; Gazda 1991).

In ancient elite literature, the evening dinner party is indeed presented as a focal point of the day and an occasion of important social interaction (Murray 1990; Slater 1991; see Dunbabin 2003 for the iconographic evidence). The excesses of Trimalchio's *cena*, as related in the surviving portion of Petronius' *Satyricon*, are as infamous as they are fictitious, but other sources reflect a hardly less extravagant reality: Apicius' (undated) cookbook of ancient haute cuisine includes recipes for peacock, parrot, and flamingo (6.1–6). Three features of these private dinner parties deserve special notice. First, the participants were all invited by the host. Their very presence was therefore a sign of social (and political) favor. Martial and other satirists play on this fact when they portray unpopular losers scouring the city's public baths or hanging about the public toilets in the hope of catching an invitation to a dinner party (Mart. 2.14, 11.77, 12.82). Second, social hierarchy was strictly maintained at table by the placement of the guests on the three-sided dining couches (the eponymous *triclinia*) and the quality of the food served. Despite an equalizing ethic at the dinner, hosts were known to serve their socially inferior guests low-class food that reflected and reinforced their inferiority (D'Arms 1990). Indeed, Cicero records how, when a friend entertained Caesar and his vast entourage in December 45 BCE at Puteoli, separate dining rooms were assigned to different classes of guests (Cic. *Att.* 13.52). Another option was to restrict invitations to guests of a comparable social status and serve food and drink of an appropriate standard to everyone. This ensured that, among the guests at least, a standard of equality prevailed, even if the host had occasionally to endure sub-standard fare as a consequence (Pliny *Ep.* 2.6). Third, the quality of the meal itself, the content and tone of the tableside conversation, and the nature of any entertainments staged for the guests' pleasure all reflected not only on the host's status but on his sense of propriety. Quality hosts invited a mix of intelligent guests who held fascinating conversations on learned issues (see Plutarch's nine books of "Table Talk," the *Quaestiones Convivales*, or the 15 extant books of Athenaeus' "Doctors at Dinner," or *Deipnosophistae*), or they put on poetry readings or displays of oratory for their guests' edification; less refined hosts mauled their guests' wives or staged gladiatorial bouts, executions, or other gross and inappropriate displays (C. P. Jones 1991). Trimalchio's vapid tableside boastings and staged excesses are the paradigm for this sort of tastelessness and form the core of Petronius' satire of Roman dinner-party culture.

Exclusivity and hierarchy are even more apparent in the Roman public banquet. Whereas, in democratic Athens, public banquets following sacrifices were open to all citizens and allotments of portions were equal (Schmitt-Pantel 1990), in Rome only persons who enjoyed the "right to dine publicly" (*ius epulandi publice*) could partake (Dosi and Schnell 1984: 299–328). Naturally, these persons tended to be priests, magistrates, and other members of the elite. The commoner was only entitled to the leftovers, which were put on sale in the market (Scheid 1988). In addition, exclusive groups could dine together as a reinforcement of their communality, such as the Arval Brethren or members of funerary clubs or other *collegia* (see, e.g., *ILS* 7212 for the regulations of a funeral club at Lanuvium, of Hadrianic date). As the euergetistic ethos gained ground in Rome with the expansion of empire, the public banquet became somewhat more open, even if it was a cause for suspicion in the minds of some. A candidate for the consulship of 62 BCE held a banquet for the populace as part of his canvass – and that act became a basis for his being prosecuted (unsuccessfully) on a charge of *ambitio* (Cic. *Mur.* 72–7).

Inscriptions reveal the popularity of public feasting in the cities of the empire (Donahue 1996; Mrozek 1987). These largely prosaic texts show that food was distributed in various guises, often described vaguely as *populo epulum dedit* ("he gave a banquet to the people") or *cena* (an evening meal), sometimes more specifically as *panis et vinum* (bread and wine) or *crustulum et mulsum* (pastries and honey-wine). Even less precise is *sportula*, a hand-out that could take the form of food portions or a monetary equivalent. Most illuminating are those inscriptions that differentiate the classes of recipient, thereby demonstrating that social distinctions were maintained (by location and/or by quality of food) as the benefaction played out (for examples, consult the tables of Donahue 1996 or Duncan-Jones 1982). From Ferentinum in Latium, for instance, comes a lengthy inscription recording the achievements of one A. Quinctilius Priscus, who had reached the highest municipal offices and then established a foundation,

> so that on his birthday in perpetuity such townspeople, inhabitants and married women as are present be given a pound of pastries and a measure of honey-wine; and where the dining-couches (*triclinia*) are concerned, that honey-wine and pastries and a hand-out of ten *sestertii* be given to the decurions; likewise for the growing boys of decurional status; and that pastries and honey-wine and a hand-out of eight *sestertii* be given to the board

of six *Augustales* and those who dine with them; and in my dining-room a further one *sestertius* per person be given ... It is better if the town's officials offer to the plebeian boys, without distinguishing free from slave, a distribution of nuts weighing thirty *modii* and a serving of drinks from six urns of wine, as befits growing youths. (*CIL* X 5853 = *ILS* 6271)

The inscription is intriguing for several reasons. First, only the decurions, their sons, and the *Augustales* (priests of the imperial cult drawn from local freedmen) are specified as reclining to eat in the aristocratic fashion (in *triclinia*), while the townspeople, inhabitants, and married women presumably sit or stand. Second, everyone gets honey-wine and pastries, but the decreasing sums of the accompanying *sportulae* may suggest that not everyone's food and drink was of the same quality. Certainly, by the time we get to the plebeian boys, nuts and limited amounts of wine are the only foodstuffs on offer. Third, the benefactor himself takes part in the event, reclining in a *triclinium*, and those selected to dine with him enjoy the privilege of an extra *sestertius* added to their hand-out. His *triclinium* has the pride of place in the whole event. In this way, the inscription tells us much about how this public banquet was staged and shows above all that, whereas many people might participate, they did not do so equally. The public banquet, like the private dinner, offered ways for the Roman social order to be made manifest with the appropriate roles of favor granting and dependency made abundantly clear to all participants (Donahue 2004).

5 Baths

If it is the case that a culture's priorities can be divined from the function of its largest public buildings, then the cityscape of ancient Rome was dominated by structures devoted to the provision of public leisure, and the same can be said of many Roman provincial cities (Dodge 1999; Coleman 2000b). The Flavian Amphitheater (Colosseum) and the Circus Maximus (seating capacity of about 200,000) were among ancient Rome's most impressive monuments (Humphrey 1986: 56–131; Bomgardner 2000: 1–31). By Constantine's day the city boasted no less than four permanent stone theaters, some with supplementary amenities attached, such as the gardens, ambulatories, porticoes, and galleries that stood behind the stage of Pompey's Theater (L. Richardson 1992, *s.v.* theatrum; *LTUR* 5.35–8, *s.v.* Theatrum Pompei [Gros]). The huge open spaces of the Roman Forum and the nearby Imperial Fora were frequently used to stage cash hand-outs, public banquets, and (before permanent amphitheaters became available) gladiatorial games and beast hunts. The fora would also regularly host market days and, it must be imagined, hucksters, snake-oil salesmen, performers, reciters, sidewalk orators, and traveling troupes of entertainers must have been a constant feature of these piazzas, as well as of other public spaces in the city (D.Chr. 20.10; Luc. *Alex.* 6; Origen, *C. Cels.* 350; Blümner 1918; Kudlien 1983).

But above the lot stood the vast public baths. When Constantine added his suite in about 315 CE, it was the eleventh set of imperial baths built in Rome since those of Agrippa, opened in 29 BCE. These buildings could cover huge areas of land (32 acres in the case of Diocletian's Baths, completed in 306 CE), comprise dozens of rooms,

Figure 19.2a and b Suburban baths, Pompeii. The establishment, located outside the Porta Marina to attract travelers as they entered or left the town, is famous for the graphic sexual frescoes in its changing room (b) Suburban baths, Herculaneum. This small bathhouse, located near the town's entrance, overlooked the sea and had a heated indoor swimming pool. The fine cut-marble floor allowed even the poorest to feel pampered for a few hours a day

and offer a great array of services, so that they were far more than places to get clean. Rather, the imperial baths were public pleasure palaces, immense cathedrals to the cult of the Roman people's *commoda* (conveniences), which the emperor and the upper classes were expected to provide by virtue of their ability to do so. The sheer scale of the imperial baths declares that public leisure was a serious business for the Romans, rulers and ruled alike.

The origins of the baths are obscure, but the developed Roman bathhouse is evidently a product of divergent cultural influences. The peculiarly Roman feature of hot bathing in communal pools deployed in carefully gradated heated spaces is coupled with manifestly Greek elements, such as exercise yards (*palaestrae*). The technology employed to facilitate these practices (the under-floor heating system called the hypocaust) also had Greek precursors in underground heating channels, but the Romans transformed it into something more ambitious and practical: the fully-fledged *suspensura*, whereby the entire floor of a room, not just a section of it, was raised on pillars and, later still, the walls rendered hollow to allow the passage of hot gases from the furnace. The available evidence points to Campania in the third century BCE as the best context for the combination of all these features into the truly Roman-style bathhouse (Fagan 2001).

Once established among the Romans by the second century BCE, the habit of public bathing became a diagnostic characteristic of Roman-ness. Newly conquered peoples adopted the habit as a sign of their embracing the new order (Tac. *Agr.* 21.2) and, indeed, baths are found in every sort of Roman settlement, no matter how large or small, central or remote. A wooden bathhouse has even been identified in a temporary fortress (occupied between 15 and 28 CE) along the German frontier which, if the structure is correctly identified, constitutes startling testimony as to the centrality of bathing in Roman daily life by this time (Bosman 1999). The enormous volume of allusions, anecdotes, metaphors, and similes drawn from the world of the baths by Roman authors only further reflects the importance of the habit. For example, satirists of Roman society, such as Martial, set many of their pungent jokes in the familiar setting of the baths (Fagan 1999a: 12–39), and the way emperors bathe is used to calibrate their moral characters in such works as the *Historia Augusta* (Merten 1983). We only have to read that Elagabalus held parties for the ruptured in the palace baths to know he was not a good man (*HA Heliogab.* 25.6). In contrast, the probity of Antoninus Pius is reflected in his opening to the public a set of baths he owned, and at no charge to boot (*HA Ant. Pius* 7.6).

Unlike many Roman buildings, the baths can boast a wealth of ancient evidence that allows them to be examined from a variety of perspectives. Recent studies of their physical remains have revealed much about their operation. The scale of the baths varied enormously, from tiny corner establishments to the larger community-owned facilities and up to the vast imperial pleasure palaces of the capital (Nielsen 1993). Most communities had multiple public facilities (by 79 CE Pompeii could boast seven, while Constantinian Rome had hundreds), of varying scale and quality that probably reflect the divergent preferences and means among the general population. Since the bathing habit did not follow a rigidly prescribed form in every place, the architecture of the baths also displays great variation (Yegül 1992). Local tastes would dictate the form of a community's establishments, as was the case with the great bath-gymnasia complexes common in Asia Minor that incorporated into the traditional Hellenistic gymnasium elements imported from the Roman bath of the Western Mediterranean (Yegül 1986). More focused studies of regional forms of baths are needed to elucidate variations in the bathing culture at a local level (Farrington 1995). Particularly intriguing is Roman Egypt, where Greek-style baths appear to have continued in use well into the first century CE and where a wealth of papyrological evidence remains to be fully mined for bath-related information. The requirements of heating, water supply, and drainage demanded by the Roman bath mean that it may have been the single most technologically complex structure developed in the ancient Mediterranean basin (see relevant chapters in Nielsen 1993 and Yegül 1992; see also specific studies such as De Haan 2001; Garbrecht and Manderscheid 1994; Parslow 2000). Indeed, the baths were partly a testament to the symbolic power of the Romans over nature, and especially of the emperors who built the huge complexes in the capital, in that they harnessed the threatening forces of fire and water and deployed them for the enjoyment of the masses (Zajac 1999).

The sculptural decoration of the baths appears to be aimed chiefly at evoking images of pleasure and abandon, via Venus and Bacchus, and of healthfulness, via Aesculapius and Hygeia (Manderscheid 1981; Marvin 1983). In this observation lies a clue to the popularity of the baths. They were places to have fun, but also to maintain one's health. Whatever the truth about the actual benefits of ancient hydrotherapy (Heinz 1996), the healthful properties of bathing, whether remedial or preventive, appear repeatedly in the comments and allusions of the written sources. That such notices are found in non-medical works suggests that the belief in healthy baths was not some rarified hypothetical construct restricted to elite medical treatises but a widespread and common assumption that can only have added to the popularity and attraction of the habit (Fagan 1999a: 85–103). The precise nature of ancient hydrotherapeutic practices is another area that needs further work, especially as they appear in the massive Galenic corpus.

Whatever the form of the facility or the motive for visiting it, the essence of Roman bathing was the communality of the experience, whether in private baths at home (with invited companions) or in public ones (with whoever happened by). This aspect of the baths gives them an unusual appeal, since here we can view the Romans in an informal context so often denied us by the nature of our evidence. The volume and complexity of the bath-related evidence from archaeological, literary, and epigraphic sources is formidable, and it cannot be fitted together at all neatly. Our impressions remain patchy and rooted to specific times and places, so that distinguishing the typical from the extraordinary is particularly difficult (Fagan 1999b). Nevertheless, a picture of Roman bathing culture can be painted in broad brush strokes, if not in minute detail. For instance, many private baths have been identified in the townhouses and villas of those who could afford them, although more work needs to be done on understanding these facilities and relating them to their better-studied public counterparts (see De Haan 1997; Entero 2001). What does emerge, however, is that access to private facilities did not preclude the use of public baths by the elite. Even if it was deemed preferable to bathe "without the mob" (Petron. *Sat.* 73.2), being seen at the public baths of one's community was part of what declared membership in it. Thus the *Digest* defines a person's legal *domicilium* for tax purposes as that place where he takes part in public life, which includes use of the public baths (*D.* 50.1.27.1). The communality of life in Roman towns, and the centrality of public bathing to that communality, is made clear by this ruling.

The vibrancy of the atmosphere at the baths shines through in dozens of sources, but perhaps most famously from Seneca's complaints about the din emanating from a bathhouse over which he rented a room in Baiae (Sen. *Ep.* 56.1–2). Other aspects of the bathing experience as alluded to in the sources – mixed bathing, sex, snacking, drinking, or the use of baths as places to meet dinner guests – only confirm Seneca's portrayal (Fagan 1999a: 12–39). That thieves habitually lurked in the baths, ready to snatch the belongings of the unwary, is a sufficient indication in itself of their being crowded and busy places (Plaut. *Rud.* 382–85; *D.* 47.17.1). The baths were thus nodes of social interaction for the Romans, but the nature of that interaction is not self-evident. It has long been recognized that Romans of all classes gathered together in the baths. Emblematic is the anecdote told by Pliny the Younger about the ex-praetor Larcius Macedo, who was accidentally struck in the face while bathing in public at Rome because his slave touched an *eques* who reacted violently (Pliny *Ep.* 3.14.6–8). The story puts a slave, a senator, and a knight in close proximity in the baths, and it is by no means a unique notice. All sorts of evidence point to a wide social mix at the typical public bathing facility (e.g. Cic. *Cael.* 61–7; *ILS* 5672). The problem lies in what we are to make of such scenarios. A common response has been to see the baths as "leveling" agents, where social distinctions broke down and moral norms were threatened. On this model, the baths were places which "threatened to undermine existing social identities" (Toner 1995: 53–64, quote at 57). While the moral ambiguity of the baths is clear enough, the supposed status anxiety they harbored seems unlikely, or, at least, as no more intensely experienced at the baths than in any other open public setting where the elite could expect to confront the non-elite (in the forum, the street, the circus, etc.). When they moved about in public, the self-important employed various strategies to make their status clear to all, and the baths seem no different. Slave retinues, quality of towels or wine or bathing accoutrements, the wearing of expensive jewelry and the application of exotic perfumes, or the very posture and accents of the well-to-do – all of these would have ensured that status distinctions were maintained inside the bathhouse as carefully as they were outside of it. Further, epigraphy reveals that the local elites were often responsible for the provision and maintenance of a Roman community's public baths. Can we really believe that such people would provide baths, have their names inscribed on the commemorative inscription, and then face possible humiliation and loss of face when they went inside? Is it plausible that when the ex-consul Pliny the Younger entered one of the modest public baths in the small town near his Laurentine villa, he risked demeaning his rank (Pliny *Ep.* 2.17.26)? Far from being social levelers, then, the baths more likely provided one more environment where the elite declared their status to all, in this instance in an intimate setting, and so reinforced their claim to leadership in a Roman community all the more forcefully.

6 Conclusion

The picture we gain of Roman leisure is necessarily sketchy, since the evidence has survived in so uneven a manner. Given the scale and longevity of the empire, there must have been tremendous variation across time and space in the habits reviewed above. We must not think, for instance, that tavern life in every Roman city, town, or hamlet was static over the centuries of Roman rule. At the same time, some conditions must have remained basically similar, and continuities surely persisted. This applies equally to the use(s) of the public baths and the nature and mode of staging public banquets. Investigating regional and chronological variations (and continuities) more closely is a task that remains for future studies. Through such investigations, we can only deepen and refine our understanding of the role of leisure in Roman life. Theoretical models and comparative data are useful avenues by which to approach such thematic issues as addressed above, so long as the temptation is resisted to maintain a model in the face of ambiguous evidence rather than adapt the model to explain the evidence. In the last analysis, little can compensate for what the Romans themselves tell us about their *otium*, patchy and selective as the surviving written sources may be.

Despite these methodological difficulties, some salient points can be made. When viewed from the perspective of the wider cultural history of the Mediterranean basin, Roman public leisure appears to be a "popularizing" of what had for many centuries been the preserves of the privileged. If elaborate dinner parties had previously been a feature of life for a limited few, the Roman public banquet offered them to the masses, on a less luxurious scale. The public baths made sensations widely available that few in earlier societies had had the opportunity to enjoy. The hunts in the amphitheaters and circuses did likewise for this formerly royal pursuit, and the once-aristocratic sport of chariot racing became under the Romans a mass spectator event (see ch. 20). It is a hallmark of Roman culture that it not only prioritized *otium* conceptually – "business" was *negotium* ("not-leisure"), as we have seen – but that it opened access to it to so many.

When reading the sources, there is an impression of a profound disconnect between what the elite did in their spare time (namely, involvement in literature) and what the masses did (worthless appeasement of bodily urges). This impression, however, is built on the public posturing of the morally upright and socially superior, whose blusterings we should always be wary of accepting at face value. Seneca the Younger, for all his public pronouncements about his frugality, simplicity, personal asceticism, and contempt for contemporary bathing culture died an enormously rich man, in one of his country villas, in a private bathhouse in that villa (Dio 61.10.2–6; Tac. *Ann.* 15.63–4). If members of the elite *pronounced* that anyone who mattered ought to spend their spare time among their scrolls and *tabellae*, it does not mean that they habitually did so. They too could be found at the banquets, taking pleasure in the games, slumming in the taverns, and sharing the baths like everyone else.

In making this observation, however, we must not fall into the trap of supposing that Roman leisure was somehow a "leveling" or "democratizing" valve in an otherwise status-obsessed social hierarchy. Just because many shared it, does not mean they shared it in equal measure. Even if there were exceptions, it is still the case that a status-obsessed senator would not want to be caught dead in a back-street tavern, playing dice with those who made disgusting sounds with their noses and talked endlessly about chariots and horses, as the fourth-century historian Ammianus Marcellinus presents it (Amm. Marc. 14.6.25). Even at literary recitations, which ostensibly united the cultured in a shared appreciation for higher art, hierarchy was maintained by means of quality of seating and proximity to the reader (Juv. 7.39–47). The same sorts of divisions applied at private dinner parties. In its leisure time also, Roman society was obsessed with maintaining the proper distinctions.

The upper classes provided the masses with the means to enjoy many of their *voluptates*, even as they publicly denigrated those pursuits. It was they who built the public spaces where *commoda* were offered and it was they who funded the events themselves. Indeed, they were expected to do so: "the masses are more hostile to a rich man who does not give them a share of his wealth than a poor man who steals from the public funds, for they think that the former's conduct is due to arrogance and contempt of them, but the latter's to necessity" (Plut. *Mor.* 822A). In the face of such attitudes, by which the commoners interpreted as contempt a rich person's reluctance to spend money on them, it is hardly surprising that the elite erected permanent records of their generosity in prominent public places, in the form of the honorific inscriptions that survive for us to read today. These inscriptions represent the essence of euergetism's social contract: the exchange of private expenditure for public recognition (Veyne 1976). In such a context, we can hardly doubt that the crowds in a town's baths or the beneficiaries at a public banquet knew who was who. The commemoratory inscriptions themselves are monuments to this fact, in that they stood in prominent spots (often accompanying statues) as permanent reminders to everyone that someone's largesse had been deployed for the enjoyment of all. Roman leisure, therefore, bears all the indicators of status and hierarchy, of obligation and reciprocity that are the enduring characteristics of the Roman Empire over its long duration. To paraphrase Pliny's assertion cited in the epigraph of this chapter: by its leisure is the essential character of Roman society revealed.

CHAPTER TWENTY

Spectacle

David S. Potter

1 Introduction

The Roman concept of leisure is deeply implicated in Roman notions of status – the rich might spend their *otium* in literary pursuits; the poor spent their time eating, drinking, and having sex (Fagan, this volume). Even in areas such as a bathhouse where members of different orders might share space, distinctions still had to be observed. When we turn to the world of spectacle, the same divisions will at first seem to apply. Before the end of the republic, seating at the theater was divided by class, a distinction that was extended to the amphitheater and the circus in the course of the first century CE. Many spectacles were associated with civic events; their provision was the duty of city magistrates. To offer a spectacle was to assert superiority in the symbolic system of exchange that governed social relations within the Greco-Roman city. That at least was the theory.

In practice the realm of spectacle was much less orderly than the theory would suggest. Just as members of the aristocracy might break the rules of *otium* through over-indulgence in the pleasures of the table, or by wandering the streets to seek the company of prostitutes, so too the divisions of class asserted in the organization of spectacle were liable to break down. Virtually every aspect of Roman hierarchy was open to challenge – public executions could go awry if the crowd demanded the release of the condemned, gladiators could become heroes, charioteers could become millionaires, and actors might challenge the order of society by the way they chose to utter their lines. To be successful, a spectacle had to offer an opportunity for radical changes of fortune; it had to stir the passions of the viewers.

To understand Roman spectacle it is perhaps best to begin with the emotional response that was expected of engaged viewing, and the Roman fascination with sharp contrast. Ancient thought often appears to be binary – chastity can only be demonstrated in the context of sexual temptation, honor implies the risk of dishonor, courage of cowardice. To know that one was strong, one had to be tempted. To be an aristocrat was to be free from the base desires of the common person, yet it was also to provide for those desires. To be an aristocrat was to be in thorough control of one's passions (Gleason 1999a: 70–8). To do so one had to be victorious in the constant struggle with the incitements to passion with which one was surrounded. One needed to empathize with powerful emotions, to recognize their effect upon others, and at times, one had to run the risk of experiencing them.

Just as the rhetorician Philostratus of Lemnos, in describing the pictures on display at a gallery on the Bay of Naples in the later second century CE, enters into the emotions of each picture, members of an imperial audience expected, or feared, involvement in the emotions of the moment. As he describes the pictures, Philostratus seems to have felt the passion of Polyphemus for the nymph Galatea, the grief of Antigone for her brother, or the drama of a boxing match between the carnivorous Phorbas and Apollo. In his descriptions he reveals what it was that people of his age expected to happen when one was confronted with an effort to escape the experience of quotidian reality (*Imag.* 2.18.3, 30.3, 19.3). So too, Augustine would write much later that he became aroused at the theater, and would tell of his friend Alypius, who thought that he could attend a gladiatorial combat and avoid being caught up in the emotions of the moment. Even though he closed his eyes, he could not close his ears and was soon screaming with the rest of the crowd. The amphitheater was, for Alypius, a test of self-mastery failed (August. *Conf.* 6.8). Others would not have bothered to attempt such a test: it was precisely in order to become lost in the emotions of the moment that they went.

To experience the passion of others, to delight in seeing the past come alive – these are factors in the classical experience of spectacle, be it theatrical, amphitheatric, athletic, or in the circus. So too could be the desire to test oneself, either as Alypius did, or to see if one could measure up to the contestants. Self-restraint is only impressive if the strong possibility exists that people will not exercise it, if peers gave way to their passions, allowed their status to be called into question, even admitted that they actually liked the games.

The vast range of possible spectacles in the Roman world has made it difficult to appreciate similarities that linked their audiences, to understand how a person could move with seeming ease from the theater to the amphitheater and then to the circus. Those who deplored gladiatorial spectacle (or professed to deplore it) were likewise liable to deplore, at least in public, the events of the circus and to be deeply ambivalent about the stage. They might also pour scorn upon professional athletes. So too, a person who liked the games would not be limited to enjoyment of just one sort. In thinking about Roman entertainment then it is perhaps best to put aside the divisions between the different sorts of events that we will see in the next section of this chapter, and concentrate on similarities: fascination with technical skill and, consequently, with celebrity performers, interest in recreating events from the distant past, the desire to cap earlier performances, and sympathetic engagement with the passions presented by the participants. Finally, we need to consider how all of these factors might have contributed to one of the most important developments during the imperial period: the increasing role of women as performers in a wide range of venues.

2 The Events

The principal public entertainments of the Roman imperial period fall into six categories: horse/chariot racing, theatrical events, unarmed contests between humans, armed contests between humans, contests involving beasts, and events in which criminals were put to death. Each of these events has its own particular history, and the evolution of the full spectrum of entertainments available between the first and fourth centuries CE reflects the considerable ability of the imperial system both to absorb and to influence the choices of the empire's population.

Horse and chariot racing reflect the different practices that evolved in Rome and the Greek world at very early stages in their history. Horse races in the Greek world were for big-spenders, be they individuals or cities seeking publicity for themselves by sponsoring a race team. In all cases credit for the victory would go first to whomever it was that paid for the horses. In some cases it appears that the sponsor might actually run the horses himself, and some prominent men did so, but this was not necessary to gain credit for the triumph. The coincidental result of this was that affluent women who sought to exalt their position in the world might well do so by paying for race teams. Nearly all the women listed as victors in athletic competitions gained their victory in equestrian events.

The first point upon which Roman racing differed from Greek was the use of a specific race course. This should not be surprising since Greek racing traditions developed in accord with the topography at different sites, while the Roman tradition was shaped by the terrain at one spot in the urban landscape: the area of the Circus Maximus at Rome. The restricted space available in the Circus Maximus meant that, if a satisfactory race was to be run, it needed to involve multiple laps around a pair of turning posts. Restricted space also meant that the Roman system could not involve a massive starting mechanism such as that at Olympia, which could accommodate up to 48 contestants (Humphrey 1986: 8–9). The Olympic start involved the horses running along a track until they reached the first turning post, at which point they would turn onto another track, with a second turning post, to run their laps (we do not know how many). The Roman race was run on a single track, which may have restricted the number of entries to 12. Here though we run into a classic chicken and egg problem – was the choice of the number 12 (still somewhat impractical) the result of the fact that there were four factions that were charged with running the races from an early date, or were there four factions because there was enough space to run 12 chariots? We cannot know for certain, but we do know that by the mid fourth century BCE the first set of permanent starting gates erected in the Circus presumed 12 teams; in the early second century we get the first – admittedly somewhat ambiguous – evidence for the factions themselves in a fragment of Ennius (Livy 8.20.2; Enn. 1 fr. xlvii, 79–83 Skutsch; Potter 1999b: 291–2). The fact that we do not get possible evidence for the factions before the controversial passage of Ennius is not in and of itself a problem – there being virtually no contemporary evidence for any Roman institutions before this time. I believe that the organization of the ground in the Circus Maximus confirms the existence of these groups, referred to by the colors worn by their members as the Reds, Whites, Blues, and Greens, by the middle of the fourth century BCE.

The particular requirement of Roman-style racing – a large stadium that could accommodate a huge crowd – is likely the reason why it took so long for the sport to spread around the empire. It is not until the third century CE that we start finding circuses in cities other than Rome, and then only in major cities. By the end of this century, however, the fact that the circus at Rome had become the primary venue for communication between the emperor and his subjects made a circus the mandatory accompaniment of an imperial palace, wherever these were built.

In thinking about theatrical and athletic events, the most important distinction is between agonistic and epideictic, that is between those that took place in the context of an *agon*, or contest, and those that were presented at an *epideixis*, or recital (Robert 1982: 36 = 1989b: 710). Amongst the *agones*, there was a further distinction, between local contests where monetary prizes were often awarded along with the crowns for victory, and the great "panhellenic" festivals, connected with the celebration of divinities and awarding only a crown. In the archaic and classical period there were four such contests – the Olympic, Pythian, Nemean, and Isthmian games – forming the "periodic cycle," organized in a four-year cycle based on the Olympics (an "Olympiad"). Like the Olympics, the Pythian games took place every four years, in the third year of each Olympiad; the Isthmian and Nemean were held every two years, in the second and fourth year of each Olympiad.

The expansion of *agones* beyond the "periodic" cycle may be traced in the century after the death of Alexander the Great. The model followed for these new games appears to have been established by Ptolemy II, who created the first festival outside the classical cycle in honor of his father. This Ptolemaia, as it was called, asserted that it was "isolympic," or "equal to the Olympics." Ptolemy's lead was followed 30 or so years later by the League of the Aetolians, which re-founded the Sôtereia, originally established to commemorate the defeat of Gallic raiders at Delphi in 279, as a "crowned" festival (Robert 1982: 37 = 1989b: 711).

After the re-foundation of the Sôtereia, the typical format for the creation of a crowned festival involved some great event – either a victory in war or some manifestation of divine power. The event, and the establishment of the festival, was then announced by the city to the Greek world as a whole. Cities would decide if they would accept the festival as being on a par with other "crowned" and sacred games. For a victor in such a contest – this is an important distinction between the "crowned" games and local contests where prizes might also be given for second and third place – there might be a ceremonial entry into his home city. In some cases this might involve the home city making a breach in its walls through which the victor would enter (in other cases he would simply come through a city gate), and place his crown on the statue of a local god. The victor would then be eligible for a maintenance grant. Games which gave the victor the right of such an entry were known as *eiselastikos* (Robert 1982: 42–3 = 1989b: 716–17). By the beginning of the second century CE, it appears as if the imperial government had stepped in to try and bring some order to these events and to their prizes (especially since cities were continuously trying to enhance the status of their games by having them granted *eiselastic* status). The most significant evidence for this development is in an exchange between the younger Pliny and the emperor Trajan. Pliny wrote that:

Athletes, Lord, think that they ought to be awarded those rewards that you have established for *eiselastic* contests on the day that they are crowned; they claim that the date upon which they are carried into their home city does not matter, rather the date on which they won the victory for which they won the right to be carried in. I responded by pointing to the title "*eiselastiskos*," so I think that the date upon which they make their entry must be relevant.

They also claim maintenance grants from a contest that was given *eiselastic* status by you, although they won before that happened. They say it is fair, since they do not receive maintenance grants from those games that ceased to be *eiselastic* after they won, if they receive maintenance grants from those that afterwards acquire them. I think that this is nonsense since there should be no retrospective claim for something that did not exist when they won. (*Ep.* 10.118)

Trajan agreed with Pliny, but that is scarcely the end of the story. The situation that Pliny confronted arose as a result of the fact that the imperial government was taking a close interest in what happened on the local level with these entertainments. Despite Trajan's refusal to support the position of the athletes, the imperial government had granted very great favors to professional athletes, and relied upon what had become, by this period, the one international association of crowned athletes to bring order to the ever-expanding range of games that had come into being after Actium. These games provided a critical venue for the exposition of imperial ideology, and of communication between the court and provincial communities.

The distinction between agonistic and epideictic performance is also crucial for understanding the competitive events that took place in the theater. Some events had long been part of agonistic festivals, and they remained, in the Greek world, events that drew performers from the upper classes – victors in these games were people who might reasonably be expected to be honored by public decrees, and, from the late fourth century BCE onwards they formed their own professional associations, the so-called *technîtai* of Dionysus (Lightfoot 2002: 212). Epideictic performances on the stage, and alongside it, involved a wide range of other performances, of which the most significant were mime (a form of ancient sitcom) and pantomime (dance on a mythological theme). Unlike the performers in agonistic events, the performers of epideictic drama did not form professional associations in the east, and did not draw upon members of the higher orders as performers. In the west, where there was no tradition of agonistic performance before the first century CE (Robert 1982: 40–1 = 1989b: 714–15; 1970: 7–10 = 1989a: 648–51), we do find professional associations of entertainers in mime and pantomime. Membership in these groups was restricted to individuals of low social status, in keeping with the Italian tradition that performers were clients of the aristocrats who dominated civic life. In this sense they were similar to gladiators.

Gladiatorial combat was but one of a number of entertainments that were characteristic of the amphitheater. These entertainments developed at different times, and appear to have derived from quite different sources. Gladiators are first attested in the archaeological record from south-central Italy (in tomb paintings at Paestum) in the middle of the fourth century BCE. The first exhibition of gladiators at Rome is said to have taken place at the funeral of Lucius Junius Brutus Pera in 264 BCE (Livy *Per.* 16; Val. Max. 2.4.7). The context is significant, for it placed gladiatorial combat firmly in the context of aristocratic *munera* rather than community *ludi*: a *munus* was intended to celebrate the individual's relationship with the community, while *ludi* were events whereby the community celebrated itself. As a general rule, *ludi* tended to include entertainments with a very long history at Rome – theatrical events and chariot racing – and to exclude relative novelties, of which gladiatorial combat was one, and wild beast hunts another. *Ludi* could, however, be venues for public punishments, as is clear from Fabius Pictor's account of one of the earliest, which centered on the story of the flogging of a slave (*FGrH* 809 Fr. 13, with Bernstein 1998: 87–96).

Despite their late arrival on the Roman scene, gladiators rapidly came to be identified with the martial virtues of the Roman people, though our best evidence for this comes from well outside of Rome itself. This evidence is provided by a performance in 167 BCE that shows how Antiochus IV of Syria, who had spent some time in Rome as a hostage, "read" the gladiatorial combats he had witnessed: he thought that they inspired young men with thoughts of valor on the battlefield. By the end of the second century the connection between gladiators and martial glory was reified when Gaius Marius introduced elements of gladiatorial training into that of legionaries. The connection continued into the first century, and it is in the *African War*, an account of Julius Caesar's North African campaign of 46 BCE, that we find Caesar explicitly compared to a gladiatorial trainer as he shouted instructions to the raw troops under his command (*B. Afr.* 71).

The connection between gladiators and military virtue may have enhanced the popularity of gladiatorial entertainment throughout the rest of peninsular Italy. A gladiatorial training ground, evidently to supply gladiators for the local market, is known to have been established at Capua in the 70s BCE, and, at the same time, we begin to find permanent stone amphitheaters throughout municipal Italy. These amphitheaters seem to have been modeled on the temporary wooden structures that were mandatory at Rome, and they appear first in cities settled by veterans of Sulla's army, victorious in the civil war of the late 80s (Welch 1994: 79–80). Thanks to the ample evidence available for the generation of Cicero and Caesar, we gain important perspectives not only on the ever-expanding scale of gladiatorial combat – leading to a law limiting the number of pairs that could be exhibited at any one time when Caesar tried to exhibit 320 of them – but also of the role of gladiators outside the arena (Plut. *Caes.* 6.5; Ville 1981: 60, 290–2). They made admirable bodyguards for the politicians of the era, and appear to have been a good investment even for members of the Senate like Cicero, who rented them out (*Att.* 4.8.2; 4.4a.2). Julius Caesar also appears to have remained a major investor: his troupe in Campania was regarded as a threat to public order when the civil war broke out in 49 BCE, and he spent part of the day before crossing the Rubicon inspecting a training ground in northern Italy (Caes. *BC* 1.14.4–5; Cic. *Att.* 7.14.2; Suet. *Jul.* 31.1).

By the time Augustus emerged victorious from the civil wars, gladiatorial combat appears to have been well established throughout the empire. Antony had established gladiatorial training grounds in the east, and there is some evidence to suggest that local aristocrats had been employing gladiators in civic festivals before Actium (Dio 51.7.2). After Actium, the primary venues for gladiatorial exhibitions included celebration of the imperial cult and the annual *munera* that civic magistrates had to offer as the price for their office. By the third century CE, there is good evidence that some cities might seek permission from an emperor to stage gladiatorial combats and beast hunts, rather than more traditional Greek style events, as a way of demonstrating their attachment to Rome (Nollé 1992/3).

As early as the reign of Augustus, it appears that costs, at least as measured against the perceived value returned from the expenditure on games, sky-rocketed at Rome. Augustus had difficulty in finding people willing to hold the aedileship and pay for their aedilician games; the result was that he had to fund some of these events himself and offer advantages in the senatorial career for people willing to undertake the cost themselves (Dio 49.16; 53.2.2, 33.3; 55.24.9; Hammond 1933: 135). He also had to limit the opportunities for competition with games that he funded on the part of very wealthy members of the aristocracy who might challenge his domination of spectacle. When Lucius Domitius Ahenobarbus (the emperor Nero's grandfather) advertised a particularly violent display of gladiators, Augustus stepped in to ban *munera* in which a fight to a defined conclusion was demanded – the so-called *munera sine missione* (Suet. *Aug.* 45.3; *Nero* 4). Tiberius, who paid a staggering sum in appearance money for some famous gladiators (see below), would later institute empire-wide restrictions on the money that could be spent on local *munera*, as well as, presumably, at Rome. The controls instituted by Augustus and Tiberius over the violence and expenditure on games continued throughout the imperial period. These controls, which could be lifted by decree of the Senate, or by imperial fiat (both are attested), enabled the imperial government to intervene at the local level to grant favors to people who, for their own reasons, might want to exceed the statutory limits.

The economics of gladiatorial exhibitions had a profound effect on the nature of the games. By the second century, two systems of acquiring performers for amphitheatric events are attested. One involved the outright purchase of the performers by the prospective *munerarius*, the other involved rental. The jurist Gaius mentions a penalty clause that appears to have been standard for gladiatorial rentals, according to which a person in whose games a gladiator was killed had to repay 50 times the rental cost, while a pair of inscriptions, one from Sardis in Asia Minor, the other from Italica in Spain, record a discussion in the Senate of a measure by Marcus Aurelius to fix the purchase price of gladiators according to the financial capacities of cities across the empire (Gaius *Inst.* 3.146; Mommsen 1892: 414). The survival of the vast majority of gladiatorial combatants is implied by both these schemes. Survival was not, however, the order of the day for people condemned to fight in the amphitheater as a result of the judicial process (see below), and it may be that restrictions on the danger of gladiatorial combat enhanced the appeal of these spectacles of public punishment.

The exhibition of wild beasts, both fighting each other and fighting humans, developed in the course of the republican period, and did so separately from gladiatorial combat (see below). By the imperial period there appears to have been a well-developed network to supply animals for contests, enabling a person who had obtained the requisite imperial permission to collect the animals himself. Beast handlers (*bestiarii*), who would also be charged with delivering human victims for the animals, and beast hunters, *venatores*, appear to have been organized separately, and, as was the tradition with events that developed under Roman influence, were supposed to be people of lower status (but see below).

All the forms of entertainment outlined in the last few pages flourished throughout the first three centuries CE, a sign of the importance of these events in the cultural and political life of the empire (Robert 1982: 45 = 1989b: 719; van Nijf 2001: 334). Fiscal crises at the end of the third century appear to have impaired athletic contests as endowments that supported many of them were probably wiped out in the currency reforms of the period, while gladiatorial combat seems to have declined in popularity as Christian emperors withdrew their direct support (though they did not ban them). At the same time the spread of circus buildings throughout the major cities of the empire, and the direct connection between circuses and imperial palaces, meant that chariot racing would enter a golden age in the later empire. The theater, despite howls of protest from local bishops, would likewise remain very popular as long as civic life endured.

3 Technical Skill

An inscription from Letoon in Lycia (southwestern Turkey) records a rather unpleasant festival that took place about 100 BCE in which inadequate numbers of contestants showed up for several of the events, and many of those who did appear were disqualified either for cheating or because they were not judged worthy of a prize (Robert 1978: 282–6 = 1990: 686–90; Crowther and Frass 1998: 58–65). The meaning of some of the technical language used for failure in the competitions mentioned in this text may be unraveled with the aid of various authors of the imperial period, who likewise record that people who were booed off the stage might be flogged. Comments like these invite us to read with some skepticism a letter written at some point in the first decade of the second century CE by the younger Pliny, in which he observes that:

> I have spent this whole time with my writing tablets and books. "How can you do that in the city?" you ask. Chariot races are going on, and I am not the least bit interested in that sort of entertainment. There is nothing new, nothing different, nothing that it does not suffice to have seen but once. For this reason I am all the more astonished that so many thousands of people desire so childishly to watch horses run, and see men ride chariots again and again. If they were drawn by the speed of the horses or the skill of the drivers, that would be one thing; now, however, they cheer for a piece of cloth, they love a piece of cloth, and if, in the middle of a race this color would be transferred to that man, and that color to this one, the partisanship and favor would change with it, and suddenly they would leave those charioteers and those horses, that they recognize at a distance and whose names they shout. (*Ep.* 9.6.1–2)

Pliny's suggestion that the games would be more interesting if people were interested in displays of skill is deeply misleading: he is trying to draw a contrast between what would be acceptable to an aristocrat such as himself as opposed to the debased passions of a crowd incapable of appreciating the finer points of a particular activity. Loyalty to a faction was a powerful factor in the enjoyment of the games, but so too was the desire to have charioteers take on new challenges and show off their skill in new ways (Potter 1999b: 292). The grandest of all inscriptions commemorating the career of a charioteer describes a career that began about a decade after Pliny's death

(*ILS* 5287). The text honors a man named Gaius Appuleius Diocles, and tells us that by the time he died at the age of 42, he had won 1463 races; of these victories, 83 came in special "races of champions" featuring one entrant from each of the four factions instead of the usual three, and another 347 victories in races involving just two teams from each faction. He also tells of victories in races with chariots that had six horses, one with seven horses, of races in which the horses were not yoked, races where riders switched teams with those of other factions, and so forth. While he did indeed switch factions, and thus, one may presume, like any modern free agent who changes teams, acquired new fans when he did so (as well as hatred from the supporters of his former faction), this should not be taken as confirming what Pliny has to say. Fans were loyal to their faction, and they expected that their faction would field drivers of talent that they could appreciate. As the inscription for Diocles also reveals – he sets his career in the context of other charioteers, comparing his victory totals with theirs – fans would have been well aware of a charioteer's statistics.

While Pliny may position himself at one end of the aristocratic mode of discourse, others were less snobbish. As early as the second century BCE, the poet Lucilius might use imagery drawn from a chariot race – hold back your chariot and horses like a good driver – and as late as the fifth century CE, Sidonius Apollinaris could put a chariot race into verse with considerable appreciation for the details of a driver's tactics (Lucil. fr. 1249; Sid. Apoll. *Carm.* 23.315–427). It is of particular interest that in Sidonius' poem we see one of Diocles' races of champions with one team from each faction, and clear understanding of the role of teams, with a driver from one faction working to ensure the victory of one from the faction paired with his own (Blues and Whites were matched against Greens and Reds) (Cameron 1976: 63–4). Sidonius writes of his charioteer's teammate who sets the pace to wear out the rival teams; in the meantime the charioteer holds back:

> You, bent double with the effort, hold back the four-horse team, and with the greatest skill hold back for the last lap. Now, with the return of the sixth lap completed, and now with the crowd calling for the prizes, the other side (*pars contraria*), not fearing your strength, was running the safe tracks in front, suddenly tightening the reins, tightening your chest, with your foot planted firmly, you pull in the mouths of your swift steeds just like that ancient charioteer, sweeping past Oenomaeus with Pisa trembling. (*Carm.* 23.385–93)

The driver cuts inside the second place chariot, and then slips ahead of the first place driver who, thinking victory within his grasp, had taken too wide a turn. Trying to recover, this driver tries to run Sidonius' hero from the track and crashes. The victory is owed to a combination of teamwork and skill. While we cannot know how a driver went from being the sort of "chariot fodder" who cleared the way for the star to being the star himself, we may imagine any number of scenarios in which the sudden failure of the expected champion led to a radical change in race strategy. This would have been one of the things that the audience wanted to see: victory, to be meaningful, had to be difficult.

The educated fan was not above attempting to handicap races on his or her own, and it is of particular interest – again as an example of how misleading Pliny's letter is when it comes to the actual conditions of the race – that curse tablets tend to be directed at specific charioteers. Thus in one case, replete as well with the technical language of the race, a petitioner of the demons asks:

> Most holy Lord Charakteres, tie up, bind the feet, the hands, the sinews, the eyes, the knees, the courage, the leaps, the whip, the victory and the crowning of Porphyry and Hapsicrates, who are in the middle left, as well as his co-drivers of the Blue colors in the stable of Eugenius. From this very hour, from today, may they not eat or drink or sleep; instead from the (starting) gates may they see *daimones* (of those) who have died prematurely, spirits (of those) who have died violently, and the fire of Hephaestus... in the hippodrome at the moment they are about to compete may they not squeeze over, may they not collide, may they not extend, may they not force us out, may they not overtake, may they not make sharp turns for the entire day when they are about to race. May they be broken, may they be dragged on the ground, may they be destroyed.... (SEG 34 no. 1437)

The list of tactics in this spell would appear to pretty much summarize the moves that might be expected of a charioteer once he had managed to avoid the spirits of those who had died prematurely or violently and go speeding around the racetrack. Like the charioteer in Sidonius' poem, he might push over to an inside lane, he might sprint (the meaning here of "extend"), overtake, and make good sharp turns. The charioteers themselves, as suggested in the inscription honoring Diocles, would be well known, as would their teams. To race with a different or new team, as Diocles suggests, would place special demands on the driver, and again this was something that fans would like to see, at least in the case of someone who had shown himself especially skillful. The interested fan wanted to know: was it just the horses, or was it Diocles?

Chariot racing enables us to observe the tendency to applaud the star in a team context. In other areas, where the star system is just as pronounced, we may see how it altered the very nature of the entertainment. This is especially true of theatrical events. Plays, both tragic and comic, continued to be written in both Greek and Latin into the imperial period, sometimes taking their cue from forms of literature that developed in the imperial period; such is the case with the extraordinary fragment of a mime dealing with a theme that is characteristic of the Greek novel (*P.Oxy.* 413). In the early imperial period, it was plainly possible for a writer of traditional tragedy, at least in Latin, to make a great deal of money: in 29 BCE Varius Rufus received one million sesterces for a *Thyestes*. Later we have evidence for the continued production of new tragedies at Athens (Lebek 1996: 35; C. P. Jones 1993: 44–5). Well into the second century, rich men who wanted to make a splash at that city would assume the traditional role of sponsor, or *choregos*, bearing the cost of the performance at one of the civic festivals. At times the playwright might act in one of his own dramas, as did the author of one comedy. But these events need to be interpreted with some caution: all known actors and victors in new dramas put on at Athens in the imperial period are native Athenians. The wealthy who are noticed for their contributions are members of the elite functioning in an agonistic context. It may be that we should view their activity as a feature of the cultural antiquarianism of the period whereby classical events were recreated precisely because they were classical: drama was as characteristic of classical Athens as was, for instance, the traditional training of young men through the *agogê* at Sparta, where tourists watched naked young men undergo severe floggings (Cartledge and Spawforth 1989: 201–7; Smith, this volume). The Spartan system, as it was known in the imperial period, was a creative anachronism instituted some time after 146 BCE, long after Sparta had any pretence of being a power in Greece.

Outside of Athens, older plays, classics, seem to have been more to the taste of major artists. This may, perhaps reflect the fact that old drama was part of the curriculum for new rhetoricians – Marcus Aurelius thought that Old Comedy (comedy written in the fifth century BCE) was particularly beneficial (*Med.* 11.6; C. P. Jones 1993: 44). Orators read these plays so that they could practice the crucial art of *ethopoesis*, necessary for success in their own performances. It is the connection with rhetorical training that perhaps sparked an interest in actually appearing on stage not only on the part of Nero, but also on that of Thrasea Paetus, who often attacked Nero for his conduct (with results both utterly predictable and fatal) (Dio 62.26.4). Marcus' interest in Old Comedy seems also to have been stimulated by his education.

If one could make a case for performing on the stage as an aristocrat in old style drama, no such case ever seems to have been made for participating in drama that fell in the epideictic tradition. Although we know that Augustus and other emperors delighted in pantomime, we do not know of any aristocrat who ever desired to play a part in a mime. Before turning to these events, it needs to be noted that star performers in traditional tragedy and comedy were less well paid than performers in either mime or pantomime, and that actors might also choose to perform "greatest hits" from selected plays. A papyrus containing a portion of Euripides' *Chresphontes* appears to be marked up so that actors could find selected excerpts; the same appears to be the case with a play written during the imperial period that features Priam and members of his family (*P.Oxy.* 409; 2458; 2746). In altering their scripts, actors were assimilating, at least to a degree, to the performances of pantomime; it appears that they would sing their parts as soloists in company with a chorus and a flute player (Plut. *Mor.* 63a; D.Chr. 19.5; E. Hall 2002: 12–24). A variation on this form of performance in the agonistic context would involve fresh settings of choruses from tragedies to music where the stress would appear to have been on the skill of the composer(?)/flautist who accompanied the chorus. A victory monument from Isthmia celebrates the triumphs of one Gaius Aelius Themision, who set the choruses of Sophocles, Euripides, and Timotheus to music, while a papyrus from Oxyrhynchus records the contract for just such a performer, a man named Epagathus (*BE* 1954 n. 111; Cockle 1975: 59–65).

Pantomime was the ultimate soloist event. It may have been the personal interest of the emperor Augustus that first established pantomimes as the superstars of the theater. It was in his reign that two great dancers – Bathyllus and Pylades – competed to dominate the art form. Bathyllus appears to have represented a more traditional style in which the dancer sang to limited musical accompaniment, and may have performed routines that could include comic themes. Pylades is said to have been the first pantomime who had a singer and may have changed the style of music to include a significant percussion element. The characteristics of Pylades' performance are said to have been "passion and variety of character" (Ath. *Deip.* 20d), while another observer – Lucian – notes that the dancer tried to present, and enact, both characters and emotions (*Salt.* 67). Sometimes the material might be adapted directly from plays by classical dramatists (*TrGF* 1 p. 344); at other times, it was a fresh composition on a traditional theme. With the passing of time, competition for new scripts appears to have been fierce; Juvenal remarks with some bitterness that Statius made lots of money for producing the libretto on the theme of *Agave* for a famous pantomime, and nothing for his great epic poem, the *Thebaid* (Juv. 7.82–7). Equally interesting is that Statius, who was not shy about describing his own career as a competitive poet, never mentions works of this sort. The *Agave*, which would have told the tale of the mother of Pentheus, who in a Bacchic rage unwittingly participated in the gruesome murder of her son, was a typically demanding role for a pantomime.

A successful pantomime, despite the epideictic context of his performance, might become virtually immortal as those who performed in his tradition took his name. The Augustan Pylades was succeeded by as many as six other Pyladeses between the first and third centuries (Leppin 1992: 284–8). Another potent name was Apolaustus: the earliest on record performed in the mid-first century CE; the latest of whom we know was dancing in the age of Commodus (Leppin 1992: 204–10). The first dancer named Paris whom we know to have become famous worked in the reign of Nero, the third was active under Commodus, while the second Paris was still remembered in the reign of Hadrian as a potent figure (it was he who bought the *Agave* from Statius) (Leppin 1992: 270–6). The point of these names – it appears that only one person in each generation might hold it – was to assert primacy in the field, and, though the evidence for this is scanty, quite possibly to claim to be the head of a particular school of dance. In the imperial period, as in the republic, famous actors would train others to follow in their footsteps. To be identified as a favored pupil appears to have been sufficient to put someone on the fast track to riches and fame (Lebek 1996: 38–9; Potter 1999b: 269–70).

Membership in a professional association was as important to athletes as it was to actors as a mark of status. Despite critics who regarded professional athletes as blockheads who would have been better off attending lectures in philosophy, or who regarded the regimen of athletic training as unhealthy (Poliakoff 1987: 93–103), those whose victories enabled them to gain a place in the international synod of athletes would enjoy privileges comparable to those of major cultural figures. The extensive certificates of membership provided by the synod asserted the special status of athletes by offering a potted history of their relationship with the imperial government. By the third century CE a typical document attesting the induction of a person would include a copy of a letter from Claudius, an edict of Hadrian, two letters from Septimius Severus, and one from Severus Alexander, all attesting the privileges of the synod, as well as a letter from an official of the synod attesting that the new member should enjoy them (Frisch 1986: no. 1).

Documents such as those certifying admission to the synod stand as stunning reminders that, contrary to a view once common in scholarship, Greek games were not considered inferior by the imperial government. Not only would members of the international synod gain a wide range of exemptions from local responsibilities, they might also be drafted into the upper-level organization of their sport. It is common to find that a retired athlete will serve as a *xystarch*, or leader of a gymnasium, by imperial appointment. Other athletes would have comprised the staff of the central office of the synod at Rome. Indeed, one of the interesting features of the extensive career inscriptions that honor athletes for their accomplishments around the empire is that they link local dignity with fame (and office) won abroad. Although these texts are rarely informative about the way that a person won, Marcus Aurelius Asclepiades proclaims that he won all the contests for which he registered, was never disqualified for stalling, and never appealed a judge's decision – something that may be connected with his further claim never to have won by "royal" favor (Moretti 1953: no. 79, with Poliakoff 1987: 126 n. 21). In another case, an inscription honoring Tiberius Claudius Rufus of Smyrna reproduces a letter from the *hellenodikai* (tournament officials) at Olympia explaining that he was declared the winner in a match that technically ended in a draw because he contended against an opponent who had benefited from a bye (SIG^3 1073). Elsewhere there is ample evidence that people discussed the specifics of matches well after they had happened. Philostratus of Athens (writing in the early third century) has his fictional character, Protesilaus – a Homeric hero who gives oracles from the region of his tomb on the Gallipoli peninsula – describe specific advice that he gave pancratiasts as to what moves will be successful. Perpetua (on whom see Evans Grubbs, this volume) dreamed that she had become a pancratiast and seems to have been able to envision a fight in some detail. The Philostratus who is the author of the *Pictures* tells us that:

> Pancratiasts engaging in wrestling that is fraught with peril, for they are subject to blows in the face that are dangerous for wrestlers, and clinches which they can only win by pretending to fall, and they must have the skill to choke an adversary in various ways at various times, they are both wrestling with the ankle and twisting the opponent's arm, dealing a blow and leaping upon him; all these things, save only biting and gouging, can be done in pankration. (*Imag.* 2.6.3)

This Philostratus seems to have had a passion for these sports – describing elsewhere a group of wrestling (and cheating) cupids, boys wrestling in an Arcadian gymnasium (again stating that the form of wrestling combined with boxing is best), or Apollo as a boxer (*Imag.* 1.6.4; 2.32.2, 19.3). He is less interested in other sports, though he can provide a portrait of a discus thrower in great detail (*Imag.* 1.24.2). His interests seem to reflect those of contemporaries who honored pancratiasts, boxers, and wrestlers more highly than those who competed in the less violent track and field events.

Man and beast

Delight in displays of skill as one human pummeled another was matched by delight in the demonstration of skill in defeating savage beasts. Public beast hunts were initiated at Rome after the Second Punic War (218–201 BCE) and, by the lifetime of Cicero (106–43 BCE), had become a crucial component of games that an aspiring politician hoped to offer – hence the extensive correspondence in 51 BCE between Cicero and M. Caelius Rufus, who hoped that Cicero would provide him with some Cilician panthers for his games (Ville 1981: 88–93). Here, as in chariot racing, the beasts could be stars in their own right. Just as mosaics depicting chariot races might include the names of the horses, so too might mosaics and other monuments depicting beast hunts give the names of well-known animals. Not all "fierce" animals contended with humans. Some popular events involved staging fights between the animals themselves, and the animals would receive special training for their events – in the *Acts of Paul and Thecla*, Thecla is assailed by a lion who is said to have been trained to fight against men. This beast is overcome by the lioness who seems to have been trained to fight other animals (*A. Paul. et Thecl.* 33). In some cases, perhaps reflecting the fact that some animals might be too smart to engage in these sports without external stimulation, beasts would be chained together by *bestiarii*, professional beast handlers. Lions and other large cats would be turned loose on "herbivores."

The star quality of fierce animals was such that there were restrictions on their hunting and use. Only people operating under an imperial license could hunt lions and the like unless the beast was a noted threat to a community. Once in captivity, "fierce animals" would be kept in special zoos – we hear of one outside of Rome – and they could only be used under special circumstances with imperial permission (Sabbatini Tumolesi 1988: nos. 8–10). *Munerarii* who obtained an exemption from the general restriction against putting on shows with wild animals would be limited in the number of days upon which they could use them, and quite possibly limited in the way they could use them (Robert 1940: 274). Thus the man who put on the games that led to the arrest of Polycarp, a noted Christian of Smyrna, in 157 CE, said that he could not use a lion against Polycarp because he only had permission to employ the beast for executions on the two previous days (*M. Pol.* 12.2). Other animals might be trained for mock combats of some sort; a legal text makes reference to a *leo mansuetus*, a tame lion, that would evidently put on displays in the amphitheater (*D.* 3.1.1.6; see also Juv. 7.77–8), while the lion trained to attack humans that appears in the *Acts of Paul and Thecla* is said to have been the personal property of the civic magistrate responsible for Thecla's persecution. There could also be animal imitators, albeit outside the amphitheater, such as the woman of Ostia who dressed as a leopard and engaged in mock duels with patrons of whatever establishment employed her (Dio 75.8.2).

We hear of the *leo mansuetus* in a discussion of the circumstances under which an aristocrat would suffer *infamia* if he fought against animals. It is recognized that members of the aristocracy had a powerful interest in putting on public displays of their hunting skills. The jurist Ulpian, the author of this ruling, states that people will only suffer *infamia* if they do this for a prize, thereby reducing themselves to the level of ordinary entertainers (*D.* 3.1.1.6). His opinion on this matter cannot reasonably be separated from the antics of two emperors, Commodus and Caracalla, both of whom put on displays of their hunting prowess. Commodus did this as part of his performance in the *ludi Romani* of 192 CE, and insisted on payment (Dio 72.19.3). Caracalla was explicit that his displays were not comparable to those of Commodus, presumably (although we are not told this) because he did not take a prize (*HA Carac.* 5.5; 9). Both men saw beast hunting as a way to demonstrate their skills, and the text of Ulpian suggests that they were merely the most visible members of the elite to do so.

Gladiators

No activity in the spectrum of Roman entertainment aroused such vigorous protest from members of the elite as gladiatorial combat. Men like Plutarch and Dio Chrysostom register objections to these spectacles on the grounds that they were Roman intrusions into the world of Greek culture (Wiedemann 1992: 128–46). The member of the Roman Senate who suggested some emendations to a proposal of Marcus Aurelius on the pricing of gladiators proposed that the imperial *fiscus* should not benefit from bloody sport (*ILS* 5163, 5–6). Severus, however, asked how members of the Senate dared criticize Commodus for appearing as a gladiator when they had bid up the price of his equipment at auction – implying that they wanted to use it themselves (Dio 75.8.3). Objections to gladiatorial combat by members of the elite need to be read with care: they are not expressions of an otherwise absent sensitivity to human suffering. The problem with gladiatorial combat must be seen in a very different light. Unlike the unfortunates who were condemned *ad ludos* or *ad gladium*, two penalties that required the condemned to fight to the death in the amphitheater with minimal training or armor, gladiators exemplified the martial virtues of the Roman people. Their skill, courage, and training appropriated the very virtues that created the empire of the Roman people to individuals of the lowest social class. Martial virtue remained one of the defining features of Roman aristocratic ideology at least until the third century, yet in the public eye it had to be shared with gladiators.

The star system that emerged in the context of gladiatorial combat was every bit as pronounced as that in any other area. Inscriptions of the second century reveal rankings according to six *pali* ranging from the first time fighter to the champion, or *primus palus* (Potter 1999b: 317–21). In the case of slave gladiators, their prices were regulated in the course of the second century, ranging from 3,000 to 15,000 sesterces (*ILS* 5163, 29–34). In the case of free men – by implication free men with experience – an effort was made to limit what they could charge for their services to 12,000 sesterces. To put this number in perspective, prizes for victors in the pancration in festivals at Aphrodisias range from 6,000 to 20,000 sesterces (Roueché 1993: nos. 52 i; 52 iii; 52 iv). In other words, champion gladiators were on a financial par with top-tier athletes. As was not, however, the case with prizes for athletes, the price for the services of a gladiator (who, it is important to remember, did not have to win) needed to be set by the imperial government to prevent the sort of price gouging by gladiatorial free agents that is attested in the first century CE, when Tiberius had to pay 100,000 sesterces for famous free gladiators (Suet. *Tib.* 7.1). Gladiators also recognized that the people who came to watch them fight were genuinely their fans. In cases where gladiators died as a result of their wounds, texts honoring them do not blame the fans – dead gladiators were "deceived" or victimized by fate or Nemesis (Robert 1940: 302). When Caracalla compelled a famous gladiator named Bato to fight three successive bouts – the third of which proved fatal to Bato – he won no plaudits from the crowd. Cassius Dio, no friend to the masses, presents the event as an outrage (Dio 77.6.2). In 238 CE, when the praetorian guard was attempting to repress the Senate, which was then in revolt against Maximinus Thrax, gladiators from the Ludus Magnus at Rome emerged to drive the guard back to their camp and lay siege to it (Herod. 7.11.9). Just as was the case with other performers, gladiators felt entitled to commemorate their accomplishments with monuments that they commissioned. The artistic style of gladiatorial monuments echoes those erected by *munerarii* and, in the Greek world, the commemorative vocabulary suggests that they wished to be seen on a par with star athletes (Robert 1940: 302). This might outrage aristocratic athletes and their sympathizers, but we must allow that the gladiators had

4 Reenactment and Competitive Recreation

No spectacle was offered in a vacuum. Well before the reign of Augustus, games and spectacles had been seen as ways for men to advertise their magnificence to domestic and foreign audiences. Thus in 167 BCE, Aemilius Paullus staged a spectacle including athletic and theatrical performances, executions, public banquets, and a massive procession to display the booty taken from the defeated Perseus of Macedon (Edmondson 1999: 78–81). The spectacle may well have been modeled on earlier displays by Hellenistic monarchs, and it inspired two further spectacles within the next year. One was the triumph, at Rome, of L. Anicius Gallus, who varied the standard triumphal fare – the procession of the army through Rome, displaying booty and captives, while the soldiers sang rude songs about the general, who was carried through the city in the guise of Jupiter on earth – by including Greek plays on a specially constructed stage in the Circus Maximus (Polyb. 30.22.1–12; Livy 45.43.1). A few months later Antiochus IV, the ruler of the Seleucid kingdom, celebrated a procession of his own at Daphne outside of Antioch. In this case he included gladiators – a novelty for the local audience – in the hope that their displays of skill would inspire the youth of his realm with dreams of martial valor. One of the most interesting features of this competition is that the events, and the buildings that supported them, were ephemeral; people came to compete in festivals that they had never seen, but which were recorded by public works of art. Power was asserted by vast expenditure on *ephemera* (Kuttner 1999: 100–2). When Cleopatra appeared before Antony at the Cydnus in 40 BCE in the guise of Aphrodite, inviting him to appear in the role of Dionysus, she was appealing to Italic representations of a banquet revel (Kuttner 1999: 114–15). The theater that Aemilius Scaurus built for his aedilician games in 58 BCE was said by the elder Pliny to be "the greatest work of art ever accomplished by the hand of man," and was intended to recall the fact that he was the stepson of Sulla (*Nat.* 36.114). His theater dwarfed those constructed in earlier generations, such as the one built by Mummius to commemorate the destruction of Corinth, and itself inspired competition from Gaius Curio, who needed something new since he lacked a stepfather like Sulla. Curio built two wooden theaters back-to-back that could be turned so that they formed an amphitheater (Plin. *Nat.* 36.116). He did this even though the theater of Pompey was already standing. The point was not that he needed a building, but rather that he needed a building that people would remember as having been his; it would be the building that set his spectacle apart from all that had gone before if people would recall it later.

Spectacular competition continued even after the establishment of the principate. Caesar had constructed a basin, either in Trastevere or the Campus Martius, in which he staged a naval battle between the Egyptians and Phoenicians, perhaps as a way of helping people visualize the naval battles that took place in the Alexandrian war, as well, perhaps, as for the pleasure of producing an unparalleled spectacle (Suet. *Jul.* 39.4; Festus p. 50 L; Dio 43.23, with Coleman 1993: 50). His basin was filled in after his death, but people do not seem to have forgotten it. Sextus Pompey staged a naval battle off Sicily as a way of mocking Augustus in 40 BCE (Dio 48.19.1). Although the evidence is very late, it may be that Augustus had staged other naval battles at Cumae to celebrate his victories over Sextus (reversing the point of the spectacle of 40 BCE) and Antony (Auson. *Mos.* 208–10, with Coleman 1993: 71–2).

It remained, however, to replicate the feat of Caesar at Rome. In 19 BCE Agrippa built an artificial pool measuring 180 meters wide by 220 or 300 meters long in which boats could be floated. In 2 BCE Augustus himself constructed a vast *stagnum*, nearly double the size of Agrippa's, to stage a reenactment of the battle of Salamis in the games that marked the dedication of the temple of Mars Ultor and the departure of Gaius Caesar for the east. Interestingly, the pond seems to have been used only once after that: by Philip the Arab in his celebration of the millennium in 248 CE (Smith, this volume). Philip had reason to return to the site of Augustus' triumph, since he was concerned to establish the legitimacy of his dynasty through his celebration of the Secular Games. Other rulers, closer in time to Augustus, looked to naval battles as symbols of their own munificence. Claudius staged a battle on the Fucine Lake to inaugurate his effort to drain that body of water (Tac. *Ann.* 12.56–7; Suet. *Claud.* 21.6). Nero tried something completely different when he flooded a wooden amphitheater in 57 CE, and included mythological impersonators who seem to have swum about as the battle took place. Both the mythological impersonators and the naval battles recur under Titus and Domitian: in Titus' case the event was staged as part of the inauguration of the Flavian amphitheater (though it remains an open question whether it took place in the Colosseum itself), while Domitian appears to have staged his as a way of doing his brother one better. The later Julio-Claudian and Flavian developments are particularly interesting when seen in light of the fact that they were not directly connected with imperial triumphs. They did not choose to re-fight battles that could be directly connected with contemporary events – e.g. a war with Persia – and their mythological re-enactors bring the events in line with contemporary tastes in drama. On the one hand they illustrated the power of rulers who could turn land into sea, and put the gods on display (Coleman 1993: 73–4). On another they echo the mythological themes of pantomime; spectacles on this scale were literally of epic proportion, intended to subsume other genres of entertainment.

Those who filled the boats for these reenactments were prisoners, and these may also be seen as an extension of the system of public punishment that was integrated into public entertainment. Two of the sentences that could result in a person's death in the amphitheater – *damnatio ad bestias* and *damnatio ad gladium* – presumed that the convict would die a horrible death as soon as possible, and there appears to have been no limit, other than taste, as to how it would be imposed (Ville 1981: 234–5). People might be burned at the stake or suffer other horrific fates in addition to exposure to the beasts or fighting. Martial and others provide ample evidence for people being dressed up in mythological garb, either to be incinerated on a pyre in the guise of Hercules, or crucified and attacked by a beast, or given a lyre and the garb of Orpheus before being turned loose in an amphitheater filled with carnivores: there was a penalty where once there was a legend (Mart. *Sp.* 7.12, with Coleman 1990: 62–3). To see a woman raped by a bull on the floor of the amphitheater, as Martial put it, was to know that the story of Pasiphae and the bull could be true (*Sp.* 5.1–2). The thought is the same as that of Philostratus, who would have his reader believe that he could recapture the emotions of a mythological moment through a good painting.

A further element that played into the emotions of execution was the fact that most of the condemned were slain near where they had committed their crimes. In such cases many in the audience may well have been present at the trial and have demanded the penalty, thereby becoming participants in the judicial process. Furthermore, on the evening before a spectacle the condemned would be on display at the *cena libera* so that people would be informed of the reasons why they were to suffer, and their crimes would be announced in the amphitheater before the execution. The point was that the crowd would participate in exacting the penalty (Potter 1996b: 147–55). In other cases, where the condemned were not locals – the state appears to have kept a supply of *damnati* on hand to sell to prospective *munerarii* (*ILS* 5163, 56–7; Robert 1940: 320–1; Ville 1981: 236–40). Before they were executed their crimes would also be recited so as to let people know why they deserved what befell them.

A different group of condemned, those condemned *ad ludos*, had a slightly better chance of survival, and could be put to different uses. A person sentenced *ad ludos* would receive minimal training before being sent out to fight, often in groups – this being the most reasonable explanation for the curious description of some combatants as priced at the same rate as people condemned to the beasts, who are said to fight *ad signum*, or "at the standard" (*ILS* 5163, 36, 56–7). These are likely to have been the people who fought in recreations of battles such as the naval encounters discussed above.

In addition to those condemned through the judicial process, prisoners of war might also be offered up to the beasts and other forms of spectacular death – allowing the audience to participate in Rome's victory. It is tempting to think that the people who played the Britons in Claudius' spectacular reenactment of a battle from his British campaign were in fact prisoners of war (Suet. *Claud.* 21; Smith, this volume). Displays of this sort should be seen as updating the traditional form of the triumph, as they would enable viewers to take an even greater part in celebrating the victory by making them, in a virtual sense, participants.

Those sponsoring games were not the only ones who would find themselves in competition with the past. The obsessive record keeping that appears to have been a feature of the star system meant that individual competitors defined their achievements in terms of great champions of early years. Diocles, for instance, is explicit in setting his accomplishments in the context of earlier charioteers (see above, section 3). Athletes might wish to be compared with great heroes – and their fans might encourage them in this. Cassius Dio tells of a man named Helix, who won both the pancration and wrestling events at the Capitoline games in the early third century. He was then the first person ever to do this. When, however, he sought to repeat his triumph at the Olympics, the Eleans did not hold the wrestling event because they did not want him to be able to claim the title "eighth after Hercules" to have done this (Dio 80.10.2, with C. P. Jones 1998: 295). As was the case in so many other cultural endeavors, the definition of success was often in terms of successful competition with the past. The thrill of capping a past performance was especially meaningful in a culture where competition with the past was a fundamental feature of the educational system.

Another form of reenactment is exemplified in the papyrus containing the contract of a charioteer named Aurelius Demetrius:

I agree voluntarily and of my own choice to act as charioteer for you with your horses in the sacred Capitoline games to be celebrated in the same city of the Oxyrhynchites. (*P.Oxy.* 3135)

The original Capitoline games were Greek-style contests, initiated in the course of the first century CE at Rome, which drew many of the best members of the synods (Roueché 1993: no. 51). That games in a Greek-speaking province, such as the ones in which Aurelius Demetrius will appear, should be modeled on the Roman imitation of a traditional Greek festival is a sign of the desire of local magnates to link their games with the imperial power. They were not alone. Games called Actian, alluding to the games founded by Augustus at Nicopolis after his defeat of Antony, also appear at diverse places, including Bostra in Jordan. These festivals represent a continuation of a trend evident well before the completion of Roman domination of the eastern Mediterranean for cities to claim that their games were "equal to" one or another of the games that made up the periodic cycle of classical Greece.

5 Engagement

Engaging the emotions of the crowd was a significant feature of any entertainment. In the case of pantomime and the theater, people wanted to see "realistic" miming of powerful emotion; they also showed up to participate in the triumphs of their favorites. While Pliny may have overstated his claim that factional success was all that interested a crowd, it nonetheless remains true that people were deeply involved in the success of their champion charioteers. Actors had supporters who were notoriously prone to riot in support of their favorites, and we have evidence for gladiatorial fan clubs. At Ephesus, for instance, there was a group known as the Philovedii, who were devoted to the fortunes of the members of the *familia* owned by the Vedii (Robert 1940: 24–7). Inscriptions recording the membership of gladiators in *collegia* might also list *pagani*, or outsiders, who were presumably great supporters of the group (Sabbatini Tumolesi 1988: no. 45; Robert 1940: 85). The senatorial decree of 19 CE that imposed penalties upon people of the senatorial and equestrian orders who appeared as actors and gladiators lists as banned activities not only fighting in the arena, but also a number of support roles (Levick 1983: 101–2). While this might seem a bit extreme, it is yet another sign of the fact that personal identity in the Roman world could be tied to the success or failure of entertainers one admired. It is also a sign of the fact that while the arenas of public entertainment were often thought to reinforce the social order, they could also be venues for transgressive behaviors to challenge it.

People might not limit their passion for participation to the venue of the entertainment itself. Clay models of gladiators look very much as if they were sold as "action figures," so that children could play "gladiator" at home (Köhne and Ewigleben 2001: 45–6, though without consideration of their function). Grownups could go much further. We have already seen how people might play at being gladiators and indulge their skill in real or simulated hunts. There are also places where we can see aristocrats trying to imagine what it would be like actually to be a gladiator. Lucilius, for instance, writes in the late second century BCE from the perspective of a gladiator, while the author of a rhetorical work of the imperial period writes from the perspective of a young man of good family who has suddenly found himself sold as a slave into a *ludus* and from there into the arena (Lucil. fr. 176–81; [Quint.] *Decl.* 9.6). Juvenal seems to be talking about a real person who went beyond simple imitation and acts of imagination when he describes a senator of good standing who fought as a *retiarius* (Juv. 2.143–8; 8.199–210). Likewise Nero and Caracalla were certainly not the only members of the aristocracy to take a keen interest in chariot racing. Tigellinus, the evil genius behind the last years of Nero's reign, seems to have risen to the emperor's attention because he supplied good chariot horses; Vitellius, briefly emperor in 69 CE, is said to have enjoyed visiting the stables of the factions (Potter 1999b: 295). We have already seen how members of the aristocracy enjoyed acting; here it should be noted that they also enjoyed having actors and other performers around the house. The younger Pliny expresses disapproval of Ummidia Quadratilla, who kept a troupe of pantomimes for her personal entertainment (he thought it promoted sexual promiscuity) (*Ep.* 7.24). Other actors are found in the context of the imperial court, perhaps, like the mime Mnester, having an affair with an empress (Messalina – he was scarcely alone) or, more simply, like the Jewish mime, Halityrus, helping an embassy get access to the emperor (Leppin 1992: 261–2; 247). A professional wrestler named Narcissus was present in the palace when it looked as if Commodus would survive Marcia's effort to poison him; she enlisted him to strangle the emperor (Dio 72.22.4–6). As usual we know more about what went on in the palace simply because the evidence for goings-on there is greater than for other places. Still, there is ample evidence, and not just from a work of satire such as Petronius' *Satyricon*, for performers of all sorts being kept in the houses of the wealthy to offer dinner-time entertainment (C. P. Jones 1991; Ville 1981: 293–5).

6 Women

One – and arguably the only – area that remains thoroughly understudied in the realm of Roman spectacle is the role of women, and the discourse about that role. The most extensive discussion of any female entertainer in the Roman world, albeit one that falls outside the strict chronological limit of this chapter, is Procopius' assault on the reputation of Theodora, the future wife of Justinian. Her talent, so he claims, was puffing out her cheeks in an amusing fashion. Her official zone of performance was the theater, where, with her sister, she gave performances between chariot races. Her efforts in this regard paled in comparison with the sexual gymnastics in which she routinely engaged, if Procopius is to be believed, with a remarkable number of men. Procopius' attack on Theodora, as with other male critiques, tended to suggest that independent women must be prostitutes (Procop. *Arc.* 8). Other displays involving women, likewise described as sex shows, include the nude water ballet at Antioch deplored by John Chrysostom in the fourth century CE, or the Floralia at Rome, where prostitutes seem to have dramatized the escape of women from Lars Porsenna (Brown 1988: 316; Wiseman 1999: 197–8). In the classical Greek world, the flute girl was also assumed to be a prostitute. The same sort of critique was leveled against actors in any genre not sanctified by inclusion in the agonistic cycle (see section 2 above). In simplest terms, the view was that since they acted in plays where illicit sex was central to the plot, actors and actresses were themselves people of very loose morals (Webb 2002: 296–7).

The discourse of *infamia* occludes issues of a very different sort. By simply claiming that men and women who played in roles that excited thoughts of sex on the part of their audience were morally reprehensible, members of the upper classes evaded their own responsibility as the financial backers of these very entertainments. Like the negative discourse about gladiatorial combat pandering to the base desires of the humble, the authors of this discourse often avoided admitting that they were as fascinated by what was going on in front of them as anyone else. At the same time, there is ample evidence to suggest that a career on the stage was potentially very lucrative for women. Although it falls outside the period covered in this chapter, a rescript of Theodosius in 393 forbidding women of the stage to dress in the clothing that ordinarily could only be afforded by women of the upper classes reflects a much broader social fact (*CTh.* 15.7.11). Women of the lower classes could make very substantial sums of money from their trade: centuries earlier, Cicero reports that a good female dancer could make 200,000 sesterces for a single appearance, and Volumnia with whom Mark Antony (and others) had affairs in the forties BCE was able to move in upper-class circles because she had made a great deal of money (Lebek 1996: 44).

If the popularity of public spectacle freed some women from dependence upon individual males to advance economically, it also challenged the restrictions placed on women of good family. Women as well as men were the object of the *senatus consultum* of 19 CE that forbade people of equestrian and senatorial status from appearing on the stage or in the arena. At the same time, of course, it reveals that this was a choice that women could make if they wanted to. The range of possibilities in such a career was very great. It extended from wretched careers that might be compared to those of strippers or other workers in modern industries that appeal primarily to male sexual fantasy, to careers that might reasonably be compared to those of modern pop idols in terms of their financial success. At the same time, it also appears that the desire to compete with the past opened up performance opportunities for girls of aristocratic families that were unparalleled in any other period of antiquity. The discourse concerning these careers (which were intended to end with marriage) shows a definite admission that women could participate in some spectacles without damaging their status, and further suggests that in the Greek east (though not in the Latin west) parental support could be found for girls who wanted to perform in a variety of stage and athletic events.

The impetus for this movement appears to have come from Sparta. A feature of the refoundation of the traditions of the *agôgê* after 146 BCE was the creation of an extended course of athletic training for girls (Cartledge and Spawforth 1989: 206; Mantos 1995: 134). In the twenties BCE Propertius wrote:

> Sparta, I marvel at many of the rules of your wrestling ground, but most of all at the many delights of gymnasia where girls train, because a girl exercises her naked body without shame amidst wrestling men, when the ball deceives the arms with a swift throw, and the hooked rod clanks against the rolling hoop, and the dust-covered woman stands at the end of the track, and endures the wounds from harsh pancration: now she ties joyful arms to the boxing-glove with thongs, now she turns the flying weight of the discus in a circle. (3.14.1–10)

Propertius' vision of female athleticism offers important insight into some aspects of the account of the reforms of Lycurgus, the legendary Spartan lawgiver, written by Plutarch toward the beginning of the second century CE. In composing his account, Plutarch was plainly influenced by contemporary admiration for what were felt to be the benefits, both in terms of health and morality, of the existing Spartan system. Thus Plutarch says:

> He [Lycurgus] exercised the bodies of young women in footraces, wrestling, the casting of the discus, and of the javelin, so that the product of their wombs would have a strong beginning in strong bodies and come better to maturity so that they would have easy pregnancies and deliveries... nor was there anything disgraceful in the nudity of young girls for they were modest and wantonness was banished. (*Lyc.* 14.2, 4)

That Plutarch's understanding was not derived from some earlier source is strongly suggested by the fact that discussions of Spartan women in the fifth century BCE imply that the system of female education then in place created nymphomaniacs, and by the fact that it corresponds to medical theory current in the imperial, though not the classical, period (Oribasius 18.11–15; 21.4 [quoting Rufus of Ephesus]; Galen 9.109 Kühn).

The competitive recreation of archaic Sparta would prove to have important consequences for young women who lived outside of Sparta. General admiration for Spartan virtue, an admiration that increased the further the reality of classical Sparta receded into the past, seems to have inspired imitation of the Spartan training system for girls. One of the speakers in Athenaeus' *Doctors at Dinner*, a work with a dramatic date at the beginning of the third century CE, observes:

> The Spartan habit of showing naked girls to strangers is praised, and, on the island of Chios, it is pleasant to walk into the gymnasia and along the race courses to see young men wrestling with girls. (*Deip.* 13.366e)

In this case it is probably correct to press the point that the speaker refers to the young men who are wrestling with girls as *neoi*, indicating that this training was continued for girls, whom we may assume to be of roughly the same age as the *neoi*, into older adolescence. This view is also necessitated by the fact that Plutarch explains the advantage of the Spartan system in terms of its impact on girls' reproductive lives.

The result of the reformed Spartan system, and its imitation elsewhere, was thus to create a cadre of teenaged women who were capable athletes, and could participate in a range of sports that was unthinkable in the classical period, when female athletes seem to have been early adolescents, and participated only in footraces. It also gave rise to new festivals in which these women could participate. At Sparta, for instance, an inscription records a female victor in a footrace at the Livia, a festival in honor of the wife of Augustus, who had sought refuge at Sparta in the triumviral period before her engagement to the future emperor (*SEG* 11 no. 861; Mantos 1995: 134). The extent of these contests is further suggested by an inscription from Delphi honoring the three daughters of a man named Hermesianax, who had won victories in races at a variety of festivals in the Peloponnese in the first half of the first century CE (*SIG*³ 802). Their victories in events such as the Asclepeia at Epidauros, the Pythian,

Nemean, and Isthmian games, as well as at a lesser festival at Sicyon, reveals the extent of the efflorescence of footraces for young women; when Menander Rhetor says that "in some festivals, such as at Olympia, women do not appear at all," he could be read as saying that at many they did (Men. Rh. 364.5–6). Other sources reveal that these festivals included events other than footraces. Nero appears to have brought Spartan female wrestlers to Rome, possibly in the context of his Capitoline games in the sixties. We know little of the impression they made, save that a scandal ensued when a member of the Senate named Palfurius Sura convinced one of these women to engage him in a wrestling match. We do not know who won, and Nero does not seem to have objected. Vespasian did, and expelled Palfurius from the Senate (*Schol. ad Juv.* 4.53). Women were not included when Domitian refounded the Capitoline games, and female athletes appear to have been restricted in their activity to the east. To judge from the remarkable account offered by John Malalas of the Olympic Games refounded by Commodus at Antioch in 181 CE, the Spartan-inspired range of female events remained very much an activity for girls of aristocratic background. It is worth quoting Malalas' account because it seems to be influenced by archival material (Schenk 1931: 419 n. 13, *contra* Mantos 1995: 142), including, possibly, a civic decree that spelled out the connection, for the Greek world, between athletic participation and virtue:

> Well born young people came from every city and district to the sacred contest of the Olympic games, competing under an oath, and they contended against each other. Receiving no money from any source, they conducted themselves chastely and with great moderation; they were rich, having their own slaves as attendants, each according their own wealth, and many of them were maidens. ... There were maidens who practiced philosophy and were present under a vow of chastity; competing, wrestling in leggings, running, declaiming and reciting various Greek hymns. These women competed against other women and the competition was intense, whether it was in wrestling, the races or recitation. (Malal. 12.10)

Septimius Severus seems to have respected these traditions. When he brought women's games to Rome – he may even have been present at the Antiochene Olympics that took place during his term as a legate to Pertinax in Syria – he was deeply disappointed to discover that a Roman audience, used to regarding female entertainers as curiosities, greeted the event by chanting lewd acclamations. Severus was not amused: he banned the exhibition of female gladiators altogether, perhaps thinking that such exhibitions had so corrupted Roman taste that a Roman audience could not appreciate what female athletes were doing (Dio 75.16.1). The confusion in the Roman audience between women who engaged in athletic contests and female gladiators reflects the fact that there was no widespread western adaptation of the Spartan myth.

We have no text that provides much information on the history of female gladiators. It is likely that their emergence reflects the ongoing desire to find something new with which to titillate the fancy of spectators in the amphitheater. Since their existence is implied by the *senatus consultum* of 19 CE, while Cicero does not mention them (one may well imagine that Clodia would have appeared as a *gladiatrix* as well as everything else in Cicero's defense of Caelius if female gladiators existed at that time), it is likely that they are a creation of the expanding spectacle culture of the

Augustan age. At no time do they appear to have been common. To judge from comments in Petronius' *Satyricon*, and an inscription found at Ostia which records their first appearance there in the second century, female gladiators were regarded as a special treat for the fans (Fora 1996: no. 29). As for how they fought, a monument erected in commemoration of some games at Halicarnassus records that a duel between two women, named, appropriately enough, Amazon and Achillea, ended in a draw (Coleman 2000a). The significance of this object (aside from providing the only representation of female gladiators that has survived) is that it shows that women fought according to the same rules as men. It would be possible for women to fight only if they had access to some sort of professional training.

In roles ranging from athletes to gladiators, in performances ranging from the routines of veiled castanet dancers in Egypt (Webb 2002: 286) to nude water ballet at Antioch, women came to play a significant role in Roman spectacle. Careers are likely to have been short: female athletes were evidently supposed to give up competitive performance upon marriage, while the evidence for stage performers likewise suggests that they were younger women. But they were still careers, and while some of them were exploitative, the extreme interest in performances by women (one young man was so fascinated by castanet dancers that he fell from a window: *P.Oxy.* 475) stands as a powerful illustration of the main point of this survey: that public spectacle thrived because it challenged the norms of hierarchical society. The role of women is an important reminder that the study of Roman spectacle must concentrate not only on the role of the games in supporting the social order, but also on the ways in which these same spectacles could offer opportunities to those who wished to escape its constraints.

It is unlikely that we will ever be able to understand the role of spectacle in Roman life if we concentrate on public venues and legal distinctions; likewise it is very difficult to understand any one style of entertainment in isolation from others. There were plainly people who were not interested in any of this; some people genuinely shared the attitudes expressed by the younger Pliny and preferred to attend poetry recitals, or even listen to Pliny recite his rhetorical works. Since their voices are expressing approved aristocratic attitudes toward leisure activity, they may often drown out other voices, voices that expressed a majority opinion. Pliny never suggests that he would have a gladiator or actor around the house, but there is enough evidence to suggest that plenty of other people would have. Roman spectacle extends across a spectrum ranging from private indulgence to local festival, from local festival to provincial event, and finally to the grandiose events in which emperors displayed their magnificence to their people.

The imperial government played a significant role in shaping the tastes of its subjects; one of the most striking features of the urban landscape of the Roman Empire is the ubiquity of buildings associated with all manner of entertainments. While some emperors might fine-tune the system by expressing particular interest in one form of entertainment over another, in the long run the Roman state, by supporting local government based upon a model of civic benefaction, encouraged the spread of the full range of entertainment. The result was that between the first and fourth centuries CE a spectacle culture arose in the territory of the Roman Empire that helped forge a common urban culture unmatched prior to the modern era.

PART V

Intellectual Life

CHAPTER TWENTY-ONE

The Construction of the Past in the Roman Empire

Rowland Smith

More than any men known to us, the Romans love their city and strive to protect all their ancestral treasures so that nothing of Rome's ancient glory will be obliterated.... [Even in the wake of the recent siege and occupation by the Goths] they preserved the city's buildings and such adornments as could withstand a long lapse of time, and all such memorials of their race, among them the ship of Aeneas, the founder of the city, a quite incredible sight: for they built a ship-house in the middle of the city on the bank of the Tiber and deposited it there, and have preserved it from that time. I have seen it myself and can describe it.... None of its timbers has rotted or gives the least sign of being unsound; intact throughout, as if newly constructed by the hand of its builder – whoever he was – it has retained its strength in a marvellous way up to my own time. Such are the facts about Aeneas' ship. (Procop. *Goth*. 8.22.3–17 [abbreviated])

Writing this passage in the mid-sixth century CE, Procopius is a striking witness to the depth of the Romans' concern for their national past – and also to the wishfulness, or credulity, of an antique writer's report of it: ancient chronographers placed Aeneas's voyage to Italy around 1200 BCE, which would make the pristine nautical relic Procopius saw – had it been genuine – over eighteen hundred years old. An "incredible sight," indeed – but perhaps for Procopius and his Byzantine readers that was just the point: to acknowledge the continuity of *Roma Aeterna* as a uniquely powerful historical ideal, a marvel that overrode one's normal experience of time (Cameron 1985: 191–2; cf. Matthews 1989: 280, 470). For us, anyway, "Aeneas' ship," so implausibly well-preserved and so willingly pronounced authentic, offers a neat emblem for the subject of this chapter. Our interest lies less with raw events of Roman history than with ancient representations of it, and "the construction of the past" – a title that begs to be deconstructed – signals that our discussion will emphasize the role of human artifice and imagination in this connection. We are not discussing some fortuitous product of random accumulation akin to a coral reef. To treat the past as "constructed," rather than just "retrieved," or "recorded," suggests narration and "emplotment," and individual or collective human agents shaping material purposefully in some degree – if not with the panoptic vision of a master architect, at least in the manner of a building gang that has some notion, however hazy, of what is being produced or added to, and of the end-product's likely utility. And that purposive impulse suggests in turn a process in which historical "fact" may be distorted or concealed, or simply invented, to suit the end in mind.

1 The Construction of Roman History

What the idea of a "constructed" past might imply about the epistemological status of historical events is a question for philosophers (e.g. Mink 1987; H. White 1984: 1–57). For a hardcore deconstructionist, it may be, "the past" is indeed just a juice secreted by present discourse, and history-writing a species of fiction. But one need not subscribe to any branch of post-structuralist theory to find "the construction of the past" an apt phrase to use in the study of Roman antiquity; one need only attend to empirical fact. The events of Roman history are plainly accessible now only through traces they have left in material remains and in texts produced and transmitted by supervening hands. And while some textual traces may survive as material remains nearly contemporaneous with the event at issue (an imperial edict, say, inscribed on stone for public display), very many others occur in writings composed well after the event: the crucial extant account, say, of Tiberius' accession in 14 CE – a critical moment in the emergence of the principate – is owed to Tacitus, writing a century afterwards (*Ann.* 1.5–13). And even when contemporaneous traces of an event survive, material or textual, they often call for interpretation in the light of later texts. In what was ancient Rome's Campus Martius, for instance, substantial remains survive of a structure readily identifiable from memorial inscriptions found nearby as a Julio-Claudian mausoleum; but many familiar "facts" about this building – the date it was built, the depositing there of Augustus' ashes, the erection at its entrance of bronze pillars bearing a copy of his *Res Gestae* – are not known to us now from any of the material remains or extant inscriptions, but only from later texts (chiefly from Suetonius' biography of Augustus [*Aug.* 100–1], again written a good century after the event). For us, in short, countless "facts" about Roman history are in practice inseparable from the ancients' own textual representations of it, and any informed modern study of the ancient Roman past must be in good part a study of the ways in which it was remembered, evaluated, and reshaped for further transmission by ancient writers.

For ancient students of the Roman past, of course, a far larger body of primary evidence was available than now survives: abundant monuments and inscriptions intact and *in situ*, public records, family archives, living witnesses for the recent past – and sometimes earlier tranches of oral memory, too, preserved indirectly in antiquarian works. It needs to be stressed, though, that imperial historiographers were themselves frequently working under a constraint similar to that which affects modern studies of ancient Rome. In their case, admittedly, it was partly a self-imposed cultural constraint: their notion of what constituted the proper subject-matter of history was narrowly framed, and their view of how it should be written, and to what purpose, did not predispose them to undertake research from primary documents in the modern way; they were usually content to work mainly from earlier historians' accounts, and dealt only rarely with primary documentary material in an unmediated form. But "primary evidence" is itself a slippery category, and little that goes by the name is an innocent witness to the past: the problem of the representation of the past begins with human memory (Ricoeur 2000), and all monuments or texts or stories generated by a commemorative impulse construct the past in a form deemed proper by those who create them. For the retrieval of data, then – not to mention the process of selection and shaping needed to produce historical narrative – imperial writers depended chiefly in practice on their interpretation of earlier writers' representations of the Roman past. Moreover, the spread of "primary" and literary evidence alike was uneven, much more surviving for some periods than for others; and for the early period it was desperately sparse (Wiseman 1979: 9–26; Cornell 1995: 4–18). Livy in the 20s BCE, beginning his history of Rome "from the foundation of the City," relied heavily for his account of archaic Rome on a line of earlier historians writing in the second and first centuries BCE – a chain of texts transmitting the varying presuppositions and biases of authors who themselves had had little but legend and folktale to work with for Rome's earliest history. In Livy's own view (6.1), any public records that might have once existed for this early period had perished long ago, when the Gauls sacked Rome c.390 BCE, and he was clear that a narrative reaching back more than 700 years to Rome's notional foundation in the mid eighth century BCE must be a construction that went beyond "the facts": the spectral Romulean and regal subject matter of his opening book, he acknowledged, rested on "stories with more of the charm of poetry than a sound historical record" (Livy *pr.* 6, with Miles 1995: 8–74).

For an imperial historian of the relatively recent past, the issue was less acute. Tacitus, writing up Tiberius' reign (14–37 CE) at a century's distance, demonstrably had access to much else besides the narratives of previous historians, most of it now quite gone: imperial speeches and memoirs, records of senatorial debates, biographies of famous men, the reminiscences of men he had talked to in his youth. But the difference still remains one of degree, not kind: even in the case of Tacitus – by ancient standards, an unusually assiduous researcher – it is hard to establish that his *Annals* represent an attempt to write up the Julio-Claudian age on a method that systematically privileged primary evidence over what intervening historians and scholars had recorded (*pace* Syme 1958a: 278). In his view, credulity and lies in the later accounts had obscured the truth about important events – but where they fell short, he judged, they often only compounded obscurities which arose from unreliability and contradiction in the contemporary evidence itself (*Ann.* 3.20). For Tacitus, both categories of evidence were suspect in principle; nor were the later writers invariably liars or dupes one could afford to discount.

Imperial historians themselves, then, could well recognize that much of the evidence they worked with was patchy or inherently tendentious. How severe a problem that posed in their eyes is another question: it depends on what they took the nature and aim of their discourse to be. Ancient historians frequently affirm in their prefaces that they mean to supply a "true" account, but "the Roman past was never a neutral, value-free area for the exercise of objective research" (Wiseman 1998: 76): aesthetic and ethical and broadly political aims were also strongly in play, and recent scholarship had vigorously questioned whether the ancient conception of historical truth was really much the same as ours, or whether it paradoxically allowed for inventions going well beyond what we call "the facts" (Woodman 1988: 70–116; Wiseman 1979: 9–53). On one view, the Roman historical tradition had developed largely out of the popular dramas (*fabulae praetextatae*) on Roman historical subjects performed at theatrical games and the quasi-dramatic celebrations of family histories enacted at aristocratic funerals (Wiseman 1998: 1–16; Flower 1996: 91–127). For the ancients, certainly, to write history was to compose in a literary genre; and just as with poetry or oratory, there were generic proprieties to be respected. History narrated, and its narration needed to be aptly constructed to give literary pleasure: a much-discussed passage in Cicero (*Orat.* 2.52–4, 62–4) scorns mere compilation of facts as dull and artless, insisting that to write history proper is to raise a pleasing "building" or "superstructure" (*exaedificatio*) by elaborating on "content" and blending it with "style." This was a fundamental artistic imperative, no matter how extensive the data for the period being treated, and no imperial historiographer ever ignored it. Beyond that, as with architecture, dictates of utility impinged. Cicero's prescription borrowed from rhetorical theory, and assumed that historical discourse, like oratory, would serve a pragmatic present purpose: it was meant to be instructive not just of fact, but of the attitudes and conduct expected of a Roman. Imperial historians of Rome wrote not only to describe but to justify what Rome had become by their day – a world power that had eclipsed all Mediterranean rivals – and in doing so they implicitly endorsed the political and social structure that maintained her power. The persons and events they treated offered *exempla*, ideal models of Roman virtue for the present to contemplate, and models of aberrance to be condemned (Chaplin 2000). In short, the program of Roman historiography was suffused by a patriotic ideology; it was written to admonish and inspire, and the heart of the enterprise was the articulation and reaffirmation of an idealized cultural and national identity.

In highlighting these ideological and cultural drives, we characterize the imperial "construction" of the past only partially, of course, and in the roughest outline. Before we pass to closer discussion, the outline needs to be qualified and refined. As presented, it sketches the narratives of Roman imperial historiography very loosely, without allowance for differences between individual writers; in practice, as we shall see, some showed a keener appetite than others for reliable evidence, and a keener critical sense in their interpretation of it. In any case, "Roman imperial historiography" was not exclusively a Roman or Italian cultural product: our picture will need to accommodate histories written by authors from a provincial background whose attitude to Rome and its empire was likely to be more complex than we have so far implied. Moreover, although narrative historiography will take pride of place in our discussion, it was clearly just one strand in a broader imperial discourse about the past in which many besides historians were implicated. Poets and philosophers, antiquarians and orators, state officials and drafters of decrees, all might look to Rome's past; their perspectives and motives could vary, and the ideological assumptions and aims prevailing in historiography would not always obtain with equal force across and within these groups. Epic poetry, for instance, clearly shared a great deal with historiographic narrative in its representation of the Roman past (Feeney 1991: 250), but even in epic the complexion of the affinity can still vary strikingly from poet to poet: a positive ideological affinity seems clear in the case of Livy and Vergil; a more problematic one, though, if the poem at issue is Lucan's *Pharsalia* – to many modern critics an "anti-*Aeneid*" whose subversive presentation of "history as nightmare" voices deep disenchantment with the claims of Julio-Claudian Caesarism (Conte 1994: 443–6; John Henderson 1998: 165–211; Myers, this volume) – or Silius' *Punica*, which on one view configures Livy and Vergil as competing intertextual presences (M. Wilson 1993: 218–19). Antiquarian scholarship was far less constricted than history or epic by the demands of literary genre; it was a field in which sheer curiosity about the past might operate for no particular purpose beyond itself. On the other hand, antiquarianism need not be innocent, and there is an affinity of sorts to be found, say, between Augustan imperial ideology and the appropriating urge to organize knowledge encyclopaedically in the Augustan scholar Verrius Flaccus (tutor to the *princeps*' grandsons, and probably the compiler of the *annales maximi* [see below, section 2]). Moreover, antiquarian works could themselves be important sources for poets as well as historians: the *Aeneid* and Ovid's *Fasti* are obvious Augustan cases. As for philosophers and moralists, like the historians they could find in the past ethical *exempla* for present conduct – but sometimes also, as we shall see (see below, section 3), less upbeat lessons that chimed less well with the memorializing impulse of the historian. In sum, "the construction of the past" is a shorthand expression for what was really a plurality of representations shaped by a variety of cultural perspectives and values. Depending on the perspective from which it was viewed, the Roman past could still look different, and could imply different lessons.

With this basic point in mind, we can look more closely at a selection of specific cases, their similarities and their differences. Latin historiography – and two exceptionally rich cases in particular – will naturally figure prominently in much of what follows, but the discussion aims to convey how the past was "usefully" constructed at different times across a range of cultural and social contexts in the empire. Starting with an emphatically Romanocentric construction of the past in Augustan Rome, it moves on in time through the early and high empire up to the mid-third century, broadening the focus as it goes to embrace some provincial viewpoints, then reverts briefly to Rome at the close, glancing forward to the fourth century, and a changed world.

2 The Utility of the Roman Past: The Livian Vision

The articulation of Roman cultural and national identity through historiography required a comprehensive story of Rome *ab origine* which could be presupposed, evoked, or re-told; and where evidence was lacking, invention could fill the vacuum. It was under this guiding impulse that a succession of Roman historians from c.200 BCE onwards had readily tackled the history of archaic Rome, notwithstanding the absence of reliable records for much of the period at issue. To give the story a suitably portentous start, they connected, and then variously embellished and rationalized, two originally quite separate myths: one the Greek tradition recounting a migration of Trojans to Italy under Aeneas, the other the indigenous story of the twins Romulus and Remus (a foundation legend, we may add, that was probably only devised in its developed form in the fourth century BCE, and was itself ideologically driven from the first in its projection of fourth-century political developments back into a distant past [Wiseman 1995; Cornell 1995: 60–8]). For the subsequent early republican history of "post-regal" Rome down to the third century there was potentially a skeletal guide in the form of an official list recording annual magistrates and outlines of key events (Cic. *Leg.* 1.5), but the detailed narratives of this period that the late republican historians composed were arguably little more than creatively invented expansions from minimal data (Wiseman 1979: 9–26).

This "expansionist' representation of early Roman history culminated in the opening books of Livy. Livy's *From the Foundation of the City* only barely qualifies as imperial historiography – work on it may have started a little before Augustus' "first settlement" of 27 BCE (perhaps even before the defeat of Mark Antony in 31 BCE), and the founding emperor may have narrowly outlived the historian (Krauss 1994: 1, 6) – but it is a text of central importance for any account of the imperial construction of the past, both in its own right and for its subsequent influence in antiquity. Its literary excellence, and the massive scale on which it was composed (142 books, running "from earliest times" to 9 BCE), quickly put the works of predecessors in the shade, and helped make Livy's account of archaic and republican Rome the standard one in the eyes of a broad antique readership for centuries afterwards. But these features cannot be divorced from a more basic ground of appeal: patriotism. In its moralizing vision of civic virtue and an empire justly won, Livy's history offered an idealized Rome in which many readers dearly wanted to believe. The work was soon a staple of public libraries, a prime source for the authors of later historical handbooks, and a boon for poets in search of an epic subject (notably, Lucan on Caesar's *Civil War*, and Silius on the war with Hannibal). Epitomes of the individual books made for casual or busy readers further extended its reach – but nostalgic Roman aristocrats were still lovingly perusing the whole work in the fifth century. For them, it had become not just the standard account of its chosen period, but a treasured memorial too to Livy's own day; like Vergil's epic, it seemed to them to distil the spirit of a golden Augustan age (R. A. Markus 1974: 1–21).

Livy's narrative of events close to his own time is now effectively lost (the relevant books are among the many extant only in barest epitome), but the early books were written as the Augustan regime was taking shape, in the immediate wake of the triumviral wars and within a generation of the fall of the republic, and recent history and a current political context were plainly a touchstone from the outset (Moles 1993). In his *Preface* (9–10), Livy calls his own day a time "when we can endure neither our vices nor the remedies needed to cure them," and advertises his history as a medicine to assuage present ills. On one view, that diagnosis discloses a firm supporter of Augustus' prescription for political and social reform obliquely chiding contemporary dissenters – and Livy's work reportedly earned him the *princeps*' friendship. On any view, a substantial ideological affinity between Livy's version of history and the proclaimed ideals of the Augustan regime is indisputable: an aside early in the work welcomes Augustus' victory at Actium as the harbinger of worldwide peace (1.19.3), and Livy's patriotic vision, charting a city's pre-destined rise to world power under leaders whose inspiring conduct the present is invited to ponder and emulate, certainly chimes well with the traditionalist and "conservative" style of Augustan publicity in the 20s BCE. But it does not follow that Livy unequivocally endorsed the new principate in all its aspects as a panacea for the age, and it is crude to treat him as its licensed propagandist (Walsh 1961: 10–19; Krauss 1994: 6–9). The "republicanism" of his history, it is true, seems nostalgic rather than actively engaged: it evokes an ideal of harmonious civic virtue projected onto earlier days when exemplary leaders – a Camillus, a Scipio Africanus, a Fabius Maximus – could check elite ambition and demagoguery, guide a rebellious commons, and see off external enemies. Some readers have treated Livy's "great men" of the past as ciphers for Augustus, symbolic prefigurations of a future national savior: his Camillus, for instance (5.49–50), is a second "Romulus" and the "Father of his Country," a "new Founder of the City" who foils a plan to transfer the state capital away from Rome, and a diligent restorer of her temples – all features, these, with parallels in Augustan claims or titles. But that view surely underplays Livy's textual nuances, and perhaps also the reach of the pessimistic strand in his preface. Livy's better modern readers find a subtler texture in his work. At first sight, for instance, his gallery of heroic leaders may seem to have an evident counterpart in the statues of Rome's great men which lined the Forum of Augustus dedicated in 2 BCE. With inscriptions attached to them to identify the subjects and their achievements, these statues offered viewers a visual lesson in officially sanctioned history (Ov. *Fast.* 5.551–68, with Zanker 1988: 210–15) – and for the compilers of the inscriptions Livy was easily to hand, and an obvious source to consult. A close reading, though, suggests that the compilers were positively disinclined to follow Livy: instead, they preferred to cull their data from another source, an antiquarian work almost certainly undertaken in Augustus' day, and with his blessing (Luce 1990: 135–6). Arguably, this pointed neglect reflects Livy's failure to lend unambiguous support to the key lesson the compilers wished to impart, that Augustus had surpassed all predecessors and constituted the acme of Roman history; Livy may have admired Augustus, but he says nothing in the extant books to raise him that high – and nothing which contemplates a permanent dynastic autocracy as the final and proper harvest from the Roman past (Luce 1990: 136–8). The Roman heroism celebrated in Livy's history, that is to say, resides fundamentally not in any individual leader, however great, but rather in the collective self-discipline and resilience which had repeatedly provided great leaders when the times demanded: this is the implied message of the famous interlude in Book 9 which poses the counterfactual question, What would have happened if Alexander the Great had thought to invade Italy? The tried and tested worth of the Roman people, it avows, would have supplied "many Romans who could have been Alexander's match in glory and achievement – and without themselves posing a threat to the public good"; a thousand Alexanders could never overcome Rome, provided its people maintained its love of internal peace and civic harmony (9.16.19–19.17; Morello 2002).

Collective resilience is a defining mark of Roman-ness in the Livian vision of history, and its basic expression is the inseparability of a people from a place. As its title implies, *From the Foundation of the City* is a deeply Romanocentric text, and its own metaphors and structure – its "rising up" or "refounding" of a written Rome, its block-grouping of books to mirror key shifts in an unfolding story, its progressively expansive accounts of year-on-year events as Rome grows larger and more powerful – seem to mimic and keep company with the growth of the physical city and the broadening aspirations of its inhabitants (Jaeger 1997). This literary procedure has been nicely likened to Augustus' own practice in his constitutional and architectural enterprises, which took shape gradually and cumulatively, and with artful evocation of historical precedents and styles to link his emergent principate with traditional public values; Livy's project, too, was to "re-build" Rome through an idealizing reconstruction of the past – in his case, a written Rome reconstructed from earlier writers (Krauss 1994: 8–9). The parallelism points to an ideological affinity of sorts, and the Livian account of early Roman history certainly has touches which evoke recent Augustan developments, but they are nuanced allusions, and they do not justify the view that Livian historiography merely projected onto the past an Augustan recipe for political virtue.

An apt illustration is the treatment of Romulus early in Book 1. Legend identified Romulus with the god Quirinus, and Augustan religious imagery was to make great play with this idealized figure, associating him with the *princeps*' adoptive father Julius Caesar: his ancient temple was rebuilt, and the awkward charge of fratricide was mitigated or refuted. The Livian account is similarly idealized in some of its features: the founding king's providential survival as an infant, his military successes, his raising of the first temple to Jupiter, his creation of a senate, all prefigure a divinely sanctioned Roman future that had already come to pass when Livy wrote, fate having long ago decreed "that such a great city should arise, and a start be made on the road to the greatest empire that has ever been" (1.4). In other details, though, the Livian account runs rather against the Augustan grain: it seems unconcerned to exculpate Romulus from the stain of a fratricide committed in pursuit of autocratic power, and is studiedly agnostic both about his supposedly divine parentage (was his father really Mars?) and about his mysterious final disappearance from men's eyes (may not his rumored ascent to heaven conceal a bloodier fate – assassination by disapproving senators?) (1.4, 16). These touches could not fail to put Livy's contemporaries in mind of a case much closer to their own time: they evoke Julius Caesar's path to autocracy through civil war, his subsequent assassination, and his posthumous deification as Divus Julius. Their uncommitted tone, though, is hardly that of Augustan publicity – and at the end of Book 1 Caesar's assassins will reappear, allusively but unmistakably, in the guise of the virtuous band of senators that swears to rid Rome of the outrageous tyranny of Tarquin, and thereby ushers in the momentous transition from monarchy to republic (1.59.1, with Ogilvie 1965: *ad loc.*). On this reading, the evocations of Caesar that open and close Livy's account of Rome's ancient kings point up – and pointedly leave hanging – the fundamental political question posed by Augustus the *princeps*: was one-man-rule at Rome just a temporary expedient, or was it henceforth to be a permanent fixture?

3   After Livy: Latin Historians of the Early Empire

Livy's nuanced reservations about the permanence of autocracy at Rome arguably gave his history a sharper resonance in his own day than is often assumed, but for most post-Augustan readers, for whom rule by emperors had become a brute fact of life, the question came to lack edge; for them, the appeal of Livy's history would lie rather in its patriotic triumphalism and pageantry – and on that score, we have noted, it exerted a shaping influence on a broad imperial readership's notion of the Roman past. An influence on subsequent historiography is evident, too, but in this field there were critical as well as admiring reactions, and the picture is more complicated. A contemporary of Livy's, the historian Pollio, famously criticized his work for its "Paduanness." Padua was Livy's home town, and regional traces in his literary diction may have been at issue, but the charge arguably went deeper, resting on a sense that Livy's idealized Rome was tainted by "small-town" sentimentality and political naiveté (Syme 1939: 486): a product of Italy's municipal gentry, never a senator and never a holder of public office or military command, Livy lacked the elite insider's political antennae. On these counts Pollio was just what Livy was not – but almost nothing of his own history of the Civil Wars of 60–42 BCE survives to test the claim that it stood as a rebuke to Livian naiveté (modern conjectures to that effect rely heavily on Pollio's reputedly prickly independence of mind in his personal dealings with Augustus [Bosworth 1972]). A little more is known of the work of another near-contemporary, Trogus, a Romanized Gaul and the author of a "universal" history whose emphasis was markedly at odds with Livy's Romanocentric narrative: of its 44 books, the bulk dealt with the Macedonian-Hellenistic kingdoms, and only the final two with Rome – coolly viewed, it would seem, as just the latest in a long line of hegemonic powers (Momigliano 1987: 45–6; Conte 1994: 378–9). Whether Trogus was consciously reacting against Livy's focus is unclear, but his case – like Pollio's – is a reminder of a significant fact: even if we confine our attention only to Latin historiography, leaving the poets and Greek writings aside, we will not find in the writers working in Augustus' reign any single and uncontentious "Augustan view" of Roman history. The reality – subsequently obscured, perhaps, by Livy's literary popularity – was a range of voices, variously chiming and contending.

However they judged Livy, neither Pollio nor Trogus was a direct rival. For ancient readers, most works of historiography fell under one of three broad headings: "local" histories focusing on a particular state or community, often with an antiquarian bent; "universalizing" histories like Trogus', aspiring to treat the past kingdoms of the Mediterranean/Near Eastern world; and "contemporary" histories of events close in time to the author, like Pollio's. Livy's history, in tracing Rome from its Romulean origins to its current standing under Augustus as the undisputed Mediterranean superpower, had expanded to embrace "universal" and contemporary subject matter, but the underlying theme and focus remained the origin and growth of a particular city and its community. On that score, subsequent Latin historiographers were not disposed to try to rewrite his chosen period at equivalent length, and left archaic matters largely to antiquarian scholarship: the very passing of time, moreover, as it confirmed the permanence of the new monarchic system, inevitably affected historiographical perspectives, and interest tended to tilt more towards recent, or "contemporary" history. In their different ways, two very different writers – one a mediocre product of the Tiberian age, Velleius Paterculus, the other an outstanding genius, Cornelius Tacitus – can exemplify the shift.

Velleius' two-book summary of Roman history was a hastily produced work by an intellectually undiscriminating author (*pace* Woodman 1977: 50–6), but it gives an interesting insight into the way the national past was pictured at the time of writing by a Tiberian loyalist of equestrian stock who had soldiered under the emperor and had won high senatorial office early in the reign (Damon, this volume). Like Livy, Velleius began with "earliest times," but, unlike Livy, he hurried from the outset "like a spinning wheel or down-rushing stream" (1.16) to reach the more recent events which chiefly preoccupied him. His first book (much of which is now lost) was effectively a rapid scene-setter, packing in the writer's slapdash notion of the essentials of a thousand years of Roman (and for that matter, Greek) history, from the siege of Troy down to the destruction of Carthage (146 BCE); the second, by contrast, covered just a century and a half, from the age of the Gracchi to the Tiberian present. In this division of material Velleius followed an already familiar (Sallustian) periodization which viewed the final demise of Carthage as the precursor of a new and critical phase in Rome's history, a prolonged era of moral decline and civil war within the state. In Velleius' optimistic version, though, there is a happy outcome which justifies and idealizes the Julio-Claudian principate: in his account, Julius Caesar is no tyrant but a magnanimous statesman murdered by myopic ingrates, and his ascendancy and adoption of his nephew Octavian point the way to a general recovery of peace and imperial prosperity forged under Augustus, and finally secured by Tiberius; it is Tiberius above all – first as Augustus' intimate colleague, then as designated successor – who dominates the later stretches of the work.

On these counts, Velleius nicely illustrates how dynastic autocracy, once normalized, could color imperial representations of the past: writers who had adjusted themselves to a world in which the personality of the ruler had become inseparable from the process of government were inclined to project their experience back in time and to associate a given historical period closely with some dominating individual. An emphasis on the individual person is evident throughout Velleius' history, and its culminating treatment of Tiberius reads more like imperial biography than narrative history as practiced by Livy a generation earlier. More like panegyric, too (*pace* Woodman 1977: 52): Velleius writes history in praise and service of the Tiberian regime – and in closing his story he patently engages *parti pris* with an issue of acute political sensitivity at the time of writing (30 CE). Observing that the "best of emperors," having selflessly presided over 16 years of justice, peace, and plenty, has now found in Aelius Sejanus an "incomparable associate" to share the princeps' burden, Velleius rounds off his effusive praises of Tiberius and his helper with a dark allusion to perversely disloyal elements lately unmasked in high places, and a closing prayer: long may the gods preserve the current arrangements and the current *princeps* – and let them grant equally outstanding and long-ruling successors (2.131). The matter here touched on was explosive – the aging Tiberius' designation of the equestrian Sejanus as his fellow consul for 31 CE, and its bearing on the succession – and the rosily sycophantic representation contrasts notably with the later tradition, which reviled Sejanus as a sinister upstart and would-be usurper justifiably loathed by the senatorial elite. To affirm both the propriety of the role of "associate" and Sejanus' fitness to fill it, Velleius looks to past precedent: the great Scipio Africanus' choice of a non-noble as his intimate counsellor in republican days, and more recently – the key case, clearly – Augustus' own raising of an equestrian, Agrippa, to highest eminence; so now, the *princeps* in his wisdom has recognized the indispensable merits of Sejanus, and has guided the Senate and Roman people accordingly (2.127–8). It is tempting to guess that Velleius wrote as a committed adherent of Sejanus in celebration of his imminent consulship, perhaps even in expectation of his nomination as successor (Agrippa, after all, had married Augustus' daughter, and later sources report that Sejanus was now angling for a Julio-Claudian princess). The sequel, anyway, is famous, and underlines the risk inherent in writing an overtly partisan history of contemporary events. The year after Velleius published his work, Sejanus was denounced by Tiberius and executed, and the purge of his alleged supporters that ensued made the last years of the reign a by-word for tyrannical savagery in the literary tradition. Whether Velleius was himself a victim is unknown, but his book seems to have quickly ceased to find a significant readership and goes unmentioned in later writers.

If Tacitus knew Velleius' work at all, it will have been as an egregious example of the sort of Julio-Claudian writing on Julio-Claudian emperors he scorns at the start of his *Annals* – false, flattering, and fear-driven. Tacitus' own representation of the period – the work of a vastly more intelligent and painstaking historian, writing expansively and with the benefit of hindsight – draws a much bleaker picture, not least in its famously mordant account of Tiberius. Taken together, his two major works – the *Histories* and *Annals*, composed in 30 books over two decades, between c.100 and c.117/120 CE – offered a continuous account of the principate over most of the preceding century (14–96 CE), viewed from the seasoned perspective of a senator who had come through dangerous times under the emperor Domitian (81–96 CE) to reach the consulship, and later the governorship of Asia. Moreover, as we noted earlier, Tacitus was an unusually diligent researcher. Recent epigraphic discoveries in Spain put it beyond question that he readily consulted primary source material for important episodes; they restore to us senatorial decrees of 19–20 CE relating to the death of the prince Germanicus and its aftermath (Damon, this volume). The circumstances of the death were murky, and among much else the new discoveries reveal the depth of Tiberius' concern to publicize across the empire an official account of events in a version designed to dispel suspicions of his complicity and to stress his own person as an exemplar of Augustan civic virtue. A comparison with the relevant chapters of the *Annals* (3.12–18) leaves no doubt that Tacitus wrote with detailed knowledge of the decrees – or that he scrutinized their content with a penetrating and sceptical intelligence (M. Griffin 1997b: 258–61; Potter 1999a: 81).

Our interest here, however, lies less with Tacitus' historical reliability than with the cultural outlook implicit in his representation of the Roman past. On that score, the vision of that past enshrined in Livy was clearly still influential, but for a thoughtful senatorial writer in the early second century CE, it was partly as a vision to react against. Tacitus admired it as a picture beautifully drawn by an honest hand (*Ann.* 4.35), and perhaps saw himself in a way as Livy's continuator: his *Annals* start roughly at the point where Livy had left off, with the last years of Augustus, and he pointedly chose to adhere to a key Livian formal feature in retaining an annalistic structure for his narrative. His purpose in keeping to this structure for a history of a period in which emperors had displaced annually-appointed senatorial magistrates as the locus of power and authority is obvious: it pitched against the sort of biographically-tilted approach – already presaged in Velleius, but best-known now through the *Lives* of Tacitus' younger contemporary, Suetonius – which by the mid-second century CE was to constitute the dominant mode of Latin literary discourse about the past (after Tacitus, indeed, no Latin author would produce grand narrative history until Ammianus in the late fourth century). His retention of the annalistic form does not, of course, entail that the literary structure of the *Annals* was entirely untouched by biographical techniques, still less that Tacitus was blind to the central importance of imperial personalities (Syme 1958a: 253–70); on the contrary, his characterizations of individual emperors are extraordinarily penetrating. It was rather that, in his eyes, the lessons to be drawn from the history of the first-century principate encompassed more than the doings of emperors, and called for more than a sequence of imperial biographies.

The structural affinity notwithstanding, the mood of Tacitean history was distinctly un-Livian. When writing about old times, Livy avowed, the spirit of those times had somehow taken him over (43.13): his expansive and romantic picture of ancient days could console readers in a decayed age, and there was a hope that under Augustus the glory-days of civic virtue might perhaps be revived. Tacitus' picture of the post-Augustan principate takes the fatuity of such a hope as axiomatic – under Domitian, after all, the mere possession of a personal anthology of inspiring speeches culled from Livy had cost a senator his life (Suet. *Dom.* 10) – and a famous digression in the *Annals* regrets that its subject-matter, unlike that of earlier historians, must be almost unrelievedly inglorious and distasteful, perhaps only tolerable for the insight it offers into the moral effect of autocracy (*Ann.* 4.32–3). Even in his allusions to pre-imperial history, Tacitus tends to shun an easy romanticizing of the past: ever since a social hierarchy had first emerged among men, he judges, an instinctual drive for self-aggrandisement had constituted the basic constant in human affairs (*Hist.* 2.38); the institution of civic law from which the republic grew had been successful for a time in diverting its more pernicious effects, but had always been potentially vulnerable to wider historical contingencies; viewed in context, rule by emperors was just the latest turn, regrettable for its curtailing of earlier liberties, but indispensable in practice as the only means currently available to secure the continuing existence of Rome and its empire: the price of peace in the state was the *princeps* (*Ann.* 3.28). The lesson, that monarchy was both repugnant and necessary, suggests no cheerful view of the present. Early in his career, Tacitus had a mind to write a contemporary history contrasting the "slavery" recently endured under Domitian with the "present blessings" enjoyed under the current emperor, Trajan (*Agr.* 3). Tellingly, he never wrote it: what came to preoccupy Tacitus was rather the issue of the elite's progressive "enslavement" under Domitian's predecessors, and the direction of his interest drew him further back into the first century in successive stages, first to the Flavian age (69–96 CE) in the *Histories*, then to the Julio-Claudians from Tiberius to Nero (14–68 CE) in the *Annals*, and finally back to Augustus himself (the projected subject of a work that in the event Tacitus did not live to write: *Ann.* 3.24).

The account of the Julio-Claudian age in the *Annals* shows this preoccupation in full bloom. Behind the hostile accounts of the individual emperors, a deeper subject is implicit: the morally enfeebling impact of dynastic monarchy, particularly on the elite at Rome (Syme 1958a: 408–19, 545). Tacitus' personal experience of the Senate's collective passivity in the face of Domitian's persecution of suspected dissenters helps to explain the prominence of this theme in his work, and on one view it predisposed him to paint Julio-Claudian times more blackly than the facts warranted. There was certainly a moral agenda: his prime task, Tacitus avowed (*Ann.* 3.65), was to preserve a record of good and wicked deeds (the latter, sadly, far more redolent of the time), serving notice to evil men that posterity, at least, will know and revile what they do. Modern readers will compare this with the impulse driving classic accounts of ghastlier twentieth-century horrors – Gilbert's *Holocaust*, say, or Solzhenitsyn's promise in *Gulag Archipelago* that "all *will* be told." Like theirs, Tacitus' moral agenda surely answered to a gnawing anxiety about the vulnerability of true memory – in his case, an anxiety that the elite's passivity under repressive emperors presaged a collective slide into historical amnesia at Rome (*Agr.* 3). It is highly telling in this connection that the Tiberian section of the *Annals* contains an item unparalleled in ancient historiography: the speech of a historian, one Cremutius Cordus, on trial in the Senate for high treason, simply on the strength, we are told, of passing praises of Brutus and Cassius in his *History*. Tacitus gives the accused a stirring defense of free speech in historiography, recounts his suicide in advance of the inevitable verdict, and ends by emphasizing that the authorities' efforts to suppress his works failed to stop them circulating subsequently in *samizdat* (*Ann.* 4.34–6). Tacitus himself clearly found Cremutius an inspirational figure, and his imaginative empathy with a martyred fellow-historian has perhaps obscured the trial's original political context. But to elite contemporaries his account also imparted a broader lesson on the need to sustain critical historical consciousness in the face of long habituation to autocratic rule. The issue had a particular edge for Tacitus, perhaps, in the years the *Annals* were composed (Syme 1958a: 475): a younger generation was entering the Senate in relatively untesting times, and a growing proportion of senators were men from the provinces, non-Italians. The speech that Tacitus placed in Cremutius' mouth was surely his own apologia for history: the message was that the republic was indeed long gone, but that the vitality of the elite's collective memory of the Roman past was all the more essential for that; its continuance could at least do something to deter an autocrat from arbitrary actions that utterly disregarded traditional precedents, and it thereby offered the senatorial class the hope of retaining at least a measure of dignity and self-respect in the imperial present.

This central conviction gives particular point to the comments on Roman antiquarian matters found in the *Annals*. Digressions on this theme were conventional in the genre, but Tacitus could signal more by them than his own adherence to a traditional annalistic technique: an artful deployment of antiquarian material would nourish and sharpen the contemporary memory of earliest Rome and the old *res publica* (Syme 1958a: 311). Thus an obituary notice for a long-serving urban prefect is an occasion to trace the office's beginnings to emergency appointments that once had covered for a temporarily absent king or consul (*Ann.* 6.11), an enlargement under Claudius of Rome's city boundary prompts topographical comment on its original extent and gradual expansion (*Ann.* 12.24), and a fire on the Caelian Hill yields the observation that it owed its name to an Etruscan ally granted residence there by an archaic king (*Ann.* 4.65). Or recent and distant past can be set in telling counterpoint: grotesque abuse of legal process by Tiberian informers sends us back to the noble origin of Roman law in the Twelve Tables (*Ann.* 3.27), and the report for the year in which an emperor kills his own mother does not forget the wilting of an ancient fig-tree "under which Romulus and Remus had sheltered 830 years previously" (*Ann.* 13.58).

Authorial "construction" of the past is evident in such comments – but they can offer significant evidence, too, of the Julio-Claudian authorities' own efforts, from various motives, to harness and shape perceptions of the past. An aging ruler's edginess may partly explain Tiberius' intervention when a supposedly long-lost book of Sibylline prophecies was mysteriously rediscovered and approved by senatorial vote for inclusion with the authorized collection: he referred the matter back to an expert committee with a sharp reminder to senators that mischievous forgery was rife in the field, and that Augustus had forbidden private retention of such texts (*Ann.* 6.12); the wishes of contemporary malcontents, he knew, were easily dressed up as "ancient" wisdom (Potter 1994: 95–6, 150–1, 175). But not all such imperial interventions were so patently self-interested. In Claudius' case, for instance, a deep and long-standing personal interest in Roman history and antiquities impinged on an emperor's public style – a feature of the reign nicely conveyed in Tacitus' account by the frequency of its antiquarian comments, many of which were derived from Claudius' own writings and speeches (Syme 1958a: 704–10). That scholarship nourished a traditionalist streak in Claudius seems clear from his anxious eye for endangered custom, as when he lectured the Senate on the need to safeguard the old Italian art of soothsaying (*Ann.* 11.15). So too, his attention to public ceremonial: the eight-hundredth anniversary of Rome's foundation in 47 CE was celebrated with special games and the re-enactment of an archaic pageant (*Ann.* 11.11). But there are also hints that an informed sense of history's broad sweep inclined him to favor innovative political action at times. The prime example is a Claudian speech supporting the petition of Gallic aristocrats to be enrolled as Roman senators. Artfully reworked in the Tacitean version (the original, only partly extant, meanders by comparison), it deflects objections to the proposal by appeal to history (*Ann.* 11.24). Ever since Romulus' time, it argues, Rome's growth has rested on its readiness to integrate its neighbors and former enemies into the body politic: men descended from old Etruscan or Samnite stock have long since entered the Senate and nowadays constitute a good proportion of its members; soon enough, the sight of a Gallic senator will have come to seem just as normal. That was indeed so by Tacitus' time, and Tacitean hindsight probably read into the speech a more ambitious and coherent policy-innovation, and greater powers of imperial historical insight, than the Claudian original merited (M. Griffin 1982). But the basic thrust of the argument – its appeal to Roman history's long march to justify a seeming innovation – was not just a Tacitean projection, and on this occasion at least, an emperor's course of action in a practical political connection perhaps really was decided by his own belief in history's guiding logic. If nothing else, it is clear from the episode that iconic moments in the Roman past offered ready rhetorical ammunition in a political controversy – and not to one side only. Chauvinist opponents of Claudius' proposal complained that the admission of Celtic upstarts would cheapen the Senate's ancient dignity, and darkly recalled an earlier influx from Gaul well known to all readers of Livy (*Ann.* 11.23; cf. Livy 5.39–41): had not the very ancestors of those now seeking senatorial rank once overrun and sacked the city?

4 Greeks and the Greek Sense of the Past

Antiquarian comment in the *Annals* naturally deals mainly with Rome and its institutions, but in reporting provincial matters where they impinged on the Julio-Claudian elite's political and military experience, Tacitus does afford occasional glimpses of non-Italian communities in the Greek East constructing a past angled to their own perspective and interests. When delegates from several Greek cities are summoned to the Senate under Tiberius to justify their retention of existing civic privileges, they base their case on the antiquity of the cities and their long record of service to Rome, citing local mythological foundation-traditions and submitting charters granted by Rome in republican days (*Ann.* 3.60–3). The same happens when inter-city rivalries or disputes are put to the ruling power for a decision: to win the privilege of housing a new temple to the emperor, Smyrna asserts an earlier civic origin than its rival Sardis, the latter's claimed Etruscan connections notwithstanding, and cites proofs of unswerving loyalty to Rome since the days of Cato the Elder two centuries back (*Ann.* 4.55); Messene similarly prevails over Sparta in a territorial dispute by establishing a more ancient claim on the strength of local inscriptions, the testimonies of poets and historians, and the favorable previous judgments of a line of Roman governors and Greek kings reaching back to the father of Alexander the Great (*Ann.* 4.43). What counted for most with the imperial authorities in such cases, Tacitus implies (*Ann.* 3.63), was the checkable evidence of charters and treaties, but even vague appeals to mythological antiquity or to a connection with some iconic person or event could still have a practical utility, particularly if they linked to a Roman interest: thus Troy won immunity from taxes under Claudius for its reputation as "founder of the future Roman race" – a privilege foreshadowed, it was said, in an ancient senatorial document composed in Greek (Suet. *Claud.* 25); and when Germanicus visited Athens on his way to reorder the Eastern frontier, its public orators flattered him all the more effectively by seasoning their compliments with frequent evocations of the far-off glory-days when Athens had seen off the great Persian invasions and forged an Aegean empire (*Ann.* 2.53).

If such episodes often show Greek subject-communities adroitly manipulating national and local traditions to gain immediate advantage or favor, they also mark the deeper role their sense of history played in the construction of Greek self-definition in the empire. The seed-bed of the diplomatic tactic was the local elites' own attachment to local historical tradition, witnessed in a wide range of day-to-day cultural practice in their cities: the images on locally minted coinage evoking legendary foundations by a god or hero, the processions and festivals of ancestral civic cult, the care of ancient buildings and statues, the textual representation of the past in commemorative inscriptions and civic archives – not to mention works of local history. The epigraphic, archaeological, and numismatic testimony of a great many Greek cities could be cited to illustrate how the celebration and creative adaptation of local tradition helped to sustain a sense of distinctive cultural identity in the face of Roman power, but here we shall focus on a particularly suggestive example which demonstrates that "Greek" and "Roman" were by no means straightforwardly contrasting or oppositional categories in such practices (Gleason, this volume). At Ephesus in 104 CE the council and *demos* made detailed arrangements for two new civic rituals which a wealthy resident, one Vibius Salutaris – the holder of both Ephesian and Roman citizenship, and a Roman equestrian to boot – was proposing to fund: an annual sequence of lotteries and cash distributions, and a "procession of statues" to be performed every few weeks each year. The relevant decrees, comprising nearly 600 lines as extant, were prominently inscribed on a wall of the city's theater and on the Artemision, the famous temple to its patron divinity, and recent study has demonstrated how carefully they shaped the rituals to mesh with the city's historical traditions, topography, and social hierarchy while simultaneously honoring the power of Rome and its emperors. Thus the complex arrangements for participation in the lottery and cash distributions classified Ephesian citizens by their tribal units – the five tribes of the ancestral Ionian foundation, and the sixth later added to commemorate Augustus – and privileged them according to their status in the traditional civic hierarchy as Councillors, Elders, magistrates, priestly officials, and members of youth associations; and the distributions themselves were timed to take place in Artemis' temple during the annual festival celebrating her birthday (Rogers 1991a: 39–79). So too, the procession of statues began and ended at her temple after a tour in which statuettes were paraded through the city's main streets on a route shaped around a sequence of progressively more ancient monumental landmarks. Rome was honorably represented in the processional statuary with images of Augustus, the reigning emperor, Trajan, and personifications of the Roman Senate and people, but the heart of the show was local: images of Ephesus' legendary founder Androclus and its Hellenistic conqueror and re-founder King Lysimachus, personifications of its tribes and civic institutions – and above all, the nine statues of Artemis herself, the goddess whose local nativity in Ephesian myth gave the city a divine proto-founder and an ultimately sacred identity within which its subsequent history could be framed (Rogers 1991a: 80–126).

For those who participated in them, especially perhaps the youth associations, these rituals offered a living lesson in their civic past, but the past they constructed was clearly not merely an exercise in archaism that wishfully ignored an uncongenial present; rather, it was envisaged as a source of power for the city in its dealings with Rome. For us, the rituals exemplify the complex interplay of Greek and Roman elements in the cultural self-definition of a Greek city under Roman rule. The temple of Artemis on which they focused, after all, had doubled as a center of emperor worship since Augustus' time, and over the succeeding century the provision for imperial cult at Ephesus, and the inroads of Roman administrative and commercial activity, had effectively transformed the architectural profile of a whole section of the upper city (Rogers 1991a: 9, 141–2). Rome was smoothly accommodated as a manifest and well-disposed presence both in the rituals themselves – the procession of statues marched Augustus' image through an Augustan basilica on days consecrated to deified emperors – and in the procedures that established them: the inscription commemorating the local decrees of foundation emphasizes that they had been referred to the proconsul of Asia for approval, and it hails the local benefactor Salutaris as a Roman citizen and equestrian and as "a lover of both Artemis and Caesar" (Rogers 1991a: 152–4, 180). Tellingly, it is unclear whether the family background of this man was local, or even Greek at all: Ephesus' economic boom under the emperors had attracted immigrants from a wide field, Italians among them, and Salutaris' family had conceivably settled quite recently; he could have been a prosperous newcomer, keen to make a splash. That said, the individual's personal origin and motives are less significant for our purposes than the pains that were taken to shape the new rituals around a traditional template, and to record their content as the outcome of a decision collectively reached by the Ephesians and warmly endorsed by the Roman governor. In a major Greek city of Trajan's day, it is plain, civic identity was still closely connected to the elite's carefully-constructed representation of a local past reaching back to the city's earliest foundation. Needless to say, it was a representation nicely calculated to endorse the elite's own continuing domination of local politics and society as a status quo sanctioned by history and enjoying the active support of the Roman authorities in the present.

The Greek past, then, could function as a common frame for discourse between Greek elites and the Roman authorities – provided that it was configured in terms acceptable to the ruling power. If appeals to local tradition were generally unproblematic in Roman eyes, one reason was surely that the civic patriotism and inter-city rivalries fueling them signaled the absence of a "pan-Hellenic" politicized consciousness of a kind that might otherwise have undermined Rome's imperial claim on the eastern Mediterranean. The broader "history of the Greeks" was accordingly a more delicate topic – and of considerable interest to elite Romans (Dionisotti 1988: 37). Roman elite culture was thoroughly Hellenized: the education of the well-to-do predisposed them to idealize ancient Greece, and on their travels as tourists and administrators they looked for the past they wished to find – a land of glorious memory, but now nestling safe and obedient under Rome's enlightened wing. The Greek mainland, as opposed to Greek Asia, was especially privileged: "Remember," Pliny advises an official assigned to Achaia, "that you are going to the pure and genuine Greece, where civilization and literature are said to have originated.... Honor its people's ancient glory, its very age.... Remember that their land gave us justice and laws (not after conquering us, but at our own request).... Remember it is Athens that you reach, Sparta that you rule: to rob them of the name and shadow of 'freedom,' which is all that now remains for them, would be cruel..." (*Ep.* 8.24). Sparta, and especially Athens, were potent names, partly because of their leading roles in the Greeks' resistance to the Persian invasions and their subsequently conflicting hegemonic aspirations in the fifth century BCE, and partly as cultural icons – Sparta for its traditional "austerity," Athens for its brilliant artistic and intellectual record. In the imperial age, both were "museum cities" attracting many cultural tourists, Roman and Greek (and among the latter, many visitors from Roman Asia), and in both the past was shrewdly manipulated to appeal on that score (Swain 1996: 74). Sparta's major tourist attraction – the enactment of the "Lycurgan" training of youths with its brutal (sometimes fatal) endurance contests – was in good part a spectacle reinvented in the Flavian age (Cartledge and Spawforth 1989: 202–11; Potter, this volume). Athens could show visitors fragmentary wooden tablets purportedly preserving enactments of the law-giver Solon as first inscribed in the sixth century BCE (Plut. *Sol.* 25), not to mention an architectural feast now augmented by Attic monuments painstakingly disassembled and relocated to the city center. Romans and Greeks alike could admire the austere model of civic discipline the "Lycurgan" show commemorated, and for elite Greek visitors – particularly in the Greek cultural "renaissance" flowering in the high empire under Hadrian and the Antonines – it came to epitomize an "old-world" Sparta now claimed as a part of the Greeks' common heritage (Cartledge and Spawforth 1989: 209). But above all – as the "Atticizing" literary purism cultivated in that renaissance suggests – it was Athens that offered the prime emblem of "Greekness": the memory of her cultural pre-eminence in the classical age, and of her legendary role in the original colonization of Ionia, seemed to constitute the Greeks' best claim to possess a history expressive of a unitary cultural identity (Alexander, as a Macedonian, constituted a more ambiguous case).

The Roman imperial authorities readily colluded in the construction of a Greek past slanted to an idealized Athens. Roman tradition had already acknowledged her special luster in a legend insisting on a propitious start to Roman-Athenian contacts:

in her Periclean heyday, the story ran, Athens had welcomed a Roman commission sent out to make a copy of the laws of Solon – a constitutional model, it was hoped, that might settle the early republican "conflict of the [patrician and plebeian] orders" (Livy 3.31). Awkwardnesses in Athens' more recent past – her siding with Mithridates against Rome, and with Antony against Octavian – were diplomatically side-stepped with rare exceptions (Tac. *Ann.* 2.55); emphasis was placed rather on her championing of the Greeks against Persia, an alien power conveniently cast as the classical analogue of Rome's own oriental bugbear, Parthia (Spawforth 1996). This tactical elision of the Persian and Parthian empires had an obvious utility in the imperial present: in representing a barbarian East as the "natural" historical enemy of the Mediterranean world, and as still a standing threat, it implied that Romans and Greeks shared a fundamental cultural affinity and a basic practical interest. On this reading of the past, Rome's empire was the bulwark, not the oppressor, of the Greeks, and it was probably in this spirit that around 114–17 CE, as Trajan marched against Parthia, a local festival at Sparta honoring the heroes of Thermopylae was thoroughly re-vamped (Cartledge and Spawforth 1989: 192–3). But again, it was perhaps a reading tending to privilege Athens particularly. Augustus, and later Nero, staged re-enactments at Rome of Athens' naval victory at Salamis to coincide with military ventures in the East (Dio 55.10.7, 61.9.6; Potter, this volume), and at Athens itself a canny local initiative placed an honorific inscription to "the Greatest Emperor Nero" on an architrave of the Parthenon, artfully associating his current Armenian campaign with the glories of the old Persian Wars (Spawforth 1996: 234–7). Under Hadrian (117–38 CE), a philhellene emperor's idealizing vision of the Greek past gave Athens pride of place in specific public initiatives. Not only did he augment the powers of her own archaic, pre-democratic council, the Areopagus (to the benefit, surely, of a local elite well-trusted by Rome), but in 131/2 CE, Athens became the seat of a newly instituted "pan-Greek" council, the Panhellenion. This council was apparently devised as a means of reasserting "old Greece" as the heart of Greek cultural identity, and as a theater for a "pan-Greek" imperial cult: one of its key functions was the celebration of the emperor as "Hadrian Panhellenius," perhaps in association with Eleusinian Demeter (Spawforth 1999: 340–1). Cities aspiring to membership were expected to show a record of good relations with Rome, and to lay claim to an ethnic link with the "true" Greek homeland; Athens was plainly a highly effective name to cite in that "ethnic" connection, and some cities lacking a real historical link with her readily concocted one. At quite whose initiative the Panhellenion was founded remains a debated question. On one view, the idea originated with Greek urban elites (C. P. Jones 1996; Romeo 2002); on another, it more likely came from the emperor Hadrian himself, and the particular image of "pan-Greek" ethnic identity that it institutionalized probably had limited appeal (perhaps was never intended to appeal) to Greeks in the empire at large: the "old Greece" membership test ignored many cities of the Alexandrian-Hellenistic diaspora, and even cities that passed it with ease might wonder about their implicit subordination in the council's structure to "the Benefactress, the most brilliant city of the Athenians" (as a Lydian city's record of membership puts it) (Spawforth 1999: 340). What the Panhellenion witnesses, on this view, is a Roman construction of an idealized Greek past, and its application to the present in a ceremonial form which naturalized the Roman emperor's power over Greeks and dignified the Greek elites' self-interested participation in the arrangement. Such elites might themselves have preferred to configure the Greek past differently, but they could recognize what a Roman emperor wanted it to be, and that what he wanted must be accommodated. On that score, Greek cities outside the old homeland and lacking traditional links with it could perhaps at least welcome Athens' privileged place in the Panhellenion inasmuch as it allowed them to construe Greekness as a cultural condition that cut across the Panhellenion's own ethnically restrictive membership criterion: many more such cities, it seems telling, sent delegates to honor Hadrian during his stay at Athens in 131/2 CE than would ever actually join his "pan-Greek" council (Spawforth 1999: 347–8).

An aside in the *Annals* (2.88) chides unnamed "Greek annalists" as blinkered admirers of the Greek past only – a Romanocentric complaint (although Tacitus proceeds to fault Roman historians, too, for dwelling myopically on antiquarian subjects), and unspecific in reference, but perhaps not utterly vacuous. Neither the local patriotism of Greek elites nor their broader concern with Greek identity in a Roman empire could fail to register in some degree in Greek writing about the past. Whether they remained in the home-town or pursued careers as sophists or lawyers or agents of the imperial administration in a wider world, the writers in question were themselves typically products of the local elites, and educated in Atticizing literary ideals which entailed close familiarity with classical Athenian prose: many had honed their skills as speakers with historical declamations, often ingeniously counter-factual, on iconic themes drawn from Thucydides, Xenophon, Demosthenes, and their like (Swain 1996: 89–96; Gleason, this volume). On one view, this harking back to the glories of the fifth and fourth centuries BCE by educated Greeks expressed a widespread dissatisfaction with their present lack of autonomy (Bowie 1970). Whether such covertly anti-Roman feelings were anything like so widespread as the claim implies is very doubtful (C. P. Jones 1971: 126–30; Potter 1999a: 55–6), though we can grant the possibility that, for *some* Greeks of the "Second Sophistic," archaism could still channel suppressed resentments (the travel writer Pausanias arguably supplies an instance: Swain 1996: 347–56). In Augustus' reign, at least, Greek rhetor-historians active at Rome had taken sharply differing views of the ruling power's claim to a cultural standing worthy of the Greeks' respect – an issue with a particular edge for Greeks in the immediate aftermath of a war in which Augustus had represented himself as championing the Italian homeland against the Greek-Egyptian Cleopatra. On the one hand, Timagenes of Alexandria had written a "universal" history, *Kings*, with a provocatively anti-Roman slant, disparaging "barbarian" Rome's success as attributable more to luck than to intrinsic strength or merit (it was probably a remark of Timagenes that prompted Livy's excursus denying the claim that Alexander the Great, if he had looked west, would have overwhelmed Rome: Gabba 1991: 192). Dionysius of Halicarnassus, by contrast – a contemporary of Livy, and an early "Atticizer" – had offered Greek readers a *Roman Antiquities* justifying Roman rule on ethnic and ethical grounds: it painstakingly reaffirmed what some earlier Greek writers had disputed (Bickerman 1952: 65–8) – a respectable (pre-Trojan) Greek origin for the Roman race – and argued that the Roman state had been consistently organized from the first in accordance with the moral and civic virtues extolled in classical Greek philosophy; for Dionysius, in short, history taught that Rome was a Greek city and that her empire was governed by the descendants of Greek emigrants on the best Greek principles (Gabba 1991: 107–18).

Timagenes' overtly unconciliatory stance perhaps owed something to his Alexandrian provenance. As inhabitants of the largest city in the empire after Rome – a great center of Hellenistic culture, and (until Cleopatra's defeat) the independent capital of a Macedonian dynasty – Alexandrian Greeks were rather a special case, and all the readier to assert their Greekness for the presence in the city of a large Jewish community. Well after Timagenes' day, their dealings with Rome would still exhibit a peculiar volatility, veering from effusive flattery of the emperor to prickly claims that their special merits were insufficiently appreciated. For instance, to honor Claudius as the author of two histories composed in Greek (on the Etruscans and Carthaginians respectively), the Alexandrians made arrangements for annual public recitations of both works in their famous Library, and even named a new wing of the building after him (Suet. *Claud.* 41); nonetheless, Claudius would still figure as one of several "tyrant" emperors out to deny Greek Alexandrians their historic rights in the so-called "Acts of the Alexandrian Martyrs," a set of dramatic fictions locally produced in the first and second centuries (Musurillo 1954). The thrust of some of these texts seems vehemently anti-Roman, but as we have noted, Alexandria's case was special, and hardly a basis from which to generalize: in fact, the hostility to Roman rule evinced in Timagenes and in some of the "Acts" finds no substantial echo in the post-Augustan Greek writers of the "Second Sophistic" at large. That is hardly surprising. By Hadrian's day, it was clear to elite Greeks that, if they wished, they could cooperate with Romans in friendship and government without sacrifice of national integrity; and very many did so wish. Antiquity and archaism dominated the literary activity of Greeks and Romans alike at this time, and both naturally looked first to their own traditions in this connection: "the mood," it is well said, "was common, its expression appropriately diverse; [but] to see a serious nationalistic split in (at any rate) the cultivated classes of the Roman Empire in the second century would be to miss the most striking feature of the age" (Bowersock 1969: 16).

A Greek could participate willingly in Roman rule, of course, while still preserving a sense of his own Greekness and of Romans as "foreign," and on this score close readings of the major Greek writers of the Second Sophistic (e.g. Swain 1996) can disclose fine distinctions between individual cases, but neither point really diminishes the basic force of Bowersock's judgment that perceptions of cultural distinctiveness did not entail substantial divergence between the outlooks of Greek and Roman elites at the political level. Plutarch, for instance, when he composed a sequence of historical biographies pairing Roman and Greek subjects in Trajan's day, found Dionysius of Halicarnassus a useful source, but he felt no need to persuade Greek readers of Rome's historical respectability, as Dionysius had a century earlier (C. P. Jones 1971: 91–2): by now most were well content to live in a Roman empire which delivered security, prosperity, and due dignity to the eastern elite – and so was Plutarch. He wrote biography as a philosophic moralist, not a conciliator, and though he clearly felt himself Greek, he also clearly took a sympathetic interest in Roman history in its own right (C. P. Jones 1971: 103). For Plutarch, doubtless, Romans could be called civilized only insofar as they had assimilated Greek culture, and he perhaps sensed an "un-Greek" potential for barbarism persisting among them (Russell 1973: 8, 132); his diagnosis of the present political realities in Greek cities, at least, was blunt: "Observe the proconsul's boots above your head" (*Prae. ger. reip.* 814e). But the Greek statesmen treated in the *Parallel Lives* win no special credit simply for being Greek – they are judged on the same ethical criteria as their Roman partners – and the lessons Plutarch drew from history (not least, his hint that the principate was sanctioned by divine providence: Swain 1996: 151–61) were intended to speak to elite Romans and Greeks alike: the dedicatee of the *Lives* was an eminent Roman friend, a general and twice a consul under Trajan (C. P. Jones 1971: 54–6, 103–9). So too, Greek historians in the high empire happily pursued parallel careers in the imperial service, and their works treated Roman as readily as Greek subjects – and with no sign of resenting Roman rule. In the second and third centuries, indeed, the narrative historiography of Rome became effectively a Greek literary province. Whereas its Latin counterpart collapsed into biography, the genre continued to flourish in Greek in various branches: local histories aside, there were re-workings of major themes in the Greeks' pre-Roman past (most notably, Arrian of Nicomedia's *Anabasis of Alexander*), large-scale accounts of the history of Rome from its origin down to the writer's time (by Appian of Alexandria, down to c.120 CE; and by Cassius Dio, to 229 CE), and "contemporary" histories of varying scope (Arrian again, for instance, on Trajan's Parthian War, or Herodian's account of the empire over the half-century since Marcus Aurelius' death [180 CE]). All of the writers named held imperial posts, some in shining senatorial careers (Arrian and Dio held consulships and governed provinces), and their works give no hint of any privately harbored distaste for the Roman Empire: for Dio, the Roman legions are "our" army (Dio 80.4.1), and Appian applauds the "happy present" of peace under the principate (*BC* 4.16.64).

In the case of Arrian, his subject in the *Anabasis* was emphatically Greek, with a Homeric grandeur especially inspiring to the writer – "for me," he wrote, "[the essence of] fatherland, family and public honors resides in these stories [of Alexander's campaigns]" (*Anab.* 1.12.5, with Moles 1985) – and his treatment of it played off an emphatically classical Greek model, Xenophon's "March of the Ten Thousand" (as a pupil of Epictetus, Arrian had philosophic as well as historical interests, and in several works he identifies strongly with Xenophon as a kindred spirit). Nothing in the *Anabasis*, though, suggests that Arrian covertly chafed at or wished to belittle Roman rule, and the collocation of Trajan's and Alexander's eastern wars as subjects on which he chose to write substantial histories is eloquent in its way. The glamor of Alexander's energy and military success was as potent for imperial Romans as for Greeks, and had perhaps already inspired a highly romanticized narrative in Latin by Curtius Rufus (of disputed date, but usually assigned to Claudius' reign: Conte 1994: 383). Augustus himself had crowned Alexander's mummified remains and had used his portrait as a personal seal for correspondence (Suet. *Aug.* 18, 50), and Alexander's eastern conquests had obvious resonance for the publicity of any subsequent Roman emperor who campaigned against the Parthians, or in later days against their Sasanian successors: they colored Trajan's dispatches to Rome from Mesopotamia, and his regret that India remained beyond his reach (Dio 68.29.1), and in the fourth century they would prompt Emperor Julian to make an honorary Roman emperor of Alexander in his fiction *The Caesars* (R. B. E. Smith 1995: 12–13, 168). Like evocations of the Athenian repulse of the Persian invader at Salamis, then, Alexander's conquests could offer an image of Romans and Greeks as fellow Mediterraneans sharing basic interests and affinities, and a common alien enemy in the East. In Alexander's case, further, the image was more aggressively slanted and was plainly predicated on monarchy – and on both counts, particularly apt to appeal to propagandists in the high empire (Spawforth 1996: 242–3). On this score, it hardly mattered if philosophers, Arrian's own teacher among them, judged Alexander a less than virtuous king (Brunt 1977a); his image epitomized the acme of military glory and success, and memories of Alexander arguably helped to shape the political reality of the high empire in a basic connection, "surely influenc[ing] not only [Trajan] and Caracalla [as individuals], but the overall importance given to the eastern frontier in imperial military policy" (Millar 1969: 13).

On a broader front, it can be argued similarly that in the "crisis" of the mid-third century, when imperial arrangements for military protection were often found wanting, the persistence of Greek memories of former glory could at times be of practical advantage to local Greek communities in their efforts to resist barbarian incursions. Athens, tellingly, offers the best grounds for the claim: a century after Arrian settled there in honorable retirement (he was made an Athenian citizen, and became an archon), historiography was still thriving at Athens in the person of a well-born native and holder of high local office, Herennius Dexippus (c.205–c.280 CE). Dexippus' works included a history of Alexander's "Successors" and a substantial "universal" history from mythical Greek times to the reign of Claudius Gothicus (268–70 CE), but special interest attaches to his *Scythian History* for the fact that it recounted Dexippus' own leading role in organizing the resistance after the capture of Athens by Herulian invaders in 267/8 CE. If the relevant fragment reflects reality, he gathered a band of Athenians and exhorted them in a speech shot through with echoes of Thucydides to live up to their proud past and recover the city (which they did): "it is a noble fate to spread the glory of our city and to be an example of courage and love of freedom to the Greeks...showing by our actions that even in disaster the resolution of the Athenians is unbroken." Unless the written version of the speech was simply a post-bellum literary invention, it seems that on this occasion the memories on which ingenious historical declaimers in Athens' lecture halls rang their variations had a very practical application in a local emergency (Millar 1969: 20–9).

5 Other Voices: The Witness of Josephus

Dexippus' speech touches on the broad (and difficult) issue of the reception of elite historical consciousness outside the ranks of the elite. It is plain that the imperial representations of the past discussed in this chapter, Roman or Greek, stem chiefly from persons equipped by a liberal education to participate as readers or writers in a sophisticated literary discourse, and reflect the attitudes and interests of a well-to-do social class. In what form and with what force they permeated down to the urban population at large is a difficult question, one we can only glance at here. For the literate, the inscribed word was clearly important; we hear of "history walls" in the provinces, collections of texts of local interest inscribed on some central civic monument, and quite often presenting official communications between Rome and the city concerned in summarized or excerpted form (Potter 1994: 117–19). At Rome, theatrical games still drew the crowds (Tac. *Ann.* 11.13) and were possibly a conduit, though proof is lacking that historical drama as such featured in that setting (the only extant item of possible relevance is the pseudo-Senecan *Octavia*, a treatment of Nero's matrimonial crimes written in the 70s with the stage arguably in mind; Wiseman 1998: 53). Mythological rather than historical scenarios seem to characterize the Colosseum's "fatal charades" (Coleman 1990), but the Campus Martius saw ad hoc "historical" shows like Claudius' "sack of a town and the surrender of British kings" (Suet. *Claud.* 21.6; Potter, this volume), and his conquest of Britain was visually commemorated in far-off Asia in an Aphrodisian relief personifying a female Britannia fallen at the feet of the divine emperor (R. R. R. Smith 1988). And there were always spectacles and visual imagery of the sort we have noticed earlier: the Augustan and Neronian recreations at Rome of the battle of Salamis; the sculptures of "great men" in the Augustan Forum; the friezes on the emperors' triumphal arches, and the coin images commemorating imperial victories; the statues led in procession through Trajanic Ephesus; the festivals of "Hadrian Panhellenios" at Athens – all of these could speak clearly enough to persons hardly literate. So, for that matter, could monumental inscriptions: many were impressive physical objects in their own right, and needed no close reading to impart a sense of the continuity of imperial power. It seems likely, too, that local tradition would count specially strongly with the humbler provincial classes, and the accommodation of its observances to the imperial present – most notably, by the linking of imperial cult to the festivals of civic cult – signals the concern of local elites to advertise the consonance of local patriotism with the imperial status quo. There are hints on this score of an awareness that popular feeling for the past, unless channeled, was potentially disruptive of civic order. Plutarch's elite Greek readers were advised to tailor their praises of the past according to the audience being addressed: to dwell on inspiring victories like Marathon was acceptable in the lecture hall, but "liable to make the common people swell with vain pride" and best avoided in public speeches (*Praec. ger. reip.* 814c). Even at Rome itself, a plebeian historical consciousness with a potentially anti-aristocratic slant apparently still existed for Sejanus to exploit in his bid for the consulship (Syme 1956), and traces of it arguably persist in the late fourth century (R. B. E. Smith 2002: 159). We have also noted Tiberius' worries over an unauthorized "Sibylline" book; its content is not specified, but it is well known that disaffected versions of "history" could masquerade as prophecy: several of the texts now extant as the "Sibylline Oracles" were second- or third-century CE Christian and Jewish forgeries whose content was shaped by their authors' hopes for the fall of the empire (Momigliano 1987: 114–15, 138–41; Potter 1994: 87–90, 171). That said, not all oracles were eschatologically-obsessed, and not all who read them were rabidly anti-Roman. Some could offer readers "potted history" in a picturesque form owing little to elite historiography, but much to what a local writer might cull from the sorts of epigraphic and visual material we have just mentioned: their stylized representations of imperial power have been aptly related to the images their authors encountered on coins and sculpture (Potter 1994: 110–30). "Alternative" history, then, did not always express active disaffection. The power of elite discourse to control the views of "the many" had its limits, and the concern of the Roman and provincial elites to head off potential recalcitrants is a reminder that to control is not to achieve total consensus; but it is implicit in the fundamental stability of imperial social structures up to the mid-third century that the cooperation of the elite effectively protected the basic interests of their class.

It is also plain that the representations of the past we have treated reflect the views of persons who identified themselves in cultural terms as Roman or Greek. But by no means all of the emperor's subjects, of course, even if they spoke Latin or Greek, identified themselves that way: to pick random examples from the frontier provinces, there were Celts, Germans, Berbers, Jews, Nabataean Arabs, each a culturally distinctive group. "Greekness" itself, for that matter, was an elastic cultural badge: the Panhellenion, as we noted, configured Greekness in Athenocentric terms that favored the old Greek homeland as against the Greek settlements in the east in the Hellenistic age – and among the latter were Egyptian Alexandria and Syrian Antioch, both great cities and cultural centers in their own right. Like the question of "non-elite" historical consciousness, the ways in which these subject-communities "constructed" their past under Roman rule is a large and difficult subject (Millar 1993a), and largely outside the compass of a chapter focused on elite Greco-Roman discourse.

One extraordinary witness to the Jewish case, though, the historian Josephus, is too important to pass unmentioned here. Greeks and Romans themselves sensed that the historical consciousness of the Jews constituted a special case on various counts – its religious nationalism and exclusiveness, the authority it assigned to sacred texts, its very longevity, and its bearing on the rebellions in Judea under Nero and Hadrian sharpened its interest for them (e.g. Tac. *Hist.* 5.1–13). Josephus (37–c.100 CE) wrote partly with gentile readers in mind, and presents us with a fascinating case of divided loyalties: a rebel general who surrendered to and later served the Romans in the catastrophic first revolt; an aristocratic and priestly Jew from Palestine writing history in Greek on Jewish subjects – writing at Rome, moreover, as a beneficiary of the Flavian dynasty's patronage, and a Roman citizen by imperial grant, but remaining a Jew by religion, and always concerned to defend and extol Judaism. Unsurprisingly, both his personal integrity and his honesty as a historian are often debated (Rappaport 1994), but for us the prime interest of the case lies elsewhere: Josephus' works reflect the power of Greco-Roman representations of the past to affect the historical outlook of a writer raised in a Palestinian Jewish cultural tradition, but equally, the resilience of the Jewish sense of history, and the ability of a resourceful writer to spot cracks in the Greco-Roman cultural facade.

On the first count, both of Josephus' major works disclose not just a general engagement with Greek historiographic models, but significant intellectual debts to specific Greek historical texts. In the *Jewish War*, for instance, the borrowings from Thucydides go deeper than the sort of literary play which makes Jerusalem respond to the news that Jotapata has fallen as the Athenians had to the Sicilian disaster (*BJ* 3.432, echoing Thuc. 8.1); a prime aim of the work was to exonerate the bulk of the Jews from the charge of disloyalty to Rome by emphasizing the pernicious role of a faction-riven extremist minority, and Josephus' notion of the workings of Jewish factionalism in this connection draws on Thucydides' famous analysis of revolutionary stasis at Corcyra (Rajak 1983: 84, 92–4). As for the *Jewish Antiquities*, written in the 90s and narrating Jewish history from the Creation to the start of the revolt in 20 books, it has been called "the first great achievement of Greek historiography in the imperial period" (Millar 1969: 14); a debt to Dionysius of Halicarnassus' *Roman Antiquities* is patent in its title and structural arrangement, and probably also at a deeper level: a central preoccupation in both works is the issue of how a non-Roman ethnic culture could hope to be accommodated within a "universalizing"

Roman Empire (Gabba 1991: 214–16). For Jews and Romans alike, this question had a very practical edge in the wake of the revolt of 66–70 CE. The Flavians' claim to dynastic power was intimately linked to their victory in Judea, and both Vespasian and Titus wrote reports of their campaigns that Josephus, and presumably others, could consult (Rajak 1983: 215–16). His own *Jewish War* was composed in the 70s for a mixed readership of gentiles and Jews of the Diaspora (his earlier version in Aramaic, Josephus observes [*BJ* 1.3–6], had catered to oriental readers, among them the Jews of Mesopotamia). A major contention of the work was that Judaism and Roman power were now compatible, the war having eliminated the "bad" Jews who had led their nation to ruin. Similarly, Josephus offered his *Antiquities* to gentile readers in the conviction that it would interest and benefit them to learn the entire course of Jewish history "up to the last war involuntarily waged against Rome"; Mosaic Law, they would find, chimed well with their own philosophers' best prescriptions for virtue (*BJ* 1.5–7, 15–20). This line of argument was obviously appealing for the hope it offered that the rift between Rome and the Judean elite was not irreparable; it is often assumed, though, that in the *Jewish War* Josephus' argument was chiefly self serving, a contorted effort to justify his own accommodation with Rome in a work whose prime purpose was to supply his Flavian patrons with an account of the revolt that glorified their suppression of it. That assumption is vulnerable in what it takes for granted: that Josephus secretly acknowledged himself to be what his critics claimed, an opportunist turncoat and imperial lackey who had irredeemably deserted his people and religion. The *War* undeniably flatters the Flavians, but its paradoxical insistence that Judaism was not inimical to Roman power is certainly no reflection of Flavian publicity. The Flavian version of the matter was just the opposite; it is enshrined on their victory arches in the friezes depicting the crushing of the rebellion, and in the inscription placed on the Flavian Amphitheater (a recent study has disclosed that the commemorative text originally displayed on this dynastic showpiece highlighted Vespasian's funding of it *ex manubiis* – "from the spoils," that is, of the Jewish War [Alföldy 1995]).

The distance between Josephus and his imperial patrons on this point is enough to refute the notion that he wrote Flavian propaganda to order. Moreover, a distinctively Jewish theological strand plainly subsisted in his basic historical outlook, his conciliatory attitude towards gentile readers and borrowings from their historians notwithstanding. Thucydides' analysis of faction dynamics might illuminate the actions of the Jewish rebels 66–70 CE, but for Josephus it could never offer a full and definitive explanation of the rebellion and its outcome: faction was a sin and God had willed the defeat of the Jews as punishment for it, using Rome as his instrument (*BJ* 6.109, 411); Rome herself only ruled the world because God, to whom past and future are one, was presently on her side (*BJ* 5.367). And it was not only that the cause of historical events lay ultimately in God; for Josephus, the history that God willed was prophetically revealed in Scripture, and the prophets were themselves inspired historians and valuable sources: Samuel, for instance, had not needed a good memory or archive to write the history of Israel's kings – God had given him secret knowledge of future events, and Samuel had written them out before they occurred (*BJ* 6.66, with J. Barton 1986: 130). Similarly, Josephus believed that the Book of Daniel (a key text for the argument of the *Antiquities*) had accurately predicted the Roman Empire, not to mention Alexander's (*AJ* 11.337, 10.276; Momigliano 1987: 117). The logical corollary, unthinkable to a Greek or Roman, was that a historian's own clairvoyance could constitute part of his knowledge and could legitimately feature in his narrative – and for Josephus, this was not just theory. A famous passage in the *War* recounts that in 67 CE, while Nero still ruled, Josephus was brought before Vespasian as a prisoner of war, and predicted to him his future rule as emperor (*BJ* 3.401): whatever moderns care to make of it, Josephus himself unequivocally ascribes the event to his own prophetic inspiration, "dreams by night in which God had foretold to him the impending fate of the Jews and the destinies of Roman kings" (*BJ* 3.351–2; J. Barton 1986: 127–8).

Josephus, then, only ever became a "Greek historian" in a significantly qualified sense: in some of his guiding presuppositions, he interpreted the past in a way quite foreign to Greeks and Romans. If one of his purposes as a historian was to represent the Jews as fundamentally loyal to the empire by emphasizing points of consonance between Judaism and Greco-Roman culture, the extent to which he personally could feel part of that culture was surely restricted – by his own mentality as much as any prejudice in the imperial system (Goodman 1994). His engagement with Greek culture, in particular, has an ambivalent and sometimes competitive edge, and a political background in long-standing tensions between the local Greek and Jewish populations in Palestine. Josephus commends his *Jewish War* to Greek readers by archly contrasting its probity and grand contemporary theme with the disengaged exercises in nostalgia that Flavian Greek historians prefer: forgetting what made Thucydides great, they spend their time re-telling the histories of the Assyrians and Medes, "as if the old narratives were not fine enough" (*BJ* 1.12). So too, while the preface of the *Antiquities* may dress Moses as a Greek philosopher-statesman in terms congenial to Greek readers, it also pointedly tells them that that he lived 2,000 years ago, and that the Jewish scriptures embrace a history stretching back 5,000 years (*AJ* 1.13, 16). The point implicit here – that if antiquity legitimated a national culture, the Greeks could not compare – is made overtly, and overtly polemically, in a complementary late work written at Rome c.96 CE, *Against Apion* (1.19–27, 57–68): there, Josephus rebuts at length Greek critics' claims that he had exaggerated the antiquity of the Jews, and ascribes the Greeks' failure to recognize it to deficiencies in their own historiographic tradition as compared to the Jewish records (Bickerman 1952: 76–8). The particular claim lends support to the broader argument of *Against Apion* that Judaism is demonstrably superior to Greek culture, and it has been acutely observed in this connection that the qualities in Judaism which Josephus picks out for special praise bear a striking likeness to those which Latin writers of the period attach to the Roman character when they wish to compare it favorably with Greek fickleness (Goodman 1994: 335): here, arguably, we see Josephus adroitly exploiting the ingrained ambivalence of one gentile culture towards another to represent Judaism in the form best suited to win it friends at Rome.

6 Epilogue

If Josephus' defense of Judaism ever had any merit in Roman eyes, it was soon discredited by the subsequent Jewish uprisings under Trajan and Hadrian. Nor could his notion of all history unrolling as the One God's will in accordance with holy scripture hold much appeal for gentile readers before the emergence of Christian historiography in the fourth century – a major development (Momigliano 1977: 115–17), but again beyond this chapter's compass. Recast in less culturally specific terms, the idea that a supreme divinity had predetermined the detailed course of history could hope to chime faintly in some pagan minds – but they were the minds of philosophers, not history writers, and the mood engendered was different from Josephus'. There is an affinity of sorts to be found between the doctrine he ascribes to the Pharisees – "they hold that to act rightly or otherwise rests mostly with men, but that in every action Fate co-operates" – and the Stoics' idea of divine Providence (*BJ* 2.163; Rajak 1983: 100); in a thoughtful pagan, though, the notion was apt to provoke sentiments on the transience and vanity of human affairs, and a mood leaning closer to Ecclesiastes than the Book of Daniel. To the philosophically-minded emperor Marcus Aurelius, for instance, musing in the mid-second century on his imperial predecessors, it was evident that even the relatively recent past was elusive, rapidly dissolving and already beyond full or certain knowledge:

> Think of the times of Vespasian, and what do you see? Men marrying, raising children, falling ill, dying; fighting, feasting, trading, farming; flattering, boasting, suspecting, plotting; cursing, complaining, loving, hoarding; coveting offices, coveting thrones. And now, that life of theirs is no more and nowhere. Come forward to the reign of Trajan, and it is the same; that life too is dead.... The famous names once hymned are now almost archaisms: Camillus, Caeso...Scipio, Cato...even Augustus, and Hadrian, and [my father] Antoninus – everything quickly fades and turns into material for stories, and forgetfulness soon covers it all like sand.... (*Med.* 4.32–3, abbreviated)

For Marcus in this mood, the past is a halfway house on a road to oblivion in which events are preserved vestigially for a time, as stories sustained by human ingenuity (which is to say, as a "construction"). As a Stoic, though, Marcus also knew it was his duty to persevere in his allotted part as a Roman emperor (*Med.* 3.6), and his reign became golden in later eyes: Cassius Dio in the third century, and Emperor Julian in the fourth, thought Marcus the best emperor that Rome had ever had (Dio 71.34; Jul. *Caes.* 333c–35d). It is a nice question, what a resurrected Marcus would have thought in return of Rome as it stood in Dio's or in Julian's time. In 247/8 CE, 20 years on from the end-point of Dio's history, the city of Romulus celebrated its thousandth birthday: as one whose own family background lay in Spain, Marcus exemplifies in his way the "open" imperial elite predicted by the Tacitean Claudius (*Ann.* 11.24), but he might still have been surprised to find that the emperor who presided over the millennial Games was a Syrian "Arab" hailing from the Jebel Druz (Millar 1993a: 530–1). And by the mid-fourth century, change had run much deeper. By that time, Rome was no longer in practice an imperial capital; in the east there was a "New Rome," Constantinople, and in the west the imperial court had moved to Milan. The emperors residing there, and a good part of the Roman aristocracy, now professed and patronized the Christian religion that Marcus had despised; there was a pope at Rome, and a church of St. Peter on the Vatican. On the other hand, Marcus' birthday was still being celebrated by annual public games (Beard, Price, and North 1998: 2: 68), and the decorated column his successor had erected to his memory was kept in good repair, along with many other public buildings, by imperial subventions dedicated to the upkeep of the city's monuments (A. H. M. Jones 1964: 709). And with the emperor away, the aristocracy could play at being Roman senators in a bygone age, disporting themselves in their inscriptions in a style that gave mundane local business a heroic luster: one such aristocrat solves a labor dispute between two trade guilds at Ostia, and earns thanks from both "for exercising control over distribution of the corn-supply of the Eternal City so fairly as to show himself more a parent than an official"; another gets an honorific statue for restoring to the Senate a trivial privilege wanting "since the times of Julius Caesar, 381 years ago" (*ILS* 1222, 1272; R. B. E. Smith 2002: 153–5). Moreover, as we noted earlier in connection with Roman travelers in Greece, observers tend to see what they wish to see. That was often the case with fourth-century representations of Rome: the potency of Rome as a symbol and repository of the national past spoke to Christians and pagans alike. The verses inscribed to commemorate a particularly prominent Christian aristocrat can report a public funeral at which "the highest buildings of Rome appeared to weep" (*ILCV* iv, no. 90; Cameron 2002); pagan traditionalists, meanwhile, were compiling potted histories of Rome without a word on its Christians (Momigliano 1977: 121–2), and representing the city in their catalogues of monuments and geographical descriptions without a glance at the Christian architecture springing up there. "Italy," we read in a description of c.359 CE,

> has the following supreme advantage: the greatest, the most distinguished imperial city, demonstrating its merit in its very name of Rome: they say young Romulus founded it. It is adorned to the greatest extent with buildings worthy of the gods: every earlier emperor, like those of the present time, has wanted to found a building there, and each has created some monument in his own name. If you want [to be reminded of] Antoninus, there are countless monuments of his; [or if Trajan], there is what they call the Forum of Trajan.... [Rome] has a circus, too, well-sited and decorated with many bronzes.... It has the greatest senate composed of rich men, all of whom could be governors – but they prefer to enjoy their wealth in peace. They worship the gods, especially Jupiter and Sol.... (*Description of the Whole World* 55; Beard, North, and Price 1998: 2: 360)

For the writers and readers of such texts, pagan or Christian, Rome itself was becoming a museum city: we are not far away, here, from the mood in the Procopian image which opened our discussion, with a sixth-century visitor marveling at the sight of Aeneas' ship, and at the care shown by the Romans to preserve their city's buildings in the wake of a Gothic occupation. Not even a Gothic king, it would seem, was immune to the spell: in 546 CE, Procopius reports, the Goth Totila had taken the city and was planning to raze it, but was dissuaded by a timely letter brought by ambassadors from Count Belisarius:

> "Among all the cities under the sun," the letter began, "Rome is agreed to be the greatest.... For it has not been created by the ability of one man, nor has it attained such greatness and beauty by a power of short duration. A multitude of kings, many bands of the best men, a long lapse of time and an extraordinary abundance of wealth have brought together in that city all other things that there are in the whole world.... Little by little, they built the city as you see it now, leaving memorials of their excellence to men of future time...." (*Goth.* 7.22.9–12)

CHAPTER TWENTY-TWO

Imperial Poetry

K. Sara Myers

Latin literature of the empire tends to be categorized by periods referring to emperors or imperial dynasties, the most notable being the Augustan, Neronian, and Flavian ages. While this kind of periodization often obscures the continuities in the development of Latin literature (see the warning of Nisbet 1995: 391 "periodization in literature is even more misleading than it is in history"), the changing circumstances of the relationship between literature and political power under the empire make such chronological markers useful. Beginning with Augustus, Latin literature is increasingly drawn into imperial circles and literary patronage comes close to being an imperial monopoly (Wallace-Hadrill 1996: 292). Writers, like the aristocracy (and the two were usually the same), had to learn how to deal with the necessity of coping in a world that now had an emperor in it. The emperors did not commission these writers, nor did they necessarily dictate what they wrote, but they were able to exert unique pressures. Most importantly, the emperors were always present as potential readers and this changes the nature and interpretation of Latin literature profoundly. Juvenal proclaims shortly after the accession of Hadrian in 117 CE that "both the hope and the motive for writing lie with the emperor" (*Satires* 7). There were also, increasingly, consequences for what was written. The picture is not overwhelmingly glum (though it does tend to grow darker as it progresses). The emperors created great opportunities for literary achievement and there is until the mid-second century CE an impressive volume and variety of work being produced. The appellation of the late republican and Augustan age as "Golden" and the following period as "Silver" is not useful, and indicative in some ways of the long-lasting success of Augustan propaganda and imperial writers' own perceptions of decline. Literature of the later imperial period is now being re-evaluated and valued on its own terms. It is generally agreed that the Roman Empire sees the full flowering of Latin literature. It was really only after Cicero and Sallust that Greek models began to give way to Latin in Roman education. The works of Vergil and Livy passed immediately into the curriculum of Roman education (Vergil became a school author before the publication of the

Aeneid in 19 BCE). In line with the Roman elite's desire to appropriate Greek cultural authority, Latin authors were motivated to achieve mastery in all major Greek genres. So Quintilian in the 90s CE can produce a checklist of all the Greek genres which have now been mastered in Latin, including tragedy, oratory, epic, didactic, lyric, pastoral, elegy, and satire (*Inst.* 10). This dry list, however, does not do justice to the highly creative ways in which imperial poets transformed their illustrious models (and these were usually multiple) and produced works which were both artistically innovative and culturally relevant. The establishment of this canon of Latin poetry early in the empire means that post-Augustan literature increasingly responds to these Latin predecessors, as well as to Greek models.

There are certain general tendencies of the literature of the imperial period which can be sketched out. One of the most commonly cited features of imperial, especially post-Augustan, literature is its desire for striking effect. This tendency towards the "spectacularization" of literature was already in antiquity traced to two causes, which are themselves related. Tacitus and Quintilian, looking back from the late first century CE, cite the new importance attached to public declamation as the reason for the decline in Roman oratory and eloquence. Declamation (producing model speeches and exercises on a set theme) was not new, but in the empire, as opportunities for the free elite expression of political ideas decreased, its popularity vastly increased as an alternative vehicle for rhetoric in light of changing political circumstances. This public form of rhetorical display was blamed for changes in style: a craving for new, paradoxical expressions, epigrammatic brevity (pithy, memorable quotes), and striking aphorisms. In all, it amounted to a fundamental change in taste and tendencies. At the same time, the public recitation of literary works also became more popular as a new forum for self-advertisement (D. Markus 2000), and also provoked rebukes from many contemporary writers (Persius, Petronius, Juvenal, Tacitus). Authors (poets, historians, orators, philosophers) recited their works and for larger audiences than in the past. The upper classes were usually the core audience. For earlier recitations the audiences tended to be smaller and more select, often other professionals or members of the imperial family. The composition and enjoyment of literature at Rome was always for the most part limited to the wealthy leisured classes, but in the Roman Empire the pursuit of literature gains a more prominent cultural role as a marker of elite status and comes to dominate social life. As government, warfare, and the dedication of public architecture, the traditional modes of elite competition, are withdrawn into imperial hands, literature is co-opted "as a manifestation of Roman excellence and integrated into patterns of social activity" (P. White 1993: 61).

As Roman literature is essentially written by the elite for the elite, so it suffers many of the same fortunes of the aristocracy under the empire. The picture is not one of unrelenting gloom; there were better and worse periods for literature. Indeed during the reign of two of the most notoriously "bad" emperors, Nero and Domitian, literature received significant, although circumscribed, support and even flourished (at least for a while). Already with Augustus we see the emergence of encomiastic court poetry and many genres become increasingly celebratory. Roman writers will borrow from Hellenistic court poetry addressed to the king as a god in order to compose panegyric of their own recently divinized rulers. One of the difficulties of later imperial literature is how to read and understand the increasingly hyperbolic flattery. Modern sensibilities revolt against such unctuous and amplified language, and while such language was conventional, there is evidence to suggest that ancient audiences, as well as emperors, might well detect masked disaffection or encoded misgivings in excessive praise. On this problem of interpretation hinge the fortunes of many later poets such as Statius and Martial, long viewed as imperial toadies. The existence of double-entendres is a debate of current scholarship, but the detection of allusive political comment was also a life-or-death sport in Rome, especially in the vociferous atmosphere of the theater, where it had been a staple of audience activity since the late republic. We know that tragedy, especially on Roman themes, was traditionally considered a potential medium for the criticism of political authority (Bartsch 1994: 71–97). Suetonius in his *Lives of the Emperors* cites a number of occasions when actors used critical innuendo or when audiences used hostile reinterpretation of a play for either flattery or the expression of displeasure. The Atellan actor Datus was exiled for making allusions to Nero from the stage (Suet. *Nero* 39.3), Caligula had burned an Atellan poet (Suet. *Cal.* 27.4), and Domitian executed authors of farce. History remains throughout the period the most dangerous genre in which to write and Latin poetry conspicuously deals less and less with historical and contemporary themes or personages. Tacitus in his *Annals* records the beginning of persecutions of *littérateurs* already during the later and considerably more repressive years of Augustus' reign. He devotes a long passage to an account of the prosecution under Tiberius of the senator Cremutius Cordus, who wrote a history in which he praised Brutus and Cassius, the murderers of Julius Caesar. The elder Seneca records the official burning of Titus Labienus' writings under Augustus (among them possibly his histories, parts of which Labienus said could only be read after his death because of their outspokenness), claiming "it was an unheard of novelty that punishment should be exacted from literature" (*Con.* 10 pref. 5, trans. M. Winterbottom). Tacitus traces from Augustus' time the increase in treason (*maiestas*) prosecutions, which curtailed the freedom of verbal and literary expression in all forms. Many have questioned whether, in this dangerous atmosphere, we can assume that authors would have dared to introduce subversive undertones or veiled criticism. While it is never easy to identify a seeming subversive allusion as a deliberate authorial strategy, the curtailment of free speech, which is typical of absolute rulers, tends to give rise to audiences that are hyper-attuned to potentially subversive meanings (Bartsch 1994: 70; Ahl 1984). The ancients shared the same difficulty of interpretation as modern scholars; Martial repeatedly had to defend himself against allegations that he was the author of anonymous abusive epigrams (*Ep.* 7.12, 72, etc.). At the same time, writers of satire, such as Persius and Juvenal, attack only figures either deceased or fictional in order to protect themselves. Other writers must have developed strategies of polyvalence, whereby plausible alternative interpretations were possible and different readers could understand their work as either celebrating current political institutions or dissenting (cf. Hinds 1988: 29 on the "hermeneutic alibi").

While traditional forms of poetic patronage become scarcer under the emperors, new opportunities are created by the establishment of literary competitions in oratory and poetry on the Greek model (see P. White 1998). New genres, such as the novel, are produced. While Augustus was largely unsuccessful in his attempts to revive Roman drama, we know that such famous writers as Ovid wrote popular tragedies (e.g. the lost *Medea*). All that survive complete are the tragedies of Seneca on Greek mythical themes, which were in all likelihood never intended for public stage performance. Horace's *Art of Poetry* and the *Letter to Augustus* are both concerned with the theater. Augustus on his deathbed identified mime, the most popular dramatic entertainment of the period, as a metaphor for life (Suet. *Aug.* 99). Pantomime which featured solo dancing, a chorus, and often tragic subjects took over the stage (Potter, this volume), and reminds us of the richness and variety of Roman fiction in the imperial period.

1 The "Augustan Age" (44 BCE, death of Caesar–14 CE, death of Augustus)

An extraordinary literary efflorescence coincides with the rise of Augustus and the establishment of his regime. Augustus' program of national recovery and renewal dominates Augustan poetry as it both responds to and seeks to define these new political circumstances. In the years which witnessed Augustus' unrelenting rise to unchallenged control (44–31 BCE) the Roman Empire saw civil war, widespread disruptions in property, and confused allegiances. After his victory at Actium in 31 BCE ended any political challenges, Augustus embarked on an ambitious program which involved the definition of his new political power and the formulation of a national identity. Augustus widely mobilized symbolic associations to promote his image and authority. This concerted cultural policy brought about sweeping alterations in the style, content, and form of architecture, art, and literature. All the dominant poets of the period have relations with Augustus and his circle, especially through his friend Maecenas, a wealthy supporter of literature (Vergil, Horace, Propertius). The mode of the dissemination of this new program is of course central to current debates about the relationship of Latin literature to power, patronage, and the *princeps*. We should not envision a systematic agenda overseen by Augustus. Current scholarship has rightly resisted viewing Augustan texts as either simply "oppositional" or simply "orthodox" and opposes reading poetry as a prefab ideology. In seeking to move away from the terms of pro- or anti-Augustanism, scholarship has advocated a consideration of the discursive power of texts to actively participate in the articulation and construction of cultural and social values (Kennedy 1992). When the point of reception is stressed, rather than authorial or textual intent, we must acknowledge that any statement is open to appropriation for either a pro- or anti-imperial reading.

Of all the poets of the Augustan age, Vergil (70–19 BCE) is most closely associated with Augustus, although this is in no small measure due to the efforts of the *princeps* himself to appropriate both his epic and his version of the national myth. Vergil recited parts of both the *Georgics* and *Aeneid* to Augustus, and Augustus is said to have been instrumental in the posthumous publication of the *Aeneid* in 19 BCE, after Vergil's death, and it is not long before imagery from the Aeneas myth appears on public monuments such as the Ara Pacis (13–9 BCE), and in the Forum Augustum, completed in 2 BCE. The epic was hailed as an instant classic, and became part of the elite system of education, a fact which cemented Vergil's reputation as a poet of Augustus and made interpretation of his poetry even more difficult. Later poets faced with his monumental achievement also tend to construct Vergil as an Augustan, for the purposes of competition and comparison (especially Ovid and Lucan). The reality of Vergil's relationship to Augustus is doubtless much more complex than this biographical tradition suggests. Born outside the ruling class, Vergil, like his fellow poet Horace, was a small Italian landholder. Vergil may indeed have owed much to the support of Maecenas or Augustus, but all of his poetry reveals a complex, multivocal, and wholly individual interpretation of his world and times. His first work, the *Bucolics* ("Herdsmen's songs," now usually called the *Eclogues* or "Extracts"), a collection of ten poems, were written largely during the turbulent triumviral period of the late forties and early thirties BCE. The work took as its main literary model the refined pastoral poetry (*Idylls*) of the Greek poet Theocritus, who had composed at the court of the Ptolemys during the height of the scholarly and literary activity at the Alexandrian library in the third century BCE. Vergil's poems, sophisticated and refined in form and composition, present a pastoral world of shepherd-poets, but also admit elements of the political world. Recent events, such as the land confiscations in 42–41 BCE (*Ecl.* 1.9) and the assassination of Caesar (*Ecl.* 5), are acknowledged obliquely, but they are assimilated into the pastoral world and poetics of the collection. Vergil followed this with another recherché genre, the *Georgics*, a didactic treatise on farming (published in 29 BCE) which took him ten years to write. The *Georgics* are both a learned combination of a number of Greek and Roman models (Hesiod, Homer, Greek Hellenistic poetry, Lucretius, Varro, etc., see Farrell 1991; R. F. Thomas 1988) and a profound meditation on nature and the nature of the world. In the poem agriculture serves as a metaphor for man's struggles with nature, civilization, and an understanding of his universe. Many scholars have felt that Vergil's stress on the violence, violation, and struggle required in the conquering of the natural world ultimately calls into question the results of man's labors and presents a dark view of Rome's (and Octavian's) achievements (R. F. Thomas 1988, 2001; Ross 1987). In *Georgics* 1 Vergil prays for future salvation from a leader (clearly Octavian), while comparing the current situation to a charioteer being pulled along with no control over his horses (1.500–14). In the *Eclogues* Vergil had only obliquely referred to Octavian in the first poem, as the shepherd Tityrus relates how his confiscated land was restored to him through the intervention of a god-like youth; the failure to name Octavian here is perhaps a reflection of the insecurities of the time (for the argument that the eighth *Eclogue* also refers to Octavian, see Bowersock 1971). In the *Georgics* he had portrayed Octavian as a potential savior (1.500ff.) and as a divine figure (1.40ff.), and at the beginning of Book 3 he seems to promise a future work in honor of the emperor, claiming that he will build a marble temple and "place Caesar in the middle." The *Aeneid* seems to fulfil this promise, but the poem is no *Augusteid*. By choosing the legend of Aeneas Vergil liberated himself from the panegyrical tradition of national epic (Naevius, Ennius, etc.) and was able to problematize the issues of Roman history and of the principate (P. Hardie 1997a: 319). The theme is mythical, in the tradition of the Homeric epics, but at the same time historical and national, tracing the struggles of the surviving Trojan hero Aeneas to travel to Italy and found the dynasty which will lead to the foundation of Rome and directly to the family of Augustus (related to Aeneas through his son Iulus, the eponymous founder of the Julian line). Contemporary events and Augustus are mentioned in several prophecies and ecphrases; Aeneas in the Underworld is shown the future emperor: "this is the man, this one, of whom so often you have heard the promise, Caesar

Augustus, son of the deified, who shall bring once again an Age of Gold" (*Aen.* 6.791–3, trans. R. Fitzgerald). The first words of the poem, "arms and a man I sing," proclaim Vergil's intent to follow and challenge Homer's *Iliad* and *Odyssey* and create a Roman epic classic. He succeeded – indeed the poet Propertius hailed the *Aeneid* as a masterpiece greater than the *Iliad* as it was being written (2.34.66). The epic is an intertextual tour de force and his treatment of Latin hexameter verse is highly innovative and varied. Vergil's *Aeneid* seeks nothing less than to define its new age in both politico-historical and cosmological terms (P. Hardie 1986). The poem aims to explain the rise of the Roman (Augustan) state to universal dominion by tracing its origins in the past and in the process to explain the nature of Roman-ness. Aeneas' primary characteristic is a sense of duty (*pietas*), but he suffers from a lack of understanding of his mission and hence an unwillingness to pursue it ('I sail for Italy not of my own free will,' *Aen.* 4.361). In the course of the poem Aeneas suffers great personal loss, losing his father, his wife, and his lover Dido, the latter two through his own inadvertent actions. As in Vergil's other works, the voice of suffering and loss of the victims is ultimately louder than that of triumph, and he reveals again his "marked openness to the problematic elements of life and its unresolved tensions" (Conte 1994: 284). The war in Italy between the Trojans and Italians in the second half of the poem is represented as a painful civil war, causing the death of many innocent youths, calling to mind the many anxieties caused by the more recent civil wars that brought Caesar and Augustus to power. While Rome's fated destiny as world leader is guaranteed by Jupiter's concern, and at the cosmic level Rome is seen as bringing order and balance, the human cost of this victory is repeatedly called into question. In the *Aeneid* the Fury of warfare always threatens to break loose again; in Augustus' age of peace "the Gates of War will then be shut: inside, unholy Furor, squatting on cruel weapons, hands enchained behind him by a hundred links of bronze, will grind his teeth and howl with bloodied mouth" (*Aen.* 1.293–6). Already in antiquity the reception of the *Aeneid* reflects its multi-vocal nature, as poets beginning with Ovid grapple with its unresolved tensions.

In 17 BCE Vergil's contemporary Horace (65–8 BCE) was commissioned by Augustus to write a Hymn, a poem to be sung by a choir of boys and girls, in celebration of the Secular Games, a festival announcing a new age (Putnam 2000; Barchiesi 2002). This was a remarkable moment in Horace's poetic career, which had been largely devoted to more private genres, such as satire, verse letters, and, most famously, lyric odes. In his *Odes*, Horace took as his models the early Greek lyric poets (Sappho, Alcaeus) and created the first lyric poetry book in Latin (so he proudly claims at *Odes* 3.30, "I was the first to bring Aeolian song to Italian measures"), with poems on personal (erotic, sympotic, philosophical) as well as public themes. After publishing *Odes* 1–3 in 23 BCE, Horace produced a fourth book ten years later in which praise of the imperial family is prominent, but mixed with personal erotic poems. The earlier *Epodes*, poems defined by their meters and invective tone, are also profoundly engaged with both their literary antecedents (at *Epistle* 1.19.23–5 Horace claims to be the first to reveal *iambi*, Archilochean poetry, to the Romans) and the turbulent political climate of the late thirties (Oliensis 1998; Mankin 1995: 10–12). One of Horace's abiding themes in all of his work is the relationship between the poet and his great patron, whether Maecenas, with whom, like Vergil, he was closely associated, or with the emperor (Oliensis 1998). We see Horace developing strategies for preserving aesthetic and personal independence within the new social and political structure, in which there were new demands on the poet's voice. These strategies for dealing with the ever-changing conditions of speech in the empire will prove useful also for later imperial authors. His *Epistles* 2.1, a poem addressed to Augustus, articulates both a "didactics and a poetics for the Principate" (Barchiesi 2001b: 82), which reveals the central place of the emperor in the construction of imperial poetics (see Feeney 2002).

There had already developed in Rome other more personal forms of poetry, such as epigram and elegy. Catullus and the "new poets" of the early and mid-first century had written on varied personal themes, especially the erotic, and perfected a learned refinement of style and content which greatly influenced Vergil and later poets. Erotic elegy (so called because it was love poetry composed in the meter known as the elegiac couplet) was practiced in the Augustan period by the poets Propertius (c.50–16/2? BCE), Tibullus (55?–19), and Ovid (43 BCE–19 CE). In these collections the poet writes in the persona of a lover "autobiographical" poems about his erotic experiences, which follow a set of predictable rules and literary conventions. As with Catullus' Lesbia, significant poetic pseudonyms are used for the mistresses (Tibullus' Delia and Propertius' Cynthia both refer to Apolline inspiration; Ovid's Corinna, like Lesbia, is the name of a Greek poetess), about whose social status the poets are deliberately vague. These mistresses often serve as ciphers for the poet's own compositions (Wyke 1989; Keith 1994). Ovid, typically, makes this most overt in poem *Amores* 3.1 where Tragedy and Elegy appear to him as female figures.

One of the most characteristic features of elegy is its tendency to communicate at two levels; love and poetry-writing are united in the figure of the lover-poet and the two activities are made parallel. So when Propertius claims, "I was born unfit for weapons, love is the warfare the fates wish me to undergo" (1.6), he equates his life of love with the composition of elegy (defined as *not* about warfare [*armis*], that is, epic). The elegists create in their works poetic identities and a poetic code which is formulated in terms directly opposed to the prevailing moral and social ideology (Kennedy 1993). They advocate a life of love and poetry, rather than political duty and military pursuits. This oppositional strategy by which elegy defines itself also involves gender and social reversals. The poets construct their mistresses as their masters (*dominae*) and play the part of slave; so Tibullus declares, "Slave to a mistress! Yes, in recognition of my fate bidding now farewell to the freedom of my birthright I accept the harshest slavery" (2.4.1–3, trans. G. Lee). The implications of this poetic code have proven difficult to interpret. The elegiac poets seem to express dissent from and even resistance to prevailing ideals, yet opposition may be read as validation of the ideal by contrast (Conte 1989; Wallace-Hadrill 1985).

The poetics of this self-professed "lesser" genre also requires a consistent rejection of the national and celebratory themes of epic. In "apologies" or "refusals" (*recusationes*) the elegiac poets express their unwillingness or profess inability to write a grander kind of poetry (usually laudatory epic). So Propertius explains that if fate had made him capable of writing about heroes he would sing about Caesar's wars, but he has not the powers (2.1). Yet Tibullus and Propertius also include in their collections poems of praise of public figures, Tibullus of his patron Messala (1.7, 2.5), while Propertius, like Horace, eventually published a fourth book of poetry which dealt with Augustan themes in a series of poems dealing with the origins of a number of

Roman monuments. Like Horace's fourth book of odes, erotic subjects are still juxtaposed and combined with the national, such as in the tale of Tarpeia (4.4), a woman punished for love and forever associated with a Roman landmark. In this way, private concerns and space never wholly yield to the national. Finally, it is also in love elegy that we have our only example of a female poet at Rome, in the six short poems of Sulpicia, a poetess associated with Tibullus and preserved with his collection. Her first elegy reveals a distinctively female perspective in the expressed hesitation at publishing her loves: "Finally a love has come which would cause me more shame were Rumor to conceal it rather than lay it bare for all" ([Tibullus] 3.13, trans. J. Snyder).

Ovid is often viewed as a transitional poet, bridging the reigns of Augustus and Tiberius. His poetry exerted a huge influence on the development of the Latin literary language and style, even if Vergil remained the primary literary model to whom later authors respond. His exile by Augustus in 8 CE forever changed, both for Ovid and for us, how we read his earlier productions and also marks the beginning of a decline in imperial tolerance. Ovid, exiled, as he tells us, because of a poem (he is probably referring to the *Art of Love*, a how-to manual for lovers) and an "error" (*Tr.* 2.207), was never recalled by Augustus or by Tiberius. The *Art of Love* provocatively advocates adultery (against which Augustus had enacted new legislation) and suggests a number of Augustus' new public monuments as good places to pick up dates. In Book 1 Romulus is held up as a model for rape, yet in the same book appears praise of Gaius, Augustus' grandson, and this work evidently was tolerated for at least eight years or so after its publication (see B. Gibson 2003: 37–43 for a recent discussion of the dating issues of the poem). Although once regarded as politically detached, Ovid is increasingly viewed as an author very much engaged in the discourses of his times. Faced with the Augustan revolution as a *fait accompli*, Ovid responds by unmasking and revealing the underpinnings and constructions of both political and literary forms (Feeney 1991: 210–32, 247–9; Myers 1994; P. Hardie 1997b). Ovidian poetry is known for its irony or meta-literary self-consciousness and its seeming awareness of the postmodern issues of fictionality and textuality. Ovid had begun as a love poet, producing a variety of amatory elegiac works. In these he systematically exposed the generic codes of elegiac love. He began his *Amores* not, as traditionally, with a declaration of love for a mistress (see Propertius 2.1.4, "my only inspiration is a girl"), but with the choice of a genre and a lack of topic. This poem also marks the beginning of a lifelong engagement with Vergil's work; instead of telling us what the *Amores* are about, we learn first what they will *not* be about, *arma,* the first word of the *Aeneid*. In the *Heroides*, a series of verse letters written by heroines, Dido herself delivers a deadly critique of Aeneas' actions in the *Aeneid* (*Her.* 4), claiming that Aeneas was the cause of her death and that she should have learned from the fate of his wife Creusa. Typically, Ovid likes to explore different perspectives, frequently female.

Ovid's two longest works, the *Fasti* and the *Metamorphoses*, are masterpieces of great originality, and in many ways as a pair represent his response to Vergil (P. Hardie 1991: 47). The epic *Metamorphoses*, a 15-book compendium of Greek and Roman myth, challenges Vergil both in its cosmological scope and its intertextual nature. Ovid tells us in the proem that his poem will be a universal history, proceeding "from the creation of the world to his own time." The many tales of metamorphosis throughout the poem account for the origins of the natural world and the poem ends with the "metamorphosis" of Julius Caesar into a god (and looks forward to the apotheosis of Augustus). Within the scope of this epic, Ovid modulates between many genres (hymn, pastoral, didactic, elegy, tragedy, etc.) and engages with a vast range of Greek and Roman literature. When the poem reaches Italy in its final books, Ovid retells the story of Aeneas, in a manner that highlights not Rome, or fate, but rather personal stories of metamorphosis, in keeping with the rest of the poem (Tissol 1997; Myers forthcoming). Thus the Sibyl does not show Aeneas his great Roman descendants, but tells the sad tale of Apollo's love for her and his punishment of her when she refused to comply with his wishes (*Met.* 14.101–53). When prophecies of Rome's greatness appear in Book 15, they are spoken by the philosopher Pythagoras, whose main goal is to stress the mutability of all things, even eternal Rome! Ovid's depiction of this profoundly unstable world of the *Metamorphoses*, governed by arbitrary divine powers, has implications for his understanding of life under the empire.

Ovid's *Fasti*, a versification in elegiac couplets of the Roman religious calendar (of which we have only the first six months and are unsure whether he ever composed the other half [see Barchiesi 1997b]), parallels Augustus' own manipulations of the Roman religious year and challenges his appropriation of the discourses of religion and antiquarianism in the service of the dissemination of his new values. Like the *Metamorphoses*, the poem is aetiological, providing explanations and historical causes for various Roman religious rituals and festivals. In the poem praise of the imperial family alternates with erotic and fanciful myth in often contradictory and uncomfortable juxtapositions. There is the peculiarly un-balanced treatment of the Ides of March in *Fasti* 3, where Ovid devotes the greater part of his lengthy narrative to the festival celebrated on that day in honor of the minor deity Anna Perenna, whereas the apotheosis of Julius Caesar is dealt with in a mere 14 lines (697–710, see Newlands 1995). The two-faced figure of Janus which opens the poem has been suggested as a symbol of the possible dual readings of the poem, as both encomiastic and oppositional (Barchiesi 1997a: 230–7).

2 The Neronian Age (55–68)

It is during the reign of the last of the Julio-Claudians, Nero, that there is again a notable explosion of literature, due in no small measure to the encouragement and support of this young philhellenic emperor who fancied himself an artist, poet, and performer. The emperor too is directly responsible for the premature and tragic ends of the major writers of this period, Petronius, Seneca, and Lucan, all forced to commit suicide in 65–66 CE after being associated with a failed conspiracy to overthrow the emperor. As poets and emperors become closer, so poetry becomes a more dangerous enterprise. Politically-committed high poetry, such as that of Vergil and Horace, is no longer prevalent. Lucan, the one poet to write an historical epic in this period, although not on contemporary history, seems to have suffered imperial disfavor through his choice of topic. Nero himself had a predilection for epic on Trojan themes. Under Nero's campaign of artistic promotion, public competitions on the Greek model were established, furthering the expectations of literature as spectacle.

Upon his arrival at Rome the young poet Lucan (39–65 CE), from a well-connected family from Spain that included his uncle Seneca, rose meteorically to became a member of the emperor Nero's circle of friends, gaining literary fame for tragedy, occasional verse, and other compositions, as well as an early quaestorship. His fall from favor was just as abrupt. He was forced to commit suicide at age 26 in 65 CE, after being suspected of participating in the Pisonian conspiracy to overthrow the emperor. Nero had evidently before this event taken umbrage with Lucan and ended his political and poetical careers, banning his public performances. Although the versions of the rupture differ in the ancient biographies and among modern scholars, some offer the suggestion that Nero may have forbidden Lucan to publish or recite out of artistic jealousy, while others suggest that the republicanism of Lucan's loyalties expressed in the epic he was composing must have offended the emperor (perhaps only the first three books). His epic *Bellum Ciuile* (*Civil war* or *Pharsalia*), which survived underground (9 1/2 books, unfinished), is an account of the combat between Caesar and Pompey for supremacy in Rome and their final battle in Thessaly at Pharsalus in 49–8 BCE. This was a minefield of a topic, as we saw in the case of Cremutius Cordus, and Lucan must have been aware of its hazardous nature. Horace had warned Asinius Pollio of the danger of writing on the civil war of 49 BCE in *Odes* 2.1, telling him "you are walking, as it were, over still smoldering ashes." In Tacitus' *Dialogue Concerning Orators*, with a dramatic date of 75 CE (Vespasian's reign), Curatius Maternus is clearly depicted as courting ruin with his tragedy entitled *Cato*. Later, a number of writers of biographies of Cato the Younger, who committed suicide after the defeat of the republicans rather than submit to the tyranny of Caesar, were punished by Domitian. Lucan's epic is overtly political and rebellious in form and content and constitutes a strong denunciation of Caesar and his successors. Yet at the beginning of the epic (33–45) Lucan inserted fulsome praise of Nero, anticipating his apotheosis and proclaiming him his muse. This dedication has caused commentators ancient and modern acute difficulties when considered in relation to the rest of the poem (for different views on interpreting imperial panegyric, see Dewar 1994; Ahl 1984). Even ancient scholars detected irony in Lucan's expressed concern about the divinized Nero's weight tipping the balance of the heavenly sphere. More disturbingly ironic are his claims that the horrifying Roman bloodshed was a worthy price to pay for the coming of Nero, when the poem relentlessly condemns imperial power and the violence and moral turpitude of civil war. At 7.640–1 Lucan claims that at Pharsalus, "we were overthrown for all time to come; all future generations doomed to slavery were conquered by those swords." The poem is an indictment of both sides and the two leaders' desire for sole power, but Cato stands out as a moral exemplar. Lucan's epic is also in revolt against the predominant features of Vergil, namely in its omission of the traditional divine machinery of the gods. The removal of divine explanation further underlines the utter despair and incomprehension at the random victory of the wrong side (Feeney 1991: 279). In a world where values have been undermined, Lucan claims, "unspeakable crime shall be called heroism" (1.667–8).

A work of a new type appears at this time in Petronius' *Satyricon*, an innovative work of fiction written in a combination of prose and verse. This remarkable hybrid literary form has precedents in earlier Latin literary forms, but is in many ways unique and extremely difficult to interpret. Petronius (d. 66 CE) too was a member of Nero's court, consul in 65 CE and later master of court entertainment. He too died a suicide by the command of Nero. The work demonstrates above all the intense literariness of Nero's age and court, encompassing almost all genres and engaging in parody and critique of contemporary literature and literary criticism. All we have remaining of what we call the first Roman novel are excerpts and fragments, in all, the remnants of four to six books out of more than 16. A recent scholar translates its title as "A Tale of Satyr-like Lust and Depravity" (Courtney 2001). A first-person narrator, Encolpius, narrates his farcical misadventures, mostly of a sexual nature. These adventures seem to follow patterns suggesting epic parody (pursuit by an angry deity [Priapus], storms at sea, a visit to the Underworld). Others suggest that many of the topoi of the developing Greek novel tradition may be spoofed, especially in the amoral and promiscuous sexual relationships engaged in by Encolpius and his friends. Encolpius' social status is probably that of a freedman and the novel is remarkable for its inclusion of freedman society, especially in the longest surviving fragment, the dinner party of the nouveau riche Trimalchio. Petronius' use of the naïve first-person narrator allows for no reliable moral critique and the tone remains ironic and difficult to pin down, yet the work clearly exposes much of the excess of contemporary society in the tradition of satire. Contemporary literary trends, such as the popularity of declamation, pretensions to literary learning and historical epic (some have thought Lucan a target), are ridiculed. After Petronius, the only Latin novel to survive complete from antiquity is *The Metamorphoses* or *Golden Ass* by (?Lucius) Apuleius (c.125–70 CE), born in Africa (Algeria), educated in Carthage. This novel (all prose) is less a product of the Latin literary tradition than of Greek literary and philosophical traditions (see Rife, this volume).

3 The Flavians and After (96–138)

After Domitian's death in 96 CE denunciation was the order of the day. Yet during his reign, there had been support for letters. Martial, Quintilian, Statius, Silius Italicus, and Valerius Flaccus had all lavished fulsome praise on Domitian and the Flavians. Statius' reputation has suffered the most due to the fact that he did not outlive Domitian and so survive to denounce him, as did Tacitus, Pliny, Juvenal, and Martial. Juvenal and Martial both complain about the conditions of patronage of poets at this time and later, but the works of Martial and Statius and the letters of Pliny the Younger reveal a vast array of imperial and private patronage. Significantly, however, non-imperial patronage is restricted to the lesser genres of poetry; epic and encomium remain an imperial prerogative. The constraints imposed by the despotic rule of Domitian which are freely complained of after his death may also be detected in the literature written during his reign.

Juvenal's *Satires* (written between 112–30 CE) paint the darkest picture of life under Domitian and under later emperors as well, during the early years of what were heralded by many other writers as much improved times. Anger and indignation at the perceived vices of contemporary society, values, and even literature are the hallmark of Juvenal's voice. The moral corruption and degradation of Roman society impel him to write satire (*Sat.* 1). Although Juvenal writes during the reigns of the "good emperors" Trajan (98–117) and Hadrian (117–38), he writes mainly about the time of Domitian (see esp. *Sat.* 4). He explains that it is safer to write only about the dead, just as Horace in his *Satires* had declined to attack the living (2.1.39–41) and Martial claims "to spare individuals and talk about vices" (10.33.9–10). Too often taken as an accurate view of corrupt imperial society, the *Satires* should be understood to present a profoundly distorted and exaggerated picture of Juvenal's times. Taking an extreme position of traditional conservatism, based on idealized national views of a virtuous Roman past, Juvenal expresses disgust with what he sees as the perversion of traditional class and social hierarchies, indicting, among other things, effeminate men, city life, the nobility, foreigners, luxury, women, patronage, and the imperial court of Domitian. The exaggeration is deliberate, as is Juvenal's choice of an angry voice for his poetic persona, and should be recognized as a feature of the genre (see S. Braund 1988, 1996; Freudenburg 2001).

The Flavians promoted and advertised a moral restoration after the years of Nero and the ensuing struggles for power (Tac. *Ann.* 3.55) and there is in this period a revival of the highest poetic genre, epic. Domitian's own early epic composition is praised by Quintilian (*Inst.* 10.1.91) and seems to have been on historical themes (Coleman 1986: 3089–91). Certainly epic on imperial themes was highly desirable and the creation of new public contests in poetry created more venues for this type of encomiastic composition. At the Alban Games of 90 held on Domitian's estate at Alba Longa, Statius won with a poem on Domitian's wars with the Germans and Dacians (*Silv.* 4.2.65–7). All three of the major surviving Flavian epics include passages of encomium of the Flavian dynasty; their themes, however, are far removed from contemporary or recent history, and are taken mainly from Greek myth, with one exception. Imperial epics suffer from a sense of post-Vergilian belatedness, but engage in deeply intertextual and interpretive ways with their predecessors (P. Hardie 1993). Silius Italicus (25/6–101 CE, consul in 68, proconsul of Asia in c.77/8) has the dubious distinction of surviving both Nero and Domitian and of writing the longest extant Roman epic, the *Punica*, 17 books and still unfinished. The epic took as its theme the second Punic war with Hannibal, an historical event safely in the distant past. Martial curries favor with Silius by flattering him as a poet and wealthy patron of the arts (*Ep.* 4.14, 6.64), while Pliny the Younger appraises his poetry as uninspired (*Ep.* 3.7). Silius was known for his personal reverence of Vergil in his life (he worshipped at his tomb and celebrated his birthday), and his epic follows Vergilian poetic practices closely in language and imagery, with full divine participation, and constitutes in some ways a sequel to the *Aeneid*, in which the Punic war was prophesized (Feeney 1991: 303–4; P. Hardie 1993: 14–16). His conservatism is also expressed in the air of nostalgia about his work, emblematic of the overwhelming sense of decline that is typical of this period. Valerius Flaccus' *Argonautica* (eight books remain) took for its theme the familiar one of Jason's quest for the golden fleece and, though technically sound and revealing a great deal of self-awareness of the literary tradition of his theme, the poem is generally considered the least successful of the Flavian epics (new evaluations include Feeney 1991; Hershkowitz 1998; P. Schenk 1999).

Statius' *Thebaid*, published in 91 or 92 (after 12 years of composition), also expresses his reverence towards Vergil: in an epilogue he warns his epic, "do not rival the divine *Aeneid*, but follow from afar and always venerate its footsteps" (*Theb.* 12.816–17, see Pollman 2001). Yet the poem in many ways is the most original and compelling of the later epics and has received much recent attention. It relates the expedition of the Seven against Thebes, when the sons of Oedipus, Eteocles and Polynices, fought over the throne of Thebes. Statius avows his deference to Vergil, but his exposition of his theme of internecine warfare owes much to Lucan, whom we know Statius also admired (see his praise of Lucan in *Silv.* 2.7, and Ahl 1982; Malamud 1995). Statius' proem echoes Lucan in its declaration of the theme of "wars between brothers" (1.1). Like Lucan, Statius evinces an interest in setting forth the horrors of tyranny, violent passion, and family strife. His tendency to allegorize the gods heralds a significant new literary trend (Feeney 1991: 364–91). The profound pessimism of the epic in its emphasis on the inexorability of fate and the horrors of despotism have led many to see in this story of Greek myth contemporary political relevance (see Dominik 1994; McGuire 1997). The portrayal of Jupiter's autocratic rule and the struggle for power on the divine level are interesting in the light of Flavian domestic struggles and Domitian's own cultivation of his association with Jupiter (Feeney 1991: 359). This identification Statius and Martial are eager to reinforce in their short poems (see *Silv.* 4.2, Martial *Ep.* 8.36, 9.11–13, 16–17). Juvenal was later to claim that Statius recited the *Thebaid* to great popularity but that lack of financial support led him to compose mime librettos (*Sat.* 7.82–7). Juvenal suggests that Statius prostituted his art, displaying his great epic to the public, but it remains unclear whether Statius or the contemporary conditions of patronage are to blame for this behavior. Statius praises Domitian at the opening of the epic and states at its end that Domitian has deemed it worthy of recognition (12.814) – conventional praise by now, but also a request for the imperial support or favor he so desperately needs.

Statius, like Martial, relied on the support of socially prominent and wealthy patrons in a way that suggests he was more dependent than many earlier Roman poets. His social status seems to be rather anomalous among the Latin poets of his period. At a time when most poets were increasingly of higher status, we have no clear evidence that Statius or his father ever reached the equestrian rank. The fact that father and son competed in the literary festivals seems to suggest otherwise, as no other well-known poets are known to have done so. Martial advertises the social and political, as well as material, benefits he received from his patrons, such as the honorific post of military tribune by which he achieved equestrian status (*Ep.* 2.91, 3.95), although he continues to complain of the hardships of the life of poetry in an age of diminished patronage (e.g., *Ep.* 8.56, 1.107). Statius' *Silvae* and Martial's *Epigrams*, although quite different in nature, are both representative of important trends in literary taste and social patterns, revealing areas of poetic patronage open to private patrons and the lively interest in literary pursuits. Both collections contain poems written largely for specific occasions, probably first recited, then circulated in published form (Martial liked to issue his books of *Epigrams* at the time of the Saturnalia). As opportunities for public political activity in the imperial period become more circumscribed, the private social life of the elite emerges increasingly as an arena for encomiastic poetry, and the publicity potential of the "minor" genres of epigram and occasional poetry is acknowledged. The letters of Pliny the Younger especially reveal the enthusiastic dilettante poetic composition and recitation undertaken by the upper classes.

Statius' *Silvae*, a collection of occasional poetry in various meters, but mainly hexameter, reveals many of the opportunities and constraints of writing poetry under Domitian. The collection contains a number of panegyrical poems on Domitian. In 4.2 the poet describes a dinner party he has been invited to at Domitian's palace, a structure whose massive archaeological remains on the Palatine confirm its intended monumentality. In this poem Statius equates Domitian with Jupiter. Elsewhere as constructor of the *via Domitiana*, Domitian is figured as a miracle worker (4.3). But the collection also contains many poems written for private patrons and these deal primarily with private themes, from marriages, birthdays, and consolations to descriptions of luxurious possessions (P. White 1974; A. Hardie 1983). Such themes betoken the changed political climate in imperial Rome, which saw as suspect the traditional political *virtus* of the Roman elite. This new emphasis on domestic activities, both architectural and intellectual, is reflected in the work of Statius' contemporaries Martial and the younger Pliny. Pliny complains of the restricted scope for acquisition of glory by senators, now that great deeds have become the prerogative of the emperor (*Ep.* 3.21.3). Within this atmosphere we can understand the pressure on poets to provide and publicize pleasing images of upper-class domestic life. Statius' published poems display and advertise the symbolic value of villa life as a manifestation of his patrons' aristocratic investment in cultural leisure activities (Myers 2000; Newlands 2002). They also hint at the restrictions and dangers facing the elite under Domitian. Both Statius and Pliny the Younger (e.g., *Ep.* 1.3, 9.36) associate the leisure of the prominent Roman with literary activity, thus distancing their lives from suggestions of political disapproval or resistance. For Statius, this self-avowed "lesser work" was both a proud display of his artistry and literary skill, as well as a confession of his dependency on private patronage and the constrictions on his choice of themes under Domitian. Statius' prose prefaces to *Silvae* 1–4 reveal his cautious maneuverings between his dependency on patronage and his poetic independence.

The *Epigrams* of Martial (written mainly under Domitian, except for books 10–12 under Nerva and Trajan) reveal the same community of patronage as Statius, i.e. both private and imperial, although their tone is different. The emperor Domitian receives a number of poems of praise (e.g. 5.1–3, 5–6, 6.1–4, 8.1–2, 4, 11), and at the beginning of Book 4 Martial says that he has presented the poems to him before publication. Many of the same private patrons reappear and the same events are commemorated, although Martial never names Statius. Epigram traditionally takes a comic-satiric tone and Martial makes wit and the closing quip his trademark style. Martial's books contain a miscellany of themes literary, panegyrical, pornographic, and sympotic. Like the satirist, life is his stated theme ("read this, of which life itself can say 'it's mine'," *Ep.* 10.4.10), but epigram eschews a moralizing position, espousing wit rather than vitriol. After his retirement to Spain Martial issued only one further book of epigrams (Book 12). Apart from the last books of Martial and the early poems of Juvenal, no substantial Latin poetry survives from the reigns of Nerva and Trajan (see Bardon 1952 on the evidence).

CHAPTER TWENTY-THREE

Greek Fiction

Joseph L. Rife

Prose fiction is the preferred literary form of our age: we keep it in our homes, we routinely read it, we share it with our children, we turn to it for diversion and enjoyment. Modern readers might be surprised to learn that fiction flourished in the Greek world under Roman rule. Certain common fictional elements, such as separated lovers and distant travels, were already present in Homer and Herodotus, and the development of exotic ethnography, sentimentalism, and type-casting, also features of fiction, can be traced in Hellenistic literature, from the biography of Alexander the Great to love poetry and New Comedy. But it was during the first three centuries of the Roman Empire that fiction emerged as a distinct mode of narrative representation and found its voice among the educated residents of the eastern Mediterranean (Table 23.1). The efflorescence of fiction belonged to a larger cultural phenomenon known as the Greek renaissance, or the Second Sophistic (for recent surveys see Goldhill 2001a, Swain 1996, and Whitmarsh 2001). This chapter will examine Greek fiction as both a sophisticated form of entertainment and a dynamic medium for self-identification.

1 Varieties of Greek Fiction

Greek fiction will confound any critic in search of a genre because it took many shapes. The most consistent form is conveniently, albeit anachronistically, called the ancient novel. Of all the varieties of Greek fiction, the novel is perhaps most easily recognized by modern readers on account of its legacy in the vernacular traditions of western European romance. Five novels have survived intact, those by Chariton, Xenophon of Ephesus, Achilles Tatius, Longus, and Heliodorus; another attributed to Lucian about a man transformed into an ass is an epitome of a full-length picaresque; two more have survived in Byzantine epitomes, those by Antonius Diogenes and Iamblichus; and some two dozen papyri certainly or probably

Table 23.1 Timeline of Greek fiction under the Roman Empire

Date	Author, work, date
1 CE	
	Ninus romance, fragmentary novel (c.1–50?)
	Metiochus and Parthenope, fragmentary novel (c.1–100?)
50	*Chion of Heraclea*, epistolary novel (c.1–100?)
	Chariton, *Chaereas and Callirhoe*, complete novel (c.50–125)
	Xenophon of Ephesus, *Ephesian Tale*, complete novel (c.50–150)
	Antonius Diogenes, *The Wonders beyond Thule*, epitomized novel (c.75–150)
	[Lucian], *The Ass*, epitomized novel (c.90–150)
100	Dio Chrysostom, *Euboean Oration*, fictionalizing oration (c.100–15)
	Dictys of Crete, *Memoir of the Trojan War*, fictional war account (66–c.200)
	Lucian, *True Histories*, fictional travel account (c.150–80)
150	Lucian, *How to Write History*, critical essay on historiography (166)
	Iamblichus, *Babylonian Tale*, epitomized novel (166–80)
	Achilles Tatius, *Leucippe and Cleitophon*, complete novel (c.150–200)
	Alciphron, *Letters*, fictional letters (c.150–225)
	Longus, *Daphnis and Chloe*, complete novel (c.175–225)
200	Aelian, *Letters of Farmers*, fictional letters (c.190–235)
	Philostratus, *In Honor of Apollonius*, biography of a holy man (217–c.30)
	Philostratus, *Heroic Discourse*, dialogue on the heroes of the Trojan war (c.222–35)
	Heliodorus, *Ethiopian Tale*, complete novel (c.200–50)
250	Quintus of Smyrna, *Post-Homerics*, epic poem about the Trojan war (c.200–300)
300	

belonging to other novels are known. Several of these works essentially tell the same story of lovers separated and reunited after dangerous adventures in foreign lands. The protagonists come close to death as they overcome assaults by villainous bandits on land and sea, the perils of shipwreck and war, enslavement and torture, and a parade of rivals for the affection of the beloved. The novelists embellished this template with innovations in narrative design, the portrayal of sexuality and gender, and geographic and temporal setting. The earliest known novels might not have predated the early first century CE, and the seven major novels can be reasonably dated between roughly 50 and 250 CE. It is difficult to trace any organic evolution in the form over time. In any event, such a critical approach would impede or even distort the assessment of each work as a singular, deliberate product of a creative mind at work in a particular place and time (for summaries see Bowie 1985; Fusillo 1989; Reardon 1991; Bowersock 1994; Morgan and Stoneman 1994; Schmeling 2003; Swain 1996: 101–31; Swain 1999; Holzberg 2001; the Petronian Society Ancient Novel web page at www.chss.montclair.edu/classics/petron/PSNNOVEL.HTML).

Although the novels are widely considered the prime examples of Greek fiction, they can be most fully appreciated as part of a larger family of contemporary prose born from the same fictional imagination. Related works by Lucian, Dio, and Philostratus of Athens fall under the traditional rubrics of satire, rhetoric, and biography.

Lucian of Samosata was a professional orator who wrote dialogues, orations, and essays ridiculing contemporary intellectuals, religious zealots, and self-absorbed aristocrats. His most famous work (*True Histories*) is a mock travelogue of a fantastic voyage by a band of intrepid explorers who sail west as far as the Moon and the Islands of the Blessed, recalling Homer's Odysseus and adumbrating Swift's Gulliver (Bompaire 1958; Hall 1981; C. P. Jones 1986; Branham 1989). Dio of Prusa, nicknamed *Chrysostomus* ("golden-mouth"), was a famous orator of the generation before Lucian who discussed a wide range of political, moral, and literary topics. One of his speeches concerning poverty and urban society (*Oration 7 = Euboean Speech*) contains an idyllic portrait of peasant life on the Aegean island of Euboea (Russell 1992: 8–13, 109–58; Swain 2001). Flavius Philostratus of Athens was an intellectual of many talents who lived after Lucian and probably around the time of the novelist Heliodorus. His biography of Apollonius of Tyana (*In Honor of Apollonius*), the legendary neo-Pythagorean holy man, narrated the sage's expansive travels to India and throughout the Mediterranean, his thaumaturgy, his communion with ghosts, his apology to the charge of sorcery before Domitian in Rome, and his divine ascension. Philostratus also wrote a fictional dialogue (*Heroic Discourse*) between a Phoenician merchant awaiting fair winds on the Thracian Chersonese and a vine-dresser who tends the land surrounding the ancient tumulus of Protesilaus, the first Greek killed in the Trojan War, and holds conversations with the hero (Anderson 1986; Bowie 1978, 1994a; Maclean and Aitken 2001).

Two other types of fiction flourished alongside the novel: epistolography and a brand of mythography that can be called Homeric revisionism. Two younger contemporaries of Lucian, Alciphron and Aelian, wrote imaginary letters to fishermen, farmers, parasites, and courtesans living in and around classical Athens. The epistolary impulse of the age also produced pseudonymous letters by great political and intellectual figures of the Greek past, such as Themistocles, Socrates, and the Cynic philosophers Crates and Diogenes. One unknown author, probably of the first century CE, fabricated an entire dossier of 17 letters allegedly penned by the minor historical figure Chion of Heraclea in the Pontus. These described his travels to Byzantium and Athens, where he studied under Plato, and then back to Heraclea, where he led the coup d'état known from other sources (Rosenmeyer 2001). Homeric revisionism has already been noted in the dialogue on heroes by Philostratus. Another example, which probably dates to the late first or second century CE (*Memoirs*), purports to be an eyewitness account of the Trojan War written in the Phoenician alphabet by Dictys of Crete, who fought under the mythical king Idomeneus. A century or two later, around the same time as or shortly after Philostratus and probably Heliodorus, Quintus of Smyrna composed a revisionist epic in 14 books on events at Troy between the *Iliad* and the *Odyssey*, covering much of the same ground as the Epic Cycle but revising the canonical tradition (Vian 1959, 1963: vii–lv; Merkle 1989, 2003).

2 *Plasma* and Verisimilitude

The major representatives of Greek fiction during the Roman Empire comprised a spectrum of forms, hardly a coherent genre. The novel and the epistle followed conventional formats, but they overlapped thematically and stylistically with rhetorical works, dramatic dialogues, and travel accounts. It is telling that ancient readers had no single word for the novel. The novelist Chariton called his story an "erotic passion" (*pathos erôtikon*, 1.1), echoing the summaries of love stories collected by the Hellenistic elegist Parthenius (*erôtika pathêmata*). The emperor Julian (*Ep.* 89.301b) probably meant the novels when he condemned "love stories" (*erôtikas hypotheseis*), and Byzantine scholars used a similar term (*erôtika*) when referring to specific novels (Socr. *Hist. Eccl.* 5.22; *Suda s. vv.* Ach. {S}tat., Xen. Eph.; cf. Iamb.). In contrast, the ninth-century epitomator Photius used the term "story of action" (*dramatikon, syntagma dramatikon, drama*) for the novels by Heliodorus, Achilles Tatius, Iamblichus, and Antonius Diogenes (*Bib.* 50a7; 65b16; 73b24, 28–9; 109a7). Lucian's account of the fantastic voyage was simply called "stories" (*diêgêmata*). Chariton (1.1.1, 5.1.2) and Xenophon of Ephesus (1.1.16, 8.3.1, 8.5.2) used the verbal form of the same word, "to tell a story" (*diêgeisthai*), when describing their own literary activity. These words show that the novels were narratives about personal experience, but this alone does not distinguish them from many other literary forms. The names of other varieties of fiction explicitly associated them with established genres. The account of the Trojan War by Dictys was, naturally, a "commentary" (*ephêmeris*), while the writings by Dio, Philostratus, Alciphron, and Aelian bore the standard titles of speeches, biographies, and letters. This heterogeneity in nomenclature mirrors the formal diversity that is an essential quality of Greek fiction.

While these works do not share a unity of form, they do share a unity of representation (Rispoli 1988; Morgan 1993; Bowersock 1994: 1–27; Potter 1999a: 9–18). They all describe events that never happened but look as though they might have. Ancient rhetorical theory recognized three classes of narrative representation according to truth-content: "history" (Gr. *historia*, Lat. *historia*), which presents that which actually happened and is "true" (*alêthês*), "fiction" (Gr. *plasma*, Lat. *argumentum*), which presents that which did not happen but is "like true" (*hôs alêthês*), and "myth" (Gr. *mythos*, Lat. *fabula*), which presents that which did not happen and is "false" (*pseudês*). Asclepiades of Myrleia apparently developed this tripartite scheme in the early first century BCE (S.E. *M.* 252, 263–4), and critics repeated it with slight variations throughout the Roman era (Barwick 1928; Potter 1999a: 13–14, 171 n. 24 summarizes the ancient testimony, to which can be added Serv. *ad* Verg. *Aen.* 1.235 and Isid. *Etym.* 1.44.5). The choice of the word *plasma* is intriguing, because its Greek root (*plas-*), like the Latin root of "fiction" (*fing-*), connotes the creative act of molding an elastic, amorphous medium into a recognizable shape. Fiction, therefore, is not simply the antithesis of history, a discourse that inquires into the truth. A work of fiction is a literary invention that sculpts story matter into a story-form with verisimilitude, or a likeness to real, familiar, "true" experience.

The varieties of Greek fiction can be viewed within this theoretical framework. Admittedly, ancient discussions of narrative representation usually adduced comedy and mime as examples of *plasma*, and they did not explicitly apply the term to the novels or other forms of prose fiction. It should, however, be noted that Macrobius, a grammarian of Late Antique Rome, used the same critical language when he called the Latin novels by Petronius and Apuleius "realistic narratives full of the invented situations of lovers" (*argumenta fictis casibus amatorum repleta, In Somn.* 1.2.7–8). Indeed, from a modern viewpoint, the novels were remarkably under-theorized in antiquity. The only certain references to them – the letter by Julian and another by Philostratus (*Ep.* 66) addressed to a Chariton who might well have been the novelist – scorned them as insubstantial, ephemeral, and deceptive. Apparently some readers considered the novels mere diversions unworthy of serious attention. Adopting a different viewpoint, the great Christian scholar Origen was ashamed that the Trojan War, which everyone believed really happened, had been debased by fictitious stories (*C. Cels.* 1.42). Lucian himself complained that the deluge of historiography during the Armenian and Parthian campaigns of 162–6 CE was full of poetic embellishment and mythic content, comparing it to the absurd figure of a burly athlete strutting in drag (*Hist. Conscr.* 8). But, as might be expected from this sardonic wit, Lucian's hypocrisy spreads thick: he begins and ends the same tirade over bad history with fictional accounts of a deadly epidemic of Euripideanism at Abdera, a lost chapter in the life of Diogenes at Corinth, and a hitherto unknown inscription inside the lighthouse at Alexandria (*Hist. Conscr.* 1–3, 62). Whether their tone was critical or satirical, all of these readers were bothered by novels that masqueraded as histories or novel histories that rewrote actual events, like the Trojan and Parthian wars. Fiction was an ambiguous and risky diegetic (narrative) medium because it blurred the boundary between what was real and what was not. Of course, not all fictional works occupied the same place on the scale from falsehood to truth – there is a wide gap between Lucian's trip to the Moon and Dio's trip to Euboea – but they all fell somewhere between the two extremes.

The authors of Greek fiction generated verisimilitude using various tricks in imitation of the historian's craft. One favorite ploy was the citation of fabricated evidence. The novelists mastered this game, often adapting it for more than simple authentication. Xenophon wrote that the adventures of Habrocomes and Anthia had in fact been inscribed on a stone they dedicated in the Artemiseion at Ephesus (Xen. Eph. 5.15). Along similar lines, Longus wrote that, while hunting on Lesbos, he found a sacred grove where he viewed a painting with scenes of pastoral romance, which, once interpreted, told the story of his novel (Long. *pr.*). Achilles Tatius began his novel with a lavish digression on a painting of Europa and the bull he had seen in Sidon just before he met Cleitophon, the novel's hero, and heard his life story, the novel itself (Ach. Tat. 1.1–3). The imagery of the painting introduced certain dominant themes (abduction, travel abroad, the caprice and danger of Eros), and its inclusion at the outset foregrounded visual description as a hermeneutic device. The opening story of the painting and the conversation with Cleitophon also situated the fictional events of the novel within the real experience of the author.

Several authors used the related *topos* of the unexpected discovery of a forgotten text. The premise points to what must have been a popular fascination in a world where old inscriptions occasionally did turn up when fields were plowed, wells and ditches dug, and masonry recycled. Dictys reportedly wrote his account of the Trojan War on linden tablets and sealed them in his tomb near Cnossus. As the story goes, shepherds found them in 66 CE and delivered them to their landlord, who gave them to the governor, who sent them to Nero, who had them translated from Phoenician into Greek as "a more true composition on the Trojan war" (*Troiani belli verior textus*), which furnished the source for the Latin translation that survives (*pr.*). Antonius Diogenes devised another variation on this theme. He claimed that Deinias, his protagonist, had the entire story inscribed on cypress tablets that were entombed in the family vault at Tyre, but later unearthed by a soldier of Alexander the Great during his siege of that city in 332 BCE (Phot. *Bib.* 111b3–31). Both authors validated the truth of their invented stories, first, by claiming their authenticity as primary testimony and, second, by inserting them into the careers of famous men. Ironically, their elaborate efforts to guarantee historical truth are themselves pseudo-historical fabrications. A similar effect is achieved by fictitious letters attributed to real people like Themistocles, Socrates, and Chion and by the frequently quoted correspondence between the novels' protagonists.

The penchant for false documentation casts a shadow of doubt over the sources Philostratus cites for his biography of Apollonius of Tyana (*VA* 1.2–3, 1.12, 3.41, 4.19 8.29; cf. Euseb. *Hierocl.* 2.6, 3). He said that he toured cities in the footsteps of Apollonius and studied his letters, his treatise on sacrifices and his "will" (*diathêkai*), the writings of Maximus of Aegae and Moeragenes, and the personal notes of the Syrian Damis, Apollonius' close disciple. The rehearsal of sources, methods, and aims was a standard feature of introductions to historical accounts. It is quite possible that Philostratus traveled to collect evidence and even read texts connected to the holy man's life, particularly the treatise and will, the local publication by Maximus, and the *memorabilia* of Moeragenes. His other sources, however, are questionable. Apollonius' celebrity must have led to the posthumous appearance of spurious personal documents. A set of letters under the sage's name has survived, but few scholars believe that all (or even most) are genuine. As for Damis, too many suspicious details collude to discredit his historicity. Not unlike the sudden appearance of Dictys' account under Nero, an anonymous middleman, some relative of Damis, delivered the "notebooks of memoirs" (*tas deltous tôn hypomnêmatôn*) to the empress Julia Domna, who then commissioned the biography from Philostratus. The fact that Damis traveled with Apollonius everywhere he went and faithfully recorded all his judgments, speeches, prophecies (*VA* 1.3), and "scraps" (*ekphatnismata*, 1.19) is too good to be true. Apollonius supposedly met Damis in Syrian Hierapolis en route to India (1.19), an exotic journey the historical Apollonius never made. So Damis must be a figment, perhaps a stand-in for the author as dutiful researcher or an homage to the biographer's own teacher, the sophist Flavius Damianus. Philostratus used the same fictional apparatus of authorization as the novelists, even as he recounted the life of a real person from the not-too-distant past in a prose form with the pretense of veridical reporting.

Another technique for generating verisimilitude was the realistic portrayal of geography and the physical landscape. Each of the five canonical novels begins at a precise locale in the Mediterranean: Syracuse (Char.), Ephesus (Xen. Eph.), Sidon and Tyre (Ach. Tat.), Mytilene (Long.), the Heracleotic mouth of the Nile (Heliod.). Readers would have known all these places. Longus' portrayal of the climate, vegetation, geology, coastal morphology, and distribution of settlement on Lesbos is so accurate that several scholars have argued that the novelist had a personal knowledge of the island. After his arrival in Alexandria, Cleitophon, the narrator of the novel by Achilles Tatius, describes passing through the Gate of the Sun and seeing all the impressive architecture and large crowds along the city's streets (Ach. Tat. 5.1). Similarly, Alciphron sprinkles his fictitious epistles with exact references to the neighborhoods and landmarks of classical Athens. By including such details, Achilles and Alciphron transported their readers to the real streets of the two great cities.

Philostratus and Lucian charted extraordinary journeys through imaginary landscapes by citing the archaeological remains of prior travelers. As Apollonius and Damis head east, they pass the column erected by Alexander near the river Hyphasis, the terminus of his Indian conquests in 326 BCE (*VA* 2.43). In comic counterpoint, Lucian's explorers on some Atlantic island encountered a column and two adjacent footprints, one colossal, marking the extent of the travels of the god Dionysus and the hero Heracles, who had famously big feet (*Ver. Hist.* 1.7).

The novelists and epistolographers also recreated the microcosm of everyday life through the concrete depiction of objects and spaces. They tell what clothing people wear and how they look; they mention furniture, rooms, doors, and windows; they specify different fabrics, metals, and woods; they portray townhouses, farms, taverns, markets, jails, shacks, caves, and cemeteries. Once readers have recognized the tangible surroundings, they can visualize the movements and activities of the characters. In these respects, the fictional universe is not unlike a theatrical set with backdrops and stage properties. It is the narrative re-enactment of life for both reader and spectator that underlies the link between fiction and drama already noted in the late Greek terminology for the novel and the ancient rhetorical theory of *plasma*.

This intricate façade of verisimilitude raises the question of what motivated the production and consumption of such literature. Since Greek fiction was a polymorphic mode of narrative representation in which imagination and experience coalesce, it met the dual needs of its authors and readers for literary entertainment and socio-cultural identification. Beyond its fundamental capacity for telling a good story, it brought pleasure to the reader through various channels. The literary texture of these works encouraged the reader to trace stylistic and thematic evocations, allusions, and quotations to other works of literature, usually those of the classical canon. On the other hand, the plausibility of these stories, or their appearance of having happened at a specific place and time, encouraged readers to pretend that they had entered the fictional world. In this way, readers could derive pleasure from their emotional involvement in events they knew on a rational level to be imaginary. Keen readers could even enjoy the game of moving back and forth between the two dimensions of fiction and reality, picking out elements of each and observing how the author had blended them.

Fiction was not just high sport; it could also furnish moral and intellectual edification. In two speeches, Dio assured his audience that his retelling of a Libyan myth about a species of savage monsters (D.Chr. 5.1–4, 16, 22–3) and his romanticized account of the sojourn among the Euboean peasants (7.81) conveyed serious messages about human passion and poverty. Lucian denounced *plasma* in a metafictional masterstroke at the opening of his fantastic travel tales. In the dry, almost professorial exordium he characterized the rollicking fantasy both as mental amusement and as criticism of authors who lied when they claimed to recount historic events. In these "true stories" (*alêthê diêgêmata*) he imitated purveyors of falsehood, but by doing so he became the truest of all writers because he admitted to lying. Thus, ironically, Lucian's most memorable fiction was a vehicle for the truth through its revelry in untruth (*Ver. Hist.* 1.1–4).

Greek fiction was able to entertain its readers through literary texture, vicarious experience, and sophisticated critique only so long as it accommodated their full range of common interests, desires, fears, and ideals. In this sense, it was also an expression of a particular social, economic, and cultural identity. The remainder of this chapter will investigate how different Greek authors of the Roman Empire sculpted imagination and experience to invent their fictional versions of the world. First, however, it must be established whose imagination and whose experience were implicated in the creation and reception of Greek fiction.

3 Authors and Readers

The authors of Greek fiction wrote for readers of comparable socio-economic status with whom they shared similar literary tastes. As far as we can tell, these authors belonged to wealthy families and passed through a common educational system. The classical allusions and quotations in many works of fiction reflect not only the authors' schooling but also their sustained interest in reading classical literature as educated adults. The novelists Chariton and Heliodorus, for example, regularly borrowed imagery and phrases from Homer and Demosthenes, while Aelian's fictional epistles to Athenian farmers echo the poetry of Hesiod and Aristophanes. Lucian's top-ten reading list, which has been painstakingly reconstructed from over a thousand passages in his voluminous corpus, resembles a curriculum in classical philology at a modern university: Homer, comedy, Plato, Euripides, Herodotus, Thucydides, lyric poetry, Demosthenes (Householder 1941). Such a high level of literary affluence presupposes material affluence. The families of these authors must have been prosperous enough to afford not only their children's tutelage but also their free time.

The educational and professional background of writers of fiction is further reflected in their language. Many of them, particularly after the late first century CE, preferred the classicizing Attic dialect to the Hellenistic vernacular (*koinê*). The linguistic and stylistic complexity of the novels varied, but even the technically simple novels by Chariton and Xenophon avoid hiatus and use simile. The later novels by Longus, Achilles Tatius, and Heliodorus display rhetorical virtuosity, including color, *ecphrasis*, suspense, narrative involution, and distinctly mannered prose. Moreover, all works of Greek fiction employ the portrayal of individuality through behavior and speech (*êthopoiïa*), a standard rhetorical technique. As students at the secondary level, future authors would have practiced the strategy of authenticating fictional accounts by expatiating upon obscure moments in ancient history in declamations (*meletai*). These exercises required that students make up deliberations or debates based on known historical or literary episodes, as preparation for careers in the assembly and the courtroom (Russell 1983 for the context of rhetorical performance). Given these propensities in their writing, it is not surprising that many authors of fiction were orators. Chariton was a "lawyer's secretary" (*hypographeus tou rhêtoros*, Char. 1.1), not a prestigious post but hardly blue collar. According to Byzantine sources, the novelist Achilles Tatius was a rhetorician whose pursuits encompassed astronomy, etymology, and history (Eust. *Comm. Od.* 14.350; Thom. Mag. *Selection of Attic Words s.v. anabainô*; *Suda s.v.* Ach. {S}tat.). Lucian, Dio, and Philostratus are all known to have studied rhetoric and philosophy and pursued oratory for at least part of their careers.

The authors of Greek fiction were clearly distinguished from the uneducated masses as privileged individuals who enjoyed high social status on the local and regional levels. According to the authorial pendant at the close of his novel, Heliodorus belonged to a priesthood of the Sun at Emesa in Syria (Heliod. 10.41), a distinction in the civic community. If the novelist Longus was in fact related to the Pompeii Longi attested in inscriptions from Roman Mytilene (*IG* 12, ii 88, 249), which is plausible but not certain, he belonged to long-standing nobility (for the lives of the novelists see Schmeling 2003: 307–653). In his rags-to-riches autobiography, the *Dream*, Lucian retold his difficult decision as a youth to pursue a life of culture rather than his family's trade, stone carving. After his education, Lucian worked the lecture circuit in public and private venues from Asia to Rome to Gaul, often associating with powerful men, like the senator Sisenna Rutilianus (*Alex.* 30, 54; *Laps.* 12–13) and the emperor Lucius Verus, to whose mistress, Pantheia of Smyrna, he gave three pretty essays (*Images, Concerning Images, About Dancing*). It is perhaps fitting that an intellectual so well connected yet so bitterly cynical never himself achieved political prominence but ended up a minor bureaucrat in the Egyptian administration (*Apol.* 12–13; for his career see Hall 1981: 1–63; C. P. Jones 1986: 6–23; Swain 1996: 298–329). Dio and Philostratus, brilliant orators both, represent the highest echelon of Greek society who entered Rome's inner circle (on Dio see Swain 2001; on Philostratus see Anderson 1986: 1–22; Bowie 1994a; Swain 1996: 380–400). Dio quickly rose to prominence in the coterie of the eminent Stoic philosopher C. Musonius Rufus; after exile and rehabilitation, he allied with Trajan. Likewise, Philostratus was an associate of the empress Julia Domna, who commissioned his work on Apollonius (*VA* 1.3; cf. *Ep.* 73); later he dedicated his biographies of the sophists to one of the Gordians (*VS* 479, 480).

To be sure, these various authors did not occupy the same rung on the social ladder. Chariton would have enjoyed far less prestige as a law clerk than the imperial courtier Philostratus, who criticized him (*Ep.* 66). Moreover, they came from different parts of the eastern Mediterranean – Alexandria, Emesa, Samosata, Aphrodisias, Lemnos, Prusa. Despite these differences, they all belonged to a supralocal elite class of "cultured men" (*pepaideumenoi*) who shared the experience of a similar education and who appreciated a common aesthetic sensibility. Their learning, their artistic taste, and their personal style were deeply rooted in the cultural heritage of the classical world. These qualities were recognized among the urban aristocracies of the Roman East, but they also led to regional or international renown outside the home city, drawing the most celebrated individuals west to Rome. In other words, the cultural distinction of these individuals accompanied and even justified their social connections and political power, whether in the civic community or in the imperial government. Their creation of fiction was therefore an act of social and cultural self-representation. Literary production was an expression of education as well as an emblem of wealth, achievement, and refinement.

The intended readers of Greek fiction were not unlike the authors in their academic achievements and artistic preferences (Bowie 1994b, 2003; Stephens 1994; Morgan 1995). The greatest enjoyment of fiction could be gained only by those who were fluently literate and familiar with classical literature. Moreover, the most ambitious works published in the second and third centuries CE, such as Lucian's satires and the intricate novel by Heliodorus, drew their readers into a reflexive analysis of fiction as a narrative mode of mimesis. This demanded of readers not just literacy and education, which enabled pattern recognition and fostered appreciation, but also an elevated awareness of the creative process. All this does not mean that the illiterate could not enjoy fiction aurally through public performances, readings, or formulaic retellings, or that the literate who were ill-educated, uninspired, or uninterested could not enjoy fiction on the level of action and dialogue. Theoretically, fiction, and in particular the novels, could have reached a wide audience. It should, however, be stressed that there is no evidence for transmissions of such a kind, apart from the public delivery of oratory with fictional scenes. The main point is that fiction was not intended primarily for popular consumption.

The sparse evidence for the readership of fiction offers a vague but useful picture. First, as one might expect, individuals at the zenith of the social structure owned sophisticated Greek literature as a mark of prestige. Several works by Lucian and Philostratus were dedicated or addressed to powerful individuals at the provincial or Imperial level. The emperor Julian, himself an accomplished man of letters, discussed erotic fiction in a letter to the arch-priest of Asia in 363 CE (*Ep.* 89.301b). Philostratus wrote that Hadrian kept a few epistles of Apollonius in his villa at Antium (*VA* 8.20), and Nero supposedly had a copy of the Greek translation of Dictys' account of the Trojan War (Dict. Cret. *pr.*). At a lower elite level, Dio and Lucian wrote mostly for eastern *litterati* and their western admirers, men of considerable wealth and status who did not necessarily occupy top offices. It is this faceless, nameless crowd of *pepaideumenoi* who read the novels. There is no substance or persuasion in the curious, once trendy theory that the novels were written chiefly for children or women. Their literary and linguistic artifice presupposes literacy, education, and participation in (or aspiration to participate in) elite culture and society, which largely excludes both those classes of reader. Undoubtedly certain women did read novels, but surely not as frequently as men, or with any favored status. The novels would have been accessible to children only through readings by parents or slaves, though this is nowhere attested. Students at grammar school were too busy reading their Euripides and Isocrates. The novelists provide some sense of their readers' profile through the ideal characterization of their own fictional personae. The aristocratic, educated protagonists write, exchange, and read letters without the assistance of scribes. Antonius Diogenes dedicated his novel to his sister Isidora, "being a lover of learning" (*philomathôs echousêi*, Phot. *Bib.* 111a30–b31). In other words, she was an appropriate reader not *qua* woman but *qua* learned person.

Papyrology and archaeology provide concrete evidence for the social world of the novels' readers. One index of the breadth of the novel's readership is the distribution by author or genre of literary papyri from Roman Egypt written during the first six centuries CE. Of the total published sample, novels account for only 42 discrete texts, whereas over a thousand fragments are attributed to Homer and well over a hundred to Demosthenes. Sheer numbers prove that the novels could not have had a mass market, as was once argued. Rather, they constituted a narrow subset of all literature read by the educated. The excavation of two lavish villas near Syrian Antioch and Alexandretta has revealed four mosaic pavements depicting legendary figures who appear in the early novels, the couple Metiochus and Parthenope, and Ninus. These mosaics have been frequently cited as evidence that the readers of the novels belonged to the class of affluent landowners. It should, however, be noted that these same characters appear in mythology and drama, and it has also been plausibly proposed that at least some of these scenes might depict mimes. Even so, one can safely assume that individuals who were well enough educated to appreciate fully the literary sophistication of Antonius Diogenes and Longus were prosperous enough to own and decorate homes such as these.

Although Greek fiction was primarily written for an eastern audience, it was also read by westerners. Apart from Nero, Hadrian, and Julia Domna, who valued artistic refinement, philhellenism, or Orientalism at court, various Roman authors also responded to Greek literary currents. It has been cogently, if not decisively, argued that both the famous story of Pyramus and Thisbe in Ovid (*Met.* 4.55–166) and the burlesque exploits of the anti-heroes in Petronius' *Satyricon* are parodies of the idealized Greek novels. Persius might have also known Chariton's novel (Pers. 1.134). If these authors did have in mind the novels and not other realistic genres, such as New Comedy, then, remarkably, the nascent literary form in the eastern provinces was already influencing Latin literature in the first century CE. A century later, the Latin novel *Metamorphoses*, or *The Golden Ass*, rewrote the lost Greek novel *Lucius or the Ass*. The author, Apuleius, was a native African, but, like many aristocrats, he was immersed in the classical heritage during his "college years" at Athens. The appreciation of Greek fiction by western contemporaries of comparable social status reveals that the reception of the form was not restricted to a region but was a pan-Mediterranean phenomenon. Nevertheless, there is no indication that Greek fiction was ever written with the particular interests or tastes of western readers in mind.

Now that the nature of Greek fiction and the identity of its authors and readers have been outlined, it is possible to explore how authors of Greek fiction blended imagination and reality to entertain, educate, and validate a common identity. To do this, it will be worthwhile to discuss two distinct views of the world in this body of literature, one internal and one external. The novels and other fictional works of rhetoric, biography, and epistolography examine the society of cities and their surrounding countrysides where the characters reside, a sphere familiar to both author and reader. They also explore the exotic realms to which their characters travel, a sphere unfamiliar to both author and reader.

4 Town and Country

Since Greek fiction was at once a literary product for sophisticated entertainment and a textual channel for self-representation, the depiction of the city and the country might be expected to reveal something significant, if distorted, about the social world of the *pepaideumenoi*. It is not surprising that the cities of the eastern provinces are the bases for the main characters in the novels, because that was where the authors and their readers lived (see Saïd 1994). Most were urban centers that prospered under the empire, like Miletus, Ephesus, Tarsus, and Alexandria. The fictional people who inhabit these cities all conform to a basic profile of ideal characteristics that varies only slightly from work to work. These traits are wealth, nobility (*eugeneia*), beauty, education, erotic self-restraint (Gr. *sôphrosynê*, Lat. *pudicitia*), and piety (*eusebeia*). Within the civic community, these traits distinguish the protagonists as members of the ruling class. In the novels, wealth is evident in the conspicuous display and consumption of precious metals and expensive materials, such as furniture, clothing, and food, in public venues, from banquets, weddings, and funerals to formal acts of largesse. It is also apparent in the ownership of palatial homes in the city and productive rural villas outside it, always prominently situated, extravagantly furnished, and well staffed (see Scarcella 2003). Aristocratic families educate their children by means of private tutors (*paidagôgoi*), and many of the protagonists are eloquent speakers. They excel in various gendered pursuits: men are athletic and prove to be sturdy combatants and successful leaders in war, while women know poetry and music. The novels idealize fidelity between lovers (though allowing men a degree of sexual freedom), virginity (particularly in women), and, above all, the reciprocal attachment of man and woman in marriage. The emphasis on conjugality and the well ordered household in part reflects the importance of intermarriage in securing the posterity of elite prestige and power. Piety is expressed by respect for divine providence, participation in public rituals and festivals, and sacred dedications. Since the characters are typically youths, they do not hold public office, but their parents or other adults sometimes do. The testimony of contemporary orators and the moralizing language of honorary inscriptions prove that this homogeneous profile of attributes was a current construction to which members of the bouleutic classes of the eastern cities commonly aspired. Lucian finds humor in the hypocrisy of aristocrats who claim personal virtue but fail to show it, such as proud hosts who try to speak eloquently but make grammatical slips, grandees who waste their fortunes on massive mausolea that are empty symbols of self worth, or charlatans who prey upon the gullibility of religious fanatics.

While the main characters in fiction embody or aspire to this aristocratic ideal, rarely does the reader meet the rest of the population. This simplification of the actual social structure is evident in the novels, where civic communities have essentially two tiers, a group of preeminent families and a univocal populace. This collective entity is a constant spectator to the public behaviors of the elite. Sometimes individuals of different professions or moral qualities appear: comic parasites, itinerant magicians, priests and lawyers, police and soldiers. These figures tend to be one-dimensional, fitting literary stereotypes or playing specific roles in the plot. The reader of the novels is seldom drawn to sympathize with secondary characters, and their activities and movements are strictly peripheral to the experience of the protagonists.

The social identity of the elite was charged with meaning most potently in the physical environs of the city. Greek orators like Dio and Aelius Aristides viewed their cities as dynamic arenas for the creation, operation, and maintenance of religious cults, cultural events, political bodies, and commercial and social interchange. They pictured them as architectural networks of harbors, circuit walls and gates, waterlines, tombs, temples, baths, gymnasia, hippodromes, theaters, stoas, streets, and houses. Even in his account of the fantastic voyage, Lucian imagines a miniature Greek settlement in similar terms. The farm of the old Cypriot marooned in the belly of the whale is represented as a grouping of functional spaces and buildings: a domicile, the adjacent field, a graveyard, a temple, and a mooring for a skiff (*Ver. Hist.* 1.32–4). The monumental program of the cities was a metaphor for the living community, so that the different physical structures were organs of a social structure. In both novels and orations, aristocrats frequent the gymnasium and the temple, their ancestors inhabit the graves, and the urban masses fill the theater and the agora. Thus while civic landscapes were an important venue for the action of fictional stories, they were also the topographical substrate for the definition of social classes. It makes sense that, once the protagonists of the novels leave their cities, they lose their identity and become unlikely outlaws, prisoners, slaves, or shepherds.

In Greek fiction, the countryside beyond the city and the extramural cemetery was a strange place where urban aristocrats never stayed very long. The countryside of the novels has two faces, one attractive and one horrific, both distorted pictures from an elite viewpoint (see Saïd 1999). It was a landscape full of possibilities both good and bad, where characters either realized their fear of anonymity and dispossession or fulfilled their desire for blissful repose and financial stability. The novels often show the productive estates that were the cornerstone of the urban economy, such as those near Miletus and Ephesus in the novels by Chariton and Achilles Tatius. These *villae rusticae* consisted of expansive fields with several buildings that could be reached by land or sea. Owners visited their properties to oversee affairs, but they largely entrusted the day-to-day management to servants. The landlord's trip to his suburban properties was a veritable pageant, as he rode in his carriage decked out in finery and accompanied by family, friends, and personnel in a long retinue. In reality these agricultural units depended on the cultivation of vine, olive, and cereal grains and on raising livestock, but the novels almost never portray real labor. Villas in the novels exist chiefly as a symbol of inherited wealth. They were also getaways where the wealthy escaped the daily grind and enjoyed their favorite pastime, hunting. In sharp contrast to this image, the novelistic countryside could also be a bleak, trackless wilderness. Once the protagonists had advanced beyond the safety of the city walls, they were vulnerable to either predatory bandits who dwelled in caves or, if they were at sea, the twin perils of piracy and shipwreck. It is seldom clear who these outlaws are or where they come from, but their characterization is antithetical to that of the ideal aristocrat. Certain groups, such as the infamous "rangers" (*boukoloi*), a legendary population of insurgents who occupied the marshy expanse of the Nile delta, were portrayed by Achilles Tatius and Heliodorus as a race apart, with their own physiognomy and language.

Longus, author of the most influential of the novels, furnishes a singular view of the relationship between the city and the country. The countryside of Lesbos, where his story takes place, fuses the world of rural estates with the world of bucolic poetry (Effe 1999; Cresci 1999). In a unique twist, the novel is set almost exclusively among the farmers and herdsmen who occupy the estate of a wealthy landowner from the city of Mytilene. Daphnis and Chloe, their families, and other villagers enjoy a life of bucolic tranquility, sharing wine, cheese, and milk, singing and playing their pipes, communing with plants and animals, and worshipping Pan and the Nymphs. The characterization of the country folk as ignorant, poor, unrefined, and inexperienced hints at urban prejudice, but this is tempered by a sense of sentimental longing for their sweet simplicity. Longus cleverly grafts bucolic scenery onto the romantic stock. Since Daphnis and Chloe never leave the estate for long periods, temporality replaces the geographic vector of novelistic narrative, and they travel through the seasons, not overseas. Pirates and hostile foreigners must therefore be imported to the estate from abroad. As it turns out, the protagonists are outsiders to this seeming paradise: they are the children of urban aristocrats who exposed them at birth in the wild. The dénouement comes when Daphnis and Chloe discover their true nobility and at last achieve full enculturation in marriage and sexual union. They decide not to move to the city but to remain in the country and partake of its simple pleasures and regenerative energy. Ultimately this urbanocentric view of the country is not so different from that of the other novelists, but Longus surpasses them by viewing the problematic relationship between his own world and the rural sphere through the lens of pastoral myth.

The fictional letters of Alciphron and Aelian also evoke an artificial rusticity, but their farmers and fishermen inhabit the fields and waters of classical Attica. Some of these letters, like Longus' novel, celebrate the quaint country life. There a goatherd can recline in the shade at midday and play his pipes for his herd (Alciphr. 2.9), and a farmer can go to bed at night satisfied that he planted his vines, figs, and olives well (Ael. 4). But these folk are hardly rugged, and they complain too much about creature comforts, money and property, and personal safety. Bad weather, sore arms, failing crops, thin catches, crushing debt, hungry wolves, and noisy roosters are genuine concerns, but preoccupation with them is unnatural. This is because Alciphron and Aelian view the countryside from the city. Their fictional letters voice the worries of the urban aristocrat who tries with some difficulty to imagine himself farming and fishing for a living. If the Athenian working class had really been so soft, it would not have survived the routines of a pre-industrial subsistence economy, let alone the disastrous unpredictability of epidemic, famine, and drought.

These authors manipulated the ambiguities of epistolary fictionality for sophisticated entertainment. Alciphron and Aelian spoiled the pastoral quietude by dropping hints of harsh reality. In one exchange between a daughter and a mother, the girl rejects the husband whom her fisherman father has chosen, the son of a Methymnian helmsman, who seemed to be a perfect match. Instead she has fallen in love with an ephebe from a distinguished Athenian family, to judge from the fact that he led the procession at the Oschophoria. She describes his beauty in her own language, laced with charming similes of the sea and shellfish. But her mother scolds her harshly, seeing through the childish fantasies of marriage across class boundaries (Alciphr. 1.11–12). In another epistle, readers of the novels will be interested finally to learn the origin of that subculture of bandits who permanently stalk the hills and sail the seas. One desperate fisherman, down on his luck and out of money, writes a letter to his wife in which he ponders joining a band of Lycian corsairs (Alciphr. 1.8). In contrast, a lazy Athenian parasite, true to his city-grown depravity, voluntarily chooses to set up shop as a highway robber at the Scironian rocks over a life of farm labor (Alciphr. 3.34). Finally, a four-letter exchange inspired by the comic poet Menander portrays two opposing personalities in the country (Ael. 13–16). Callipides begins with a trite encomium on the gentle pace of rustic life. Then in friendly tones he tries to persuade his misanthropic neighbor, Cnemon, to stop throwing dirt and pears at passers-by and join in a local sacrifice to Pan and the banquet to follow. Cnemon, who refuses to tend his yard and insists on conversing through messengers, hates crowds and spurns the rural hospitality. Daphnis and Chloe would be horrified at such boorish behavior.

Dio's *Euboean Speech* employs fictional invention to convey a moral message concerning the city–country dichotomy. The orator describes a pseudo-historical event in his own life when, shipwrecked on the treacherous southern coast of Euboea, he meets an amicable huntsman and accompanies him to his modest abode (7.1–10). There the narrator enjoys the kindness of the huntsman's family, their rustic cuisine and pleasant conversation, and even the wedding of two teenage lovers. These people are by nature gentle and kindhearted, their home harmonious and happy (64–80). So far the romantic scene resembles the pastoral world of Daphnis and Chloe. But next the speech exposes a rift between city and country in a direct clash between humble rusticity and the urban sphere of Dio and his audience. The huntsman tells that his land had once belonged to a wealthy magnate, upon whose death it was confiscated. Thereafter, the huntsman and his family continued to live in a cluster of huts, surviving on only a few crops and whatever they could catch (10–21). In time the nearby city summons him to face the charge of squatting on public land (22–63). An ensuing debate in the assembly sharply articulates the contrary viewpoints of city-dwellers and country folk. To the huntsman, the town is a garish, unnatural creation, its people loud, threatening, and corrupt. To the oligarchic assemblymen, the country is untamed and perilous, its inhabitants violent and malicious. Later in his speech, Dio lauds the rural population as a bastion of traditional values in the face of moral and intellectual decay in urban society (80–152, with Desideri 2001: 99–101). Of course, Dio's voice wins the fictional debate, and the citizens adjudicate in favor of the hapless huntsman, who is thoroughly baffled by their language and procedures. The city's decisions regarding its territory are naturally expressed in terms of its own peculiar social system. By decree the huntsman is granted the disputed land, a meal, new clothing, and cash, all at public expense, in honor of his selfless acts of rural euergetism, namely, the recovery of the shipwrecked and the provision of warm porridge and venison by the fire (54–63). This miniature ecclesial drama recalls the democratic machine of classical Athens and the conventional rhetoric of the Attic orators (Ma 2001). Epigraphy also reveals that the operations and terminology in the oration are equally appropriate to the conservative political culture of Greece and Asia Minor during the Roman Empire. What is most significant is that Dio chose a fictional mode for his discursive critique of contemporary society.

5 Exotic Peoples and Places

The authors of Greek fiction also looked beyond the safe confines of the cities to peoples and places beyond the "inhabited world" (*oikoumenê*). Stories of travels to faraway places were influenced not only by heroic journeys to mythic lands recounted by classical authors beginning with Homer, but also by geography, ethnography, and paradoxography, genres emanating from Hecataeus and Herodotus that flourished during the Hellenistic age. Moreover, the ancient notion of a Greek-barbarian polarity resonates in fiction under various guises, such as the Persian and Mesopotamian portraits in the novels of Chariton and Iamblichus. Against this traditional scenery, authors of fiction invented new places for their characters on the road. These journeys of exploration, pilgrimage, and self-discovery were not only exercises in literary imagination but also articulations of Greek cultural identity through the delineation of outsiders (see in general Romm 1992: 202–14; Bowersock 1994: 29–53).

The epitomized novel by Antonius Diogenes (Phot. *Bib.* 109a–112a) and the travel tales by Lucian (*Ver. Hist.*) related fictitious travels to places far to the west of the

Mediterranean, beyond continental Europe and outside the Pillars of Hercules, as the ancients called Gibraltar (Bompaire 1958: 658–77; Morgan 1985; Fusillo 1999). After Alexander's conquest of the Orient, Hellenistic and Roman geographers considered the western Ocean the next unexplored frontier. The choice of this realm as the destination of the brave voyageurs in both works granted the authors considerable license to roam freely in the borderlands of scientific description and pseudo-scientific fantasy. Diogenes' *The Wonders beyond Thule* was not a formulaic novel but the amalgam of an itinerary, a romance, and a tale of persecution. Deinias is driven to travel not by love but by the pursuit of knowledge. He moves north past the Black Sea to Scythia, skirts the world's edge, and reaches Thule, a land probably located in the North Atlantic (Iceland?) that was purportedly discovered by Pytheas of Massilia in the late fourth century BCE (Strabo 2.4.1). On Thule his path converges with that of his lover-to-be, Dercyllis, who had fled her home in Tyre with an evil Egyptian sorcerer in hot pursuit. Most of the work's novelistic décor – magical spells, false deaths, erotic attraction, jealous rivalry – fills the episode on Thule. But before he returns to Tyre to join Dercyllis, Deinias' expedition continues westward beyond Thule, the end of the known world. In the great unknown he witnesses endless nights and even approaches the moon (Phot. *Bib.* 110b39–111a11). Diogenes offers both an entertaining variation on the traditional formula of the novel and a parodic exposé of the slippery claims to scientific accuracy by prior geographers.

Lucian too chose the fantastic journey of westward exploration as a way to criticize geographers and historians who related make-believe journeys as true accounts. His imaginary travelers, driven by a series of tempests, see much more than Deinias: they reach the Moon, they are swallowed by a giant whale, and they visit the Islands of the Blessed and Ogygia. The satirist plays in many registers at once. Some of his humor, such as sexual obscenity and the invention of otherworldly creatures, is coarse and obvious. At other times he parodies other authors by casting absurd discoveries behind a transparent veneer of veracity. In his account of the battle between the forces of the Moon under Endymion and the forces of the Sun under Phaethon (*Ver. Hist.* 1.12–21), Lucian describes with mock precision the composition, size, and maneuvering of the armies, which are astronomically large and absurdly diverse, like an international coalition. He then reproduces the text of their peace treaty, modeled on the famous Athenian settlement with Mytilene (Thuc. 3.36, 3.49). In this way he blends Herodotean and Thucydidean historiography to narrate a war between celestial bodies as though they were competing polities in classical Greece. Later the travelers reach the Islands of the Blessed, where they encounter a menagerie of figures from mythology, literature, and philosophy, all mingling for eternity as though in a "School of Athens" centuries before Raphael (*Ver. Hist.* 2.5–28). The narrator even interviews Homer and resolves several uncertainties about the bard: he could see, he was Babylonian, he did write all the obelized lines, and he composed the *Iliad* before the *Odyssey*.

Philostratus also applied layers of literary tradition to an exotic landscape in his account of the journey of Apollonius of Tyana to India (Anderson 1986: 199–226; Stoneman 1995; Elsner 1997). Apollonius, accompanied by Damis, made a pilgrimage to consult the great sages, the Brahmans. He set out from Syrian Antioch (*VA* 1.18), passed through Ctesiphon and Babylon, over the Caucasus, and across the Indus to the city of Taxila (2). From there he crossed the Hydraotes and the Hyphasis into the uncharted land of the Brahmans, who occupy a citadel enclosed by a magical cloud, where he stayed for four months (3.1–50). Thereafter he traveled straight to the Arabian Sea and embarked for a return voyage along a coastal route to Mesopotamia and, eventually, Ionia (3.50–8).

The biographer relied on diverse sources to create his fictional India. At a basic level he imagined a real geography that could be accurately documented. India was not an unknown place, like Thule. Communication between the Mediterranean and the subcontinent had been established in prehistory, and commercial exchange with the Far East flourished during the first centuries of the Roman Empire. Philostratus used various devices to validate his account as documentation of a historical journey. He noted geographic features and gave their dimensions, and he included the text of two letters to the Brahman high priest Iarchas (2.41, 3.51). Moreover, Apollonius followed in the path of other famous travelers both mythical and historical, including Prometheus, Dionysus, Hercules, and, of course, Alexander the Great (e.g., 2.3, 2.8–10, 2.13, 2.20, 2.24, 2.33, 2.42–3, 3.13, 3.53). The conscientious biographer even corrected earlier writers on India, such as Scylax, Nearchus, Orthagoras, and Juba (e.g., 2.13, 2.17, 3.47, 3.53). Finally, he recorded the deltas and islands that Apollonius passed on his return journey along the southern coasts of Pakistan and Iran, naming the natural products of each region, from seafood to bronze, dates, and pearls (3.52–7). This section is very much like a merchants' manual, such as one on trade between Egypt, East Africa, Arabia, and India that has survived from the first century CE (cf. *Peripl. M. Rubr.* 36–7). In these carefully selected details Philostratus portrays for his readers an India that is credible.

On the other hand, even in the early third century CE India remained a land enshrouded in myth. Philostratus, as an educated author with no firsthand knowledge of the region, turned to three major traditions: geography and ethnography, ranging from early paradoxographical works by Ctesias and Megasthenes to more scientific accounts by Strabo and Arrian in the Roman era; the stories of Alexander's conquests beyond Persepolis; and Neo-Pythagorean philosophy. The author devised a triptych structure within which passages derived from the first tradition typically resolved into passages from the second, and these concluded with a philosophical discussion. So, for example, early in Apollonius' journey, Philostratus describes Mount Nysa and the crag of Aornus, then recounts the local legends concerning Dionysus and Alexander, and ends with a lecture on the intelligence of elephants (*VA* 2.8–16). In this way, the referential scheme of the Indian travels of Apollonius traces a narrowing series of concentric fields, like a bull's-eye, with philosophy at the center. This organization also operates on the scale of the entire episode. Apollonius' conversations with Iarchas and the Brahmans are the focal point; they are directly preceded and succeeded by reminiscences of Alexander's journey; and before and after are extended expositions of geographic and ethnographic data. By superimposing layers of literary tradition in such a pattern, like an orator building an argument, Philostratus reminds the attentive reader that the central goal of the sage's journey is not merely exploration or conquest but the acquisition of wisdom as embodied by the Brahmans.

Philostratus invented not only a fictional landscape with a realistic appearance for Apollonius to traverse but also a fictional people for him to meet. The Brahmans, who appear in several accounts of India, including the Alexander-Romance, were naked ascetics whose shifting persona preserves a kernel of historical truth, perhaps representing real Brahmans, Jains, or Buddhist monks. While Indians were known to Mediterranean peoples through occasional embassies to the Roman emperor, the Brahmans portrayed by Philostratus were completely fictional. They inhabit a philosophical utopia that is not alien but oddly Hellenized. Their citadel resembles the Athenian Acropolis, and as Apollonius ascends he sees statues from the local cults of ancient Greece (3.13–14). The Brahmans converse like sophists and speak impeccable Greek (3.12, 3.16), they sing a paean of Sophocles in a levitating chorus (3.17), and they keep in their dining room a statue of Tantalus in Argive dress and a Thessalian mantle and Pythian tripods like Homer described (3.25, 3.27). The Brahmans' wisdom primarily consists in their transcendent knowledge of Greek culture, which enables them to interpret Greek mythology, morality, and history (e.g., 3.19, 3.22, 3.25, 3.30–2). Author and reader understand the exotic landscape and its people in terms of their own traditions. As in the case of Lucian's fantastic journey, Philostratus' fictional history of the Indian travels of Apollonius transports the reader to a distant land. In fact, the reader is never very far from the classical library.

Heliodorus, like Philostratus, preferred to view exotic peoples not as savages or curiosities but as cohabitants of a polyethnic world (see in general Bowersock 1994: 48–50; Whitmarsh 1998a). The Ethiopians in his novel are outsiders to Greek culture but sympathetic to its values. Just as Philostratus in his picture of India, the novelist describes the capital Meroë, which historically communicated with Roman Egypt, both as a real city on an island of known size and as a place full of marvels, like enormous date palms, giant elephants, and griffins (Heliod. 10.4, 5). When the king, Hydaspes, grants audience to delegations from his subject nations, he receives as gifts, among other things, gold produced by ants, silk textiles, and an impressive giraffe (10.22–7). Despite his foreign origin, the king Hydaspes is a good-hearted ruler who possesses Greek virtues. In skirmishes with the Persian satrap in Egypt over emerald mines, the Ethiopian king spares the life of the vanquished general, orders that his wounds be tended, and manages a peace settlement (9.21–2, 9.27; cf. 10.34). Hydaspes in court at Meroë, just like Apollonius in India, is advised by a council of naked ascetics (9.2, 10.4, 10.6, 10.9–10). Moreover, at the novel's climax, Hydaspes bends to the will of the people when they respond vocally to his decisions (10.30–1, 10.38–41). He is a merciful and wise leader who values philosophy and appeases the masses, hardly a wanton, tyrannical barbarian.

The novel's main female character, Charicleia, is another complex figure who transforms with the changing scenery. She grew up at Delphi, but she must embark on a long journey of hardship to discover her true origins. Eventually she finds that she is an Ethiopian princess whom the queen Persinna had orphaned at birth. Nonetheless, Charicleia is in every respect an idealized Greek aristocrat and an appropriate spouse for the hero Theagenes. She is a paragon of femininity, unfailingly devoted to Artemis, protective of her virginity, faithful to her husband, and surpassingly beautiful. Most remarkably, her skin is milky-white, not dark black, the complexion of her biological parents. This is explained by the arcane phenomenon whereby her mother at the moment of conception spied a painting of the pale Andromeda on the bedroom wall in the palace at Meroë (4.8, 10.14–15). Even when the protagonists reach Ethiopia, join in marriage, and assume the priesthoods of the Sun and the Moon, the astronomical counterparts of Apollo and

Artemis (10.41), they are fulfilling an oracle from Delphi, one of the most venerable of Greek religious institutions (2.35). It would be wrong to conclude that Heliodorus' view of the Ethiopians is Hellenocentric. He envisions a world marked by ethnic and genealogical ambiguity, and these tensions continuously challenge the reader's perception of who the characters really are. The slippage between the ethnic categories "Greek" and "Ethiopian" seen in the figures of Hydaspes and Charicleia could be best exploited in a fictional medium.

6 The Classical Past and the Roman Present

By now it is clear that the Greek authors of the Roman Empire often turned to their classical heritage as a source of inspiration for fictional invention. This literary preference was inculcated by the educational system and reinforced by the demands of cultural elitism. Authors mined classical literature for proofs of authenticity or models of urban, rural, and exotic landscapes. It will be worthwhile to examine more closely historical novels and Homeric revisionism, which showcased the interpenetration of the historical or imaginary past of literature and the experience or imagination of author and reader.

Several novelists spun their stories off footnotes or forgotten chapters in ancient history, as if they were revealing lost or secret histories of great importance. One of the earliest novels, the fragmentary *Ninus*, derived its story from oriental, not classical, history. It recounted the love between Ninus, the Assyrian king and eponymous founder of Nineveh, and (probably) Semiramis, the Assyrian queen and founder of Babylon, even though these legendary figures supposedly lived in different millennia. A similar chronological discrepancy is found in the fragmentary *Metiochus and Parthenope*, which is set in Archaic Greece and adapts events recorded by Herodotus (3.124–51, 6.39–41). The four central characters in the preserved passages are Polycrates, tyrant of Samos from 540–522/1 BCE, his daughter Parthenope, Metiochus, the son of Miltiades the Athenian general, and the Milesian philosopher Anaximenes. These individuals lived in two separate generations, but the novel depicts them as contemporaries. Other fictional works were launched from obscure moments in the past. The epistolary novel *Chion of Heraclea* portrays the feelings and relations of a Pontic aristocrat otherwise known only as the assassin of the tyrant Clearchus in 353/2 BCE. The author, however, is concerned foremost to recreate the personal experience of Chion, and as a result the historical frame is inconsistent. Although Chion meets the historian Xenophon in Byzantium, which, given Xenophon's career, could only have been in c.400/399, he returns to Heraclea for the conspiracy against Clearchus after only five years.

One well documented example of this historicizing tendency in prose fiction is the novel by Chariton. Certain characters and events in this work recall events in the classical historians. Hermocrates, the father of Callirhoe, is the Syracusan general who defeated the Athenian expedition of 415–13 BCE, while Ariston, the father of Chaereas, was a helmsman in the Syracusan navy (Thuc. 7.39.2). The Persian king Artaxerxes was most likely based on Artaxerxes II, who ruled 405/4–359/8 BCE and was also married to a Statira. The siege of Tyre (Char. 7.4.3–9) parallels either the siege in 360 BCE, during an Egyptian revolt, as in the novel, or Alexander's siege in

332 BCE. Chariton has thus combined several historical events and figures from the late fifth and fourth centuries BCE into a synchronic pastiche. The educated and attentive reader would have noted these signals of dramatic date and delighted in finding the learned anachronisms (Bompaire 1977; Hägg 1987; Hunter 1994).

The historical setting of this novel, however, was merely atmospheric. The experiences of the characters – their private lives, religion and morality, social position, commercial and civic activity – still mirrored the world of author and reader. Classical Syracuse is only a *mise en scène* for the narrative foreground of Greek urban society under the Roman Empire. Callirhoe's father Hermocrates is historical only inasmuch as he shares his name with the general who fought the Athenians. The circumstances of the Peloponnesian War, or any social, political, or economic effect it had on life in the Sicilian colonies, are irrelevant to the actions and thoughts of the actors. Rather, Chariton's Syracuse is like any Roman provincial city: there are popular acclamations at the theater (1.1.11, 8.7.1), the pirate Theron is interrogated and crucified outside the walls (3.4.7–18), and the civic assembly grants honorary citizenship and farmland to the veterans from Chaereas' Egyptian campaign (8.8.13–14). But the novelist, who was from Aphrodisias in southwestern Asia Minor and had probably never been to Roman Syracuse, portrayed the city's topography imprecisely. His picture of the harbor is unusually specific, if inaccurate (3.3.18, 3.4.2, 8.6), presumably because it was the site of the great battle of 413 BCE, one of the most memorable episodes in Thucydides (Thuc. 7.31–41).

In order not to disrupt this historicizing ambience the novelists eschewed direct references to Roman rule. The capital city itself never appears among the many cities both large and small mentioned in the novels. Provincial institutions and administrative officials that were well known to the novelists and their readers were cited only obliquely and in classicizing language. For instance, Xenophon of Ephesus includes two characters who are unequivocally identified by their activities as a municipal policeman from Tarsus (Xen. Eph. 2.13.3; cf. 3.9.5) and the governor of Egypt (3.12.6, 4.2.1, 4.2.9, 4.4.1, 4.4.2, 5.3.1, with Rife 2002). But when the novelist refers to their posts, he does not use the technical terminology abundantly attested in papyri, inscriptions, and Roman literature. He instead chooses oblique periphrases from the classical Attic lexicon, "the one presiding over the peace in Cilicia" (*ho tês eirênês tês en Kilikiai proestôs*) and "the ruler of Egypt" (*ho archôn Aigyptou*). The novelist Achilles Tatius referred to the same provincial governorship using a word with stronger connotations, "satrap," the title of the Persian official (Ach. Tat. 3.13–4.14 *passim*). The novelists invented dramas of contemporary life familiar to their readers but fictionalized them by infusing historical reminiscences and classicizing geography and language.

Homeric revisionism also confounded past and present, but its method turned the novelistic creation of a classicized present upside-down. The revisionists relocated the fictional world of Homer in the present through the depiction of concrete details, familiar settings, and personal emotions. These devices validated the basic premises of this type of literature, namely, that the Trojan War was an historical event, that the Homeric heroes were historical persons, and that the truth about what happened to these people in that place and time could be uncovered through historical research. Moreover, if his veracity was accepted, Homer could provide historical data just like the classical historians or even eyewitness reports. This was the assumption of

Philostratus in his description of Apollonius' Indian travels. The biographer cited Homer (*Il.* 2.308) as a source for the species of dragons like those indigenous to India (*VA* 3.6), while Apollonius and the Brahmans revered Achilles and Ajax as philosophical luminaries (3.19), and considered an Indian youth the reincarnation of the hero Palamedes (3.22).

Three speeches by Dio illustrate how the historical truth of mythical subjects was a matter for rhetorical contestation (Saïd 2001: 174–86). In two works (D.Chr. 60–1) Dio rewrote the original version of the death of Hercules by Archilochus and Sophocles and reinvents Chryseis as a sentient being, far from the mute pawn in the power struggle among the Homeric warlords. In a third work (D.Chr. 11) Dio went so far as to refute systematically the Greek capture of Troy. Just like Dictys, he devises a fictional source to authorize his account. He asserts that he heard the story from an old Egyptian priest at Onuphis who preserved an oral tradition stretching back to Menelaus, who, according to Homer, had returned to Greece from Troy by way of Egypt (*Od.* 3.299–302). This tradition was inscribed in a temple, but, like so many epigraphic texts, several slabs had broken and the account was fragmentary (D.Chr. 11.37–8). Modern critics have debated whether this speech functioned as literary showpiece, political propaganda, or moral polemic. In any case, it demonstrates a profound interest in the literary construction of truth. A "true" account (*alêthês*), as Dio defines it (D.Chr. 11.70, 11.76, 11.88, 11.90, 11.107, 11.139; 60.3, 60.5, 60.9; cf. 61.18, Plut. *Thes.* 10.4, 26.1, 31.2, 32.2), is one that is "credible" (*pithanos*), "plausible" (*eikos*), and "similar to actual events" (*homoios gegonosi*). His definition recalls the verisimilitude of *plasma*.

Lucian, in his guise as critic of false intellectualism, has given us the most outrageous revisions of the Homeric poems. He asserts that he wrote his travel tales as a lighthearted critique of authors who passed off myths as truthful histories, such as Odysseus when he recounted his journey in the court of Alcinous (*Ver. Hist.* 1.3). Lucian's fantastic voyage includes several episodes involving Homer or the Homeric heroes as historical figures. For instance, Thersites indicts Homer on a charge of slander (2.21), and Odysseus writes a love letter to Calypso professing how much he misses her (2.35). Lucian also wrote a comic dialogue between a poor cobbler and his rooster that lampoons Homeric revisionism founded on bogus autopsy, such as the *ephêmeris* of Dictys (*Gall.* 17). The bird claims to be the reincarnation of the Trojan hero Euphorbus and judges that Homer was completely wrong on many things, because at the time of the war Homer himself was actually a Bactrian camel!

One of the most compelling resurrections of the classical past in the contemporary experience of the Greek provinces is Philostratus' *Heroic Discourse*. This dialogue between a Phoenician traveler and a native vinedresser takes place in the Thracian Chersonese, but the staging evokes a novelistic scene. Like Dio's *Euboean Speech*, Philostratus portrays a confrontation between a wealthy foreigner from the city and a simple peasant in the country that teaches the outsider something unexpected but important. The vinedresser tends the plot around Protesilaus' tumulus in the territory of Elaious. The ghost of the hero appears to him regularly and instructs him on sundry matters, from gardening and philosophical virtue to the true history of the Trojan War and the inaccuracies of Homer. Furthermore, the vinedresser asserts, the ghosts of several other heroes – Ajax, Hector, Palamedes, Patroclus, Achilles – still haunt the Trojan plain where their tombs and other memorials are to be seen, talking with local residents and exacting retribution on those who disregard their cults (*Her.* 18.1–23.1, 52.3–54.1). The vinedresser convinces the skeptical Phoenician of the heroic presence by citing the discovery of giant bones, some in tombs, near Troy and throughout the Greek world (6.7–8.18; cf. *VA* 5.16, Dict. Cret. 6.10). At the end of the catalog of marvelous finds, the Phoenician considers himself fortunate to have heard the vinedresser's "truthful account" (*historia*: 8.18).

The monuments and cults of the heroes of the Trojan War were venerated during the Roman Empire. Hadrian restored the decrepit tomb of Ajax when he visited the site probably in 124 CE (Philostr. *Her.* 8.1), and Caracalla in imitation of Alexander sacrificed to Achilles there in 214 CE (Dio 78.16.7). Even Apollonius of Tyana performed obsequies at the tombs of the Achaeans (Philostr. *VA* 4.11), and encountered the ghost of Achilles, who complained that the Thessalians had failed to keep his cult (4.16; cf. 4.23). The existence of these tombs inspired the composition of epigrams fashioned as epitaphs on the actual graves of the heroes or as graveside dedications to them (e.g., *AP* 7.136, 7.137, 7.140, 7.142, 7.145, 7.146, 7.148). During the early empire, the geographer Strabo recorded numerous ancient landmarks like those described by Philostratus' vinedresser in the real territory of the Roman colony of Ilium, citing the events of the Trojan War among references to Sulla, Mithridates VI, Antony, and Augustus (Strabo 13.1.24–50). This intense fascination in the archaeology and topography of the Trojan plain shows how the mythical past of fictional literature, namely, the Homeric tradition, was revived in Roman history. Works such as the *Heroic Discourse* encouraged readers to travel to Troy and communicate with the heroes themselves, or at least imagine themselves in the place of the Phoenician. Tombs, bones, and landmarks all played a crucial part in this experience. As sacred relics for cultic veneration they were the portal between the present and the past; as historical artifacts they verified the truth of the experience (see now, in general, Zeitlin 2001).

One late Greek poem exhibits many of these fictional developments, despite the fact that its literary form is appropriated from the very tradition it is revising. The epic by Quintus of Smyrna mostly catalogues the deaths of numerous heroes at Troy during the period between the *Iliad* and the *Odyssey*. This gap in the Homeric narrative was particularly susceptible to revision because no master-text existed. Quintus employed Homeric language and meter and adapted many of the original characters and events, but he also turned to Greek tragedy and Hellenistic writers, like Apollonius of Rhodes and Lycophron. Furthermore, as a professed native of Smyrna in the Roman province of Asia (Q.S. 12.306–13), Quintus reveals his knowledge of the civic realities and political sphere of the empire, despite its incongruity with the temporal setting of his story. In one simile, Quintus compares the sons of Atreus on the battlefield with beasts in a gladiatorial show at the amphitheater (6.531–7). As Aeneas escapes a burning Ilion with his father and son, the seer Calchas prophesies that he will found a city by the Tiber destined for far-flung dominion (13.334–41). Like Philostratus and Strabo, Quintus treats the vicinity of Troy as a concrete landscape that can be retraced through its natural and artificial features. Dominant among the monuments of the war are the tombs of the great warriors, the exact form and location of which he provides, including those of Achilles (3.718–42, 9.47–9), and Ajax, son of Telamon (5.653–6). Just as in the *Heroic Discourse*, the poet imagines encounters between the living and the dead that might remind readers of participation in a contemporary cult. The heroes visit the tombs to leave dedications and to mourn, as do Achilles and Ajax at the grave of Patroclus (1.376–9). The ghost of Achilles comes to his son Neoptolemus to give him advice and demand the proper observation of funerary rites, in particular the sacrifice of Polyxena (14.179–223). This scene had been written long before by Euripides (*Hec.* 35–44, 220–4, 534–40; cf. *Tr.* 39–40), but Philostratus also portrayed Achilles' spirit dictating sacrifices, and Caracalla saw fit to pay his respects at the most popular cult site in the Troad. There is no evidence that Quintus ever in fact visited the site of Troy; he could have extracted these details from his reading. Regardless of its accuracy, his Trojan geography maps out a monumental space that his readers could imagine themselves traversing.

Another strategy Quintus employs to resituate the past in the present is his strikingly un-Homeric treatment of human experience and private, ordinary events. He depicts the daily preparations for battle at Troy, when men don their equipment with the aid of tearful wives and little children. They are sorry to leave their loved ones but heartened by fatherly pride; sometimes they are spurred to bravery by their elderly fathers who once fought too and have the scars to show for it (Q.S. 9.110–24). The arming scene was an epic set piece, and readers of Homer would have immediately remembered the poignant, tragic image of Hector's last farewell to his wife Andromache and his infant son Astyanax (*Il.* 6.369–502). But in the latter-day epic, soldiers were nameless and voiceless, their actions and feelings not heroic but mundane. Later, the poet described the Trojans' return homeward after a day on the battlefield. Their wives and children help them remove the gory armor and bathe their wearied limbs. Some seek medical care for their painful wounds, others relax at dinner while their stabled horses loudly chomp on fodder (Q.S. 11.316–29). Quintus examines the physical and emotional effects of war on the human body and psyche. His subject in these vignettes is the experience of everyman, not the deadly competition for status among commanders. He draws the reader into the fictional events of his story through his sensitive use of such personal detail.

All these works insert the imaginary world of the classical past into the historical world of the reader. On the one hand, historicizing novels and fictional letters transport the present into the past by applying historical decoration, such as allusions to historical persons and events. On the other, Homeric revisionism brings the past into the present by generating high realism and sympathetically depicting physical and emotional states. The commingling of past and present is only possible in the medium of fiction, which manipulates the boundaries between what is true and what is not true to produce a vision that is "like true." This world could be either so like the truth that it elicited religious devotion, such as the tombs and bones of the Homeric heroes, or so unlike the truth that it was comically absurd, such as Lucian's revisionist rooster.

There remains the fundamental question of why Greek authors of the Roman Empire indulged in fictional creation. It could not have been a game of happy escapism from a gloomy present or a movement of resistance against foreign subjugation. These works were reflections, however distorted or fragmentary, of the world of the authors and their readers. Moreover, Greek-ness was not a nationality, and it should not be implicated in the political relations between rulers and ruled. Indeed, westerners read Greek fiction, and eastern authors associated with powerful Romans and enjoyed their patronage. Greek fiction served instead as a channel for expressing intellectual, social, and moral values, and the preferred mode of expression was antiquarianism, or the reinvention of the classical past in the Roman present. Cultural identity was constructed through the process of literary creation and reception. Writing and reading fiction thus signaled participation in a supralocal elite that was defined by a common educational system and a shared aesthetic taste. A similar creative ethos marked the prose narratives of nascent Christianity, from the evangelical biography of Jesus to the apostolic acts, martyrology, and hagiography. Much like Greek fiction, early Christian literature offered the imaginary or the unreal as the truth, in this case not the classical past but the mortally impossible – miracles, god in man, death transcended. But those works traced a strange new nexus of identities and relations in Greco-Roman society.

ACKNOWLEDGMENTS

I express my sincere gratitude to my teachers and friends Ewen Bowie, Ludwig Koenen, and David Potter for helping me better to understand Greek fiction in its socio-cultural and literary historical contexts. For introducing me to ancient fiction I am indebted to William E. McCulloh, with whom I first read Herodotus, Lucian, and Philostratus in the idyllic countryside of central Ohio. This chapter germinated during the fall of 2001 in a spirited seminar at Cornell. Those students taught me what a joy it can be to teach fictional polyphony.

CHAPTER TWENTY-FOUR

Roman Law and Roman History

John Matthews

1 Introduction

At the beginning of the twentieth century it would have been surprising to find a Roman historian who did not possess some knowledge of Roman law. If this is so, it was a legacy of the great historian Theodor Mommsen, whose last project, an edition of the Theodosian Code, was published in 1905, two years after Mommsen's death at the grand old age of 85. This late masterpiece complemented the edition of Justinian's *Corpus Iuris Civilis* which, in collaboration with Paul Krüger, began to appear in 1876. The Theodosian Code, and especially its commentary by James Godefroy (Gothofredus), had already been among the most important influences in the reading, and later on the writing, of Edward Gibbon. Gibbon recalled this in his fascinating *Memoirs of My Life*, where, however, he described it as a "work of history, rather than Jurisprudence," evidence above all for the *political* state of the empire in the fourth and fifth centuries (Gibbon 1966: 147). In due course, Gibbon included as chapter 44 of *The Decline and Fall of the Roman Empire* a description of the work of Justinian in legal codification, incorporating a long account of the principles of Roman law (beginning with a waspish complaint about the arcane system of reference employed by "the civilians of the darker ages") (Gibbon 1994: 2: 778–844). He had done the same, on a smaller scale, in chapter 38, with an account of the legal enterprises of the barbarian kings of the fifth and early sixth centuries, with the strange result that we read about the law of the barbarian territories of the west in an earlier chapter – originally in an earlier volume – than we read about the Roman law from which it partly derived (Gibbon 1994: 2: 472–85). But there is a vast difference between Gibbon's and Mommsen's approaches to the subject. Gibbon had made no use of the *Digest* (or *Pandects*, as he referred to this part of the *Corpus Iuris Civilis*) to illuminate the history of the period to which its assembled texts actually referred, and his description of the principles of Roman law derives not from the *Digest* but from the textbook account of Justinian's Institutes (his catalogues list only a volume on ante-Justinianic law and an edition of Justinian's *Institutes* – followed by six editions or translations of Juvenal [Keynes 1940: 164–5]). Gibbon made no attempt to integrate the subject with the history of the Roman Empire as a whole, and his treatment of Roman law has only a shadow of the impact of his great digressions, for example on the Germans and Persians, or on the early history of Christianity and its treatment by the Roman state.

The gulf between Gibbon and Mommsen is not only one of times and temperaments, but between different assumptions about the nature of research and the academic environment. Gibbon was a gentleman of private means, a self-educated man, whose university education had notoriously little influence on his intellectual formation. He was a genius, whose work still impresses us for its accuracy of judgment, its sustained intelligence, its breadth of learning, and its respect for the learning of others. A German review of *Decline and Fall*, however, already noted its undeveloped sense of source criticism, a response that expresses the different academic traditions of continental Europe (Momigliano 1966a: 40). There, historians were professionals trained in techniques, who did not just read and respond to texts, but analyzed them. The learning of Mommsen, as of his historian predecessor Niebuhr, and, in literary studies, the Homeric scholar Friedrich August Wolf, was founded on research and teaching based in public institutions, on scholarly collaboration and systematic publication, and a syllabus of study designed to train the skills of criticism. For these scholars, the study of ancient culture was based on the analysis of the sources on which it was based. It was also focused on the institutions of Roman society as much as on its narrative history, and this led them to an interest in Roman law even if they did not, like Mommsen, consider themselves primarily students of law rather than Classics; already in his doctoral dissertation, Mommsen, with all the intellectual arrogance that would serve him so well later, pronounced that the study of Greek was essentially philological, that of Latin essentially legal (Wiedemann 1996a: 40). Among Mommsen's earliest writings, which arose from his studies at Kiel University (where Niebuhr too had studied), were dissertations on the Roman *collegia* (trade associations), on the citizen tribes, and on certain minor magistracies (the doctoral dissertation just referred to). It was Niebuhr, already the author of a published history of Rome and editor of the second-century writer Fronto, and the future founder of the academic journal *Rheinisches Museum* (from 1827), who discovered at Verona and published the text of Gaius' *Institutes*, to which we will return below. In the special field of Roman law, Friedrich Bluhme, whose research produced the still fundamental analysis of the mode of preparation of Justinian's *Digest*, published his work in 1818 (Kunkel 1973: 158–9; Honoré 1978: 150–70).

Two other elements strengthened Mommsen's interest in Roman law and the history of Roman institutions. The first was his early involvement in the discovery and publication of inscriptions. These were important because they presented an alternative to the literary sources, and because they offered an approach to the institutional patterns in Roman society, which in turn generated a new, and already modern way of approaching its history – through the description of its social and political order rather than the narrative of its events. The second element was the movement, in Germany as elsewhere in Europe, towards unification around a national identity, to be implemented not by the hereditary monarchies but by a strong leader who would give political expression, like Mommsen's hero Julius Caesar, to the institutional and social changes that were taking place. Along with this movement went a complex debate about the relations between law and political reform, one strand of which concerned the relations between the Roman law, enshrined in the *Digest*, that had been inherited from the Middle Ages, and the European codes of the early nineteenth century (Whitman 1990: 212–28). There was an issue of jurisprudence at stake in this debate: whether the law should be codified in the interests of clarity and consistency, or left in its natural state, in order to be more sensitive to the needs of individuals and unforeseen situations. Mommsen's belief in law as an instrument of change has an obvious bearing on the politics of the nineteenth century, and, no less obviously, on his view of the Roman Empire.

Such motivation and emphasis lead more strongly to the study of public than of private law, as can certainly be said of Mommsen's two late masterpieces on Roman law. *Römisches Staatsrecht* (*Roman Public Law*), published over the years 1870/88, traced the sources and processes of public law and administration as they led the transition from republican to imperial government; and *Römisches Strafrecht*, of 1899, was about the criminal law of Rome. This does not mean that private law was not studied, far from it. Roman private law remained an essential component of the curriculum of law schools, not only in continental Europe, where the Roman model was relevant to modern practice (Mommsen's dissertation on the Roman trade guilds qualified him to practice law), but in Great Britain, where it was not. Even there, Roman law ceased to be a compulsory discipline in the syllabuses of university law faculties only within the last few decades.

Twentieth-century Roman historians writing in English, who unlike their European counterparts were never deeply involved in Roman legal studies (political debates in nineteenth-century Britain were very unlike their counterparts in continental Europe), moved away from Mommsen's concern for public law as the foundation of political institutions. This detachment was underlined by the experience of their own times. Two world wars, and the rise of dictatorships in the interwar years, showed how the institutions of a society could be manipulated by those who seized power, and how the law could as easily be made to support tyranny as to offer protection against it. The real issue, emerging one might say from the unsentimental, disillusioned tradition of Thucydides, Sallust, and Tacitus, concerned the nature of power and its manipulation by propaganda and deception. The Roman Empire, presented by Mommsen as a system of law, was really a system of power, which emerged through the murderous rivalries of dynasts (the term of the historian Appian), not the least of them Octavian who later became Augustus. One only has to read some of the chapter titles in Ronald Syme's *The Roman Revolution* of 1939, to hear the march of the fascist dictators of the 1920s and 1930s: "Dux," "Crisis in Party and State," "The National Programme," "The Organization of Opinion." The eloquent but fruitless political philosophy of Cicero, sponsoring conservatism under the guise of unity, left stranded by the flow of events from Pompey to Julius Caesar and surrendered by Octavian to the revenge of Mark Antony, is dismissed in a phrase: "Political Catchwords." Yet it was Mommsen's hero Julius Caesar, practical as well as brilliant, who planned the codification of Roman law, and one of whose supporters wrote the first detailed commentary on the Praetor's Edict (Suet. *Jul.* 44.3, with D.1.2.2.44 on Aulus Ofilius, *Caesari familiarissimus*).

Another influence in twentieth-century historical writing, emerging from a different strand in nineteenth-century thought, was an interest in social history, and in the experience of the ordinary people of the Roman Empire. This was not just a curious antiquarianism but part of a search for a historical dialectic built upon on socio-economic determinants, that would correspond to the logic of development inherent in biological studies – it is not just a coincidence that Marx's *Preface to a Contribution to the Critique of Political Economy* and Darwin's *Origin of Species* were published in the same year, 1859. This severe philosophical quest combined however with the discovery of new materials in the form of archaeology, inscriptions, and in due course papyri, to produce a practical appreciation of the diversities of life in the regions of the Roman world. The central chapters of Rostovtzeff's *Social and Economic History of the Roman Empire* (1957) are arranged, not around the central organization of the empire, but under its regions, under the general theme of town and country and the gulf of economic standing and privilege that divided them. Some texts of the *Digest* are cited in the source indexes of that great work, and Roman law (or rather, individual laws) are discussed from time to time, but the texts are concentrated on specific issues such as agrarian, commercial, and maritime law, the organization of town councils and the preservation of peace in the cities and countryside. Inscriptions and papyri are many times more numerous, and the legal texts do not form a central theme. The realization of just how far the populations of the empire, including the vast majority who lived in the country, might have been in terms of distance and culture from the city-based central authorities, might well encourage a sense that the resources of Roman law were peripheral to all but a minority of the people, and therefore to Roman history itself, as it was now understood. Yet the tendency to isolation is not all on one side. There is no shortage of textbooks and monographs on Roman law from which the physical realities of the Roman Empire seem no less remote than is the law from the pages of Rostovtzeff. This is not in all cases an outcome of neglect, but of a principled debate among legal historians themselves as to the nature of the connection between Roman law and the realities of Roman society. Alan Watson is the most recent to argue that the development of Roman law is to be understood from within the juristic tradition itself, without reference to an everyday society with which it had little connection (Watson 1995). It is an austere view, which does not seem at present to be the prevailing one among legal historians (Johnston 1999: 9–11; Frier 2000a). In any case, the argument would apply to juristic thinking rather than to the many primary texts that clearly relate to real conditions in the empire (see below, section 5).

2 Recent Developments: The *Digest*

The last three or four decades have shown an increasing eagerness among Roman historians to use the evidence of legal texts, both to address questions of a specifically legal nature, and to enrich the general understanding of the character of Roman society. John Crook's *Law and Life of Rome*, headed by the wry epigraph "Iuris consultus abesto" ("Jurisconsults Keep Off!"), appeared in 1967 and was quite explicit in its aim "to strengthen the bridge between two spheres of discourse about ancient Rome by using the institutions of the law to enlarge understanding of the society and bringing the evidence of social and economic facts to bear on the rules of law" (Crook 1967: 7). Since then has appeared a great number of studies representing the same way of thinking, on topics to which the legal evidence contributes – social and legal privilege, the status and duties of town councilors, marriage and the position of women, sexuality and prostitution, the food supply and commerce, city administration, the agrarian economy, landowners and tenants, the origin and character of the jurists themselves – not to mention those more specifically legal issues, such as crime and punishment, the Roman citizenship, testamentary succession, slavery and manumission, and others, for which the legal evidence has always been understood to be central. This work has been complemented by books in which specialists in Roman law have explained without compromise the technical character of issues in their field to a more general audience.

The single most important development in making Roman law accessible to the wider constituency of Roman historians is however the translation, by a team of translators assembled by Alan Watson, of the *Digest*, the most substantial of the four works that make up the *Corpus Iuris Civilis* of Justinian. This book, a still more massive achievement than the translation of the Theodosian Code produced by Clyde Pharr and a team of collaborators 50 years ago, should in time have a similar effect on Roman studies.

The *Digest* is one of the most important intellectual legacies of the ancient world, in bulk and variety exceeding most of them (perhaps only the Hebrew Bible and its legal commentaries contain so much of interest on so many different things). It was produced in 533 after a mere four years of work, a true reflection of the astonishing burst of energy that marks the early years of the reign of Justinian (Honoré 1978:138–86). It was accomplished under the guidance of the great jurist (and hated politician) Tribonian, by editorial committees who reduced to a mere 150,000 lines a total of 3 million lines of text contained in nearly 2,000 books (*libri*, in the sense of an ancient book division). At the head of their text the editors listed the 204 works of the 38 jurists they had read, including 13 by Gaius, 23 by Ulpian, and 71 by Paul. These works could be very substantial in their own right; Ulpian's and Paul's *Commentaries on the Edict*, for example (on which see below), consisted of 83 and 80 books respectively. To give some sense of proportion, the combined lengths of these two works alone easily exceed the original number of 142 books into which Livy – the Patavine historian, as Syme described him, "sunk by his bulk" – divided his history. Despite the scale of reduction, the emperor, no doubt giving voice to Tribonian's opinion, remarked that the completed work seemed to contain more law than anyone knew existed (*Const. "Tanta,"* 17). Like other ventures at consolidation, the *Digest* put paid to the specialist works from which it was derived and it was the *Digest*, not the works of the jurists themselves, that was the foundation of the rediscovery of Roman law in the eleventh-century schools of Bologna.

The majority of the jurists whose names occur in the *Digest* lived in the later second and early third centuries, with outliers such as Q. Mucius Scaevola and P. Alfenus Varus from the republican period and Hermogenianus and Aurelius Arcadius Charisius from the late third and early fourth century of the empire. It is ironic that the period of the jurists coincides with one that, apart from ecclesiastical writers in the shape of Tertullian and Cyprian, has left hardly any Latin literature. The *Cambridge*

History of Latin Literature produces no significant author between Fronto, Aulus Gellius, and Apuleius in the second century and the fourth century, and is totally silent on jurists. Yet jurists were invariably men of a literary education, which was the foundation of a legal education and always preceded it; they frequently rise to eloquence even in the excerpted form in which we have them, and their writings are in play in dictionaries of the Latin language. It is not obvious why juristic culture should have less of a presence in a history of Latin literature than an astrologer and the author of a handbook on military science.

The *Digest* is such a monumental book as to defy summary, beyond saying that it is divided into 50 long books, that it covers the full range of public and private law, and that in translation it fills two very large volumes in fine print. Not that it is entirely unknown, for a privileged few texts have long been in play for their contribution to specific topics and have entered into the general literature on them. No one would address such fundamental questions in political philosophy as the definition and purpose of law, or the distinctions between "civil law," "the law of nations," and "natural law," without studying the first chapter of the *Digest* and the related definitions at the beginning of Justinian's *Institutes*. Also in the first book of the *Digest* is a passage from Pomponius' "Manual in One Book," which is a plausible elementary guide to the historical development of Roman law (1.2.2). A substantial extract from Ulpian's "On the Duties of a Proconsul" explains very carefully how a governor should treat his province, to the extent of advising him that he may take his wife though it is preferable for him not to, asking him to ensure that he enters his province by the most important city (mentioning Ephesus, the metropolis of Asia), reminding him that he must listen patiently to endless speeches of welcome since the provincials expect it of him, and warning him to be careful to strike a balance between accepting too many gifts and seeming offhand through refusing them. On this last point a letter of the emperor Caracalla is quoted, expressing his opinion with an apt Greek proverb. In any discussion of provincial life in its relations with the ruling power, this text is essential reading (1.16.4, 1.16.6–7, 1.16.9–10). So too in the matter of demographic trends is the "life-table" cited by the jurist Aemilius Macer from Ulpian, giving figures for life expectancy from various base points, from birth to 60, in order to calculate the tax consequences that arise for the future in the case of usufructs and annuities received as inheritances (35.2.68). It is a complicated law, much debated by scholars, but on any account is an essential component in any discussion of life expectancy in the Roman Empire (Frier 1982; Parkin 1992: 27–41). A ruling, again by Ulpian, that *fideicommissa* might be expressed in any language, whether Latin or Greek, "Gallic" (that is, Celtic), Punic, or "Assyrian" (which we know as Syriac), or "any other language," so long as it was understood by the participants, through an interpreter if necessary, has an obvious bearing on the use of the non-Classical languages in the Roman provinces (32.11 or 45.1.1), as, on the broad question of literacy, does his opinion as to the length of time, physical conditions, and language in which a notice must be displayed to allow it to come to public attention (14.3.11). We learn too from the *Digest* that it was common practice in dispute settlement to avoid litigation by taking oaths, on the basis that "the taking of an oath is a species of settlement and has greater authority than a judgment," and that "it is an indication of manifest wickedness and an admission, to refuse to swear or to counter-tender" (Paul *D.* 12.2.2.38). If widely practiced, this custom would have a great impact on our understanding of the conduct of law in the Roman Empire, and on the law itself.

To such texts as these, we may add the endless individual circumstances, real or imagined, that arise in the course of legal discussion. What are we to make of the slave fishermen who "attended a testator and followed him everywhere" (the question arose because at the time of the testator's death the slaves were not on his farm and so did not seem to be part of his property)? Are plant pots full of earth and containing plants part of the house? (They are, provided they are fastened to the house permanently.) This whole title of the *Digest* (33.7), on farms and their equipment or *instrumenta*, reads like a physical archaeology of the rural household; another, with a similar variety in the situations found or imagined, considers the uses of and damage caused by rain, ditches and water channels, rivers and standing water (39.3). The Roman Empire, and not just the life of its richest classes, comes to life in these pages. Some of the circumstances that arise would not be out of place in Petronius or Apuleius (to which it is worth adding that the *Dinner of Trimalchio* contains an informative parody of a Roman will, and that Apuleius' *Apology* is the best example that we have of a Roman lawsuit in the provinces). One text considers the value of a slave with a mental rather than a physical defect, such as being "addicted to watching the games or studying works of art or lying" (21.1.65); another considers the consequences that arise when two carts being pushed up the slopes of the Capitol run out of control back down the hill and knock down a slave boy belonging to someone else (9.1.52.2); another asked what would happen if freedom had been given to two slaves on condition that they had painted a room and built a ship, and one completed his task but the other not (40.4.13). Whether real, or imagined in order to illustrate points of law, such situations are part of the thought-world of the writers, and so part of the history of their society.

Behind the whole question of the nature of legal texts and the way in which they can be used by historians is that of the legal procedures from which they arise. This is another way of putting the question of the sources of law, and it is to this that we turn next.

3 Sources of the Law and Forms of Legislation

The term "sources of law," has two senses (cf. Johnston 1999: 1). The first is a practical question, better expressed in terms of "transmission" than "sources": how do we, as historians, recover our knowledge of the law? The answer, easier to state than to implement given the multiplicity of sources, comprises the writers of literature, legal texts, inscriptions, papyri, and so on, on which we base our knowledge (O. Robinson 1997: 54–78). In reading these sources, we must always be alert to the agendas, whether overt or hidden, that they contain. This is especially true of literary texts, which often describe legal processes, in anecdotes expressing the writer's judgment, in matters not directly to do with the law; they were not written to tell *us* about the law, but with concerns of their own. An example is the story of the emperor Claudius, who was extremely devoted to hearing legal cases and did it with such disregard for proper procedure that on one occasion an infuriated defendant, a Roman knight, hurled his sharpened pen and writing tablets at the emperor, badly cutting his cheek (Suet. *Claud.* 15). Another anecdote shows Augustus as judge, questioning a man accused of parricide in such a way that the defendant would have to insist on his own guilt in order to be condemned: "You surely did not kill your father?" (Suet. *Aug.* 33). Both stories are told in order to illustrate the character of the main protagonists – Augustus conscientious and lenient, Claudius willful and stupid – rather than to make a legal point. They are evidence, however, for the emperor's role in jurisdiction.

An especially important source of information is inscriptions, either put up by imperial instruction in order to publicize the law or by successful petitioners who were anxious to record decisions in their favor and the services of the individuals who had secured them – that is to say that these too have their agendas, in the need to secure publicity. There are papyrus and other records of legal proceedings, which are interesting because they may take us to parts of the empire beyond the normal reach of the central government and into the domain of local law; and many individual documents in the class known as *negotia* (business transactions): agreements, leases, and contracts of different sorts. The main single source is of course the massive compilations of extracts made by jurists, to which we shall return.

The question of the sources of law in its second sense – what, in the Romans' view, gave authority to the law – can most easily be addressed as a law student in the later second century would address it, from a standard textbook. The opening sentences of Gaius' *Institutes* go straight to the heart of the matter. The sources of law are as follows: in the first place are laws (*leges*) and plebiscites; then there are *senatusconsulta*, imperial edicts and the edicts of other magistrates, especially the praetors and *aediles*; and the opinions of those jurists who were permitted to "establish" it (the Latin word is *condere*). His formulation is echoed by the early third-century jurist Papinian: "the civil law (*ius civile*) is that which comes in the form of statutes, plebiscites, senatus consulta, imperial decrees, or authoritative juristic statements" (*D.* 1.1.7).

From the point of view of the authority of the law, it does not matter that Gaius and Papinian were giving a composite picture as it had developed to their own day, since Roman law was cumulative, and in all the forms which they mentioned had left some law that was still in active use. For example, Gaius explains the historical distinction between statute laws and plebiscites, observing that the latter were given the status of laws by the *Lex Hortensia* (of 267 BCE). By Gaius' time, the distinction was a matter of history only. It was still the case, however, that some of the "laws" that he and his contemporary jurists had to deal with were in fact plebiscites. The *Lex Aquilia*, of the later third century BCE, concerned liabilities and remedies for damage to property, an extremely important subject. It merits an entire title in the *Digest*, in the first extract of which Ulpian notes the historical point that the "law," which superseded all previous laws, was in fact a plebiscite, on a motion introduced by a tribune (9.2.1).

Statute law, in whatever form, was uncommon under the Roman Empire. After the many "*Leges Iuliae*" and others introduced or instigated by Augustus on various subjects (a sort of Indian summer of statute legislation), few statutory *leges* emerged from the Roman assemblies. Those that did, tended to reflect the political and dynastic needs of the ruling house and were often ceremonial in character, such as the series of laws setting out the posthumous honors to be paid to the princes Gaius and Lucius in 5 CE, and to Germanicus and Drusus after their premature deaths in 19 and 23 CE respectively. The law of 19, previously known in part and recently supplemented by one of several spectacular discoveries of inscriptions from Spain, has been somewhat over-interpreted because of its apparent reference to reforms in the procedures for electing consuls and praetors, but in its complete version it emerges as an essentially ceremonial – though very interesting – enactment (Jones 1955: 9–21; González 1984). After this, the list of *leges* promulgated by the Roman people peters out very quickly. The best known is the so-called *Lex de Imperio Vespasiani* ("Law Concerning the Imperial Power of Vespasian") of 70 CE, part of which survives in a fine bronze inscription now displayed in the Palazzo dei Conservatori at Rome, recording with precedents the concatenation of powers bestowed upon Vespasian upon his accession to the imperial office; whether it is taken to be ceremonial or substantive legislation depends on the view taken of the institutions of the early principate (Brunt 1977b). The last statutory legislation issued by the people is from the time of Nerva in 97 CE, but existing laws, many of them very ancient, continued to underlie the legal processes of the Roman Empire.

It is evident from the law of 19 honoring Germanicus, that its origin was a resolution of the Senate inviting legislation from the people, and this raises the next item in Gaius' list of sources, decrees of the Senate. So partisan was the role of the Senate in the later republic that it could hardly then have been claimed as a legal authority by a conscientious jurist. Under the empire, however, despite complaints in some quarters of its loss of political liberties, the legal authority of the Senate was increased, through its relations with the people in the way we have just seen, and with the emperors (Talbert 1984: 431–59). We find the Senate issuing regulatory provisions in the form of *senatus consulta*, on matters such as public games at Syracuse (Tac. *Ann.* 15.49), the establishment of a market in north Africa (Riccobono, *FIRA*^{2}, I, No. 47), and the cost of gladiators in the provinces (*FIRA*^{2}, I, No. 49: Oliver and Palmer 1955). Some *senatus consulta*, which were often, but not always, responses to an imperial request for legislation, had a permanent effect upon important issues, such as the *senatus consultum Claudianum* on the marriage of partners of free and slave status, and the *senatus consulta Orfitianum* and *Tertullianum* on the inheritance and testamentary rights of women. The *s.c. Claudianum*, a set of regulations framed, ironically, by Claudius' freedman Pallas, was not repealed (through disuse) until the time of Justinian.

Until the emergence of the emperors as lawgivers, Roman legal development owed more to the implementation and adaptation of existing rules than to substantive change in the law. This was done by the interventions of magistrates in the judicial process, and especially the Praetor's Edict. This was the annual statement by which the urban praetor (also the *praetor peregrinus* in matters concerning resident aliens, and the *aediles* in matters affecting the markets) announced his forthcoming policy in the administration of the law – what types of case he would hear, what defenses he would admit, what exceptions he would allow, and so on. Each year the praetor would review the policy of his predecessor, accepting arguments and grounds of procedure that had been found satisfactory and rejecting or reviewing those that had not (Watson 1974b).

Praetorian jurisdiction was a cumbersome procedure, but it allowed for the application of the law to be changed even when the law itself was not. The most interesting example of this is the "legal fiction" whereby the prohibition of a non-citizen from taking legal action against a citizen was circumvented by the "fiction" that the non-citizen was in fact a citizen, a counterfactual assertion that allowed the law to develop in the interests of a broader conception of justice. Another was the procedure of "restoration" (*restitutio in integrum*), whereby under certain circumstances – if a victim had been unable to reach a court to defend his interests, for example, or could claim intimidation or fraud – a praetor could set aside a legal transaction in the interests of justice. A comical but still instructive example of the praetor's powers is cited by Aulus Gellius (Gel. 20.1.13) from the writings of the Augustan jurist Labeo on the Twelve Tables. An offensive Roman by the name of L. Veratius was in the habit of accosting free Romans and slapping them in the face. He would then take 25 *asses* from a slave following him and give them to the person he had insulted, this being the fine, by now of no value, laid down by the Twelve Tables. The praetors added to their Edict the provision that the question of damages in such a case would be henceforth submitted to a board of "recoverers" (*recuperatores*) for appraisal, and this became the law in future. And to take an example from statute law, almost the whole title in the *Digest* relating to the *Lex Aquilia* mentioned earlier consists of extracts from juristic commentaries on the edicts of the praetors and provincial governors (*D.* 9.2.1–57). The law itself was neither changed nor repealed, but was progressively modified in its application by magisterial edict and juristic interpretation.

In the time of Hadrian, the Edict was consolidated as a statement of private law by the great jurist Salvius Julianus. It was the subject of the massive commentaries by Gaius, Ulpian, and others mentioned earlier, and in its organization of subject matter underlies the private law sections of the Theodosian Code, the *Codex Justinianus*, and the *Digest* itself. The text of the Edict, which does not survive in its complete state, was reconstituted by Otto Lenel from the references to it made by the commentaries cited in the *Digest* and other sources.

Long before its codification by Julianus, the Edict had been superseded by a new set of procedures deriving from the concentration of magisterial powers in the hands of the Roman emperors. The emperor was now expected to remedy deficiencies in the law by changing it substantively, and he did so by all the means mentioned by Gaius – by decree, edict, and letter, all of which became known collectively by the single term, "constitution." Modern discussions are often content to describe them by the single term "pronouncement," or even "law," but they differ in character. Decrees (*decreta*) are strictly understood as legal rulings arising from the emperor's role as judge. Edicts were open communications directly addressed to the people at large or to individual communities, while letters were addressed to governors with instructions to enforce them within their jurisdictions. The best-known example of legislation by edict is probably the set of edicts issued by Augustus to the province of Cyrene on various aspects of local jurisdiction (Sherk 1984: 127–32), while the tenth book of Pliny's letters, those exchanged with Trajan from the province of Bithynia, provides an excellent example of lawmaking by letters addressed to a provincial governor (Sherwin-White 1966: 525–8). Trajan's reply to Pliny on the subject of the trial and punishment of Christians, for instance, is founded on an assertion of sound legal principles – only actual crimes are to be punished, alleged Christians are not to be sought out, and anonymous denunciations are not to be admitted (Pliny *Ep.* 10.96–7).

Gaius' claim, with which Ulpian agreed (*D.* 1.4.1), that imperial edicts possessed the force of law because they were an exercise of his imperium that was bestowed on him by law has been criticized as unsatisfactory. However, the formulation is only meant to provide an underpinning in constitutional theory for a right that the emperor was clearly understood to possess. Ulpian offered an enlargement of the theory, in the form of the proposition, "anything decided by the emperor has the force of law" (*D.* 1.4.1 pr.). This is not quite so bald a statement as it looks. Ulpian defined the categories of authoritative imperial pronouncements as whatever the emperor had decided "by letter over his signature or decreed on judicial investigation, or pronounced in an interlocutory manner or prescribed in an edict;" in sum, "what we commonly call constitutions." The word used for "decided," *placet*, is the formal word for a decision taken in due order by a properly constituted body, and there could hardly be any doubt that the emperor was such. We have also to take into account the expectation in every area of Roman life, that when serious decisions were taken, they were taken seriously and with relevant advice. The emperor's rulings possessed legal force because of the emperor's authority *as properly exercised*, namely with the advice of jurists. For the whole process of change and innovation in the law, whether this was done by procedural intervention by praetors or by substantive changes brought in by emperors, the contribution of jurists was essential.

4 The Nature of the Material

In using the evidence of legal texts, historians need to be aware of two distinctions of form. The first is between imperial pronouncements that were meant to be valid in all relevant situations, and those that were not intended to create precedent. The first category, that of "general laws," was defined as those pronouncements issued as edict, decree, or letter to a public authority or official, and made known by posting in public places, usually in association with an edict of the governor of a province (Matthews 2000: 65–70). Many laws so issued and published were very specific and even eccentric in content; nevertheless, and this is the essence of their definition as "general laws," the rule was to be applied whenever similar situations might recur in future.

The Theodosian Code is a collection of more than 2,700 (originally 3,500) "general laws" on all imaginable matters, legal, political, and administrative, from the reign of Constantine down to the time of compilation in the 430s. The material is incomplete, since it could only contain those texts that were actually found by the editors, and it is clear that they missed many (Matthews 2000: 291); not only this, but the manuscript tradition of the first five books of the code – those on the private law – is incomplete, with the paradoxical result that the most important source for the content of these books is the *Lex Romana Visigothorum* published in southern Gaul in 506. Despite these deficiencies, the code as we have it is a fuller and better organized collection of imperial constitutions than was available to any individual of the fourth or early fifth centuries who was living under the law, or to any emperor who was actually making it. The modern historian using the code, and indeed the legal material in general, must always remember that while he has the material in codified form, its ancient subjects did not.

It is difficult to weigh these considerations in assessing the force or effectiveness of any particular text. A. H. M. Jones' much-quoted observation in the Preface to his *The Later Roman Empire* that the laws preserved in the Theodosian Code "are clues to the difficulties of the empire, and records of the aspirations of the government and not its achievement" (1964: viii) is salutary, but less helpful than it seems. Take for instance the longest title of the Theodosian Code, which contains 192 laws originating between 313 and 436 on the subject of city councils (*CTh.* 12.1). Even allowing for the fact that some of these texts are cited from the same original law and should be reassembled into a smaller number, this is still a lot of legislation; but the Roman Empire was immense, and contained thousands of cities. It is the role of governments to confront problems, and governments are always at odds with taxpayers; it seems impossible to say whether this number of laws spread over this period is larger or smaller than one would expect, or whether the laws do more than document an unresolved battle of interests between government and (the better-off) governed. Apart from their general legislation, there is a second and very numerous category of legal rulings, given by the emperor or in his name, in the form of replies to individual petitioners on matters they brought forward for decision. From the start, the emperors had given rulings and benefits to all sorts of petitioners who managed to reach them (Millar 1977: 465–549), and Ulpian made the necessary distinction between general constitutions and those which, being issued to individuals, were not considered to set precedent (*D.* 1.4.2). That there seems to have been an increase of rescripts during the third century may be a trick of the evidence for the reasons to be described below, but there may also be a substantive cause, in the form of Caracalla's enactment of 212 CE, the famous *constitutio Antoniniana*, to the effect that all free inhabitants of the Roman Empire, whatever their social status, would become Roman citizens. Caracalla's critics claimed that his motive was simply to extend tax liability to a greater sector of the population, but whether this is true or not, a consequence of the change was an immediate increase in the numbers of people who fell under Roman law and reaped the benefits – or were exposed to the disadvantages – of its procedures.

Our main source of rescripts consists of two legal codes of the late third century, the *Codex Gregorianus* and its close successor the *Codex Hermogenianus*, both named after jurists who held court office under Diocletian and his colleagues (the system of government known as the tetrarchy). Neither code is extant in its own right, but both were excerpted for general rules in the *Codex Justinianus*, published in successive editions in 529 and 534, and can partly be reassembled from that source. The Gregorian Code contained rescripts going back from the jurist's own day to the later second and early third centuries. The Hermogenian Code collected rescripts issued by the tetrarchs – the vast majority by Diocletian himself, under whom Hermogenianus served as *Magister Libellorum* (Master of Petitions); more precisely, he collected texts from just two years, 293–4, of the reign of Diocletian (Honoré 1994: 163–81). The result is a challenge to the imagination. Even in their excerpted state, the two codes preserve more than 2,500 texts from the period they cover, and more than 850 from these two years of the reign of Diocletian (Honoré 1994: 189). It is perhaps going a little too far to describe the situation, with Honoré, as a "legal advisory service" provided by the emperor, but the scale on which the emperor, or his judicial department, was prepared to respond to his subjects' legal enquiries is very surprising, and has implications for our understanding of the imperial office itself. Diocletian cannot realistically be claimed to have personally weighed every judicial response made to his petitioners in these two years. The sheer numbers of rescripts and the technicality of many of them imply delegation to the people – again, the jurists – who would know how to handle them.

Rescripts, as we saw, were not in principle meant to apply to other than the cases for which they were issued. The very existence of the Gregorian and Hermogenian codes shows however that in practice this could not be so, for the obvious reason that, even in specific cases, the emperor or his jurists would state the grounds for their decisions. Legal thinking, like all organized thinking, is a matter of defining categories of understanding within which individual situations can be evaluated, and it is in the nature of law to justify action in a particular case by appealing to principles larger than the case itself. If the emperor gave a good reason for a decision issued to an individual, this would take its place in the thinking about the subject.

5 *Leges* and *Ius*

The second distinction, which has pervaded this chapter, is between different types of text – between the substantive pronouncements of legal authorities, in our period mainly the emperors, and the law that was written from the texts, which was the work of jurists.

Legal codification before the *Digest* had a limited aim. It consisted simply in the collection and publication of the verbatim pronouncements of the emperors, classified by topic and set in order, without general indications of the law that could be inferred from them. This is true of the Gregorian and Hermogenian codes, of the Theodosian Code which imitated their arrangement although not their principles of selection (since it contained only general law), and of the *Codex Justinianus*, which excerpted the earlier codes and added material from the period after the Theodosian Code down to Justinian's own day. The texts were edited to identify the substantive point at issue, which essentially means that the supportive rhetoric often attached to imperial pronouncements, together with any rationale the emperors may have offered to justify them, was omitted; the substantive text was left unchanged, though it might be divided into sections appropriate for the different titles under which the texts were arranged, or repeated if it were relevant to more than one. An incidental benefit to the historian is that, in the absence of any critical evaluation of the points of law that were involved, the texts were simply set out in chronological order, under the basic principle "the later, the more valid" (*CTh.* 1.1.5). Since the place of issue and recipient of the communications are also recorded, they provide us with the fullest information about imperial movements and the identity of their supporters that is available for any period of Roman history (Seeck 1919; Jones, Martindale, and Morris 1971; Martindale 1980; Barnes 1982).

The distinction before us is that between, on the one hand, *leges* or *constitutiones* in the various forms referred to, the primary pronouncements of Roman emperors, and, on the other hand, *ius*, the "law" itself, as deduced by the jurists from their scrutiny of the texts. It was part of the original plan of Theodosius II to add a compendium of "law" to the collection of *leges* that we possess in the Theodosian Code itself. The projected volume would be closer to a modern idea of codification, an authoritative statement of the "law" as it stood. It would present "no error, no ambiguities, [but would show] what must be followed and what must be avoided by all" (*CTh.* 1.1.5). No trace survives of progress on this ambitious project. In the meantime, Roman courts worked with an extremely restricted range of juristic writing, notably Papinian, Gaius, Ulpian, Modestinus, and Paul, and epitomes of these writers (*CTh.* 1.4.3). When the early sixth-century editors of the *Lex Romana Visigothorum* annotated their texts, which they selected from the Theodosian Code, to the effect that they needed supplementation from *ius*, they meant precisely this, that the pronouncements of emperors needed setting in the context of legal writing. It was left to Tribonian and his colleagues to complement the collection of laws in the *Codex Justinianus* by a critical presentation of the law as considered by jurists, in the *Digest* and *Institutes*.

In considering the role of the jurists, one question that has not been mentioned so far, but is of very great importance for the closer study of legal texts, is the extent of interpolation. The editors of the Theodosian Code were forbidden to do more than adjust texts in order to preserve their sense as they excerpted them, but it would be natural for jurists working on the legal texts of the past to modify them in the light of their own later knowledge, and all legal scholars agree that in the *Digest* this has taken place, to a greater or lesser extent (Johnston 1999: 17–22). The point of high fashion in interpolation was reached in the nineteenth century, when literary texts too were exposed to the suspicions of editors who put their own judgment of what an author should have written above the evidence for what he actually did write, but that ancient legal texts were subject to interpolation is beyond doubt. How else, for example, did the provision in the *Lex Julia de Maiestate* that provincial governors may not act in certain ways "without the instruction of the senate and Roman people" become transformed into the formula "without the instruction of the Princeps," except by the silent correction of Marcian or some other jurist (*D.* 48.4.3)? It is not conceivable that the wily, clever Augustus made such a change, and he is the latest possible author of a *Lex Julia* (on any subject). In the same way Constantine's suspension of gladiatorial combat recorded in the Theodosian Code, which refers to the end of civil war and onset of domestic peace after the defeat of Licinius and is known only from the copy posted at Beirut, appears in the *Codex Justinianus* as the sole text of a title referring to a "total ban" of the institution (*CTh.* 15.12.1, *CJust* 11.44). Too many historians of Constantine accept the stronger interpretation without asking whether it may be an interpolation of the time of Justinian, by which time gladiatorial combat had indeed come to an end.

6 Conclusion

In his Prolegomena to the Theodosian Code, Mommsen remarked that their laws were collected by the Romans as a matter of public initiative only twice in their history; in the Twelve Tables, published at Rome at the outset of the republic, and in the Theodosian Code, published at Constantinople at the close of the empire. He clearly regarded the work of Justinian as falling outside the true period of Roman history (or, worse, as a project of Greek inspiration). It is equally clear, however, that neither Theodosius nor Justinian thought of their work as a legacy of a dying empire for the future, but as a contribution to its continuing life. In that sense the readers closest to the original intentions of the codes and the *Digest* are those historians who aspire to use it to reconstruct the life of the Roman Empire in all its available dimensions.

Roman law, in the fine words of Bruce Frier, is an "intricate and honored discipline" (Frier 2000a: 446), and the historian must respond with both an awareness of the intricacy and a respect for the discipline. Some of the challenges have been described in this chapter: the question of precedent, the extent to which laws addressing one situation are intended to apply to others, whether they "map onto" social reality, whether they portray a social ideal in the minds of legislators, or simply reveal the imperfections of society as perceived by them, whether, in many cases, they are real or imagined situations and, if the latter, what difference this makes; the sources of jurisdiction, the distinctions between procedural and substantive change, between *leges* and *ius*; the sheer technicality of much of the literature. All of these issues present difficulties which the historian must address by establishing rules of procedure and in difficult cases by principled judgment; which is, after all, how the law itself developed.

CHAPTER TWENTY-FIVE

Roman Medicine

Ann Hanson

1 Roman Medicine and its Antecedents in the Greek World

As with many other arts and sciences Greek achievements in secular medicine during the Classical and Hellenistic periods served as a backdrop for the medicine that developed in Rome. The transplantation of Greek medicine to Rome, followed by its recasting to better suit the tastes and demands of Roman society and the subsequent spread of that medicine throughout the Roman Empire, was one of the important events in the history of medicine (Nutton 2004: 157). Although we can be very certain that such a transfer did take place, it is difficult to trace the process prior to the middle of the second century BCE, a time when Greek practitioners were beginning to be well established at Rome.

The earliest Roman contacts with Greek healing involved the importation of cults of healing gods as a response to the plague epidemics that were devastating Rome and Latium. A temple was dedicated to Apollo in 431 BCE, ordered by the Sibylline books (Livy 4.25.3); the temple was built on the site of a preexisting shrine to Apollo, signaling Roman awareness that this foreign god could be useful in fighting pestilence. Roman envoys journeyed farther afield in 292 BCE, when the Sibylline books again prescribed the transference of the healing god Asclepius to combat another plague. After reaching the god's most important shrine at Epidaurus in the northeastern Peloponnese, they found the god, whom they called Aesculapius, more than willing to return with them in the form of a snake. The envoys watched in horror as the snake slithered away once they reached the coast of Italy – first at the port of Antium and again upon their arrival in Rome. It eventually reappeared on the Tiber Island where the god's sanctuary was then established (Val. Max. 1.8.2; Ov. *Met.* 15.622–744; Livy, *Per.* 11). Both the temple to Apollo Medicus and that to Aesculapius were situated outside the sacred boundary of Rome (*pomerium*), as was customary for temples dedicated to foreign gods. The site of Aesculapius' temple was considered particularly salubrious with its clean air and plentiful supply of fresh, clear water, and, as at Epidaurus, patients slept in the temple in the expectation the god would visit them in a dream with information about a cure (incubation). Romans may have learned about these healing deities from the Greeks of south Italy or Sicily with whom they were in contact, or from the Etruscans to the north, but whether any of the sophisticated and secular medicine that was being practiced in the fifth and fourth centuries BCE in the Greek world came to Rome with the snake of Aesculapius is unclear.

According to the Roman annalist Lucius Cassius Hemina (mid-second century BCE), it was Archagathus, summoned from Sparta in 219 BCE, who introduced the Romans to Greek medicine; he was invited at public expense, given citizenship rights (*ius Quiritium*), and a work-space in which to practice his art at an important crossroads in the city. At first, Romans referred to him as a "wound-healer" (*uolnerarius*), apparently because of special skills in dealing with accidents and war wounds, and he was said to have been wonderfully popular. Soothing plasters attributed to Archagathus for healing wounds and medicating skin diseases are occasionally quoted for centuries to come (Celsus, *Med.* 5.19.27; *P.Merton* I 12; Cael.Aur., *TP* 4.1.7). Hemina's account, however, is preserved for us by Pliny the Elder, the encyclopedist of the *Natural Histories* who perished in the eruption of Vesuvius in 79 CE, and he located Archagathus' story in the midst of his own tirade against the medical profession and the enormous profits Greek doctors were reaping in the Rome of his day. He castigated not only their greed for fees, but pointed to the adulteries they were committing with Roman matrons and wives of emperors, and the malpractice and murders they carried out with impunity, as they went about intervening in many aspects of Roman private life (*Nat.* 29.1.1–29.8.28, especially 29.6.12–8.15). Pliny intended his as a negative account of medicine, beginning with a version of the Asclepius myth that had the god struck by lightning for bringing a dead mortal back to life and continuing with the implication that Hippocrates copied out inscriptions set up at the temple of Asclepius on Cos by grateful patients in order to use the remedies in the construction of his own medicine. Thus, Pliny was pleased to add Hemina's tale about the career of Archagathus at Rome, for, because of the cruelty he displayed through his surgery and cautery, cutting and burning the bodies of his Roman patients, they changed his name to "Executioner" (*carnifex*). As a result, "the entire art of medicine and all (Greek) doctors became objects of loathing." The alternative, according to Pliny, consisted of the simple remedies Romans had always used, and their application required no intervention by a professional healer; instead, the Roman head of the household, the *pater familias*, was to doctor his own family, as he had done from Rome's earliest days. Pliny noted with approval the notebook of recipes by which Marcus Porcius Cato the Elder (consul, 195 BCE; censor, 184 BCE) had once kept himself and his wife healthy into old age, as well as their young son, the family's slaves, and entire household. In his work on estate management, *On Agriculture*, Cato claimed to cure a dislocated joint through chants and the application of a long reed that had been split, then rejoined over the bone, and affixed to the dislocation (*Agr.* 160). By contrast, a Greek medical writer of the *Hippocratic Corpus* in the late fifth century BCE concentrated in his surgical treatise "Joints" on various methods of extension by which to reset a dislocated shoulder, and he appealed to specialized equipment, such as leather straps, boards, and ladders, to facilitate the doctor's efforts, along with his hands, his head, even his heel to achieve the extension, as his assistant applied counter-pressure. He advised cautery of the skin under the armpit in cases of repeated dislocations of the shoulder (Hippoc. *Art.* 2–12). Greek treatments could seem violent and were no doubt initially shocking to Roman patients, but they were also far more likely to return the limb to normal use in the case of a dislocation or a fracture (Nijhuis 1995).

Cato himself stood in the vanguard of those who argued that Rome's traditional values were being attacked by those Romans who advocated further conquest in the Greek world of the eastern Mediterranean. Romans told themselves that the defeat of Hannibal in the Second Punic War (218–201 BCE) bereft them of the strenuous and mighty Carthaginian foes who for decades had exercised them and forced them to stay strong. With Hannibal gone, the influx of Greeks, their cultural products, their luxurious habits, and their medicine were making Romans soft, and thus in need of more elaborate doctoring. The attitude of Cato, whose political career was rooted in opposition to his contemporaries, the Philhellenes, nonetheless appealed nearly three centuries later to Pliny, despite the fact that Greek doctors dominated the medical scene at Rome around the time of Cato's death. It is thus clear that not all Romans took so dim a view of the Greek practitioners in their midst as did Cato, and having Greek medical personnel attached to one's household was becoming fashionable in the middle decades of the second century BCE. The very successful playwright Plautus, an older contemporary of Cato, thought his Roman audience would find a Greek doctor and his methods humorous, for he put one on stage in a scene from his popular comedy of mistaken identity, the *Menaechmus Twins*. The scene may well have been inspired by an earlier play in Greek that Plautus was using as his model, but by including the Greek doctor in his own comedy Plautus demonstrated his confidence that such a doctor would make Romans laugh. The action of Plautus' play was set in the Greek city of Epidamnus, where the pair of like-named twins, accidentally separated when they were seven, were reunited unbeknownst to anyone, including themselves; so identical were they in appearance that the Epidamnian family of the one continually mistook the twin newly arrived from Syracuse for their husband and son-in-law. A Greek doctor was brought on stage to diagnose madness in the Epidamnian Menaechmus, because in previous scenes the Syracusan Menaechmus refused to recognize members of the Epidamnian family, for he had, of course, never seen them before. Much as a Greek physician operating in the Hippocratic tradition might do, Plautus' doctor began to build a case history, questioning his prospective patient in the presence of his father-in-law:

> Doctor: Do you drink white wine or red?
> Menaechmus: Why don't you go hang yourself?
> Doctor (*aside*): My goodness, he is really beginning to go mad!
> Menaechmus: Why don't you ask me if I usually eat purple bread, or red or yellow bread? Or how about birds with scales, or fish with feathers?
> Doctor: Tell me, do your eyes ever seem hard and fixed?
> Menaechmus: What do you think I am, a lobster, you jerk?
> Doctor: Well, do your innards ever make a rumbling noise, as far as you can tell?
> Menaechmus: When I am full, they never rumble at all, but when I am hungry, they do.

Doctor (*aside*): That hardly seems the response of a crazy man. (*To Menaechmus*) Do you sleep through the night, falling asleep easily?

Menaechmus: Sure, I sleep through the night when I've paid my bills. Damn you, and your questioning!

Doctor (*aside*): Now he's beginning to be insane. (Plaut. *Men.* 914–56, condensed)

Both doctor and father-in-law concluded from the increasing violence of Menaechmus' responses that the Epidamnian twin had, in fact, gone mad, although he mused to himself that he was certainly in good health and always had been. In his view the members of his own Epidamnian family were the crazy ones as they recounted their exasperating experiences with the Menaechmus from Syracuse. Nonetheless, Epidamnian Menaechmus was dragged offstage all unwilling by four slaves to the doctor's quarters for treatment with a potion of hellebore for the next 20 days, a conventional remedy for insanity throughout the Greek world.

The immigrant doctors who first arrived in Rome apparently brought with them from their homelands the latest medical practices and theories, including not only the achievements of the medical writers whose treatises appeared in the *Hippocratic Corpus* of the fifth and early fourth centuries BCE, but also the advances in anatomy and physiology pioneered by doctors in Ptolemaic Alexandria, who were for the first time performing systematic dissections and even vivisection on the bodies of criminals condemned to death (von Staden 1989: 26–31, 139–53). The "cutting and cauterizing" attributed to Archagathus no doubt startled Romans at first, but Archagathus was soon followed by an increasing number of Greek-speaking practitioners, and the more successful of them became better attuned to the culture and society of the Romans, more adept at catering to distinctly Roman habits and preferences. For example, Asclepiades of Bithynia (early first century BCE) popularized his non-invasive therapeutics – massage, bathing, and passive exercise, such as riding horseback, or in a boat or litter, and reading aloud – and mild medicaments, such as wine and water for the management of diet, rather than recourse to drugs; his prescriptions were famous for being more pleasant and also less damaging to the stomach. To Pliny, Greek doctors were "hunting for popular favor by advertising their novel cures" (*Nat.* 29.5.11), and, while this criticism was perhaps apt for some, the later Greek doctors whose writings have come down to us displayed considerable sensitivity to the hierarchical power structure operative within the Roman family, expending considerable efforts to educate the *pater familias* about their medicine and emphasizing his responsibility for choosing those who would doctor in his household. In his *Gynecology* Soranus (c.60–130 CE) instructed the *pater familias* on how to select the best-qualified nurse and wet nurse for the females and infants over whom his authority extended (*Gyn.* 1.2–5); in his medical autobiography *Prognosis* Galen (129–c.216 CE) explained to another *pater familias* the theory and authority behind the treatments he would use for the man's wife and young son in this consular household and again on another occasion to the chamberlain in the imperial household how and why he medicated the emperor's son Commodus as he did, since the chamberlain was in charge of the boy in the absence of his father, Marcus Aurelius (*Praecog.* 7–8, 12). Galen also wrote a short treatise on methods for choosing a competent doctor, *Examinations of the Best Physicians*, now lost in Greek, but surviving in Arabic translation; in it Galen argued that proper questioning meant interrogating a physician first about medical theory and the doctrines espoused by the best among previous practitioners, including Hippocrates, and then by testing him in the clinical diagnosis of specific cases and their therapies (*Examin.* 9).

2 Sources for Roman Medicine: Authors, Texts, and Artifacts

Our views about the medicine practiced at Rome from the second century BCE until the collapse of the empire in the seventh century CE are heavily influenced by the medical writings that survived to modern times. Additional information about the profession from an empire-wide perspective and the healing methods employed throughout the Mediterranean world can be drawn from a variety of other sources. There are accounts of illnesses in non-medical writers; the inscriptions *medici* and *medicae* placed on their tombs in the Latin-speaking west, or *iatroi* and *iatrinai* in the Greek-speaking east; the papyri of medical content from the dry sands of the province of Egypt which provide a glimpse of medical literature otherwise lost; amulets and charms that claimed healing properties which have been found throughout the empire. Nonetheless, the writers, such as the Greeks Soranus of Ephesus and Galen of Pergamum, both of whom journeyed from towns whose ruins still grace the coast of modern Turkey to practice at Rome, tell us much, and Greek names dominate among medical professionals and other healers, not only in the city and eastern provinces, but even in western ones (Korpela 1987; Nutton 2004, 164–6). Latin writers are not totally absent, but their own texts reveal the great extent to which doctoring among Romans had absorbed and assimilated the Greek antecedents. Two authors of the Julio-Claudian period, Aulus Cornelius Celsus and Scribonius Largus, will be investigated here in some detail together with Soranus and Galen.

In the reign of the emperor Tiberius (14–37 CE) Cornelius Celsus wrote a Latin encyclopedia on the four *Artes*, agriculture, military science, rhetoric, and medicine (Quint. *Inst.* 12.11.24). Only the seven-book "On medicine" (*De medicina*) survives to our time, and this work went virtually unmentioned after the late first century CE, although it was copied a number of times in the ninth and tenth centuries CE, thus testifying to continued interest by some in Celsus' text; when these manuscript copies were rediscovered in the early fifteenth century, they created quite a stir (Reeve 1986a: 46–7). Celsus was remarkably knowledgeable about Greek secular medicine up to his own day, giving mostly favorable mentions to many of the important practitioners, such as Hippocrates in the world of Classical Greece, the anatomists Erasistratus and Herophilus in Ptolemaic Alexandria, and among those Greeks who made a reputation for themselves at Rome, Meges and Aesclepiades of Bithynia. Never once, however, did Celsus identify himself as a member of the medical profession, nor did he claim that he practiced medicine, although he did at times refer to visits he made to the ill and injured, the weak and dying (Nutton 2004: 166–7; von Staden 1996: 401). Celsus' stance was not that of a professional, but closer to that of a Cato, in that he was an educated Roman whom necessity compelled to acquire broad technical knowledge in many fields of human endeavor. He learned medicine to advise members of his household and those within his circle of his friends on how to preserve their health, or at least how to regain it if they should fall ill (*Med.* 3.4.9–10). His medical studies enabled Celsus to explain his own medical preferences in order to aid other *paters familias* in establishing their strategies for health care within their own households, and he passed judgment on what Greeks had said over generations concerning foodstuffs, therapies and drugs, and surgeries. His concern was to point out the more efficacious among the multitude of medical choices then available at Rome. For example, when examining maladies that afflict specific body parts and offering remedies, he noted with regard to diarrhea that Asclepiades of Bithynia had defied earlier authorities when he advocated drinks as cold as possible to ameliorate loose bowels, concluding with the observation, "Yet I myself think that each person should trust himself as to whether or not he should use a hot drink or a cold one" (*Med.* 4.26.4). The story that this same Asclepiades was famous for once having encountered a funeral procession conveying for burial a man still alive impelled Celsus to assert that medicine was a kind of educated guesswork (*ars coniecturalis*) in which experienced practitioners, although not immune to deceptive symptoms and wrong guesses, were nonetheless to be relied upon in most instances, more often able to benefit the sick than not (*Med.* 2.6.13–18). Celsus also found room in his survey for therapies drawn from folk traditions. After listing doctors' remedies for toothache, including extraction, he finished off with a therapy developed by country people that involved a steam bath with an herb from the mint family (*mentastrum*), roots and all, for this not only caused profuse sweating and a flow of phlegm from the mouth, but "ensured good health for a year or longer" (*Med.* 6.9.7). Professional medical men may have been embarrassed when abscesses in the lymphatic glands called *strymata* recurred after treatment, but Celsus again interjected the experience of country-folk who cured these by eating a snake (*Med.* 5.28.7b). Some even freed themselves from epilepsy (for which disease Celsus employed the Latin term *morbus comitialis*) by drinking the blood of a gladiator whose throat had been cut (*Med.* 3.23.7), a remedy also recorded by Pliny (*Nat.* 28.2.4).

Celsus underscored in his preface the fact that it was men who led their lives in luxury and indolence that required elaborate doctoring: "This happened first among the Greeks and then later among us Romans" (*Med. praef.* 4–6). He also began his text proper by reiterating that the man in good health of body and mind had no need for doctors, while the weak did, for these latter were, for the most part, modern city-dwellers immersed in literary pursuits (*Med.* 1.1–1.2). Pliny shared Celsus' dream of a bygone Golden Age of healthy and hearty Romans, free of Greek doctors, and Pliny's boast that few Romans practiced medicine alone of the Greek arts, despite the great profits to be had (*Nat.* 29.8.17), seems born out not only by the predominance of Greek names among medical practitioners known to have doctored at Rome, as well as by Celsus' own *On Medicine* (Nutton 2004: 164–6). On the one hand, there is much Greek medicine in Celsus' text, for he easily included Greek words for diseases, bodily parts, therapeutic agents, and surgical instruments into his Latin narrative, explicitly identifying them as such on nearly 200 occasions (von Staden 1996: 394–6). When his description of bodily parts and their ailments descended down from the head to the male genitalia, he emphasized the appropriateness of Greek words for anatomical parts, for these were everywhere met and were not only preferable to the coarseness of Latin's sexual vocabulary, but they enabled patients to discuss more freely a complaint such as a swollen penis (*Med.* 6.18.1). Yet Celsus made clear that the educated Roman should be discriminating in his use of Greek medicine, maintaining his health and vigor through the hard work of sailing, hunting, and attending to matters on his country estates, as was the Roman way. Celsus' aim was to record, evaluate, and arrange for Roman use what Greek medical writers had produced. Still his careful compendium never circulated as widely as Pliny's *Natural History*, and medical excerpts from the latter's more garrulous work remained particularly popular (L. D. Reynolds 1986b: 309–16; Reeve 1986b: 352–3).

Scribonius Largus was, by contrast, a medical professional and he accompanied the emperor Claudius to Britain in 43 CE, perhaps as private physician to a member of the emperor's entourage, since Claudius' personal physician was a Greek from the island of Cos, Gaius Stertinius Xenophon. Largus was well known in the imperial household, for he not only dedicated his Latin work on drugs (*Compositiones*) to Gaius Julius Callistus, one of Claudius' most trusted freedmen, but he also included recipes for medicaments employed by members of the Julio-Claudian family, such as a restorative salve used by Augustus' wife Livia and the younger Antonia (mother of Claudius) that countered arthritic pain and, when rubbed on joints, made them warm and supple (*Comp.* 271, 268). Largus wrote his drug book after his return from Britain, dividing it into three sections: medicaments for diseases in a "head-to-toe" arrangement, from headache to gout; theriac remedies for insect stings, snake bites, and antidotes for poisons; and a final section on plasters, many of them named for the Greek surgeons who invented or popularized them. Largus was apparently born in Sicily and trained there before moving to Rome, for his teacher was from the Sicilian town of Centuripae. In addition, Largus occasionally mentioned medical practices of the island, noting, for example, that the pointed trefoil grew in plentiful quantities in Sicily, but not elsewhere, despite its usefulness against snakebites; he first recorded the Latin name of the plant (*trifolium acutum*) and then the Greek (*oxytriphyllon*, *Comp.* 94, 163). As a native of Sicily, he was most likely bilingual, and some 22 of his recipes were quoted in Greek by Galen in his own drug books, suggesting that Largus himself may have written a now lost Greek version in addition to the Latin drug book we now have (Sconocchia 1983). Largus' Latin version served as basis for the pharmaceutical treatise by Marcellus of Bordeaux at the end of the fourth century CE, now expanded with remedies from Marcellus' native Gaul. A printed text of Largus' *Compositiones* was produced in Paris in 1529, but the manuscript used for that edition soon disappeared, and only in the latter decades of the twentieth century has a manuscript of the *Compositiones*, copied at the beginning of the sixteenth century, been discovered in the library of the cathedral of Toledo, Spain (Reeve 1986b: 352–3).

Like Celsus, Largus often glossed names for diseases and medicinal plants with their Greek names, underscoring once again the extent to which Greek medicine had become naturalized in a Roman setting. He likewise shared Celsus' interest in popular remedies, including a therapeutic recipe for epilepsy (*morbus comitalis*), advocated by a certain Roman lady, that required fresh blood from a male turtle or a male dove if the patient were a boy, but from the female, if a girl. Largus looked with distaste, however, upon remedies in which epileptics were ordered to drink blood from their own veins or eat bites from the liver of a dead gladiator, declaring such practices outside the professional practice of medicine (*Comp.* 17). Largus' elaborate dedicatory letter to Callistus began with the much-quoted statement by the Alexandrian Herophilus that medicaments were "the hands of the gods" (*Comp. praef.* 1; von Staden 1989: 416–18). "And a reasonable view, in my opinion," Largus went on, "for the healing which divine touch brings about, medicaments long in use and tested can also effect." He went on to argue that remedies from plants and their roots were the oldest branch of medicine, because the race of men was essentially cowardly and did not willingly undergo the healing that involved cutting or cautery. Largus chastised those doctors who eschewed pharmacy, for they were violating the promise medicine declared in its oath – that it would come to the aid of all who asked for help on an equal basis and never bring harm to anyone, not even giving an evil medicament to one's foreign enemies. Not only do these statements make clear that Largus viewed doctors as moral men, bound by a common code of ethics, but he was paraphrasing for the first time from our point of view portions of what we refer to as the Hippocratic *Oath*:

> Hippocrates, the founder of our profession gave us the beginnings of our endeavors through that *Oath* in which one promises not to give a medicament to a pregnant woman that will expel her fetus. Each doctor must make this clear to his students, shaping their minds from the outset toward the good of mankind. Anyone who thought it criminal to damage the precarious hope for a human being before its birth is certain to judge it all the more criminal to harm the living. Hippocrates therefore considered it of great importance that each doctor preserve the reputation and honor of medicine with his spirit pious and holy, conducting himself in accordance with his precept that medicine is a science of healing, not of destroying. (*Comp. praef.* 5)

Appealing to the fifth-century BCE Greek doctor Hippocrates of Cos as an authority figure in medical matters became increasingly common during the Hellenistic period, and by the time of both Celsus and Largus he had been accepted at Rome as the "Father of Medicine." About two generations after Largus, Soranus of Ephesus, then practicing at Rome, also discussed the prescribing of abortives and contraceptives (*Gyn.* 1.60–5). Because nothing was known about the ovulatory cycle or the early events in pregnancy, Soranus repeated the kind of advice most medical writers gave throughout antiquity, yet by no means the advice a modern gynecologist would give. Namely, that fruitful intercourse, designed to result in conception, should take place as menstruation was abating and an appetite for coitus present (*Gyn.* 1.43–5). Soranus thought it better for a woman who did not want to conceive to take contraceptive precautions and he advised such measures as holding her breath and drawing back a bit as the man ejaculated, so that his generating seed not be thrust too deeply into her uterus; a douche after intercourse might also be useful, or a forceful sneeze. Soranus' prescriptions for precoital insertions with contraceptive intent included ingredients that were styptic, clogging, and cooling, so as to make the *os uteri* close before intercourse took place. He listed other contraceptive remedies that were more potent and, in his view, potentially dangerous, since they not only irritated the interior of the uterus, but destroyed a fetus, if one had already been conceived (*Gyn.* 1.60–5). Soranus knew two abortive methods; the *phthorion* destroyed a fetus through drugs and the *ekbolion* expelled the fetus through shaking and leaping. When Soranus explained his practice with regard to abortion, he too quoted the *Oath*, "I will give no one an abortive," adding that it was medicine's task to protect what nature engendered, but he also turned to another treatise in the multi-authored *Hippocratic Corpus*, "Nature of the Child," for here the medical writer counseled a pregnant flute-girl, a slave who belonged to one of his household, to leap into the air and kick her buttocks with her heels (Hippoc. *Nat. puer.* 13). On her seventh leap the conceptus fell out with a plop, and the girl stared at it in surprise. From this latter example that Soranus also attributed to the "Father of Medicine," he concluded that abortion was advisable if allowing a pregnancy to proceed to term endangered the mother's life, especially if she were too young and her uterus underdeveloped. Soranus refused, however, to prescribe abortives if the motive were to hide an adulterous affair or to preserve youthful beauty. Both the prostitute and the adulteress may well have looked to abortive techniques as a way out of inconvenient pregnancies (Kapparis 2002: 97–120). By contrast, married couples worried about their ability to leave behind them two adult children as replacements at parents' deaths, because the levels of infant mortality were high. Wives in the Roman world appear to have given birth throughout their fertile lives, rather than deliberately restricting their childbearing years primarily through contraceptive procedures, as is currently done in developed countries of the West (Frier 1994). Prolonged nursing of an infant by the mother for two or three years, as was the habit in the Roman world, did have a dampening effect on the mother's fertility, and for those who wished to conceive again Soranus advised the employment of a wet nurse. Even better, he thought, was to have several wet nurses available to suckle the child, lest a single wet nurse become ill or die (*Gyn.* 2.19–20).

Soranus practiced his medicine in accordance with the principles of Methodist physicians who concentrated on treatment and eschewed theorizing about unseen happenings inside the human body, or worrying overmuch about the kind of imbalance in bodily humors causing an illness. It did not matter to Methodists whether the patient's body contained a dearth or surplus of a particular bodily fluid, such as phlegm and black or yellow bile; rather they simply investigated whether the body was too constricted, as in constipation, or too relaxed, as in diarrhea, and set about rectifying the state of the patient's body in order to return it to health. This medical approach appealed to Romans, and the sect remained popular into late antiquity, especially in the provinces of North Africa. Soranus' *Gynecology* is his only treatise to survive to modern times in Greek, and it did so in a single copy made in the thirteenth century. In the fifth century CE Caelius Aurelianus, a Methodist of African birth, produced Latin translations of Soranus' *On Chronic Diseases, On Acute Diseases*, and also his *Gynecology*; these were read and revised throughout the earlier Middle Ages, until superseded at the beginning of the thirteenth century by medical texts being produced at the new medical center of Salerno (Hanson and Green 1994: 1045–61).

Galen of Pergamum spent the majority of his long adult career in Rome, doctoring, philosophizing, and climbing the city's social ladder to become one of the physicians who regularly attended the emperors and the imperial household – from Marcus Aurelius to Septimius Severus (161–c.216 CE). In his medical autobiography *Prognosis* Galen took great pleasure in recounting the night he was summoned to sleep at the imperial palace and successfully diagnosed that the emperor's current ailment was only an upset stomach, due to the cold food he ate for lunch that caused a flow of phlegm into his stomach. Thus this was not the attack of fever the emperor feared, and, according to Galen, Marcus Aurelius responded to the diagnosis by asserting,

"We have one doctor, and he is a consummate gentleman." Galen then claimed, "He was always speaking of me as the first among physicians and the only genuine philosopher" (*Praecog.* 11). As a Methodist, Soranus paid scant attention to bodily humors, and, while Celsus occasionally mentioned a superfluity of phlegm and bile as disease agents, he did so in a way reminiscent of many Hippocratic writers, with phlegm predominant in diseases afflicting the eyes and head, but black bile, "which the Greeks called *melancholia*," appearing not only in cases of ophthalmia, but in abscesses all over the body (*Med.* 2.1.6). It was Galen who set the four humors (phlegm, yellow bile, black bile, blood) into prominence in physiology and nosology, and although he asserted that this was what Hippocrates had done, it was principally the treatise "Nature of Man" within the *Hippocratic Corpus* that likewise insisted on these four particular fluids. The four humors and the four qualities (hot/cold and wet/dry) served as organizing principles for Galen's classifications of foodstuffs, for some foods were heating, others cooling, moistening, or drying, in various degrees; some made the humors thicker, others thinned them. Phlegm was more likely to dominate the body in winter, blood in summer, with the biles relegated to fall and spring. The humoral theory, as formulated by Galen, remained central in physiology and nosology for more than a millennium and a half thereafter, and the four resulting temperaments for human beings – phlegmatic, bilious (or "choleric"), melancholic, and sanguine – were, for example, one shorthand means Shakespeare used to sum up the personalities of his characters.

Galen not only considered Hippocrates the greatest of medical authorities, repeatedly citing him, but his picture of Hippocrates as practicing physician and author of medical texts increasingly meshed with Galen's own view of himself and his experiences to a degree not known elsewhere (Nutton 2004: 216–29; A. E. Hanson 1998a). Galen's long active career of some 60 years, his strict work habits, and his intellectual restlessness resulted in a mammoth output of treatises on medical, philosophical, and linguistic topics. It has been estimated that his writings in Greek represent ten percent of all surviving Greek literature written before 360 CE and that he must have written or dictated to a scribe about two or three pages every day of his working life (Nutton 2004: 390). Determining the exact number of items in Galen's bibliography, however, is a complicated matter: towards the end of his life, Galen composed a descriptive catalog of what he had written, *On His Own Books*, and a companion volume, *On the Order of His Own Books*, explaining the order in which readers at varying degrees of medical sophistication, especially in anatomy, should approach them. Galen, however, neglected to mention a number of works he thought lost, and the ninth-century Arabic translator of Galen, Hunain ibn Ishaq, listed 50 works known to him in Baghdad that Galen had omitted from his catalogue. The standard edition of Galen's works by C. G. Kühn runs to some 16,000 pages, but in the nearly two centuries since it was printed in the 1830s, discoveries of works by Galen previously thought lost have been made, especially in translations into Arabic, Syriac, Armenian, Hebrew, or Latin, increasing the number of pages by at least one quarter (Nutton 2002: vii). Galen dominated the medicine of the Greek-speaking east for the next millennium, as the number of languages into which his works were translated makes clear. The breadth of his learning and his passion for anatomy resulted in a medical system whose conservative teleology appealed to learned men, pagan, Christian, and Muslim alike. With the revival of learning in the late Middle

Ages and throughout the Renaissance his writings were studied afresh, first through Latin translations from the Arabic and then through the Greek books that their owners carried with them from Constantinople to the west after the city's capture in 1453. Galen's enthusiasm for Hippocrates revived interest in the *Hippocratic Corpus*, and these texts also made their way back to Italy and the west.

Galen began his study of medicine at age 17, when Asclepius appeared to his father in a dream, urging him to add medicine to his son's studies in philosophy, and for the next 11 years Galen journeyed around the eastern Mediterranean in pursuit of important teachers, training first in Pergamum and then at Smyrna, Corinth, and finally Alexandria. Little wonder, then, that Galen heaped scorn on Thessalus, a Methodist physician and contemporary of the emperor Nero (54–68 CE), who boasted he could teach medicine to his pupils in six months. Galen's first professional appointment was as physician to the gladiatorial school at Pergamum, and from gladiators' wounds and fractures he not only became skilled in practical surgery, but also acquired a fascination with anatomy and physiology. In his *Examinations of the Best Physician*, Galen drew attention to the fact that only two wounded gladiators died in his care, while 16 had perished at the hands of his predecessor (9.7).

Once arrived and established in Rome, Galen gave anatomical demonstrations for a time before crowds of invited guests; at one such session he demonstrated the mechanisms of speech by ligating nerves in the muscles of a pig's larynx, disabling the animal's ability to squeal (*Praecog.* 5). Galen continued to dissect and vivisect animal bodies, for the intellectual and moral climate of Rome had little tolerance for the opening of human bodies, as had once been the case for the anatomists of Alexandria in the mid-third century BCE. Galen usually preferred to work with pigs, goats, or oxen, rather than apes, because one thus avoided seeing the unpleasant expression on the ape's face when it was being vivisected and because demonstration of vocal apparatus worked better on animals with a loud cry, "a thing one does not find with apes" (*Anat. admin.* 9.11–15). In his *Anatomical Procedures* Galen described how to open the mid-section of a pregnant goat, revealing a fetus still contained in the womb; the discussion is impressive not only for its surgical skills, for the mother goat was stitched back up to live another day, but also for the demonstration that a fetal heart beat independently from the heart of the mother (12.4–6). Galen also corrected Herophilus' mistaken analogy from male anatomy that a woman's ovarian tubes implanted into the neck of her bladder, just as spermatic ducts did in men, noting instead that they grew from the ovaries into the body of the uterus (*Sem.* 2.1). Debates as to which organ was in control of the human body (*hegemonikon*) continued in Galen's time, and, although he was convinced that it was the brain, others still argued for the heart. Galen, however, adopted the erroneous view from Hellenistic predecessors that there was a confluence of nerves and blood vessels at the base of the human brain which resembled layers of fishermen's nets, the retiform plexus (or *rete mirabile*, as it came to be called), and, confident that this convoluted vascular structure existed in humans, he assigned it a physiological function important to him – that of transforming life-giving breath (vital *pneuma*) that flowed in the arteries into the animated breath (psychic *pneuma*) that activated the brain and nerves to govern both sensation and motion (*Usu puls.* 2, *Anat. admin.* 9.8; Rocca 2003: 202–19, 249–53). But the retiform plexus is not found in either humans or apes, but exists in mammals such as the ox, goat, or pig, animals Galen preferred to dissect and vivisect. What Galen said about cranial and cerebral anatomy is accurate for oxen. By the early sixteenth century some Renaissance anatomists were stating openly that they could not find the Galenic *rete mirabile* in the cadavers they dissected. For example, Berengario da Carpi (c.1460–c.1530), a lecturer at the flourishing medical center of Bologna, denied its anatomical existence in human bodies, but retained Galen's physiology by transferring the function of the *rete mirabile* to the pial arteries; and despite his anti-Galenic rhetoric, based on an awareness that Galen's anatomy derived for the most part from his dissections of animals, Andreas Vesalius (1514–64) nonetheless also reassigned Galen's physiological functions for the *rete mirabile* to the cerebral arteries. Galen never anticipated the domination he would achieve over subsequent medicine, but threads of ambition and self-promotion run through his many writings, underscoring his hope that he would be recognized as having created a medical system which summarized and obviated the need for others to read his predecessors. His treatises survived intact the process of epitomization into the works of the Byzantine compendiasts, while those of his approximate contemporaries Archigenes, Rufus, and Philumenus did not.

The medical texts from antiquity we read today survive because they continued to be read century after century and were recopied by hand in sufficient numbers up to the time when the printing press was invented in the mid-fifteenth century. Thereafter, multiple copies of ancient physicians' books became increasingly available to Renaissance readers. The writings of many, however, were early lost, and we know only their names from mentions in Celsus, Soranus, and Galen. Material objects from the Roman past afford us some notion of the medical personnel who functioned outside the city and hint at the medicine they were practicing. About 140 CE, a midwife named Scribonia Attice had an attractive brick tomb constructed for herself, her husband Marcus Ulpius Amerimnus, and members of their *familia*, both blood kin and freedmen, in the cemetery that lined a road leading out from Trajan's newly built harbor for Rome at Portus (Isola Sacra, tomb #100). She had the tomb decorated with terracotta plaques: the one at right depicted Scribonia Attice herself, in attendance at a birth; she knelt in front of a birth chair on which the parturient sat and she held out her arms to receive the neonate, who would soon drop from her mother and through the perforated seat in the birth chair. The birth chair was slanted gently backwards, had handles for the parturient to grip, and an attendant behind to support her back, the very equipment and helper called for by Soranus (*Gyn.* 2.3.1–2) (Figure 25.1a). The plaque on the left shows that Scribonia Attice's husband Amerimnus was a surgeon; he was in the act of drawing blood from a patient's leg, while various of his specialized instruments (scalpels of various sizes, hooks, and probes) lay spread out in the background (Figure 25.1b). Both husband and wife were of Greek origin, as their *cognomina* (*Attice* and *Amerinmos*) and the name of Attice's mother *Callityche* demonstrate, but their *nomina* (*Scribonia* and *Ulpius*) were thoroughly Roman, and the dedicatory inscription on their tomb was written in Latin. The couple was likely to have acquired their *nomina* when they were manumitted, with Amerimnus' *praenomen* and *nomen* (Marcus Ulpius) implying that he was probably an imperial freedman of Trajan. Attice and Amerimnus took pride in their work as medical practitioners, for their skills enabled them to become full participants in the world in which only Roman citizens were legally privileged and socially advantaged. They themselves owned slaves, despite their servile origins, and had manumitted

Figure 25.1a Relief of Scribonia Attice assisting with a birth

Figure 25.1b Relief of Marcus Ulpius Amerimnus drawing blood

some of them. It was nonetheless for their medical skills that they wished to be remembered in the cemetery of Isola Sacra, where many others also advertised the trades they practiced in life.

Elaborate collections of medical instruments (*instrumentaria*) have been found all over the Roman Empire, as well as in Italy and the vicinity of Rome, consisting not only of scalpels, hooks, and probes, but also forceps of various design for specialized tasks, wound retractors, needles, and cupping vessels (Jackson 1988: 112–23; Jackson 2003). Many scalpels were finely crafted in different shapes, with blades of steel from the Alpine province of Noricum, and the assemblages unearthed from the towns of Pompeii and Herculaneum, destroyed by the eruption of Vesuvius in 79 CE, have provided particularly large and elegant examples (Bliquez 1994). Some *instrumentaria* were buried with their owners, while others were excavated from the military hospitals (*valetudinaria*) that became an essential part of the permanent fortresses housing the legionary and auxiliary troops who guarded the edges of the empire. From the days of Julius Caesar's wars in Gaul, special areas of a military camp were set aside in which wounded and ailing soldiers were cared for (*BG* 6.38), and well known are the hospital facilities later constructed in the forts of Britain and along the Rhine–Danube frontier. The wooden writing tablets that survive from the fort at Vindolanda adjacent to Hadrian's Wall include an interim strength report for the auxiliaries in the First Cohort of Tungrians stationed there in the early second century CE, listing those away from the fort on army business (*absentes*) and those at the fort currently unfit for active service – the sick (*aegri*), the wounded (*volnerati*), and those with ophthalmic diseases (*lippientes*; Bowman and Thomas 1994, *T.Vindol.* 2.154). Similar strength reports are known from the First Veteran Cohort of Spaniards, stationed in the early second century in Moesia on the lower Danube; from the First Equestrian Cohort of Lusitanians, stationed in Egypt (dated to August 31, 156 CE); and from the Twentieth Cohort of Palmyrenes, stationed in the early third century at Dura-Europus on the middle Euphrates (Fink 1971, text nos. 63, 64, 8). The general public was not serviced by hospital facilities until the empire had become Christian and charity for the sick and dying was considered part of the Christian's duty. Galen's appointment as doctor to the Pergamene school of gladiators demonstrates, however, that specialized groups were likewise cared for; Galen noted that gladiators were wounded in ways similar to soldiers in the army and also ordinary people, especially hunters. In his commentary to the Hippocratic treatise "Fractures" he drew attention to the bandages and plasters he applied to patients' wounds, always soaking the freshly stitched-up ones with dry, red wine (*Hipp. Fract. comment.* 3.21; cf. *Comp. med. per gen.* 2.17 and 3.9). Meticulous treatment of this nature would have lessened the likelihood of infection.

Papyri from the Roman province of Egypt likewise clarify other aspects of the medicine being practiced outside of Rome itself, for the desert sands preserved written texts of all kinds in great numbers. Galen boasted that his treatises were being read throughout the empire, and his claim was bolstered somewhat by finding a copy of his *Opinions of Hippocrates and Plato* in circulation in Egypt no later than a generation after his death, and perhaps even during his lifetime (A. E. Hanson 1985: 32–47). Illustrated herbals, describing the plants pictured and clarifying their medicinal properties, were popular in the province from the second century onwards (A. E. Hanson 2001: 585–604). Some of the earliest parchment codices to survive from late antiquity were also elegantly illustrated herbals – the Greek *Materia medica* by the mid-first-century CE pharmacologist Dioscorides of Anazarbus, which was copied and illustrated in or near Constantinople about 512 CE as a wedding present for an emperor's daughter (MS Vindobonensis med. gr. 1), and, in the west, the Latin pseudo-Apuleian *Herbarium* (MS Leidenensis Voss. Lat. Q.9) copied later in the same century. Greek texts intended to provide summaries of medical information were also common in Egypt, sometimes as a list of medical definitions and sometimes in a question-and-answer format, and, like the herbals, they offered some degree of medical self help to the literate, as well as being tools in medical education. Much attention was paid in these texts to diseases of the eye, and while this may be due in part to the ancient medical habit of discussing diseases in a "head-to-toe" arrangement (*a capite ad calcem*), in part to the hot, dry, and dusty climate of Egypt that exacerbated ophthalmic maladies, and in part to the absence of powerful antiseptics that facilitated disease transmission, eye diseases were nonetheless conditions that medical practitioners of the Roman period were able to ameliorate with considerable success through their compound salves (*collyria*) and eyewashes. The auxiliary troops at Vindolanda suffering from eye disease (*lippientes*) most likely had their inflamed eyes and conjunctivitis treated with salves that arrived in camp in dried form, imprinted with a *collyrium* stamp explaining its precise use (Jackson 1988: 83–5). More than 300 *collyrium* stamps made of stone have survived from the northern provinces of Britain, Gaul, and Germany. In the warmer and drier climates bordering on the Mediterranean, the salves no doubt circulated in moist form in vials and jars. Directions for preparing eye salves and washes also dominated the papyri from Egypt that contained recipes, underscoring the likelihood that many in the populations of the Roman Empire suffered from ophthalmias and relied on such medicaments to ease them (Marganne 1994: 173–6; Andorlini 2001: 139–47). The medical definitions and questions-and-answer texts enjoyed empire-wide popularity, for not only do we find papyrus fragments of them in Greek-speaking Egypt throughout antiquity, but beginning in the tenth century CE copies on parchment appear in the west, now translated into Latin and not infrequently attributed to Soranus. The following excerpt from a Latin version paraphrased the Hippocratic *Oath*, manipulating it in a manner similar to Scribonius Largus' discussion:

> Let us, moreover examine what kind of man ought to be a doctor. He must be kindly in his habits and moderate with the expected honorable qualities, nor should a certain holiness be lacking to him, nor should he be haughty. He must give treatment equally to poor and rich, slave and free. Among doctors medicine is a unity. If indeed they are paid money, let them accept it and not refuse; but if pay is not forthcoming, let them not demand it, for however much a person has paid cannot be equated with the benefits medicine conveys. Into whatever homes the doctor enters, he must have before his eyes curing to the extent of his ability. Let him be mindful of the *Oath* of Hippocrates so that he hold himself off from all blame and especially from sexual and criminal acts, and what ever is said or done in the house he should conceal as he would a sacred mystery. As a result, he will acquire more abundant praise for himself and for his art. (*Quaest. med.*, 245.10–20 Rose)

3 The Parts of Medicine: Dietetics, Drugs, and Surgeries

We learn of the tri-partite division of medicine first and most elaborately from Celsus; he labeled each branch according to the Greek name, thereby underscoring that these formal divisions had been carried out previously by Greek-speakers. Cures were accomplished through dietetics (*diaitêtikê*), through drugs (*pharmakeutikê*), and through surgery (*chirourgia*), and the doctors who practiced at Rome from the mid-second century BCE onwards contributed significantly to each of the three branches. Dietetics became increasingly more elaborate, as special daily regimens to preserve health or, in the sick, to restore it, were described not only for adult men, as in the *Hippocratic Corpus*, but also for children, young girls approaching puberty, adult women, and old men (Flemming 2000: 220–8). The eastern conquests of Alexander the Great of Macedon and the successor kingdoms, especially that of the Ptolemaic monarchs in Egypt, had brought many new spices and minerals to the attention of physicians and pharmacologists of the Hellenistic world. With Rome's expansion into the eastern Mediterranean exotic medicaments became available in ever more plentiful quantities in the city's markets via the caravan routes from the east (Houston 2004). The Christian moralist and writer Clement of Alexandria heaped scorn about 200 CE on the women of Egypt who smeared their faces and bodies with substances taken from the intestines of the crocodile in order to make their complexions luminous and wrinkle-free (*Paidagogos* 3.2.5). But it was not only in Egypt, native home of the crocodile, where the cosmetic was readily available, for Galen reported that wealthy women of Rome were likewise wont to use it for the same purpose (A. E. Hanson 1998b: 91). While the therapeutic recipes of the *Hippocratic Corpus* seldom specified amounts to be employed in a medicament compounded from numerous ingredients, and almost never named a recipe for the practitioner who invented or popularized it, Celsus' recipes gave exact amounts for ingredients and often named the medical person closely associated with it; his Greek and Latin successors did likewise. Perhaps the greatest advances at Rome were those made in surgery, despite the fact that it remained the choice of last resort behind diet and regimen on the one hand, and the prescription of *pharmaka* on the other, unless accidents or other emergency situations compelled a practitioner either to perform the needed surgical procedure himself, or to call in another specially skilled in such matters.

Dietetics and regimen in Celsus and others

Celsus claimed that dietetics was the most important of medicine's three branches. The first book of his *On Medicine* probed one part of dietetics – those daily habits which were prophylactic and contributed to the maintenance of health, such as reading aloud, military exercises, handball, running, and walking (*Med.* 1.2.6). Celsus cautioned against daily vomiting for the sake of gourmandizing (*Med.* 1.3.21), and when plague struck the best recourse in his opinion was to go abroad, but if this were not possible, one must avoid fatigue, indigestion, extremes of temperature, and sexual intercourse (*Med.* 1.10.1–4). The second book of *On Medicine* surveyed symptoms of impending disease, first charting the personal and environmental factors that impinged upon an individual's experience of a sickness. As for the seasons of the year, spring was the most salubrious, autumn the most dangerous; settled weather with temperate sunshine was healthier than a foggy and cloudy day. The worst weather for the sick was that which caused the illness in the first place. Middle age was the healthiest time of life, provided one was neither overly fat nor overly thin; children and adolescents enjoyed the best health in spring and were most free from disease in early summer, but old people were better off in summer and early autumn (*Med.* 2.1.1–23). Celsus' discussion of symptoms antecedent to illnesses was heavily indebted to the Hippocratic treatise *Prognostikon*, including the facial signs of the patient about to die (*facies Hippocratis*): nose pointed, temples sunken, eyes hollow, ears cold and flaccid, skin on the forehead hard and stretched tight. In common with his Hippocratic predecessors, Celsus considered as diseases some items we now classify as symptoms, such as fevers, dropsy (retention of fluid), diarrhea, etc. His general overview of dietetic therapies included a glowing account of phlebotomy's usefulness, and he explained in detail how, when, and why blood was to be drawn. He also considered useful the therapies of massage and anointing, rocking, sweating, and bathing (*Med.* 2.10.1–17.10). Only at the end of the second book did Celsus turn to food and drink which have become for us the central facet of modern dietetics, a discipline with medical aspects, but by no means so central to medicine as the broader concept of regimen was to Celsus and his medical colleagues. He classified foods as strong, medium, or weak, whether or not they were easy to digest and nourishing, and whether they heated or chilled the body. Heating foods included pepper, salt, stewed meat, garlic, onion, and strong wines; cooling ones were endive, lettuce, cucumber, cooked squash, cherries, sour apples, boiled meat, and vinegar. Celsus admitted that medical men did not agree on the precise benefits of the different foods, because each man tended to follow his own prejudices, rather than what the combined experience of many had made clear over the years. Conservative as Celsus' statement sounds, he was far less impressed with the qualities of cabbage (*brassica*) than was either Cato or Pliny. As this quotation from Cato's *On Agriculture* makes clear, he considered the entire cabbage family as both a foodstuff and a medicinal drug:

> It is the cabbage which surpasses all other vegetables. It can be eaten either cooked or raw. If you eat it raw, dip it into vinegar. It is a marvelous aid to digestion and a good laxative, while the urine is salubrious for everything. If you want to eat and drink a lot at a dinner party, eat as much raw cabbage with vinegar as you please before the dinner, and after dinner again eat about five leaves. This will make you think you ate virtually nothing and you will continue to drink as much as you wish.... If you save urine from someone who eats cabbage frequently, heat it, and immerse a sick person in it, you will speedily make him healthy, as experience has shown. Likewise, if you wash babies with this urine, they will never become sickly. (*Agr.*156.1 and 157.10)

When discussing cabbages and kales (*olus caulesque*) as plants, Pliny mentioned the high esteem Cato had expressed for these, adding, however, that he himself did not find Greeks so generous in their praise of the vegetable (*Nat.* 19.136). By the time Pliny turned to medicinal uses of garden vegetables in the next book of the *Natural History*, he had discovered in addition an entire book devoted to cabbage by the Greek Chrysippus, as well as a discussion by another Greek, the third-century BCE physician Dieuches. Still it was the opinions of Cato on cabbage that Pliny paraphrased, for he wanted it known, as he said, that the Roman people had used cabbage as their medicine for over 600 years (*Nat.* 20.78–83). So impressed was he by Cato's remark about bathing babies in "cabbage urine" that he quoted those lines in full.

Celsus' third book gave detailed information about the treatment of diseases that affected the entire body, with the majority of his attention devoted to fevers. There were ones that spiked every other day (tertian), or every second day (quartan), and those that did not remit (quotidian), or were extremely high and accompanied by chill. He carefully rehearsed the opinions held by his predecessors as to when the feverish patient should receive food and drink; his own opinion was that fasting was appropriate at the onset of the fever, with solid food introduced again only on the fourth day thereafter (*Med.* 3.4.10). Malaria was endemic in many low-lying, swampy regions around the Mediterranean, and within Italy it impacted the peoples along the western coast, from Etruria, Latium, Campania, down to Magna Graecia, exercising an awesome effect on mortality and morbidity. It is likely that most cases of tertians and quartans represented periodic malarial fevers (Sallares 2002: 2: 283–5). Celsus also paid attention to mental problems, such as insanity, depression caused by black bile (*melancholia*), and lethargy, as well as physical ones, such as dropsy (*leukophlegmasia*), wasting disease (*phthisis*, probably pulmonary tuberculosis), epilepsy (*comitialis*), and jaundice. He cautioned that news potentially upsetting to the patient must be suppressed in the case of the very ill, and, in general, ought not to be delivered to anyone directly after a meal, but saved until the morning of the next day (*Med.* 3.5.11). In the fourth book, Celsus turned to treatment of diseases that affected particular parts of the body, beginning with the head, paralysis of the tongue and coughs, and moving downwards in the body to end at gout (*podagra*). Although the feverish and swollen feet of those suffering from gout required refrigerants, should these symptoms be absent, Celsus counseled hot fomentations, and at night a heating plaster, especially one of mallow root (*hibiscum, malva*) boiled in wine (*Med.* 4.31.4). Pliny named Celsus among the Greek and Latin authors he consulted for his *Natural History* and he clearly noted the detail about the efficacy of mallow root boiled in wine for cases of gout without swelling when reading Celsus, because he set the information at the end of his discussion of the plant *hibiscum*. Immediately preceding, however, he mentioned another use for mallow root: it healed suppurated, scrofulous sores, if dug up before sunrise, perhaps with a golden trowel, and wrapped in wool from a ewe that had given birth to a ewe (*Nat.* 20.26). As the latter passage underscored, Pliny was not so much interested in medical practice and healing of the sick as he was in the accumulation of facts about the known world and everything in it (Scarborough 1986: 60–3).

Pharmaceuticals in Celsus and others

Celsus turned to drugs in the fifth and sixth books of his *On Medicine*, following a pattern similar to the one he had established in his third and fourth books – a wide-ranging general discussion, coupled with specific recipes for medicaments, and then a "head-to-toe" discussion of individual ailments and the prescriptions appropriate for them. Because he saw all branches of medicine as interconnected, he cautioned at the outset that just because one was combating a disease principally with drugs this did not mean regimen could be neglected. In medicating lesions and wounds, it was important to examine not only the surface, but also to estimate as best as possible the extent of the injury unseen within the body. The prudent practitioner, in Celsus' opinion, ought not to attempt to cure the man he could not save, nor should he, on the other hand, overestimate the difficulties merely to magnify his own achievements. Wounds affecting the major organs (brain, heart, stomach, liver, spinal marrow, middle of the lung, intestines, kidneys) and the large blood vessels and arteries of the throat Celsus deemed most likely to be fatal (*Med.* 5.26.1A–36B; cf. 5.27.1A–12C for bites and 5.28.1A–19D for lesions).

After surveying major uses of unmixed ingredients, the simples, at the beginning of the fifth book, Celsus turned to compounded drugs, to be administered as emollients or softeners (*malagmata*), or as plasters, or pills (*pastilli, trochiscoi*). The plasters and pills were particularly likely to include metallic ingredients, in addition to substances derived from plants and animals. As Galen would also do more than a century later, Celsus relied for prescriptions on earlier Greek physicians, including the "wound-healer" Archagathus for a soothing plaster (*Med.* 5.27). He quoted a mildly astringent plaster from Heras of Cappadocia, who had migrated to Rome and practiced there between 20 BCE and 20 CE:

> There is also the compound of Heras which contains 8 grams each of myrrh and copper ore (*chalcitis*); 16 grams each of aloes, frankincense, split alum (*alumen scissile*); 32 grams each of aristolochia and unripe oak galls; and 40 grams of ground pomegranate rind. (*Med.* 5.22.3; cf. Fabricius 1972: 183–5)

Recipes for Heras' plasters were still circulating in Roman Egypt in the early fourth century CE (Youtie 1996: 36–8). Celsus borrowed the recipe for compounding a pill to soothe a cough from the early first-century BCE Heracleides of Tarentum:

> When coughing prevents sleep, the pill of Heracleides ameliorates both: .66 of a gram of saffron; 1 gram each of myrrh, pepper, costmary (*costus*), galbanum; 4 grams each of cinnamon, castoreum, poppy tears. (*Med.* 5.25.10)

Celsus also included a theriac called "Mithridatium" after King Mithridates VI Eupator of Pontus (120–63 BCE), for that monarch was said to have consumed the compounded drug every day in order to render himself immune to poisons; there were 38 ingredients in Celsus' recipe, including myrrh and poppy tears, moistened with honey. Against poisons it was administered with wine in a dosage equivalent to the size of a hazelnut. For other affections unspecified by Celsus an amount corresponding to an Egyptian bean was sufficient (*Med.* 5.23.3; Totelin 2004). Scribonius Largus also included a recipe for Mithridatium, specifying more than 22 ingredients, for the beginning of his ingredient list has been lost, and he offered an expanded number of conditions Mithridatium could alleviate beyond merely serving as an antidote against poisoning – snake bites, liver and kidney problems, coughs, eye disease, pains in the side and belly, fevers, tetanus, and spasms (*Comp.* 170). A pair of father-and-son physicians, both named Andromachus, were active at the court of the emperor Nero, and according to Galen both tinkered with the recipes for Mithridatium, adding and subtracting ingredients to produce their own versions. Galen quoted the some 120-line elegiac poem in which the senior Andromachus described his revised version of the theriac and offered it to Nero, now labeling it "Calmness" (*Galene*). Galen himself reproduced recipes for Calmness, Mithridatium, and other theriacs the younger Andromachus had included in his own books of drugs (*Antid.* 1.6–7, 2.1–2). Pliny mentioned Mithridatium in the course of his tirade against Greek physicians and while he noted that it was compounded from 54 ingredients, he failed either to list them or to explain what conditions the antidote medicated. For Pliny, the prescription was an example of physicians' absurdities of the kind against which Cato had long ago campaigned, and, he unconvincingly offered as proof the fact that the amounts of each of the many ingredients employed in Mithridatium were not the same, but it was one gram of this, five grams of that, and ten grams of something else. Nonetheless, Galen's collection underscored that versions of Mithridatium continued to be developed at Rome, more as a "cure-all" than as antidote. He specifically noted that theriacs in general and Mithridatium in particular were widely used by the Roman aristocracy while the emperor Marcus Aurelius was alive, because they wished to emulate imperial tastes. When the emperor died (180 CE), however, few continued to have it prepared for them (*Antid.* 1.4). Galen assured his readers that Mithridatium rendered not only King Mithridates' body immune to poisoning, for he had to resort to a sword when, as prisoner of Pompey and the Romans, he wished to commit suicide (*Antid.* 2.13; *Ther. ad Pis.* 16), but the body of Marcus Aurelius was also thus protected by it (*Antid.* 1.1).

Celsus' version of the Mithridatium included poppy tears (*Papaver rhoeas*, Scarborough 1995: 5), while in the Calmness recipes both father and son Andromachus included poppy juice, likely to be opium latex (*Papaver somniferum* L.), and thus considerably stronger than poppy tears (Scarborough 1995: 11). Poppy juice was a frequent ingredient for Scribonius Largus in prescriptions for eye salves (*collyria*), chronic coughs, and colic (*Comp.* 21–33, 89–93, 120–1), yet he was well aware that ingesting poppy juice could likewise prove fatal, recommending vomiting and prohibiting sleep when a patient presented signs of opium poisoning (*Comp.* 180). Galen personally compounded a number of theriacs for Marcus Aurelius, ranging from a four-ingredient one invented by Heras to versions of Andromachus' Calmness with some 40 or 50 ingredients. When preparing Mithridatium for the emperor Galen knew well how to vary the dosage, the amount, and the means of administering, so as to achieve the desired result for Marcus' bodily type and whether he required a stimulant or a potion to help him go to sleep (*Antid.* 1.1; Scarborough 1995: 17–18).

The most influential discussion of Greek and Roman pharmaceuticals was produced by Dioscurides of Anazarbus (mid-first century CE). Galen borrowed extensively from his *Materia medica* for his own drug books. Oribasius of Pergamum (c.325–400 CE), physician at the court of the emperor Julian, produced at his emperor's behest a 70-book collection of the best writings in medicine up to his own time; only 30 books of his *Medical collections* (*Collectiones medicae*) survive, three of which were excerpts Oribasius drew from Dioscorides (*Coll. med.* 11–13). Copies of Dioscorides on papyrus circulated in Roman Egypt, and the drug book was eventually translated into Latin, Syriac, and Arabic. The first printed edition was issued by Aldus Manutius of Venice in 1499, and editions of Latin translations continued to be printed until the early nineteenth century. The *Materia medica* dealt one by one with the simples, derived from plants and products from trees, from animals and animal products, from minerals, with a section also on wines. In writing the preface to his work Dioscorides was careful to explain the virtues of his compilation: his were the results of careful observations of many plants throughout their growing season, so that he knew when to harvest for greatest efficacy; he advised on the best methods for extracting their juices and on the storage of drugs (Scarborough and Nutton 1982). Dioscorides emphasized the close ties between pharmacology and medicine and was particularly proud of the method he devised for arranging the drugs he catalogued, "according to the properties of the individual drugs." He took a dim view of arranging medicinal plants and other simples in alphabetical order, although later copyists did alphabetize his work, and they did so early, for the copies we possess are alphabetized, including Oribasius' excerpts. As a result, our knowledge of the original arrangement remains hazy, although Dioscorides' attention to what drugs accomplished for the sick throughout the *Materia medica* suggests that similarities in efficacy were important to his original arrangement.

Dioscorides did not mention Mithridatium, not even in passing, perhaps because of its manifold ingredients, although he discussed the opium poppy (*mekon*), beginning with the use of its seeds in bread and as an alternate for sesame seeds in drinks prepared with honey. Additionally, he provided elaborate directions on how to extract poppy juice (*opos mekonos, mekoneion*; *MM* 4.64.1–7). Among Latin speakers the diminutive form of the Greek word for juice (*opion*, "dear little juice") became the word *opium*. At some ten points in Dioscorides' text he noted what poppy juice accomplished medically when mixed with the other simples he was cataloguing.

Both Dioscorides and Galen attributed medicinal properties to stones of various kinds, but they expressed skepticism that markings and engravings on the stones themselves enhanced their efficacy. Dioscorides tended to distance himself from information he was repeating, but did not endorse himself, by beginning with such phrases as "they say" and "it is said." Thus, in regard to the stone called serpentine he reported that one type was dense, another ashen in color and spotted, while yet another had white markings. "All types are useful against snakebite and headache when worn on the person, but those with the markings *are said* to help the headache of lethargy in particular" (*MM* 5.143). Galen was even more outspoken in the case of green jasper:

> Some authorities attribute to certain stones a peculiar quality which is actually possessed by the green jasper. When worn as an amulet, green jasper benefits the stomach and esophagus. Some men also set it in a ring, and engrave on it the radiate serpent, just as King Nechepsos prescribed in his fourteenth book. I myself have made a satisfactory test of this stone: I fashioned a necklace of small stones of that variety and hung it from my neck at just the length that placed the stones near the opening of my stomach. These seemed totally efficacious even though they had not been carved with the design that Nechepsos prescribed. (*Simpl. med. temp.* 10.19)

Surgery in Celsus and others

Surgery involved, as Celsus reported at the beginning of his seventh book, cures effected by the doctor's hands, and what the surgeon accomplished was more visible than in the other two branches of medicine. This comment highlighted the fact that the much of ancient surgery was performed on the surface of the body or on areas available to the touch, with medical instruments extending and facilitating what the surgeon could accomplish. Accidents, of course, confronted the physician with interior parts that were normally hidden within. In the seventh book of *On Medicine* Celsus described surgical procedures in the soft parts of the body in the usual head-to-toe arrangement, while the eighth book concentrated on wounds and injuries to bones. Considerable progress had been made in surgical techniques in Hellenistic Alexandria and late republican Rome, and these are on display in Celsus' account, especially in operations on the surface of the eyeball and on the eyelids, including couching a cataract (*Med.* 7.7). Still, in his catalogue Celsus jumped from tumors in the neck between skin and trachea to the lower body, skipping for the most part surgical interventions in the central trunk. He did describe procedures for the drainage of retained fluids through insertion of a bronze tube in cases of dropsy and for prolapse of the intestine (*Med.* 7.14–17). Reversing the effects of circumcision was probably a procedure originally developed in the Hellenistic world of the eastern Mediterranean, when those who had been circumcised wished to participate in Greek gymnastic contests performed in the nude. Celsus reported that the prepuce was to be raised from the penis with a scalpel and the foreskin fastened to its proper place by a threaded needle (*Med.* 7.25). The procedure was in his view neither very painful nor did it result in profuse bleeding, two of the worries that punctuated most surgical accounts along with the fear of infection (Salazar 2000: 43–4).

In the eighth book Celsus seems to have been somewhat more dependent upon surgical treatises in the *Hippocratic Corpus* than in his other discussions, for not only was the greatest period in Roman surgical experimentation just getting underway in the early first century, but techniques Hippocratic doctors employed for dealing with fractures clearly remained useful. Hippocratic knowledge of the larger bones of the human skeleton and their crucial joints was relatively sophisticated, when compared with their knowledge of organ anatomy and general physiology, although their nomenclature for individual bones was closer to "the knee-bone connected to the thigh-bone" than was the case in Hellenistic times and in Celsus, when specific bones were increasingly likely to have individual names. In a similar vein, the Hippocratic author of "Wounds in the Head" spoke of the act of trephination only through the verb meaning "saw" and its compounds "saw through," and "saw out" (*priein, diapriein, ekprien*), cautioning that when trepanning, it was frequently necessary to stop, "for sawing heats because of the rotation, and by heating and drying the bone, scorches it and causes more of the bone surrounding the site to separate than would normally do so" (*Cap. vuln.* 21). While Celsus was likewise concerned that instruments employed to penetrate the skull in the treatment of head wounds be kept cool by dipping them in water, his description proceeded in terms of the two instruments employed, the "crown trephine" (*modiolus, choinikis*), which bored through the bone, and the "perforator" (*terebra*), which chiseled and separated bone segments for subsequent excising. Celsus' language implied that both instruments were in use in contemporary Rome, as was the *meningophylax*, a metal plate to protect the *dura mater* during surgery on the head (*Med.* 8.3). A treatise in the Galenic corpus, but clearly not by Galen, claimed that surgeons no longer used the crown trephine, but by the early second century CE were content solely to perforate and chisel their way through the skull (*Introd.* 19).

The works of the important surgeons at Rome, such as Heliodorus and Antyllus, have largely been lost, except for excerpts in Oribasius' massive collection and in later compendia by Aetius of Amida in the early sixth century, and Paul of Aegina, who lived to see the Arab conquest of Alexandria in the seventh century; fragments from Heliodorus have also been preserved on papyrus. Heliodorus was a contemporary of the social critic and poet Juvenal (early second century CE), as we know from

Heliodorus' appearance in the misogynist sixth *Satire*, in which Juvenal called Heliodorus a castrator of young slave boys, asserting that he did so for the sexual pleasure of their Roman mistresses (6.366–73). Castration, after all, removed the possibility of an unwanted pregnancy as the result of intercourse. Heliodorus' seriousness as a surgeon can be observed in his discussion of treatments for intestinal incontinence with which the fourth book of his *Surgery* closed (Marganne 1998: 96–109). Although little more than a single column of the treatise survived on the fragmentary papyrus, it is clear that Heliodorus was concerned with etiology and he distinguished three causes for the fact that an anal sphincter was no longer functioning properly, but continuously discharged excrement: either the sphincter had been incised by mistake, or a pathologic condition had eroded its musculature, or paralysis impeded its functioning. Oribasius relied heavily on Heliodorus for his excerpts on surgical topics and a brief look at Heliodorus' directions for examining head wounds dispels any notion that he was merely a society doctor catering to the whims of an elite clientele. "Every wound is to be subjected to personal inspection and probing, discovering thereby whether it is simple, or if there is bruising of the entire mass; probing ascertains its depths, whether superficial or deep" (Heliodorus apud Orib. *Coll.* 46.7). Or again, when Heliodorus confronted distension of the skull's sutures after a blow or a fall:

> Use your hands immediately, pressing on either side in order to reunite the separated skull bones at the suture; then dry out the entire head and apply a plaster with non-inflammatory, fastening properties; finally tie with a bandage capable of complementing the closure of the sutures, the bunny bandage; untie it during the first day, or the second, and introduce a drying vapor bath, subsequently reapplying the same plaster and bandaging. The skull usually reunites and solidifies..., although occasionally suppuration ensues. (Heliodorus apud Orib. *Coll.* 46.26)

Heliodorus was apparently the inventor of the bunny bandage, used for wounds in the head, sometimes "without ears" and sometimes "with ears," with the ears apparently providing the means by which greater or lesser pressure was to be exerted on the skull through the bandaging. When treating the head fracture called *rhogme*, Heliodorus acknowledged how dreadful an experience surgery on the skull was for the patient: he used restraints to hold the patient down during the surgery, as well as an assistant to keep his head motionless. When removing bone from the skull by chiseling and chipping, he plugged the patient's ears lest echo from the chisel terrify him (apud Orib. *Coll.* 46.11). The surgeon Antyllus practiced at Rome subsequent to Heliodorus and he observed with regard to penetrating the skull in cases of hydrocephalus:

> If the fluid collects under the skull, whether the sutures distend or not, we forswear surgery, for the dura is impossible to manage when it lies in a sorry state surrounded by fluid; distension of the sutures cannot then be treated at all. If the skull is swollen even without distension, surgery is useless, for while we displace the fluid when we perforate through, how could anyone dissipate the deformity caused by the skull's upward movements? If someone wants to chisel out a skull that has separated upward, he will totally denude the dura and abandon his patient to spasm. (Antyllus apud Orib. *Coll.* 46.28)

Expressing concern for the patient's comfort, as well as his survival, was present already in Celsus' discussion of surgery, and the thought punctuated later surgical practice at Rome, for Heliodorus too repeatedly spoke of abandoning the knife when there was no hope of the patient's recovery, because this brought only additional suffering. In common with his Hippocratic predecessors Celsus was also concerned that the surgeon be youthful and strong, with steady and ambidextrous hands and sharp vision; at the same time, Celsus' surgeon was also to be filled with pity, because his greatest desire was to make the patient well. Nonetheless, he must not be so moved by the patient's cries that he rush along and cut less than necessary, ever reacting to cries of pain without emotion (*Med.* 7 proem. 4). The emphasis on concern for the patient found echo in a fragmentary papyrus from the Egyptian town of Oxyrhynchus, copied in the third century CE: "...The best surgeon needs at times to be one who consoles" (*P.Oxy.* 3.437.12–13). Galen was certainly one of the most accomplished of the surgeons at Rome, yet once he left his position in the gladiatorial school at Pergamum, he seldom operated on human beings, except in emergencies, and perfected his skills largely by cutting open and stitching up the animals he vivisected (*Meth. med.* 6.4).

4 Gynecology and Pediatrics

Celsus' attention to diseases of women was jejune and scattered throughout Books 2–4, with a short section in his seventh book on gynecological surgery, including the procedure for removing a dead fetus from the mother's womb (*Med.* 7.28–9). His gynecological material was drawn for the most part from the fifth book of "Aphorisms," an extensive gnomic treatise in the *Hippocratic Corpus* that remained popular throughout antiquity and beyond, but there is no indication Celsus ever consulted the larger gynecological works of the *Corpus*, such as "Diseases of Women," with its elaborate discussion of dystocia and excision of the dead fetus (*Morb. mul.* 1.68–70). In the next century Soranus and Galen also drew considerable gynecological material from "Aphorisms 5" (A. E. Hanson 2004a: 281–2). Nonetheless, both amply demonstrated that the join between childbearing and women's health that characterized Hippocratic gynecology had been severed, at least in medical theory. Male health in the *Hippocratic Corpus* largely involved an esthetic balancing of the food and drink ingested against what was expended in exercise as sweat or evacuated as urine and feces. In the case of women, however, the refrain "If she becomes pregnant, she will be healthy" was oft repeated in the gynecological treatises (e.g. Hippoc. *Morb. mul.* 2.137), and "old virgins and widows too young in their widowhood" were declared particularly prone to illnesses (A. E. Hanson 2000: 149–50; cf. Hanson and Flemming: 1998). Quotations from Herophilus' now lost treatises suggest that he was an important figure in the assimilation of men's and women's bodies, whether one looked to his employment of the same nomenclature for male and female generative parts that underscored similarity, not difference, or his judgment that the uterus was made of the same stuff as the rest of the body (Fragments 105–109 and 193 von Staden). The Hellenistic anatomists demystified the uterus Hippocratics had medicated and rendered old-fashioned their etiology for "hysterical suffocation" (*hysterike pnix*), the disease caused by the wandering of the uterus around the woman's body, wreaking havoc and preventing her from breathing (e.g. Hippoc. *Morb. mul.* 2.123–53; H. King 1998: 205–46). Hellenistic anatomists' ability to isolate and see the ligaments that held the uterus in place did not mean that this disease of the womb disappeared or lost its prevalence among those women not so sexually active as they should be. Rather, Soranus thought hysterical suffocation was caused by tensions on uterine ligaments resulting from miscarriage and long widowhood (*Gyn.* 3.26–9), and Galen attributed suffocation to retention of generating seed and menses, followed by their subsequent putrefaction (*Loc. affect.* 6.5). Perhaps more significant, Galen thought those men who retained seed in excess might also exhibit hysteric symptoms, albeit less frequently than women (*Diff. resp.* 3.10). The notion that the uterus roamed the woman's body kept its hold on the popular imagination, as uterine amulets, magic charms, and its reappearance in the *Gynaecia* of Mustio, another late antique translator of Soranus from North Africa, demonstrated (*Gen.* 2.4.26).

Soranus readily dismissed Hippocratic confidence in the salubriousness of pregnancy, maintaining rather that perpetual virginity was healthful for men and women, while repeated childbirth was exhausting (*Gyn.* 1.30–3; 42); his evidence came not only from female animals who were more healthy and sleek once their sexual organs were removed, but also from Rome's Vestal virgins who were less susceptible to disease, because they renounced sexual intercourse and were kept active and thin by their perpetual service to the gods. Soranus viewed menstruation as harmful, albeit a necessary antecedent to pregnancy, and considered amenorrhea as natural in the young, the menopausal, and female athletes, for the latter expended their bodily fluids in strenuous activities, thus leaving no surplus to be evacuated (*Gyn.* 1.23–9). Soranus' views were nonetheless juxtaposed to instructions on promoting healthful pregnancies and successful birthing. At the same time, Soranus also marked the fact that male and female pathologies and physiologies were drawing closer together by noting that diseases previously thought to afflict only men, such as gonorrhea (in the ancient sense, a continuous flow of seed) and satyriasis (continuous erection of the penis, or engorgement of the clitoris), might afflict women as well (*Gyn.* 3.28; 45–6). Galen endorsed the Aristotelian position that the female body possessed less innate heat than the male body. He was nevertheless able to construct a gendered thought-experiment comparing pulses, which were, in turn, determined by interior body heat, and he came to the conclusion that the pulse of a particular woman under a specific set of circumstances could beat more strongly than the pulse of a particular man:

> Have the man dwell in Pontus, but the woman in Egypt; he should pass the day indoors and idle, eating cold and luxurious food. By contrast have the woman spend her days out of doors, exercising strenuously and maintaining a modest intake of hot foods. This woman's pulse is surely greater than that man's. (*Caus. puls.* 3.2)

Medicine at Rome was deliberately distancing itself from the gender asymmetry that had characterized the medicine of fifth-century Greece and the *Hippocratic Corpus*. Roman therapeutics, however, remained conservative in gynecological practice, retaining the many old recipes, sometimes enhanced by exotic ingredients from faraway places, as well as introducing new therapies and procedures. Providing cures for infertility and amenorrhea, preventing miscarriage, and medicating all manner of uterine complaints remained a high priority. Both wet and dry fumigations that delivered vapors directly into the uterus continued to be popular and would be for a millennium to come. Cato had prescribed as a gynecological cure-all boiling the urine from a cabbage eater in a pan and sending the fumes through a reed into the woman's uterus, as she sat above on a chair with a pierced seat, her garments enveloping her lest the fumes escape (*Agr.* 107.11). Similar methods for fumigations punctuated the gynecological treatises of the *Hippocratic Corpus*, for the application of odoriferous vapors was often a therapy of choice for drawing a traveling uterus back to its proper position in the body. Old fashioned as the procedure seems, so sophisticated a woman as the empress Agrippina the Younger (15–59 CE) gave herself fumigations, once she recovered from her misadventure in the collapsible boat her son Nero had had built in order to kill her and her swift swim to shore, and after she applied medicaments to her bruises (Tac. *Ann.* 14.6). Agrippina would no doubt have employed more exotic ingredients in her fumigations than Cato's cabbage urine.

Archeologists have unearthed uterine amulets, usually made of hematite, from the length and breadth of the Roman Empire, from Britain to Syria; common features of the amulets included a stylized image of the uterus as a rounded globe with a foreshortened vagina, closed at the mouth by a lock; an *ouroboros* (snake eating its tail) usually encircled the image; and the name *Ororiouth* was carved somewhere on its surface. The lock facilitated the closing of the uterus when menses were to be retained during gestation for nourishing the fetus, while its opening permitted the uterus' contents to be expelled – an infant, or monthly accumulation of menses (A. E. Hanson 1995). A specialized sub-type of uterine amulet was carved on red, orange, or yellow gemstones (red jasper, yellow jasper, carnelian). These were "quick-birthers" (*okytokia*), and women employed them over the course of two millennia, from the time of the *Hippocratic Corpus* until the sixteenth century (A. E. Hanson 2004b). A "quick-birther" from the Taubman collection at the University of Michigan was probably carved in the third century CE and, in common with late antique and medieval examples, it summoned the fetus to stride into this world with its words "Onto your little feet" (*epi podia*, Bonner 1950: 274, no. 134) (Figure 25.2). Both pagan and Christian versions of the "quick-birthers" addressed the fetus directly, instructing it to come out, for by the time of birth a fetus was thought sufficiently sentient to respond to commands. Although it lacked sense and feeling at conception, the fetus gradually acquired these characteristics *in utero*, and this gradualist view of embryonic and fetal development was widespread among medical professionals, as well as the general populace. The messages of the quick-birthers shared in this assumption. The writers of the *Hippocratic Corpus* had been unaware of uterine contractions and attributed the pains of labor to the movements of the baby, as it punched and jabbed its way down and out in the effort to be born (e.g. Hippoc. *Nat. puer.* 30; A. E. Hanson 1999b). Galen knew all about uterine contractions, describing in elaborate detail the ability of the uterus to retain its contents through a retentive faculty and its ability to deliver the baby through an expulsive faculty, yet he continued to endorse the Hippocratic view that the fetus of term initiated birth when it recognized that its food supply *in utero* was inadequate. In a restlessness born of hunger the fetus broke the membranes that surrounded it in the womb, thus causing birth to take place (*Nat. fac.* 3.3–12).

Infancy and childhood had begun to attract serious attention from both philosophers and medical writers in the Roman republic, and by the time of the empire rules proliferated as to how responsible adults should best prepare children for the later life that hopefully awaited them. The second book of Soranus' *Gynecology* discussed neonates and small children up to their being weaned, probably at age two or three, and the time a pedagogue or other child minders took charge of them. Galen supplied fulsome information on pediatric theory and practices that Greek doctors were purveying at Rome in the first book of his *Hygiene* and at various points in his *Habits*, another treatise preserved only in Arabic (*Sanit.* 1; *Mor.*). Contracts for the hire of wet nurses from the Roman province of Egypt exhibited some of the same concerns about the care of infants and young children, thus tempering, to some extent, the notion that Soranus or Galen wrote about babies and small children only from books and the perspective of the elite (Masciadri and Montevecchi 1984; A. E. Hanson 2003). Roman babies were swaddled for months after birth, and Soranus provided elaborate instructions for massaging and swaddling, for female neonates were to be bound more tightly in the breast, but loosely in the hips, since this promoted the shape attractive for women (*Gyn.* 2.14–16). He was also preoccupied with the damaging effects premature standing and walking had on the legs of small children, lashing out at Roman mothers who failed to devote sufficient attention to child rearing, as Greek women did, but

Figure 25.2 An *okytokia*, or "quick birth" amulet, beseeching the gods for a birth in which the child appeared feet first (C. Bonner, *Studies in Magical Amulets, Chiefly Graeco-Egyptian*, Ann Arbor, 1955, n. 134. Photo courtesy of the A. Alfred Taubman Medical Library, University of Michigan)

Figure 25.2 (*Cont'd*)

allowed little children to stand and walk before they were physically ready. As a result, the child's legs became distorted, bowing outward, as the weight of its body rested on the still pliant limbs, and the ground of Rome, solid and hard because paved with stones, did not give way (*Gyn.* 2.43–4). Soranus advised clothing that supported the child's back, whenever the baby tried to sit up, and a chair with wheels, when it first tried to walk. He claimed that Romans attributed the bowing of small children's legs to the cold waters flowing beneath the city, an explanation that faulted no one, although he had heard stories attributing the cause to the fact that Roman women had intercourse too frequently, and did so when drunk. Galen boasted of having diagnosed what ailed a crying baby when its nurse was at a loss as to how to quiet her charge; his inspection of the baby's bed revealed its clothes and linens were dirty, and after ordering the nurse to bathe the baby and provide clean garments, the baby stopped crying (*Sanit.* 1.8.30–2). Galen saw three- and four-year olds as separating into two groups – those amenable to discipline, who loved praise for its own sake, and those who resisted out of naughtiness:

> [W]e sometimes see one of them hurt by a playmate, and... we see some of them take pity on him and help him, and others laugh at him, gloat over him, and sometimes join in and take part in hurting him. We also see some children rescue others from difficulties,

and others push playmates into dangerous places, poke their eyes out or choke them. Some are reluctant to give away anything they have in their hands, some are envious, others are not. (*Mor.*)

Galen deemed vigorous exercises appropriate for older children who attended school and were learning sports, such as riding on horseback, but by then frequent bathing was no longer salubrious (*Sanit.* 1.8.5–6).

5 The Medical Sects at Rome

It is also from Celsus that we first learn about disagreements in medicine as to what knowledge doctors must rely upon in order to cure patients: some held that experience and awareness of the evident cause of the illness were the essential ingredients, while others claimed that a thorough knowledge of human anatomy and physiology was required in addition to experience, so that a cause arising from deep within the body could be identified through reasoning (*Med. proem.* 9–53). The quarrel Celsus referred to was that between "Empiricists" and "Rationalists" (or "Dogmatists"), and while this essentially epistemological argument among doctors originated among Greek-speakers of the eastern Mediterranean, it too transferred to Rome and was a part of the medical scene there from Celsus' day to the time of Galen. When Celsus came to describe beliefs of the two medical sects, he switched from past tense verbs to the present tense and continued to do so when he added the third way of looking at what was essential to medical practice. These latter were the doctors of the Method, a sect which developed subsequent to the other two and did so primarily at Rome, classifying diseases according to bodily states and applying rules the Method established for treating each state (*Med. proem.* 54–73). While Soranus was a Methodist, Galen considered himself an eclectic, choosing what was best from the Empiric and Rationalist points of view; he gave the quarrel full coverage and even claimed to have seen a doctrinal dispute erupt into fisticuffs at the bedside of a patient (*Diff. puls.* 1.1). Nonetheless Galen's insistence on combining information gained from both empiric and dogmatic points of view and the influence he wielded over subsequent centuries seem to have lessened the vehemence in doctors' epistemological arguments.

6 Overall Roman Health and Life Expectancy

At the end of the eighteenth century, Edward Gibbon began his *History of the Decline and Fall of the Roman Empire* by observing that the empire's inhabitants in the years 98–180 CE were reaping the benefits of the peace and prosperity initiated by the emperor Augustus, "a happy period of more than fourscore years." Gibbon's assertion that these inhabitants "enjoyed and abused the advantages of wealth and luxury" is reminiscent of Celsus' view that townspeople were more sickly than country-folk because of their sedentary lifestyle and improper diet, both of which sprang from the omnipresent luxuries then available (*Med.* 1.2). The average citizen of Rome and those inhabiting urban centers throughout the empire certainly lived more varied and more interesting lives than those in centuries past. Traditions of euergetism flourished, and the emperors, as well as local elites, undertook many individuals projects that enhanced the quality of daily life (Gleason, this volume). In addition to entertainments, spectacles and doles of food stuffs, public libraries and parks, and magnificent buildings, there were aqueducts bringing water to fountains, bathing establishments, and public latrines; drainage projects attempted to clean sewers and clear unhealthy swamps; expanded harbor facilities ensured supplies of basic foods; cemeteries, crematoria, and professions associated with disposing of the dead were deliberately confined to the areas outside the walls (Bodel 2000; Patterson 2000). Public doctors, along with teachers and professors, were at times hired by individual communities, especially in the cities of the eastern provinces; emperors awarded these learned professions immunities from some tax burdens, yet they also strictly limited the numbers so benefited (Parsons 1976: 438–46). Still, it remains unclear the extent to which those labeled public physicians were concerned about the entire community, since the concept of public health did not exist in the ancient world. Policies designed to ameliorate an urban population's health would come into being only with the Enlightenment of the eighteenth century (Nutton 2000: 71). The environmental factors classified as salubrious in the Hippocratic treatise "Airs, Waters, Places," were adhered to and repeated by Roman authors: it was best to build in a locality that received the benefits of air and waters that were clear, bright, and light. Such advice was useful largely for those intending to locate a city or a villa on virgin territory, while those who lived in an unhealthy location with brackish water and stifling winds that brought bad air had either to fortify their bodies as best they could, or move elsewhere. If many sickened at once, the winds were faulted for bringing insalubrious conditions. The etiologies proffered for the diseases that killed in medical and lay writers of the Roman period more often centered on the capacity of the individual's body to withstand assaults from malfunctions within the body than on the pernicious effects of one's surroundings. Celsus frequently advised the sick to visit the baths without a thought for how this might compromise the health of other bathers (Fagan 1999: 179–88). There can be no question but that infective agents, such as worms, amoebas, bacteria, and viruses, lurked everywhere in Rome and other ancient cities, but they went unseen and unsuspected. It was the filth and squalor omnipresent in the crowded neighborhoods where dwelt the urban poor that those who would preserve their own health must avoid (Scheidel 2003). The wealthy did so in all seasons, building their urban houses on the hills of Rome and deserting the city altogether for country villas when the air of summer turned oppressive. Slaves and the poor had no choice but to remain where circumstances placed them; whether those who found themselves in slavery or poverty in the countryside found life less short and less nasty than that of their urban counterparts is uncertain.

Demographers who study the ancient Mediterranean work with admittedly jejune evidence that is sometimes a bit more full for the populations of the Roman Empire, especially that of Roman Egypt. Average life expectancy at birth was most likely between 22 and 25 years, and the level of infant mortality was high, with perhaps nearly half the babies born dying before their fifth birthday (Bagnall and Frier 1994: 103–10; Bagnall, Frier and Rutherford 1997: 100). Children who survived to their tenth birthday had on average a life expectancy of some 36 to 38 additional years, taking the surviving female past menopause and the male to nearly age 50. Life span among Romans was apparently similar to our own, yet only a little over one percent of the Roman population reached their eightieth birthday, and people were dying at all ages (Bagnall and Frier 1994: 81–103; Frier 2000b). Good genes were perhaps less essential to longevity than good nourishment in infancy and early childhood, and avoidance not merely of injuries that penetrated the skin and brought pernicious infections, but also of the potentially lethal diseases that antibiotics and other synthecized medications now cure.

7 Attitudes Towards Medicine and Physicians in the Roman World

Medical practitioners had long been aware they were unable to cure all the sick persons who sought their help. Medicine's fallibilities were equally known to the Roman public and elicited from them, in turn, a variety of responses beyond the anger and frustration of a Cato or a Pliny. The Neronian courtier and Stoic philosopher Seneca the Younger spoke most warmly about his doctor, claiming that because he devoted his attentions to him alone and deserted his other patients to attend him, his doctor was his friend, not merely some salaried professional (*Ben.* 6.16). Seneca's insistence on exclusivity tempers the warmth and gratitude he was expressing, such that his stance seems more that of a patron towards a reliable dependent and a social inferior. The Roman satirist Martial (c.40–104 CE) saw the doctor as someone to poke fun at, playing upon Roman suspicions that the Greek doctor, admitted into the center of the Roman household, had designs on corrupting a young wife:

> Leda told her aged husband that she was suffering from a womby disease
>   and lamented that only intercourse would cure her.
> But she wept and groaned that her own health did not matter
>   and preferred to die than submit to disgrace.
> Her husband begged her to live and preserve her life and youthful beauty,
>   giving permission for others to do what he could not.
> The female practitioners departed, and the doctors ran over to her:
>   up went her legs – this is serious medicine. (11.71)

A common response to the professional medicine of the day was to pursue multiple paths for restoration of health, either simultaneously or serially, rather than to place exclusive reliance on doctors and doctoring. The alternatives available to Roman patients were many and manifold, and the shrines of Asclepius at Pergamum and Cos clearly flourished, for both were extensively rebuilt during the earlier Roman Empire. Stories such as that of the woman in the Gospels suffering from a chronic flow of blood for 12 years who reached out to touch Jesus' robe as he passed testified to the appeal of healing by faith. In one moment she felt herself cured. Her illness and cure were told three times (Mt 9: 20–2; Mk 5: 25–9; Lk 8: 43–8), but the narrative in Mark's versions began with the observation that she had spent her money on doctors to no avail, and some copies of Luke opened in the same fashion. Helios-Sarapis, the Bringer of Victory, an oracular deity resident at the Egyptian town of Oxyrhynchus, was asked in the second century CE whether or not he advised the petitioner to make use of Hermeinos, doctor at Hermopolis, to cure his eyes (*P.Oxy.* 42.3078). We do not know whether Helios-Sarapis responded, "Yes, your should consult Hermeinos," or "No, you should not," but we can guess with some confidence that, if consulted, Hermeinos was likely to prescribe soothing eye salves (*collyria*) for the petitioner's ophthalmia. The fact that the petitioner wanted reassurance from the god that he should visit the Hermopolite doctor in the first place underscores yet once again the fact that neither the medical practitioner nor his craft held the trust and authority in the Roman world that is today awarded physicians, with their vast array of tools for diagnosis and their ever-expanding repertory of cures. Medicine's impressive successes in the early twenty-first century have not only expanded average life expectancy at birth to near or into the low eighties for those in the affluent west, but have also pushed many alternative medicines to the fringes. The Hippocratic "Epidemics" enjoined the physician to help his patients, or at least not to harm them (Hippoc. *Epid.* 1.11), and the doctors of the Roman world endeavored to follow this injunction from the "Father of Medicine" with the limited tools at their disposal. There can be no doubt but that medicine offers an interesting lens through which to examine a society and its social preferences.

CHAPTER TWENTY-SIX

Philosophy in the Roman Empire

Sara Ahbel-Rappe

1 Introduction: How Roman is Imperial Philosophy?

Philosophical developments in the Roman Empire deeply influenced how we conceive of Ancient Greek philosophy today. In the high empire Hellenistic philosophy (especially Stoicism) was immensely popular, but increasingly revitalized forms of Aristotelian and Platonic philosophies came to dominate the intellectual field. In particular, it was the scholastic reading of the treatises and dialogues, the advent of the exegetical tradition, that resulted in an almost scriptural status accorded to the works of Aristotle and Plato (Tarrant 2000; J. Barnes 1993; Sedley 1997b). Ironically, for those who associate the Roman Empire with Hellenistic philosophy, it was precisely at this time that the Hellenistic schools began to be eclipsed.

These centuries saw the resurgence of Aristotle's school, of Pythagoreanism, and of course, the development of Middle Platonism (Dillon 1977), followed by Neoplatonism. There were also revelatory traditions of a multiethnic origin, including the *Hermetica*, the *Chaldean Oracles*, and Philo's particularly Jewish brand of Stoic Platonism. Because the Roman Empire embraced a world whose intellectual aspirations always returned to Greek as the language of choice, we shall see that the majority of the philosophers in this period wrote in Greek. There were few Latin exceptions, of course: the Stoic Seneca, the Platonist Calcidius, and the novelist and author of a Platonist handbook, Apuleius of Madaura (perhaps only marginally an original philosopher). More typical are the Latin writers who chose to write in Greek though they lived in Rome or were themselves Roman. Marcus Aurelius wrote his *Meditations* in Greek and other native Italians such as Musonius Rufus wrote in Greek as well (Inwood 1995; Sedley 1997c; M. Griffin 1992, 1997a). Our period gives birth to mottos that sound anything but self-evident to the modern ear. Numenius (a second-century Pythagorean from Syria) quips, "what is Plato but a Moses who speaks Greek, or Moses but a Jew who Platonizes?" (Numen. fr. 8 des Places). This *bon mot* epitomizes the spirit of imperial philosophy, as Hebrew is eclipsed in favor of Greek, and Classical philosophy is displaced by the revelations of the God of Israel.

In the earlier part of our story, in the first century CE, philosophy from the viewpoint of someone living in Rome could have looked plausibly familiar, especially as the Stoics and Epicureans had already come to be Latinized in the works of Cicero and then of Lucretius and Seneca. Cicero notoriously published the *Academica*, a dialogue featuring the statesmen Lucullus, Catulus, and Hortensius expounding abstruse epistemological problems. Miriam Griffin persuasively writes of this period, "there is considerable evidence that, to many Romans, Stoicism as a moral philosophy seemed like a rationalization of (or a poor substitute for) Rome's own traditional ideals" (M. Griffin 1997a: 8, citing Cic. *Tusc.* 1.2, *Fin.* 2.67). By contrast, it was the composite identity of the empire, the very fact that the empire itself exceeded anything peculiarly Roman, that coincided with the new spirit of imperial philosophy. For imperial philosophy was decidedly Hellenic, even if this very Hellenism was born in the distant reaches of the Empire, beyond Rome and beyond Athens (Millar 1997: 243). The powerful ideas of the Platonic and Aristotelian schools found voices in the brilliant exegetical works of Alexander of Aphrodisias, the Alexandrians Philo and Plotinus, and the Syrian-born Iamblichus. Beyond this philosophic geography there was a theoretical component to the cosmopolitanism that characterized imperial philosophy.

We glimpse this idea in Celsus' *On the True Doctrine*. Celsus was a Middle Platonist philosopher of the second century who penned what was perhaps the first systematic philosophical attack on Christianity (Frede 1994, 1997; Dörrie 1987). From what can be constructed of this treatise through Origen's reply (written some 70 years after Celsus' original), it seems that Celsus adapted certain Stoic doctrines concerning the natural revelation afforded by reason, to suggest that there was one primordial and universal wisdom tradition. This true doctrine was attested among the highest and most ancient civilizations, including Egypt, Assyria, Persia, India, and various other tribes (Origen *C.Cels.* 1.16). The Jewish nation, however, corrupted and distorted this doctrine through the botched efforts of Moses, who offered a misleading account of reality to his followers. In fact, the uneducated shepherds and goatherds who constituted the followers of Moses actually worshipped the cosmos (*C.Cels.* 1.24.4) and not the transcendent god at all. Christians further embraced and amplified the mistakes introduced by the Jews (Frede 1997; *C.Cels.* 1.26). The Christian claim to possess a uniquely privileged revelation of the truth, resulting in a refusal to accord the same status to the gods of other nations or to recognize the universal monotheism (and what amounts to a largely Middle Platonist metaphysical scheme) of the world's great religions, betrayed its intellectual inferiority.

Therefore the Roman Empire, as an amalgam or collective unity of the ancient nations, was providentially disposed to preserve and uphold this true doctrine. Imperial philosophy, insofar as it embraced the Syrian, Babylonian, Egyptian, and Greek traditions that came to inform it, was inherently multi-ethnic and could never be provincial (Frede 1997: 247; *C.Cels.* 1.16: "Linus, Musaeus, Orpheus, Pherecydes, the Persian Zoroaster, and Pythagoras collected [these teachings] and preserved their own teachings in the books [they wrote], preserving them until the present day"). Celsus was a Platonist, but his notion of a universal wisdom lineage has roots in the theories of allegory promoted by the Stoa and the Cosmopolis, promoted by the Cynics. Other Platonists of this era were also inclined to see the Roman Empire as a providential dispensation meant to provide for the flourishing of wisdom. Simon Swain has shown that many passages in Plutarch's *Parallel Lives* touch on this theme, and that Plutarch cautiously embraced the idea that "the Platonic god had brought about the present political ordering of the world" (Swain 1997: 186–7; 1996). Although Swain sees in this pro-imperial attitude a gesture of appropriation (Romans need Greek divinity), Michael Frede (1997) is more accurate in noticing the universalizing tendency of Roman imperial philosophy. Rome became a gathering place, a meeting of minds that perhaps first benefited from the Athenian brain drain. But this cosmopolitanism grew as Rome in its military assimilation of other cultures stumbled on the great treasure troves of Hellenic wisdom (Millar 1993a, 1997; Potter 1994).

A quick glance at two of the most influential philosophers in the empire reveals an international cast. One, Alexander of Aphrodisias, dedicated his *Concerning Fate* to Septimius Severus and Caracalla c.198 CE. Whether the teaching post Alexander filled was one of Marcus Aurelius' chairs in philosophy, and hence whether Alexander actually taught in Athens, is unknown. Among the successive members of the Aristotelian Commentator tradition of late antiquity (along with, e.g., Philoponus,

Table 26.1 Names and dates of important philosophers

Antiochus of Ascalon	c.130 BCE	Academic
Apuleius	c.123 CE	Middle Platonist and Rhetorician
Arcesilaus	c.316–241 BCE	Head of Skeptical Academy
Celsus	active c.200 CE	Platonist philosopher
Damascius	c.467–540 CE	Last head of the Neoplatonist Academy
Epictetus	c.50 CE	Stoic teacher
Iamblichus	active c.245 CE	Neoplatonist
Marcus Aurelius	c.161–80 CE	Roman emperor and Stoic
Numenius	active c.150 CE	Middle Platonist/Pythagorean
Philo of Alexandria	c.20 BCE	Middle Platonist
Philo of Larissa	c.159 BCE	Academic
Plotinus	c.204–70 CE	Neoplatonist
Plutarch	c.45 CE	Middle Platonist and *litterateur*
Porphyry	active c.270 CE	Neoplatonist
Proclus	c.412–85 CE	Neoplatonist
Pyrrho	c.360 BCE	Philosopher associated with skepticism
Sextus Empiricus	Uncertain dates. Perhaps second century CE	Neo-Pyrrhonist
Seneca	c.1 BCE–65 CE	Stoic essayist
Zeno	Third century BCE	founder of Stoicism

Simplicius, Ammonius, all of whom were Neoplatonists), Alexander was known as the dean of commentators. Nevertheless, Alexander wrote his commentaries and independent treatises as the last purely Aristotelian scholar. He made his appearance before the rise of Neoplatonism, and yet the theory for which he was best known, his doctrine of the active intellect, is rightly identified as an antecedent to Plotinus' theory. Alexander taught that "our own higher thoughts were really the activity of a single, non-human *nous*" (Lloyd 1990: 183; cf. Sharples 1987; Schroeder and Todd 1990). Thus Alexander indirectly influenced the formation of Neoplatonic noetics, and directly inspired the largest body of philosophical literature to have survived from antiquity – a group of works masterfully edited by Kalbfleish as the *Corpus Aristotelicum Graecum* (CAG) and now being translated under the direction of Richard Sorabji.

Another influential individual from the eastern provinces is Iamblichus, who was born in Syria and migrated to Apamea in northern Syria; there, in a city full of Platonist history – Numenius, whom we have already met, was also from Apamea – he radically transformed the shape of Neoplatonic philosophy and infused a religiosity into what might have collapsed into a purely scholastic tradition. Iamblichus' only surviving works, *The Life of Pythagoras* and *On the Mysteries of the Egyptians*, are set in the worlds of Magna Graecia and of Egypt, respectively, thus traversing the borders of the Roman Empire. Along the way, Iamblichus manages to transform what we might think of as the ordinary structure of pagan ritual into a rite of self-transformation, known as theurgy, or "divine activity." As Iamblichus explains in *On the Mysteries*, theurgy relies on the resonances between the human soul and the divine world. This resonance is captured in the lexical idea of the *sunthema* or *symbolon*, the corresponding tokens that, when united, reveal a complete meaning. *Sunthemata* are ritual objects employed in theurgic rites. Theurgists attributed their efficacy to causal structures initiated by *Henads*, the unifying principles of reality whose proper characteristics manifest themselves at every level of being, including the material order. The use of *Henads* in rites of ascent involves the installation of a given deity or divine energy in the *sunthema*, which functions as a cosmic switch and allows the soul of the practitioner to unite with the deity invoked. Likewise, certain dimensions of the soul are divinely complemented by corresponding functions, powers, and even virtues that exist among the gods whose assistance provides the foundation for theurgic ascent.

The example of Iamblichus' school in Apamea allows us once more to consider the multi-ethnic quality of imperial philosophy, for this city is also associated with the *Chaldean Oracles* (Athanassiadi 1999a: 153–4). These hexameter verses, written in archaizing Greek, were traditionally attributed to Julianus the Theurgist, a contemporary of Marcus Aurelius and a medium who succeeded in "channeling" Plato's soul! The *Oracles* achieved canonical status in the third century CE, and were celebrated as a sacred text by members of the Neoplatonist school. The extant fragments of this work are preserved for the most part in commentaries on the *Parmenides* by Proclus and Damascius. There are two kinds of fragments: those that reveal magical practices or theurgic rites, and those that discuss Platonic doctrine in terms of a Middle-Platonist scheme. The word Chaldean connoted Babylonian, and there are indeed several links to Babylonian religion in the texts of the *Oracles*, as in for example Proclus' *Commentary on the Parmenides*, which plays on a Syrian word, *Ad* "one" (Procl. *In Prm.* 7.58). At any rate, whether or not the Chaldean oracles participate in only a fabricated "Orientalism," as many Western scholars insist, for our purposes it is enough to note that imperial philosophy is a philosophy that originates to a large extent at the margins of empire. It would seem that there is hardly anything Roman about philosophy in the Roman Empire.

2 The Athenian Brain Drain

In the final years of the Roman Republic, people still went to graduate school in Athens to study philosophy. Certainly Cicero did: we know that he listened to the lectures of Antiochus of Ascalon for six months during his student years (*Brut.* 315). So did his brother Quintus, his friend Atticus – though he became an Epicurean (*Ac.* 14) – and his associates Varro (*Ac.* 12) and Brutus (*Tusc.* 5.21) (J. Barnes 1997: 59–61; M. Griffin 1997a: 4–7; Brittain 2001: 64–6). But after the Mithridatic War, the philosophical fortunes of Athens waned and philosophers in large numbers arrived in Rome. According to Brittain (2001: 58–63), the evidence suggests that the officially sanctioned schools of philosophy were simply shut down in 88 BCE (Ath., *Deip.* 5.213d). Cicero tells us in his *Brutus* of the flight of Philo of Larissa to Athens along with the other "optimates" (*Brut.* 306). Philo of Larissa, Antiochus of Ascalon, the Epicurean Phaedrus, and the Peripatetic Cratippus all arrived in the Eternal City. Cicero himself attended on Philo with great enthusiasm, a fact which he attributes to the dismal political situation of Rome during the Social Wars:

> Stirred by an amazing enthusiasm for philosophy I gave myself wholly to Philo. The reason I spent so long in this study – although the variety and the magnitude of the subjects themselves held me with great delight – was that the order of the law courts seemed to have disappeared forever. (*Brut.* 306, with Brittain 2001: 65)

Many of Cicero's circle came to have connections with household philosophers who, exiled from the great Athenian schools, had ended up in Roman villas. Lucullus associated with Antiochus, Brutus with Antiochus' brother, Aristus, Cato the younger with the Stoic Athenodorus, Calpurnius Piso with Philodemus (J. Barnes 1997: 60–2). In the early empire, Augustus himself patronized Stoic philosophers, while Tiberius sponsored the esoteric Pythagorean Thrasyllus as his court astrologer, although he later tried to kill him (Tac. *Ann.* 6.20–1; for Tiberius' plot against Thrasyllus see Tarrant 1993: 216–19). Much later, Plotinus and Porphyry also found themselves in Rome (Porph. *VP* 5.1–7 discusses Porphyry's arrival in Rome and so marks the beginning of Plotinus' residency as a teacher there).

Before we leave this overview of Roman philosophical history, it will be useful to dwell for a moment on Cicero's dialogue, the *Academica* (Brittain 2001; Tarrant 1985; Inwood and Mansfeld 1997). In it we find Cicero confessing his own philosophical allegiances to Academic skepticism. Cicero's dialogue also shows the increasing importance of the history of philosophy in our period. Specifically, the *Academica* attempts to offer a uniform history of the Academy that makes skepticism, rather than dogmatism or doctrinal philosophy, central to the enterprises of both Plato and Socrates (Brittain 2001). Book Two of the *Academica* features Lucullus expounding the philosophy of the Academic renegade, Antiochus. Lucullus explains that he spent time with Antiochus in Alexandria while serving as quaestor (2.11). Whether their acquaintance could have qualified Lucullus to explicate the minutia of Antiochean doctrine that Cicero has him expound in the *Academica* is another story. Certainly Cicero caught flack for this representation. Romans could be cruel about intellectuals, as their word, *baro*, "egg-head," suggests (M. Griffin 1997a: 14). At issue in the dialogue is the content of Philo's so-called Roman books (Brittain 2001: 129–68). Evidently Philo began to embrace a qualified form of dogmatism while he was the scholarch of the Academy, which for generations had maintained a radical form of skepticism. *Akatalepsia*, the principle that nothing can be known or rather that, so far, no one has succeeded in showing that knowledge is attainable, became central to the epistemology and ethics of the Academy under Arcesilaus and then Carneades, while at the same time detailed study of Plato's dialogues had fallen out of favor in the Hellenistic Academy. Philo's break meant a return to the limited affirmation that some things can be known. Largely due to the puzzling nature of Cicero's account, Antiochus himself has recently become a philosophical legend, the supposed founder of the Alexandrian metaphysical school of Platonism and the first Academic philosopher to reintroduce Plato's philosophy of the ideas (but see J. Barnes 1997, who considerably deflates the reputation of Antiochus).

Well and good, one might say, but why are these quibbles of any interest to a student of Roman imperial history? Because they show that philosophy was subject to shifting tides even before it reached Rome. The move to (a dogmatic) Plato was building momentum at a time when ordinary citizens and then emperors still affiliated themselves with the Hellenistic schools. The scriptural reverence for Plato's dialogues was just on the horizon, as the intellectual vigor of the schools waned through lack of mutual antagonism. At any rate, while Philo modified his skepticism, two thinkers broke away from the Academy altogether. The first was Aenesidemus. Perhaps disgusted by the mediocrity of Philonian skepticism, Aenesidemus sponsored a return to the philosophy of Pyrrho, a fourth-century BCE eccentric who wrote nothing, but who evidently maintained that the world was not such that anything could be known about it. Later, Sextus Empiricus was to champion the cause of Neo-Pyrrhonism with his monumental works, *Against the Grammarians* and *Outlines of Pyrrhonism*, perhaps relying extensively on the now lost works of Aenesidemus (for the relationship between Pyrrho, Aenesidemus, and Neo-Pyrrhonism, see Bett 1997). Second, though, was Antiochus himself, who (as we hear from Cicero's *Lucullus*) actually went so far as to embrace Stoic epistemology. Did he have a doctrine of ideas or concepts that echoed Plato's own epistemology, however dimly? Did he anticipate the return to the *cosmic noetos*, the intelligible order valorized in Middle Platonism? The jury is still out on this question.

This transition from the skepticism of the Hellenistic period to a more dogmatic Platonism anticipates the general movement of philosophy back to the classical authors and away from the Hellenistic schools. But this shift was gradual, and it is certainly true that in the first century CE, Stoicism, followed by Epicureanism as a distant second, defined the philosophical spirit of Romans more popularly. Already we have seen that Antiochus, a popularizer of Academic skepticism, was willing to accept the Stoa's central epistemology, which was entirely empiricist. According to the Stoics, the mind formed its concepts through repeated experience of the objects encountered through the senses, and the accuracy of this process was assured through the device of the so-called "cognitive impression." In other words, our minds receive as their very birthright a true and accurate assurance (the clear and distinct mark of the cognitive impression) that the world just is how we find it through ordinary sense experience (Frede 1983). This native ability of the mind to discern the truth becomes the focus of the Roman Stoa's emphasis on the deity within, as we shall see when we come to Epictetus.

3 Popular Philosophy in Rome: Self-Improvement

It was ethics, and not epistemology however quotidian, that formed the heart and soul of Hellenistic popular philosophy in the High Empire. Philosophy at this period was largely conceived along the lines of therapy, a way to burnish the character flaws from one's personality and to find peace amidst the surging tides of worldly misfortune (Hadot 1995). This philosophical therapy cut across school and class divisions, as everyone from the lowliest slave to the emperor himself could benefit from a proper understanding of the emotions.

Stoic therapy was both cognitive and practice-oriented. The theoretical component comprised a psychology of mind that originated in the Ancient Stoa (with perhaps some modifications by Panaetius); the practical component was elaborated as a series of meditations or philosophical exercises meant to be cultivated in everyday life. Pierre Hadot, Martha Nussabuam, and Richard Sorabji have done much to familiarize us with these practical therapies that Cicero, Seneca, Epictetus, and Marcus Aurelius deploy extensively throughout their writings (Nussbaum 1994; Sorabji 2000; Hadot 1995). In the next section, we shall see how the epistemology of the Stoa combines with its psychology and creates a context in which the "therapy of desire," as Nussbaum has famously called it, can be applied in ordinary settings.

For the early Stoa (the Stoa of Zeno and Chrysippus), the emotions originated as cognitive dispositions to evaluate states of affairs in terms of the advantage or disadvantage that they possessed. Thus Stoicism in general is characterized by a radical rejection of Plato's tripartite psychology according to which emotion and desire operate independently of reason. Yet for the Stoics, emotion can be defined as consisting in an incorrect opinion, to the effect that a given situation is inherently good or bad (Inwood 1985: 130–1). We find a good summary of Zeno's doctrine in Cicero's *Tusculan Disputations*: "pain is an opinion about a present evil, and in this opinion there is this element, that it is right to feel pain" (*Tusc.* 3.74; Inwood 1985: 148). All emotions, as for example greed, anger, lust, cowardice, etc., flow from this one central channel, viz., the belief that states of affairs can be, in themselves, either good or bad (Stob. 2.90). Not so, for the later Stoics. In fact there was only one good, moral virtue, and one bad, moral vice. These terms ("good" and "bad"), then, refer in the strict sense only to states of affairs in the human soul. Every other state of affairs, that is the conditions or objects of infinite variety, falls technically under the heading of "indifferent." Nevertheless, one may and ideally should prefer certain kinds of "indifferents," viz., those which fully accord with nature, such as health or wisdom.

The sage alone is able to treat indifferent things as truly indifferent; ordinary people experience emotions as a result of their ability or inability to acquire items in the category of "indifferents," that is, things that are preferable, although not inherently objects of moral choice. Therefore the Stoic sage is able to see things from the point of view of Zeus. As Seneca puts it, the sage is not just a part of nature, but becomes an ally of Zeus himself (*Ep.* 92.30; Inwood 1999: 683). All things form part of a seamless universal nexus of events, the *heimarmenê* or fate that is identical with the body and will of Zeus, the ultimate rational principle. Although every human mind is a spark or *apospasma* of this rational principle, only the sage is able to live a life in accord with this fact. The sage alone recognizes that since all things are willed by Zeus, this universe is the best possible world. Everything that happens within this world is necessarily a part of the total perfection. Stoic philosophy is designed, at the highest end of the philosophical spectrum, to help the practitioner acquire the mind of the sage who constantly attends to the perfection (Long 2002: 38–66). Epictetus' favorite saying was a quotation from Cleanthes' *Hymn to Zeus*:

> Lead me, Zeus, and you Fate, wherever you have ordained for me. For I shall follow unflinching. But if I become bad and unwilling, I shall follow none the less. (*Ench.* 53)

Sagacity is the *summum bonum* of the Stoic school. The sage represents the human quest for perfection, expressed in the Platonic curriculum as the culminating stage of one's studies, when one attains "likeness to god." The very concept of the sage looks backwards in time, to the charismatic influence of particular philosophers such as Socrates, Zeno, Epicurus, or Diogenes. As David Sedley has shown in an important article, Hellenistic school philosophy was very much grounded in the philosophical circle that developed around a central intellectual figure who inspired imitation, if not emulation, in his or her students (Sedley 1997a). Yet the sage also anticipates Christian ideas of the blessed person or saint, one who shares properties of the deity and leads other human beings in developing these same qualities.

At the lower end of the philosophical spectrum, one can at least practice the therapies, that is, cultivate *apatheia*, or detachment from emotional conditioning, even if perfection remains on the distant horizon: the Stoics referred to the ordinary person's career in philosophical training as "making progress" (*prokopton*) (Sorabji 2000: 194–227). For such students, the handbook was a useful tool. In works like Epictetus' *Encheiridion*, extracted from the *Discourses* by Arrian and meant to serve as a constant companion for the aspirant, or in Marcus Aurelius' *Meditations*, we find self-help techniques designed with the learner in mind. These passages contain instructions on how to calm the savage fires of anger or greed, or how to get through the bouts of grief and loss that inevitably come our way as human beings.

The student is reminded to treat indifferent things with indifference, to attend to the character of her representations, not assenting to the suggestions of emotion, and to label all thoughts appropriately. Some meditations help the reader/disciple more readily attain to this emotional detachment through the themes of impermanence, mortality, death, and human insignificance more generally:

> Set before your eyes all the plays and sets, all alike, that you know from your own experience or from the history of older times: for instance, the whole course of Hadrian and the whole course of Antoninus and the whole court of Philip, Alexander, Croesus – for all of those were just the same only different actors played the parts. (Marc. Aurel. *Med.* 10.57, with R. Rutherford 1989: 166)

Attention, watchfulness, looking over the condition of one's mind, categorizing thoughts – all of these techniques would not be out of place in a Christian or Buddhist meditation manual. Even though some of the practices look more like our own *Chicken Soup for the Soul* manuals than truly serious philosophy, in fact they were profoundly influential in the development of monastic and desert spirituality. Some 700 years after Zeno, we find Evagrius Ponticus, a fourth-century Cappadocian renegade, turning up in Nitria, possibly fleeing from a scandal at home. But after a period of adjustment he made great progress in the deserts near Alexandria. Evagrius' instructions for monastics have come down to us under the name of St. Nilus – Evagrius himself was excommunicated during the fifth-century Origenist controversy (see E. Clark 1992 and Edwards, this volume) – as *Treatise on Prayer* and *On Evil Thoughts*. Evagrius uses Stoic teaching on emotions as a foundation for a system designed to help monks battle the eight demons or evil thoughts that block the way to tranquility (*apatheia*). In fact, Evagrius' Stoic-inspired manual has become the basis for the contemporary Christian tradition of the seven deadly sins (Sorabji 2000: 357–71).

Even Neoplatonists employed meditation techniques to help their students assimilate their difficult metaphysics and radical teachings on the illusoriness of our ordinary world (Rappe 2000: 45–66). Many such meditations can be found in Plotinus' *Enneads*, Porphyry's compilation of his master's essays that perhaps owes something of its stylistic difficulties to Plotinus' method of personal instruction. In one very well known passage, Plotinus appears to be leading the student in a just such an exercise:

> So far as possible, try to conceive of this world as one unified whole, with each of its parts remaining self-identical and distinct. So that whatever part of, for example, the outer sphere is shown forth, there immediately follows the image of the sun together with all of the other stars, and earth and sea and all sentient beings are seen, as if upon a transparent sphere. (*Enn.* 6.8.9.1–6)

Invoking the cosmic spirituality that enjoyed a long tradition in Platonic writings but also more generally prevailed in the religiosity of the empire, Plotinus brings the student into a vision of an immaterial world (Fowden 1977). These meditations, whether on time or on the cosmos, offer us a firsthand look at how philosophy was taught in the second and third centuries of the Roman Empire. Although philosophy involved the study of texts, there was as well an emphasis on personal training, on seeing the truth for oneself, and on assimilation to the truth seen (as Plotinus exhorts his students, "make yourself the vision!").

It is time to turn from generalization and spend a few moments dwelling on a figure who perhaps epitomizes Roman philosophy in the first and second centuries CE. Epictetus was born c.50–60 CE in what is now Turkey, near Ephesus. He was a slave by birth, but as fortune would have it, was purchased by Epaphroditus, Nero's secretary. While still a slave Epictetus began to listen to the lectures of Musonius Rufus. He moved to Greece, to Nicopolis, after Domitian banned all philosophers from the Italian continent. A. A. Long has written instructively about the contrast between the Stoicism of the former slave, Epictetus, and that of his older contemporary, Seneca:

> Epictetus without any [social climbing] achieved renown simply by being a dedicated teacher, impervious to all external markers of success. In this he contrasted radically with

the immensely wealth and powerful Seneca, who was not a practicing teacher and whose Stoicism, though certainly sincere, was fully tested only in old age when Nero forced him to commit suicide. (Long 2002: 11)

As Long points out, Epictetus' own experience of slavery surfaced in his lifelong habit of taunting his freeborn students with the jibe, "slave." His style with the interlocutors who appear in the *Discourses* is rough, haranguing, and in the manner of the Cynic diatribe:

> *I have to die!* Do I also have to die groaning? *I have to be fettered.* While moaning too? *I have to go into exile.* Does anyone prevent me from going with a smile, cheerful and serene? *Tell your secrets.* I refuse, because that is up to me. *Then I will fetter you.* What do you mean, fellow? Fetter me? You can fetter my leg but not even Zeus can overcome my volition. (Arr. *Epict.* 1.1.21–3)

Epictetus, like his spiritual ancestor, Socrates, taught groups of wealthy youths in public, writing nothing, but directly ministering to the spiritual needs of his students. His was a philosophy of self-transformation consistent with the Socratic exhortation to virtue. Perhaps the greatest affinity with Socrates, however, lay in Epictetus' emphasis on the god within.

In Greek, the word that Epictetus uses as the focal point for his philosophical instruction is *prohairesis* (Long 2002: 27–31). We might literally translate this word as "choice," which in turn might raise in the modern reader some analogous notion of freedom of the will. But for Epictetus, *prohairesis* refers to the authentic self, the character that one has come to form, and the possibility to realize one's identity as an *apospasma* (spark) of Zeus:

> My friend, you have a *prohairesis* that is by nature unimpeded and unconstrained. This is inscribed here in the entrails. I will prove it to you, first in the sphere of assent. Can anyone prevent you from assenting to a truth? No one can. Can anyone compel you to accept a falsehood? No one can. (*Epict.* 1.17.21–2, with Long 2002: 209)

This faculty of assent is fundamental to the whole structure of Stoic psychology and epistemology. In assent (Greek *katathesis*) lies the essence of our rationality and the essence of our freedom (Inwood 1985: 76–7). It is the faculty of assent that distinguishes humans from other animals and hence brings us into the sphere of the divine. One way of understanding this faculty is to consider that for the Stoics, there are actually two parts to any given thought. The first aspect is the presentation (Greek *phantasia*), which is something like a thus-ness or so-ness. All thoughts flow through the mind as presenting certain qualities. The other part is the affirmation, the assent to the presentation as true. The affirmation is like an inner voice that stamps a kind of inner commitment on the presentation. This inner voice says, "It *is* like this! This *is* how things truly are." This ability to say "yes" or to withhold our inner commitment is our *prohairesis*. For Epictetus this faculty, and only this faculty, lies in our power: no one can compel our inner commitment to the truth of an appearance. Epictetus identifies this inherent capacity to recognize the truth, the mind's inner light, as the inner deity:

> Whenever you are in company, whenever you take exercise, whenever you converse, don't you know that you are nursing God, exercising God? You are carrying God around, you poor things, and you don't know it. (*Epict.* 2.8.12–13; Long 2002: 142)

This style of face-to-face teaching is clear on every page of Epictetus' discourses. Here we see it employed in the context of inculcating a specific doctrine, the god within, that is particularly suited to the method of personal instruction. This inner light and its location at the center of human consciousness is a theme that ran throughout imperial philosophy. Though Epictetus' *Discourses* have little in common with the speculative metaphysics that developed in Middle and Neoplatonism, in fact, just this god within is the focus of Neoplatonic contemplative *askesis*, a topic to which we shall return shortly. We move in the meantime to another feature of imperial philosophy that applies across school divisions, the student–teacher relationship.

4 The Teacher

In imperial philosophy the bond of one who searches for wisdom with a teacher is valorized as the fulfillment of a lifelong quest, as the foundation for exegetical traditions, and most importantly as a golden chain, a transmission of knowledge that can truly take place only outside of all texts. For the later Neoplatonists, teaching and learning were thought to constitute a sacred rite. Proclus begins the *Platonic Theology* with an allusion to the doctrine that there is an eternal chain of transmission that extends from Plato. Wisdom, he writes, abides in an eternal storehouse but is manifested temporally when conditions are ripe, or human beings are capable of receiving this wisdom: "residing with the gods eternally, [wisdom] from there is revealed temporally to those who are able to appreciate it" (Procl. *PT* 1.1.5–6). Moreover, this possibility of receiving divine wisdom is continually present with each successive generation, and the transmission is accomplished out of gratitude for those who made it available: "one must … also make available the signs of the blessed vision for the next generation" (*PT* 1.1.7.13–14). One of the most important traditional celebrations of the *diadoche*, or transmission of the teacher's mantle, is to be found in a text that, unfortunately, is somewhat late for this chapter's historical range. The work is the *Philosophical History* of Damascius, a kind of *Who's Who* of the late pagan world, but also a scathing critique of those entrusted to uphold what Damascius understood as the sacred institutions of Hellenic philosophy, that is, those who occupied the title of Scholarch of the Platonic academy.

Students spent long decades with their teachers; the philosophical partnership could become a lifelong association. Plotinus studied with his teacher Ammonius for 11 years; Amelius had been with Plotinus for 18 years when Porphyry joined them at the age of 30. According to Longinus, esteemed members of the Platonic school engaged primarily in oral teaching, devoting themselves to refining their students' understanding; Plotinus' own teacher, Ammonius, wrote nothing and possibly enjoined his followers to maintain a similar practice (*VP* 3.30). If Porphyry's *Life of Plotinus* is credible, Plotinus himself committed nothing to writing until almost the age of 50, and instead concerned himself with the difficulties presented by individual students during the course of personal instruction:

> In the tenth year of the reign of Gallienus Plotinus was about fifty-nine years old. I, Porphyry, when I first joined him was thirty. From the first year of Gallienus Plotinus had begun to write on the subjects that came up in the meetings of the school. (*VP* 4.10.12, tr. Armstrong)

Although Plotinus and Epictetus engaged whoever wished to attend the lectures (evidently chaos reigned in Plotinus' classroom, with answers to objections dragging on for days), it seems clear that this public teaching style was modified by two factors. The first qualification for a student of philosophy was basic familiarity with the textual tradition that maintained the philosophical lineage. Famously, Émile Bréhier reconstructed a typical day in the classroom of Epictetus, which began with an oral recitation of one of the old Stoics. In the afternoon Epictetus extemporized from the day's readings. Bréhier compared this procedure to what he imagined went on in the classroom of Plotinus, based on some passages of *The Life of Plotinus*:

> In the classes, they read for him the commentaries, whether those of Severus, or those of Cronius or Numenius or Gaius or Atticus, and among the Peripatetics those of Aspasius, Alexander and Adrastus, and whichever ones came up. (*VP* 14.10–14)

Whether or not the *Enneads* are a kind of record of such collective reading practices, the point remains that texts remained an integral tool, yet texts were never enough, as Epictetus tells his students:

> You have merely picked up the words themselves and utter them. Are the words in themselves sacred? One needs to approach these things with a certain attitude: the matter is of great magnitude, a solemn rite, not something ordinary or granted to just anyone. (*Epict.* 3.21.16–17)

The other constraint on discipleship has to do with a ranking system that Porphyry intimates was present in Plotinus' own circle. Porphyry tells us that Plotinus "had numerous auditors (*akroatai*), but of devoted followers drawn to him by a commitment to philosophy (*zelotai*) there were Amelius... [and roughly six others]" (*VP* 7.1, with Lamberton 2001: 440). Senators, doctors, politicians, indeed, as Porphyry tells us, "whoever wished" to listen to Plotinus was welcome. But the life of philosophy set one apart, as in the case of Plotinus' student Rogatianus, a senator who renounced his office and became "an example for those who engage in the life of philosophy" (*VP* 7.45–6, with Lamberton 2001: 440). In his *Exhortation to Philosophy*, Iamblichus discusses the distinction between esoteric and exoteric doctrines, pointing to the Pythagorean separation of mere auditors from actual followers of Pythagoras, as well as to the Pythagorean rule of silence and nondisclosure to the uninitiated. In the following passage Iamblichus interprets the Pythagorean saying, "Avoid the highways and take the short-cuts":

> I think this saying tends in the same direction. For it exhorts one to keep away from the vulgar and merely human life, and thinks it better to follow the detached, divine life, and it asserts that one ought to ignore *communis opinio* and value instead one's own thoughts, which are secret. (*Prot.* 21.4)

5 Exegesis

Curriculum is central to the ancient classroom and it was during the reign of Tiberius, if we are to believe the work of Harold Tarrant (1993), that Platonism started to be transmitted in terms of a cycle of reading the dialogues. Here again we see how influential the imperial method of studying ancient philosophy has proved to be, since even today the standard Greek text of Plato's dialogues (the Oxford Classical Text) is printed according to the tetralogic classificatory scheme of Thrasyllus. Hence in the Oxford edition nine tetralogies comprise the total of 36 dialogues that Thrasyllus considered genuinely Platonic.

For his detective work, Tarrant makes use of a passage in Diogenes Laertius (3.56–61), which functions as an introduction to reading a specific collection of the dialogues (that of Thrasyllus). The details of the groupings are difficult to follow, involving as they do both Pythagorean number theory and a strange mechanism, whereby one member of the tetralogy functions as the "odd man out" (Tarrant 1993: 85–107, esp. 95). Thrasyllus grouped the dialogues under headings such as "ethical," "logical," and "maieutic," evidently trying to shape and mold the intellect of the potential reader in a pattern that closely followed Plato's own provisions for the Guardians of his *Republic*. Preparation of the student involves basic inculcation of ethics, study of mathematics, followed by the final three stages of a sacred transmission of wisdom: the highest vision of the Ideas, preparing others for the same visions, and likeness to god (*Rep.* 540a6–c2).

The idea that Plato's dialogues are to be read in a fixed order is preserved in another introduction to the reading of Plato, the so-called *Anonymous Prolegomena to the Study of Plato*, written in the sixth century, but containing evidence for the curricula used in the third (Westerink 1962; cf. Tarrant 1998: 11–15). The *Prolegomena* list a considerably scaled-down reading program, tending to exclude the aporetic dialogues as incomplete and lacking sufficient doctrinal content. We know that Porphyry's younger colleague, the Syrian-born Iamblichus, promoted this curriculum, which correlated closely with the Neoplatonic system of ranking kinds of virtue. The *Alcibiades* (a dialogue hardly recognized as genuine among scholars today) came first in the schedule, since it promoted self-knowledge. It was followed by the *Gorgias* (constitutional virtues) and the *Phaedo* (purificatory virtues). The first *decad* of dialogues was crowned by the *Philebus* (study of the Good), a theological dialogue, and followed by the two "perfect" dialogues, the *Timaeus* (all reality via physics) and the *Parmenides* (all reality via metaphysics).

Two dialogues that had particular importance in the history of exegesis were Plato's *Timaeus* and *Parmenides*. So important are these two dialogues for the development of imperial philosophy that one could realistically claim to find them at the center of virtually every philosophical or religious sect in Late antiquity. Unfortunately, there is no space here to discuss the import of these dialogues for the development of Gnostic or Hermetic traditions. Much less is there space to discuss the Jewish Alexandrian philosophy of Philo Judaeus, whose commentary on *Genesis, On the Creation of the World* (*De opificio mundi*) leans heavily on the account of creation found in the *Timaeus*. I can try instead only to give some brief indications of the importance of exegesis for the development of imperial philosophy as a whole.

Above I mentioned the Iamblichean commentary on the Pythagorean saying, "avoid the highway." The context for this passage speaks volumes for how Platonic philosophy was conceived in Apamea, the town in Syria that had long developed a reputation for esoteric studies. Iamblichus finds an esoteric Plato connected to Pythagorean tradition, as we have seen in the passage already quoted. In fact, Iamblichus, Numenius, and Moderatus thought that anything of value in Plato had already been taught by Pythagoras. Insofar as Plato was an original philosopher, he could only be approached as a renegade Pythagorean.

Recently, Michael Frede (1987) has again drawn our attention (after Dillon and other pioneers in the field) to a wonderfully amusing work by the Middle Platonist/ Pythagorean Numenius, a colleague of Julianus the Theurgist and predecessor of Iamblichus. *On the Divergence of the Academy from Plato* is yet another history of the Academy, this time presented from a Pythagorean point of view:

> Socrates asserted the existence of three gods, and philosophized about them in expressions suited to each single auditor... Plato, who followed Pythagoras, knew that Socrates had derived his teachings from no one else. But Plato did not [teach] in the ordinary way nor did he [reveal his Pythagorean doctrines] openly. (Numen. fr. 24 des Places, abbreviated)

Numenius says that Plato is actually a combination of Socrates and Pythagoras (fr. 24), which is why he confused his auditors and why the chain of Pythagorean transmission had to break down in the Academy. It is a little confusing as to which "three gods" Numenius refers to in the teaching of Socrates. Does he mean the Middle Platonist system of Being, Creator, and Creation, or some similar triad? This triadic theology already anticipates the work of Plotinus, generally considered the founder of the Neoplatonic school in Alexandria.

Rather than presenting themselves as innovators or original thinkers, ancient philosophers tended to present themselves as exegetes of previous texts or doctrines, and the Neoplatonists were no exception (on Plotinus as exegete of Plato, see most recently Gatti 1996). Perhaps the most famous example of this traditional claim to orthodoxy is found in *Ennead* 5.1.8, Plotinus' doxography concerning his doctrine of the three primary hypostases: "our present doctrines are an exegesis of those [ancient teachings], and so the writings of Plato himself provide evidence that our doctrines are of ancient origin" (*Enn.* 5.1.8.11–15). What exactly does Plotinus mean when he calls his doctrines an exegesis of Plato's text, especially in the context of *Ennead* 5.1? To answer this question is to gain a theoretical foothold in the often abstract world of Neoplatonic metaphysics.

The Neoplatonists held that Plato's *Parmenides* was a theological disquisition that charted not only the fundamental principles of reality but also the emergence of any possible form of being from one transcendent source. Plotinus launched the tradition. As we have just seen, in *Ennead* 5.1 he interprets the three initial hypotheses in the second half of Plato's *Parmenides* as adumbrating his own metaphysical doctrine, according to which reality has different levels: the One, Intellect, and Soul. Plotinus refers the first hypothesis ("if the one is," *Prm.* 137c4) to the One beyond being, the transcendent source of all. The second hypothesis refers to a subsequent stage of reality, the level of Being/Intellect (the intelligible world that consists of intellects each contemplating all the other intellects, rather like a hall of mirrors). Transitory being (Greek *genesis* or "becoming") originates in the third hypostasis, at the level of Soul, which is present both on a cosmic level and within individuals as the entryway into the life of the One. Plotinus left it for his followers to iron out the details of precisely how the entire dialogue mapped onto the universe as a whole. Proclus Diadochus, the fifth-century scholarch of the Platonist academy in Athens, left a catalogue of these attempts in Book 6 of his *Commentary on the Parmenides* (col. 1052.31–1064). There he set forth in astonishing detail the evolution of this exegetical tradition, ending with the interpretation of his own teacher, Syrianus (Morrow and Dillon 1987: xxiv–xxxiv; Saffrey 1968).

Likewise the cosmological and theological debates of the imperial period survive in his *Commentary on the Timaeus*, written when Proclus was 28. This work documents centuries of an interpretive tradition that no doubt began as soon as the *Timaeus* was written. Proclus refers back to the lost commentaries of a number of predecessors, including Plotinus' disciples, Amelius and Porphyry, the Academic Crantor, the Middle Platonist Moderatus, and the Neoplatonists Iamblichus and Syrianus, the latter Proclus' own teacher. The *proemium* of the *Timaeus* (*Ti.* 27d6–29d5) forms the basis for the bulk of Proclus' discussion. In Plato's text, we find 'Timaeus' asking a timeless cosmological question: "Has the world always been in existence... or did it arise, taking its origin from some beginning?" (28b5–7). "Timaeus" answers his own question in the next line: "It came into existence," he says (*gegonen*, 28b7). But this use of the word *gegonen* ("came into existence," "was generated") is actually problematic for the Platonists, since the orthodox Neoplatonist position held that the world was eternal, a point that they disputed hotly with their Christian contemporaries. Proclus' predecessors grappled mightily with this exegetical problem. Proclus cites Alcinous/Albinus, some anonymous Platonists, and Porphyry and Iamblichus, all on this particular Greek word.

In fact, Neoplatonists kept lists of exegetical solutions to those contradictions of Plato's text which seemed to suggest that the world did begin from a certain point in time. An earlier, more strictly Platonic explanation of the text assumes that by "generated" Plato must mean composite. Or again, the world could be generated in the sense that it was dependent on a higher, external cause. Or, once more, one could distinguish between eternity and sempeternity (or indefinite duration as opposed to unchanging existence). Proclus concludes that the world is "in virtue of its body, wholly becoming, and yet Plato bestows on it another aspect, its quality of being not originated, since the world is also a god" (*in Ti.* 1.276; for a discussion of these lists, see Sorabji 1987; J. F. Phillips 1997: 173–96).

6 Conclusion: Philosophy, the Sacred Activity

It would be wrong, however, to end on this scholastic point, though the issue of the world's eternity was actually highly fraught and became the basis of a heated dispute between philosophers and Christians at the very end of Late antiquity. In fact, it looks like the last members of the Platonist school in Alexandria had to compromise with Christian authorities on just these cosmological questions in order to stay in business. Nevertheless, we should keep in mind that for philosophers of the imperial period, philosophy was conceived as a sacred rite: learning, teaching, belonging in the transmission of wisdom – all of this is part of a larger conception of philosophic activity, one that has its place, ultimately, in the cosmic scheme.

No doubt the philosopher who best illustrates this merging of scripture and exegesis is Philo Judaeus, the first century Alexandrian philosopher and statesman who undertook a vast (48 works survive; the majority are in Greek, but a significant group only survives in Armenian) defense of Jewish religion in the form of a sprawling commentary on the Five Books of Moses. Philo belonged to the elite of Alexandrian Jewish society. His brother was one of the wealthiest men in Alexandria; supposedly the grandson of Herod the Great had to borrow money from him. His nephew became the Prefect of Alexandria, and we know that it was the very prominent social status of Philo that allowed him to form part of the embassy to Gaius Caesar in 38, an event we learn about from Philo's own *Embassy to Gaius*. Philo wrote this political essay in the aftermath of a pogrom that resulted in the massacre of countless Jews living in Alexandria.

For our purposes, it is important to approach Philo with the realization that he believes that Moses literally composed the entire Pentateuch, the first five books of the Jewish Scripture. According to Philo, Moses, like Philo himself, received a thoroughly "Greek" education in both science and philosophy in Egypt at the court of Pharaoh. This education in the Greek curriculum was possible because it was Pythagoras, who as we saw founded Platonic philosophy, that brought the Hellenic tradition to Egypt during his travels. Thus the two traditions, Jewish and Hellenic, are really branches of the same primordial stream of wisdom.

His *On the Creation of the World*, actually a commentary on *Genesis*, follows the Antiochean interpretation of the *Timaeus* (recall that Antiochus was that notorious synthesizer of Platonic and Stoic tenets whom we first met in the *Academica* of Cicero), according to which two constituent principles, an active or divine cause, and a passive or material substrate, are completely fused and present in each other throughout the whole of nature (Cic. *Ac.* 1.24, with Sedley 2002: 48–50). Compare these excerpts from Philo's *On the Creation* and Cicero's summary of Antiochean physics:

When it came to nature...they spoke in such a way as to divide it into two things, so that one was active, the other at this one's disposal, as it were, and acted upon by it in some way. In the active one they held that there was a power, in the one which was acted upon just a kind of matter. (*Ac.* 1.24.1–5, tr. Sedley)

But Moses, who had early reached the very summits of philosophy and who had learnt from the Oracles of God the most numerous and important of the principles of nature, was well aware that it is indispensable that in all existing things there must be an active cause, and a passive subject; and that the active cause is the intellect...(*Op.* 8.1–5, tr. Younge)

Philo takes the Stoic and already odd interpretation of the *Timaeus*, which posits a pantheist or immanentist account of deity vis-à-vis the world, and inserts it into a Judeo/Middle Platonist retelling of the Creator's tale. Here the Forms supply a blueprint for the creative aspect of God, our divine architect, who uses the blueprint to provide a model for the temporal world. Now Plato's Forms have become the thoughts of the divinity; a feature that is absent from Plato's text. Nevertheless, in Philo's account the craftsman, or *logos*, is really just a power of the highest God. For

Philo, God brings the intelligible order, the blueprint, into being on day one of creation. Hence although it is intelligible and in strictly Platonic terms should be an aspect of eternal being, in fact Philo finds that Moses understands that the blueprint, i.e. the Forms, actually occupies a space in genesis, the world of becoming. This example shows us that Philo uses Platonic conceptions in order to penetrate beneath the surface of the Mosaic text and uncover a theological doctrine that suggests that God is at once the creator of the universe but also utterly transcends any created nature. Moreover, God's activity as Creator is only one aspect of the deity, one of the seven powers, as Philo calls them, that communicate but do not exhaust the divine substance (Runia 2002: 304–6). In turn, Philo's apophatic and positive theologies that center on his appropriation of the Stoic *logos* via the transformations of Middle Platonism also form a foundation for his emphasis on the contemplative knowledge of God, which forms the destiny of every human soul.

The example of Philo reminds us that the Platonisms of the imperial era are not just an exegetical metaphysics that attempt to reify the hypotheses of Plato's *Parmenides* or to spin theologies out of the *Timaeus*. There is also a dynamic aspect of the philosophy that can be expressed in terms of what A. C. Lloyd has called the spiritual circuit (Lloyd 1990). Procession, remaining, and reversion are the three moments of this cosmic respiration or universal pulse that constantly sends forth beings from the One into a state of manifestation, and at the very same time, unifies all things back into the One. This manifestation is just the life of the soul, as it undertakes the journey of awakening to its source in the One, and also its cosmic mission of returning the multiplicity back into the source. Porphyry ends the *Life of Plotinus* with the dying words of the sage: "Strive to bring the One in yourself back to the One."

Iamblichus formally introduced a language to convey some of the aspects of this spiritual life; the name he gave to it was theurgy, which he discussed in his work *On the Mysteries of the Egyptians*. The book opens with Iamblichus adopting the persona of an Egyptian prophet who will attempt to answer Porphyry's objections concerning the ritual efficacy of certain symbols for the purpose of uniting the individual soul with the gods. Knowledge or intellection does not deliver the soul from the constraints of embodiment. To complete its cosmic task, the soul must win over the whole chain of being that links our ordinary world with the ultimate principles of reality. "Thinking does not connect theurgists with divine beings, for what would prevent those who philosophize theoretically from having theurgic union with the gods? Rather... it is the power of ineffable symbols comprehended by the gods alone, that establishes theurgical union" (Iamb. *Myst.* 96).

For other philosophers of the imperial era, the most sacred rite was to engage with the text of Plato, since the Plato of this period was no longer just an Athenian philosopher but a vessel of divine knowledge. So, for example, Proclus: "I beg all the gods and all the goddesses to... open up the doors of my soul and allow it to receive the divinely inspired doctrine of Plato" (*in Prm.* 1.617.1). How far we have wandered in this prayer, from the skeptical Academy that burst on the scene in Cicero's Rome. Here we find the Platonists doing theology and no longer truly philosophy. At the same time, perhaps it is in the words of this Greek philosopher from Lycia, who lived at a time when Rome had at last repudiated its traditional gods, that philosophy in the Roman Empire was able to preserve an element that echoed the Roman Empire's inclusion of every nation's gods.

PART VI

Religion

CHAPTER TWENTY-SEVEN

Traditional Cult

David Frankfurter

1 "Traditional Cult" in the Roman Empire: Introduction

For centuries the Mediterranean world of the Roman period has captured the interest of historians, professional and amateur alike, as an era of transition and transformation. It involved, of course, the period and places in which Christianity formed and spread, and hence it constituted a kind of *inter-regnum* between Classical Greek civilization (a golden age for many scholars of antiquity) and the rise of Christianity, with all its prophetic passion, conviction, and mystery. Given these key transitions, the *interpretation* of religious life in this period and its various remains depends to a large extent on whether one sees this shift from Classical world to Christendom as a triumph or a decline. The great historian Edward Gibbon, of course, mapped out one perspective with great detail between 1776 and 1788 in his *Decline and Fall of the Roman Empire*. But the inevitable ecclesiastical and theological interests of many ancient historians have pressed the "triumph" perspective with equal vehemence.

These biases, which we will shortly address in more depth, were not entirely preconceived but also responded to a curiosity in the data itself. For the historian of religion in the Roman period encounters a profusion of ancient writers, like Plutarch, Apuleius, and Lucian, who not only captured ancient religion in detail but also could convey a tone of satire and skepticism somehow recognizable to modern readers, directed especially towards the theatrical elements of traditional cult: priesthoods, oracles, ritual activities. Other ancient writers on religion seemed to promote a higher, almost pantheistic "spirituality" that belonged to no place or god but sought union with an ineffable Divine (e.g. Philo, Iamblichus, Philostratus).

In a post-Reformation world, historians could find in these authors – anachronistically, to be sure – resonances of their own anti-ecclesiastic sentiments or spiritual aspirations. And thus they would construct a religious mentality of the Roman period that conformed to some historical pattern they deemed necessary, such as the dawning awareness of Christian truth, the consolidation of superstition in Christian guise, the ethereal ascents of pure philosophy, or the indiscriminate blending of great classical traditions in popular ritual.

It is to alert the reader of this chapter to this legacy of scholarship on religions of the Roman Empire that we begin our survey of "traditional cult" by scrutinizing some of the biases and idealizations that have gone into past interpretations of this topic. Following this review of "methodological pitfalls" will be a discussion of some more productive approaches available to historians.

Terms of generalization: "paganism"

Casting religion of the Roman period as a movement towards the triumph of Christianity or as the end of Classical culture, or even as the dissipation of original Christian ideals, has historically been facilitated by the term "paganism," which claims the monolithic capacity to represent all religious things outside Christianity (and, to some degree, Judaism). As a catch-all for the vast world of philosophies, local and migratory cults, and religious traditions in the Roman Empire, "paganism" (and its recent replacement, "polytheism") has allowed simplistic contrasts between Christianity and prevailing religions of a region (Brown 1998: 639–42). Christianity, for example, might provide "salvation," whereas "paganism" only offered "ritual." Thus "paganism" as an idea allowed the possibility of deducing *influences* on Christianity – to its perfection or pollution. Most of all, "paganism" has allowed historians to assume that Christianity – still in the third century but a loose assortment of warring apocalyptic sects with only the most general overlaps in ritual and belief – was *essentially* distinct from its immediate environment (rather than being a part of it, interacting thoroughly with other religions). The term creates a standard of imprecision that easily leads to theologically-based judgments about religion "apart from" Christianity.

It must be acknowledged that the third and fourth centuries saw the consolidation, in various social arenas, of a religious-cultural identity juxtaposed to Christianity and called *hellênê*, after the Greek culture to which it laid claim. For many scholars, the fact that both Christians and non-Christians spoke of a unified religious realm opposed to Christianity and consisting essentially of "Hellenic" heritage and devotion to all things traditional, justified the modern use of the term "pagan" or its facile substitutes (cf. Trombley 1993/4). However, these predominantly fourth-century efforts at defining an intellectually coherent non-Christian religiosity were idiosyncratic hybrids, not extensions, of indigenous piety, often the inventions of philosophers and imperial programs, and hardly indicative of a common "pagan*ism*" across the diverse and far-flung religious cultures of the Roman world. Often these intellectual pagans had more in common with the Christian fathers they opposed than with the villagers and pilgrims who crowded shrines in an effort to resolve quotidian crises (Geffcken 1978; Fowden 1982; Athanassiadi 1993; Beard, North, and Price 1998: 312; Frankfurter 2000a: 184–92). When one seeks terms of generalization like "paganism" to cover the non-Christian religions of a period and place, one needs to consider the general (cross-cultural) applicability of such a word. In this case it should be noted that studies of comparatively modern religious worlds – African, Asian – do not employ such categories as "paganism" or "polytheism," since – apart from missionary interests – these terms would not be appropriate to describe the variety of regional religious traditions.

Traditional cult as a point of comparison with Christianity

Jonathan Z. Smith's 1990 book *Drudgery Divine: On the Comparison of Early Christianities and the Religions of Late Antiquity* provided an important glimpse into the history of the study of ancient "paganism." Smith showed above all that scholarly attempts to grasp the nature of religions of the Roman Empire besides Christianity were inevitably – and often explicitly – motivated by an anti-Catholic polemic, in which a pure, inspired Christian message became gradually "paganized" through the early centuries. Smith also observed that the categories by which scholars would label the principal features of the religions of the Roman Empire – "priest," "sacrifice," "god," "sanctuary," "theology" – were so loaded with Christian theological and liturgical meaning that they tended to obscure the data under examination: a Roman priest was not a man consecrated to God; few religions of the empire held communal "theologies"; and "sacrifice" did not emphasize the violent, guilt-inducing blood-bath that scholars often placed as the backdrop to Christ's "perfect sacrifice."

It is notable that many of the scholars most prone to accepting theologically-loaded terminology and repeating old Protestant biases have come not from religious studies but from disciplines like classics and history that claim a preference for ostensibly "native" terms ("magic," "baptism") over critically-informed "comparative" categories ("ritual expertise," "initiation drama"). But any student of ancient religions must inevitably rely on comparative categories to make sense of primary materials, explain them in understandable ways, and assemble larger conclusions. Hence, to study the religions of the Roman Empire requires a willingness to abandon blatantly theological categories (e.g. "salvation"), to rectify and define critically such inevitable categories as "priest" or "god," and to develop new categories that more fittingly represent the religious worlds and experiences of people beyond a putative Christian fold. Ultimately, Christianity should emerge as one trend among many in the religious world of the Roman Empire. Indeed, it should be treated as a source of comparative data in its own right – for example, for new locations for shrine-centers or prevailing trends in the use of scripture for talismanic functions – rather than as the endpoint of ancient religious longing (see now Beard, North, and Price 1998).

Romantic and triumphalist perspectives

The Protestant, anti-Catholic agenda that Smith discovered in past studies of religion in the Roman Empire has a fundamentally romantic perspective: an original prophetic Christian message became polluted and "paganized," to become the obscurantist "mystery religion" that the Catholic church represented to these scholars. Examples of this romanticism pervade scholarship: for the Reverend Blomfield Jackson, a late-nineteenth-century translator of ancient Christian writers, "Christianity relapsed into paganism" as iconography became increasingly plentiful in a church that had gone out of its way to destroy the images in temples (*NPNF* 3:148 n. 1); for more recent scholars Christianity was losing its original spiritual energy to convention and formalism (Helgeland 1980; compare Luck 2000: 52). But such lamentations also go back to late antiquity, when some Christian writers themselves felt a cooling of the Church's (imagined) primal passions (Brown 1998: 662–4).

For some classical scholars who romanticized an originally "pure" Greek (or Egyptian or Babylonian) culture, the Roman period posed a similar decline. In the opinion of A. A. Barb, the "economic upheaval and moral decadence" of Greco-Roman times led to the democratization, the cheapening, and the wholesale mutation of the great classical cults of the empire, whose grotesque remains, preserved in magical spells and mysteries, resembled once-fresh food that had rotted (Barb 1963, 1971; also Luck 2000: 204).

In contrast to these romantic perspectives, which viewed the religious trends of the Roman Empire as amounting to a progressive decline, another perspective sought to discover a kind of anticipation of Christian truth – a *praeparatio evangelica* – in the scope or nature of religious movements in the Mediterranean world. Scholars of this inclination have claimed to identify a pervasive anxiety or existential yearning, a need for "salvation," a general dissatisfaction with tradition, which Christianity was then supposed to have resolved. Such evaluations are inevitably motivated by theological assumptions about the "needs" that Christianity uniquely answered, such as the salvation of the individual or anxiety about evil. Christianity's rise could thus be seen as historically or culturally timely, even necessary, given the lamentable state of the great temples or the chaotic marketplace for mysteries and magic. These kinds of evaluations about Christianity's ultimate inevitability all underscore the dangers in broad generalizations, especially those with an eye towards "Christian triumph." Thus the papyrologist H. I. Bell concluded his lectures on the Greco-Roman transformation of Egyptian religion:

> Later paganism ... died with a kind of mellow splendour, like a beautiful sunset, but dying it was. It had been conquered by the truer and finer religion, for which it had itself prepared the way, a religion which at last brought the solution of problems which paganism had posed but to which it had found no answer. (Bell 1953: 105)

Study of the religions of the Roman Empire must avoid preconceptions about spiritual needs, their fulfillment, and the capacity of historical Christian groups to address them. Christianization itself was a diverse, regionally-specific, and socially-contextual process. More importantly, Christianity attracted adherents for many reasons apart from personal needs for "salvation": healing, protection against demons, prophecy, and social organization, none of which reasons justify a triumphalist conclusion (Brown 1978; MacMullen 1984a; Stark 1996; Frankfurter 1998a: 23–33, 265–84).

New approaches to ancient religions

The study of religions in the Roman Empire has profited immeasurably from anthropological work on religious identity and change in other periods and places, particularly those cultures undergoing centralization, Christianization, or modernization. In these situations, the dynamics of interchange between *local* and *broad* religious discourses – between the intimate local goddess or saint in her centrally placed shrine and the cosmic authority or transcendent capacity of Sanskritic Hinduism or official Catholicism – emerge much more visibly than we can discern in antiquity. By illustrating analogous patterns and dynamics, such modern studies help us to answer such questions as: how *does* a Syrian village embrace a Roman god, an Egyptian or Gallic village accept Christianity, or an Anatolian village assert the importance of its traditional oracle?

Studies of local religion in Spain (Christian 1981) and in the Andes (MacCormack 1991; Sallnow 1987), *inter alia*, have demonstrated the importance of landscape and traditional sacred topographies in giving structure and orientation to religion. They have shown the concentric spheres of religious action and identity, from the local (and domestic) to the urban, the regional, and the trans-regional or national. Within and across these spheres of religious action people would seek resolution to misfortune and engage new religious identities and ideas. Shrines and cults assume meaning according to their location in home, district, village, city – or on the periphery of settled society, requiring pilgrimage and a consequent openness to the distant, the novel, and the alien. While we may be aware only of the great temple whose ruins are excavated, we must approach religion with the assumption that there were many smaller spheres of religious action and many more shrines that were all equally (if not more) constitutive of religion in a region. To discover these further religious arenas we must look to inscriptions, papyri, and crude domestic figurines for information.

This regional approach to religions offers fresh insight into religious change, for it is *within* the context of competing or overlapping shrines and *across* landscapes effervescent with gods and oracles that the altogether traditional mentality of village religion changes in dialectic with "modern" schemes of divinity and sacred representation, like Hellenism, Christianity, and ultimately Islam (V. Turner 1974; Eade and Sallnow 1991). These schemes are embraced to the extent that they offer new authority and meaning for traditional religious experience. Moreover, such studies have demonstrated that abstract concepts of "belief," divinity, salvation, and supernatural mediation, such as historians used to discuss as constitutive of "religion," instead must be understood as *functions of* shrine placement, ritual action, economic pursuit, institutional competition, and local or urban identity. The scholar interprets religion according to what people do (and where and when) rather than in terms of belief systems and theories (C. R. Phillips 1986: 2697–711; Frankfurter 1998a; Derks 1998).

2 Centers

Religions of the Roman Empire were fundamentally expressions of "place" – evolving combinations of rites, myths and legends, and structures located at a particular site in the landscape and articulating the traditional power of that site. Because of their still-visible remains, we are most accustomed to imagining great temples – the centers of official ritual – as the epitome of religious center. Often temples did represent a point of orientation for people over very large territories: for example, the Jerusalem temple was very much the center of the cosmos for Jews around the Roman world. But individual temples could fluctuate in their political importance;

many Near Eastern temple cults comprised ritual operations entirely separate from the lives of those who paid occasional homage there. For these reasons, as well as the comparative guidance provided by modern ethnography, we must consider a more complex series of overlapping and concentric "centers" for religious activity in the Roman world: minor temples, modest shrines, cultic places afforded by the landscape (springs, mountaintops), and the home itself – the perennial anchor of religious activity even when it involves pilgrimage to distant temples. This section will cover three "concentric" aspects of religious center: the official temple, the shrine (covering both natural sites and minor temples), and domestic altars. We will use the word "cult" here to designate a set of traditions governing the collective ritual devotion to a deity, usually including both a rank of experts or leaders and an established place for this ritual devotion to take place.

Temples

In Rome itself, religious practice, experience, and cultural significance rested on the location of cult sites – within or beyond Rome's sacred *pomerium*, or city boundary, for example – and on the myths that legitimized these places in the names of heroes and gods. Restorations of earlier temples with new iconography might link a traditional cult with the increasingly central figure of the emperor. The inclusion of new temples and cults within the *pomerium* signified the broadening of supernatural protectorship for a holy city: Magna Mater, Apollo, Isis. In a city like Ostia, "foreign" cult sites were likewise set off on the urban periphery, while the chief temples deemed traditional occupied the center forum (Beard, North, and Price 1998: 167–210; Scheid 2003: 60–76).

Cult places in Rome, its environs, and colonies served primarily as the locations for public ritual – sacrifice, feasting, prayer, vows – and their layouts reflected this "occasional" function. Raised on a platform, a cult statue was partially enclosed in a *cella*, a house for the divinity (conceptualized according to regional ideals of domestic habitation) with a porch (*pronaos*) and stairs, before which stood one or more sacrificial altars. The "priests" who officiated in these rituals invariably came from the ranks of the civic elite – who combined cultic with political leadership – rather than a segregated class of ritual experts. In the precinct of the cult place might be found votive stelae, rooms for feasting in honor of the god, theaters, and, in the case of healing sanctuaries, rooms for incubants (Derks 1998: 185–213; Scheid 2003: 66–73). Outside Rome, the location of temples and sanctuaries depended on landscape features (hilltops, rivers and springs, forests), economy (the edges of cultivated areas, towns and districts seeking the favors of particular gods), and cultural or local identity (the boundaries or pilgrimage centers of agricultural, pastoral, warrior, or mercantile peoples). In this way, cult places both integrated and demarcated social identity (Mitchell 1993: 19–31; Derks 1998: 132–44). Furthermore, while Hellenized or Romanized cultures tended to adopt Greek or Roman names for their indigenous gods – Zeus, Heracles, Diana – the strongly regional character of cult places remained, whether through localizing titles – Zeus Narenos or Mên Selmeanos – or iconographic features or simply through local meanings (on Asia Minor, Mitchell 1993: 19–31; on Gaul, Derks 1998: 73–130). In this way, as anthropologists have observed for village India, the shrine images function as both local versions of a "great" deity and universalizing forms of a local deity (see Redfield 1956: 67–104; Frankfurter 1998a: 97–106).

In the Near East, temples had a more distinct separation from economic and civic life, supported as they were by full-time priestly institutions and often maintaining essential rites and images of gods beyond public view. In the extensive cult precincts of Egypt and Syria, often comprising sanctuaries to several gods, ritual professionals would adorn images of gods and carry them in procession, perform prayers and hymns for cosmic protection on a perpetual cycle, study and copy ancient texts, and manage an often thriving temple economy. A popular piety also flourished by such temples, oriented towards specific shrines in the precinct and conducted through the literate, creative facilities of certain priests.

For Roman and Greek observers the temples of Hierapolis in Syria, Jerusalem in Palestine, and Thebes in Egypt were the awesome spectacles of the ancient world, radiating antiquity, mystery, and authority (e.g. on Egypt: Strabo 17.1; on Hierapolis: Luc. *Syr. D.*; on Jerusalem: *Ep. Aristeas* 83–120; Mk 13:1). Temple professionals sought to cultivate Roman popular and imperial patronage both by showing their disinclination to rebellion and through innovations: the development of new oracles (e.g. that of Bes at Abydos in upper Egypt), the proffering of "mysteries" to spiritual pilgrims, the translation of traditions and texts into Greek, and the "syncretism" of temple gods with Greek or Roman divinities – an endeavor often facilitated through iconography (Egyptian Isis as Demeter, Syrian Atargatis as Hera). Here was a more active, systematic attempt to mediate between "great" (Hellenistic) and local forms of divinity than what one finds in Asia Minor and the western Roman colonies, where the indigenous gods did not have a millennium of temple-based traditions behind them and thus profited considerably from a Roman guise. Moreover, established temple cultures, such as the Egyptian, Syrian, and (before 70 CE) Jewish, were able to retain traditional iconography – or, in the Jewish case, a relative aniconicity – while still absorbing aspects of Hellenism and offering due attention to the Roman emperors.

Shrines

Large temple precincts might house shrines to additional gods, but the landscapes of the Roman Empire were filled with shrines of major and minor scope: lone altars on hill tops, sacred precincts marked out with stones, pillars, miniature temples, and in the forests, no doubt, the votive detritus around trees or rocks that might signal to a traveler that spirits were near (much as one sees in contemporary India or Greece) (see Derks 1998: 132–85; Scheid 2003: 73–5). Such minor shrines provided the location for myth (that is, stories that begin or culminate "here"), for village or family tradition, and for the occasional sacrifices and ritual communications that occupied popular religious life as much as the principal gods and their official feasts.

In some cases shrines exemplify a popular piety beyond the world of official temples: outside the walls of the temple of Atargatis at Hierapolis (Syria) stood two pillars on which designated people from local villages would invoke the gods – separately from the priestly cult within the walls (Luc. *Syr. D.* 28–9; Frankfurter 1990: 169–77). Just outside Jerusalem a healing shrine with two pools continued into the second century CE, eventually to be Christianized beneath a basilica (Jn 5:2–9;

ABD s.v. "Beth-Zatha"). Egyptian temples were likewise surrounded by shrines to local gods who "heard" supplicants' appeals and vows (Frankfurter 1998a: 46–52). Gallo-Roman temples often included minor shrines, votive stelae, and sacred wells in their precincts (Derks 1998: 206–9). One notable type of shrine in temple precincts of the Roman Mediterranean had long been the incubation or voice oracle, a room in which a pilgrim might sleep to receive a divine message in a dream or simply wait for a "voice" to emit from a divine image (Frankfurter 1998a: 150–2, 162–9; Lane Fox 1986: 150–67).

Even without priestly or institutional leadership, some established regional shrines could function as common centers for diverse religious or economic communities: nomadic, pastoral, agricultural, warrior. Devoted sometimes to several gods in the same place, these "common shrines" allowed various types of ritual activity (ecstatic, sacrificial, processional) around the same geographical point. One such cult, at Mamre in Palestine, continued to provide a center for regional piety through the fourth century (Kofsky 1998; Maraval 1985: 133–5):

> Here the inhabitants of the country and of the regions round Palestine, the Phoenicians, and the Arabians, assemble annually during the summer season to keep a brilliant feast; and many others, both buyers and sellers, resort thither on account of the fair. Indeed, this feast is diligently frequented by all nations: by the Jews, because they boast of their descent from the patriarch Abraham; by the Pagans, because angels there appeared to men; and by Christians, because He who for the salvation of mankind was born of a virgin, afterwards manifested Himself there to a godly man. This place was moreover honored fittingly with religious exercises. Here some prayed to the God of all; some called upon the angels, poured out wine, burnt incense, or offered an ox, or he-goat, a sheep, or a cock.... No one during the time of the feast drew water from [the well there]; for according to Pagan usage, some placed burning lamps near it; some poured out wine, or cast in cakes; and others, coins, myrrh, or incense. (Soz. *Hist. Eccl.* 2.4, tr. Hartranft, *NPNF* 2: 261)

Due to the dynamic character of these regional shrines – their multiple interpretations and rituals – new legends of angels or holy people inevitably sprang up around them to preserve their vitality in the landscape. Christianization (and subsequently Islamization) often took root in the landscape through reinterpreting such common shrines and either extirpating prior traditions or, as in the case of Mamre above, allowing them to persist (Maraval 1985: 51–60; Trombley 1985; Flint 1991: 254–73; Frankfurter 1998b).

A new kind of urban shrine that gained increasing importance after the third century was the tomb. Traditional Roman civic religion (both in Rome and its colonies) regarded the place of the dead as properly outside the city boundaries. But the Christians' propensity to extend the community to include the dead – the martyrs, who might intercede for the living – required a more intimate spatial connection (Rv 6:9–11; *M. Pol.* 17; *P. Perp.*). Consequently, by the end of the fourth century, tombs and gravesites had moved inside the cities' boundaries, as basilicas housing specific holy relics became cultic centers and badges of urban authority (Brown 1981; Caseau 1999: 40–4), and as the faithful increasingly sought to be buried *ad sanctos* ("by the saints"). Many of the devotional and festival activities characteristic of regional shrines like Mamre and Beth-Zatha, such as dance, healing, and oracles, came also to typify the cult of saints at their tombs (e.g. for Egypt: Montserrat 1998a; Frankfurter 1998a: 267–72; Papaconstantinou 2001: 313–67).

Homes

Archaeology of homes of even modest size in the Roman world has demonstrated the integral importance of domestic cult, which involves the various rites and ritual centers devoted to protective gods, ancestral gods, and immediate ancestors. The evidence includes wall niches and miniature shrines, divine images, and evidence of offerings (usually liquids, grains and foodstuffs, and incense, rather than animal parts). In Rome, the two main orders of domestic deities were the *lares* and the *penates*, which carried various protective functions. In addition, rituals were devoted to the *genius*, the sacred power behind the family and its current patriarch (Orr 1978). In Roman Egypt, domestic forms of great deities (Harpocrates, Isis) as well as deities specific to household protection (Bes) were represented in homes and received ritual devotion (Frankfurter 1998a: 131–42).

Household images functioned both as miniature representations of major temple gods and as appropriations of these gods and their powers for domestic functions: fecundity, militant protection from demonic beings, or the magnification of food. While animal offerings were rare in domestic cult, representations of animal offerings near the shrine niche (or stamped on festival food) offered vicarious participation in official temple sacrifices (Orr 1978: 1577–85). The niches and portable shrines that housed these images, often modeled on temples, reinforced the sense that the object of household devotion "contained" the power of the temple god. It is likely that domestic figurines (and accoutrements like lamps) were procured from merchants by the temple precincts. Domestic shrines also provided a domestic link with temple festivals and processions, for it is here that one would place holiday food offerings, newly blessed objects from festal shrine visits, and sometimes lamps lit for the goddess or god. Festival foods are particularly represented for domestic religion in Roman Egypt, for example, with evidence for ritual vessels, bread stamps, and honey offerings. Lamps likewise seem to have played an integral role in linking the fortune of the household and the power of a regional god during festival time (Dunand 1976). In this way there was a perpetual dialogue between domestic and central religious worlds (Frankfurter 1998a: 131–42).

This dialogue is most apparent in the miniaturizations discussed above and in the home's centrifugal reception of the central cult's power, but representation could go the other direction as well. In Rome, the sacred fire that the Vestal Virgins tended in the temple of Vesta represented a symbolic *expansion* – to the Roman cosmic sphere – of the domestic hearth and the various protective rites that women maintained there (their virginal status signifying the powerful ambiguity necessary to raise domestic cult to cosmic status: Beard, North, and Price 1998: 51–4).

Domestic cult also comprised the care for and invocation of the ancestral dead. In most cultures of the Roman Mediterranean these responsibilities were fulfilled at gravesites, necessarily located outside city boundaries, and involved offerings and feasts in communion with the deceased (more elaborate tombs had banquet rooms built inside). Often the feasts of the dead took place on common holidays, just as the deceased were often understood to join the ranks of a particular supernatural society – in Rome, the *Di Manes* – or to be assimilated to a particular god, such as Osiris in Egypt. Thus the domestic reverence for the dead, like the veneration of domestic gods, had a civic dimension (J. M. C. Toynbee 1971: 48–55, 61–4; Beard, North, and Price 1998: 270–1; Kákosy 1995: 2997–3023; Scheid 2003: 167–70).

The importance of memorializing the dead is reflected in epitaphs and grave decoration throughout the Roman world, as well as in the rich archaeology of grave offerings. Neglecting one's ancestors might bring havoc down on the household (or, in Egypt, lurid suffering for the deceased in the liminal zones of the post-mortem world); yet mortuary rites were performed less out of fear than a desire for contact with the deceased. One of the first crises among the Thessalonian Jesus-devotees, for example, was the believers' fear (c.50 CE) that their recently deceased family members might not be able to join them in the heavenly world (1 Thes 4:13–17). In Roman Egypt, the use of portraits of the deceased to individualize mummies has been taken as evidence of some kind of domestic display: either the portrait alone, before affixing it to the mummy, or the entire mummy for a period, in some room in the house, as ancient authors suggest (Montserrat 1997; Borg 1997). Maintaining contact with the dead was thus critical to domestic fortune.

Due to its largely private sphere of performance, domestic cult in general could persist apart from anti-"pagan" repression. Indeed, as critical as it is to the maintenance of social life, domestic cult may well be the most resilient form of traditional religion. Christian writers describe domestic cult practices continuing well after central and regional shrines had been destroyed (*CTh*. 16.10.12 [392 CE]; Martin of Braga, *De corr. rust*. 16 [VI CE]; cf. Flint 1991: 226–8, 286–8; MacMullen 1997: 61–4, 109–12; Frankfurter 1998a: 27–30, 62–5, 131–2). Moreover, the relative independence of households to interpret domestic rites, especially in times of religious decentralization or repression, allows these same rites to assume new meaning under the hegemony of new religious systems like Christianity or Islam.

3 Experts

Religions of the Roman world were "performed" as much as "placed," and a considerable degree of expertise went into the performance of religious tradition. The range of ritual experts extended from those who officiated and served in a central, "priestly" capacity – whether by virtue of professional training or social status – to those who provided occasional ritual services as itinerant specialists (often designated "magicians"), or on the periphery of cities, like prophets and oracles. Their range of functions (sacrifice on behalf of social order or the providing of amulets), meaning to society (stability or threat), and dynamics of change (conservative or protean) depended on these various ritual experts' location in the center or periphery.

Priests

Scholars have long imposed anachronistic stereotypes on the official ritual experts of the ancient world, based on positive and negative caricatures of religious leaders of their own day. A "priest" might represent a mystically-inclined and far-thinking hierophant, capable of satisfying the quotidian needs of the simple at the same time as directing the spiritual aspirations of the devout. Or a "priest" might represent a mindless functionary, a cynical producer of spectacle and deceit, or even – as blood sacrifice enters the equation – a cruel inducer of innocents' pain for strange and uncompromising gods. To the degree that the reconstruction of Mediterranean religions involved the retrojection of anti-Catholic sentiments, the latter model might prevail; and to the degree that it involved an invented "pagan-romanticism," the former might (for both, see above, section 1). Of course, the diverse sorts of priests in the Roman Empire and their functions in society were far more complex than modern caricatures allow. The interpreter of religions must begin with the perspective that, despite the many ways in which a "priest" might be set apart from other people in a culture, he or she will also perform duties within and on behalf of society.

In places like Rome and Carthage, "priesthood" was essentially a civic office. But in (e.g.) Egypt and the Jewish temple in pre-70 CE Jerusalem, the higher priestly offices were passed down through family lineages (*Zadokim, Kohanim, Leviim*) and even the lower ranks carried popular prestige in the wider community. In these and many other Near Eastern religions it was priests alone who had access to the interior of temple complexes, performing sacrifices and other ritual gestures apart from the wider population. Rome, on the other hand, while noted for a highly organized series of priestly institutions (*collegia*), allowed entrance to priesthood through *election* from the ranks of the free, usually male, and invariably elite citizenry. This fluidity between priestly rank and elite civic culture translated into a general overlap between political and religious spheres, at least as an outsider might demarcate these spheres. Priesthood was a form of prestige – a fact underlined when Roman emperors began to claim for themselves increasing numbers of priestly offices. Furthermore, the priestly functions extended to areas of law, the calendar, and civic order that historians might not typically categorize as "religious." Yet Romans clearly invested the priestly spheres – their books, rites, authority, and responsibility – with religious importance. The lives of the *flamen dialis* and the Vestal Virgins, each unique priestly ranks responsible for certain public rituals, were in fact hedged in by taboos – where they could go, what they could do – in ways similar to other priesthoods of the ancient Mediterranean world, but only as long as the individual might inhabit the post. (It has been suggested, indeed, that the taboos around the *flamen* might derive merely from his unique performative position, since this priest served alone, without a *collegium* of alternates to replace him: Beard, North, and Price 1998: 29.)

The Roman priesthoods' primary functions involved the performance of public sacrifices and divination, both as an extension of other forms of civic authority. Sacrifices, required to be performed in established places according to established procedures, signified civic cooperation with the gods at a great variety of events and crisis points in the life of the city and its colonies. Divination encompassed the interpretation of the books of the Sibylline oracles (*collegium* of the *quindecemviri*), the observation and interpretation of prodigies like disasters and remarkable bird-flights (*augures*), and such deliberate forms of divination ritual as the examination of the entrails of sacrificial victims (*haruspices*). Roman divination integrated notions of sacred boundary and divine authority – that is, what the gods wanted and where they might speak – with political and military decision making (Beard, North, and Price 1998: 19–24, 36–9; Scheid 2003: 111–26).

Elsewhere in the Mediterranean world, priestly responsibilities corresponded to the special status of the priests. Jewish priests in Jerusalem performed sacrifices on behalf of worshippers but according to biblically-established codes of ritual purity; others would sing hymns or blow trumpets to receive or celebrate the presence of the aniconic Jewish god. The purity and holiness of priests is likened to that of angels in the literature of the Dead Sea Scrolls, where hymns and hymnic descriptions of sacrifice are understood as substitutes for blood sacrifices. Egyptian priests likewise performed sacrifices (more often libations and food offerings than blood sacrifices), as well as caring for divine images and uttering prayers, invocations, and curses, always as representatives of the Pharaoh, the chief priest of the land. Such duties were usually performed within the temple's private confines. Priests were also responsible for carrying divine images in procession among the various temples and shrines in the landscape. During such processions, movements of the image on the shoulders of the bearer-priests were understood as oracular (often occurring in answer to a particular question) and would be interpreted by a senior priest. In these ways, priests maintained the gods' protection of the land and also brought the gods into public contact with its people.

For the more ancient Mediterranean priesthoods, texts represented the words of gods, and their interpretation and application were primary activities of priesthoods. In Palestine, Egypt, Mesopotamia, and Syria, as well as Rome, books and scribal institutions had become essential to the priestly maintenance of religion. Often the texts were deemed historically authoritative, providing either insight into current events or guidance in their interpretation. Priestly scribes around the Mediterranean produced a rich flow of new interpretive or revelatory texts on the basis of ancient authorities: Thoth, Hermes, Enoch, Zarathustra, Orpheus, and others. Genres included chronicles, often recounting legendary oracular pronouncements with commentary (Jewish Book of Genesis and its Roman-era apocalyptic interpretations; Egyptian *Oracle of the Potter*), collections of oracular pronouncements or divine omens (Sibylline Oracles), and manuals for interpreting portents and omens in the world. If the priestly consultation of texts in Rome carried comparatively less mystique than in Egypt or Palestine, it was all the more important for seeking and interpreting the "actual" communications of gods through omens – procedures essential for the maintenance of convention and civic order (see in general Gordon 1990a; Potter 1994; Daumas 1961; Frankfurter 1998a: 145–97, 238–64).

In those Mediterranean cultures where priests and literacy itself tended to be set apart as holy, priestly status carried with it a certain charisma in the wider social environment; and priestly training in ritual utterance, gesture, writing, and divination might thus be applied to everyday concerns outside the world of the temple: scorpion stings, childbirth, sexual attraction, competition. It has been suggested that Babylonian priests were carrying their techniques internationally already by the Classical Greek period, synthesizing new versions of temple lore for new lands and publics (Burkert 1992). Jewish priests seem to have been adept at providing amulets and spells in the early Roman period (Schwartz 2001: 82–7), and Egyptian priests – especially those of the "lector priest" rank – had long carried their facility with magical language beyond temple walls. Indeed, their additional appeal to exotically-minded Roman youths is documented both in Greco-Roman novels and in the body of Greek "magical papyri," which reflect Egyptian priests' endeavors to remarket temple traditions for a wider clientele (Frankfurter 1998a: 198–237; 2000a).

Freelance ritual experts

As spell manuals like the Greek Magical Papyri moved beyond the provenance of priesthoods to circulate in Greek, they became sources of authority for individuals whose primary ritual expertise was their literacy. The Roman Empire saw an international circulation both of spells and of self-defined ritual experts who relied on the medium of the text to ply their trades (Dickie 2001: 73, 117–23, 314–19). Of course, the exotic or antiquarian allure of the temple remained in the spells' pedigrees, which often claimed to derive from particular priests or sanctuaries, as well as in the ostensible pedigrees of the ritual experts themselves. The second-century author Celsus remarks caustically on "the accomplishments of those who are taught by the Egyptians, who for a few obols make known their sacred lore in the middle of the market-place and drive daemons out of men and blow away diseases and invoke the souls of heroes" (in Origen *C. Cels.* 1.68, tr. Chadwick 1965); novelists like Lucian and Apuleius depict young Roman literati anxious to learn priestly secrets in order to set themselves up as ritual specialists.

An interest in the diverse possibilities for divination in the Roman world also led to the establishment of new learned divinatory traditions like astrology, dream interpretation, and collections of lost oracles. If divination had locally been associated with priestly rituals and incubation shrines (see below, section 4), the tides of Mediterranean culture now brought specialists in the use of lamps, mirrors, and corpses to discern divine intent, future success, and the power of new gods (Graf 1997: 194–200; S. I. Johnston 2001). As these traditions became consolidated and specialized they spawned their own hybrid literatures and authoritative pedigrees, separate from both Near Eastern temple traditions and official Roman divination traditions.

If literate ritual experts become an increasingly prominent part of the religious landscape during the Roman period, especially in the cities, the types of rituals that they purveyed – love, healing, cursing, amulet manufacture, and the "binding" of others' urges – had long been the responsibility also of non-literate members of society: wise women and cunning men, who employed ritual traditions passed down as family heritages, and professionals in competitive trades who sought ritual means for advantage: athletes, merchants, prostitutes (Dickie 2001: 162–201). These were quotidian pursuits, which anthropologists attribute to that typical human tendency to hedge around crisis points in life with procedures that create certainty or safety. The ritual expert thus constituted an inevitable role in society, but also an ambiguous one, offering danger and disruption as well as assurance and health (Gager 1992; Meyer and Smith 1994; Frankfurter 2002). To comprehend the ritual expert's inevitability *and ambiguity* there had long existed in the Greek world stereotyped constructions of the wizard and witch and the "magic" they worked (Gordon 1999: 191–219). But by the second century CE an increasingly anxious Roman attitude towards the subversive potential of alien ritual led to official attempts to legislate against "magic" and suspicious religious movements. Concern for "magic" and ritual subversion as obstacles to civic and imperial stability became ever more fraught through the fourth and fifth centuries, even as literary and documentary evidence shows a continuing fascination with the literary figure of the wizard – even in Christian literature, where he remained an essential foil to the saint. The same evidence points, moreover, to people's ongoing dependence on real ritual experts at all levels of society (Liebeschuetz 1979: 126–39; Kippenberg 1997; Graf 1997; Beard, North, and Price 1998: 211–44; Dickie 2001: 251–321).

Prophets and inspired oracles

In a world that craved the authoritative presence of actual deities, it was natural that one of the many idioms of ritual expertise was inspired prophecy, whereby a person would become possessed by a god and speak as the god's vessel. The Greco-Roman world had a number of oracles that had worked this way for so long that they had become effectively temple cults, with priesthoods on hand both to interpret the speech of the prophets and to direct festivals and the devotions of pilgrims. But inspired prophets appeared continually in the cities, towns, and villages of the Roman world: "Many... are nameless," the Roman author Celsus described, "and prophesy at the slightest excuse for some trivial cause both inside and outside temples; and there are some who wander about begging and roaming around cities and military camps; and they pretend to be moved as if giving some oracular utterance. It is an ordinary and common custom for each one to say: 'I am God (or a son of God, or a divine Spirit). And I have come. Already the world is being destroyed. And you, O men, are to perish because of your iniquities. But I wish to save you...' " (in Origen *C. Cels.* 7.9, tr. Chadwick 1965).

In their ecstatic performances, in their claims to direct divine mediation, and in their pretense to authority over civic and domestic cultic issues, prophets and inspired oracles sought to function as "regional cults," standing at the periphery of social centers and traditional cultic domains as a source of supreme religious authority. Drawing clients from a broad catchment area, they might (as in Celsus' description above) denounce all religious activities, or establish a new cult to supersede others, or propose reform of traditional cults. Regional cults in the ancient world and modern Africa have functioned in this way, sometimes demonizing, sometimes revitalizing tradition, generally from the social margins (Lane Fox 1986: 168–261; Potter 1994: 29–57; Frankfurter 1998a: 184–93; 2002: 170–3).

Perhaps the most important example of such a figure is Alexander of Abonuteichos, who established an oracle and healing cult in an Asia Minor town in the mid-second century. He accomplished this notoriety, so his satirical biographer Lucian tells it, through the force of personality and by a series of clever devices for "manifesting" the god Glycon, a hybrid of Asclepius (Luc. *Alex.*; Lane Fox 1986: 241–50). The phenomenon was widespread in Asia Minor: prophecy distinguished one kind of Christianity, elevating direct vision and divine presence, well into the fourth century (Revelation; Ascension of Isaiah; 5, 6 Ezra) and spreading westward during the second century in the form of "New Prophecy" or Montanism (Lane Fox 1986: 375–418; Frankfurter 1998c: 426–30, 435–6; Edwards, this volume). In Palestine, Roman writers like Celsus (above) portray a continuing stream of prophets acting in imitation of ancient Israelite prophets, some with enormous followings (Jos. *AJ* 20.97–8, 167–70); and popular prophets are reported elsewhere in the Roman world (Acts 16:16; Plut. *de Def. or.* 421; cf. Potter 1994: 29–37). Still in the later fourth century the intellectual pagan Antoninus, having set himself up as a holy man by an Egyptian temple outside Alexandria, began to utter memorable oracles about the imminent fate of traditional cult (Eun. *VS* 471–2; Frankfurter 1998a: 185–6;

2000a: 186–9). By this time it was Christianity that was bestowing special legitimacy on inspired prophets, dubbing them saints even if (as modern historians have noted) church officials were often unable to pull them in from the moral and social periphery: John of Lycopolis, Antony of the desert, and others serve explicitly as seers and regional prophets in their hagiographies (Frankfurter 1998a: 186–93). In all such cases, modern historians have examined the geographical and moral position of the prophet vis-à-vis central cults, his impact on traditional cults in the area, and the context of his often highly partisan literary portrayals.

4 Rites and Practices

The study of religion has come increasingly to emphasize practice and performance as the central feature of religions; and despite past efforts to discuss the beliefs and doctrines that led to – or resisted – Christianity, the Roman world also requires a practice-centered approach to religion. In Rome, North Africa, Gaul, Syria, Asia Minor, and elsewhere, "religion" revolved around action – gesture, performance, and the fulfillment of ritual responsibilities – whether in the public realm of civic drama or in the privacy of a "magical" rite. "Irreligion" and atheism were understood in similar terms: not disbelief or philosophical skepticism but rather the avoidance of ritual responsibilities or even the pursuit of ritual practices that could subvert the social order. Only with the rise of Christian orthodoxy in the fourth century does "right belief" come – in some quarters – to carry the same critical importance for civic and cosmic stability as did *orthopraxy* in the Roman Empire (C. R. Phillips 1986: 2697–711, 2746–52; Beard, North, and Price 1998: 42–54).

Although there is an enormous range of culturally-inscribed gestures and utterances that allow people effective mediation with holy things, we may capture much of this range through three general patterns. The official cult of temples and cities revolved around sacrifice, often an elaborate public drama, or around the festival presentation and procession of the god's image. Divination, sometimes (as in Rome) an extension of official cult, comprised those ritual means by which gods' intentions might be known (and across the Mediterranean world these means were as diverse as they were vital to quotidian life). And pilgrimage and devotion cover private, familial, or group expressions of allegiance to a god in a shrine. Whether carrying supplicants to distant lands or – more often – involving the festive or desperate visit to a regional shrine, pilgrimages and the appeals or vows people made on them reflect the "popular" dimension of religious expression in the Roman world.

Official cult: sacrifice, offerings, festivals

Central to public ritual was some kind of sacrifice or offering, which a priest or official, rigorously purified for the act, might present on an altar as a way of communicating with a god. Many studies of sacrifice – from the nineteenth-century sources for Freud's *Totem and Taboo* to twentieth-century authors like René Girard – have focused on the blood and violence intrinsic to animal sacrifice, but this emphasis has tended to distort the meaning of sacrificial rituals in their cultural and performative contexts. Indeed, such violence-oriented interpretations have often served explicitly to frame the Christian myth of Christ's ultimate sacrifice (cf. discussion in Hammerton-Kelly 1987). More recent examinations of the place of sacrifice in public ritual have stressed the *meal* elements in sacrifice, which appear not only in the choice of offering (edible animals) and the mode of "rendering sacred" (through cooking and burning), but also the use of the remains: shared and eaten or, for gods, sprinkled as ashes or blood at a sacred location. Even in their largest scales (such as the continual offering cycle in the Jewish temple of pre-70 Jerusalem: Schürer 1973–87: 2: 295–308), sacrifices essentially constituted meals that the human community shared with gods. Divine and human "portions" were strictly designated according to tradition, and those portions meant for humans were subsequently eaten among an authorized group, priesthood, or cult society, often in a state of marked purity. This feast represented not a sharing *of* the god or his essence but rather *with* the god, as the blessed remnant of a lord's meal (Beard, North, and Price 1998: 36–7; Scheid 2003: 79–110).

The omnipresence of sacrifice in religions of the Roman Empire obscures the fact that in most Mediterranean cultures "sacrifice" involved grain, oil, and bread offerings far more than meat. Conversely, ritual slaughters of animals were not necessarily "sacrifice": Plutarch describes annual slaughters of crocodiles in one part of Egypt, conducted in order to expel disorder from the cosmos (*de Is. et Os.* 50); and evidence from Egyptian animal necropolises suggests that ibises, cats, and other animals were killed simply to produce mummies for pilgrims' devotions (Charron 1990). The exceedingly rare evidence for human sacrifice in the Roman world points to communities attempting ritual mediation under extraordinary stress (as in a siege). The *imagery* of human sacrifice, however, which was often coupled with allegations of cannibalism, commonly served to designate the anti-human or subversive; and all manner of subcultures – from the pacifist (Christians) to the foreign (Jews, Egyptian herders) to the weird (Bacchantics, Gnostics) – fell under such accusations over the course of late antiquity (Beard, North, and Price 1998: 80–2; Scheid 2003: 95; Rives 1995).

Public sacrificial ritual and domestic offerings alike were performed to mark critical events in civic life, to maintain the fortune of city and home, and to celebrate in common at festival occasions. In such cases, the actual killing and eating of an animal would be part of a much more elaborate ritual process. Whereas in Rome sacrificial rites intrinsically involved divination, as *haruspices* examined the entrails of the offering, and came in imperial times to signify the emperor's cosmic authority (Gordon 1990b), in Egypt blood sacrifices were far less central in the total theater of festival than, for example, the procession of the divine image beyond the temple doors. Furthermore, the importance of public sacrifices notwithstanding, much of the "life" and meaning of these occasions was borne in music, song, particular festival foods, and pantomimes (MacMullen 1981: 16–42; Lane Fox 1986: 91–2; Frankfurter 1998a: 52–65).

Under the anxious third-century edicts of the emperors Decius and Valerian, sacrifice – in the simple form of pouring libations and sharing in ritually killed and dedicated meat – became the symbol of the *orthopraxy* without which the empire would descend into chaos and invasion. It is now certain that these edicts were not meant to persecute Christians – who might or might not participate in these rites (Wipszycka 1987) – but rather to establish a common ritual for the sake of social order and cosmic harmony; even priests and priestesses of traditional religions were sometimes called in to perform the required gestures (Beard, North, and Price 1998: 239–43; Knipfing 1923: 364–5; Fredriksen, this volume).

Divination

Divination covers a diversity of rites, from the most public and institutionally prescribed to the most private and informal, that provide the supernatural world a means of communication and intervention in human affairs. Cross-culturally, divination constitutes one of the primary vehicles for applying the authority of religious tradition to the vicissitudes and potentialities of social life. It was central to Roman administration (with several *collegia* of priests devoted specifically to divination), to the functioning of Egyptian temples (where it took place during festival processions as well through rituals of private consultation), and to the development of new Mediterranean cults like that of Alexander of Abonuteichos and Christianity (Beard, North, and Price 1998: 19–23; Scheid 2003: 111–26; Frankfurter 1998a: 145–97; Johnston and Struck 2005).

Divination rites generally involve the layout of some materials or the definition of some circumstance as a "pallette" on which a range of patterns can result. The range of patterns can be small, as in certain types of "lot" oracles; it can be broad yet delimited, as in the shape of an animal's liver or an arrangement of birds in flight; or it can be enormous, as in the ecstatic medium's utterances or some astronomical event. Experts – priests, freelance specialists, or simply the owner of a divination manual – interpret the resulting patterns as the encoded communications of gods, spirits, or some greater supernatural order. Hence, the materials or circumstances – lots, livers, flying birds, or running children – amount to a code through which the supernatural beings transmit their message. The pattern emergent in the code, the *omen* proper, precedes the interpretation – the pattern rendered meaningful – which is the *oracle* proper. The chance patterns or responses emerge, through interpretation, as the nuanced expression of a divinity's will. From the recognition of a sheep liver's peculiar lobes to the inference of a divine military strategy, or from a series of dice rolls to the "instruction" to go to Alexandria, there is a sequence of stages: preparation of the random "pallette," observation of the omen, and translation as an oracle.

Divination is ultimately a social drama, both in its ritual elements and its capacity to criticize or legitimate acts of social significance. Divination rituals are often quite dynamic, maintaining cultural stability in placid times, while in more complex times reaching out to new materials and idioms to aid people's transitions to new social realities. Thus in the Roman period we find both quite archaic, temple-based forms of *haruspices* and augury and entirely new types of oracle, like astrology, lots, dream interpretation, and divination by sacred text. Yet ancient divination always involved the creative use of *tradition*, a sense of authority that could be brought to bear on a situation at hand. This tradition might comprise the performative style of a medium, the identity of the speaking god, the divination materials themselves, the expertise of the diviner, or simply the shrine at which divination could occur. Tradition provided the framework, the fixed and sacred theater, for the coded pattern or occurrence that signaled the god's own communication. The preeminence of tradition is particularly evident in Rome, where volumes of ancient Sibylline oracles and augury interpretation guided priests' divination, and in Egypt, where the archaic rite of the processional oracle still in the Roman period brought the power and presence of the god out of the temple and into a context of public communication, where it could be seen to move around on its bearers' shoulders. Tradition likewise undergirded astrology as it took root in temples and developed among freelance experts of the Mediterranean world. Whether freelance or priestly, astrologers worked hard to assimilate the omens of planets and stars to indigenous gods and epistemologies. Divination inevitably involved a close combination of the traditional and authoritative, on the one hand, and the innovative, on the other.

Many cultures had long accorded a role to *writing* in their central divination procedures in one form or another: Israel's adultery ordeal, in which the accused had to drink the letters of a curse to prove her guilt or innocence (Nm 5:11–31); Egypt's "ticket" oracles, in which supplicants would deliver questions to the god in positive and negative alternatives, expecting the correct answer to be returned as the divine will; and of course the written records of ancient oracles that many temples preserved for later interpretation (Champeaux 1997). But the Greco-Roman era saw a profusion of new divinatory texts. For example, there circulated a variety of manuals for preparing the divinatory "pallette" using dreams, mirrors, or bowls of water (sometimes using a pure youth as the discerner), or for inviting a god's direct apparition. In this way one could gain authoritative oracles apart from traditional temple space (J. Z. Smith 1978a; Eitrem 1991; Frankfurter 2000a: 180–2; S. I. Johnston 2001). Furthermore, we find a profusion of "new" oracles attributed to ancient sibyls, kings (like the Persian Hystaspes), gods (Egyptian Hermes Trismegistos), or sages (Jewish Seth or Enoch), collected and even cited as authoritative, even though historians can date these oracles clearly to the Greco-Roman or late antique periods (Himmelfarb 1993: 95–104; Potter 1994: 58–97). There also developed a form of text-based oracle, the *Sortes Astrampsychi*, whereby a client might find an answer to a particular question by thinking of a number, which would lead (through a technique known only to the *Sortes*' owner) to the authoritative answer in the pages of the book. In this way, the book itself became the multipurpose repository of mantic guidance (Frankfurter 1998a: 170–84; van der Horst 1998).

The capacity of foreign divination traditions to invade politics, much as official Roman divination was intended to do, led to its occasional proscription and even fullscale purges of astrologers and oracles, as the Roman historian Ammianus Marcellinus says took place in 359 CE in upper Egypt (Amm. Marc. 19.12.3; see Frankfurter 2000b and in general Liebeschuetz 1979: 119–26).

Pilgrimage and devotion

Inasmuch as religion was conceived spatially in the Roman world, the most basic form of ritual act in Mediterranean cultures involved movement to, through, or among the various concentric "centers" that gave meaning to the landscape, and then in the concrete acts of devotion one performed to signify one's presence at a place. Processions followed routes that symbolically involved specific shrines in city or countryside. Domestic cult itself comprised acts of devotion before images in a particular part of the house, as well as trips to local and regional shrines to avail of their gods' favors. In general, one's social and personal relationship to a temple or even to a regional prophet was inevitably expressed through some form of travel (Belayche 1987; Frankfurter 1998b: 13–28). Even the imagery of otherworldly vision, which often guaranteed the authority of a seer, was played out across a heavenly landscape of deities, angels, the dead, and mysterious sights (Himmelfarb 1987).

It has been debated whether the term "pilgrimage" ought to be used to designate travel in such religious contexts, since in the ancient world "religious" travel could not be easily distinguished from what the modern scholar might call "tourism" (Bernand 1988; Elsner and Rutherford 2005). But for our purposes, the recognition of certain patterns in religious travel in the Roman period obviate the larger categories. Shrines with regional catchment areas receive regular visitors seeking resolution of concrete crises: health, advice, blessing. At Egyptian shrines like that of Bes at Abydos, or that of saints Cyrus and John at Menouthis, or even the aerie of a regional prophet like the Syrian Simeon Stylitês, devotees come from area villages to resolve illnesses, agricultural dilemmas, and social conflicts (MacMullen 1981: 26–9; Dunand 1991, 1997; Montserrat 1998a; Derks 1998: 215–39). Some of these shrines and seers also gained international clienteles: in Egypt, for example, the Mandulis shrine at Talmis (Kalabsha) and the Amun shrine of Siwa, both on the very boundaries of Egypt, and by the fifth century the shrine of Saint Menas; in Palestine an entire "holy land" of Jewish and Christian sacred sites; Hierapolis in Syria; and the many oracle shrines in Greece and Asia Minor (Volokhine 1998: 82–97; I. Rutherford 1998; and in general Maraval 1985:105–15). Appeals to these shrines, as we find in inscriptions and literary sources, often tended towards the "spiritual" – the acquisition of some revelatory experience – and reflected the hybrid religious sentiments of urbane Roman travelers, not just regional peasants (Nock 1934; Hohlwein 1940; Frankfurter 1998a: 217–21; Moyer 2003).

Upon reaching such shrines, travelers would express their presence and particular appeals: in graffiti – called *proskynêmata*, "devotions" – on the walls of the shrine, occasionally in elaborate verse prayers; by leaving votive images of afflicted body parts, much as in healing shrines today; by endowing commemorative stelae; and by sleeping as close as possible to the holy place, a need for which many shrines, both pre-Christian and Christian, provided facilities. Pilgrimages at festival times would encounter processions, dramas, spectacles of all sorts, and various collective devotions: at Syrian Hierapolis, for example, one might witness the priestly sacrifice amidst "holy men, flute players as well as pipers and *Galli* [ecstatics who castrate themselves], and frenzied and deranged women" (Luc. *Syr. D.* 43; in general see Maraval 1985: 213–45).

The concentration of such activities at a traditional center, often following a difficult journey from one's home village, invites the analytic approach of the anthropologist Victor Turner, who emphasized the religious experience particular to "liminal" situations – away from home, as part of a like-minded party, in or en route to an extraordinary place, during festival time (V. Turner 1974). Thus spatially, socially, and temporally dis-located, the pilgrim might find her perception of sacred or "real" things heightened; she might achieve deeper bonds with others similarly disposed; and she might undergo some permanent psychological transformation. Travel and pilgrimage literature of the Roman period alike emphasized the boundaries and frontiers of imperial civilization, the inhuman dangers, spiritual potentialities, and odd spectacles that lay beyond familiar territory; to the elite Roman, the archaic temple off on the periphery was heavy with an exotic allure that could not but have influenced his experience on arrival. Of course, literature describing such experiences often served to promote particular shrines, and regional or local pilgrimages tended to function on more of a continuum with local religious experience than international pilgrimages, which involved more of a departure.

5 Metamorphoses

The Mediterranean world of the Roman Empire saw a number of religious changes, some of which contributed to the position Christianity assumed in many regions, while others were far more gradual, stretching back to the beginning of Hellenism itself. Many changes revolved around the assimilation of "foreign" religious ideas and cults within zones hitherto restricted to indigenous priestly traditions. As Beard, North, and Price have observed, the Foreign – albeit dangerous in some circumstances – could be appropriated and located "as established *ways of thinking* at Rome about the most central human values" (1998: 166). Gods of Asia Minor and Egypt were enthusiastically Romanized in ritual, architecture, and civic function and thus celebrated within the *pomerium*. Emperors co-opted the priestly accoutrements of foreign gods and sponsored their festivals. And elsewhere – Palestine, Egypt, Syria – priesthoods sought ever more quickly to indigenize the symbols of Hellenism while asserting – even promoting – cultural distinctiveness.

Centers

While many archaic cults held fast through late antiquity, the Roman period saw numerous shifts to new centers. The consolidation of Roman authority in some Mediterranean regions led to a view of Rome itself as the religious center, a shift away from the traditional sacred city (Jerusalem is thus left behind in the early Christian Book of Acts). Yet for Romans themselves the archaic cults of the "Orient" began to look increasingly like centers – origins, sources – of religious meaning by virtue of their profound differences from Roman religion, their textual traditions, and the exotic "wisdom" proffered by their ritual experts (Beard, North, and Price 1998: 196–201, 263–6, 278–87). In the countryside there is evidence of shifts from ancient temple cults to seers and holy men, although this evidence is inconsistent and must be compared to the evidence for temples thriving into the Christian period (Brown 1978: 1–26; Frankfurter 1998a: 153–79). With the Christianization of mortuary space and the triumph of the saintly relic came abundant new religious centers in the necropolises or, by the mid-fourth century, in the martyria and basilicas built at the center of cities (Caseau 1999; Frankfurter 2005).

Another shift was intellectual: the eschewing of terrestrial centers for the goals of mystical ascent: union with the divine, the heavenly city of God, or a perfection independent of place (A. Segal 1980; Himmelfarb 1993; Athanassiadi 1993; S. I. Johnston 1997; Smith 2003: 30–4). Of course, these sentiments were hardly typical of intellectuals in late antiquity, who usually revered traditional holy places (Frankfurter 2000a: 184–92). For rabbinic Judaism, which began to form in the late first century following the destruction of the Jerusalem temple (see Eliav, this volume), the "center" was supposed to be the Torah, the book from God, placed at the front of some synagogues and celebrated in study; yet Jews continued to venerate tombs and regional holy places. Economic decline of major regional temples in some parts of the empire occasionally led to a centrifugal shift of religious authority and orientation-points to local shrines and subsequently, if these too dwindled (or suffered destruction by Christian monks), to the domestic shrine. At this point, traditional rites maintained only in the domestic sphere could be revitalized through Christian idioms of power (Frankfurter 1998a: 142–4).

Experts

Mediterranean cultures had long held the "foreign" ritual expert alluring and would credit him with particular magical powers (Burkert 1992), yet *religious* authority was based squarely in the traditional and familiar. However, in the imperial period, as part of the importation of new cults into zones hitherto reserved for the quintessentially Roman, priests and ritual experts with foreign credentials apparently began to be credited with religious authority as well. Their forms of divination rivaled that of the *haruspices* and *augures*; their texts appeared more ancient; their rites and teachings originated in archaic temple cities off in the mysterious east. Egyptian priests were particularly alluring in this sense, depicted in novels like Heliodorus' *Ethiopian Story* as peripatetic dispensers of enlightenment and wizardry and even appearing historically as court wizards (Dio 72.8.4; cf. Frankfurter 1998a: 224–37); but Babylonian, Syrian, and Jewish priests also carried the potential for such roles. Submission to – or simply participation in – a foreign priest's religious authority could thus bring new powers, new religious experiences, and new ways of orienting oneself in an enormous, culturally complex world while still under the aegis of Roman identity.

Rites and practices

Along with new rites for binding, cursing, healing, and divining, foreign ritual experts brought new forms of religious experience and community that centered not so much on traditional civic performance as on a psychological–emotional *transformation* (Beard, North, and Price 1998: 278–91; Smith 2003: 30–6). As described in both fiction and epigraphy, the experiences gained (and repeated) through participating in these "mysteries" – a kind of intensive dramatization of some myth (Isis/Osiris, Attis/Magna Mater, Mithras/Sol) – led to a sense of power, control, and unity with an incomprehensible cosmos (Nock 1934; Beck 2000). Participation in the societies that celebrated the mysteries and maintained their hybrid traditions also offered security in a hitherto ambiguous afterlife and, in this world, a new experience of religious *community* – one no longer based on family, residence, and civic status. These new social–ritual worlds were popular and successful, and it is in the context of their appeal that scholars have long explained the rapid expansion of the Christian movement and even the abundance of proselytes to Judaism. Both religious subcultures not only promoted rituals for safety in the cosmos but also defined social boundaries as crucial to participation and benefits.

But the legitimation of foreign religiosity in these social and personal domains was the corollary of – and might quickly revert to – an intense anxiety about foreign religious subversion in political and civic domains. A religious movement like Christianity, whose adherents (officially) refused allegiance to Roman religious traditions of sacrifice and devotion, was easily cast as subversive group of atheists whose very presence in the cities and countryside caused cosmic havoc (by the fifth century "pagans" and "heretics" were construed in the same manner: Rives 1995). "Magic," an idea that by imperial times intrinsically denoted foreignness, was officially proscribed – and was even the subject of inquisitions – while virtually everyone sought its benefits and powers from the perennial ranks of ritual experts (Beard, North, and Price 1998: 218–25; Dickie 2001: 142–321). Divination, which offered the power to discern prospects for the most mundane crises and the most sensitive political situations, could appear uniquely dangerous to the stability of the empire, and frightened emperors and officials tried at various times to eliminate even old, indigenous oracles. Expulsion of the foreign – whether wizards, modes of divination, cults, or religious societies – reflected a general anxiety about boundaries, but this anxiety only increased over the third and subsequent centuries as the empire's political structures and centers splintered. In their dramatic, often violent character, purges of foreign influence offered participants the possibility of renewed tradition and renewed commitment to the old centers (Brown 1970; Beard, North, and Price 1998: 228–44).

CHAPTER TWENTY-EIGHT

Jews and Judaism 70–429 CE

Yaron Z. Eliav

By a conservative estimate, scholars assess the population of the Roman Empire at the beginning of the first millennium CE to have been 50–60 million, inhabiting the lands around the Mediterranean basin. An educated guess counts among them about five million Jews, more or less (Hopkins 1998; Schwartz 2001: 10–11, 41; cf. McGing 2002). Something between 10 and 20 percent of the empire's Jewish population lived in the area now called Israel or Palestine, in those days a Roman province first called Judaea and later Syria-Palestina. The rest lived in cities and villages throughout the Mediterranean world, from Egypt and North Africa, through Syria, Asia Minor, and Greece, to Rome and even beyond it in Gaul (modern-day France) and the Iberian peninsula, non-contiguous islands of Jewish habitation usually referred to as the Diaspora. These numbers, imprecise as they may be, and their geographical distribution, establish the Jews as the largest and most widely dispersed ethnic minority under Roman rule. This immediately raises questions about the nature of this community, which in turn takes us from geography and statistics to politics, society, culture, and religion. The answers to these questions are not as simple as one might think.

1 The Sources and their Problems

A variety of different but interrelated factors undermines the historian's efforts to recount straightforwardly the story of ancient Judaism and the Jewish people in the centuries following the destruction of the Second Jewish Temple (in 70 CE). First and foremost stands the situation of the sources. The last three centuries BCE and the first two generations of the first century CE – a time span known in Jewish history as the Second Temple period (more broadly dated from 586 BCE to 70 CE) – produced a large number of documents that have come down to us, in Hebrew, Aramaic, and Greek. These include historiographical works, such as the books of the Jewish historian Flavius

Josephus, as well as a rich variety of other writings – wisdom literature, philosophy, exegesis, polemics, apocalyptic works, fiction, and poetry (Stone 1984; Schürer 1973–87: 3: 177–889). This wealth of sources enabled scholars to reconstruct a vibrant picture of an era riven with controversies, some of them violent.

After 70 CE, the evidence soon becomes far less plentiful. True, we have a series of compositions that articulate the world of those who believed in Jesus as the messiah – people who should, through most of this period, be viewed as Jews in every sense of the word (Fredriksen, this volume). But other than texts relating to the followers of Jesus, and a small number of other works, most of what has survived is the corpus known today as Rabbinic literature. This category comprises some 40 documents of various sizes, most of them of a legal nature (called *halakha*, from the Hebrew verb "to go" – in the sense of "the way in which we live"). Some of these, labeled "*midrash*," are commentaries on the scriptures; the other non-legal material – stories, homilies, parables, proverbs, and other genres – are grouped under the general heading of *aggadah* ("telling"). Through a long and convoluted process spanning the first centuries of the common era, about which much remains a mystery, the figures we call rabbis produced, and then gathered, collected, and edited these works (S. Safrai 1987; Strack and Stemberger 1996). The utility of these sources for the reconstruction of Jewish life at this time poses grave challenges to the modern historian.

The "Rabbinic Movement" (in Hebrew *ḤAZAL*, an acronym for "our sages may their memory be blessed") is the anachronistic term given to the men who created this literature. The term intends to exalt and set them apart as a homogeneous group with a distinct ideology and systematic philosophy of life that shaped the character of Judaism, its institutions, and its way of life from then until now. According to this view, Rabbinic literature contains within it the essence of Judaism after the destruction of the Temple, a way of life developed, honed, and led by those who wrote these works – the rabbis. Hence the common label of the centuries after 70 CE in collective Jewish memory – the Rabbinic Period (or, in some cases, the Period of the Mishnah and the Talmud[s], after the two major Rabbinic texts). The foundation of this view lies in the Middle Ages, when most segments of the Jewish population accepted Rabbinic literature as a cornerstone of Jewish life and as the very soul of Judaism. The leaders of Jewish communities in the medieval Jewish Diaspora (and in many cases until our day) viewed themselves as the successors and followers of the Rabbinic sages (the *ḥakhamim*) who created this literature. Accordingly, they adopted for themselves the collective title of "rabbi" that they had bestowed on their predecessors.

The veneration of Rabbinic texts ensured their preservation from one generation to the next – first as hand-written codices, and finally printed in thousands of copies. Yet this very process of perpetuation undermined the ability of modern scholars, many of whom came from circles that revered the rabbis, to reconstruct the context in which their texts were composed. In fact, the process of composition often completely distorted that context. The result is that most members of the current generation of scholars now reject the view that emerged in the nineteenth and early twentieth century, that Jews in the ancient world defined themselves and lived their lives according to the ideas and instructions to be found in Rabbinic literature (Hezser 1997: 1–42, 353–404). To this we must add the recognition that the Rabbinic literature was never intended to be read as if it were history. The sages sought mostly to record and document their intellectual, legal, and midrashic discussions, not to tell future generations what happened during their time. This makes even more challenging the work of the modern investigator who seeks to draw out details from Rabbinic literature and assemble them into a historical narrative.

The sages' status in antiquity was much more modest and their authority – if they had any at all – more meager than the traditional view would allow. The creators of Rabbinic literature were learned Jews – scholars – who were active in Palestine in the generations after the destruction of the Second Temple, and later, from the third century, also in the Persian Empire ("Babylonia" as they called what is now Iraq and Iran). Like other intellectuals (whether Jewish or not) throughout history, the rabbis were animated by their personalities, in particular the natural proclivity towards learning that singles out some individuals early in life. They devoted their lives to scholarship and erudition. The focus of their studies, the foundation texts of their curriculum, consisted of the Jewish scriptures, which later became the Bible. Their preferred "field" of study centered on legal discourse (unlike other ancient Jewish scholars, who engaged in other branches of learning, such as philosophy and mysticism). Accordingly, Rabbinic sages endeavored to channel what they believed to be the eternal truth of God, as articulated in the Torah (the first five, most important, books of the Bible), into meticulous and well-structured legal formulae. In a long and gradual process, extending well beyond the limits of this chapter, Rabbinic legal scholarship grew into an all-embracing legal system. They named it *Halakha*, "the way" – God's way of life (cf. S. Safrai 1987: 121–209).

The small group of intellectuals who crafted the Rabbinic tradition had limited, if any, impact on the Jewish public in Palestine, and even less on the Jewish communities elsewhere in the Mediterranean regions. There were never more than a few dozen of them active at any given time, and sometimes even fewer (L. I. Levine 1989: 66–9). Moreover, it is not at all clear, during the 150 years after the Temple's destruction, whether the sages were an organized movement, with self-awareness, well-defined political goals, and a coherent conceptual outlook on Jewish life. It seems more likely to me that the opposite is true (Hezser 1997: 185–224). At first, and through several generations, the sages functioned as individual scholars, teachers who gathered small numbers of students around them on a personal basis. Whatever links existed among them were loose and limited, and generally restricted to intellectual interests and scholarly debates. The situation began to change, slowly, only at the beginning of the third century CE with the project of redacting and publishing the Mishnah, the first comprehensive compilation of Rabbinic legal material. Judah the Patriarch, the official political leader of Jewish Palestine, who exercised considerable authority and prestige among Diaspora communities as well, initiated, and to a great extent funded, this huge undertaking. It was only by chance that this particular patriarch also belonged to the circle of the sages. In my view the Mishnah was the creator rather than the creation of the Rabbinical movement.

These seemingly minute nuances greatly affect our interpretation of Rabbinic texts. For one, they clog the traditional channels of information about this period. Almost no one in scholarly circles nowadays would accept Rabbinic material as a straightforward representation of contemporary Jewish life in antiquity; many Rabbinic depictions tend to exaggerate (or idealize) the role and stature of the rabbis, their practices, and their legal rulings. Other material, also of a legal nature, addresses highly theoretical issues, far removed from real life. This does not mean that one should ignore Rabbinic sources altogether. On the contrary – Rabbinic material, if properly used, contains a wealth of information about Jewish life in antiquity. But it must be studied with caution and within the wider context of the ancient world.

Downgrading the role of the rabbis in ancient Jewish society requires rethinking the nature of the Jewish world in the High Empire and Late Roman periods. If the sages did not set the agenda for Jewish life, and if their worldview was not generally held by their coreligionists, how did Jews live in those days? As it happens, these questions are much more complicated than we once thought. Although we would now tend to reject the centrality of Rabbinic thought to Judaism in the Roman and Byzantine periods, it must also be conceded that efforts to replace that model have not won universal assent. For example, Jacob Neusner, one of the first and sharpest critics of the old view, reconstructs many "Judaisms" that, in his view, existed side by side in those days. His approach, based on methodology from the school of intellectual history (heavily influenced by Protestant scholarship) links texts to social groups. According to Neusner, different works, even within the Rabbinic corpus, as well as certain artistic depictions (for example the mosaic floors of synagogues), represent all-inclusive religious and even social entities with independent conceptions and identities of Judaism. This equation is artificial and forced, and thus has not found many supporters in the scholarly community (e.g. Neusner 1995: 1: 117–72; S. Cohen 1983).

Archaeological discoveries add another important layer to our understanding of the period, but do not reduce its ambiguities. The most significant remains belong to ancient synagogues (L. I. Levine 2000), a subject I will deal with in greater detail below. The synagogue originated as an institution during the Second Temple period, but after 70 CE it gradually filled the vacuum left by the destroyed Temple as the central space for the performance of Jewish ritual and worship and as the prime location for communal organization. But even here the picture remains vague. Archaeologists differ about the dating of the dozens of synagogues that have been excavated throughout the Mediterranean basin, many of them in modern Israel. The artwork found in these structures presents researchers with another series of challenges. Many of the mosaic floors contain manifestly pagan motifs. The image of Helios mounted on his chariot, or the 12 signs of the Zodiac, all quite popular images in synagogue iconography, often accompany biblical motifs and narratives (such as the binding of Isaac), depictions of Temple vessels (such as the Menorah and other objects associated with this institution), and illustrations of its liturgy. What conclusions are we to draw from this about the character of the Jews who used these buildings and about the nature of the Judaism they practiced? Seth Schwartz has proposed that Judaism entirely evaporated in the early centuries after the destruction of the Temple, and was reborn only under the sponsorship and at the initiative of the Byzantine rulers. He bases his claim largely on, first, a late dating of most of the excavated synagogues and, second, on the "pagan" character of the early material evidence, such as coins from cities generally thought to have had vast Jewish populations (such as Tiberias and Sepphoris), and burial inscriptions from the 150 years after the destruction (Schwartz 2001). But his view is equally untenable (Eliav 2004). Beyond some serious methodological flaws that undermine Schwartz's thesis, many sources, especially Roman legal material (such as Linder 1987: 103–6), as well as abundant archaeological information, demonstrate a vibrant Jewish existence during this period.

Figure 28.1a Mosaic "carpet" from the fourth-century synagogue at Ḥamat Tiberieas featuring in the top panel the Ark of the Torah surrounded by liturgical items (the Temple menorah, the four species of Sukkot, and more); in the central panel is the zodiac with month signs and the four personifications of the seasons at the corners identified with Hebrew terms, and at the center Helios mounting a chariot and holding a globe; the bottom panel (the closest to the entrance) shows two lions embracing a Greek inscription mentioning the donors (one of which is designated as "Friend of the Patriarchs")

Another question that causes researchers a great deal of trouble is the nature of Jewish–Christian encounters. Modern scholars have often projected the medieval picture of two diametrically opposed religions separated by a theological abyss, not to mention hostility, loathing, and violence backwards into the Roman period. Excessive reliance on the contentious rhetoric of the church fathers has also contributed to the common view that colors the religious and social milieu of late antiquity in bold shades of segregation and conflict. Many of these dichotomies have come under attack in the last generation. The problem, as Daniel Boyarin states, is that Judaism and Christianity in this period "shared crisscrossing lines of history and

Figure 28.1b The interior of a fourth-century synagogue at Sardis which is built into a huge gymnasium/bath complex. The picture looks east at the three entrances to the main hall; in the back of the central door one can still see the marble basin for washing that stood in the atrium (probably the "fountain of the Jews" that is mentioned in one of the city's municipal inscriptions); flanking the central portal on the inside are two *aediculae*, one of which surely functioned as an Ark for the Torah scroll (archaeologists debate the function of the other). At the front of the picture is a massive stone table, perhaps for the reading of the Torah, with two eagles engraved to its legs (not shown) and a pair of lions flanking its sides. A closer look shows also the remains of pillars that divided the interior space into a central nave and two aisles, as well as the remains of the numerous mosaics that decorated the floors

religious development." Therefore, he wrote, "one could travel, metaphorically, from Rabbinic Jew to Christian along a continuum where one would hardly know where one stopped and the other began" (Boyarin 1999: 8–9; Becker and Yoshiko-Reed 2003).

All this leads, in my opinion, to the need for a radical change in our historiographic expectations. We must recognize that, given the sources currently available to us, certain questions, some of them central and fundamental, must remain unanswered. On the other hand, such an understanding allows for a more cautious, and thus more balanced, evaluation of Jewish history in this era.

2 The Historical Framework

The contours of the era are reasonably clear. It begins with two generations of violent confrontations between Jews and the Roman Empire. Decades of unstable provincial rule in Judaea, accompanied by ethnic tensions between Jews and other national groups in the region (Samaritans, the inhabitants of the Phoenician-Greek coastal cities, and others), erupted in a local–national revolution, called the Great Rebellion, in 66 CE. Fighting broke out in Judaea and adjacent areas to the north and the east. The Romans, at the time preoccupied with their internal affairs – after Nero's suicide in 68, the imperial throne bounced between four men in just 18 months – took close to four years to suppress the uprising. It was not until 70 CE that four legions under the command of the future emperor Titus conquered Jerusalem and burned the Jewish Temple.

We know almost nothing about the state of affairs related to the Jews or the substance of their lives in the Roman Empire during the generation and a half after the destruction of the Temple, beyond haphazard archaeological finds that merely testify to their existence here and there. But in 115, at the peak of the emperor Trajan's campaign in Mesopotamia (today's Iraq), a second Jewish rebellion broke out. This time it started in Egypt and Cyrenaica in North Africa, ignited by violent clashes between Jews "and their Greek fellow-citizens" (Euseb. *Eccl. Hist.* 4.2.2; Schürer 1973–87: 1.529–34). The uprising quickly spread to other Jewish communities throughout the Mediterranean region, and compelled the emperor Trajan to appoint one of his best generals, Marcius Turbo, to suppress it.

The last, most ferocious, and best-planned of the insurgencies broke out in 132, during the reign of Hadrian, and is known from the name of its leader as the Bar Kokhba rebellion. The few lines that the historian Cassius Dio devotes to documenting this clash convey the intensity and horror of the conflict (Dio 69.12.1–14.3). Tens if not hundreds of thousands died on both sides, entire villages were razed, and once densely-populated Jewish areas in Palestine were only sparsely inhabited for many generations thereafter (Isaac and Oppenheimer 1985).

These 60 years of bloody confrontation between Jews and the Roman Empire find no parallel anywhere else in the Roman world. Although the threat posed by the Germanic and Scythian tribes, for example, during the second century far exceeded the trouble caused by the Jews, and although the Romans also faced many other upheavals within the empire's borders (including Boudicca's rebellion in Britain and serious uprisings in Gaul), the Jewish uprisings were more persistent and extensive. Scores of Jewish communities throughout the Mediterranean suffered from the conflicts, or encountered the suffering of fellow Jews, whether through the death of family members, their sale into slavery or prostitution, or the official confiscation of property and land. Imperial propaganda, especially of the Flavians but also of Hadrian, spread the word of Jewish defeat and hardship even further in the form of "Judaea Capta" coinage and by legislation; it was also advertised through triumphal art and architecture (the arch of Titus being the most famous example). The horrendous outcome of these conflicts became a fundamental component of the experience and consciousness of the generations that followed, shaping the Jewish historical heritage, collective memory, and sense of identity. In my view, it is impossible to understand the history of the Jews in the early centuries of the Common Era without reference to this context. Many historians who address the tension between early Christianity and the empire as expressed, for example, in the phenomenon of martyrdom, often forget that the discord between the Jews and the Romans was harsher and far bloodier.

Figure 28.2a Imperial celebration of the capture of Jerusalem is reflected in the issue of Judaea Capta coinage under Vespasian (*RIC* Vespasian 424; ANS 1947.2.430-rev) (Photo courtesy of the American Numismatic Society)

Figure 28.2b The imperial issues were echoed on local coinages in the reign of Titus. Coin of Caesarea with Titus on the obverse, and Nike holding a shield on the reverse with the legend IOUDAIAS (H)ELAKÔSUIAS [Judaea Capta] (editor's collection)

The violent intensity that characterized the history of the Jews throughout the Mediterranean in the first century CE and the first half of the second century stands in stark contrast to the political tranquility of the next 200 years, persisting, to a large extent, although not absolutely, through the rest of late antiquity. The political and economic unrest throughout the empire, especially in its eastern portions, during the third century (see Potter, chapter 8, this volume), offered myriad opportunities to cast off the yoke of the central government and join in any of the frequent insurrections that surfaced during this time. The silence of the sources regarding any participation of the Jews in these upheavals is telling. Likewise, unlike the Samaritans, who rebelled on numerous occasions in the fifth and sixth centuries to contest restrictions imposed on them by the Byzantine authorities, the Jews remain quiescent. We can only speculate as to the reasons for this peculiar reconciliation, but the outcome is clear – serenity facilitates prosperity. The archaeological and epigraphical record from the period, in the form of many dozens of Jewish villages, both in northern Palestine and in numerous cities along the Mediterranean coast, testifies to a cultural and communal flowering of Judaism.

3 Leadership

Misled by the harmonious portrait of Jewish society discussed above, modern scholars overrated the question of leadership after the destruction of the Second Temple. The view of Jews in that era as a homogeneous group with the rabbis at the helm compelled modern investigators to seek factors to account for this situation. This effort is superfluous. In the Second Temple period, especially during the final generations of that period (for which there is a broad spectrum of documentation), the Roman regime recognized the Temple in Jerusalem as the central institution of the Jewish minority throughout the Roman Empire. Thus they allowed the collection, both in Judaea and in the Diaspora, of the half-shekel, an annual tax which funded the daily and public sacrifices, as well as the day-to-day operations of the Temple (Schürer 1973–87: 2: 570–2). The natural corollary of this, which is also in keeping with a Jewish tradition that goes back to the beginning of the Second Temple period, is that the Temple's premier official, the high priest, functioned as the formal leader of the Jewish public in Judaea. He also enjoyed great influence, even if less formal power, in the Diaspora (Goodblatt 1994: 6–56). After the Temple was destroyed, Roman authorities decided, unlike their practice in regard to temples demolished elsewhere, not to allow the renewal of the sanctuary in Jerusalem. As a result, the institution of the high priest lost its base of power and legitimacy. This does not mean, however, that the priesthood ceased to exist. A variety of sources testify to the persistence of the priestly status and its high social prestige up until the end of antiquity and beyond. The hope to rebuild the Temple continued to beat in the hearts of many generations of Jews (manifesting itself, for example, in the Bar Kokhba revolt), thus sustaining the role of the priests. On the other hand, we no longer hear of priests holding any official position, at least not in the three centuries discussed in this chapter (Irshai 2004).

By the same measure, there is no need to assume that an alternative leadership of the entire Jewish "nation" emerged immediately, whether by Roman fiat or spontaneously from within the populace. The Roman imperial system had always functioned, along the ancient Greek-Hellenistic model, as a two-headed system integrating local government, in the form of city councils and assemblies with municipal administrative powers as well as the right to enforce (to a certain extent) indigenous constitutions, and imperial rule, in the form of the provincial management headed by a governor and his entourage, with an army (most of the time) under his command (Ando, this volume; Lintott 1993). On occasion, the Romans bestowed power and authority on individual local figures, whether "as kings and friends of the Roman People" (what are sometimes misleadingly called client-kings) or as priests. This was the case in Judaea, when Julius Caesar recognized the high priesthood office of the Hasmonean Hyrcanus II. He also granted him the status of ethnarch of the Jews, and at the same time designated the local Jewish-Iudamaean Antipater a procurator of Judaea (Jos. *AJ* 14.143–91). By the same token, the Roman Senate acknowledged Herod's loyalty and promoted him to the rank of king of the Jews (Jos. *AJ* 14.385); later, the Jewish patriarch (*nasi*) also held the title of ethnarch (see discussion below). The same set of recognitions resonates in the official status of the high priests during the final generations of the Second Temple.

It seems, however, that the centuries immediately following the destruction witnessed a different situation. In Palestine, the Roman governor managed the province's business from his capital in Caesarea, while city councils along the coastal plain, the central hill region, Galilee, and Transjordan oversaw local affairs. When it comes to the multitudes living outside Palestine, since Jewish existence in antiquity should not be reconstructed as a monolithic, homogeneous entity (like the Jewish nation imagined in the romantic-nationalist historiography of the nineteenth and early twentieth century), we need not amalgamate all its constituents into a single coherent hierarchy. Jews were both scattered through and embedded in the multicultural and multiethnic landscape of the Roman world, in the cities of the Mediterranean basin. They were known as an ancient and honorable, if sometimes annoying, minority, united, like other religious groups and municipal associations, principally around their cultic institutions (synagogues) and communal life. The vast amount of epigraphic material from all over the Roman Empire, sporadic and vague as it may be, offers occasional glimpses into the administrative textures of these local, self-contained communities. Honorary and burial inscriptions mention time and again the "father (and at times the mother?) of the community of the Jews," "archon of the Jews," "head of the synagogue (*archisynagogus*)," as well as other Jewish dignitaries, many of whom also hold high offices in the municipal administration of their cities (conveniently and exhaustively collected in Horbury and Noy 1992; Noy 1993–5; Noy et al. 2004).

As early as the Second Temple period some informal (i.e. for the most part lacking official recognition) elements in Jewish society amassed status and power. The best known of these are the Pharisees, of which Josephus writes that their influence "is so great with the masses" that the people adhere to their guidance over the commands of the king (*AJ* 13.288). Yet the direct link that modern scholars created between Second Temple Pharisees and post-70 sages does not stand up on close examination (e.g. S. Cohen 1984a: 36–43; 1999a). Excluding instances of their self-portrayal (which tend to be found in later texts), nowhere do we find that the Rabbinic sages held the official reins of leadership in the early generations after the destruction, although they might have enjoyed some sporadic communal influence in Palestine, especially in "religious" (i.e. not civil or criminal) matters and over their own disciples/followers (Goodman 1983: 93–111; S. Cohen 1992; Hezser 1997: 329–489).

At some point – the earliest well-founded sources date to the beginning of the third century – a new form of leadership emerged: the patriarch (Jacobs 1995). The origins

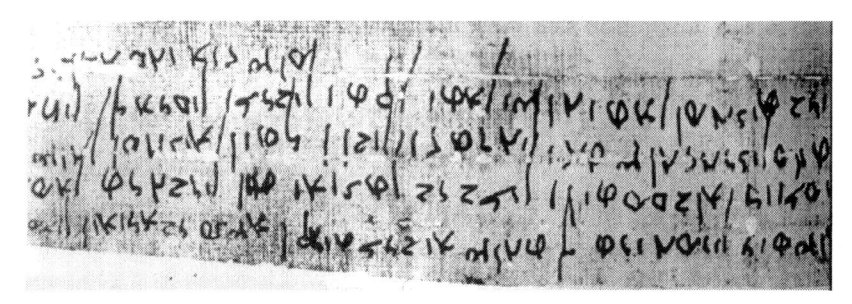

Figure 28.3 An Aramaic letter written on papyrus from the so called "Cave of the Letters" at the Judaean Desert (known as *P.Yadin 57*), communicating an order from Simeon, the famous leader of the 132 revolt against Rome, also known as Bar Kokhba, to his Lieutenant (one Yehuda the Son of Menasheh). It instructs to send him the four species required by Jewish law for the celebration of the holiday of Sukkot (note that the same four species appear in the top panel of the Ḥamat Tiberieas synagogue, flanking the two sides of the Tiberias synagogue)

of this institution, its nature, and the source of the patriarch's authority remain unclear, and are the object of speculation by modern scholars. Some believe that the Romans created the position in order to fill the vacuum left in the local government of the Jews in Palestine after the destruction of the Temple (Goodblatt 1994: 218–31). Others argue that the patriarchate was created from below, from the Jewish public (Goodman 1992), or as others maintain, only from the Rabbinic circles, and was only afterwards accorded *de facto* recognition by the Romans (Schwartz 1990). Advocates of all these views link the patriarchate intimately, at least at its beginning, to what is generally called "the Rabbinic movement." But this hardly needs to be taken as unassailable fact. Presenting a strong and early bond between the patriarch and the sages served the latter's agenda in the third and fourth centuries, as a self-conscious group seeking to strengthen their positions in society and increase their influence over Jewish life. Good relations with the patriarch, whose authority was of greater antiquity, scarcely hindered such aspirations. But the question of whether to believe this image, which derives from ostensibly historical traditions in Rabbinic literature about early patriarchs who came from among the sages, remains open at best. Simeon Bar Kosiba, the leader of the Bar Kokhba revolt, signed his letters, some of which have been uncovered in the Judaean desert, with the Hebrew title *nasi*, or patriarch (e.g. Yadin et al. 2002: 44, 45, 46, 54), and he certainly did not belong to the circle of the sages.

The later history of the patriarchate, between the fourth century and the elimination of the post by Christian emperors in the third decade of the fifth century, is easier to reconstruct. Roman law recognized the patriarchs' power to collect special taxes, as well as to appoint and remove community leaders both in Palestine and the Diaspora (e.g., Linder 1987: 132–8, 186–9, 196–7, 204–11). A variety of sources, both hostile – such as the writings of Christians like Eusebius, Epiphanius, and Jerome – and more sympathetic and admiring ones – such as the letters of the well-known Syrian-Greek rhetorician Libanius of Antioch – testify to the growing eminence and wide sway of the patriarchs over the generations, and about the expansion of their political and economic networks. Jewish inscriptions from synagogues and cemeteries in Palestine and the Diaspora supplement the picture, demonstrating the appreciation and admiration that most, though not all Jews had for this institution (Jacobs 1995).

4 Identity and Lifestyle

The question "who is a Jew?" has been answered in myriad ways over the generations. Defining Jewish identity in the ancient world involves no less difficulty, and perhaps even more. The rubric "Jewish" (*yehudi*) which began as a geographical–tribal marker (a person living in the territory called Judaea or belonging to the tribe of Judah) had by the second century BCE (2 Mc 2:21 offers the earliest testimony) developed into a signifier of cultural, religious, and national identity. Roman law (and before that Hellenistic imperial correspondence), as well as many non-Jewish authors, acknowledged a Jewish reference group with unique characteristics, and a respectable historical heritage anchored in ancient times (Pucci ben Zeev 1998; Linder 1987; M. Stern 1974–84). These sources confirm the existence of a definable Jewish identity, while at the same time assailing the signifiers of Judaism. But, more importantly for our purposes, the texture and content of that identity continued to be fluid for centuries more. Jewish identifying marks, such as dress and language, that later in history demarcated the boundaries between the members of this group and others, had not yet matured and were not sharp identifiers in antiquity. In a cultural environment in which identity is not hermetic, a person can be a good Jew, at least in his own eyes, while also being an Idumaean and a Roman, all at the same time (S. Cohen 1999b; Herod, the Jewish king of the last part of the first century BCE, represents a classic example: S. Cohen 1999b: 13–24). Alternatively, a Jew could also be a Christian and vice versa (Boyarin 2004).

Theologically, and with the aid of hindsight, it may be possible to locate clusters of ideas that could epitomize the epistemological nucleus of ancient Judaism, or at the very least denote a certain strand within it. Beyond a very superficial level, however, no consensus has ever been reached on such notions; various groups and sects differed among themselves, and within themselves, about any number of principles. Even if all of them acknowledged the importance of a given tenet in the world of Judaism, such as the belief in the God of Israel and in the traditions that the scriptures convey about him (that he created the world, brought Israel out of Egypt, gave the Torah, and so on), different people perceived the nature and essence of this God in contradictory ways. Philo of Alexandria's philosophical divinity, for example, modeled on the high god of Greek *paideia* and his subordinate agent (the *logos*), was nothing like the concrete, almost flesh-and-blood God that nearly rubs shoulders with Bar Kokhba's armies, according to some Rabbinic tales (Philo, *Quod Deus est immutabilis; PT* Ta'an. 68d). Both of these, in turn, are far from the heavenly, sometimes dualistic God that stands out in many mystical and apocalyptic works. Yet it seems to me that if we could bring Philo and Bar Kokhba together (even though historically impossible) and overcome the language gap between them (Philo spoke and thought in Greek, whereas Bar Kokhba's mother tongue was Aramaic), the two of them would have agreed that they believe in the same deity – the God of Abraham, Isaac, and Jacob, who granted the Torah to Israel.

But even this kind of consensus does not resolve the problem of identity. Diversity and flexibility characterized the ancient marketplace of faiths and views, and people mixed and matched their spiritual groceries eclectically and with no product loyalty (at least not in modern terms). Instances of unabashed gentiles who believed in the God of Israel and took part in his worship in synagogues are well documented (Trebilco 1991: 127–66). Likewise, many of those who professed Jesus' messianic status retained their adherence to the God of Israel and continued to observe his laws in later generations, even when criticized by other Christians who felt that the very meaning of their faith involved separation from Judaism (Fredriksen, this volume). Finally, many (all, in my opinion) Jews took part in the Roman experience (*romanitas*) that pervaded the Mediterranean at one level or another, and did not necessarily see this as something that contradicted their Judaism. For example, some Jews who held official positions in municipal administrations must have actively and centrally participated in the city cult, the common norm in those days, even if certain Roman legislation pronounced their exemption from such obligations (Linder 1987: 103–7, 120–4). Jewish communities that chose to depict the image of the sun god Helios mounted on his chariot and bearing identifying attributes on the mosaic floors of their synagogues offer another example (Goodman 2003). All this points to the messiness of the cultural environment of the ancient world. In such a context, it seems to me that the very act of searching for a coherent ancient Jewish theology is fundamentally mistaken, perhaps an outgrowth of the theological intensity of Christianity. For reasons that lie outside the scope of the current study, Christian thinkers tended, already in late antiquity and even more so in the Middle Ages, to arrange the set of ideas that defined their way of life into an organized system (see Edwards, this volume). In this sense, pre-medieval Judaism was, with a handful of exceptions, a non-theological religion, and to the extent that a certain framework exists it encompassed amorphous and non-compulsory traits.

More than theology, in my opinion, Judaism features a shared historical heritage, based freely and without concrete obligation on the biblical ethos. Jews identified themselves and were perceived by their gentile neighbors as the descendants of Abraham, Isaac, and Jacob, members of a nation that had been enslaved in Egypt, that had been taken out of bondage with signs and wonders, that had received the Torah at Sinai, and whose twelve tribes had inherited the land of Canaan.

In this pre-theological environment, Jewish experience centered on a way of life, a long list of details, small and large, that shaped the time and space of the individual and the family, weaving the practitioners, even if only very loosely, into what was called the Jewish people. Aside from the Temple, which in the time under discussion already lay in ruins, and the Jewish God, who naturally attracted much attention, Greek and Roman authors who wrote about the Jews took note of the unique law (the *nomos*) that set this group apart (a full collection of the material in M. Stern 1974–84); as mentioned before, Hellenistic and then Roman legislation recognized this way of life and alluded to its importance to Jews (Pucci ben Zeev 1998; Linder 1987). Its central components were:

1 The Sabbath, the seventh day of the week on which labor was prohibited, a day devoted to prayer, to family feasts, and to rest;

2   Dietary laws, which proscribed certain foods, in particular specific types of meat and especially pork, a common ingredient in the Roman diet;
3   Circumcision.

These core practices are frequently supplemented in our sources with references to burial practices, the sabbatical year, and annual festivals. Jewish writers of different traditions articulate this almost obsessive tendency to encapsulate Judaism in legal paradigms, and itemize its essence in (what we now call after the Rabbis) "halakhic" details. The roots of this legal propensity go back to the sacred writings that Second Temple Jews revered as their foundation texts; first among them are the Five Books of Moses, known as the Torah. At their core, these scriptures convey the God of Israel's requirement that his subjects strictly observe his instructions, God's precepts (the *mitsvot*). The Torah communicates these guidelines as legal strictures, dictating permitted and forbidden actions for God's people. Through the *mitsvot* the Torah endeavors to shape the Jew's entire way of life – from his diet to his farming, from his family to the marketplace and economy, not to mention his army and its wars. Of course, the Torah also devotes much attention to the laws laying out the proper procedures for the sacrificial process of the Temple, the highest institution in the life of ancient Jews (more on this below). It also specifies a series of annual feasts that created a link between agriculture and the changing seasons of the year on the one hand and the nation's mythological-historical heritage on the other, producing a Jewish dimension of time, a calendar. These holidays included festivals in memory of the exodus from Egypt (Passover), receiving the Torah (Shavu'ot), and later also the victories of the Hasmoneans (Ḥanukah), as well as fasts and days of mourning commemorating the destruction of the Temple and the exile of the nation.

Many Jewish writers from the Second Temple period recognize the importance of the divine law. Philo endows the laws with allegorical–philosophical meaning, Josephus explains them in language comprehensible to his Greco-Roman readership, while other books, such as *Jubilees*, address a solely Jewish audience (Philo, *Spec. Leg.*; Jos. *AJ* 4.196). The brevity and ambiguity with which the Torah formulates its laws stimulated different Jewish groups in the Second Temple era to interpret and shape them in different ways, each differing and disputing the interpretations of the other. The Judaean Desert ("Dead Sea") scrolls provide a lively example of such a legal–polemical discourse (esp. in the text known as the Halakhic Letter [*MMT*; *4Q394–399*]). Many of the messages that the authors of the canonical Gospels put in the mouth of Jesus also express his disagreement with the legal interpretations that the Pharisees, one of the central groups at the end of the Second Temple period, bestowed upon the Torah. Yet, at the same time, they confirm the centrality of legalistic behavior (the *mitsvot*) in his world (Fredriksen 2000: 98–106; in contrast to later Christian claims that Jesus rejected the Torah's practical commandments and advocated their replacement with a spiritual doctrine). The sages, as will be shown below, built on this legalistic mentality and enhanced it in the generations after the destruction.

One caveat is necessary in this regard: many modern scholars are not sufficiently sensitive to the distinctions between the function of Jewish law in ancient Judaism and the supremacy of Rabbinic *halakha* in the medieval and early modern world. Clear-cut and considerable differences set these two historical moments and their legal systems apart. Ancient Jewish law existed in a relatively rudimentary, and therefore amorphous state; consider only the fact that at the time, no one had yet produced a legal code that would regulate Jewish life beyond the important but rather vague statements of the Torah, whereas through the Middle Ages the great Rabbinic legal scholars including Rabbi Isaac of Fez (1013–1103), Maimonides (1135–1204), and Rabbi Jacob *ba'al haturim* (died c.1340) produced countless codices, each expanding, elaborating and clarifying its predecessors. Jews in antiquity lived in a relatively flexible and unenforceable legal environment. They were able to navigate much more freely than could their medieval descendants, who lived according to a well-organized written system of *halakha* that predominated and determined Jewish religious experience. Jewish life in antiquity should be seen as a diversified and porous continuum on which individual Jews and groups (families, communities, geographical settings) located themselves differently, appropriating some aspects of Jewish law and rejecting others, either intentionally or obliviously.

Yet another characteristic of Jewish life in the Roman world distinguished it from both later and earlier periods. Like other minorities at the time, and unlike the Jews of the medieval world (when firm boundaries, encompassing many facets of daily routines, alienated Jews from Christians), Jews in the Roman era lived in a relatively seamless cultural environment which extended to even the far edges of the empire and embraced its members regardless of their ethnic or religious orientation. Here are two examples from Asia Minor: at Aphrodisias in Caria some high-ranking non-Jewish city officials (whom this Jewish inscription calls *theosebeis*, i.e. God-fearers) cooperated with their Jewish neighbors in the establishment of a public kitchen for the needy (Reynolds and Tannenbaum 1987: 5 line 1, 26–7). In the inland city of Acmonia, one Julia Severa, a high priestess of the house of the divine emperors and president of the city's competitive games, donated the "house" of the local synagogue (Rajak 2002: 463–78).

The same social and cultural dynamics emerge from the examination of the Roman bathhouse. Scholars who have reconstructed Jewish life in the Roman world by applying norms that developed later on could not conceive of Jews being part of the cultural milieu that existed in the bathhouse. After all, this institution encapsulated the very essence of the Roman way of life (*romanitas*), with its nudity, sports, and the hedonistic fixation on the human body (Fagan, this volume). In fact, the opposite is true: not only did Jews visit the bathhouse regularly, they also lauded its benefits and partook of its cultural proceedings (Eliav 2000). This flexibility applied even to features of Roman life that at first glance seem to be highly problematic for Jews, such as the numerous statues that permeated the Graeco-Roman landscape. Rabbinic literature expresses surprisingly lenient and diverse attitudes to these statues. Even more importantly, the rabbis' views about three-dimensional sculpture are articulated in accordance with common modes of viewing sculpture throughout the Mediterranean (Eliav 2002). Magic is yet another feature that Jews happily shared with other constituents of the ancient world, as is perfectly apparent from the many magical texts (a full Jewish recipe book of magic formulae survived in the Cairo Genizah – *Sefer ha-Razim*), amulets, and curse tablets that exhibit Jewish traits, as well as numerous references to magic, not all unfavorable, in Rabbinic literature (Schaefer 1997). Such shared cultural textures undermine the prevalent modern view which reconstructs the encounter between Jews and Graeco-Roman culture as two distinct and predominantly hostile entities that at the most negotiate with and influence each other. At least with regard to late antiquity, this model must be revised.

5 Ritual

The worship of gods was one of the basic and indispensable elements of human experience in the ancient world. The period under discussion here witnessed a total revision of the ritual system in the Jewish world, one of the most significant revolutions that any religion has ever undergone. At their core, Israelite and subsequent Second Temple Judaism were cultic religions, which means that they encompassed two basic ingredients:

1. the existence of a Temple(s);
2. the worship of God through offerings – mainly animal sacrifices but also vegetarian offerings (called "meal offerings," especially all kinds of grain breads) and liquids (like oil and wine, called "libations").

In this respect, Judaism resembled all other religious systems in the ancient Near East and the Graeco-Roman world, which respectively formed the cultural environments for the Israelite tradition and Judaism. While sacrifices and offerings may well seem fetishistic, not to say primitive and absurd, to the modern observer, to ignore them is to overlook a fundamental aspect of ancient Jewish experience. To put it bluntly: on a daily basis, on the grounds of the Temple, up to a hundred animals a week (rising to thousands during the major holidays) were butchered, skinned, and finally burned on a huge altar. Try to imagine, for example, the odor – of flowing blood, of quantities of meat left out for too long without refrigeration, and the smell of thousands of pounds of scorched livestock. This is what ancient religious procedures entailed. For people of the past, these smells were sweeter than the finest perfume. In fact, a Jewish tradition configured the spatial layout of the Temple as "Mount Moriah," from the Hebrew "*mor*" – myrrh, a kind of perfume. Ancient texts tell us that the appearance of the smoke coiling up from the altar prompted the highest joy to the populace (*Sir.* 50:16–19 [Ziegler 359–40]). After all, it meant that God had received their sacrifice. This seemingly simple act embodied no small achievement in a world that had not yet witnessed the modern age's dramatic advances in the natural sciences, technological–industrial revolution, and its replacement of devout belief by secularism, all of which have radically transformed the religious landscape. In the ancient Mediterranean, gods supplied the necessary safety nets in an environment replete with agony and insecurity. They helped people interpret, understand, and control their fate. Everyone strived to be on their good side.

Ancient people in general and Israelites and then Jews in particular conceived a temple as the house of a god, any god. Within this domestic conception of sacred space, sacrifices functioned as the "communication lines" through which the public, standing outside the house (a gap representing the cosmological breach between the human and the divine), could connect with the godly entity who resided inside (*GenR* 68:12 [Theodor and Albeck 784–6] is one Rabbinic articulation of this idea). Conceptualized as doctor, lawyer, financial advisor, and psychiatrist all in one,

God existed beyond immediate reach, but remained accessible nevertheless. Accordingly, the common belief in those days held that God must dwell among his people. Judaism differed from the other religions throughout the Roman Mediterranean in that the latter viewed their gods as human or semi-human figures and therefore placed their images in the temples. The Torah insisted on the non-anthropomorphic nature of God, and thus prohibited its depiction. So the Temple in Jerusalem stood naked, devoid of statues. Instead, ancient Israelite thinkers formulated the elusive concept of *Shekhina* ("presence"), meaning that only the intangible essence of God inhabited the sanctuary (this notion finds an intriguing parallel in the Graeco-Roman conceptualization of the divine presence in statues; see Eliav 2003). Beyond this difference, however, all ancient religions shared common practices in regard to the spatial organization of worship. The Jewish Temple resembled a huge house, consisting of two main chambers: the Holy of Holies, where the Ark of the Covenant stood and God's presence resided, and the outer chamber called *kodesh* or *heikhal*, containing the sacred vessels (furniture) – the *menorah* (a seven-branched candelabrum lit with oil), a golden table holding a dozen loaves of bread, and a small bronze altar for incense (analogous in the domestic metaphor to electricity, a pantry with food, and a ventilation system; the smell was, after all, quite potent). The huge altar for sacrifice stood just outside the entrance to the building (Busink 1970–80).

Another important aspect of the cultic religion involved the location of the masses while conducting worship. They were neither permitted to enter the Temple, which was considered "sacred" (i.e. extra-territorial, off limits), nor were they allowed to participate in the sacrifice of their own offerings. These privileges were exclusively granted to the priests (Hebrew: *kohanim*), who were seen as God's servants and were in charge of maintaining the house (Temple) and taking care of the entire sacrificial process. The populace would gather in the courts and the huge compound that surrounded the Temple and bring their offerings to a certain point only to hand them over to the priests and watch the procedures from a distance. Such measures resulted in the separation of the individual from the core of religious activity, the encounter with God remaining indirect through a sacrifice that was handled by someone else.

Nevertheless, in the ancient world almost everyone seemed happy with this arrangement. Jews everywhere revered the Temple of God, even if some – like Jesus, who according to the Gospel writers overturned the tables in the Temple's court (Mk 11:15–19 and parallels) – criticized the priests who controlled it or disapproved of the corruption that developed around it (C. A. Evans 1992; Larsson 1993). Notwithstanding these occasionally dissonant voices, the Temple had, by the last centuries of the First Temple period (seventh and sixth centuries BCE), become the most beloved institution of the people of Israel. This popularity reached an unprecedented peak during the days of the Second Temple. Hundreds of thousands flocked to its compound during the Jewish holidays to be in the vicinity of God. From all over the world Jews voluntarily raised a special annual levy, called the "half-shekel," for the maintenance of the Temple (Schürer 1973–87: 2: 270–2). On the conceptual level, the Temple served as a fundamental and, in their minds, irreplaceable element of the encounter with God, the hub of the religious experience. Prayers were directed towards the Temple, sins were absolved through the offering of sacrifice, and in general the practice of Judaism was dependent on its existence. It is no surprise, therefore, that the Temple exceeded its practical religious status and became the best-known emblem of the nation of Israel (Horbury 1991).

All this changed, though not instantly, after the destruction of the Temple. Beyond the horrendous physical blow – tens if not hundreds of thousands of dead (a number that was doubled and tripled by later rebellions), the loss of property and land – the Jews remained without the institution that in their mind made life possible. It is no wonder, then, that many of them (although surely not all) concluded that Judaism had reached its end. In their mind, with the eradication of the mechanism that had linked them with God, Israel's connection with its protector had been cut off and the way of life that had been nourished by that union had terminated (e.g. 2 Bar 10 [Charles 39–41], 44 [Charles 60–1]; *tSotah* 15:10–15 [Lieberman 4.242–4]). The paucity of sources from this period does not allow us to fully measure the circulation of such beliefs. I surmise that it is no coincidence that it is in this period that Jewish groups that believed in Jesus formulated their first comprehensive narratives about his teaching. These accounts should be seen, in my view, at least in part, as responses to the vacuum created by the destruction. The gospel accounts offer a formula of redemption in place of the security that the Temple had provided. The halakhic framework of the sages also sought, in a fundamental way, to redeem the loss of the Temple by providing an answer to the question of what constituted a Jewish way of life in its absence.

In time, the synagogue filled the spatial void left by the Temple's destruction (much of the following is loosely based, although not without disagreement, on L. I. Levine 2000; S. Cohen 1984b; Fine 1997; Rajak 2002: 301–499). The origins of this institution stretch back to the centuries prior to the Temple's destruction, which explains the stories about Jesus that are set in synagogues. At that time, the synagogue was a gathering place for a local community, mainly for the sake of reading the Torah publicly on the Sabbath. But after 70 CE the synagogue's appearance and role changed dramatically. Although we cannot firmly date the stages of its development, it is safe to say that the synagogue gradually became, as it remains today, the prime locus for the Jewish worship of God, and unquestionably the most important institution in Jewish life. This role, grafted on to its original function, makes the synagogue a fascinating combination of apparent contradictions.

On one level, the synagogue seems to reverse the attributes of the Temple. Whereas the Temple occupied an exclusive and remote location that required worshipers to make a special effort to reach it, synagogues can be found in every Jewish community. A standard city averaged more than a few. In the Temple, a priestly caste served as mediators between the common people and God, while synagogue worship allowed each devotee to approach the divine equally and directly. The institution's name, combining the Greek *syn* ("together") and *agoge* ("bringing in"), literally meaning a coming together of people, or the place in which this occurred, reflects this egalitarian tendency. The congregation as a whole invokes God within the building and plays an equal part in his worship. This probably amounts to one of the most significant changes in the history of religions, and signals an important departure from the ancient hierarchical cultic world to the new, although not yet modern, anthrocentric religious system. Finally the liturgical routine and its agents also changed dramatically. The destruction of the Temple marks the termination of the sacrificial system, and eventually prayer replaced animal offerings. This change embodies a second, no less radical transformation, inasmuch as it replaces a physical means of worship with a spiritual one. Finally, without sacrifices, the priestly class lost its unique status as well as its base of social power and wealth.

On another level, however, despite these contrasts, many traits of the synagogue deliberately recall the Temple, and are meant to sharpen the sense of its loss. In doing so they necessarily fuel the expectation of the Temple's return. Despite their diversity in structure, art, and probably, although less documented, in content, almost every level of synagogue experience patently exhibits Temple-oriented elements, from the organization of the synagogue's spatial layout to the substance of its rituals. Many, although admittedly not all, synagogue buildings face Jerusalem, fixing the attention of the attendants on that distant ruin that they all expect to be rebuilt "soon, in our own days," as the closing pericope of the popular *'amidah* prayer states. Prayer procedures in the synagogue (preserved only in Rabbinic compilations and thus to be treated with caution) were modeled on, and thus propagate the memory of, the Temple's daily sacrificial liturgy. The services borrowed their names from the two main daily offerings of the Temple worship – *shaḥarit* (morning) and *minḥah* (afternoon) sacrifices. Sabbaths and festivals included an additional service, *musaf*, named for the extra sacrifice offered on those days. Even more significantly, the content of the prayers evoked the Temple sacrifice and fostered an emotional longing for its return (Fine 1997: 79–94). Finally, the synagogue's furnishings duplicated the Temple's in many, although not uniform, ways. At the front of the hall, placed on a platform (and usually enclosed by a chancel screen: Fine 1998) separating it from the congregation, stood the ark of the Torah, reminiscent of the Ark of the Covenant that resided, also removed from the public, in the Temple's Holy of Holies. A freestanding Menorah, a replica of the Temple's, decorated many synagogues in the past and to this day. Even more significantly, synagogue art in the shape of numerous mosaic floors, the most common ornamentation of these buildings, regularly depicted sacred objects associated with the Temple, as well as motifs from its liturgy (such as the binding of Isaac, with its strong connotations of sacrifice).

Was the synagogue meant to be a definitive replacement for the Temple, or was it intended to be a temporary substitute that kept the memory of the real, beloved institution fresh in the minds of the Jews? The answer is probably both. Rabbinic literature, the sole literary evidence from this period, reflects this complexity and sophistication. (It should be noted that we have no clear evidence to support the traditional claim that the rabbis shaped the institution of the synagogue; many of the available sources actually seem to contradict this notion: L. I. Levine 2000: 440–70). The rabbis simultaneously embraced two opposite tendencies. They praised and exalted the past eminence and glory of the Temple, yet at the same time created a new future without it. Such an approach proved essential for people who felt they had lost everything with the destruction, and even more for a religious system that lacked its most prominent institution. Thus the synagogue embodies two utterly contrasting claims. On the one hand, the Temple is not lost, it is here in miniature (and indeed a Rabbinic tradition labels the synagogue "a little/lesser temple," *bMegilah* 29a). On the other hand, refashioning the Temple as the synagogue actually presupposes and institutionalizes its absence forever. But there was more to it. The rabbis read the historical map correctly and understood the huge changes of their time. The Jewish people who were scattered all over the world lacked a strong center to look to. Other religious systems, like Christianity, were eschewing animal sacrifice and creating spiritualized forms of worship. In this context, the rabbis felt that an existential mode consisting of two conflicting registers – longing for the past and strong assurance about the present – epitomized the formula that could keep Judaism going.

Stepping back from Rabbinic sensibilities, the ancient synagogue emerges as a multi-functional cultic and communal establishment, diversified in its appearance and substance. Alongside the worship of God through prayer and the housing of the Torah scroll in a special ark, some communities in the Bosporan kingdom, for example, practiced and documented the manumission of slaves in this institution (E. L. Gibson 1999). Other synagogues housed the public archives of the people associated with it (non-Jews included?) and other functions of community life such as schools for the youth. Most of all, the building embodied the spatial layout so central for ancient identity – its iconography, most of which, but not all, is later than the period discussed here, brought to life and perpetuated the memories of the shared past as communicated by the scriptures, and its space provided for the various Jewish celebrations such as the Sabbath, annual holidays, marriages, and other local festivities, as well as for the enactment of local hierarchy and power (who sat where, whose honor was inscribed on stone or mosaic, etc.).

6 The Intellectual Dimension: The Sages and Their Literature

A discussion of Judaism in antiquity must include an evaluation of the sages' literary and intellectual endeavor. As noted above, the social power and political prestige that later rabbis gained, in particular after the Muslim conquest, and the canonical status of their writings at that later time, complicates any examination of their origin and development in the period under discussion here. As mentioned above, we need not accept the somewhat romantic and certainly anachronistic position voiced in the past, according to which the sages became the leaders of the Jewish people immediately or soon after the destruction of the Temple, constituting a kind of supreme council that steered the ship of Judaism and shaped its way of life. Even so, one cannot ignore the enormous literary project of the rabbis and their profound, mainly intellectual, achievements in the first centuries of the Common Era (S. Safrai 1987; Strack and Stemberger 1996).

First and foremost stands the Mishnah, the earliest known literary accomplishment of the sages. Dating from approximately 200 CE, it is a comprehensive legal text, a type of compendium (or legal anthology) to which we have but few parallels from this early period. The quality and precision of its phraseology and scrupulous editing combined with its intellectual vigor rank the Mishnah at the top of the ancient world's legal documents. The view, embraced by some modern scholars (as well as orthodox Jews), that sees the Mishnah as a type of legal codex, a charter or rule of behavior addressed to the public at large, meant to lay out and dictate the Jewish way of life, should be roundly rejected (Goldberg 1987: 213–14). Texts of such pragmatic nature are well known in the Middle Ages, for example Maimonides' *Mishneh Torah* and later on Joseph Karo's *Shulḥan Arukh*. The earliest such works date back to the end of the Byzantine period and were discovered in the Cairo Genizah (a repository of ancient Jewish texts that was discovered in the nineteenth century), and the genre continued to evolve in Persia after the rise of Islam under the guidance of a group known as the Gaonim, hundreds of years after the Mishnah. The editors of the Mishnah executed an entirely different agenda, evident in the simple fact that the work does not provide a clear and unambiguous legal ruling on nearly any subject. On the contrary, its editors gathered and then offered several opposing positions on each and every issue. Those who wish to conduct their life according to the Mishnah would quickly find themselves at a dead end. Whose views are they to follow? Rabbi Eliezer's, Rabbi Yehoshua's, Rabbi Meir's, or Rabbi Shimon Bar Yoḥai's? Lacking the sophisticated hermeneutic tools that developed in much later generations which would enable them to choose between opposing positions, there is no way of deciding between the disagreeing voices of the Mishnah, and the editors were apparently uninterested in reaching such a verdict. Furthermore, from the work's first line, the text ignores the larger public (most of whose members did not, in those days, know how to read: Hezser 2001). It requires prior knowledge of nuances and complex legal concepts that the sages had developed. The Mishnah itself does not convey this preliminary knowledge, and without it the text is accessible only to those conversant with the sages' legal thinking – a doctrine so difficult to grasp that the untrained person could hardly understand it. The Mishnah contains no hint that its editors presumed, expected, or hoped that their text would turn out to be what it eventually became, a Jewish foundation document of the same, and in some cases even higher, standing than the Torah itself.

Apparently, the original target audience of the Mishnah was the sages themselves. The work sought to collect and summarize their legal project. Understanding this is inextricably linked to a balanced appreciation of the sages' position in Jewish society after the destruction of the Second Temple. As noted above, I view them as individual intellectuals, with at most a handful of them gathered at any given time around a revered teacher (Hezser 1997). They were legally inclined, erudite scholars who devoted their lives to the study of the Jewish scriptures, and to examining them through legal paradigms. They developed methods for explicating and interpreting texts, some very original; others had been known to previous learned Jews in the Second Temple period (such as the people of Qumran); still others were borrowed from the Mediterranean non-Jewish intellectual milieu, which itself had a long tradition of textual and legal analysis (Lieberman 1941: 47–82; and somewhat differently in the articles collected in Hezser 2003). The destruction of the Temple, and the fact that the Romans prevented its rebuilding, produced an existential challenge that spurred and nourished the sages' creative work. It posed a key question that lay at the foundation of their enterprise: What constitutes Jewish life in the absence of the Temple?

Individual sages pursued their study for several generations until, at the end of the second and the beginning of the third centuries, the conditions were right for the collection, editing, and production of a summary document. It was a huge undertaking that required intense organization and significant financial support. Emissaries had to be sent out to gather the material; scholars had to elucidate, arrange, organize, and edit it; scribes had to copy it and produce drafts. Carrying out this endeavor required a figure of authority and vision. Apparently all these conditions came together in the persona of Rabbi Judah "the Prince" (*ha-Nasi*, also translated "the

Patriarch"). Peeling away the myths and legends that collected around this character in later generations, we encounter a member of the patriarchal family, perhaps the richest clan in Palestine, who found his way to Rabbinic circles, first as a student and later as an esteemed teacher. I have already argued that the production of the Mishnah supplied the impetus for the amalgamation of the class of sages, rather than vice versa. The Mishnah wove the fabric that brought together individual intellectuals who had previously been linked, if at all, only loosely and informally, and turned them into a group founded on recognition of the importance of the text it had created.

The third century opened a new stage in the history of the sages. First, they diverted their intellectual focus from the scriptures to the Mishnah itself. Some of the rabbis, apparently displeased with the final product, launched a supplementary work, the *Tosefta*. But this new composition assumed the Mishnah's internal organization – six "orders," each covering a large category of subjects, and further divided into subsections called tractates – so acknowledging its appreciation of the older work. In the third century we also hear, for the first time, of organized centers of learning – the yeshiva – some with dozens of students, who arrived from distant communities, like Persia, to hear the teachings of the sages and study the Mishnah (L. I. Levine 1989: 25–9; cf. Hezser 1997: 195–214). Some of them even transported the Mishnah outside the borders of the Roman Empire and founded centers of study in Sasanid Persia. Other works amassing the sages' commentaries on the Bible – called "*midrash*" – began to appear at this time as well. It is in the third century that we can first really talk about a movement led by the sages, even if they still had a long way to go until they were accepted by all strata of the Jewish public and the legal products of their scholarship – the *halakha* – became the obligatory infrastructure of Jewish life. That happened only after the rise of Islam, outside the traditional borders of the Roman world, in Persia, and from there back to Palestine, and thence to North Africa and Europe.

CHAPTER TWENTY-NINE

Christians in the Roman Empire in the First Three Centuries CE

Paula Fredriksen

1 Prelude: The Fourth-Century Watershed

Our view of Christians in the Roman Empire during their first three hundred years is profoundly affected by what happened both to Christianity and to the empire in the course of the fourth century. In 312 CE, Constantine began Christianity's conversion to a form of imperial Roman religion. Becoming the patron of one branch of the church, he used his prestige, his authority, and a good deal of publicly-funded largesse on behalf of this now-favored community. As Constantine consolidated his own power, so too did those urban bishops upon whom he increasingly relied as ad hoc administrators of welfare and justice (Drake 2000: 309–440). Throughout the course of the fourth century, interrupted dramatically but only briefly by the reign of Constantine's pagan nephew Julian (361–3), imperial and ecclesiastical politics grew increasingly entwined. The emperors were always unambiguously supreme. Their support for projects important to the bishops, however, ultimately enabled the bishops to have a profound effect not only on their own contemporaries, whether Christian, Jewish, or pagan (Fowden 1978; Bradbury 1994), but also on their distant cultural descendants, modern historians of ancient Christianity.

The long shadow cast by these bishops gives the measure of their commitment to the ideology of orthodoxy. "Orthodoxy" means "right opinion." In the period before Constantine, this term might serve as a self-designation for any Christian group: "orthodoxy" is always "*my* doxy." All the various Christian communities, in their rivalry with each other, claimed to represent the "true faith," the only way. We see this as early as the late first century, when Matthew's Jesus, in the Sermon on the Mount, repudiates other Christians whose views and practices are, presumably, different from those of Matthew's community (Mt 7:15–23). And we see this in the generation after Constantine, when the political split between East and West Rome corresponded to differing theological constructions of the person of Christ. Each side viewed itself as "orthodox," and accused the other of heresy (Hunt 1998: 7–43).

What changed with Constantine, however, was the nature, and thus the consequences, of the argument. Earlier, the intra-Christian polemic between different groups had fundamentally been name calling; now, the invective of one side could inform government policy. The first Romans to feel the negative effects of Constantine's new religious allegiance, in short, were other Christians. The emperor ordered them to disband, outlawing their assemblies, exiling their bishops and burning their books (Euseb. *Eccl. Hist.* 10.5.16, 6.4, 7.2; *VC* 64–6; cf. *CTh.* 16.5.1). Such legislation, difficult to enforce, clearly met with uneven success, and "heretical" (that is, non-enfranchised) churches long continued to exist (T. D. Barnes 1981: 224). But an atmosphere of intimidation could easily be conjured, and various Christian communities could be and were targeted. By the early fifth century, in North Africa, imperial legislation and even military force would impose the policies of the orthodox or "catholic" ("universal") bishops against Christians of a rival church (Frend 1952: 227–74; Brown 1967: 226–43).

The imperial bishops' battle against Christian diversity affected more than the lives of their contemporaries. It affected, as well, both the past and the future. By banning the texts of "deviant" Christians, burning their books, or simply ceasing to allow them to be copied, the bishops got to remake the past in their own image. The only documents to survive were the ones that they approved. Countless gospels, apocryphal acts, sermons, letters, commentaries, and theological treatises simply disappeared. Some lucky manuscript finds in the twentieth century – most spectacularly, the Nag Hammadi library in Egypt, on which more below – have off-set this ancient triage. But the loss has been immense, and much of the record of the Christian past was simply effaced by the church itself.

The bishops filled this void of their own making by recreating the past in their own image, the "true" history of the "true" church – that is, of their church. Through biblical exegesis and ecclesiastical histories, they constructed a genealogy of orthodoxy that stretched from the prophets of ancient Israel (in their view, witnesses to Christ) through the appearance in the flesh of God's son, through his apostles (who in their view were their early counterparts, the first bishops), and ultimately to themselves. Christians outside of their own communities they condemned as excessively influenced by Judaism, or by pagan philosophy, or by pride. "Heretics" were innovators; the orthodox, guardians of true tradition. Orthodoxy, in this view, was stable across the ages and prior to all other confessions. Discernible in the Jewish Bible (if that were interpreted "correctly"), it was revealed once for all by Christ, and preserved unchanging and uniquely, from his time to theirs, in his true church, the church of the imperial bishops. Diversity was simple – and damnable – deviance.

The language of modern scholarship witnesses to the continuing power of this ancient orthodox rhetoric. Surveys of pre-Constantinian Christianity perforce identify these other Christian communities, marginalized only in the fourth century, as "heretical" already in the late first, the second, and the third centuries (Chadwick 2001). Such an approach implicitly takes "orthodoxy" to mean "intrinsically authentic," somehow in some special way "true." What primarily distinguished the orthodox from their rivals, however, was power. After 312, one group won in the imperial patronage sweepstakes, and the others lost. To think otherwise is simply to recapitulate in academic language the claim of the orthodox bishops themselves.

Even scholars sensitive to this problem nonetheless continue to identify these communities, as did the orthodox before them, by the names of their prominent leaders – "Marcionites" (followers of Marcion), "Valentinians" (followers of Valentinus), "Montanists" (followers of Montanus), and so on. This practice has the virtue of easily distinguishing these communities from their proto-"orthodox" contemporaries. But it only reinforces the orthodox victory, for these people, in their own eyes, were simply followers of Christ, and thus, Christians. Finally, even the terms of ancient polemic have passed into modern scholarship as categories of analysis. Historians have also described various Christian sects as overly influenced by classical philosophy, or by esoteric forms of Judaism, or by oriental cults. They do so seemingly unaware of the degree to which their views and even their analytic terms derive from and recapitulate the perspective of the orthodox, whose texts often provide our only glimpse of these otherwise lost and silenced communities (K. L. King 2003).

If the fourth century so obscures our view of earlier intra-Christian diversity, it obscures no less our view of how these ancient Christians interacted with their Jewish and pagan neighbors. Orthodoxy presents a story of almost universal hostility directed against the true church, stretching from the murder of Christ through the persecution of his saints until, miraculously, history reached a moment of dramatic reversal with Constantine's conversion. It foregrounds an image of heroic resistance to relentless attacks from furious Jews and murderous pagans, while belittling non-orthodox Christians and denying that they showed such resolve. It presents orthodox identity as distinct, unambiguous, and unchanging, preserved through a principled separation from the world, with "true" Christians assiduously avoiding synagogue and civic rituals, and any sort of friendly – or even normal – contact with pagans and Jews.

The messiness of real life rarely obliges the clarity of ideology. Embedded in the very texts that promulgate the orthodox view lies the evidence of a more complicated – and more interesting – story. To understand and appreciate the diverse practices, experiences, and commitments of these many different sorts of ancient Christians in the period before any one group could impose its own views is the goal of this chapter. To re-imagine them, we have to place ourselves back in their world: a world thick with gods and different ethnic (thus, religious) groups; a world where communal eating and public celebration were the measure of piety, which was a concern of the state. Further, and despite its roots in the farming villages of the Galilee, Christianity as soon as we meet it in its earliest texts – the letters of Paul (c.50 CE) and the writings of the canonical evangelists (c.70–100) – was essentially and already an urban phenomenon. And for its first three centuries, Christianity in all its varieties remained an urban phenomenon. To re-imagine these ancient Christians, then, we also have to place ourselves in a world where life and time were measured by the rhythms of the Greco-Roman city.

2 Gods and Humans in Mediterranean Antiquity

People in the modern West tend to think of religion as a detachable aspect of personal (and even of national) identity. We also tend to think of religion as something largely personal or private, a question first of all of beliefs. And "God" in modern monotheisms functions as a unique, transcendent, somewhat isolated metaphysical point.

What of "religion" in Mediterranean antiquity? The word, first of all, scarcely translates at all. Its closest functional equivalent would be "cult," those rituals and offerings whereby ancients enacted their respect for and devotion to the deity, and thereby solicited heaven's good will. While individual households and, indeed, persons might have their own particular protocols of piety, much of ancient worship was public, communal, and (at the civic and imperial levels) what we would call "political." Modern religion emphasizes psychological states: sincerity or authenticity of belief, the inner disposition of the believer. Ancient "religion" emphasized acts: how one lived, what one did, according to both inherited and local custom. Ancient religion was thus intrinsically communal and public: performance-indexed piety.

In this world filled with gods, some ancient communities – Jewish; eventually, Christian; also pagan (Athanassiadi and Frede 1999) – worshiped a single god as the highest one, the one to whom they particularly owed allegiance and respect. But ancient monotheists did not doubt that other gods also existed. In antiquity, divinity expressed itself along a gradient, and the Highest God (be he or it pagan, Jewish, or Christian) hardly stood alone. Many lesser divine personalities, cosmic and terrestrial, filled in the gap between the High God and humanity. The question for the ancient monotheist was how to deal with all these other gods. Different groups – and different individuals within the same group – had, as we shall see, different answers to this question. But as we imagine both Judaism and, later, Christianity within ancient Mediterranean culture, we should not conceive them as "monotheism" standing against "polytheism." By modern measure, all ancient monotheists were polytheists. It was their behavior, not their beliefs, that distinguished these groups from others.

A useful way to contrast ancient and modern conceptualizations of "religion" is to consider, in antiquity, the embeddedness of divinity. Ancient gods were local in a dual sense. First, they attached to particular places, whether natural or man-made. Groves, grottos, mountains; cities, temples and, especially, altars: all these might be visited or inhabited by the god to whom they were sacred (Lane Fox 1986: 11–261). Gods tended to be emotionally invested in the precincts of their habitation. Humans, in consequence, took care to safeguard the purity, sanctity, sacrifices, and financial security of such holy sites, because, in a simple way, the god was there. We catch a nice statement of this common ancient idea in the Gospel of Matthew, wherein Jesus observes that "he who swears by the Temple [in Jerusalem], swears by it and by *him who dwells in it*" – that is, the god of Israel, who abides in his temple (Mt 23:21; cf. similarly Paul, Rom 9:4).

Second, gods also attached to particular peoples: "religion" ran in the blood. Put differently: cult was a type of ethnic designation, something that identified one's people or kinship group, the *genos*. Herodotus, in his *Histories*, gives a clear example of this way of thinking, when he defines "Greekness" in terms of shared blood, gods, cults, and customs (Hdt. 8.144.2–3; Malkin 2001); centuries later, the apostle Paul likewise described Jewishness in strikingly similar terms (Rom 9:4–5; see below). More commonly, deities were identified through reference to the peoples who worshiped them: the god of Israel, the gods of Rome, the god at Delos, and so on (cf. Acts 19:28: "Great is Artemis of the Ephesians!").

This family connection between gods and their humans could be expressed or imagined in terms of descent. Rulers – kings of Israel, or Alexander the Great, or Julius Caesar, for example – were deemed the "son" of their particular god. Alexander was descended from Heracles; the Julian house, through Aeneas, from Venus. Jewish scriptures used similar language, designating Israelite kings the sons of Israel's god (e.g., 2 Sm 7:14; Ps 2:7, and frequently elsewhere. Later Christian exegesis referred such passages to Jesus.) Divine connections were politically useful.

Whole peoples, also, saw themselves in family relationships with their gods. Hellenistic and later Roman diplomats wove intricate webs of inter-city diplomacy through appeals to consanguinity inaugurated, in the distant past, by prolific deities (C. P. Jones 1999). Jewish scriptures frequently referred to Israelites as the sons of their god. The apostle Paul, repeating this biblical commonplace of Israel's sonship, distinguished his *genos* in terms reminiscent of Herodotus. To them, he said, through the gracious gift of their god, belong the presence of the deity (*doxa*, a reference to the divine presence at the altar in the Jerusalem temple), customs ("covenant" and "law," that is, Torah), and cult (*latreia*, a reference as well to the Temple, where the cult was performed: Rom 9:4). Later in the second and third centuries, when non-Jewish Christian communities sought to formulate their identity, they too would fall back on this native Mediterranean language of divinity and blood-kinship or ethnicity (Buell 2002).

What did these ideas about gods and humans mean practically for the way in which ancient people lived? They meant that, first, in an age of empire, gods bumped up against each other with some frequency, even as their humans did. The larger the political unit, the greater the number of different peoples, and thus the greater the plurality of gods. And the greater the number of gods and peoples, the greater the plurality of cultic practices, since different peoples had their own ancestral customs. Ancient empires, in other words, accommodated as a matter of course a wide range of religious practices. To see this accommodation as "religious tolerance" is to misunderstand it. Ancient society simply presupposed religious difference, since many subject peoples *eo ipso* meant many customs and many gods.

Second, the existence or non-existence of the gods of outsiders (those of a different *genos* or *natio*) was not at issue: people generally assumed that various gods existed, just as various humans did. The Roman practice of *evocatio* makes this point nicely. When besieging a city, Romans would call out the city's gods to come over to them, promising to continue their cult. Jewish traditions also presupposed the existence of other gods, e.g., Micah 4:5: "All the peoples walk, each in the name of its god, but we will walk in the name of the Lord *our* god forever and ever." Jews living in the Hellenistic Diaspora lived with a different pantheon than the Canaanite/Philistine ones frequently reviled in their prophet texts, and the translators of the Jewish Bible, rendering their sacred Hebrew text into Greek, seem to have taken account of this shift. When they came to the Hebrew of Exodus 22:28, they altered "Do not revile God," to "Do not revile the gods (*tous theous*)." Paul too acknowledges the existence and influence of these other gods: he demands, however, that his gentiles, if they want to be included in the coming redemption, worship only the god of Israel, and no longer these lower divine powers (2 Cor 4:4; Gal 4:8–9; 1 Cor 15:24). Short of extreme situations (like siege in our first example, or apocalyptic convictions in the second), what mattered to ancient people was the practical question how to deal with these other gods, while dealing with their humans as well. In general, a sensible display of courtesy, showing and (perhaps as important) being seen to show respect, went a long way towards establishing concord both with other gods (who, if angered, could be dangerous) and with their humans (ditto).

Third, the index of respectable cult within this culture was precisely ethnicity and antiquity. To be pious meant to honor one's own gods according to ancestral custom. People might well choose to honor gods who lay outside their inherited ones. Isis, Mithras, and Sarapis were new deities; emperors (and occasionally even governors) were themselves the object of cult (Price 1984; Gradel 2002); some pagans, continuing in their native cults, nonetheless joined with Jews both in diaspora synagogues and, until 70 CE, in the Temple in Jerusalem, to worship the Jewish god as well (Reynolds and Tannenbaum 1987; L. I. Levine 2000). Diaspora Jews also, to the degree that they engaged in athletics, higher education, the military, civic politics, drama, or music, were involved in activities entwined with the gods of majority culture (Schürer 1973–87: 3: 1–149; Gruen 2002: 105–32; Fredriksen 2003: 38–56). But this openness to other cult in principle did not loosen the ties of obligation and respect that bound people, first of all, to their own gods. Conversion to Judaism, however, and later to Christianity, demanded the convert's renouncing the worship of his native gods and pledging exclusive allegiance to the god of Israel. As we shall see, such activity did indeed lead to social disruption.

The dense religious multiplicity of the Roman world was offset by the binding power of civic organization and the imperial cult. Both were the political and religious legacy of Alexander the Great (d. 323 BCE). In the wake of his conquests, which stretched from the eastern Mediterranean and Egypt to the edges of Afghanistan, Alexander established cities settled by Greek colonists and organized along lines reminiscent of the ancient *polis*. Civic altars, the agora, city councils, schools, libraries, theaters, gymnasia – the organs of the polis, widely transplanted abroad, gave rise to the West's first experiment in cultural "globalization," namely Hellenism. At a practical level, this meant that Greek became the international language *par excellence*, whether for trade, for government, or for high cultural endeavor (*paideia*) – philosophy, poetry, music, drama. (So enduring was this linguistic accomplishment that most of the Christian documents that we shall review, even those composed in the "Latin" West, were in fact written in Greek.) Hellenism, its myriad local variations notwithstanding, facilitated communication and cultural coherence across vast distances. Adapting and adopting it, Rome extended this civilization even further. By the end of the first century CE, the expanse from Britain in the west to the edge of Persia in the east, from the Danube in the north to the African breadbasket in the south, formed an identifiable (if not uniform) cultural whole.

Through the Hellenistic city, at another equally practical level, Alexander had a lasting effect on Roman religion and politics. These cities were themselves religious institutions. Through innumerable public and communal rituals – processions, blood sacrifices, dancing, hymns, competitions both athletic and musical – citizens and residents displayed their respect to the heavenly patrons of their city, thereby ensuring continued divine favor. Further, the opening of a city council, the convening of a court of law, the enjoyment of and participation in cultural events – all these activities, which seem religiously neutral to moderns, in fact acknowledged and honored the traditional gods. (This is why later Christian moralists, such as Tertullian, inveighed against Christians' frequenting the theater, the baths, and the competitions: these were tainted with the worship of pagan deities. Diaspora Jews – and as the heat of

Tertullian's invective reveals, most gentile Christians – evidently made their peace with this level of engagement with "idolatry.") Public displays of piety measured civic responsibility. Impiety risked divine anger, which could be manifest in any number of dangerous ways: drought, flood, plague, earthquake, invading armies. Proper cult pleased gods; and when gods were happy, cities prospered.

Finally, the cult of the ruler, introduced to the West through Alexander, was adapted and adopted by Rome. The emperors, from Augustus on, ruled and protected the commonwealth as heaven's special agent on earth. After death, translated to a higher realm, they continued to serve as the empire's special agent in heaven (Gradel 2002; cf. Euseb. *LC* I.1.1: after death, Constantine too continued to exercise this protective celestial function). Such worship served to bind the empire's far-flung municipalities together both politically and religiously (again, the terms are virtually synonymous in this context). Politically, establishing an imperial cult brought honor to one's city and the potential for more direct imperial patronage. Religiously, to offer to the emperor was to offer as well for the empire.

3 The Diaspora Synagogue and the Origins of Christianity

When, where, and how, within this culture, did Christianity begin? The question is more difficult to answer than it might seem. The mission and message of Jesus of Nazareth, Christianity's retrospective founder, was addressed almost entirely to fellow Jews in the Galilee and Judaea. Jesus' message of the imminent arrival of the Kingdom of God sounded themes long traditional in biblical and post-biblical Jewish prophecy: the expectation of God's radical intervention in history, the ingathering of the 12 tribes of Israel, the righting of wrongs, the consolation of the oppressed, the resurrection of the dead (Sanders 1985, 1993; Meier 1991; Fredriksen 1999). After the trauma of Jesus' execution, some 500 of his followers (so Paul) reassembled, convinced that they had seen Jesus again, raised from the dead (1 Cor 15:5–6). They saw their experience as a miracle confirming Jesus' message: the Kingdom really *was* at hand, the general resurrection of the dead was nigh, the liberation from bondage to the evil cosmic powers of the age about to begin (1 Cor 15 *passim*).

By the forties of the first century, what would become Christianity was still a form of messianic Judaism, with a necessary and idiosyncratic twist. The messiah, they held, would establish God's Kingdom (that much is traditionally messianic). But since they now identified this figure with Jesus, they believed that the establishment of God's Kingdom would actually mark their messiah's *second* coming, since his first coming had ended in the crucifixion/resurrection. His original disciples evidently expected this final event – again, on the strength of their experience of Jesus' resurrection – to occur within their own lifetimes (Fredriksen 2000: 133–42). So too did that apostle who joined the movement a few years after Jesus' death, and whose name history most associates with the mission to the gentiles: Paul.

We know more about Paul than we do about any other member of this first generation of the Christian movement. His letters – seven undisputed ones, six more attributed to him by tradition – date from the late forties–early fifties CE. They are thus a generation earlier than the earliest gospel, Mark. Paul's letters dominate the New Testament collection, and preserve the oldest stratum of evidence available to us.

Despite his prominence in later Christian tradition, however, Paul's cultural formation differed in significant ways both from that of Jesus and from that of Jesus' earliest followers. Jesus' first language had been Aramaic. His audiences were fellow Jews in the villages of Galilee and Judaea: the only major city of his acquaintance was the capital, Jerusalem. Jesus' teachings were exclusively oral, his formal education most probably slight (Meier 1991: 253–315). The version of the Bible familiar to him would have been in Semitic languages, whether Hebrew or Aramaic. The other Jews whom he gathered as disciples from Galilee and Judaea were similar in language, culture, and experience.

Paul, by contrast, was cosmopolitan. A Jew of the Diaspora, his vernacular and his scriptural tradition were Greek. Literate, well-educated in Greek rhetoric as well as in his own religious culture (the "traditions of my fathers," Gal 1:14), Paul left behind not just teachings, but writings. He traveled broadly throughout the great cities of the eastern Mediterranean. And – perhaps the most significant contrast of all – Paul's audiences, unlike those of Jesus and, initially, of his disciples, were *not* primarily fellow Jews, but rather "gentiles," the Jewish term for non-Jews. In other words, Paul's hearers were pagans.

Until Paul had brought them his message (*evangelion*), these non-Jews had, naturally, worshipped their own native gods. Paul dismisses their former practice as idolatry, the futile worship of lower powers. "When you did not know God, you were enslaved to beings that by nature are not gods," he tells his communities in Galatia (Gal 4:8; so too 1 Cor 6:10–11; 1 Thes 1:9). Through baptism into Christ, Paul tells them, they have been freed from their bondage to these lower gods in order to worship Christ's father, the God of Israel. Purged of their idol worship and its attendant sins (fornication, drunkenness, and so on: Paul takes a dim view of the morality of pagan culture, Rom 1:18–32), these formerly pagan gentiles-in-Christ can now worship "the true and living God" while awaiting his Son from heaven (1 Thes 1:9–10). Being brought into the redemption promised to Israel through their incorporation into Christ (Rom 15), these ex-pagans will be spared the "wrath of God" which will fall upon sinners in the last days. The returning Christ, whom Paul and his congregations expect to live to see (1 Thes 4:15–17), will raise the dead, transform the living, vanquish evil, and finally establish the Father's Kingdom (1 Cor 15:23–5).

Who were these people? How did Paul find them? And how did they, as pagans, make sense of, and ultimately commit themselves to, Paul's fundamentally Jewish message? To answer these questions, we have to situate ourselves within the ancient Greco-Roman city. We have to consider, in particular, one of the most well-established groups living within the ancient city: the Jews.

The Greek diaspora caused by Alexander the Great's victories had brought the Jewish one in tow. Alexander's conquests led to the wholesale resettlements of Greek veterans, merchants, and travelers in his new territories. They drew new immigrants with them, among them ancient Jews. Unlike Israel's experience of exile, when Nebuchadnezzar took ancient Judaeans as captives to Babylon, this later Diaspora was for the most part voluntary. By the dawn of the Christian era, Jews had been settled for centuries everywhere in the Mediterranean world. Strabo the geographer and historian, and elder contemporary of Jesus of Nazareth, remarked that "this people has made its way into every city, and it is not easy to find any place in the habitable world which has not received [them]" (in Jos. *AJ* 14.115).

Establishing themselves in their new cities of residence, these Jews, over the course of four centuries, absorbed and adapted Greek language and culture. As their vernacular shifted from Aramaic to Greek, their scriptures shifted too. By about 200 BCE, Jews in Alexandria had completed the Septuagint (LXX), the translation of their sacred texts into Greek. Through this medium, Jewish ideas about divinity, worship, creation, ethics, piety, and practice came to be broadcast in the international linguistic frequency. And due to this same fact of translation, the vocabulary of *paideia* – Greek ideas about divinity, cosmology, philosophy, and government – was established in these texts. Their creative interpenetration would have enormous consequences for Western culture, as we shall see.

Living in foreign cities put Jews in a potentially awkward situation. Like everyone else, Jews had their own ancestral, thus ethnic, traditions. But unlike anyone else, because of these traditions, Jews in principle were restricted to worshiping only their own god. Some pagan observers commented irritably on this fact, complaining of Jewish civic irresponsibility, or disloyalty, or impiety, or at least discourtesy. But majority culture was extremely capacious, and respect for ancestral tradition was the bedrock of Mediterranean religious, political, and legal civilization. Thus ancient pagans by and large were prepared to respect Jewish religious difference, and even to make social allowances for it, precisely because of Judaism's ethnicity and antiquity. Where awkwardness might result – Jewish members of town councils, Jewish athletes, Jewish military men, all of whose activities necessarily involved them with cultic activities dedicated to other gods – Jews negotiated exemptions as they could, and so found ways to serve both their city and their own traditions. Eventually, once Rome ruled the entire Mediterranean, such exemptions were written into imperial law (Linder 1987; Pucci ben Zeev 1998).

The city provided one context for shared social and religious activity between pagans and Jews. Another was that singular institution common to Jewish populations wherever they were found: the synagogue.

Ancient synagogues functioned as community centers and as a type of ethnic reading-house, where Jews could gather at least once every seven days to hear instruction in their ancestral laws. Literary and epigraphical evidence – donor inscriptions in particular – afford us a glimpse of the mixed population that frequented, and supported, this Jewish institution. Pagans as well as Jews attended synagogue activities. Some, like the professional magicians whose recipes relay "magic" Hebrew words and garbled biblical images, might drop by simply to hear stories about a powerful god read aloud in the vernacular. Other pagans, called "godfearers" in inscriptions and literature, voluntarily assumed some Jewish practices: ancient witnesses most frequently mention lighting lamps on the Sabbath (Friday evening), avoiding pork, or keeping community fasts or feasts. Some wealthy pagans, prominent in their own religious communities, contributed conspicuously to Jewish ones, too: Julia Severa, a noblewoman and priestess of the imperial cult, built a synagogue; Capitolina, a wealthy woman and self-described "god-fearer" furnished an interior; nine town councilors among the godfearers of Aphrodisias contributed to the synagogue fund drive (Fredriksen 2003: 48–55).

The point, for our present purpose, is that these pagans participated *as pagans* in Jewish communal activities. The diaspora synagogue evidently welcomed the interest and beneficence of sympathetic outsiders: good will made for good neighbors. Nor did these Jews impose on sympathetic pagans a demand that they commit to the exclusive worship of the Jewish god: that was a command given to them by their god for Israel alone. Within the religious ecosystem of the ancient city, in brief, pagans and Jews mixed and mingled in the schools and in the baths, in the courts and in the curiae, and in the synagogues as well. The synagogue fit comfortably into the religiously open environment of the Greco-Roman city, welcoming outsiders while, at the same time, structuring and facilitating Jewish communal life.

Enter Paul, and other Jewish *apostoloi* of the first generation of the Christian movement. Its initial stage was radioactively apocalyptic – partly continuous with Jesus of Nazareth's own message of the coming Kingdom, partly amplified by this generation's conviction that they worked in a brief wrinkle in time, between Christ's resurrection and his imminent second coming (Fredriksen 1991a, 1999: 78–119). In the mid-30s, as the movement spread out from Judaea into Asia Minor and the cities of the western Diaspora, its apostles followed the paths laid out by the network of Diaspora synagogues. These synagogues, unlike their counterparts in Galilee and Judaea, held significant numbers of pagans familiar with the idea of Israel, and with the Jewish scriptures. These pagans responded to earliest Christianity's apocalyptic message too.

Traditions concerning gentiles are scarce in the gospels: gentiles did not figure prominently among Jesus' hearers, and accordingly occupied no major place in Jesus' teachings. But the ultimate fate of gentiles at the end of the world was a theme well-developed within other Jewish apocalyptic traditions. These traditions varied. Some prophecies predicted the final submission of the nations to Israel, others their punishment for having oppressed Israel, and still others their voluntary destruction of their idols and final acknowledgment of the God of Israel once he revealed himself in glory (Sanders 1985: 212–21). The gentiles' destruction of their idols, in these traditions, does not imply their conversion to Judaism (which would mean, for men, receiving circumcision; also, becoming responsible for maintaining Jewish customs and laws, and so on; Fredriksen 1991a: 544–8). Rather, when God established his Kingdom and redeemed Israel, according to this tradition, gentiles would be included *as gentiles*. They simply would not worship any other gods any more.

It was this last tradition, evidently, that helped the apostles to improvise in their unanticipated situation. Apostles in the Diaspora received pagans together with Jews into their new messianic movement. The non-Jews, once baptized, were "in Christ." This meant that they were in a sense already, proleptically, in the vanguard of the Kingdom. The apostles had empirical evidence of this: these gentiles were now released from bondage to their former gods and evil cosmic agents, empowered by God's spirit to prophesy and to perform "works of power," capable of discerning between good and evil spirits (e.g. 1 Cor 12:6–10). And, consistent with both the traditions of Jewish apocalyptic inclusivism and with general Jewish social practice, these sympathetic gentiles were neither asked nor encouraged to convert to Judaism as a condition for joining this new movement forming within the penumbra of the synagogue.

Their acceptance into the Christian movement was provisional, however. The proviso was this: these pagans could not continue in their native religions. Here this first generation of apostles, creatively applying an element of apocalyptic hope to their present situation, directly violated long-standing, and eminently pragmatic, Jewish practice regarding sympathetic gentiles. By the same measure, these apostles also threatened to undermine the centuries-long stability of Jewish-pagan relations not only within the synagogue but also within the larger urban diaspora community. By *not* converting to Judaism, these Christian gentiles maintained their public status, and in a sense their "legal" status, as pagans. But by exempting themselves from the public worship of those gods who were theirs by birth and blood, they walked into a social and religious no-man's-land. Exemption from public worship was a protected right only of Jews, and that only on account of their ancestral customs. These gentiles-in-Christ were violating their own ancestral customs. They were thus open to the charge of atheism and impiety, thus to suspicion of public endangerment: gods, deprived of the cult due them, grew angry.

The Book of Acts, written c.100 CE, offers a vivid and realistic description of early responses to the socially disruptive message of this tiny messianic Jewish sub-culture. Itinerant apostles were actively repudiated by their host synagogues, run out of town by irate gentile citizens, and occasionally punished by cautious Roman authorities attempting to keep the peace (Acts 13:50; 14:2, 4–6, 19; 16:20–4; 17:5–9; 18:12–17 before Gallio in Corinth; 19:23–41 tumult in Ephesus. Cf. Paul's description of his woes, inflicted variously by Jews, gentiles, and Romans, 2 Cor 4:8–9; 6:4–5; 11:24–6; also Mk 13:6, 11). In the thirties and forties, this unprecedented and disruptive policy of separating gentiles-in-Christ from their native cults gives the measure of the apocalyptic mind-set, and indeed of the time frame, of the earliest apostles. Christ would return soon; all would be finally resolved.

But as Christ delayed and the Kingdom tarried, improvisations and confusions mounted within the movement itself. Baptized gentiles began again to participate in pagan public cult, perhaps confused because, as godfearers, their ancestral worship had caused no problem for the synagogues (e.g., 1 Cor 5:11; 8:7–12; cf. 10:14; Fredriksen 1999: 128–37). By the late 40s some apostles suggested that Christian gentiles should convert to Judaism (Gal *passim*; cf. Phil 3:2–11: Paul did not like his colleagues' idea). Such a policy would be no less socially destabilizing to Diaspora synagogue communities, which might still bear the brunt of their neighbors' resentment. But at least in the instance of conversion to Judaism, these gentiles-in-Christ, socially and religiously, would have some place to stand: pagan culture had long acknowledged conversions to Judaism.

What happened next is difficult to say. As early as we have evidence of the Christian movement – which is to say, with Paul's letters – so too do we have evidence of loud and roiling internal debate. Vigorous variety characterized this moment of Christian history no less than it characterized the Judaism that was its matrix. This variety – and these arguments – only increased with time. We know that gentile Christians continued for centuries to frequent synagogues and to co-celebrate Jewish festivals and fasts, just as their pagan neighbors did (Fredriksen and Irshai 2004). We know that there were Christians who were traditionally religious Jews. (Justin *Trypho* 47.3 refers to Torah-observant Christian Jews in the Diaspora; for Christian Jews in the Galilee up through the Talmudic period, see Boyarin 1999.) We know that, by the early second century, purely gentile forms of Christianity were also evolving. We know that well-educated, formerly pagan intellectuals, turning to the Jewish Bible in Greek as the textual ground for their speculations, invented many different forms of Christian *paideia*. We know that those gentile Christians who refused to worship their ancestral gods became the target of pagan anxieties and, eventually, of pagan persecutions. And we know that a vivid and energetic expectation of Christ's imminent Second Coming proved paradoxically long-lived, characterizing many different sorts of Christianity throughout this period – and, indeed, continuing into our own day.

This inner-Christian variety, and all these continuing Christian–Jewish–pagan connections, were masked by the triumph of the imperial church. To continue our investigation of Christians in the first three centuries, I would like to trace three topics in particular that convey something of the intellectual, social, and spiritual vitality of Christianity in the pre-Constantinian period. The first is birth and growth of Christian *paideia*, what we might think of as "theology." The second is that great anomaly in Mediterranean culture, religious persecution. The third is Christian millenarianism both charismatic and erudite: prophecies of the End, and learned calculations of when the End would come. Interrelated and synchronous, these three phenomena will provide us with a sense of how Christianity developed within the context of the empire.

Christian paideia

"*Theos*" is Greek for "god." "*Logos*" means "order, reason, word." Theology is ordered, rational discourse on the nature of divinity. As such, theology was not native to any ancient religion, pagan, Jewish, or Christian.

Theology began not in temples or around altars, but within the ancient academy. It was in this sense a "secular" subject, a special branch of philosophy, and philosophy was quite distinct from traditional Greek cult. The ways in which philosophers conceived the nature of divinity coordinated with their views on the nature of time, matter, cosmos, reason, and so on. "God" as a concept was a part of a larger, ideally coordinated and rational system.

Again thanks to Alexander, these Greek intellectual ways of thinking were imported on a grand scale: Hellenistic cities had gymnasia, and gymnasia had philosophy among the subjects – literature, rhetoric, mathematics, music – of their curriculum. Rome spread this culture westwards. As a result, educated urban elites from one end of the Roman world to the other shared a common literary culture mediated by this sort of education.

Philosophical thought (especially in those forms that owed most to Plato) complicated traditional religiousness in interesting ways. "God" in such systems tended to be radically stable and transcendent, immaterial, perceptible only through mind. Though the source of everything else (in the sense that all else was contingent upon him, or it), "god" was in no active sense its creator. Defined as "perfect," *theos* was also necessarily immutable, since change (within this system) implied imperfection. While lower gods with visible bodies might seem more involved with time, the highest god, their ultimate source, lay beyond both time and matter.

Revered ancient poems and dramas that conveyed the gripping stories of gods and men clashed directly with these philosophical modes of conceiving divinity. Young men of the urban elite encountered both literatures, philosophical and narrative, in the course of their higher education. Those of an intellectual bent might resolve the tension between the two ways of conceiving divinity through *allegory*. Allegory could relate narrative to the categories of theology by reading beyond what the text merely said (say, that the god Chronos devoured his children) to divine its deeper, intellectual meaning (here, that time divides into sub-units). Traditional cult – the worship due the lower gods, for those who thought this way – in any case continued, financed precisely by these same elites.

Hellenistic Jews, themselves educated in these literatures, applied the principles of *paideia* to their own ancient epic of divine/human interaction, the Bible. They were obliged in their efforts by having their text available to them in Greek. Thus, when God created with a "word" (Ps 32[33]:6: Hebrew *davar*), he made the heavens with his *logos*. When God announced his name to Moses (Ex 3:14), the Hebrew *ehyeh* ("I am") became, in Greek, *ho ôn*, "the being" – a sound philosophical response. Diaspora Jews produced a tremendous out-pouring of literary and philosophical creations, based on their readings of the Bible. Biblical theology properly so-called commenced with their work.

The LXX or Septuagint was the Bible for Christians as well as for Jews in the Western Diaspora. For the first century of the movement, Christians whether Jewish or gentile had no other texts that they considered sacred scripture. By the turn of the late first/early second century CE, we begin to find Christian authors who define their views of God, of Christ, and of their own communities through allegorical readings of select biblical texts (*Epistle of Barnabas*). The social provenance of these biblical texts – a bulky collection of scrolls, not an individual "book" – was the synagogue, and we do not know how copies of these books came to travel into non-Jewish communities. The intense interest in biblical hermeneutics on the part of outsiders, however, gives us an intriguing measure of the availability of the LXX by the early second century CE: in the Hellenistic period, Jewish texts did not command gentile interest in nearly the same way (Momigliano 1971: 74–96). What we do know is that, by the mid-second century, forms of Christianity had captured the allegiance of members of that tiny articulate minority, the erudite pagan urban elite. These formerly pagan intellectuals applied their commitment to systematic rational thought and their individual convictions about the Christian message to the Greek text of the Jewish Bible. An eruption of intra-Christian theological dispute ensued.

The key point of debate among all these contesting Christian theologians – as, indeed, among pagan and among Jewish theologians – was the relation of the High God to matter. As these Christian thinkers defined that relationship, so too did they define the figure of Christ, the revelatory status of the LXX, and the relationship of Jews and Judaism to their own movement (Fredriksen and Lieu 2004). Three prominent second-century Christian theologians, considered together, can give us a sense of the scope of these issues. All three defined the High God, or "the Father," according to the criteria of *paideia*. Accordingly, all three agreed that only a lower god, and certainly not the High God himself, could be the immediate author of material creation. All three identified the High God as the father of Jesus Christ. All three held that the LXX, interpreted correctly, with spiritual understanding, could provide knowledge of revelation. And all three agreed that Jewish religious practice, which enacted the precepts of these scriptures – keeping the Sabbath, the food laws, circumcision, the holy days, and so on – exposed the

Jews as fundamentally unenlightened readers. In the view of these gentile Christian theologians, this intrinsic Jewish inability to read "spiritually" explained why the Jewish people had failed to grasp the essentially Christian, gentile significance of their own text.

The earliest commentaries both on Genesis and on the Gospel of John came from the church of the first theologian, Valentinus (fl. 130). The second, Marcion (fl. 140), first conceived the idea of a "new testament" as an authoritative collection of specifically Christian texts comprising a gospel and the letters of Paul. But only the third, Justin Martyr (fl. 150), was deemed "orthodox" in the perspective of the church that won Constantine's support in the fourth century. In consequence, only Justin's writings have survived. Thanks to the manuscript find at Nag Hammadi, fourth-century Coptic translations of some of Valentinus' originally Greek texts have been recovered. *The Antitheses*, Marcion's great work contrasting Jewish scriptures ("Law") with Christian, especially Pauline writings, has been utterly lost. Marcion's other great idea, however, though repudiated in his own lifetime, eventually "won." Christians did develop a "new testament," a separate canon of specifically Christian writings. But even here, Marcion lost, because his opponents' New Testament was linked to and combined with the Jewish Bible or LXX (which Marcion had rejected: see Edwards, this volume), in its turn conceived as superseded and "old."

Sharing a common cosmology from *paideia*, these three gentile Christian theologians differed in their assignment of moral value both to the lower god who made matter and, accordingly, to matter itself. For Valentinus as for Marcion, this lower god was the chief character in Genesis and, accordingly, the god of the Jews. Both saw him as the cosmic opponent of the High God, Christ's father, and thus of Christ. Thus matter itself, the chief medium of this lower god, was morally derelict. Justin also saw this lower god as the deity described in Genesis (*Trypho* 56). And this *heteros theos*, as Justin calls him, is thus properly the god of the Jews. But Justin also identifies this same lower deity with the pre-Incarnate Christ, the framer of material creation. For Justin, then, the moral valence of matter shifts from negative to positive, because Christ is its author. Consequently, Justin's Christ truly does take on flesh; the Christ of Valentinus and Marcion, matter's opponent, only "seems" to (cf. Phil 2:5–11). Justin also takes the redemption of the flesh, the resurrection of the believer in the last days, as the measure of salvation, whereas Valentinus and Marcion see salvation in terms of the soul's escape from the material cosmos. Their theological differences are all variations on a theme. That theme, however, is set not by the Bible or by the Christian message (howsoever construed), but by the philosophical problem of relating the changeless and perfect High God to cosmos, thus to time and matter.

Much more bound these thinkers together than drove them apart. But they did not see things this way. Trained in philosophy, dedicated to intellectual rigor and systematic reflection, they concentrated, with precision, on their differences. As a result of their debate, characteristic of this stratum of learned Christian writers, the old word for "philosophical school," *haeresis*, took on new meaning: heresy. What had once implied "choice" now meant "error." Diversity was lamented and delegitimated. Eventually, once one group finally had legal power, in the fourth century, such diversity would be outlawed.

The persecution of religious minorities

As soon as we have Christian writings, we have evocations of Christian suffering. Paul's version of "Nobody Knows the Trouble I've Seen" – imprisonments, beatings, Jewish juridical lashing, Roman beating with rods, a stoning (2 Cor 11:23–7) – coheres well with the picture presented later in Acts: early Christian apostles (who were themselves Jews) often met with hostility and energetic rejection both in synagogues and in the larger urban context of their mission. In the Gospel of Mark (written sometime after 70 CE), Jesus "prophesies" that his followers will experience similar harsh receptions: "They will deliver you up to councils; and you will be beaten in synagogues, and you will stand before governors and kings for my sake" (Mk 13:9; Mark's reference to "beating in synagogues" attests to his envisioning a predominantly Jewish movement: synagogues had no jurisdiction over gentiles). Such measures can be viewed as improvised and ad hoc attempts on the part of urban communities, both Jewish and gentile, to contain and control the potential disruptiveness of the early Christian mission.

By the turn of the first century, however, we already find a startling change: evidence of coercion, now directed specifically against *gentile* Christians, and exercised by government agents, civic and imperial. Throughout the second century and into the third, this pattern sporadically continues, rising to a crescendo with anti-Christian persecutions under Diocletian in 303. After 312, with the progressive Christianization of the government – and "governmentalization" of the church – religious persecutions continue, for much the same reasons as during their pagan phase. In its post-Constantinian Christian phase, however, religious coercion targeted a more diverse population. Gentile Christians (now identified as "heretics") continue to be harassed, but pagan public worship, and pagan worshipers, also joined the roll (MacMullen 1997). Whether under pagan or, later, Christian persecutors, however, Jews and the practice of Judaism for the most part remained free from government harassment, and continued to be protected by imperial law (Fredriksen and Irshai 2004).

How can we account for the origin and development of such persecution, given the practical and principled religious pluralism long native to Mediterranean culture? We should orient ourselves by thinking of "religion" in the terms that mattered to these ancient people: ethnicity and antiquity; standing obligations to one's own people's gods; the importance of public cult acts, showing – and being seen to show – respect; the importance for public security of maintaining the *pax deorum*, the concordat between heaven and earth that guaranteed the well-being of city and empire.

The problem, then, in the view of majority culture, was not that gentile Christians were "Christians." The problem was that, whatever religious practices these people chose to assume, they were still, nonetheless, "gentiles." That is, the Christians were still members of their own *genos* or *natio*, with the standing obligations to the gods of their *genos*, who were the gods of the majority. From roughly the end of the first century until 250 CE, these Christians could be the object of local resentments and anxieties precisely because they were not honoring the gods upon whom their city's prosperity depended. As Tertullian famously complained, "if the Tiber overflows to the walls, if the Nile does not rise to the fields; if the sky does not move or the earth does; if there is famine or plague, the cry goes up at once, 'The Christians to the lion!'" (*Apol.* 40.2). Jewish Christians were not so persecuted, because as Jews their exemption from public cult was ancient, traditional, and protected by long legal precedent. Ancestral obligation was what mattered.

Popular fear of this strange new group fed also on rumor, which attributed terrible anti-social crimes to Christians – infanticide, cannibalism, incestuous intercourse – all accusations that the different Christian sects also made against each other, and that medieval Christianity would ultimately fix upon the Jews. Such stories eventually lost their force: courts discounted and disproved them (e.g. Pliny *Ep.* 10.95–6 [112 CE]). Once a Christian was in court, before the governor, the matter turned upon showing respect both for authority and for the *mos Romanorum*. Would the accused defer to the governor's request? Would he honor the emperor's image? Would she eat meat offered to the gods? Some Christians complied; others refused. And as canons 2, 3, and 4 of the Council of Elvira (303 CE) make clear, not all gentile Christians saw the problem: this church council had to legislate against Christians who nonetheless continued to serve as *flamines*, that is, as priests of the imperial cult. The stalwart might end their days in the arena, robed as characters from classical mythology, sacrificed in spectacles recalling the stories of the same gods whom these Christians had refused more conventionally to honor (Coleman 1990; Potter 1993).

This first phase of anti-Christian persecution was random, sporadic, and local. The contributing role of social factors seems clear, though the actual legal grounds for persecution remain foggy. Evidence of significant freedom of movement – Christians freely visiting and supporting those arrested in jail, or Christians in custody (in the case of Ignatius of Antioch) visiting churches despite having been arrested – implies what the correspondence between Pliny and Trajan clearly states: simply *being* a Christian did not suffice to have action brought. The admiring many, who recorded and preserved acts of the martyrs, surely outnumbered the heroic (and perhaps voluntary) few.

With the emperor Decius, in the mid-third century, both the issues and the evidence become clearer. In response to the decades of turmoil that had gripped the empire, Decius mandated that all citizens participate in public cult. The protocols most especially emphasized blood sacrifices and honoring the emperor (Rives 1999). (Jews – and thus Jewish Christians – were once again exempt: Euseb. *Eccl. Hist.* 6.12.1.) The emperor did not forbid the practice of Christianity. Rather, he ordered that gentile Christians, whatever their peculiar practices, also observe those rites that ensured the gods' goodwill. His goal was not religious uniformity but the preservation of the commonwealth.

More Christians were caught in this imperial net than in the earlier, local, uncoordinated efforts. The chief consequence of Decius' initiative and of the other occasional imperial efforts that followed was an internal crisis of authority within the church over the question of those who had lapsed – an indirect measure, perhaps, of the relative proportion of Christian resistance to accommodation. Churches of various orientations continued, nonetheless, to settle into Roman society: on the eve of the "great persecution" of 303, a large basilica stood just across the way from Diocletian's own palace.

The persecution of its own citizens is to a society what an auto-immune disease is to an individual: it wastes resources, squanders solidarity, and ultimately leaves the whole much weakened. Within Mediterranean culture in particular, religious persecution was an anomaly. Yet from the mid-third century on, the Roman government, whether pagan or Christian, pursued such policies. The imperial church, once the object of persecution, shifted roles with equanimity. Augustine of Hippo (354–430), directing the persecution of Donatist Christians in North Africa, even made a reasoned theological defense of coercion as a sort of muscular pastoral care. Despite its changed role – indeed, perhaps because of it – the church nevertheless clung to the idea that the true church was the church of the martyrs (though by its own definition, those contemporaries currently subject to coercion were, *ipso facto*, "false" Christians).

Religious persecution was the expression of insecurity, and a socially enacted form of theodicy: if bad things happened, it must be that the good gods (or God) were rightly angry. In their imperial phase, these persecutions were wed to a sense of declining political fortune. Christian emperors sought to preserve the *pax dei* just as purposefully as their pagan predecessors had sought to preserve the *pax deorum*. Christian emperors persecuted those whom they deemed to be dangerous outsiders – or false insiders – for the same reasons that pagan ones had: the hope of averting heaven's wrath, and of soliciting divine goodwill (Liebeschuetz 1979: 277–308, esp. 297). Thus in 430, calling for the Third Ecumenical Council, the Christian emperor Theodosius II expressed his hope that "the condition of the church might honor God and *contribute to the safety of the Empire*" (*Acts of the Ecumenical Councils* I.1.1, 114). One year later, the same emperor wrote in his constitution against pagans, Samaritans, and Jews: "Why has the spring lost its accustomed charm? Why has the summer, barren of its harvest, deprived the laboring farmer? ... Why all these things, unless nature has transgressed the decree of its own law *to avenge such impiety?*" (*NTh.* 3.; cf. Tert. *Apol.* 40.2, quoted above, for the pagan enunciation of exactly the same sensibility).

Waiting for the End

Christianity began with the announcement that time was about to end. Paul expected to see God's Kingdom established by the Risen and Returning Christ in his own lifetime, and he proclaims this good news from his earliest surviving letter (1 Thes 1:10) to his last (Rom 13:11). Even generations after Jesus' lifetime, evangelists continued to repeat a prophecy of Jesus given to his own generation in the Gospel of Mark: "There are some standing here who will not taste death before they see the Kingdom of God come with power" (Mk 9:1; cf. Mt 16:28, Lk 21:32). Justin in the mid-second century, Irenaeus in the early third, Lactantius in the early fourth, Hesychius in the early fifth: these writers, each situated within the orthodox stemma, all asserted their conviction that Christ would return soon to establish his father's Kingdom. Much of the social and doctrinal development of ancient Christianity can be understood as ways of coping with history's persistent failure to end on time (Fredriksen 1991b).

Whence this constant conviction in the face of such unimpeachable and repeated disconfirmation? We see here the effects of the continuing combination of post-biblical apocalyptic Jewish traditions about God's final intervention in history, of the traumatic experience of persecution (which reinforced the idea that the End was at hand), and of the appeal to both learned and unlearned methods of decoding the Bible and figuring out what time it was on God's clock.

Post-biblical Jewish apocalyptic prophecy provided the material for much of Jesus' own teachings (Sanders 1985). Jewish apocalyptic hope, amplifying themes already in biblical prophecy, affirmed *inter alia* the belief that God would redeem his people, raise the dead, vindicate the righteous, turn gentiles to himself, and gather humanity together in Jerusalem. In light of Jesus' death, and then the belief that he had been raised, the earliest community added to these themes the expectation of Jesus' imminent return or *Parousia*, which would itself accomplish the founding of the Kingdom (1 Thes; 1 Cor 15; Rom 11, 15; Mk 13). The stirrings of persecution, whether as simple rejection, social harassment, or actual executions, reinforced the new community's sense of beleaguered righteousness and certain, ultimate vindication. Towards the end of the first century, John of Patmos contributed a further refinement: that the martyrs ("those who had been beheaded for their testimony to Jesus and for the word of God") would rise bodily at Christ's Second Coming to reign with him for a thousand years on earth, before a second, general resurrection to judgment (Rv 20:1–6). John concluded his vision speaking for Christ: "Surely I am coming soon" (22:20).

This last formulation touches on the formal definition of millenarianism: the belief in the terrestrial, thousand-year reign of the saints. In the course of the second century, this idea became virtually definitive of proto-orthodox eschatologies. This was so, in part, because these developed against those other forms of Christianity (such as Valentinus' and Marcion's) that asserted that Christ himself had only "appeared in the form of man" and in the "likeness" of flesh (cf. Phil 2:5) without having actually had a fleshly body. Redemption, as these other Christians conceived it, was neither terrestrial nor historical. "Time" would not end; the saved Christian would pass, as had the Risen Christ, from the lower material cosmos to the upper *plêrôma*, the realm of light and spirit, to the Father. Flesh, time, the earthly Jerusalem: all these ideas, said these Christians, showed the unhappy influence of carnal, Jewish thought, and a carnal reading of Jewish texts, on Christ's message of redemption.

By contrast, millenarianism cohered effortlessly with the points of principle in proto-orthodox doctrine. Its emphasis on bodily resurrection and historical redemption, and its focus on Jerusalem in particular, resonated with these churches' affirmation of Christ's incarnation, his bodily resurrection, and the physical resurrection of believers. Millenarianism was also stimulated by the experience of persecution. The linkage between the suffering of the righteous and their impending vindication – a tradition taken directly from Judaism (e.g., Dn 7:21; 12:2–13; 2 Mc 6:12–7:38) – supported the hope that the brute fact of persecution itself signaled the imminent return of Christ, who would punish the wicked and reward the faithful. More generally, the prophetic and evangelical lists of pre-apocalyptic disasters – plagues, famine, earthquakes, flood, or drought – studied and decoded, could be and were continuously found to fit the times. Indeed, since gentile Christians were often accused of bringing on such disasters because of their refusal to honor the gods, disaster and persecution might often coincide.

This link between keen millenarian expectation and pagan persecution gave early Christian apocalyptic writings a decidedly political slant (Fredriksen 1991b: 152–7). John of Patmos, around the turn of the first century CE, unforgettably described his vision of the great Whore of Babylon who fornicated with the kings of the earth, drank the blood of the saints, and sat on seven hills – a clear reference to Rome

(Rv 17:1–6, 9). Irenaeus, a century later, decoded the Fourth Beast of Daniel 7 and the Beast from the Sea of Revelation 13 as "the empire that is currently reigning" (*imperium quod nunc regnat*). The name encoded in the apocalyptic number 666 (Rv 13:18) was LATINUS. The "lawless one" prophesied in 2 Thessalonians 2:3–7, claimed Irenaeus, was the emperor (*AH* 5.26.1, 30.3). A century later still, Victorinus of Pettau awaited "the destruction of Babylon, that is, the city of Rome" (*ruina Babylonis, id est civitatis Romanae*) (*On the Book of the Apocalypse* 8.2, 9.4).

A vivid expectation of the end tends to be enormously destabilizing. Many Christians of various denominations during the course of the second century – the period coinciding with the onset of serious persecutions – saw visions, uttered apocalyptic prophecies, and acted on their convictions by deserting their fields, and even their towns, to greet the Second Coming. With the conversion of (one denomination of) Christianity to a form of imperial religion, the anti-Roman tenor of orthodoxy's earlier apocalyptic writings relaxed. For those other Christian communities now persecuted by the imperial church, the earlier correspondence of persecution and millenarian hope remained: "beneath the purple and scarlet robes of the apocalyptic whore...[they] could still recognize Rome" (R. A. Markus 1970: 55).

Some learned churchmen gained some purchase on millenarian enthusiasms by devising elaborate calculations establishing the age of the world. The End could not come and Christ would not return, so went the argument, until 6,000 years of Creation were accomplished. These calculations, based on creative readings of biblical numbers and symbols, have been revised continually from antiquity on into the present (Landes 1988). But apocalyptic convictions themselves remained unchanged. Stimulated formerly by civic or imperial aggression, they could later, in the post-Constantinian period, be agitated by signs of imperial decline. Thus, after 410, when Rome fell to Gothic invaders, Augustine reported a surge in millenarian expectation: "Behold, from Adam all the years have passed," Augustine exclaimed, quoting these people, "and behold, the 6,000 years since Creation are complete, and now comes the Day of Judgment!" (*Serm.* 113.8). Christian apocalypticism, the most mythological ancient belief, and the one so readily vulnerable to unambiguous empirical disconfirmation, has paradoxically remained one of the most characteristic convictions of Western Christian culture.

4 Conclusion

Energetic variety characterized the first three centuries of the Christian movement. We might, indeed, even query the use of the singular "movement" to describe what we have just surveyed. Some forms of Christianity remained comfortably within the ambit of the synagogue; others became virulently anti-Jewish. Some Christians expressed their convictions through elaborate intellectual constructions, creatively re-conceiving the theological project of post-classical *paideia*, others did so by putting themselves forward to be martyred, and still others by distilling the age of the world from the signs in their revelatory texts. Some continued to constitute their Christianity as a studied otherworldliness and defiance of imperial authority, still others by becoming the most effective urban power-brokers of the late empire. "Christiani*ties*," or "Christian movement*s*," might seem more adequate to the task of description.

Yet all of these highly various Christians, their behavioral and doctrinal differences notwithstanding, saw themselves as the recipients of salvation (howsoever defined) thanks to the mission and message of Jesus Christ (howsoever constructed). Our historical perspective can allow us to see beyond the narrowness of fourth-century orthodox retrospect, and to appreciate the wider Christian world of which "orthodoxy" itself was only a small part. It is precisely the heat of their internal debate, the contesting self-definitions of all these different Christian communities, that gives us the measure of their more fundamental kinship.

CHAPTER THIRTY

Christian Thought

Mark Edwards

Under the Roman Empire Christianity was but one of the religions – if indeed it was one religion and not a family. It grew under persecution and flourished under patronage; some authors wrote theology of set purpose, while others, as it were, stumbled on their own beliefs in works of casuistry, apologetic, exhortation, and controversy. It often happened that one man's apology was another man's heresy, one man's philosophical speculation another man's dogma, one man's defense of orthodoxy another man's gratuitous polemic. Sometimes a Christian sovereign would publish his own opinion; sometimes, in trying to appease two factions, he would be surprised to find himself the leader of a third. There is therefore no one stream of Christian thought in the early period, and a history of it cannot be a history of dogmatics. At the same time, it is a salient fact, which sets Christianity apart from the other creeds of the Roman Empire, that it formed a church, that this church was governed by councils, and that councils made pronouncements which it was dangerous for a Christian to oppose. In this chapter, therefore, I shall not relegate dogmatics to the margins, as some classicists do when writing about the church within the empire, but at the same time I shall try to deal an even hand to heresy and orthodoxy, while taking due account of the ambient culture and the plasticity of personal conviction under political duress.

1 The Uniqueness of Christianity

Whatever else is doubted – and most everything in the history of the early church is doubtful – it can hardly be denied that Christianity originates in the preaching of a Jew to other Jews. All four of the canonical Gospels indicate that Jesus proclaimed the kingdom of God to his countrymen in Palestine, thus exciting fears – or at least a charge – of insurrection, and that when he was crucified by Pontius Pilate, procurator of Judaea, a mocking rubric, "Jesus the Nazarene, King of the Jews" was inscribed above his head (Mk 15:26 etc.). This testimony is certainly disinterested, for the four evangelists are at one with Paul in holding the Jews accountable for the death of Jesus, though it is not clear from their narratives whether the chief cause of their enmity lay in his blasphemous pretensions, his infringements of the Sabbath and the dietary code, his irreverent demonstrations in the temple, or his strictures on the hypocrisy of the Pharisees, the most rigorous exponents of the Law. Gentile Christians at an early period were allowed to waive not only the ceremonial ordinances but circumcision as well (Acts 15:29); we should not conclude too hastily, however, that the Jesus of the gospels is entirely the creation of gentile churches. Although the Jewish neophytes included a number of Pharisees, and the Christian way of life was often styled a law or *nomos* (Jas 1:25; Rom 8:2), it was agreed on all sides that faith was the price of entry to the kingdom, and that love, displayed above all in the relief of the weak and indigent, was the fulfilling of the whole law (Rom 13:10). The object of faith was Jesus, as the anointed representative of God the Almighty Father; the Greek for the anointed one is *Christos*, and when outsiders coined the epithet "Christian" (Acts 11:26), it was quickly embraced by members of the sect. No doubt there were some who stopped short of worship, some who doubted the resurrection, some whose faith demanded no support from the expectation of his imminent return; nonetheless it would seem that the petition *maranatha* ("Lord, come quickly") was common tender in Aramaic-speaking churches, and Paul assured the Greeks that every knee in earth and heaven had already bowed to the "Name above all names" (1 Cor 16:22; Phil 2:9). Not that Paul the Pharisee had renounced the strict monolatry of his teachers: for him the acclamation of the One God was now inseparable from that of "One Lord Jesus Christ" (1 Cor 8:4), and the image of God had never been so plainly manifested as in the ignominy of a sinner's cross.

It is evident (or ought to be) that this cult of a "crucified sophist" (Luc. *Peregr.* 13) was as alien to Greek or Roman as to Jewish practice. A favorite might be deified by an emperor, an emperor by the Senate, and a prodigy like Alexander of Macedon by himself; a Pythagoras might leave a school of followers who spoke of him in an undertone, and statues of a thaumaturge might be credited with the power of working miracles; but no inherited paradigm – not even the death of Hercules or Romulus – can explain how a man who never professed to be more than the Messiah of Israel came to be invoked as the creator and the bearer of salvation to every people under heaven. Adoration must have been inspired by the life of Jesus, or at least by the first accounts of his resurrection; the gradual apotheosis postulated by many modern scholars lacks all precedent, and would have been, if anything, more offensive to the commonsense of gentiles than to the piety of Jews. After all, the claim that Jesus sits at God's right hand (Mk 14:62; Acts 7:56) was barely intelligible to pagans, but would have caused no perplexity to a reader of the Psalms, the Book of Daniel, or Hellenistic Jewish literature.

As a sect that took its name from its founder, Christianity was easily distinguished from the two groups that are now most often suggested as its prototypes – the Cynics and the rigorists of Qumran. The Cynics in the first century were popular exponents of frugality, who upheld the law of nature by flouting sexual and dietary conventions, by upbraiding the rich and mighty, and by mocking archaic notions of the gods. A wilful vagabond with no companion but his staff and wallet, the Cynic (if there were any such in the Jewish parts of Palestine) might have fallen in unnoticed with the seventy whom Jesus sent to preach in the kingdom of God in Galilee. Nonetheless, there was no place in the Christian communion for this king without a kingdom: there was never a school of Cynicism which lived by a common law, revered its founder, or endeavoured to build a new faith on the ruins of superstition. Numerous parallels have been discovered between the maxims of the sect and those of Jesus; no Cynic, however, was ever heard to say "Bless them that persecute you," and it was never said of one that "being reviled he reviled not again" (Mt 5:44; 1 Pt 2:23). Cynics defied the emperor, Christians made a boast of loyalty; Cynics pursued simplicity in this life, Christians prayed for a reversal of their fortunes in the next.

The Christians of this age had more in common with the Jewish recusants, possibly a community of Essenes, who settled in the caves about Qumran and left the so-called Dead Sea Scrolls as their memorial. These separatists, like the church of Jerusalem, held all goods in common; like Christ, and in the tradition of the prophets, they denounced the profanations of the Temple while insisting on obedience to the spirit of the Law. Styling themselves the Sons of Light, they claimed that they alone understood the scriptures and denied that more than a remnant of the Jews would be admitted to the kingdom. They seem to have traced their origin to a Teacher of Righteousness who was done to death by a wicked priest, and whose disciples may have suffered crucifixion. Nevertheless, although their writings entertain the hope of both a kingly and a priestly Messiah, the Teacher was not expected to rise again in either role, and there is no evidence of a cult. Nor do the Dead Sea Scrolls show that indifference to religious forms which marks the earliest phase of Christianity: the laborious prescriptions of the Temple Scroll and Damascus Document savor more of Pharisaic righteousness than the law of love enjoined by Christ and Paul.

Whether or not it was they who formed the colony at Qumran, it was the common, though not universal, practice of the Essenes to create their own societies at a distance from the centers of population. Christians, by contrast, lived anonymously in cities (*Epistle to Diognetus* 5), and there is no trace in our sources of any period when they did not participate in civic life: those who hold that Jesus came to found a band of wandering ascetics must explain why he sent his 70 ambassadors through the cities of Galilee (Lk 10:1), why the most Jewish stratum of his teaching alludes to sacrifice and ostentatious piety at street corners (Mt 5:23 and 6:5), and why the most itinerant of the apostles, Paul of Tarsus, should have thought that it was his task to build up churches in the great cities of Asia, Greece, and Italy. For all that, early Christian morality did not coincide with the civic ideals of paganism, even for those few Christians who were citizens of Rome or of some provincial commonwealth. The New Testament does not enjoin that love of all humanity for its own sake which the Stoics and their Hellenistic overlords called *philanthrôpia*; members of the church were to live and die for one another, loving their neighbors only as prospective sons of God. Idolatry and polytheism were always to be shunned; Paul deprecated, and others forbade, the eating of meat from beasts that had been sacrificed to idols (1 Cor 8:9; Rev 2:14). While edifying similes might be drawn from martial discipline or athletic competition, the teachers of the church before Constantine were inclined to frown on Christian service in the army or participation even in bloodless games (Tertullian, *On the Military Crown, On Spectacles*). The Christian magistrate was required to exercise his office with a cumbersome discretion; the conventional, and largely self-serving, practice of euergetism (see Gleason, this volume) or public liberality was deemed inferior to private charities, performed in the sight of God alone, and chiefly for the benefit of those who would not be able to repay.

Abraham, the forefather of Israel, set an example to all believers when he left Chaldaea and sought the unseen city (Heb 8–10); yet Christians did not imitate the Jewish exegete Philo in describing him as a citizen of the world. Even Roman citizenship – which Paul, a Greek of Tarsus and a Jew of the tribe of Benjamin, was not ashamed to plead for his own protection (Acts 22:25) – was of no account when set against the franchise of the heavenly Jerusalem. The price of becoming Roman, for those who were not already so by origin, sank to nothing in 212 when Caracalla granted citizenship to every freeborn person in the empire; the privileges of Christians, on the other hand, were "bought at a great price" (1 Cor 6:20; cf. Acts 22:28) even when they lived in peaceful times. "My kingdom," Jesus said, "is not of this world" (Jn 18:36), but his people were; prohibited by devotion to the one Lord Christ from offering sacrifices to the emperor, they pre-empted, and therefore challenged, Rome by abolishing the distinctions between barbarian, Jew, and Greek. While the church made no attempt to part slaves from their masters, it taught that all were free in Christ, and ecclesiastical rank was not determined by position in society. This was a religion born in prophecy, and, though the desire to suppress false prophecy would in the end result in the extinction of the living voice, no book in the second century was of more authority than Revelation. Here Rome was personified as Babylon the great whore, and it was widely held that a name associated with the city was connoted by the cipher 616 or 666 (Rv 17:5 and 13:18).

2   The Era of Debate

All surviving Christian literature after the apostolic period was produced by gentiles. Their first task, then, was not to refute or assimilate Judaism but to define the belief and practice of the church itself; their second was to prove that a gentile convert had good reason to abandon the religion of his childhood. Modern talk of identity, self-definition, apologetic, and polemic often threatens to obscure the fact that when a person adopts a new philosophy, he will feel, before he starts to vindicate it to outsiders, that he needs to justify it to himself and to harmonize it with those elements of his previous education that he wishes to retain. Second-century churchmen made pronouncements that can now be cited in histories of dogma; their aim, however, was not to resolve intestine controversies, but to strengthen perseverance and to demonstrate to pagans that the God of Jesus Christ, having made the world and thus the empire, would infallibly be its judge.

Ignatius, Bishop of Antioch, was perhaps the earliest writer to say explicitly that Christ was God and man, and to make obedience to the clergy a condition of salvation. Those who belittled Christ were the docetics who maintained that he was man in appearance only and had therefore never suffered; the factions of the church included celebrants of a private Eucharist and Judaizers who displayed the outward works without circumcision (Ign., *Phld.* 6). It is possible that all the schismatics formed a single party; certainly it was equally convenient in a season of tribulation to deny that Christ had suffered, to secede from the visible church and to conform to the practice of the synagogue. To all three errors Ignatius gave the same answer as he passed through Asia to martyrdom in Rome. If Christ had been a phantom or an angel, why should his human followers submit to pains that he had only pretended to undergo? How can a congregation be divided in its worship if the Eucharist is the flesh and blood of the undivided Savior? How can we let a Judaizer challenge us for a proof from the so-called archives when our archive is the one Lord Jesus Christ (Ign., *Phld.* 8)? Should it be said that Christ is now invisible, and the episcopate is our guarantee of unity; by presiding at the Eucharist, the bishop reminds the people that they are all one body in the Christ who died for them, sustaining them with a medicine of immortality, in contrast to the medicine of death that is purveyed by those who stand outside the altar (Ign., *Eph.* 20; *Tr.* 6). The bishop is the apex of a threefold order of ministry: after him come the presbyters or elders and then the deacons, who, as servitors to the clergy and the laity, are an earthly type of Christ (Ign., *Tr.* 3).

Ignatius was the first spokesman of a "catholic" church (*Sm.* 8.3), and the only one of the Apostolic Fathers who came close to the formulation of a creed. For a comparable fusion of Christology with the doctrines of salvation and the church we must look, not to these contemporaries, but to a generation of innovators, then decried as heretics and now conventionally labeled Gnostics. As the Fathers insisted, however, Gnosticism was no more a single heresy than its putative helpmeet Middle Platonism was a school. Most scholars now know better than to caricature every Gnostic as an arch-dualist, who equated matter with evil, regarded incarnation and resurrection as degrading to the spirit, and substituted nebulous myths for the plain sense of the scriptures. Even before the discovery of the Nag Hammadi Codices in 1945, it was all too clear that these simple notions were incompatible with the ancient charges that Apelles attributed eternal flesh to Christ, that Valentinus foisted the properties of matter on the Godhead, and that Marcion put too literal a construction on the prophets and the Law. If we believe Hippolytus, the first men to describe themselves as Gnostics (he prefers to call them serpent-folk, or Naassenes) professed a *gnôsis* or knowledge not primarily of God or of the soul, but of the truths concealed in the mysteries, mythologies, and scriptures of the nations (Hipp., *Ref.* 5.6–11). The theme of the Naassene Sermon – a catena of testimonies from all religions, not excluding Christianity – is that matter and spirit were at first a "single blessed substance," an undifferentiated sea of being. Now that the waters have parted, a benevolent Creator sits above, a fiery Demiurge below, and seeds of spirit are in constant pilgrimage from one side of the firmament to the other. The initiate in the lower realm will yearn to ascend, but rather by the sublation than the rejection of the body, as the Naassenes taught by adopting the symbolism of alchemy.

It has been maintained that Gnosticism was not so much a heresy as a Hellenization of Christian thought, or else a distinct, more primitive religion of the Mediterranean world. Such theories may commend themselves to those who think it possible to distinguish between the Palestinian yolk of Christianity and the Hellenistic albumen which nourished it; but since most scholars now acknowledge almost as many varieties of Judaism as of Hellenism, it seems wiser to assume that Christianity was complex even in embryo, and kept pace as it matured with the development of the womb that gave it birth. If there was ever an independent Gnosticism, it left no trace of itself in archaeology or in the works of any heresiarch who did not purport to be a

Christian. If their doctrines had been too exotic to be reconciled with the apostolic literature, such teachers could not have hoped to gain a following, and they would not have been the ones to set a precedent for treating the works of Paul and the evangelists as scripture. Basilides of Egypt, for example, was a pioneer in the fertile vein of negative or apophatic theology, which denies that even the most exalted predicates can be applied to God (Hipp., *Ref.* 7.2–27). Nevertheless, he says, the ineffable Father has revealed himself through three descending Sonships, each of which brings order to the ferment of creation, then assumes its destined place, with its proper retinue, on one side or another of the heavens. Much remains obscure, but as Basilides is alleged to have composed the earliest commentary on John's Gospel, we may plausibly surmise that his three Sons are also those of the Evangelist: the Son of God in the bosom of the Father, the Son of Man ascending where he was before, and the Son of Man as he toils with the elect.

Salvation is thus prefigured in cosmogony – a trope which may reveal that Basilides understood both the pagan mysteries and the Book of Genesis better than his orthodox co-religionists. A similar reading seems to be demanded by the tragedy of Sophia, which was always associated in antiquity with another Egyptian Christian, Valentinus. It probably originates, however, in Ignatius' bold description of the incarnate Christ as the "word who proceeds from silence" (*Mg.* 8.2) – that is to say, from the virgin womb and the secret counsel of God. In the Valentinian myth this silence is personified as the consort of the Father, now conceived as an unfathomable abyss (Iren., *AH* 1.1–5). The aeons or ages springing from their union make up the *plêrôma*, or fullness, of the Godhead. The last of these, Sophia or "wisdom," falls from the *plêrôma* when she endeavors to create without a consort or to plumb the ineffable being of the Father. She spawns a son, the Demiurge, who proclaims himself the only God and fashions the material world as a feeble copy of the divine original. This pretender is evidently the Yahweh of the Old Testament, the totem of the Jews and of "psychic" Christians who possess soul but not spirit and remain in willing bondage to the Law. Meanwhile the entire *plêrôma* brings forth Christ and the Holy Spirit for the redemption of Sophia, but it is her task to emancipate her spiritual children, the Valentinian elect. The story of the fall of Eve is thus turned into an allegory of our common human tendency to fall into idolatry by overreaching the limits of our wisdom; as in Paul the fullness of the Godhead dwells in Christ, but only the spiritual perceive this, while the psychics put their faith in Moses or some other creature. Whereas Paul declared that the crucifixion was a stumbling block to the wisdom of Jews and gentiles, Valentinus postulates two crosses – first a heavenly one, dividing the other aeons from Sophia, then an earthly one on which the embodied Christ (in the *Gospel of Truth*) became the first fruits of the *plêrôma*. Purified flesh is promised in the *Letter to Rheginus* to those who enter into the aeon; a purified understanding of the Old Testament reveals that it is partly inspired and partly consummated in the New.

Less mythical in form, and thus more obviously at odds with the mind of the primitive church, is Marcion's dichotomy between the God of Moses and the father of Jesus Christ. The first is just, the second good; the second redeems the spirit from the world that the first created for the flesh. Marcion's canon allegedly consisted of a few truncated letters of Paul and the tatters of Luke's Gospel; his strictures on the Old Testament, which he rejected in its entirety, were fully, though obliquely answered in Justin Martyr's *Dialogue with Trypho*. This work was designed ostensibly to convince a Jew that Christ was the Messiah, and his church therefore the Israel, of the prophets. The tone, like that of an earlier text ascribed to Paul's friend Barnabas, is hostile to Judaism: where Barnabas maintains that the outward rite was a misconstruction of a precept addressed to the inner man, Justin argues that it foretold the severance of the Jews from God (*Barn.* 9.4; Justin, *Trypho* 16). He further enhanced the authority of the Old Testament – or at least the Greek version of it – in his *Apologies*, where he urged that the loftiest thoughts of the philosophers had been stolen from the prophets. Justin's "spermatic logos" works primarily through this licensed plagiarism, not by direct inspiration (*1 Apol.* 44). Despite his Platonic schooling, he is therefore not the humanist that he is often supposed to be; when he uses Logos as a title of Christ it means to him what it means in the Gospel of John – the word of God in creation and in prophecy – rather than what the Platonists meant by this term or by *nous*. Still less is the Christian Logos derived from that of the Stoics, which is not a subaltern deity but Zeus himself, though at the same time (as Justin protested at *2 Apol.* 7) immanent in and coeval with the world.

Martyred around the year 165, Justin was a touchstone of orthodoxy in the eyes of Irenaeus, Bishop of Lyons, two decades later. In his skilful "Refutation of Gnôsis falsely so-called," Irenaeus accuses the Valentinians of slighting the incarnation, the resurrection, and the unity of God. Rejecting the possibility of change or emanation in the Godhead, he foreshadows the later doctrine that the three hypostases (Father, Son, and Spirit) are coeternal (Iren., *AH* 2.12–13); he also threatens to turn a commonplace into a heresy, for most of the second-century apologists had preserved their monotheism by maintaining that the Logos was initially no more than the immanent thought of God the Father, and had become distinct from him only when the thought was enunciated as the edict of creation. Irenaeus is equally innovative in anthropology, for he urges (against the Gnostics, and indeed most future Christians) that the whole of the human frame, including the body, has been fashioned in the image of its Creator (Iren., *AH* 5.6.1). He must therefore suppose that the Logos was eternally resolved to become incarnate – his argument implies, indeed, that without this manifestation of divinity, the human race could not achieve its end. Adam and Eve in Eden, he contends, were only capable of perfection, not yet perfect, and, as he believes perfection to consist in virtue freely chosen, he grants to the Valentinians that God would be unjust if he deprived us permanently of the knowledge of good and evil. To eat the fruit of knowledge was therefore not an act of wickedness but, like the sin of Sophia, a premature striving for the good (Iren., *AH* 4.38–9). Now that Adam's offense has made us mortal, the way to immortality is to exercise our freedom in obedience to God, and thus to mature into the likeness which was not initially given with the image. In our present condition this would be impossible, had not Christ by his free obedience reversed the disobedience of Adam, conquered Satan, and released us – by persuasion, not by force – from the toils of hell (Iren., *AH* 5.1; 5.20). The fall is not so catastrophic, the cross not so divisive, the world not quite so demon-ridden in the sober exposition of Irenaeus as in the myths of his adversaries; it was thanks to him, however, and therefore thanks to them, that these themes were restored to the central place in Christian thought that they had occupied in Paul.

3 The Era of Dogmatic Formulation

It cannot be true, as many have asserted, that the Christian world had no criterion of orthodoxy before the third century. The Fatherhood of the one God and the Lordship of Christ were universal axioms, though contention might arise when different parties undertook to render these axioms more persuasive to themselves or to outsiders. So far as we know there was never a congregation without some notion of a scripture: most groups claimed the authority of at least one of the apostles, and Marcion was perhaps the only teacher who rejected the Old Testament *in toto*. The letters of Ignatius do not indicate, as Bauer supposed (1972), that some desired a church without any bishop, though it would seem that not everyone held so high a view of the bishop's office. Irenaeus feels obliged to defend the fourfold canon of the Gospels, but he implies that this was the norm in churches governed, like his own, by a strong episcopate; wherever we find evidence of such an institution at the end of the second century, we also find, as Irenaeus himself predicts, a common rule of faith (Iren., *AH* 3.2–3).

In the third century, while it was the bishops who maintained this rule of faith, it was the task of laymen or dissentient clerics to expound it, to confirm it from the scriptures, and to elaborate it with ratiocination. Tertullian of Carthage was the first and most belligerent of Latin theologians. He is often called a schismatic, but to him the true schismatics were the "psychics" who were not quickened by the "new prophecy" of the Phrygian Montanus. Even when he began to shun his lukewarm co-religionists, he did not attempt to form a rival clergy; he had no cause to do so, for he could preach new fasts, forbid remarriage even after widowhood, and refuse forgiveness to sinners whom the episcopate absolved without being thought to lay a new foundation for Christian belief. In his *Apology* of 197, he ridicules the manmade gods of Rome and pleads that Christians are innocent of any act that would warrant persecution. From Moses, whom he proves to be more ancient than any pagan source, he demonstrates the unity of God; Christ he represents, in the manner of the Greek apologists, as a supervenient being, the latent reason of the Father taking shape as concrete speech for the creation and redemption of humanity (*Apol.* 21). He upholds the same view with the vigor of the new prophecy in his strident work *Against Praxeas* (c.207), where he also coins the word *trinitas* and bequeaths at least a lexical norm to western Christianity by distinguishing the one substance of the Godhead from the three persons who are Father, Son, and Spirit. Praxeas was one of a numerous party of "monarchians" who maintained that the three were merely different phases of one being; Tertullian's case for the Trinitarian view proceeds with a confident inconsistency – sometimes tending to tritheism, sometimes threatening to reduce the Son and Spirit to epiphenomena of the Father – which suggests that he saw himself as the mouthpiece of an established dogma. Even his premise that God, like every actual being, must be a *corpus* or body, does not seem to have been derived from the Stoics, for he implies that this is not a body of matter (*Adv. Prax.* 8). On the other hand, he draws openly and freely on the Stoics in his lengthy treatise *On the Soul*, with the aim of proving that the soul, being as material as the body, is not naturally immortal and disposed to transmigration as the Platonists affirmed. Tertullian was a Montanist when he wrote this catholic masterpiece, as he was when he completed his five books *Against Marcion*, arguing, with greater skill than any previous writer, for the salvation of the body, the authority of the Old Testament, and the integrity of Luke.

Tertullian therefore cultivates philosophy in fields that he believes to have been left fallow by the apostles. His Greek-speaking contemporary Hippolytus maintained in his *Refutation of all Heresies* that every pagan system was both false in itself and fatal to the orthodoxy of Christian adherents. In Alexandria the eminent theologians were at once less contumacious to the episcopate and more generous to Greek culture. Clement, head of the Catechetical School, set out to demonstrate, in the eight books of his *Strômateis* or *Miscellanies*, that the best thoughts of the Greeks concurred with the biblical revelation, and conversely that philosophy was a serviceable discipline for those who wished to graduate from simple faith to the wisdom of the true Gnostic. Those who condemn his "intellectualism" fail to see that, just as philosophy for its zealots was not merely a school of reason but a way of life, so *gnôsis* in Clement signifies the perfection of obedience and not merely a refinement of theology. Nor, though he admired Plato more than any of his rivals, does he deserve to be called a Platonist: he never accepts a doctrine on the authority of Plato, seldom borrows Plato's vocabulary except when quoting him, and attributes his discoveries not to native shrewdness or direct inspiration, but to a holiday in Egypt where he stumbled across the Book of Jeremiah. Philosophy may help us to elucidate the truth, but it is God who has revealed it through the Logos. It is true that Clement says little of a historical Incarnation, of a bodily resurrection, or of anything else that cannot be harmonized with pagan doctrines; but that is because the object of the *Strômateis* is to illustrate this harmony, and if we had more of his *Hypotypôseis*, or *Outlines of Theology*, we might find the peculiar tenets of Christianity discussed with less reserve. He was not always deferential to the philosophers, for even when he contends in his *Protrepticus* that they too despised the atrocities of popular religion, he implies that, not being Christians, they lacked the courage to die for their beliefs.

Nor should we be too eager to make a Platonist of Origen, who is said to have succeeded Clement as president of the Catechetical School. His reputation as commentator and preacher flourished after he decamped to Palestinian Caesarea and was illegally ordained as a presbyter. He was persecuted, however, by the jealous Bishop Demetrius of Alexandria, and suspected by some contemporaries of heresy; in 553 the Fifth Oecumenical Council denounced 15 propositions widely associated with his name. Of these the one that has come to define Origenism states that souls exist before embodiment, and descend by their own inertia into the bodies of angels, human beings, or devils after tiring of the contemplation of God. The evidence of his own works, however, suggests that he entertained at most the first half of this thesis, which by itself is neither Platonic nor heretical; he certainly did not accept the transmigration of souls, and he maintained that the body, suitably attenuated and purified, participates in the sanctification of the inner man (*C. Cels.* 5.18–23 etc.). His purpose, as he states in the introduction to his treatise *On First Principles*, is to uphold the rule of faith, speculating only where the apostles left a matter undetermined, and he admonishes a pupil that the function of Greek learning – whether in grammar, rhetoric, history, or philosophy – is to elucidate the obscurities of scripture (*Ph.* 13). With these auxiliaries we may arrive at a consistent and intelligible paraphrase of the letter, but the sacred book must be its own interpreter in the quest for the higher or mystical intention. This is present and mandatory even where the literal construction is untenable, since every word is a manifestation of Christ the Word of God (*Ph.* 4). Most passages have a threefold signification by analogy with the threefold division of the human person into body, soul, and spirit (*De princ.* 4.2.4); 1 Thessalonians 5:23 is the source of this trichotomy, which a Platonist could only have elicited with difficulty from the *Axiochus*. In any case the Platonists had only begun to flirt with allegory, and neither they nor the Stoics (who are invidiously associated with Origen by Porphyry at Euseb. *Eccl. Hist.* 6.19) had yet shown such assiduity in the exposition of a classic text. His only predecessor in this marriage of exegesis with philosophy was Philo of Alexandria, in this respect not so much a Middle Platonist as a Jew.

In Alexandria, as elsewhere, it was necessary to urge against the monarchians that such titles as Wisdom, Word, and Power did not imply that the Son was less substantial than the Father. On the contrary, says Origen, since God cannot change, the distinctions that we express by the formula "three hypostases" must be eternal; and if Christ is the Wisdom of God there was no time when he was not, or there would have been a time when God was without his wisdom. This reasoning entails that the three hypostases are coeternal, not that they are equal: commenting on John 1:1, where the Father is styled *ho theos* (God) and the Logos merely *theos* (god), Origen calls the Father *autotheos*, as the one who is by nature what the Son and the Spirit are by derivation (*In Joh.* 2.2). With Proverbs 8:22 in mind, he can even say that the Son is the one true creature of the Father, whereas everything in the world is not so much created as made by the Son himself (Justinian, *Letter to Mennas*). He has, however, no term (other than *theos*) to express the common essence of the three hypostases, and he seems at times to imply that they are united not in essence but in will (*C. Cels.* 8.12).

An extreme proponent of the monarchian doctrine, Paul of Antioch (more commonly known as Paul of Samosata), was condemned by a council of his fellow bishops in 268. An extreme proponent of the three hypostases, the Alexandrian presbyter Arius, went so far as to say that the Son was created out of nothing, and perhaps (though this is not certain) that he was quite unlike the Father. In 325 the Christian Emperor Constantine, having recently become master of the east, convened a council of about 200 bishops at Nicaea in Asia Minor to adjudicate a number of controversies, including the one provoked by Arius. The bishops agreed to designate what the Father and Son had in common by the adjective *homoousios*. This was not the last word but the first of many, for there was no accord on the meaning of the term. The Alexandrian bishops Alexander and Athanasius took it to mean that the two were identical in nature, while Eusebius of Caesarea, the great historian and apologist, insisted that it betokened only a similarity of attributes (Socr., *Hist. Eccl.* 1.6–8). Some objected that it was unscriptural, or had hitherto been used only to say that two material things were of the same stuff; others, like Marcellus of Ancyra, may have inferred that, since *hypostasis* and *ousia* were almost synonyms in ordinary usage, there was only one hypostasis in the Godhead. Small wonder then that in 341 a council held in Antioch drafted four new creeds without the word *homoousios*, and that 40 years of internecine wrangling intervened before the Second Oecumenical Council in 381 was able to proclaim in the name of Christendom that the Son (though not the Spirit) was consubstantial with the Father, light from light and God from God.

4 The Era of Dogmatic Speculation

In the third century presbyters had acted at synods as spokesmen for the bishops; the council of Antioch laid it down as an axiom that bishops take the lead. As the bishop was above all the head of the worshipping congregation, creeds and liturgical practices were now regularly cited as ancillaries to biblical exegesis. At the same time, as the clergy gathered privileges and subsidies under Christian rule, their ranks were swelled by men who had received a professional schooling in philosophy and rhetoric. Eunomius, Bishop of Cyzicus, was (perhaps unfairly) decried as an Aristotelian when he reasoned that the Godhead contains two essences, since at least one attribute, that of being ingenerate (*agennêtos*) is reserved for the Father alone. In reply the three Cappadocian Fathers (Basil of Caesarea, Gregory Nyssen, and Gregory Nazianzen) are at their strongest when they argue that whatever we predicate of the inscrutable Godhead is a feeble adumbration of its real properties, which cannot be unveiled in the present life. Even if, with Nyssen, we propose that the terms "begotten," "unbegotten," and "proceeding" denote relations rather than substances, we must refrain from inferring, as we would in any other instance, that beings who are related to one another cannot also be the same. A false desire for philosophical clarity lures both Basil and Nyssen into the assertion that the three hypostases are all God because they share divinity as an essence or *ousia*, just as any three men share the common essence of humanity. To forestall the charge of tritheism, Nyssen perversely argues in his *Letter to Ablabius* that an accurate use of words would allow us only to speak of "man" in the singular, never of a plurality of men. Perhaps he is taking for granted his own contention in *The Making of Man* that the image of God, as undivided intellect, resides identically in all human beings; to explain the peculiar logic of the term "God," however, one needs, as Basil's friend Apollinarius told him, to postulate not so much a generic as a "genarchic" unity, which consists in the descent of Son and Spirit from the Father, as men are united by their descent from David or from Adam (Basil, *Ep.* 362). It was in fact the Cappadocian Fathers who put the stamp of orthodoxy on this position, while the Second Oecumenical Council of 381 condemned the over-subtle Apollinarius for denying a human intellect to Christ.

The paradoxical union of God and man in Jesus became all the more perplexing with this settlement of the Trinitarian question, for the Cappadocians – unlike Origen, Arius, or even Athanasius – affirmed that the three hypostases were not only one in kind but fully equal in rank and power – as indeed they must be if they are all to be identical with the one God. If that is so, the Logos himself would share the impassibility of the Father, and could not have been the subject of the ignorance and weakness that are attributed to the Savior in the Gospels. On the other hand, if the man in Christ were merely a companion of the Logos, had the Word of God indeed become flesh, as John the Evangelist proclaimed? Apollinarius held that he inhabited a human body and soul in place of the intellect; Theodore of Mopsuestia and his "Antiochene" followers objected that in that case God himself would be a prisoner to the flesh. Nor could man be said to have overcome his own jailer, Satan, if the Logos were the sole agent of the victory; Nazianzen added that the human mind, not having been assumed in the incarnation, would not have been redeemed from its fallen state (Greg. Naz. *Ep.* 102). Cyril of Alexandria, however, thought (or at least affected to think) that his contemporary Nestorius, a follower of Theodore and Bishop of Constantinople, had posited so loose an association between the Logos and humanity as to make two Christs of one (*Second Letter to Nestorius*). At the Council of Ephesus in 431, Nestorius, who refused to confess that Mary was the mother of God, that the flesh of Christ was life-giving in the Eucharist, and that the Word of God had tasted death (Cyril, *Ep.* 3 anathemas 11 and 12), was deposed by a phalanx of Egyptian prelates. The partisans of Nestorius, led by Bishop John of Antioch, arrived too late and retaliated by deposing Cyril. An accord between John and Cyril, signed in 433, declared that Christ was consubstantial in his divinity with God and in his humanity with all other human beings. When a monk named Eutyches denied this, he was condemned by Flavian of Constantinople, but in 449, at the second Council of Ephesus, the Egyptian bishops carried the day against Flavian by force. At the instance of the emperor and the Bishop of Rome, an oecumenical council in 451 reversed this verdict and laid down that Christ existed in two natures, though he remained a single person or hypostasis; whatever we predicate of the man we predicate of the Logos, and conversely, though we do not say of him *as man* what we say of him *as God*.

There was little philosophy in these altercations, and in the west the career of Augustine illustrates the maxim that the one who makes the most of his education is the one who shows it least. In his youth he imbibed a material notion of God from the Manichaean heresy, which, because it taught that the spirit alone was worthy of redemption, made him tolerant of impurity in the flesh. He embraced philosophy as a moral discipline after reading the *Hortensius* of Cicero, and study of the Platonists reconciled him to catholic teaching on the incorporeality of God (*Conf.* 7 etc.). Augustine in his early prime was enough of a Neoplatonist to maintain, in his *Soliloquies*, that the soul must be immortal because it sees eternal objects, and to the end of his long life he remained indebted to Plotinus for the axiom that evil is a deficiency of being (though not, for Christians, a deficiency in matter). His literary mentor was the philosopher and rhetorician Marius Victorinus, a late convert to Christianity who had previously translated Plotinus and Porphyry into Latin. In his tracts against the Arians, Victorinus states that Father and Son are one because the former is everything in potentiality that the latter is in act. He also adapted the Neoplatonic doctrine that the mind is an "intelligible triad," in which being, the proper object of cognition, takes the form of cognitive intellect through the medium of life. In the exposition of Victorinus, being corresponds to the Father, life and intellect (less consistently) to the Son and Spirit. Yet the mature Augustine, in his 15 books *On the Trinity*, takes only passing notice of the intelligible triad, grounding his vindication of divine unity on the Johannine dictum "God is love," together with two psychological triads – mind, knowledge, love, and memory-understanding-will – which are dimly, if at all, anticipated in either Christian or pagan literature. These similes, drawn as they are from the incorporeal realm, have a clear advantage over those of Basil and Gregory Nyssen; and Augustine holds a stricter monotheism than any Platonist when he stipulates that the divine *essentia* is simply God (*De Trin.* 5.2.3).

Even less Platonic is the theory of divine predestination which was worked out against Pelagius and Celestius in the last two decades of Augustine's life. Where they held that God has created humans with the ability to do good works and the freedom to reject or choose the Gospel, Augustine taught that Adam's fall has rendered us incapable of exercising either faith or charity without divine assistance. Since God may will that his grace should be irresistible (and has so willed, according to the scriptures), it does not lie with the creature to accept or to refuse the offer: whoever is saved is saved by God alone (*To Simplicianus*, c.397 CE). So little does Pelagian freedom matter to Augustine that he conceives the final state of the elect as one in which sin has become impossible (*City of God*, Book 13 etc.); in this one tenet he is still a Platonist, who identifies freedom with the full possession of one's nature, and deduces that an agent is not truly free so long as he can compromise his own nature by wrongdoing. A Platonist would not have said, however, that the righteous man is one who acts in charity, observes the rule of charity in interpreting the scriptures and cements the bond of charity by joining the Catholic Church. Platonists, says Augustine, are too proud to see the incarnate Word, and thus do not know what it is for Christ, the invisible fund of truth in every human intellect, to pour himself as sacrificial love into the soul.

Disputes over free will barely touched the east, where Pelagius was acquitted in 415. Nevertheless Celestius was condemned at Ephesus in 431, and Cyril intimates that the death of God was rendered necessary by the plight of Adam's children. In the Christological debates that followed Chalcedon in 451, the question was rather "Whom do I worship?" than "How can I be saved?". In the last years of the fifth century this question was addressed by one who purports to be Paul's convert Dionysius the Areopagite, though he gives himself away when he quotes passages from Proclus the Neoplatonist (again under a pseudonym) to extol the providential love of God. The treatise *On the Divine Names* and the *Mystical Theology* mark the climax in antiquity of the apophatic method which contends that the nature of God is better described by the negation than by the affirmation of properties. Whether his plagiarisms were intended to disguise the priority of the Neoplatonists or to hint that Christianity should befriend them, the first citation of Dionysius almost coincides with the famous edict of Justinian, which temporarily closed the schools of Athens. Although the Alexandrian school of Platonism survived for a generation, and even the Athenians came back, the expropriation of Greek culture was now complete, and from Justinian to the renaissance there was no academy of pagan thought outside the church.

Bibliography

Abramenko, A. 1993. *Die munizipale Mittelschicht im kaiserzeitlichen Italien: Zu einem neuen Verständnis von Sevirat und Augustalität*. Frankfurt.
Absil, M. 1997. *Les préfets du prétoire d'Auguste à Commode*. Paris.
Adam, J.-P. 1992. *Roman building: Materials and techniques*. Trans. A. Matthews. Bloomington, IN.
Adams, C. E. P. 2001. Who bore the burden? The organization of stone transport in Roman Egypt. In Mattingly and Salmon 2001a: 171–92.
Ager, S. 1996. *Interstate arbitrations in the Greek world, 337–90 BC*. Berkeley.
Ahl, F. M. 1982. Lucan and Statius. In Luce, T. J. (ed.), *Ancient writers*. New York. 914–41.
Ahl, F. M. 1984. The rider and the horse: Politics and power in Roman poetry from Horace to Statius, with an Appendix by J. Garthwaite. *ANRW* 2.32.1: 40–124.
Alarcão, A., Étienne, R., and Golvin, J.-C. 1997. Le centre monumental du forum de Conimbriga: réponse à quelques contestations. In Étienne, R. and Mayet, F. (eds.), *Itinéraires lusitaniens. Trente années de collaboration archéologique luso-française*. Paris. 49–68.
Alarcão, J. 1988. *Roman Portugal. I. Introduction*. Warminster.
Alarcão, J. and Étienne, R. 1977. *Fouilles de Conimbriga. I. Architecture*. Paris.
Alba Calzado, M. 2004. Arquitectura doméstica. In Dupré Raventós: 67–83.
Alcock, S. E. 1993. *Graecia Capta: The landscapes of Roman Greece*. Cambridge.
Alcock, S. E. 2002. *Archaeologies of the Greek past: Landscape, monuments, and memories*. Cambridge.
Alcock, S. E., Day, H. W., and Parker, G. 2001. Sitting down with the Barrington atlas. *JRA* 14: 454–61.
Aldrete, G. and Mattingly, D. J. 1999. Feeding the city: The organization, operation and scale of the supply system for Rome. In Potter and Mattingly: 171–204.
Alföldi, M. R. 1958/9. Epigraphische Beiträge zur römischen Münztechnik bis auf Konstantin den Grossen. *SNR* 39: 35–48.
Alföldy, G. 1968. Septimius Severus und der Senat. *Bonner Jahrbücher* 168: 112–60.
Alföldy, G. 1974. The crisis of the third century as seen by contemporaries. *GRBS* 15: 80–111. (Rpr. in Alföldy 1989: 319–42.)
Alföldy, G. 1985. *The social history of Rome*. London.

Alföldy, G. 1987. *Römisches Städtewesen auf der neukastilischen Hochebene. Ein Testfall für die Romanisierung*. Abhandlungen der Heidelberger Akademie der Wissenschaften, Philosophisch-Historische Klasse. Heidelberg.
Alföldy, G. 1989. *Die Krise des Römischen Reiches. Geschichte, Geschichtsschreibung und Geschichtsbetrachtung. Ausgewählte Beiträge*. Stuttgart.
Alföldy, G. 1995. Eine Bauinschrift aus dem Colosseum. *ZPE* 109. 195–226.
Alföldy, G. 2000. Das neue Edikt des Augustus aus El Bierzo in Hispanien. *ZPE* 131: 177–205.
Alföldy, G. and Halfmann, H. M. 1973. Cornelius Nigrinus Curiatius Maternus, General Domitians und Rivale Trajans. *Chiron* 3: 331–73.
Allison, P. M. 1992. Artefact assemblages: Not the "Pompeii premise." In Herring, E., Whitehouse, R., and Wilkins, J. (eds.), *Papers of the Fourth Conference of Italian Archaeology*. London. 49–56.
Allison, P. M. 2001. Using the material and written sources: Turn of the millennium approaches to Roman domestic space. *AJA* 105: 181–208.
Allison, P. M. 2004. *Pompeian households: An analysis of the material culture*. Cotsen Institute of Archaeology Monograph 42. Los Angeles.
Al-Salihi, W. 1987. Palmyrene sculptures found at Hatra. *Iraq* 49: 53–61.
Alston, R. 1994. Roman military pay from Caesar to Diocletian. *JRS* 84: 113–23.
Alston, R. 1995. *Soldier and society in Roman Egypt: A social history*. London.
Alston, R. 1999. The ties that bind: Soldiers and societies. In Goldsworthy and Haynes: 175–95.
Álvarez Martínez, J. M. 1983. *El puente romano de Mérida*. Monografías Emeritenses 1. Badajoz.
Álvarez Martínez, J. M. and Nogales Basarrate, T. 2003. *Forum Coloniae Augustae Emeritae: "Templo de Diana."* Mérida.
Amandry, M. 1988. *Le monnayage des duovirs corinthiens*. BCH Suppl. 15. Athens.
Amouretti, M. C. and Brun, J. P. (eds.) 1993. *La production du vin et de l'huile en Méditerranée*. BCH Suppl. 36. Paris.
Amphores 1989 = *Amphores romaines et histoire économique. Dix ans de recherches*. CEFR 114. Paris.
Anderson, G. 1986. *Philostratus: Biography and* belles lettres *in the third century* AD. London.
Ando, C. 1999. Was Rome a *polis*? *CA* 18: 5–34.
Ando, C. 2000. *Imperial ideology and provincial loyalty in the Roman Empire*. Berkeley.
Ando, C. forthcoming. *Administration and acculturation in the Roman Empire*.
Andorlini, I. (ed.) 2001. *Greek medical papyri* 1. Firenze.
André, J-M. 1966. *L'Otium dans la vie morale et intellectuelle romaine, des origines à l'époque augustéenne*. Paris.
Andreau, J. 1999. *Banking and business in the Roman world, 310* BC *to* AD *284*. Cambridge.
Andreau, J. 2000. Commerce and finance. In *CAH*² 11: 769–86.
Ankarloo, B. and Clark, S. (eds.) 1999. *Witchcraft and magic in Europe: Ancient Greece and Rome*. Philadelphia.
Archer, L. J., Fischler, S., and Wyke, M. (eds.) 1994. *Women in ancient societies*. London.
Aristides, Aelius 1981. *The complete works*. Edited by C. A. Behr. Leiden.
Arjava, A. 1996. *Women and law in late antiquity*. Oxford.
Arjava, A. 1998. Paternal power in late antiquity. *JRS* 88: 147–65.
Armstrong, A. H. 1966. *Porphyry: On the life of Plotinus and the order of his books*. Cambridge, MA.
Athanassiadi, P. 1993. Dreams, theurgy and freelance divination: The testimony of Iamblichus. *JRS* 83: 115–30.
Athanassiadi, P. 1999a. The Chaldean Oracles: Theology and theurgy. In Athanassiadi and Frede: 149–84.

Athanassiadi, P. 1999b. *Damascius. The philosophcal history.* Text with Translation and Notes. Athens.
Athanassiadi, P. and Frede, M. (eds.) 1999. *Pagan monotheism in late antiquity.* Oxford.
Atherton, C. 1998. Children, animals, slaves and grammar. In Too and Livingstone: 214–44.
Aubert, J.-J. 1994. *Business managers in Ancient Rome: A social and economic study of Institores 200 BC–AD 250.* Leiden.
Aulock, H. von. 1968. Kleinasiatische Münzstätten. I. Die vermeintliche Stade Sebaste in Paphlagonien; II. Korynai in Paphlagonien. III. Aizanoi. *JNG* 18: 43–8.
Aulock, H. von. 1969. Kleinasiatische Münzstätten. IV. Kolbasa; V. Die Homonoia-Münzen von Mytilene. *JNG* 19: 79–88.
Aulock, H. von. 1970. Kleinasiatische Münzstätten. VI: Die römische Kolonie Komama in Pisidien. *JNG* 20: 151–9.
Aulock, H. von. 1977. *Münzen und Städte Pisidiens Teil I.* DAI Istanbuler Mitteilungen Beiheft 19. Tübingen.
Aulock, H. von. 1979. *Münzen und Städte Pisidiens Teil II.* DAI Istanbuler Mitteilungen Beiheft 22. Tübingen.
Aulock, H. von. 1980. *Münzen und Städte Phrygiens Teil I.* DAI Istanbuler Mitteilungen Beiheft 25. Tübingen.
Aurenhammer, M. 1995. Sculptures of gods and heroes from Ephesos. In Koester, H. (ed.), *Ephesos, metropolis of Asia: An interdisciplinary approach to its archaeology, religion, and culture.* Harvard Theological Studies 41. Valley Forge, PA. 251–80.
Badian, E. 1972. *Publicans and sinners.* Ithaca.
Badian, E. 1989. History from square brackets. *ZPE* 79: 59–70.
Bagnall, R. S. 1977. Army and policy in Roman Upper Egypt. *JARCE* 14: 67–86.
Bagnall, R. S. 1985. *Currency and inflation in fourth-century Egypt. BASP* Suppl. 5. Atlanta.
Bagnall, R. S. 1992. Landholding in late Roman Egypt: The distribution of wealth. *JRS* 82: 128–49.
Bagnall, R. S. 1995 *Reading papyri, writing ancient history.* London.
Bagnall, R. S. 1997. *The Kellis agricultural account book.* Oxford.
Bagnall, R. S. 2000. A note on P. Oxy. 4527 and the Antonine plague in Egypt: Death or flight? *JRA* 13: 288–92.
Bagnall, R. S. and Frier, B. W. 1994. *The demography of Roman Egypt.* Cambridge.
Bagnall, R. S., Frier, B. W., and Rutherford, I. C. 1997. *The census register P.Oxy. 984: The reverse of Pindar's paeans.* Brussels.
Baharal, D. 1996. *Victory of propaganda. The dynastic aspect of the imperial propaganda of the Severi. The literary and archaeological evidence AD 193–235.* Oxford.
Bakels, C. and Jacomet, S. 2003. Access to luxury foods in Central Europe during the Roman period: The archaeobotanical evidence. In van der Veen, M. (ed.), *Luxury Foods. World Archaeology* 34.3: 542–57.
Baldus, H.-R. 1969. *MON(eta) VRB(is) ANTIOXIA: Rom und Antiochia als Prägestätten syrischer Tetradrachmen des Philippus Arabs.* Frankfurt.
Baldus, H.-R. 1971. *Uranius Antoninus.* Bonn.
Balsdon, J. P. V. D. 1969. *Life and leisure in ancient Rome.* London.
Balty, J.-Ch. 1987. Nouvelles données sur l'armée romaine d'orient et les raids sassanides du milieu du IIIe siècle. *CRAI*: 213–41.
Balty, J.-Ch. 1988. Apamea in Syria in the second and third centuries AD. *JRS* 78: 91–104.
Balty, J.-Ch. 1992. *Curia ordinis: recherches d'architecture et d'urbanisme antiques sur les curies provinciales du monde romain.* Brussels.
Balty, J.-Ch. and Cazes, D. 1995. *Portraits impériaux de Béziers: le groupe statuaire du forum.* Toulouse.

Balty, J.-Ch. and van Rengen, W. 1993. *Apamea in Syria: The winter quarters of Legio II Parthica: Roman gravestones from the military cemetery.* Brussels.
Banaji, J. 2001. *Agrarian change in late antiquity: Gold, labour, and aristocratic dominance.* Oxford.
Barb, A. A. 1963. The survival of magic arts. In Momigliano 1963: 100–25.
Barb, A. A. 1971. Mystery, myth, and magic. In J. R. Harris 1971: 138–69.
Barchiesi, A. 1997a. *The poet and the prince: Ovid and Augustan discourse.* Berkeley.
Barchiesi, A. 1997b. Endgames: Ovid's *Metamorphoses* 15 and *Fasti* 6. In Roberts, D. H., Dunn, F. M., and Fowler, D. (eds.), *Classical closure: Reading the end in Greek and Latin literature.* Princeton. 181–208.
Barchiesi, A. 2001a. Horace and Iambos: The poet as literary historian. In Cavarzere, A., Aloni, A., and Barchiesi, A. (eds.), *Iambic ideas: Essays on a poetic tradition from archaic Greece to the late Roman Empire.* Lanham, MD: 141–64.
Barchiesi, A. 2001b. Teaching Augustus through allusion. In Barchiesi, A. (ed.), *Speaking volumes: Narrative and intertext in Ovid and other Latin poets.* London. 79–104.
Barchiesi, A. 2002. The uniqueness of the *Carmen saeculare* and its tradition. In Woodman and Feeney: 107–23.
Bardon, H. 1952. *La littérature latine inconnue.* Paris.
Barker, G. W. (ed.) 1996. *Farming the desert: The UNESCO Libyan Valleys Archaeological Survey,* vol. 1. *Synthesis.* London.
Barker, G. W., Adams, R., and Creighton, O. H. 2000. Archaeology and desertification in the Wadi Faynan: The fourth (1999) season of the Wadi Faynan Landscape Survey. *Levant* 32: 27–52.
Barker, G. W. and Lloyd, J. (eds.) 1991. *Roman landscapes. Archaeological survey in the Mediterranean region.* British School at Rome Archaeological Monograph 2. London.
Barker, G. W. (ed.), with major contributions by Hodges, R., Hunt, C., Lloyd, J., Suano, M., Taylor, P., and Wickham, C. 1995. *A Mediterranean valley: Landscape archaeology and Annales history in the Biferno Valley.* London.
Barnes, J. 1993. Imperial Plato. *Apeiron* 26: 129–51.
Barnes, J. 1997. Antiochus of Ascalon. In Griffin and Barnes: 51–96.
Barnes, J. and Griffin, M. (eds.) 1997. *Philosophia Togata II: Plato and Aristotle at Rome.* Oxford.
Barnes, T. D. 1981. *Constantine and Eusebius.* Cambridge, MA.
Barnes, T. D. 1982. *The new empire of Diocletian and Constantine.* Cambridge, MA.
Barnes, T. D. 1985. Constantine and the Christians of Persia. *JRS* 75: 126–36.
Barnes, T. D. 2001. Monotheists all? *Phoenix* 55: 142–62.
de la Barrera, J. L. and Trillmich, W. 1996. Eine Wiederholung der Aeneas-Gruppe vom Forum Augustum samt ihrer Inschrift in Mérida (Spanien). *Rheinisches Museum* 103: 119–38.
Bartman, E. 1999. *Portraits of Livia: Imaging the imperial woman in Augustan Rome.* Cambridge.
Barton, J. 1986. *Oracles of God.* London.
Barton, T. 1994. *Power and knowledge: Astrology, physiognomics, and medicine under the Roman Empire.* Ann Arbor.
Bartsch, S. 1994. *Actors in the audience: Theatricality and doublespeak from Nero to Hadrian.* Cambridge.
Barwick, K. 1928. Die Gliederung der Narratio in der rhetorischen Theorie und ihre Bedeutung für die Geschichte des antiken Romans. *Hermes* 63: 260–87.
Baskin, J. R. 1991. *Jewish women in historical perspective.* Detroit.
Bauer, W. 1972. *Orthodoxy and heresy in earliest christianity.* London.
Bay, A. 1972. The letters S C on Augustan *Aes* Coinage. *JRS* 62: 111–22.

Beard, M. and Henderson, J. 1997. With this body I thee worship: Sacred prostitution in antiquity. *Gender and History* 9: 480–504.
Beard, M. and North, J. (eds.) 1990. *Pagan priests: Religion and power in the ancient world*. Ithaca.
Beard, M., North, J., and Price, S. 1998. *Religions of Rome*. 2 vols. Cambridge.
Beck, R. 2000. Ritual, myth, doctrine, and initiation in the mysteries of Mithras: New evidence from a cult vessel. *JRS* 90: 145–80.
Becker, A. H. and Yoshiko-Reed, A. (eds.) 2003. *The ways that never parted: Jews and Christians in late antiquity and the early Middle Ages*. Tübingen.
Bek, L. 1983. *Quaestiones conviviales*: The idea of the triclinium and the staging of convivial ceremony from Rome to Byzantium. *AnalRom* 12: 81–107.
Belayche, N. 1987. Les pèlerinages dans le monde romain antique. In Chelini and Branthomme: 136–54.
Bell, H. I. 1953. *Cults and creeds in Graeco-Roman Egypt*. Liverpool. (Rpr. Chicago, 1975.)
Benabou, M. 1976. *La résistance africaine à la romanisation*. Paris.
Ben Lazreg, N., Bonifay, M., Drine, A., and Trousset, P. 1995. Production et commercialisation des salsamenta de l'Afrique ancienne. In Trousset, P. (ed.), *Productions et exportations africaines*. Paris. 103–42.
Bennett, J. M. 2000. "Lesbian-like" and the social history of lesbianisms. *Journal of the History of Sexuality* 9.1–2: 1–24.
Berchem, D. van. 1952. *L'armée de Dioclétien et la réforme Constantinienne*. Paris.
Bergmann, B. and Kondoleon, C. (eds.) 1999. *The art of ancient spectacle*. New Haven.
Bernand, E. 1988. Pèlerins dans l'Égypte grecque et romaine. In Mactoux, M. M. and Geny, E. (eds.), *Mélanges Pierre Lévêque 1: religion*. Paris. 49–63.
Bernario, H. W. 1980. *A commentary on the* Vita Hadriani *in the* Historia Augusta. Chico.
Bernhardt, R. 1971. *Imperium und Eleutheria*. Dissertation: Die Universität Hamburg.
Bernhardt, R. 1985. *Polis und römische Herrschaft in der späten Republik (149–31 v. Chr.)*. Berlin.
Bernstein, F. 1998. Ludi Publici. *Untersuchungen zur Entstehung und Entwicklung der öffentlichen Speile im republikanischen Rom*. Historia Einzelschriften 119. Stuttgart.
Berriman, A. and Todd, M. 2001. A very Roman coup: The hidden war of imperial succession, AD 96–8. *Historia* 50: 312–31.
Berry, J. 1997. Household artifacts: Towards a re-interpretation of Roman domestic space. In Laurence and Wallace-Hadrill: 183–95.
Besly, E. and Bland, R. 1983. *The Cunetio treasure: Roman coinage of the third century AD*. London.
Bett, R. 1997. *Sextus Empiricus. Against the ethicists*. Oxford.
Bett, R. 2000. *Pyrrho, his antecedents and his legacy*. Oxford.
Bianchi-Bandinelli, R. 1970. *Rome: The centre of power: Roman art to AD 200*. Trans. P. Green. London.
Bickerman, E. 1952. Origines gentium. *CPh* 47: 63–81.
Bierbrier, M. L. (ed.) 1997. *Portraits and masks: Burial customs in Roman Egypt*. London.
Bintliff, J. L. (ed.) 1991. *The "Annales" School and archaeology*. New York.
Bird, D. G. 1972. The Roman gold mines of north-west Spain. *Bonner Jahrbucher* 172: 36–64.
Birley, A. R. 1981. *The* Fasti *of Roman Britain*. Oxford.
Birley, A. R. 1987. *Marcus Aurelius. A biography*. 2nd edn. London.
Birley, A. R. 1988. *The African emperor. Septimius Severus*. 2nd edn. London.
Birley, A. R. 1997. *Hadrian. The restless emperor*. London.
Birley, A. R. 1998. Decius reconsidered. In Frézouls, E. and Jouffroy, H. (eds.), *Les empereurs illyriens: actes du colloque de Strasbourg (11–13 octobre 1990), organisé par le Centre de Recherche sur l'Europe centrale et sud-orientale*. Strasbourg. 57–80.

Bisel, S. C. and Bisel, J. F. 2002. Health and nutrition at Herculaneum: An examination of human skeletal remains. In Jashemski and Meyer 2002. 451–75.
Bishop, M. C. and Coulston, J. C. N. 1993. *Roman military equipment: From the Punic wars to the fall of Rome*. London.
Bland, R. 1988. Normanby, Lincolnshire. *Coin hoards from Roman Britain* 8: 114–215.
Bland, R. 1991. The last coinage of Caesarea in Cappadocia. In *Studia Ermanno A. Arslan dicata* (Glaux 7). Milan. 213–58.
Bland, R. 1996. The development of gold and silver coin denominations, A.D. 193–253. In King and Wigg 1996: 63–100.
Blazquez Martinez, J. M. and Remesal Rodriguez, J. (eds.) 1999/2003. *Estudiois sobre el Monte Testaccio (Roma)*. 3 vols. Barcelona.
Bliquez, L. J. 1994. *Roman surgical instruments and other minor objects in the National Archaeological Museum of Naples*. Mainz.
Bloomer, W. M. 1997. *Latinity and literary society at Rome*. Philadelphia.
Blümner, H. 1918. Fahrendes Volk im Altertum. *Sitzungsberichte der Bayerischen Akademie der Wissenschaften* 6: 3–53.
Boak, A. E. R. 1959. Egypt and the plague of Marcus Aurelius. *Historia* 8: 248–50.
Boatwright, M. T. 1991. Imperial women of the early 2nd century AD. *AJP* 112: 513–40.
Boatwright, M. T. 2000. *Hadrian and the cities of the Roman Empire*. Princeton.
Bodel, J. 2000. Dealing with the dead: Undertakers, executioners and potters' fields in ancient Rome. In Hope and Marshall: 128–51.
Bodel, J. 2001. *Epigraphic evidence: Ancient history from inscriptions*. London.
Boffo, L. 1995. Ancora una volta sugli "archivi" nel mondo Greco: conservazione e "publicazione" epigrafica. *Athenaeum* 83: 91–130.
Bollmann, B. 1998. *Römische Vereinshäuser. Untersuchungen zu den Scholae der römischen Berufs-, Kult- und Augustalen-Kollegien in Italien*. Mainz.
Bomgardner, D. L. 2000. *The story of the Roman amphitheatre*. London.
Bompaire, J. 1958. *Lucien écrivain: imitation et creation*. Paris.
Bompaire, J. 1977. Le décor sicilien dans le roman grec et dans la littérature contemporaine. *REG* 90: 55–68.
Bonneau, D. 1972. *Le fisc et le Nil. Incidences des irrégularités de la crue du Nil sur la fiscalité foncière dans l'Égypte grecque et romaine*. Publications de l'Institut de Droit romain de l'Université de Paris. N.S., No. 2. Paris.
Bonneau, D. 1993. *Le régime administratif de l'eau du Nil dans l'Égypte grecque, romaine et byzantine*. Probleme der Ägyptologie 8. Leiden.
Bonner, C. 1950. *Studies in magical amulets chiefly Graeco-Egyptian*. Ann Arbor.
Borg, B. 1997. The dead as guest at table? Continuity and change in the Egyptian cult of the dead. In Bierbrier: 26–32.
Bosman, A. V. A. J. 1999. Possible baths at the fort of Velsen 1: A provisional interpretation. In DeLaine and Johnston: 245–50.
Boswell, J. 1980. *Christianity, social tolerance, and homosexuality*. Chicago.
Boswell, J. 1988. *The kindness of strangers: The abandonment of children in Western Europe from late antiquity to the Renaissance*. New York.
Bosworth, A. B. 1972. Asinius Pollio and Augustus. *Historia* 21: 441–73.
Bouby, L. and Marinval, P. 2004. Fruits and seeds from Roman cremations in Limagne (Massif Central) and the spatial variability of plant offerings in France. *Journal of Archaeological Science* 31: 77–86.
Bouet, A. 2001. Les collèges dans la ville antique: le cas des *subaediani*. *RA*: 227–78.
Bowersock, G. W. 1969. *Greek Sophists in the Roman Empire*. Oxford.
Bowersock, G. W. 1971. A date in the eighth Eclogue. *HSCP* 75: 73–80.

Bowersock, G. W. 1973. *The social and economic history of the Roman Empire*, by Michael Ivanovich Rostovtzeff. *Daedalus*: 15–23.
Bowersock, G. W. 1983. *Roman Arabia*. Cambridge, MA.
Bowersock, G. W. 1991. Momigliano's quest for the person. In Steinberg: 27–36.
Bowersock, G. W. 1993. "Ronald Syme," *Proceedings of the British Academy* 84 (1994), 539–63.
Bowersock, G. W. 1994. *Fiction as history from Nero to Julian*. Berkeley.
Bowie, E. L. 1970. Greeks and their past in the Second Sophistic. *Past and Present* 46: 3–41. (Rpr. in Finley 1974: 166–209).
Bowie, E. L. 1978. Apollonius of Tyana: Tradition and reality. *ANRW* 2.16.2: 1652–99.
Bowie, E. L. 1982. The importance of Sophists. *YCS* 27: 29–59.
Bowie, E. L. 1985. The Greek novel. In Easterling, P. E. and Knox, B. M. W. *The Cambridge history of classical literature* 1 *Greek literature*. Cambridge. 683–99. (Rpr. Swain 1999: 39–59).
Bowie, E. L. 1994a. Philostratus: Writer of fiction. In Morgan and Stoneman 1994: 181–99.
Bowie, E. L. 1994b. The readership of the Greek novels in the ancient world. In Tatum 1994: 435–59.
Bowie, E. L. 2003. The ancient readers of the Greek novels. In Schmeling: 87–106.
Bowman, A. K. 1971. *The town councils of Roman Egypt*. ASP 6. Toronto.
Bowman, A. K. 1976. Papyri and Roman imperial history, 1960–75. *JRS* 66: 153–73.
Bowman, A. K. 1986. *Egypt after the pharaohs*. London.
Bowman, A. K. 1994. *Life and letters on the Roman frontier. Vindolanda and its people*. London.
Bowman, A. K. 1996. Egypt. In CAH^2 10: 676–702.
Bowman, A. K. 2001. Documentary papyrology and ancient history. *Atti del XXII Congresso Internazionale di Papirologia, Firenze 1998*. Florence. Vol. 1: 137–45.
Bowman, A. K. and Rathbone, D. W. 1992. Cities and administration in Roman Egypt. *JRS* 82: 107–27.
Bowman, A. K. and Thomas, J. D. 1994. *The Vindolanda writing-tablets*. Vol. 2. London.
Bowman, A. K., Champlin, E. J., and Lintott, A. (eds.) 1996. *The Augustan Empire 43 B.C.–A.D. 69*. CAH^2 10. Cambridge.
Bowman, A. K., Garnsey, P. D. A., and Rathbone, D. 2000. *The high empire AD 70–192*. CAH^2 11. Cambridge.
Boyancé, P. 1941. Cum dignitate otium. *REA* 43: 171–92.
Boyarin, D. 1993. *Carnal Israel: Reading sex in Talmudic culture*. Berkeley.
Boyarin, D. 1999. *Dying for God: Martyrdom and the making of Christianity and Judaism*. Stanford.
Boyarin, D. 2004. *Border lines: The partition of Judaeo-Christianity*. Philadelphia.
Boyle, A. J. (ed.) 1993. *Roman epic*. London.
Bradbury, S. 1994. Constantine and the problem of anti-pagan legislation in the fourth century. *CPh* 89: 120–39.
Bradley, K. R. 1991. *Discovering the Roman family*. Oxford.
Bradley, K. R. 1993. Writing the history of the Roman family. *CPh* 88: 237–50.
Bradley, K. R. 1994. *Slavery and society at Rome*. Cambridge.
Bradley, K. R. 2003. Sacrificing the family: Christian martyrs and their kin. *Ancient Narrative* 3: 1–32.
Branham, R. B. 1989. *Unruly eloquence: Lucian and the comedy of traditions*. Cambridge, MA.
Branham, R. B. and Goulet-Caze, M.-O. (eds.) 1996. *The Cynics*. Berkeley.
Braudel, F. 1972–3. *The Mediterranean and the Mediterranean world in the age of Philip II*. Trans. of 2nd French edn. by S. Reynolds. 2 vols. New York.
Braund, D. 1988. *The administration of the Roman Empire 241 B.C.–A.D. 193*. Exeter.

Braund, S. 1988. *Beyond anger*. Cambridge.
Braund, S. 1996. *The Roman satirists and their masks*. Bristol.
Bremen, R. van. 1994. A family from Sillyon. *ZPE* 104: 43–56.
Bremen, R. van. 1996. *The limits of participation: Women and civic life in the Greek East in the Hellenistic and Roman periods*. Amsterdam.
Bremmer, J. 2002. Perpetua and her diary: Authenticity, family and visions. In Ameling, W. (ed.), *Märtyrer und Märtyrerakten*. Altertumswissenschaftliches Kolloquium 6. Stuttgart. 77–120.
Brendel, O. 1979. *Prolegomena to the study of Roman art*. New Haven.
Brennan, T. C. 1990 [2000]. Princeps and plebs. Nerva's reign as a turning-point? *AJAH* 15: 40–66.
Brenner, A. (ed.) 1995. *A feminist companion to the latter prophets* (= *The feminist companion to the Bible* 8). Sheffield.
Brewster, E. H. 1917. *Roman craftsmen and tradesmen of the early empire*. New York.
Briand-Ponsart, C. 1999. Summa honoraria et les resources des cités d'Afrique. In *Il capitolo delle entrate nelle finanze municipali in Occidente ed in Oriente: Actes de la Xe rencontre franco-italienne sur l'épigraphique du monde romain, Rome, 27–29 mai 1996*. CEFR 256. Rome. 217–34.
Brittain, C. 2001. *Philo of Larissa. The last of the Academic Sceptics*. Oxford.
Bromwich, J. 1993. *The Roman remains of southern France: A guidebook*. London.
Brooten, B. J. 1996. *Love between women: Early Christian responses to female homoeroticism*. Chicago.
Brown, P. 1967. *Augustine of Hippo*. Berkeley.
Brown, P. 1970. Sorcery, demons, and the rise of Christianity from late antiquity into the Middle Ages. In Douglas: 17–45.
Brown, P. 1971. *The world of late antiquity* A D 150–750. London.
Brown, P. 1978. *The making of late antiquity*. Cambridge, MA.
Brown, P. 1981. *The cult of the saints: Its rise and function in Latin Christianity*. Chicago.
Brown, P. 1988. *The body and society: Men, women, and sexual renunciation in early Christianity*. New York.
Brown, P. 1995. *Authority and the sacred: Aspects of the Christianisation of the Roman world*. Cambridge.
Brown, P. 1998. Christianization and religious conflict. *CAH*^{2} 13: 632–64.
Bruns, K. G. (ed.) 1909. *Fontes Iuris Romani Antiqui*. 7th edn. by O. Gradenwitz. Tübingen. (Rpr. Aalen, 1969.)
Brunt, P. A. 1961. Charges of provincial maladministration under the early principate. *Historia* 10: 189–227. (Rpr. in Brunt 1990: 53–95.)
Brunt, P. A. 1966. Procuratorial jurisdiction. *Latomus* 25: 461–87. (Rpr. in Brunt 1990: 163–87.)
Brunt, P. A. 1974a. C. Fabricius Tuscus and an Augustan dilectus. *ZPE* 13: 161–85.
Brunt, P. A. 1974b. Conscription and volunteering in the Roman imperial army. *SCI* 1: 90–115. (Rpr. in Brunt 1990: 188–214.)
Brunt, P. A. 1975. The administrators of Roman Egypt. *JRS* 65: 124–47. (Rpr in Brunt 1990: 215–54.)
Brunt, P. A. 1977a. From Epictetus to Arrian. *Athenaeum* 65: 19–48.
Brunt, P. A. 1977b. Lex de Imperio Vespasiani. *JRS* 67: 95–116.
Brunt, P. A. 1980. Evidence given under torture in the principate. *ZSS* 97: 256–65.
Brunt, P. A. 1984. The role of the Senate in the Augustan regime. *CQ* 34: 423–44.
Brunt, P. A. 1987. *Italian manpower 225 B.C.–A.D. 14*. 2nd edn. Oxford.
Brunt, P. A. 1988. *The fall of the Roman Republic and related essays*. Oxford.
Brunt, P. A. 1990. *Roman imperial themes*. Oxford.

Bruun, P. M. 1966. *Roman imperial coinage vol. 7. Constantine and Licinius (AD 313–337)*. London.
Buell, D. 2002. Race and universalism in early Christianity. *JECS* 10: 429–68.
Burford, A. 1972. *Craftsmen in Greek and Roman society*. London.
Burkert, W. 1992. *The Orientalizing revolution: Near eastern influence on Greek culture in the early Archaic age*. Trans. M. E. Pinder and W. Burkert. Cambridge, MA.
Burnett, A. M. 1977. The authority to coin in the late republic and early empire. *NC*[7] 17: 37–63.
Burnett, A. M. and Amandry, M. (with P. P. Ripollès). 1992. *Roman provincial coinage. I. From the death of Caesar to the death of Vitellius*. London and Paris.
Burnett, A. M. and Amandry, M. (with I. Carradice). 1999. *Roman provincial coinage. II. From Vespasian to Domitian*. London and Paris.
Burnett, A. M. and Craddock, P. 1983. Rome and Alexandria: The minting of Egyptian tetradrachms under Severus Alexander. *ANSMN* 28: 109–18.
Burnham, B. C. and Wacher, J. S. 1990. *The small towns of Roman Britain*. London.
Burton, G. P. 1975. Proconsuls, assizes and the administration of justice under the empire. *JRS* 65: 92–106.
Burton, G. P. 1979. The *curator rei publicae*: Towards a reappraisal. *Chiron* 9: 465–87.
Burton, G. P. 2000. The resolution of territorial disputes in the provinces of the Roman Empire. *Chiron* 30: 195–215.
Burton, G. P. 2001. The imperial state and its impact on the role and status of local magistrates and councillors in the provinces of the empire. In De Blois: 202–14.
Busink, T. A. 1970–80. *Der Tempel von Jerusalem von Salomo bis Herodes; Eine archäologisch-historische Studie unter Berücksichtigung des westsemitischen Tempelbaus*. 2 vols. Leiden.
Butcher, K. 1988. *Roman provincial coinage. An introduction to the "Greek imperials."* London.
Butcher, K. and Ponting, M. 1995. Rome and the east: Production of Roman provincial coinage for Caesarea in Cappadocia under Vespasian, AD 69–79. *Oxford Journal of Archaeology* 14.1: 63–77.
Butler, S. 1998. Notes on a *membrum disiectum*. In Joshel and Murnaghan: 236–55.
Buttrey, T. V. 1992. The denarii of Pescennius Niger. *NC* 152: iv–xxii.
Buttrey, T. V. 1993. Calculating ancient coin production: Facts and fantasies. *NC* 153: 335–51.
Buttrey, T. V. 1994. Calculating ancient coin production II: Why it cannot be done. *NC* 154: 341–52.
Caballos Rufino, A. 1984. P. Acilius Attianus. *Habis* 15: 237–51.
Caballos Rufino, A. and León Alonso, P. (eds.) 1997. *Itálica MMCC. Actas del las jornadas del 2.200 aniversario de la fundación de Itálica (Sevilla, 8–11 noviembre 1994)*. Seville.
Callataÿ, F. de. 1995. Calculating ancient coin production: Seeking a balance. *NC* 155: 289–311.
Cameron, A. 1976. *Circus factions: Blues and greens at Rome and Constantinople*. Oxford.
Cameron, A. 1998. Love (and marriage) between women. *GRBS* 39: 137–56.
Cameron, A. 2002. The funeral of Junius Bassus. *ZPE* 139: 288–92.
Cameron, Averil. 1985. *Procopius and the sixth century*. London.
Cameron, Averil. 1997. Eusebius' *Vita Constantini* and the construction of Constantine. In Edwards and Swain: 145–74.
Cameron, Averil and Garnsey, P. D. A. 1998. *The late empire A.D. 337–425. CAH*[2] 13. Cambridge.
Camodeca, G. 1999. *Tabulae Pompeianae Sulpiciorum (TPSulp.)*. 2 vols. Rome.
Campbell, J. B. 1978. The marriage of soldiers under the empire. *JRS* 68: 153–66.
Campbell, J. B. 1984. *The emperor and the Roman army, 31 BC–AD 235*. Oxford.

Campbell, J. B 1994. *The Roman army 31 BC–AD 337: A sourcebook*. London.
Campbell, J. B. 2000. *The writing of the Roman land surveyors. Introduction, text, translation and commentary*. London.
Campbell, J. B. 2002. *Warfare and society in imperial Rome c. 31 BC–AD 280*. London.
Capasso, L. 2000. Herculaneum victims of the volcanic eruptions of Vesuvius in 79 AD. *Lancet* 356. 1344–6.
Capasso, L. 2001. *I fuggiaschi di Ercolano: Paleobiologia delle vittime dell'eruzione vesuviana del 79 d.C.* Rome.
Carandini, A. 1983. Pottery and the African economy. In Garnsey and Whittaker 1983: 145–62.
Carandini, A. 1989. La villa romana e la piantaggione schiavistica. In Momigliano, A. and Schiavone, A. (eds.), *Storia di Roma*. Turin. 4: 101–200.
Carandini, A. (ed.) 1984. *Settefinestre. Una villa schiavistica nell'Etruria romana*. Modena.
Carlsen, J., Ørsted, P., and Skydsgard, J. (eds.) 1994. *Land-use in the Roman Empire*. Rome.
Carreras Montfort, C. 2002. The Roman military supply during the principate. Transportation and staples. In Erdkamp: 70–89.
Carson, R. A. G. 1956. System and product in the Roman mint. In Carson and Sutherland: 227–39.
Carson, R. A. G. 1962. *Coins of the Roman Empire in the British Museum. Volume VI, Severus Alexander to Balbinus and Pupienus*. London.
Carson, R. A. G. 1965. The reform of Aurelian. RN^6 7: 225–35.
Carson, R. A. G. 1990. *Coins of the Roman Empire*. London.
Carson, R. A. G. and Sutherland, C. H. V. (eds.) 1956. *Essays in Roman coinage presented to Harold Mattingly*. Oxford.
Cartledge, P. and Spawforth, A. J. 1989. *Hellenistic and Roman Sparta: A tale of two cities*. London.
Caruso, G. and Volpe, R. 2000. Preesistenze e persistenze delle Terme di Traiano. In Fentress: 42–56.
Caseau, B. 1999. Sacred landscapes. In Bowersock, G. W., Brown, P., and Grabar, O. (eds.), *Late antiquity: A guide to the postclassical world*. Cambridge, MA. 21–59.
Casey, P. J. 1986. *Understanding ancient coins: An introduction for archaeologists and historians*. London.
Casey, P. J. 1994. *The British usurpers: Carausius and Allectus*. New Haven.
Casson, L. 1974. *Travel in the ancient world*. Baltimore.
Chadwick, H. 1965. *Origen: Contra Celsum*. Cambridge.
Chadwick, H. 1966. *Early Christian thought and the classical tradition*. Oxford.
Chadwick, H. 2001. *The church in ancient society from Galilee to Gregory the Great*. Oxford.
Champeaux, J. 1997. De la parole à l'écriture: Essai sur le langage des oracles. In Heintz: 405–38.
Champlin, E. J. 1985. The glass ball game. *ZPE* 60: 159–63.
Chaniotis, A. 1985. Eine neue lateinische Ehreninschrift aus Knossos. *ZPE* 58: 182–8.
Chaniotis, A. 2003. Vom Erlebnis zum Mythos: Identitätskonstruktionen im kaiserzeitlichen Aphrodisias. In Schwertheim, E. and Winter, E. (eds.), *Stadt und Stadtenwicklung in Kleinasien*. Bonn. 69–84.
Chaplin, J. 2000. *Livy's exemplary History*. Oxford.
Charron, A. 1990. Massacres d'animaux à la Basse Époque. *Revue d'Égyptologie* 41: 209–13.
Chastagnol, A. 1967. Les années régnales de Maximien Hercule en Égypte et les fêtes vicennales du 20 novembre 303. RN^6 9: 54–81.
Cheesman, G. L. 1914. *The auxilia of the Roman imperial army*. Oxford.
Chelini, J. and Branthomme, H. (eds.) 1987. *Histoire des pèlerinages non chrétiens*. Paris.
Chevallier, R. 1958. Essai de chronologie des centuriations romaines de Tunisie. *MÉFRA* 70: 61–128.

Christian, W. 1981. *Local religion in sixteenth-century Spain.* Princeton.
Christol, M. 1975. Les règnes de Valérien et de Gallien (253–268). Travaux d'ensemble, questions chronologiques. *ANRW* 2.2: 803–27.
Christol, M. 1977. La carrière de Traianus Mucianus et l'origine des *protectores*. *Chiron* 7: 393–408.
Christol, M. 1980. À propos de la politique extérieure de Trébonien Galle. *RN* 22: 68–74.
Christol, M. 1986. *Essai sur l'évolution des carrières sénatoriales dans la seconde moitié du IIIe siècle ap. J.C.* Paris.
Christol, M. 1994. Pline l'Ancien et la *formula* de la province Narbonnaise. In Démougin: 45–63.
Christol, M. and Loriot, X. 1997. À propos de l'inscription d'Augsbourg: remarques liminaires. *Cahiers Glotz* 8: 223–7.
Ciarallo, A. 2001. *Gardens of Pompeii.* Trans. L.-A. Touchette. Los Angeles.
Cité 1989. *La cité antique? A partir de l'oeuvre de M. Finley.* (Special edition of) *Opus* 6–9 (1987–9).
Clark, E. A. 1989. Devil's gateway and bride of Christ: Women in the early Christian world. In O'Barr: 81–102.
Clark, E. A. 1992. *The Origenist controversy.* Princeton.
Clark, P. A. 1998. Women, slaves, and the hierarchies of domestic violence: The family of St Augustine. In Joshel and Murnaghan: 109–29.
Clarke, J. R. 1998. *Looking at lovemaking: Constructions of sexuality in Roman art 100 BC–AD 250.* Berkeley.
Clarke, J. R. 2003. *Art in the lives of ordinary Romans: Visual representation and non-elite viewers in Italy, 100 BC–AD 315.* Berkeley.
Clavel-Lévêque, M. 1983. Pratiques impérialistes et implantations cadastrales. *Ktema* 8: 185–251.
Cockle, H. 1975. The Odes of Epagathus the Choral Flautist: Some documentary evidence for dramatic representation in Roman Egypt. *Proceedings of the XIV International Congress of Papyrologists, Oxford, 24–31 July 1974*: 59–65. Greco-Roman Memoirs 61. London.
Cockle, H. 1981. Pottery manufacture in Roman Egypt: A new papyrus. *JRS* 71: 87–97.
Cockle, H. 1984. State archives in Graeco-Roman Egypt from 30 BC to the reign of Septimius Severus. *JEA* 70: 106–22.
Cohen, D. and Saller, R. 1994. Foucault on sexuality in Greco-Roman antiquity. In Goldstein: 35–59, 262–6.
Cohen, H. 1880–92. *Description historique des monnaies frappées sous l'Empire romain communément appellées, médailles impériales.* 2nd edn. 8 vols. Paris.
Cohen, S. J. D. 1983. Jacob Neusner, Mishnah, and counter-Rabbinics: A review essay. *Conservative Judaism* 37: 48–63.
Cohen, S. J. D. 1984a. The significance of Yavneh: Pharisees, rabbis, and the end of sectarianism. *Hebrew Union College Annual* 55: 27–53.
Cohen, S. J. D. 1984b. The Temple and the synagogue. In Madsen, T. G. (ed.), *The Temple in antiquity: Ancient records and modern perspectives.* Religious Studies Monograph Series 9. Provo, UT. 151–74.
Cohen, S. J. D. 1991. Menstruants and the sacred in Judaism and Christianity. In Pomeroy: 273–99.
Cohen, S. J. D. 1992. The place of the rabbi in Jewish society of the second century. In L. I. Levine: 157–73.
Cohen, S. J. D. 1997. Why aren't Jewish women circumcised? *Gender and History* 9: 560–78.
Cohen, S. J. D. 1999a. Were pharisees and rabbis the leaders of communal prayer and Torah study in antiquity? The evidence of the New Testament, Josephus, and the early church

fathers. In Kee, H. C. (ed.), *Evolution of the synagogue: Problems and progress.* Harrisburg, PA. 89–105.
Cohen, S. J. D. 1999b. *The beginnings of Jewishness: Boundaries, varieties, uncertainties.* Berkeley.
Coleman, K. 1986. The emperor Domitian and literature. *ANRW* 2.32.5: 3087–115.
Coleman, K. 1990. Fatal charades. *JRS* 80: 44–74.
Coleman, K. 1993. Launching into history: Aquatic displays in the early Roman Empire. *JRS* 83: 48–78.
Coleman, K. 2000a. *Missio* at Halicarnassus. *HSCP* 100: 487–500.
Coleman, K. 2000b. Entertaining Rome. In Coulston, J. N. C. and Dodge, H. (eds.), *Ancient Rome: The archaeology of the Eternal City.* Oxford. 205–52.
Collins, J. J. (ed.) 1998. *Encyclopedia of apocalypticism*, vol. 1: *Jewish and Christian Origins of Apocalypticism.* New York.
Colson, F. H. 1935. *Philo.* Vol. 7. Loeb Classical Library. London.
Connolly, J. 2001. Problems of the past in imperial Greek education. In Too: 339–72.
Conte, G. B. 1989. Love without elegy: The *Remedia Amoris* and the logic of a genre. *Poetics Today* 10: 441–69.
Conte, G. B. 1994. *Latin literature: A history.* Baltimore.
Cooley, A. (ed.) 2000a. *The epigraphic landscape of Roman Italy.* BICS Suppl. 73. London.
Cooley, A. (ed.) 2000b. *The afterlife of inscriptions: Reusing, rediscovering, reinventing, and revitalizing ancient inscriptions.* BICS Suppl. 75. London.
Cooper, K. 1996. *The virgin and the bride: Idealized womanhood in late antiquity.* Cambridge, MA.
Corbier, M. 1991a. Divorce and adoption as Roman familial strategies. In B. Rawson: 47–78.
Corbier, M. 1991b. City, territory and taxation. In Rich and Wallace-Hadrill: 211–39.
Corbier, M. 1994. La Maison des Césars. In Bonte, P. (ed.), *Epouser au plus proche: inceste, prohibitions, et stratégies matrimoniales.* Paris. 243–91.
Corbier, M. 1995. Male power and legitimacy through women: The *domus Augusta* under the Julio-Claudians. In Hawley, R. and Levick, B. M. (eds.), *Women in antiquity. New assessments.* London. 178–93.
Corbier, M. 2001. Child-exposure and abandonment. In Dixon: 52–73.
Corcoran, S. 1993. Hidden from history: The legislation of Licinius. In Harries, J. and Wood, I. (eds.), *The Theodosian Code.* Ithaca. 97–119.
Corcoran, S. 2000. *Empire of the tetrarchs.* 2nd edn. Oxford.
Cornell, T. 1995. *The beginnings of Rome.* London.
Cornell, T. and Lomas, K. (eds.) 1995. *Urban society in Roman Italy.* New York.
Cornell, T. and Lomas, K. (eds.) 1997. *Gender and ethnicity in ancient Italy.* London.
Cotton, H. M. 1995. The papyrology of the Roman near east: A survey. *JRS* 85: 214–35.
Cotton, H. M. 1999. The impact of the documentary papyri from the Judaean desert on the study of Jewish history from 70 to 135 CE. In Oppenheimer, A. and Müller-Luckner, J. (eds.), *Jüdische Geschichte in hellenistisch-römischer Zeit: Wege der Forschung – vom alten zum neuen Schürer.* Munich. 221–36.
Coulton, J. J. 1987. Roman aqueducts in Asia Minor. In Macready and Thompson 1987: 72–84.
Courtney, E. 2001. *A companion to Petronius.* Oxford.
Crawford, D. 1976. Imperial estates. In Finley, M. I. (ed.), *Studies in Roman property.* Cambridge. 35–70.
Crawford, M. H. 1974. *Roman republican coinage.* Cambridge.
Crawford, M. H. 1975. Finance, coinage and money from the Severans to Constantine. *ANRW* 2.2: 560–93.

Crawford, M. H. 1983. Roman coin types and the formation of public opinion. In Brooke, C. N. L. et al. (eds.), *Studies in numismatic method presented to Philip Grierson*. Cambridge. 47–64.
Crawford, M. H. 1985. *Coinage and money under the Roman Republic. Italy and the Mediterranean economy.* Berkeley.
Crawford, M. H. (ed.) 1986. *L'Impero romano e le struture economiche e sociali delle province.* Biblioteca di Athenaeum 4. Como.
Crawford, M. H. 1988. The laws of the Romans: Knowledge and diffusion. In González, J. and Arce, X. (eds.), *Estudios sobre la Tabula Siarensis*. Madrid. 127–40.
Crawford, M. H. (ed.) 1996. *Roman Statutes*. 2 vols. BICS 64. London.
Cresci, L. R. 1999. The novel of Longus the sophist and the pastoral tradition. In Swain 1999: 210–42.
Crook, J. A. 1967. *Law and life of Rome*. London.
Crook, J. A. 1971. Arnold Hugh Martin Jones, 1904–1970. *Proceedings of the British Academy* 57: 425–38.
Crowther, N. B. and Frass, M. 1998. Flogging as a punishment in ancient games. *Nikephoros* 11: 51–82.
Culham, P. 1997. Did Roman women have an empire? In Golden and Toohey: 192–204.
Cumont, F. 1926. *Fouilles de Doura-Europos (1922–1923)*. Paris.
Cunliffe, B. 1988. *Greeks, Romans and barbarians: Spheres of interaction*. New York.
Curtis, R. I. 1991a. *Garum and Salsamenta: Production and commerce in materia medica*. Studies in Ancient Medicine 3. Leiden.
Curtis, R. I. 1991b. Salt-fish products around the Strait of Gibraltar. *JRA* 4: 299–305.
Curtis, R. I. 2001. *Ancient food technology.* Leiden.
Dalzell, A. 1955. Asinius Pollio and the introduction of recitation at Rome. *Hermathena* 86: 20–8.
Damon, C. 2003. *Tacitus, Histories 1*. Cambridge.
Damon, C. and Takács, S. (eds.) 1999. *The Senatus Consultum de Cn. Pisone Patre: Text, translation, discussion. AJP* 120. Baltimore.
Daniel, R. W. and Maltomini, F. (eds. and trans.) 1990. *Supplementum Magicum*, vol. 1. = *Abhandlungen der Rheinisch-Westfälischen Akademie der Wissenschaften, Sonderreihe Papyrologica Coloniensia*, vol. 16.1. Opladen.
Daniélou, J. 1964–77. *A history of early Christian doctrine before the Council of Nicaea*. 3 vols. London.
D'Arms, J. 1981. *Commerce and social standing in ancient Rome*. Cambridge, MA.
D'Arms, J. 1984. Control, companionship and clientela: Some social functions of the Roman communal meal. *EchCl* 28: 327–48.
D'Arms, J. 1990. The Roman *convivium* and the idea of equality. In Murray: 308–20.
D'Arms, J. 1995. Heavy drinking and drunkenness in the Roman world: Four questions for historians. In Murray and Tecusan: 304–17.
D'Arms, J. 1999. Performing culture: Roman spectacle and the banquets of the powerful. In Bergmann and Kondoleon: 301–19.
D'Arms, J. 2000. Memory, money and status at Misenum: Three new inscriptions from the collegium of Augustales. *JRS* 90: 126–44.
Daumas, F. 1961. Littérature prophétique et exégétique égyptienne et commentaires esséniens. In *A la rencontre de Dieu (Mémorial Albert Gelin)*. Le Puy. 203–21.
Davidson, J. 2001. Dover, Foucault and Greek homosexuality: Penetration and the truth of sex. *Past and Present* 170: 3–51.
Davies, J. K. 2005. Greek archives: From record to monument. In Brosius, M. (ed.), *Ancient archives and archival traditions: Concepts of record-keeping in the ancient world*. Oxford. 323–43.

Davies, R. W. 1974. The daily life of the Roman soldier. *ANRW* 2.1: 299–338.
De Blois, L. (ed.) 2001. *Administration, prosopography and appointment policies in the Roman Empire*. Amsterdam.
De Blois, L. and Rich, J. (eds.) 2002. *The transformation of economic life under the Roman Empire*. Amsterdam.
De Blois, L., Pleket, H., and Rich, J. 2002. Introduction. In De Blois and Rich 2002: ix–xx.
De Felice, J. 2001. *Roman hospitality: The professional women of Pompeii*. Warren Center, PA.
De Haan, N. 1997. *Nam Nihil Melius Esse Quam Sine Turba Lavari*: Privatbäder in den Vesuvstädten. *Mededelingen van het Nederlands Instituut te Rome* 56: 205–26.
De Haan, N. 2001. *Si Aquae Copia Patiatur*: Pompeian private baths and the use of water. In Koloski-Ostrow: 41–9.
Deininger, J. 1965. *Die Provinziallandtage der römischen Kaiserzeit von Augustus bis zum Ende des dritten Jahrhunderts n. Chr.* Vestigia, Beiträge zur alten Geschichte 6. Munich.
De Laet, S. 1949. Portorium. *Étude sur l'organisation douanière chez les romains, surtout à l'époque du haut-Empire*. Brugge.
DeLaine, J. 1997. *The baths of Caracalla: A study in the design, construction, and economics of large-scale building projects in imperial Rome*. JRA Suppl. 25. Portsmouth, RI.
DeLaine, J. 2000. Building the Eternal City: The construction industry of imperial Rome. In Coulston, J. and Dodge, H. (eds.), *Ancient Rome. The archaeology of the Eternal City.* Oxford. 119–41.
DeLaine, J. 2001. Bricks and mortar. Exploring the economics of building techniques at Rome and Ostia. In Mattingly and Salmon 2001a: 230–68.
DeLaine, J. and Johnston, D. E. (eds.) 1999. *Roman baths and bathing*. JRA Suppl. 37. Portsmouth, RI.
De Ligt, L. 1993. *Fairs and markets in the Roman Empire: Economic and social aspects of periodic trade in a pre-industrial society*. Amsterdam.
De Ligt, L. 1998–9. Studies in legal and agrarian history I: The inscription from Henchir Mettich and the *Lex Manciana*. *Ancient Society* 2: 219–39.
Démougin, S. (ed.) 1994. *La mémoire perdue. À la recherche des archives oubliées, publiques et privées, de la Rome antique*. CNRS – Série Histoire Ancienne et Médiévale 30. Paris.
De Neeve, P. W. 1984. *Colonus: Private farm-tenancy in Roman Italy during the republic and the early principate*. Amsterdam.
De Neeve, P. W. 1990. A Roman landowner and his estates: Pliny the Younger. *Athenaeum* 78: 363–402.
Derks, T. 1998. *Gods, temples and religious practices: The transformation of religious ideas and values in Roman Gaul*. Amsterdam.
De Romanis, F. and Tchernia, A. (eds.) 1997. *Crossings: Early Mediterranean contacts with India*. New Delhi.
Derow, P. S. 1989. Rome, the fall of Macedon and the sack of Corinth. *CAH*[2] 8: 290–323.
Desideri, P. 2001. City and country in Dio. In Swain 2001: 93–107.
Des Places, É. (ed. and trans.) 1973. *Numenius*. Paris.
De Vos, A. and De Vos, M. 1982. *Pompei, Ercolano, Stabia*. Guide archeologiche Laterza 11. Bari.
De Vos, M. (ed.) 2001. *Rus Africum: Terra acqua olio nell'Africa settentrionale. Scavo e recognizione nei dintorini di Dougga* (Alto Tell tunisino). Trento.
Dewar, M. 1994. Laying it on with a trowel: The proem to Lucan and related texts. *CQ* 44: 199–211.
Dickie, M. W. 2001. *Magic and magicians in the Greco-Roman world*. London.
Dietz, K. 1980. *Senatus contra principem: Untersuchungen zur senatorischen Opposition gegen Kaiser Maximinus Thrax*. Munich.

Dihle, A. 1994. *Greek and Latin literature of the Roman Empire: From Augustus to Justinian.* London.
Dilke, O. 1971. *The Roman land surveyors. An introduction to the Agrimensores.* Newton Abbott.
Dillon, J. M. 1977. *The middle Platonists.* London.
Dillon, J. M. 1982. Self-definition in later Platonism. In Meyer and Sanders: 60–75.
Dillon, J. M. 1989. Tampering with the Timaeus: Ideological emendations in Plato, with special reference to the *Timaeus. AJP* 110: 50–72.
Dionisotti, A. 1988. Nepos and the generals. *JRS* 78: 35–49.
Dixon, K. R. and Southern, P. 1992. *Roman cavalry.* London.
Dixon, S. 1988. *The Roman mother.* Norman, OK.
Dixon, S. 1991. The sentimental ideal of the Roman family. In B. Rawson 1991: 99–113.
Dixon, S. 1992. *The Roman family.* Baltimore.
Dixon, S. (ed.) 2001. *Childhood, class and kin in the Roman world.* London.
Dobbin, R. 1998. *Epictetus, Discourses Book II.* Oxford.
Dobney, K. 2001. A place at the table: The role of vertebrate zooarchaeology with a Roman research agenda for Britain. In James, S. T. and Millett, M. (eds.), *Britons and Romans: Advancing an agenda for Britain.* York. 36–45.
Dodge, H. 1988. Decorative stones for architecture in the Roman Empire. *Oxford Journal of Archaeology* 7.1: 65–80.
Dodge, H. 1991. Ancient marble studies: Recent research. *JRA* 4: 28–50.
Dodge, H. 1999. Amusing the masses: Buildings for entertainment and leisure in the Roman world. In Potter and Mattingly 1999: 205–55.
Dodge, H. and Ward-Perkins, B. 1992. *Marble in antiquity.* British School at Rome Monog. 6. London.
Domaszewski, A von. 1914. *Geschichte der römischen Kaiser.* 2nd edn., vol. 2. Leipzig.
Domergue, C. 1990. *Les mines de la péninsula ibérique dans l'antiquité romaine.* Rome.
Dominik, W. J. 1994. *The mythic voice of Statius: Power and politics in the Thebaid.* Leiden.
Dominik, W. J. (ed.) 1997. *Roman eloquence: Rhetoric in society and literature.* London.
Donahue, J. F. 1996. Epula publica: *The Roman community at table during the principate.* PhD dissertation, University of North Carolina at Chapel Hill.
Donahue, J. F. 2004. *The Roman community at table during the principate.* Ann Arbor.
Dörrie, H. 1987. *Der Platonismus in der Antike.* Vol. 1. Stuttgart.
Dosi, A. and Schnell, F. 1984. *A tavola con i romani antichi.* Rome.
Douglas, M. (ed.) 1970. *Witchcraft confessions and accusations.* London.
Downing, F. G. 1994. *Cynics and Christian origins.* Cambridge.
Drake, H. A. 2000. *Constantine and the bishops.* Baltimore.
Drerup, H. 1959. Bildraum und Realraum in der römischen Architektur. *Römische Mitteilungen* 66: 147–76.
Driel-Murray, C. van. 1999. And did those feet in ancient time... Feet and shoes as a material projection of the self. In Baker, P., Forcey, C., Jundi, S., and Witcher, R. (eds.), *TRAC 98: Proceedings of the Eighth Annual Theoretical Roman Archaeology Conference, Leicester 1998.* Oxford. 131–40.
Drinkwater, J. F. 1987. *The Gallic empire: Separatism and community in the north-western provinces of the Roman Empire, AD 260–274.* Historia Einzelschriften 52. Stuttgart.
Drinkwater, J. F. 2001. The Gallo-Roman woollen industry and the great debate. The Igel column revisited. In Mattingly and Salmon 2001a: 297–308.
Drinkwater, J. F. 2002. Prologue and epilogue. The socio-economic effect of Rome's arrival and departure from Gaul. In de Blois and Rich: 128–40.
Dunand, F. 1976. Lanternes gréco-romaines d'Égypte. *Dialogues d'histoire ancienne 1976*: 71–95.

Dunand, F. 1991. Miracles et guérisons en Égypte tardive. In Fick and Carrière: 235–50.

Dunand, F. 1997. La consultation oraculaire en Égypte tardive: L'oracle de Bès à Abydos. In Heintz: 65–84.

Dunbabin, K. M. D. 1989. *Baiarum grata voluptas*: Pleasures and dangers of the baths. *PBSR* 57: 6–46.

Dunbabin, K. M. D. 1999. *Mosaics of the Greek and Roman world*. Cambridge.

Dunbabin, K. M. D. 2003. *The Roman banquet: Images of conviviality*. Cambridge.

Duncan-Jones, R. P. 1976. Some configurations of landholding in the Roman Empire. In Finley, M. I. (ed.), *Studies in Roman property*. Cambridge. 7–33 [revised at Duncan-Jones 1990: 121–42].

Duncan-Jones, R. P. 1982. *The economy of the Roman Empire*. Rev. edn. Cambridge.

Duncan-Jones, R. P. 1990. *Structure and scale in the Roman economy*. Cambridge.

Duncan-Jones, R. P. 1994. *Money and government in the Roman Empire*. Cambridge.

Dupré Raventós, X. (ed.) 2004. *Mérida. Colonia Augusta Emerita* (Las capitales provinciales de *Hispania* 2). Rome.

Duthoy, R. 1974. La fonction social de l'augustalité. *Epigraphica* 36: 134–54.

Duthoy, R. 1978. Les *Augustales*. *ANRW* 2.16.2: 1254–309.

Dyson, S. L. 2003. *The Roman countryside*. London.

Eade, J. and Sallnow, M. J. (eds.) 1991. *Contesting the sacred: The anthropology of Christian pilgrimage*. London.

Easterling, P. E. and Hall, E. (eds.) 2002. *Greek and Roman actors: Aspects of an ancient profession*. Cambridge.

Ebel, C. 1973. *Transalpine Gaul. The emergence of a Roman province*. Leiden.

Eck, W. 1970. *Senatoren von Vespasian bis Hadrian. Prosopographische Untersuchungen mit Einschluss der Jahres und Provinzialfasten der Statthalter*. Munich.

Eck, W. 1979. *Die staatliche Organisation Italiens in der hohen Kaiserzeit*. Munich.

Eck, W. 1984. Senatorial self-representation: Developments in the Augustan period. In Millar and Segal: 129–67.

Eck, W. 1985. *Die Statthalter der germanischen Provinzen vom 1.–3. Jahrhundert*. Cologne-Bonn.

Eck, W. 1998. Inschriften auf Holz. Ein unterschätztes Phänomen der epigraphischen Kultur Roms. In Kneissl, P. and Losemann, V. (eds.), *Imperium Romanum. Festschrift für Karl Christ*. Stuttgart. 203–17.

Eck, W. 1999. Zur Einleitung römische Provinzialadministration und die Erkenntnismöglichkeiten der epigraphischien Überlieferung. In Eck and Müller-Luckner: 1–15.

Eck, W. 2000. Provincial administration and finance. CAH^2 11: 266–92.

Eck, W. 2002. An emperor is made: Senatorial politics and Trajan's adoption by Nerva in 97. In Clark, G. and Rajak, T. (eds.), *Philosophy and power in the Graeco-Roman world. Essays in honour of Miriam Griffin*. Oxford. 211–26.

Eck, W., Caballos, A., and Fernández, F. 1996. *Das senatus consultum de Cn.Pisone patre*. Vestigia 48. Munich.

Eck, W. and Müller-Luckner, E. (eds.) 1999. *Lokale Autonomie und römische Ordnungsmacht in den kaiserzeitlichen Provinzen vom 1. bis 3. Jahrhundert*. Munich.

Edmondson, J. C. 1996a. Roman power and the emergence of provincial administration in Lusitania during the republic. In Hermon, E. (ed.), *Pouvoir et Imperium. L'exercice du pouvoir et l'administration provinciale dans l'Empire romain républicain*. Naples and Quebec. 163–211.

Edmondson, J. C. 1996b. Dynamic arenas: Gladiatorial presentations in the city of Rome and the construction of Roman society during the early empire. In Slater 1996: 69–112.

Edmondson, J. C. 1999. The cultural politics of spectacle in the Greek east, 167–66 BCE. In Bergmann and Kondoleon: 77–96.

Edwards, C. 1993. *The politics of immorality in ancient Rome*. Cambridge.
Edwards, C. 1997. Unspeakable professions: Public performance and prostitution in ancient Rome. In Hallett and Skinner: 66–95.
Edwards, M. J. and Swain, S. (eds.) 1997. *Portraits: Biographical representation in the Greek and Latin literature of the Roman Empire*. Oxford.
Effe, B. 1999. Longus: Towards a history of bucolic and its function in the Roman Empire. In Swain 1999: 189–209.
Ehrhardt, C. T. H. R. 1984. Roman coin types and the Roman public. *JNG* 34: 41–54.
Eilberg-Schwartz, H. and Doniger, W. (eds.) 1995. *Off with her head*. Berkeley.
Eitrem, S. 1991. Dreams and divination in magical ritual. In Faraone, C. A. and Obbink, D. (eds.), *Magika Hiera: Ancient Greek magic and religion*. New York. 175–87.
Eliav, Y. Z. 2000. The Roman bath as a Jewish institution: Another look at the encounter between Judaism and the Greco-Roman culture. *Journal for the Study of Judaism* 31: 416–54.
Eliav, Y. Z. 2002. Viewing the sculptural environment, shaping the Second Commandment. In Schäfer, P. (ed.), *The Talmud Yerushalmi and Graeco-Roman culture* III. TSAJ 93. Tübingen. 411–33.
Eliav, Y. Z. 2003. On idolatry in the Roman bath house – two comments. *Cathedra* 110: 173–80. (Heb.)
Eliav, Y. Z. 2004. The matrix of ancient Judaism: A review essay of Seth Schwartz's *Imperialism and Jewish society 200 BCE to 640 CE*. *Prooftexts* 24: 116–28.
Ellis, S. P. 1988. The end of the Roman house. *AJA* 92: 565–76.
Ellis, S. P. 1997. Late-antique dining: Architecture, furnishings, and behaviour. In Laurence and Wallace-Hadrill: 41–52.
Ellis, S. P. 2002. *Roman housing*. London.
Elsner, J. 1995. *Art and the Roman viewer: The transformation of art from the pagan world to Christianity*. Cambridge.
Elsner, J. (ed.) 1996. *Art and text in Roman culture*. Cambridge.
Elsner, J. 1997. Hagiographic geography: Travel and allegory in the *Life of Apollonius of Tyana*. *JHS* 117: 22–37.
Elsner, J. and Rutherford, I. (eds.) 2005. *Seeing the gods: Pilgrimage in Graeco-Roman and early Christian antiquity*. Oxford.
Elsom, H. E. 1992. Callirhoe: Displaying the phallic woman. In Richlin 1992e: 212–30.
Elton, H. 1996a. *Frontiers of the Roman Empire*. London.
Elton, H. 1996b. *Warfare in barbarian Europe, AD 350–425*. Oxford.
Entero, V. G. 2001. *Los balnea de las villae Hispanoromanas provincia tarraconense*. Madrid.
Erdkamp, P. P. M. 2001. Beyond the limits of the consumer city. A model of the urban and rural economy in the Roman world. *Historia* 50: 332–56.
Erdkamp, P. P. M. (ed.) 2002. *The Roman army and the economy*. Amsterdam.
Errington, R. M. 1988. Aspects of Roman acculturation in the east under the republic. *Festschrfit K. Christ*. Darmstadt. 140–57.
Estiot, S. 1987. *Ripostiglio di Venerà nuovo catalogo illustrato. II/2. Tacito e Floriano*. Verona.
Estiot, S. 1995. *Ripostiglio di Venerà nuovo catalogo illustrato. II/1. Aureliano*. Rome.
Étienne, R. 1958. *Le culte impérial dans la péninsule ibérique d'Auguste à Dioclétien*. Bibliothèque des Écoles Françaises d'Athènes et de Rome 191. Paris.
Evans, C. A. 1992. Opposition to the Temple: Jesus and the Dead Sea Scrolls. In Charlesworth, J. H. (ed.), *Jesus and the Dead Sea Scrolls*. New York. 235–353.
Evans, R. 1999. Ethnography's freak show: The grotesques at the edges of the Roman earth. *Ramus* 28.1: 54–73.
Evans Grubbs, J. 1995. *Law and family in late antiquity: The emperor Constantine's marriage legislation*. Oxford.

Evans Grubbs, J. 2002. *Women and the law in the Roman Empire: A sourcebook on marriage, divorce, and widowhood*. London.
Fabricius, C. 1972. *Galens Exzerpte aus älteren Pharmakologe*. Berlin
Fagan, G. G. 1999a. *Bathing in public in the Roman world*. Ann Arbor.
Fagan, G. G. 1999b. Interpreting the evidence: Did slaves bathe at the baths? In DeLaine and Johnston. 25–34.
Fagan, G. G. 2001. The genesis of the Roman public bath: Recent approaches and future directions. *AJA* 105: 403–26.
Fant, J. C. (ed.) 1988. *Ancient marble quarrying and trade*. BAR S453. Oxford.
Fant, J. C. 1989. Cavum antrum Phrygiae: *The organization and operations of the Roman imperial marble quarries in Phrygia*. BAR S482. Oxford.
Fant, J. C. 1993. Ideology, gift and trade: A distribution model for the Roman imperial marbles. In W. V. Harris 1993a: 145–70.
Fantham, E. 1991. *Stuprum*: Public attitudes and penalties for sexual offences in republican Rome. *EchCl* 35, n.s. 10: 267–91.
Fantham, E. 1996. *Roman literary culture from Cicero to Apuleius*. Baltimore.
Farrell, J. 1991. *Vergil's Georgics and the traditions of ancient epic: The art of allusion in literary history*. New York.
Farrington, A. 1995. *The Roman baths of Lycia: An architectural study*. Ankara.
Fedeli, P. 1989. Il "Panegirico" di Plinio nella critica moderna. *ANRW* 2.33.1: 387–515.
Feeney, D. 1991. *The Gods in epic*. Oxford.
Feeney, D. 2002. *Una cum scriptore meo*: Poetry, principate and the traditions of literary history in the Epistle to Augustus. In Woodman and Feeney: 172–87.
Feissel, D. 1985. Une dédicace en l'honneur de Constantin II César et les préfets du prétoire de 336. *Travaux et Mémoires* 9: 421–34.
Feissel, D. 1991. Praefatio chartarum publicarum; l'intitulé des actes de la préfecture du prétoire du IVe au VIe siècle. *Travaux et Mémoires* 11: 437–64.
Feissel, D. and Gascou, J. 1995. Documents d'archives romains inédits du Moyen Euphrate (IIIe s. après J.C.). *Journal des Savants*: 65–119.
Fentress, E. (ed.) 2000. *Romanization and the city: Creation, transformations, and failures*. JRA Suppl. 38. Portsmouth, RI.
Ferris, I. M. 2000. *Enemies of Rome: Barbarians through Roman eyes*. Sutton.
Fick, N. and Carrière, J.-C. (eds.) 1991. *Mélanges Étienne Bernand*. Paris.
Fine, S. 1997. *This holy place: On the sanctity of the synagogue during the Greco-Roman period*. South Bend, IN.
Fine, S. 1998. "Chancel" screens in late antique Palestinian synagogues: A source from the Cairo Genizah. In Lapin, H. (ed.), *Religious and ethnic communities in later Roman Palestine*. Studies and Texts in Jewish History and Culture 5. Bethesda, MD. 67–85.
Fink, R. O. 1971. *Roman military records on papyrus*. Philological Monographs of the American Philological Association, no. 26. Cleveland.
Finley, M. I. 1965. Technical innovation and economic progress in the ancient world. *Economic History Review* 18: 29–45. (Rpr. in Shaw, B. D. and Saller, R. P. [eds.], *Economy and society in ancient Greece*. 1981. London. 176–95.)
Finley, M. I. (ed.) 1974. *Studies in ancient society*. London.
Finley, M. I. 1977. The ancient city: From Fustel de Coulanges to Max Weber and beyond. *Comparative Studies in Society and History* 19: 305–27. (Rpr. in Shaw, B. D. and Saller, R. P. [eds.], *Economy and society in ancient Greece*. 1981. London. 3–23.)
Finley, M. I. 1985. *The ancient economy*. Rev. edn. London.
Fisher, N. R. E. 1988. Roman associations, dinner parties and clubs. In Grant and Kitzinger: 2: 1199–225.
Fishwick, D. 1995. The Temple of Divus Claudius at Camulodunum. *Britannia* 26: 11–27.

Fishwick, D. 2002. *The imperial cult in the Latin west. Studies in the ruler cult of the western provinces of the Roman Empire. III. Provincial cult. 2. The provincial priesthood.* Religions in the Graeco-Roman World 146. Leiden.

Fitz, J. and Fedak, J. 1993. From Roman Gorsium to late-antique Herculia: A summary of recent work at Tác (NE Pannonia). *JRA* 6: 261–73.

Flach, D. 1978. Inschriftenuntersuchungen zum römischen Kolonat in Nordafrika. *Chiron* 8: 441–92.

Flemming, R. 2000. *Medicine and the making of Roman women: Gender, nature, and authority from Celsus to Galen.* Oxford.

Fleming, S. 2001. *Vinum: The story of Roman wine.* Glen Mills, PA.

Flint, V. I. J. 1991. *The rise of magic in early medieval Europe.* Princeton.

Flower, B. and Rosenbaum, E. 1958. *Apicius: The Roman cookery book.* London.

Flower, H. 1996. *Ancestor masks and aristocratic power in Roman culture.* Oxford.

Fontana, S. 2001. Leptis Magna. The Romanization of a major African city through burial evidence. In Keay and Terrenato: 161–72.

Fora, M. 1996. *Epigrafia anfiteatreale dell' occidente romano.* Vol. 4. Rome.

Forni, G. 1953. *Il reclutamento delle legioni da Augusto a Diocleziano.* Milan.

Foti-Talamanca, G. 1974. *Ricerche sul processo nell'Egitto greco-romano I: L'organizzazione del "conventus" del "praefectus Aegypti."* Rome.

Foucault, M. 1988. *The care of the self.* Trans. R. Hurley. New York.

Fowden, G. 1977. The Platonist philosopher and his circle in late antiquity. *Philosophia* 7: 359–83.

Fowden, G. 1978. Bishops and temples in the eastern Roman Empire, AD 320–435. *JTS* 29: 53–78.

Fowden, G. 1982. The pagan holy man in late antique society. *JHS* 102: 33–59.

Fowden, G. 1993. *Empire to commonwealth: Consequences of monotheism in late antiquity.* Princeton.

Foxhall, L. 1990. The dependent tenant: Land leasing and labour in Italy and Greece. *JRS* 80: 97–114.

Francovich, R., Patterson, H., and Barker, G. W. (eds.) 2000. *Extracting meaning from ploughsoil assemblages.* Oxford.

Frank, T. (ed.) 1933–40. *An economic survey of ancient Rome.* Baltimore.

Franke, P. R. 1968. *Kleinasien zur Römerzeit. Griechisches Leben im Spiegel der Münzen.* Munich.

Frankfurter, D. 1990. Stylites and *Phallobates*: Pillar religions in late antique Syria. *VC* 44: 168–98.

Frankfurter, D. 1998a. *Religion in Roman Egypt: Assimilation and resistance.* Princeton.

Frankfurter, D. 1998b. Introduction: Approaches to Coptic pilgrimage. In Frankfurter 1998d: 3–48.

Frankfurter, D. 1998c. Early Christian apocalypticism: Literature and social world. In Collins: 415–53.

Frankfurter, D. (ed.) 1998d. *Pilgrimage and holy space in late antique Egypt.* Leiden.

Frankfurter, D. 2000a. The consequences of Hellenism in late antique Egypt: Religious worlds and actors. *Archiv für Religionsgeschichte* 2.2: 162–94.

Frankfurter, D. 2000b. The zenith and destruction of a native Egyptian oracle in 359 C.E. In Valantasis: 476–80.

Frankfurter, D. 2002. Dynamics of ritual expertise in antiquity and beyond: Towards a new taxonomy of "Magicians." In Mirecki and Meyer: 159–78.

Frankfurter, D. 2005. Urban shrine and rural saint in fifth-century Alexandria. In Elsner and Rutherford.

Frayn, J. M. 1993. *Markets and fairs in Roman Italy.* Oxford.

Frede, D. and Laks, A. (eds.) 2002. *Traditions of theology: Studies in Hellenistic theology, its background and aftermath*. Leiden.
Frede, M. 1983. Stoics and skeptics on clear and distinct impressions. In Burnyeat, M. (ed.), *The skeptical tradition*. Berkeley. 65–93.
Frede, M. 1987. Numenius. *ANRW* 2.36.2: 1034–75.
Frede, M. 1994. Celsus. Philosophicus Platonicus. *ANRW* 2.36.7: 5183–213.
Frede, M. 1997. Celsus' attack on the Christians. In Barnes and Griffin: 218–40.
Frede, M. 1999. Stoic epistemology. In Algra, K. et al. (eds.), *The Cambridge history of Hellenistic philosophy*. Cambridge. 295–322.
Fredrick, D. 1995. Beyond the atrium to Ariadne: Erotic painting and visual pleasure in the Roman house. *CA* 14: 266–87.
Fredrick, D. 1997. Reading broken skin: Violence in Roman elegy. In Hallett and Skinner: 172–93.
Frederiksen, M. W. 1965. The republican municipal laws: Errors and drafts. *JRS* 55: 183–98.
Fredriksen, P. 1991a. Judaism, the circumcision of gentiles, and apocalyptic hope: Another look at Galatians 1 and 2. *JTS* 42: 536–64.
Fredriksen, P. 1991b. Apocalypse and redemption in early Christianity, from John of Patmos to Augustine of Hippo. *VC* 45: 151–83.
Fredriksen, P. 1999. *Jesus of Nazareth, King of the Jews*. New York.
Fredriksen, P. 2000. *From Jesus to Christ*. 2nd edn. New Haven. (1st edn. 1988.)
Fredriksen, P. 2003. What "parting of the ways"? Jews, gentiles, and the ancient Mediterranean city. In Becker, A. and Reed, A. Y. (eds.), *The ways that never parted*. Tübingen. 36–63.
Fredriksen, P. and Irshai, O. 2004. Christian anti-Judaism: Polemics and policies, from the second to the seventh century. In Katz, S. T. (ed.), *Cambridge history of Judaism*. Vol. 4. Cambridge.
Fredriksen, P. and Lieu, J. 2004a. Rival traditions: Christian theology and Judaism. In Evans, G. R. (ed.), *The first Christian theologians*. Oxford. 85–101.
Freeman, P. W. M. 1997. Mommsen through to Haverfield: The origins of Romanization studies in late 19th-century Britain. In Mattingly 1997: 27–50.
French, R. and Greenaway, F. (eds.) 1986. *Science in the early Roman Empire: Pliny the Elder, his sources and influence*. Totowa, NJ.
Frend, W. H. C. 1952. *The Donatist Church*. Oxford.
Frend, W. H. C. 1956. A third-century inscription relating to *Angareia* in Phrygia. *JRS* 46: 46–56.
Freudenburg, K. 2001. *Satires of Rome: Threatening poses from Lucilius to Juvenal*. Cambridge.
Friedland, E. A. 2003. The Roman marble sculptures from the north hall of the East Baths at Gerasa. *AJA* 107: 413–48.
Friedländer, L. 1922. *Darstellungen aus der Sittengeschichte Roms*. 10th edn. 4 vols. Leipzig. (Translation as Friedländer, L. 1908–13. *Roman life and manners under the early empire*. 4 vols [tr. Freese, J. H., A. B. Gough, and L. A. Magnus]. New York.)
Frier, B. W. 1979. Law, technology, and social change: The equipping of Italian farm tenancies. *ZSS* 96: 204–28.
Frier, B. W. 1982. Roman life expectancy: Ulpian's evidence. *HSCP* 86: 213–51.
Frier, B. W. 1985. *The rise of the Jurists*. Princeton.
Frier, B. W. 1989–90. Law, economics, and disasters down on the farm: "Remissio Mercedis" revisited. *Bullettino dell'Istituto di diritto romano*^{3} 31–2: 237–70.
Frier, B. W. 1991. Pompeii's economy and society. *JRA* 4: 243–7.
Frier, B. W. 1992. Statistics and Roman society. *JRA* 5: 286–90.
Frier, B. W. 1994. Natural fertility and family limitation in Roman marriage. *CPh* 89: 318–33.
Frier, B. W. 1999. Roman demography. In Potter and Mattingly: 85–109.

Frier, B. W. 2000a. Roman law's descent into history (review of Robinson 1997 and Johnston 1999). *JRA* 13: 446–8.
Frier, B. W. 2000b. Demography. *CAH*² 10: 787–816.
Friesen, S. J. 1993. *Twice Neokoros: Ephesus, Asia, and the cult of the Flavian imperial family*. Religions in the Graeco-Roman world 116. Leiden.
Frisch, P. 1986. *Zehn agonistische Papyri*. Opladen.
Frost, F. 1999. Sausage and meat preservation in antiquity. *GRBS* 40: 241–52.
Frye, R. N. 1984. *The history of ancient Iran*. Munich.
Fulford, M. 1987. Economic interdependence among urban communities of the Roman Mediterranean. *World Archaeology* 19.1: 58–75.
Fulford, M. 1989. To east and west: The Mediterranean trade of Cyrenaica and Tripolitania in antiquity. *Libyan Studies* 20: 169–91.
Fulford, M. 1992. Territorial expansion and the Roman Empire. *World Archaeology* 23.3: 294–305.
Fulford, M. 2004. Economic structures. In Todd, M. (ed.), *A companion to Roman Britain*. Oxford. 309–26.
Fulle, G. 1997. The internal organization of the Arretine *terra sigillata* industry: Problems of evidence and interpretation. *JRS* 87: 111–55.
Funaioli, I. 1920. Recitationes. *REA* 1: 435–46.
Fusillo, M. 1989. *Il romanzo greco: Polifonia ed eros*. Venice.
Fusillo, M. 1999. Lucian's *A True Story* – from satire to utopia. In Swain 1999: 351–81.
Gabba, E. 1991. *Dionysius and the history of archaic Rome*. Berkeley.
Gager, J. (ed.) 1992. *Curse tablets and binding spells from the ancient world*. New York.
Gagos, T. and Sijpesteijn, P. J. 1996. Towards an explanation of the typology of the so-called "orders to arrest." *BASP* 33: 77–97.
Galinsky, K. 1996. *Augustan culture. An interpretive essay*. Princeton.
Galsterer, H. 1986. Roman law in the provinces: Some problems of transmission. In Crawford: 13–27.
Galsterer, H. 1988. Municipium Flavium Irnitanum: A Latin town in Spain. *JRS* 78: 78–90.
Galsterer, H. 1996. The administration of justice. *CAH*² 10: 397–413.
Galsterer, H. 1999. Kolonisation im Rheinland. In Dondin-Payre, M. and Raepsaet-Charlier, M.-T. (eds.), *Cités, municipes, colonies: les processus de municipalisation en Gaule et en Germanie sous le Haut Empire romain*. Paris. 251–70.
Garbrecht, G.-H. and Manderscheid, H. 1994. *Die Wasserbewirtschaftung römischer Thermen: Archäologische und hydrotechnische Untersuchungen*. 3 vols. Mitteilungen aus dem Leichtweiß-Institut f. Wasserbau der Technischen Universität Braunschweig 118. Braunschweig.
Gardiner, I. and Lieu, S.N.C. 1996. From Narmouthis (Medinet Madi) to Kellis (Ismant El-Kharab): Manichaean Documents from Roman Egypt. *JRS* 86: 146–69.
Gardner, J. F. 1986. *Women in Roman law and society*. London.
Gardner, J. F. 1993. *Being a Roman citizen*. London.
Gardner, J. F. 1998. *Family and* familia *in Roman law and life*. Oxford.
Gardner, J. F. 2001. Making citizens: The operation of the *Lex Irnitana*. In De Blois: 215–29.
Garlick, B., Allen, P., and Dixon, S. (eds.) 1992. *Stereotypes of women in power*. Westport.
Garnsey, P. D. A. 1970. *Social status and legal privilege in the Roman Empire*. Oxford.
Garnsey, P. D. A. 1971. Honorarium decurionatus. *Historia* 20: 309–25.
Garnsey, P. D. A. 1974. Aspects of the decline of the urban aristocracy in the empire. *ANRW* 2.1: 229–52. (Rpr. in Garnsey 1998: 3–27.)
Garnsey, P. D. A. 1980. *Non-slave labour in the Greco-Roman world*. Cambridge.
Garnsey, P. D. A. 1988. *Famine and food supply in the Graeco-Roman world*. Cambridge.
Garnsey, P. D. A. 1998. *Cities, peasants and food in classical antiquity: Essays in social and economic history*. Ed. with addenda, W. Scheidel. Cambridge.

Garnsey, P. D. A. 1999. *Food and society in classical antiquity.* Cambridge.
Garnsey, P. D. A. 2000. The land. In *CAH*² 10: 679–709.
Garnsey, P. D. A., Hopkins, K., and Whittaker, C. R. (eds.) 1983. *Trade in the ancient economy.* London.
Garnsey, P. D. A. and Humfress, C. 2001. *The evolution of the late antique world.* Cambridge.
Garnsey, P. D. A. and Saller, R. 1987. *The Roman Empire. Economy, society and culture.* London.
Garnsey, P. D. A. and Whittaker, C. R. 1983. *Trade and famine in classical antiquity.* Cambridge.
Garnsey, P. D. A. and Whittaker, C. R. 1998. Trade, industry and the urban economy. In *CAH*² 13: 312–37.
Gascou, J. 1983. *Pagus* et *castellum* dans la confédération cirtéenne. *Ant.Afr.* 19: 175–207.
Gascou, J. 1999. Unités administratives locales et fonctionnaires romains: les données des nouveaux papyrus du Moyen Euphrate et d'Arabe. In Eck and Müller-Luckner: 61–74.
Gatti, M. L. 1996. Plotinus: The Platonic tradition and the foundation of Neoplatonism. In Gerson, L. P. (ed.), *The Cambridge companion to Plotinus.* 10–37.
Gawlikowsky, M. 2000. Un nouveau mithraeum récemment découvert à Huarté près d'Apamée. *CRAI*: 161–71.
Gazda, E. K. (ed.) 1991. *Roman art in the private sphere.* Ann Arbor.
Geffcken, J. 1978. *The last days of Greco-Roman paganism.* Trans. S. MacCormack. Amsterdam.
George, M. 1997. Servus and domus: The slave in the Roman house. In Laurence and Wallace-Hadrill: 15–24.
Giard, J.-B. 1976–98. *Bibliothèque Nationale. Catalogue des monnaies de l'empire romaine.* 3 vols. Paris.
Giard, J.-B. 1995. *Ripostiglio di Venerà nuovo catalogo illustrato. I. Gordiano III-Quintillo.* Rome.
Giardina, A. 1993a. *The Romans.* Trans. L. Cochrane. Chicago.
Giardina, A. 1993b. The merchant. In Giardina 1993a: 245–71.
Gibbon, E. 1966. *Memoirs of my life.* Ed. G. A. Bonnard. London.
Gibbon, E. 1994. *The history of the decline and fall of the Roman Empire.* Ed. with introduction by D. Womersley. 3 vols. Harmondsworth.
Gibson, B. 2003. *Ovid, Ars Amatoria Book 3.* Cambridge.
Gibson, E. L. 1999. *The Jewish manumission inscriptions of the Bosporus kingdom.* TSAJ 75. Tübingen.
Gleason, M. W. 1986. Festive satire: Julian's *Misopogon* and the new year at Antioch. *JRS* 76: 106–19.
Gleason, M. W. 1995. *Making men: Sophists and self-presentation in ancient Rome.* Princeton.
Gleason, M. W. 1999a. Elite male identity in the Roman Empire. In Potter and Mattingly: 67–84.
Gleason, M. W. 1999b. Truth contests and talking corpses. In Porter, J. I. (ed.), *Constructions of the classical body.* Ann Arbor. 287–313.
Goldberg, A. 1987. The Mishnah – A study book of Halakha. In Safrai, S. (ed.), *The literature of the sages.* Compendia Rerum Iudaicarum ad Novum Testamentum 2:3. Assen. 211–62.
Golden, M. and Toohey, P. (eds.) 1997. *Inventing ancient culture: Historicism, periodization, and the ancient world.* London.
Goldhill, S. 1995. *Foucault's virginity: Ancient erotic fiction and the history of sexuality.* Cambridge.
Goldhill, S. (ed.) 2001a. *Being Greek under Rome: Cultural identity, the Second Sophistic and the development of empire.* Cambridge.
Goldhill, S. 2001b. The erotic eye: Visual stimulation and cultural conflict. In Goldhill 2001a: 154–94.

Goldstein, J. (ed.) 1994. *Foucault and the writing of history.* Oxford.
Goldsworthy, A. 1996. *The Roman army at war 100 BC–AD 200.* Oxford.
Goldsworthy, A. and Haynes, I. (eds.) 1999. *The Roman army as a community.* JRA Suppl. 34. Portsmouth, RI.
Golvin, J. C. 1988. *L'amphithéâtre romain. Essai sur la théorisation de sa forme et de ses functions.* Paris.
González, J. 1984. Tabula Siarensis, Fortunales Siarenses et municipia civium Romanorum. ZPE 55: 55–100. (Text translated in Sherk 1988, no. 36.)
González, J. 1986. The *Lex Irnitana*: A new Flavian municipal law. *JRS* 76: 147–243.
González, J. 1988. The first oath *Pro Salute Augusti* found in Baetica. *ZPE* 72: 113–27 (AE 1988, no. 723).
Goodblatt, D. 1994. *The monarchic principle: Studies in Jewish self-government in antiquity.* TSAJ 38. Tübingen.
Goodman, M. D. 1983. *State and society in Roman Galilee, AD 132–212.* Totowa, NJ.
Goodman, M. D. 1987. *The ruling class of Judaea. The origins of the Jewish revolt against Rome, AD 66–70.* Cambridge.
Goodman, M. D. 1992. The Roman state and the Jewish patriarch in the third century. In L. I. Levine: 127–39.
Goodman, M. D. 1994. Josephus as a Roman citizen. In Parente and Sievers: 329–38.
Goodman, M. D. (ed.) 1998. *Jews in a Graeco-Roman world.* Oxford.
Goodman, M. D. 2003. The Jewish image of God in late antiquity. In Kalmin, R. and Schwartz, S. (eds.), *Jewish culture and society under the Christian Roman Empire.* Interdisciplinary Studies in Ancient Culture and Religion 3. Leuven. 133–45.
Gordon, P. 1997. The lover's voice in *Heroides* 15: Or, why is Sappho a man? In Hallett and Skinner: 274–91.
Gordon, P. and Washington, H. C. 1995. Rape as a military metaphor in the Hebrew Bible. In Brenner: 308–25.
Gordon, R. 1990a. From republic to principate: Priesthood, religion and ideology. In Beard and North: 177–98.
Gordon, R. 1990b. The veil of power: Emperors, sacrificers and benefactors. In Beard and North: 199–231.
Gordon, R. 1999. Imagining Greek and Roman magic. In Ankarloo and Clark: 159–275.
Goudineau, C. and Peyre, C. 1993. *Bibracte et les Éduens. À la découverte d'un peuple gaulois.* Paris.
Gowers, E. J. 1993. *The loaded table: Representations of food in Latin literature.* Oxford.
Gowing, A. M. 1992. *The triumviral narratives of Appian and Cassius Dio.* Ann Arbor.
Gradel, I. 2002. *Emperor worship and Roman religion.* Oxford.
Graf, F. 1997: *Magic in the ancient world.* Trans. F. Philip. Cambridge, MA.
Grant, Mark. 2000. *Galen on food and diet.* London.
Grant, M. 1946. *From Imperium to Auctoritas. A historical study of* aes *coinage in the Roman Empire 49 BC–AD 14.* Cambridge.
Grant, M. 1953. *The Six main* aes *coinages of Augustus. Controversial studies.* Edinburgh.
Grant, M. and Kitzinger, R. (eds.) 1988. *Civilization of the ancient Mediterranean: Greece and Rome.* 3 vols. New York.
Graver, M. 1998. The manhandling of Maecenas: Senecan abstractions of masculinity. *AJP* 119: 607–32.
Green, A. (ed.) 1997. *Jewish spirituality I: From the Bible through the Middle Ages.* New York.
Greene, E. 1998. *The erotics of domination: Male desire and the mistress in Latin love poetry.* Baltimore.
Greene, K. 1986. *The archaeology of the Roman economy.* London.
Greene, K. 1992. *Roman pottery.* London.

Greene, K. 1994. Technology and innovation in context: The background to medieval and later developments. *JRA* 7: 22–33.
Greene, K. 2000a. Industry and technology. In *CAH* 10^2: 741–68.
Greene, K. 2000b. Technological innovation and economic progress in the ancient world. *Economic History Review* 53: 29–59.
Grewe, K. 1993. Augusta Emerita/Mérida: Eine Stadt römischer Technikgeschichte. *Antike Welt* 24.3: 244–55.
Gricourt, D. 2000. *Ripostiglio di Venerà nuovo catalogo illustrato. IV. Caro-Diocleziano.* Verona.
Griffin, J. 1984. Augustus and the poets: "Caesar qui cogere posset." In Millar and Segal: 189–218.
Griffin, M. 1982. The Lyons Tablet and Tacitean hindsight. *CQ* 32: 404–18.
Griffin, M. 1992. *Seneca: A philosopher in politics.* 2nd edn. Oxford.
Griffin, M. 1997a. Philosophy, politics, and politicians at Rome. In Griffin and Barnes. 1–37.
Griffin, M. 1997b. The Senate's story. *JRS* 87: 249–63.
Griffin, M. and Barnes, J. (eds.) 1997. *Philosophia Togata I: Essays on philosophy and Roman society.* Oxford.
Grigg, D. B. 1974. *The agricultural systems of the world: An evolutionary approach.* Cambridge.
Grillmeier, A. 1975. *Christ in Christian tradition I: From the Apostolic age to Chalcedon.* Atlanta.
Grimm, V. E. 1996. *From feasting to fasting, the evolution of a sin.* London.
Groningen, B. A. van. 1932. Projet d'unification des systèmes de signes critiques. *Cd'É* 7: 262–9.
Gros, P. 1984. L'*Augusteum* de Nîmes. *Revue archéologique narbonnaise* 17: 123–34.
Gros, P. 1987. Un programme augustéen: le centre monumental de la colonie d'Arles. *Jahrbuch des Deutschen Archäologischen Instituts:* 339–63.
Gros, P. 1990a. Le premier urbanisme de la Colonia Julia Karthago: mythes et réalités d'une fondation césaro-augustéenne. In *L'Afrique dans l'Occident romain (Ier siècle av. J.-C.–IVe siècle ap. J.-C.).* CEFR 134. Rome. 547–73.
Gros, P. 1990b. Théâtre et culte impériale en Gaule Narbonnaise et dans la Péninsule ibérique. In Trillmich and Zanker: 381–90.
Gros, P. 1991. *La France gallo-romaine.* Paris.
Gros, P. 1996. *L'architecture romaine du début du IIIe siècle av. J.-C. à la fin du Haut Empire. 1. Les monuments publics.* Paris.
Gros, P. 2001. *L'architecture romaine du début du IIIe siècle av. J.-C. à la fin du Haut Empire. 2. Maisons, palais, villas et tombeaux.* Paris.
Gros, P. and Torelli, M. 1988. *Storia dell'urbanistica: Il mondo romano.* Rome/Bari.
Gruen, E. 2002. *Diaspora. Jews amidst Greeks and Romans.* Cambridge, MA.
Guarducci, M. 1924. Poeti vaganti e conferenzieri dell'età ellenistica: Ricerche de epigrafia greca nel campo della letteratura e del costume. *Rendiconti. Accademia nazionale dei Lincei* 6.2: 627–75.
Gwilt, A. and Haselgrove, C. (eds.) 1997. *Reconstructing Iron Age societies.* Oxbow Monograph 71. Oxford.
Habermann, W. 1998. Zur chronologischen Verteilung der papyrologischen Zeugnisse. *ZPE* 122: 144–60.
Habicht, C. 1975. New evidence on the province of Asia. *JRS* 65: 64–91.
Habinek, T. N. 1992. An aristocracy of virtue: Seneca on the beginnings of wisdom. *YCS* 29: 187–203.
Habinek, T. N. 1997. The invention of sexuality in the world-city of Rome. In Habinek and Schiesaro: 23–43.
Habinek, T. N. 1998. *The politics of Latin literature: Writing, identity, and empire in ancient Rome.* Princeton.

Habinek, T. N. and Schiesaro, A. (eds.) 1997. *The Roman cultural revolution*. Cambridge.
Hadot, P. 1995. *Philosophy as a way of life: Spiritual exercises from Socrates to Foucault* (ed. with introduction by A. Davidson, trans. J. M. Chase). Oxford.
Haensch, R. 1992. Das Statthalterarchiv. *ZSS* 109: 209–317.
Haensch, R. 1994. Die Bearbeitungsweisen von Petitionen in der Provinz Aegyptus. *ZPE* 100: 487–546.
Haensch, R. 1997. Zur Konventsordnung in Aegyptus und den übrigen Provinzen des römischen Reiches. In Kramer et al.: 320–91.
Hägg, T. 1987. *Callirhoe* and *Parthenope*: The beginning of the historical novel. *CA* 6: 184–204.
Haines, C. R. (ed.) 1919. *The correspondence of Marcus Cornelius Fronto*. Vol. 1. London.
Hales, S. 2003. *The Roman house and social identity*. Cambridge.
Hall, E. 2002. The singing actors of antiquity. In Easterling and Hall: 3–28.
Hall, J. 1981. *Lucian's satire*. New York.
Hallett, J. P. 1977. *Perusinae Glandes* and the changing image of Augustus. *AJAH* 2: 151–71.
Hallett, J. P. 1989. Female homoeroticism and the denial of Roman reality in Latin literature. *Yale Journal of Criticism* 3.1: 209–27. (Rpr. in Hallett and Skinner: 255–73.)
Hallett, J. P. 1992. Martial's Sulpicia and Propertius's Cynthia. *CW* 86.2: 84–95.
Hallett, J. P. and Skinner, M. B. (eds.) 1997. *Roman sexualities*. Princeton.
Halperin, D. M. 1990. *One hundred years of homosexuality*. New York.
Halperin, D. M. 1992. Historicizing the sexual body: Sexual preferences and erotic identities in the pseudo-Lucianic *Erotes*. In Stanton: 236–61.
Halperin, D. M. 2002. Forgetting Foucault: Acts, identities, and the *History of Sexuality*. In Nussbaum and Sihvola: 21–54.
Hammerton-Kelly, R. G. (ed.) 1987. *Violent origins: Ritual killing and cultural formation*. Stanford.
Hammond, M. 1933. *The Augustan principate in theory and practice during the Julio-Claudian period*. New York.
Hansen, M. H. 2001. What is a document? An ill-defined type of source. *Classica et Mediaevalia* 52: 317–43.
Hansen, W. (ed.) 1998. *Anthology of Greek popular literature*. Bloomington, IN.
Hanson, A. E. 1985. Papyri of medical content. *YCS* 28: 25–47.
Hanson, A. E. 1994. Topographical arrangement of tax documents in the Philadelphia tax archive. In Bälno-Jacobsen, A. (ed.), *20th International Congress of Papyrology*. 210–18.
Hanson, A. E. 1995. Uterine amulets and Greek uterine medicine. *Medicina nei secoli* 7: 281–99.
Hanson, A. E. 1998a. Galen: Author and critic. In Most, G. (ed.), *Editing texts/Texte edieren* (= *Aporemata* II). Göttingen. 22–53.
Hanson, A. E. 1998b. Talking recipes in the Hippocratic corpus. In Wyke, M. (ed.), *Parchments of gender: Deciphering the body in antiquity*. Oxford. 71–94.
Hanson, A. E. 1999a. The Roman family. In Potter and Mattingly: 19–66.
Hanson, A. E. 1999b. A hair on her liver has been lacerated. In Garofalo, I. et al. (eds.), *Aspetti dela terapia nel Corpus Hippocraticum. Atti del IXe Colloque international hippocratique, Pisa 25–29 settembre 1996*. Florence: 235–54.
Hanson, A. E. 2000. Widows too young in their widowhood. In Kleiner, D. E. E. and Matheson, S. B. (eds.), *I, Claudia II: Women in Roman art and society*. Austin. 149–65.
Hanson, A. E. 2001. Text and context for the illustrated herbal from Tebtunis. *Atti del XXII Congresso Internazionale di Papyrologia, Firenze 1998*. Florence. 585–604.
Hanson, A. E. 2003. "Your mother nursed you with bile": Anger in babies and small children. *YCS* 32: 185–207.
Hanson, A. E. 2004a. *Aphorismi* 5.28–63 and the gynaecological texts of the *Corpus Hippocraticum*. In Horstmanshoff, H. F. J. and Stol, M. (eds.), *Magic and rationality in ancient near eastern and Graeco-Roman medicine*. Leiden. 277–304.

Hanson, A. E. 2004b. A long-lived "quick-birther" (*okytokion*). In *Naissance et petite enfance dans l'Antiquité, Actes du colloque de Fribourg, 28 novembre–1er décembre 2001*. Göttingen. 265–80.
Hanson, A. E. and Flemming, R. 1998. Hippocrates' *Peri Parthenîon* ("Diseases of Young Girls"): Text and translation. *Early Science and Medicine* 3: 241–52.
Hanson, A. E. and Green, M. H. 1994. Soranus, Methodicorum princeps. *ANRW* 2.37.2: 968–1075.
Hanson, R. P. C. 1988. *The search for the Christian doctrine of God*. Edinburgh.
Hanson, W. S. 1988. Administration, urbanisation and acculturation in the Roman west. In D. Braund: 53–68.
Hardie, A. 1983. *Statius and the Silvae. Poets, patrons and epideixis in the Graeco-Roman world*. Liverpool.
Hardie, P. 1986. *Vergil's Aeneid: Cosmos and imperium*. Oxford.
Hardie, P. 1991. The Janus episode in Ovid's *Fasti*. *Materiali e discussioni per l'analisi dei testi classici* 26: 47–64.
Hardie, P. 1993. *The epic successors of Virgil: A study in the dynamics of a tradition*. Cambridge.
Hardie, P. 1997a. Virgil and tragedy. In C. Martindale 1997: 312–26.
Hardie, P. 1997b. Questions of authority: The invention of tradition in Ovid's *Metamorphoses* 15. In Habinek and Schiesaro: 182–98.
Harl, K. W. 1987. *Civic coins and civic politics in the Roman east, AD 180–275*. Berkeley.
Harl, K. W. 1996. *Coinage in the Roman economy, 300 BC–AD 700*. Baltimore.
Harnack, A. 1908. *The mission and expansion of Christianity in the first three centuries*. 2 vols. London.
Harries, J. 1988. The Roman imperial quaestor from Constantine to Theodosius II. *JRS* 78: 148–72.
Harries, J. 1999. *Law and empire in late antiquity*. Cambridge.
Harris, J. R. (ed.) 1971. *The legacy of Egypt*. 2nd edn. Oxford.
Harris, W. V. 1993a. *The inscribed economy*. JRA Suppl. 6. Ann Arbor.
Harris, W. V. 1993b. Between archaic and modern: Some current problems in the history of the Roman economy. In W. V. Harris 1993a: 11–29.
Harris, W. V. 1994. Child-exposure in the Roman Empire. *JRS* 84: 1–22.
Harris, W. V. 1999. Demography, geography and the sources of Roman slaves. *JRS* 89: 62–75.
Harris, W. V. 2000. Trade. In *CAH*[2] 10: 710–40.
Hartmann, U. 2001. *Das palmyrenische Teilreich*. Stuttgart.
Hauken, T. 1998. *Petition and response: An epigraphic study of petitions to Roman emperors 181–249*. Bergen.
Haynes, I. 1999. Military service and cultural identity in the *Auxilia*. In Goldsworthy and Haynes: 165–74.
Heather, P. J. 1994. New men for new Constantines? Creating an imperial elite in the eastern Mediterranean. In Magdalino: 11–33.
Heffernan, T. 1995. Philology and authorship in the *Passio Sanctarum Perpetuae et Felicitatis*. *Traditio* 50: 315–25.
Heintz, J.-G. (ed.) 1997. *Oracles et prophéties dans l'antiquité*. Paris.
Heinz, W. 1996. Antike Balneologie in späthellenisticher und römischer Zeit: Zur medizinischen Wirkung römischer Bäder. *ANRW* 2.37.3: 2411–32.
Hekster, O. 2001. All in the family: The appointment of emperors designate in the second century AD. In De Blois: 35–49.
Hekster, O. 2002. *Commodus: An emperor at the crossroads*. Amsterdam.
Helgeland, J. 1980. Time and space: Christian and Roman. *ANRW* 2.23.2: 1285–305.
Hellegouarc'h, J. 1972. *Le vocabulaire latin des relations et des partis politiques sous la république*. 2nd edn. Paris.

Henderson, Jeffrey. 1992. *The Maculate muse*. Rev. edn. of 1975. Oxford.

Henderson, John. 1988. Lucan/The word at war. In Boyle, A. J. (ed.), *The imperial muse: To Juvenal through Ovid*. Berwick, Victoria, Australia. 122–64. (Rpr. in Henderson 1998: 165–211.)

Henderson, John. 1998. *Fighting for Rome*. Cambridge.

Hendy, M. 1970. On the administrative basis of the Byzantine coinage c. 400–c. 900 and the reforms of Heraclius. *Historical Journal (Birmingham)* 12: 129–54.

Hendy, M. 1972. Mint and fiscal administration under Diocletian, his colleagues and his successors, AD 305–24. *JRS* 62: 59–74.

Hendy, M. 1985. *Studies in the Byzantine monetary economy*. Cambridge.

Henry, M. M. 1992. The edible woman: Athenaeus's concept of the pornographic. In Richlin 1992e: 250–68.

Hermansen, G. 1981. *Ostia: Aspects of Roman city life*. Edmonton.

Hermon, E. 1993. *Rome et la Gaule Transalpine avant César, 125–59 av. J.-C.* Diáphora 3. Naples and Québec.

Herrmann, P. 1990. *Hilferufe aus römischen Provinzen. Ein Aspekt der Krise des römischen Reiches im 3. Jhdt.n.Chr.* Göttingen.

Hersh, C. A. 1977. Review of Crawford 1974. NC^7 17: 19–36.

Hersh, C. A. and Walker, A. 1984. The Mesagne hoard. *ANSMN* 29: 103–34.

Hershkowitz, D. 1998. *Valerius Flaccus' Argonautica: Abbreviated voyages in silver Latin epic*. Oxford.

Herz, P. 2000. Die römische Kaiserzeit (30 v. Chr. bis 284 n. Chr.). In Gehrke, H.-J. and Schneider, H. (eds.), *Geschichte der Antike. Ein Studienbuch*. Stuttgart-Weimar. 301–75.

Hezser, C. 1997. *The social structure of the Rabbinic movement in Roman Palestine*. TSAJ 66. Tübingen.

Hezser, C. 2001. *Jewish literacy in Roman Palestine*. TSAJ 81. Tübingen.

Hezser, C. 2002. The social status of slaves in the Talmud Yerushalmi and in Graeco-Roman society. In Schaefer 1998–2002: 91–137.

Hezser, C. (ed.) 2003. *Rabbinic law in its Roman and near eastern context*. TSAJ 97. Tübingen.

Hill, J. D. 1997. The end of one kind of body and the beginning of another kind of body? Toilet instruments and "Romanization." In Gwilt and Haselgrove: 96–107.

Himmelfarb, M. 1983. *Tours of hell: An apocalyptic form in Jewish and Christian literature*. Philadelphia.

Himmelfarb, M. 1987. From prophecy to apocalypse: *The Book of the Watchers* and tours of heaven. In Green: 145–65.

Himmelfarb, M. 1993. *Ascent to heaven in Jewish and Christian apocalypses*. New York.

Hinds, S. E. 1988. Generalising about Ovid. In Boyle, A. J. (ed.), *The imperial muse: To Juvenal through Ovid*. Berwick, Victoria, Australia. 4–31.

Hinds, S. E. 1998. *Allusion and intertext: Dynamics of appropriation in Roman poetry*. Cambridge.

Hingley, R. 2000. *Roman officers and English gentlemen: The imperial origins of Roman archaeology*. London.

Hirschfeld, O. 1905. *Die kaiserlichen verwaltungsbeamten bis auf Diocletian*. Berlin.

Hitchner, R. B. 1993. Olive production and the Roman economy: The case for intensive growth. In Amouretti and Brun: 499–508.

Hodge, A. T. 2002. *Roman aqueducts and water supply*. 2nd edn. London.

Hoffer, S. 1999. *The anxieties of Pliny the Younger*. Atlanta.

Hohlwein, N. 1940. Déplacements et tourisme dans l'Égypte romaine. *Chronique d'Égypte* 30: 253–78.

Hohlwein, N. 1969. *Le stratège du nome*. Pap. Brux. 9. Brussels.

Holder, P. A. 1980. *Studies in the* auxilia *of the Roman army from Augustus to Trajan*. BAR International Series 70. Oxford.
Holder, P. A. 1982. *The Roman army in Britain*. London.
Holzberg, N. 2001. *Der antike Roman: Eine Einführung*^{2}. Düsseldorf.
Hong, S., Candelone, J.-P., Patterson, C. C., and Boutron, C. F. 1994. Greenland ice evidence of hemispheric lead pollution two millennia ago by Greek and Roman civilizations. *Science* 265: 1841–3.
Hong, S., Candelone, J.-P., Patterson, C. C., and Boutron, C. F. 1996a. History of ancient copper smelting pollution during Roman and medieval times recorded in Greenland ice. *Science* 272: 246–9.
Hong, S., Candelone, J.-P., Soutif, M., and Boutron, C. F. 1996b. A reconstruction of changes in copper production and copper emissions to the atmosphere during the past 7000 years. *The Science of the Total Environment* 188: 183–93.
Honoré, A. M. 1978. *Tribonian*. London.
Honoré, A. M. 1994. *Emperors and lawyers*. 2nd edn. Oxford.
Hope, V. M. 2000. Inscription and sculpture: The construction of identity in the military tombstones of Roman Mainz. In Oliver, G. J. (ed.), *The epigraphy of death: Studies in the history and society of Greece and Rome*. Liverpool. 155–86.
Hope, V. M. 2003. Trophies and tombstones: Commemorating the Roman soldier. In Gilchrist, R. (ed.), *The Social Commemoration of Warfare*. World Archaeology 35.1: 79–97.
Hope, V. M. and Marshall, E. (eds.) 2000. *Death and disease in the ancient city*. London.
Hopkins, K. 1978a. The political power of eunuchs. In Hopkins 1978b: 172–96.
Hopkins, K. 1978b. *Conquerors and slaves*. Cambridge.
Hopkins, K. 1978c. Rules of evidence. *JRS* 68: 178–86.
Hopkins, K. 1978d. Economic growth and towns in classical antiquity. In Abrams, P. and Wrigley, E. A. (eds.), *Towns in societies*. Cambridge. 35–79.
Hopkins, K. 1980. Taxes and trade in the Roman Empire. *JRS* 70: 101–25.
Hopkins, K. 1983a. Introduction. In Garnsey et al. 1983: ix–xxv.
Hopkins, K. 1983b. Models, ships and staples. In Garnsey et al. 1983: 84–109.
Hopkins, K. 1983c. Murderous games. In Hopkins 1983d: 1–30.
Hopkins, K. 1983d. *Death and renewal*. Cambridge.
Hopkins, K. 1994. Novel evidence for Roman slavery. *Past and Present* 138: 3–27.
Hopkins, K. 1995/6. Rome, taxes, rent and trade. *Kodai* 6/7: 41–75.
Hopkins, K. 1998. Christian number and its implications. *JECS* 6.2: 185–226.
Hopkins, K. and Burton, G. 1983. Ambition and withdrawal: The senatorial aristocracy under the emperors. In Hopkins 1983d: 120–200.
Horbury, W. (ed.) 1991. *Templum Amicitiae: Essays on the Second Temple presented to Ernst Bammel. Journal for the Study of the New Testament* Suppl. 48. Sheffield.
Horbury, W. and Noy, D. 1992. *Jewish inscriptions of Graeco-Roman Egypt: With an index of the Jewish inscriptions of Egypt and Cyrenaica*. Cambridge.
Horden, P. and Purcell, N. 2000. *The corrupting sea: A study of Mediterranean history*. Oxford.
Hornblower, S. and Spawforth, A. 1996. *Oxford classical dictionary*. 3rd edn. Oxford.
Horsfall, N. 1983. Some problems in the "Laudatio Turiae." *BICS* 30: 85–98.
Horst, P. W. van der. 1998. *Sortes*: Sacred books as instant oracles in late antiquity. In Rutgers et al.: 143–73.
Householder, Jr., F. W. 1941. *Literary quotation and allusion in Lucian*. New York.
Houser, J. S. 1998. *Eros* and *Aphrodisia* in the works of Dio Chrysostom. *CA* 17: 236–58.
Houston, G. W. 2003. Galen, his books, and the Horrea Piperataria at Rome. *Memoirs of the American Academy in Rome* 48: 45–51.
Houston, G. 2004. Galen and the Horrea Pipperiana. In Corbeill, A. (ed.), *Memoirs of the American Academy in Rome*. Rome.

Howe, L. L. 1942. *The praetorian prefect from Commodus to Diocletian (AD 180–305)*. Chicago.
Howgego, C. 1985. *Greek imperial countermarks: Studies in the provincial coinage of the Roman Empire*. Royal Numismatic Society Special Publication 17. London.
Howgego, C. 1992. The supply of money in the Roman world 200 BC–AD 300. *JRS* 82: 1–31.
Howgego, C. 1994. Coin circulation and the integration of the Roman economy. *JRA* 7: 5–21.
Howgego, C. 1995. *Ancient history from coins*. London.
Hubbard, T. K. 2003. *Homosexuality in Greece and Rome: A sourcebook of basic documents*. Berkeley.
Huchthausen, L. 1974. Kaiserliche Rechtsauskünfte an Sklaven und in ihrer freiheit angefochtene Personen aus dem *Codex Iustinianus*. *Wissenschaftliche Zeitschrift der Wilhelm-Pieck-Universität Rostock* 22: 251–7.
Humphrey, J. H. 1986. *Roman circuses: Arenas for chariot racing*. Berkeley.
Hunt, D. 1998. The successors of Constantine. In *CAH*² 13: 1–43.
Hunter, R. L. 1994. History and historicity in the romance of Chariton. *ANRW* 2.34.2: 1055–86.
Hunter R. L. (ed.) 1998. *Studies in Heliodorus*. Cambridge Philosophical Society Suppl. vol. no. 21. Cambridge.
Hurlet, F. 1997. *Les collègues du prince sous Auguste et Tibère. De la légalité républicaine à la légitimité dynastique*. Rome.
Hurlet, F. 2001. L'image du pouvoir impérial et sa localisation dans la ville: la singularité de la province d'Afrique aux deux premiers siècles de notre ère. In Molin, M. (ed.), *Images et représentations du pouvoir et de l'ordre social dans l'Antiquité*. Paris. 277–89.
Hurst, H. (ed.) 1999. *The* coloniae *of Roman Britain: New studies and a review*. JRA Suppl. 36. Providence, RI.
Hurst, H. 2000. The fortress *coloniae* of Roman Britain: Colchester, Lincoln and Gloucester. In Fentress: 105–14.
Ihm, M. 1891. Delle tavole lusorie romane. *Rheinisches Museum* 6: 208–20.
Inwood, B. 1985. *Ethics and action in early Stoicism*. Oxford.
Inwood, B. 1995. Seneca in his philosophical milieu. *HSCP* 97: 63–76.
Inwood, B. 1999. Stoic ethics. In Algra, K. et al. (eds.), *The Cambridge history of Hellenistic philosophy*. Cambridge. 675–738.
Inwood, B. and Mansfeld, J. (eds.) 1997. *Assent and argument: Studies in Cicero's* Academic Books. Leiden.
Irshai, O. 2004. The priesthood in Jewish society of late antiquity. In Levine, L. I. (ed.), *Continuity and renewal: Jews and Judaism in Byzantine-Christian Palestine*. Jerusalem. 67–106. (Heb.)
Isaac, B. 1992. *The limits of empire. The Roman army in the east*. 2nd edn. Oxford.
Isaac, B. and Oppenheimer, A. 1985. The revolt of Bar Kokhba: Ideology and modern scholarship. *Journal of Jewish Studies* 36: 33–60.
Jackson, R. 1988. *Doctors and diseases in the Roman Empire*. London.
Jackson, R. 2003. The Domus "del chirurgo" at Rimini: An interim account of the medical assemblage. *JRA* 16: 312–21.
Jacobs, M. 1995. *Die Institution des jüdischen Patriarchen: Eine quellen und traditionskritische Studie zur Geschichte der Juden in der Spätantike*. TSAJ 52. Tübingen.
Jacques, F. 1972. *La politique municipale de l'Empire romain en Afrique Proconsulaire de Trajan à Septime-Sévère*. CEFR 8. Rome.
Jacques, F. 1984. *Le privilège de liberté. Politique impériale et autonomie municipale dans les cités de l'Occident romain*. CEFR 76. Rome.
Jaeger, M. 1997. *Livy's written Rome*. Ann Arbor.

James, S. 2003. Roman archaeology: Crisis and revolution. *Antiquity* 77: 178–84.
Jashemski, W. F. 1979. *The gardens of Pompeii*. Vol. 1. New Rochelle, NY.
Jashemski, W. F. and Meyer, F. G. (eds.) 2002. *The natural history of Pompeii*. Cambridge.
Johns, C. 1982. *Sex or symbol: Erotic images of Greece and Rome*. Austin.
Johnson, A. C., Coleman-Norton, P. R., and Bourne, F. C. 1961. *Ancient Roman statutes*. Austin.
Johnston, A. 1974. New problems for old: Konrad Kraft on die-sharing in Asia Minor. *NC*^{7} 14: 203–7.
Johnston, A. 1985. The so-called "pseudo-autonomous" Greek imperials. *ANSMN* 39: 89–112.
Johnston, D. 1999. *Roman law in context*. Cambridge.
Johnston, D. E. (ed.) 1977. *The Saxon shore*. London.
Johnston, S. I. 1997. Rising to the occasion: Theurgic ascent in its cultural milieu. In Schäfer and Kippenberg: 165–94.
Johnston, S. I. 2001. Charming children: The use of the child in ancient divination. *Arethusa* 34: 97–117.
Johnston, S. I. and Struck, P. (eds.) 2005. *Mantikê: Studies in ancient divination*. Leiden.
Jones, A. H. M. 1952. Michael Ivanovich Rostovtzeff, 1870–1952. *Proceedings of the British Academy* 38: 347–61.
Jones, A. H. M. 1955. The elections under Augustus. *JRS* 45: 9–21. (Rpr. in Jones 1960: 29–50.)
Jones, A. H. M. 1956. Numismatics and history. In Carson and Sutherland: 13–33. (Rpr. in Jones 1974: 61–81 with an additional note by M. H. Crawford.)
Jones, A. H. M. 1960. *Studies in Roman government and law*. Oxford.
Jones, A. H. M. 1964. *The later Roman Empire, 284–602: A social, economic and administrative survey*. 3 vols. Oxford. (Rpr. in 2 vols., 1973.)
Jones, A. H. M. 1971. *The cities of the eastern Roman provinces*. 2nd edn. Oxford.
Jones, A. H. M. 1974. *The Roman economy: Studies in ancient economic and administrative history*. Oxford.
Jones, A. H. M., Martindale, J. R., and Morris, J. (eds.) 1971. *The prosopography of the later Roman Empire*. Vol. I, AD 260–395. Cambridge.
Jones, B. 2000. Aerial photography around the Mediterranean. In Pasquinucci, M. and Trément, F. (eds.), *Non-destructive techniques applied to landscape archaeology*. The Archaeology of Mediterranean Landscapes 4. Oxford: 49–60.
Jones, B. W. 1992. *The emperor Domitian*. London.
Jones, C. P. 1971. *Plutarch and Rome*. Oxford.
Jones, C. P. 1978. *The Roman world of Dio Chrysostom*. Cambridge.
Jones, C. P. 1986. *Culture and society in Lucian*. Cambridge, MA.
Jones, C. P. 1991. Dinner theatre. In Slater 1991: 185–98.
Jones, C. P. 1993. Greek drama in the Roman Empire. In Scodel: 39–52.
Jones, C. P. 1996. The Panhellenion. *Chiron* 26: 29–56.
Jones, C. P. 1998. The pancratiasts Helix and Alexander on an Ostian mosaic. *JRA* 11: 293–8.
Jones, C. P. 1999. *Kinship diplomacy in the ancient world*. Cambridge, MA.
Jones, G. D. B. and Mattingly, D. J. 2002. *An atlas of Roman Britain*. Oxford.
Jongman, W. 1988. *The economy and society of Pompeii*. Amsterdam.
Jongman, W. 2002. The Roman economy: From cities to empire. In de Blois and Rich: 28–47.
Joshel, S. R. 1992. *Work, identity, and legal status in Rome*. Norman, OK.
Joshel, S. R. and Murnaghan, S. (eds.) 1998. *Women and slaves in Greco-Roman culture*. London.
Jouguet, P. 1911. *La vie municipale dans l'Égypte romaine*. Bibliothèque des Écoles françaises d'Athènes et de Rome 104. Paris.

Kákosy, L. 1995. Probleme der Religion im römerzeitlichen Ägypten. *ANRW* 2.18.5: 2894–3049.
Kampen, N. B. (ed.) 1996. *Sexuality in ancient art*. Cambridge.
Kampen, N. B. 2003. On writing histories in Roman art. *Art Bulletin* 85: 371–86.
Kapparis, K. 2002. *Abortion in the ancient world*. London.
Keay, S. 1988. *Roman Spain*. London.
Keay, S. and Terrenato, N. (eds.) 2001. *Italy and the west. Comparative issues in Romanization*. Oxford.
Keegan, J. 1976. *The face of battle*. London.
Kehoe, D. P. 1988a. *The economics of agriculture on Roman imperial estates in North Africa*. Göttingen.
Kehoe, D. P. 1988b. Allocation of risk and investment on the estates of Pliny the Younger. *Chiron* 18: 15–42.
Kehoe, D. P. 1992. *Management and investment on estates in Roman Egypt during the early empire*. Bonn.
Kehoe, D. P. 1997. *Investment, profit and tenancy: The Jurists and the Roman agrarian economy*. Ann Arbor.
Keith, A. M. 1994. *Corpus eroticum:* Elegiac poetics and elegiac *Puellae* in Ovid's *Amores. CW* 88: 27–40.
Keith, A. M. 1997. *Tandem venit amor*: A Roman woman speaks of love. In Hallett and Skinner: 295–310.
Keith, A. M. 2000. *Engendering Rome: Women in Latin epic*. Cambridge.
Kelly, J. N. D. 1977. *Early Christian doctrines*. 5th edn. London.
Kennedy, D. 1992. "Augustan" and "anti-Augustan": Reflections on terms of reference. In Powell: 26–58.
Kennedy, D. 1993. *The arts of love: Five studies in the discourse of Roman love elegy*. Cambridge.
Kenney, E. J. 1984. Moretum: *The Ploughman's Lunch, a poem ascribed to Virgil*. Cambridge.
Kent, J. P. C. 1978. *Roman coins*. London.
Kent, J. P. C. 1981. *Roman imperial coinage vol. 8: The family of Constantine I, AD 337–364*. London.
Kent, J. P. C. 1987. The monetary system. In Wacher 1987: 568–85.
Kent, J. P. C. 1994. *Roman imperial coinage vol. 10: The divided empire and the fall of the western parts, AD 395–491*. London.
Kent, J. P. C., Overbeck, B., and Stylow, A. U. (eds.) 1973. *Die römische Münze. Aufnahme von Max und Albert Hirmer*. Munich.
Keppie, L. J. F. 1983. *Colonisation and veteran settlement in Italy, 47–14 BC*. London.
Keppie, L. J. F. 1984. *The making of the Roman army: From republic to empire*. London.
Kettenhofen, E. 1979. *Die syrischen Augustae in der historischen Überlieferung. Ein Beitrag zum Problem der Orientalisierung*. Bonn.
Kettenhoffen, E. 1984. Die Einforderung des Achämeniderbes durch Ardasir: Eine Interpretatio Romana. *Orientalia Lovaniensa Periodica* 15: 177–90.
Kettenhoffen, E. 1995. Die Eroberung von Nisibis und Karrhai durch die Sāsāniden in der Zeit Kaiser Maximins (235/236 n. Chr.). *Iranica Antiqua* 30: 159–77.
Keynes, G. 1940. *The library of Edward Gibbon*. 2nd edn. London, 1980.
King, A. 1999. Diet in the Roman world: A regional inter-site comparison of the mammal bones. *JRA* 12: 168–202.
King, A. 2001. The Romanization of diet in the western empire: Comparative archaeozoological studies. In Keay and Terrenato: 210–23.
King, C. E. and Walker, D. R. 1976. The earliest Tiberian tetradrachms and Roman monetary policy towards Egypt. *ZPE* 21: 265–9.

King, C. E. and Wigg, D. (eds.) 1996. *Coin finds and coin use in the Roman world. The thirteenth Oxford Symposium on Coinage and Monetary History 25–27.3.1993*. Berlin.

King, H. 1998. *Hippocrates' woman*. London.

King, K. L. (ed.) 1988. *Images of the feminine in gnosticism*. Philadelphia.

King, K. L. (ed.) 1997. *Women and goddess traditions*. Minneapolis.

King, K. L. 2003. *What is gnosticism?* Cambridge, MA.

Kinsey, A. C., Pomeroy, W. B., and. Martin, C. E. 1948. *Sexual behavior in the human male*. Philadelphia.

Kingsley, S. and Decker, M. (eds.) 2001. *Economy and exchange in the east Mediterranean during late antiquity*. Oxford.

Kippenberg, H. G. 1997. Magic in Roman civil discourse: Why rituals could be illegal. In Schäfer and Kippenberg: 137–63.

Kleberg, T. 1957. *Hôtels, restaurants et cabarets dans l'antiquité romaine: études historiques et philologiques*. Uppsala.

Kleiner, D. E. E. 1992. *Roman sculpture*. New Haven.

Klose, D. O. A. 1987. *Die Münzprägung von Smyrna in der römischen Kaiserzeit*. Antiken Münzen und Geschnittene Steine 10. Berlin.

Knipfing, J. R. 1923. The Libelli of the Decian persecution. *HTR* 16: 345–90.

Knox, B. M. W. 1968. Silent reading in antiquity. *GRBS* 9: 421–35.

Kofsky, A. 1998. Mamre: A case of a regional cult? In Kofsky and Stroumsa: 19–30.

Kofsky, A. and Stroumsa, G. G. (eds.) 1998. *Sharing the sacred: Religious contacts and conflicts in the Holy Land*. Jerusalem.

Köhne, E. and Ewigleben, C. (eds.) 2001. *Gladiators and Caesars: The power of spectacle in ancient Rome*. Trans. R. Jackson. Berkeley.

Kolb, A. 2002. Impact and interaction of state transport in the Roman Empire. In de Blois and Rich: 67–76.

Kolb, F. 1987. *Diocletian und der erste Tetrarchie. Improvisation oder Experiment in der Organisation monarchischer Herrschaft?* Berlin.

Kolendo, J. 1991. *Le colonat en Afrique sous le haut-Empire*. 2nd edn. Paris.

Koloski-Ostrow, A. O. 2001. *Water use and hydraulics in the Roman city*. Dubuque.

Komnick, H. 2000. Die flavischen Fundmünzen aus dem Bereich des "sottosuolo urbano" der Stadt Rom: Eine Vergleichsanalyse. In *XII Internationaler Numismatischer Kongress Berlin 1997*. 1: 544–51.

König, D. 1981. *Die gallischen Usurpatoren von Postumus bis Tetricus*. Munich.

Konstan, D. 1994. *Sexual symmetry: Love in the ancient novel and related genres*. Princeton.

Korpela, J. 1987. *Das Medizinalpersonal im antiken Rom: Eine sozialgeschichtliche Untersuchung*. Helsinki.

Kraemer, R. S. 1988. *Maenads, martyrs, matrons, monastics*. Philadelphia.

Kraemer, R. S. 1991. Jewish women in the Diaspora world of late antiquity. In Baskin: 43–67.

Kraemer, R. S. 1992. *Her share of the blessings: Women's religions among pagans, Jews, and Christians in the Greco-Roman world*. Oxford.

Kraft, K. 1972. *Das System der kaiserzeitlichen Münzprägung in Kleinasien–Materialien und Entwürfe*. Berlin.

Kramer, B., Luppe, W., and Maehler, H. (eds.) 1997. *Akten des 21. internationalen Papyrologenkongresses, Berlin 1995*. Archiv für Papyrusforschung, Beiheft 3. Leipzig.

Krauss, C. 1994. *Livy, Ab Urbe Condita VI*. Cambridge.

Kreuz, A. 2000. Functional and conceptual archaeobotanical data from Roman cremations. In Pearce, J., Millet, M., and Manuela Struck, M. (eds.), *Burial, society and context in the Roman world*. Oxford. 45–51.

Krinzinger, F. (ed.) 2002. *Das Hanghaus 2 von Ephesos: Studien zu Baugeschichte und Chronologie*. Archäologische Forschungen 7. Vienna.

Krueger, D. 1996. The bawdy and society: The shamelessness of Diogenes in Roman imperial culture. In Branham and Goulet-Caze: 222–39.

Kruse, T. 2002. *Der königliche Schreiber und die Gauverwaltung. Untersuchungen zur Verwaltungsgeschichte Ägyptens in der Zeit von Augustus bis Philippus Arabs (30 v.Chr.–245 n.Chr.)*. ArchPF. Beiheft 11, 1–2. Munich.

Kudlien, F. 1983. Schaustellerei und Heilmittelvertieb in der Antike. *Gesnerus* 40: 91–8.

Kuefler, M. 2001. *The manly eunuch: Masculinity, gender ambiguity, and Christian ideology in late antiquity.* Chicago.

Kunkel, W. 1973. *An introduction to Roman legal and constitutional history*. 2nd edn. Trans. J. M. Kelly. Oxford.

Kunst, C. 2000. Die Rolle der römischen Kaiserfrau. Eine Einleitung. In Kunst, C. and Riemer, U. (eds.), *Grenzen der Macht. Zur Rolle der römischen Kaiserfrauen*. Stuttgart. 1–6.

Kuttner, A. 1999. Hellenistic images of spectacle, Alexander to Augustus. In Bergmann and Kondoleon: 97–124.

Lacey, W. K. 1996. *Augustus and the principate. The evolution of the system*. Leeds.

Laffi, U. 1966. *Adtributio e contributio. Problemi del sistema politico-administrativo dello stato romano*. Pisa.

Lamberton, R. 2001. Schools of platonic philosophy in the Roman Empire: The evidence of biographies. In Too: 433–58.

Lancel, S. 1995. *Carthage, a history*. Trans. A. Neville. Oxford.

Landes, R. 1988. "Lest the millennium be fulfilled": Apocalyptic expectations and the patttern of Western chronography, 100–800 CE. In Verbeke, W., Verhelst, D., and Welkenhuysen, A. (eds.), *The use and abuse of eschatology in the Middle Ages*. Louvain. 141–211.

Lane Fox, R. 1986. *Pagans and Christians*. Harmondsworth.

Lang-Auinger, C. 2003. *Hanghaus 1 in Ephesos: Funde und Ausstattung*. Forschungen in Ephesos 8.4. Vienna.

Langhammer, W. 1973. *Die rechtliche und soziale Stellung der Magistratus Municipales und der Decuriones in der Übergangsphase der Städte von sich selbstverwaltenden Gemeinden zu Vollzugsorganen des spätantiken Zwangsstaates (2.–4. Jahrhundert der römischen Kaiserzeit)*. Wiesbaden.

Larmour, D. H. J., Miller, P. A. and Platter, C. (eds.) 1998. *Rethinking sexuality: Foucault and classical antiquity*. Princeton.

La Rocca, E. 2000. L'affresco con veduta di città dal colle Oppio. In Fentress: 57–71.

Larsson, E. 1993. Temple-criticism and the Jewish heritage: Some reflections on Acts 6–7. *New Testament Studies* 39: 379–95.

Laurence, R. 1994. *Roman Pompeii: Space and society*. London.

Laurence, R. 1997. Space and text. In Laurence and Wallace-Hadrill: 7–14.

Laurence, R. 1998. Land transport in Roman Italy: Costs, practice and the economy. In Parkins and Smith: 129–48.

Laurence, R. and Wallace-Hadrill, A. 1997. *Domestic space in the Roman world: Pompeii and beyond*. JRA Suppl. 22. Portsmouth, RI.

Lauwerier, R. C. G. M. and Robeerst, A. (J.) M. M. 2001. Horses in Roman times in the Netherlands. In Buitenhuis, H. and Prummel, W. (eds.), *Animals and man in the past, Essays in honour of Dr. A. T. Clason Emeritus Professor of Archaeozoology Rijksuniversiteit Groningen, the Netherlands*. ARC-Publicatie 41. Groningen.

Lazer, E. 1997. Pompeii AD 79: A population in flux? In Bon, S. E and Jones, R. (eds.), *Sequence and space in Pompeii*. Oxford. 102–20.

Leadbetter, B. 1998. "Patrimonium Indivisum"? The empire of Diocletian and Maximian. *Chiron* 28: 213–28.

Lebek, W. D. 1996. Moneymaking on the Roman stage. In Slater 1996: 29–48.

Le Bohec, Y. 1989a. *La troisième légion Auguste*. Paris.

Le Bohec, Y. 1989b. *Les Unités auxiliaires de l'armée romaine en Afrique proconsulaire et Numidie sous le Haut Empire*. Paris.
Le Bohec, Y. 2000. *The imperial Roman army*. London.
Le Bohec, Y. and Wolff, C. 2000. *Les légions de Rome sous le haut-Empire. Actes du Congrès de Lyons (17–19 septembre 1998)*. Lyons.
Le Glay, M. 1990a. La place des affranchis dans la vie municipale et dans la vie religieuse. MEFRA 102: 621–38.
Le Glay, M. 1990b. Évergétisme et vie religieuse dans l'Afrique romaine. In *L'Afrique dans l'occident romain (Ier siècle av. J.-C.–IVe siècle ap. J.-C.)*. CEFR 134. Rome. 77–88.
Lendon, J. E. 1997. *Empire of honour. The art of government in the Roman world*. Oxford.
Lenel, O. 1889. *Palingenesia Iuris Civilis*. Leipzig.
Lenel, O. 1927. *Das Edictum Perpetuum: Ein Versuch zu seiner Wiederherstellung*. 3rd edn. Leipzig. (Rpr. 1956.)
León Alonso, P. 1988. *Traianeum de Italica*. Seville.
León Alonso, P. 1995. *Esculturas de Itálica*. Seville.
Lepelley, C. (ed.) 1998. *Rome et l'intégration de l'Empire (44 av. J.-C.–260 ap. J.-C.). Tome II. Approches régionales du haut-Empire romain*. Paris. Trans with updates as Lepelley, C. (ed.) 2001. *Rom und das Reich in der Hohen Kaiserzeit 44 v. Chr.–260 n. Chr. Band II. Die Regionen des Reiches*. Stuttgart-Leipzig.
Leppin, H. 1992. *Histrionen: Untersuchungen zur sozialen Stellung von Bühnenkünstlern des Römischen Reiches zur Zeit der Republik und des Principats*. Bonn.
Le Roux, P. 1982. *L'armée romaine et l'organisation des provinces ibériques d'Auguste à l'invasion de 409*. Paris.
Le Roux, P. 1986. Municipe et droit latin en Hispania. *Nouvelle revue historique de droit français et étranger* 64: 325–50.
Levick, B. 1982. Propaganda and the imperial coinage. *Antichthon* 16: 104–16.
Levick, B. 1983. The *Senatus Consultum* from Larinum. *JRS* 73: 97–115 (AE 1991, no. 515).
Levick, B. 1990. *Claudius*. London.
Levick, B. 2000. *The government of the Roman Empire: A sourcebook*. London.
Levine, L. I. 1989. *The Rabbinic class of Roman Palestine in late antiquity*. Jerusalem.
Levine, L. I. (ed.) 1992. *The Galilee in late antiquity*. New York.
Levine, L. I. 2000. *The ancient synagogue: The first thousand years*. New Haven.
Levine, M. M. 1995. The gendered grammar of ancient Mediterranean hair. In Eilberg-Schwartz and Doniger: 76–130.
Lewis, N. P. 1970. Greco-Roman Egypt: Fact or fiction? *Proceedings of the Twelfth International Congress of Papyrology, Ann Arbor 1968*. ASP 8: 3–14. (Rpr. in Lewis 1995: 138–49.)
Lewis, N. P. 1981. The prefect's *conventus*: Proceedings and procedures. *BASP* 18: 119–29.
Lewis, N. P. 1983. *Life in Egypt under Roman rule*. Oxford. (Rpr. Atlanta, 1999.)
Lewis, N. P. 1984. The Romanity of Roman Egypt: A growing consensus. *Atti del XVII Congresso Internazionale di Papirologia (Napoli, 19–26 maggio 1983)*. Naples. Vol. 3: 1077–84. (Rpr. in Lewis 1995: 298–305.)
Lewis, N. P. 1995. *On government and law in Roman Egypt*. Ed. A. E. Hanson. ASP 33.
Lewis, N. P. 1997. *The compulsory public services of Roman Egypt*. 2nd edn. Papyrologica Florentina 28. Florence.
Lewis, N., Yadin Y., and Greenfield, J. (eds.) 2002. *The documents from the Bar Kokhba Period in the Cave of the Letters: Hebrew, Aramaic, and Nabatean-Aramaic papyri*. 3 vols. Jerusalem.
Lieberman, S. 1941. *Hellenism in Jewish Palestine*. (Rpr. New York and Jerusalem, 1994.)
Liebeschuetz, J. H. W. G. 1979. *Continuity and change in Roman religion*. Oxford.
Liebeschuetz, J. H. W. G. 2002. Unsustainable development: The origin of ruined landscapes in the Roman Empire. In de Blois and Rich: 232–43.

Lieu, S. N. C. and Montserrat, D. (eds.) 1996. *From Constantine to Julian: Pagan and Byzantine views*. London.
Lieu, S. N. C. and Montserrat, D. (eds.) 1998. *Constantine: History, historiography and legend*. London.
Lightfoot, J. B. 1889–90. *The apostolic fathers* (text, translation and commentary). 5 vols. London.
Lightfoot, J. L. 2002. Nothing to do with the *technītai* of Dionysus. In Easterling and Hall: 209–24.
Linder, A. 1987. *The Jews in Roman imperial legislation*. Detroit.
Ling, R. 1991. *Roman painting*. Cambridge.
Ling, R. 1995. The decoration of Roman *Triclinia*. In Murray and Tecusan: 239–51.
Lintott, A. R. 1993. *Imperium Romanum: Politics and administration*. London.
Lintott, A. R. 1999. *The constitution of the Roman Republic*. Oxford.
Lloyd, A. C. 1990. *Anatomy of Neoplatonism*. Oxford.
Loane, H. J. 1938. *Industry and commerce of the city of Rome*. Baltimore.
Lo Cascio, E. 1999. *Census* provinciale, imposizione fiscale e amministrazione cittadine nel Principato. In Eck and Müller-Luckner: 197–211.
Lomas, K. 1993. *Rome and the western Greeks, 350 BC–AD 200: Conquest and acculturation in southern Italy*. London.
Lomas, K. and Cornell, T. (eds.) 2002. *"Bread and circuses": Euergetism and patronage in Roman Italy*. London.
Long, A. A. 2002. *Epictetus*. Oxford.
Long, A. A. and Sedley, D. 1987. *The Hellenistic philosophers: The principal texts in translation with philosophical commentary*. Cambridge.
López Vilar, J. and Currula Ferré, O. 2001. Nous elements religiosas a Tàrraco: inscripció al geni del *Conventus Tarraconensis*, ares i restes de bucranis. *Butlletí Arqueològic* 23: 249–58.
Lopuszanski, G. 1951. La police romaine et les chrétiens. *L'Antiquité Classique* 20: 5–46.
Loriot, X. 1975. Les premières années de la grande crise de III siècle. De l'avènement de Maximin le Thrace (235) à la mort de Gordien III (244). *ANRW* 2.2: 657–787.
Love, J. R. 1991. *Antiquity and capitalism: Max Weber and the sociological foundations of Roman civilization*. London.
Luce, T. 1990. Livy, Augustus and the Forum Augustum. In Raaflaub and Toher: 123–38.
Luck, G. 2000. *Ancient pathways and hidden pursuits: Religion, morals, and magic in the ancient world*. Ann Arbor.
Luttwak, E. N. 1976. *The grand strategy of the Roman Empire*. Baltimore.
Lutz, C. E. 1947. Musonius Rufus, "The Roman Socrates." *YCS* 10: 3–151.
Ma, J. 2001. Public speech and community in the *Euboicus*. In Swain 2001: 108–24.
MacAdam, H. I. 1983. Epigraphy and village life in southern Syria during the Roman and early Byzantine periods. *Berytus* 31: 103–15.
MacAlister, S. 1992. Gender as sign and symbolism in Artemidoros' *Oneirokritika*: Social aspirations and anxieties. *Helios* 19.1–2: 140–60.
MacCormack, S. 1981. *Art and ceremony in late antiquity*. Berkeley.
MacCormack, S. 1991. *Religion in the Andes: Vision and imagination in early colonial Peru*. Princeton.
MacDonald, W. L. 1982. *The architecture of the Roman Empire I: An introductory study*. New Haven.
MacDonald, W. L. 1986. *The architecture of the Roman Empire II: An urban appraisal*. New Haven.
MacKinnon, M. 2004. *Production and consumption of animals in Roman Italy: Integrating the zooarchaeological and textual evidence*. JRA Suppl. 54. Portsmouth, RI.
Maclean, J. K. and Aitken, E. B. 2001. *Flavius Philostratus*: Heroikos. Atlanta.

MacMullen, R. 1970. Market days in the Roman Empire. *Phoenix* 24: 233–41.
MacMullen, R. 1974. *Roman social relations 50 BC to AD 284.* New Haven.
MacMullen, R. 1976. *Roman government's response to crisis AD 235–337.* New Haven.
MacMullen, R. 1981. *Paganism in the Roman Empire.* New Haven.
MacMullen, R. 1984a. *Christianizing the Roman Empire,* A.D. *100–400.* New Haven.
MacMullen, R. 1984b. The Roman emperor's army costs. *Latomus* 43: 571–80.
MacMullen, R. 1984c. The legion as a society. *Historia* 33: 440–56. (Rpr. in MacMullen 1990: 225–35.)
MacMullen, R. 1986. Judicial savagery in the Roman Empire. *Chiron* 16: 147–66. (Rpr. in MacMullen 1990: 204–17.)
MacMullen, R. 1990. *Changes in the Roman Empire: Essays in the ordinary.* Princeton.
MacMullen, R. 1997. *Christianity and paganism in the fourth through eighth centuries.* New Haven.
Macready, S. and Thompson, F. H. (eds.) 1987. *Roman architecture in the Greek world.* London.
Magdalino, P. (ed.) 1994. *New Constantines: The rhythm of imperial renewal in Byzantium, 4th–12th centuries.* Aldershot.
Magie, D. 1950. *Roman rule in Asia Minor, to the end of the third century after Christ.* Princeton.
Malamud, M. 1995. Happy birthday dead Lucan: (P)raising the dead in *Silvae* 2.7. *Ramus* 24: 1–30.
Malkin, I. (ed.) 2001. *Ancient perceptions of Greek ethnicity.* Washington, DC.
Manderscheid, H. 1981. *Die Skulpturenausstattung der kaiserzeitlichen Thermenanlagen.* Berlin.
Mankin, D. 1995. *Horace,* Epodes. Cambridge.
Mann, J. C. 1977. *Duces* and *comites* in the fourth century. In D. E. Johnston 1977: 11–15.
Mann, J. C. 1983. *Legionary recruitment and veteran settlement during the principate.* Institute of Archaeology Occasional Publications 7. London.
Mantos, K. 1995. Women and athletics in the Roman east. *Nikephoros* 8: 125–44.
Mar, R. 1993. El recinto de culto imperial de Tarraco y la arquitectura flavia. In Mar, R. (ed.), *Els monuments provincials de Tàrraco: Noves aparticions al seu coneixement.* Documents d'arqueologia clàssica 1. Tarragona. 107–56.
Maraval, P. 1985. *Lieux saints et pèlerinages d'Orient.* Paris.
Marganne, M.-H. 1994. *Ophtalmologie dans l'Égypte gréco-romaine d'aprés les papyrus.* Leiden.
Marganne, M.-H. 1998. *La chirurgie dans l'Égypte gréco-romaine d'aprés les papyrus littéraires.* Leiden.
Markus, D. 2000. "Performing the book": The recital of epic in the first century CE Rome. *CA* 19: 138–79.
Markus, R. A. 1970. Saeculum: *History and society in the theology of St. Augustine.* Cambridge.
Markus, R. A. 1974. Paganism, Christianity and the Latin classics. In Binns, J. W. (ed.), *Latin literature of the fourth century.* London. 1–21.
Marquardt, J. 1886. *Das Privatleben der Römer.* 2nd edn. Leipzig.
Marrou, H. I. 1964. *Mousikos anêr. Étude sur les scènes de la vie intellectuelle figurant sur les monuments funéraires romains.* Rome.
Marsden, E. W. 1969. *Greek and Roman artillery: Historical development.* Oxford.
Marsden, E. W. 1971. *Greek and Roman artillery: Technical treatises.* Oxford.
Marshall, A. J. 1964. The structure of Cicero's edict. *AJP* 85: 185–91.
Marshall, A. J. 1966. Governors on the move. *Phoenix* 20: 231–46.
Marshall, A. J. 1980. The survival and development of international jurisdiction in the Greek world under Roman rule. *ANRW* 2.13: 626–61.
Martin, A. 1992. Archives privée et hachettes documentaries. *Proceedings of the 20th International Congress of Papyrologists. Copenhagen 23–29 August, 1992.* Copenhagen. 569–77.

Martin, D. 1996. The construction of the ancient family: Methodological considerations. *JRS* 86: 40–60.
Martindale, C. (ed.) 1997. *The Cambridge companion to Virgil*. Cambridge.
Martindale, J. R. (ed.) 1980. *The prosopography of the later Roman Empire II: AD 395–527*. Cambridge.
Marvin, M. 1983. The freestanding sculptures from the baths of Caracalla. *AJA* 87: 347–84.
Masciadri, M. M. and Montevecchi, O. (eds.) 1984. *I contratti di baliatico*. Milan.
Mason, S. (ed.) 2000–. *Flavius Josephus, translation and commentary*. Leiden.
Masterson, M. A. 2001. *Roman manhood at the end of the ancient world*. PhD dissertation, University of Southern California.
Mateos Cruz, P. 2001. Augusta Emerita. *Archivo español de arqueología* 74 (183–4): 183–208.
Mateos Cruz, P., Ayerbe Vélez, R., Barrientos Vera, T., and Feijoo Martínez, S. 2002. La gestión del agua en *Augusta Emerita*. *Empúries* 53: 67–88.
Mathisen, R. (ed.) 2001. *Law, society and authority in late antiquity*. Oxford.
Mattern, S. P. 1999. *Rome and the enemy imperial strategy in the principate*. Berkeley.
Matthews, J. F. 1984. The tax law of Palmyra: Evidence for economic history in a city of the Roman east. *JRS* 74: 157–80.
Matthews, J. F. 1989. *The Roman Empire of Ammianus*. London.
Matthews, J. F. 1998. Eternity in perishable materials: Law-making and literate communities in the Roman Empire. In Hillard, T. W. (ed.), *Ancient history in a modern university*. 2 vols. Grand Rapids, MI. 2: 253–65.
Matthews, J. F. 2000. *Laying down the law: A study of the Theodosian Code*. New Haven.
Mattingly, D. J. 1988a. Oil for export: A comparative study of Roman olive oil production in Libya, Spain and Tunisia. *JRA* 1: 33–56.
Mattingly, D. J. 1988b. Megalithic madness and measurement. Or how many olives could an olive press press? *Oxford Journal of Archaeology* 7.2: 177–95.
Mattingly, D. J. 1988c. Olea mediterranea? *JRA* 1: 153–61.
Mattingly, D. J. 1989. Olive cultivation and the Albertini Tablets. *L'Africa Romana* 6: 403–15.
Mattingly, D. J. 1990. Paintings, presses and perfume production at Pompeii. *Oxford Journal of Archaeology* 9.1: 71–90.
Mattingly, D. J. 1993. Maximum figures and maximizing strategies of oil production? Further thoughts on the processing capacity of Roman olive presses. In Amouretti and Brun: 483–98.
Mattingly, D. J. 1994. *Tripolitania*. Ann Arbor.
Mattingly, D. J. 1996a. First fruit? The olive in the Roman world. In Shipley, G. and Salmon, J. (eds.), *Human landscapes in classical antiquity. Environment and culture*. London. 213–53.
Mattingly, D. J. 1996b. Olive presses in Roman Africa: Technical evolution or stagnation? *L'Africa Romana* 11: 577–95.
Mattingly, D. J. (ed.) 1997. *Dialogues in Roman imperialism*. JRA Suppl. 22. Portsmouth, RI.
Mattingly, D. J. 2003. Family values: Art and power at Ghirza in the Libyan pre-desert. In Scott, S. and Webster, J. (eds.), *Roman imperialism and provincial art*. Cambridge. 153–70.
Mattingly, D. J. and Hitchner, R. B. 1993. Technical specifications of some North African olive presses of Roman date. In Amouretti and Brun: 439–62.
Mattingly, D.J. and Hitchner, R. B. 1995. Roman Africa: An archaeological review. *JRS* 85: 165–213.
Mattingly, D. J. and Salmon, J. 2001a. *Economies beyond agriculture in the classical world*. London.
Mattingly, D. J. and Salmon, J. 2001b. The productive past. Economies beyond agriculture. In Mattingly and Salmon 2001a: 3–14.

Mattingly, D. J., Stone, D., Stirling, L., and Ben Lazreg, N. 2001. Leptiminus (Tunisia): A "producer" city? In Mattingly and Salmon 2001a: 66–89.
Mattingly, H. 1923. *Coins of the Roman Empire in the British Museum*. 5 vols. London.
Mattingly, H. 1940. *Coins of the Roman Empire in the British Museum. Volume IV, Antoninus Pius to Commodus*. London.
Mattingly, H. 1950. *Coins of the Roman Empire in the British Museum. Volume V, Pertinax to Elagabalus*. London.
Mattingly, H. 1960. *Roman coins from the earliest times to the fall of the western empire*. 2nd edn. London.
Mattingly, H. B. 1977. Coinage in the Roman state. NC^7 17: 199–215.
Maxfield, V. A. 1981. *The military decorations of the Roman army*. Berkeley.
Maxfield, V. A. 1986. Pre-Flavian forts and their garrisons. *Britannia* 17: 59–72.
Maxfield, V. A. 2001. Stone quarrying in the eastern desert with particular reference to Mons Claudianus and Mons Porphyrites. In Mattingly and Salmon 2001a: 143–70.
Maxfield, V. and Peacock, D. P. S. 2001. *Survey and excavation Mons Claudianus 1987–1993. I. Excavations*. Cairo.
McCann, A. M. and Freed, J. 1994. *Deep water archaeology. A late Roman ship from Carthage and an ancient trade route near Skerki bank off northwest Sicily*. JRA Suppl. 13. Ann Arbor.
McGing, B. 2002. Population and proselytism: How many Jews were there in the ancient world? In Bartlett, J. R. (ed.), *Jews in the Hellenistic and Roman cities*. London. 88–106.
McGinn, T. A. 1989. The taxation of Roman prostitutes. *Helios* 16: 79–110.
McGinn, T. A. 1998. *Prostitution, sexuality, and the law in ancient Rome*. Oxford.
McGinn, T. A. 2004. *The economy of prostitution in the Roman world: A study of social history and the brothel*. Ann Arbor.
McGuire, D. 1997. *Acts of silence: Civil war, tyranny, and suicide in the Flavian epics*. Hildesheim.
McKechnie, P. 1992. Tertullian's *De Pallio* and life in Roman Carthage. *Prudentia* 24.2: 44–66. = www.tertullian.org/articles/mckechnie_pallio.htm.
Meadows, K. 1999. The appetites of households in early Roman Britain. In Allison, P. (ed.), *The archaeology of household activities*. London. 101–20.
Meier, J. P. 1991. *A marginal Jew: Rethinking the historical Jesus*. Vol. 1. New York
Meijer, F. and van Niff, O. 1992. *Trade, transport and society*. London.
Mellor, R. 1993. *Tacitus*. London.
Merkle, S. 1989. *Die* Ephemeris belli Troiani *des Diktys von Kreta*. Frankfurt.
Merkle, S. 2003. The truth and nothing but the truth: Dictys and Dares. In Schmeling: 563–80.
Meshorer, Y. 1985. *City-coins of Eretz-Israel and the Decapolis in the Roman period*. Jerusalem.
Merten, E. W. 1983. *Bäder and Badegepflogenheiten in der Darstellung der Historia Augusta*. Bonn.
Metcalf, W. E. 1982. The Flavians in the east. In Hackens, T. and Weiller, R. (eds.), *Actes du ix Congrès international de numismatique, Berne, septembre 1979*. Louvain-la-Neuve. 321–39.
Metcalf, W. E. 1989. Rome and Lugdunum again. *AJN* 1: 51–70.
Metcalf, W. E. 1993. The emperor's liberalitas: Propaganda and the imperial coinage. *RIN* 95: 337–46.
Metcalf, W. E. 1995. Review of Duncan-Jones 1994. *SNR* 74: 145–59.
Metcalf, W. E. 1996. *The silver coinage of Cappadocia: Vespasian–Commodus*. New York.
Meyer, B. T. and Sanders, E. P. 1982. *Jewish and Christian self-definition*. 3 vols. Philadelphia.
Meyer, E. A. 1990. Explaining the epigraphic habit in the Roman Empire: The evidence of epitaphs. *JRS* 80: 74–96.
Meyer, E. 2004. *Legitimacy and law in the Roman world*. Cambridge.
Meyer, M. and Smith, R. (eds.) 1994. *Ancient Christian magic: Coptic texts of ritual power*. San Francisco.

Meyer-Zwiffelhoffer, E. 2002. *Politikós archein: zum Regierungsstil der senatorischen Statthalter in den Kaiserzeitlichen greischischen Provinzen.* Stuttgart.
Miles, G. 1995. *Livy: Reconstructing early Rome.* Ithaca.
Milik, J. T. 1972. *Dédicaces faites par des dieux (Palmyre, Hatra, Tyr) et des thiases sémitiques à l'époque romaine.* Paris.
Millar, F. 1964a. *A study of Cassius Dio.* Oxford.
Millar, F. 1964b. Some evidence on the meaning of Tacitus Annals XII.60. *Historia* 13: 180–7.
Millar, F. 1965. The development of jurisdiction by imperial procurators: Further evidence. *Historia* 14: 362–7.
Millar, F. 1966. The emperor, the Senate and the provinces. *JRS* 56: 156–66.
Millar, F. 1969. P. Herennius Dexippus: The Greek world and the third century invasions. *JRS* 59: 12–29.
Millar, F. 1977. *The emperor in the Roman world.* London.
Millar, F. 1981. The world of the Golden Ass. *JRS* 71: 63–75.
Millar, F. 1983. Empire and city, Augustus to Julian: Obligations, excuses and status. *JRS* 73: 76–96. (Rpr. in Millar 2004: 336–71.)
Millar, F. 1984. State and subject: The impact of monarchy. In Millar and Segal: 37–60.
Millar, F. 1993a. *The Roman near east 31 BC–AD 337.* Cambridge, MA.
Millar, F. 1993b. The Greek city in the Roman period. In Hansen, M. H. (ed.), *The ancient Greek city-state.* Copenhagen. 232–60.
Millar, F. 1996. Emperors, kings and subjects: The politics of two-level sovereignty. *SCI* 15: 159–73.
Millar, F. 1997. Porphyry: Ethnicty, language, and alien wisdom. In Barnes and Griffin: 241–62.
Millar, F. 1998. *The crowd in Rome in the late republic.* Ann Arbor.
Millar, F. 1999a. The Greek east and Roman law: The dossier of M. Cn. Licinius Rufinus. *JRS* 89: 90–108.
Millar, F. 1999b. Civitates liberae, coloniae and provincial governors under the empire. *Mediterraneo Antico* 2: 95–113.
Millar, F. 2000. Trajan: Government by correspondence. In González, J. (ed.), *Trajano emperador de Roma.* Madrid. 363–88. (Rpr. in Millar 2004: 23–46.)
Millar, F. 2002. *Rome, the Greek world, and the east. 1. The Roman Republic and the Augustan revolution* (eds. H. Cotton and G. M. Rogers). Chapel Hill.
Millar, F. 2004. *Rome, the Greek world, and the east. 2. Government, society and culture in the Roman Empire* (eds. H. Cotton and G. M. Rogers). Chapel Hill.
Millar, F. and Segal, E. (eds.) 1984. *Caesar Augustus: Seven aspects.* Oxford.
Millett, M. 1990. *The Romanization of Britain.* Cambridge.
Millett, M. 2001. Roman interaction in northwestern Iberia. *Oxford Journal of Archaeology* 20: 157–70.
Millett, P. 2001. Productive to some purpose? The problem of ancient economic growth. In Mattingly and Salmon 2001a: 17–48.
Milnor, K. 2000. On silence: History, hermeneutics, and the lost lesbian voice of *CIL* 4.5296. Paper presented at "Feminism and Classics 3," University of Southern California.
Milnor, K. 2002. Sulpicia's (corpo)reality: Elegy, authorship, and the body in [Tibullus] 3.13. *CA* 21: 259–82.
Mink, I. 1987. *Historical understanding.* Ithaca.
Minnen, P. van. 2000. An official act of Cleopatra (with a subscription in her own hand). *Ancient Society* 30: 29–34. (*P.Bingen* 45)
Mirecki, P. and Meyer, M. (eds.) 2002. *Magic and ritual in the ancient world.* Leiden.
Mitchell, S. 1976. Requisitioned transport in the Roman Empire: A new inscription from Pisidia. *JRS* 66: 106–31.

Mitchell, S. 1988. Maximinus and the Christians in AD 312: A new Latin inscription. *JRS* 78: 105–24.
Mitchell, S. 1990. Festivals, games, and civic life in Roman Asia Minor. *JRS* 80: 183–93.
Mitchell, S. 1993. *Anatolia: Land, men, and gods in Asia Minor.* 2 vols. Oxford.
Mitchell, S. 1995. *Cremna in Pisidia: An ancient city in peace and war.* London.
Mitchell, S. 1999. The administration of Roman Asia 133 BC–AD 250. In Eck and Muller-Luckner: 17–46.
Mitchell, S. 2000. Ethnicity, acculturation and empire in Roman and late Roman Asia Minor. In Mitchell, S. and Greatrex, G. (eds.), *Ethnicity and culture in late antiquity.* Swansea. 117–50.
Mitteis, L. 1891. *Reichsrecht und Volksrecht in den östlichen Provinzen des römischen Kaiserreichs.* Leipzig.
Mitteis, L. and Wilcken, U. 1912. *Grundzüge und Chrestomathie der Papyruskunde.* Leipzig.
Moatti, C. 1993. *Archives et partage de la terre dans le monde romain (IIe siècle avent–Ier siècle après J.-C.).* CÉFR 173. Rome.
Mócsy, A. 1962. Ubique res publica. Zu den Autonomiebestrebungen und Uniformierungstendenzen am Vorabend des Dominats. *Acta Antiqua Academiae Scientiarum Hungaricae* 10: 367–84.
Moles, J. 1985. The second preface in Arrian's Anabasis. *JHS* 105: 162–8.
Moles, J. 1993. Livy's Preface. *PCPS* 39: 141–68.
Momigliano, A. (ed.) 1963. *The conflict between paganism and Christianity in the fourth century.* Oxford.
Momigliano, A. 1966a. Gibbon's contribution to historical method. In Momigliano, A., *Studies in Historiography.* London. 40–55. (First published in *Historia* 2 [1953–4]: 450–64.)
Momigliano, A. 1966b (1994). Julius Beloch. In Momigliano, A., *Studies on modern scholarship.* Eds. G. W. Bowersock and T. J. Cornell. Berkeley. 97–120.
Momigliano, A. 1971. *Alien wisdom. The limits of Hellenization.* Cambridge.
Momigliano, A. 1977. *Essays in ancient and modern historiography.* Oxford.
Momigliano, A. 1987. *On Pagans, Jews and Christians.* Middletown, CT.
Mommsen, T. 1885. *Römische Geschichte, vol. 5: Die Provinzen des römischen Reich von Caesar bis Diocletian.* Berlin. Trans. W. P. Dickson as *The provinces of the Roman Empire from Caesar to Diocletian.* London. 1886.
Mommsen, T. 1887/8. *Römisches Staatsrecht^3.* Leipzig. (Rpr. Graz, 1965.)
Mommsen, T. 1889. *Römisches Strafrecht.* Leipzig. (Rpr. Graz, 1955.)
Mommsen, T. 1892. Senatus consultum de sumptiis ludorum gladiatoriorum minuendis factum A.P.C. 176/7. *Ephemeris Epigraphica* 7: 388–416.
Montevecchi, O. 1988. *La Papirologia.* 2nd edn. Milan.
Montserrat, D. 1996. *Sex and society in Graeco-Roman Egypt.* London.
Montserrat, D. 1997. Death and funerals in the Roman Fayum. In Bierbrier: 33–44.
Montserrat, D. 1998a. Pilgrimage to the shrine of Ss. Cyrus and John at Menouthis in late antiquity. In Frankfurter 1998d: 257–79.
Montserrat, D. (ed.) 1998b. *Changing bodies, changing meanings: Studies on the human body in antiquity.* London.
Moore, S. D. 2001. *God's beauty parlor and other queer spaces in and around the Bible.* Stanford.
Morello, R. 2002. Livy's Alexander Digression (9.17–19): Counterfactuals and apologetics. *JRS* 92: 62–85.
Moretti, L. 1953. *Iscrizioni agonistiche greche.* Rome.
Morgan, J. R. 1982. History, romance, and realism in the *Aithiopika* of Heliodoros. *C* 1: 221–65.

Morgan, J. R. 1985. Lucian's *True Histories* and the *Wonders Beyond Thule* of Antonius Diogenes. *CQ* 35: 475–90.
Morgan, J. R. 1993. Make-believe and make believe: The fictionality of the Greek novels. In Gill and Wiseman: 175–229.
Morgan, J. R. 1995. The Greek novel: Towards a sociology of production and reception. In Powell 1995: 130–52.
Morgan, J. R. and Stoneman, R. (eds.) 1994. *Greek fiction: The Greek novel in context*. London.
Morley, N. 1996. *Metropolis and hinterland: The city of Rome and the Italian economy 200 BC–AD 200*. Cambridge.
Morris, I. 1992. *Death-ritual and social structure in classical antiquity*. Cambridge.
Morrow, G. R. and Dillon, J. M. 1987. *Proclus' commentary on Plato's* Parmenides. Princeton.
Mouritsen, H. 2001. *Plebs and politics in the late Roman Republic*. Cambridge.
Moyer, I. 2003. Thessalos of Tralles and cultural exchange. In Noegel et al.: 39–56.
Mrozek, S. 1987. *Les distributions d'argent et de nourriture dans les villes italiennes du haut-Empire romain*. Brussels.
Münzer, F. 1999. *Roman aristocratic parties and families*. Trans. T. Ridley. Baltimore.
Murray, O. 1990. *Sympotica: A symposium on the Symposium*. Oxford.
Murray, O. 1991. Arnaldo Momigliano in England. In Steinberg: 49–64.
Murray, O. and Tecusan, M. 1995. *In vino veritas*. London.
Musurillo, H. 1954. *Acts of the pagan martyrs*. Oxford.
Myers, K. S. 1994. *Ovid's causes: Cosmogony and aetiology in the Metamorphoses*. Ann Arbor.
Myers, K. S. 1999. The metamorphosis of a poet: Recent work on Ovid. *JRS* 89: 190–204.
Myers, K. S. 2000. *Miranda fides*: Poet and patrons in paradoxographical landscapes in Statius' Silvae. *Materiali e discussioni per l'analisi dei testi classici* 44: 103–38.
Myers, K. S. forthcoming. Latin myth in *Metamorphoses* 14. *Hermathena*.
Nathan, G. 2000. *The family in late antiquity: The rise of Christianity and the endurance of tradition*. London.
Nauta, R. 2002. *Poetry for patrons: Literary communication in the age of Domitian*. Leiden.
Navarro Caballero, M. 2001. Les femmes de l'élite hispano-romaine, entre la famille et la vie publique. In Navarro Caballero, M. and Demougin, S. (eds.), *Élites hispaniques*. Bordeaux. 191–201.
Nelis-Clément, J. 2000. *Les* beneficiarii: *militaires et administrateurs au service de l'Empire (1er s. a.C.–VIe s. p.C.)*. Paris.
Neusner, J. (ed.) 1995–2001. *Judaism in late antiquity*. 5 vols. Leiden.
Newlands, C. 1995. *Playing with time: Ovid and the* Fasti. Ithaca.
Newlands, C. 2002. *Statius' Silvae and the poetics of empire*. Cambridge.
Nicholas, B. 1962. *An introduction to Roman law*. Oxford.
Nicolet, C. 1980. *The world of the citizen in republican Rome*. Berkeley.
Nicolet, C. 1991. *Space, geography and politics in the early Roman Empire*. Ann Arbor.
Nicolet, C. 1996. *Financial documents and geographical knowledge in the Roman world*. Oxford.
Nicolet, C. 2000. *Censeurs et publicains: économie et fiscalité dans la Rome antique*. Paris.
Nielsen, I. 1993. *Thermae et balnea: The architecture and cultural history of Roman public baths*. 2nd edn. Aarhus.
Nijf, O. M. van. 1997. *The civic world of professional associations in the Roman east*. Dutch monographs on ancient history and archaeology 17. Amsterdam.
Nijf, O. M. van. 2000. Inscriptions and civic memory in the Roman east. In Cooley 2000b: 21–36.
Nijf, O. M. van. 2001. Local heroes: Athletics, festivals and elite self-fashioning in the Roman east. In Goldhill 2001a: 306–34.

Nijhuis, K. 1995. Greek doctors and Roman patients: A medical anthropological approach. In van der Eijk, P. J., Hosrtmanshoff, H. F. J., and Schrijvers, P. H. (eds.), *Ancient medicine in its socio-cultural context* 1. Amsterdam. 49–66.

Nisbet, R. G. M. 1995. The survivors: Old style literary men in the triumviral period. In Nisbet, R. G. M., *Collected papers on Latin literature*. Ed. S. J. Harrison. Oxford. 390–413.

Nixon, C. E. V. and Rodgers, B. S. 1994. *In praise of later Roman emperors: The* Panegyrici Latini. Berkeley.

Nock, A. D. 1934. A vision of Mandulis Aion. *HTR* 29: 53–104. (Rpr. in Nock, A. D., *Essays on religion and the ancient world*. Ed. Z. Stewart. Oxford. 1: 356–400.)

Nodelman, S. 1975. How to read a Roman portrait. *Art in America* 63: 26–33.

Noegel, S., Walker, J., and Wheeler, B. (eds.) 2003. *Prayer, magic, and the stars in the ancient and late antique worlds*. University Park, PA.

Nogales Basarrate, T. 2000. Un altar en el foro de Augusta Emerita. In León Alonso, P. and Nogales Basarrate, T. (eds.), *Actas de la III Reunión sobre Escultura romana en Hispania (Córdoba 1997)*. Madrid. 25–46.

Nollé, J. 1992/3. Kaiserliche Privilegien für Gladiatorenmunera und Tierhetzen. Unbekannte und ungedeute Zeugnisse auf städtischen Münzen des grieschischen Ostens. *Jahrbuch für Numismatik und Geldgeschichte* 42/43: 49–82.

Noreña, C. 2001. The communication of the emperor's virtues. *JRS* 91: 146–68.

Norman, N. J. 2003. Death and burial of Roman children: The case of the Yasmina cemetery at Carthage – Part II, The archaeological evidence. *Mortality* 8: 36–47.

Novick, P. 1988. *That noble dream: The "objectivity question" and the American historical profession*. Cambridge.

Noy, D. 1993–5. *Jewish inscriptions of western Europe*. 2 vols. Cambridge.

Noy, D., Alexander Panayotov, A., and Bloedhorn, H. 2004. *Inscriptiones Judaicae Orientis*. 3 vols. Tübingen.

Nussbaum, M. 1994. *The therapy of desire*. Princeton.

Nussbaum, M. 2002. The incomplete feminism of Musonius Rufus, Platonist, Stoic, and Roman. In Nussbaum and Sihvola: 283–326.

Nussbaum, M. and Sihvola, J. (eds.) 2002. *The sleep of reason*. Chicago.

Nutton, V. 1986. The perils of patriotism: Pliny and Roman medicine. In French and Greenaway: 30–58.

Nutton, V. 1990. The patient's choice: A new treatise by Galen. *CQ* 40: 236–57.

Nutton, V. 1995. Roman medicine, 250 BC to AD 200; Medicine in late antiquity and the early Middle Ages. In Conrad, L. I. et al. (eds.), *The western medical tradition: 800 BC to AD 1800*. Cambridge. 31–91.

Nutton, V. 2000. Medical thoughts on urban pollution. In Hope and Marshall: 65–73.

Nutton, V. (ed.) 2002. *The unknown Galen*. BICS Suppl. 77. London.

Nutton, V. 2004. *Ancient medicine*. London.

O'Barr, J. F. (ed.) 1989. *Women and a new academy*. Madison.

O'Connor, C. 1993. *Roman bridges*. Oxford.

Oertel, F. 1917. *Die Liturgie. Studien zur ptolemäischen und Kaiserlichen Verwaltung Ägyptens*. Leipzig.

Ogilvie, R. 1965. *A commentary on Livy I–V*. Oxford.

Oliensis, E. 1998. *Horace and the rhetoric of authority*. Cambridge.

Oliver, J. H. 1966. A Roman governor visits Samothrace. *AJP* 87: 75–80.

Oliver, J. H. 1971. Epaminondas of Acraephia. *GRBS* 12: 221–37.

Oliver, J. H. 1979. Greek applications for Roman trials. *AJP* 100: 543–58.

Oliver, J. H. and Clinton, K. 1989. *Greek constitutions of early Roman emperors from inscriptions and papyri*. Memoirs of the American Philosophical Society 178. Philadelphia.

Oliver, J. H. and Palmer, R. E. A. 1955. Minutes of an act of the Roman Senate. *Hesperia* 24: 320–49.
Orr, D. G. 1978. Roman domestic religion: The evidence of the household shrines. *ANRW* 2.16.2: 1557–91.
Ørsted, P. 1985. *Roman imperial economy and Romanization. A study in Roman imperial administration and the public lease system in the Danubian provinces from the first to the third century AD*. Copenhagen.
Osborn, E. 1993. *The emergence of Christian theology.* Cambridge.
Osborne, R. 2004. *Studies in ancient Greek and Roman society.* Cambridge.
Osiek, C. 2002. Perpetua's husband. *JECS* 10: 287–90.
Ostenfeld, E. N. and Blomqvist. 2002. *Greek Romans and Roman Greeks: Studies in cultural interaction.* Aarhus studies in Mediterranean antiquity 1. 3. Aarhus.
Packer, J. E. 1975. Middle and lower class housing in Pompeii and Herculaneum: A preliminary survey. In Andreae, B. and Kyrieleis, H. (eds.), *Neue Forschungen in Pompeji.* Recklinghausen. 133–46.
Packer, J. E. 1978. Inns at Pompeii: A short survey. *Cronache Pompeiane* 4: 5–53.
Papaconstantinou, A. 2001. *Le culte des saints en Égypte des Byzantins aux Abbassides. L'apport des sources papyrologiques et épigraphiques grecques et coptes.* Paris.
Parente, F. and Sievers, J. (eds.) 1994. *Josephus and the history of the Greco-Roman period: Essays in memory of Morton Smith.* Leiden.
Parker, A. J. 1990. The wines of Roman Italy. *JRA* 3: 325–31.
Parker, A. J. 1992. *Ancient shipwrecks of the Mediterranean and Roman provinces.* BAR S580. Oxford.
Parker, H. N. 1992a. Love's body anatomized: The ancient erotic handbooks and the rhetoric of sexuality. In Richlin 1992e: 90–111.
Parker, H. N. 1992b. Other remarks on the other Sulpicia. *CW* 86.2: 89–95.
Parker, H. N. 1997. The teratogenic grid. In Hallett and Skinner: 47–65.
Parker, W. H. 1988. Priapeia: *Poems for a phallic God*. London.
Parkin, T. G. 1992. *Demography and Roman society.* Baltimore.
Parkin, T. G. 2001. On becoming a parent in later life: From Augustus to Antonio Agustin via Saint Augustine. In S. Dixon: 221–34.
Parkins, H. (ed.) 1997a. *Roman urbanism. Beyond the consumer city?* London.
Parkins, H. 1997b. The consumer city domesticated? The Roman city and elite economic strategies. In Parkins 1997a: 83–111.
Parkins, H. 1998. Time for change? Shaping the future of the ancient economy. In Parkins and Smith: 1–15.
Parkins, H. and Smith, C. (eds.) 1998. *Trade, traders and the ancient city.* London.
Parrish, D. 1999. House (or Wohneinheit) 2 in Hänghaus 2 at Ephesos: A few issues of interpretation. In Friesinger, H. and Krinzinger, F. (eds.), *100 Jahre Österreichische Forschungen in Ephesos, Akten des Symposions Wien 1995.* Vienna. 507–13.
Parslow, C. 2000. The hydraulic system in the Balneum Venerium et Nongentum of the Praedia Iuliae Felicis in Pompeii. In Jansen, G. C. M. (ed.), *Cura Aquarum in Sicilia.* Leiden. 201–9.
Parsons, P. J. 1976. Petitions and a letter: The Grammarian's Complaint. In Hanson, A. E. (ed.), *Collectanea Papyrologica: Texts published in Honor of H. C. Youtie*, 2. Bonn. 409–46.
Parsons, P. J. 1994. Summing up. *Proceedings of the 20th International Congress of Papyrologists, Copenhagen August 23–29, 1992.* Copenhagen. 118–23.
Paterson, J. 1982. Salvation from the sea: Amphorae and trade in the Roman west. *JRS* 72: 146–57.

Paterson, J. 1998. Trade and traders in the Roman world: Scale, structure and organization. In Parkins and Smith: 149–67.
Patterson, J. 1987. Crisis, what crisis? Rural change and urban development in imperial Appenine Italy. *PBSR* 55: 115–46.
Patterson, J. R. 2000. On the margins of the city of Rome. In Hope and Marshall: 85–103.
Pavis d'Escurac, H. 1980. Flaminat et société dans la colonie de Timgad. *Ant.Afr.* 15: 183–200.
Peachin, M. 1990. *Roman imperial titulature and chronology, AD 235–284*. Amsterdam.
Peachin, M. 1996. Iudex vice Caesaris. *Deputy emperors and the administration of justice during the principate*. Stuttgart.
Peachin, M. 2001. Jurists and the law in the early Roman Empire. In De Blois: 109–20.
Peacock, D. P. S. 1982. *Pottery in the Roman world: An ethnoarchaeological approach*. Harlow.
Peacock, D. P. S and Maxfield, V. 1997. *Survey and excavation Mons Claudianus 1987–1993. I. Topography and Quarries*. Cairo.
Peacock, D. P. S. and Williams, D. F. 1986. *Amphorae and the Roman economy: An introductory guide*. Harlow.
Pearce, J., Millet, M., and Struck, M. (eds.) 2001. *Burial, society and context in the Roman world*. Oxford.
Pelikan, J. 1993. *Christianity and classical culture*. New Haven.
Pelling, C. B. R. 1997. Biographical history? Cassius Dio on the early principate. In Edwards and Swain: 117–44.
Peña, J. T. 1998. The mobilization of state olive oil in Roman Africa: The evidence of late 4th-c. ostraca from Carthage. In Peña, J. T., Rossiter, J. J., Wilson, A. I., and Wells, C. M. (eds.), *Carthage papers. The early colony's economy, water supply, a public bath, and the mobilization of state olive oil*. JRA Suppl. 28. Portsmouth, RI. 117–238.
Percival, J. 1976. *The Roman villa*. Berkeley.
Perkins, J. 1995. *The suffering self: Pain and narrative representation in the early Christian era*. London.
Peskowitz, M. B. 1997. *Spinning fantasies: Rabbis, gender, and history*. Berkeley.
Petersen, L. H. 2003. The baker, his tomb, his wife, and her breadbasket: The monument of Eurysaces in Rome. *Art Bulletin* 85: 230–57.
Pflaum, H.-G. 1940. Essai sur le cursus publicus sous le haut-Empire romain. *Monuments et mémoires publiés par l'Académie des inscriptions et belles-lettres* 14: 189–391.
Pflaum, H.-G. 1950. *Les procurateurs équestres sous le haut-Empire romain*. Paris.
Pflaum, H.-G. 1960–1. *Les carrières procuratoriennes équestres sous le haut empire romain, I–IV*. Paris.
Plaum, H. G. 1976. Zur Reform des Kaisers Gallienus. *Historia* 25: 109–17.
Phang, S. E. 2001. *The marriage of Roman soldiers, 13 BC–AD 235: Law and family in the Roman army*. Leiden.
Pharr, C. (ed. and trans.) 1952. *The Theodosian Code and novels, and the Sirmondian Constitutions; A translation, with commentary, glossary and bibliography*. Princeton. (Rpr. New York, 1969.)
Phillips, C. R. 1986. The sociology of religious knowledge in the Roman Empire to AD 284. *ANRW* 2.16.3: 2677–773.
Phillips, J. F. 1997. Neoplatonic exegeses of Plato's cosmogony (*Timaeus* 27c–28c). *Journal of the History of Philosophy* 35.2: 173–97.
Pinault, J. R. 1992. The medical case for virginity in the early second century CE: Soranus of Ephesus, *Gynecology* 1.32. *Helios* 19.1–2: 123–39.
Pintabone, D. T. 2002. Ovid's Iphis and Ianthe: When girls won't be girls. In Rabinowitz and Auanger: 256–83.

Pleket, H. W. 1993a. Rome: A pre-industrial megalopolis. In Barker, T. and Sutcliffe, A. (eds.), *Megalopolis. The giant city in history.* London. 14–35.

Pleket, H. W. 1993b. Agriculture in the Roman Empire in comparative perspective. In Sancisi-Weerdenburg et al.: 317–42.

Polanyi, K., Arensberg, C. M., and Pearson, H. W. 1957. *Trade and market in the early empires.* Glencoe, IL.

Poliakoff, M. 1987. *Combat sports in the ancient world: Competition, violence, and culture.* New Haven.

Pollard, N. 1996. The Roman army as "total institution" in the near east? In Kennedy, D. (ed.), *The Roman army in the east.* JRA Suppl. 18. Ann Arbor. 211–27.

Pollard, N. 2000. *Soldiers, cities and civilians in Roman Syria.* Ann Arbor.

Pollmann, K. F. L. 2001. Statius' *Thebaid* and the legacy of Vergil's *Aeneid. Mnemosyne* 54.1: 10–30.

Pomeroy, S. B. (ed.) 1991. *Women's history and ancient history.* Chapel Hill.

Potter, D. S. 1987. The Tabula Siarensis, Tiberius, the senate, and the eastern boundary of the Roman Empire. *ZPE* 69: 269–76.

Potter, D. S. 1990. *Prophecy and history in the crisis of the Roman Empire. A historical commentary on the thirteenth Sibylline oracle.* Oxford.

Potter, D. S. 1991. The inscriptions on the bronze Herakles from Mesene: Vologeses IV's war with Rome and the date of Tacitus' *Annales. ZPE* 88: 277–90.

Potter, D. S. 1993. Martyrdom and spectacle. In Scodel: 53–88.

Potter, D. S. 1994. *Prophets and emperors: Human and divine authority from Augustus to Theodosius.* Cambridge, MA.

Potter, D. S. 1996a. Palmyra and Rome: Odaenathus' titulature and the use of the *Imperium Maius. ZPE* 113: 271–85.

Potter, D. S. 1996b. Performance, power, and justice in the high empire. In Slater 1996: 129–59.

Potter, D. S. 1999a. *Literary texts and the Roman historian.* London.

Potter, D. S. 1999b. Entertainers in the Roman Empire. In Potter and Mattingly: 256–325.

Potter, D. S. 2001. Roman history and the American Philological Association, 1900–2000. *Transactions of the American Philological Association* 131: 315–27.

Potter, D. S. 2004. *The Roman Empire at bay AD 180–395.* London.

Potter, D. S. and Mattingly, D. J. (eds.) 1999. *Life, death, and entertainment in the Roman Empire.* Ann Arbor.

Powell, A. (ed.) 1992. *Roman poetry and propaganda.* Bristol.

Pray Bober, P. 1999. *Art, culture and cuisine: Ancient and medieval gastronomy.* Chicago.

Price, S. 1984. *Rituals and power: The Roman imperial cult in Greece and Asia Minor.* Cambridge.

Provost, M. and Mennessier-Jouannet, C. 1994. *Clermont-Ferrand.* Carte archéologique de la Gaule 63.1. Paris.

Pucci, G. 1983. Pottery and trade in the Roman period. In Garnsey et al. 1983: 105–17.

Pucci, J. 1998. *The full-knowing reader: Allusion and the power of the reader in the western literary tradition.* New Haven.

Pucci ben Zeev, M. 1998. *Jewish rights in the Roman world: The Greek and Roman documents quoted by Josephus Flavius.* TSAJ 74. Tübingen.

Purcell, N. 1983. The *apparitores*: A study in social mobility. *PBSR* 51: 125–73.

Purcell, N. 1985. Wine and wealth in ancient Italy. *JRS* 75: 1–19.

Purcell, N. 1987. Tomb and suburb. In von Hesberg, H. and Zanker, P. (eds.), *Römische Gräberstraaen: Selbstdarstellung, status, standard. Kolloquium in München vom 28. bis 30 Oktober 1985.* Munich. 25–42.

Purcell, N. 1990. The creation of provincial landscape: The Roman impact on Cisalpine Gaul. In Blagg, T. and Millett, M. (eds.), *The early Roman Empire in the west*. Oxford. 6–29.

Purcell, N. 1995. Literate games: Roman urban society and the game of *alea*. *Past and Present* 147: 3–37.

Putnam, M. C. P. 2000. *Horace's Carmen Saeculare. Ritual magic and the poet's art*. New Haven.

Quinn, K. 1982. The poet and his audience in Augustan Rome. *ANRW* 2.30.1: 76–180.

Raaflaub, K. and Toher, M. (eds.) 1990. *Between republic and empire: Interpretations of Augustus and his principate*. Berkeley.

Rabinowitz, N. S. and Auanger, L. (eds.) 2002. *Among women: From the homosocial to the homoerotic in the ancient world*. Austin.

Radice, B. 1969. *Pliny: Letters and panegyricus*. 2 vols. Cambridge, MA.

Raepsaet-Charlier, M.-T. 1987. *Prosopographie des femmes de l'ordre sénatorial (Ier–IIe siècles)*. Louvain.

Rajak, T. 1983. *Josephus: The historian and his society*. London.

Rajak, T. 2002. *The Jewish dialogue with Greece and Rome: Studies in cultural and social interaction*. Leiden.

Rakob, F. (ed.) 1993. *Simitthus 1, Die Steinbrüche und die antike Stadt*. Mainz.

Rakob, F. 2000. The making of Augustan Carthage. In Fentress: 72–82.

Ramage, E. S. 1987. *The nature and purpose of Augustus' "Res Gestae."* Historia Einzelschriften 54. Stuttgart.

Ramallo Asensio, S. 2003. Las ciudades de *Hispania* en época republicana: Una aproximación a su proceso de monumentalización. In Abad Casal, L. (ed.), *De Iberia in Hispaniam. La adaptación de las sociedades ibéricas a los modelos romanos*. Alicante. 101–49.

Ramírez Sádaba, J. L. 1994. Epigrafía del anfiteatro romano de Mérida. In Álvarez Martínez, J. M. and Enríquez Navascués, J. J. (eds.), *El anfiteatro en la Hispania romana*. Mérida. 285–99.

Rappaport, U. 1994. Where was Josephus lying – in his *Life* or the *War*? In Parente and Sievers: 279–89.

Rappe, S. 2000. *Reading Neoplatonism*. Cambridge.

Rathbone, D. W. 1981. The development of agriculture in the "ager cosanus" during the Roman republic: Problems of evidence and interpretation. *JRS* 71: 10–23.

Rathbone, D. W. 1991. *Economic rationalism and rural society in third century AD Egypt: The Heroninos archive and the Appianus estate*. Cambridge.

Rathbone, D. W. 1993. Egypt, Augustus, and Roman taxation. *Cahiers Glotz* 4: 81–112.

Rathbone, D. W. 1996. The imperial finances. *CAH*^{2} 10: 309–23.

Rawson, B. (ed.) 1991. *Marriage, divorce, and children in ancient Rome*. Oxford.

Rawson, B. 2001. Children as cultural symbols: Imperial ideology in the second century. In S. Dixon: 21–42.

Rawson, E. 1985. *Intellectual life in the late Roman Republic*. London.

Rawson, E. 1991. *Roman culture and society. Collected papers*. Oxford.

Reardon, B. P. (ed.) 1989. *Collected ancient Greek novels*. Berkeley.

Reardon, B. P. 1991. *The form of Greek romance*. Princeton.

Redfield, R. 1956: *Peasant society and culture: An anthropological approach to civilization*. Chicago.

Rees, R. 1993. Images and image: A re-examination of tetrarchic iconography. *Greece and Rome* 40: 181–200.

Reeve, M. D. 1986a. Celsus. In Reynolds 1986: 46–7.

Reeve, M. D. 1986b. Scribonius Largus. In Reynolds 1986: 353.

Remesal Rodriguez, J. 2002. Baetica and Germania. Notes on the concept of "provincial interdependence" in the Roman Empire. In Erdkamp: 293–308.

Rengen, W. van. 2000. La IIe légion Parthique à Apamée. In Le Bohec and Wolff: 407–10.
Reynolds, J. 1982. *Aphrodisias and Rome*. JRS Monograph 1. London.
Reynolds, J. 1988. Cities. In D. Braund: 15–51.
Reynolds, J. and Tannenbaum, R. 1987. *Jews and godfearers at Aphrodisias*. Cambridge.
Reynolds, L. D. (ed.) 1986a. *Texts and transmission: A survey of the Latin classics*. Oxford.
Reynolds, L. D. 1986b. The elder Pliny. In L. D. Reynolds 1986a: 307–16.
Reynolds, L. G. 1986. *Economic growth in the third world: An introduction*. New Haven.
Reynolds, P. 1995. *Trade in the western Mediterranean, AD 400–700: The ceramic evidence*. BAR S604. Oxford.
Ribera i Lacomba, A. 1995. La primera evidencia arqueológica de la destrucción de Valentia por Pompeyo. *JRA* 8: 19–40.
Riccobono, S., Baviera, J., and Furlani, J. (eds.) 1968–72. *Fontes Iuris Romani AnteJustiniani*. 2nd edn. 3 vols. Florence.
Rich, J. W. and Wallace-Hadrill, A. (eds.) 1991. *City and country in the ancient world*. London.
Rich, J. W. and Williams, J. H. C. 1999. *Leges et ivra P. R. restitvit*: A new *aureus* of Octavian and the settlement of 28–27 BC. *NC* 159: 169–213.
Richardson, J. S. 1996. *The Romans in Spain*. Oxford.
Richardson, Jr., L. 1992. *A new topographical dictionary of ancient Rome*. Baltimore.
Richlin, A. 1981a. Approaches to the sources on adultery at Rome. *Women's Studies* 8.1–2: 225–50.
Richlin, A. 1981b. The meaning of *Irrumare* in Catullus and Martial. *CPh* 76: 40–6.
Richlin, A. 1984. Invective against women in Roman satire. *Arethusa* 17: 67–80.
Richlin, A. 1991. Zeus and Metis: Foucault, classics, feminism. *Helios* 18: 160–80.
Richlin, A. 1992a. *The garden of Priapus: Sexuality and aggression in Roman humor*. New York. (Rev. edn. of 1983.)
Richlin, A. 1992b. Julia's jokes, Galla Placidia, and the Roman use of women as political icons. In Garlick et al.: 65–91.
Richlin, A. 1992c. Reading Ovid's rapes. In Richlin 1992e: 158–79.
Richlin, A. 1992d. Sulpicia the satirist. *CW* 86.2: 125–40.
Richlin, A. (ed.) 1992e. *Pornography and representation in Greece and Rome*. Oxford.
Richlin, A. 1993. Not before homosexuality: The materiality of the *Cinaedus* and the Roman law against love between men. *Journal of the History of Sexuality* 3.4: 523–73.
Richlin, A. 1995. Making up a woman: The face of Roman gender. In Eilberg-Schwartz and Doniger: 185–213.
Richlin, A. 1997a. Carrying water in a sieve: Class and the body in Roman women's religion. In K. L. King: 330–74.
Richlin, A. 1997b. Towards a history of body history. In Golden and Toohey: 16–35.
Richlin, A. 1997c. Gender and rhetoric: Producing manhood in the schools. In Dominik: 90–110.
Richlin, A. 1997d. Pliny's brassiere: Roman medicine and the female body. In Hallett and Skinner: 197–220.
Richlin, A. 1998. Foucault's *History of Sexuality*: A useful theory for women? In Larmour et al: 138–70.
Rickman, G. 1980. *The corn supply of ancient Rome*. Oxford.
Ricoeur, P. 2000. L'ecriture de l'histoire et la representation du passé. *Annales*: 731–48.
Rife, J. L. 2002. Officials of the Roman provinces in Xenophon's *Ephesiaca*. *ZPE* 138: 93–108.
Riggsby, A. 1997. "Public" and "Private" in Roman culture: The case of the Cubiculum. *JRA* 10: 36–56.
Riley, D. N. 1987. *Air photography and archaeology*. Philadelphia.
Rispoli, G. 1988. *Lo Spazio del verisimile: Il racconto, la storia e il mito*. Naples.
Rives, J. B. 1995. Human sacrifice among pagans and Christians. *JRS* 85: 65–85.

Rives, J. B. 1996. The piety of a persecutor. *JECS* 4: 1–25.
Rives, J. B. 1999. The decree of Decius and the religion of the empire. *JRS* 89: 135–54.
Rives, J. B. 2003. Magic in Roman law: The reconstruction of a crime. *CA* 22: 313–39.
Robert, L. 1930. Pantomimen im griechischen Orient. *Hermes* 1930: 106–22. (Rpr. in Robert 1969a: 654–70.)
Robert, L. 1936. ΑΡΧΑΙΟΛΟΓΟΣ. *REG*. 235–54. (Rpr. in Robert 1969a: 671–90.)
Robert, L. 1940. *Les gladiateurs dans l'Orient grec*. Paris.
Robert, L. 1948. Épitaphe de provenance inconnue faisant mention des barbares. *Hellenica* 6: 117–22. Paris.
Robert, L. 1949. Le culte de Caligula à Milet et la province d'Asie. *Hellenica* 7: 206–38.
Robert, L. 1954. Les fouilles de Claros. Paris. (Rpr. in Robert 1989b: 523–49.)
Robert, L. 1960. Αἰτησάμενος sur les monnaies. *Hellenica* 11–12: 53–62.
Robert, L. 1961. Les épigraphies et l'épigraphie grecque et romaine. *L'histoire et ses méthods*. *Encyclopédie de la Pléaide*. Paris. 3–47 = *OMS* 5: 65–119.
Robert, L. 1967. Sur les inscriptions d'Éphèse. Fêtes, athlètes, empereurs, épigrammes. *Revue de philologie* 41: 7–84. (Rpr. in Robert 1989a: 347–424.)
Robert, L. 1969a. *Opera Minora Selecta* 1. Amsterdam.
Robert, Louis. 1969b. Inscriptions d'Athènes et la Grèce centrale. *Archaiologike Ephemeris* 108: 1–58. (Rpr. in Robert 1990: 707–64.)
Robert, L. 1970. Deux concours grecs à Rome. *CRAI*: 6–27. (Rpr. in Robert 1989a: 647–68.)
Robert, L. 1971. Un oracle gravé à Oenoanda. *CRAI*: 597–619. (Rpr. in Robert 1989a: 617–39.)
Robert, L. 1977. La titulature de Nicée et de Nicomédie: la gloire et la haine. *HSCP* 81: 1–39. (Rpr. in Robert 1989b: 211–49.)
Robert, L. 1978. Catalogue agonistique des Romaia de Xanthos. *RA*: 277–90. (Rpr. in Robert 1990: 681–94.)
Robert, L. 1982 Discours d'ouverture du VIIIe Congrès international d'épigraphie grecque et latine à Athènes, 1982. *Actes du VIIIe Congrès international d'épigraphie grecque et latine*. Vol. 1. Athens. 31–42. (Rpr. in Robert 1989b: 709–19.)
Robert, L. 1987. *Documents d'Asie mineure*. Paris.
Robert, L. 1989a. *Opera minora selecta* 5. Amsterdam.
Robert, L. 1989b. *Opera minora selecta* 6. Amsterdam.
Robert, L. 1990. *Opera minora selecta* 7. Amsterdam.
Robert, L. 1992. Décret de Colophon pour un chresmologue de Smyrne appelé à diriger l'oracle de Claros. *BCH* 116: 279–91.
Robert, L. and Robert, J. 1989. *Claros I. Décrets hellénistiques*. Paris.
Robinson, M. 2002. Domestic burnt offerings and sacrifices at Roman and pre-Roman Pompeii, Italy. *Vegetation history and archaeobotany* 11: 93–9.
Robinson, O. F. 1997. *The sources of Roman law*. London.
Rocca, J. 2003. *Galen on the brain: Anatomical knowledge and physiological speculation in the second century AD*. Leiden.
Roddaz, J.-M. 2003. De l'oppidum indigène à la ville romaine: l'évolution de l'urbanisme dans la péninsule Ibérique à la fin de la Republique. In Reddé, M., Dubois, L., Briquel, D., Lavagne, H., and Queyrel, F. (eds.), *La naissance de la ville dans l'antiquité*. Paris. 157–70.
Rodriguez Almeida, E. 1984. *Il monte Testaccio*. Rome.
Rodríguez Hidalgo, J. M., Keay, S. J., Jordan, D., and Creighton, J. 1999. La Itálica de Adriano. Resultados de las prospecciones arqueológicas de 1991 y 1993. *Archivo Español de Arqueología* 72: 73–97.
Rogers, G. 1991a. *The sacred identity of Ephesus: Foundation myths of a Roman city*. London.
Rogers, G. 1991b. Demosthenes of Oenoanda and models of euergetism. *JRS* 81: 91–100.
Roller, L. E. 1997. The ideology of the eunuch priest. *Gender and History* 9: 542–59.

Romeo, I. 2002. The Panhellenion and ethnic identity in Hadrianic Greece. *CPh* 97: 21–40.
Romm, J. S. 1992. *The edges of the earth in ancient thought: Geography, exploration, and fiction.* Princeton.
Rose, C. B. 1997. *Dynastic commemoration and imperial portraiture in the Julio-Claudian period.* Cambridge.
Rosenmeyer, P. A. 2001. *Ancient epistolary fictions: The letter in Greek literature.* Cambridge.
Rosman, K. J. R., Chisholm, W., Hong, S., Candelone, J.-P. and Boutron, C. F. 1997. Lead from Carthaginian and Roman Spanish mines isotopically identified in Greenland ice dated from 600 BC to 300 AD. *Environment, Science and Technology* 31: 3413–16.
Ross, D. O. 1987. *Virgil's elements: Physics and poetry in the Georgics.* Princeton.
Rostovtzeff, M. 1957. *Social and economic history of the Roman Empire.* 2nd edn., rev. P. M. Fraser. Oxford.
Roth-Congès, A. 1992. Nouvelles fouilles à Glanum (1982–1990). *JRA* 5: 39–55.
Roth-Congès, A. 2000. *Glanum: De l'oppidum salyen à la cité latine.* Paris.
Rotondi, G. 1912. *Leges publicae populi Romani.* Milan.
Roueché, C. 1989. *Aphrodisias in late antiquity.* JRS Monograph 5. London.
Roueché, C. 1993. *Performers and partisans at Aphrodisias in the Roman and late Roman periods: A study based on inscriptions from the current excavations at Aphrodisias in Caria.* JRS Monograph 6. London.
Rougé, J. 1981. *Ships and fleets of the ancient Mediterranean.* Middletown, CT.
Rousselle, A. 1988. *Porneia: On desire and the body in antiquity.* Trans. F. Pheasant. Oxford.
Rousset, D. 1994. Les frontières des cités grecques. Premières réflexions à partir du recueil des documents épigraphiques. *Cahiers Glotz* 5: 97–126.
Rowe, G. 2002. *Princes and political cultures.* Ann Arbor.
Rowlandson, J. 1996. *Landowners and tenants in Roman Egypt: The social relations of agriculture in the Oxyrhynchite nome.* Oxford.
Rowlandson, J. (ed.) 1998. *Women and society in Greek and Roman Egypt: A sourcebook.* Cambridge.
Roxan, M. M. 1978. *Roman military diplomas 1954–1977.* Institute of Archaeology Occasional Publication No. 2. London.
Roxan, M. M. 1985. *Roman military diplomas 1978–1984.* Institute of Archaeology Occasional Publication No. 9. London.
Roxan, M. M. 1994. *Roman military diplomas 1985–1993.* Institute of Archaeology Occasional Publication No. 14. London.
Roxan, M. M. and Holder, P. A. 2003. *Roman military diplomas 4.* BICS Suppl. 82. London.
Runia, D. T. 2002. The beginnings of the end: Philo of Alexandria and Hellenistic theology. In Frede and Laks: 281–316.
Russell, D. A. 1973. *Plutarch.* London.
Russell, D. A. 1983. *Greek declamation.* Cambridge.
Russell, D. A. 1992. *Dio Chrysostom: Orations VII, XII, XXXVI.* Cambridge.
Russell, D. A. and Wilson, N. G. 1981. *Menander Rhetor* (edited with translation and commentary). Oxford.
Rutgers, L. V., Van der Horst, P. W., Havelaar, H. W., and Teugels, L. (eds.) 1998. *The use of sacred books in the ancient world.* Leuven.
Rutherford, I. 1998. Island of the extremity: Space, language, and power in the pilgrimage traditions of Philae. In Frankfurter 1998: 229–56.
Rutherford, R. 1989. *The meditations of Marcus Aurelius: A study.* Oxford.
Sabbatini Tumolesi, P. 1988. *Epigrafia anfiteatrale dell' occidente romano.* Vol. 1. Rome.
Saffrey, H. 1968. Introduction to *Proclus: théologie platonicienne.* Livre I. Paris. ix–cxcii.
Saffrey, H. 1986. Neoplatonist spirituality II. From Iamblichus to Proclus and Damascius. In Armstrong, A. (ed.), *Classical Mediterranean spirituality.* New York. 250–68.

Safrai, S. (ed.) 1987. *The literature of the sages.* Compendia Rerum Iudaicarum ad Novum Testamentum 2:3. Assen.
Safrai, Z. 1994. *The economy of Roman Palestine.* London and New York.
Sahin, S. 1995. Studien zu den Inschriften von Perge I. Germanicus in Perge. *Epigraphica Anatolica* 24: 21–36.
Saïd, S. 1994. The city in the Greek novel. In Tatum: 216–36.
Saïd, S. 1999. Rural society in the Greek novel, or the country seen from the town. In Swain 1999: 83–107.
Saïd, S. 2001. Dio's use of mythology. In Swain 2001: 161–86.
Ste. Croix, G. E. M. de. 1981. *The class struggle in the ancient Greek world.* Ithaca.
Salazar, C. F. 2000. *The treatment of war wounds in Graeco-Roman antiquity.* Leiden.
Salisbury, J. 1997. *Perpetua's passion: The death and memory of a young Roman woman.* London.
Sallares, R. 1991. *The ecology of the ancient Greek world.* Ithaca.
Sallares, R. 2002. *Malaria and Rome: A history of malaria in ancient Italy.* Oxford.
Saller, R. P. 1982. *Personal patronage under the early empire.* Cambridge.
Saller, R. P 1984. *Familia, domus,* and the Roman conception of family. *Phoenix* 38: 336–55.
Saller, R. P. 1987. Slavery and the Roman family. In Finley, M. I. (ed.) *Classical slavery.* London. 65–87.
Saller, R. P. 1990 [2000]. Domitian and his successors. Methodological traps in assessing emperors. *AJAH* 15: 4–18.
Saller, R. P. 1994. *Patriarchy, property and death in the Roman family.* Cambridge.
Saller, R. P. 2001. The non-agricultural economy: Superceding Finley and Hopkins? *JRA* 14: 580–4.
Saller, R. P. 2002. Framing the debate over growth in the ancient economy. In Scheidel and von Reden: 251–69.
Saller, R. P. and Shaw, B. D. 1984. Tombstones and Roman family relations in the principate: Civilians, soldiers and slaves. *JRS* 74: 124–56.
Sallnow, M. J. 1987. *Pilgrims of the Andes: Regional cults in Cusco.* Washington, DC.
Salway, B. 2000. Prefects, *patroni,* and decurions: A new perspective on the album of Canusium. In Cooley 2000a: 115–71.
Sánchez-Palencia, F.-J. 2000. *Las Medulas (Léon). Un paisaje cultural en la Asturia Augustana.* Léon.
Sánchez Palencia, F.-J., Montalvo, A., and Gijón Gabriel, E. 2002. El circo de *Augusta Emerita.* In Nogales Basarrate, T. and Sánchez Palencia, F.-J. (eds.), *El circo en Hispania romana.* Madrid. 75–95.
Sancisi-Weerdenburg, H., van der Spek, R. J., Teitler, H. C., and Wallinga, H. T. (eds.) 1993. *De Agricultura: In memoriam Pieter Willem de Neeve (1945–1990).* Amsterdam.
Sanders, E. P. 1985. *Jesus and Judaism.* Philadelphia.
Sanders, E. P. 1993. *The historical figure of Jesus.* London.
Sartre, M. 1983. Les voyages d'Aurelius Gaius, soldat de Dioclétien, et la nomenclature provinciale. *Epigraphica Anatolica* 2: 25–32.
Sartre, M. 1984. Le *Dies Imperii* de Gordien III: une inscription inédite de Syrie. *Syria* 61: 4961.
Sartre, M. 1991. *L'Orient romain: provinces et sociétés provinciales en Méditerranée orientale d'Auguste aux Sévères (31 avant J.-C.–235 après J.-C.).* L'Univers historique. Paris.
Sartre, M. 1995. *L'Asie mineure et l'Anatolie, d'Alexandre à Dioclétien: IVe s. av. J.-C.–IIIe s. ap. J.-C.* Paris.
Sartre, M. 1997. *Le haut-Empire romain: les provinces de Mediterranee orientale d'Auguste aux Severes 31 av. J.-C. –235 apr. J.-C.* Nouvelle histoire de l'antiquite 9. Paris.
Satlow, M. L. 1995. *Tasting the dish: Rabbinic rhetorics of sexuality.* Brown Judaic Studies 303. Atlanta.

Satlow, M. L. 1996. "Texts of Terror": Rabbinic texts, speech acts, and the control of mores. *Association for Jewish Studies Review* 21.2: 273–97.

Satlow, M. L. 1997. Jewish constructions of nakedness in late antiquity. *Journal of Biblical Literature* 116.3: 429–54.

Satlow, M. L. 1998a. Rhetoric and assumptions: Romans and rabbis on sex. In Goodman 1998: 135–44.

Satlow, M. L. 1998b. "One who loves his wife like himself": Love in Rabbinic marriage. *Journal of Jewish Studies* 49: 67–86.

Sauer, E. 1998. M. Annius Florianus: Ein Drei-Monate-Kaiser und die ihm zu Ehren aufgestellten Steinmonument (276 n. Chr.). *Historia* 47: 174–203.

Scarborough, J. 1986. Pharmacy in the *Natural History*. In French, R. and Greenaway, F. (eds.), *Science in the early Roman Empire: Pliny the Elder, his sources and influence*. Totowa, NJ. 59–85.

Scarborough, J. 1995. The opium poppy in Hellenistic and Roman medicine. In Porter, R. and Teich, M. (eds.). *Drugs and narcotics in history*. Cambridge. 4–23.

Scarborough, J., and Nutton, V. 1982. The preface of Dioscorides' *Materia Medica*: Introduction, translation, commentary. *Transactions and studies of the College of Physicians of Philadelphia* 4: 187–225.

Scarcella, A. M. 2003. The social and economic structure of the ancient novels. In Schmeling: 221–76.

Schaad, D. et al. 1992. *Le trésor d'Eauze: bijoux et monnaies de IIIe siècle après J.-C.* Toulouse.

Schaefer, P. 1981. *Der Bar Kokhba-Aufstand: Studien zum zweiten jüdischen Krieg gegen Rom*. TSAJ 1. Tübingen.

Schaefer, P. 1997. Magic and religion in ancient Judaism. In Schaefer and Kippenberg: 19–43.

Schaefer, P. (ed.) 1998–2002. *The* Talmud Yerushalmi *and Graeco-Roman Culture*. 3 vols. Tübingen.

Schaefer, P. and Kippenberg, H. G. (eds.) 1997. *Envisioning magic: A Princeton seminar and symposium*. Leiden.

Scheid, J. 1988. La spartizione sacrificale a Roma. In Grottanelli, C. and Parise, N. F. *Sacrificio e società nel mondo antico*. Rome. 167–92.

Scheid, J. 1998. *Commentarii fratrum arvalium qui supersunt*. Paris.

Scheid, J. 2003. *An introduction to Roman religion*. Trans. J. Lloyd. Bloomington, IN.

Scheidel, W. 1994. *Grundpacht und Lohnarbeit in der Landwirtschaft des römischen Italien*. Frankfurt.

Scheidel, W. 1997. Quantifying the sources of slaves in the Roman Empire. *JRS* 87: 159–69.

Scheidel, W. 2003. Germs for Rome. In Edwards, C. and Woolf, G. (eds.), *Rome the cosmopolis*. Cambridge. 158–76.

Scheidel, W. and Reden, S. von. (eds.) 2002. *The ancient economy*. Edinburgh.

Scheithauer, A. 1987. *Kaiserbild und literarisches Programm. Untersuchungen zur Tendenz der Historia Augusta*. Frankfurt.

Schenk, A. 1931. *Die Römische Kaisergeschichte bei Malalas; Griechischer Text der Bücher IX–XII und Untersuchungen*. Stuttgart.

Schenk, P. 1999. *Studien zur poetischen Kunst des Valerius Flaccus*. Zetemata 102. Munich.

Scherrer, P. (ed.) 2000. *Ephesus, the new guide*. Trans. L. Bier and G. M. Luxton. Turkey.

Schlumberger, D. 1942–3. L'inscription d'Hérodien: remarques sur l'histoire des princes de Palmyre. *Bulletin des études orientales* 11: 36–50.

Schlüter, W. and Wiegels, R. (eds.) 1999. *Rom, Germanien und die Ausgrabungen von Kalkriese*. Osnabrück.

Schmeling, G. (ed.) 2003. *The novel in the ancient world*. Mnemosyne Suppl. 159. Leiden.

Schmitt-Pantel, P. 1990. Collective activities and the political in the Greek city. In Murray, O. and Price, S. (eds.), *The Greek city from Homer to Alexander*. Oxford. 199–213.

Schmitt-Pantel, P. 1992. *La Cité au banquet: histoire des repas publics dans les cités grecques.* Paris.

Schmitt-Pantel, P. 1997. Public feasts in the Hellenistic city: Forms and meanings. In Bilde et al.: 29–67.

Schmitz, G., Sahin, S., and Wagner, J. 1988. Ein Grabaltar mit einer genealogischen Inschrift aus Kommagene. *Epigraphica Anatolica* 11: 81–95.

Schmitz, T. 1997. *Bildung und Macht: Zur sozialen und politischen Funktion der zweiten Sophistik in der griechischen Welt der Kaiserzeit.* Zetemata Heft 97. Munich.

Schönert-Geiss, E. 1965. *Griechisches Münzwerk: Die Münzprägung von Perinthos.* Deutsche Akademie der Wissenschaften zu Berlin. Schriften der Sektion für Altertumswissenschaft 45. Berlin.

Schönert-Geiss, E. 1970. *Griechisches Münzwerk: Die Münzprägung von Byzantion.* Schriften zur Geschichte und Kultur der Antike 2. Berlin.

Schönert-Geiss, E. 1975. *Griechisches Münzwerk: Die Münzprägung von Bisanthe, Dikaia, Selymbria.* Schriften zur Geschichte und Kultur der Antike 13. Berlin.

Schönert-Geiss, E. 1987. *Griechisches Münzwerk: Die Münzprägung von Maroneia.* Schriften zur Geschichte und Kultur der Antike 26. Berlin.

Schönert-Geiss, E. 1991. *Griechisches Münzwerk: Die Münzprägung von Augusta Traiana und Traianopolis.* Schriften zur Geschichte und Kultur der Antike 31. Berlin.

Schroeder, F. and Todd, R. 1990. *Two Greek commentaries on the intellect.* Toronto.

Schürer, E. 1973–87. *The history of the Jewish people in the age of Jesus Christ (175 BC–AD 135).* 3 vols. Rev. edn. by G. Vermes et al. Edinburgh.

Schwartz, S. 1990. The patriarchs and the Diaspora. *Journal of Jewish Studies* 50: 208–22.

Schwartz, S. 2001. *Imperialism and Jewish society, 200 B.C.E. to 640 C.E.* Princeton.

Scodel, R. (ed.) 1993. *Theater and society in the classical world.* Ann Arbor.

Sconocchia, S. (ed.) 1983. *Compositiones.* Leipzig.

Scott, S. and Webster, J. (eds.) 2003. *Roman imperialism and provincial art.* Cambridge.

Sedley, D. 1997a. Philosophical allegiance in the Greco-Roman world. In Griffin and Barnes: 97–119.

Sedley, D. 1997b. Plato's *Auctoritas* and the rebirth of the commentary tradition. In Barnes and Griffin: 110–29.

Sedley, D. 1997c. The ethics of Brutus and Cassius. *JRS* 87: 41–53.

Sedley, D. 2002. The origins of the Stoic god. In Frede and Laks: 41–85.

Seeck, O. 1919. *Regesten der Kaiser und Päpste.* Stuttgart. (Rpr. Frankfurt, 1984.)

Seeck, O. 2000. *Geschichte des Untergangs der antiken Welt.* Ed. S. Rebinich. 6 vols. Darmstadt.

Segal, A. 1980. Heavenly ascent in Hellenistic Judaism, early Christianity and their environment. *ANRW* 2.23.2: 1333–94.

Segal, C. 1995. *Greece in Rome: Influence, integration, resistance.* Cambridge, MA.

Seyrig, H. 1963. Les fils du roi Odainat. *Les Annales archéologiques de Syrie* 13: 159–72. Also in Seyrig, H. *Scripta Varia: Mélanges d'archéologie et d'histoire.* Paris, 1985. 265–78.

Sharp, M. 1999. Shearing sheep: Rome and the collection of taxes in Egypt, 30 B.C.–A.D. 200. In Eck and Müller-Luckner: 213–41.

Sharples, R. W. 1987. Alexander of Aphrodisias. *ANRW* 2.36.2: 1176–243.

Shaw, B. D. 1981a. Rural markets in North Africa and the political economy of the Roman Empire. *Ant.Afr.* 17: 37–83.

Shaw, B. D. 1981b. The Elder Pliny's African geography. *Historia* 30: 424–71.

Shaw, B. D. 1982. Lamasba: An ancient irrigation community. *Ant.Afr.* 81: 61–103.

Shaw, B. D. 1983. Soldiers and society: The army in Numidia. *Opus* 2: 133–59.

Shaw, B. D. 1984a. Bandits in the Roman Empire. *Past and Present* 105: 5–52. (Rpr. in Osborne 2004: 326–74.)

Shaw, B. D. 1984b. Water and society in the ancient Maghrib: Technology, property and development. *Ant.Afr.* 20: 121–73.
Shaw, B. D. 1988. Roman taxation. In Grant and Kitzinger: 2: 809–27.
Shaw, B. D. 1993. The passion of Perpetua. *Past and Present* 139: 3–45. (Rpr. in Osborne 2004: 286–325.)
Shaw, B. D. 1996. Seasons of death: Aspects of mortality in imperial Rome. *JRS* 86: 100–38.
Shaw, B. D. 1997. Agrarian economy and the marriage cycle of Roman women. *JRA* 10: 57–76.
Shaw, B. D. 2000. Rebels and outsiders. *CAH* 11^2: 361–403.
Shaw, B. D. 2001. Challenging Braudel: A new vision of the Mediterranean. *JRA* 14: 419–53.
Sherk, R. K. 1984. *Rome and the Greek east to the death of Augustus.* Translated Documents of Greece and Rome, 4. Cambridge.
Sherk, R. K. 1988. *The Roman Empire: Augustus to Hadrian.* Translated Documents of Greece and Rome, 6. Cambridge.
Sherwin-White, A. N. 1966. *The letters of Pliny: A historical and social commentary.* Oxford.
Sherwin-White, A. N. 1973. *The Roman citizenship.* 2nd edn. Oxford.
Sherwin-White, S. M. 1985. Ancient archives: The edict of Alexander to Priene, a reappraisal. *JHS* 105: 69–89.
Sillar, S. 2001. Caracalla and the senate: The aftermath of Geta's assassination. *Athenaeum* 89: 407–23.
Sirks, A. J. B. 1991. *Food for Rome: The legal structure of the transportation and processing of supplies for Rome and Constantinople.* Amsterdam.
Sirks, A. J. B. 2001. Making a request to the emperor: Rescripts in the Roman Empire. In De Blois: 121–35.
Sitwell, N. H. H. 1981. *Roman roads of Europe.* New York.
Skinner, M. B. 1979. Parasites and strange bedfellows: A study in Catullus' political imagery. *Ramus* 8: 137–52.
Skinner, M. B. 1996. Zeus and Leda: The sexuality wars in contemporary classical scholarship. *Thamyris* 3.1: 103–23.
Slater, W. J. (ed.) 1991. *Dining in a classical context.* Ann Arbor.
Slater, W. J. (ed.) 1996. *Roman theater and society.* Ann Arbor.
Smallwood, E. M. 1966. *Documents illustrating the principates of Nerva, Trajan, and Hadrian.* Cambridge.
Smith, J. Z. 1978a. The Temple and the magician. In Smith 1978b: 172–89.
Smith, J. Z. (ed.) 1978b. *Map is not territory: Studies in the history of religions.* Leiden.
Smith, J. Z. 1990. *Drudgery divine: On the comparison of early Christianities and the religions of late antiquity.* Chicago.
Smith, J. Z. 2003. Here, there, and anywhere. In Noegel et al.: 21–36.
Smith, R. B. E. 1995. *Julian's gods.* London.
Smith, R. B. E. 2002. Restored utility, eternal city: Patronal imagery at Rome in the fourth century AD. In Lomas and Cornell: 142–66.
Smith, R. R. R. 1988. Simulacra gentium: *Ethne* from the Sebasteion at Aphrodisias. *JRS* 78: 50–77.
Smith, R. R. R. 1990. Late Roman philosopher portraits from Aphrodisias. *JRS* 80: 127–55.
Smith, R. R. R. 1998. Cultural choice and political identity in honorific portraits in the Greek east in the second century AD. *JRS* 88: 56–93.
Sorabji, R. 1987. Infinity and the creation. In Sorabji, R. (ed.), *Philoponus and the Rejection of Aristotelian Science.* Ithaca. 164–78.
Sorabji, R. 2000. *Emotions and peace of mind.* Oxford.
Southern, P. and Dixon, K. 1996. *The late Roman army.* London.

Spawforth, A. 1996. Symbol of unity? The Persian wars tradition in the Roman Empire. In Hornblower, S. (ed.), *Greek historiography.* Oxford. 233–47.
Spawforth, A. 1999. The Panhellenion again. *Chiron* 29: 339–52.
Spawforth, A. and Walker, S. 1985. The world of the Panhellenion I: Athens and Eleusis. *JRS* 75: 78–104.
Spawforth, A. and Walker, S. 1986. The world of the Panhellenion II: Three Dorian cities. *JRS* 76: 88–105.
Speidel, M. A. 1992. Roman army pay scales. *JRS* 82: 87–106.
Speidel, M. P. 1973. The pay of the auxilia. *JRS* 63: 141–7.
Speidel, M. P. 1975. The rise of ethnic units in the Roman imperial army. *ANRW* 2.3: 202–31.
Speidel, M. P. 1994. *Riding for Caesar: The Roman emperors' horse guards.* London.
Sperber, D. 1970. On pubs and policeman in Roman Palestine. *Zeitschrift der Deutschen Morgenländischen Gesellschaft* 120: 257–63.
Spurr, M. S. 1986. *Arable cultivation in Roman Italy, c. 200 BC–c. AD 100.* JRS Monograph 3. London.
Srejovi, D. 1994. The representations of tetrarchs in Romuliana. *Antiquité Tardive* 2: 143–52.
Staden, von, H. 1989. *Herophilus: The art of medicine in early Alexandria.* Cambridge.
Staden, von, H. 1996. Liminal perils. Early Roman receptions of Greek medicine. In Ragep, F. J. and Ragep, S. P. (eds.) *Tradition, transmission, transformation.* Leiden. 369–418.
Stadter, P. W. 1992. *Plutarch and the historical tradition.* London.
Stark, R. 1996. *The rise of Christianity: A sociologist reconsiders history.* Princeton.
Stanton, D. C. (ed.) 1992. *Discourses of sexuality.* Ann Arbor.
Steinberg, M. P. 1991. *The presence of the historian: Essays in memory of Analdo Momigliano. History and Theory,* Beiheft 30.
Stephens, S. A 1994. Who read ancient novels? In Tatum: 405–18.
Stephens, S. A. and Winkler J. J. (eds.) 1995. *Ancient Greek novels: The fragments.* Princeton.
Stern, E. M. 1999. Roman glassblowing in a cultural context. *AJA* 103: 441–84.
Stern, H. 1954. Remarks on the *adoratio* under Diocletian. *Journal of the Warburg and Courtauld Institutes* 17: 184–9.
Stern, M. 1974–84. *Greek and Latin authors on Jews and Judaism.* 3 vols. Jerusalem.
Stirling, L. M. 2004. Archaeological evidence for food offerings in the graves of Roman North Africa. In Egan, R. and Joyal, M. (eds.), Daimonopylai*: Essays in classics and the classical tradition presented to Edmund G. Berry.* Winnipeg. 427–51.
Stirling, L. M. 2005. *The learned collector: Mythological sculpture and classical taste in late-antique Gaul.* Ann Arbor.
Stirling, L. M., Mattingly, D. J., and Ben Lazreg, N. 2001. *Leptiminus (Lamta): A Roman port city in Tunisia, report no. 2, the east baths, Venus mosaic, cemeteries and other studies.* JRA Suppl. 41. Portsmouth, RI.
Stolte, B. H. 2001. The impact of Roman law in Egypt and the near east in the third century A.D.: The documentary evidence. In De Blois: 167–79.
Stolte, B. H. 2003. Jurisdiction and representation of power, or the emperor on circuit. In De Blois et al. *The representation and perception of Roman imperial power.* Leiden. 261–8.
Stone, L. 1972. Prosopography. In Gilbert, F. and Graubard, S. *Historical studies today.* New York. 107–40. (Rpr. in Stone, L. *The past and the present revisited.* 1981. London. 45–73.)
Stone, M. E. (ed.) 1984. *Jewish writings of the Second Temple period.* Compendia Rerum Iudaicarum ad Novum Testamentum 2:2. Aassen.
Stoneman, R. 1995. Naked philosophers: The Brahmans in the Alexander historians and the Alexander Romance. *JHS* 105: 99–114.
Storey, G. R. 1999. Archaeology and Roman society: Integrating textual and archaeological data. *Journal of Archaeological Research* 7: 203–48.

Strack, H. L. and Stemberger, G. 1996. *Introduction to the Talmud and Midrash*. Trans. M. Bockmuel. 2nd edn. Edinburgh.

Strobel, K. 1993. *Das Imperium Romanum im "3. Jahrhundert." Modell einer historischen Krise? Zur Frage mentaler Strukturen breiterer Bevölkerungsschichten in der Zeit von Marc Aurel bis zum Ausgang des 3. Jh. n. Chr.* Historia Einzelschriften 75. Stuttgart.

Strubbe, J. H. M. 1984–6. Gründer kleinasiatischer Städte, Fiktion und Realität. *Ancient Society* 15–17: 253–304.

Sullivan, J. P. 1985. *Literature and politics in the age of Nero*. Ithaca.

Sullivan, J. P. 1991. *Martial: The unexpected classic. A literary and historical study*. Cambridge.

Sünskes Thompson, J. 1990. *Aufstände und Protestaktionen im Imperium Romanum. Die severischen Kaiser im Spannungsfeld innenpolitischer Konflikte*. Bonn.

Sünskes Thompson, J. 1993. *Demonstrative Legitimation der Kaiserherrschaft im Epochenvergleich. Zur politischen Macht des stadtrömischen Volkes*. Stuttgart.

Sutherland, C. H. V. 1967. *Roman imperial coinage vol. 6. From Diocletian's reform (AD 294) to the death of Maximinus (AD 313)*. London.

Sutherland, C. H. V. 1974. *Roman coins*. London.

Swain, S. 1996. *Hellenism and empire: Language, classicism, and power in the Greek world, AD 50–250*. Oxford.

Swain, S. 1997. Plutarch, Plato, Athens, and Rome. In Barnes and Griffin: 165–87.

Swain, S. (ed.) 1999. *Oxford readings in the Greek novel*. Oxford.

Swain, S. (ed.) 2001. *Dio Chrysostom: Politics, letters, and philosophy*. Oxford.

Swarney, P. R. 1970. *The Ptolemaic and Roman* idios logos. ASP 8. Toronto and Amsterdam.

Syme, R. 1939. *The Roman revolution*. Oxford.

Syme, R. 1956. Seianus on the Aventine. *Hermes* 84: 257–66. (Rpr. in Syme 1979–91: 1: 305–14.)

Syme, R. 1958a. *Tacitus*. Oxford.

Syme, R. 1958b. *Colonial elites: Rome, Spain and the Americas*. Oxford.

Syme, R. 1968. *Ammianus and the* Historia Augusta. Oxford.

Syme, R. 1971a. *Emperors and biography: Studies in the* Historia Augusta. Oxford.

Syme, R. 1971b. *The* Historia Augusta*: A call of clarity*. Bonn.

Syme, R. 1973. The Titulus Tibertinus. *Akten des VI Internationalen Kongress für Greischiche und Lateinische Epigraphik*. Munich. 585–601. (Rpr in Syme 1979–91: 3: 869–84.)

Syme, R. 1977. La richesse des aristocraties de Bétique et de Narbonnaise. *Ktema* 2: 373–80. (Rpr. in Syme 1979–91: 3: 977–85.)

Syme, R. 1978. *History in Ovid*. Oxford.

Syme, R. 1981. Rival cities, notably Tarraco and Barcino. *Ktèma* 6: 271–85. (Rpr. in Syme 1979–91: 4: 74–93.)

Syme, R. 1983. Historia Augusta *papers*. Oxford.

Syme, R. 1984. Some neglected children on the Ara Pacis. *AJA* 88: 583–9. (Rpr. in Syme 1979–91: 4: 418–29.)

Syme, R. 1979–91. *Roman papers*. Eds. E. Badian and A. R. Birley. 7 vols. Oxford.

Syme, R. 1995. *Anatolica. Studies in Strabo*. Ed. A. R. Birley. Oxford.

Syme, R. 1999. *The provincial at Rome and Rome and the Balkans 80 BC–AD 14*. Ed. A. R. Birley. Exeter.

Talbert, R. J. A. 1984. *The Senate of imperial Rome*. Princeton.

Talbert, R. J. A. (ed.) 2000. *Barrington atlas of the Greek and Roman world*. Princeton.

Tarpin, M. 2002. *Vici et pagi dans l'Occident romain*. CEFR 299. Rome.

Tarrant, H. 1985. *Scepticism or Platonism? The philosophy of the Fourth Academy*. Cambridge.

Tarrant, H. 1993. *Thrasyllan Platonism*. Ithaca.

Tarrant, H. 1998. Introduction. In *Olympiodorus: Commentary on Plato's* Gorgias. Leiden. 1–52.

Tarrant, H. 2000. *Plato's first interpreters*. London.
Tatum, J. (ed.) 1994. *The search for the ancient novel*. Baltimore.
Tausend, K. 1999. Bemerkunden zum Wandaleneinfall des Jahres 271. *Historia* 48: 119–27.
Tchernia, A. 1983. Italian wine in Gaul at the end of the republic. In Garnsey et al. 1983: 87–104.
Tchernia, A. and Brun, J. P. 1999. *Le vin romain antique*. Grenoble.
TED'A (Taller Escola d'Arqueologia). 1989. El foro provincial de Tarraco, un complejo arquitectónico de época flavia. *Archivo Español de Arqueología* 62: 141–91.
Temin, P. 2001. A market economy in the Roman Empire. *JRS* 91: 169–81.
Thomas, J. D. 1975. The introduction of Dekaprotoi and Comarchs into Egypt in the third century AD. *ZPE* 19: 111–19.
Thomas, J. D. 1983. Compulsory public service in Roman Egypt. In Grimm, G., Heinen, H., and Winter, E. (eds.), *Das römish-byzantinish Ägypten, Akten des internationalen Symposions 26–30 September 1978 in Trier*. Aegyptiaca Treverensia. Trier. Vol. 2: 35–9.
Thomas, J. D. 1999. Communication between the Prefect of Egypt, the procurators and the *nome* officials. In Eck and Müller-Luckner: 181–95.
Thomas, J. D. 2001. The administration of Roman Egypt: A survey of recent research and some outstanding problems. *Atti del XXII Congresso Internazionale di Papirologia, Firenze 1998*. Florence. Vol. 2: 1245–54.
Thomas, R. F. 1988. *Virgil, Georgics*. 2 vols. Cambridge.
Thomas, R. F. 2001. The *Georgics* of resistance: From Virgil to Heaney. *Vergilius* 47: 117–47.
Throckmorton, P. (ed.) 1987. *The sea remembers: Shipwrecks and archaeology*. London.
Tissol, G. 1997. *The face of nature: Wit, narrative, and cosmic origins in Ovid's* Metamorphoses. Princeton.
Tomlin, R. S. O. 1992. The Twentieth Legion at Wroxeter and Carlisle in the first century: The epigraphic evidence. *Britannia* 23: 141–58.
Toner, J. P. 1995. *Leisure and ancient Rome*. Cambridge.
Too, Y. L. (ed.) 2001. *Education in Greek and Roman antiquity*. Leiden.
Too, Y. L. and Livingstone, N. (eds.) 1998. *Pedagogy and power: Rhetorics of classical learning*. Cambridge.
Totelin, L. M. V. 2004. Mithradates' antidote – A pharmacological ghost. *Early Science and Medicine* 9.1: 1–19.
Touratsoglou, I. 1988. *Die Münzstätte von Thessaloniki in der römischen Kaiserzeit (32/31 v.Chr. bis 268 n.Chr.)*. Antiken Münzen und Geschnittene Steine 12. Berlin.
Toynbee, A. J. 1965. *Hannibal's legacy*. Oxford.
Toynbee, J. M. C. 1971. *Death and burial in the Roman world*. Baltimore.
Trebilco, P. R. 1991. *Jewish communities in Asia Minor*. Cambridge.
Treggiari, S. 1991a. *Roman marriage:* Iusti Coniuges *from the time of Cicero to the time of Ulpian*. Oxford.
Treggiari, S. 1991b. Divorce Roman style: How easy and how frequent was it? In B. Rawson: 31–46.
Trillmich, W. 1995. Gestalt und Ausstattung des "Marmorforums" in Mérida: Kenntnisstand und Perspektiven. *Mitteilungen des Deutschen Archäologischen Instituts* (Madrid) 36: 269–91.
Trillmich, W. and Zanker, P. (eds.) 1990. *Stadtbild und Ideologie. Die Monumentalisierung hispanischer Städte zwischen Republik und Kaiserzeit*. Munich.
Trombley, F. R. 1985. Paganism in the Greek world at the end of antiquity: The case of rural Anatolia and Greece. *HTR* 78: 327–52.
Trombley, F. R. 1993/4. *Hellenic religion and Christianization c. 370–529*. 2 vols. Leiden.
Turner, E. G. 1936. Egypt and the Roman Empire: The DEKAPROTOI. *JEA* 22: 7–19.
Turner V. 1974. *Dramas, fields, and metaphors: Symbolic action in human society*. Ithaca.

Valantasis, R. (ed.) 2000. *Religions of late antiquity in practice.* Princeton.
Varner, E. R. 2001. Punishment after death: Mutilation of images and corpse abuse in ancient Rome. *Mortality* 6: 45–64.
Veen, M. van der. 1998. A life of luxury in the desert? The food and fodder supply to Mons Claudianus. *JRA* 11: 101–16.
Veyne, P. 1976. *Le pain et le cirque: Sociologie historique d'un pluralisme politique.* Paris. (Trans. O. Murray and B. Pearce. 1990. *Bread and circuses: Historical sociology and political pluralism.* London.)
Veyne, P. 1979. Mythe et réalité de l'autarcie à Rome. *REA* 81: 261–80.
Veyne, P. (ed.) 1987. *A history of private life I: From Pagan Rome to Byzantium.* Cambridge, MA.
Vian, F. 1959. *Recherches sur les* Posthomerica *de Quintus de Smyrne.* Paris.
Vian, F. (ed.) 1963. *Quintus de Smyrne: le Suite d'Homère tome I, livres I–IV.* Paris.
Ville, G. 1981. *La gladiature en Occident des origenes à la mort de Domitien.* Paris.
Vinson, M. 1998. Gender and politics in the post-iconoclastic period: The *Lives* of Antony the Younger, the Empress Theodora, and the Patriarch Ignatios. *Byzantion* 68: 469–515.
Virlouvet, C. 1997. Existait-il des registres de décès à Rome au Ier siècle ap. J.-C.? In Virlouvet, C. (ed.), *La Rome impériale: démographie et logistique.* CÉFR 230. 77–88.
Vittinghoff, F. 1951. *Römische Kolonisation und Bürgerrechtspolitik unter Caesar und Augustus.* Wiesbaden.
Volokhine, Y. 1998. Les déplacements pieux en Égypte pharaonique: sites et pratiques cultuelles. In Frankfurter 1998d: 51–98.
Wacher, J. (ed.) 1987. *The Roman world.* London. (2nd edn., London, 2001.)
Walbank, F. W. 1979. *A historical commentary on Polybius.* Vol. 3: Commentary on books XIX–XL. Oxford.
Walbank, M. E. H. 2003. Aspects of Corinthian coinage in the late 1st and early 2nd centuries AD. In Williams III, C. K. and Bookidis, N. (eds.), *Corinth, the centenary 1896–1996.* Corinth vol. 20. Princeton. 337–49.
Walker, D. R. 1976. *The metrology of the Roman silver coinage. Part I: From Augustus to Domitian.* BAR Supplementary Series 5. Oxford.
Walker, D. R. 1977. *The metrology of the Roman silver coinage. Part II: From Nerva to Commodus.* BAR Supplementary Series 22. Oxford.
Walker, D. R. 1978. *The metrology of the Roman silver coinage. Part III: From Pertinax to Aemilian.* BAR Supplementary Series 40. Oxford.
Walker, D. R. 1988. *Roman coins from the sacred spring at Bath.* Oxford.
Wallace, S. 1938 *Taxation in Egypt from Augustus to Diocletian.* Princeton University Studies in Papyrology 2. Princeton.
Wallace-Hadrill, A. 1981. Family and inheritance in the Augustan marriage laws. *PCPS* 207: 58–80.
Wallace-Hadrill, A. 1982. *Civilis Princeps*: Between citizen and king. *JRS* 72: 32–48.
Wallace-Hadrill, A. 1983. *Suetonius, the scholar and his Caesars.* London.
Wallace-Hadrill, A. 1985. Propaganda and dissent? Augustan moral legislation and the love poets. *Klio* 67: 180–4.
Wallace-Hadrill, A. 1986. Image and authority in the coinage of Augustus. *JRS* 76: 66–87.
Wallace-Hadrill, A. 1990. Patronage in Roman society: From republic to empire. In Wallace-Hadrill, A. (ed.), *Patronage in ancient society.* London. 61–87.
Wallace-Hadrill, A. 1993. *Augustan Rome.* London.
Wallace-Hadrill, A. 1994. *Houses and society in Pompeii and Herculaneum.* Princeton.
Wallace-Hadrill, A. 1995. Public honour and private shame: The urban texture of Pompeii. In Cornell and Lomas 1995: 39–62.
Wallace-Hadrill, A. 1996. The imperial court. In *CAH*^{2} 10: 283–308.

Walsh, P. G. 1961. *Livy: His historical aims and methods.* Cambridge.
Walters, J. 1993. "No more than a boy": The shifting construction of masculinity from ancient Greece to the Middle Ages. *Gender & History* 5.1: 20–33.
Walters, J. 1997a. Soldiers and whores in a pseudo Quintilian declamation. In Cornell and Lomas 1997: 109–14.
Walters, J. 1997b. Invading the Roman body: Manliness and impenetrability in Roman thought. In Hallett and Skinner: 29–43.
Waltzing, J.-P. 1895–1900. *Étude historique sur les corporations professionelles chez les romains.* Louvain.
Ward-Perkins, J. B. 1970. From republic to empire: Reflections on the early provincial architecture of the Roman west. *JRS* 60: 1–19.
Ward-Perkins, J. B. 1993. *The Severan buildings of Lepcis Magna: An architectural survey.* Society for Libyan Studies Monograph 2. London.
Watson, A. 1974a. *Law making in the later Roman Republic.* Oxford.
Watson, A 1974b. The development of the Praetor's Edict. In Watson: 31–62. (First published *JRS* 60 [1970]: 105–19.)
Watson, A. 1984. *Sources of law, legal change, and ambiguity.* Philadelphia. (Rpr. 1998.)
Watson, A. 1985a. *The digest of Justinian.* English translation edited by Alan Watson, 4 vols. with Latin text. Philadelphia. (English translation only, 2 vols., 1998.)
Watson, A. 1985b. *The evolution of western private law.* Baltimore. (Expanded edn, 2001.)
Watson, A. 1995. *The spirit of Roman law.* Athens, GA.
Webb, R. 2001. The Progymnasmata as practice. In Too: 289–316.
Webb, R. 2002. Female entertainers in late antiquity. In Easterling and Hall: 282–303.
Weber, M. 1958. *The city.* Trans. D. Martindale and G. Neuwirth. New York.
Webster, J. 2001. Creolizing the Roman provinces. *AJA* 105: 209–25.
Webster, J. and Cooper, N. (eds.) 1996. *Roman imperialism: Post-colonial perspectives.* Leicester Archaeology Monographs 3. Leicester.
Wegner, J. R. 1988. *Chattel or person? The status of women in the Mishnah.* Oxford.
Wegner, J. R. 1991. The image and status of women in classical Rabbinic Judaism. In Baskin: 68–93.
Weinstock, S. 1971. *Divus Julius.* Oxford.
Welch, K. 1994. The Roman arena in late-republican Italy: A new interpretation. *JRA* 7: 59–80.
Welch, K. 2003. A new view of the origins of the Basilica: The Atrium Regium, Graecostasis, and Roman diplomacy. *JRA* 16: 5–34.
Wesch-Klein, G. 1998. *Soziale Aspekte des römischen Heerwesens in der Kaiserzeit.* Stuttgart.
Weßel, H. 2003. *Das Recht der Tablettes Albertini.* Berlin.
Westerink, L. G. 1962. *Anonymous prolegomena to Platonic philosophy.* Amsterdam.
White, H. 1984. *The content of the form.* Baltimore.
White, K. D. 1970. *Roman farming.* Ithaca.
White, K. D. 1977. *Country life in classical times.* London.
White, K. D. 1984. *Greek and Roman technology.* London.
White, P. 1974. The presentation and dedication of the *Silvae* and the *Epigrams*. *JRS* 64: 40–61.
White, P. 1993. *Promised verse: Poets in the society of Augustan Rome.* Cambridge, MA.
White, P. 1998. Latin poets and the *Certamen Capitolinum*. In Knox, P. and Foss, C. (eds.), *Style and tradition: Studies in honor of Wendell Clausen.* Stuttgart/Leipzig. 84–95.
Whitehouse, D., Barker, G., Reece, R. and Reese, D. 1982. The *Schola Praeconum* I: The coins, pottery, lamps and fauna. *PBSR* 5: 53–101.
Whitman, J. Q. 1990. *The legacy of Roman law in the Romantic era.* Princeton.

Whitmarsh, T. 1998a. The birth of a prodigy: Heliodorus and the genealogy of Hellenism. In Hunter, R. (ed.), *Studies in Heliodorus*. Cambridge Philological Society Suppl. 21. Cambridge. 93–124.

Whitmarsh, T. 1998b. Reading power in Roman Greece: The *Paideia* of Dio Chrysostom. In Too and Livingstone: 192–213.

Whitmarsh, T. 2001. *Greek literature and the Roman Empire: The politics of imitation*. Oxford.

Whittaker, C. R. 1985. Trade and the aristocracy in the Roman Empire. *Opus* 4: 49–75.

Whittaker, C. R. (ed.) 1988. *Pastoral economies in classical antiquity*. Cambridge Philological Society Suppl. 14. Cambridge.

Whittaker, C. R. 1990. The consumer city revisited. *JRA* 3: 110–18.

Whittaker, C. R. 1993. Do theories of the ancient city matter? In Whittaker, C. R. (ed.), *Land, city and trade in the Roman Empire*. Aldershot. 1–20.

Whittaker, C. R. 1994. *Frontiers of the Roman Empire: A social and economic study*. Baltimore.

Whittaker, C. R. 1996. Moses Finley, 1912–1986. *Proceedings of the British Academy* 94: 459–72.

Whittaker, C. R. and Garnsey, P. D. A. 1998. Rural life in the later Roman Empire. In CAH^2 13: 277–311.

Wickham, C. 1988. Marx, Sherlock Holmes and late Roman commerce. *JRS* 78: 183–93.

Wiedemann, T. E. J. 1992. *Emperors and gladiators*. London.

Wiedemann, T. E. J. 1996a. Mommsen, Rome and the German *Kaiserreich*. In Mommsen, T. *A history of Rome under the emperors* (based on the lecture notes of Sebastian and Paul Hensel, 1882–6). Eds. Barbara and Alexander Demandt. English translation by Clare Krojzl. London.

Wiedemann, T. E. J. 1996b. Tiberius to Nero. CAH^2 10: 198–255.

Wilcken U. (with the assistance of Mitteis, L.) 1912 = *Grundzüge und Chrestomathie der Papyrusurkunde*. Leipzig.

Wilfong, T. 1998. Reading the disjointed body in Coptic: From physical modification to textual fragmentation. In Montserrat 1998b: 116–36.

Wilkes, J. J. 1999. The Roman army as a community in the Danube lands. In Goldsworthy and Haynes: 95–104.

Wilkes, J. J. 2003. The towns of Roman Dalmatia. In Wilson, P. (ed.), *The archaeology of Roman towns: Studies in honour of John S. Wacher*. Oxford. 233–41.

Wilkins, J., Harvey, D., and Dobson, M. (eds.) 1995. *Food in antiquity*. Exeter.

Williams, C. 1995. Greek love at Rome. *CQ* 45: 517–39.

Williams, C. 1997. *Pudicitia* and *Pueri*: Roman concepts of male sexual experience. In Duberman: 25–38.

Williams, C. 1999. *Homosexuality and the Roman man*. Oxford.

Wilson, A. 1999a. Commerce and industry in Roman Sabratha. *Libyan Studies* 30: 29–52.

Wilson, A. 1999b. Deliveries *extra urbem*: Aqueducts and the countryside. *JRA* 12: 314–31.

Wilson, A. 2001. Timgad and textile production. In Mattingly and Salmon 2001a: 271–96.

Wilson, A. 2002a. Machines, power and the ancient economy. *JRS* 92: 1–32.

Wilson, A. 2002b. Urban production in the Roman world: The view from North Africa. *PBSR* 70: 231–73.

Wilson, M. 1993. A Flavian variant history. Silius' *Punica*. In Boyle 1993: 218–36.

Winter, E. 1988. *Die sasanidisch-römischen Friedensverträge des 3. Jahrhunderts n. Chr. – Ein Beitrag zum Verstandnis der auaenpolitischen Beziehungen zwischen de bieden Groamächten*. Frankfurt.

Winterbottom, M. 1982. Schoolroom and courtroom. In Vickers, B. (ed.), *Rhetoric revalued*. Binghamton, NY. 59–70.

Wipszycka, E. 1987. Considérations sur les persécutions contre les chrétiens: qui frappaient-elles? In *Poikilia: études offertes à Jean-Pierre Vernant*. Paris. 397–405.

Wiseman, T. P. 1979. *Clio's cosmetics*. Leicester.
Wiseman, T. P. 1995. Remus: A Roman myth. Cambridge.
Wiseman, T. P. 1998. *Roman drama and Roman history*. Exeter.
Wiseman, T. P. 1999. The games of Flora. In Bergmann and Kondoleon: 197–203.
Wistrand, E. 1976. *The so-called* Laudatio Turiae. Studia Graeca et Latina Gothoburgensia 34. Goteburg.
Witschel, C. 1999. *Krise – Rezession – Stagnation? Der Westen des römischen Reiches im 3. Jahrhundert n. Chr.* Frankfurt.
Wolters, R. 1999. *Nummi Signati. Untersuchungen zur römischen Münzprägung und Geldwirtschaft. Vestigia* 49. Munich.
Woodman, A. J. 1977. *Velleius Paterculus: The Tiberian narrative*. Cambridge.
Woodman, A. J. 1988. *Rhetoric in classical historiography*. London.
Woodman, A. J. and Feeney, D. (eds.) 2002. *Traditions and contexts in the poetry of Horace*. Cambridge.
Woods, A. 1987. Mining. In Wacher: 611–34.
Woolf, G. 1992. Imperialism, empire and the integration of the Roman economy. *World Archaeology* 23.3: 283–93.
Woolf, G. 1994. Becoming Roman, staying Greek: Culture, identity and the civilizing process in the Roman east. *PCPS* 40: 116–43.
Woolf, G. 1996. Monumental writing and the expansion of Roman society in the early empire. *JRS* 86: 22–39.
Woolf, G. 1998. *Becoming Roman: The origins of provincial civilization in Gaul*. Cambridge.
Wörrle, M. 1975. Zwei neue Inschriften aus Myra zur Verwaltung Lykiens in der Kaiserzeit. In Borchhardt, J. (ed.), *Myra. Eine Lykische Metropole in antiker und byzantinischer Zeit*. Istanbuler Forschungen 30. Berlin. 254–300.
Wörrle, M. 1988. *Stadt und Fest im kaiserzeitlichen Kleinasien: Studien zu einer agonistischen Stiftung aus Oinoanda*. Vestigia 39. Munich.
Wrede, H. 1981. Consecratio in formam deorum: *vergöttlichte Privatpersonen in der römischen Kaiserzeit*. Mainz.
Wyke, M. 1989. Mistress and metaphor in Augustan elegy. *Helios* 16: 25–47.
Wyke, M. 1994. Woman in the mirror: The rhetoric of adornment in the Roman world. In Archer et al.: 134–51.
Wyke, M. 2002. *The Roman mistress: Ancient and modern representations*. Oxford.
Yavetz, Z. 1969. Plebs *and* princeps. Oxford.
Yegül, F. 1986. *The bath-gymnasium complex at Sardis*. Cambridge, MA.
Yegül, F. 1992. *Baths and bathing in classical antiquity*. Cambridge, MA.
Yegül, F. (with Couch, T.) 2003. Building a Roman bath for the cameras. *JRA* 16: 153–77.
Youroukova, I. 1973. *Griechisches Münzwerk: Die Münzprägung von Deultum*. Berlin.
Youroukova, I. 1982. *Griechisches Münzwerk: Die Münzprägung von Bizye*. Schriften zur Geschichte und Kultur der Antike 18. Berlin.
Youtie, H. C. 1973a. The papyrologist: Artificer of fact. *Scriptiunculae* 1. Amsterdam. 9–23.
Youtie, H. C. 1973b. Text and context in transcribing papyri. *Scriptiunculae* 1. Amsterdam. 25–33.
Youtie, L. C. 1996. *P.Mich*. XVII 758. *The Michigan medical codex*. ASP 35. Atlanta.
Zach, B. 2002. Vegetable offerings on the Roman sacrificial site in Mainz, Germany – short report on the first results. *Vegetation History and Archaeobotany* 11: 101–6.
Zajac, N. 1999. The *thermae*: A policy of public health or personal legitimation? In DeLaine and Johnston: 99–105.
Zanker, P. 1988. *The power of images in the age of Augustus*. Ann Arbor.
Zanker, P. 2000. The city as symbol: Rome and the creation of an urban image. In Fentress: 25–41.

Zeitlin, F. 2001. Visions and revisions of Homer. In Goldhill 2001a: 195–266.

Ziegler, R. 1985. *Städisches Prestige und kaiserliche Politik: Studien zum Festwesen in Ostkilikien im 2. und 3. Jahrhundert n. Chr.* Düsseldorf.

Ziegler, R. 1993. *Kaiser, Heer und staedtisches Geld: Untersuchungen zur Muenzprägung von Anazarbos und anderer ostkilikischer Städte.* Oesterreichische Akademie der Wissenschaften, Philosophisch-Historische Klasse Denkschriften 234 = Ergänzungsbände zu den Tituli Asiae Minoris 16. Vienna.

Zienkiewicz, J. D. 1986. *The legionary fortress baths at Caerleon.* Cardiff.

Zimmermann, M. 1999. *Kaiser und Ereignis. Studien zum Geschichtswerk Herodians.* Munich.

Zuckerman, C. 1994. Les campagnes des tetrarques, 296–298. Notes de chronologie. *Antiquité Tardive* 2: 65–70.

Index

abortion/contraception, 320, 351, 499–500
Achilles Tatius (novelist), 336, 458, 460, 465
actors, 394–6, 404–5, 408, 441
Aelian (novelist), 455, 466
Aelius Aristides (rhetorician), 239–40, 464
Aeneas: in *Aeneid*, 250–1, 443–4; example of *pietas*, 313; ship of, 411; statue group, 261, 266 (fig. 13.4)
agones: Capitoline, 402–3; conduct of, 392; development of, 388–9, 391
Agrippa, M. Vispanius: and Emerita, 261; Augustus' *elogium* for, 116, 121; in Velleius, 420
Agrippa Postumus, M. Vipsanius, 118
Alciphron (novelist), 455, 466
Alexander of Abonuteichos (prophet), 556, 559; *see also* Glycon
Alexander of Aphrodisias (philosopher), 526–7
Alexandria (in Egypt): "Acts of the Alexandrian Martyrs," 430; in Cleitophon, 458; and history of medicine, 495, 502; Jewish population of, 121, 242–3; population, 231
amphitheaters, 80–2, 261, 390, 400; *see also* Colosseum
amulets: birth, 517–19 (fig. 25.2); healing, 512; Jewish, 554

Antioch, in Syria: mint at, 38, 40; mosaics, 462; Olympic Games at, 407; population, 231, sacked (252), 158
Antoninus Pius (emperor 138–161), 131–2, 182
Antonius Diogenes (novelist), 453, 467–8
Antony (triumvir): and Augustus, 116, 207; coinage of, 36
Apicius (writer on food), 359, 377
Appian (historian), 26
aqueducts, 83–4, 230, 261
army, Roman: *Aerarium militare*, 118, 188, 208; archaeology of, 91–3; and Augustus, 118, 207–9, 211; *Auxilia*, 118, 208, 211–15; "barbarization" of, 201, 225; and civilian population, 223–5; Christians in, 199–200, 609; *Comitatenses*, 226; conscription, 208, 225; disposition of legions, 209–11; donatives, 220–1, 227; dynastic loyalty, 142, 154–5; economic impact of, 219–21, 287, 296; frontier defenses, 118, 201, 209–10, 226–7; length of legionary service, 208; medical care, 505; officers, 213; pay, 124, 219–21, 227, 298; as police, 191, 210–11; recruitment, 211, 222–3; and selection of emperors, 138–43, 151, 155, 164–5; settlement of veterans, 118, 189, 207–8, 211–12, 220, 259–60; size of, 208–11, 225; tactical doctrine, 154, 165, 193,

army, Roman: (*cont'd*)
  213–15, 226; weapons, 193, 214, 226; see *also* praetorian guard
Arnouphis (magician), 146
Arrian: *Anabasis*, 431–2; *Order of battle against the Alans*, 214–15
art: *see* mosaics; sculpture; wall painting
Asinius Pollio (senator), 371–2, 419, 448
Athens, 234, 378, 395, 427–8, 432–3, 458, 467, 528
athletes, Greek, 388–9, 396–7, 399, 402–3; women as, 405–7, 516
Augustus (emperor 31 BC–AD 14): accusations of personal cowardice, 207, 431; and Alexander the Great, 391; aquatic spectacles, 484; coinage, 36–7, 39 (with fig. 2.1), 42–3 (with fig. 2.2), 115; dynastic ambitions of, 117–18, 153, 127, 261, 417, 442, 446; early career, 77, 274, 315–16, 329, 417, 433; Forum of, 77–8, 261, 274, 315–16, 329, 417, 433, 446; and gladiators, 439–47; and Latin literature, 395; marriage legislation, 315–16, 374; as model for later emperors, 147–9; moral legislation, 316, 351, 493, 522, 560; name, 115–16; and pantomime, 186; *pater patriae*, 148; as proconsul, 117; and provincial census, 15, 298; "Restoration of the Republic," 42–3, 115–17, 147; and senators, 314; senators executed by, 117; and "Turia," 401; veteran colonies, 207–8, 259–60; *see also* Agrippa, M. Vispanius; *Res Gestae Divi Augusti*; Syme, R.; tribunician power
Aulus Gellius: on *coloniae*, 259–60
Aurelian (emperor 270–275): coinage reform, 38, 165, 203; reign, 164–6
Aurelius, Marcus (emperor 161–180): and Arnouphis, 145–6; and Avidius Cassius, 139; creates new legions, 209; and Fronto, 336; and Galen, 500, 511; marriages of children, 129–30; and Old Comedy, 395; pays accession bonus, 140, 220; philosophic interests, 524, 531; and predecessors, 131, 437; preferred medication, 511
Aurelius Victor (historian), 29–30, 203, 218

banking, 121–2, 292
banquets: private, 356–60, 372, 376–8; public, 235, 247–8, 276, 354, 378–9, 558

Bar Kokhba (Simeon ben Kosiba), 571, 575–6 (with fig. 28.3)
bars, 373–6
baths and bathing, 82–3, 96, 230, 277, 379–83, 521, 579
beast hunt, *see* venatio
benefaction, *see* euergetism
biography: political, 27–9, 421, 430; *see also Historia Augusta*; Suetonius
Boeckh, Karl August, 48
breast-feeding, 322
brothels, 376
Brown, Peter L., 8
Brunt, Peter A., 5–6, 59

Cagnet, René, 49, 51
Caligula (emperor 31–41), 121, 242–3
Calpurnius Piso, Gnaeus, *see* Piso, Gnaeus Calpurnius; *senatus consultum Pisonianum*
Caracalla (emperor 211–217): and Bato the gladiator, 399; and Egypt, 66; hunting exhibitions, 398; interest in magic, 146; portrait of, 83; reign of, 141–2, 146; and Roman citizenship, 178, 228; and Tipasa, 184; and Troy, 474
Carausius (usurper), 167
Carthage: Roman, 80, 251
Cassius Dio, *see* Dio, L. Cassius
Celsus (medical writer): career, 496–7, 520; on drugs, 510–11; on fevers, 508–9; on folk remedies, 497; on food, 361, 508; on Greek medicine, 497–8, 506–8; gynecology, 515; on surgery, 512–15
Celsus (philosopher), 525–6, 555, 556
Chaldean Oracles, 524, 527–8
chariot racing: history, 387–8, 392, 404; techniques, 393–4; *see also* Circus Maximus
Chariton (novelist), 456, 460–1, 465, 467, 471–2
childbirth: amulets, 517–19 (fig. 25.2); dangers, 516; family planning, 320, 499–500, 514, 516; midwives, 503–4 (fig. 25.1); miscarriages, 320
Christians/Christianity: in army, 199–200; Arian controversy, 171, 197–8, 616–17; asceticism, 366–7; bishops, 588, 617; and classical culture, 110–11, 476, 532, 589, 596–7, 609, 611–12, 615–16; conception of God, 171, 197–8, 599–600, 608, 611–19; Donatist controversy, 171, 204, 603; early growth of, 595–6; and Judaism,

566, 569–70, 577, 589–90, 593, 595–7, 608–10; intellectual attacks upon, 525; Marcion, 600, 604, 611, 612–14; martyrdom, 321–4, 366, 398, 550, 562, 602; Messianism, 593–4, 596–7, 603–5; millenarian beliefs, 604–5; Montanism, 556, 589, 614–15; Nag Hammadi, 600, 611; orthodoxy, 557, 587–9, 600, 611; and "paganism," 544–7, 550; persecution of, 168, 197, 558, 589, 597, 601–3; and sexuality, 324, 338, 340–1, 347–8; and Sibylline Oracles, 433; Torah-observant, 597, 602; urbanism of, 609–10; Valentinus, 589, 600, 604, 612–13; *see also* Constantine; Council of Nicaea; Jesus of Nazareth; Paul of Tarsus; Perpetua, Vibia

Cicero, Marcus Tullius: on dinner with Caesar, 377; on historical writing, 414; on *otium*, 370; philosophic works, 525, 528–30; on provincial government, 178, 190, 241

cinaedi, 337, 340–1

circumcision, 351–2

Circus Maximus: demonstrations in, 144; development of, 387–8

cities, Greek: archives, 46–7, 184, 425, 432; assemblies in, 182, 231, 233–4; benefactions, 232–4, 237–40, 244, 247–9, 425–6; coinage, 39–40; *collegia* (associations), 233–4, 246–7; councils, 181, 234–7, 244, 426, 463–4; cults, 230, 232, 246–8, 425–6, 591–2; disputes between, 246, 425; distributions in, 233, 425; entertainments, 230, 235, 247–9, 388, 433, 592; freedom, 184, 231, 240, 464–5, 574; idealized, 239–40; immunities, 232; *koina*, 71, 233–7, 247–8; liturgies, 182, 232; *metropoleis*, 230, 425, 446; mythological founders, 161, 182, 242–4, 425, 591; negotiations with emperors, 235–6, 240, 246; revenues, 187, 235–9; Roman preference for oligarchies in, 181–2, 234, 245; territory, 183, 465, 467; typical buildings, 230, 251–3, 464; unrest in, 247, 433; *see also* Antioch; Athens; Ephesus; euergetism; provincial government

cities, western: benefactions, 254, 258, 265, 274–8, 378–9; *collegia* (associations), 274, 376, 378; corvée labor, 255; councils, 255, 258, 272–6, 278; ideal components, 250–3, 260–9, 279–80; fora, 79–80; negotiations with emperors, 258, 267–71; plebs, 273–4; priesthoods, 255, 273–5, 553; rivalries between, 277–8; Roman attitude towards, 182; temples, 80; statuses, 256–60; territory, 183, 254, 256; *see also* Carthage; *coloniae*; euergetism; Herculaneum; Italic rights; *Lex Irnitana*; municipal status; Pompeii; provincial government

citizenship, Roman: and epigraphic habit, 57; spread of, 121, 178, 184, 211–12, 223, 228–9, 255, 264, 424

Claudius (emperor 41–54) Nero: and Alexandria, 430; and doctors, 498; donatives paid by, 220; exhibition on the Campus Martius, 402, 433; exhibition on the Fucine lake, 401; expansionist policies, 121–2, 216; freedmen of, 121; as judge, 483; and Roman citizenship, 272, 424; scholarship of, 424; temple to (in Britain), 271

Claudius, Marcus Aurelius (emperor 268–270), 164

Cleopatra, 116

client kings, 121, 123, 212–13

Colonia Augusta Emerita, 260–5

coloniae, 231, 254, 258–60

Colosseum, 80–1 (with fig. 4.3), 123, 401, 435

Commodus (emperor 180–192): accession, 135; in amphitheater, 15, 398–9; and Clodius Pompeianus, 15; murder of, 140, 404; and Perennis, 139; quality of, 135, 139–40; and *saltus Burunitanus*, 139

Constantine (emperor 306–337): accession, 153; administrative reforms, 200; and Constantinople, 171; conversion to Christianity, 170, 587; Council of Nicaea, 170–1, 198, 616; and Donatists, 171, 204; edicts restoring Christian property, 170, 197; and gladiators, 490; image of, 194; letter to orcistus, 52, 188, 199; marriage legislation, 325; sources for, 27–8, 32; succession plans, 166, 171, 194–5

Constantinople, 171, 197

Constantius I (Caesar 293–305, Augustus 305–306), 166–9, 196

convivium, 356–7, 372; *see also* banquets, private

corruption: in provincial administration, 16–17, 179–80, 188, 242, 308–9, 482
Council of Nicaea, 170–1, 198, 616
countryside: development of, 286–90, 302–4; methods for study of, 84–5, 93–4, 103, 303–4; *see also* villages
Crawford, Michael H., 35, 42, 52
Cremutius Cordus (historian), 32, 423, 441, 448
Crispus (Caesar 317–326), 32, 169, 171
culture, Roman: artistic, 77–8, 93–7, 106; literary, 107, 413–24, 439–52, 481–2, 525–6, 528; self understanding, 228, 385–6, 411–24, 444, 562
curse tablets, 394
Cursus publicus, *see* provincial administration

Decius (emperor 249–251), 156, 558, 602
declamation: Greek, 107, 239–40, 244–5, 460; Latin, 371–2, 440; *see also epideixis*
demography, 57, 104–5, 283–4, 482, 520–1; *see also* family; marriage
Dessau, Hermann, 3, 51–2
Dexippus, P. Herennius (historian), 432
Dictys (Homeric revisionist), 456–7
Didius Julianus (emperor 193), 140, 141
diet: archaeological evidence for, 88, 91–2, 284, 288, 368; beer, 289; categorization of food, 360–1; cereals, 289, 355, 361; class distinctions, 355, 359–60; fish sauce, 295, 355; and health, 360–1, 508; meat, 91, 289, 293, 361, 367–8; olive oil, 290, 301–2; religious strictures concerning, 354, 368, 578, 609; vegetables, 360–2; vegetarianism, 362–4, 367–8; wine, 301–2
Dio, L. Cassius: on Ardashir, 157; on Augustus, 34, 42; on Caracalla, 66, 399; on Commodus, 15; on Macrinus, 16–18; on Marcus Aurelius, 135, 437; scope of his history, 26–7, 431; on senators, 15–17; on Trajan, 129; on Vitellius, 358; use of sources, 33–4
Dio "Chrysostom": on assembly at Prusa, 182; as benefactor, 237; career, 461–2; on cities, 231, 464; *Euboean Speech*, 455, 459, 466–7, 473; and Homer, 473; on sex between men and boys, 335
Diocletian (emperor 284–305): and army, 225–6; coinage reform, 38–9, 168, 203; and court ceremonial, 199; creates imperial college, 166–7, 194–6, 198; family, 154; image of, 194; and Manichaean books, 160; and Nicomedia, 168, 602; persecutes Christians, 168, 197, 601–3; on rent remission, 310; sources for, 30–1; succession plans, 168–9; *see also* law, Roman
Dittenberger, Wilhelm, 50–1
divination, 559–60, 563–4; *see also* oracles
Domitian (emperor 81–96): administration, 124–5, 422; declared public enemy, 128; and Latin literature, 441, 450–2; spectacles, 401
drunkenness, 373–4; *see also* bars; gluttony
Dura Europus: and Rostovtzeff, 7; garrison of, 212, 224–5; sack of, 158

Eck, Werner, 15, 52
economy, Roman: agricultural, 283–5, 288–90, 299–311, 465; demography and, 286–7; growth, 283–5, 299; imperial coinage, 36–9, 291–3; mining, 291–2; technological development, 287–8, 291, 299–300; trade, 285–6, 293–4; *see also* Finley, Moses; Rostovtzeff, Michael
Egypt: bathing in, 381; close-kin marriages, 312; coinage, 40; cosmetics, 507; cults, 522–3, 549–50, 554, 556, 559, 561; funerary practices, 89, 552; imperial estates, 299; liturgies, 70–2, 304; priests, 554; quarries, 292, 296; Roman administration of, 45–6, 63–71, 117, 178, 202, 283, 286, 289–90, 472; rural economy, 303–4; under Zenobia, 186; *see also* Alexandria (in Egypt); revolts
Elagabalus (emperor 217–222), 136, 142–3, 154, 381
emperor, Roman: accession ceremonies, 120–1, 123, 144–5; *acta* of, 47; *adventus* ceremonials, 196; and adoption, 117, 120, 128, 130–2, 135, 153; "Bad," 168, 171, 196; capitals (outside Rome), 180, 298–9, 306–9; *comitatus*, 196, 200–1; and Egypt, 439–40; *fiscus*, 13–14, 123, 147–52; "Good," 117–18, 129–38, 167, 193, 196; household, 76–7, 129, 148, 151, 194; image of, 193–4, 196, 199–200, 215–16, 230; imperial cult, 198, 230, 232, 246, 263, 268–9, 273–5, 425, 593; journeys, 156, 180; and literary patronage, 267–9; and native cities, 64, 66; *patrimonium*, 69, 73; petition and response, 145–7, 204,

486, 488–9; and senatorial career, 14, 215–16; and soldiers, 135, 151, 357, 440; supreme legal authority, 146, 486–7; Tetrarchic iconography, 167, 194, 198; victory titles, 216

Ephesus: asserts status, 182, 482; Philovedii, 403; population, 231; Salutaris and, 425–6; Terrace Houses at, 86–7, 352

Epictetus (philosopher), 431, 531–5

epideixis, 388–9

epigraphy, *see* inscriptions

Epitome of the Emperors, 29–30

equestrians/equestrian order: auxiliary prefects, 51, 53, 58–60, 118; centurions, 213; epigraphic evidence for, 213, 256; equestrian census, 118; legionary legates, 213; military tribunes, 120, 128, 138–40, 156; Praetorian Prefects, 63, 66–7, 117, 200; Prefect of Egypt, 58–60, 67–8; procurators, 122, 156, 180; promotion, 59; as provincial *legati*, 180; replace senators, 164–5, 201, 298; secretaries, 58, 200–1

euergetism: theory, 356, 370–1, 384, 385; in civic contexts, 232–4, 237–40, 244, 247–9, 254, 258, 264–5, 274–8, 378–9, 383, 389–90, 394, 425–6, 521, 609–10

eunuchs, 199, 352, 513–14, 561

Eusebius of Caesarea, 616; *Chronological Canons*, 30; *Ecclesiastical History*, 31; *Life of Constantine*, 27, 32, 196

Eutropius (historian), 29–30

executions: in amphitheaters, 254, 324–5, 401–2, 433

family, Roman: care of children, 517–20; diversity of practices, 312; extended, 56–7; infant mortality, 521; nuclear, 56; *patria potestas*, 314, 318, 322, 356, 493, 495; "testamentary adoption," 317; *tutores*, 317; *see also* childbirth; funerary practices; marriage

Fausta, wife of Constantine, 32

Favorinus (rhetorician), 108

Festus (historian), 29–30

field survey, *see* countryside

Finley, Moses: career, 6–7, 9; on the ancient economy, 7, 283–4, 286–7, 290

Florus (historian), 30–1

freedmen: as *Augustales*, 273, 277, 297, 379; under Claudius, 122; as medical professionals, 503–4; *vicesima libertatis*, 187

Frier, Bruce W.: on demography, 57, 104, 482; on Roman law, 491

funerary practices, 56–7, 88–91, 550–2

Gaius (emperor 37–41), *see* Caligula

Gaius (jurist): *Institutes*, 484; on provincial edict, 178

Galba, Sulpicius (emperor 68–69), 33, 123, 218

Galen (doctor): career, 502–3, 520; on children's health, 517–20; corpus, 501–3; on doctors, 495–6; on drugs, 510–12; on food, 361–2; gynecology, 515–17; and imperial family, 495, 500–1; view of Hippocrates, 501–2

Galerius (Caesar 293–305, Augustus 305–311): defeats Persians, 167, 196; and Diocletian, 168; persecutes Christians, 197; retirement palace, 167

Gallienus (emperor 253–268): coinage, 38, 41; reign, 156–7, 162–5, 226

Gallus, Cornelius, 117

Gallus, Trebonianus (emperor 251–253), 156

gambling, 375–6

games, *see agones*; chariot racing; gladiators

Gelzer, Matthias, 4

Germanicus Caesar, 120; *see also tabula Siarensis*

Gibbon, Edward: on Antonine age, 126–7, 520; use of sources, 100, 477–8

gladiators: becoming, 120, 403–5; blood of, as cure, 497; decree on prices of in 177 AD, 46, 52, 391, 399, 485; development of, 389–91, 399, 407; female, 407–8; financial rewards, 399; ideology of, 81; restrictions on numbers of, 278; restrictions on senators and equestrians wounds, 502, 505

gluttony, 357–8; *see also* drunkenness

Glycon, 87, 556

Gnosticism, 611–12

Gordian III (emperor 238–244), 155, 202

Goths, 156, 161, 164

grain distributions: at Interpromium, 121; at Rome, 121, 148–9

Greeks, under Roman rule: and their cultural heritage, 94–6, 105–7, 183, 228–31, 398–9, 424–32, 434, 455, 471–6, 592;

Greeks, under Roman rule: (*cont'd*)
Roman attitude towards, 93, 228–9, 241–2, 245, 396–7, 425, 429, 443–4, 447, 463, 493–7, 525, 562, 592; *see also* cities, Greek; *paideia*

Hadrian (emperor 117–138): accession, 130, 138; on civic immunities, 239; construction of wall in Britain, 34, 92; criticism of, 216; dynastic plans, 131–2, 135; family, 130–1; founds Panhellion, 214; and Hispalis, 267; interest in magic, 145; and Jews, 571, 575; praises *auxilia*, 428–9; and Troy, 474
Heliodorus (doctor), 513–15
Heliodorus (novelist), 345, 461, 465, 470–1, 563
Herculaneum: baths, 380 (fig. 19.2b); bodies found at, 89
Herodian (historian), 27, 66, 157
Historia Augusta: nature of, 28; political theory, 129; scope, 28–9
Homer: revisionism, 397, 455–7, 473–5; Roman poets and, 443–4
Hopkins, Keith: and *Life of Aesop*, 12; on the Roman economy, 283–4; on the Roman imperial senate, 104–5
Horace (poet): corpus, 444–5; on literature, 442; on sex between men and boys, 334
houses, 86–8, 107–8, 263–4, 265, 377, 382, 551
humors, theory of, 360–1

Iamblichus (novelist), 453, 464
Iamblichus (philosopher), 527–8, 535–7, 540
Ignatius of Antioch (bishop), 601, 611–12, 614
imperial cult, *see* emperor, imperial cult
Imperium Galliarum, 163–5
India, 160, 287, 469–70
inscriptions: collections of, 48–53, 100–1; domestic objects, 293; editorial conventions, 54–5; erasure of, 128; funerary, 56–71; honorary, 233, 237–40; graffiti, 339, 346, 376; military diplomas, 211–12; public, 46–7, 244, 425, 432–3; restoration of, 54–5; *see also Laudatio Turiae*; *Lex de imperio Vespasiani*; *Lex Irnitana*; *Lex portoria provinciae Asiae*; *Res Gestae Divi Augusti*; *senatus consultum Pisonianum*; *tabula Siarensis*
Irenaeus (Christian theologian), 605, 613
Italic rights, 259–60

Jerome: *Chronological Canons*, 30–1
Jerusalem: healing shrine at, 549; Temple at, 121, 243, 547, 553, 558, 565–6, 573, 575, 580–2, 592
Jesus of Nazareth: and contemporary Judaism, 578, 581, 593–4, 596, 607–9; in Christian theology, 171, 197–8, 610–11; narratives concerning, 582, 590, 593–4, 601, 603, 608–10
Jews: and Caligula, 121, 242; attitudes towards sexuality, 332–4, 339–42, 344–5, 349, 350–1; conception(s) of God, 576–7, 580–1, 591, 599; diaspora, 576–80, 595–7; festivals, 578, 581, 583; identity, 578, 592, 595, 599–600; and magic, 579; numbers, 565; Patriarch of, 574–6, 581–2; priests, 553–4, 573–4; and Sibylline Oracles, 433; Theosebeis, 579, 595; veneration of tombs, 563; *see also* Josephus; Judaism; revolts
Jones, A. H. M., 5–6, 8, 41–2
Josephus, Flavius, 566, 578; *Against Apion*, 436; *Jewish Antiquities*, 434–6; *Jewish War*, 31–2, 434–7
Judaism: apocalyptic literature, 110, 604; attacks upon, 525; and Christianity, 566, 569–70, 577, 590–1, 593, 596–7; Dead Sea Scrolls/Qumran sect, 578, 609; Rabbinic, 562–3, 566–9, 583–6; Roman attitude towards, 571, 573–4, 576–7; synagogues, 568–9, 582–4, 592, 595–6; Temple cult, 580–3; Temple tax, 571, 581; Torah, 578–9, 581–2, 591; *see also* Mishnah; Talmud, Babylonian; Talmud, Jerusalem
Jupiter Optimus Maximus, cult of, 122, 127, 129
Juvenal (satirist): corpus, 449–50; on eunuchs, 513–14; on sexuality, 340

Labor/labores, 369–70
Lactantius: *On the Deaths of the Persecutors*, 31–2; on Diocletianic army, 225; on Diocletianic provinces and taxation, 202–3; on "Edict of Milan," 197; on the end of the world, 603

languages, non-classical: reflected in cult titles, 548; in religious contexts, 554; used in provinces, 183, 482, 584
Last, Hugh, 3, 5, 8
Latin rights, 189–90, 257–8, 267
Laudatio Turiae, 313–16
law, Roman: *Codex Gregorianus*, 203, 488–9; *Codex Hermogenianus*, 203, 488–9; *Codex Theodosianus*, 203–4, 477, 487, 489–90; *Corpus Iuris Civilis*, 477–8, 481; *Digest*, 481–3, 490; Praetor's Edict, 485–6; role in modern curricula, 478–9; sources of, 483–90; use of in provinces, 189–90, 305–7, 323–4, 481–2
leisure, *see otium*
Lepcis Magna: and Oea, 278; and Septimius Severus, 268–9
lesbianism, 338–9, 341, 346–8, 351
Lex Hadriana de rudibus agris, 146
Lex de imperio Vespasiani, 146, 485
Lex Irnitana, 124, 185, 189–90, 257–8
Lex Manciana, 307
Lex portoria provinciae Asiae, 122, 184
Licinius (Augustus 308–324), 169–70, 197
Livia Augusta: portrait of, 77–9 (with fig. 4.1); position of, 117
Livy: on Aemilius Paullus, 177–8, 400; *Periochae*, 30; on sources, 413, 417; view of Roman history, 415–18
Longus (novelist), 465–6
love: idealized, 315, 318–19; in novels, 456; poetic images, 319, 445–6; same-sex, 333–43, 346–8
Lucan (poet), 415, 447–8
Lucian (satirist): career, 461–2; on cities, 464; on historical writing, 457; on sexuality, 336, 340; *True Histories*, 455, 459, 464, 468, 473
ludi: *privati*, 276–7; *scaenici*, 254, 276
luxury, 356–8, 363, 520

Macrinus (emperor 217–218): accession of, 136, 142, 154; and the senate, 16
Mani (religious leader), 160
Marcus Aurelius, *see* Aurelius, Marcus
marriage: adultery, 316, 350, 493, 522, 560; age at, 318; age discrepancies between partners, 318; in art, 89, 345; divorce, 314–15, 321; and family structure, 56–7, 274; forms of (Roman), 313; sexual relations within, 343–5, 350, 499–500; of soldiers, 219, 223
Mars Ultor, temple of, 77, 123
Martial (poet): corpus, 372, 451–2; and Domitian, 441; on sexuality, 335, 344, 347, 522; on spectacles, 401
Masada, 92
Maxentius (usurper 306–312), 168–70
Maximianus (Caesar 285–286, Augustus 286–305), 166–9
Maximinus (emperor 235–238), 143, 154–5, 219–20
Mishnah, 332, 584–6
Mithras/Mithraism, 160
Momigliano, Arnaldo, 8–9
Mommsen, Theodor: and *CIL*, 48–9, 101, 478; and *Corpus Iuris Civilis*, 477–8, 490–1; on role of soldiers, 138; *Staatsrecht*, 2, 479
monotheism, 590
Montanism, *see* Christians/Christianity
mosaics: depicting novels, 462; in synagogues, 568–9 (with fig. 28.1a)
municipal status, 189–90, 257–8, 264, 268
Münzer, Friedrich, 3
Musonius Rufus (philosopher): and Epictetus, 532; on sexuality, 344

Neoplatonism, 524, 527–8, 532, 534–8, 540, 619
Nero (emperor 54–68): finances under, 67; habits, 122, 395, 404, 517; and Latin literature, 447–9; overthrow of, 67, 123; preferred drug, 510; spectacles, 401, 428
Nerva (emperor 96–98), 127–8
New College, Oxford: importance of for ancient history, 6–7
Nicomedia: and Diocletian, 168, 197; dispute with Nicaea, 246
Nîmes: Augusteum, 265; as mint, 39
Numenius (philosopher): influence of, 527, 535, 537; on Plato and Moses, 524

Odaenathus, of Palmyra, 162–4
oracles/books, 423–4, 433, 554–5; *see also Chaldean Oracles*
oracles/oracular sites, 232, 470–1, 522–3, 550, 555, 559–61
Origen (Christian theologian), 457, 525, 615–16

Orosius (historian), 31
otium, 82, 369–71, 385
Ovid (poet): *Amores*, 445; *Art of Love*, 446; *Fasti*, 446–7; *Medea*, 441; *Metamorphoses*, 446–7; on sexuality, 334, 343, 346

"paganism," 544–5; *see also* Christianity
Paideia, 95, 243–5, 460–4, 469–70, 592, 595, 599; *see also* "Second Sophistic"
Palmyra: auxiliary units, 213; as *colonia*, 161; population, 231; trade, 160, 187; *see also* Odaenathus; Zenobia
pantomime, 389, 395–6
papyri: archives, 61–3, 304–5; census returns, 57, 178; collections of, 53–4; distribution of, 60–1, 179, 284; editorial conventions, 55; and history of medicine, 505–6, 513–15, 522–3; literary texts, 462; magical, 554–5; restoration of, 54–5; *see also* Vindolanda writing tablets
passions: control of, 356, 386
patronage: of groups, 233, 239, 274; of individuals, 18, 59, 86, 180–1, 356–7; literary, 439–40
Paul of Tarsus (a.k.a. Paul, St.), 147, 247, 331, 339, 590–1, 593–4, 596–7, 601, 603, 608, 610
pederasty, 334–43, 349
Perpetua, Vibia, 321–5, 330, 397
Persia (Parthian and Sassanian), 154, 157–63, 167–8, 428, 431
Pertinax (emperor 193), 140
Pescennius Niger (usurper): coinage, 38; and Septimius Severus, 141
Petronius Arbiter: *Satyricon*, 334–5, 359, 372, 376–7, 448–9, 463
Pflaum, Hans-Georg, 53, 58–60
Philip (emperor 244–249): celebration of millennium, 401, 437; government of, 68, 156
Philo of Alexandria (philosopher): on Abraham, 610; conception of God, 576; embassy to Caligula, 242–3; on Moses, 540; *On the contemplative life*, 365; Platonism of, 536, 539–40; on sexuality, 331, 334; and Torah, 578
Philo of Larisa (philosopher), 528–9
Philostratus of Athens: *Erotic Letters*, 337; *Heroic Discourse*, 397, 455, 473–4; *In Honor of Apollonius*, 455, 458–9, 468–70,
474; on novels, 457; social standing, 461–2; on sophists, 245
physiognomics, 108
pilgrimage, 560–2
Piso, Gnaeus Calpurnius (consul 2 BC), 33–4, 120
Plasma (fiction), 455–60
Plato/Platonism: developments in the imperial period, 525–9, 532, 536–7, 539–40, 615–16, 618–19; on the good life, 365; *see also* Celsus (philosopher); Neoplatonism; Philo of Alexandria; Plotinus
plays: Greek, 394–5; Latin, 254, 394, 413, 432–3, 441–2; *see also* pantomime
Pliny, the Elder: on Greek doctors, 493, 495, 497, 510–11; on medicinal value of cabbage, 508; on theater of Aemilius Scaurus, 400; and the Younger Pliny, 317
Pliny, the Younger: on Achaia, 427; on athletic victors, 388–9; on chariot racing, 392–3, 403; and Christians, 320, 486, 602; estates, 298, 303, 306, 309, 317; as governor, 237; his published letters, 317; on *labor* and *otium*, 369–71; marriages, 13, 316–20; *Panegyric* on Trajan, 127, 129, 147–5; as patron, 18, 181; as prosecutor, 17; on Ummidia Quadratilla, 404
Plotinus (philosopher): arrival in Rome, 528; and Augustine, 618; and Plato, 537–8, 540; as teacher, 532, 534–5
Plutarch: advice on governing cities, 182, 237, 278, 433; advice on marriage, 344; on Platonism, 526; *Parallel Lives*, 27–8, 430; theory of biography, 27–8
Polemo (rhetorician), 108, 244
Pompeii: bars, 373, 375; baths, 381; brothels, 376; bodies found at, 90; houses at, 88, 372; workshops, 290; *see also* wall painting
Porphyry (philosopher): career, 528, 534; *On Abstinence from Animal Food*, 364
Praetorian guard: accession bonuses for, 140, 217; and Augustus, 208–9; and Claudius, 121, 217; and Domitian, 128; and Elagabalus, 143; and Nero, 122–3, 217; and Nerva, 128, 138, 217; and Pertinax, 140–1, 217; recruitment of, 141, 216–17; and Septimius Severus, 140–1

Probus, Marcus Aurelius (emperor 276–282), 166
Propertius (poet), 445
prosopography, 3–4
prostitution, 335, 339, 376, 500; *see also* brothels
provincial government: Augustan organization, 117, 254; assize districts, 183, 190–1, 241, 255; *cursus publicus*, 188; after Diocletian, 201–3; in Egypt, 67–73, 186; establishment of, 177–8; "freedom" of cities, 184, 231, 278; governors' staffs, 180–1; in Judaea, 573–4; lottery for governors, 16; loyalty oaths, 118; policing, 191–2; production of provincial coins at Rome, 40; provincial census, 183–4, 186; provincial militias, 161; relations between provincials and governors, 17, 179, 240–2, 278–9; respect for precedent, 182, 184–5; sons of governors as hostages at Rome, 139; sources for, 178–9, 183–4; taxation, 67–72, 185–8, 122, 243, 254–7, 308; use of Roman law, 189–90, 202–3; *see also* equestrians; Romanization; Verona List
Pythagoreanism, 524, 528, 535–7

Quintus of Smyrna (poet), 474–5

rape, 351, 353, 446
reading, 371–2, 461–3; *see also* declamation
record keeping: archives, 46–7, 62–3, 67, 184, 304–5, 425, 432; by emperors on campaign, 196; errors in transcription, 54; "verbatim transcription," 46–7, 191–2; *see also* inscriptions; papyri
Res Gestae Divi Augusti, 42, 116, 147–9, 412
revolts: against Severus Alexander, 143, 155, 162; in 238, 155; of Avidius Cassius, 139; of Carausius, 167–8; of Egypt under Diocletian, 168, 196; of Galba, 123; of Jews under Hadrian, 571, 575 (with fig. 28.3); of Jews under Nero, 80, 92, 123, 212, 214, 434–6, 571; of Jews under Trajan, 69, 571, 573; provincial in third century, 161–3, 166
"Right of three children" (*ius trium liberorum*), 274, 301, 316, 320
Robert, Louis: on epigraphy, 46, 49–50, 52, 54–5; and the Greek city, 9–10, 40
Roman culture, *see* culture, Roman

Roman economy, *see* economy, Roman
Romanization, 56–7, 93–7, 108–10, 123, 182, 189–90, 192, 222, 228–9, 253, 255, 260–9, 279–80, 303, 380–1, 424
Rome (city of): *Aeterna*, 411, 438; banquets, 378, baths, 379–80, Capitoline Games, 403; economic impact of, 285, 296; emperors and people of, 123–4, 144–5, 148, 437–8; "foreign cults" at, 548; Forum of Augustus, 77–8, 262, 274, 315–16, 329, 417, 433, 446; foundation myths, 77, 411, 415–18, 429, 438; healing cults at, 492–3; Monte Testaccio, 293, 295; plebeian consciousness, 433; provincial view of, 357; Vestal Virgins, 551, 553; *see also* Augustus, Forum of; Circus Maximus; Colosseum; Trajan, Forum of
Rostovtzeff, Michael: and archaeology, 7; *Social and Economic History of the Roman Empire*, 4–5, 101–2, 286, 480

sacrifice, 557–9
sculpture: Avezzano relief, 251; in baths, 83, 381; Jewish attitudes towards, 579, 581; portrait, 78–9, 105–6; representing Aeneas, 105–6, 261; on Sebasteion at Aphrodisias, 86–7; in Terrace Houses at Ephesus, 352; on triumphal arches, 76–7; "Weary Hercules," 95–7 (fig. 4.6a–b); *see also* Augustus, Forum of; Trajan, column of
Scribonius Largus (medical writer), 498–9, 506, 510
"Second Sophistic," 107, 243–5, 425–32
Sejanus, 120–1, 216, 420–1, 433
Senate, Roman: and Augustus, 116–17; and Commodus, 135; as court, 16–17, 485; and Didius Julianus, 144; and Domitian, 128; and Maximinus, 155; and Nero, 122–3; and provincial government, 116–17, 179; publication of decrees, 46–7, 117; recruitment, 272; structure, 12–13; and Tiberius, 120–1; *see also senatus consultum Pisonianum*; *tabula Siarensis*; tribunician power
senators, Roman: career pattern, 12–17; dining habits, 356–7; and "edict" of Gallienus, 164; expectations of emperors, 13–15, 149–1, 145–51; and gambling, 375–6; and imperial tastes, 511; income of, 298; involvement in commerce, 284; as patrons of individuals, 18, 145; philosophic

senators, Roman: (cont'd)
  interests, 528–9, 535; as provincial
    governors, 116, 117, 179–80, 184–5;
    priesthoods, 553; trials of, 16–17, 117,
    120, 150–1; triumphs of, 117
Senatus consultum Pisonianum (a.k.a. senatus
    consultum de Pisone patre), 34–5, 54, 120
Seneca, the Younger: diet, 364; on *otium*,
    371; on the Stoic sage, 531
Septimius Severus (emperor 193–211):
    accession, 140–1; and army, 141, 209,
    218–21; cruelty of, 146, 150; dynastic
    ambitions of, 136; and Egypt, 70–1; and
    Lepcis Magna, 268–9; and Palmyra, 161;
    and the senate, 16; on provincial
    government, 16
Severus Alexander (emperor 222–235):
    accession of, 136, 143; murder of, 143,
    154, 162; and Sasanians, 157, 162; on
    tenants' rights, 310
shipwrecks, 293–4
Sibylline Oracles, 423–4, 433, 553–4, 559
Silius Italicus (poet), 450
slavery: employment of, 234, 274, 288,
    300–1, 306, 483; *Life of Aesop*, 12; sexual
    abuse, 339, 349; slave tenants, 305;
    sources, 301; taxes on slaves, 187;
    treatment, 301–2, 483; *see also* freedmen
Soranus of Ephesus (medical writer): on care
    of children, 517–20; on sexual intercourse,
    499–500, 516; on women's health,
    516–17
Sparta, 394–5, 405–6, 427
Statius (poet): *Agave*, 396, 451; and
    Domitian, 441, 450; *Silvae*, 451–2;
    Thebaid, 450–1
Stoicism, 356, 362–5, 525, 529–34
Suetonius Tranquillus (biographer): on
    Augustan army reforms, 207; *Caesars*, 28;
    career, 18, 28; on senatorial decrees, 34;
    and Trajan, 18; on Vitellian cuisine, 358;
    and the Younger Pliny, 18
Syme, Ronald: and art and archaeology, 7–8;
    background, 2–3; and literature, 7; *The
    Roman Revolution*, 2–4, 479; *Tacitus*,
    4, 422

Tabula Siarensis, 47, 77, 120, 485
Tacitus, Cornelius (historian): *Agricola*, 27,
    279–80, 380; on Cremutius Cordus, 32,
    423, 441; *Dialogue Concerning Orators*,
    448; family, 26, 421; on historical
    narrative, 23–4, 32; narrative technique,
    24, 33–4, 99, 413, 421–5; scope of his
    work, 26–7; on sexuality, 335, 339; on
    Tiberius and the senatorial career, 14, 16,
    125; on Vitellius, 357–8; view of the
    imperial system, 4, 18, 141, 217, 421–4
Tacitus, Marcus Aurelius (emperor
    275–276), 40, 165
Talmud, Babylonian, 332–3, 345, 347
Talmud, Jerusalem, 341, 343–5
taxation, *see* provincial government; *Lex
    portoria provinciae Asiae*
Tertullian (Christian theologian): on
    lesbianism, 347; on martyrdom, 601;
    theology, 614–15
Teutoberger Wald, battle of, 93
theater, Roman: seating in, 151, 254, 275;
    temporary, 400
Tiberius (emperor 14–37): accession of,
    120; coinage, 37; early career, 117–18,
    120; and the senatorial career, 14, 16,
    120; and Sibylline Oracles, 423–4; on
    triumphal arch at Orange, 77; *see
    also senatus consultum Pisonianum*;
    Sejanus
Tibullus (poet), 445–6
Trajan (emperor 98–117): attitude towards
    laws, 147; on civic building projects, 243;
    and civic statuses, 259; column of, 76,
    214–15; Forum of, 77, 123; and imperial
    coinage, 41; invasion of Parthia, 157, 431;
    selection of as emperor, 127, 129, 138,
    218; succession to, 130–1, 138–9; and
    Suetonius Tranquillus, 18; and the
    Younger Pliny, 18, 602
Tribunician power, 117
triumphal arches: at Glanum, 76–7; at
    Orange, 76

Ulpian: on domiciles, 277; on general
    constitutions, 488; life table, 482; murder
    of, 155, 217; on powers of an emperor,
    146; on provincial government, 16,
    179–80, 191
Uranius Antoninus (ursurper), 161–2

Valerian (emperor 253–260): capture of, 158,
    161–2; coinage, 41; reign of, 156, 558;
    Rescript to Baetocaece, 47
Valerius Flaccus (poet), 450

Vedius Pollio (friend of Augustus), 116
Velleius Paterculus (historian): history, 29, 419–21; on *novi homines*, 120, 420–1; as a senator, 15
venatio, 391, 397–8
Vergil (poet): *Aeneid*, 250–1, 443–4; and Augustus, 414–15, 439–40, 442–4; *Eclogues*, 443; *Georgics*, 443; and later Latin poetry, 448, 450
Verona List, 202
Verus, Lucius (emperor 161–168), 131–3
Vespasian (emperor 69–79): coinage, 37, 571–2; and Colosseum, 80, 401, 435; and Latin rights, 258–9, 264; reign of, 123–4, 218
villages: administration of (Egypt), 70–2; architecture (Africa), 87; architecture (Syrian), 548–9, 561; cults of, 87; economic role of (Egypt), 304–5; taxes collected from, 187; in western provinces, 254
Vindolanda writing tablets, 45, 179, 212, 221, 296, 505–6

wall painting: in novels, 457; Philostratus of Lemnos on, 386, 397; at Pompeii, 372, 376
work, *see labor/labores*

Xenophon (novelist), 456, 460, 472

Zanker, Paul: *Augustus und die Macht der Bilder*, 8, 42, 105
Zenobia of Palmyra, 160, 164–5
Zonaras, John (historian), 31
Zoroaster, 160
Zosimus (historian), 29–30